Concordance To The Doctrine and Covenants

Compiled by

John V. Bluth

A COMPLETE CONCORDANCE TO THE DOCTRINE AND COVENANTS

A

Adam   Abideth

Sec.	Vs.	
		AARON
8	6	which is the gift of A.
	7	that can cause gift of A. to be with you
13	1	I confer the priesthood of A.
27	8	might be called and ordained as A.
28	3	which I shall give unto him even as A.
68	15	except they be literal descendants of A.—18; 107:16
	16	if they be literal descendants of A.; the first born among the sons of A.
	19	when no literal descendant of A.—107:17
	20	a literal descendant of A. must be
84	18	confirmed a priesthood also upon A.
	27	to continue with the house of A.
	30	priesthood confirmed upon A. and his
	31	the sons of A. shall offer an
	32	sons of Moses and of A. shall be
	34	they become sons of Moses and of A.
107	13	called priesthood of A. because conferred on A.
	69	unless a literal descendant of A.—70
	73	bishop not literal descendant of A.
	76	literal descendant of A. has legal
	87	president over the priesthood of A.
132	59	called of my Father as was A.
		AARONIC
107	1	the Melchizedek and A. including—107:6
	20	the authority of the A. priesthood
		ABASE
124	114	let him therefore A. himself that he
		ABASED
101	42	that exalteth himself shall be A.
112	3	inasmuch as thou hast A. thyself
		ABASETH
101	42	that A. himself shall be exalted
		ABEL
84	16	from Enoch to A. who was slain by

Sec.	Vs.	
		ABIDE
35	18	time of my coming if he A. in me
	21	and shall A. the day of my coming
38	8	is not purified shall not A. the
43	3	none to receive commandments if he A.
45	57	shall not be hewn down but shall A.
61	39	that you may A. the day of his
67	12	no man can A. in presence of God
	13	ye are not able to A. the presence
88	3	that the Comforter may A. in your
	22	he who is not able to A. the law cannot A.
	23	cannot A. law of a terrestrial cannot A.
	24	cannot A. law of a telestial cannot A.; must A. a kingdom which is not a
	26	A. power by which it is quickened
	35	that which willeth to A. in sin
	39	beings who A. not in those conditions
	66	A. ye in the liberty with which
97	4	inasmuch as he continueth to A. in me
98	14	whether you *will* A. in my covenant
	15	if ye *will* not A. in my covenant
112	22	inasmuch as they shall A. in me
119	5	shall not be found worthy to A.
128	24	who can A. the day of his coming
132	4	and if ye A. not that covenant
	5	shall A. the law which was appointed
	6	shall A. the law or be damned
	17	these angels did not A. my law
	19	and if ye A. in my covenant
	21	except ye A. in my law ye cannot
	25	neither do they A. in my law
	54	A. and cleave unto my servant; if she A. not in my law
	55	if she *will* not A. this commandment.—54
	64	all those who receive and A. in my
		ABIDETH
1	39	the truth A. forever and ever

Sec.	Vs.		Sec.	Vs.	
84	18	A. forever with the priesthood			**ABOUT**
88	25	earth A. the law of a celestial	4	1	marvelous work is A. to come forth.
	35	and A. not by law; and A. in sin, cannot be			—6:1; 11:1; 12:1; 14:1
	66	truth A. and hath no end	17	4	bring A. my righteous purposes. —17:9
97	3	servant Parley P. Pratt for he A.	19	40	canst thou run A. longer as a
132	27	he that A. not this law can in no	27	16	having your loins girt A. with truth
		ABILITY	109	38	judgments thou art A. to send in
134	81	use their A. in bringing offenders	111	5	concern not yourselves A. your debts
		ABLE		6	concern not yourselves A. Zion
8	8	no power shall be A. to take it	121	22	millstone hanged A. their necks
27	15	that ye may be A. to withstand the; having done all ye may be A. to stand	124	6	I am A. to call upon them to give
			127	8	I am A. to restore many things
	17	be A. to quench all the fiery darts	132	3	instructions that I am A. to give
60	7	I am A. to make you holy and your	135	1	were shot A. five o'clock p.m.
	11	he that is A. let him return it by			See *Round*
61	16	none is A. to go up to the land of			**ABOVE**
63	4	who is A. to cast the soul down to	6	10	it is sacred and cometh from A.
64	20	tempted above that which he is A.	18	45	the blessings are A. all things.
67	13	not A. to abide the presence of	20	6	white A. all other whiteness
76	118	they may be A. to bear his presence	29	14	greater signs in heaven A. and in
84	107	that you are not A. to fill	45	40	shown forth in the heavens A.
	109	how shall the body be A. to stand	49	20	possess that which is A. another
88	22	he who is not A. to abide the law	58	33	lurketh beneath and not from A.
89	11	men shall not be A. to stand		61	exceedingly blessed even A. measure
111	11	as fast as ye are A. to receive	59	4	crowned with blessings from A.
124	30	wherein ye are not A. to build a	60	4	I rule in the heavens A. and
130	16	left without being A. to decide	63	59	I am from A. and my power lieth
		ABLE-BODIED		64	that which cometh from A. is sacred
136	7	choose a sufficient number of A.	64	20	not be tempted A. that which he is
		ABODE	67	9	righteous cometh down from A.
48	1	remain in your places of A. as it	78	14	independent A. all other creatures
132	37	given him and he A. in my law	84	100	hath brought down Zion from A.
		ABOLISHMENT	88	41	he is A. all things and in all
84	114	utter A. which await them if they	125		A. all things clothe yourselves
		ABOMINABLE	89	16	whether in the ground or A. the
29	21	that great and A. church which is	101	34	things that are A. and things that
		ABOMINATION	102	13	according to the form A. written
84	117	desolation of A. in the last days	110	3	his countenance shone A. the brightness
88	85	desolation of A. which awaits the	112	11	partial in love A. many others
		ABOMINATIONS	122	7	A. all, if the very jaws of hell
3	18	because of the iniquities and A.	124	143	the A. offices I have given
10	21	their hearts are full of A.	128	4	believes the A. statement to be
29	21	as I live for A. shall not reign	132	20	then shall they be A. all because
35	7	A. shall be made manifest in the			**ABOVE-NAMED**
45	12	they found it not because of A.	68	21	under the hands of the A. presidency
50	4	I have seen A. in the church that	102	4	the A. councilors were asked
88	94	mother of A. that made all nations		5	in appointing the A. councilors were
97	24	kindled against their A. and all		6	to act without seven of the A.
117	11	secret A. and of all his littleness		8	whenever any one of the A. councilors
124	48	A. which you practice before me			**ABRAHAM**
		ABOUND	27	10	with Isaac and A., your fathers, by
45	27	wax cold and iniquity shall A.	84	13	Esaias lived in the days of A. and
88	50	you are in me or ye could not A.		14	which A. received the priesthood
	66	if truth be in you it shall A.		34	and of Aaron and the seed of A.
107	31	if these things A. in them they	98	32	this is the law I gave unto A.
112	11	let thy love A. unto all men			

Sec.	Vs.		Sec.	Vs.	
101	4	chastened and tried even as A.	45	17	long A. of your spirits from your
103	17	for ye are of the seed of A.	102	11	in the A. of one or both of those
109	64	which thou didst give unto A.			**ABSENT**
110	12	the dispensation of gospel of A.	102	7	in the place of A. councilors
124	19	who sitteth with A. at his right		11	in case he himself is A. the other
	58	as I said unto A. conserning the			**ABSTAIN**
132	1	wherein I justified A., Isaac and	49	18	forbiddeth to A. from meats that
	29	A. received all things whatsoever			**ABUNDANCE**
	30	A. received promises concerning; and as touching A. and his seed	49	19	and that he might have in A.
	31	ye are of A. and promise was made to A.	70	13	which A. is multiplied unto them
	32	go ye and do the works of A.		14	the A. of the manifestations of
	33	the promise which he made to A.	101	75	there is an A. to redeem Zion
	34	God commanded A. and Sarah gave Hagar to A.	104	18	if any man shall take of the A.
	35	was A. therefore under condemnation	117	7	to blossom and bring forth in A.
					ABUNDANTLY
	36	was commanded to offer his son; A. did not refuse	61	32	their labors are wanted more A.
	37	A. received concubines and they bear	70	13	even more A. which abundance
			71	6	given more A. even power
	49	in kingdom of my Father with A. your			**ABUSE**
	50	as I accepted the offering of A.	134	11	where personal A. in inflicted
	51	to prove you all as I did A.			**ABUSES**
	57	I am with him as I was with A.	123	1	all the sufferings and A. put upon
	65	who administered to A. when I commanded A.			**ACCEPT**
			98	35	did not A. the offering of peace
133	55	with A., Isaac and Jacob, shall be in	105	19	heard their prayers and *will* A.
136	21	the God of A., Isaac and Jacob	109	4	O Lord A. of this house the
	37	from the days of Adam to A.; from A. to Moses		78	A. the dedication of this house
			115	15	I *will* not A. it at their hands
		ABRIDGMENT		16	then *will* I A. it at the hands of
10	44	an A. of the account of Nephi	124	17	work he hath done which I A.
		ABROAD		49	but to A. of their offerings
45	72	keep these things from going A.		75	I *will* A. of his offerings
50	1	the spirits which have gone A.	132	9	*will* I A. of an offering saith the
52	14	Satan is A. in the land and he			**ACCEPTABLE**
69	5	servants who are A. in the earth	63	56	his writing is not A. to the Lord
88	79	things which are A., the wars and	72	17	rendereth every man A. and
102	24	High Priests when A. have power	84	31	shall offer an A. offering and
	28	this council of High Priests A.	93	51	proclaim the A. year of the Lord
	29	traveling High Priests A. have	124	2	your prayers are A. before me
	30	distinction between High Priests A.		30	this ordinance cannot be A. to me
105	8	speak concerning my churches A.		31	your baptisms shall be A. unto me
109	29	spread lying reports A. over the		32	baptisms for dead shall not be A.
112	1	to send it A. among all nations		33	baptisms for dead cannot be A.
	16	hold the keys of my kingdom A.		35	baptisms for dead are not A.
115	3	scattered A. in all the world		37	how shall your washings be A.
124	3	nations of the earth scattered A.	104		if he will offer unto me an A.
	35	baptism by those scattered A. are	126	1	for your offering is A. to me
134		different stakes scattered A.			**ACCEPTANCE**
126	3	command you to send my word A.	109	10	be done to thy divine A.
		ABSENCE			**ACCEPTATION**
20	56	lead of meetings in the A. of the	124	23	a good house worthy of all A.
			128	24	records of dead worthy of A.

Sec.	Vs.	
		ACCEPTED
52	15	is A. of me if he obey mine
72	18	he shall not be A. of the bishop
96	6	whose offering I have A. and whose
97	8	command, they are A. of me
	27	I have A. of her offering
102	4	whether they A. their appointments; they all answered that they A.
110	7	I have A. of this house
124	51	for this cause have I A. the
132	50	as I A. the offering of Abraham
		ACCLAMATIONS
109	79	with A. of praise singing Hosanna
		ACCOMPANYING
102	26	of the testimony A. their decision
	33	evidences and statements A. it
		ACCOMPLISH
5	34	means whereby thou mayest A.
10	14	not suffer that Satan shall A. his
	31	they shall not A. their evil
11	19	be patient until you shall A. it
38	40	A. the things which I have commanded
43	13	whatsoever thing he needeth to A.
45	72	that ye may A. this work in the eyes
58	58	to A. the residue of the work
78	13	A. the commandments which are
105	37	shall have power to A. all things
124	79	to A. the work that my servant
		ACCOMPLISHED
10	34	have A. the work of translation
19	2	having A. and finished the will of
45	72	until ye have A. the thing which
77	10	when are these to be A.; they are to be A. in the sixth
	13	when are they to be A.; to be A. after the opening of the
109	40	until this be A. let not thy
		ACCOMPLISHING
90	27	thereby you are hindered in A.
		ACCORD
104	62	shall belong to all with one A.
128	12	that one principle might A. with
	13	that they may A. one with another
		ACCORDING
1	10	unto every man A. to his work; A. to the measure which he has measured—19:3; 76:11; 101:65; 112:34
6	9	A. to my commandments and you—59:1; 76:51
7	8	ye shall both have A. to your
8	11	A. to your faith so shall it be

Sec.	Vs.	
9	1	because you did not translate A.
10	47	granted them A. to their faith
	52	A. to their faith in their prayers
11	9	bring forth my work A. to my
	17	A. to your desires, even A. to
	23	all things shall be added A. to
15	5	which I have given you A. to my—16:5
18	7	A. to that which I have commanded
	29	A. to that which is written—30; 24:14; 29:50
	32	A. to power of the Holy Ghost; A. to the callings and gifts of—20:60
20	4	A. to the grace of our Lord and
	24	A. to the will of the Father
	35	A to the revelations of John
	41	Holy Ghost, A. to the scriptures
	45	Holy Ghost A. to the commandments
24	16	smite them A. to your words in
	19	shall do even A. to this pattern
25	7	A. as it shall be given thee by
	9	revealed unto them A. to their
28	14	A. to the covenants of the church
29	6	united in prayer A. to my command
	21	A. as it is spoken by the mouth
	48	A. to my own pleasure
38	23	teach one another A. to the
42	3	assembled yourselves A. to the—57:1
	33	receive A. to his wants
	55	that all things may be done A.—44:6
	60	he that doeth A. to these things
	79	dealt with A. to laws of; proved A to the laws of the land—51:6
	81	dealt with A. to the law of God
44	4	organize A. to laws of man
46	15	A. as the Lord will, suiting his mercies A.
	30	he that asketh A. to the will of
48	6	every man A. to his family; A. to his circumstances; A. to laws and commandments which—51:3
49	4	not A. to that he has received of, but A. to that which shall be taught him
	13	A. to the holy commandment for the
	17	A. to his creation before the world
50	1	A. as ye have asked and are
51	2	be organized A. to my laws.
	4	A. to the laws and covenants
	8	A. to the wants of this people
	11	again A. as they shall agree
	15	organizing themselves A. to my
52	2	are heirs A. to the covenant
	17	A. to revelations and truth which
	18	fruits even A. to this pattern
	20	A. to men's faith it shall be done
53	3	preach faith and repentance A. to

| According | | 5 | | Account |

Sec.	Vs.		Sec.	Vs.	
	4	A. to the commandments which shall		13	A. to the form above written
	6	A. to your labor in my vineyard		16	speak A. to equity and justice
56	12	A. to that which they do—56:13		19	decision A. to the understanding
58	18	A. to the laws of the kingdom—70:8		27	conducted A. to the former pattern
	20	A. to the counsel of his own will	104	18	A. to the law of my gospel
	36	do. with his moneys A. as the law		21	A. to the counsel of the order—104:36
	56	done A. to the knowledge which they		26	A. as my servant Gazelam (Joseph Smith)
59	22	A. to the law and the prophets		81	Write A. to that which shall be
61	22	A. to their judgments hereafter		86	I have laid before you A. to my
62	8	do A. to judgment and the direction	105	4	united A. to the union required
63	21	transfigured even A. to the		25	execute justice for us A. to law
	44	let him do A. to wisdom		29	A. to the laws of consecration
64	11	reward thee A. to thy deeds		40	A. to the voice of the spirit
	29	do A. to the will of the Lord	107	72	shall be laid before him A. to the
68	14	to minister even A. to the first		79	testimony A. to the laws of the
	24	A. to the covenants and commandments—107:63		84	A. to truth and righteousness
				85	edifying one another A. to the
71	1	A. to that portion of spirit		89	teach them A. to the covenants
72	15	for A. to the law every man must		93	it is A. to the vision showing
75	4	A. to the revelations and	109	3	thy servants have done A. to thy
76	73	judged A. to men in the flesh—81:99		15	organized A. to thy laws and be
	111	be judged A. to their works; A. to his own works—128:6, 7, 8		41	let it be upon that city A. to
			121	25	time appointed for every man A. as
82	15	done A. to the laws of the Lord		32	A. to that which was ordained
	17	every man A. to his wants and his	124	115	A. to the contract which he has
	21	A. to the laws of my church	128	8	A. to the ordinances which God has; A. to the records which they have kept
83	3	remain upon their inheritances A.			
84	6	A. to the Holy Priesthood which he		9	A. to the decrees of the great
	39	A. to the oath and covenant	130	4	A. to the planet on which they
	57	A. to that which I have written	132	26	marry a wife A. to my word and; A. to my appointment
	99	A. to the election of grace			
86	9	lawful heirs A. to the flesh		37	A. to the promises and sit upon
88	60	A. as his lord had commanded		40	it shall be given you A. to my
	61	A. to the decree which God hath		48	by my word and A. to my law it—132:59
	68	in his own way and A. to his own			
	141	gird himself A. to the pattern		63	replenish the earth A. to my
90	1	thy sins are forgiven thee A. to		65	administer unto him A. to my word; administered unto Abraham A. to
93	42	taught your children light A.			
	52	even A. to the prayer of faith	133	52	bestowed upon them A. to his goodness and A. to his
94	2	A. to the pattern which I have—94:5, 6, 12		61	A. to the mind and will of the Lord
	6	A. to the order of the priesthood	134	8	punished A. to the nature of the offence; A. to their criminality
	15	build mine houses A. to the—115:14, 15, 16		10	A. to the rules and regulations of
96	3	divided into lots A. to wisdom	136	8	equal proportion A. to the dividend
97	26	will visit her A. to all her works			
98	31	rewardest him A. to his works—101:65			**ACCORDINGLY**
			102	21	the decision shall be altered A.
101	22	worship me A. to my everlasting	134	5	and should be punished A.
	65	A. to the parable of the wheat			**ACCOUNT**
	77	A. to the laws and constitution; A. to just and holy principles	10	38	an A. of these things that you
	78	A. to the moral agency I have		39	that a more particular A. was given
102	4	act A. to the law of heaven; A. to the grace of God		40	the A. which is engraven upon the; to knowledge of people in this A.
	10	A. to the dignity of his office		44	an abridgement of the A. of Nephi
	12	organized A. to the foregoing	50	34	let him A. it of God and rejoice

Sec.	Vs.		Sec.	Vs.	
63	21	of which A. the fullness ye have			**ACKNOWLEDGE**
70	4	an A. of this stewardship will I	5	28	except he humble himself and A.
72	3	to render an A. of his stewardship —72:5	81	3	I A. him and will bless him and
			105	32	constrained to A. that the kingdom
	11	to take an A. of the elders	109	13	A. that thou hast sanctified
	13	an A. shall be taken and handed			**ACKNOWLEDGED**
	16	every elder must give an A. of his	102	3	were A. presidents by the voice
	19	who shall give an A. to the bishop		9	A. in his administration by the voice
104	12	that every man may give an A.			**ACKNOWLEDGMENTS**
		ACCOUNTABILITY	124	1	I am well pleased with your A.
18	42	have arrived to the years of A.—20:71	104		offer unto me acceptable A.
		ACCOUNTABLE			**ACQUAINTANCE**
29	47	begin to become A. before me	111	3	form A. with men in this city
42	32	every man shall be made A. unto			**ACQUAINTED**
101	78	every man A. for his own sins	20	84	if the member is personally A.
104	13	make every man A. as a steward	84	52	receiveth not my voice is not A.
134	1	he holds men A. for their acts	90	15	become A. with all good books
		ACCOUNTED			**ACT**
50	34	A. of God worthy to receive	43	8	that ye may know how to A. and direct, how to A. upon—103:1
51	4	and is not A. worthy by the voice			
	5	not A. worthy to belong to the		9	bind yourselves to A. in all
72	4	A. worthy to inherit the mansions	51	17	let them A. upon this land as for
	22	and be A. as wise stewards	77	4	a representation of power to A.
	26	shall not be A. as a wise steward	82	9	directions how you may A. before
90	5	lest they are A. as a light thing	93	30	God has placed it to A. for itself
	6	are A. as equal with thee in	95	4	I may bring to pass my strange A.—101:95
98	24	A. unto you as being meted out a			
101	39	they are A. as the salt of the	96	1	may know how to A. concerning this
124	122	shall be A. unto them for stock			
132	36	it was A. unto him for righteousness—132:37	101	78	that every man may A. in doctrine
			102	4	whether they would A. in that
		ACCOUNTS		6	cannot have power to A. without
69	5	should send forth the A. of their		7	capable to A. in the place of
72	19	render himself and his A. approved		8	to A. in the name of the church
		ACCURATE		13	convenes to A. upon any case
128	3	qualified for taking A. minutes	107	34	the seventy are to A. in the name
		ACCURSED		75	they shall A. in the same office
124	71	they shall be A. and shall be		76	to A. in the office of bishop
		ACCUSATION		99	let every man learn his duty and A.
50	33	not with railing A. that ye be	124	69	by their own free will and A.
		ACCUSATIONS		95	that he may A. in concert also
122	6	accused with all manner of false A.			**ACTING**
		ACCUSED	68	8	A. in the authority which I have
102	15	the A. in all cases has a right			**ACTS**
	17	stand up in behalf of the A.	1	3	their secret A. shall be revealed
	18	the accuser and A. shall have	88	108	and reveal the secret A. of men—88:109
	19	after accuser and A. have spoken			
122	6	if thou art A. with all manner of	134	1	holds men accountable for their A.
		ACCUSER			**ACTUAL**
102	18	the A. and the accused shall have	128	9	to any man by A. revelation or any
	19	after the A. and accused have			**ADAM**
			27	11	with Michael, or A., the father of all

Sec.	Vs.		Sec.	Vs.	
29	34	neither A. your father whom I created		24	in A. to the laws of the kingdom
	36	A. being tempted of the devil, for the devil was before A.	83	1	in A. to the laws of the church—107:59
	40	the devil tempted A. and he partook			**ADDITIONAL**
	42	I gave unto A. and his seed that	102	21	if any A. light is shown upon the
84	16	by hand of his father A. who was the		22	but in case no A. light is given
107	41	was instituted in the days of A.	128	2	I have had a few A. views in
	42	from A. to Seth, ordained by A.			**ADDRESSED**
	44	Enos was ordained by hand of A.	127	10	I desired to have A. them from the
	45	Cainan met A. in journeying to the			**ADJOINING**
	46	Mahalaleel was ordained by hand of A.	105	28	in the A. counties round about
	47	Jared was ordained under hand of A.	106	2	in his own place, but in A. counties
	48	Enoch was ordained by A. and A. blessed him			**ADJOURNED**
	50	Methuselah was ordained under hand of A.	102	34	after prayer the conference A.
	53	three years previous to death of A.			**ADMINISTER**
	54	they rose up and blessed A. and	20	40	and to A. the bread and wine
	55	the Lord administered comfort unto A.		46	and baptize and A. the sacrament
	56	A. stood up in midst of congregation		58	no deacons have authority to A.
116	1	where A. shall come and visit his		76	elder or priest shall A. it; and after this manner shall he A.
117	8	or the land where A. dwelt	38	35	and shall A. to their relief—44:6
128	18	and be revealed from the days of A.	42	33	to A. to those who have not
	21	from A., or Michael, down to present		34	to A. to the poor and needy
136	37	from the days of A. to Abraham	70	12	A. spiritual things; to A. in
		ADAM-ONDI-AHMAN	72	11	and to A. to their wants—84:112
78	15	who hath established foundations of A.	77	11	to A. the everlasting gospel
107	53	into the valley of A. and there	84	71	and if any man shall A. poison
116	1	A., because it is where Adam shall	107	8	to A. in spiritual things—107:12
117	8	room enough upon the mountains of A.		20	to A. in outward ordinances
	11	come up to the land of A. and be a	124	21	he may A. blessings upon the heads
		ADAM'S		98	who would A. unto him deadly
107	42	blessed by him three years previous to A. death	132	64	then shall she believe and A.
		ADAPTED		65	because she did not A. unto him
89	3	A. to the capacity of the weak	134	3	such as *will* A. the law in equity
		ADDED			**ADMINISTERED**
11	22	shall all things be A. thereunto—106:3	20	72	baptism to be A. in the following
	23	A. according to that which is just	88	140	washing of feet is to be A. by
43	10	glory shall be A. to the kingdom	107	55	the Lord A. comfort unto Adam and
78	19	things of this earth shall be A.	109	4	whose name alone salvation can be A.
		ADDING	132	65	law of Sarah who A. unto Abraham
20	35	neither A. to nor diminishing from			**ADMINISTERETH**
		ADDITION	84	19	greater priesthood A. the gospel
5	11	and in A. to your testimony the			**ADMINISTERING**
68	13	items in A. to the covenants	20	78	the manner of A. the wine
72	9	in A. to the law which has been	72	14	A. the gospel and the things
			76	88	telestial receive it of the A. of
			107	10	in A. spiritual things and also
				14	power in A. outward ordinances
				38	calls for preaching and A. the
				67	A. of ordinances and blessings
				68	office of a bishop is in A. all
			134	1	either in making laws or A. them

Administration 8 Afflicted

Sec. Vs.
ADMINISTRATION
46	15	to know the differences of A. as
90	7	through your A. the keys of the
	9	through your A. they may receive; through their A. the word may go.
	11	by the A. of the comforter shed
102	9	acknowledged in his A. by the
129	9	you may know whether any A. is

ADMIT
104	53	as your circumstances *will* A.
127	1	or as the circumstances may A. of

ADMONISH
6	19	A. him in his faults and also
112	12	A. them sharply for my name's sake

ADMONISHED
90	17	be A. in all your high-mindedness
112	12	let them be A. for all their sins

ADMONITION
6	19	admonish him and also receive A.

ADORNED
109	74	and be A. as a bride for that day

ADULTERERS
63	14	there were among you A. and
76	103	these are they who are liars and A.

ADULTERY
42	24	thou shalt not commit A.; he that committeth A. shall
	25	that has committed A. and repents
	75	their companions for the sake of A.
	80	if any man or woman shall commit A.
59	6	neither commit A. nor kill nor do
63	16	shall commit A. in their hearts
66	10	commit not A., a temptation which
132	41	as ye have asked concerning A; hath committed A. and shall
	42	with another man she has committed A.
	43	broken his vow and committed A.
	44	if she hath not committed A.; give her to him that hath not committed A.
	61	he cannot commit A. for they—132:62
	63	committed A. and shall be destroyed

ADULTRESSES
63	14	there were among you A.

ADVANCE
78	4	to A. the cause which ye have

ADVANTAGE
63	27	you may have A. of the world
130	19	much the A. in the world to come

Sec. Vs.
ADVERSARIES
133	42	make thy name known to thine A.

ADVERSARY
3	8	against the fiery darts of the A.
50	7	which has given the A. power
82	5	watch, for the A. spreadeth his
101	83	saying, avenge me of mine A.

ADVERSITY
121	7	thine A. shall be but a small

ADVICE
30	5	give heed unto the words and A.

ADVOCATE
29	5	I am your A. with the Father—32:3; 110:4.
45	3	listen to him who is the A. with
62	1	Jesus Christ, your A. who knoweth

AFAR
1	1	hearken ye people from A. and—70:1
45	74	they shall stand A. off and tremble
63	1	your hearts and give ear from A.
101	54	enemy while he was yet A. off
124	23	strangers may come from A. to
	25	let all my saints come from A.
133	8	unto the nations that are A. off

AFFAIRS
38	36	to govern the A. of the property
78	3	establishing the A. of the storehouse
82	12	to manage the A. of the poor
90	13	preside over the A. of the church
	16	set in order all the A. of this
107	33	and regulate all the A. of the—107:34
	36	equal in authority in the A. of—107:37
112	27	concerning the A. of my church
127	1	I have left my A. with agents and

AFFIDAVITS
123	4	to take statements and A. and

AFFIXED
82	4	the penalty A. unto my law
135	7	is a broad seal A. to Mormonism

AFFLICTED
30	6	be you A. in his afflictions
52	40	remember the sick and the A.
64	8	for this evil they were A.
98	3	things wherewith you have been A.
101	1	your brethren who have been A.
	2	I have suffered them to be A.
105	1	the redemption of mine A. people
	3	to the poor and A. among them
109	48	oppressed and A. by wicked men
	55	the needy and A. ones of the earth

Afflicted   9   **After**

Sec.	Vs.	
	72	with all their sick and A. ones
133	53	in all their afflictions he was A.

AFFLICTION

Sec.	Vs.	
66	9	be patient in A.
93	42	this is the cause of your A.
97	26	with sore A., with pestilence
101	2	I have suffered the A. to come
104	81	out of their minds to bring A.
109	47	break off this yoke of A. that
	49	suffer this people to bear this A.
124	16	stand by you in the hour of A.
	76	turn away their hearts from A.

AFFLICTIONS

24	1	have lifted thee up out of thine A.
	8	in A. for thou shalt have many
25	5	in his A. with consoling words
30	6	be you afflicted in all his A.
31	2	you have had many A. because of
	9	be patient in A., revile not
109	68	all his A. and persecutions
121	7	thine A. shall be but a small
133	53	in all their A. he was afflicted

AFFORDED

134	11	be made to the laws and relief A.

AFFRIGHTED

101	51	servants of the nobleman were A.

AFLOAT

123	4	libelous publications that are A.

AFRAID

45	75	all nations shall be A. because of
98	14	be not A. of your enemies for I
103	27	let no man be A. to lay down his

AFTER

.1	16	and A. the image of his own God
	24	A. the manner of their language
	29	and A. having received the record
3	4	follows A. the dictates of his own
9	6	I have dealt with you A. this
17	3	A. that you have obtained faith
18	43	A. that you have received this—
		18:46
20	5	A. it was truly manifested to
	6	A. repenting and humbling himself
	18	male and female A. his own image
	26	A. he came in the meridan of time
	27	as those who should come A., who
	68	duty of members A. they are
	76	A. this manner shall he administer
24	3	and A. thou hast sowed thy fields
26	1	until A. you shall go to the west
28	10	not leave this place until A. the
42	23	looketh upon a woman to lust A.
		—63:16

Sec.	Vs.	
	32	A. they are laid before the bishop;
		A. he has received these testimonies
	33	A. this first consecration which is
46	6	earnestly seeking A. the kingdom
48	5	A. your brethren come from the
54	9	and A. you have done journeying
55	1	A. thou hast been baptized by
56	3	A. I have commanded and the
58	3	shall follow A. much tribulation
	4	for A. much tribulation cometh—
		103:12
	11	A. that cometh the day of my power
	46	A. that let them return to their
	58	A. that let my servants Sidney
60	14	A. thou hast come up unto the land
61	22	mattereth not unto me A. a little
	24	A. they leave the canal they shall
63	12	you who have sought A. signs
	49	from the dead and shall not die A.
	53	speaking A. the manner of the—
		64:24
64	18	Sidney Gilbert A. a few weeks
	22	A. that day I will not hold any
	24	for A. today cometh the burning
67	12	neither A. the carnal mind
73	4	A. that it is expedient to continue
76	22	now, A. the many testimonies which
	35	denied the Holy Spirit A. having
	38	A. the sufferings of his wrath
	43	who deny the Son A. the Father has
	51	A. the manner of his burial being
	57	A. the order of Melchizedek; A. the order of Enoch; A. the order of the Only Begotten—124:123
77	13	A. the opening of the seventh seal
	15	Jews, A. they are gathered and
83	5	and A. that they have claim upon
84	18	which is A. the holiest order of God
	41	whoso breaketh this covenant A.
	112	searching A. the poor to administer
85	2	apostatize A. receiving their
86	3	and A. they have fallen asleep
	7	and A. the gathering of the wheat
87	4	A. many days slaves shall rise up
88	19	for A. it hath filled the measure
	88	A. your testimony cometh wrath
	89	A. your testimony cometh testimony
	95	immediately A. shall the curtain; unfolded A. it is rolled up
	99	A. this another angel shall sound
	132	when any shall come in A. him
	141	A. partaking of bread and wine
95	13	built, not A. the manner; to live A. manner of the
	14	A. the manner which I shall show
98	39	A. thine enemy has come upon thee
99	7	and A. a few years if thou desirest
101	8	day of their trouble they feel A.

After   10   Again

Sec.	Vs.	
	53	A. ye had planted the vineyard
	62	A. many days all things were
	75	who call themselves A. my name—101:97; 103:4
102	10	appointed A. the same manner that
	16	present the case A. the evidence
	18	A. the evidences are heard—102:19
	20	A. hearing the evidences and
	21	and if, A. a careful re-hearing
	24	organize a council A. the manner
	33	A. examining the appeal and the
	34	A. prayer the conference adjourned
103	13	blessing which I have promised A.
	24	A. these testimonies ye shall curse
104	22	and his seed A. him—103:24, 25, 37, 40, 41, 42; 124:59
	32	and their seed A. them—104:33
	48	your brethren A. they are organized
105	29	and A. they are purchased that my
	30	A. these lands are purchased I will
	34	and fulfilled, A. her redemption
	37	shall have power A. many days to
107	3	A. the order of the Son of God
	4	A. Melchizedek or the M. priesthood
	9	A. the order of Melchizedek—107:10, 29, 71, 73, 76; 124:123
	80	A. this decision it shall be had
110	11	A. this vision closed—110:13
	12	A. this Elias appeared and committed; all generations A. us should be blessed.
112	5	day A. day let thy warning voice
	13	A. their temptations I will feel A. them
119	4	A. that, those who have been tithed
121	21	nor their posterity A. them from
122	1	earth shall inquire A. thy name
	7	gape open the mouth wide A. thee
124	2	which is A. the similitude of a
	33	A. you have had sufficient time
	35	A. this time, your baptisms for
	57	head of his posterity A. him
	69	for himself and his generation A.—124:74, 77, 81, 82, 117
	128	and A. that to send my word to
132	7	in and A. the resurrection from the
	13	shall not remain A. men are dead; nor A. the resurrection
	19	if it be A. the first resurrection
	27	assent unto my death A. ye have
	63	if, A. she is espoused she shall
133	35	A. their pain shall be sanctified
135	1	both shot A. they were dead in a
	4	the same morning, A. Hyrum had made

AFTERWARD

| 101 | 84 | but A. he said within himself |
| 128 | 14 | natural, and A. that which is spiritual |

Sec.	Vs.	
		AFTERWARDS
76	74	in the flesh but A. received it
121	43	showing forth A. an increase of

AGAIN

1	34	A. verily I say unto you—29:12, 22, 49; 37:2; 38:25, 28, 40; 42:2, 10, 11, 19, 76; 43:13, 15; 45:2; 46:5, 6, 10, 17,31; 47:2, 3; 49:15, 22; 50:25; 52:7, 22, 35, 38; 53:5; 55:5; 56:8; 57:8, 11; 61:21,30; 63:57; 64:20; 67:10; 75:14, 28; 82:8; 84:77, 103; 88:25, 34, 42, 62; 89:10; 90:6, 28; 92:2; 94:1, 10; 96:6; 98:22, 39; 101:63, 76, 96; 104:78; 105:38; 106:4, 6; 107:78, 85; 112:21; 115:17; 117:12, 16; 124:12, 15, 18, 20, 25, 37, 55, 70, 91, 103, 111, 115, 119, 121, 131, 141, 142; 132:18, 19, 47, 48, 56, 57, 64; 133:7.
3	10	thou art A. called to the work
5	23	and now, A. I speak unto you
	30	thou shalt stop until I command thee A., then thou mayest translate A.
9	1	did commence A. to write for my
10	3	it is now restored unto you A.
	15	asking to translate it over A.
	16	he will also give him power A.
	17	if God giveth him power A., or if he translates A.
	30	you shall not translate A. those
13	1	this shall never be taken A. from; offer A. an offering unto the Lord
18	12	he hath risen A. from the dead
19	7	A. it is written eternal damnation
	20	I command you A. to repent, lest I
	25	and A. I command thee that thou—19:26, 28
20	5	he was entangled A. in the vanities
	23	crucified, died and rose A. the
	37	and A. by way of commandment
	74	come forth A. out of the water
28	11	A., thou shalt take thy brother
29	22	and men A. begin to deny their God
	32	and A., first temporal—secondly
37	3	and A., a commandment I give—104:54
38	17	A. I will stand upon it
	20	ye shall possess it A. in eternity
39	23	and A., it shall come to pass—42:48
41	7	and A., it is meet that my servant—41:8
	9	and A., I have called my servant
42	12	and A., the elders, priests and
	26	but if he doeth it A. he shall
	33	A., if there shall be properties

Again | 11 | Against

Sec.	Vs.	
	37	and shall not receive A. that
	40	A., thou shalt not be proud.
	78	A., every person who belongeth
43	18	stay and sleep until I shall call A.
	22	and A., when the lightnings shall
	23	and A., the Lord shall utter his
	31	and when he is loosed A. he shall
45	25	but they shall be gathered A.
46	15	and A., to some it is given by the. —46:16, 19, 21, 24.
50	19	A., he that receiveth the word of
51	11	let them pay unto this church A.
	13	and A., let the bishop appoint.
52	14	A., I will give unto you a pattern
	17	A., he that trembleth under my
	18	A., he that is overcome and
	23	and A., let my servant—52:24, 41; 55:6; 72:20; 104:24, 27, 34, 39, 43; 124:16
53	7	A., I would that ye should learn
54	10	A. be patient in tribulation
55	4	and A., you shall be ordained
56	12	I will pay it unto him A. in the; that those may be rewarded A.
58	16	and it shall not be given A.
	54	A., inasmuch as there is land
61	23	let them come not A. upon the waters
68	22	A., no bishop or high priest who
	25	A., inasmuch as parents have children
73	3	it is expedient to translate A.
75	8	I forgive him and say unto him, A.
	13	A. verily thus saith the Lord.—75:23; 127:4.
	15	A., I say unto my servant.—75:17.
76	47	but straightway shut it up A.
	50	and A, we bear record, for we saw
	71	A., we saw the terrestrial world
	81	A., we saw the glory of the telestial
79	1	Jared Carter should go A. into the
	3	I will crown him A. with sheaves
84	29	A., the offices of elder and bishop
	30	A., the offices of teacher and
	64	I say unto you A. that every soul
	92	return not A. unto that man
	95	wo, I say A., unto that house
	99	the Lord hath brought A. Zion
88	26	it shall die, it shall be quickened A.
	27	they also shall rise A. a spiritual
	32	they shall return A. to their own
	80	I shall send you A. to magnify
	100	and A., another trump shall sound
	101	live not A. until, neither A. until the end of the earth
	105	A., another angel shall sound —88:106
	108	then shall the first angel A. sound
	127	A., the order of the house prepared
	140	A., the ordinance of washing feet
89	7	A., strong drinks are not for the

Sec.	Vs.	
	8	A., tobacco is not for the body
	9	A., hot drinks are not for the body
93	38	men became A. in their infant state
96	3	A., let it be divided in lots
98	13	shall find it A. even life eternal
	17	A., the hearts of the Jews unto the
	25	A., if your enemy shall smite you —98:26
	33	A., this is the law that I gave
103	27	layeth down his life shall find it A.
104	67	A., there shall be another treasury
107	89	A., the duty of the president over —107:91
110	11	the heavens were A. opened unto us
113	8	power of priesthood to bring A. Zion
117	1	before I send A. the snows upon
	13	when he falls he shall rise A.
121	9	they shall hail thee A. with warm
123	1	A., we would suggest for your
124	9	A., I will visit and soften their
	28	restore A. that which was lost
	55	I command you A. to build a house
	104	he shall lift up his voice A. on
	133	A., I give unto you Don C. Smith
	138	A., I give unto you Joseph Young
127	1	were A. in pursuit of me; then I will return to you A.
	5	A., I give unto you a word in
	9	A., let all the records be had in
128	10	A., for the precedent, Matthew 16: 18, 19.
	17	A., in connection with this quotation
	20	and A., what do we hear? Glad
	21	A., the voice of God in the chamber
	23	A., I say, how glorious is the
132	61	A., as pertaining to the law of
133	67	when I called A. there was none
136	26	thou shalt deliver it to him A.

AGAINST

3	8	supported you A. all the fiery darts
5	8	mine anger is kindled A. them—56:1; 60:2; 63:2; 82:6; 84:24.
	18	if they harden their hearts A. them
6	34	let earth and hell combine A. you
10	20	stirreth them up to iniquity A. that
	24	stirreth up their hearts to anger A.
	31	evil designs in lying A. those words
	32	stir them up to anger A. you
	68	the same is not of me but is A. me
	69	gates of hell shall not prevail A.—17:8; 18:5; 21:6; 33:13; 98:22; 128:10.
18	20	contend A. no church save it be the
19	30	reviling not A. revilers
24	13	A. poisonous serpents and A. deadly
	15	casting off the dust of your feet A. —60:15
29	8	A. the day when tribulation and

| Against | 12 | Agency |

Sec.	Vs.		Sec.	Vs.	
	19	that they shall not utter A. me		24	inasmuch as mine enemies come A. you; after these testimonies brought A. them
	36	he rebelled A. me saying, Give me			
31	8	prepare them A. the time when they	109	27	if any people shall rise A. this people; that thine anger be kindled A. them.—121:5
	9	revile not A. those that revile			
32	3	and nothing shall prevail A. them			
37	3	assemble together A. the time		29	lying reports A. thy servant
42	80	every word shall be established A.		30	lyings and slanders A. thy people
	81	church shall lift up their hands A.		46	prepared A. the day of burning
45	33	men will harden their hearts A. me; take up the sword A. another	112	13	and stiffen not their necks A. me
				15	rebel not A. my servant Joseph
	68	not take his sword A. his neighbor		26	and have blasphemed A. me in the
	70	let us not go up to battle A. Zion	121	10	thy friends do not contend A. thee
50	32	you shall proclaim A. that spirit		16	that shall lift up the heel A. mine
59	21	A. none is his wrath kindled save		18	those who swear falsely A. my
60	15	testimony A. them in day of		23	that murder, and testify A. them
61	31	lift up their voices unto God A.— anger kindled A. their wickedness		38	left to himself to kick A. the pricks, and to fight A. God
			122	1	derision, and hell shall rage A. thee
63	28	to anger A. you and to the shedding		3	thy people shall never be turned A.
64	6	sought occasion A. him without cause		7	if billowing surge shall conspire A.
			127	1	getting up prosecutions A. me
	8	my disciples sought occasion A.	132	27	the blasphemy A. the Holy Ghost
71	8	bring forth their strong reasons A.		39	none of these things did he sin A. me
	9	no weapon that is formed A. you shall.—109:25		56	wherein she has trespassed A. me
			134	8	bringing offenders A. good laws to
	10	if any man lift his voice A. you he	136	8	ears of the Lord A. this people
75	20	off your feet as a testimony A. them		36	which crieth from the ground A. them
76	25	who rebelled A. the Only Begotten			
	28	the devil—who rebelled A. God			
82	3	he who sins A. the greater light		**AGE**	
	21	the soul that sins A. this covenant. and hardeneth his heart A.	20	11	in this A. and generation as well
			63	50	appointed to him to die at the A.
84	76	for their rebellion A. you at the	83	4	maintenance until they are of A.
85	3	prepare them A. the day of vengeance	101	30	life shall be as the A. of a tree
				55	young men and they that are of middle A.
87	3	Southern States shall be divided A.; defend themselves A. other nations	107	42	was ordained by Adam at the A. of
				43	distinguished from him only by his A.
	4	slaves shall rise up A. their			
88	113	come up to battle A. Michael and		44	Enos was ordained at the A. of
95	3	ye have sinned A. me a very grievous		45	in the fortieth year of his A.
				56	he was bowed down with A. being
97	24	kindled A. their abominations and	122	6	although but six years of A.
98	23	bear it patiently and revile not A.	135	6	from A. to A. shall their names go down.
	25	and you revile not A. your enemy			
	27	three testimonies shall stand A.		**AGED**	
	33	not go out unto battle A. any nation	90	20	let mine A. servant, Joseph Smith
	34	should proclaim war A. them		25	especially mine A. servant Joseph
	36	going out to battle A. that nation	124	19	also mine A. servant Joseph Smith
	39	as a testimony A. thine enemy		**AGES**	
	40	wherewith he has trespassed A. thee. —98:44	76	7	from days of old and for A. to come
			107	8	the church in all A. of the world
	41	if he trespass A. thee and repent.—98:42, 43	128	9	nevertheless in all A. of the world
	48	as a testimony before the Lord A.		**AGENCY**	
99	4	by the way for a testimony A. them	29	36	away from me because of their A.
	5	deeds which they have committed A.	64	18	to his A. in the land of Zion.
101	58	inasmuch as they gather together A.	93	31	behold, here is the A. of man
	98	grievous sin A. me and A. my people	101	78	according to the moral A. which I
103	6	begin to prevail A. mine enemies			
	8	the world shall prevail A. them			

Sec.	Vs.	
		AGENT
29	35	he should be an A. unto himself
51	8	let there be an A. appointed unto: 58:49
	12	done through the bishop or the A.
53	4	to be an A. unto this church—57:6
57	15	let the bishop and the A. make
58	51	of himself or the A. as seemeth
	55	by the bishop or the A. of the
60	11	let him return it by way of the A.
63	45	let him be ordained an A. unto the
70	11	the A. who keepeth the Lord's
84	113	he should employ an A. to take
90	22	search diligently to obtain an A.
104	41	him and his A. and his seed after
		AGENTS
29	39	could not be A. unto themselves
58	28	wherein they are A. unto themselves
64	29	as ye are A. and ye are on the
104	17	men to be A. unto themselves.
127	1	I have left my affairs with A.
128	8	or by means of their own A.
		AGHAST
123	10	and to stand A. and pale, and the
		AGREE
10	18	therefore, they *will* not A. and we
41	2	together to A. upon my word
51	11	church again according as they shall A.
61	12	needful with him, as you shall A.
		AGREEABLE
20	1	established A. to the laws of our
	69	that there may be works and faith A.
42	32	the church A. to my commandments
85	3	consecration A. to this law.
92	1	organized A. to commandment
107	12	A. to the covenants and commandments.—107:20
	33	A. to the institution of heaven
	58	A. to the revelation which says:
	77	A. to the commandment which says:
		AGREED
27	18	be A. as touching all things
29	33	ye have asked it of me and are A.
42	3	are A. as touching this one thing
50	1	are A. as touching the church
104	53	as shall be A. by this order
107	27	every member must be A. to its
124	121	as shall be A. among themselves
		AGREEING
128	7	the principles A. precisely with
		AHASHDAH
78	9	let my servant A. (N. K. Whitney)—96:2; 104:39

Sec.	Vs.	
82	11	expedient for my servants, Alam and A.
104	40	all this I have appointed unto A.—41
		AHMAN
78	20	saith your Redeemer, even the Son A.
95	17	school of mine apostles, saith Son A.
		AIR
		See Fowls
		ALAM
82	11	expedient for my servants, A. and
		ALBANY
84	114	let the bishop go to city of A. and
		ALERT
127	11	for the enemy is on the A.
		ALIKE
51	9	be A. among this people and receive A.
		ALIVE
88	96	who are A. shall be quickened
		ALL
1	11	that A. that will hear may hear
	18	and A. this that it might be fulfilled
	37	which are in them shall A. be
	38	but shall A. be fulfilled.
3	8	against A. the fiery darts of the
4	2	serve him with A. your heart, might
8	11	knowledge from A. those ancient
10	46	A. the remainder of this work does contain A. those parts of my gospel
	48	A. that had become Lamanites.
	49	this is not A.—their faith in their
	51	that it might be free unto A.
	56	and A. those that do wickedly
11	19	cleave unto me with A. your heart
	20	keep my commandments with A. your
	22	until you have obtained A. which I
	27	I speak unto A. who have good desires.—12:7
15	2	mine arm is over A. the earth—16:2
18	15	if you should labor A. your days in
19	3	retaining A. power even to the
	16	I have suffered these things for A.
	18	even God, the greatest of A., to
	30	do it with A. humility, trusting
	34	impart A. save the support of thy
	37	and speak freely to A.
20	4	to whom be A. glory, both now and
	6	white above A. other whiteness
	26	A. those from the beginning even as
	31	A. those who serve God with A. their

Sec.	Vs.		Sec.	Vs.	
	37	A. those who humble themselves have truly repented of A. their sins	41	1	with the greatest of A. blessings; with the heaviest of A. cursings
	44	and to take lead of A. meetings		9	spend A. his time in the labors
	47	and attend to A. family duties—51	42	15	A. this ye shall observe to do
	52	in A. these duties the priest is		22	love thy wife with- A. thy heart
	55	see that A. members do their duty		25	and repents with A. his heart
	57	assisted always in A. his duties		29	keep A. my commandments—43:35; 46:9; 136:2
	59	invite A. to come to Christ		40	let A. thy garments be plain
	72	baptism—unto A. those who repent		43	nourished with A. tenderness
	77	bread to the souls of A. those who		72	just remuneration for A. their.—42:73
	79	wine to the souls of A. those who		74	testify before you in A. lowliness
	82	a regular list of A. the names		76	be careful, with A. inquiry
	84	A. members removing from the church		77	they shall repent of A. their sins
21	4	shalt give heed unto A. his words walking in A. holiness before me	43	9	to act in A. holiness before me
	5	own mouth, in A. patience and faith		21	speaking to the ears of A. that live
	9	I will bless A. those who labor		22	utter forth their voices unto A., make the ears of A. tingle
22	1	A. old covenants have I caused to		25	the voice of mercy A. the day long
23	6	pray, among your friends and in A.	45	12	a day sought for by A. holy men
24	5	expounding A. scriptures unto the— 24:9; 68:1; 97:5.		23	shall not pass away until A. shall
	7	shalt devote A. thy service in Zion		44	glory, with A. the holy angels
	12	at A. times and in A. places he		49	A. the ends of the earth shall hear
	19	A. those whom thou hast ordained	46	2	conduct A. meetings as directed by
25	1	A. those who receive my gospel		7	should do in A. holiness of heart
	16	this is my voice unto A. Amen.		9	that A. may be benefited that
27	6	spoken by the mouth of A. the— 86:10.		11	A. have not every gift given unto
	11	Adam, the father of A., the prince of A.		12	that A. may be profited thereby
	14	A. those whom my father hath given		18	that A. may be taught to be wise
	15	having done A. ye may be able to stand	48	4	save A. the money that ye can; obtain A. that ye can in righteousness
	17	to quench A. the fiery darts of	49	2	know the truth in part but not A.
28	4	to speak, or teach, or at A. times		8	for A. are under sin
	16	must open thy mouth at A. times		16	and A. this that the earth might
29	9	A. the proud and they that do		23	A. this when the angel shall sound
	11	from heaven with A. the hosts		26	repent of A. your sins.
	13	and A. the earth shall quake	50	26	he is least and the servant of A.
	21	the whore of A. the earth shall be		28	be purified and cleansed from A. sin—29
	24	and A. the fulness thereof	52	21	this commandment is given unto A. elders
	26	shall A. the dead awake, even A.		33	let A. these take their journey—75:18
	30	A. my judgments are not given to men	54	3	let them repent of A. their sins
30	6	be afflicted in A. his afflictions	56	4	A. this to be answered upon the heads
	11	labor in Zion with A. your soul	57	6	buy lands in A. the regions round
31	5	thrust in your sickle with A. your —33:7	58	47	bear testimony in A. places
33	4	priestcrafts, A. having corrupt		54	workmen sent forth to A. kinds
35	8	unto A. those who believe on my		60	chastened for A. his sins
	24	keep A. the commandments and covenants—42:78	59	2	shall rest from A. their labors—124:86
38	1	A. the seraphic hosts of heaven		5	with A. thy heart, with A. thy
	10	ye are clean but not A.		11	on A. days and at A. times
	11	presence of A. the hosts	60	9	A. this for the good of the churches
	12	and A. eternity is pained.	61	1	the voice of him who has A. power
	19	if you seek it with A. your hearts		8	until you are chastened for A. your
39	1	who is from A. eternity to A.		18	what I say unto one I say unto A. 61:36; 82:5; 92:1; 93:49

Sec.	Vs.		Sec.	Vs.	
	26	you shall give unto A. your brethren		87	to reprove the world of A. their 84:117
	27	by the spirit to know A. his ways		98	until A. shall know me who remain
63	17	the unbelieving and A. liars		104	A. those who have not families
	40	let A. the moneys that can be spared		106	he may be edified in A. meekness
	43	let him impart A. the money which		110	that A. may be edified together
	59	I am over A., and in A., and through A.	85	1	of A. those who consecrate properties
64	24	tomorrow A. the proud and they that—133:64	88	9	A. who are not found written in the
66	3	William, you are clean but not A.		5	even of God, the holiest of A.
	10	forsake A. unrighteousness.		18	sanctified from A. unrighteousness
68	2	this is an ensample unto A. those		36	A. kingdoms have a law given.
	7	unto A. the faithful elders of my		39	A. beings who abide not in those
	19	to officiate in A. lesser offices		43	comprehend the earth and A. the planets
	30	to labor in A. faithfulness		44	A. these are one year with God
69	3	making a history of A. important		47	A. these are kingdoms and any man
72	23	ensample for A. the extensive		56	tarried with him A. that hour
74	2	circumcision was had among A. Jews		58	thus they A. received the light of
75	26	A. such as can obtain places for		60	that they A. might be glorified
76	7	reveal A. mysteries, A. the hidden		61	will I liken A. these kingdoms
	22	this is the testimony, last of A.		98	A. this by the sounding of the trump
	31	concerning A. those who know my power		108	in the ears of A. living and reveal
	39	A. the rest shall be brought forth		118	as A. have not faith seek ye diligently—109:7
	41	cleanse it from A. unrighteousness		120	that A. your salutations may be in
	42	through him A. might be saved		121	cease A. your light speeches, A. laughter, A. lustful desires, A. pride and A. your wicked doings
	43	saves A. the works of his hands		122	let not A. be spokesmen at once; let A. listen unto his sayings; when A. have spoken that A. may be edified of A.
	44	wherefore, he saves A. except them			
	52	washed and cleansed from A. their			
	53	which the Father sheds forth upon A.			
	66	heavenly place, holiest of A.		127	for A. the officers of the church
	68	God and Christ are the judge of A.		133	walk in A. the commandments
	70	the glory of God, the highest of A.		137	give utterance in A. your doings
	89	which surpasses A. understanding—76:114	89	2	temporal salvation of A. saints
	102	last of A., these A. are they who		3	weak and the weakest of A. saints
	110	these A. all shall bow the knee and every		8	herb for bruises and A. sick
77	11	out of A. the tribes of Israel		10	A. wholesome herbs God hath ordained
78	14	independent above A. other creatures		11	A. these to be used with thanksgiving
82	2	A. of you have sinned, but beware		14	A. grain is ordained for the use; A. wild animals that run
	6	A. have gone out of the way		16	A. grain is good for the food
	18	A. this for the benefit of the church		17	and for A. the beasts of the field; barley for A. useful animals
83	4	A. children have claim upon their		18	A. saints who remember to keep and
84	5	this generation shall not A. pass	90	5	A. they who receive the oracles
	28	in whose hand is given A. power		15	acquainted with A. good books
	35	A. who receive this priesthood—84:40		16	mission in A. your lives; set in order A. the affairs of
	38	A. that my Father hath shall be given		17	be admonished in A. your highmindedness
	42	A. who come not unto this priesthood	92	2	faithful in keeping A. former
	56	upon the children of Zion, even A.	93	17	he received A. power both in heaven
	75	and the gospel is unto A.		22	A. those who are begotten through me
	76	A. those to whom the kingdom has			
	82	in A. their glory are not arrayed			
	86	this commandment is unto A. the			

Sec.	Vs.		Sec.	Vs.	
	26	a fullness of truth, yea even of A.		62	A. the sacred things shall be; it shall belong to you A. with one
	30	A. truth is independent, as is A.		68	A. moneys that you receive in
	53	A. this for the salvation of Zion		78	you should pay A. your debts
97	2	mercy unto A. the meek and upon A.	105	3	full of A. manner of evil
				7	are not A. under this condemnation
	8	A. among them who know their hearts		28	purchasing of A. the lands in
			107	5	A. other authorities or offices
	13	place of thanksgiving for A. saints; place of instruction for A. those; in A. their several callings and		8	power over A. the offices in the church in A. ages of the
				9	right to officiate in A. the offices—107:12
	16	A. the pure in heart that shall		17	to officiate in A. the lesser
	21	while A. the wicked shall mourn		18	keys of A. the spiritual blessings
	24	their abominations and A. their		30	to be made in A. righteousness
	26	visit her according to A. her works		33	regulate A. the affairs of the same —107:34
98	5	belongs to A. mankind and is		36	equal in authority in A. their decisions—107:37
	11	forsake A. evil and cleave unto A.			
	20	forsake A. their detestable things		39	in A. large branches of the church
	22	I will turn away A. wrath and		53	who were A. high priests
	32	A. mine ancient prophets and		57	these things were A. written in the
	45	forgive him with A. thine heart		58	set in order A. the other officers
	46	children of A. them that hate me		64	High Priesthood, the greatest of A.
	47	turn to the Lord with A. their hearts, with A. their might, mind and; restore four-fold for A. their		99	act in the office in A. diligence
			108	7	strengthen your brethren in A. your conversations, A. your prayers, A. your exhortations, A. your doings
99	5	to convince A. of their ungodly			
100	1	for in me there is A. power	109	1	before thee, with A. their hearts
	11	be mighty in expounding A. scriptures		9	that A. your salutations may be in —109:19
	17	A. that call on the name of the Lord—101:22		14	that A. those who shall worship
				17	that A. the incomings of thy people
101	5	A. those who will not endure chastening		18	that A. the outgoings of thy people
				29	A. those who have spread lying reports
	12	A. who are found upon the watchtower; A. mine Israel shall be saved			
				30	that A. their works may be brought
	14	A. they who have mourned shall		38	for A. those judgments thou art
	15	A. they who have given their lives		56	may obtain favor in the sight of A.
	24	that dwell upon A. the face of the		57	that A. the ends of the earth may
	25	glory may dwell upon A. the earth		58	that from among A. these thy servants
	35	A. they who suffer persecution; shall partake of A. his glory			
				67	may A. the scattered remnants of
	41	children of Zion, even many but not A.		68	A. his afflictions and persecutions
				70	A. their immediate connections—109:71, 72
	55	take A. the strength of mine house; among A. my servants who are of the			
				71	remember A. the presidents of thy church with A. their families
	70	purchase A. the lands by money			
	71	A. the land which can be purchased		72	remember A. thy church, A. their families, A. their sick with A. the poor
	72	gather together A. their moneys			
102	4	to which they A. answered that			
103	7	hearkening to observe A. the words		76	reap eternal joy for A. our sufferings
	8	hearken not to observe A. my words	112	3	A. thy sins are forgiven thee
	36	A. victory and glory is brought		11	and unto A. who love my name
104	1	concerning A. the properties which		12	be admonished for A. their sins
	7	A. this that the innocent among you		14	I say unto A. the Twelve, arise
	34	A., save the ground which has been		17	door of the kingdom in A. places
	40	A. this I have appointed unto my		24	shall come upon A. the face of the
	55	A. these properties are mine or else			

Sec.	Vs.		Sec.	Vs.	
	31	hold in connection with A. those		48	and by A. your abominations
	32	last of A. being sent down from		49	go with A. their might and with A.
114	1	settle up A. his business		53	your consolation concerning A. those
115	5	I say unto you A., arise and shine		54	will save A. those of your brethren
117	4	let them repent of A. their sins and A. their covetous desires		76	I will forgive A. his sins—124:78
	6	destinies of A. the armies of the		106	in A. his journeyings let him lift
	11	A. their secret abominations and of A. his littleness of		116	let him repent of A. his folly and lay aside A. his hard speeches
	16	let A. my servants in the land of		121	wages for A. their labors which
118	3	do this in A. lowliness of heart		144	you should fill A. these offices
119	1	I require A. their surplus property		145	prepare room for A. these offices
	4	one tenth of A. their interest	125	4	let A. those who come from the east; and in A. the stakes which I have
	5	A. those who gather unto the land			
	7	ensample unto A. the stakes of Zion	127	1	are A. founded in falsehood of the; I would say to A. those with whom; who will transact A. business in a; see that A. my debts are cancelled
121	8	shalt triumph over A. thy foes			
	16	cursed are A. those that shall lift			
	23	wo unto A. those that discomfort my			
	24	mine eyes know A. their works; swift judgment for them A.		2	my common lot A. the days of my life; it A. has become a second nature to; delivered me out of them A.
	29	A. thrones and dominions and A. who have endured valiantly for			
	31	A. the times of their revolutions; A. the appointed days, months and; A. the days of their days. months; A. their glories, laws and set		3	let A. the saints rejoice, therefore; upon the heads of A. their oppressors
				4	A. the works which I have appointed; for A. this there is a reward in heaven
	32	Eternal God of A. other Gods			
122	6	accused with A. manner of false		7	that in A. your recordings it may —128:7
	7	A. the elements combine to hedge up; above A.. if the very jaws of hell			
				9	let A. the records be had in order
	8	hath descended below them A.		10	I will say to A. the saints that
123	1	the propriety of A. the Saints; gathering up a knowledge of A.		12	that you A. may be saved
			128	3	at A. times and do A. the business
	2	also of A. the property and amount		4	and A. the attending witnesses
	3	also the names of A. persons who		9	in A. ages of the world, whenever
	5	A. that are in the magazines; A. the libelous histories that are		17	this most glorious of A. subjects
				21	through A. the travels and tribulations; A. declaring their dispensation
	6	in A. their dark and hellish hue			
	7	very mainspring of A. corruption		23	and A. ye valleys cry aloud; A. ye seas and dry lands tell the; A. the trees of the field praise the; A. the sons of God shout for joy
	11	A. the rising generations and A. the pure			
	12	among A. sects, parties and denominations			
			130	9	A. kingdoms of a lower order
	13	bringing to light A. hidden things		20	upon which A. blessings are predicated
124	3	made to A. the kings of the world			
	7	A. their glory as the flower	131	7	A. spirit is matter, but it is more
	23	worthy of A. acceptance—128:24		8	we shall see that it is A. matter
	25	let A. my saints come from afar	132	3	A. those who have this law revealed
	26	come with A. your gold and your; and with A. your antiquities; A. who have knowledge of antiquities; together with A. the precious trees		5	A. who will have a blessing at my
				7	A. covenants, contracts, bonds; for time and A. eternity; A. contracts that are not made—132: 18, 19
	27	with A. your precious things of the			
	31	command you, A. ye my saints			
	39	endowment of A. her municipals		17	their saved conditions to A. eternity
	44	if ye labor with A. your might		19	dominions. A. heights and depths

Sec.	Vs.	
	20	then shall they be above A.; Gods, because they have A. power
	26	and A. manner of blasphemies
	49	end of the world, and through A.
	50	I will forgive A. your sins
	51	to prove you A. as I did Abraham
	52	let Emma Smith receive A. those
	64	magnify my name upon A. those who
133	2	upon A. the ungodly among you
	3	A. the ends of the earth shall see
	4	A. you that have not been commanded
	51	and stained A. my raiment
	52	A. that he has bestowed upon them
	53	in A. their afflictions he was; and carried them A. the days of old
134	3	we believe that A. governments
	5	A. governments have a right to enact
	7	laws for the protection of A. citizens
	8	the general peace, in A. respects
	10	A. religious societies have a right
	11	redress of A. wrongs and grievances; and encroachment of A. persons
135	7	blood of A. the martyrs under the
136.	4	in A. the ordinances of the Lord
	5	with A. the teams, wagons and
	10	every man use A. his influence
	11	if ye do this in A. faithfulness
	20	keep A. your pledges one with another
	37	if ye are faithful in keeping A.
	42	be diligent in keeping A. my

See Cases, Churches, Enemies, Flesh, Generations, Gifts, Hosts, Men, Nations, People, Things, World

ALLOW
107	98	as their circumstances shall A.

ALLOWANCE
1	31	sin with the least degree of A.

ALLOWING
134	12	every government A. human beings

ALMIGHTY
19	14	it is by my A. power that you have
	20	lest I humble you with my A. power
20	21	the A. God gave his only Begotten
	24	to reign with A. power according
76	106	suffer the wrath of A. God, until
	107	fierceness of the wrath of A. God—88:106
84	96	I, the A., have laid my hands upon
	118	for with you, saith the Lord A., I
87	6	chastening hand of an A. God, until
109	77	O Lord God A., hear us in these our
121	4	O Lord God A., maker of the heavens
	33	hinder the A. from pouring down

ALMOST
121	39	nature and disposition of A. all men

ALMS
88	2	the A. of your prayers have come up
112	1	thine A. have come up as a memorial

ALONE
15	3	no man knoweth save me and thee A.—16:3
28	11	between him and thee A. and tell —42:88
76	107	and have trodden the wine-press A.—88:106; 133:50
82	23	leave judgment A. with me, for it is
84	92	go away from him A. by yourselves
109	4	in whose name A. salvation can be
124	102	my servant Hyrum, and for them A.

ALONG
10	26	flattereth and leadeth them A. until
78	18	good cheer, for I will lead you A.

ALOUD
109	80	thy saints shout A. for joy
124	101	let my servant William cry A. and
128	23	and all ye valleys cry A.

ALPHA AND OMEGA
19	1	I am A., Christ the Lord—63:60; 112:34; 132:66
35	1	A., the beginning and the end—38:1; 45:7; 54:1; 61:1; 84:120
68	35	I am A. and I come quickly
75	1	I am A. your Lord and your God
81	7	these are the words of A., even Jesus

ALPHUS
95	17	saith Son Ahman, or A., or Omegus

ALREADY
4	4	the field is white A. to harvest—6:3; 11:3; 12:3; 14:3; 31:4; 33:3, 7
19	27	look not for a Messiah who has A. come
35	16	for even now A. the summer is nigh
101	75	even now A. in store a sufficient

ALTAR
135	7	martyrs under the A. that John saw

ALTER
10	10	to A. the words which you have

ALTERED
10	11	because they have A. the words they

Sec.	Vs.	
	17	have the same with us and we have A.
	29	they have A. the words because Satan
	42	confound those who have A. my words
102	21	the decision shall be A. accordingly

ALTHOUGH

Sec.	Vs.	
3	4	A. a man may have many revelations
	7	A. men set at naught the counsels of
22	2	A. a man should be baptized an
100	13	A. she is chastened for a little
122	4	A. their influence shall cast thee
	6	elder son, A. but six years of age

ALTOGETHER

Sec.	Vs.	
19	7	children of men, A. for my name's
62	5	bear record, even A., or two by two
84	41	and A. turneth therefrom, shall not
88	35	and A. abideth in sin, cannot be
103	4	they did not hearken A. unto the

ALWAYS

Sec.	Vs.	
1	33	my Spirit shall not A. strive with
10	5	pray A. that you may come off
	37	you cannot A. judge the righteous; you cannot A. tell the wicked from the
19	38	pray A. and I will pour out my
20	33	pray A. lest they fall into temptation—31:12; 61:39
	53	to watch over the church A.
	57	to be assisted A. in all his duties
	77	and A. remember him that they may A. have his spirit—20:79
32	4	pray A. that I may unfold them to
33	17	be faithful, praying A., having
46	2	it A. has been given to the elders of
	8	A. remembering for what they are given
	10	I would that ye should A. remember and A. retain in your minds
62	9	I am with the faithful A.
75	11	praying A. that they faint not—88:126
81	2	which belongeth A. unto the presidency
	3	in prayer A., vocally and in thy heart
90	24	pray A. and be believing
93	49	pray A. lest that wicked one have
	50	pray A. or they shall be removed
101	38	seek the face of the Lord A.
	81	men ought A. to pray and not faint
103	31	but men do not A. do my will
124	39	which my people are A. commanded to
128	9	this power has A. been given

Sec.	Vs.	
		AMBASSADOR
135	7	is an A. for the religion of Jesus
		AMBER
110	2	work of pure gold in color like A.
		AMBITION
121	37	gratify our pride, our vain A., or
		AMEN
88	135	or by saying A. in token of the same
121	37	A. to the priesthood of that man
		AMENABLE
134	4	men are A. to Him and to Him only
		AMISS
80	3	it mattereth not for ye cannot go A.
		AMONG
1	14	shall be cut off from A. the people —133:63
4	1	is about to come forth A. the children—11:1; 12:1
5	14	same testimony A. this generation
	19	scourge shall go forth A. the
7	5	a greater work yet A. men than what
10	53	establish my church A. them
11	22	hath gone forth A. the children of
18	44	work a marvelous work A. the
19	29	declare glad tidings A. every people
21	1	shall be a record kept A. you
23	6	pray in your family and A. your friends
24	12	strength such as is not known A. men
27	4	except it is made new A. you
28	8	cause my church to be established A.
	14	take thy journey A. the Lamanites
29	15	weeping and wailing A. the hosts of
30	6	build up my church A. the Lamanites
32	2	into the wilderness A. the Lamanites
35	7	even A. the Gentiles, for their folly
36	5	everlasting gospel A. the nations
38	11	prevail upon the earth A. the
	26	what man A. you having twelve sons
	33	shall go forth A. all nations
	34	certain men A. them shall be appointed
	42	go ye out from A. the wicked
39	15	blessing such as is not known A. men
41	5	shall be cast out from A. you—42:75
42	39	those who embrace my gospel A. the
	43	whosoever A. you are sick, and have
	74	whatever persons A. you, having; shall not cast them out from A. you

Sec.	Vs.		Sec.	Vs.	
	76	receive none such A., you if they are		134	he shall not have place A. you
	79	if any persons A. you shall kill		138	not receive any A. you into this school
43	11	purge out iniquity which is A. you	89	5	drinketh wine or strong drink A. you
	19	lest ye be found A. the wicked	93	4	and dwelt A. the sons of men
45	19	scattered A. all nations—45:24		11	dwelt in the flesh and dwelt A. us
	28	a light shall break forth A. them	95	5	many who have been ordained A. you
	32	A. the wicked men shall lift up	96	2	the place which is named A. you
	68	A. the wicked, every man that will		3	determined in council A. you
	70	it shall be said A. the wicked		9	that are upon the house named A. you
	71	gathered out from A. all nations	97	8	all A. them who know their hearts are
46	27	be any A. you professing and yet be			
49	11	that ye go A. this people and say	101	6	lustful and covetous desires A. them
50	7	there are hypocrites A. you, who		47	they began to say A. themselves—101:48
	16	he that is weak A. you shall be		55	also A. all my servants, who are
	25	that you may chase darkness from A.		90	their portion A. hypocrites and
	37	go forth A. the churches and strengthen	104	7	that the innocent A. you may not be; that the guilty A. you may not escape
51	9	and be alike A. this people		10	if any man A. you, of the order
60	4	I rule A. the armies of the earth		61	appoint one A. you to keep the
	8	A. the congregations of the wicked—60:13, 14; 61:32, 33; 62:5		62	no man A. you shall call it his own
61	6	he that is faithful A. you shall not		69	if any man A. you obtain five talents
62	6	that the faithful A. you should be		70	let not any man A. you say that it is
	7	if any A. you desire to ride		72	any man A. you say unto the treasurer
63	8	there are those A. you who seek signs	105	3	to the poor and afflicted A. them
	12	those A. you who have sought after	107	21	from A. those who are ordained
	14	there were A. you adulterers and		72	will choose A. the elders of the church
	19	because these things are A. you		74	common judge A. the inhabitants
	54	there will be foolish virgins A. the	98		responsibility to travel A. all
64	3	those A. you who have sinned—82:2	109	58	that from A. these, thy servants
65	4	his wonderful works A. the people	112	1	send it abroad A. all nations
67	6	even the least that is A. them; appoint him that is most wise A. you		6	publishing my name A. the children
				7	thy path lieth A. the mountains and A. many nations
	7	if there be any A. you that shall		16	abroad A. all nations
68	16	if they are the firstborn A. the sons		26	first A. those A. you, saith the Lord
	31	for there are idlers A. them	113	10	scattered condition A. the Gentiles
	32	must be done away from A. them	114	2	there are those A. you who deny my name
74	2	circumcision was had A. all the Jews	119	5	not be found worthy to abide A. you
	3	there arose a great contention A.	122	5	if thou art in perils A. false; if thou art in perils A. robbers
	5	law of Moses should be done away A.	123	12	A. all sects, parties and denominations
	6	for it was had A. the Jews	124	8	of the oppressor A. hypocrites
81	3	proclaiming the gospel A. thy brethren		79	Isaac Galland he appointed A. you
84	27	A. the children of Israel until John		121	as shall be agreed A. themselves
	86	therefore, let no man A. you	130	2	same sociality which exists A. us here will exist A. us there
	106	if any man A. you be strong in the			
	112	travel A. all the churches, searching	132	34	fulfilling, A. other things, the promises
85	9	shall be appointed them A. unbelievers			
	11	shall not find an inheritance A. the	133	2	upon all the ungodly A. you
86	7	gather out the wheat from A. the tares			
88	84	go forth A. the Gentiles for the last			
	102	there are found A. those who remain			
	122	appoint A. yourselves a teacher			

Sec.	Vs.		Sec.	Vs.	
	7	gather ye out from A. the nations		106	another A. shall sound his trump which is the seventh A.
	10	let the cry go forth A. all people		108	shall the first A. sound his trump
	12	let them who are A. the Gentiles flee		109	shall the second A. sound his trump
	14	go ye out from A. the nations		110	until the seventh A. shall sound
	21	his voice shall be heard A. all		112	Michael, the seventh A., even the
	36	these things might be known A. you	89	21	the destroying A. shall pass by
	66	no man A. you received me	103	19	mine A. shall go before you, but
134	8	their tendency to evil A. men	128	20	Moroni, an A. from heaven. declaring; devil as he appeared as A. of light
135	6	be classed A. the martyrs of religion	129	5	if he be an A. he will do so
	7	hearts of honest men A. all nations		8	if it be the Devil as an A. of light
		AMOUNT	133	17	A. crying through the midst of
123	2	and A. of damages that they have		36	A. flying through the midst of
124	68	in proportion to the A. of stock		53	the A. of his presence saved them
		AMPLY			**ANGELS**
42	33	who has need may be A. supplied	13	1	keys of the ministering of A. 84:26; 107:20
		ANARCHY	20	10	confirmed by the ministering of A.
134	6	harmony would be supplanted by A.		35	come by the ministering of A.
		ANCIENT	27	16	I have sent mine A. to commit unto
8	1	engravings of old records which are A.	29	28	prepared for he devil and his A.
	11	receive knowledge of all those A.		37	thus came the devil and his A.
27	11	the prince of all, the A. of days		42	God should send forth A. to declare
58	17	like as it was in A. days to divide	38	12	A. are waiting to reap down the earth
84	108	way that mine apostles in A. days	42	6	declaring my word like unto A.
98	32	all mine A. prophets and apostles	43	25	called upon you by the ministering of A.
107	4	they, the church, in A. days, called	45	44	great glory, with all the holy A.
111	9	A. inhabitants and founders of this	49	7	no man knoweth, neither the A. in
116	1	where the A. of days shall sit	62	3	recorded for the A. to look upon
135	3	most of the Lord's anointed in A.	63	54	will I send mine A. to pluck out
		ANCIENTLY	67	13	neither the ministering of A.
107	29	a quorum of three presidents were A.	76	21	saw the holy A. and they who are
		ANCIENTS		33	with the devil and his A. in eternity—76:44
98	33	law that I gave unto mine A.		36	brimstone, with the devil and his A.
		ANGEL		67	an innumerable company of A., to
7	6	as flaming fire and a ministering A.		88	receive it of the administering of A.
20	6	ministered unto him by an holy A.	77	8	are we to understand by the four A. they are four A. sent forth from God
45	45	an A. shall sound his trump—88:94, 99		9	he crieth unto the four A. having
49	23	when the A. shall sound his trumpet		11	by the A. to whom is given power
76	25	an A. of God who was in authority		12	sounding of the trumpets of the seven A.
77	9	what are we to understand by the A. ascending from the east	84	42	mine A. charge concerning you
84	28	ordained by the A. of God at the time		88	A. round about you to bear you up
88	98	sounding of the trump of the A. of God	86	5	A. are crying unto the Lord, day and
	103	fifth A. who committeth the gospel	88	2	and the A. rejoice over you.—90:34
	105	another A. shall sound his trump which is the sixth A.		92	A. shall fly through the midst of
				107	then shall the A. be crowned with
			103	20	mine A. shall go before you
			109	22	and thine A. have charge over them
			121	27	by the A., as held in reserve

Sec.	Vs.		Sec.	Vs.	
123	7	duty that we owe to God, to A.			**ANNOUNCE**
128	21	divers A., from Michael or Adam	135	1	we A. the martyrdom of Joseph Smith
129	1	A. who are resurrected personages			**ANNUALLY**
130	5	are no A. who minister to this earth	119	4	one-tenth of all their interest A.
	6	A. do not reside on a planet like			**ANNULLED**
132	16	but are appointed A. in heaven; A. are ministering servants, to	128	9	and could not be A. according to
					ANOINTED
	17	these A. did not abide my law; not Gods, but are A. of God forever	68	20	designated and found worthy and A.
	18	A. and the Gods are appointed there	109	53	when thou lookest upon the face of thine A.
	19	they shall pass by the A. and the		80	let these thine A. ones be clothed
	20	and the A. are subject unto them	121	16	that lift up the heel against mine A.
	37	and are not A. but are Gods	124	76	I have chosen him and A. him
136	37	whom I did call upon by mine A.		91	be appointed, ordained and A. as a
		ANGEL'S	132	7	spirit of promise, of him who is A. through the medium of mine A.—132:19
130	4	is not the reckoning of A. time			
		ANGER		18	through him whom I have A. and
1	13	the A. of the Lord is kindled	135	3	like most of the Lord's A. in ancient
5	8	mine A. is kindled against them—60:2; 84:24			**ANOINTING**
10	24	stirreth up their hearts to A.—10:32	68	21	they may claim their A. if at any
19	15	lest I smite you by mine A. and	109	35	let the A. of thy ministers be
56	1	mine A. is kindled against the rebellious	124	57	for this A. have I put upon his head
61	5	have decreed in mine A. many destructions	132	41	appointed unto her by the holy A.
					ANOINTINGS
	20	but today mine A. is turned away	124	39	your A., your washings and your
	31	A. is kindled against their wickedness—63:2			**ANOTHER**
63	27	that they may not be stirred up to A.	8	6	you have A. gift, which is the gift
	28	putteth it into their hearts to A.	10	28	because he supposeth that A. lieth
82	6	the A. kindleth against the inhabitants	18	35	you can read them one to A.
			28	7	until I shall appoint unto them A.
101	90	in his fierce A., in his time	35	18	A. will I plant in his stead
109	27	that thine A. be kindled against.—121:5	38	23	teach one A. according to the office
	30	thou wilt send upon them in thine A.	42	10	A. shall be appointed in his stead—104:77
	52	may thine A. be kindled and thine	43	4	except to appoint A. in his stead
133	51	I did tread upon him in mine A.	45	20	not be left one stone upon A.
		ANGRY		33	take up the sword one against A., and they will kill one A.
61	20	I was A. with you yesterday		69	shall not be at war one with A.
63	11	with whom God is A. he is not well	46	12	and to some is given A., that all
	32	I, the Lord, am A. with the wicked		18	to A. is given the word of knowledge
64	15	I was A. with him who is my servant		25	to A. the interpretation of tongues
87	5	and shall become exceeding A.	47	3	I have appointed to A. office
88	87	the stars shall become exceeding A.	49	20	not possess that which is above A.
		ANGUISH	50	11	as a man reasoneth one with A.
124	52	wailing, and A. and gnashing of		22	understandeth one A. and both are
		ANIMALS	51	10	taken and given to A. church
89	14	all wild A. that run or creep on the		11	if A. church would receive money
	17	and barley for all useful A.	63	56	he shall make A. writing and if the

| Another | 23 | Any |

Sec.	Vs.	
64	8	sought occasion against one A. and forgave not one A.
	9	ye ought to forgive one A., for he
76	98	as star differs from A. star in glory, so differs one from A. in glory
	100	they are some of one and some of A.
82	1	inasmuch as ye have forgiven one A.
88	3	now I send upon you A. comforter
	21	must inherit A. kingdom, even a
	77	teach one A. the doctrine of the
	94	A. angel shall sound his trump —88:105, 106
	99	after this A. angel shall sound
	100	A. trump shall sound which is the —88:102, 103
	118	teach one A. words of wisdom— 109:7
	123	see that ye love one A.; impart one to A.
	124	cease to find fault one with A.
	136	for a salutation to one A. in the
90	4	through you shall the oracles be given to A.
	24	ye have covenanted one with A.
101	50	were at variance one with A.
	79	should be in bondage one to A.
	101	they shall build and A. shall not
104	67	there shall be A. treasury prepared
107	85	edifying one A. as it is given
110	13	A. great and glorious vision burst
124	130	A. may be appointed unto the same —124:132
128	6	and A. book was opened which was the—128:7
	13	that they may accord one with A.
	16	I will give you A. quotation of Paul
	25	continue the subject A. time
130	19	through his obedience than A., the
132	39	for I gave them unto A., saith the
	41	if she be with A. man, she hath— 132:42, 63
	43	if her husband be with A. woman
	61	virgin, and desire to espouse A.
133	6	speak often one to A.
134	9	and A. proscribed in its spiritual
136	20	keep all your pledges one with A.
	23	cease to contend one with A.; cease to speak evil one of A.
	24	let your words tend to edifying one A.

ANOTHER'S

| 52 | 33 | not build upon A. foundation, neither journey in A. track |

ANSWER

| 49 | 16 | earth might A. the end of its creation |
| 50 | 16 | ye shall A. this question yourselves |

Sec.	Vs.	
72	14	shall A. the debt unto the bishop in
101	7	A. them in the day of their trouble
109	77	A. us from Heaven, thy holy
	78	A. these petitions, and accept
112	10	give thee A. to thy prayers
124	2	in A. to them I say unto you,
	52	I *will* A. judgment, wrath and
128	4	shall A. the ordinance just the same
	5	it is only to A. the will of God
	12	to A. to the likeness of the dead
130	4	In A. to the question, "Is not the
	5	I A., yes. But there are no angels
132	2	*will* A. thee as touching this matter
133	65	this shall be the A. of the Lord
	67	there was none of you to A.

ANSWERED

25	12	it shall be A. with a blessing
41	12	they are to be A. upon your souls
56	4	to be A. upon the heads of the
102	4	they all A. that they accepted their
133	41	it shall be A. upon their heads
134	6	to be A. by man to his Maker

ANSWERETH

| 72 | 17 | and A. all things for an inheritance |

ANTHEMS

| 128 | 22 | let the dead speak forth A. of |

ANTIQUITIES

| 124 | 26 | precious stones and with all your A.; all who have knowledge of A. |

ANXIOUS

| 121 | 27 | have waited with A. expectation |

ANXIOUSLY

| 58 | 27 | men should be A. engaged in a good |

ANY

6	12	make not thy gift known unto A.
20	83	if A. have been expelled from the
28	12	appointed unto A. of this church
42	92	if A. shall offend in secret, he
43	5	receive not the teachings of A.
46	4	and if A. have trespassed
	5	shall not cast A. out of your
	6	if there be A. that are not of the
	27	lest there be A. among you professing
62	7	if A. among you desire to ride
63	16	if A. shall commit adultery in their
64	22	I will not hold A. guilty that shall go
	24	I will not spare A. that remain
67	7	if A. among you shall make one like it

Sec.	Vs.	
68	25	A. of her stakes which are organized—68:26
76	3	neither are there A. who can stay his
84	105	if A. man shall give unto A. of you a coat
85	4	found on A. of the records or history
88	47	A. man who hath seen A. or the least
	132	when A. shall come in after him, let
	138	shall not receive A. among you in
94	8	not suffer A. unclean thing to come —97:15
	9	A. unclean thing, my glory shall not
102	8	whenever A. vacancy shall occur by
	13	convenes to act upon A. case
	20	who have not spoken or A. one of them
	21	if A. additional light is shown
	33	whether A. such case is entitled to
104	62	no man shall call it his own or A. part
	64	not taken out of the treasury by A.
	70	let not A. say it is his own nor A. part of it
	71	shall not A. part of it be used
109	21	when thy people transgress A. of them
121	37	in A. degree of unrighteousness
124	24	not suffer A. pollution to come upon
	49	give commandment to A. of the sons
	68	shall not receive A. stock in that
	69	if A. pay stock into their hands, it
	70	receive A. stock into their hands
	71	if they do appropriate A. portion; I cannot be mocked in A. of these
127	6	when A. of you are baptized for your
128	3	if there be A. present who can at A.
129	9	know whether A. administration is of God
130	17	will not be A. sooner than that time
132	15	not bound by A. law when they are
134	10	not believe that A. religious society; or to inflict A. physical

See *Blessing, Branch, Call, Court, Crime, Decision, Elder, Eye, Further, Harm, Individuals, Man, Manner, Member, More, Nation, Office, One, Other, People, Persons, Portion, Power, Set, Sin, Time, Trespassed.*

ANYTHING

Sec.	Vs.	
28	12	neither shall A. be appointed unto
35	11	without faith shall not A. be shown
58	29	he that doeth not A. until he is
59	6	nor kill, nor do A. like unto it
88	65	if ye ask A. that is not expedient
115	12	shall not A. remain that is not finished
129	8	his hand, and you will not feel A.
132	59	if he do A. in my name and according

ANYWHERE

| 124 | 71 | appropriate any portion of that stock A.; stock which they appropriate A. else |

APART

42	31	appointed and set A. for that
68	14	other bishops to be set A. unto the
	19	provided he is called and set A.—107:17
	22	who shall be set A. for this ministry.—107:74
107	71	set A. unto ministering temporal

APOCRYPHA

| 91 | 1 | concerning the A. there are many |
| | 3 | not needful A. should be translated |

APOLLOS

| 76 | 99 | they who are of Paul, and of A. and |

APOSTATE

| 86 | 3 | the A., the whore, even Babylon |

APOSTATES

| 85 | 2 | all the A. who apostatize after |

APOSTATIZE

| 85 | 2 | apostates who A. after receiving |

APOSTATIZED

| 85 | 11 | that are found to have A. or to |

APOSTLE

18	9	even as unto Paul mine A. for you
20	2	Joseph Smith ordained an A. of
	3	who was also called of God an A.
	38	an A. is an elder and it is his duty
21	1	thou shalt be called an A. of
	10	ordained by you O. Cowdery, mine A.
49	11	like unto mine A. of old whose name
74	5	for this cause the A. wrote unto

APOSTLES

| 1 | 14 | neither give heed to words of the A. |
| 19 | 8 | meet to know even as mine A. |

Sec.	Vs.	
27	12	I have confirmed you to be A.
29	10	that which was spoken by mine A.
	12	mine A. which were with me at Jerusalem
35	6	laying on of hands as the A. of old
52	9	which the prophets and A. have written
	36	declaring none other things than the A.
63	21	which was shown unto mine A. on the mount
	52	for this cause preached A. resurrection
64	39	they who are not A. shall be known
66	2	written by the A. in days of old
74	2	in the days of the A. the law of
84	63	as I said to mine A. so I say unto; for you are mine A. even God's High—84:64
	108	this is the way that mine A. in
86	2	the A. were the sowers of the seed
95	4	prepare mine A. to prune my
	9	tarry as mine A. at Jerusalem
	17	for the school of mine A. saith Son
98	32	this is the law I gave unto mine A.
102	30	High Council composed of the Twelve A.
107	23	are called to be the Twelve A.
	26	equal in authority to the Twelve A.
124	139	wherever my A. shall send them
133	55	the holy A. with Abraham, Isaac and
136	3	under the direction of the Twelve A.
	37	from Moses to Jesus and his A.; from Jesus and his A. to Joseph Smith

APPAREL

Sec.	Vs.	
133	46	clothed in his glorious A., traveling
	48	the Lord shall be red in his A.

APPEAL

Sec.	Vs.	
11	18	hold your peace, A. unto my spirit
102	27	they may A. to the High Council of
	31	from the decision there can be an A.
	33	after examining the A. and the
107	32	otherwise there can be no A. from
134	11	men should A. to the civil law for; where immediate A. cannot be made

APPEALED

Sec.	Vs.	
102	33	whether such a case as may be A. is

APPEAR

Sec.	Vs.	
45	74	when the Lord shall A. he shall be
88	93	there shall A. a great sign in heaven
110	8	I *will* A. unto my servants and speak
129	6	that is the only way he can A.
130	1	when the Saviour shall A. we shall see
133	36	who shall A. unto many that dwell

APPEARANCE

Sec.	Vs.	
130	3	of the Father and Son, is a personal A.

APPEARED

Sec.	Vs.	
107	54	Lord A. unto them and they rose up
110	11	Moses A. before us and committed
	12	after this, Elias A. and committed
128	20	devil when he A. as an angel of light
133	36	who hath A. unto some and hath

APPEARETH

Sec.	Vs.	
128	24	who can stand when he A.; for he is

APPEARING

Sec.	Vs.	
130	3	A. of Father and Son is a personal
	16	millennium or some previous A., or

APPENDAGE

Sec.	Vs.	
107	14	it is an A. to the greater or the

APPENDAGES

Sec.	Vs.	
84	29	are necessary A. belonging to the—30
107	5	all other authorities are A. to this

APPLY

Sec.	Vs.	
8	4	A. unto it, and blessed art thou

APPOINT

Sec.	Vs.	
20	61	meet as said conferences shall A.
	82	elders shall A. from time to time
28	7	until I shall A. unto them another
29	43	A. unto man the days of his probation
42	31	such as he shall A. or has
43	4	not have power except to A. another
	12	A. ye my servant Joseph Smith and
46	27	such as God shall A. and ordain to
51	3	A. unto this people their portion
	4	when he shall A. a man his portion
	13	let the bishop A. a storehouse
54	7	A. whom you will to be your leader
57	13	whatsoever place I shall A. unto him
67	6	A. him that is the most wise among you
70	9	shall hereafter A. to any man
78	21	and A. every man his portion
88	122	A. among yourselves a teacher
95	14	three of you whom ye shall A. and
101	21	I have other places which I *will* A.
	90	A. them their portion among hypocrites
102	7	shall have power to A. other High

Appoint   26   Appointed

Sec.	Vs.	
	25	power to A. one of their own number
104	11	A. every man his stewardship
	61	ye shall A. one to keep the treasury
105	21	as my servant Joseph shall A. unto
	22	whatsoever he shall A. shall be fulfilled
109	51	didst A. a Zion unto thy people
	59	we ask thee to A. other stakes
124	8	A. the portion of the oppressor among
	62	A. one of them to be a president
	94	I A. unto him that he may be a prophet
125	2	gather unto the places which I shall A.
132	11	and *will* I A. unto you saith the Lord
136	15	A. presidents and captains of hundreds

APPOINTED

28	2	no one shall be A. to receive—43:3
	10	Joseph shall be A. to preside over
	12	these things have not been A. unto: neither shall anything be A. unto
30	7	none have I A. to be his counselor
32	2	that which I have A. unto him is
38	23	office wherewith I have A. you—42:10; 54:2; 63:56; 81:3
	34	shall be A. and they shall be A. by the voice of the church
41	9	he should be A. by the voice of
	10	to see to all things as it shall be A.
42	10	another shall be A. in his stead—104:77
	31	A. and set apart for that purpose
	34	as shall be A. by the High Council
	48	not A. unto death, shall be healed
	56	scriptures shall be given as I have A.
	71	High Priests who are A. to assist
43	2	through him whom I have A. unto you—43:7; 132:18
	4	none else shall be A. unto this gift
	15	elders of my church whom I have A.
45	65	inheritance which shall hereafter be A.
47	3	A. unto him to keep the church record; Cowdery I have A. to another
48	5	there are to be certain men A.
	6	A. to purchase the lands and to make; as is A. by the presidency and the
49	25	unto the place which I have A.—53:4; 101:67
50	26	the same is A. to be the greatest
	30	as ye are A. to the head, the spirits
	38	that which I have A. unto them

Sec.	Vs.	
51	7	let that which belongs, be A. unto this people
	8	let there be an agent A. unto this—58:49
	12	agent, which shall be A. by the voice
56	7	to the land which I have A.—57:1
	9	he shall be A. still to go to the
57	6	stand in the office which I have A.—57:7; 58:40; 81:5
	7	those whom he has A. to assist him
58	14	have A. unto him his mission in
	17	whoso standeth in his mission is A.
	24	whom he has A. for his counselors; whom I have A. to keep my storehouse
	44	only as it shall be A. of the Lord
	46	they who are not A. to stay in this land
	58	accomplish the work which I have A.
59	10	this is a day A. unto you to rest
61	24	I have A. a way for the journeying
63	40	sent up to whom I have A. to receive
	50	is A. to him to die at the age of man
64	5	through the means which I have A.
68	2	whose mission is A. unto them to go
	15	shall be A. by the first presidency
	30	inasmuch as they are A. to labor
70	3	I have A. and ordained them to be
	5	wherefore I have A. them and this is
	9	his stewardship, even as I have A.
	11	neither he who is A. in a
	12	he who is A. to administer spiritual; those who are A. to a stewardship
72	2	it is expedient for a bishop to be A.
	5	the bishop who shall be A. of me
	8	Whitney is the man who shall be A.
	20	let my servants who are A. stewards
	24	they that are A. to go up unto Zion
76	15	translation which the Lord had A.
	88	who are A. to minister for them; or A. to be ministering spirits
78	16	who hath A. Michael your prince
82	20	this order I have A. to be an
84	3	A. by the finger of the Lord in the
	31	consecrated spot as I have A.
	111	deacons and teachers should be A.
85	1	Lord's clerk, whom he has A. to keep
	8	man who was called of God and A.
	9	their portion shall be A. them among
88	128	he that is A. to be president
94	15	may do the work that I have A.
101	20	there is none other place A. than that which I have A.; neither shall there be any other place A. than that which I have A.
	55	save those whom I have A. to tarry
	70	A. to be the land of Zion for

Sec.	Vs.	
	73	let honorable men be A. even wise
	96	my storehouse which I have A. unto
	97	let not that which I have A. be polluted
	99	hold claim upon that which I have A.
102	2	High Council was A. by revelation
	6	or their regularly A. successors
	9	president of the church A. by revelation
	10	two other presidents A. after the same manner that he himself was A.
	11	absence of one of those who are A.
	14	if thought difficult four shall be A.; in no case shall more than six be A.
	16	councilors A. to speak before the—102:18
104	12	his stewardship which is A. unto him—104:30, 32, 37, 41, 44, 54, 63
	20	let my servant, have A. unto him—104:24, 39, 43
	40	all this I have A. unto my servant
	57	I have A. unto you to be stewards
	67	a treasurer A. to keep the treasury
	68	improving the properties which I have A.
105	7	who are A. to lead my people—124:45
	27	Baurak Ale whom I have A. shall
106	1	should be A. and ordained a presiding
107	21	growing out of, or A. of or from
	22	A. and ordained to that office
	63	from priest to elder as they are A.
	65	must needs be that one be A. of
	75	as there are other bishops A. they
	99	act in the office in which he is A.
108	1	receive counsel of him whom I have A.
109	59	besides this one which thou hast A.
112	30	unto you and those who are A. with you
115	1	who are and shall be A. hereafter
	18	that other places should be A. for stakes
118	1	let men be A. to supply the places
	6	A. to fill the places of those who
121	25	there is a time A. for every man
	31	all the A. days, months, years
123	4	perhaps a committee can be A. to
124	23	the cornerstone I have A. for Zion
	24	if the governor which shall be A.
	36	those places which I have A. for refuge
	46	voice of these men whom I have A.
	79	Isaac Galland be A. among you and
	91	let my servant William be A.;

Sec.	Vs.	
		which was A.-unto him by his father
	109	out of the city which I have A. unto
	111	hands of those whom I have A. to build
	130	another may be A. unto the same calling—124:132
	134	who shall be A. standing presidents
125	4	in all the stakes which I have A.
127	4	all the works which I have A.
128	3	a recorder A. in each ward of the
132	5	shall abide the law which was A.
	7	whom I have A. on the earth to hold; I have A. unto my servant Joseph to
	10	will I receive that which I have not A.
	16	but are A. angels in heaven which
	18	angels and gods are A. there
	19	unto whom I have A. this power
	41	and I have not A. unto her by the
136	16	servants that have been A. go and teach

APPOINTING
| 102 | 5 | in A. the above named councilors |

APPOINTMENT
109	39	to her stakes, the places of thine A.
118	6	be officially notified of their A.
124	32	at the end of this A. your baptisms; if you do not these things at end of A.
128	4	general character and A. of those men
132	26	they are sealed according to mine A.
	40	I gave unto thee, Joseph, an A.

APPOINTMENTS
| 84 | 107 | send them before you to make A. prepare the way and to fill A. |
| 102 | 4 | asked whether they accepted their A.; answered they accepted their A. |

APPROPRIATE
| 124 | 70 | shall not A. any portion of that stock |
| | 71 | if they do A. any portion of that stock; which they A. anywhere else |

APPROVE
| 124 | 144 | A. of those names which I have |

APPROVED
72	19	render himself and his accounts A.
	22	render themselves A. in all things
107	100	he that shows himself not A. shall

APRIL
| 20 | 1 | sixth day of the month called A.—21:3 |

Sec.	Vs.		Sec.	Vs.	
118	5	in Far West on 26th day of A. next			**ARMED**
		ARCHANGEL	109	22	from this house A. with thy power
29	26	Michael, mine A. shall sound his trump	135	1	shot by an A. mob, painted black
88	112	A. shall gather together his armies			**ARMIES**
107	54	called him Michael, the Prince, the A.	60	4	I rule among the A. of the earth
128	21	and the voice of Michael, the A.	88	111	that he may gather together his A.
		ARCHIVES		112	and Michael shall gather together his A.
127	9	put in the A. of my Holy Temple		113	devil shall gather together his A.; battle against Michael and his A.
		ARISE		114	devil and his A. shall be cast away
39	10	A. and be baptized, and wash away	105	30	will hold the A. of Israel guiltless
43	18	ye saints A. and live; ye sinners	117	6	do I not hold destinies of all A. of
82	14	Zion must A. and put on her beautiful			**ARMOR**
88	124	A. early that your bodies may be	27	15	take upon you my whole A. that ye
	132	let the teacher A. and with uplifted			**ARMS**
101	89	then *will* the Lord A. and come forth	6	20	will encircle thee in the A. of my love
102	2	difficulties which might A. in the			**ARMY**
108	3	A. *up* and be more careful henceforth	5	14	terrible as an A. with banners—109:73
112	14	A. and gird up your loins, take up	105	26	until the A. of Israel becomes great
115	5	A. and shine forth, that thy light		31	let my A. become very great and let
117	2	let them awake and A. and come forth	136	8	those who have gone in the A.
124	103	let him A. and come and stand in the			**AROSE**
130	13	it may A. through the slave question	74	3	there A. a great contention among
133	10	A. and go forth to meet the bridegroom	95	10	contentions A. in the school of the
			101	51	servants of the nobleman A. and were
		ARK			**AROUND**
85	8	putteth forth his hand to steady the A.	109	79	shining seraphs A. thy throne, with
			122	6	if enemies prowl A. thee like wolves
		ARM			**ARRANGE**
1	14	the A. of the Lord shall be revealed—90:10	63	38	A. their temporal concerns, which
	19	neither trust in the A. of flesh	85	7	A. by lot the inheritances of the
3	8	he would have extended his A. and			**ARRAYED**
15	2	mine A. is over all the earth—16:2	84	82	are not A. like one of these
29	1	whose A. of mercy hath atoned for			**ARRIVE**
35	8	God, and mine A. is not shortened	61	30	until they A. in Cincinnati
	14	their A. shall be my A. and I will			**ARRIVED**
45	45	before the A. of the Lord shall fall	18	42	who have A. to years of accountability—20:71
	47	then shall the A. of the Lord fall			**ARTICLES**
56	1	they shall know mine A. and indignation	33	14	remember the church A. and covenants
103	17	by power, and with a stretched-out A.	42	13	observe the covenants and church A.
109	51	make bare thine A. O Lord, and			**ASCEND**
121	33	man stretch forth his puny A. to stop	109	49	cries of their innocent ones to A. *up*
123	6	send forth the power of his mighty A.			**ASCENDED**
	17	God, and for his A. to be revealed	20	24	A. into heaven to sit down on the
133	3	he shall make bare his holy A. in	88	6	he that A. *up* on high as also
	67	yet my A. was not shortened at all			
136	22	my A. is stretched out in last days			

Sec.	Vs.	
		ASCENDING
77	9	understand by the angel A. from; the angel A. from the east is he to
		ASCERTAIN
68	21	A. it by revelation from the Lord
102	12	thereby A. who shall speak first—102:34
		ASCRIBED
84	102	glory, honor and power be A. to our
		ASHAMED
10	19	that we may not be A. in the end
29	27	wicked on my left will I be A. to own
42	91	that he or she may be A.
90	17	be not A.; neither confounded
117	11	be A. of the Nicolaitane band and of
		ASHERY
104	39	on which the Shule (A.) is situated
		ASHLY, MAJOR N.
75	17	I say unto my servant A., let them take
		ASIDE
25	10	lay A. the things of this world
124	116	lay A. all his hard speeches
		ASK
4	7	A. and ye shall receive—6:5; 11:5; 12:5; 14:5; 49:26; 66:9; 75:27; 88:63; 103:31, 35
7	1	A. what you will it shall be granted—50:29; 132:40
8	1	whatsoever you shall A. in faith—29:6
	9	whatsoever you shall A. me to tell you
	10	therefore A. in faith; do not A. for that which you ought not
	11	A. that you may know the mysteries
9	7	took no thought save it was to A. me
	8	then you must A. me if it be right
10	21	therefore they *will* not A. of me
14	8	A. the Father in my name in faith believing—18:18
20	77	we A. thee, in the name of thy son—20:79
27	18	be agreed as touching whatsoever ye A.
35	9	whoso shall A. it in my name in faith
42	56	A., and my scriptures shall be given
	61	A., thou shalt receive revelation
	62	A., and it shall be revealed unto you
	68	A. of me and I will give liberally
46	7	A. of God who giveth liberally
50	9	that A. of me, that A. not for a sign
	13	I the Lord, A. you this question
	30	shall be given you what you shall A.
	31	A. of the Father in the name of Jesus
64	7	confess their sins and A. forgiveness
88	64	A. the Father in my name it shall be
	65	if ye A. anything not expedient it
101	27	whatsoever any man shall A. it shall
109	4	we A. thee, Holy Father in the name; we A. Thee to accept this house
	10	we A. thee to assist us thy people
	22	we A. thee that thy servants may go
	24	we A. thee to establish the people
	29	we A. thee to confound and astonish
	47	we A. thee to remember those who
	59	we A. thee to appoint unto Zion
	62	we A. thee to have mercy on the children
124	95	keys whereby he may A. and receive—124:97
129	7	A. him to shake hands with you
	8	when you A. him to shake hands he
		ASKED
6	6	as you have A. behold I say keep—11:6; 12:6
29	33	because ye have A. and are agreed—50:1
42	3	and have A. the Father in my name
45	16	ye have A. concerning the signs of
102	4	were A. whether they accepted their
124	73	for they have A. it at my hands
132	41	ye have A. concerning adultery
		ASKETH
46	28	he that A. in spirit shall receive
	30	he that A. in the spirit A. according to the will; it is done as he A.
		ASKING
10	15	tempt thy God in A. to translate over
		ASLEEP
35	21	shall see me and shall not be A.
86	3	after they have fallen A. the great
101	53	not have fallen A. lest the enemy
		ASPIRE
121	35	their hearts A. to the honors of men
		ASPIRETH
124	84	he A. to establish his counsel
		ASSASSINATION
135	4	three days previous to his A. he said
		ASSAULTS
134	11	from unlawful A. and encroachments
		ASSEMBLE
37	3	should A. together at the Ohio

Assemble   30   Attain

Sec.	Vs.
39	15 people shall A. themselves to Ohio
41	2 ye shall A. yourselves together—45:64; 52:42; 58:46; 63:24; 88:74
44	2 in the day that they A. themselves
62	4 A. yourselves upon the land of Zion
128	13 where the living were wont to A.

ASSEMBLED

Sec.	Vs.
42	1 who have A. yourselves together—42:3; 57:1; 67:1; 72:1; 78:1; 88:1; 105:1
43	8 when ye are A. together ye shall
49	25 A. unto the place which I have
61	2 ye elders who are A. upon this spot
63	36 I will that my saints should be A.
89	1 Council of High Priests A. in Kirtland
102	1 twenty-four High Priests A. at the house

ASSEMBLIES

Sec.	Vs.
124	39 your solemn A., your memorials
133	6 call your solemn A. and speak often

ASSEMBLING

| 89 | 5 only in A. yourselves together to offer up |

ASSEMBLY

Sec.	Vs.
76	67 general A. and church of Enoch
88	70 call a solemn A.—88:117; 95:7; 109:6
107	19 to commune with the general A. and
	32 it may be brought before a general A.
108	4 wait patiently until the solemn A.
109	10 assist us in calling our solemn A.

ASSENT

| 132 | 27 innocent blood and A. unto my death |

ASSIST

Sec.	Vs.
6	9 A. to bring forth my work according—11:9
	27 A. in bringing to light with your gift—11:19
9	2 that you may A. to translate
12	8 no one can A. in this work except
14	11 David, and thou art called to A.
20	52 priest is to A. the elder if
28	14 thou shalt A. to settle all these
42	71 appointed to A. the bishop as counselors
47	1 and A. you my servant Joseph
55	4 ordained to A. my servant Oliver
57	7 whom he has appointed to A. him
	13 let my servant Oliver Cowdery A. him
75	24 A. in supporting the families of
96	8 A. in bringing forth my word unto
102	11 those who are appointed to A. him
107	79 even twelve to A. as counselors
109	10 we ask thee to A. us thy people

Sec.	Vs.
124	107 let him A. my servant Joseph and also let William Law A.

ASSISTANCE

Sec.	Vs.
58	18 by the A. of his counselors—107:72
69	4 that he receive counsel and A. from
72	20 have claim for A. upon the bishop
107	38 call upon seventy when they need A.

ASSISTANT

| 102 | 11 power to preside without an A. |

ASSISTED

Sec.	Vs.
20	57 to be A. always in all his duties
102	10 to be A. by two other presidents
107	82 who shall be A. by twelve counselors

ASSISTING

| 109 | 44 to say, with thy grace A. them, thy |

ASSOCIATIONS

| 132 | 7 all A. that are not made and sealed |

ASSURANCE

Sec.	Vs.
106	8 I will give him grace and A. wherewith
123	17 then may we stand still with utmost A.

ASSURE

| 128 | 15 let me A. you that these are principles |

ASSUREDLY

Sec.	Vs.
8	1 A. as the Lord liveth who is your
43	3 know A. that none other is appointed
52	36 seen and heard and most A. believe
58	59 bear record of that he most A. believes

ASTONISH

| 109 | 29 we ask thee to A. and bring to shame |

ASUNDER

Sec.	Vs.
6	2 to the dividing A. of both joints—11:2; 12:2; 14:2; 33:1
85	9 they shall be cut A. and their portion

ATHIRST

| 84 | 80 shall not go hungry neither A. |

ATONED

| 29 | 1 whose mercy hath A. for your sins |

ATONEMENT

Sec.	Vs.
74	7 being sanctified through the A. of
76	69 who wrought out this perfect A.

ATTAIN

Sec.	Vs.
130	18 whatever we A. unto in this life
132	21 my law, ye cannot A. to this glory

Sec.	Vs.	
		ATTEMPT
135	1	and was shot dead in the A.
		ATTEND
20	47	A. to all family duties—20:51
	81	to A. the several conferences held
24	9	A. to thy calling and thou shalt
30	4	you shall A. to the ministry
50	1	A. to the words of wisdom which shall
88	78	my grace shall A. you that you may
		ATTENDED
123	14	should be A. to with great earnestness
124	120	shall be A. with cursings and not
128	4	A. with certificates over their own
	8	whether they themselves have A. to
		ATTENDING
128	4	certificates and all A. witnesses
		AUTHORITIES
102	32	called in question by the general A.
107	5	all other A. are appendages to this
	12	where there are no higher A. present
	32	which constitute the spiritual A.
124	5	my will concerning those kings and A.
	118	hearken unto the A. which I have
		AUTHORITY
1	6	this is mine A. and the A. of my servants
20	58	teachers nor deacons have A.
	73	person who has A. from Jesus Christ
28	3	with power and A. unto the church
42	11	ordained by some one who has A.; and known to church he has A.
63	62	and use it in vain, having not A.
68	8	acting in the A. which I have given
	17	holds the keys or A. of the same—107:15
	19	has A. to officiate in all the lesser—107:17
76	25	angel of God who was in A. rebelled
84	21	and without the A. of the priesthood
101	76	placed as rulers and are in A. over
107	8	has power and A. over all offices
	18	power and A. of the higher or
	20	power and A. of the lesser or
	24	form a quorum equal in A. and power—107:26, 36, 37
113	8	to put on the A. of the priesthood
121	37	amen to the priesthood or A. of
	39	as soon as they get a little A. they
122	2	virtuous shall seek counsel and A.
124	128	Twelve hold keys to open up the A.
128	9	whatsoever those men did in A. in
134	10	no religious society has A. to try

Sec.	Vs.	
		AUTHORIZE
20	64	which shall A. to him to perform the
		AUTHORIZED
68	20	otherwise they are not legally A.
112	21	duly A. by you shall have power to
		AVAILETH
22	2	baptized an hundred times it A. nothing
		AVAILS
104	64	the A. of the sacred things shall be
	65	thus shall ye preserve the A. of
		AVENGE
98	45	the Lord *will* A. thee of thine enemy
101	58	A. me of mine enemies that by
	83	saying, A. me of mine adversary
	84	I *will* A. her lest by her continual
103	25	ye shall A. me of mine enemies
121	5	with thine sword A. us of our wrongs
		AVENGED
87	7	from the earth, to be A. of their enemies
98	37	until they had A. themselves on all
		AVENGES
135	7	till he A. that blood on the earth
		AVENGING
103	26	even in A. me of mine enemies—105:30
		AVOID
107	4	to A. the too frequent repetition
		AWAIT
34	9	great destructions A. the wicked
45	62	I say unto you, great things A. you
84	114	utter abolishment which A. them if
124	88	A. patiently and diligently further
		AWAITED
121	27	forefathers A. with anxious expectation
		AWAITS
88	85	desolation of abomination which A.
		AWAKE
29	26	then shall all the dead A. for their
117	2	let them A. and arise and come forth
124	11	A. O, kings of the earth! Come ye
133	10	A. and arise and go forth to meet
		AWARE
3	9	if thou art not A. thou wilt fall
121	38	ere he is A. he is left unto himself

Sec.	Vs.		Sec.	Vs.	
		AWAY	68	32	these things must be done A. from
1	38	though the heavens and earth pass A. my word shall not pass A.—45:22; 56:11	74	5	except law of Moses should be done A.
				6	that the tradition might be done A.
5	19	until inhabitants are consumed A.	76	36	they shall go A. into the lake
	31	I will take A. the things which I		44	shall go A. into everlasting
8	8	no power shall be able to take it A.	78	10	to turn their hearts A. from the truth
9	5	I have taken A. this privilege from	84	5	this generation shall not all pass A.
10	7	he has sought to take A. the things		92	go A. from him alone by yourselves
	29	flattereth them A. to do iniquity	88	69	cast A. your idle thoughts and
22	1	old covenants have I caused to be done A.		114	devil and his armies shall be cast A.
29	23	earth shall be consumed and pass A.	93	39	wicked one cometh and taketh A. light
	24	all old things shall pass A. and all—63:49	96	9	seek diligently to take A. incumbrances
	26	before the earth shall pass A.	98	22	I will turn A. all wrath and indignation
	36	hosts of heaven turned he A. from me		47	thine indignation shall be turned A.
38	20	in eternity no more to pass A.	104	81	taken A. out of their minds to bring
39	10	wash A. your sins, calling on my	109	30	and be swept A. by the hail
42	74	having put A. their companions for		52	that they may be wasted A. both root
43	32	earth shall pass A. so as by fire		53	merciful, and wilt turn A. thy wrath
	33	wicked shall go A. into unquenchable		70	and swept A. as with a flood
45	21	generation of Jews shall not pass A.	121	11	their prospects shall melt A. as the
	23	not pass A. until all shall be	124	28	lost or which he hath taken A.
56	11	these words shall not pass A.		69	convey the stock A. out of their hands
60	3	taken A. even that which they have		76	turn A. their hearts from affliction
	13	Thou shalt not idle A. thy time	133	73	these shall go A. into outer darkness
61	20	but today mine anger is turned A.			**AX**
63	13	turned A. from my commandments	97	7	A. is laid at the root of the trees
	14	some of whom have turned A. from			
64	35	the rebellious shall be sent A.			
66	1	have turned A. from your iniquities			

B

Sec.	Vs.		Sec.	Vs.	
		BABBITT, ALMON	31	5	laden with sheaves upon your B.
124	84	my servant B. aspireth to establish	67	14	let not your minds turn B.; and when ye are
		BABES	77	6	sealed on the B. with seven seals
128	18	shall be revealed unto B. and sucklings	133	15	he that goeth let his not look B.
		BABYLON		23	great deep shall be driven B. into
1	16	shall perish in B., even B. the great		24	land of Zion shall be turned B. into
35	11	except desolations upon B.			**BACKS**
64	24	I will not spare any that remain in B.	33	9	laden with sheaves upon your B.
86	3	the apostate, the whore, even B.			**BACKBITING**
133	5	go ye forth from B., be ye clean	20	54	see that there is no B. nor evil
	7	go ye out of B., gather ye out from			**BACKWARD**
	14	even from B., from wickedness, which is spiritual B.	128	22	go forward and not B. Courage
		BACK			**BAD**
6	26	records kept B. because of wickedness	127	2	ordained for some good end or B. as; God knoweth whether it be good or B.

Sec.	Vs.	
		BAKER, JESSE
124	137	I give unto you B., and, which priesthood
		BALDWIN, WHEELER
52	31	let B. and, take their journey
		BALLOT
102	34	proceeded to cast lots or B.
		BALLS
135	1	brutal manner, and both received four B.
	2	in a savage manner with four B.
		BAND
117	11	be ashamed of the Nicolaitane B.
123	8	it is an iron yoke, it is a strong B.
		BANDS
88	94	her B. are made strong, no man can
101	66	B. made strong that they may be burned
113	9	loosing herself from the B. of her
	10	B. of her neck are the curses of God
		BANEEMY
105	27	and B. (mine elders) whom I have
		BANKS
128	20	Michael on the B. of the Susquehanna
		BANNER
135	7	innocent blood on the B. of liberty
		BANNERS
5	14	terrible as an army with B.—109:73
105	31	her B. may be terrible to all nations
		BAPTISM
13	1	B. by immersion for remission of sins
19	31	remission of sins by B. and by fire
20	37	commandment concerning manner of B.; shall be received by B. into his church
	41	laying on of hands for the B. of fire
	68	after they are received by B.
	72	B. is to be administered in the following
	73	presented him or herself for B.
33	11	then cometh the B. of fire and the Holy Ghost—39:6
39	6	this is my gospel: repentance and B.
55	2	remission of sins by way of B. in the
68	25	of B. and the gift of the Holy Ghost
84	27	gospel of repentance and of B. and
107	20	letter of the gospel—the B. of
127	5	in relation to the B. for your dead—128:16
	10	addressed them on the subject of B.
128	1	now resume subject of B. for the dead
	12	the ordinance of B. by water to be; relationship with ordinance of B. for dead
	17	most glorious of all subjects, B. for dead
	18	what is that subject? B. for the dead
		BAPTISMS
124	31	your B. shall be acceptable unto me
	32	B. for your dead shall not be acceptable
	33	B. for dead cannot be acceptable
	35	after this time your B. for the dead
	36	places for your B. for your dead
	39	your B. for the dead are ordained
127	6	let him be eye-witness of your B.
		BAPTISMAL
124	29	a B. font there is not upon the earth
128	13	B. font was instituted as a simile
		BAPTIZE
18	29	ordained of me to B. in my name
20	38	apostle, it is his calling to B.
	42	to teach, expound, exhort, B., and—20:50
	46	to B. and administer the sacrament
	58	teachers nor deacons have authority to B.
	73	who has authority from Jesus to B.; I B. you in the name of the Father
35	5	thou didst B. by water unto repentance
	6	thou shalt B. by water and they shall
39	23	as many as ye shall B. with water
134	12	neither preach the gospel to nor B. them
		BAPTIZED
18	7	as thou hast been B. by the hands of
	22	as many as repent and are B. in my name
	41	saying, you must repent and be B. in
	42	for all men must repent and be B.
20	25	as many as would believe and be B.
	37	all those who desire to be B. and come
	41	to confirm those who are B. into the
22	2	although a man should be B. an hundred
33	11	repent and be B. every one of you; be B. even by water, and then cometh
39	10	arise and be B. and wash away your
49	13	repent and be B. in the name of Jesus
55	1	and after thou hast been B. by water
68	9	he that believeth and is B. shall be—112:29
	27	their children shall be B. for the
76	51	B. after the manner of his burial

Sec.	Vs.		Sec.	Vs.	
84	28	he was B. while yet in his childhood		35	that my servant B. may go with you
	64	every soul who is B. by water for the	105	16	I have commanded my servant B. to say
	74	they who are not B. in water shall		27	until my servant B. shall have time
112	29	he that is not B. shall be damned			**BEAR**
124	29	may be B. for those who are dead	19	15	yea, how hard to B. you know not
127	6	when any of you are B. for your dead		22	they cannot B. meat now, but milk
128	16	else what shall they do which are B.; why are they then B. for the dead	20	16	have heard and B. witness to the words
		BAPTIZING	27	12	and B. the keys of your ministry
39	20	go forth B. with water, preparing—42:7	38	42	be ye clean that B. the vessels of the Lord—133:5
52	10	in every congregation B. by water	42	52	thou shalt B. their infirmities
68	8	B. in the name of the Father and of	50	40	ye cannot B. all things now—78:18
124	33	wherein the ordinance of B. for the dead	58	6	hearts might be prepared to B. testimony
		BARE	47		B. testimony of the truth in all places
109	51	if they will not, make B. thine arm		59	except he B. record by the way of
133	3	he shall make B. his holy arm in the	61	4	I suffered it that ye might B. record
		BARLEY	62	5	then you may return to B. record
89	17	and B. for all useful animals and for	64	20	tempted above that he is able to B.
		BARNS	66	7	B. testimony in every place
59	17	for B. or for orchards, or for gardens	67	8	under condemnation if ye do not B. record
121	20	their houses and B. shall perish	68	6	ye shall B. record of me, even Jesus
		BARREN		12	of as many as the Father shall B.
133	29	in B., deserts shall come forth pools	71	4	B. record and prepare the way
		BARS	76	14	of whom we B. record and the; record which we B. is the fulness
122	4	cast thee into trouble and into B.		25	this we saw also and B. record
		BASKET		41	to B. the sins of the world and to
121	20	their B. shall not be full, their		50	we B. record for we saw and heard
		BASSET, HEMAN		118	they may be able to B. his presence
52	37	let that which was bestowed on B. be taken	84	88	angels round about you to B. you *up*
				92	B. testimony of it unto your Father
		BATHED	90	2	that B. the keys of the kingdom given
1	13	his sword is B. in heaven and it shall		28	receive money to B. her expenses
88	87	the moon shall be B. in blood	93	11	I, John, B. record that I beheld his
		BATTLE		15	I, John, B. record, heavens were opened
45	70	let us not go up to B. against Zion		16	I, John, B. record, he received a
88	113	hosts of hell shall come up to B.	98	23	B. it patiently and revile not against—98:25
	114	then cometh the B. of the great God		24	but if ye B. it not patiently it shall
98	33	they should not go out unto B.		26	and ye B. it patiently
	36	and justify them in going out to B.	109	23	they may B. exceedingly great and
109	28	fight as thou didst in the day of B.		49	wilt thou suffer this people to B. this
		BATTLES		56	out from thy house to B. testimony
88	115	for Michael shall fight their B.	112	1	who were chosen to B. testimony of
98	37	I, the Lord, would fight their B. and their children's B.		4	thou shalt B. record of my name
105	14	to fight the B. of Zion; I will fight your B.	114	1	B. glad tidings unto all the world
			118	4	fulness thereof and B. record of my
		BAURAK ALE (JOSEPH SMITH, JR.)	124	18	I will B. him *up* as on eagles' wings
103	21	B. is the man to whom I likened		38	they should B. it with them in the wilderness
	22	therefore let B. say unto the strength		96	Hyrum may B. record of the things
				122	let every man B. his proportion of the
				139	traveling elders to B. record of my

Sec.	Vs.	
128	20	three witnesses to B. record of the book
132	63	that they may B. the souls of men
136	8	let each company B. an equal proportion
	31	he that will not B. chastisement
	37	ye cannot B. my glory; but ye shall

BEARETH

Sec.	Vs.	
1	39	Spirit B. record and the record is true
20	27	Holy Ghost which B. record of the
42	17	B. record of the Father and the Son
59	24	I have spoken·it and the Spirit B.

BEARING

Sec.	Vs.	
1	8	B. these tidings unto inhabitants
21	11	this church of Christ B. my name
24	10	shall continue in B. my name before
58	7	B. record of the land upon which
	63	B. record of things which are revealed
76	23	we heard a voice B. record that he is
84	61	B. testimony to all the world of
100	8	shall be shed forth in B. record
109	31	innocent before thee in B. record

BEAST

Sec.	Vs.	
77	2	as also the spirit of the B.

BEASTS

Sec.	Vs.	
29	20	B. of the forest shall devour them
	24	both men and B., the fowls of
49	19	B. of the field and fowls of the air—59:16; 101:24
77	2	understand by the four B.; happiness of man and of B.
	3	are the four B. limited to individual B.; are limited to four individual B.
	4	eyes and wings which the B. had.
89	12	flesh also of B. and of the fowls
	14	for the use of man and of B.; not only for man but for the B. of the
	17	for swine and for all B. of the field
101	26	enmity of B. shall cease from before
117	6	have I not the B. of the mountains

BEAT

Sec.	Vs.	
90	5	when rains descend and B. upon their

BEAUTIFUL

Sec.	Vs.	
82	14	Zion must put on her B. garments
88	130	this is B. that he may be an example
128	19	how B. upon the mountains are the feet

BEAUTY

Sec.	Vs.	
42	40	their B. the B. of the work of thine own hands

Sec.	Vs.	
82	14	Zion must increase in B. and in holiness

BECAME

Sec.	Vs.	
10	2	and your mind B. darkened
20	20	man B. sensual and devilish and B. fallen man
29	40	wherein he B. subject to the will
	41	wherein he B. spiritually dead
74	4	believed not, wherein they B. unholy
93	38	men B. again in their infant state
101	50	they B. slothful and hearkened not
128	9	it B. a law on earth and in heaven

BECAUSE

Sec.	Vs.	
3	9	but B. of transgression, if thou art not
	18	dwindled in unbelief B. of iniquity; destroy, B. of their iniquities and
5	32	B. I foresee the lying in wait to
6	10	blessed art thou B. of thy gift
	20	spoken unto thee B. of thy desires
	26	been kept back B. of the wickedness
	27	which have been hidden B. of iniquity
7	3	B. thou desirest this thou shalt tarry
9	1	B. you did not translate according to
	5	B. you did not continue as you commenced
10	1	B. you delivered up those writings—10:8
	11	B. they have altered the words, they read
	21	than light, B. their deeds are evil
	28	that lieth to deceive B. he supposeth
	29	altered these words B. Satan saith unto
	34	and B. I show unto you wisdom
	40	B. the account which is engraven
	48	become Lamanites B. of dissensions
17	5	he has seen them B. he had faith
18	1	B. of the thing which you have desired
19	18	greatest of all to tremble B. of pain
22	3	it is B. of your dead works that I
23	3	and this B. of thy family. Amen
25	4	murmur not B. of the things which
29	17	B. of the wickedness of the world
	33	B. ye have asked it of me
	36	away from me B. of their agency
	40	devil, B. he yielded unto temptation
	41	from my presence B. of transgression
	44	spiritual fall, B. they repent not
31	1	blessed are you B. of your faith in
	2	had many afflictions B. of your family
33	4	err in many instances B. of priestcrafts
34	4	blessed are you B. you have believed
	5	blessed are you B. you are called

Sec.	Vs.		Sec.	Vs.	
37	1	and this B. of the enemy and for your	116	1	B. it is the place where Adam shall come
38	14	not B. of your iniquity, neither	121	13	also B. their hearts are corrupted
	30	tell you these things B. of your prayers		17	do it B. they are the servants of sin
				19	B. they have offended my little ones
39	9	rejected me many times B. of pride		35	B. their hearts are set so much upon
41	11	this B. his heart is pure before me	122	4	fierce lion, B. of thy righteousness
45	12	they found it not B. of wickedness	123	12	kept from the truth B. they know not where
	29	hearts from me B. of precepts of men	124	15	I love him B. of the integrity of his; B. he loveth that which is right before
	53	shall they weep B. of their iniquities; B. they persecuted their king		20	he may be trusted B. of the integrity
	75	nations shall be afraid B. of terror		46	not be blest B. they pollute mine holy
50	12	understood of man B. he reasoneth as		87	family B. of the sickness of the land
			129	7	he will not move B. it is contrary to
56	14	are not pardoned B. you seek to counsel	132	18	B. they are not joined by me, saith: B. the angels and Gods are appointed
60	2	hide the talent B. of the fear of man		20	shall they be Gods B. they have no end; be from everlasting to, B. they continue; above all, B. all things are subject; be Gods B. they have all power
63	19	not justified B. these things are			
64	13	not B. ye forgive not, having not			
	43	nations of the earth shall tremble B. of her; shall fear B. of her terrible ones			
				22	few find it B. ye receive me not
84	50	bondage of sin B. they come not unto me		25	B. they receive me not neither do they
	54	B. of unbelief; B. you have treated lightly the things		31	promise is yours B. ye are of Abraham
88	32	B. they were not willing to enjoy		34	B. this was the law and from Hagar
	66	wilderness, B. you cannot see him; my voice B. my voice is spirit		37	B. they were given unto him; B. they did none other things
93	4	Father B. he gave me of his fulness; the Son B. I was in the world and		65	B. she did not administer unto him
			135	5	and B. thou hast seen thy weakness
	9	B. the world was made by him	136	39	many have marveled B. of his death
	14	called Son of God B. he			**BECOME**
	31	condemnation of man B. that which was	3	11	delivered up and B. as other men
	39	B. of tradition of their fathers	10	48	all that had B. Lamanites because
101	29	no sorrow B. there is no death	11	30	give power to B. the sons of God
	84	yet B. this widow troubleth me I will	29	24	all things shall B. new, even the— 63:49; 101:25
103	4	chastisement, B. they did not hearken		47	until they begin to B. accountable
			33	4	my vineyard has B. corrupted every whit
104	7	B. I have promised unto you a crown		8	you shall B. even as Nephi of old
107	2	B. Melchizedek was such a great High	34	3	would believe might B. sons of God
			35	2	believe on my name that they may B. sons
	13	B. it was conferred upon Aaron and his	38	39	pride, lest ye B. as the Nephites of old
	14	B. it is an appendage to the greater	39	4	gave I power to B. my sons—45:8
	31	B. the promise is, if these things		18	inasmuch as they B. sanctified I will
	43	B. he (Seth) was a perfect man and his	42	52	believe in me have power to B. my sons
108	1	forgiven you B. you have obeyed my	43	9	ye shall B. instructed in the law of
109	38	in thy wrath B. of their transgressions	49	23	for the rough places to B. smooth
			54	3	and B. truly humble before me
	48	sorrow, B. of their grievous burdens		4	it has B. void and of none effect
	65	smitten B. of their transgression	63	51	children shall grow up until they B. old
112	5	let not inhabitants slumber B. of thy speech			

Sec.	Vs.	
70	8	inasmuch as they B. heirs according
74	3	and B. subject to the law of Moses
78	10	they B. blinded and understand not
82	4	ye be transgressors and justice and
	18	to B. the common property of the whole
84	34	they B. the sons of Moses and of
	77	that ye B. even as my friends in days
	106	that he may B. strong also
87	5	shall B. exceeding angry and shall vex
88	35	seeketh to B. a law unto itself
	68	that your minds B. single to God
	87	the stars shall B. exceeding angry
	137	that it may B. a sanctuary, a tabernacle
90	15	and B. acquainted with all good books
96	8	he should B. a member of the order
97	18	Zion shall B. very glorious very great
105	31	let my army B. very great; that it may B. fair as the sun
	32	let us B. subject unto her laws
109	72	kingdom may B. a great mountain
112	23	all flesh has B. corrupt before my face
122	7	if fierce winds B. thine enemy
127	2	it all has B. a second nature to me
130	10	white stone *will* B. a Urim and
133	23	and the islands shall B. one land
	28	their enemies shall B. a prey unto
	58	the little one B. a strong nation

BECOMES

105	26	until the army of Israel B. great
107	74	B. necessary to have other bishops
132	65	she then B. the transgressor

BECOMETH

88	81	it B. every man who hath been warned
105	3	impart of their substance as B. saints

BED

88	124	retire to thy B. early that ye may

BEFALL

101	98	and are soon to B. the nations
107	56	predicted what should B. his posterity
124	5	even what shall B. them in a time to come

BEFORE

1	23	ends of the world and B. kings and
2	1	B. the coming of the great and dreadful—128:17
3	13	promises which were made B. God
4	2	that ye may stand blameless B. God
5	21	repent and walk more uprightly B. me

Sec.	Vs.	
	24	does not humble himself sufficiently B. me; but if he will bow down B. me
.	27	covenant which he has B. covenanted
7	3	shalt prophesy B. nations, kindred
	5	greater work than what he has B. done
18	17	you have my gospel B. you and my rock
	30	you have that which is written B. you
	31	you must walk uprightly B. me—46:7; 68:28
19	28	pray B. the world as well as in secret—23:6
	41	and conduct thyself wisely B. me
20	8	by the means which were B. prepared
	26	even as many as were B. he came
	37	those who humble themselves B. God and witness B. the church
	69	members shall manifest B. the church and also B. the elders; walking in holiness B. the Lord—21:4
	70	bring them unto the elders B. the church
	71	years of accountability B. God, and is
21	6	powers of darkness from B. you
	12	preacher B. the world, yea B. the Gentiles
23	2	make known thy calling B. the world
	4	not yet called to preach B. the world
24	10	continue in bearing my name B. the
25	2	walk in the paths of virtue B. me
28	14	B. thou shalt take thy journey among
29	2	as many as will humble themselves B.
	14	B. this great day shall come, the sun—34:9; 45:42; 49:24
	26	B. the earth shall pass away, Michael
	27	will I be ashamed to own B. the Father
	36	the devil was B. Adam for he rebelled
	47	they begin to become accountable B. me
30	4	attend to the ministry B. the world
35	4	to prepare the way B. me and B. Elijah
36	5	as many as shall come B. my servants
38	1	hosts of heaven B. the world was made
	2	all things are present B. mine eyes
	4	have I pleaded B. the Father for them

Sec.	Vs.		Sec.	Vs.	
	11	for all flesh is corrupted B. me—112:23		37	you have humbled yourselves B. me
	14	some of you are guilty B. me	63	16	as I have said B., he that looketh
	16	the poor have complained B. me		49	receive an inheritance B. the Lord
	24	practice virtue and holiness B. me—46:33	64	7	who confess their sins B. me and ask
39	8	thine heart is now right B. me		9	standeth condemned B. the Lord
	12	I will be with thee and go B. thy face—84:88		12	ye shall bring him B. the church
	20	preparing the way B. my face for the—77:12	67	1	whose desires have come up B. me
				4	commandments which are lying B. you
40	1	servant James Covill was right B. me		10	humble yourselves B. me—104:79
41	3	and have all things right B. me—57:13	68	22	save it be B. the first presidency
				23	found guilty B. this presidency
	6	or the pearls to be cast B. swine		30	idler shall be had in remembrance B.
	11	because his heart is pure B. me		33	observeth not his prayers B. the Lord; remembrance B. the judge of my people
	12	words are given and they are pure B.			
42	31	shall be laid B. the bishop of my	72	11	take an account of the elders as B.
	32	after they are laid B. the bishop		15	must lay all things B. the bishop
	41	things be done in cleanliness B. me	76	9	B. them the wisdom of the wise shall
	71	for other purposes as B. mentioned		13	were from the beginning B. the world
	74	shall testify B. you in all lowliness			
	80	shall be tried B. two elders of the		21	who are sanctified B. his throne
	81	the elders shall lay the case B. the		39	in the bosom of the Father B. the world
	83	do in all cases which shall come B. you		93	B. whose throne all things bow
				116	who purify themselves B. him
	89	done in a meeting, not B. the world	77	13	seventh seal, B. the coming of Christ
	90	he or she shall be chastened B. many	78	2	thing which you have presented B. me
43	5	teachings of any that shall come B. you		20	who prepareth all things B. he taketh
	7	be ordained as I have told you B.			
	9	to act in all holiness B. me	82	9	directions how you may act B. me
	11	sanctify yourselves B. me	84	28	straight the way of the Lord B. the
	12	uphold him B. me by the prayer of faith		73	neither speak them B. the world
				107	send them B. you to make appointments
	14	unto myself a pure people B. me			
	33	until they come B. me in judgment	88	40	judgment goeth B. the face of him
45	3	who is pleading your cause B. him		41	all things are B. him and about him
	9	messenger B. my face to prepare the way B. me		74	cleanse your hands and feet B. me
				131	in prayer upon his knees B. God
	16	as I stood B. them in the flesh		135	that cometh in and is faithful B. me
	45	B. the arm of the Lord shall fall	89	5	offer up your sacraments B. him
46	3	meetings which are held B. the world	90	23	brought into disrepute B. the eyes of
				36	chasten her until she is clean B. me
49	2	they are not right B. me and must	93	7	he was in the beginning B. the world
	17	his creation B. the world was made			
	27	I will go B. you and be your rearward		38	their infant state innocent B. God
				47	must needs stand rebuked B. the Lord—95:2
50	9	in truth and righteousness B. me			
54	3	become truly humble B. me and contrite	98	5	to all mankind and is justifiable B. me
				17	and all flesh be consumed B. me
55	3	if they are contrite B. me—56:7		28	that he be not brought into judgment B.
	4	receive instruction B. me as is pleasing			
				35	should bring these testimonies B. the Lord—98:44
58	5	remember this which I tell you B.			
	35	laying his moneys B. the bishop		38	your God, for justification B. me
	41	not sufficiently meek B. me		48	never be brought as testimony B. the
59	4	that are faithful and diligent B. me			
	12	confessing thy sins B. the Lord			
61	34	and they shall be spotless B. me	100	5	you shall not be confounded B. men

Sec.	Vs.		Sec.	Vs.	
101	26	enmity shall cease B. my face		32	was ordained B. this world was—128:22; 132:11, 28
	68	let all things be prepared B. you—101:69, 72; 135:15	123	6	B. we can fully and completely claim; B. he can send forth the power of his
102	16	appointed to speak B. the council; in its true light B. the council	124	2	your prayers are acceptable B. me
	18	speaking for themselves B. the council		15	he loveth that which is right B. me
103	19	mine angel shall go up B. you—103:20		18	confessing me B. the world and I will
	24	testimonies which ye have brought B.		33	instituted from B. the foundation of—132:5
104	23	inasmuch as he shall be humble B. me—106:7; 112:22		38	been hid from B. the world was
	74	and it is manifest B. the council		41	kept hid from B. the foundation of the
	86	do things which I have laid B. you		48	abominations which you practice B. me
105	12	continue in humility B. me		97	let him be humble B. me and be without
	23	be prayerful and humble B. me		103	let him humble himself B. me
	31	let it be sanctified B. me		104	and be a spokesman B. my face
107	3	B. his day it was called the Holy		107	even as I have B. said unto you
	32	may be brought B. a general assembly		139	send them to prepare a way B. my face
	49	he was B. his face continually	127	2	unless I was ordained from B. the
	72	it shall be laid B: him according		4	righteous men that were B. you
	78	B. the presidency of the High priesthood	128	1	in my letter B. I left my place
	80	in remembrance no more B. the Lord		2	make a record of a truth B. the Lord
	82	in remembrance B. the common council		5	prepared B. the foundation of the
	84	done in order and solemnity B. him		6	dead, small and great, stand B. God
109	1	uprightly B. thee with all their hearts		8	salvation from B. the foundation of
	31	servants have been innocent B. thee		11	whole subject that is lying B. us
	32	we plead B. thee a full and complete	130	7	and are continually B. the Lord
	43	their souls are precious B. thee		20	decreed in heaven B. the foundations
	49	blood come up in testimony B. thee	132	52	who are virtuous and pure B. me
	52	cause of thy people may not fail B.		63	promise given by my Father B. the
	56	prejudices may give way B. the truth	133	24	like as it was B. it was divided
	60	we have spoken B. thee concerning		26	shall come in remembrance B. the Lord
	67	and rejoice B. Thee		35	shall be sanctified in holiness B. the
110	2	upon the breastwork of the pulpit B.		54	the prophets who were B. him; Noah and they who were B. him; Moses also, and they who were B. him
	5	you are clean B. me, therefore lift up		62	repenteth and sanctifieth himself B.
	11	Moses appeared B. us and committed	135	5	we shall meet B. the judgment-seat of
	13	without tasting death, stood B. us		7	innocent as they had often been proved B.
	14	Elijah should be sent B. the great and			**BEFOREHAND**
112	1	alms have come up as a memorial B. me	84	85	neither take ye thought B. what ye
	4	be of good cheer B. my face			**BEFRIENDING**
	12	be ye faithful B. me unto my name	98	6	in B. that law which is constitutional
	28	but purify your hearts B. me			**BEGAN**
115	19	I will sanctify him B. the people	9	5	when you B. to translate, that I have
117	1	B. I send again the snows upon the	27	6	holy prophets since the world B.—86:10
	4	all their covetous desires B. me	101	46	set watchmen and B. to build a tower
	11	of all his littleness of soul B. me			
121	3	B. thine heart shall be softened toward			
	11	as hoar-frost melteth B. the burning			
	16	when they have not sinned B. me			

Sec.	Vs.	
	47	they B. to say among themselves

BEGET

Sec.	Vs.	
124	18	he shall B. glory and honor to himself

BEGGING

Sec.	Vs.	
124	90	nor his seed be found B. bread

BEGIN

Sec.	Vs.	
29	22	and men again B. to deny their God
	47	until they B. to become accountable
31	4	you shall B. to preach from this time
45	36	when the light shall B. to break forth
	37	ye say when they B. to shoot forth
48	6	shall ye B. to be gathered with your
90	34	your brethren in Zion B. to repent
103	6	shall B. to prevail against mine enemies
109	62	from this hour may B. to be redeemed
	63	yoke of bondage may B. to be broken
	64	children of Judah may B. to return
112	25	upon my house shall it B. and from
121	39	*will* B. to exercise unrighteous dominion

BEGINNING

Sec.	Vs.	
3	15	director to be trampled upon from B.
5	14	this the B. of the rising up and coming
8	12	same that spake unto you from the B.
19	1	I am the B. and the end—35:1; 38:1; 45:7; 49:12; 54:1; 61:1; 84:120
20	26	but all those from the B. even as many
22	1	even that which was from the B.—49:9; 76:13
29	32	temporal, which is the B. of my work
	33	my works have no end neither B.
	38	place prepared for them from the B.
46	2	to the elders of my church from the B.
61	14	I in the B. blessed the waters, but
	17	as I in the B. cursed the land, even
63	8	there have been such even from the
77	12	in B. of seventh thousand years will; finishing his work in the B. of the
78	16	who is without B. of days or end of—84:17
84	3	B. at the temple lot which is appointed
	4	gathering of the saints B. at this place
86	4	while the Lord is B. to bring forth the
87	1	B. at the rebellion of South Carolina

Sec.	Vs.	
	2	upon all nations B. at that place
88	59	B. at the first and so on unto the last
127		B. at the High Priest, even down to
93	7	he was in the B. before the world was
	8	in the B. the Word was, for he was the
	21	I was in the B. with the Father
	23	ye were also in the B. with the Father
	25	wicked one who was a liar from the B.
	29	man was also in the B. with God
	31	from the B. is plainly manifest unto
	38	spirit of man was innocent in the B.
94	1	preparing a B. and foundation of the; land of Kirtland B. at my house
95	7	creator of first day, the B. and end
101	70	for the B. of the gathering of my
104	32	this is the B. of the stewardship—104:37, 44
110	10	this is the B. of the blessing
112	31	at any time from the B. of the creation
115	9	let there be a B. of this work
	10	let the B. be made on the fourth day
119	3	this shall be the B. of the tithing
124	39	for the B. of the revelations
128	18	which dispensation is now B. to usher in
130	16	referred to the B. of the millennium
132	38	from the B. of the creation until this
133	45	since the B. of the world have not men

BEGOTTEN

Sec.	Vs.	
20	21	God gave his only B. son as it is
29	42	through faith on the name of mine only B.
	46	redeemed through mine only B.
49	5	I have sent mine only B. Son into the
76	13	ordained through his only B. Son
	23	he is the only B. of the Father
	24	are B. sons and daughters of God
	25	rebelled against the only B. Son
	35	having denied the only B. Son
	57	after the order of the only B. Son
93	11	as the glory of the only B. of the Father—124:123
	22	those who are B. through me are *See Only Begotten*

BEGUN

Sec.	Vs.	
10	3	work of translation as you have B.

BEHALF

Sec.	Vs.	
35	14	I will let fall the sword in their B.—101:10
102	17	stand up in B. of the accused
109	49	display of thy testimony in their B.

Sec.	Vs.		Sec.	Vs.	
112	1	in B. of those thy brethren who were			**BELIEF**
		BEHELD	134	7	free exercise of their religious B.
76	20	we B. the glory of the Son on the right			**BELIEVE**
	27	we B. and lo, he is fallen, is fallen	3	20	that they my B. the gospel and—19:27
	28	we B. Satan, that old serpent	5	7	if they *will* not B. my words they would not B. you my
93	11	I B. his glory as the glory of the	10	32	that they *will* not B. my words
		BEHIND		50	whosoever should B. in this gospel
136	9	for those who remain B. this season	11	30	even to them that B. on my name
		BEHOLD	20	25	that as many as would B. and be—29:43; 33:6; 34:3; 35:2; 66:1
5	13	that they may B. and view these things		27	who should B. in the gifts and callings
9	12	do ye not B. that I have given unto my		29	all men must repent and B. on the
34	1	hear and B. what I shall say unto you	21	9	they shall B. on his words
45	4	B. the sufferings and death of him	29	44	they that B. not unto eternal damnation
	18	ye B. this temple which is in Jerusalem	31	2	they *will* B. and know the truth
	37	ye look and B. the fig trees and ye	35	8	all those who B. on my name
	41	they shall B. blood and fire and	42	1	inasmuch as they B. on my name
	46	as you now B. me and know that I am		43	not faith to be healed but B.
50	31	if you B. a spirit manifested that you		52	not faith to do these things but B.
58	3	ye cannot B. with your natural eyes	45	5	spare these my brethren that B.
63	35	B. this is not yet but by and by	46	14	to others it is given to B. on their
84	23	that they might B. the face of God	49	12	B. on the name of the Lord Jesus
88	52	ye shall B. the joy of my countenance	52	36	seen and heard and most assuredly B.
121	2	thy pure eye B. from the eternal heavens	58	64	with signs following them that B.—84:65
136	37	ye shall B. it if ye are faithful	63	9	by signs, but signs follow those that B.
		BEHOLDEST	64	25	if ye B. me ye will labor while it is
109	3	now thou B. O Lord, that thy servants	67	3	ye endeavored to B. that ye should
		BEHOOVETH	80	4	verily B. and know to be true
21	10	it B. me that he should be ordained	84	74	they who B. not on your words
61	9	it B. me that ye should part	90	8	of the Gentiles as many as *will* B.
124	49	it B. me to require that work no more	109	67	B. in the Messiah and be redeemed
		BEING	130	17	I B. the coming of the Son of Man will
20	19	the only B. whom they should worship	132	64	then shall she B. and administer
45	1	which live and move and have a B.		65	because she did not B. and administer to
107	4	reverence to the name of the Supreme B.	134	1	we B. governments were instituted of
		BEINGS		2	we B. no government can exist in
77	3	represent the glory of the classes of B.		3	we B. all governments require civil
88	39	all B. who abide not in those conditions		4	we B. religion is instituted of God; but we do not B. that human law
129	1	there are two kinds of B. in heaven		5	we B. all men are bound to sustain
134	12	allowing human B. to be held in servitude		6	we B. every man should be honored in
		See *Fellow-beings*.		7	we B. rulers, states and governments; we do not B. that they have a right in
				8	we B. crime should be punished
				9	we do not B. it just to mingle religious
				10	we B. all religious societies have; not B. that any religious society has

Sec.	Vs.	
	11	we B. men should appeal to the civil; we B. all men justified in defending
	12	we B. it just to preach the gospel; not B. it right to interfere with bond; such interference we B. to be unlawful

BELIEVED

Sec.	Vs.	
20	26	not only those who B. after he came; who B. in the words of the prophets
34	·4	blessed are you because you have B.
38	4	as many as have B. in my name
45	8	B. on my name gave I power to obtain
74	2	who B. not the gospel of Jesus Christ
	4	traditions of their fathers and B. not
76	51	B. on his name and were baptized
133	71	ye B. not my servants and when they

BELIEVER

74	5	that a B. should not be united to an
124	119	unless he shall be a B. in the Book of

BELIEVES

58	59	which he knows and most assuredly B.
128	4	he verily B. above statement to be true

BELIEVETH

5	16	whosoever B. on my words them will I
68	9	he that B. and is baptized shall be; he that B. not shall be damned—112:29
	10	he that B. shall be blest with signs
84	64	every soul who B. on your words
112	29	that B. not and is not baptized

BELIEVING

8	1	B. that you shall receive a knowledge
11	10	B. in the power of Jesus Christ
	14	in faith B. in me that you shall receive
14	8	ask Father in my name in faith B.—18:18
90	24	pray always and be B.

BELLIES

56	17	whose B. are not satisfied and whose

BELLY

89	7	strong drinks are not for the B.
	8	tobacco not for body neither for B.
	9	hot drinks are not for the body or B.

BELONG

20	63	vote of the church to which they B.
41	6	not meet that the things which B.

Sec.	Vs.	
51	4	not accounted worthy to B. to the church—5
70	10	who B. to the church of the living God
81	2	keys of the kingdom which B. always
83	1	women and children who B. to the
90	25	to those who do not B. to your families
104	1	all properties which B. to the order
	62	for it shall B. to you all with one
107	95	first seventy to whom they B.
	98	who B. not unto the Twelve neither to
130	5	this earth but those who do B. to it
132	62	not commit adultery for they B. to him

BELONGED

77	5	who B. to the seven churches and were
130	5	angels who belong or have B. to it

BELONGETH

10	55	whosoever B. to my church need not
42	78	every person that B. to this church
46	4	not to cast anyone out who B. to
51	10	let that which B. to this people not
84	39	oath and covenant which B. to the priesthood
124	30	for this ordinance B. to my house
	33	ordinance of baptizing for the dead B.
132	61	not commit adultery with that that B.

BELONGING

84	29	appendages B. to the high priesthood
	30	appendages B. to the lesser priesthood
104	5	inasmuch as any man B. to the order
107	81	there is not any person B. to the
124	123	the officers B. to my priesthood
128	17	most glorious of all subjects B. to

BELONGS

51	7	let that which B. to this people
98	5	rights and privileges B. to all mankind
107	40	rightly B. to literal descendants
113	6	unto whom rightly B. the priesthood

BELOVED

7	1	John, my B., what desirest thou?
	5	my B. has desired that he might do more
93	15	saying, this is my B. son
123	17	dearly B. brethren, let us cheerfully
128	15	dearly B. brethren and sisters let me

Sec.	Vs.	
		BELOW
88	6	also he descended B. all things
122	8	Son of man hath descended B. them all
		BENEATH
29	14	signs in heaven above and earth B.—45:40
58	33	their reward lurketh B. and not from
63	59	I am from above, my power lieth B.
78	14	above all other creatures B. celestial
84	100	the Lord hath brought up Zion from B.
101	34	things that are above, things that are B.
		BENEFIT
42	35	for the public B. of the church
46	9	for the B. of those who love me
	26	for the B. of the children of God
59	18	made for the B. and use of man
70	15	for their B. while they remain
72	21	obtain funds which shall B. the church
82	13	for the B. of the saints of the Most
	17	for the B. of managing concerns
	18	all this for the B. of the church
84	103	or make use of it for their B.
89	1	a word of wisdom for the B. of the
91	5	whoso is—shall obtain B. therefrom
96	3	for B. of those who seek inheritances
	4	that is necessary to B. mine order
104	1	everlasting order for the B. of my
	40	for the B. of the Ozondah
111	2	in this city for the B. of Zion
117	14	merchant unto my name for the B. of my
134	1	instituted of God for the B. of man
135	3	instructions for the B. of children
		BENEFITED
46	9	that all may be B. that seek or ask
91	6	not by the spirit cannot be B.
123	16	a large ship is B. very much by a
		BENEFITS
70	5	to manage them and the B. thereof
	8	the B. shall be consecrated unto the
		BENIGHTED
121	4	dark and B. dominion of Shayole
		BENJAMIN
10	41	till you come to the reign of King B.
		BENNETT, JOHN C.
124	16	let my servant B. help you in your
		BENSON, EZRA T.
136	12	let B. and, organize a company

Sec.	Vs.	
		BENT, SAMUEL
124	132	viz., B., H. G. Sherwood, and
		BESEECH
109	42	deliver thou, O Jehovah, we B. thee
		BESIDE
76	1	B. him there is no Savior
		BESIDES
107	95	choose other seventy B. the first
109	59	appoint unto Zion other stakes B. this
133	45	neither hath eye seen, O God, B. thee
		BESPEAKETH
60	4	know what it is that B. the power of God
		BEST
42	72	as may be thought B. or decided by
46	8	seek ye earnestly the B. gifts
88	118	seek ye out of the B. books words of—109:7
109	14	taught words of wisdom out of the B.
134	5	B. calculated to secure the public
135	6	cost the B. blood of the nineteenth
		BESTOW
33	15	I *will* B. the Holy Ghost upon them
		BESTOWED
5	4	this is the first gift that I B.
39	8	I have B. great blessings upon thy
52	37	let that which was B. upon Heman
58	60	let that which has been B. upon Ziba
88	33	profit a man if a gift is B. upon
102	4	according to the grace of God B.
107	53	there B. upon them his last blessing
133	52	all that he has B. upon them according
		BESTOWS
76	116	which God B. on those who love him
107	92	all the gifts of God which he B.
		BETIMES
121	43	reproving B. with sharpness
		BETTER
25	10	and seek for the things of a B.
42	80	if more than two witnesses it is B.
54	5	B. for him that he had been drowned
76	32	B. for them never to have been born
121	22	B. for them that a millstone had
		BETWEEN
28	11	take thy brother B. him and thee alone—42:88
57	4	running directly B. Jew and Gentile
58	25	shall counsel B. themselves and me

Sec.	Vs.		Sec.	Vs.	
64	11	let God judge B. me and thee.		32	after they are laid before the B. of
101	95	that men may discern B. the righteous		33	residue to be consecrated unto the B.
				34	as shall be appointed by the B. and
102	30	distinction B. the High Council	71	who are appointed to assist the B. as; property which is consecrated to the B.
124	140	difference B. this quorum and the			
128	18	welding link B. the fathers and			
	20	in the wilderness B. Harmony, and		72	as thought best by counselors and B.
134	6	regulating our interest B. man and		73	B. also shall receive his support for
				82	it is necessary that the B. be present
		BEWARE	46	27	unto the B. of the church and unto such
23	1	B. of pride lest thou shouldst enter —25:14; 38:39	48	6	as is appointed to him by the B. of
41	12	B. how you hold them for they are to	51	5	which he has consecrated to the B.
46	8	B. lest ye are deceived		12	shall be done through the B. or the
50	9	let every man B. lest he do that		13	let the B. appoint a storehouse unto; be kept in the hands of the B.
52	12	let my servant Lyman Wight B. for			
63	15	let such B. and repent speedily	53	4	in the place appointed by the B.
	61	let all men B. how they take my name	57	15	let the B. make preparations for those
82	2	B. from henceforth and refrain from sin	58	35	in laying his moneys before the B.
				51	put into hands of B. to purchase lands
84	43	commandment to B. concerning yourselves		55	made known by the B. or the agent of
90	5	oracles of God, let them B. how they	64	40	even the B. if he is not faithful
		BEYOND	68	19	he may officiate in the office of B. —107:17
67	5	that you might express B. his language		22	no B. or high priest shall be tried
88	90	heaving themselves B. their bounds	70	11	neither the B., neither the agent
		BIBLE	72	2	expedient for a B. to be appointed
42	12	of my gospel which are in the B.		5	account of their stewardship unto the B.—16
		BID		6	to be handed over unto the B. in Zion
125	5	now I B. farewell to the Gentiles		7	duty of the B. shall be made known
		BILLINGS, TITUS		9	making known the duty of the B.
63	39	let B. who has the care thereof, dispose		13	an account shall be handed over to B.
				14	shall answer the debt unto the B. in
		BILLOWING		15	must lay all things before the B.
122	7	if the B. surge conspire against thee		17	certificate from judge or B. unto B.
		BIND		18	otherwise he shall not be accepted of B.
43	9	B. yourselves to act in all holiness		19	who shall give an account unto the B.
82	15	B. yourselves by this covenant			
88	84	to B. up the law and seal up the testimony—109:46		20	have claim for assistance upon the B.
				25	let them carry up unto the B. a certificate from the B.
124	93	whatsoever he shall B. on the earth 127:7; 128:8, 10; 132:46.	84	29	offices of elder and B. are necessary
134	4	worship to B. the consciences of men		104	send it up unto the B. in Zion or unto the B. in Ohio
		BINDING		112	the B., N. K. Whitney, should travel round
128	14	this is the sealing and B. power		113	let the B. go unto the city of New York
		BINDS	85	1	who receive inheritances legally from B.
128	9	power which records or B. on earth and B. in heaven			
			90	22	let B. search diligently to obtain an agent
		BISHOP		30	an inheritance from the hand of the B.
20	67	every B. is to be ordained by the			
41	9	should be ordained a B. unto the church		35	the B. also have many things to repent
42	31	they shall be laid before the B. of			

Bishop   45   Blessed

Sec.	Vs.	
93	50	B. of my church hath need to be chastened
99	6	sent up kindly to the B. in Zion
107	68	wherefore office of B. is not equal; office of B. is in administering temporal
	69	a B. must be chosen from High Priesthood
	73	this is the duty of a B. who is not a
	76	to act in the office of B. independently
	78	not satisfaction upon decision of B.
	88	this president is to be a B., for
117	11	be a B. unto my people, not in name
119	1	put into hands of the B of my church
120	1	composed of the B. and his council

BISHOPRIC

68	16	they have a legal right to the B. if
82	12	to manage all things pertaining to the B.
107	15	B. is the presidency of this priesthood
114	2	planted in their stead and receive their B.
124	21	I seal upon his head the office of a B.
	141	if he will receive it to preside over B; a knowledge of said B. is given.

BISHOPS

20	66	but traveling B. may have privilege
68	14	other B. to be set apart unto the church
72	20	claim for assistance upon the bishop or B.
107	74	becomes necessary to have other B.
	75	as there are other B. appointed

BISHOP'S

102	2	could not be settled in B. council

BITTER

19	18	that I might not drink the B. cup
29	39	if they never should have B. they
42	47	wo unto them for their death is B.

BLACK

135	1	by an armed mob painted B.—of from

BLACKENING

123	10	which dark and B. deeds are enough

BLACKEST

127	1	founded in falsehood of the B. dye

BLACKNESS

122	7	if the heavens gather B. and all
133	69	I clothe the heavens with B.

Sec.	Vs.	

BLADE

86	4	the B. is springing up and is yet tender
	6	pluck not up the tares while the B.

BLAMELESS

4	2	that ye may stand B. before God
38	31	righteous people without spot and B.
88	133	to walk in commandments of God, B.

BLASPHEME

105	15	not be left to B. my name upon the

BLASPHEMED

112	26	and have B. against me in the midst

BLASPHEMIES

132	26	shall commit all manner of B.

BLASPHEMY

132	27	the B. against the Holy Ghost

BLASTED

121	11	their hope shall be B. and their

BLEED

19	18	to B. at every pore and to suffer

BLESS

20	70	Jesus Christ and B. them in his name
	77	to B. and sanctify this bread to
	79	to B. and sanctify this wine to the
21	9	I will B. all those who labor in
24	3	I will B. them both spiritually and
31	2	I will B. you and your family
32	5	I will B. them—70:18; 104:31
41	1	whom I delight to B. with the greatest
49	4	by so doing I will B. him, otherwise
81	3	I acknowledge him and will B. him
97	5	I will B. him with a multiplicity—124:13, 90
	28	I will B. her with blessings
108	8	I am with you to B. you and deliver
124	55	that I may B. you and crown you with
132	47	whomsoever you B. I will B. and
	55	I will B. him and multiply him
	56	I will B. her and multiply her

BLESSED

1	28	made strong and B. from on high
6	9	my commandments and you shall be B—11:9
	10	B. art thou because of thy gift
	14	B. art thou for what thou hast done
	29	if they reject my words, B. are ye
	30	do as they have done unto me B. are ye
	31	reject not my words B. are they
8	4	apply unto it, and B. art thou for
14	11	ye shall be B. both spiritually and

Sec.	Vs.		Sec.	Vs.	
15	5	B. are you for this thing and for—16:5		46	hand of Adam who also B. him—107:47
18	8	he shall be B. unto eternal life:—30:8		48	and he was 65 and Adam B. him
19	37	B. be the name of the Lord God.—36:3; 39:19	108	54	and they rose up and B. Adam and
23	1	thou art B. and art under no condemnation	110	3	B. with exceeding great blessings
31	1	B. are you because of your faith in	117	12	all generations after us should be B.
34	4	B. are you because you have believed		10	let him be B. with the blessings of my
	5	more B. are you because you are called	124	15	B. is my servant Hyrum Smith for I
35	4	thou art B. for thou shalt do great		19	B. and holy is he for he is mine
	17	and in weakness have I B. him		58	in thy seed shall kindred of earth be B.
36	1	you are B. and your sins are forgiven		79	let my servant I. Galland be B. of him; they shall be greatly B.
38	14	ye are B. not because of your iniquity		93	whoever he blesses shall be B. and
45	46	if ye have slept in peace B. are you	136	11	if ye do this ye shall be B.; B. in your flocks and herds
46	32	for whatsoever blessing ye are B. with			**BLESSES**
50	5	B. are they who are faithful and	124	93	whoever he B. shall be blessed and
	36	B. are you who are now hearing these			**BLESSING**
52	34	faithful shall be kept and B. with	10	50	they did leave a B. upon this land
54	6	B. are they who have kept the covenant	19	38	and great shall be your B.
56	18	B. are the poor who are pure in heart	21	9	in my vineyard with a mighty B.
58	2	B. is he that keepeth my commandments	24	4	I will send a cursing instead of a B.—24:6
	61	some of whom are exceedingly B. even		15	ye shall leave a cursing instead of a B.
59	1	B. are they who have come up unto this	25	12	it shall be answered with a B. upon
	3	B. are they whose feet stand upon	39	10	receive a B. so great as you never
61	14	I in the beginning B. the waters		15	I have kept in store a B. such as is
	17	so in the last days have I B. it in	46	32	give thanks for whatsoever B. ye are
62	3	ye are B. for the testimony which ye	58	32	I revoke and they receive not the B.
63	30	and if by purchase behold you are B.	62	7	in chariots, he shall receive this B.
	49	B. are the dead that die in the Lord	67	3	believe that ye should receive the B.
	50	that liveth and has kept the faith B. is he	75	19	leave your B. upon that house
66	1	B. are you as you have turned away	96	9	ye shall ordain him unto this B.
	2	B. are you for receiving mine everlasting	101	61	this shall be my seal and B. upon you
84	13	days of Abraham and was B. of him	103	12	after much tribulation cometh the B.
	60	B. are ye inasmuch as ye receive these		13	this is the B. which I have promised
86	11	B. are ye if ye continue in my goodness	104	22	this stewardship and B. I confer; for a B. upon him and his seed after him—104:37, 40
90	2	art B. from henceforth that bear the		44	for a B. upon him and his father
92	2	commandments you shall be B. forever		61	he shall be ordained unto this B.
97	2	B. are such for they shall obtain		79	obtain this B. by your diligence and
99	3	B. are they for they shall obtain mercy	105	12	I have prepared a great endowment and B.—105:18
104	2	B. with a multiplicity of blessings	107	53	there bestowed upon them his last B.
106	7	B. is my servant Warren for I will	110	10	this is the beginning of the B. which
107	42	and was B. by him three years previous	124	57	his B. shall also be put upon the head
				91	patriarch, by B. and also by right
				95	and be crowned with the same B. and
			130	21	when we obtain any B. from God it is
			132	5	all who will have a B. at my hands, shall abide the law appointed for that B.

Blessing — 47 — Blood

Sec.	Vs.	
133	34	this is the B. of the everlasting God; and the richer B. upon the head of Ephraim

BLESSINGS

Sec.	Vs.	
18	45	B. which I give unto you are above all
21	8	manifestations of my B. upon his works
39	8	I have bestowed great B. upon thy head
41	1	I delight to bless with greatest B.
58	4	after much tribulation cometh the B.
59	4	they shall also be crowned with B.
61	37	the B. of the kingdom are yours—78:18
70	15	for a manifestation of my B. upon
78	17	not understood how great B. the Father
82	23	my B. continue with you
96	7	is partaker of the B. of the promise
97	5	I will bless him with a multiplicity of B.—124:13, 90
	28	I will bless her with B., and multiply a multiplicity of B. upon her and him—104:38
104	2	blessed with a multiplicity of B.
	13	as stewards over earthly B.
	23	I will multiply B. upon him—104:25, 31, 33, 35, 42, 46
	33	even a multiplicity of B.—104:42, 46
107	18	hold the keys of all spiritual B. of
	29	decisions not entitled to the same B.
	67	comes administering of ordinances and B.
108	3	blessed with exceeding great B.
109	21	and be restored to the B. which thou
110	9	rejoice in consequence of the B. which
117	10	let him be blessed with the B. of my
	15	let the B. of my people be on him forever
122	2	seek B. constantly from under thy hand
124	17	will crown him with B. and great glory
	21	that he may administer B. upon the heads
	48	for instead of B. ye bring cursings
	92	hold the keys of the patriarchal B.
	97	keys by which he may ask and receive B.
	120	be attended with cursings and not B.
	124	to hold the sealing B. of my church
130	20	upon which all B. are predicated
132	48	shall be visited with B. and not cursings

BLEST

Sec.	Vs.	
68	10	that believeth shall be B. with signs

Sec.	Vs.	
124	46	they shall not be B. because they pollute

BLIND

Sec.	Vs.	
19	40	canst thou run about as a B. guide
35	9	shall cause the B. to receive their sight
58	11	then shall the poor, the lame and the B.
84	69	they shall open the eyes of the B.
121	12	to B. their minds that they may not

BLINDED

Sec.	Vs.	
76	75	who were B. by the craftiness of men—123:12
78	10	they become B. and understand not

BLINDNESS

Sec.	Vs.	
58	15	which are unbelief and B. of heart

BLOOD

Sec.	Vs.	
20	40	emblems of the flesh and B. of Christ
	79	in remembrance of the B. of thy Son
27	2	my B. which was shed for remission
29	14	the moon shall be turned into B. 34:9; 45:42
	17	my B. shall not cleanse them if they
38	4	by virtue of the B. which I have spilt
45	4	behold the B. of thy Son which was shed, the B. of him whom
	41	they shall behold B. and fire and
49	21	wo unto that man that sheddeth B.
58	53	save it be by the shedding of B.
63	28	into their hearts to the shedding of B.
	29	not be obtained but by purchase or B.
	31	if by B. as you are forbidden to shed B.
64	36	rebellious are not of the B. of Ephraim
76	69	through the shedding of his own B.
87	7	the B. of the saints shall cease to
88	75	clean from the B. of this wicked
	85	their garments are not clean from the B.
	87	the moon shall be bathed in B.
	94	persecuteth saints, that shed their B.
	138	save he is clean from the B. of this
101	80	redeemed the land by the shedding of B.
109	42	and cleanse them from their B.
	49	and their B. come up in testimony
112	33	lest the B. of this generation be
122	6	like wolves for the B. of the lamb
132	19	murder whereby to shed innocent B. 132:26, 27.
133	51	their B. have I sprinkled upon my

Blood / Bondage

Sec.	Vs.	
135	3	sealed his works with his own B.
	4	he was murdered in cold B.
	5	my garments are not spotted with your B.
	6	cost the best B. of the nineteenth
	7	B. on the floor of Carthage jail. B. on the escutcheon of the State of; B. on the banner of liberty and on; B. with the innocent B. of all martyrs; till he avenges that B. on the earth
136	36	and they have shed innocent B.
	39	should seal his testimony with his B.

BLOODSHED

87	6	thus, with the sword and by B. the
109	66	may lay down their weapons of B.
130	12	difficulties which will cause much B.

BLOSSOM

49	24	Lamanites shall B. as the rose
117	7	make solitary places to bud and B.

BLOTTED

20	83	their names may be B. out of the
98	27	and shall not be B. out—98:44
109	34	and let them be B. out forever

BLOW

90	5	when the winds B. and the rains descend

BLOWN

127	1	when I learn the storm is fully B. over

BOARDING

124	23	it shall be a house for B., a house
	56	as pertaining to my B. house; for the B. of strangers
	111	I have appointed to build a house for B.

BOAST

84	73	they shall not B. themselves of
105	24	neither B. of faith nor of mighty

BOASTED

3	13	judgment, and B. in his own wisdom

BOASTING

50	33	neither with B. nor rejoicing less

BOASTS

3	4	yet if he B. in his own strength

BODIES

45	17	absence of your spirits from your B.
76	70	they whose B. are celestial
	78	are B. terrestrial and not B. celestial
84	33	by the Spirit unto renewing of their B.
88	20	that B. who are of the celestial

Sec.	Vs.	
	28	ye shall receive your B. and your glory that by which your B. are quickened
	67	your whole B. shall be filled with
	124	arise early that your B. and minds
89	7	but for the washing of your B.
129	1	having B. of flesh and bones
131	8	when our B. are purified we shall see

BODY

19	18	and to suffer both B. and spirit
20	77	in remembrance of the B. of thy Son
27	2	remembering unto the Father my B.
59	19	to strengthen the B. and enliven the Soul
84	80	neither in B., limb, nor joint
109		how shall the B. be able to stand
110		the B. hath need of every member
88	15	spirit and B. is the soul of man
	27	they shall rise again a spiritual B.
	28	shall receive the same B. which was a natural B.
	67	that B. which is filled with light
89	8	tobacco is not for the B. neither
	9	hot drinks are not for the B. or belly
101	37	care not for B. neither life of the B.
107	22	High Priests chosen by the B.
130	22	Father has a B. of flesh and bones; Holy Ghost has not a B. of flesh and

BOIL

133	41	which causeth the waters to B.

BOLD

128	9	may seem to be a very B. doctrine

BOND

43	20	both old and young, both B. and free
44	5	that every B. may be broken
78	11	organize yourselves by a B. or
82	11	bound together by a B. or covenant
88	125	clothe yourselves with the B. of charity; the B. of perfectness and peace

BONDAGE

19	35	release thyself from B.
45	17	spirits from your bodies to be a B.
84	49	under darkness and under B. of sin—84:50, 51
101	79	that any man should be in B. to another
103	17	needs be led out of B. by power
104	83	be delivered this once out of your B.
	84	loan enough to deliver yourselves from B.
109	63	the yoke of B. may begin to be broken

Sec.	Vs.	
121	18	that they might bring them into B. and

BONDS

Sec.	Vs.	
24	11	strength, whether in B. or free
78	5	equal in the B. of heavenly things
88	133	grace of God in the B. of love
132	7	all B. that are not made and entered

BOND-SERVANTS

134	12	not right to interfere with B.

BONES

29	19	flesh shall fall from off their B.
85	6	it maketh my B. to quake while it
89	18	health in their navel, marrow to their B.
129	1	having bodies of flesh and B.
	2	a spirit hath not flesh and B. as
130	22	Father has a body of flesh and B.; Holy Ghost has not a body of flesh and B.

BOOK

1	6	preface unto the B. of my commandments
17	6	he has translated the B., even that
20	35	nor diminishing from the prophecy of his B.
	82	kept in a B. by one of the elders
67	6	seek ye out of the B. of commandments
77	6	what are we to understand by the B.—77:14
85	5	written in the B. of the law of God
	7	enrolled in the B. of the law of God
	9	found written in the B of remembrance
	11	not found written in the B. of the law
88	2	recorded in the B. of the names of the
99	5	written of me in the volume of the B.
128	4	enter record on the general church B.; when this is done on general church B.; record of same on general church B.
	6	another B. was opened which was B. of life—128:7
	7	B. which was the B. of life is record
	20	of prophets—the B. to be revealed; witnesses to bear record of the B.
	24	a B. containing records of our dead
132	19	shall it be written in Lamb's B. of life
135	1	to seal the testimony of this B.

BOOK OF COMMANDMENTS

67	6	seek ye out of the B. the least among them

BOOK OF DOCTRINE AND COVENANTS

Sec.	Vs.	
124	141	of bishopric is given unto you in the B.
135	3	commandments which compose this B.
	6	B. of the church cost best blood

BOOK OF ENOCH

107	57	things were all written in the B.

BOOK OF MORMON

1	29	translate by the power of God the B.
19	26	impart it freely to printing of B.
20	8	prepared to translate the B.
24	1	called and chosen to write B.
27	5	whom I have sent unto you to reveal B.
33	16	B. and Holy Scriptures are given
42	12	gospel which are in the Bible and B.
84	57	remember new covenant even B.
124	119	unless he shall be a believer in B.
135	1	to seal testimony of this book and B.
	3	he has brought forth the B.
	4	in B. and turned down the leaf
	6	every nation will be reminded that the B.

BOOKS

55	4	selecting and writing B. for schools
88	118	seek ye out of the best B. words of wisdom—109:7
90	15	become acquainted with all good B.
109	14	taught words of wisdom out of best B.
128	6	and the B. were opened; things which were written in the B.—128:7
	7	you will discover that the B. were; which were written in the B.; B. spoken of must be B. which contained
	8	for out of the B. shall your dead be

BOOTH, EZRA

52	23	let Isaac Morley and B. take their
64	15	angry with him who was my servant B.

BORDERING

57	5	every tract B. by the prairies

BORDERS

17	1	wilderness on the B. of the Red Sea
28	9	be on the B. by the Lamanites—54:8
82	14	her B. must be enlarged; her stakes
107	74	until the B. of Zion are enlarged
133	9	that the B. of my people may be enlarged

BORE

76	40	voice out of the heavens B. record

Sec.	Vs.		Sec.	Vs.	
93	6	John saw and B. record of the fulness	29	13	for a trump shall sound B. long and—43:18; 88:94
	7	he B. record saying, I saw his glory		24	fulness thereof, B. men and beasts
	26	John B. record of me saying, He		31	created all things, B. spiritual and
132	37	concubines and they B. him children	34	6	sound of a trump B. long and loud
133	53	he redeemed them, and B. them and carried	38	40	that every man, B. elder, priest
			42	67	establish you B. here and in the New
		BORN	43	20	repent, B. old and young, B. bond and
5	16	they shall be B. of me even of water	50	22	B. are edified and rejoice together
76	32	better for them never to have been B.		27	all things are subject unto him, B. in
		BORNE	51	13	let all things, B. in money and meat
5	1	of which you have testified and B. record	52	32	let B. be ordained and also take their
62	3	testimony ye have B. is recorded in	57	16	unto the residue of B. elders and members
		BORROWED	59	18	B. to please the eye and gladden the
136	25	return that which thou hast B.	63	37	declare B. by word and by flight that
		BORROWEST	71	7	to meet you B. in public and in private
136	25	if thou B. of thy neighbor thou	72	3	stewardship, B. in time and in eternity
		BOSOM	78	3	B. in this place and in the land of
9	8	your B. shall burn within you	82	12	B. in land of Zion and in Shinehah
35	20	even as they are in mine own B.	88	85	B. in this world and in world to come
38	4	taken Zion of Enoch into mine own B.	88	104	saying to all people B. in heaven
	38	gathered unto the B. of the church	93	17	he received all power B. in heaven
76	13	who was in the B. of the father—76:25, 39	101	24	every corruptible thing, B. of man
			102	11	in case of the absence of one or B.; B. or either of them
88	13	his throne, who is in the B. of eternity	109	52	be wasted away B. root and branch
	17	in whose B. it is decreed that the	123	2	B. of character and personal injuries
109	4	Jesus Christ, the Son of thy B.	127	1	my enemies B. in Missouri and this state
122	6	tear thee from the B. of thy wife	128	11	B. as well for the dead as for the living
		BOSOMS	132	7	B. as well for time as for all eternity
38	30	treasure up wisdom in your B.		30	B. in the world and out of the world
		BOSTON	134	1	B. in making laws or administering
84	114	let the bishop go to the city of B.		6	B. to be answered by man to his Maker
		BOTH	135	1	they were B. shot after they were dead, B. received four
1	8	power given to seal B. on earth and			**BOUGHT**
6	2	dividing asunder of B. joints and marrow—11:2; 12:2; 14:2	60	5	let there be a craft made or B. as
7	8	ye shall B. have according to your; ye B. joy in that which ye have desired	101	56	I have B. it with money
			103	22	the land which I have B. with money
14	8	things which you shall B. hear and see			**BOUND**
	11	ye shall be blessed B. spiritually	35	24	keep all covenants by which ye are B.
18	6	unto repentance, B. the Gentiles and	43	31	for Satan shall be B. and when he is
	26	declare my gospel B. unto Gentile	45	55	Satan shall be B. that he shall have no
19	18	and to suffer B. body and spirit	82	10	I am B. when ye do what I say but
20	4	to whom be all glory B. now and for		11	be B. together by a bond and covenant
	36	rendered to his holy name B. now and			
24	3	I will bless them B. spiritually and			
	12	voice of a trump, B. day and night			
27	13	B. which are in heaven and which are—88:79			

Sec.	Vs.		Sec.	Vs.	
84	100	Satan is B. and time is no longer	109	52	wasted away both root and B. from
86	7	tares are B. in bundles and the field—101:66	133	64	it shall leave them neither root nor B.
88	94	she is B. in bundles, her bands are			**BRANCHES**
	110	Satan shall be B., that old serpent	72	23	ensample for all extensive B. of my
104	5	break the covenant with which ye are B.	107	39	duty of the Twelve in all large B.
	47	no longer be B. as an united order			**BRASS**
	53	you are not B. only up to this hour	124	27	with iron, with copper and with B.
124	93	he shall bind on earth shall B. in			**BREACH**
127	7	whatsoever you bind on earth may be B. in heaven—128:8, 10	134	8	theft, and B. of the general peace
132	15	they are not B. by any law when they			**BREAD**
	46	it shall be eternally B. in heavens	20	40	and to administer B. and wine
133	72	sealed up testimony and B. *up* the law		75	meet often to partake of B. and wine
134	5	all men are B. to sustain and uphold		77	to bless and sanctify this B. to the
	7	are B. to enact laws for the protection	42	42	that is idle shall not eat the B. nor
			88	141	and after partaking of B. and wine
		BOUNDARIES	124	90	nor his seed be found begging B.
84	3	in the western B. of the state of			**BREAK**
133	31	B. of the everlasting hills shall	1	19	and B. *down* the mighty and strong ones
		BOUNDS	5	27	he *will* B. the covenant he has before
88	38	unto every law there are certain B.	42	52	inasmuch as they B. not my laws
	90	heaving themselves beyond their B.	45	28	a light shall B. *forth* among them
102	8	removal from the B. of this church		36	when the light shall begin to B. *forth*
121	30	if there be B. set to the heavens	58	21	let no man B. the laws of the land; hath no need to B. the laws of the
122	9	for their B. are set they cannot pass	84	40	which he cannot B. neither can it be
		BOW	101	57	B. *down* the wails of mine enemies
5	24	but if he *will* B. *down* before me	104	5	shall B. the covenant with which ye
49	10	nations of the earth shall B. to it	109	33	B. it off, O Lord, B. it off from the
76	93	all things B. in humble reverence		47	B. off, O Lord, this yoke of affliction
	110	all shall B. the knee and every tongue—88:104	128	22	let the earth B. *forth* into singing
123	7	have been made to B. *down* with grief	133	22	which shall B. *down* the mountains
		BOWED			**BREAKETH**
106	6	when my servant Warren B. to my sceptre	78	12	he who B. it shall lose his office
107	56	notwithstanding he was B. *down* with age	84	41	whoso B. this covenant after he hath
		BOWELS	88	35	that which B. a law and abideth not
84	101	truth is established in her B.			**BREAKING**
85	7	his B. shall be a fountain of truth	101	54	kept the enemy from B. *down* the hedge
101	9	my B. are filled with compassion			**BREASTPLATE**
121	3	and thy B. moved with compassion—121:4	17	1	the B., the sword of Laban, the Urim
	45	let thy B. also be full of charity	27	16	having on the B. of righteousness
		BOX-TREE			**BREASTWORK**
124	26	bring the B. and the fir-tree	110	2	we saw the Lord standing upon the B.
		BRANCH			**BRETHREN**
10	60	they were a B. of the house of Jacob	3	18	suffered to destroy their B. the
20	65	where there is a regularly organized B.	10	48	might come unto their B. the Lamanites
	66	where there is no B. of the church	45	5	spare these my B. that believe on my
107	74	in *any* B. of the church where he shall		11	is the God of Enoch and his B.

Sec.	Vs.		Sec.	Vs.	
48	2	ye shall impart to the eastern B.	136	34	thy B. have rejected you and your
	5	but after your B. come from the east			**BRIDE**
54	3	if your B. desire to escape their	109	74	and be adorned as a B. for that day
58	60	with his own hands with the B.			**BRIDEGROOM**
59	12	confessing thy sins to thy B.	33	17	may be ready at the coming of the B.
61	18	you shall forewarn your B. concerning	65	3	supper of the Lamb, make ready for B.
	26	commandment you shall give unto all B.	88	92	the B. cometh, go ye out to meet him—133:10, 19
	32	journey for the congregations of their B.			**BRIGHAM**
75	25	inasmuch as your B. are willing to open	126	1	my servant B., it is no more required
81	3	land of the living and among thy B.			**BRIGHT**
84	76	and your B. in Zion for their rebellion	109	79	our voices with those B. shining seraphs
88	132	salute his brother or B. with these			**BRIGHTER**
	133	art thou a brother or B.	50	24	light groweth B. and B. until perfect
	135	or if they be B. they shall salute			**BRIGHTNESS**
90	1	the prayers of thy B. have come up	5	19	utterly destroyed by the B. of my coming
	6	verily I say unto thy B., Sidney	65	5	clothed in the B. of his glory
	32	say unto your B. in Zion in love	110	3	his countenance shone above the B. of
	34	your B. in Zion begin to repent			**BRIMSTONE**
97	1	my will concerning your B. in the land	63	17	lake which burneth with fire and B.
98	6	I justify you and your B. of my church	76	36	go away into the lake of fire and B.
100	14	thy B. are in my hands and inasmuch			**BRING**
101	1	your B. who have been afflicted	1	30	to B. it *forth* out of obscurity
103	1	salvation and redemption of your B.	6	6	seek to B. *forth* and establish the cause—11:6; 12:6; 14:6
	11	your B. which have been scattered		9	assist to B. *forth* my work according—11:9
	13	and the tribulations of your B. and the redemption of your B.		11	thou mayest B. many to the knowledge
	30	not return to the land of their B.		28	which shall B. to light this ministry
104	47	bound as an united order to your B.	7	2	that I may live and B. souls unto thee
	48	your B. after they are organized shall		4	he desired that he might B. souls
	53	dissolved as an united order with your B.	8	4	slay you and B. your soul to destruction
108	7	strengthen your B. in all your conversation	10	31	if you should B. *forth* the same words
110	6	let the hearts of your B. rejoice		40	I would B. to the knowledge of the
112	1	in behalf of thy B. who were chosen		52	*will* I B. this part of my gospel to the; I do not B. it to destroy that which
	11	have heard thy prayers concerning thy B.		61	I *will* B. to light their marvelous
	12	pray for thy B. of the Twelve		62	I *will* B. to light my gospel which; B. to light the true points of my
	21	by the voice of your B. the Twelve	12	7	desires to B. *forth* and establish
122	5	if thou art in perils among false B.	14	10	I must B. *forth* the fulness of my
	6	tear thee from the society of thy B.	15	6	that you may B. souls unto me—16:6
123	16	you know, B., that a very large ship			
	17	beloved B., let us cheerfully do all			
124	54	I will save all those of your B. who			
128	15	B. and sisters, let me assure you that			
	22	B., shall we not go on in so great a cause? Courage B. and			
	25	B. I have many things to say to you			
135	5	yea and also unto my B. whom I love			

Sec.	Vs.	
17	4	that I might B. about my righteous purposes—17:9
18	12	that he might B. all men unto him
	15	and B. save it be one soul unto me
	16	if you should B. many souls unto me
20	70	having children is to B. them unto
29	7	called to B. to pass the gathering
38	13	to B. to pass even your destruction
39	13	to B. *forth* Zion that it may rejoice
50	61	*will* B. them to judgment—97:2
52	17	B. *forth* fruits of praise and wisdom
58	25	let them B. their families to this land
	27	and B. to pass much righteousness
59	3	it shall B. forth in its strength
64	12	ye shall B. him before the Church
71	8	let them B. *forth* their strong reasons
76	63	they whom he shall B. with him
77	11	to B. as many as will come unto the
84	58	B. *forth* fruit meet for their Father's —101:100
86	4	is beginning to B. *forth* the word
90	26	provided for you to B. to pass my work
93	40	B. *up* your children in light and truth
95	4	that I may B. to pass my strange act—101:95
97	9	I will cause them to B. *forth* as a
98	35	they should B. these testimonies before the Lord—44
104	10	not have power to B. evil upon you
	81	taken out of their minds to B. affliction
109	29	B. to shame and confusion all those
113	8	power of the priesthood to B. again Zion
117	7	to B. *forth* in abundance saith the
121	13	which they are willing to B. upon
	18	that they might B. them into bondage
124	26	B. the box-tree and the fir-tree
	48	ye by your own works B. cursings
128	19	feet of those that B. glad tidings
133	30	they shall B. *forth* their rich treasures
135	6	to B. them *forth* for the salvation of
136	37	out of the heavens to B. *forth* my work

BRINGETH

4	4	perish not, but B. salvation to his soul
10	17	if he B. *forth* the same words we have
42	61	that which B. joy, which B. eternal life

Sec.	Vs.	
52	19	he that is overcome and B. not *forth*
63	24	confusion, which B. pestilence
90	17	for it B. a snare upon your souls
97	7	every tree that B. not *forth* good fruit

BRINGING

6	27	then shall you assist in B. to light
11	19	you may assist in B. to light those
27	6	the keys of B. to pass the restoration
84	104	consecrated for B. *forth* of revelations
96	4	B. *forth* my word to the children of men
	8	he may assist in B. *forth* my word
123	13	wear out our lives in B. to light all
134	8	use their ability in B. offenders

BROAD

132	25	B. is the gate and wide the way that
135	7	is a B. seal affixed to Mormonism

BROKE

40	3	wherefore he B. my covenant
101	51	came by night and B. *down* the hedge and B. *down* the olive trees

BROKEN

1	15	have B. mine everlasting covenant
3	13	has B. the most sacred promises
20	37	with B. hearts and contrite spirits
42	30	covenant and a deed that cannot be B.
44	5	that every band may be B. wherewith
54	4	as the covenant has been B. even so
56	3	commanded and the commandment is B.
	17	poor men, whose hearts are not B.
	18	who are pure in heart whose hearts are B.
59	8	even that of a B. heart and a contrite
78	11	everlasting covenant that cannot be B.
82	11	that cannot be B. by transgression.
97	8	their hearts are honest and are B.
101	45	that olive-trees may not be B. *down*
104	4	have B. the covenant by covetousness
	52	covenants being B. through transgression
	55	which ye have made unto me are B.
	86	master will not suffer his house to be B. *up*
109	63	begin to be B. off from the house of
	70	that their prejudices may be B. *up*
132	43	he hath B. his vow and hath committed

Sec.	Vs.	
	44	innocent and hath not B. her vow
135	7	and the B. faith of the State as

BROOKS

Sec.	Vs.	
128	23	ye rivers, and B. and rills flow down

BROOME

Sec.	Vs.	
128	20	between Harmony and Colesville, B. County

BROTHER

Sec.	Vs.	
7	7	to minister for him and thy B. James
17	1	which were given to the B. of Jared
24	10	thy B. Oliver shall continue in
28	11	thou shalt take thy B. Hiram Page
30	5	take your journey with your B. Oliver; give heed to advice of your B.
	7	except is it his B., Joseph Smith, Jr
	10	your labor shall be at your B. Philip
38	24	let every man esteem his B. as himself—25
42	54	pay for that thou shalt receive of thy B.
	88	if thy B. or sister offend thee
	90	if thy B. or sister offend many
64	9	he that forgiveth not his B. his
84	16	who was slain by the conspiracy of his B.
88	132	salute his B. or brethren with these
	133	art thou a B. or brethren? to be your friend and B.
	135	he that cometh in and is a B.
126	1	dear and well beloved B. Brigham
135	3	blood—and so has his B. Hyrum

BROTHERLY

Sec.	Vs.	
4	6	remember B. kindness, godliness
107	30	to be made in B. kindness and charity

BROTHERS

Sec.	Vs.	
132	55	hundred-fold in this world, mothers, B.

BROTHER'S

Sec.	Vs.	
42	54	shalt not take thy B. garment
136	20	covet not that which is thy B.

BROUGHT

Sec.	Vs.	
8	3	by which Moses B. the children of
18	16	with one soul that you have B. unto me
62	6	I have B. you together that the
74	4	being B. up in subjection to the law
76	39	shall be B. forth by the resurrection
84	55	hath B. the whole church under condemnation
	99	the Lord hath B. again Zion; which was B. to pass by the faith
	100	Lord hath B. down Zion from above; Lord hath B. up Zion from beneath
	101	earth hath travailed and B. forth her
88	14	Is B. to pass the resurrection from
90	5	and are B. under condemnation thereby
	23	storehouse may not be B. into disrepute
98	28	that he be not B. in judgment before
	48	never be B. any more as a testimony
103	24	testimonies which ye have B. before me
	36	all victory and glory is B. to pass
105	11	this cannot be B. to pass until
	19	they should be B. thus far for a trial
107	32	it may be B. before a general assembly
109	30	all their works may be B. to naught
112	8	many high ones shall be B. low and
123	7	with whom we shall be B. to stand
133	50	have B. judgment upon all people
135	3	he has B. forth the Book of Mormon; B. forth the revelations and commandments

BRUISES

Sec.	Vs.	
89	8	is an herb for B. and all sick cattle

BRUNSON, SEYMOUR

Sec.	Vs.	
75	33	and my servant Daniel Stanton and B.
124	132	B. I have taken to myself, no man

BRUTAL

Sec.	Vs.	
135	1	shot after they were dead in B. manner

BUCKLER

Sec.	Vs.	
35	14	I will be their shield and their B.

BUD

Sec.	Vs.	
117	7	make solitary places to B. and blossom

BUFFETINGS

Sec.	Vs.	
78	12	delivered over to the B. of Satan— 82:21; 104:10; 132:26
104	9	ye cannot escape the B. of Satan

BUILD

Sec.	Vs.	
10	52	to destroy, but to B. it up
	54	but I say this to B. up my church
	56	but B. up churches unto themselves to; and B. up the kingdom of the devil
	62	they shall B. it up and shall bring

Build   55   Built

Sec.	Vs.	
11	24	B. upon my rock which is my Gospel
18	5	if you shall B. *up* my church
21	2	to B. it *up* unto the most holy faith
30	6	B. *up* my church among the Lamanites
33	13	upon this rock I *will* B. my church 128:10
39	13	thou art called to B. *up* my church
42	8	B. *up* my church in every region
	11	to B. *up* my church except he be ordained
45	64	as they do repent, B. *up* churches unto
52	33	one man shall not B. upon another's
58	48	let them B. *up* churches inasmuch as
84	32	sent forth to B. *up* my church
94	15	to be a committee to B. mine houses
95	8	commandment that you should B. a house
	11	my will that you should B. a house; you shall have power to B. it
96	2	upon which I design to B. mine holy
97	15	inasmuch as my people B. a house
101	18	to B. *up* the waste places of Zion —103:11
	45	set watchmen and B. a tower that one
	46	the servants began to B. a tower
	64	that I may B. them *up* unto my name
	101	they shall B. and another shall not
107	33	to B. up the church and regulate all
109	2	commanded thy servants to B. a house
	4	which thou didst command us to B.
	5	given of our substance to B. a house
	58	to B. a holy city to thy name
115	8	I command you to B. a house
	10	let my people labor diligently to B.
	15	if my people B. it not according
	16	but if my people do B. it according
124	22	and others B. a house unto my name
	27	B. a house for the Most High to dwell
	30	wherein ye are not able to B. a
	31	command you all ye my saints to B.; I grant sufficient time to B. a house
	33	you have had sufficient time to B.
	38	that he should B. a tabernacle; to B. a house in the land of promise

Sec.	Vs.	
	39	always commanded to B. unto my holy
	43	ye shall B. it on the place where; spot which I have chosen for you to B.
	47	if you B. a house unto my name and do
	51	whom I commanded to B. *up* a city and
	55	I command you again to B. a house
	56	to B. for the boarding of strangers
	83	I, the Lord, *will* B. *up* Kirtland
	111	whom I have appointed to B. a house
	115	let him B. a house for my servant
	145	these offices in my house when you B. it
125	2	B. *up* cities unto my name that they
	3	let them B. *up* a city unto my name
136	19	if any man seek to B. *up* himself

BUILDETH

| 50 | 44 | he that B. upon this rock shall never |
| 63 | 4 | who B. *up* at his own will and pleasure |

BUILDING

42	35	B. houses of worship and B. *up* New
94	3	consecrated unto me for the B. of
	10	dedicated unto me for B. of a house
95	3	concerning the B. of mine house
104	34	reserved for the B. of my houses
	36	laid off for the B. *up* of the city
	39	the lot and B. on which the Ozondah
	43	laid off for the B. of my house which
	59	for the purpose of B. *up* my church
107	34	in B. *up* the church and regulating
115	13	get in debt any more for the B. of a
119	2	for the B. of mine house and for
124	43	where you have contemplated B. it
	62	for the purpose of B. that house
	63	may receive stock for the B. of that
	72	pay stock into their hands for the B.
	121	labors which they do in B. the Nauvoo

BUILDING-SPOT

| 118 | 5 | take leave on the B. of my house |

BUILT

6	34	ye are B. upon my rock, they cannot
22	3	church to be B. *up* unto me even as
27	4	kingdom which shall be B. *up* on the
28	9	knoweth where the city shall be B.
33	13	upon this rock ye are B. and if ye
41	7	should have a house B. in which to
42	62	where the New Jerusalem shall be B.

Sec.	Vs.		Sec.	Vs.	
77	15	and have B. the city of Jerusalem in	29	9	I *will* B. them *up* saith the Lord—64:24
84	3	which city shall be B., beginning at	133	64	day cometh that shall B. as an oven; day cometh that shall B. them *up*
	4	New Jerusalem shall be B. by gathering			
	5	until an house shall be B. unto the	135	6	how easy it will be to B. *up* the dry trees
	31	B. unto the Lord in this generation			**BURNED**
	108	apostles in ancient days B. *up* my church	31	4	field which is white already to be B.
94	4	it shall be B. 55 by 65 feet in	38	12	gather the tares that they may be B.
	16	these two houses are not to be B. until	64	23	he that is tithed shall not be B. at
			86	7	field remaineth to be B.
95	13	be B. not after the manner of the world	88	94	therefore, she is ready to be B.
	14	let it be B. after the manner which	101	66	may be B. with unquenchable fire
97	10	my will that a house shall be B.			**BURNETH**
	11	let it be B. speedily by tithing	63	17	in that lake which B. with fire and
	12	house B. unto me for the salvation	133	41	as the melting fire that B. and as
101	46	and B. a hedge round about and—101:53			**BURNETT, STEPHEN**
	53	and B. a tower also	75	35	also my servant Ruggles Eames and B.
	74	eastern countries when they are B. *up*	80	1	my servant, B., go ye into the world
104	14	B. the earth my very handiwork			**BURNING**
105	5	Zion cannot be B. *up* unless it is by	33	17	having your lamps trimmed and B. and
	33	which I have commanded to be B. unto	64	24	for after today cometh the B.
109	78	which we have B. unto thy name	85	3	to prepare them against the day of B.—109:46
110	6	with their might B. this house unto my	112	24	a day of wrath, day of B., a day of
115	14	let an house be B. unto my name—124:40	121	11	as hoar frost melteth before B. rays
	17	Far West should be B. *up* speedily by			**BURROUGHS, PHILIP**
124	24	habitation if it be B. unto my name	30	10	your labors shall be at your brother B.
	37	perform them in a house which you have B.			**BURST**
	42	and the place whereon it shall be B.	110	13	another great and glorious vision B. upon us
	56	let it be B. unto my name and let my			**BURY**
		BUNDLES	60	13	neither shalt thou B. thy talent
86	7	the tares are bound in B. and the—101:66			**BUSINESS**
88	94	she is bound in B. her bands are made	20	62	do whatever church B. is necessary
		BURDEN	51	14	he shall be employed in doing this B.
112	18	on them I have laid the B. for a	64	18	return upon his B. and to his agency
		BURDENS		29	to the will of the Lord is the Lord's B.
109	48	sorrow, because of their grievous B.	70	5	this is their B. in the church of God
		BURIAL	84	113	to do his secular B. as he shall direct
76	51	after the manner of his B., being	90	16	this shall be your B. and mission
		BURIED	104	49	shall do their B. in their own name—104:50
76	51	being B. in the water in his name	107	59	the church laws respecting church B.
		BURLINGTON		72	to do the B. of the church, to sit
124	88	also to the inhabitants of B.		78	the most important B. of the church
		BURN	114	1	that he settle up all his B. as soon
9	8	cause that your bosom shall B. within	117	1	let them settle up their B. speedily

| Business | 57 | Call |

Sec.	Vs.		Sec.	Vs.	
127	1	all those with whom I have B.; who will transact all B. in a prompt	57	5	as my disciples are enabled to B. lands
128	3	present at all times and do all the B.		6	to B. land in all the regions round
				8	may obtain money to B. lands for the
		BUTTERFIELD, JOSIAH	101	74	they may B. lands and gather together
124	138	I give unto you Joseph Young, B., and			**BY**
		BUY	63	35	Behold this is not yet but B. and B.
48	3	let them B. for the present time in	101	58	B. and B. I may come with the residue

C

Sec.	Vs.		Sec.	Vs.	
		CAESAR	20	11	God does inspire men and C. them
63	26	the Lord rendereth unto C. things which are C.'s		76	kneel with the church and C. upon the
		CAHOON, REYNOLDS	29	2	and C. upon me in mighty prayer
52	30	let C. and, take their journey	33	3	last time I shall C. laborers into my
61	35	let my servants C. and Samuel H. Smith	35	13	I C. upon the weak things of
				23	C. on the holy prophets to prove his
75	32	also my servant Hyrum Smith and C.	39	16	people in Ohio C. upon me in much faith
94	14	lots on the north shall C. and Jared		17	C. faithful laborers into my vineyard
		CAIN	43	18	stay and sleep until I shall C. again
124	75	shall not be unto me as offerings of C.		20	C. upon the nations to repent both old
		CAINAN		21	C. upon you to repent and ye hate me
107	45	God called upon C. in wilderness		28	for the last time C. upon the inhabitants
	53	Adam called Seth, Enos, C., who were	45	18	this temple which ye C. the house of
		CAINHANNOCH		64	C. upon the inhabitants to repent
104	81	write speedily to C., (New York)	58	47	C. upon the rich the high and the low
		CALAMITY	63	1	listen, you that C. yourselves the people
1	17	the Lord knowing the C. which should	65	4	C. upon his holy name, make known
45	50	C. shall cover the mocker and the		5	call upon the Lord that his kingdom
109	46	deliver thy people from the C. of the	71	4	C. upon the inhabitants of the earth
136	35	now cometh the day of their C.		7	C. upon them to meet you in public and
		CALCULATED	82	4	ye C. upon my name for revelations
134	5	best C. to secure the public interest	84	77	from henceforth I shall C. you friends
		CALEB	87	3	they shall C. upon other nations
84	7	Jethro received it under hands of C.	88	62	ye shall C. upon me while I am near
	8	C. received it under hand of Elihu		70	C. a solemn assembly even of those—117; 95:7; 109:6; 133:6
		CALF			
124	84	he setteth up a golden C. for the			
		CALL		71	C. on the Lord and ponder the warning
5	11	servants whom I shall C. and ordain			

Sec.	Vs.		Sec.	Vs.	
	85	until the mouth of the Lord shall C.	20	1	day of the month which is C. April—21:3
93	45	I *will* C. you friends		2	who was C. of God and ordained an—20:3
100	17	*all* that C. on the name of the Lord		66	that a vote may be C.
101	22	*all* they who C. on my name and worship		73	the person who is C. of God and has
	75	who C. themselves after my name—97; 103:4; 125:2	21	1	thou shalt be C. a seer, a translator
102	19	C. upon the twelve councilors to sanction	23	4	thou art not as yet C. to preach
	24	power to C. and organize a council	24	1	thou wast C. and chosen to write the
	28	not sufficient to C. such a council		19	thou art C. to prune my vineyard
	29	it is necessary to C. such a council or not	25	3	thou art an elect lady whom I have C.
104	62	no man among you shall C. it his own	27	8	you might be C. and ordained as Aaron
	82	humble and faithful and C. upon my name	29	7	ye are C. to bring to pass gathering
107	38	to C. upon the seventy when they need	30	2	ministry whereunto you have been C.
	79	have power to C. other high priests	33	2	ye are C. to lift up your voices as
113	8	whom God should C. in the last days		5	this church have I C. *forth* out of the
123	6	which shall C. him *forth* from his	34	5	blessed are you because you are C. of
124	6	I am about to C. upon them to give	36	1	you are C. to preach my gospel as with
	7	C. ye upon them with loud proclamation	39	13	thou art C. to labor in my vineyard
127	2	or bad as you may choose to C. it		14	art not C. to go into the eastern; thou art C. to go to the Ohio
133	6	let every man C. upon the name of	41	2	elders of my church whom I have C.—52:1
	8	C. upon all nations, firstly upon		9	I have C. my servant Edward Partridge
136	29	if thou art sorrowful C. on the Lord	42	44	two or more shall be C. and shall pray
	37	whom I did C. upon by mine angels	43	25	how oft have I C. upon you by the
			44	1	expedient that elders should be C. together

CALLED

Sec.	Vs.		Sec.	Vs.	
1	17	C. upon my servant Joseph Smith, Jr.	45	6	hear my voice while it is C. today
3	10	thou art again C. to the work		66	it shall be C. the New Jerusalem
4	3	if ye serve God ye are C. to the work		67	and it shall be C. Zion
6	4	the same is C. of God—11:4; 12:4; 14:4	47	1	until he is C. to further duties
9	4	the work which you are C. to do is to	53	1	you have C. upon me that it should be
	14	stand fast in the work wherewith I have C.	55	1	thou art C. and chosen and after thou
11	15	not suppose you are C. to preach until C.	57	3	the place which is now C. Independence
12	9	heed with your might, then you are C.	58	58	let a conference meeting be C.
14	11	thou art David and art C. to assist	60	5	for the place which is C. St. Louis
18	8	I have C. him unto mine own purpose	64	23	it is C. today until the coming of the
	9	you are C. with that same calling with which he was C.		25	ye will labor while it is C. today
	14	you are C. to cry repentance unto	68	1	was C. by his ordination to proclaim
	24	in that name shall they be C. at the		19	provided he is C. and set apart and—107:17
	25	know not the name by which they are C.	75	24	support families of those who are C.
	26	there are others who are C. to declare	76	26	and was C. perdition for the heavens
	28	they are C. to go into all the world			

Sec.	Vs.		Sec.	Vs.	
80	5	this is the will of him who hath C. you	127	118	authorities which I have C. to lay
81	1	the calling wherewith you are C.—88:80	128	2	perils which I am C. to pass through
			132	3	who can at any time when C. upon
84	32	also many whom I have C. and sent	133	59	if a man be C. of my Father as was
	86	all the faithful who are C. of God		67	when I C. again there was none of you
85	8	that man who was C. of God	·	71	when I C. to you out of the heavens
87	3	nation of Great Britain as it is C.			**CALLETH**
88	110	that old serpent who is C. the devil	93	1	every soul who C. on my name and
	127	those who are C. to the ministry—97:13	133	16	for he C. upon all men and commandeth
	137	ye who are C. to do this by prayer			**CALLING**
89	3	all saints who are or can be C. saints	18	9	called with that same C. with which
90	32	I have C. you to preside over Zion	20	38	it is his C. to baptize
93	14	he was C. the Son of God because he		64	to perform the duties of his C.
	46	I C. you servants for the world's sake		73	shall say, C. him or her by name
			23	2	make known thy C. unto the church
95	5	many are C. but few are chosen—121:34, 40		3	thy C. is to exhortation—23:4, 5
			24	5	thou shalt continue in C. upon God
99	1	thou art C. to go into the eastern		9	not have strength for this is not thy C.; attend to thy C. and thou shalt have
101	21	they shall be C. stakes for curtains			
	35	though C. to lay down their lives	25	5	thy C. shall be for a comfort unto my
	39	when men are C. to mine everlasting		9	for unto them is his C. that all things
	40	they are C. to be the savor of men			
	52	lord of the vineyard C. upon his servants	36	4	this C. and commandment give I unto you
102	28	only to be C. on the most difficult		5	embracing this C. and commandment
	32	the latter can only be C. in question			
104	48	you shall be C. the United Order; C. the United Order of the City of	39	10	wash away your sins. C. on my name
	66	this shall be C. the sacred treasury	53	1	concerning your C. and election in this
	70	it shall not be C. his nor any part	75	10	C. on the name of the Lord for the—133:40; 136:32
107	2	why the first is C. the Melchizedek			
	3	before his day it was C. the holy	81	1	hearken to the C. wherewith you are
	4	in ancient days C. that priesthood	84	33	faithful unto the magnifying their C.
	13	second priesthood is C. the priesthood		109	let every man labor in his own C.
			88	80	send you again to magnify the C.
	14	why it is C. the lesser priesthood is	100	9	I will ordain you unto this C.
	23	traveling counselors are C. to be the	105	35	there has been a day of C. but the
	25	the seventy are C. to preach the gospel	106	3	high and holy C. which I now give
	45	God C. upon Cainan in wilderness in	107	23	differing in the duties of their C.—25
	53	Adam C. Seth, Enos, Cainan, Mahalaleel	109	6	given to us, C. us thy friends
				10	assist thy people in C. our solemn
	54	blessed Adam and C. him Michael	112	33	Behold, how great is your C.
	65	he shall be C. president of the High	124	103	let him stand in the office of his C.
108	4	until the solemn assembly shall be C.		130	may be appointed unto the same C.
115	3	for thus it shall be C.		132	be ordained unto this C. in his stead
	4	for thus shall my church be C. in the		135	this is the office of their C.
	7	it shall be C. most holy for the ground			**CALLINGS**
122	5	if thou art C. to pass through tribulation	18	32	according to the C. and gifts of God—20:60
124	2	you are now C. immediately to make a	20	27	who should believe in the gifts and C.
	60	name of that house be C. Nauvoo House	84	117	go ye forth in your several C. unto
			97	13	in all their several C. and offices

Sec.	Vs.		Sec.	Vs.	
		CALLS	9	9	you C. write that which is sacred save
107	38	to fill the several C. for preaching	10	37	you C. always judge the righteous; you C. always tell the wicked
		CALM			
135	4	I am C. as a summer's morning	14	9	a light which C. be hid in darkness
		CALMLY	18	25	they C. have place in the kingdom
135	1	Hyrum was shot first and fell C.		46	keep not my commandments you C. be saved
		CAME	19	22	they C. bear meat now but milk they
6	21	I am the same that C. unto my own—10:57; 11:29; 39:3; 45:8	20	29	or they C. be saved in the kingdom
19	24	I C. by the will of the Father and I	22	2	you C. enter in at the straight gate by
20	26	not only those who believed after he C.; even as many as were before he C.	25	15	except thou do this where I am you C. come
29	36	and it C. to pass—29:36, 40; 74:3, 4; 135:5	29	29	where I am they C. come for they have
	37	thus C. the devil and his angels		44	for they C. be redeemed from their
38	3	all things C. by me		47	they C. sin for power is not given
60	1	return to land from whence they C.	38	7	I am in your midst and ye C. see me
	5	journey unto land from whence you C.		37	they that have farms that C. be sold
	8	return to churches from whence they C.	39	16	but I C. deny my word
76	15	we C. to the 29th verse of the 5th	42	30	covenant and a deed which C. be broken—78:11; 82:11
	30	thus C. the voice of the Lord unto us		32	they C. be taken from the church
	41	that he C. into the world even Jesus	45	70	of Zion are terrible wherefore we C. stand
88	48	he who C. unto his own was not	50	21	why is it that ye C. understand
93	9	who C. into the world because the world		31	spirit manifested that you C. understand
	11	which C. and dwelt in the flesh		40	ye C. bear all things now; ye must—78:18
	15	there C. a voice out of heaven saying	58	3	ye C. behold with your natural eyes
101	51	the enemy C. by night and broke down	62	6	I, the Lord, C. lie
	83	she C. unto him saying, avenge me	67	8	if ye C. make one like unto it ye are
107	41	and C. *down* by lineage in the following	68	23	by testimony that C. be impeached
133	66	in that day when I C. unto my own no	76	112	where God and Christ dwell they C. come
		CAMP	78	6	ye C. be equal in obtaining heavenly
61	29	course of the C. of the Lord to journey	80	3	it mattereth not for ye C. go amiss
136	1	will of Lord concerning C. of Israel	84	40	which he C. break neither can it be
		CANAL		62	whatsoever place ye C. go into ye shall
61	23	upon the waters, save it be upon the C.		119	ye C. see it now, yet a little while
	24	after they leave the C. they shall	88	22	he C. abide a celestial glory
		CANCELED		23	who C. abide law of terrestrial C. abide
127	1	will see that all my debts are C.		24	who C. abide law of telestial kingdom C.
		CANKER		35	abideth in sin C. be sanctified by law
56	16	your riches *will* C. your souls		66	in the wilderness because you C. see him
		CANNOT	91	6	receiveth not by Spirit C. benefited
1	31	I C. look upon sin with the least	93	34	when separated man C. receive fulness
3	1	purposes of God C. be frustrated			
6	34	built upon my rock, they C. prevail			

Sec.	Vs.	
97	19	surely Zion C. fall, neither be moved
101	5	all who deny me C. be sanctified
102	6	High Council C. have power to act
	31	from decision of latter C. be an appeal
103	32	if ye C. obtain five hundred seek
	33	if ye C. obtain three hundred seek
104	8	ye C. escape my wrath in your lives
	9	ye C. escape the buffetings of Satan
105	5	Zion C. be built up unless it is by; otherwise I C. receive her unto myself
	11	this C. be brought to pass until mine
	21	those that C. stay who have families
107	70	he C. hold the keys of that priesthood
109	52	if it C. be otherwise, may thine anger
112	17	where my servant Joseph C. come
121	36	powers of heaven C. be controlled only
122	9	for their bounds are set, they C. pass
124	30	this ordinance C. be acceptable only in
	33	baptisms for your dead C. be acceptable
	71	I C. be mocked in any of these things
	72	Joseph C. pay over $15,000 stock in
	99	where the poisonous serpent C. lay hold
128	15	principles that C. be lightly passed over; they without us C. be made perfect—128:18
131	3	if he does not he C. obtain it
	4	he C. have an increase
	8	we C. see it; but when our bodies
132	17	these angels C. be enlarged but remain
	18	when out of the world it C. be received; appointed there by whom they C. pass; they C. inherit my glory for my house
	21	except ye abide my law ye C. attain to
	33	ye C. receive the promise of my Father
	61	he C. commit adultery for they are given; he C. commit adultery with that that
	62	he C. commit adultery for they belong
134	11	where immediate appeal C. be made
135	3	left a fame and name that C. be slain
	7	seal that C. be rejected by any court; witness that all the world C. impeach

Sec.	Vs.	
136	37	ye C. yet bear my glory, but ye shall

CAN'T

| 122 | 6 | father, why C. you stay with us |

CAPABLE

20	71	unless he is C. of repentance
76	116	neither is man C. to make them known
102	7	worthy and C. to act in the place of

CAPACITY

| 89 | 3 | adapted to the C. of the weak and the |

CAPTAINS

136	3	organized with C. of hundreds, C. of fifties, C. of tens
	7	let each company with their C. decide
	15	appoint C. of hundreds of fifties and

CARE

12	8	whatsoever shall be entrusted to his C.
63	39	who has the C. thereof dispose of land
	64	is sacred and must be spoken with C.
88	72	I will take C. of your flocks
101	37	C. not for the body; C. for the soul
123	7	made to bow down with grief and C.
124	113	that shall be entrusted to his C.
126	3	take special C. of your family from

CAREFUL

42	76	ye shall be watchful and C. with all
102	21	if, after a C. re-hearing, any additional
108	3	be more C. henceforth in observing

CAREFULLY

| 88 | 129 | may hear his words C. and distinctly |
| 105 | 24 | C. gather together as much in one region |

CARES

| 39 | 9 | rejected me because of the C. of the world |
| 40 | 2 | the C. of the world caused him to reject |

CARMEL

| 128 | 19 | as the dews of C. so shall knowledge |

CARNAL

| 3 | 4 | dictates of his own will and C. desires |

Sec.	Vs.		Sec.	Vs.	
29	35	they are not temporal, neither C. nor		14	in no C. shall more than six be appointed
67	10	not with the C., neither natural mind		16	to present C. after evidence is examined
	12	neither after the C. mind		18	who are appointed to speak on the C.
84	27	and the law of C. commandments, which		19	understanding which he shall have of C.

CARRIED

				20	and the C. shall have a rehearing
107	78	C. *up* unto the council of the church		21	if additional light is shown upon C.
133	53	and C. them all the days of old		22	but in C. no additional light is shown

CARRY

				23	in C. of difficulty, if there is not a sufficiency written to make C. clear
68	32	C. these sayings unto the land of Zion		27	which C. shall there be conducted
69	1	moneys that he shall C. unto the land		28	nor ordinary C. is to be sufficient
72	25	let them C. *up* unto the bishop a certificate		32	called in question in C. of transgression
				33	determine whether any such C. is

CARTER, GIDEON

			104	76	in C. of transgression the treasurer
75	34	also my servant Sylvester Smith and C.		77	in C. treasurer is found an unfaithful

CARTER, JARED

			107	29	unless this is the C. their decisions
52	38	let C. be ordained a priest		32	in C. any decision of these quorums
79	1	C. should go again into eastern		76	except in a C. where a president of
	4	let your heart be glad my servant C.	127	1	turning out property as C. may require
94	14	lots on north shall C. receive an	128	18	it is sufficient to know in this C.
102	3	C. and, were chosen a standing High Council	132	39	save in the C. of Uriah and his wife

CASES

	34	Orson Hyde, C., etc., (signatures)	42	83	thus ye shall do in *all* C. which shall

CARTER, JOHN S.

			52	19	spirits in *all* C. under heavens
102	3	Martin Harris, C., chosen a standing	102	15	the accused in *all* C. has a right
	34	Luke Johnson, C., etc., (signatures)		18	in *all* C. the accuser and the accused

CARTER, SIMEON

				28	only to be called on most difficult C.
52	27	let Solomon Hancock, and C. take their	107	78	the most difficult C. of the church

CAST

75	30	let my servant C. and, be united in	6	22	C. your mind upon the night that you

CARTER, WILLIAM

			29	21	whore of all earth shall be C. *down*
52	31	let my servants Baldwin and C. take	41		C. *out* from the garden of Eden

CARTHAGE

			35	9	they shall C. *out* devils; they shall 84:67; 124:98
124	88	also to the inhabitants of C.	41	5	and shall be C. *out* from among you
135	1	they were shot in C. jail on the		6	or pearls to be C. before swine
	4	when Joseph went to C. to deliver	42	20	he that will not repent shall be C. *out*—42:21, 23, 24, 26, 28, 37.
	7	innocent blood on floor of C. jail		74	ye shall not C. them *out* from among you

CASE

				75	they shall be C. *out* from among you
5	29	if this be the C. I command you— 5:30	45	50	shall be hewn down and C. into the fire—97:7
42	74	testify before you that this is the C.		57	shall not be hewn down and C. into fire
	81	elders shall lay C. before the church			
102	1	three presidents as the C. might require			
	11	in C. of the absence of one or both; in C. that he himself is absent, the			
	13	council convenes to act upon any C.			

Sec.	Vs.		Sec.	Vs.	
46	3	never C. any one *out* from public meetings	88	96	shall be C. *up* to meet him—88:97 98
	4	commanded not to C. any one *out* who	101	31	C. *up* and his rest shall be glorious
	5	ye shall not C. any *out* of sacrament	109	75	we shall be C. *up* in the cloud to
	6	seeking kingdom ye shall not C. them *out*			**CAUSE**
63	4	able to C. the soul *down* to hell.	5	33	for this C. that thy days may be
	54	wicked and C. them into unquenchable fire		34	for this C. I have said stop and stand
76	106	these are they who are C. *down* to hell	6	6	seek to bring forth and establish C. of Zion—11:6; 12:6
77	8	to C. *down* to regions of darkness	7	4	for this C. the Lord said unto Peter
82	18	to be C. into the Lord's storehouse	8	7	that can C. this gift of Aaron to be
84	105	take the old and C. it unto the poor	9	8	I *will* C. that your bosom shall burn
88	69	C. away your idle thoughts and your		9	shall C. you to forget the thing which
	87	stars shall C. themselves *down* as a fig	10	7	for this C. I said he is a wicked man
	114	devil and his armies shall be C. away		53	for this C. have I said if this generation
101	1	C. out from land of their inheritance		56	C. to tremble and shake to the center
	9	I *will* not utterly C. them off	21	6	*will* C. heavens to shake for your good—35:24
	40	good for nothing only to be C. *out*—103:10		7	inspired to move the C. of Zion in
102	12	duty to C. lots by numbers thereby		8	I *will* C. that he shall mourn no longer
	34	then proceeded to C. lots or ballot	24	10	not suppose he can say enough in my C.
104	68	shall be C. into treasury as fast as	28	8	thou shalt C. my church to be established
	69	let him C. them in the treasury	29	18	and shall C. maggots to come in upon them
122	4	their influence shall C. thee into trouble	30	11	you shall ever open your mouth in my C.
	7	if thou shouldst be C. into the pit; if thou be C. into the deep	35	9	they shall C. the blind to receive their
133	27	an highway shall be C. *up* in the midst	38	6	so *will* I C. the wicked to be kept
		CASTING		32	for this C. I gave unto you commandment—95:7; 133:60
24	13	C. out devils, healing the sick	42	74	put away companions for C. of fornication
	15	C. off the dust of your feet against	45	3	who is pleading your C. before him
		CATCH	55	5	for this C. you shall take your journey
10	25	deceive and lie in wait to C. that ye; that they may C. a man in a lie that	58	6	for this C. I have sent you that you—58:14
	26	to C. themselves in their own snare		27	men should be engaged in a good C.
		CATTLE	63	52	for this C. preached the apostles unto
89	8	an herb for bruises and all sick C.	64	6	have sought occasion against him without C.
104	68	in houses, or in lands, or in C., or in		14	for this C. ye shall do these things
		CAUGHT		19	for this C. have I spoken these things
10	13	may say they have C. you in the words	74	5	for this C. the apostles wrote unto church
27	18	ye shall be C. *up* that where I am ye	78	4	to advance the C. which ye have espoused
61	18	lest faith fail and they are C. in her	88	89	earthquakes that shall C. groanings in
76	102	C. *up* unto the church of the firstborn	93	42	this is the C. of your affliction

Sec.	Vs.	
97	9	I *will* C. them to bring forth fruitful
98	13	whoso layeth down his life in my C.
101	52	why! what is the C. of this great evil
109	52	that the C. of thy people fail not
	65	and C. that the remnants of Jacob
	74	and C. the mountains to flow down at
124	38	for this C. I commanded Moses that he
	51	for this C. have I accepted offerings
	75	to plead the C. of the poor and needy
	89	with his interest support C. of poor
127	1	they pursue me without a C. and have
	2	and for what C. it seems mysterious
128	22	shall we not go on in so great a C.
130	12	difficulties which will C. bloodshed
133	57	for this C. that men might be made
134	12	to C. them to be dissatisfied with their

CAUSED

5	3	I have C. you should enter into covenant
10	10	alter words which you have C. to be written
	11	translated and C. to be written
19	18	which suffering C. myself even God
22	1	all old covenants have I C. to be done
	3	I have C. this last covenant and church
29	41	I C. that he should be cast out of the
40	2	cares of the world C. him to reject
76	18	this C. us to marvel for it was given
84	27	which the Lord C. to continue with house

CAUSETH

10	26	he C. them to catch themselves in their
38	12	which C. silence to reign and all eternity
133	41	as fire that C. waters to boil

CEASE

87	7	blood of saints shall C. to come up
88	121	C. from all your light speeches
	123	C. to be covetous
	124	C. to be idle; C. to be unclean; C. to find fault one with another; C. to sleep longer than
90	33	let them C. wearying me concerning
101	26	the enmity of all flesh shall C. from
103	7	they shall never C. to prevail until
109	50	that they may C. to spoil, that they

Sec.	Vs.	
	66	lay down their weapons and C. rebellions
112	9	let the tongue of the slanderer C.
124	49	perform that work and C. not their diligence
	87	and C. to fear concerning his family
	116	C. to do evil and lay aside all his
127	4	work be continued on and not C.
136	23	C. to contend one with another; C. to speak evil one of another
	24	C. drunkenness and let your words tend

CELESTIAL

76	70	these are they whose bodies are C.
	78	they are bodies terrestrial and not C.
	87	terrestrial through the ministration of the C.
	92	thus we saw the glory of the C.
	96	the glory of the C. is one even as
78	7	give unto you a place in the C. world
	14	above all other creatures beneath C. world
88	2	even them of the C. world
	4	even the glory of the C. kingdom
	18	that it may be prepared for C. glory
	20	bodies who are of the C. kingdom may
	22	not able to abide law of C. kingdom cannot abide C. glory
	25	the earth abideth law of a C. kingdom
	28	they who are of a C. spirit shall
	29	quickened by a portion of C. glory
101	65	crowned with C. glory when I shall
105	4	union required by law of C. kingdom
	5	by the principles of the law of C. kingdom
130	11	each of those who come into the C. kingdom
131	1	in the C. glory there are three heavens

CENTER

10	56	to tremble and shake to the C.

CENTER-PLACE

57	3	the place now called Independence is C.

CENTURY

135	6	cost the best blood of the nineteenth C.

CEPHAS

76	99	who are of Paul, and Apollos and C.

Sec.	Vs.	
		CERTAIN
38	34	C. men among them shall be appointed—48:5
88	38	unto every law there are C. bounds
101	44	a C. nobleman had a spot of land very
		CERTAINTY
100	11	that thou mayest know the C. of all
		CERTIFICATE
20	64	each priest may take a C. from him at the time, which C. when
	84	which C. may be signed by any elder
72	17	a C. from the judge or bishop in this
	25	let them carry up unto the bishop a C., or a C. from the bishop
		CERTIFICATES
128	4	being attended with C. over their own; with C. and all attending witnesses
		CERTIFY
128	2	additional views which I now C.
	3	can at any time when called upon C. to
		CERTIFYING
20	84	letter C. that they are regular members
128	3	C. in his record that he saw with his
	4	C. that the record they have made is true
		CHAFF
52	12	Satan desireth to sift him as C.
		CHAINS
38	5	wicked have I kept in C. of darkness
123	8	they are the handcuffs and C. of hell
		CHAMBER
128	21	voice of God in C. of old father Whitmer
		CHAMBERS
38	13	a thing which is had in secret C.
	28	enemy in secret C. seeketh your lives
		CHANCE
104	84	inasmuch as you obtain a C. to loan money
		CHANGE
121	12	to C. the times and seasons and to blind
124	108	let him C. their habitation
		CHANGED
43	32	C. in the twinkling of an eye— 63:51; 101:31

Sec.	Vs.	
		CHAPTER
45	60	know any further concerning this C.
76	15	we came to the 29th verse of the 5th C. of John
77	1	sea of glass spoken of by John 4th C.
	8	four angels spoken of in the 7th C.
	9	ascending from the east, Revelations 7th C.
	10	the things spoken of in this C. to be
	12	mentioned in the 8th C. of Revelations
	13	are written in the 9th C. of Revelations
	14	mentioned in the 10th C. of Revelations
	15	witnesses in 11th C. of Revelations
85	12	found recorded in 2nd C. of Ezra
88	141	pattern given in 13th C. of John's
113	1	5th verses of 11th C. of Isaiah
	3	the 1st verse of the 11th C. of Isaiah
	5	spoken of in 10th verse of 11th C.
	7	meant by the command in Isaiah 52nd C.
128	17	for Malachi says, last C., verses 5th
135	4	near the close of the 12th C. of Ether
		CHARACTER
123	2	damages sustained both of C. and personal
128	4	from his knowledge of the general C.
134	11	or the right of property or C. infringed
		CHARGE
82	7	I will not lay any sin to your C.
84	42	given mine angels C. concerning you
113		also employ an agent to take C.
96	2	let my servant Ahashdah take C. of the
109	22	and thine angels have C. over them
121	10	neither C. thee with transgression as
	11	they who do C. thee with transgression
		CHARIOTS
62	7	if any desireth to ride in C. he shall
		CHARITY
4	5	faith. hope, C. and love, qualify him
	6	remember godliness, C., humility
6	19	have patience, faith, hope and C.
12	8	having faith, hope and C., being temperate
18	19	if you have not faith, hope and C. you
88	125	clothe yourself with the bonds of C.
107	30	decisions are to be made in all C.
121	45	let thy bowels be full of C. towards

Sec.	Vs.		Sec.	Vs.	
124	116	clothe himself with C. and cease to do			**CHEERFUL**
135	5	give Gentiles grace that they might have C.; if they have not C. it mattereth not	59	15	do these things with C. hearts; with a glad heart and a C. countenance
		CHARTERS			**CHEERFULLY**
124	46	they pollute mine holy grounds, and C.	123	17	let us C. do all things that lie in our
		CHASE			**CHICKENS**
50	25	that you may C. darkness from among you	10	65	as a hen gathereth her C. under her—29:2; 43:24
		CHASTEN			**CHILD**
75	7	I C. him for the murmurings of his heart	99	3	whoso receiveth you as a little C.
90	36	*will* C. her until she overcomes and is			**CHILDHOOD**
95	1	whom I love I also C. that their sins	84	28	baptized while he was yet in his C.
98	21	I, the Lord, *will* C. them and will do			**CHILDREN**
		CHASTENED	2	2	he shall plant in the hearts of the C.; hearts of the C. shall turn to their
1	27	as they sinned they might be C. that	4	1	work to come forth among the C. of *men*—6:1; 11:1; 12:1; 14:1
42	90	he or she shall be C. before many	5	6	deliver my words to the C. of *men*
58	60	until he is sufficiently C. for his sins	8	3	Moses brought the C. of Israel through
61	8	until you were C. for all your sins	11	22	word gone forth among the C. of *men*; word which shall come forth among C. of *men*; all which I shall grant unto C. of *men*
64	8	for this evil they were sorely C.			
93	50	N. K. Whitney hath need to be C. and set			
95	2	ye must needs be C. and stand rebuked	17	4	my righteous purposes unto C. of *men*—17:9
	10	therefore I sent them forth to be C.	18	6	that C. of *men* are stirred up unto
97	6	there are those that must needs be C.		18	which are expedient unto the C. of *men*
100	13	although she is C. for a little season	42		and C. who arrived to the years of
101	4	they must needs be C. and tried even as	44		work a marvelous work among the C. of *men*
	41	therefore they must needs be C.	19	7	that it might work upon hearts of C. of *men*
103	4	C. for a little season with a sore and		19	finished my preparations unto C. of *men*
105	6	be C. until they learn obedience by	20	70	every member of church having C. is
		CHASTENING	27	9	turning hearts of fathers to C., and hearts of C. to—98:16; 110:15; 128:17
87	6	feel the C. hand of Almighty God, until			
101	5	all who will not endure C. cannot be	29	34	neither any man nor the C. of *men*
		CHASTISEMENT		39	needs be that devil should tempt C. of *men*
95	1	for with C. I prepare a way for their		46	little C. are redeemed from foundation
103	4	might be chastened with a sore C.		47	power not given unto Satan to tempt C.
136	31	he that will not bear C. is not worthy	35	10	great things to be shown forth unto C. of *men*
		CHEER	38	11	powers of darkness prevail among C. of *men*
61	36	be of good C. little children for I am		20	for the inheritance of your C. forever
68	6	be of good C. and do not fear for I			
78	18	be of good C. for I will lead you along	39	15	a blessing not known among C. of *men*
112	4	let thy heart be of good C. before my			

Sec.	Vs.		Sec.	Vs.	
41	6	things which belong to C. of the kingdom		12	done unto them as unto C. of the priest
43	15	to teach the C. of *men* the things which	89	21	pass by them as C. of Israel and not slay
45	55	Satan no place in hearts of C. of *men*	93	39	taketh away light from the C. of *men*
	58	their C. shall grow up without sin unto		40	bring up your C. in light and truth
46	15	according to conditions of C. of *men*		42	you have not taught your C. light and
	26	for the benefit of the C. of God		44	the commandment concerning his C.
50	40	ye are little C. and ye cannot bear	96	4	bringing forth my word unto C. of *men*—96:8
	41	fear not little C. for you are mine		5	my word shall go forth unto C. of *men*; subduing hearts of C. of *men* for your
55	4	that little C. may receive instruction			
58	17	divide heritage of God unto his C.	98	28	even your children's C. unto the third and
	51	an inheritance for the C. of God		29	come upon your C. or your children's C. unto
	52	Lord willeth that C. of *men* should open		30	also thy C. and thy children's C. unto
61	25	do like unto the C. of Israel pitching		46	upon his C. and children's C. of all that hate
	36	be of good cheer little C. for I am in		47	but if C. shall repent or children's C.
63	51	C. shall grow up until they become old	99	6	not go until your C. are provided for
64	22	I require the hearts of the C. of *men*	101	17	notwithstanding her C. are scattered
66	2	gospel sent forth unto the C. of *men*		18	come to inheritances they and their C.
68	25	inasmuch as parents have C. in Zion		41	here is wisdom concerning the C. of
	27	their C. shall be baptized for remission		81	unto what shall I liken the C. of Zion
	28	they shall teach their C. to pray and to		85	thus will I liken the C. of Zion
	31	their C. are growing up in wickedness	103	16	lead them like as Moses led the C. of
74	1	else were your C. unclean but now are		17	for ye are the C. of Israel and seed of
	3	desirous that his C. should be circumcised		35	establish C. of Zion upon the laws and
	4	the C. being brought up in subjection	104	17	have given unto C. of *men* to be agents
	6	that their C. might remain without; which saith that little C. are unholy	106	5	that you may be the C. of light
	7	little C. are holy being sanctified by	109	4	salvation administered to the C. of *men*
78	17	ye are little C. and ye have not as yet		61	thou hast a great love for C. of Jacob
83	1	laws concerning women and C. who belong		62	have mercy upon C. of Jacob
	4	all C. have claim upon their parents		64	C. of Judah may begin to return to the
84	23	this Moses taught to the C. of Israel		69	have mercy upon his wife and C. that
	27	continue among the C. of Israel until	112	6	publishing my name among C. of *men*
	56	condemnation resteth upon the C. of Zion	121	17	and are the C. of disobedience themselves
	58	to be poured out upon the C. of Zion		37	upon the souls of the C. of *men*
	59	shall the C. of the kingdom pollute my	123	7	duty to our wives and C. who have been; who have inherited lies upon hearts of C.—123:9
85	5	nor the names of the C. written in the			
	7	and of their C. enrolled in the book			

Sec.	Vs.		Sec.	Vs.	
128	11	in relation to salvation of C. of *men*	95	5	many are called but few are C.—121:34, 40
	18	welding link between the fathers and C.		6	they who are not C. have sinned
132	37	concubines and they bore him C.		8	endow those whom I have C. with power
	55	wives and C. and crowns of eternal lives	102	3	C. to be a standing council for church
133	30	treasures unto C. of Ephraim my servants	105	35	let those be C. that are worthy
	32	servants of Lord even C. of Ephraim		36	voice of the spirit those that are C.
135	3	instructions for the benefit of C. of *men*	107	22	presiding high priests C. by the body
136	22	I am he who led the C. of Israel out		40	to the literal descendants of the C. seed

CHILDREN'S

				42	his posterity should be C. of the Lord
98	28	even your C. children unto the third		69	a bishop must be C. from the High Priesthood
	29	come upon your children, or your C. children		72	assistance of counselors whom he has C.
	30	also thy children and thy C. children unto		93	C. out of the number of the seventy
	37	their C. battles and their C. children	112	1	brethren who were C. to bear testimony
	46	upon his children and C. children of all that hate		7	thou art C. and thy path lieth among
	47	but if children shall repent or C. children		16	thou art the man whom I have C. to

CHOICE

			121	34	and why are they not C.
101	44	nobleman had a spot of land very C.	124	26	send swift messengers, C. messengers

CHOKE

				43	spot which I have C. for you to build
86	3	the tares C. the wheat and drive church		76	I have C. him and anointed him

CHOOSE

CHRIST

37	4	let every man C. for himself until I	18	21	take upon you the name of C.
107	72	counselors whom he has chosen or *will* C.	19	1	I am Alpha and Omega, C. the Lord
	95	seven presidents are to C. other seventy	20	37	they have received of the spirit of C.
124	135	they may travel also if they. C. but		40	the emblems of the flesh and blood of C.
127	2	good end or bad as you may C. to call it		59	teach and invite all to come unto C.
136	7	C. out a sufficient number of able-bodied	38	4	for I am C., and in my own name, by the

CHOOSING

			45	26	shall say that C. delayeth his coming
105	35	time has come for a day of C. and let	46	31	all things must be done in name of C.

CHOSEN

			68	25	faith in C. the son of the living God
1	4	whom I have C. in these last days	74	4	and believed not the gospel of C.
3	9	thou wast C. to do the work of the Lord	76	28	take the kingdom of our God and his C.
	10	thou art still C. and art again called		50	this is the testimony of the gospel of C.
19	9	I speak unto you that are C. in this		59	they are Christ's and C. is God's
24	1	thou wast called and C. to write the		62	in the presence of God and his C.
29	4	that ye are C. out of the world to		68	where God and C. are the judge of all
51	3	Partridge and those whom he has C.		82	they who received not the gospel of C.
52	1	whom he hath called and C. in these last		85	until the Lord, even C. the Lamb shall
	21	unto all the elders whom I have C.—108:4		100	some of C. and some of John and some of
55	1	thou art called and C.			

Sec.	Vs.		Sec.	Vs.	
	106	when C. shall have subdued all enemies		43	confirm the C. by the laying on of hands
	112	but where God and C. dwell they cannot		53	teacher's duty to watch over C. always
77	13	seventh seal, before the coming of C.		54	see that there is no iniquity in C.
86	9	hid from the world with C. in God		55	see that the C. meet together often—20:75
88	7	this is the light of C.		57	assisted in all his duties in C. by
	21	not sanctified through the law of C.		62	conferences are to do whatever C. business
105	32	Zion is kingdom of our God and his C.		63	by a vote of the C. to which they belong
107	23	special witnesses of the name of C. in		65	to be ordained to any office in this C.; without a vote of that C.
113	2	verily thus saith the Lord, it is C.		66	where there is no branch of the C. that
	4	it is a servant in the hands of C.		69	members shall manifest before the C.
133	55	who were with C. in his resurrection		70	bring them unto elders before the C.
135	5	shall meet before the judgment-seat of C.		76	he shall kneel with the C. and call
		See Church, Jesus, Jesus Christ		82	members uniting themselves with the C.; names of the whole C. may be kept in a

CHRIST'S

76	59	all are theirs and they are C.		83	if any have been expelled from the C.; blotted out of the general C. record
88	98	they are C. the first fruits, they			
	99	redemption of those who are C. at his		84	all members removing from the C. where; if going to a C. where they are not known; signed by teachers or deacons of C.
130	9	and this earth will be C.			

CHURCH

1	1	hearken, O ye people of my C.—41:2; 45:1, 6; 46:1; 70:1; 133:1; 136:41	21	1	an elder of the C. through the will of
				3	which C. was organized and established
	30	power to lay foundation of this C.; the only true and living C. upon the; speaking to the C. collectively and not—105:2		4	wherefore, meaning the C., thou shalt
				12	the first preacher of this C. unto the C.
5	14	coming forth of my C. out of wilderness	22	3	last covenant and this C. to be built up
10	53	I will establish my C. among them	23	2	make known thy calling unto the C.
	54	not say this to destroy my C. but to build up my C.		3	to exhortation and to strengthen the C.; thy duty is unto the C. forever—23:4, 5.
	55	whosoever belongeth to my C. need not		7	your duty to unite with the true C.
	67	cometh unto me the same is my C.	24	3	go speedily unto the C. in Colesville
	68	therefore he is not of my C.		5	expounding all scriptures unto the C.
	69	whosoever is of my C. and endureth of my C.		10	before the world and also to the C.
11	16	until you shall have word, my C. and		18	the C. shall give unto thee in the hour
18	4	concerning the foundation of my C.	25	7	exhort the C. according as it shall be
	5	if you shall build up my C. upon the		9	thy husband shall support thee in C.
	20	contend against no C. save it be C. of		11	of sacred hymns to be had in my C.
20	2	to be the first elder of this C.	26	1	preaching and confirming C. at Colesville
	3	to be the second elder of this C.			
	33	let the C. take heed and pray always		2	done by common consent in the C. —28:13
	37	by way of commandment to the C.; and witness before the C. that they have; shall be received by baptism into his C.	28	1	thou shalt be heard by the C. in all
	41	confirm those who are baptized into C.			
	42	exhort, baptize and watch over the C.			

Sec.	Vs.		Sec.	Vs.	
	2	receive revelations in this C. excepting		34	appointed by the High Council of the C.
	3	with power and authority unto the C.		35	for the public benefit of the C.
	4	by way of commandment unto the C.		37	shall be be cast out of the C. and shall; unto the poor and needy of my C.—51:5
	6	at thy head and at the head of the C.		59	to be my law to govern my C.
	8	thou shalt cause my C. to be established		67	shall hereafter receive C. covenants
	12	of this C. contrary to the C. covenants		69	the keys of the C. have been given
	14	according to the covenants of the C.		73	remuneration for all his services in C.
29	21	and that great and abominable C. which		78	keep all commandments of the C.
30	4	attend to the ministry in the C.		80	by two witnesses of the C. and not of
	6	build up my C. among the Lamanites		81	elders shall lay case before the C.; the C. shall lift up their hands against
	7	no counselor over him in the C.; concerning C. matters, except		89	deliver him or her up unto the C., not
31	2	and be one with you in my C.		92	that the C. may not speak reproachfully
	7	I will establish a C. by your hand	43	2	commandment for a law unto my C.
	10	you shall be a physician unto the C.		8	know how to act and direct my C.
33	5	this C. have I established and called		9	become instructed in the law of my C.
	13	upon this rock I will build my C.—128:10	46	4	not cast out any one who belongeth to C.
	14	ye shall remember the C. articles—42:13		5	concerning those who are not of the C.
	15	having faith you shall confirm in my C.		6	if there be any that are not of the C.
37	2	strengthened up the C. whithersoever it		10	those gifts that are given unto the C.
	3	commandment I give unto the C. that it		27	unto the bishop of the C.; such as God shall appoint to watch over C., and be elders to C.
38	34	I give unto the C. in these parts a; shall be appointed by the voice of C.—41:9; 51:12	47	3	appointed to keep the C. record and
	36	govern the affairs of the property of C.	48	6	as is appointed by the bishop of the C.
	38	gathered to the bosom of the C.	50	1	as ye have asked touching the C.
39	13	to build up my C. and to bring forth		4	seen abominations in C. that profess my
41	3	that ye may know how to govern my C.		8	wo unto them who are cut off from my C.
	9	ordained a bishop unto the C.; all his time in labors of the C.	51	4	shall hold this inheritance in the C.; not accounted worthy by voice of C. to belong to the C.; according to laws and covenants of C.—68:24; 107:63, 79
42	8	ye shall build up my C. in every region		5	if not accounted worthy to belong to C.
	11	not build up my C. except he be ordained; known to C. he has authority; ordained by the heads of C.		10	not given unto that of another C.
	12	teachers of the C. shall teach the		11	if another C. would receive money of this C. let them pay unto this C.
	18	behold, I speak unto the C.		13	let bishop appoint storehouse unto this C.
	31	shall be laid before the bishop of my C.	52	41	take with them a recommend from the C.
	32	after they are laid before bishop of C.; the consecration of properties of my C.; they cannot be taken from the C.			
	33	properties in the hands of the C.			

Church

Sec.	Vs.	
53	1	your calling and election in this C.
	4	also be an agent unto this C.
55	2	to be an elder unto this C. to preach
	4	writing books for schools in this C.
56	10	and shall be cut off out of my C.
57	6	to be an agent unto the C. to buy lands
	11	be established as a printer unto the C.
58	23	from my hand are the laws of my C.
	35	Harris should be an example unto C.; laying his moneys before bishop of C.
	49	agent appointed by voice of the C., unto C. in Ohio
	55	by the bishop or the agent of the C.
	60	let him stand as a member in the C.
63	63	Let the C. repent of their sins
64	12	ye shall bring him before the C.
	26	until residue of C. shall go up unto
	37	I have made my C. in these last days
68	14	other bishops to be set apart unto C.
	22	before the first presidency of the C.
69	3	shall observe and know concerning my C.
	7	travel from place to place and from C. to C.
	8	which shall be for the good of the C.
70	5	this is their business in the C. of
	6	shall not give these things unto C.
	10	who belong to the C. of the living God
71	2	regions round about and in C. also
72	1	who are the High priests of my C.
	2	the C. in this part of the Lord's vineyard
	9	bishop ordained unto the C.
	10	to receive the funds of the C.
	12	consecrated to the good of the C.
	14	the things of the kingdom unto the C.
	15	thus it cometh out of the C.
	19	give an account unto bishop of the C.; be recommended by the C. or churches
	20	stewards over literary concerns of my C.
	21	obtain funds which shall benefit the C.
	23	ensample for all extensive branches of C.
	24	few words respecting members of the C.
74	5	for this cause the apostle wrote unto C.
75	24	duty of the C. to assist in supporting
	26	obtain support of the C. for them
	28	and let him labor in the C.

Sec.	Vs.	
	29	the idler shall not have place in the C.
76	54	they who are the C. of the first born
	67	to the general assembly and C. of Enoch
	71	differs from that of the C. of the
	94	his presence are the C. of the first-born
	102	caught up unto the C. of the first born
77	11	as many as will come unto C. of first
78	1	ordained unto high priesthood of C.
	4	everlasting order unto my C.—104:1
	12	lose his office and standing in the C.
	14	that the C. may stand independent above
	21	ye are the C. of the first-born—93:22
81	1	to be a high priest in my C.
82	18	all this for the benefit of the C.; common property of the whole C.
	21	dealt with according to laws of my C.
83	1	in addition to the laws of the C.; women and children who belong to C.—107:59
	2	they shall have fellowship in the C.
	3	they shall not have fellowship in the C.
	5	they have claim upon the C. or in other
	6	kept by consecrations of the C.
84	2	the word of the Lord concerning his C.
	17	which priesthood continueth in the C.
	32	sent forth to build up my C.
	34	the C. and kingdom and the elect of God
	55	brought whole C. under condemnation
	86	called of God in C. unto ministry
	108	in ancient days built up my C. unto me
	111	appointed to watch over the C.; to be standing ministers unto the C.
85	1	keep history and general C. record
	4	on any of the records or history of C.
	11	or to have been cut off from the C.
86	3	the great persecutor of the C.; and drive the C. into the wilderness
88	5	glory is that of the C. of first-born
	94	that great C., mother of abomination
	127	even for all the officers of the C.; those who are called to ministry in C.
	140	to be administered by the President of C.

Sec.	Vs.		Sec.	Vs.	
89	1	word of wisdom for the benefit of C.		58	set in order all other officers of C.
90	4	given to another yea even unto the C.		59	C. laws respecting C. business
	13	preside over the affairs of the C. and		65	called president of High Priesthood of C.
	16	set in order all affairs of this C.		66	High Priest over High Priesthood of C.
93	50	Whitney also a bishop of my C. hath need		67	administering blessings upon the C.
94	3	in all things pertaining to the C.		72	to do the business of the C.
97	5	edification of the school and of the C.		74	in any branch of the C. where he shall
98	6	justify you and your brethren of my C.		78	the most important business of the C.; most difficult cases of the C.; carried up unto the council of the C.
	19	not pleased with many in C. at Kirtland			
100	15	and to the sanctification of the C.		80	this is the highest council of the C.
102	2	difficulties that might arise in C. which could not be settled by the C.		81	not any person belonging to C. exempt from council of the C.
	3	chosen a standing council for the C.		82	remembrance before common council of C.
	5	who voted in the name and for the C.		91	to preside over whole C. and be like
	8	removal from bounds of this C. government: to act in the name of the C.		92	gifts which he bestows upon head of C.
	9	president of C. is appointed by revelation; acknowledged by the voice of the C.		98	whereas other officers of the C. who; hold as high and responsible offices in C.
	10	should preside over the council of C.	109	71	remember all the presidents of thy C.
	26	of the seat of first presidency of C. —102:27, 33		72	remember all thy C. O Lord with all
	28	on the most difficult cases of C. matters—107:78		73	that thy C. may come forth out of the
	32	by the general authorities of the C.		79	also this C. to put upon it thy name
104	59	for the purpose of building up my C.	112	27	concerning the affairs of my C. in this
106	1	presiding high priest over my C.	115	3	of the High Council of my C. in Zion; of my C. of Jesus Christ of Latter-day
	8	faithful witness and light unto the C.			
107	1	there are in the C. two priesthoods		4	for thus shall my C. be called, the C. of
	4	the C. in ancient days called that			
	5	other offices in C. are appendages	117	13	redemption of First Presidency of my C.
	8	authority over all offices in the C.			
	9	right to officiate in all offices of C.—107:12	119	1	put into hands of bishop of my C.
				2	for the debts of presidency of my C.
	12	agreeable to the covenants of the C.	120	1	composed of first presidency of my C.
	18	keys of all spiritual blessings of C.			
	19	to commune with the C. of the firstborn	124	32	ye shall be rejected as a C. with your
	22	upheld by faith and prayers of the C.; form a quorum of presidency of the C.		41	I deign to reveal unto my C. things hid
				84	even the Presidency of my C.
	23	differing from other officers in the C.—25		94	prophet, seer, revelator unto my C.
				124	to hold the sealing blessings of my C.
	32	constitute spiritual authorities of C.			
	33	under direction of the presidency of C.; to build up the C. and regulate affairs—34		125	presiding elder over *all* my C.
				126	receive the oracles for the whole C.
				136	quorum of High Priests of my C.
	36	equal in authority in the affairs of C.—37		137	ordained to be standing ministers to my C.
	39	in all large branches of the C.	127	12	prophet and seer of the C. of Jesus

| Church | 73 | City |

Sec.	Vs.	
128	4	C. recorder can enter record on general C. book; appointment of those men by the C.; when this is done on general C. book; made record of same on general C. book
	21	travels and tribulations of C. of Jesus
	24	let us therefore as a C. and a people
133	4	gather together O ye people of my C.
135	6	book of Doctrine and Covenants of C.
136	2	let all the people of the C. of Jesus See Elders

CHURCH, OF CHRIST

Sec.	Vs.	
20	1	the rise of the C. in these last
	38	the duty of the members of the C.
	61	elders composing this C. are to
	68	expound all things concerning C.
	70	every member of C. having children
	71	no one can be received into C.
	80	any member of C. transgressing
	81	duty of churches composing the C.
21	11	that you might be an elder unto C.
42	78	every person who belongeth to C.
102	1	to organize the high council of C.
	12	whenever a high council of C. is
107	59	to the C. in the land of Zion

CHURCHES

Sec.	Vs.	
10	56	who build up C. unto themselves to get
20	81	shall be the duty of the several C.
24	9	laying on hands and confirming the C.
45	64	build up C. unto me
50	37	go forth among the C. and strengthen
52	39	let the elders watch over the C.
58	48	let them build up C. inasmuch as the
60	8	return to the C. from whence they came
	9	and all this for the good of the C.
63	46	now speedily visit the C. expounding
72	19	be recommended by the church or C.
73	1	exhortation to the C. in the regions
77	5	who belonged to the seven C.
90	15	set in order the C., study and learn
101	74	and the C. in the eastern countries
	75	were the C. willing to hearken to my
103	29	preparing the C. to keep commandments
105	8	I speak concerning my C. abroad
109	55	remember the C., all the poor and
124	140	to preside over the C. from time to time

CHURCHES, ALL

Sec.	Vs.	
51	18	this shall be an example in all C.
58	51	to be presented to all the C.
84	112	travel round about among all the C.
101	63	wisdom in me concerning all the C.
	67	a commandment I give unto all the C.
	72	let all the C. gather together all
103	23	let all the C. send up wise men
112	18	have I laid the burden of all the C.

CINCINNATI

Sec.	Vs.	
60	6	let my servants take their journey for C.
61	30	until they arrive at C.

CIRCUMCISED

Sec.	Vs.	
74	3	desirous that his children should be C.

CIRCUMCISION

Sec.	Vs.	
74	2	in days of apostles law of C. was had
	3	contention concerning the law of C.
	6	that children might remain without C.

CIRCUMSTANCES

Sec.	Vs.	
6	18	in whatsoever difficult C. he may be
48	1	as it shall be suitable to your C.
	6	according to his family, according to C.—51:3
70	16	in whatsoever C. I shall place them
84	117	go ye forth as your C. shall permit
104	53	as your C. will admit and the voice of
107	28	when C. render it impossible to be
	98	but are to travel as their C. shall allow
127	1	turning out property as C. may admit

CITIES

Sec.	Vs.	
84	114	warn the people of those C. with the sound
	117	go unto the great and notable C. and
125	2	and build up C. unto my name

CITIZEN

Sec.	Vs.	
134	5	rebellion are unbecoming every C. so

CITIZENS

Sec.	Vs.	
134	7	enact laws for protection of all C.; to deprive C. of this privilege
	9	individual rights of members as C. denied

CITY

Sec.	Vs.	
28	9	no man knoweth where C. is to be built

Sec.	Vs.		Sec.	Vs.	
42	9	when the C. of New Jerusalem shall be		3	form acquaintance with men in this C.
45	12	a C. reserved until day of righteousness		4	I will give this C. into your hands
				9	ancient inhabitants and founder of this C.
	66	a C. of refuge, a place of safety		10	more treasures than one for you in this C.
48	4	purchase land for inheritance, even C.	115	7	let the C., Far West, be a holy and
	6	to lay the foundation of the C.		17	C. of Far West should be built up
52	43	I will hasten the C. in its time	117	10	let him preside in the C. of Far West
57	2	this is the place for the C. of Zion			
58	13	from the mouth of the C. of the heritage	118	5	take leave of my saints in the C. of
			124	51	whom I commanded to build up a C. and a
63	31	ye shall be scourged from C. to C.		109	refuge out of C. even C. of Nauvoo
	49	inheritance before the Lord in holy C.			
66	5	gospel from land to land from C. to C.	125	3	let them build up a C. opposite C. of
75	18	going from village to village from C. to C.—99:1		4	in C. of Nashville or in C. of Nauvoo
76	66	unto C. of the living God, the heavenly	128	3	recorder appointed in each ward of C.
77	15	and build the C. of Jerusalem in land	133	56	stand upon Mount Zion, upon holy C.
78	4	or in other words, the C. of Enoch	135	3	founded a great C. and left a name
79	1	go from place to place, from C. to C.			**CIVIL**
84	2	which shall be the C. of New Jerusalem	134	3	all governments require C. officers
	3	which C. shall be built beginning at		4	that the C. magistrate should restrain crime
	4	the C. New Jerusalem shall be built by		9	mingle religious influence with C.
	93	whatsoever village or C. ye enter do		11	should appeal to the C. law for redress
	94	wo unto that house, or C. that rejecteth you.—95			**CLAIM**
	114	go unto C. of New York, C. of Albany, C. of	51	5	not have power to C. that portion which; only have C. on that portion
94	1	a beginning and foundation of the C.	63	27	that you may have C. on the world
97	19	surely Zion is the C. of our God	68	21	they may C. their anointing if at any
101	82	there was in a C. a judge which feared	72	20	have C. for assistance upon the bishop
	83	and there was a widow in that C.	83	2	women have C. on their husbands for
104	36	lots laid off for building of the C.		4	all children have C. upon their parents
	48	shall be called the C. of Shinehah; United Order of the C. of Zion		5	after that they have C. upon church
109	39	whatsoever C. thy servants shall enter; and people of that C. receive testimony; let thy peace be upon that C. that they may gather out of that C. the righteous—41	101	99	my people should C. and hold C. upon
			123	6	before we can fully C. that promise
					CLAIMETH
	40	let not thy judgments fall upon that C.	88	40	on mercy and C. her own; justice continueth its course and C. its
	41	people of that C. received not testimony; let it be upon that C. according to			**CLAIMS**
			82	17	to have equal C. on the properties
	58	to build a holy C. to thy name			**CLASSED**
111	2	I have much treasure in this C.; many people in this C. whom I will	135	6	their names will be C. among martyrs

Sec.	Vs.	
		CLASSES
77	3	or do they represent C. or orders? represent glory of the C. of beings

		CLEAN
38	10	you are C. but not all—66:3
	42	be ye C. that bear the vessels of the—133:5
88	74	that I may make you C.
	75	that you are C. from the blood of this
	85	their garments are not C. from the blood
	86	let your hands be C. until Lord come
	138	save he is C. from the blood of this
90	36	chasten her until she overcomes and is C. before me
110	5	sins are forgiven, you are C. before
135	5	thou hast been faithful: thy garments are C.

		CLEANLINESS
42	41	let all things be done in C. before me

		CLEANSE
29	17	my blood shall not C. them if they
76	41	to C. it from all unrighteousness
84	92	C. your feet even with water pure
88	74	C. your hands and your feet before me
99	4	C. your feet in the secret places by
109	42	their hands, and C. them from their
112	33	C. your hearts and your garments

		CLEANSED
50	28	except he be purified and C. from all
	29	are purified and C. from all sin
76	52	be washed and C. from all their sins

		CLEANSING
24	15	C. your feet by the wayside

		CLEAR
5	14	C. as the moon, fair as the sun—105:31; 109:73
102	23	to make the case C. to the minds of

		CLEARLY
84	117	setting forth C. and understandingly

		CLEAVE
11	19	C. unto me with all your heart
25	13	C. unto the covenants that thou hast
42	22	shalt C. unto her and none else
45	48	this mount, and it shall C. in twain
98	11	forsake all evil and C. unto all good
132	54	to abide and C. unto my servant Joseph

Sec.	Vs.	
		CLEAVETH
88	40	intelligence C. unto intelligence; light C. unto light

		CLERK
85	1	it is the duty of the Lord's C. whom

		CLERKS
57	9	as C. employed in his service
102	34	Oliver Cowdery, Orson Hyde, C.
127	1	I have left my affairs with agents and C.

		CLIMBETH
59	16	that which C. upon the trees and

		CLING
122	6	thine elder son shall C. to thy garments

		CLOSE
127	11	I now C. my letter for the present—128:25
135	4	near the C. of twelfth chapter of Ether

		CLOSED
110	11	after this vision C.—110:13

		CLOTHE
84	89	who will feed you and C. you and give
88	125	C. yourselves with bonds of charity
124	116	let him C. himself with charity and cease
133	69	I C. the heavens with blackness

		CLOTHED
29	12	C. with robes of righteousness—109:76
	13	to be C. upon even as I am, to be with
38	26	be thou C. in robes; be thou C. in rags
45	44	C. with power and great glory
65	5	C. in the brightness of his glory
84	81	drink, or wherewithal ye shall be C.
101		she is C. with the glory of her God
85	7	C. with light for a covering
109	80	anointed ones be C. with salvation
133	46	C. in his glorious apparel, traveling

		CLOTHES
84	90	he who feeds you or C. you or gives

		CLOTHING
61	11	take that which is needful for C.
136	5	provide themselves with C. and other

		CLOUD
34	7	I shall come in a C. with power and

Sec.	Vs.	
45	45	shall come forth to meet me in the C.
76	102	firstborn, and received into the C.
78	21	he will take you up in a C. and appoint
84	5	a C. shall rest upon it which C. shall
109	75	we shall be caught up in the C.

CLOUDS

45	16	come in my glory in the C. of heaven
	44	they shall see me in the C. of heaven
76	63	when he shall come in the C. of heaven

CLOUDY

109	61	for a long time in a C. and dark day

CLOVEN

109	36	even C. tongues as of fire and the

COAT

84	105	if any man shall give unto you a C.

COATS

24	18	take no purse nor scrip neither two C.—84:78

COE, JOSEPH

55	6	let C. also take his journey with
102	3	C., and, were chosen standing High Council
	34	Cowdery, C., etc., (signatures)

COLD

45	27	the love of men shall wax C.
84	92	pure water, whether in heat or C.
89	13	used only in times of winter or of C.
135	4	he was murdered in C. blood

COLESVILLE

24	3	go speedily to the church in C. and
26	1	and confirming the church at C.
37	2	and more especially in C.
128	20	between Harmony, and C., Broome Co.

COLLECTIVELY

1	30	speaking unto the church C. and not

COLOR

110	2	work of pure gold in C. like amber

COLORING

127	1	not the least shadow or C. of justice

COLTRIN, ZEBEDEE

52	29	let Levi Hancock and C., take their

COMBINATION

109	26	no C. of wickedness shall have power

COMBINATIONS

42	64	and this in consequence of secret C.

COMBINE

6	34	let earth and hell C. against you for
122	7	all elements C. to hedge up the way

COMBINED

38	12	behold, the enemy is C.

COME

1	10	Lord shall C. to recompense to every—56:19
	12	prepare ye for that which is to C.—45:61
	17	knowing the calamity which should C.
	24	that they might C. to understanding
3	1	neither can they C. to naught
	16	as knowledge of a Savior has C. unto world so shall it C. unto
	18	this testimony shall C. to knowledge of
	20	that Lamanites might C. to knowledge of
5	5	wo shall C. unto inhabitants of earth
6	14	thou wouldst not have C. to the place
7	3	thou shalt tarry until I C. in glory
	4	if I will that he tarry until I C.; that thou mightest speedily C. unto me
	7	and the keys of this ministry until I C.
8	2	Holy Ghost which shall C. upon you
10	5	that you may C. off conqueror
	41	till you C. to reign of King Benjamin, or until you C. to that
	48	that my gospel might C. unto their
	66	if they *will* C. they may and partake
18	11	all men might repent and C. unto him
	44	that they may C. unto repentance; that they may C. unto the kingdom of
19	27	look not for a Messiah to C. who has already C.
	41	yea, C. unto me thy Savior
20	13	as many as shall C. to a knowledge of
	27	as well as those who should C. after
	35	revelations which shall C. hereafter
	59	teach and invite all to C. unto Christ
21	8	his days of rejoicing are C. unto the
25	4	which is wisdom in me in a time to C.
	14	and the glory which shall C. upon him

Sec.	Vs.		Sec.	Vs.	
	15	where I am you cannot C.—29:29		46	even so shall ye C. unto me and your souls
27	18	be faithful until I C. and ye shall be		56	day when I shall C. in my glory
29	3	sin no more lest perils shall C. upon		67	that the wicked *will* not C. unto it
	14	before this great day shall C.—34:9; 45:42; 49:24		71	and shall C. to Zion singing with songs
	18	shall cause maggots to C. in upon them	46	26	and all these gifts C. from God
	23	the end shall C. and the heaven and	48	5	after your brethren C. from the east
30	5	the time has C. that it is expedient	49	12	who was on the earth and is to C.
31	3	for the hour of your mission is C.	50	10	and now C. saith the Lord by the spirit
33	18	I C. quickly—34:12; 35:27; 39:24; 41:4; 49:28; 54:10; 68:35; 88:126; 99:5; 112:34	52	11	days C. that I will send forth judgment
34	7	I shall C. in a cloud with power and		20	days have C. according to men's faith
	11	I am with you until I C.	53	6	residue shall be known in time to C.
35	4	before Elijah which should C.	54	7	flee the land lest your enemies C. upon
	18	things which shall C. from this time		10	be patient in tribulation until I C.
	27	the kingdom is yours until I C.	56	14	your sins have C. *up* unto me and are
36	5	as many as shall C. before my servants	57	15	been commanded to C. to this land
	8	I shall suddenly C. to my temple	58	3	those things which shall C. hereafter
37	4	let every man choose for himself until I C.		4	after much tribulation C. the blessings
38	5	which shall C. at end of earth		6	bear testimony of things which are to C.
	22	have no laws but my laws when I C.		11	the deaf C. in unto the marriage of the; be prepared for the great day to C.—65:5
39	10	days of thy deliverance are C.		44	time has not yet C. for many years
	21	no man knoweth, but it surely shall C.	59	1	blessed are they who have C. *up* unto this
41	4	I will be your ruler when I C.		17	and good things which C. of the earth
42	9	time C. when it shall be revealed		18	all things which C. of the earth
	18	in this world nor in the world to C.—76:34; 84:41; 90:3; 93:52		23	and eternal life in the world to C.
	36	when I shall C. to my temple	60	1	it pleaseth me that you have C. up hither
	83	in all cases that shall C. before you		12	residue who are to C. unto this land
43	5	teachings of any that shall C. before		14	after thou hast C. *up* unto the land
	7	shall C. in at the gate and be ordained	61	15	days *will* C. that no flesh shall be
	22	repent for the great day of Lord is C.		16	it shall be said in days to C. that none
	26	the day has C. when the cup of the wrath		18	C. not in journeying upon them lest
	29	in my own due time *will* I C. upon the earth		23	C. not again upon the waters; they shall not C. upon the waters to
	30	for the great Millennium shall C.	63	6	the day of wrath shall C. as a
	33	until they C. before me in judgment		10	signs C. by faith not by the will of
45	5	that they may C. unto me and have		11	signs C. by faith unto mighty works
	10	C. ye unto it and with him that cometh		15	lest judgment C. upon them as a snare
	12	until a day of righteousness shall C.		20	when day of transfiguration shall C.
	16	day when I shall C. in my glory		33	fear shall C. upon every man
	17	how the day of redemption shall C.		37	desolation shall C. upon the wicked
	19	desolation shall C. upon this generation		48	also a reward in the world to C.
	24	when that day shall C. shall a remnant		49	when the Lord shall C.—63:50
	28	when the time of the Gentiles is C. in		53	in a time to C. even in day of coming
	39	looking for great day of Lord to C.			
	44	and behold, I *will* C.			

Sec.	Vs.	
64	42	shall C. unto her out of every nation
	43	day shall C. when nations of earth shall
65	6	that the kingdom of heaven may C.
67	1	whose desires have C. *up* before me
68	6	that I was, that I am, that I am to C.
71	1	the time has verily C. that it is
	4	prepare way for revelations to C.—101:23
76	7	for ages to C. will I make known unto
	8	things to C. will I show them
	9	understanding of prudent shall C. to naught
	59	present, or things to C., all are theirs
	63	when he shall C. in the clouds of
	66	they who are C. unto Mount Zion
	67	who have C. to an innumerable company
	112	where God and Christ dwell they cannot C.
77	9	this is Elias which was to C. to gather
	11	to bring as many as *will* C. to church
	14	who must C. and restore all things
78	3	the time has C. and is now at hand
	15	that you may C. *up* unto the crown prepared
84	42	those who C. not unto this priesthood
	50	bondage of sin because they C. not unto me
	74	shall not C. into my Father's kingdom
	87	teach them of the judgment which is to C.
	119	I *will* C. and reign with my people
87	2	time *will* C. that war will be poured
	7	shall cease to C. *up* into the ears of
	8	be not moved until day of Lord C.
88	2	prayers have C. *up* into the ears of the—90:1; 112:1
	49	day shall C. when you shall comprehend
	52	in the first hour I *will* C. unto you
	68	the days will C. that you shall see him
	84	the hour of judgment which is to C.
	85	both in this world and in the world to C.; call them, for their time is not yet C.
	91	for fear shall C. upon all people
	92	for the judgment of our God is C.
	100	then C. the spirits of men to be judged
	104	for the hour of his judgment is C.—133:38
	113	shall C. *up* to battle against Michael
	126	that ye may not faint until I C.
	132	when any shall C. in after him let the
93	19	that you may C. unto the Father in my
	24	as they were, and as they are to C.
94	8	no unclean thing to C. in unto it—97:15; 109:20
	9	if there shall C. in unto it any unclean; shall not C. into it
95	7	your fastings and mourning might C. *up*
97	16	I *will* C. into it and all pure in heart that shall C. into
	17	if it be defiled I *will* not C. into it; I *will* not C. into unholy temples
	23	it shall not be stayed until the Lord C.
	27	none of these things shall C. upon her
98	17	lest I C. and smite the whole earth—128:17
	28	warn him that he C. no more upon you
	29	then if he shall C. upon you or your
	39	if after thine enemy has C. upon thee; and C. unto thee praying forgiveness
	48	vengeance shall no more C. upon them
99	5	I C. quickly to judgment to convince
100	4	I have suffered you to C. unto this place
101	2	I have suffered affliction to C. upon
	3	when I shall C. to make *up* my jewels
	18	return and C. to their inheritances
	32	when Lord shall C. he shall reveal all
	45	when enemy shall C. to spoil and take
	53	lest the enemy should C. upon you
	58	by and by I may C. with residue of mine
	64	for the time of harvest is C. and my
	65	when I shall C. in the kingdom of my
	92	that these things may not C. upon them
103	15	redemption of Zion must needs C. by power
	24	as mine enemies C. against you to drive
104	1	for the salvation of men until I C.
	51	in consequence of that which is to C.
105	20	that as many as have C. *up* hither that
	35	time has C. for a day of choosing

Sec.	Vs.		Sec.	Vs.	
107	55	a multitude of nations shall C. of thee		19	much the advantage in the world to C.
109	49	and their blood C. *up* in testimony	132	12	no man shall C. unto the Father but by
	67	may C. to a knowledge of the truth		57	lest an enemy C. and destroy him
110	14	behold, the time has fully C. which; great and dreadful day of the Lord C.	133	2	who shall suddenly C. to his temple
				7	time has C. when the voice of the Lord
112	15	shall not be taken from him till I C.		15	lest sudden destruction shall C. upon
	17	where my servant Joseph cannot C.		26	shall C. in remembrance before the Lord
	24	as a whirlwind it shall C. upon all the		52	now the year of my redeemed is C.
	34	be faithful until I C. for I. C. quickly	136	8	cries of widow and fatherless C. not *up*
113	3	that should C. of the Stem of Jesse		42	lest judgment C. upon you and your faith
116	1	where Adam shall C. to visit his people			**COME DOWN**
117	9	C. *up* hither unto land of my people	1	36	C. in judgment upon Idumea or the
	11	C. *up to* the land of Adam-ondi-Ahman	49	10	if not of themselves they shall C.
			63	34	*will* C. in heaven from the presence
	14	let him C. *up* hither speedily unto the	65	5	Son of Man shall C. in heaven, clothed
120	1	time is now C. that it shall be disposed	112	32	keys of dispensation C. from fathers
121	13	may C. upon themselves to the uttermost	133	2	who shall C. upon world with a curse
	28	time to C. in which nothing shall be		40	that thou wouldst C., that mountains
124	5	what shall befall them in a time to C.		42	thou shalt C. to make thy name known
	6	for the set time has C. to favor her			**COME FORTH**
	9	that they may C. to the light of truth	1	19	weak things of world shall C. and
	11	C. ye, O, C. ye, with your gold and silver—124:26	4	1	marvelous work is about to C.— 6:1; 11:1; 12:1; 14:1
	23	a house that strangers may C. from afar	10	33	that the work may not C. in this
				46	prayers should C. unto this people
	24	not suffer any pollution to C. upon it	11	22	study my word which shall C. among
	25	let all my saints C. from afar	20	37	who C. with broken hearts and contrite
	26	all that *will* C. may C. and bring the		74	and C. again out of the water— 128:12
	28	that he may C. and restore again that	29	13	earth shall quake and they shall C.
	49	and their enemies C. upon them and hinder		26	graves shall be opened and they shall C.
	85	who has C. here assaying to keep my	36	6	C. out of the fire hating even the
	103	let him arise and C. *up* and stand in	45	45	shall C. to meet me in the cloud
	105	let him C. and locate his family in the		46	shall C. from four quarters of earth
	106	warn inhabitants to flee the wrath to C.	76	16	voice of the Son of Man and shall C.
	124	hour of temptation that may C. upon you		50	concerning them who C. in resurrection
125	2	that which is in store for a time to C.		65	shall C. in resurrection of the just
	4	let all those who C. from the east	88	97	who have slept in their graves shall C.
128	21	by holding forth that which is to C.	101	89	C. out of his hiding place and in his
129	6	made perfect, he *will* C. in his glory			
130	11	those who C. into the celestial kingdom	109	39	that they may C. unto Zion or to her

Sec.	Vs.		Sec.	Vs.	
	73	that thy church may C. out of wilderness	45	10	with him that C. I will reason as with
117.	2	let them awake. arise and C.		22	ye know that the end of the world C.
132	19	ye shall C. in the first resurrection			
	26	they shall C. in the first resurrection	49	19	and that which C. of earth is ordained
133	29	there shall C. pools of living water		22	Son of Man C. not in form of a woman
	56	they shall C. and stand on right hand	50	45	day C. that you shall hear my voice
			51	20	I am Jesus Christ who C. quickly

COME TO PASS

14	8	and it shall C.—24:16; 29:17, 20; 35:7; 39:12, 23; 42:10, 32, 37, 39, 46, 48, 63, 79; 44:2, 3; 45:21, 39, 68, 71; 46:28; 50:31; 60:3; 64:38; 85:7; 87:4, 5; 90:11; 93:1, 18; 111:4; 119:5; 124:47	54	5	wo to him by whom this offence C.
			58	4	day C. that ye shall be crowned with
				11	after that C. the day of my power
				36	every man that C. unto this land—72:15
29	10	as they spoke so shall it C.		65	and behold the Son of Man C.
	21	these things which have not C.	61	38	for he C. in an hour you think not
45	21	until every desolation shall C.	63	9	faith C. not by signs but signs follow
	35	when these things shall C.			
64	32	all things must C. in their time		54	at that hour C. entire separation
87	1	the wars that will shortly C.		59	day C. that all things shall be subject
88	79	things which must shortly C.			
101	10	even as I have said it shall C.		64	that which C. from above is sacred
			64	24	for after today C. the burning

COMES

			67	9	that which is righteous C. *down* from
49	7	nor shall they know until he C.			
88	86	until the Lord C.	72	15	thus it C. out of the church; every man that C. *up* to Zion
107	7	office of an elder C. under priesthood			
	64	then C. the High Priesthood which is	80	1	every creature that C. under sound of
	67	from the same C. the administering	84	46	every man that C. into the world—93:2
129	4	when a messenger C. saying he has a		47	hearkeneth to voice of Spirit C. to God

COMEST

				51	whoso C. not unto me is under bondage
133	44	when thou C. *down* and the mountains	87	8	for it C. quickly saith the Lord
			88	88	after your testimony C. wrath and

COMETH

				89	after your testimony C. testimony of
1	14	day C. that they who will not hear the		90	also C. testimony of voice of thunderings
	35	all men shall know that day speedily C.		92	bridegroom C. go ye out to meet him—133:10
6	10	it is sacred and C. from above		99	then C. redemption of those who are
10	67	whosoever repenteth and C. unto me		114	then C. the battle of the great God
27	5	hour C. that I will drink of the fruit		130	when he C. into the house of God
31	2	day C. that they will believe and know		135	he that C. in and is faithful before me
33	11	then C. the baptism of fire and of the—39:6	90	10	then C. the day when the arm of Lord
35	10	time speedily C. that great things are	93	1	who forsaketh sins and C. unto me
38	8	day soon C. that ye shall see me		39	wicked one C. and taketh away light and
	18	there shall be no curse when the Lord C.	97	22	vengeance C. speedily upon the—112:24
43	18	day C. that Lord shall utter his voice	98	7	whatsoever is more or less than these C. of evil—98:10; 124:120
	21	day C. when thunders shall utter their	101	21	until the day C. when there is found no
	31	and then C. the end of the earth			

Sec.	Vs.		Sec.	Vs.	
103	12	after much tribulation C. the blessing			**COMING**
112	5	when night C. let not the inhabitants	2	1	before the C. of the great and dreadful day of—128:17
124	10	day of my visitation C. speedily		3	earth would be utterly wasted at his C.
127	11	prince of this world C. but he hath	5	14	the C. *forth* of my church out of wilderness
133	46	who is this that C. *down* from God in		19	destroyed by the brightness of my C.
	64	day C. that shall burn as an oven; day that C. shall burn them up, saith	20	1	since the C. of our Lord and Savior
			29	12	at the day of my C. in a pillar of fire
136	35	now C. the day of their calamity	33	17	be ready at the C. of the bridegroom
		COMFORT	34	6	preparing way of Lord for second C.
25	5	thy calling shall be for a C. unto my		8	be a great day at the time of my C.
107	55	the Lord administered C. unto Adam	35	15	be looking forth for the time of my C.
		COMFORTED		18	from this time until the time of my C.
98	1	fear not, let your hearts be C.—100:15		21	and shall abide the day of my C.
101	14	they who have mourned shall be C.	39	20	preparing way for time of my C.
	16	let your hearts be C. concerning Zion		23	looking forth for the signs of my C.—45:39
		COMFORTER	42	64	in consequence of that which is C. on
21	9	which are given him through me by the C.	45	16	asked me concerning signs of my C.
24	5	things which shall be given thee by the C.		26	shall say that Christ delayeth his C.
28	1	thou shalt teach them by the C.	56	18	shall see kingdom of God C. in power
	4	if thou art led at any time by the C.	58	61	let the elders who are C. to this land
31	11	given you by the C. what you shall do	61	38	looking forth for the C. of the Son of
35	19	given by the C. that knoweth all things		39	that you may abide the day of his C.
36	2	C. which shall teach you peaceable things	63	39	be prepared in the C. spring to take
39	6	C. which showeth all things		53	in the day of the C. of the Son of man
42	16	shall lift up your voices by the C.	64	23	called today until C. of Son of Man; tithed shall not be burned at his C.
	17	the C. knoweth all things	68	11	signs of the C. of the Son of Man
47	4	given by C. to write these things	77	12	preparing way before the time of his C.
50	14	C. which was sent forth to teach truth		13	seventh seal, before the C. of Christ
	17	to preach the word of truth by the C.	84	28	to prepare them for the C. of the Lord
52	9	that which is taught them by the C.	88	99	those who are Christ's at his C.
75	10	C. which shall teach them all things	90	2	which kingdom is C. *forth* for last time
	27	made known by C. whither they shall go	101	84	lest by her continual C. she weary me
79	2	I will send upon him the C. which shall	106	4	the C. of the Lord draweth nigh and
88	3	I now send upon you another C.; which other C. is the same that I promised	108	1	obeyed my voice in C. *up* hither this
	4	this C. is the promise of eternal life	111	1	I am not displeased with your C. this
90	11	by the administration of the C. shed	128	12	the dead C. *forth* out of their graves
	14	time to time as shall be manifest by the C.		24	who can abide the day of his C.
124	97	C. which shall manifest unto him truth	130	12	bloodshed previous to the C. of the Son

Sec.	Vs.		Sec.	Vs.	
	14	to know the time of the C. of the Son of	133	23	he shall C. the great deep and it shall
	16	whether this C. referred to the beginning			**COMMANDED**
	17	I believe the C. of the Son will not	1	5	for I the Lord have C. them
133	17	for the hour of his C. is nigh	5	2	C. you that you should stand as witness
	19	prepare ye for the C. of the bridegroom		3	except to those persons to whom I C. you
	58	those things which are C. on the earth		4	C. that you should pretend to no other
		COMMAND		22	commandments wherewith I have C. you—42:3
5	21	I C. you my servant Joseph—5:29		34	accomplish thing which I have C. thee—38:40; 43:13; 45:72; 90:27
	26	I C. my servant Martin Harris that he	6	35	perform with soberness the work I have C.
	30	even until I C. thee again	9	13	do this thing which I C. you and you
	34	stop and stand still until I C. thee	17	6	even that part which I have C. him
6	27	I C. you that if you have good desires	18	7	according to that which I have C. him; he hath fulfilled the thing which I C.
11	15	I C. you that you need not suppose that	22	4	enter ye in at the gate as I have C.
18	9	I C. all men everywhere to repent	29	49	whoso have I not C. to repent
19	13	I C. you to repent—19:15, 20	30	2	persuaded by those whom I have not C.
	21	I C. that you preach naught but	38	35	to the place which I have C. them
	25	I C. thee that thou shalt not covet—19:26	42	15	ye shall observe to do as I have C.
	28	I C. thee that thou shalt pray vocally	46	3	ye are C. never to cast any one out—46:4
24	13	require not miracles except I shall C.		7	ye are C. in all things to ask of God
	16	ye shall C. to be smitten in my name	49	26	go forth as I have C. you
28	6	not C. him who is at thy head and at	51	9	that ye may be one even as I have C.
29	6	united in prayer according to my C.	56	3	after I have C. and commandment is broken
30	10	until I C. you to go from hence—51:16	57	7	divide their inheritance as I have C.
38	12	angels are waiting great C. to reap down		13	assist him even as I have C.
56	3	I C. and he that will not obey shall be		15	families that have been C. to come to
	4	I C. and revoke as seemeth me good	58	29	he that doeth not anything until he is C.
58	26	it is not meet that I should C. in all	60	10	unto mine elders who are C. to return
	32	I C. and men obey not, I revoke and	61	24	inasmuch as they are C. to journey
61	27	whom it is given power to C. the waters	72	11	take an account of the elders as C.
63	39	shall not go until I C. them	75	9	proclaim the things which I have C.—75:13, 15
94	10	all things whatsoever I shall C. you—94:12; 98:4; 124:55		18	take their journey as I have C. them
95	9	therefore I C. you to tarry	76	28	C. us that we should write the vision
97	8	every sacrifice which I the Lord shall C.		80	Lord C. us to write while we were in
98	22	if ye observe to do whatsoever I C.		113	we were C. to write while in the spirit
104	20	even as I will when I shall C. him		115	we were C. not to write while yet in
109	4	which thou didst C. us to build	78	7	which I have C. and require of you
113	7	what is meant by the C. in Isaiah		20	do the things which I have C. you—101:60
115	8	I C. you to build an house unto me—124:31			
117	2	let them not tarry for I the Lord C. it			
124	55	I C. you again to build a house unto			
126	3	I C. you to send my word abroad			
132	54	I C. mine handmaid Emma Smith to abide			

Sec.	Vs.	
88	60	according as his Lord had C. him
	117	call your solemn assembly as I have C.—109:6
90	7	school I have C. to be organized
93	40	C. you to bring up your children in
97	25	observe to do all things I have C. her—97:26
98	33	battle save I the Lord C. them
101	4	Abraham who was C. to offer up his—132:36
	46	the servants did as their lord C. them—101:62
	53	ought ye not to have done even as I C.
103	23	purchase lands as I have C. them
104	1	order which I C. to be organized
	2	as those whom I C. were faithful
	51	this I have C. to be done for salvation
	58	I have C. you to organize yourselves
105	16	I have C. my servants Baurak Ale
	28	wise men to fulfill that I have C.
	33	house which I have C. to be built unto
109	2	thou who hast C. thy servants to build
	58	build holy city to thy name as thou C.
121	16	but have done that which I C. them
124	38	I C. Moses that he should build a
	39	which my people are always C. to build
	51	offerings of those whom I C. to build
	53	all who have been C. to do a work and
	56	boarding house which I have C. you to
128	7	doctrine which is C. you in revelation
	13	font was C. to be in a place underneath
132	34	God C. Abraham and Sarah gave Hagar to
	35	I say unto you, nay, for I C. it
	37	none other things than that they were C.
	51	partake not of that which I C. you to
	65	when I C. Abraham to take Hagar to wife
133	4	all you that have not been C. to tarry
	60	they were C. to be kept from the world

COMMANDETH

61	28	let him do as spirit of living God C.
133	16	he C. all men everywhere to repent

COMMANDMENT

Sec.	Vs.	
3	10	contrary to the C. which I gave you
18	3	I give unto you a C. that you rely
	9	I speak unto you by way of C.
19	32	this is a great and the last C. I shall
20	37	again, by way of C. to the church
27	3	a C. I give that you shall not purchase
28	4	to speak by way of C. unto the church
	5	thou shalt not write by way of C.
	8	but write them not by way of C.
29	35	I gave unto him C. but no temporal C. gave I unto him
	40	forbidden fruit and transgressed the C.
35	6	a C. that thou shalt baptize by water
	20	a C. I give that thou shalt write for
36	4	this calling and C. give I unto you
	5	embracing this calling and C. shall
	7	this C. shall be given unto elders of
37	3	a C. I give unto the church that it is
38	16	for your salvation I give a C. for I
	32	a C. that ye should go to the Ohio
	34	a C. that certain men among them shall
	40	a C. that every man both elder and
41	2	a C. that ye shall assemble yourselves—88:74
	9	a C. that he should be appointed by
42	3	assembled yourselves according to C.
	4	this first C. that ye shall go forth
	5	C. that they shall go forth for a little
	58	a C. that then ye shall teach them unto
43	2	ye have received a C. for a law unto
	8	a C. that ye shall instruct and edify
49	1	a C. that you shall go and preach my
	11	a C. that ye go among this people and
	13	according to holy C. for remission of
52	21	this C. is given unto all elders whom
53	2	a C. that you shall forsake the world
54	6	kept the covenant and observed the C.
56	3	I have commanded and the C. is broken
	5	I revoke the C. which was given; and give a new C. unto my servant—56:6
	8	and obey the former C. which I have
58	29	that receiveth a C. with doubtful heart
	50	a C. that he shall write a description

Sec.	Vs.		Sec.	Vs.	
59	5	a C. saying thus: thou shalt love thy	101	10	decree hath gone forth by a former C.
60	13	a C. thus: thou shalt not idle away thy		67	a C. I give unto all the churches
61	13	gave a C. concerning these things		68	as I have said unto you in a former C.—103:12; 105:14
	18	a C. that what I say unto one I say		69	observe the C. which I have given
	26	this C. you shall give unto all your	103	1	a C. that you may know how to act
63	22	not by the way of C. for there are many		34	a C. that ye shall not go up unto land
64	12	either by C. or revelation	104	1	a C. concerning all the properties
	15	they kept not the law neither the C.		4	have not kept the C. but have broken
	20	I gave C. that his farm should be sold		47	a C. I give concerning Zion that you
68	33	a C. that he that observeth not his		54	a C. concerning your stewardship
70	1	W. Phelps, by way of C. unto them		64	by the voice of the order or by C.
	2	for I give unto them a C.—70:6	105	20	a C. that as many as have come up hither
	15	this C. I give unto my servants for	107	77	agreeable to the C. which says
74	5	a C., not of the Lord, but of himself	109	3	servants have done according to thy C.
75	7	a new commission and a new C. in	124	49	when I give a C. to any of the sons of
	25	this C. that ye obtain places for your		144	a C. that you should fill all these offices
76	51	according to the C. which he has given	132	7	that too most holy by revelation and C.
78	11	a C. to organize yourselves—104:11		12	this C. that no man shall come unto the
82	8	I give unto you a new C. that you may		29	whatsoever he receiveth by revelation or C.
	15	this C. that ye bind yourselves by		51	a C. that I give unto mine handmaid Emma
84	43	a C. to beware concerning yourselves		54	but if she will not abide this C.—132:55
	61	forgive you of your sins with this C.		63	replenish the earth according to my C.
	73	a C. that they shall not boast themselves			
	75	this C. is in force from this very hour			**COMMANDMENTS**
	77	it is expedient that I give this C.	1	6	my preface unto the book of my C.
	86	for this C. is unto all the faithful		17	spake unto him and gave him C.
85	3	it is contrary to will and C. of God—101:96		18	and also gave C. to others
88	62	ponder in your heart with this C.		24	these C. are of me and were given
	76	a C. that ye shall continue in prayer		30	those to whom these C. were given
	77	a C. that ye shall teach one another		32	he that repents and does the C. of the
89	2	to be sent greeting, not by C. or		37	search these C. for they are true
90	12	a C. that you continue in the ministry	3	5	but how strict were your C.
	32	ye shall write this C., and say unto		6	you have transgressed the C. and laws
92	1	organized agreeable to C. previously given, a revelation and C.	5	22	be firm in keeping the C.
93	43	a C. I give if you will be delivered		28	covenant with me that he will keep my C.
94	1	a C. I give that ye shall commence a		33	I have given unto thee these C.
	15	build mine houses according to C.		35	if thou art faithful in keeping my C.
	16	not to be built until I give unto you a C.	6	6	keep my C.—6:9, 37; 8:5; 11:6, 9, 18; 12:6; 14:6; 18:43; 25:15; 42:29; 43:35; 71:11
95	3	ye have not considered the great C.			
	7	C. that you should call your solemn			
	8	a C. that you should build a house			
98	11	a C. that ye shall forsake all evil			
	36	then I would give unto them a C. and		9	bring forth my work according to C.—11:9
100	7	a C. that ye shall declare whatsoever			

Sec.	Vs.	
	20	be diligent in keeping the C.—18:8; 30:8; 136:42
10	34	give you C. concerning these things
	56	who do not fear me neither keep my C.
11	20	this is your work to keep my C.
14	7	if you keep my C. and endure to the end
15	5	given you according to my C.—16:5
17	8	if you do these last C. of mine
18	46	if you keep not my C. you cannot be
19	13	command you to repent and keep the C.
2.	1	by the will and C. of God in the fourth
	2	which C. were given to Joseph Smith
	7	gave unto him C. which inspired him
	19	gave C. that they should love and serve
	45	according to the C. and revelations of
	77	always remember him and keep his C.
21	4	give heed unto all his words and C.
28	1	concerning the revelations and C.—109:60
	2	no one appointed to receive C.—43:3
	3	declare faithfully the C. and revelations
29	12	as many as have kept my C.
	35	for my C. are spiritual
30	4	until I give you further C.
35	24	keep all the C. and covenants
41	8	inasmuch as he keepeth my C.
42	1	as they believe on my name and keep my C.
	32	taken from church agreeable to my C.
	78	shall observe to keep all the C.
43	2	receive C. and revelations from my hand
	5	come before you as revelations and C.
	8	how to act on any law and C.
46	7	doctrines of devils or the C. of men
.	9	those who love me and keep all my C.
48	6	according to the laws and C. which ye
53	4	according to C. which shall be given
56	2	that will not keep my C. the same shall
57	1	assembled yourselves according to my C.
58	2	blessed is he that keepeth my C.

Sec.	Vs.	
	30	hold him guiltless that obeys not my C.
59	1	single to my glory according to my C.
	4	blessings from above and with C. not a few
	21	who confess not his hand and obey not his C.
63	13	I give C. and many have turned away from my C.
	22	there are many who observe not to keep my C.
	23	unto him that keepeth my C. I will give
67	4	testimony of the truth of these C. that
	6	seek ye out of the Book of C. the least
68	13	items in addition to covenants and C.
	24	according to covenants and C. of—107:12, 20, 63
69	1	not wisdom he should be entrusted with C.
70	3	ordained them stewards over C.
71	4	the C. and revelations which are to come
72	7	shall be made known by the C.
75	4	according to the revelations and C.
76	52	that by keeping the C. they might be
78	13	whereby you may accomplish the C.
84	16	who received priesthood by C. of God
	27	law of carnal C. which the Lord in his
	57	Book of Mormon and the former C. which
88	133	to walk in all C. of God blameless
89	18	walking in obedience to the C. shall
92	2	faithful in keeping all former C.
93	1	who keepeth my C. shall see my face
	20	if you keep my C. you shall receive of
	27	no fulness unless he keepeth his C.
	28	that keepeth his C. receiveth truth
	42	light and truth according to the C.
	44	not kept the C. concerning his children
	47	you have not kept the C. and must needs
95	11	if you keep my C. you shall have power
	12	if you keep not my C. the love of the
96	6	as he keepeth my C. from henceforth
97	4	until I shall give unto him other C.
100	14	as they keep my C. they shall be saved
	17	all that keep his C. shall be saved
101	50	hearkened not unto C. of their Lord

Sec.	Vs.	
103	4	did not hearken unto precepts and C.
	8	inasmuch as they keep not my C.
	29	in preparing churches to keep the C.
	35	establish children of Zion upon the C.
	40	in obtaining the fulfillment of these C.
104	42	as he is faithful in keeping my C.
	86	laid before you according to my C.
105	34	let those C. which I have given
109	68	the C. which thou hast given unto him
110	8	if my people will keep my C. and do not
124	50	transgression of my holy laws and C.
	85	who has come here essaying to keep my C.
	87	if ye love me keep my C. and the
125	2	if they will do my will and keep my C.
133	60	for this cause these C. were given
135	3	has brought forth the revelations and C.
136	2	covenant and promise to keep all C.

COMMENCE

9	1	and did C. again to write for my
30	9	thou shalt C. from this time forth
94	1	ye shall C. a work of laying out and

COMMENCED

9	5	you did not continue as you C. when
	11	it was expedient when you C. but you
88	141	it is to be C. with prayer and after

COMMENCEMENT

| 48 | 6 | make a C. to lay foundation of the city |
| 130 | 12 | the C. of the difficulties that will |

COMMENCING

| 102 | 12 | C. with number one and so in succession |

COMMISSION

75	6	I revoke the C. which I gave unto him
	7	I give unto him a new C. and a new
134	8	the C. of crime should be punished

COMMISSIONED

| 20 | 73 | having been C. of Jesus Christ I baptize |
| 88 | 80 | magnify the mission with which I have C. you |

COMMIT

| 27 | 16 | I have sent mine angels to C. unto you |
| 42 | 24 | thou shalt not C. adultery—59:6 |

Sec.	Vs.	
	80	if any man or woman shall C. adultery
63	16	if any shall C. adultery in their hearts
66	10	C. not adultery a temptation with which
77	8	everlasting gospel to C. to every
132	19	he shall C. no murder whereby to shed; if ye C. no murder whereby to shed
	26	he or she shall C. any sin or transgression, if they C. no murder
	27	is in that ye C. murder wherein ye shed
	59	he *will* not C. sin and I will justify
	61	cannot C. adultery for they are given; cannot C. adultery with that belongeth
	62	cannot C. adultery for they belong to

COMMITTED

5	7	these things which I have C. unto you
27	5	to whom I have C. the keys of the record
	6	I have C. the keys of bringing to pass
	9	have C. the keys of power of turning
	13	I have C. the keys of my kingdom
42	25	he that has C. adultery and repents
65	2	keys of kingdom of God are C. unto man
99	5	ungodly deeds which they have C. against
110	11	Moses C. the keys of the gathering of
	12	Elias appeared and C. the dispensation
	16	keys of this dispensation are C. into
132	41	she hath C. adultery—132:42, 63
	43	he hath broken his vow and C. adultery
	44	if she hath not C. adultery give her unto him who hath not C.
133	36	gospel, and hath C. it unto man who
134	8	government in which the offense is C.

COMMITTEE

| 94 | 15 | to be a C. to build mine house according |
| 123 | 4 | perhaps a C. can be appointed to find |

COMMITTETH

| 42 | 24 | he that C. adultery and repenteth not |
| 88 | 103 | fifth angel who C. the everlasting gospel |

COMMON

| 26 | 2 | all things shall be done by C. consent—28:13 |

Sec.	Vs.		Sec.	Vs.	
82	18	to become the C. property of the whole		13	not because ye forgive not, having not C.
102	28	no C. or ordinary case is to be sufficient	88	40	mercy hath C. on mercy and claimeth
104	71	only by voice and C. consent of order	101	9	my bowels are filled with C. towards
	72	this shall be the voice and C. consent	121	3	bowels moved with C. towards them—121:4
	85	by giving your names by C. consent			**COMPELLED**
107	74	a C. judge among the inhabitants of	58	26	he that is C. in all things is slothful
	82	had in remembrance before C. council			**COMPLAINED**
127	2	wrath of man have been my C. lot all	38	16	the poor have C. before me and the rich

COMMOTION

					COMPLETE
45	26	the whole earth shall be in C. and	77	12	sanctify earth and C. salvation of man
88	91	and all things shall be in C.	109	32	we plead a full and C. deliverance
		COMMUNE	128	18	that a whole and C. and perfect union
107	19	to C. with the general assembly			**COMPLETED**
		COMMUNICATED	84	97	until I have C. my work which shall be
84	61	those things which are C. unto you			**COMPLETELY**
		COMMUNION	123	6	before we can fully and C. claim that
107	19	to enjoy the C. and presence of God			**COMPOSE**
		COMPANIES	135	3	commandments which C. this Book of
103	30	until they have obtained C. to go up			**COMPOSED**
136	2	be organized into C. with a covenant	102	30	traveling High Council C. of the Twelve
	3	let the C. be organized with captains	120	1	a council C. of the First Presidency
	6	when the C. are organized let them go			**COMPOSING**
		COMPANION	20	61	several elders C. this church of Christ
80	2	inasmuch as you desire a C. I will	81		several churches C. the church of Christ
121	46	Holy Ghost shall by thy constant C.	102	5	the number C. the council who voted
		COMPANIONS			**COMPREHEND**
42	74	put away their C. for cause of fornication	88	43	which C. the earth and all the planets
	75	have left their C. for adultery and their C. are living		49	day shall come when you shall C. God
		COMPANY			**COMPREHENDED**
61	3	not needful for this whole C. of elders	88	6	in that he C. all things that he might
	9	take their former C. and let them take		48	he who came unto his own was not C.
76	67	come to an innumerable C. of angels			**COMPREHENDETH**
114	1	perform a mission in C. with others	6	21	shineth and darkness C. it not— 10:58; 34:2; 39:2; 45:7; 88:49
136	5	let each C. provide themselves with	88	41	He C. all things and all things are
	7	let each C. with their captains, decide		67	which is filled with light C. all things
	8	let each C. bear an equal proportion			
	9	let each C. prepare houses and fields			
	12	let my servants—organize a C.—136:13, 14			

COMPASSION

64	2	wherefore I will have C. upon you

Sec.	Vs.		Sec.	Vs.	
		COMPULSION		57	thou shouldst hold thy peace C. them
121	37	to exercise control, dominion or C.	45	16	asked me C. signs of my coming in
		COMPULSORY		21	desolation which I have told you C. them
121	46	without C. means it shall flow unto		24	this I have told you C. Jerusalem
		CONCATENATION		56	which I spake C. the ten virgins
123	5	present whole C. of diabolical rascality		60	to know any further C. this chapter
		CONCERN	46	5	C. those who are not of the church
111	5	C. not yourselves about your debts		6	C. your confirmation meetings that if
	6	C. not yourselves about Zion for I will	53	1	C. your calling and election in this
			56	8	C. the place upon which he lives
		CONCERNED	57	15	and now C. the gathering
93	50	more diligent and C. at home and pray	58	1	what I will C. you and also C. this land
		CONCERNING		3	C. the things which shall come hereafter
5	23	C. the man that desires the witness		24	as I spake C. my servant Edward
	26	say no more unto them C. these things		34	I give further direction C. this land
	29	nor trouble me any more C. this matter—59:22		38	other direction C. my servant Martin
6	22	that you might know C. the truth of		44	C. the residue of the elders of my church
	23	speak peace to your mind C. the matter	60	5	speak unto you C. your journey
8	1	knowledge C. engravings of old records		17	shall be made known C. Sidney Rigdon
	9	and you shall have knowledge C. it	61	13	I gave a commandment C. these things
10	34	give you commandments C. these things		18	forewarn your brethren C. these waters
	37	all things known unto world C. matter		21	let those C. whom I have spoken
	40	Nephi is more particular C. the things		23	now, C. my servants Sidney Rigdon and
	63	contention C. the points of my doctrine		33	now C. the residue let them journey
18	4	all things written C. foundation of	63	1	word of the Lord and his will C. you
19	2	and finished the will of Father C. me		24	the will of the Lord C. his saints
	32	the last commandment C. this matter	64	1	hear and receive my will C. you
20	37	to the church C. the manner of baptism	66	4	will show unto you what I will C. you, or what is my will C. you
	68	expound all things C. the church	68	13	now C. the items in addition to the
25	2	a revelation I give C. my will		21	by virtue of decree C. their right of
27	6	since the world began C. the last days	69	3	he shall observe and know C. my church
28	1	C. the revelations and commandments	74	3	contention C. the law of circumcision
30	7	in the church C. church matters	75	12	this is the will of the Lord C. you
32	1	now C. my servant Parley P. Pratt		23	that you might know his will C. you
36	4	commandment I give unto you C. all men	76	7	good pleasure of my will C. all things
42	15	as I have commanded C. your teaching		16	C. those who shall hear the voice of
	28	thou knowest my laws C. these things		31	C. all those who know my power
	32	testimonies C. the consecration of		34	C. whom I have said there is no forgiveness
				50	C. them who come forth in resurrection
			77	6	his economy C. this earth during the

Sec.	Vs.	
82	8	that you may understand my will C. you
83	1	laws of church C. women and children
84	2	the word of the Lord C. his church
	31	as I said C. the sons of Moses
	42	given mine angels charge C. you
	43	commandment to beware C. yourselves
	94	that rejecteth your testimony C. me
86	1	C. the parable of wheat and of tares
87	1	C. wars that will shortly come to pass
88	1	assembled to receive his will C. you
	141	13th chapter of John's testimony C. me
90	33	cease wearying me C. this manner
91	1	saith Lord unto you C. the Apocrypha
92	1	commandment C. my servant Shederlaomach
93	44	not kept commandments C. his children
94	16	built until I give commandment C. them
95	3	C. the building of mine house
96	1	ye may know how to act C. this matter
97	1	my will C. your brethren in land of
	3	C. the school in Zion I the Lord am
98	4	C. the laws of the land it is my will
	23	I speak unto you C. your families
100	13	I give unto you a word C. Zion
101	1	C. your brethren who have been afflicted
	16	let your hearts be comforted C. Zion
	41	here is wisdom C. children of Zion
	43	my will C. the redemption of Zion
	63	wisdom in me C. all the churches
	69	observe the commandments C. these things
103	1	discharge your duties C. salvation and
	29	C. the restoration and redemption of Zion
104	1	C. all the properties which belong to
	19	C. the properties of the order
	47	commandment I give C. Zion
	54	commandment I give C. your stewardship
	78	I say unto you C. your debts
105	1	that you may learn my will C. redemption
	2	speaking C. church and not individuals
	7	I speak not C. those who are appointed
	8	I speak C. my churches abroad

Sec.	Vs.	
	10	and know more perfectly C. their duty
	22	I will counsel him C. this matter
	28	C. the purchasing of all lands in
	34	let commandments I have given C. Zion be
107	83	shall be an end of controversy C. him
108	2	be at rest C. your spiritual standing
109	23	mouths of the prophets C. last days
	45	spoken terrible things C. the wicked
	60	C. the revelations and commandments
111	9	inquire diligently C. the more ancient
112	11	have heard thy prayers C. thy brethren
	27	trouble not yourselves C. affairs of my
124	5	to know my will C. those kings and
	53	consolation C. all those who have been
	58	said unto Abraham C. kindreds of earth
	73	who wish to know my will C. them
	74	C. my servant Vinson Knight if he will
	87	cease to fear C. his family because of
125	1	what is the will of the Lord C. saints
	2	keep my commandments C. them
127	6	thus saith the Lord C. your dead
128	2	revelation to you C. a recorder
	8	records which they have kept C. dead
	15	as Paul says C. the fathers "that they
132	30	Abraham received promises C. his seed
	41	as ye have asked C. adultery, I say
133	1	hear the word of the Lord C. you
136	1	will of the Lord C. Camp of Israel in
	9	this is will of the Lord C. his people

CONCERNS

63	38	arrange their temporal C. which dwell
70	5	to manage them and the C. thereof
72	20	appointed stewards over the literary C.
82	17	managing the C. of your stewardships
134	6	prescribing rules on spiritual C.

CONCERT

122	95	that he may act in C. also with my

CONCUBINES

132	1	of their having many wives and C.

Sec.	Vs.		Sec.	Vs.	
	37	Abraham received C. and they bore him			**CONDITION**
	38	David also received many wives and C.	109	65	be converted from wild and savage C.
	39	David's wives and C. were given him of	113	10	remnants of Israel in their scattered C.
		CONDEMN	132	17	without exaltation in their saved C.
6	35	I do not C. you, go your ways and sin no			**CONDITIONS**
75	21	shall be judges of that house and C. them	18	12	bring men unto him on C. of repentance
136	25	tell thy neighbor lest he C. thee	46	15	suiting his mercies according to C. of
		CONDEMNATION	86	38	there are certain bounds also and C.
5	18	go forth unto the C. of this generation		39	all who abide not in those C. are not
10	23	turn to their shame and C. in day of	132	5	shall abide the law and the C. thereof
20	15	reject it, it shall turn to their own C.		7	the C. of this law are these
23	1	thou art under no C.—23:3, 4, 5			**CONDUCT**
63	11	showeth no signs only unto their C.	19	41	C. thyself wisely before me
	62	many there be who are under this C.	20	45	the elders are to C. the meetings as
	64	and in this there is no C. and ye; without this there remaineth C.	42	93	and thus shall ye C. in all things
	66	weight of glory, otherwise a greater C.	46	2	to C. all meetings as they are directed
67	8	ye are under C. if ye do not bear record	134	10	deal with their members for disorderly C.
76	48	except them who are ordained unto this C.			**CONDUCTED**
82	3	greater light shall receive greater C.	102	27	which case shall there be C. according
84	55	hath brought the whole church under C.			**CONFER**
	56	this C. resteth upon the children of	13	1	I C. the priesthood of Aaron which holds
	57	they shall remain under this C. until	104	22	this stewardship and blessing I C.
88	65	not expedient, it shall turn unto your C.			**CONFERENCE**
	100	judged and are found under C.	20	61	to meet in C. once in three months
90	5	and are brought under C. thereby		64	or he may receive it from a C.
93	31	here is the C. of man because that		67	direction of a high council or general C.
	32	receiveth not the light is under C.		82	uniting with church since the last C.
	41	you have continued under this C.	26	1	go to the west to hold the next C.
105	7	for they are not all under this C.	28	10	shalt not leave this place until after C.; to preside over the C. by the voice of it
132	35	was Abraham therefore under C.	52	2	do from this time until the next C.
	48	and shall be without C. on earth and	58	58	let a C. meeting be called and after
136	33	sent forth to the C. of the ungodly		61	also hold a C. upon this land
		CONDEMNED		62	direct the C. which shall be held by
5	27	if he deny this behold he is C.	72	7	by commandments and voice of the C.
9	12	and neither of you have I C.	73	1	in the regions round about until C. 73:4
42	81	he or she shall be C. by the mouth of		2	made known unto them by voice of the C.
64	9	he standeth C. before the Lord	102	34	after prayer the C. adjourned
	16	they C. for evil that thing in which	118	1	let a C. be held immediately
	40	not faithful in stewardships shall be C.	124	88	further instructions at my general C.
68	22	no bishop shall be tried or C. for any		144	or else disapprove of them at general C.
	23	cannot be impeached he shall be C.			
104	7	that innocent may not be C. with unjust			
136	39	honored, and the wicked might be C.			

Sec.	Vs.	
		CONFERENCES
20	61	as said C. shall direct or appoint
	62	said C. are to do whatever business
	63	to which they belong or from the C.
	81	to attend the several C. held by elders
58	56	as counseled by elders of church at C.
	58	residue as shall be ruled by the C.
		CONFERRED
67	14	see and know that which was C. upon
97	14	keys of which kingdom have been C. upon
107	13	because it was C. upon Aaron and his
121	37	that they may be C. upon us is true
132	7	and the keys of this priesthood are C.
	45	I have C. upon you the keys and power
		CONFESS
19	20	C. your sins lest you suffer these
42	88	if he or she C. thou shalt be reconciled
	89	if he or she C. not thou shalt deliver
	91	if he or she C. not he or she shall be
	92	may have opportunity to C. in secret
58	43	he *will* C. them and forsake them
59	21	those who C. not his hand in all things
61	2	merciful unto those who C. their sins
64	7	forgive sins unto those who C. their
76	110	every tongue shall C. to him who sits
88	104	every knee shall bow, every tongue C.
		CONFESSED
45	13	and C. they were strangers and pilgrims
		CONFESSETH
58	60	for he C. them not and thinketh to hide
64	12	repenteth not of his sins and C. them not
		CONFESSING
59	12	C. thy sins unto thy brethren and
124	18	C. me before the world and I will bear
		CONFIDENCE
107	22	upheld by the C., faith and prayer of
121	45	then shall thy C. wax strong in the
124	112	that he may obtain the C. of men

Sec.	Vs.	
		CONFINED
135	7	were only C. in jail by the conspiracy
		CONFIRM
20	41	to C. those who are baptized into the
.	43	to C. the church by the laying on of
33	15	you shall C. in my church by laying on
84	42	which I now C. upon you who are present
		CONFIRMATION
46	6	I say concerning your C. meetings
		CONFIRMED
20	10	is C. to others by ministering of
	68	being C. by the laying on of hands of
27	12	ordained and C. you to be apostles.
84	18	the Lord C. a priesthood also upon Aaron
	30	which priesthood was C. upon Aaron and
	48	covenant which he has renewed and C. upon you which is C.
107	40	order of this priesthood was C. to be
		CONFIRMING
24	9	laying on of hands and C. the churches
26	1	and to C. the church at Colesville
128	21	that which is to come, C. our hope
		CONFORMING
128	5	by C. to ordinance and preparation
	13	that which is earthly C. to that which
		CONFOUND
10	42	thus I *will* C. those who have altered
71	7	C. your enemies; call upon them to
109	29	we ask thee to C. and astonish and
133	58	day when the weak should C. the wise
		CONFOUNDED
35	25	be led, and no more be C. at all
49	27	in your midst and you shall not be C.
71	10	he shall be C. in mine own due time
84	116	trust in me and he shall not be C.
90	17	be not ashamed neither C., but be
93	52	you shall not be C. in this world nor
100	5	and you shall not be C. before men.
		CONFUSION
63	24	not in haste lest there should be C.
109	29	bring to shame and C. all those who
123	7	and filled the world with C. and has
132	8	house of order and not a house of C.

Sec.	Vs.	
		CONGREGATION
52	10	let them preach by the way in every C.
88	129	that the C. in the house may hear his
107	56	Adam stood up in the midst of the C.
		CONGREGATIONS
60	8	among the C. of the wicked.—60: 13, 14; 61:30, 32, 33; 62: 5; 68:1
61	32	journey for the C. of their brethren
103	29	lift up his voice in C. in the eastern
		CONNECTED
93	33	spirit and element inseparably C.
121	36	rights of priesthood inseparably C. with
		CONNECTION
112	31	which power you hold in C. with all
128	17	in C. with this quotation I will give
		CONNECTIONS
109	70	have mercy upon all their immediate C.
	71	exalt them with their immediate C.
	72	remember all their immediate C.
132	7	all C. that are not made and entered
		CONQUER
10	5	that you may C. Satan and that you
		CONQUEROR
10	5	pray always that you may come off C.
		CONSCIENCE
134	2	to each individual free exercise of C.
	4	restrain crime but never control C.
	5	holding sacred the freedom of C.
135	4	I have a C. void of offense towards
		CONSCIENCES
134	4	rules of worship to bind the C. of men
		CONSECRATE
42	30	C. of thy properties for their support
	39	I *will* C. of the riches of those who
51	16	I C. unto them this land for a season
52	2	the land which I *will* C. unto my people
58	57	let Sidney Rigdon C. and dedicate this
85	1	of all those who C. their properties
104	60	prepare a treasury and C. it unto my
124	44	I *will* C. that spot that it shall be

Sec.	Vs.	
		CONSECRATED
42	33	which is a residue to be C. unto bishop
	37	not receive again that which he has C.
	71	out of property which is C. to bishop
51	5	not claim that portion he has C. unto
57	1	land which I have C. for the gathering
70	8	benefits shall be C. unto inhabitants
72	12	this also may be C. to the good of
82	13	I have C. the land of Shinehah in
84	31	upon the C. spot as I have appointed.
104		that it may be C. for bringing forth
90	29	residue of money may be C. unto me
94	3	let first lot on the south be C. unto
103	22	bought with money that has been C.
	24	which I have C. to be the land of Zion
	35	organize the kingdom upon the C. land
104	66	that it may be holy and C. unto Lord
105	15	lands which I have C. for gathering of
109	12	that it may be sanctified and C. to be
115	7	let the city be a holy and C. land
		CONSECRATION
42	32	concerning C. of properties of my church; that which he has received by C.
	33	after this first C. which is a residue
85	3	who receive not their inheritance by C.
105	29	according to laws of C. which I have
		CONSECRATIONS
83	6	kept by the C. of the church
124	21	that he may receive C. of mine house
		CONSENT
26	2	done by common C. in the church. 28:13
93	51	by your prayer of faith with one C.
101	97	by the C. of those who call themselves
104	21	united C. or voice of the order
	71	only by the voice and common C. of the
	72	shall be the voice and common C.
85		by giving your names by common C. or
124	71	without the C. of the stockholder
132	61	espouse another and the first give her C.
		CONSEQUENCE
42	64	in C. of that which is coming on earth
52	37	in C. of transgression let that which
56	6	in C. of the stiff-neckedness of my

Sec.	Vs.		Sec.	Vs.	
89	4	in C. of evils and designs which do			**CONSTANT**
101	2	afflicted in C. of their transgressions	121	46	Holy Ghost shall be thy C. companion
104	98	in C. of those things which I have			**CONSTANTLY**
104	51	in C. of their being driven out	122	2	seek blessings C. from under thy hand
105	9	in C. of transgression of my people			
110	9	thousands shall greatly rejoice in C.			**CONSTITUTE**
		CONSEQUENTLY	107	32	which C. spiritual authorities of church
128	7	C. the books spoken of must be the	124, 126		that these may C. a quorum and First
	13	C. the baptismal font was instituted			
		CONSIDER			**CONSTITUTION**
45	73	that they may C. these things	89	10	for the C. nature and use of man
84	82	for C. the lilies of the field how	101	77	according to the laws and C. of people
102	7	whom they may C. worthy and capable		80	I established C. of this land by hands
	13	shall C. whether it is a difficult one	109	54	nobly defended, viz. C. of our land
		CONSIDERATION	124	63	they shall form a C. whereby they may
123	1	we would suggest for your C. the propriety			**CONSTITUTIONAL**
		CONSIDERED	98	5	that law of the land which is C.
95	3	ye have not C. the great commandment		6	befriending that law which is the C.
101	94	and know that which they have never C.			**CONSULTED**
			101	48	and C. for a long time saying among
		CONSIDERING			**CONSUME**
46	7	C. the end of your salvation, doing all	46	9	a sign that they may C. it upon their lusts
		CONSIST	63	34	C. the wicked with unquenchable fire
102	1	which was to C. of twelve high priests			**CONSUMED**
128	14	keys of kingdom which C. in key of	5	19	the inhabitants thereof are C. away
		CONSISTENTLY	29	23	heaven and earth shall be C. and pass
105	24	as can be C. with feelings of the people	45	50	the scorner shall be C. and they that
		CONSISTS	98	17	and all flesh be C. before me
128	8	nature of this ordinance C. in power	101	24	dwell upon face of earth shall be C.
	11	C. in obtaining power of Holy Priesthood			**CONSUMPTION**
		CONSOLATION	87	6	until the C. decreed hath made an end
124	53	for your C. concerning all those who			**CONSTRAINED**
128	21	giving us C. by holding forth that	105	32	C. to acknowledge that kingdom or Zion
		CONSOLING	109	13	feel C. to acknowledge that thou hast
25	5	husband in his afflictions with C. words			**CONSTRAINT**
		CONSPIRACY	63	64	spoken with care and by C. of spirit
84	16	Abel who was slain by C. of his brother	89	2	greeting, not by commandment or C., but
134	7	opinions do not justify sedition or C.			**CONTAIN**
135	7	confined in jail by C. of traitors	3	19	plates preserved which C. records
		CONSPIRE	6	26	records which C. much of my gospel
122	7	if the billowing surge C. against thee			
		CONSPIRING			
89	4	which will exist in hearts of C. men			

Sec.	Vs.		Sec.	Vs.	
8	1	which C. those parts of my scripture			**CONTINUAL**
10	46	remainder of this work does C. all those	101	84	lest by her C. coming she weary me
		CONTAINED			**CONTINUALLY**
9	1	many things C. therein are true	23	3	and to strengthen the church C.
	2	many things C. therein are not true		7	give your language to exhortation C.
128	7	books which C. record of their works; revelation C. in letter I wrote	25	15	keep my commandments C. and a crown
135	3	sent fulness of gospel which it C.	46	33	practice virtue and holiness before me C.
		CONTAINING	47	3	keep church record and history C.
27	5	Book of Mormon C. fulness of gospel	84	85	treasure up in your minds C. the word
128	24	a book C. the records of our dead	107	49	and was before his face C.
		CONTAINS	109	12	that thy holy presence may be C. in
9	26	Book of Mormon which C. truth and word	124	140	one is to travel C. and the other is
20	9	which C. a record of a fallen people	130	7	future, and are C. before the Lord
77	6	it C. revealed will, mysteries, works			**CONTINUANCE**
	7	the first seal C. the things of the first	77	6	during seven thousand years of its C.
		CONTEMPLATE			**CONTINUATION**
124	23	while he shall C. word of the Lord	132	19	which glory shall be a fulness and C.
	60	that he may C. the glory of Zion		22	leadeth unto exaltation and C. of lives
		CONTEMPLATED		31	by this law are the C. of the works of
124	43	the place where you have C. building it			**CONTINUE**
		CONTEMPLATING	5	19	shall C. to be poured out from time to
128	6	John the revelator was C. this subject	9	1	C. until you have finished this record
		CONTEND		5	because you did not C. as you commenced
18	20	C. against no church save it be the	10	3	see that you are faithful and C. on to
90	36	I will C. with Zion and plead with her	24	5	thou shalt C. in calling upon God
112	5	C. thou morning by morning and day after		9	and C. in laying on of hands and
117	13	let him C. earnestly for redemption of		10	Oliver shall C. in bearing my name
121	10	thy friends do not C. against thee	25	14	C. in the spirit of meekness and
136	23	cease to C. one with another	33	13	if ye C. the gates of hell shall not
		CONTENTION	46	14	have eternal life if they C. faithful
10	63	that there may not be so much C.; C. concerning the points of my doctrine	49	23	be not deceived but C. in steadfastness
74	3	there arose a great C. among the people	62	4	and now C. your journey
		CONTENTIONS	66	12	C. in these things even unto the end
95	10	C. arose in the school of the prophets	67	13	C. in patience until ye are perfected
101	6	there were jarrings and C. and strifes	69	3	he shall C. in writing and making
		CONTINENTS	73	1	they should C. preaching the Gospel
135	3	been the means of publishing it on two C.		4	C. the work of translation until it be
			82	23	my blessings C with you.
			84	27	caused to C. with the house of Aaron
				80	and fail not to C. faithful in all
			86	11	blessed are ye if ye C. in my goodness
			88	76	ye shall C. in prayer and fasting
				85	let elders C. in the vineyard until
			90	12	that you C. in ministry and presidency

Sec.	Vs.		Sec.	Vs.	
	20	C. with his family upon the place where			**CONTRADICTED**
95	12	the love of the Father shall not C.	10	31	translate, but that you have C. yourself
97	4	he shall C. to preside over the school			**CONTRARY**
99	8	thou shalt C. proclaiming my gospel	3	10	done that which is C. to commandment
100	12	C. your journey and let your hearts	10	11	they read C. from that you translated
101	64	that the gathering of my saints may C.	28	12	of this church C. to church covenants
	67	C. to gather unto the places which I	85	3	it is C. to the will and commandment of
	76	should C. to importune for redress	101	96	it is C. to my commandment and my will
105	12	faithful and C. in humility before me	129	7	C. to order of heaven for a just man
	18	endowment for them if they C. faithful	134	12	C. to the will and wish of their masters
106	8	if he C. to be a faithful witness			**CONTRITE**
108	5	promise of Father unto you if you C.	20	37	come forth with broken hearts and C.
118	3	let the residue C. to preach from that	21	9	for remission of sins unto C. heart
124	17	work which I accept if he C.	52	15	he that prayeth whose spirit is C. the
	18	Wight should C. preaching for Zion		16	he that speaketh whose spirit is C.
	86	labors here and shall C. their works	54	3	become truly humble before me and C.
128	25	close for present and C. subject another	55	3	if they are C. before me you shall have
132	20	from everlasting to; because they C.	56	7	as many as will go may go that are C.
	30	were to C. so long as they were in world, and out of the world they should C. as innumerable		17	wo unto poor men whose spirits are not C.
		CONTINUED		18	blessed are poor whose spirits are C.
84	26	and the lesser priesthood C. which	59	8	that of a broken heart and a C. spirit
86	8	with whom the priesthood hath C. through	97	8	their hearts are honest and spirits C.
93	13	but C. from grace to grace until he	136	33	to enlighten the humble and C. and to
	41	you have C. under this condemnation			**CONTROL**
127	4	let the work of my temple be C. and	21	37	or to exercise C., or dominion, or
132	63	herein is the work of my Father C.	134	2	as will secure right and C. of property
		CONTINUES		4	restrain crime but never C. conscience
42	60	doeth them not shall be damned if he C.			**CONTROLLED**
		CONTINUETH	121	36	powers of heaven cannot be C. only upon
50	24	he that receiveth light and C. in God			**CONTROLLEST**
84	17	which priesthood C. in the church of	121	4	who C. and subjectest the devil and
	18	which priesthood C. and abideth forever			**CONTROVERSIES**
88	40	justice C. its course and claimeth its	107	80	final decision upon C. in spiritual
97	4	inasmuch as he C. to abide in me he			**CONTROVERSY**
		CONTRACT	107	83	their decision shall be an end of C.
124	115	according to the C. which he has made			**CONVENED**
		CONTRACTED	102	8	council of High Priests C. for that
19	35	pay the debt thou hast C. with the printer			**CONVENES**
		CONTRACTS	102	13	Whenever this council C. to act upon
132	7	all C. that are not made and entered; all C. that are not made unto this end			

Sec.	Vs.	
		CONVERSATION
20	69	manifest by a godly walk and C. that
108	7	strengthen your brethren in all your C.
		CONVERSATIONS
124	39	wherein you receive C. and your
		CONVERSED
76	14	with whom we C. in heavenly vision
		CONVERTED
42	64	teach them that be C. to flee to west
44	4	many shall be C. insomuch that ye shall
109	65	be C. from their wild and savage condition
	70	that they may be C. and redeemed with
112	13	they shall be C. and I will heal them
		CONVEY
124	69	do not sell and C. the stock away out
		CONVINCE
6	11	yea, C. them of the error of their ways
99	5	to C. all of their ungodly deeds which
		CONVINCING
11	21	power of God unto the C. of men
18	44	unto the C. of many of their sins
90	10	be revealed in power in C. the nations
		COPPER
124	27	and with iron, with C. and with brass
		COPY
57	13	to C. and to correct and select that
102	26	transmit immediately C. of proceedings
		COPYING
69	8	preaching and expounding, writing, C.
		CORDS
121	44	faithfulness is stronger than C. of death
		CORINTHIANS
8	13	as Paul hath declared in First C.
	16	quotation of Paul, First C. 25:29
		CORN
89	17	wheat for man, C. for the ox, and oats
		CORNER
104	39	the lot which is on the C. south of

Sec.	Vs.	
		CORNERS
124	3	proclamation to the four C. thereof
128		my kingdom upon four C. of the earth
		CORNER-STONE
115	12	finished from the C. thereof unto top
124	2	which I have planted to be a C. of Zion
	23	and the C. I have appointed for Zion
	60	and the glory of this the C. thereof
131		a High Council for the C. of Zion
		CORRECT
57	13	to copy, and to C. and select that all
		CORRECTLY
91	1	and it is mostly translated C.
		CORRILL, JOHN
50	38	and C., or as many as are ordained
52	7	let Lyman Wight and C. take their
		CORRUPT
10	21	and their hearts are C. and full of
53	4	because of priestcrafts all having C. minds
112	23	all flesh has become C. before my face
		CORRUPTED
33	4	my vineyard has become C. every whit
38	11	for all flesh is C. before me
121	13	because their hearts are C. and things
		CORRUPTIBLE
101	24	every C. thing shall be consumed
		CORRUPTIBLENESS
19	38	obtain treasures of earth and C. to the
		CORRUPTION
123	7	is now the very mainspring of all C.
134	12	to save themselves from C. of the world
135	6	to purify the vineyard of C.
		COST
135	6	C. best blood of the 19th century
		COUNCIL
42	34	appointed by the bishop and his C.
78	9	sit in C. with the saints which are in
89	1	for the benefit of C. of High Priests
90	16	to preside in C. and set in order all
96	3	as it shall be determined in C. among
102	1	this day a general C. of 24 High priests
	2	not be settled by church or bishop's C.

Council 97 Counsel

Sec.	Vs.	
	3	acknowledged presidents by voice of C; chosen to be standing C. for church by unanimous voice of C.
	5	the number composing the C. who voted
	8	sanctioned by the voice of general C.
	9	who is also president of the C.
	10	he should preside over the C. of church
	11	preside over C. without an assistant
	13	whenever this C. convenes to act upon
	15	accused has a right to one-half of C.
	16	councilors appointed to speak before C.; in its true light before the C.
	18	speaking for themselves before the C.
	22	majority of C. having power to
	23	make the case clear to the minds of C.
	24	have power to call and organize a C.
	25	said C. shall have power to appoint; to preside over such C. for time being
	26	duty of said C. to transmit a copy
	27	be dissatisfied with decision of C.
	28	this C. is only to be called on most; no ordinary case sufficient to call C.
	29	whether it is necessary to call such C.
104	53	as shall be agreed by this order in C.; admit and the voice of the C. direct
	74	manifest before the C. of the order
	76	treasurer shall be subject unto the C.
	77	he shall be subject to C. or voice of
107	78	carried up unto the C. of the church
	79	presidency of C. of High Priesthood
	80	this is the highest C. of the church of
	81	not any who is exempt from this C. of
	82	had in remembrance before common C.
	85	to sit in C. with them.—107:86, 87, 89
120	1	it shall be disposed of by a C. composed of; and the bishop and his C. and by my High C.
121	32	ordained in midst of C. of Eternal God
124	127	be president over twelve traveling C.
		See also High Council

COUNCILORS

102	4	above-named C. were then asked if they
	5	appointing above-named C. were 43 as
	6	not have power to act without seven C.

Sec.	Vs.	
	7	capable to act in place of absent C.
	8	vacancy occur by death of any one of C.
	12	it shall be the duty of the twelve C.
	13	the twelve C. shall consider whether; two only of the C. shall speak upon it
	16	the C. appointed to speak before
	17	those C. who draw even numbers
	18	after C. have finished their remarks
	19	after C. have spoken the president; call upon the twelve C. to sanction
	20	should the remaining C. discover an
	34	the twelve C. proceeded to cast lots

COUNCILS

| 107 | 37 | equal to the C. of the Twelve at |
| | 77 | the decision of either of these C. |

COUNSEL

1	19	man should not C. his fellow man
3	15	suffered C. of thy director to be trampled
22	4	seek not to C. your God
56	14	you seek to C. in your own ways
58	20	according to the C. of his own will
	25	they shall C. between themselves and me
63	55	he received not C. but grieved my
64	20	and C. wrongfully to your hurt I gave
69	4	that he receive C. and assistance from
78	2	listen to the C. of him who hath ordained
	16	under the C. and direction of the Holy
81	3	inasmuch as thou art faithful in C.
100	2	listen to the C. which I shall give
101	8	in day of peace they esteemed lightly my C.
	74	if they will hearken to his C. they
103	5	inasmuch as they hearken unto the C.
	40	whithersoever my servants shall C. them
104	1	my friends I give unto you C.
	21	done according to C. of the order—104:36
105	22	I *will* C. him concerning this matter
	37	inasmuch as they follow the C. they
108	1	coming hither this morning to receive C.
122	2	virtuous shall seek C. from under thy
124	13	let him hearken to your C. and I will
	16	reward shall not fail if he receive C.
	61	that he may receive also the C. from
	84	he aspireth to establish his C. instead of the C. which I

Sec.	Vs.	
	89	let him hearken to C. of my servant—124:112
	95	he shall receive C. from my servant
	118	hearken unto the C. of my servants
136	19	and seeketh not my C. he shall have no

COUNSELED

24	1	out of thy afflictions and have C. thee
58	56	let it be done as it shall be C. by

COUNSELETH

58	20	him that C. or sitteth upon judgment seat

COUNSELOR

30	7	none have I appointed to be his C.
81	1	a C. unto my servant Joseph Smith, Jr.
90	19	for the family of thy C. and scribe
	21	let my C. Sidney Rigdon remain where
124	91	let my servant William be appointed a C.
	103	if Sidney will serve me and be C. unto

COUNSELORS

42	31	laid before bishop of my church and C.
	71	to assist the bishop as C. in all things
	72	thought best by the C. and bishop
58	18	by the assistance of his C. according
	24	those whom he has appointed for his C.
64	40	bishop and C. if they are not faithful
107	23	the twelve traveling C. are called to
	72	by assistance of C. whom he has chosen
	76	act in office of bishop without C.
	79	call other High Priests to assist as C.; its C. shall have power to decide upon
	82	who shall be assisted by twelve C.
112	20	whom I have made C. for my name's sake
	30	to be your C. and your leaders
115	1	your C. who are and shall be appointed
	2	my servant E. Partridge and his C.
	16	my servant Joseph and his C.
124	126	I give unto him for C. my servants
	136	give A. Lyman and N. Packard for C.
	142	Samuel Rolfe and his C. for priests; president of teachers and his C.; president of deacons and his C.; president of the stake and his C.

Sec.	Vs.	
136	3	with a president and his two C. at head

COUNSELS

3	4	if he sets at naught the C. of God
	7	although men set at naught the C. of
	13	who has set at naught the C. of God
19	33	misery if thou wilt slight these C.

COUNT

123	15	let no man C. them as small things
132	30	if ye were to C. the sand upon the

COUNTED

107	100	he that is slothful shall not be C.

COUNTENANCE

20	6	whose C. was as lightning and
59	15	but with a glad heart and cheerful C.
88	52	shall behold the joy of my C.
	53	I will visit you with the joy of my C.
	56	made glad with light of his C.
	58	all received the light of his C.
110	3	his C. shone above the brightness of

COUNTENANCES

59	15	do these with cheerful hearts and C.

COUNTIES

101	71	land which can be purchased in C. round
105	28	purchased in adjoining C. round about
106	2	his own place but in adjoining C.

COUNTRIES

38	29	ye hear of wars in far C. and say; there will soon be great wars in far C.
39	14	art not called to go into eastern C.
45	64	go ye forth into the western C., call
75	6	commission to go unto eastern C.
	8	say unto him again go ye into south C.
	13	take their journey into eastern C.—75:14
	15	take their journey unto western C.
79	1	Carter should go again into eastern C.
88	79	knowledge also of C. and kingdoms
93	53	obtain a knowledge of histories and C.
99	1	thou art called to go into eastern C.
101	74	every church in the eastern C. when
103	29	shall lift up his voice in eastern C.
133	23	shall be driven back into the north C.
	26	they who are in the north C. shall come

Sec.	Vs.		Sec.	Vs.	
		COUNTRY	38	20	this shall be my C. with you
20	1	established agreeable to laws of our C.	39	11	the C. which I have sent forth in these
58	52	to purchase this whole region of C.	40	3	he broke my C. and it remaineth with
75	17	take their journey also into south C.	42	30	impart unto them with a C. and a deed
		COUNTY		36	that my C. people may be gathered in
101	71	land which can be purchased in Jackson C.	45	9	I have sent mine everlasting C.—49:9
105	28	purchasing all lands in Jackson C.	52	2	those who are heirs according to the C.
109	47	driven by inhabitants of Jackson C.	54	4	the C. which they made unto me has
124	51	build a house unto my name in Jackson C.		6	blessed are they who have kept the C.
128	20	in wilderness of Fayette, Seneca C.; wilderness between Harmony, Susquehanna C. and Colesville, Broome C.	66	2	blessed are you for receiving mine C.
	21	old father Whitmer in Fayette, Seneca, C.	76	69	Jesus the mediator of the new C.—107:19
		COUPLED	101		received not gospel neither the C.
130	2	only it *will* be C. with eternal glory	78	11	organize by a bond or everlasting C.
		COURAGE	82	11	to be bound together by a bond and C.
128	22	C. brethren, and on, on to victory		15	that ye bind yourselves by this C.
		COURSE		21	the soul that sins against this C.
3	2	his C. is one eternal round—35:1	84	39	this is according to the oath and C.
61	29	unto you is given the C. for the saints		40	receive this oath and C. of my Father
88	40	justice continueth its C. and claimeth		41	whoso breaketh this C. after he hath
121	33	stop Missouri river in its decreed C.		48	teacheth him of the C. which he has
		COURSES		57	repent and remember the new C. even
52	33	unto one place in their several C.		99	by the faith and C. of their fathers
88	43	their C. are fixed even the C. of	88	131	in remembrance of the everlasting C.—88:133
		COURT		133	in which C. I receive you to fellowship
94	4	in the length thereof in the inner C.—94:11; 95:15		135	with this same prayer and C. or by
	5	there shall be a lower C. and a higher C.—94:11	90	24	remember C. wherewith ye have
95	16	let lower part of inner C. be dedicated	98	3	an immutable C. that they shall be
	17	let higher part of inner C. be dedicated		14	whether you will abide in my C. unto
135	7	that cannot be rejected by *any* C. on		15	if ye will not abide in my C. ye are
		COURT-HOUSE	101	39	when men C. with an everlasting C.
57	3	upon a lot which is not far from the C.	104	4	have broken the C. through covetousness
		COVENANT		5	inasmuch as any man shall break C. with
1	15	have broken mine everlasting C.	109	1	who keepest C. and showest mercy unto
	22	that mine everlasting C. might be		38	put upon thy servants the C. that when
5	3	you should enter into a C. with me	131	2	meaning the everlasting C. of marriage
	27	he will break the C. which he has	132	4	I reveal unto you a new, everlasting C.; if ye abide not that C. then are ye damned; no one can reject this C. and enter
	28	and C. with me that he will keep my			
22	1	this is a new and everlasting C.			
	3	I have caused this last C. and this			

Sec.	Vs.	
	6	as pertaining to the new C.
	15	and he C. with her so long as he is in; their C. and marriage are not of force
	18	make a C. with her for time and for all; if that C. is not by me or by my word
	19	marry by the new and everlasting C.; and if ye abide in my C. and commit no
	26	any sin or transgression of the new C.
	27	after ye have received my new C.
	41	if a man receiveth a wife in the new C.
	42	if she be not in the new and, C.
	51	offering at your hand by C. and sacrifice
133	57	fulness of gospel. his everlasting C.
136	2	with a C. and promise to keep all
	4	and this shall be our C. that we will

COVENANTED

5	27	covenant which he has before C. with me
40	1	he C. with me that he would obey my
91	24	wherewith ye have C. one with
109	68	how he has C. with Jehovah and vowed

COVENANTS

22	1	all old C. have I caused to be done
25	13	cleave unto the C. which thou hast made
28	12	appointed to any contrary to church C.
	14	according to the C. of the church—68:24; 107:63
33	14	remember the church articles and C. to
35	24	keep all the commandments and C. by—42:78
42	13	observe the C. and church articles to
67		ye shall herafter receive church C.
51	4	according to the laws and C.
68	13	items in addition to the C. and
97	8	willing to observe C. by sacrifice
104	52	C. being broken through transgression
	55	C. which ye have made unto me are
107	12	agreeable to the C. and commandments—107:20
	85	as it is given according to the C.—107:86, 87
	89	teach them according to the C.
132	7	all C. that are not made and entered

COVER

45	31	desolating sickness shall C. the land

Sec.	Vs.	
	50	calamity shall C. the mocker and scorner
121	37	when we undertake to C. our sins

COVERED

121	4	let thy hiding place no longer be C.

COVERETH

112	23	darkness C. the earth and gross darkness
121	1	where is the pavilion that C. thy

COVERING

85	7	clothed with light for a C.
101	23	when the veil of the C. of my temple
124	8	when I shall unveil the face of my C.
133	69	and make sackcloth their C.

COVET

19	25	thou shalt not C. thy neighbor's wife
	26	thou shalt not C. thine own property
117	8	that thou should C. that which is but
136	20	and C. not that which is thy brother's

COVETOUS

88	123	cease to be C., learn to impart one to
101	6	lustful and C. desires among them
117	4	let them repent of all their C. desires

COVETOUSNESS

98	20	for they do not forsake their C. and
104	4	but have broken the covenant by C.—104:52

COVILL, JAMES

40	1	my servant C. was right before me

COWDERY, OLIVER

8	1	C., I say unto you, assuredly as
18	1	the thing you, C. have desired to know
	9	and now, C., I speak unto you and also
	37	I give unto you C., and, that you
20	3	and C. who was also called of God
21	10	he should be ordained by you, C.
25	6	that I may send my servant, C.
27	8	sent Smith and C., to ordain you
32	2	go with my servants C. and Whitmer
37	3	against the time that C. shall return
47	3	for C. I have appointed to another
52	41	let there be one obtained for C. also

Sec.	Vs.		Sec.	Vs.	
55	4	to assist C. to do the work of printing	88	19	after it hath filled measure of its C.
57	13	let C. assist as I have commanded		25	it filleth the measure of its C.
58	58	return, and also C. with them	112	31	at any time from the beginning of the C.
60	6	and C., take their journey for	132	38	from the beginning of C. until this time
	17	made known concerning Rigdon and C.			**CREATIONS**
61	23	concerning my servants C., let them	128	23	let the eternal C. declare his name
	30	my servants, C., shall not open			**CREATOR**
63	46	expounding these things with C.	95	7	by interpretation, the C. of first day
68	32	let C. carry these sayings unto land			**CREATURE**
69	1	for my servant C.'s sake	18	28	preach my gospel unto every C.—68:8; 80:1; 112:28
	2	Whitmer should go with my servant C.	58	64	gospel must be preached to every C.
	4	that he receive counsel from C.	77	2	every other C. which God has created
70	1	which I give unto C., and also to	84	62	into all the world unto every C.
82	11	expedient for Oliah (C.) and, to be	124	128	to send my word to every C.
102	3	C. and, be chosen standing High Council			**CREATURES**
	34	C., Joseph Coe, etc. (signatures), C. and Orson Hyde, Clerks	78	14	may stand independent above all other C.
104	28	let Oliah (C.) have the lot which	104	13	I have made and prepared for my C.
	29	and let O. (C.) have printing office			**CREEDS**
	34	lots which have been named for C.	123	7	so strongly riveted the C. of the fathers
124	95	once put upon him that was my servant C.			**CREEP**
		COWDERY, WARREN A.	89	14	wild animals that run or C. on earth
106	1	I will that C. be appointed and ordained			**CREEPING**
		CRAFT	77	2	and of beasts and of C. things
60	5	let there be a C. made or bought			**CRIED**
		CRAFTINESS	6	22	night that you C. unto me in your heart
76	75	who were blinded by the C. of men—123:12			**CRIES**
121	12	and take them in their own C.	101	92	their ears may be opened unto your C.
		CRAFTS	109	49	the C. of their innocent ones to ascend
106	6	separated himself from the C. of men	121	2	thine ears be penetrated with their C.
		CREATED	136	8	that the C. of the widow and fatherless
14	9	Jesus who C. the heavens and the earth			**CRIETH**
20	18	he C. man, male and female, after his; in his own likeness C. he them	77	9	he C. unto the four angels having the
29	30	in all things whatsoever I have C.	136	36	innocent blood which C. from the ground
	31	by the power of my spirit C. I them			**CRIME**
	34	neither Adam your father whom I C.	68	22	tried or condemned for *any* C. save it
76	24	through him the worlds are and were C.	134	4	civil magistrate should restrain C.
77	2	every other creature which God has C.		8	commission of C. should be punished
88	20	for this intent was it made and C.			
93	29	intelligence was not C. or made			
		CREATION			
49	16	earth might answer the end of its C.			
	17	according to his C. before the world			
77	3	in their destined order or sphere of C.			

Sec.	Vs.	
135	7	they were innocent of *any* C. as they

CRIMINALITY

Sec.	Vs.	
134	8	should be punished according to their C.

CROPS

29	16	hailstorm shall destroy the C. of the
136	7	to prepare for putting in spring C.

CROOKED

3	2	God doth not walk in C. paths neither
33	2	declare my gospel unto a C. generation
34	6	cry repentance to a C. generation

CROSS

23	6	you must take up your C. in the which
56	2	he that will not take up his C. and
112	14	take up your C., follow me and feed my

CROWN

20	14	shall receive a C. of eternal life—66:12
25	15	a C. of righteousness thou shalt receive
29	13	to receive a C. of righteousness and
52	43	I *will* C. the faithful with joy and
59	2	shall receive a C. in the mansions of—106:8
75	28	he shall in nowise lose his C.
76	79	wherefore they obtain not the C. over
	108	be crowned with a C. of his glory
78	15	come up unto the C. prepared for you
79	3	I *will* C. him again with sheaves
81	6	thou shalt have a C. of immortality
104	7	I have promised unto you a C. of glory
124	17	I *will* C. him with blessings and great
	55	that I may C. you with honor and

CROWNED

58	4	day cometh that ye shall be C. with
59	4	they shall also be C. with blessings
75	5	laden with sheaves and C. with honor
76	108	shall be C. with the crown of his glory
88	19	it shall be C. with glory even with
	107	then shall the angels be C. with glory
101	15	given their lives for my name shall be C.
	65	and be C. with celestial glory
124	95	and be C. with the same blessing and glory
133	32	there shall they fall down and be C.

CROWNS

Sec.	Vs.	
29	12	with C. upon their heads—109:76
132	55	and C. of eternal lives in eternal

CRUCIFIED

20	23	he was C., died and rose again the
21	9	manifesteth that Jesus was C. by sinful
35	2	who was C. for the sins of the world—53:2; 54:1
45	52	I am Jesus that was C. I am the Son of
46	13	to know that he was C. for the sins
76	35	having C. him unto themselves and put
41		he came into the world to be C. for

CRY

18	14	you are called to C. repentance unto
34	6	C. repentance to a perverse generation
87	7	that the C. of the saints shall cease
121	16	and C. they have sinned when they have not
	17	those who C. transgression do it because
124	101	C. aloud and spare not, with joy and
128	23	all ye valleys C. aloud and all ye seas
133	9	this shall be their C. and the voice
	10	let the C. go forth among all people
135	7	their innocent blood will C. unto Lord

CRYING

18	15	labor all your days in C. repentance
19	37	C. Hosanna, blessed be the name of
36	6	C. repentance, saying save yourselves
39	19	go forth C. with a loud voice, C. Hosanna
65	3	a voice C., prepare ye the way of the
86	5	angels are C. unto the Lord day and night
88	66	as the voice of one C. in wilderness
	92	through midst of heaven C. with a loud
133	17	angels C. through the midst of heaven

CRYSTAL

130	9	this earth will be made like unto C.

CUMBERED

66	10	seek not to be C.

CUMORAH

128	20	glad tidings from C.

CUNNING

10	12	devil has sought to lay a C. plan
	23	thus he has laid a C. plan thinking to

Sec.	Vs.	
	43	my wisdom is greater than C. of devil

CUP

Sec.	Vs.	
19	18	would that I might not drink the bitter C.
20	78	he shall take the C. also and say
29	17	for the C. of mine indignation is full—43:26
86	3	maketh all nations to drink of her C.
101	11	will I do when C. of iniquity is full
103	3	iniquities, that their C. might be full

CURSE

27	9	whole earth may not be smitten with C.
38	18	there shall be no C. when Lord cometh
41	1	ye that hear me not *will* I C.
45	32	lift up their voices and C. God and die
98	17	lest I smite the whole earth with a C.—110:15; 128:17
103	24	after these testimonies ye shall C. them
	25	whomsoever ye C. I *will* C. and ye—132:47
104	4	with a very sore and grievous C.
128	18	earth will be smitten with a C. unless
133	2	come down upon world with a C. and

CURSED

24	17	go to law with thee shall be C. by law
29	28	depart from me ye C.—29:41
61	14	in the last days I C. the waters
	17	in the beginning I C. the land
104	4	I have C. them with a very sore and
	5	he shall be C. in his life and shall
109	65	remnants of Jacob who had been C. and
121	16	C. are all those that shall lift up
124	93	whoever he curses shall be C.

CURSES

113	10	the bands of her neck are the C. of God
124	93	whoever he C. shall be cursed

CURSING

24	4	will send them a C. instead of blessing—24:6
	15	ye shall leave a C. instead of blessing
104	3	not faithful they were nigh unto C.

CURSINGS

41	1	will I curse with the heaviest of all C.
124	48	instead of blessings ye bring C., wrath
120		and shall be attended with C. and not
132	48	be visited with blessings and not C.

CURTAIN

88	95	after shall the C. of heaven be unfolded

CURTAINS

101	21	called stakes, for the C. or strength

CUT

1	14	shall be C. off from among the people—133:63
45	44	that watches not for me shall be C. off
50	8	hypocrites shall be C. off either in; woe unto them who are C. off from my
51	2	if otherwise they *will* be C. off
52	6	not faithful they shall be C. off—63:63
	11	*will* C. my work short in righteousness—84:97; 109:59
56	3	he that will not obey shall be C. off
	10	shall be C. off out of my church
64	35	rebellious shall be C. off out of land
65	2	stone which is C. out of mountain
85	9	they shall be C. asunder and their
	11	apostatized or have been C. off from
101	90	*will* C. off those wicked, unfaithful
104	9	inasmuch as ye are C. off by transgressions
121	14	disappointed and their hopes may be C. off

CUTLER, ALPHEUS

124	132	viz., David Fullmer, C., and William

D

Sec. Vs.
DAILY
19 32 this shall suffice for thy D. walk
DAMAGES
123 2 amount of D. they have sustained both
DAMNATION
19 7 again, it is written eternal D.
29 44 that believe not unto eternal D. for
121 23 vipers shall not escape D. of hell
DAMNED
42 60 he that doeth them not shall be D. if
49 5 he that receiveth him not shall be D.
58 29 with slothfulness the same shall be D.
68 9 he that believeth not shall be D.
84 74 shall be D. and shall not come into my
112 29 and is not baptized shall be D.
132 4 abide not that covenant then are ye D.
6 shall abide the law or he shall be D.
27 nowise enter into my glory but shall be D.
DAMNING
123 7 under the most D. hand of murder, tyranny
DANCING
136 28 praise the Lord with singing, with D.
DANGEROUS
134 12 unlawful, unjust and D. to peace of
DANGERS
61 4 there are many D. upon the waters
DANIEL
116 1 as spoken of by D. the prophet
DARK
109 61 for a long time in a cloudy and D. day
121 4 the D. and benighted dominion of Sheol
123 6 present them in all their D. and hellish hue
10 which D. and blackening deeds are
DARKENED
10 2 at the same time and your mind became D.

Sec. Vs.
29 14 the sun shall be D. and the moon shall be—34:9; 45:42
84 54 your minds in times past have been D.
80 not be weary in mind, neither D., neither
DARKNESS
1 30 bring it forth out of obscurity and D.
6 21 I am the light which shineth in D. and D. comprehendeth it not— 10:58; 11:11; 34:2; 39:2; 45:7; 88:49
10 21 they love D. rather than light— 29:45
14 9 a light which cannot be hid in D.
21 6 the Lord will disperse the powers of D.
24 1 thou hast been delivered from D.
38 5 wicked have I kept in chains of D.
8 the veil of D. shall soon be rent
11 powers of D. prevail upon the earth
45 28 break forth among them that sit in D.
50 23 doth not edify is not of God and is D.
25 that you may chase D. from among you
57 10 may be preached unto those who sit in D.
77 8 or to cast down to regions of D.
82 5 spreadeth his dominions and D. reigneth
84 49 world lieth in sin and groaneth under D.
53 groaneth under sin and D. even now
88 67 there shall be no D. in you and that
95 6 they are walking in D. at noon-day
12 therefore you shall walk in D.
101 91 even in outer D. where there is
109 73 come forth out of the wilderness of D.
112 23 D. covereth the earth and gross D. the
123 13 to light all hidden things of D.
133 72 ye were delivered over unto D.
73 these shall go away into outer D. where
DARTS
3 8 against all the fiery D. of adversary
27 17 quench all the fiery D. of wicked

Sec.	Vs.	

DATE
| 128 | 3 | giving the D. and names and history |

DAUGHTER
| 25 | 1 | speak unto you, Emma Smith, my D., for |

DAUGHTERS
25	1	who receive my gospel are my sons and D.
76	24	are begotten sons and D. of God
124	11	come to the house of the D. of Zion

DAVID
14	11	thou art D., and art called to assist
30	1	I say unto you D. you have feared
109	63	to be broken off from house of D.
132	1	as also Moses, D., Solomon, my
	38	D. also received many wives and
	39	D.'s wives and concubines were given

DAVIES, AMOS
| 124 | 111 | let my servant D. pay stock into |

DAY
1	9	seal them up into the D. when the wrath
	10	unto the D. when the Lord shall come
	14	D. cometh that they who will not hear
	35	all men shall know that D. speedily
2	1	the great and dreadful D. of the Lord
4	2	blameless before God at the last D.
5	35	thou shalt be lifted up at the last D.—9:14; 17:8; 52:44; 75:16, 22
6	3	reap while the day lasts—11:3; 12:3; 14:3
10	23	to their condemnation in D. of judgment
18	24	that name shall they be called at last D.
19	3	and the last great D. of judgment
20	1	on the sixth day of the month—21:3
	23	died and rose again the third D.
24	12	with the voice of a trump both D. and night
27	15	may be able to withstand the evil D.
29	8	the D. when tribulation and desolation
	9	the D. soon at hand when earth is ripe
	12	at my right hand at D. of my coming
	14	before this great D. shall come—34:9; 45:42; 49:24; 110:14; 128:17
31	2	day cometh that they will believe and
34	8	great day at the time of my coming
35	21	shall abide the D. of my coming
38	5	great D. which shall come at the end
	8	D. soon cometh that ye shall see me; not purified shall not abide the D.—50:45
39	21	the D. nor the hour no man knoweth—49:7
41	10	my laws in the D. that I shall give them
	12	upon your souls in D. of judgment
42	36	may be gathered in one in that D. when
43	17	great D. of the Lord is nigh at hand
	18	D. cometh that Lord shall utter his
	20	prepare for great day of Lord—43:21; 58:11; 133:10
	21	D. cometh when thunders shall utter
	22	for the great D. of the Lord is come
	25	by the voice of mercy all the D. long
	26	D. has come when cup of the wrath of
44	2	in the D. that they assemble themselves
45	12	city reserved until a D. of righteousness; a D. sought for by all holy men
	16	the D. when I shall come in my glory—45:56
	17	how the D. of redemption shall come
	24	when that D. shall come shall a remnant
	26	in that D. shall be heard of wars and
	38	in that D. when they shall see all
	39	looking forth for the great D. of Lord
	57	they shall abide the D.
50	24	brighter and brighter until perfect D.
51	17	the hour and the D. is not given unto
56	1	in the D. of visitation—124:8, 10
	16	lamentation in the D. of visitation
58	4	D. cometh that ye shall be crowned
	11	after that cometh the D. of my power
59	9	offer up sacraments upon my holy D.
	10	this is a D. appointed unto you to rest
	12	on this the Lord's D. thou shalt offer
	13	on this D. thou shalt do none other

Day 106 Day

Sec.	Vs.
60	4 the D. when I shall make up my jewels—101:3
	15 as a testimony against them in D. of
61	39 that you may abide D. of his coming
63	6 D. of wrath shall come as whirlwind
	20 when D. of transfiguration shall come
	53 in D. of the coming of Son of man
	54 in that D. will I send mine angels to
	58 D. of warning and not a D. of many words
	59 D. cometh that all things shall be
64	22 after that D. I will not hold any
	23 it is a D. of sacrifice and a D. of tithing for my people
	43 D. shall come when nations of earth
68	29 observe the Sabbath D. to keep it holy
70	4 require of them in the D. of judgment
75	21 in D. of judgment you shall be judges
	22 tolerable for heathen in D. of judgment
77	12 on seventh D. he finished his work
78	12 of Satan until D. of redemption—82:21; 104:9; 132:26
84	42 confirm upon you who are present this D.
85	3 prepare them against D. of vengeance
	9 shall find none inheritance in that D.—85:9
86	5 crying unto the Lord D. and night
87	8 be not moved until the D. of the Lord come
88	45 the sun giveth his light by D. and
	49 D. shall come when you shall comprehend
	102 are to remain until great and last D.
90	10 D. when the arm of the Lord shall be
	11 in that D. every man shall hear fulness
95	7 the Creator of the first D., beginning
97	23 scourge shall pass over by night and D.
101	7 answer them in D. of their trouble
	8 in D. of their peace they esteemed lightly; in D. of their trouble they feel after
	9 in D. of wrath I will remember mercy
	12 in that D. all who are found upon watch
	21 until D. cometh when there is no room

Sec.	Vs.
	26 in that D. enmity of man shall cease
	27 in that D. whatsoever man shall ask it
	28 in that D. Satan shall not have power
	30 in that D. an infant shall not die
	32 in that D. when the Lord shall come
	78 for his own sins in D. of judgment
102	1 this D. a general council of 24 high
105	35 there has been a D. of calling; time has come for a D. of choosing
106	5 that D. shall not overcome you as a thief
107	3 before this D. it was called the Holy
108	6 shall be fulfilled upon you in that D.
109	28 as thou didst in the D. of battle
	36 as upon those on the D. of Pentecost
	38 may not faint in the D. of trouble
	46 be prepared against the D. of burning
	61 for a long time in cloudy and dark D.
	74 D. when thou shalt unveil the heavens
110	16 dreadful D. of the Lord is near even
112	5 D. after D. let thy warning voice go
	24 D. of wrath, D. of burning, D. of desolation
115	10 let beginning be made on 4th D. of
	11 in one year from this D. let them
118	5 take leave on the 26th D. of April
124	124 sealed up unto the D. of redemption
127	2 to this D. has the God of my fathers
128	24 great D. of the Lord is at hand; who can abide D. of his coming
133	11 ye know neither the D. nor the hour
	35 dwell in his presence D. and night
	40 calling upon name of Lord D. and night
	51 for this was the D. of vengeance
	56 sing the song of the Lamb D. and night
	58 in the D. when the weak should confound
	60 kept from the world in D. they were
	64 D. cometh that shall burn as an oven; D. cometh that shall burn them up
	66 in that D. when I came unto my own
136	35 now cometh the D. of their calamity

DAYS

1	4 whom I have chosen in these last D.—52:1

Sec.	Vs.	
5	33	that thy D. may be prolonged I have
10	48	gospel that they might preach in their D.
18	15	labor all your D. in crying repentance
20	1	rise of church of Christ in last D.
21	8	for his D. of rejoicing are come
22	3	built up unto me even as in D. of old
24	8	I am with thee unto the end of thy D.
27	6	holy prophets concerning last D.
	11	the prince of all, the ancient of D.
29	43	appoint unto man the D. of his probation
39	10	the D. of thy deliverance are come if
	11	which I have sent forth in last D.
45	10	I will reason as with men in D. of old—61:13
	15	I will prophecy as unto men in D. of old
52	11	D. cometh that I will send forth judgment
	20	D. have come; according to men's faith
53	1	which I have raised up in these last D.
58	17	in Israel, like as it was in ancient D.
59	11	offered up in righteousness on all D.
61	14	in the last D. I cursed the waters
	15	D. will come that no flesh shall be
	16	it shall be said in D. to come that none
	17	even so in the last D. have I blessed it
63	58	I am not to be mocked in the last D.
64	8	my disciples in D. of old sought occasion
	30	to provide for his saints in the last D.
	34	eat the good of land of Zion in last D.
	37	made my church in these last D. like
65	5	be prepared for the D. to come in
66	2	written by prophets and apostles in D.
	6	tarry not many D. in this place
74	2	in D. of apostles law of circumcision
76	7	mysteries of my kingdom from D. of old
77	12	as God made the world in six D. and
	15	raised up to Jewish nation in last D.
78	16	who is without beginning of D. or or end of life—84:17
84	2	church established in the last D. for
	13	Esaias lived in the D. of Abraham
	28	at the time he was eight D. old

Sec.	Vs.	
	77	in D. when I was with them traveling
	108	in ancient D. built up my church unto
	117	desolation of abomination in last D.
86	4	in the last D. even now while the Lord
87	4	after many D. slaves shall rise up
88	44	in their D., in their weeks, in their
	68	the D. will come that you shall see him
	87	not many D. hence the earth shall reel
89	2	salvation of all saints in the last D.
	4	hearts of conspiring men in last D.
90	31	not be idle in her D. from thenceforth
101	62	after many D. all things were fulfilled
105	37	they shall have power after many D. to
107	4	the church in ancient D. called that
	41	this order was instituted in days of Adam
	46	Mahalaleel was 496 years and 7 D. old
109	23	spoken concerning the last D.
	45	concerning the wicked in the last D.
112	30	this priesthood given for the last D.
113	6	gathering of my people in last D.
	8	those whom God should call in last D.
115	4	shall church be called in the last D.
116	1	where the ancient of D. shall sit
121	31	all appointed D., months and years, and all the D. of their D.; shall be revealed in the D. of the
122	9	thy D. are known and thy years shall
124	30	only in the D. of your poverty wherein
127	2	my common lot all the D. of my life
128	17	glories to be revealed in the last D.
	18	from the days of Adam to present time
132	7	Joseph to hold this power in the last D.
133	24	as it was in D. before it was divided
	53	and carried them all the D. of old
135	4	three D. previous to his assassination
136	22	in the last D. to save my people Israel
	35	even the D. of sorrow like a woman that
	37	given from the D. of Adam to Abraham

DEACON

	20	6	every D. is to be ordained according
		64	each D. may take a certificate from

Sec.	Vs.		Sec.	Vs.	
84	30	offices of teacher and D. are necessary		6	thus saith the Lord concerning your D.; when any are baptized for your D. let
107	10	also in the office of a D. and member		10	subject of baptism for the D.—128:1
	63	from D. to teacher and from teacher to	128	5	for the salvation of the D. who should
	85	duty of president over office of a D		6	this very subject in relation to the D.; and I saw the D. great and small stand; the D. were judged out of those—128:7

DEACONS

				8	out of the books shall your D. be judged; the records kept concerning their D.
20	38	duty of elders, priests, teachers, D.		11	both as well for the D. as for living
	39	to ordain other D.—20:48		12	to answer to the likeness of the D.; in likeness of resurrection of the D.; ordinance of baptism for the D. being in likeness of the D.
	57	assisted in all his duties by D.			
	58	neither teachers nor D. have authority			
	84	it may be signed by D. of the church		13	to show forth the living and the D.
84	111	but the D. should be appointed to watch		14	the records in relation to your D.
88	127	High Priests, even down to the D.		15	these are principles in relation to D.; neither can we without our D. be made
107	62	in like manner and also the D.			
	85	is to preside over twelve D., to sit		16	what shall they do which are baptized for D. if D. rise not; why are they then baptized for the D.
124	142	also the president of the D. and his			

DEAD

				17	most glorious of all, baptism for the D.
18	12	he hath risen again from the D.		18	it is the baptism for the D.
22	2	by law of Moses neither by your D. works		19	glad tidings for the D.; a voice of gladness for living and D.
	3	it is because of your D. works that I		22	let the D. speak forth anthems of praise
29	13	even the D. which died in me and shall		24	a book containing the records of our D.
	26	then shall all the D. awake from their	132	7	after the resurrection of the D.; contracts have an end when men are D.
	41	wherein he became spiritually D.			
63	49	blessed are the D. that die in the Lord; they shall rise from the D.		13	shall not remain after men are D.
				15	marriage are not of force when they are D.
	52	preached apostles the resurrection of D.	135	1	calmly, exclaiming "I am a D. man"; and was shot D.; they were both shot after they were D.
76	16	speaking of the resurrection of the D.			
	39	brought forth by the resurrection of D.		5	the testators are now D. and their

DEADLY

77	5	work of the ministry and were D.	24	13	and against D. poisons
88	14	brought to pass resurrection from D.	124	98	who would administer unto him D. poison
	16	resurrection from D. is redemption of			

DEAF

	101	these are the rest of the D. and			
109	75	when trump shall sound for the D.	35	9	they shall cause the D. to hear
124	29	may be baptized for those who are D.	58	11	then shall the lame, the blind, the D.
	32	baptisms for D. shall not be acceptable; rejected as a church with your D.	84	69	they shall unstop the ears of the D.

DEAL

	33	ordinance of baptizing for D. belongeth; baptisms for D. cannot be acceptable			
			51	9	let every man D. honestly and be
	35	after this time your baptisms for D.	111	6	for I will D. mercifully with her
	36	be places for baptisms for your D.	134	10	societies have a right to D. with their
	39	baptisms for your D. are ordained by			
	100	if I will that he should raise the D.			
127	5	in relation to baptism for your D.—128:16			

Sec.	Vs.	
		DEALINGS
134	10	provided that such D. be for fellowship
		DEALT
9	6	wisdom in me that I have D. with you
20	80	overtaken in a fault shall be D. with
42	79	D. with according to laws of the land
	81	D. with according to the law of God
82	21	D. with according to laws of my church
		DEAR
126	1	D. and well-beloved brother Brigham
		DEARLY
123	17	D. beloved brethren let us cheerfully
128	15	D. beloved brethren and sisters let me
		DEATH
7	2	give unto me power over D. that I may
18	11	your Redeemer suffered D. in the flesh
29	41	which is the first D., even that same D. which is the last D.
	42	they should not die as to temporal D.
42	46	that die in me shall not taste of D.
	47	wo unto them for their D. is bitter
	48	not appointed unto D. shall be healed
45	2	hearken unto my voice lest D. overtake
	4	behold the sufferings and D. of him
50	5	endure whether in life or D. for they
	8	shall be cut off either in life or in D.
57	10	who sit in the region and shadow of D.
58	2	commandments whether in life or in D.
61	39	abide his coming whether in life or D.
63	17	and brimstone which is the second D.
64	7	forgiveness, who have not sinned unto D.
76	37	on whom second D. shall have any power
	59	all things are theirs whether in life or D.
85	8	shall fall by the shaft of D. like as
87	1	will eventually terminate in D. and

Sec.	Vs.	
88	116	and they shall not any more see D.
98	14	abide in my covenant even unto D. that
101	29	shall be no sorrow because there is no D.
	36	wherefore, fear not even unto D.
102	8	whenever any vacancy shall occur by D.
107	42	three years previous to Adam's D. —107:53
110	13	who was taken to heaven without tasting D.
121	18	might bring them into bondage and D.
	44	thy faithfulness is stronger than cords of D.
122	7	and sentence of D. passed upon thee
132	27	innocent blood and assent unto my D.
135	3	in D. they were not separated
136	39	many have marveled because of his D.
		DEATHS
132	25	wide the way that leadeth to the D.
		DEBT
19	35	pay the D. thou hast contracted with
64	27	forbidden to get in D. to thine enemies
72	13	shall pay the D. out of that which the
	14	shall answer the D. unto the bishop in
90	23	he may be enabled to discharge every D.
104	80	of those to whom you are in D.— 104:81
115	13	let not my servant get in D. any more
		DEBTS
104	78	concerning your D. it is my will you shall pay all your D.
111	5	concern not yourselves about your D.
117	5	properties of Kirtland be turned out for D.
119	2	for D. of the presidency of my church
127	1	I will see that all my D. are canceled in
		DECEIVE
10	25	D. and lie in wait to catch that ye
	28	wo be unto him that lieth to D. because another lieth to D.
50	3	Satan hath sought to D. you that he
123	12	whereby they lie in wait to D.
129	7	contrary for a just man to D.

Sec.	Vs.		Sec.	Vs.	
		DECEIVED			final D. upon controversies in spiritual
10	29	Satan saith unto them, He hath D. you	83		their D. upon his head shall be an end
43	6	that you may not be D., that you may			**DECISIONS**
45	57	spirit for guide and have not been D.	102	30	there is a distinction in their D.
46	8	beware lest ye are D., and that ye may not be D. seek ye	107	27	each quorum must be agreed to its D. in order to make their D. valid
49	23	be not D. but continue in steadfastness		29	unless this is the case D. not entitled to same blessings which D.
50	7	hypocrites among you who have D. some		30	D. of these quorums are to be made in
52	14	pattern in all that ye may not be D.		36	equal in authority in all their D. —107:37
		DECEIVERS			**DECLARE**
50	6	wo unto them that are D. and hypocrites	5	12	for from heaven *will* I D. it unto them
		DECEIVETH	11	21	seek not to D. my word but first seek
28	11	are not of me and that Satan D. him	14	8	D. repentance unto this generation
		DECEIVING	15	6	D. repentance unto this people.—16:6
50	2	gone forth in the earth D. the world	18	26	others who are called to D. my gospel
52	14	he goeth forth D. the nations		32	to D. my gospel according to power of
		DECEMBER	19	29	thou shalt D. glad tidings—31:3
130	13	on the subject, D. 25th, 1832		31	thou shalt D. repentance and faith on
135	6	Joseph Smith was 38 in D., 1843		37	D. the truth even with a loud voice
		DECIDE	24	12	he shall open his mouth and D. gospel
107	79	shall have power to D. upon testimony	28	3	D. faithfully the commandments and the
130	16	I was left thus without being able to D.	29	4	ye are chosen out of world to D. gospel
136	7	presidents D. how many can go next spring		42	forth angels to D. unto them repentance
		DECIDED		50	I D. no more unto you at this time
42	72	as may be thought best or D. by the	30	5	open your mouth to D. my gospel
		DECISION	31	4	D. the things which have been revealed
102	19	the president shall give a D. according		6	D. my word and I will prepare a place
	20	discover an error in the D. of the	32	1	I will that he shall D. my gospel and
	21	the D. shall be altered accordingly	33	2	D. my gospel unto a crooked and perverse
	22	the first D. shall stand, the majority	36	3	you shall D. it with a loud voice
	26	the testimony accompanying their D. to	52	39	D. the word in the regions about them
	27	be dissatisfied with the D. of said; as though no D. had been made	60	7	D. my word without wrath or doubting
	31	from D. of former there can be appeal but from D. of latter	61	33	let them journey and D. the word among
107	27	every D. made by either of these	62	5	only be faithful and D. glad tidings
	32	in case *any* D. of these quorums is; there can be no appeal from their D.	63	37	D. both by word and by flight that
	77	the D. of either of these councils	64	31	I D. unto you and my words are sure
	78	as there is not satisfaction upon D.			
	80	after this D. it shall be had in;			

Sec.	Vs.		Sec.	Vs.	
80	4	D. the things which ye have heard and	101	98	consequence of things which I have D.
99	2	you shall have power to D. my word	103	5	I have D. a decree which my people
100	7	D. whatsoever things ye D. in my name		6	they shall, for I have D. it, begin to
128	23	let eternal creations D. his name		11	I have D. that your brethren which have

DECLARED

			104	16	I have D. to provide for my saints
20	10	which is D. unto the world by them	121	33	stop Missouri river in its D. course
29	29	never at any time have I D. from mine	130	20	there is a law irrevocably D. in heaven
128	2	it was D. in my former letter that			
	6	when he D. as you will find recorded			**DECREES**
	13	that which is heavenly as Paul hath D.	128	9	according to D. of the great Jehovah
130	13	this a voice D. to me while I was			**DEDICATE**
			58	57	consecrated and D. this land and spot
		DECLARETH	109	12	thy house which we now D. to thee
10	68	whosoever D. more or less than this			**DEDICATED**

DECLARING

28	16	D. my gospel with the sound of rejoicing	84	3	D. by the hand of Joseph Smith, Jr.
42	6	D. my word like unto angels of God	94	6	it shall be D. unto the Lord from the
52	36	D. none other things than the prophets		7	it shall be wholly D. unto the Lord —94:12
128	20	D. the fulfillment of the prophets; D. the three witnesses to bear record; D. themselves as possessing the keys		10	second lot on the south shall be D.
			95	16	inner court be D. unto me for sacrament
				17	D. unto me for the school of mine
	21	D. their dispensation, their rights			**DEDICATION**
			109	78	accept the D. of this house unto thee

DECREE

					DEED
29	8	the D. hath gone forth from the Father—101:10	42	30	with a D. which cannot be broken
	12	it hath gone forth in a firm D. by the	105	32	Zion is in very D. the kingdom of our
61	19	I revoke not the D.	117	11	be a bishop not in name but in D. saith
68	21	by virtue of the D. concerning their			
88	61	according to the D. which God hath made			**DEEDED**
103	5	I have decreed a D. which my people	51	5	claim on that portion that is D. unto

DECREED

					DEEDS
1	7	what I have D. shall be fulfilled	10	21	than light because their D. are evil —29:45
49	5	have D. that he that receiveth him	19	3	his works and D. which he hath done
61	5	I have D. in mine anger many	64	11	and reward thee according to the D.
	19	I have D. and the destroyer rideth	84	87	reprove world of all their unrighteous D.—84:117
63	33	I have D. wars upon the face of the			
	36	I have D. all these things upon face a	99	5	to convince all of their ungodly D.
87	6	until the consumption D. hath made	123	10	which dark and blackening D. are enough
88	17	it is D. that the poor and the meek			**DEEP**
98	2	Lord hath D. that they shall be granted	122	7	if thou be cast into the D.
	14	I have D. in my heart saith the Lord—104:5	127	2	D. water is what I am wont to swim in
			133	20	upon the mighty ocean, even the great D.

Sec.	Vs.	
	23	he shall command the great D. and it
	27	highway cast up in midst of great D.

DEFEND

Sec.	Vs.	
87	3	in order to D. themselves against

DEFENDED

Sec.	Vs.	
109	54	those principles which were so nobly D.

DEFENDING

Sec.	Vs.	
134	11	all men are justified in D. themselves

DEFENSE

Sec.	Vs.	
115	6	may be for a D. and for a refuge

DEFERENCE

Sec.	Vs.	
134	6	to laws all men owe respect and D.

DEFILED

Sec.	Vs.	
93	35	whatsoever temple is D. God shall destroy
97	15	thing to come into it that it be not D.
	17	if it be D. I will not come into it

DEFY

Sec.	Vs.	
76	31	to deny the truth and D. my power

DEGREE

Sec.	Vs.	
1	31	look upon sin with least D. of allowance
19	20	even in the least D. you have tasted
121	37	in any D. of unrighteousness the

DEGREES

Sec.	Vs.	
131	1	in celestial glory there are three D.

DEIGN

Sec.	Vs.	
38	18	I D. to give you greater riches
124	41	I D. to reveal unto my church things

DELAYETH

Sec.	Vs.	
45	26	they shall say Christ D. his coming

DELIGHT

Sec.	Vs.	
25	14	let thy soul D. in thy husband and
41	1	ye whom I D. to bless with the greatest
76	5	I D. to honor those who serve me in
109	43	we D. not in the destruction of our

DELIGHTETH

Sec.	Vs.	
25	12	my soul D. in the song of the heart

DELIGHTFUL

Sec.	Vs.	
124	60	let it be a D. habitation for man and

DELIVER

Sec.	Vs.	
5	6	go forth and D. my words unto children
8	4	it shall D. you out of the hand of thine

Sec.	Vs.	
42	89	thou shalt D. him or her *up* unto the
76	107	when he shall D. *up* the kingdom and
104	10	ye shall D. him over to buffetings of
	84	you shall loan enough to D. yourselves
105	8	he will D. them in time of trouble
108	8	I am with you to bless you and D. you
109	42	but D. thou, O Jehovah, we beseech
	46	D. thy people from the calamity of the
127	2	and *will* D. me from henceforth
129	7	but he *will* still D. his message
133	67	could not redeem, neither my power to D.
	71	there are none to D. you for ye obeyed
135	4	Joseph went to Carthage to D. himself
136	26	till thou shalt D. it to him again

DELIVERANCE

Sec.	Vs.	
30	6	in prayer and faith for his and your D.
39	10	the days of thy D. are come if thou
56	18	coming in power and glory unto their D.
95	1	I prepare a way for their D.
104	80	shall send means unto you for your D.
109	32	complete D. from under this yoke

DELIVERED

Sec.	Vs.	
3	11	thou shalt be D. *up* and become as
10	1	because you D. *up* those writings which
	8	you have D. writings into his hands
	9	therefore, you have D. them *up*; yea
24	1	thou hast been D. from all thine; thou hast been D. from power of Satan
42	79	D. *up* to the laws of the land—42:84, 85, 86, 87
	91	shall be D. *up* unto the law of God
78	12	D. over to the buffetings of Satan —82:21, 132:26
93	43	if you will be D. you shall set in order
98	29	I have D. thine enemy unto thine hands
104	62	all sacred things shall be D. into the
	83	you shall be D. this once out of your
109	28	that they may be D. from the hands of
124	98	be D. from those who would administer

| Delivered | | 113 | | Describing |

Sec.	Vs.	
127	2	has the God of my fathers D. me out of
133	72	and ye were D. over unto darkness
136	40	have I not D. you from your enemies

DELIVEREDST

3	12	when thou D. *up* that which God had; thou D. *up* that which was sacred into

DEMONSTRATION

99	2	declare my word in D. of Holy Spirit

DENIED

76	35	having D. the holy spirit after; having D. the only begotten Son of the
134	9	individual rights of its members D.

DENIETH

11	25	wo unto him that D. these things

DENOMINATIONS

23	12	there are many yet among all D. who are

DENY

5	27	if he D. this he will break covenant
10	62	they shall not D. that which you have
11	25	D. not the spirit of revelation nor
29	22	men again begin to D. their God then
39	16	but I cannot D. my word
42	23	woman to lust after her shall D. faith—63:16
76	31	to D. the truth and defy my power
	43	who D. the Son after the Father has
	83	these are they who D. not Holy Spirit
101	5	those who D. me cannot be sanctified
114	2	there are those among you who D. my name

DEPART

20	32	fall from grace and D. from living God
20	28	D. from me ye cursed—29:41
75	20	D. speedily from that house and shake
118	4	next spring let them D. to go over

DEPENDED

3	13	has D. upon his own judgment and

DEPENDS

123	15	much which D. upon these things

DEPRIVE

134	7	to D. citizens of this privilege

Sec.	Vs.	

DEPTH

54	5	had been drowned in the D. of the sea—121:22
76	48	D. and misery thereof they understand

DEPTHS

132	19	shall inherit thrones all heights and D.

DERISION

122	1	fools shall have thee in D. and hell

DESCEND

78	14	the tribulation which shall D. upon
88	98	they who shall D. with him first
90	5	when the storms D. and the rains D.
128	19	so shall the knowledge of God D. upon
130	23	it may D. upon him and not tarry with

DESCENDANT

68	18	except he be a literal D. of Aaron —107:16, 69, 70
	19	when no literal D. of Aaron can be —107:17
	20	a literal D. of Aaron must be designated
96	7	for he is a D. of Seth, (Joseph) and a
107	73	duty of a bishop who is not literal D.
	76	a literal D. of Aaron has a legal right
113	4	who is partly a D. of Jesse as well as
	6	it is a D. of Jesse as well as of Joseph

DESCENDANTS

68	15	except they be literal D. of Aaron
	16	literal D. of Aaron have a legal right
107	40	belongs to the literal D. of chosen

DESCENDED

88	6	ascended on high as also he D. below
93	15	Holy Ghost D. upon him in the form of
122	8	Son of man hath D. below them all

DESCENDING

68	21	the priesthood D. from father to son

DESCENDS

49	6	reign till he D. on the earth to put

DESCRIBING

77	2	used by Revelator John in D. heaven

Sec.	Vs.	
		DESCRIPTION
58	50	he shall write a D. of the land of Zion
		DESERTS
133	29	in the barren D. there shall come forth
		DESIGN
10	14	Satan shall not accomplish his evil D.
58	3	for the present time the D. of your God
95	4	I D. to prepare mine apostles to prune
	8	I D. to endow those whom I have chosen
96	2	upon which I D. to build mine holy house
		DESIGNATED
68	20	must be D. by this presidency
107	39	as they shall be D. by revelation
		DESIGNED
107	90	and is D. for those who do not travel
		DESIGNS
3	1	the works, D. and purposes of God
10	31	they shall not accomplish their evil D.
89	4	in consequence of evils and D. which
		DESIRE
6	8	even as you D. so shall it be unto; if you D. you shall be the means of—11:8
	22	if you D. a further witness cast your
	25	grant unto you a gift if you D. of me
	27	a D. to lay up treasures for yourself
7	5	this was a good D. but my beloved has
11	10	have a gift if thou wilt D. of me in faith
	14	know all things whatsoever you D. of
	21	if you D. you shall have my spirit
18	27	who shall D. to take upon them my name
	28	if they D. to take upon them my name
19	36	when thou shalt D. to see thy family
20	37	and D. to be baptized and come forth
24	14	required of you by them who D. it
43	12	if ye D. the glories of the kingdom
	13	if ye D. the mysteries of the kingdom

Sec.	Vs.	
49	2	they D. to know the truth in part but
54	3	if your brethren D. to escape enemies
58	44	except they D. it through prayer of
62	7	if any among you D. to ride upon
63	57	those who D. in their hearts to warn
80	2	as you D. a companion I will give unto
127	10	great D. to have addressed them from
132	61	and D. to espouse another and the first
		DESIRED
5	1	Martin Harris has D. a witness at my
7	4	he D. of me that he might bring souls
	5	my beloved has D. that he might do more
	8	ye both joy in that which ye have D.
9	1	translate according to that which you D.
10	46	D. in their prayers should come forth
15	4	many times you have D. of me—16:4
18	1	Cowdery have D. of me I give unto you
127	10	I D. with exceedingly great desire to have
		DESIREDST
7	4	but thou D. that thou mightest speedily
		DESIRES
3	4	dictates of his own will and carnal D.
4	3	if ye have D. to serve God ye are
5	23	concerning the man that D. witness
	24	a view of the things which he D. to see
6	20	spoken unto thee because of thy D.
	27	command you, that if you have good D.
7	8	ye shall both have according to your D.
11	17	according to your D. shall it be done
	27	I speak unto all who have good D.—12:7
18	37	who shall have the D. of which I have
	38	their D. and works you shall know them
67	1	whose D. have come up before me
88	121	cease from all your lustful D.

Sec.	Vs.	
95	16	offering up your most holy D. unto me
101	6	there were covetous D. among them
117	4	let them repent of all their covetous D.
125	4	all that have D. to dwell therein take

DESIREST

7	1	John, my beloved, what D. thou?
	3	because thou D. this thou shalt tarry
99	7	if thou D. of me thou mayest go up

DESIRETH

6	3	whoso D. to reap let him thrust in his sickle—11:3; 12:3; 14:3
52	12	for Satan D. to sift him as chaff

DESIROUS

74	3	unbelieving husband was D. that children

DESOLATE

84	115	their house shall be left unto them D.

DESOLATING

5	19	a D. scourge shall go forth among the
45	31	a D. sickness shall cover the land

DESOLATION

29	8	and D. are sent forth upon the wicked—63:37
45	19	D. shall come upon this generation as a
	21	until every D. shall come to pass
84	114	D. and utter abolishment which await
	117	D. of abomination in the last days
88	85	D. of abomination that awaits wicked
112	24	a day of D., of weeping, of mourning

DESOLATIONS

35	11	not anything shown forth except D. upon
45	33	earthquakes in divers places and many D.

DESPISE

3	7	counsels of God and D. his words
117	15	let no man D. my servant Oliver Granger
124	21	let no man D. my servant George

DESPISED

35	13	those who are unlearned and D. to thresh
121	20	they shall be D. by those that flattered

Sec.	Vs.	

DESTINED

77	3	classes of being in their D. order or

DESTINIES

117	6	do I not hold the D. of all the armies

DESTROY

3	18	suffered to D. their brethren, Nephites
5	32	I foresee the lying in wait to D. thee
	33	there are many that lie in wait to D.
10	6	they have sought to D. you; whom you have trusted has sought to D.
	7	he has also sought to D. your gift
	12	a cunning plan that he may D. this work
	19	we *will* D. him and also the work
	23	thinking to D. the work of God
	25	lie in wait to catch that ye may D.; catch a man in a lie that they may D.
	27	seeking to D. the souls of men
	43	I will not suffer that they shall D. my
	52	I do not bring it to D. that which they
	54	I do not say this to D. my church but
29	16	sent forth to D. the crops of the earth
44	5	wherewith the enemy seeketh to D. my
64	17	hath sinned and Satan seeketh to D. his soul
77	8	of the earth to save life and to D.
82	22	of unrighteousness, and they *will* not D. you
86	6	faith is weak, lest you D. the wheat also
93	35	whatsoever temple is defiled God shall D.
105	15	forth to D. and lay waste mine enemies
132	54	I *will* D. her if she abide not
	57	lest an enemy come and D. him; for Satan seeketh to D.
	64	for I *will* D. her

DESTROYED

5	19	utterly D. by the brightness of my
17	4	that Joseph Smith, Jr., may not be D.
45	19	this people shall be D. and scattered
101	51	the enemy D. their works and broke down
132	14	not by me shall be shaken and D.
	26	they shall be D. in the flesh and
	41	committed adultery and shall be D. —132:63

Sec.	Vs.	
	52	said they were pure shall be D. saith
	54	she shall be D. saith the Lord
	64	administer unto him or she shall be D.

DESTROYER

Sec.	Vs.	
61	19	the D. rideth on the face thereof and
101	54	saved my vineyard from hands of the D.
105	15	the D. I have sent forth to destroy

DESTROYETH

Sec.	Vs.	
63	4	who buildeth up and D. when he pleases

DESTROYING

Sec.	Vs.	
19	3	even to the D. of Satan and his works
89	21	the D. angel shall pass by them as the

DESTRUCTION

Sec.	Vs.	
5	20	I told the people of the D. of Jerusalem
8	4	would slay you and bring your soul to D.
10	22	that he may lead their souls to D.
19	33	even the D. of thyself and property
38	13	bring to pass your D. in process of time
61	31	who are well nigh ripened for D.
109	43	we delight not in D. of our fellow-men
133	15	lest sudden D. shall come upon him

DESTRUCTIONS

Sec.	Vs.	
34	9	great D. await the wicked
61	5	decreed many D. upon the waters

DETECT

Sec.	Vs.	
129	8	not feel anything; you may therefore D. him

DETECTED

Sec.	Vs.	
50	8	but the hypocrites shall be D. and shall

DETECTING

Sec.	Vs.	
128	20	Michael D. the devil when he appeared

DETERMINATION

Sec.	Vs.	
20	37	having a D. to serve him to the end
88	133	in a D. that is fixed, immovable to be your

DETERMINE

Sec.	Vs.	
102	22	Council having power to D. the same
	33	shall have power to D. whether any such

DETERMINED

Sec.	Vs.	
96	3	as shall be D. in council among you

DETESTABLE

Sec.	Vs.	
98	20	covetousness and all their D. things

DETROIT

Sec.	Vs.	
52	8	unto same place by way of D.

DEVIATING

Sec.	Vs.	
128	25	humble servant and never D. friend

DEVIL

Sec.	Vs.	
1	35	D. shall have power over his own
10	12	D. has sought to lay a cunning plan
	43	my wisdom is greater than cunning of D.
	56	and build up the kingdom of the D.
18	20	contend against no church save church of D.
29	28	fire prepared for D. and his angels
	36	Adam being tempted of the D., for the D. was before Adam
	37	and thus came the D and his angels
	39	needs be that D. should tempt children of men
	40	D. tempted Adam and he partook the; he became subject to the will of the D.
76	28	even the D. who rebelled against God
	31	through the power of D. to be overcome
	33	with the D. and his angels in eternity
	36	fire and brimstone with the D. and his
	44	to reign with the D. and his angels
	85	who shall not be redeemed from the D.
88	110	that old serpent who is called the D.
	113	the D. shall gather together his armies
	114	the D. and his armies shall be cast away
121	4	who controllest and subjectest the D.
123	10	hands of the very D. to tremble and
128	20	detecting the D. when he appeared as an
129	8	if it be the D. as an angel of light

DEVILISH

Sec.	Vs.	
20	20	man became sensual and D. and became

DEVILS

Sec.	Vs.	
24	13	except casting out D., healing the sick
35	9	they shall cast out D.
46	7	seduced by evil spirits and doctrines of D.; some are of men and others of D.
84	67	in my name they shall cast out D.

Sec.	Vs.		Sec.	Vs.	
124	98	he shall cast out D. and shall be		44	if they D. they shall D. unto me
		DEVOTE		45	weep for the loss of them that D.
24	7	thou shalt D. all thy service in Zion		46	those that D. in me shall not taste of
104	26	D. his moneys for the proclaiming of		47	they that D. not in me wo unto them
106	3	D. his whole time in this high and holy	45	32	lift up voices and curse God and D.
		DEVOTED	59	2	those that D. shall rest from all their
26	1	let your time be D. to the studying of	63	49	blessed are the dead that D. in the; rise from dead and shall not D. after
		DEVOTION		50	appointed to him to D. at the age of
134	4	dictate forms for public and private D.		51	until they become old, old men shall D.
		DEVOTIONS	88	26	notwithstanding it shall D. it shall be
59	10	to pay thy D. unto the most high		27	notwithstanding they D. they shall rise
		DEVOUR	101	30	an infant shall not D. until he is old
29	20	fowls of the air shall D. them *up*	124	86	if they D. let them D. unto me
		DEVOURING	128	5	dead who should D. without a knowledge
29	21	shall be cast down by D. fire	130	16	whether I should D. and thus see his face
97	26	with sword, with vengeance, with D. fire	133	68	their fish stink and D. for thirst
		DEWS	135	4	I shall D. innocent and it shall yet be
121	45	distil upon thy soul as the D. of heaven			**DIED**
128	19	as the D. of Carmel so shall knowledge	20	23	he was crucified, D. and rose again
		DIABOLICAL	29	13	even the dead which D. in me to receive
123	5	whole concatenation of D. rascality	76	72	these are they who D. without law
		DICTATE	128	18	without those who have D. in the gospel
134	4	nor D. forms for public or private	135	3	he D. great in the eyes of God and his
		DICTATED		6	they lived for glory; they D. for glory
104	81	write that which shall be D. by my spirit			**DIES**
		DICTATES	101	31	when he D. he shall not sleep, that is
3	4	follows after D. of his own will and			**DIETH**
		DID	76	44	where the worm D. not and the fire is
10	61	marvelous works which they D. in my			**DIFFER**
45	4	sufferings and death of him who D. no sin	76	78	and D. in glory as the moon differs
101	46	servants of nobleman went and D. as their			**DIFFERENCE**
	62	servant went straightway and D. all	124	140	the D. between this quorum and the
128	9	whatsoever those men D. in authority and D. it truly			**DIFFERENCES**
132	37	Jacob D. none other things than that because they D. none other things than	46	15	to know the D. of administration as it
	51	for I D. it to prove you all as I D.			**DIFFERENT**
		DIE	124	134	presidents or servants over the D. stakes
29	42	they should not D. as to temporal death	128	8	taking a D. view of the translation
42	19	he that killeth shall D.			

Sec.	Vs.	
		DIFFERING
107	23	thus D. from other officers—107:25
		DIFFERS
76	71	whose glory D. from that of the church; as the moon D. from the sun—76:78
81		stars D. from that of the glory of moon
98		as one star D. from another star in glory, even so D. one from
		DIFFICULT
6	18	in whatsoever D. circumstances he may
102	13	consider whether it is a D. one or not
	14	if it is thought to be D. four shall be appointed; if more D., six
	28	only to be called on most D. cases of
107	78	and the most D. cases of the church
128	3	it would be very D. for one recorder
		DIFFICULTIES
102	2	for purpose of settling important D.
	24	to settle D. when the parties or
130	12	commencement of the D. which will cause
		DIFFICULTY
102	23	in cases of D. respecting doctrine or
128	3	to obviate this D. there can be a
	11	there is no D. in obtaining knowledge
		DIG
88	51	sent forth servants into the field to D.
		DIGGETH
109	25	he who D. a pit for them shall fall
		DIGNITY
102	10	it is according to the D. of his office
		DILIGENCE
4	6	remember godliness, charity, humility, D.
21	7	his D. I know and his prayers I have
70	15	for a reward of their D. and for their
103	36	brought to pass through your D.
104	79	obtain this blessing by your D. and
107	99	in which he is appointed, in all D.
124	49	to perform that work and cease not their D.
127	4	let your D. and your perseverance
130	19	through his D. and obedience than
		DILIGENT
6	18	therefore be D.—6:20; 30:8; 136:42

Sec.	Vs.	
10	4	be D. to the end
18	8	if he shall be D. in keeping my
59	4	they that are faithful and D. before
75	29	let every man be D. in all things
84	43	give D. heed to the words of eternal
93	50	see that they are more D. at home
104	80	inasmuch as they are D. and humble
136	26	thou shalt make D. search till thou
	27	thou shalt be D. in preserving what
		DILIGENTLY
84	23	sought D. to sanctify his people that
94		search D. and spare not
88	63	seek me D. and ye shall find me
	78	teach ye D. and my grace shall attend
84		tarry ye and labor D. that you may
118		seek ye D. and teach one another words—109:7
90	22	let the bishop search D. and obtain an
	24	search D., pray always and be believing
96	9	he shall seek D. to take away incumbrances
97	1	seeking D. to learn wisdom and to find
98	10	wise men should be sought for D.
	16	seek D. to turn hearts of their children
103	32	seek D. and peradventure you may —103:33
106	3	seeking D. the kingdom of heaven
111	9	inquire D. concerning the more ancient
115	10	labor D. to build a house unto my name
	12	labor D. until it shall be finished
124	88	await patiently and D. for further
		DIMINISHING
20	35	adding to nor D. from the prophecy of
		DIRECT
20	61	as said conferences shall D. or appoint
	80	shall be dealt with as the Scriptures D.
43	8	that ye may know how to act and D. my
57	6	in righteousness and as wisdom shall D.
58	51	as seemeth him good or as he shall D.
	62	let E. Partridge D. the conference
84	103	for their benefit as the Lord shall D.
	113	to do his secular business as he shall D.
104	26	as my servant Gazelam shall D.
	53	and the voice of the council shall D.

Sec.	Vs.	
		DIRECTED.
42	13	as they shall be D. by the spirit
46	2	conduct all meetings as they are D. by
63	46	obtaining moneys even as I have D.
		DIRECTION
20	67	to be ordained by D. of a High Council
78	16	under counsel and D. of the Holy One
107	10	officiate under D of the Presidency —107:33
	34	under the D. of the Twelve or traveling
136	3	under D. of the Twelve Apostles
		DIRECTIONS
51	1	I will speak and give unto him D.; it must need be that he receive D. how
57	16	further D. shall be given hereafter
58	34	I give unto you further D. concerning
	38	other D. concerning my servant Martin
62	8	to do according to D. of the spirit
82	9	I give unto you D. how you may act
		DIRECTLY
57	4	line running D. between Jew and Gentile
88	132	even D. salute his brother or brethren
		DIRECTOR
3	15	suffered counsel of thy D. to be trampled
		DIRECTORS
17	1	miraculous D. that were given to Lehi
		DIRECTS
58	36	do with his moneys according as law D.
		DISAPPOINTED
121	14	that they may be D. also and their
		DISAPPROVE
124	144	or else D. of them at my general conference
		DISCERN
46	27	given unto them to D. all those gifts
63	41	he shall be enabled to D. by the spirit
101	95	that men may D. between the righteous

Sec.	Vs.	
		DISCERNED
131	7	and can only be D. by purer eyes
		DISCERNER
33	1	is a D. of the thoughts and intents of
		DISCERNING
46	23	and to others the D. of spirits
		DISCHARGE
90	23	he may be enabled to D. every debt
103	1	know how to act in D. of your duties
		DISCIPLE
41	5	and doeth it the same is my D.; and doeth it not the same is not my D.—84:91
52	40	that doeth not these things is not my D.
103	28	down his life for my sake is not my D.
		DISCIPLES
1	4	by the mouths of my D. whom I have
6	32	as I said unto my D., where two or three
10	46	which my D. desired in their prayers
	59	I am he who said unto my D., and many
18	27	the Twelve shall be my D., and they shall
45	16	as I showed it unto my D. as I stood
	32	my D. shall stand in holy places
	34	when I had spoken these words unto my D.
57	5	as my D. are enabled to buy lands
	8	obtain whatsoever things the D. may
58	52	Lord willeth that the D. and children
63	38	let my D. in Kirtland arrange their
	41	those of my D. who shall tarry
	45	an agent unto D. that shall tarry and
64	8	my D. in days of old sought occasion
	19	made known unto my D. that they perish not
84	91	by this you may know my D.
88	3	the same that I promised unto my D. as
		DISCIPLINED
87	4	who shall be marshaled and D. for war
		DISCOMFORT
121	23	wo unto all that D. my people

Sec.	Vs.	
		DISCOVER
102	20	D. an error in the decision of the
111	4	they shall not D. your secret parts
128	7	you *will* D. in this quotation that the
		DISOBEDIENCE
93	39	taketh away light and truth through D.
121	17	and are the children of D. themselves
		DISORDERLY
134	10	deal with their members for D. conduct
		DISPENSATION
27	13	a D. of the gospel for the last times
110	12	committed D. of gospel of Abraham
	16	the keys of this D. are committed into
112	30	which is D. of fulness of times
	31	with all who have received a D. at any
	32	keys of the D. which ye have received
121	31	in the days of the D. of the fulness
124	41	things that pertain to the D. of the
128	9	whenever the Lord has given a D. of the
	18	necessary in the ushering in of the D.; which D. is now beginning to usher in; unto babes and sucklings in this the D.
	20	possessing keys of kingdom and of D. of
	21	all declaring their D., their rights
		DISPENSATIONS
128	18	welding together of D. and keys and
		DISPERSE
21	6	God will D. the powers of darkness
		DISPLAY
109	49	make a D. of thy testimony in their
		DISPLEASED
111	1	I am not D. with your coming this journey
		DISPLEASURE
101	90	in his hot D. and in his fierce anger
		DISPOSE
63	39	let my servant D. of the land that he
		DISPOSED
120	1	it shall be D. of by a council composed
		DISPOSITION
114	1	make a D. of his merchandise that he

Sec.	Vs.	
121	39	it is the nature and D. of almost all
		DISREPUTE
90	23	that the storehouse may not be brought into D.
		DISSATISFIED
102	27	or either of them be D. with decision
134	12	to cause them to be D. with situations
		DISSENSIONS
10	48	had become Lamanites because of their D.
		DISSOLVED
104	53	you are D. as an United Order with your
		DISTIL
121	45	shall D. upon thy soul as the dews from
		DISTINCT
107	90	this presidency is a D. one from that
		DISTINCTION
102	30	there is a D. between the High Council
		DISTINCTLY
88	129	may hear his words carefully and D.
		DISTINGUISHED
107	43	and could be D. from him only by his age
		DISTURB
10	56	it is they that I *will* D. and cause to
		DIVERS
45	33	be earthquakes also in D. places
128	21	and at sundry times and in D. places; and of D. angels from Michael down
		DIVERSITIES
46	16	to know the D. of operations whether
		DIVIDE
57	7	to D. the saints their inheritance
58	17	to D. the lands of the heritage of God
		DIVIDED
87	3	Southern States shall be D. against the
96	3	let it be D. in lots according to
133	24	as it was in the days before it was D.
135	3	in life they were not D., in death they

Sec.	Vs.		Sec.	Vs.	
		DIVIDEND	11	12	which leadeth to do good, to do justly
136	8	according to the D. of their property	14	11	which thing if ye do and are faithful
		DIVIDING	17	4	this you shall do that my servant
6	2	to the D. asunder of both joints and marrow—11:2; 12:2; 14:2; 33:1		8	if you do these last commandments of
		DIVINE	19	24	by will of the Father and I do his will
109	10	to thy honor and to thy D. acceptance		30	thou shalt do it with all humility
134	6	and D. laws given of heaven	20	55	see that all the members do their duty
		DIVISIONS		62	conferences are to do whatever church
56	9	there shall be no D. made upon land		79	that they may D. it in remembrance
107	6	but there are two D. or grand heads	24	14	these things ye shall not do except; ye shall do according to that which is
		DO		19	they shall do according to this pattern
3	4	have power to do many mighty works	25	15	except thou do this where I am you
	9	thou wast chosen to do the work of the	26	1	shall be made known what you shall do
	11	except thou do this thou shalt be	27	2	if ye do it with an eye single to my
5	22	if you do this I grant unto you eternal	28	15	it shall be given thee what thou shalt do—31:11
	29	he shall do no more nor trouble me any	29	9	they that do wickedly shall be as stubble—64:24; 133:64
	31	except thou do this thou shalt have no		50	it remaineth in me to do as—40:3
6	13	if you wilt do good and hold out	30	11	not fearing what man shall do for I
	29	they can do no more unto you than	35	4	thou shalt do great things
	30	if they do unto you as they have done	38	33	be told them what they shall do—52:2, 4
	33	fear not to do good, my sons	39	11	if thou do this I have prepared thee
	34	fear not little flock, do good	42	13	observe the covenants to do them
	35	I do not condemn you; go your ways and		15	all this ye shall observe to do
7	5	my beloved desired that he might do more		27	of thy neighbour nor do him any harm
8	8	in your hands and do marvelous works		31	unto the poor ye *will* do it unto me
	10	without faith you can do nothing —18:19		36	this I do for the salvation of my people
9	4	work which you are called to do is to		38	inasmuch as ye do it unto the least of these ye do it unto me
	13	do this thing which I have commanded		52	they who have not faith to do these
10	13	he has put into their hearts to do this		83	thus ye shall do in all cases
	19	we *will* do this that we may not be		87	if he or she do any manner of iniquity
	29	he flattereth them away to do iniquity	43	10	as ye do this glory shall be added; as ye do it not it shall be taken
	34	concerning the things what you shall do		14	if ye do it not he shall remain unto
	56	all those that do wickedly and build up	45	8	gave I power to do many miracles and to
	63	this I do that I may establish my; in these things they do err; they do wrest the scriptures; and do not understand	46	7	I would that ye should do in all holiness
				9	and him that seeketh so to do
				31	whatsoever you do in the spirit
			50	9	beware lest he do that which is not in
			55	1	which if ye do with an eye single

Sec.	Vs.		Sec.	Vs.	
	4	assist my servant to do work of printing		26	if she observe not to do whatsoever I—98:22
	5	land of your inheritance to do this work	98	4	my people should observe to do all
56	9	if he *will* do this as there shall be		21	I *will* do whatsoever I list if they do
	12	rewarded according to that which they do		45	if he do this thou shalt forgive him; if he do not this I will avenge thee
	13	according to that which they do they	100	1	I will do with them as seemeth me good
	14	you have many things to do and to repent		8	as ye do this the Holy Ghost shall be
57	14	to do those things as I have spoken	101	11	this *will* I do when the cup of mine
58	27	should do many things of their own free		60	go straightway and do *all* things
	28	inasmuch as men do good they shall in	103	31	but men do not always do my will
	36	he shall do with his moneys according	104	49	they shall do their business in their —104:50
	53	let them do this lest they receive none		69	or an hundred let him do likewise
59	6	nor kill nor do anything like unto it		86	if you proceed to do the things which
	13	on this day thou shalt do none other	107	72	to do the business of the church
	15	as ye do these things with thanksgiving	109	33	in midst of this generation and do thy work
	16	as ye do this the fulness of earth is		68	he hath sincerely striven to do thy will
61	25	they shall do like unto the children	112	6	I have a great work for thee to do
	28	let him do as spirit commandeth; as it remaineth with me to do hereafter	118	3	if they *will* do it in all lowliness
			122	6	what are the men going to do with you
	34	as they do this they shall rid their		9	fear not what man can do for God shall
62	8	do according to judgment and directions	123	17	let us cheerfully do all things that
63	44	let him do according to wisdom	124	17	for he shall be mine if he do this
64	12	do with him as the scripture saith		32	if you do not these things at the end
	13	this ye shall do that God may be glorified		47	if you do not do the things I say
	14	for this cause ye shall do these things		49	commandment to do a work unto my name
	29	whatever ye do according to will of		53	who have been commanded to do a work
69	6	a place to receive and do all these		69	if you *will* do my will saith the Lord
75	11	as they do this I will be with them			
78	20	do the things which I have commanded		74	if he *will* do my will—124:83, 89, 108
81	4	thou wilt do the greatest good unto		90	if he *will* do this I will bless him
82	10	I am bound when ye do what I say; when ye do not what I say ye have no		112	this let him do if he will have an
				116	cease to do evil and lay aside all his
84	57	do according to that which is written		121	labors which they do in building the
	66	they shall do many wonderful works	125	2	if they *will* do my will and keep
	93	whatsoever village ye enter do likewise	127	10	as it is out of my power to do so I
			128	3	at all times and do all the business
	113	to do his secular business as he shall		16	else what shall they do which are
88	137	ye are called to do this by prayer	129	5	if he be an angel he *will* do so and you
89	18	who remember to keep and do these			
94	15	that they may do the work which I have	132	32	go ye therefore and do the works of
97	18	if Zion do these things she shall prosper		34	and why did she do it? because this was
	25	if she observe to do all things			

Sec.	Vs.		Sec.	Vs.	
	55	then shall my servant do all things for		60	he that D. according to these things shall be saved and that D. them not
	59	if he do anything in my name and			
	60	for he shall do the sacrifice which I	49	14	whoso D. this shall receive the gift of
136	11	if ye do this with a pure heart ye			
	17	go thy way and do as I have told you	52	40	he that D. not these things is not my—84:91
	30	and I *will* do my pleasure with them	58	29	he that D. not anything until he is
			59	23	he who D. the works of righteousness

DOCTRINE

			63	20	and D. my will the same shall overcome
10	62	bring to light true points of my D., the only D. which is in me			

DOGS

	63	contention concerning points of my D.	41	6	to them that are not worthy or to D.
	67	this is my D.			

DOING

11	16	that you may know of a surety my D.	6	8	you shall be means of D. much good in—11:8
68	25	to understand the D. of repentance	21	6	by D. these things the gates of hell
88	77	teach one another the D. of the kingdom	46	7	D. all things with prayer and thanksgiving
	78	instructed in principle, in D. in—97:14	49	4	by so D. I will bless him, otherwise he
101	78	that every man may act in D. and principle	50	35	by giving heed and D. these things
102	23	is cases of difficulty respecting D.		38	let no man hinder them of D. that which
121	45	the D. of the priesthood shall distil			
128	7	principle agreeing precisely with the D.	51	14	shall be employed in D. this business
	9	it may seem a very bold D. that we talk	76	15	while we were D. work of translation
132	1	D. of their having many wives and	78	7	prepare yourselves by D. the things
			81	4	in D. these things thou wilt do greatest

DOCTRINES

46	7	seduced by evil spirits or D. of devils	82	19	D. all things with an eye single to

DOINGS

			76	2	extent of his D. none can find out

DOCUMENTS

135	3	many other wise D. and instructions	88	121	cease from all your wicked D.
				137	in all your D. in the house of Lord

DODDS, ASA

75	15	D. and, shall also take their journey	108	7	strengthen your brethren in all your D.

DOES

DOLLARS

1	32	he that repents and D. the commandments	104	69	obtain five talents, D., let him
	46	this work D. contain all those parts		73	if it be five talents, D., or ten D.
131	3	and if he D. not he cannot obtain it	124	64	shall not receive less than fifty D.; to receive 15,000 D. from any one man

DOEST

				65	not permitted to receive over 15,000 D.
133	43	when thou D. terrible things, things they		66	not permitted to receive under 50 D.
				72	Joseph cannot pay over 15,000 D. stock nor under 50 D.

DOETH

DOMINION

33	4	there is none which D. good save it be—35:12; 82:6	1	35	devil shall have power over his own D.
41	5	he that receiveth my law and D. it is; receiveth it and D. it not is not my	76	91	excels in power, in might and in D.
				95	equal in power, in might and in D.
42	25	and D. it no more thou shalt forgive		111	receive according to his own D. in the
	26	if he D. it again he shall not be			

Dominion 124 Doors

Sec.	Vs.		Sec.	Vs.	
	114	surpasses all understanding in D.	74	5	except law of Moses should be D. away
	119	to God be glory and D. forever		6	that the tradition might be D. away
109	77	thou sittest enthroned with glory, D.	76	17	they who have D. good in resurrection of; D. evil, in resurrection of the unjust
121	4	the dark and benighted D. of Sheol			
	37	or to exercise control or D. or			
	39	will begin to exercise unrighteous D.	78	8	that all things be D. unto my glory
	46	thy D. shall be an everlasting D. and	82	15	it shall be D. according to laws of
			85	12	D. unto them as unto children of priest

DOMINIONS

82	5	watch, for the adversary spreadeth his D.	94	2	must be D. according to pattern which
121	29	all thrones and D. shall be revealed	101	53	ought ye not to have D. as I commanded
132	19	and shall inherit thrones, powers, D.		72	let these things be D. in their time

DONE

3	10	repent of that thou hast D.	104	16	must needs be D. in my own way
5	28	acknowledge unto me the things he has D.		21	let all things be D. according to counsel
6	14	blessed art thou for what thou hast D.		51	commanded to be D. for your salvation
	30	unto you even as they have D. unto me	109	3	thy servants have D. according to thy
7	5	among men than what has before D.		5	we have D. this work through tribulation
8	11	according to your faith so shall it be D.—11:17		10	that it may be D. to thy honor and to
11	8	as you desire so shall it be D.		44	thy will be D., O Lord, and not ours
19	2	having D. this that I might subdue	121	16	have D. that which was meet in mine
	3	his works and deeds which he hath D.	124	17	I have seen the work which he hath D.
20	62	church business necessary to be D. at		78	I love him for the work he hath D.
	68	that all things may be D. in order	128	4	when this is D. on the general church
22	1	old covenants have I caused to be D. away	132	19	it shall be D. unto them in all things
26	2	all things shall be D. by common consent—28:13	135	3	Joseph Smith has D. more for salvation
27	15	having D. all ye may be able to stand			
42	41	let all things be D. in cleanliness			

DOOM

38	6	and wo, wo, wo, is their D.

DOOMED

76	33	D. to suffer wrath of God with devil

	55	that all things may be D. according to
	89	it shall be D. in a meeting and that
44	6	until all things may be D. according
46	30	wherefore it is D. even as he asketh
	31	all things must be D. in name of Christ

DOOR

100	3	an effectual D. shall be opened—112:19; 118:3
107	35	to open the D. by proclamation of Gospel
112	17	to unlock the D. of the kingdom in all
	21	have power to open D. of my kingdom
124	115	as the D. shall be open to him from

49	6	they have D. unto Son of man as they
50	29	ask what you will it shall be D.
51	12	this shall be D. through the bishop
52	20	according to men's faith it shall be D.
54	9	after you have D. journeying I say
57	6	as can be D. in righteousness
58	55	let all things be D. in order—107:84
	56	let it be D. as it shall be counseled
68	32	these things must be D. away from
70	17	have D. well as they have not sinned
72	3	in this thing ye have D. wisely

DOORS

45	63	they are nigh even at your D.
110	16	day of Lord is near even at the D.

Sec.	Vs.		Sec.	Vs.	
		DORT, DAVID			**DRAGGETH**
124	132	viz., Newel Knight, D., and Dunbar	10	26	until he D. their souls down to hell
		DOUBLED			**DRAW**
98	26	your reward shall be D., unto you four	88	63	D. near unto me and I *will* D. near
		DOUBT	102	17	those counselors who D. even numbers
6	36	D. not, fear not			**DRAWETH**
8	8	D. not for it is the gift of God	35	26	your redemption D. nigh
		DOUBTFUL	106	4	the coming of the Lord D. nigh
58	29	receiveth a commandment with D. heart			**DRAWN**
		DOUBTING	122	6	if with a D. sword thine enemies tear
60	7	with loud voices, without wrath or D.			**DREADFUL**
		DOVE	2	1	coming of great and D. day of Lord—110:14; 128:17
93	15	descended upon him in the form of a D.	110	16	the great and D. day of Lord is near
		DOWN			**DRINK**
10	26	he draggeth their souls D. to hell	19	18	that I might not D. the bitter cup
	27	thus he goeth up and D. to and fro in	20	79	the souls of all those who D. of it
	41	D. even till you come to the reign of	27	2	it mattereth not what ye shall D.
20	24	ascended into heaven to sit D. on right		3	neither strong D. of your enemies
	73	shall go D. into the water with person		5	I *will* D. of the fruit of the vine
27	2	my body which was laid D. for you	35	11	has made all nations D. of the wine of—88:94, 105
81	5	lift up the hands which hang D.	84	81	take no thought for what ye shall D.
84	100	Lord hath brought D. Zion from above	86	3	maketh all nations to D. of her cup
88	127	High Priests, even D. to the deacons	89	5	any man drinketh wine or strong D.
90	31	that she may settle D. in peace			**DRINKETH**
101	57	throw D. their tower	89	5	any man D. wine or strong drink among
104	5	shall be trodden D. by whom I will			**DRINKS**
105	16	throw D. the towers of mine enemies—105:30	89	7	strong D. are not for the belly but for
107	40	to be handed D. from father to son		9	hot D. are not for the body or belly
109	12	that my glory may rest D. upon thy		17	for useful animals and for mild D.
112	32	being sent D. from heaven unto you			**DRIVE**
121	33	hinder Almighty from pouring D. knowledge	86	3	and D. the church into the wilderness
128	21	from Adam D. to the present time, all	103	24	against you to D. you from my goodly
135	4	and turned D. the leaf upon it	121	23	wo unto all those that D. and murder
	5	even unto sitting D. in the place			**DRIVEN**
	6	their names shall go D. to posterity	103	2	being D. and smitten by the hands of
		See Break, Breaking, Bow, Bowed, Broke, Broken, Came, Cast, Come, Comest, Cometh, Fall, Flow, Hewn, Lay, Layeth, Reap, Sent, Thrown, Thrust.	104	51	in consequence of their being D. *out*
			109	47	remember those who have been D. by the
		DRAGGED		50	that wicked mob who have D. thy people
122	6	and thou be D. to prison, and thine			

Sec.	Vs.	
	67	who have been D. to ends of the earth
133	23	it shall be D. back into north countries
	66	none received me, and you were D. out
136	34	even the nation that has D. you *out*

DROP

117	8	that you should covet that which is but the D. and neglect

DROWNED

54	5	better that he had been D. in depth of the sea—121:22

DRUNKEN

49	23	reel to and fro as a D. man—88:87

DRUNKENNESS

136	24	cease D. and let your words tend to

DRY

8	3	through the Red Sea on D. ground
121	30	or to the D. land or to the sun, moon
128	23	all ye seas and D. lands tell the
133	68	at my rebuke I D. *up* the sea
135	6	how easy it will burn up the D. trees

DUE

24	16	in mine own D. time—35:25; 42:62; 43:29; 56:3; 67:14; 71:10; 82:13; 90:29, 32; 117:16; 136:18
68	14	in the D. time of the Lord—76:38
93	19	and in D. time receive of his fulness
107	57	are to be testified of in D. time
111	2	whom I will gather out in D. time
	4	it shall come to pass in D. time
117	14	in D. time he shall be made a merchant
127	1	that all my debts are canceled in D. time
132	45	make known unto you all things in D. time

DULY

112	21	D. recommended and authorized by you

DUMB

35	9	the deaf to hear and the D. to speak
84	70	and the tongue of the D. shall speak

DURING

77	6	D. 7,000 years of its continuance
124	31	D. this time your baptisms shall be

DUST

24	15	by casting off the D. of your feet
60	15	shake off the D. of thy feet against —75:20

Sec.	Vs.	
63	51	but they shall not sleep in the D.
77	12	formed man out of the D. of the earth

DUTIES

20	47	and attend to all family D.—20:51
	52	in all these D. the priest is to assist
	57	assisted always in all his D. in
	64	authorize him to perform the D. of his
47	1	until he is called to further D.
103	1	how to act in the discharge of your D.
107	23	in the church in the D. of their calling—107:25
	86	teaching them the D. of their calling
	87	to teach them the D. of their office
	88	this is one of the D. of this priesthood

DUTY

20	38	the D. of the elders, priests, teachers
	46	the priest's D. is to preach, teach
	53	the teacher's D. is to watch over the
	55	see that all members do their D.
	68	the D. of the members after they are
	81	it shall be D. of the several churches
23	3	thy D. is unto the church forever
	5	this is thy D. from henceforth and
	7	it is your D. to unite with the true
72	7	the D. of the bishop shall be made known
	9	making known the D. of the bishop
75	24	is D. of church to assist in supporting
85	1	it is D. of the Lord's clerk to keep
102	12	it shall be D. of the Twelve councilors
	26	shall be D. of said council to transmit
105	10	know more perfectly concerning their D.
107	38	it is D. of traveling high council
	39	it is D. of the Twelve in all large
	58	it is D. of Twelve to ordain and set
	73	this is D. of bishop who is not literal
	85	D. of president over office of deacon; and to teach them their D.
	86	D. of president over office of teacher
	87	D. of president over priesthood of Aaron
	89	D. of president over office of elders
	91	D. of president of office of High
	99	now let every man learn his D. and to
	100	he that learns not his D. shall not be

Sec.	Vs.		Sec.	Vs.	
123	7	it is an imperative D. that we owe —123:9, 11	125	4	that have desires to D. therein take up
		DWELL	130	3	the idea that Father and Son D. in man's
6	30	you shall D. with me in glory		9	Thummim to inhabitants who D. thereon; will be manifest to those who D. on it
7	6	heirs of salvation who D. on the earth			
8	2	Holy Ghost which shall D. in your heart		22	the Holy Ghost could not D. in us
			133	35	to D. in his presence day and night
29	11	and D. in righteousness with men on earth		36	who shall appear unto many that D. on
63	38	let my disciples which D. upon this farm			**DWELLS**
			1	1	saith the voice of him who D. on high
	39	with those that D. upon the face thereof			
			101	24	every corruptible thing that D.
76	62	these shall D. in the presence of God	104	27	have the place upon which he now D.
	94	they who D. in his presence are church			**DWELT**
			93	4	tabernacle, and D. among the sons of men
	112	where God and Christ D. they cannot			
				11	which came and D. in the flesh and D.
96	9	that he may D. therein			
101	25	knowledge and glory may D. upon all		17	was with him for he D. in him
			117	8	or the land where Adam D.
	99	should not be permitted to D. thereon			**DWINDLED**
			3	18	who D. in unbelief because of iniquity
	100	I do not say they shall not D. thereon; meet for my kingdom they shall D. thereon			
					DYE
			127	1	founded in falsehoods of the blackest D.
104	21	the order which D. in land of Shinehah			
					DYED
	59	when I shall D. with them	133	46	cometh down from God with D. garments
105	23	let all my people who D. in regions of			
124	24	or the Lord your God *will* not D. therein			
	27	for the Most High to D. therein			

E

Sec.	Vs.		Sec.	Vs.	
		EACH	134	2	as will secure to E. the free exercise
20	47	and visit the house of E. member—51			
			136	5	let E. company provide teams, wagons
	54	neither hardness with E. *other*			
	64	E. priest, teacher, may take certificate		7	let E. company decide how many can go
43	8	ye shall instruct and edify E. *other*		8	let E. company bear an equal proportion
88	44	they give light to E. *other* in their			
107	27	every member in E. quorum must be agreed		9	let E. company prepare houses and fields
					EAGLES
128	3	a recorder appointed in E. ward of city	124	18	I will bear him up as on E. wings
130	10	become a Urim and Thummim to E. individual		99	imagination of thoughts as on E. wings
	11	a white stone is given to E. of those			

Sec.	Vs.	
		EAMES, RUGGLES
75	35	and also my servants E. and Stephen
		EAR
1	2	neither E. that shall not hear
43	1	give an E. to the words which I shall
45	1	give E. to him who laid foundation
50	1	give E. to the voice of the living God
58	1	give E. to my word and learn of me
63	1	open your heart and give E. from afar
76	1	hear O ye heavens and give E. O earth
	10	which eye has not seen nor E. heard
88	104	for every E. shall hear it and every
121	2	and thine E. be penetrated with their cries
	4	let thine E. be inclined
133	45	have not men heard nor perceived by E.
		EARLY
54	10	who sought me E. shall find rest to
88	83	he that seeketh me E. shall find me
	124	retire to thy bed E. that ye may not; arise E., that your bodies
		EARNEST
93	48	give more E. heed unto your sayings
		EARNESTLY
46	5	who are E. seeking the kingdom—46:6
	8	seek ye E. the best gifts
68	31	they seek not E. riches of eternity
103	35	pray E. that peradventure my servant
117	13	let him contend E. for redemption of
130	13	while I was praying E. on subject
	14	I was once praying E. to know the time
		EARNESTNESS
123	14	these should be attended to with great E.
		EARS
33	1	open ye your E. and hearken to voice
38	30	speak in your E. with a voice louder
43	21	speaking to the E. of all that live
	22	make the E. of all tingle that hear
78	2	speak in your E. the words of wisdom
84	69	they shall unstop the E. of the deaf
87	7	cry of saints shall cease to come up in E.
88	2	alms of your prayers have come up in E.
108		shall sound his trump in E. of all
90	1	thy prayers have come up into my E.—98:2
95	7	that your mourning might come up in E.
97	27	let it be read this once in their E.
101	92	pray ye that their E. may be opened to
109	29	when gospel shall be proclaimed in E.
	49	cries of innocent ones ascend up in thine E.
127	6	let him hear with his E. that he may—128:2, 3, 4
128	23	proclaiming in our E. glory, salvation
136	8	that cries of widow come not up in E.
	32	and his E. opened that he may hear
		EARTH
1	6	O inhabitants of the E.—1:34; 133:16, 36
	8	bearing tidings to inhabitants of E.; to seal both on E. and in heaven—62:5; 109:23
	11	voice of Lord is unto ends of E.
	13	it shall fall upon inhabitants of E.
	17	calamity come upon inhabitants of E.
	21	that faith also might increase in E.
	30	the only true church upon whole E.
	35	when peace shall be taken from the E.
	38	though heavens and E. shall pass away—29:23; 45:22; 56:11
2	3	were it not so whole E. would be wasted
5	5	woe shall come unto inhabitants of E.
	19	scourge shall go forth among, of the E., until the E. is empty
	33	many lie in wait to destroy thee from E.
6	34	let E. and hell combine against you
7	6	minister for those that dwell on E.
10	27	he goeth up and down to and fro in E.
13	1	this shall never be taken from the E.
14	9	I, who created the heavens and the E.
15	2	for mine arm is over all the E.—16:2
19	38	more than if you should obtain treasure of E.
20	17	God, the framer of heaven and E.
27	4	kingdom which shall be built up on E.
	5	drink of fruit of vine with you on E.
	9	that E. may not be smitten with curse

Sec.	Vs.		Sec.	Vs.	
	13	both which are in heaven and on E.		58	E. shall be given them for an inheritance
29	9	day soon at hand when E. is ripe; wickedness shall not be upon the E.	49	6	he will reign till he descends on E.
				10	the nations of the E. shall bow to it
	11	dwell in righteousness on E. a thousand		12	Jesus who was on the E. and is to come
	13	and all the E. shall quake		16	that the E. might answer end of its creation
	14	signs in heaven above and in E. beneath—45:40		19	that which cometh of E. is ordained
	16	great hailstorm to destroy crops of E.		22	neither of a man traveling on E.
	18	God will send forth flies upon the E.		23	the E. to tremble and to reel
	21	church which is the whore of all the E.	50	1	spirits which have gone abroad in E.—50:2
	22	then will I spare E. but for a little		27	all things subject unto him on E.
	23	there shall be a new heaven and new E.	55	1	yea, even the Lord of the whole E.
			56	18	the fatness of E. shall be theirs
	24	all things shall become new even the E.		20	their generations shall inherit the E.
	26	before the E. shall pass away, Michael	58	8	that E. may know that mouths of prophets
30	2	your mind has been on things of E.		45	push people together from ends of E.
33	6	gather elect from four quarters of E.		48	inasmuch as inhabitants of E. repent
38	5	of the great day at the end of the E.		64	go forth unto uttermost parts of E.
	11	powers of darkness prevail upon the E.	59	2	those that live shall inherit the E.
	12	angels are waiting to reap down the E.		3	for their reward the good things of E.
	17	I have made the E. rich		16	fulness of E. is yours, beasts, fowls and that which walketh upon E.
	20	your inheritance while E. shall stand		17	the good things which come of the E.
	30	voice louder than that, shall shake E.		18	all things which come of the E. in
	39	the riches of the E. are mine to give	60	4	I rule among the armies of the E.
42	64	in consequence of what is coming on E.	63	20	shall receive an inheritance upon E.
43	18	heavens shall shake and E. shall tremble—45:48; 88:87		21	when the E. shall be transfigured
				32	I am holding my spirit from inhabitants of E.
	21	shall utter their voices from ends of E.		33	I have deceed wars on the face of E.
	23	Hearken O ye nations of E.—43:24		36	I have decreed all these things on E.
	28	for last time call on inhabitants of E.		37	lift a warning voice unto inhabitants of E.
	29	I will come upon the E.; and shall reign with me on E.	64	43	nations of E. shall tremble because of
	31	and then cometh the end of the E.	65	1	whose going forth is unto ends of E.
	32	E. shall pass away so as by fire		2	keys of kingdom committed to man on E.; gospel shall roll forth unto ends of E.; roll forth until it has filled whole E.
	33	their end no man knoweth on E.			
45	1	him who laid the foundation of the E.			
	12	who were separated from E. and received		5	his kingdom may go forth upon E.; to meet kingdom of God set up on E.
	13	they were strangers and pilgrims on E.		6	mayest be glorified in heaven so on E.
	26	the whole E. shall be in commotion; delayeth his coming until end of E.	67	2	heavens and E. are in mine hands
			69	5	my servants who are abroad in the E.
	46	come forth from four quarters of E.	71	4	call upon inhabitants of the E.
	49	all the ends of the E. shall hear it; the nations of the E. shall mourn	72	21	that revelation may go forth to ends of E.
			76	1	hear O ye heavens and give ear O E.

Sec.	Vs.		Sec.	Vs.	
	63	to reign on the E. over his people		39	they are accounted as salt of the E.
	75	these are honorable men of the E.		40	if that salt of the E. lose its savor
	104	these suffer the wrath of God on E.	103	7	until E. is given to the saints to
77	1	it is the E. in its sanctified state	104	14	I stretched out heavens and built E.
	6	hidden things of economy concerning E.		17	for E. is full and there is enough and
	8	given power over four parts of E.		59	for purpose of building up kingdom on E.
	9	saying hurt not the E. neither the sea	105	39	proclamation for peace unto ends of E.
	11	angels given power over nations of E.	107	42	they should be preserved unto end of E.
	12	formed man out of dust of the E.; the Lord God will sanctify the E.	109	38	judgments upon the inhabitants of the E.
78	19	things of this E. shall be added unto		54	have mercy upon all nations of E.
82	6	anger of God kindleth against inhabitants of E.		55	remember the great ones of the E., and afflicted ones of E.
84	97	plagues shall not be taken from E.		57	that all ends of E. may know that we
	101	E. hath travailed and brought forth her		67	who have been driven to ends of the E.
	118	I will not only shake the E. but the		72	remember all poor and meek of E.; that the kingdom may fill the whole E.
87	6	by bloodshed inhabitants of E. shall; inhabitants of E. made to feel wrath of		74	that thy glory may fill the E.
	7	that the cry of saints from the E. shall	110	11	gathering of Israel from four parts of E.
88	10	the E. also, even the E. upon which you stand	112	4	shalt send forth my word unto ends of E.
	17	poor and meek of E. shall inherit it		5	let not inhabitants of E. slumber
	25	E. abideth law of celestial kingdom		23	darkness covereth E. and gross darkness
	43	courses of heaven and E. which comprehend E. and all planets		24	vengeance cometh speedily upon E.; as a whirlwind it shall come upon all E.
	45	the E. rolls upon her wings	115	6	when it shall be poured out upon whole E.
	79	things in the E. and under the E.	117	1	before I send again snows upon the E.
	92	prepare ye O inhabitants of E.		6	have I not made E.; do I not hold destinies of all armies of E.
	94	she is the tares of the E.	121	4	God, maker of heaven, E. and seas
	96	saints that are upon E. who are alive	122	1	ends of E. shall enquire after thy name
	98	they who are on E. and in their graves	123	7	whole E. groans under weight of iniquity
	101	live not again until the end of E.		12	there are many yet on E. who are blinded
	104	saying to all people in E. and under E.	124	1	show wisdom through weak things of E.
89	14	wild animals that run or creep on E.		3	to all nations of E. scattered abroad
90	9	that word may go forth unto ends of E.		11	Awake! O kings of the E.! Come ye
93	17	received all power in heaven and E.		16	in sending my word to kings of E.
97	14	pertaining to kingdom of God on E.		26	together with all precious trees of E.
	19	the nations of the E. shall honor her		27	with zinc and all precious things of E.
98	17	lest I smite whole E. with a curse 110:15; 128:17		28	there is not a place found on E. that
100	11	things pertaining to my kingdom on E.		29	a baptismal font there is not upon E.
101	23	when the veil which hideth the E. shall		58	I said concerning kindreds of the E.; in thy seed shall kindreds of E. be blessed
	24	everything upon all E. shall be consumed			
	25	that my knowledge may dwell upon all E.			
	31	he shall not sleep that is to say in E.			
	33	things of the E. by which it was made			
	34	things that in E., upon E., and in heaven			

Earth — 131 — Easy

Sec.	Vs.	
	89	publish translation unto inhabitants of E.
	93	whatsoever he shall bind on E. shall be bound in heaven, whatsoever he shall loose on E.—127:7; 128:8, 10; 132:46
	106	warn inhabitants of E. to flee wrath
	107	making solemn proclamation to kings of E.
	128	my kingdom upon four corners of E.
127	8	I am about to restore many things to E.
128	7	refer to records which are kept on E.
	8	whatsoever you record on E. shall be recorded in heaven; and whatsoever you do not record on E.
	9	a power which binds on E. and binds in! it became a law on E. and in heaven
	14	the first man is of E. earthy; as are the records on E. in relation to
	18	E. will be smitten with a curse unless
	19	a voice of truth out of the E.
	22	let the E. break forth into singing
130	5	there are no angels who minister to E.
	6	angels reside not on planet like E.
	9	this E. in immortal state will be made; this E. will be Christ's
132	7	whom I have appointed on E. to hold; there is never but one on E. at a time
	46	whosoever sins you remit on E. shall; whosoever sins you retain on E. shall
	48	whatsoever you give on E.; to whomsoever you give any one on E., it shall be without condemnation on E.
	63	given him to multiply and replenish E.
133	3	ends of E. shall see salvation of their
	24	E. shall be as it was before it was
	36	shall appear unto many that dwell on E.
	39	worship him that made heaven and E.
	58	those things which are coming on E.
	59	by weak things of E. the Lord should
134	12	believe it just to preach gospel to nations of the E.
135	3	sent fulness of gospel to four quarters of E.
	7	cannot be rejected by any court on E.; till he avenges the blood on the E.

Sec.	Vs.	
		EARTHLY
78	5	that you may be equal in E. things
	6	if ye are not equal in E. things ye
104	13	accountable as steward over E. blessings
128	13	that which is E. conforming to that
		EARTHQUAKES
43	25	and by the voice of E. and great
45	33	there shall be E. in divers places
87	6	with famine, plague and E. shall they
88	89	after your testimony cometh E. that
		EARTHY
128	14	the first man is of the earth, E.; as is the E. such are they that are E.
		EASILY
69	7	he may the more E. obtain knowledge
		EAST
42	63	shall be sent forth to the E. and to
	64	let him that goeth to the E. teach
43	22	when lightnings shall streak from E.
44	1	called together from the E. and from
48	5	after your brethren come from the E.
75	26	go into the world whether to the E. or
77	9	angel ascending from E. is he to whom
80	3	preach my gospel whether to the E. or
105	21	those who have families in E. let them
125	4	let all those who come from the E.
		EASTERN
39	14	thou art not called to go into E. countries
45	64	gather ye out from the E. lands
48	2	ye shall impart to the E. brethren
52	35	take their journey into the E. lands —75:13, 14
66	7	go unto the E. lands, bear testimony
75	6	gave unto him to go unto E. countries
79	1	go again into the E. countries—99:1
100	3	effectual door shall be opened in E.
101	74	every church in E. countries when they
103	29	shall lift up his voice in E. countries
124	83	let him not take his family unto E. —124:108
		EASY
135	6	how E. it will be to burn up dry trees

Sec.	Vs.	
		EAT
20	77	that they may E. in remembrance of
27	2	it mattereth not what ye shall E. or
29	18	shall E. their flesh and shall cause
42	42	he that is idle shall not E. the bread
49	18	meats, that man should not E. thereof
64	34	the obedient shall E. the good of land
84	81	take no thought for what ye shall E.
101	101	they shall E. the fruit thereof
		EATEN
77	14	little book which was E. by John
		ECONOMY
77	6	the hidden things of his E. concerning
		EDEN
29	41	cast out from the Garden of E.
		EDIFICATION
88	137	a tabernacle of Holy Spirit to your E.
97	5	in expounding mysteries to E. of school
		EDIFIED
50	22	both are E. and rejoice together
84	106	that he may be E. in all meekness
	110	that all may be E. together
88	122	that all may be E. of all
		EDIFIETH
52	16	he whose language is meek and E.
		EDIFY
43	8	ye shall instruct and E. each other
50	23	that which doth not E. is not of God
		EDIFYING
107	85	E. one another as it is given according
136	24	let your words tend to E. one another
		EDWARD
36	1	my servant E., you are blessed
		EFFECT
54	4	it has become void and of none E.
		EFFECTUAL
100	3	an E. door shall be opened in— 112:19; 118:3
		EFFICACY
132	7	are of no E., virtue, or force after
		EFFORT
123	6	as the last E. enjoined on us by our

Sec.	Vs.	
		EGYPT
136	22	who led Israel out of the land of E.
		EIGHT
68	25	laying on of hands when E. years old
	27	children shall be baptized when E.
84	28	ordained at the time he was E. days old
102	17	who draw even numbers, six, E., ten
		EIGHTEEN
128	10	for the precedent, Matthew 16:E.
		EIGHTH
77	12	mentioned in the E. chapter of Revelations
113	10	see 6th, 7th and E. verses
		EIGHTY-FIVE
130	15	if thou livest until E. years old
		EIGHTY-SEVEN
107	45	he was E. years old when he received
		EITHER
42	72	E. a stewardship or otherwise as thought
50	8	shall be cut off E. in life or death
61	3	inhabitants on E. side are perishing
64	12	as scripture saith, E. by commandment
88	37	E. a greater or lesser kingdom
102	11	power to preside, both, or E. of them
	24	when the parties or E. of them shall
	27	should E. of them be dissatisfied with
107	27	every decision made by E. of these
	30	decisions of these quorums or E. of
77		decision of E. of these councils
132	63	but if one or E. of the ten virgins
134	10	to put them in jeopardy of E. life or
		ELDER
20	2	to be the first E. of this church
	3	to be the second E. of this church and
	5	after it was manifested to this first E.
	38	an apostle is an E. and it is his
	49	lead of meetings when there is no E.
	50	but when there is an E. present he is
	52	is to assist the E. if occasion requires
	56	in the absence of the E. or priest
	60	every E. is to be ordained according

Sec.	Vs.		Sec.	Vs.	
	64	which certificate when presented to an E.	52	1	thus saith the Lord unto the E. whom
	67	every presiding E. is to be ordained		21	this commandment is given unto all E.
	76	and E. or priest shall administer it		39	let residue of E. watch over churches
	84	certificate may be signed by *any* E.; personally acquainted with E. or priest	57	16	unto residue of both E. and members
21	1	thou shalt be called an E. of church	60	10	mine E. who are commanded to return
	11	you are an E. under his hand; that you might be an E. unto church	61	3	not needful for this company of mine E.
38	40	that every E. go to with his might	72	11	to take an account of the E. as
53	3	even that of an E. to preach faith	73	5	let this be a pattern unto the E. until
55	2	thou shalt be ordained to be an E.			
72	16	every E. in this part of the vineyard	77	5	what are we to understand by 24 E.; these E. whom John saw were E. who had
	19	let every E. who shall give an account			
84	29	offices of E. and bishop are necessary	84	1	a revelation unto Joseph Smith and 6 E.
88	140	to be administered by presiding E. of		111	and also the E. and lesser priests
107	7	office of an E. comes under priesthood	88	72	I will raise up E. and send unto them
	10	also in the office of an E., priest		85	let those who are not first E. continue
	11	an E. has right to officiate in	102	5	were 43, as follows: 17 E., 4 priests
	12	and E. are to administer in spiritual	105	9	expedient that mine E. should wait—105:13
	60	preside over those of office of an E.			
	63	wherefore from priest to E., severally		11	until mine E. are endowed with power
122	6	and thine E. son, although but 6 years		27	until Baurak Ale and Baneemy, (mine E.)
124	125	Joseph to be presiding E. over church	107	60	there must needs be presiding E. to
				89	duty of president over office of E. is to preside over 96 E.
		ELDERS	108	4	be remembered with first of mine E., with the rest of mine E.
20	38	the duty of E., priests, teachers			
	39	and to ordain other E. priests, teachers	115	3	unto *all* E. and people of my church
	45	E. are to conduct the meetings as they	124	137	to preside over the quorum of E.
	61	the several E. composing this church		139	quorum is instituted for traveling E.
	63	E. receive their licenses from other E.		140	difference between this quorum and E.
	66	presiding E., and E. may have privilege			**ELDERS OF THE,** *or* **ELDERS OF MY CHURCH**
	68	the E. are to have sufficient time to; confirmed by laying on of hands of E.			
	69	also before the E. by a godly walk	20	16	we the E. have heard and seen
	70	bring them unto E. before the church		81	conferences held by the E.
	82	kept in a book by one of E., whoever other E. appoint from	36	7	commandments given unto E.
42	12	the E. shall teach principles of my	41	2	Hearken O ye E.—42:1; 43:1, 15; 50:1; 57:1; 58:1; 62:1; 64:1; 67:1; 75:23
	31	two of the E. or high priests such as			
	71	E. who are appointed to assist bishop	42	44	the E., two or more, shall lay
	81	the E. shall lay the case before church		80	shall be tried before the E.
	89	not to the members but to the E.	44	1	it is expedient that the E.
45	6	ye E. listen together and hear my	45	64	assemble yourselves ye E.
46	27	E. unto the church are to have it given	46	2	given to E. from beginning
			49	14	laying on of hands of E.
			50	10	thus saith the Lord unto E.—60:1; 61:2
			58	44	concerning the residue of E.
				56	be counselled by the E.

Sec.	Vs.		Sec.	Vs.	
	61	let the residue of the E.		14	testifying that he (E.) should be sent
68	7	unto all the faithful E.	128	17	I will send you E. the prophet
72	5	I say unto the E. in this	133	55	from Moses to E.; from E. to John
	25	a certificate from three E.			

ELSE

105	7	those who are the first E.	5	14	to none E. will I grant this power
	33	that the first E. should	6	16	there is none E. save God that knowest
107	72	or will choose among the E.	29	12	as have kept my commandments and none E.
133	8	send forth the E. unto	38	10	there is none E. with whom I am pleased
	16	listen ye E. together—136:41	42	22	thou shalt cleave unto her and none E.

ELECT

25	3	thou art an E. lady whom I have called	43	4	none E. shall be appointed unto this
29	7	gathering of mine E. for mine E. hear	74	1	E. were your children unclean but now
33	6	I will gather mine E. from the four	104	55	E. your faith is vain and ye are found
35	20	to the salvation of mine own E.	124	71	appropriate stock anywhere E., only
84	34	the church and kingdom and E. of God	144		or E. disapprove of them at my general

ELECTION

53	1	concerning your calling and E. in this	128	16	E. what shall they do which are baptized
84	99	according to E. of grace which was	132	54	cleave unto Joseph and to none E.
				61	that belongeth to him and to no one E.

ELEMENT

ELSEWHERE

93	33	spirit and E. inseparably connected	107	74	to have other bishops in Zion or E.
101	25	that of E. shall melt with fervent heat			

EMBARK

| | | | 4 | 2 | O ye that E. in the service of God see |

ELEMENTS

EMBLEMS

93	33	the E. are eternal and spirit and	20	40	the E. of the flesh and blood of Christ
	35	the E. are the tabernacle of God			
122	7	and all E. combine to hedge up thy way			

EMBRACE

			36	7	every man which will E. it with
			42	39	those who E. my gospel among Gentiles

ELEVENTH

33	3	and it is the E. hour, and the last
77	15	two witnesses in E. chapter of
113	1	in the E. chapter of Isaiah, 3rd
	5	in 10th verse of the E. chapter of

EMBRACETH

| 88 | 40 | truth E. truth |

ELIAS

EMBRACING

27	6	with E. to whom I have committed	36	5	as many E. this calling and commandment
	7	which Zacharias he (E.) visited; be filled with spirit of E.			

EMPLOY

76	100	some of E., some of Esaias, some of	84	113	he should E. an agent to take charge
77	9	if you will receive it, this is E.			

EMPLOYED

	14	this is E., who, as it was written	51	14	as he shall be E. in doing this business
110	12	after this, E. appeared and committed	57	9	as clerks E. in his service

ELIHU

EMPTY

84	8	Caleb received it under hand of E.	5	19	until the Earth is E. and inhabitants
	9	and E. under hand of Jeremy			

ELIJAH

2	1	by the hand of E. the prophet
27	9	also E. to whom I have committed keys
35	4	and before E. which should come
110	13	glorious vision burst upon us for E.

Sec.	Vs.	
		ENABLE
10	4	means provided to E. you to translate
109	46	E. thy servants to seal up the law and
128	22	would E. us to redeem them out of prison
		ENABLED
44	5	that you may be E. to keep my laws
48	4	that ye may be E. to purchase land
57	5	as my disciples are E. to buy lands
63	41	he shall be E. to discern by the spirit
90	23	he may be E. to discharge every debt
		ENACT
134	5	governments have a right to E. laws
	7	governments are bound to E. laws for
		ENCIRCLE
6	20	I will E. thee in the arms of my love
		ENCOMPASSETH
76	29	he maketh war and E. them round about
		ENCROACHMENTS
134	11	from unlawful assaults and E. of all
		ENCYCLOPEDIAS
123	5	all that are in the E. and all the
		END
6	13	hold out faithful to the E.—31:13
10	4	but be diligent to the E.
	19	that we may not be ashamed in the E.
	69	and endureth of my church to the E.
14	7	if you endure to the E. you shall have
18	22	as many as endure to the E.—20:25
19	1	I am the beginning and the E.—35:1; 38:1; 45:7; 49:12; 54:1; 61:1; 84:120
	3	destroying Satan and his works at the E.
	6	it is not written there shall be no E.
	32	this shall suffice unto E. of your life
20	28	one God infinite, eternal, without E.
	29	all men must endure in faith to the E.
	37	having determination to serve him to E.
24	8	I am with thee even unto the E.—100:12; 105:41; 132:49
	10	lo, I am with him to the end.

Sec.	Vs.	
29	23	the E. shall come and heaven and earth
	33	my works have no E. neither beginning
38	5	great day which shall come at the E. of
43	31	then cometh the E. of the earth
	33	their E. no man knoweth on earth nor
45	22	ye know that the E. of world cometh
	26	Christ delayeth his coming until E. of
46	7	considering the E. of your salvation
49	16	earth might answer E. of its creation
53	7	he only is saved who endureth to E.
56	20	now I make an E. of speaking—72:23
59	20	unto this E. were they made to be used
66	12	continue in these things unto the E.
75	11	I will be with them unto the E.—75:13, 14
76	5	those who serve me in truth unto the E.
	45	the E. thereof neither the place thereof
	48	the E. width, height, depth and misery
	49	the E. of the vision of sufferings of
	80	E. of the vision we saw of terrestrial
	112	they cannot come, worlds without E.
	113	this is E. of vision which we saw
77	12	sealed all things unto E. of all things
78	16	without beginning of days or E. of life
81	6	if thou art faithful unto the E.
84	17	without beginning of days or E. of years
87	6	hath made a full E. of all nations
88	66	truth abideth and hath no E.
	101	neither again until E. of the earth
	102	until that great and last day, even the E.
	139	unto this E. was ordinance of washing
95	7	Creator of first day, beginning and E.
101	33	made, and the purposes and E. thereof
107	42	should be preserved unto E. of the earth
	83	shall be an E. of controversy concerning
109	30	that there may be an E. to lyings
121	32	reserved unto finishing and E. thereof
124	1	for unto this E. have I raised you up

Sec.	Vs.		Sec.	Vs.	
	32	at the E. of this appointment your; if you do not these things at the E.		23	by weak and simple unto E. of the world
127	2	for some good E. or bad as you may	45	21	shall utter their voices from E.
131	4	but that is the E. of his kingdom	45	49	all the E. shall hear it
132	7	contracts not made unto this E. have an E. when men are dead	58	45	push people together from E.
	20	shall be Gods for they have no E.	65	1	whose going forth is unto E.
133	7	from one E. of heaven to the other		2	shall gospel roll forth unto E.
			72	21	published and go forth unto E.
			90	9	the word may go forth to the E.

ENDANGERED

			105	39	make proclamation for peace to E.
98	31	and thy life is E. by him, thine enemy	109	23	bear glorious tidings unto the E.
			57		that all E. may know that we, thy
			67		Israel who have been driven to E.

ENDEAVOURED

			112	4	send forth my word unto the E.
67	3	ye E. to believe that ye should receive	122	1	the E. shall enquire after thy
			133	3	all E. shall see salvation of

ENDED

ENDURE

29	22	when the thousand years are E. and men	14	7	if you E. to end you shall
45	2	the harvest E. and your souls not saved	18	22	as many as E. to end shall be saved—20:25
56	16	summer is E. and my soul is not saved	20	29	must E. to end or they cannot be
88	101	live not again until thousand years E.	24	8	many afflictions; but E. them for I am
			50	5	blessed are they who are faithful and E.
			84	24	they could not E. his presence therefore

ENDLESS

19	4	for I, God am E.	101	5	those who *will* not E. chastening cannot
	6	but it is written E. torment		35	E. in faith though they are called to
	10	I am E., punishment given from my hand is E., for E. is my name	121	8	if thou E. it well God shall exalt thee
	12	E. punishment is God's punishment			
76	44	everlasting punishment which is E.			

ENDURED

ENDOW

			121	29	all who have E. valiantly for gospel
95	8	I design to E. those whom I have chosen			

ENDURETH

ENDOWED

			10	69	whosoever E. of my church to the end
38	32	there you shall be E. with power from	53	7	he only is saved who E. to the end
	38	when men are E. with power from on	63	20	he that E. in faith and doeth my will
43	16	ye shall be E. with power that ye may		47	he that E. shall overcome the world

ENEMIES

105	11	not until mine Elders are E. with	8	4	deliver you out of hands of your E.
110	9	with which my servants have been E. in	27	3	shall not purchase wine of your E.
132	59	I have E. him with the keys of the	35	14	their E. shall be under their feet
			44	5	that your E. may not have power over

ENDOWMENT

105	12	I have prepared a great E.—105:18	45	18	your E. say this house shall never fall
	33	the first elders should receive their E.		72	in eyes of the people and in eyes of E.
110	9	the E. with which my servants have been	52	42	which is now the land of your E.
124	39	for the E. of all her municipals are	54	3	if your brethren desire to escape E.
				7	flee the land lest your E. come upon

ENDS OF THE EARTH

			63	31	your E. are upon you and ye shall be
1	11	voice of the Lord is unto the E.	64	27	it is forbidden to get in debt to E.
			65	6	that thy E. may be subdued

Sec.	Vs.		Sec.	Vs.	
71	7	wherefore confound your E.		27	these testimonies shall stand against E.
87	7	from earth to be avenged of their E.		28	if that E. shall escape my vengeance
98	14	be not afraid of your E.—136:17, 30		29	I have delivered thine E. into thine
101	57	break down the walls of thine E.		31	thine E. is in thine hands and thou art
	58	avenge me of mine E.—103:25, 26; 105:30		39	if after thine E. has come upon thee; no more as a testimony against thine E.
	76	those who have been scattered by E.		40	as oft as thine E. repenteth thou shalt
	96	should not sell into hands of mine E.		45	I will avenge thee of thine E. an
	97	let it not be polluted by mine E.	101	45	when the E. shall come to spoil
103	2	driven and smitten by hands of mine E.		51	the E. came by night and broke down; the E. destroyed their works
	6	they shall prevail against mine E.		53	lest the E. should come upon you
	24	as mine E. come against you to drive		54	watchman would have seen the E. while; and kept the E. from breaking down the.
105	15	have sent forth to lay waste mine E.	121	43	lest he esteem thee to be his E.
	16	throw down the towers of mine E.—105:30	122	7	if fierce winds become thine E.
121	5	let thine anger be kindled against E.	127	11	the E. is on the alert and as the
122	4	thy voice shall be more terrible in midst of thine E.	132	57	lest an E. come and destroy him
	6	if thine E. fall upon thee: if thine E. tear thee from the bosom; and E. prowl around thee like			**ENFORCE**
			134	3	magistrates to E. the laws of the same
124	49	if their E. come upon them and hinder			**ENGAGED**
	51	and were hindered by their E.—124:53	58	27	men should be anxiously E. in a good
127	1	my E. both in Missouri and this State			**ENGRAVEN**
128	1	since I have been pursued by my E.	10	38	are E. upon the plates of Nephi
133	28	their E. shall become a prey unto them		40	because the account which is E. upon
136	40	have I not delivered you from your E.		45	there are many things E. on the plates
	42	your faith fail you and your E. triumph			**ENGRAVINGS**
		ENEMIES, ALL	8	1	concerning the E. of old records which
24	1	delivered from all thine E.	10	41	you shall translate the E. which are
49	6	to put all E. under his feet		45	translate the first part of the E. of
58	22	subdues all E. under his feet—76:61, 106			**ENJOINED**
98	37	avenged themselves upon all their E.	123	6	the last effort which is E. on us by
109	28	from the hands of all their E.			**ENJOY**
127	2	I shall triumph over all my E.	88	32	to E. that which they are willing to; because they were not willing to E. that
		ENEMY	107	19	to E. the communion and presence of God
37	1	this because of the E. and for your	130	2	eternal glory which glory we do not now E.
38	9	kingdom is yours and E. shall not overcome			**ENJOYMENT**
	12	behold, the E. is combined	77	3	in the E. of their eternal felicity
	28	the E. in secret chambers seeketh your			**ENLARGE**
	31	that ye might escape power of the E.	121	42	which shall greatly E. the soul
42	43	and that not by the hand of an E.			
	80	two witnesses of church and not of E.			
44	5	wherewith the E. seeketh to destroy my			
86	3	in whose hearts the E., even Satan			
98	25	if your E. shall smite you a second; and you revile not against your E.			

Sec.	Vs.	
		ENLARGED
82	14	her borders must be E.
107	74	until the borders of Zion are E.
132	17	therefore they cannot be E. but remain
133	9	that the borders of my people may be E.
		ENLIGHTEN
6	15	I did E. thy mind
11	13	spirit, which shall E. your mind
76	10	by my spirit will I E. them
136	33	sent forth to E. humble and contrite
		ENLIGHTENED
6	15	thou hast been E. by spirit of truth
76	12	our understandings were E. so as to see
91	5	whoso is E. by the Spirit
		ENLIGHTENETH
84	46	the spirit E. every man through the
88	11	is through him who E. your eyes
		ENLIVEN
59	19	to strengthen the body and E. the soul
		ENMITY
101	26	in that day the E. of man, E. of beasts, E. of all flesh shall cease from
		ENOCH
38	4	have taken Zion of E. into my bosom
45	11	whom ye say is the God of E.
76	57	which was after the order of E.
	67	the general assembly and church of E.
	100	some of Esaias, some of Isaiah, some of E.
78	1	the Lord spoke unto E., saying
	4	or in other words the city of E.
	9	and my servant, Gazelam or E.
84	15	and from Noah till E. through the
	16	and from E. to Abel who was slain
107	48	E. was 25 years old when ordained
	53	Adam called Seth, Enos, E. and, into
	57	these were all written in Book of E.
133	54	E. also and they who were with him
		ENOS
107	44	E. was ordained at age of 134 years
	53	Adam called Seth E., Cainaan and, into
		ENOUGH
24	10	not suppose that he can say E. in my
104	17	earth is full and there is E. and to
	84	until you shall loan E. to deliver

Sec.	Vs.	
117	8	is there not room E. upon the mountains
123	10	which deeds are E. to make hell shudder
		ENROLLED
85	3	should have their names E. with people
	7	E. in the book of the law of God
		ENSAMPLE
68	2	this is an E. unto all those who were
	3	this is the E. unto them that they
72	23	this shall be an E. for all branches
	26	this is also an E.
78	13	the E. which I give unto you whereby
88	136	this is an E. for a salutation
98	38	this is an E. unto all people saith the
119	7	this shall be an E. unto all stakes of
		ENSIGN
64	42	she shall be an E. unto the people
105	39	and lift up an E. of peace and make a
113	6	and the keys of the kingdom for an E.
		ENTANGLE
88	86	E. not yourselves in sin but let your
		ENTANGLED
20	5	he was E. again in the vanities of
		ENTER
5	3	you should E. into a covenant with me
19	9	that you may E. into my rest
22	2	you cannot E. in at the strait gate
	4	E. ye in at the gate as I have
23	1	lest thou should E. into temptation —31:12; 61:39
24	15	in whatsoever place ye shall E.— 75:19, 20; 84:93; 109:39, 41
51	19	he shall E. into the joy of his Lord
70	18	they shall E. into joy of these things
84	24	swore they should not E. into his rest
109	13	all people who shall E. upon threshold
121	32	when every man shall E. into his presence
128	4	can E. the record on general church book
131	2	a man must E. into this order of priesthood
	4	he may E. into the other but that is
132	4	and be permitted to E. into his glory

| Enter | 139 | Escape |

Sec.	Vs.	
	26	they shall E. into their exaltation
	27	he can in nowise E. into my glory
	32	E. into my law and ye shall be saved
	33	but if ye E. not into my law ye cannot

ENTERED

Sec.	Vs.	
76	10	nor yet E. into the heart of man
98	2	your prayers have E. into the ears of
132	7	that are not made and E. into, sealed
	29	Abraham hath E. into his exaltation
	37	they have E. into their exaltation

ENTHRONED

| 109 | 77 | holy habitation where thou sittest E. |

ENTIRE

| 63 | 54 | at that hour cometh an E. separation of |

ENTITLE

| 20 | 64 | certificate shall E. him to a license |

ENTITLED

| 102 | 33 | whether it is justly E. to a rehearing |
| 107 | 29 | their decisions are not E. to the same |

ENTRUSTED

3	5	you have been E. with these things
5	9	those things which I have E. to you
	31	take away things which I have E.—10:7
9	1	this record which I have E. unto him
12	8	whatsoever shall be E. to his care
69	1	not wisdom he should be E. with moneys
124	113	faithful in all things E. to his care

ENVY

| 127 | 2 | the E. and wrath of man have been my |

ENVYINGS

| 101 | 6 | there were E. and strifes among you |

EPHRAIM

27	5	the record of the stick of E.
64	36	the rebellious are not of blood of E.
113	4	a descendant of Jesse as well as E.
133	30	unto the children of E. my servants
	32	of the Lord, even the children of E.
	34	richer blessings upon the head of E.

EPISTLE

| 58 | 51 | an E. and subscription to be presented |

EQUAL

| 51 | 3 | every man E. according to their families |

Sec.	Vs.	
70	14	in your temporal things you shall be E.
76	95	he makes them E. in power, might and
78	5	that you may be E. in bands of heavenly
	6	if ye are not E. in earthly things, ye cannot be E. in obtaining
82	17	you are E.; you are to have E. claims
88	107	receive inheritance and be made E. with
	122	that every man may have an E. privilege
90	6	they accounted as E. with thee in
107	24	they form a quorum E. in authority —107:26, 36, 37
	68	office of a bishop is not E. unto it
136	8	let each company bear an E. proportion

EQUITY

| 102 | 16 | every man is to speak according to E. |
| 134 | 3 | as will administer the law in E. and |

ERR

| 10 | 63 | in these things they do E. for they |
| 33 | 4 | and they E. in many instances because |

ERRAND

61	7	be in haste on their E. and mission
64	29	ye are on the Lord's E.
133	58	to prepare the weak for the Lord's E.

ERRED

| 1 | 25 | as they E. it might be made known |

ERROR

| 6 | 11 | convince them of the E. of their ways |
| 102 | 20 | discover an E. in decision of president |

ESAIAS

76	100	some of Elias, some of E., some of Isaiah
84	11	and Gad under hand of E.
	12	and E. under the hand of God
	13	E. also lived in days of Abraham

ESCAPE

1	2	unto all men and there is none to E.
10	5	that you may E. hands of the servants
38	31	that ye might E. power of enemy
54	3	if your brethren desire to E. enemies
63	34	the saints also shall hardly E.
88	85	that their souls may E. wrath of God
97	22	vengeance cometh speedily, who shall E. it

Sec.	Vs.	
	25	Zion shall E. if she observe to do all
98	28	if that enemy shall E. my vengeance
104	7	that the guilty among you may not E.
	8	ye cannot E. my wrath in your lives
	9	ye cannot E. buffetings of Satan until
121	23	generation of vipers shall not E.
132	50	I make a way for your E. as I accepted

ESCAPED
135	2	the latter E. without even a hole in

ESCUTCHEON
135	7	their innocent blood on E. of the State

ESPECIAL
27	12	apostles and E. witnesses of my name
107	25	to be E. witnesses unto the Gentiles
126	3	take E. care of your family
128	17	in an E. manner this most glorious of

ESPECIALLY
37	2	and more E. in Colesville
42	45	more E. for those that have not hope of
61	4	more E. hereafter
	5	yea, and E. upon these waters
90	25	let your families be small. E. mine aged

ESPOUSE
132	61	if any man E. a virgin and desire to E. another; and if he E. the second

ESPOUSED
78	4	the cause which ye have E. to salvation
132	63	after she is E. shall be with another

ESSAYING
124	85	who has come here E. to keep my
125	2	if those who are E. to be my saints will

ESSENTIAL
128	15	their salvation is E. to our salvation

ESTABLISH
1	16	they seek not to E. his righteousness
6	6	seek to E. the cause of Zion—11:6; 12:6; 14:6
10	53	I *will* E. my church among them
	63	this I do that I might E. my gospel
	69	him *will* I E. upon my rock and the
12	7	who have desires to E. this work
31	7	I *will* E. a church by your hand
42	67	such as shall be sufficient to E. you

Sec.	Vs.	
57	8	let Sidney Gilbert E. a store that he
88	119	E. a house even a house of prayer—109:8
101	74	in this way they may E. Zion
	75	to redeem Zion and E. her waste places
103	35	E. the children of Zion upon the laws
109	24	we ask thee to E. the people that
124	84	he aspireth to E. his counsel instead

ESTABLISHED
1	22	that mine covenant might be E.
6	28	three witnesses shall every word be E.—128:3
	31	which shall be E. by testimony which
20	1	it being regularly organized and E.—21:3
28	8	cause my church to be E. among them
33	5	this church have I E. and called forth
42	80	every word shall be E. against him by
57	11	and be E a printer unto the church
72	23	in whatsoever land they shall be E.
78	15	who E. foundations of Adam-ondi-Ahman
	16	who appointed Michael and E. his feet
84	2	his church E. in the last days for the
101	1	and truth is E. in her bowels
88	127	school of the prophets E. for their
101	77	people which I have suffered to be E.
	80	I have E. constitution of this land
103	13	to be E., no more to be thrown down
104	1	the order which I commanded to be E.
	40	my order which I have E. for my stake
109	54	may constitution of our land be E. forever

ESTABLISHING
78	3	in regulating and E. the affairs of the
84	104	the printing thereof and for E. Zion

ESTABLISHMENT
78	4	for a permanent and everlasting E. and
104	39	for Ozondah (mercantile E.)—104:40, 41

ESTEEM
38	24	let every man E. his brother as himself—38:25
121	43	lest he E. thee to be his enemy

ESTEEMED
101	8	in peace they E. lightly my counsel

Sec.	Vs.	
		ETERNAL
3	2	his course is one E. round—35:1
5	22	I grant unto you E. life
6	7	he that hath E. life is rich—11:7
10	50	in this land might have E. life
14	7	you shall have E. life—101:38; 133:62
18	8	he shall be blessed unto E. life—30:8
19	7	it is written E. damnation
	11	E. punishment is God's punishment
20	14	shall receive a crown of E. life—66:12; 81:6
	17	there is a God who is infinite and E.
	26	should have E. life
	28	they are one God, infinite and E., without
	77	O God, the E. father, we ask thee—20:79
29	27	gathered on my right hand unto E. life
	43	be raised in immortality unto E. life
	44	they that believe not unto E. damnation
42	61	mayest know that which bringeth life E.
43	25	glory, honor, and the riches of E. life
45	8	unto them gave I power to obtain E. life
46	14	that they also might have E. life
50	5	for they shall inherit E. life—51:19
59	23	peace in this world and E. life in the
63	66	such may receive an E. weight of glory
68	12	given power to seal them up unto E. life
75	5	crowned with immortality and E. life
76	6	and E. shall be their glory
	44	endless punishment, which is E. punishment
	86	receive not of his fulness in E. world
	105	they who suffer vengeance of E. fire
77	1	it is the earth in its E. state
	3	in the enjoyment of their E. felicity
84	43	give diligent heed to words of E. life
85	7	whose mouth shall utter words, E. words
88	4	this comforter is promise of E. life
93	33	the elements are E.
96	6	unto whom I give a promise of E. life
98	13	shall find it again, even life E.
	20	and observe not the words of E. life
101	65	secured in garners to possess E. life

Sec.	Vs.	
109	76	and reap E. joy for all our sufferings
121	2	thy pure eye behold from E. heavens
	32	ordained in midst of council of E. God; every man shall enter into his E. presence
124	55	that I may crown you with E. life
128	12	herein is glory, honor and E. life
	22	let the dead speak anthems of E. praise
	23	tell the wonders of your E. king; let the E. creations declare his name; proclaiming in our ears glory and E. life
130	2	only it will be coupled with E. glory
131	5	knowing that he is sealed up unto E. life
132	16	worthy of a far more E. weight of glory
	24	this is E. lives to know the only wise
	55	and crowns of E. lives in the E. worlds
	63	for their exaltation in the E. worlds
135	6	died for glory, and glory is their E. reward
		ETERNALLY
132	46	it shall be E. bound in the heavens; sins shall be remitted E. in heavens
		ETERNITY
38	1	which looked upon wide expanse of E.
	12	all E. is pained and angels are
	20	ye shall possess it again in E.
	39	ye shall have the riches of E.
39	1	voice of him who is from all E to all E.
	22	gathered unto me in time and E.
43	34	let solemnities of E. rest upon your
67	2	the riches of E. are mine to give
68	31	they seek not earnestly the riches of E.
72	3	render an account both in time and E.
76	4	from E. to E. he is the same
	8	the wonders of E. they shall know
	33	with devils and his angels in E.—76:44
78	18	riches of E. are yours
88	13	who is in the bosom of E., who is in
109	24	to all generations and for E.
132	7	who is anointed for time and all E.
	17	remain in their saved condition to all E.
	18	make a covenant with her for time and E.
	19	it shall be done unto them in time and E.
	49	unto end of world and through all E.

Sec.	Vs.		Sec.	Vs.	
		ETHER		31	and by fire, yea E. the Holy Ghost
135	4	near close of twelfth chapter of E.		32	for thy daily walk, E. unto end of life
		EVANGELICAL		33	yea, E. the destruction of thyself and
107	39	to ordain E. ministers as they shall		34	yea, E. part of thy lands and all save
		EVEN		37	declare the truth, E. with a loud voice
1	16	shall perish in Babylon, E. Babylon the		38	yea, E. more than if you should obtain
	20	the Lord, E. the Savior—133:25	20	13	E. as many as shall hereafter come to
	29	ye E. my servant Joseph Smith, Jr.		26	E. as many as were before he came
	33	from him shall be taken E. the light		34	E. let those who are sanctified take heed
3	16	E. so shall knowledge of a Savior come	22	1	covenant, E. that which was from beginning—49:9
5	16	born of me, E. of water and the spirit		3	built up unto me, E. as in the days of old
	20	E. as I told people of destruction of	24	8	I am with thee, E. to end of thy days
	22	eternal life E. if you should be slain		19	mighty pruning, E. for the last time; shall do E. according to this pattern
	30	stop for a season E. until I command			
6	8	E. as you desire so it shall be—11:8	27	8	be called and ordained E. as Aaron
	25	to translate E. as my servant Joseph	28	2	for he receiveth them E. as Moses
	30	E. do unto you E. as they have done unto me		3	which I shall give unto him E. as Aaron
	32	E. so am I in the midst of you	29	2	E. as a hen gathereth her chickens; E. as many as will hearken to my
8	1	E. so surely shall you receive knowledge		12	in glory, E. as I am; E. as many as have loved me
9	1	E. so I would that ye should continue		13	long and loud, E. as upon Mount Sinai; E. the dead which died in me; clothed upon E. as I am
10	6	yea E. the man in whom you have trusted			
	41	down E. till you come to reign of king		24	shall become new, E. heaven and earth
11	17	E. according to your faith shall it be		26	they shall come forth; yea E. all
	30	E. to them that believe on my name		30	E. so shall they be fulfilled
17	2	obtain a view of them E. by that faith		41	the first death, E. that same death
	5	E. as my servant Joseph has seen them		43	E. as many as would believe—33:6; 35:2; 38:4; 45:8; 66:1
	6	translated the book, E. that part which		48	it is given unto them E. as I will
18	9	I speak unto you, E. as unto Paul mine; E. with that same calling	31	13	these words are of me, E. Jesus Christ
	27	yea, E. Twelve; and the Twelve shall be	33	6	E. so will I gather mine elect
19	1	yea, E. I am he, the beginning and end		8	you shall become E. as Nephi of old
	2	the will of him whose I am, E. the Father		11	be baptized E. by water, and then cometh
	3	retaining all power, E. to destroying of	34	1	what I shall say unto you, E. Jesus
	8	meet unto you to know, E. as mine apostles	35	1	listen to the Lord, E. Alpha and Omega—61:1
	9	that are chosen in this thing, E. as one		2	E. one in me as I am in the Father
	17	they must suffer, E. as I		4	sent forth E. as John to prepare the
	18	which caused myself, E. God, to tremble		6	laying on of hands, E. as apostles of old
	20	which in the smallest, E. in the least		7	great work in land, E. among the Gentiles
				16	for E. now already summer is nigh
				18	E. things which were from foundation of

Sec.	Vs.		Sec.	Vs.	
	20	given E. as they are in my own bosom		18	bringeth not forth fruits, E. according to
	21	shall be purified E. as I am pure		26	preach by the way, E. unto this land
36	2	E. the Comforter which shall teach		42	thus, E. as I have said, if ye are
	6	hating E. the garments spotted with	53	3	mine ordinances, E. that of an elder
	7	E. as I have spoken—43:16, 57:14	54	1	E. he who was crucified for the sins of
38	1	saith the Lord, E. Jesus Christ—54:1; 62:1; 66:13; 79:4		4	has-been broken, E. so it has become void
	6	E. so will I cause the wicked to be kept	55	1	yea—E. the Lord of the whole earth
	13	to bring to pass E. your destruction and		6	made known hereafter, E. as I will
	18	greater riches, E. a land of promise	56	13	receive, E. in lands for their inheritance
	27	a parable and it is E. as I am	57	4	E. unto the line running directly
39	1	the Great I Am, E. Jesus Christ		7	divide inheritance, E. as I commanded
	4	E. so will I give unto as many as will		9	unto the people. E. by whom he will
	6	and the Holy Ghost, E. the Comforter		13	assist him E. as I have commanded
42	1	in my name, E. Jesus Christ the Son of	58	52	open their hearts, E. to purchase this
	3	asked in my name E. so ye shall receive		61	exceedingly blessed E. above measure
	64	E. now let him that goeth to the east	59	8	sacrifice E. that of a broken heart
	70	have their stewardships E. as the members		23	E. peace in this world and eternal life
	87	delivered up unto the law, E. that of God	61	17	E. so in the last days have I blessed
43	10	it shall be taken, E. that which ye have—60:3		32	their labors E. now are wanted more
45	9	E. so have I sent mine everlasting	62	5	return, E. altogether or two by two as
	11	let me show it unto you, E. my wisdom	63	3	who willeth to take E. them whom he will
	38	E. so shall it be in that day when they		8	there have been such, E. from beginning
	39	looking forth E. for the signs of the		21	transfigured, E. according to pattern
	46	E. so shall you come unto me and your		46	obtaining moneys, E. as I have directed
	63	they are nigh, E at your doors		53	time to come, E. in day of coming of
46	7	E. so I would that ye should do in all		60	I am Alpha and Omega, E. Jesus Christ
	30	wherefore it is done E. as he asketh	64	40	E. the bishop who is a judge and his
48	4	purchase land for inheritance, E. the city	66	2	covenant, E. the fullness of my gospel
49	1	preach my gospel E. as ye have received		12	continue in these things E. unto end
	6	done unto Son of man E. as they listed	67	6	E. the least that is among them
50	8	in life or in death, E. as I will	68	6	bear record of me, E. Jesus Christ
	11	let us reason E. as a man reasoneth		10	E. as it is written—73:5
	12	E. so will I reason with you that you		14	to minister E. according to the first
	14	E. the Comforter which was sent forth	70	9	stewardship, E. as I have appointed
51	4	that he shall hold it, E. this right		12	worthy of his hire, E. as those who are
	9	that ye may be one, E. as I have commanded		13	yea, E. more abundantly, which
52	6	they shall be cut off E. as I will	71	1	power given unto you E. as I will
				2	for a season, E. until it shall be
				6	shall be given more abundantly, E. power
			75	1	speak E. by the voice of my spirit; E. Alpha and Omega your Lord and God—81:7

Sec.	Vs.		Sec.	Vs.	
	11	I will be with them E. unto end—75:13, 14; 100:12; 105:41; 132:49		57	new Covenant, E. the Book of Mormon
	15	proclaim my gospel, E. as I have		63	you are mine apostles, E. God's High
	27	made known from on high, E. by comforter		77	that ye become E. as my friends in days
76	8	E. the wonders of eternity; E. the things of many generations		92	cleanse your feet E. with water, pure
	10	E. those things which eye has not seen		98	who remain, E. from least unto greatest
	13	E. those things which were from beginning; in bosom of Father, E. from beginning	86	3	the apostate, the whore, E. Babylon; E. Satan sitteth
	23	we saw him, E. on the right hand of God		4	E. now while the Lord is beginning to
	27	he is fallen, E. a son of morning	87	3	on other nations, E. Great Britain
	28	that old serpent, E. the devil who	88	2	E. them of the celestial world
	41	he came in the world, E. Jesus, to		3	E. upon you my friends, E. Holy spirit of
	58	they are Gods, E. the sons of God		4	E. the glory of the celestial kingdom
	70	whose glory is that of sun, E. glory of God		5	E. of God the holiest of all
	71	E. as that of the moon differs from		10	E. the earth upon which you stand
	81	E. as the glory of the stars differs		13	E. the power of God who sitteth upon
	85	until the Lord, E. Christ, shall have		19	E. with the presence of God, the Father
	91	excels in all things, E. in glory, power		21	E. the law of Christ, E. of a terrestrial
	92	where God, E. the Father, reigns upon		28	E. ye shall receive your bodies
	96	E. as the glory of the sun is one		29	receive of the same, E. a fulness—88:30, 31
	97	E. as the glory of the moon is one		41	all things are by him, E. God, forever
	98	E. as the glory of the stars is one; E. so differs one from another in glory		43	E. the courses of the heaven and earth
	107	E. the wine-press of the fierceness of—88:106		49	day come when you shall comprehend E. God
77	12	E. so, in beginning of the 7000th		60	E. according as his lord had commanded
78	19	added unto him, E. a hundred-fold		61	E. according to the decree which God
	20	saith your Redeemer, E. the Son Ahman		70	call a solemn assembly, E. of those who
79	1	of great joy, E. everlasting gospel		102	E. the end, who shall remain filthy still
80	5	your Redeemer, E. Jesus Christ		112	E. the archangel shall gather his armies, E. hosts of heaven
81	1	called, E. to be a High Priest in my		113	devil shall gather E. the hosts of hell
82	1	trespasses, E. so I forgive you		115	who sitteth upon the throne, E. the lamb
	2	yea, E. all of you have sinned		118	seek learning E. by study and also by—109:7, 14
	18	other talents, yea, E. an hundred-fold		119	establish a house, E. a house of prayer—109:8
	24	for E. yet the kingdom is yours		127	E. for all officers, E. down to deacons
84	4	at this place, E. the place of the temple		132	yea, E. directly, salute his brother or
	5	which cloud shall be E. the glory of	89	19	treasures of knowledge, E. hidden treasures
	14	lineage of his fathers E. till Noah	90	4	oracles be given, E. unto church
	19	E. the key of the knowledge of God		19	counselor and scribe, E. Frederick
	22	see face of God, E. the Father, and live		21	let my counselor, E. Sidney Rigdon
	42	and E. I have given heavenly hosts			
	45	whatsoever is light is spirit E. spirit of			
	47	cometh unto God, E. the Father			
	53	world groaneth under darkness E. now			
	56	resteth upon children of Zion, E. all			

Sec.	Vs.	
93	8	the Word, E. the messenger of salvation
	11	full of grace and truth, E. spirit of
	23	which is spirit, E. the spirit of truth
	26	a fulness of truth, E. of all truth
	35	man is tabernacle of God, E. temples
	52	given, E. according to prayer of faith
95	9	tarry, E. as mine apostles at Jerusalem
	17	in other words Omegus, E. Jesus Christ
97	1	my voice, E. the voice of my spirit
98	13	shall find it again, E. life eternal
	14	abide in my covenant, E. unto death
	28	your family, E. your children's children
100	9	this calling, E. to be a spokesman unto
101	4	must be tried, E. as Abraham, who was
	10	E. as I have said it shall come to pass
	36	fear not E. unto death; for in this
	41	children of Zion, E. many, but not all
	44	my vineyard, E. upon this very choice
	53	ought ye not to have done E. as I
	73	let men be appointed, E. wise men and
	75	there is E. now in store a sufficient, yea, E. abundance to
	91	E. in outer darkness where there is
102	17	those councilors who draw E. numbers
103	13	E. their restoration to land of Zion
	18	E. so shall the redemption of Zion be
	23	purchase lands, E. as I have commanded
	24	to drive you, E. from your own land
	26	my presence shall be with you, E. in avenging
104	20	E. as I will when I shall command him
	33	multiply, E. a multiplicity of blessings—104:42, 46
	41	E. this whole Ozondah (mercantile)
	57	over mine house, E. stewards indeed
	58	organize yourselves, E. to shinelah
	84	E. until you shall loan enough to deliver
105	2	they might have been redeemed E. now
	14	as I said, E. so will I fulfill
	16	strength of my house, E. my warriors
107	74	shall he be a judge, E. a common judge

Sec.	Vs.	
	79	call other High Priests, E. twelve
109	16	a house of glory, E. thy house
	36	E. cloven tongues as of fire and the
	71	remember E. all the presidents of thy
110	3	E. the voice of Jehovah, saying
	16	day of the Lord is near, E. at the doors
114	1	in company with others, E. twelve
115	4	called, E. church of Jesus Christ of
	16	their presidency, E. my servant Joseph
117	9	unto the land of my people, E. Zion
124	5	know E. what shall befall them in time to
	16	stand by you, E. you my servant Joseph
	19	receive him unto myself, E. as I did my
	28	taken away, E. fulness of priesthood
	55	build a house, E. in this place
	58	E. so say I unto my servant Joseph
	83	unto eastern lands, E. unto Kirtland
	84	which I have ordained, E. presidency of
	97	receive of my spirit, E. the comforter
	107	E. as I have before said unto you—124:108
	109	which I have appointed, E. city of Nauvoo
	110	E. now, if he will hearken, it shall be
	111	a house for boarding, E. Nauvoo House
	113	faithful, yea, E. in a few things, he
	123	keys thereof, E. the priesthood which is
	124	of my church, E. Holy Spirit of promise
128	18	from the days of Adam E. to present time
132	11	E. as I and my Father ordained unto you
	55	do all things for her, E. as he said
	57	E. unto his exaltation and glory
133	14	go out from among nation, E. Babylon
	20	the mighty ocean, E. the great deep
	32	crowned with glory E. in Zion; E. the children of Ephraim
135	2	without E. a hole in his robe
	5	made strong, E. to sitting down in place
136	21	God, E. God of your fathers, God of
	31	for them, E. the glory of Zion, and he
	34	E. the nation that has driven you out
	35	day of calamity, E. the days of sorrow

Eventually   146   **Every**

Sec.	Vs.	
		EVENTUALLY
87	1	which will E. terminate in death and
		EVER
20	36	rendered to his holy name both now and E.
30	6	E. lifting up your heart unto me in
	11	you shall E. open your mouth in my cause
43	33	no man knoweth nor E. shall know until
46	2	given from beginning and E. shall be, to
109	75	that we may E. be with the Lord
128	25	I am, as E., your humble servant and
135	3	than any other man that E. lived in it

See Forever and Ever

EVERLASTING

1	15	they have broken my E. covenant
	22	that mine E. covenant might be established
6	3	treasure up for his soul E. salvation—11:3; 12:3; 14:3
20	17	who is infinite and eternal, from E. to E.
22	1	is a new and E. covenant
27	5	containing the fulness of my E. gospel
29	28	depart, ye cursed, into E. fire
36	5	sent forth to preach the E. gospel
43	25	would have saved you with E. salvation
45	5	they may come unto me and have E. life
	9	so I have sent mine E. covenant into
	71	singing with songs of E. joy—66:11; 101:18; 109:39; 133:33
49	9	I have sent unto you mine E. covenant
57	5	that they may obtain it for E. inheritance
61	1	him who is from E. to E., even Alpha
63	23	living water springing up unto E. life
66	2	blessed for receiving mine E. covenant
68	1	called to proclaim the E. gospel—99:1; 124:88
76	44	they shall go away into E. punishment
	101	received not prophets, neither E. covenant
77	8	who have the E. gospel to commit to
	9	the four angels having the E. gospel
	11	ordained to administer E. gospel

Sec.	Vs.	
78	4	for a permanent and E. establishment
	11	an E. covenant that cannot be broken
79	1	tidings of great joy, even E. gospel
82	20	appointed to be an E. order unto you
84	103	who goes forth to proclaim my E. gospel
88	103	fifth angel who committeth E. gospel
	131	in remembrance of the E. covenant—88:133
101	22	worship me according to my E. gospel
	39	called unto mine E. gospel with E. covenant
104	1	to be an E. order for the benefit of
106	2	and should preach my E. gospel
109	29	will not repent when E. gospel shall be
	65	to the fulness of the E. gospel
	71	be perpetuated and had in E. remembrance
	77	an infinity of fulness from E. to E.
121	46	thy dominion shall be an E. dominion
128	17	all subjects belonging to E. gospel
131	2	meaning new and E. covenant of marriage
132	4	I reveal unto you a new and E. covenant
	6	as pertaining to the new and E. covenant
	19	marry by the new and E. covenant
	20	therefore shall they be from E. to E.
	26	any transgression of new and E. covenant
	27	after ye have received my E. covenant
	41	if a man receiveth a wife in E. covenant
	42	if she be not in the E. covenant
133	31	boundaries of the E. hills shall
	34	this is the blessing of the E. God
	36	in the midst of heaven having E. gospel
	57	the Lord sent forth his E. covenant
135	3	has sent the fulness of E. gospel
	7	a witness to truth of the E. gospel

EVERMORE

98	1	rejoice E. and in everything give thanks

EVERY

1	10	to recompense unto E. man according to—112:34
	16	but E. man walketh in his own way
	20	that E. man might speak in the name of
3	8	been with you in E. time of trouble

Sec.	Vs.	
6	28	three witnesses shall E. word be—128:3
	36	look unto me in E. thought
18	28	to preach my gospel unto E. creature—58:64; 68:8; 80:1; 112:28
19	3	judging E. man according to his works—76:111; 101:65
	4	surely E. man must repent or suffer
	18	to bleed at E. pore and to suffer
	29	upon E. high place and among E. people
20	60	E. elder, priest, teacher or deacon
	67	E. president of the High Priesthood
	70	E. member of the Church of Christ
33	4	my vineyard has become corrupted E. whit
	11	repent and be baptized E. one of you
36	7	that E. man that will embrace it with
37	4	let E. man choose for himself until
38	24	let E. man esteem his brother—38:25
	40	that E. man go to with his might
	41	warning voice E. man to his neighbor
42	4	go forth in my name E. one of you
	8	build up my church in E. region
	32	E. man shall be made accountable unto
	33	that E. man who has need may be
	78	E. person who belongeth to this church
	80	E. word shall be established against
43	25	famines and pestilences of E. kind
44	5	that E. bond may be broken wherewith
45	21	until E. desolation shall come to pass
	68	E. man that will not take his sword
	69	out of E. nation under heaven—64:42
46	11	all have not E. gift; to E. man is given a gift
	16	given to E. man to profit withal
	29	that E. member may be profited thereby
48	6	gathered, E. man according to his family—51:3
50	9	let E. man beware lest he do that
51	9	let E. man deal honestly and be alike
52	10	preach by the way in E. congregation
56	19	he shall reward E. man and the poor
57	4	also E. tract lying westward
	5	also E. tract bordering by the prairies
58	36	this is a law unto E. man that cometh
63	33	fear shall come upon E. man
	37	E. man should take righteousness in his

Sec.	Vs.	
66	7	bear testimony in E. place, unto E.
	8	shall be made strong in E. place
70	9	Lord requires of E. man in his stewardship
72	3	is required at the hand of E. steward
	15	E. man must lay all things before the
	16	as E. elder must give an account
	17	a certificate rendereth E. man acceptable
	19	let E. elder who shall give an account
75	28	E. man who is obliged to provide for
	29	let E. man be diligent in all things
76	110	and E. tongue shall confess to him
77	2	and E. other creature which God has
	8	gospel to commit to E. nation, kindred
	11	12,000 out of E. tribe; ordained out of E. nation, kindred
78	21	he will appoint E. man his portion
82	17	E. man according to his wants
	18	that E. man may improve his talent; E. man may gain other
	19	E. man seeking the interest of his
84	44	you shall live by E. word that proceedeth—98:11
	46	spirit giveth light to E. man that; spirit enlighteneth E. man through
	47	E. one that hearkeneth to the voice of
	62	go into all the world unto E. creature
	64	that E. soul who believeth on your words
	85	portion that shall be meted to E. man
	103	it is expedient that E. man who goes
	109	let E. man stand in his own office
	110	the body hath need of E. member
88	38	unto E. kingdom is given a law, unto E. law there
	58	E. man in his hour and in his time
	60	E. man in his order until his hour
	61	E. kingdom in its hour and in its
	81	it becometh E. man who hath been warned
	104	E. ear shall hear; E. knee shall bow; E.
	119	prepare E. needful thing and establish—109:8
	122	that E. man may have an equal privilege
89	11	E. herb in the season thereof; E. fruit
90	11	E. man shall hear the fulness of the
	23	he may be enabled to discharge E. debt

Sec.	Vs.		Sec.	Vs.	
93	1	E. soul who forsaketh his sins shall		21	than light because their deeds are E.—29:45
	2	that lighteth E. man that cometh into		20	54 neither lying, backbiting, nor E. speaking
	32	E. man whose spirit receiveth not the		27	15 ye may be able to withstand the E. day
	38	E. spirit of man was innocent in the		42	27 thou shalt not speak E. of thy neighbor
97	7	E. tree that bringeth not forth good		46	7 that ye be not seduced by E. spirits
	8	yea, E. sacrifice which I shall command		64	8 for this E. they were afflicted
101	24	E. corruptible thing shall be consumed			16 they sought E. in their hearts; condemned for E. that in which was no E.
	78	E. man may act in doctrine and principle; E. man accountable for his own sins			17 repent of the E. they shall be forgiven
102	16	E. man is to speak according to equity	76	17	they who have done E., in the resurrection
104	11	appoint E. man his stewardship	84	76	repent of their former E. works; upbraided for their E. hearts
	12	that E. man may give an account of his	93	37	light and truth forsake that E. one
	13	I should make E. man accountable	98	7	whatsoever is more or less cometh of E.—98:10; 124:120
107	27	E. decision made by either of these; E. member in each quorum must be		11	ye shall forsake all E. and cleave
	99	let E. man learn his duty and act	101	52	what is the cause of this great E.
109	15	be prepared to obtain E. needful thing	104	10	if any man repenteth not of the E.; not have power to bring E. upon you
121	25	there is a time appointed for E. man	105	3	but are full of all manner of E.
	32	E. man shall enter into his presence	124	116	cease to do E. and lay aside all his
124	122	let E. man who pays stock bear his	134	8	and their tendency to E. among men
	128	after that send my word to E. creature	136	21	keep yourselves from E.
133	6	let E. man call upon the name of the Lord		23	cease to speak E. one of another
	37	gospel shall be preached to E. nation			**EVILS**
134	5	rebellion are unbecoming E. citizen	89	4	in consequence of E. and designs
	6	E. man should be honored in his station			**EXALT**
	12	dangerous to peace of E. government	109	71	that thy right hand may E. them with
135	6	the reader in E. nation will be reminded	112	15	E. not yourselves; rebel not against
136	10	let E. man use all his influence and	121	8	God shall E. thee on high
		EVERYTHING			**EXALTATION**
98	1	rejoice and in E. give thanks	124	9	Gentiles to E. and lifting up of Zion
132	13	E. in this world, whether it be ordained	132	17	remain separately and singly without E.
		EVERYWHERE		19	pass by the angels to their E. and
18	9	I command all men E. to repent—133:16		22	narrow the way that leadeth unto E.
		EVIDENCE		23	then shall ye know me and receive your E.
102	16	present the case after E. is examined		26	and shall enter into their E.
		EVIDENCES		29	and hath entered into his E. and
102	18	after the E. are heard—102:19, 20		37	they have entered into their E. and are
	33	after examining the appeal and E.		39	therefore he hath fallen from his E.
		EVIL		49	I seal upon you your E. and prepare
10	14	shall not accomplish his E. design—10:31		57	Abraham, thy father, unto his E. and

Sec.	Vs.	
	63	for their E. in eternal worlds

EXALTED

Sec.	Vs.	
49	10	that which is now E. of itself shall
	23	for the valleys to be E. and for—109:74
63	55	he E. himself in his heart and
101	42	he that abaseth himself shall be E.
104	16	that the poor shall be E. in that the
109	69	that they may be E. in thy presence
112	3	hast abased thyself thou shalt be E.
	8	by thy word many low ones shall be E.
124	114	let him abase himself that he may be E.

EXALTETH

101	42	he that E. himself shall be abased

EXALTS

5	24	he E. himself and does not humble

EXAMINED

102	16	present the case after evidence is E.

EXAMINING

102	33	after E. the appeal and the evidences

EXAMPLE

51	18	this shall be an E. unto my servant
58	35	Martin Harris should be an E. to church
88	130	this is beautiful that he may be an E.
124	53	this I make an E. unto you

EXCEEDING

63	66	a more E. weight of glory—132:16
87	5	and shall become E. angry—88:87
108	3	blessed with E. great blessings

EXCEEDINGLY

58	61	some of whom are E. blessed
82	2	those among you who have sinned
109	23	they may bear E. glorious tidings
127	3	let saints rejoice and be E. glad
	10	I desired with an E. great desire to
128	22	let your hearts rejoice and be E. glad

EXCEL

58	41	not pleased with him for he seeketh to E.

EXCELS

76	91	which E. in all things the glory—76:92

EXCEPT

3	11	E. thou do this thou shalt be delivered
5	3	not show them E. to those persons; no power over them E. I grant it
	26	E. he shall say I have seen them
	28	now, E. he humble himself and acknowledge
	31	E. thou do this thou shalt have no gift
12	8	no one can assist E. he be humble
19	36	E. when thou desire to see thy family
24	13	require not miracles E. I shall command; E. casting out devils
	14	these things ye shall not do E. it be
25	15	E. thou do this where I am you cannot
27	4	partake of none E. it is made new
30	7	none appointed over him E. it is his
35	11	nothing shown forth E. desolations upon
	12	none that doeth good E. those who are
42	11	E. he be ordained by some one who has
43	4	none appointed unto this gift E. it be; E. to appoint another
49	8	all are under sin E. those which I have
50	28	no man is possessor of all things E. he
58	44	E. they desire it through prayer of
59		let no man return E. he bear record
67	11	in the flesh E. quickened by the spirit
68	15	E. they be literal descendants—68:18; 107:16
69	1	one go with him who will be true
74	5	not united to an unbeliever E. law of
75	29	E. he repents and mends his ways
76	43	E. those sons of perdition who
	44	wherefore he saves all E. them
	46	not revealed unto man E. to them who
	48	neither any man E. those who are ordained
	90	no man knows it E. him to whom God has
77	12	redeem all things E. that which he hath
82	11	cannot be broken E. judgment shall
107	76	E. in a case where a president of the
124	37	E. ye perform them in a house which ye
	67	E. the same shall pay his stock into
132	11	will I appoint unto you E. it be by law
	21	E. ye abide my law ye cannot attain
134	2	not exist in peace E. such laws are

Sec.	Vs.	
		EXCEPTING
28	2	none appointed E. my servant Joseph
42	4	go forth, every one of you E. my servants
63	39	E. those whom I shall reserve to myself
		EXCESS
59	20	to be used with judgment, not to E.
88	69	cast away idle thoughts and E. of laughter far
89	15	only in times of famine and E. of hunger
		EXCHANGE
104	24	obtained in E. for his former inheritance
		EXCHANGERS
101	49	might not this money be given to E.
		EXCLAIMING
135	1	Hyrum was shot first, E.; Joseph was shot dead, E.
		EXCLUSIVE
104	63	use stewardship, E. of sacred things
		EXCOMMUNICATE
134	10	they can only E. them from their society
		EXCUSABLE
24	2	thou art not E. in thy transgressions
		EXCUSE
1	38	I have spoken and I E. not myself
88	82	they are left without E. and their sins
101	93	that all men may be left without E.—124:7
123	6	that whole nation may be left without E.
		EXECUTE
105	25	E. judgment and justice for us
		EXECUTED
105	34	let her law be E. and fulfilled
		EXECUTETH
88	40	him who governeth and E. all things
		EXEMPT
10	28	such are not E. from the justice of God
70	10	none are E. from this law who belong
107	81	there is not any who is E. from this
132	65	he is E. from the law of Sarah who

Sec.	Vs.	
		EXEMPTED
107	84	none shall be E. from the justice and
		EXERCISE
5	28	if he will E. faith in me I say unto
6	11	thou shalt E. thy gift, that thou
44	2	as they are faithful and E. faith in me
104	80	as they E. the prayer of faith
121	37	when we undertake to E. control
	39	immediately begin to E. unrighteous
134	2	to each individual free E. of conscience
	4	for the E. of it unless their religious
	7	in the free E. of their religious belief
		EXERT
84	119	my hand to E. powers of heaven
		EXHORT
19	37	preach, E., declare the truth
20	42	teach, expound, E., baptize—20:46, 50
	47	E. them to pray vocally and in secret
	59	they are, however, to warn, expound, E.
25	7	to E. the church according as it shall
		EXHORTATION
23	3	thy calling is to E.—23:4, 5
	7	give your language to E. continually
50	37	strengthen them by word of E.
73	1	preaching the gospel in E. to churches
		EXHORTATIONS
108	7	strengthen your brethren in all your E.
		EXHORTED
113	10	scattered remnants are E. to return
		EXHORTING
20	51	E. them to pray vocally and in secret
		EXIGENCY
134	11	in times of E. where immediate appeal
		EXIST
89	4	designs which do and *will* E. in the
130	2	sociality which exists here *will* E. there
134	2	no government can E. in peace except
	11	where such laws E. as will protect
		EXISTENCE
77	6	during 7,000 years, or its temporal E.

Sec.	Vs.	
93	30	all truth is independent otherwise there is no E.

EXISTS
130	2	same sociality which E. here will

EXPANSE
38	1	looked upon the wide E. of eternity

EXPECT
124	47	neither fulfill promises which ye E.

EXPECTATION
121	27	forefathers have awaited with anxious E.

EXPECTATIONS
132	7	all covenants and E. that are not made

EXPEDIENT
9	3	not E. that you should translate—9:10; 37:1
	11	it was E. when you commenced, but it is not E. now
18	18	which manifesteth all things that are E.
20	75	it is E. that church meet together often
30	5	it is E. in me—37:3; 44:1; 45:72; 47:1; 61:7; 64:18; 71:1; 72:2; 73:1; 78:8; 96:1, 5, 6, 8; 100:4, 9; 105:9, 13, 19, 33.
42	57	it is E. thou shouldst hold thy peace
47	2	lift up his voice whenever E.
73	3	now it is E. to translate again
	4	it is E. to continue the work
75	10	teach them all things that are E.
82	11	it is E. for my servant Alam
84	77	it is E. that I give you commandment
	103	it is E. that every man who goes forth
88	64	given unto you that is E. for you
	65	if ye ask anything that is not E.
	78	in all things that are E. for—88:127
99	6	it is not E. that you should go until
104	13	E. that I should make every man
111	3	E. that you should form acquaintance
127	1	I have thought it E. and wisdom

EXPELLED
20	83	if any have been E. from the church

EXPENSES
90	28	receive money to bear her E. and go up

EXPERIENCE
Sec.	Vs.	
105	10	taught more perfectly and have E.
121	39	we have learned by sad E. that it is
122	7	all these things shall give thee E.

EXPERT
136	7	sufficient number of able-bodied and E. men

EXPLAIN
19	8	I *will* E. unto you this mystery

EXPOUND
20	42	to teach, E., exhort—20:46, 50, 59
	68	have sufficient time to E. all things
24	9	to E. all scriptures, and continue
25	7	ordained under his hand to E. scriptures

EXPOUNDING
24	5	E. all scripture unto the—68:1
63	46	E. these things unto them
69	8	preaching and E., writing and
71	1	E. the mysteries thereof out of the
97	5	in E. all scriptures and mysteries
100	11	be mighty in E. all scriptures

EXPRESS
19	7	it is more E. than other scriptures
67	5	that you might E. beyond his language
107	43	his likeness was the E. likeness of his
134	6	laws being instituted for E. purpose of

EXPRESSIONS
77	2	they are figurative E. used by the

EXQUISITE
19	15	sufferings be sore; how E. you know not

EXTENDED
3	8	he would have E. his arm and supported

EXTENSIVE
72	23	ensample for all E. branches of church

EXTENT
19	38	of earth and corruptibleness to the E.
76	2	the E. of his doings none can find out

EXTORTION
59	20	to be used with judgment, not by E.

EYE
1	2	there is no E. that shall not see

Eye · Face

Sec.	Vs.	
4	5	with an E. single to the glory of God—27:2; 55:1; 59:1; 82:19; 88:67
43	32	shall be changed in twinkling of an E.—63:51; 101:31
59	18	to please the E. and to gladden heart
76	10	things which E. hath not seen—133:45
84	98	and shall see E. to E. and lift up
121	2	and thine E., yea thy pure E. behold
	4	let thine E. pierce
128	17	who had his E. fixed on the restoration
		See *Eye-witness*

EYES

Sec.	Vs.	
1	1	whose E. are upon all men
17	3	after you have seen them with your E.
29	19	their E. shall fall from their sockets
35	7	made manifest in E. of all people—63:15
38	2	all things are present before mine E.
	7	mine E. are upon you—62:2; 67:2
45	37	fig-trees, ye see them with your E.
72		in E. of people and in E. of your enemies
56	17	whose E. are full of greediness—68:31
58	3	ye cannot behold with your natural E.
64	13	that ye may be justified in E. of law
67	5	your E. have been upon my servant
76	12	our E. were opened and our understandings
	19	the Lord touched E. of our understandings

Sec.	Vs.	
77	4	what are we to understand by the E.; the E. are a representation of light
84	69	they shall open E. of the blind
88	11	him who enlighteneth your E.
90	23	brought into disrepute before E. of people
	30	it is meet in mine E. that he should
104	18	lift up his E. in hell being in torment
105	25	I will give you favor in their E.
	26	in this way you may find favor in E. of
110	1	E. of our understanding were opened
	3	his E. were as a flame of fire
121	16	have done that which was meet in mine E.
	24	mine E. see and know all their works
124	9	that ye may find grace in their E.
	13	he shall be great in mine E.
128	3	that he saw with his E. and heard
	4	as if he had seen with his E. and
131	7	can only be discerned by purer E
133	3	holy arm in E. of all nations
135	3	he died great in the E. of God and
136	32	that his E. may be opened that he may

EYE-WITNESS

Sec.	Vs.	
127	6	let him be an E. of—128:2

EZEKIEL

Sec.	Vs.	
29	21	spoken of by the mouth of E. the

EZRA

Sec.	Vs.	
33	1	my servants E. and Northrop, open ye your
85	12	2nd chapter 61st and 62nd verses of E.

F

FACE

Sec.	Vs.	
1	30	only true church upon F. of whole earth
5	33	to destroy thee from F. of the earth
17	1	when he talked with the Lord F. to F.
29	8	gathered unto one place upon F. of
	18	will send forth flies upon F. of earth
39	12	I will go before thy F.—84:88

Sec.	Vs.	
	20	preparing the way before my F.—124:139
45	9	to be a messenger before my F.
50	11	as man reasoneth with another F. to F.
61	19	destroyer rideth upon the F. thereof
63	33	decreed wars upon the F. of the earth
	36	decreed all these things upon F. of
	39	with those that dwell upon F. thereof

Face   153   Faith

Sec.	Vs.	
84	22	no man can see F. of God and live
	23	that they might behold the F. of God
	28	make straight the way before F. of
88	40	judgment goeth before the F. of him
	68	he will unveil his F. unto you
	87	the sun shall hide his F.—133:49
	95	the F. of the Lord shall be unveiled
93	1	shall see my F. and know that I am
95	2	must stand rebuked before my F.
101	24	everything that dwells upon all the F.
	26	enmity shall cease from before my F.
	38	seek the F. of the Lord always
107	49	he was before his F. continually
109	53	thou lookest upon F. of thine anointed
112	4	be of good cheer before my F.
	23	all flesh become corrupt before my F.
	24	as whirlwind it shall come upon F.
124	8	when I shall unveil F. of my covering
	104	he shall be spokesman before my F.
130	15	thou shalt see F. of the Son of Man
	16	whether I should die and see his F.

FACTS

123	1	gathering up knowledge of all F.
128	11	no difficulty in obtaining knowledge of F.

FAIL

35	19	watch over him that his faith F. not
45	26	men's hearts shall F. them—88:91
58	8	mouths of the prophets shall not F.
61	18	lest their faith F. and they are
64	31	my words are sure and shall not F.
75	26	let not such F. to go into world
76	3	his purposes F. not
	4	and his years never F.
84	80	and F. not to continue faithful
109	52	that cause of thy people may not F.
124	16	his reward shall not F. if he
	75	and let him not F., neither
136	42	your faith F. you and your enemies

FAINT

75	11	praying always that they F. not—88:126
89	20	and shall walk and not F.
101	81	ought always to pray and not to F.
103	19	let not your hearts F.
109	38	that thy people may not F. in day
124	75	neither let his heart F.

FAIR

5	14	F. as the sun—105:31; 109:73

Sec.	Vs.	
		FAITH
1	21	that F. also might increase
3	20	glorified through F. in his name
4	5	F., hope, charity and love
	6	remember F., virtue, knowledge
5	24	humble himself in mighty prayer and F.
	28	and will exercise F. in me
6	12	save those who are of thy F.
	19	have F., hope, and charity—12:8
8	1	whatsoever you shall ask in F.—29:6
	10	without F. you can do nothing; ask in F.—18:19
	11	according to your F. shall it be—10:47, 52; 11:17; 25:9; 52:20; 93:52
10	48	this was their F. that my gospel
	49	their F. in their prayers was
11	10	if thou wilt desire of me in F.
	14	in F., believing in me
14	8	ask the Father in F. believing—18:18
17	2	by your F., even by that F.
	3	after that you have obtained F.
	5	it is because he had F.
	7	you have received the same F.
19	31	declare repentance and F. on—53:3
20	6	through F. God ministered unto him
	14	those who receive it in F.
	25	that as many as endure in F.
	29	all men must endure in F.
	69	that there may be works and F.
21	2	build it up unto most holy F.
	5	his word ye shall receive in all F.
26	2	all things shall be done by F.; all things you shall receive by F.—28:13
27	17	taking the shield of F. wherewith
29	42	through F. on the name of mine only
30	6	lifting up your heart in F.
31	1	blessed are you because of your F.
33	12	they shall have F. in me
	15	whoso having F. you shall confirm
35	9	ask it in my name in F.
	11	without F. shall not anything be shown
	19	watch over him that his F. fail not
37	2	they pray unto me in much F.—39:16
39	12	thou shalt have great F.
41	3	by prayer of F. ye shall receive
42	14	spirit given by prayer of F.
	23	to lust after her shall deny F.—63:16
	43	sick and hath not F. to be healed
	48	that hath F. in me to be healed
	49	he who hath F. to see shall see
	50	who hath F. to hear shall hear

| Faith | | 154 | | Faithful |

Sec.	Vs.		Sec.	Vs.	
	51	lame who hath F. to leap	44	2	inasmuch as they are F.—47:4; 52:4, 5; 61:10; 71:7; 75:13; 79:3; 81:3; 92:2; 104:2, 25, 31, 33, 35, 38, 42, 46, 82; 105:12
	52	they who have not F. to do these			
43	12	uphold him by prayer of F.			
44	2	inasmuch as they exercise F.			
46	19	given to have F. to be healed	46	14	eternal life if they continue F.
	20	given to have F. to heal	50	5	blessed are they who are F.
52	9	taught them through prayer of F.—58:44	51	19	whoso is found F., a just steward—78:22
61	9	through F. they shall overcome	52	6	inasmuch as they are not F.—83:3 104:3
	18	lest their F. fail and they are—136:42		13	that is F. shall be made ruler
63	9	F. cometh not by signs but by		34	F. shall be blessed with much fruit
	10	signs come by F., not by the will—11		42	if ye are F. ye shall assemble
	11	without F. no man pleaseth God		43	will crown the F. with joy
	12	who have sought after signs for F.	58	2	he that is F. in tribulation
	20	he that endureth in F.—101:35	59	4	they that are F. and diligent
	50	he that hath kept the F., blessed	60	3	if they are not more F. unto me
68	25	that teach them not F. in Christ	61	6	he that is F. among you shall
76	53	and who overcome by F., and are	62	5	only be F. and declare glad
84	99	which was brought to pass by F.		6	that the F. should be preserved; I promise the F. and cannot lie
85	2	their manner of life, their F.		9	I am with the F. always
86	6	verily your F. is weak	63	47	he that is F. and endureth shall
88	118	as all have not F. seek ye; seek learning by study, also by F.—109:7, 14	64	40	if they are not F. in stewardships
			66	8	he that is F. shall be made strong
				11	these sayings are true and F.—68:34; 71:11
	119	establish a house of F.—109:8, 16	68	7	unto all F. elders of my church
90	22	a man of God, and of strong F.	69	1	go with him who will be true and F.
93	51	your prayer of F. with one consent	70	17	have been F. over many things
103	36	all victory through prayers of F.	72	4	he who is F. and wise in time
104	55	or else your F. is vain		14	the F. who labor in spiritual things
	79	obtain this blessing by prayer of F.		17	to be received as a F. laborer
	80	exercise the prayer of F.	75	5	if ye are F. ye shall be laden
105	19	brought thus far for trial of F.		16	who is F. shall overcome all
	24	neither boast of F.		22	gird up your loins and be F.
107	22	upheld by confidence, F. and	77	5	elders who had been F. in the
	30	the decisions are to be made in F.	81	5	be F., stand in the office which
121	45	and to the household of F.	84	33	F. unto obtaining these Priesthoods
134	6	prescribing rules for F. and worship		80	and fail not to continue F.
135	7	with broken F. of the State		86	this commandment is unto all the F.
		FAITHFUL	88	135	he that cometh in and is F. unto me
1	37	for they are true and F.	90	31	inasmuch as she is F. and not idle
3	8	you should have been true and F.	93	18	if F. you shall receive the fulness
5	35	if thou art F. in keeping—34:11; 81:6; 136:37	98	12	give unto F. line upon line
6	13	hold out F. to the end	101	61	a F. and wise steward in the midst
	20	be F. and diligent in keeping—37; 9:13	104	75	but so long as he is F. and wise
			105	18	endowment for them if they continue F.
10	3	see that you are F. and continue		23	let all my people be very F.
14	11	which thing if ye do and are F.	106	8	continue to be a F. witness
25	2	if thou art F. and walk in paths	108	5	promise if you continue F.
27	18	be F. until I come and ye shall—112:34	112	12	be ye F. before me unto my
31	13	be F. unto the end—105:41	115	3	also unto my F. servants
33	17	be F., praying always	117	10	let Wm. Marks be F. over
39	17	call F. laborers into my vineyard	124	13	let him be F. and true in all
42	66	observe the laws and be F.		55	prove that ye are F. in all things
				113	when he shall prove himself F. in

| Faithful | 155 | Family |

Sec.	Vs.	
128	9	kept a proper, and F. record of; this is a F. saying
132	44	but hath been F., be made ruler
	53	he hath been F. over few things
135	5	thou hast been F., thy garments
136	38	he was F. and I took him to myself

FAITHFULLY

6	18	stand by my servant Joseph, F.
28	3	declare F. the commandments
128	9	they did it truly and F. and kept

FAITHFULNESS

63	37	take F. upon his loins and lift
68	30	they are appointed to labor in F.
103	36	all glory brought to pass through F.
121	44	that he may know that thy F. is
136	11	if ye do this in all F. you

FALL

1	13	it shall F. on inhabitants of
	16	Babylon the great which shall F.
3	4	he must F. and incur the
	9	if thou art not aware thou wilt F.
5	32	that he will F. into transgression
18	40	you shall F. *down* and worship
20	32	there is possibility that man may F.
	33	lest they F. into temptation
29	14	stars shall F. from heaven—34:9; 45:42
	19	flesh shall F. from off their bones
	44	cannot be redeemed from spiritual F.
35	14	I will let F. the sword in their behalf—101:10
45	18	enemies say this house shall never
	45	the arm of the Lord shall F.—45:47
50	44	buildeth upon this rock shall never F.
58	15	let him take heed lest he F.
82	2	lest sore judgments F. upon your
	24	if you F. not from your steadfastness
84	80	hair of his head shall not F.—84:116
85	8	shall F. by the shaft of death
88	89	men shall F. upon the ground
90	5	lest they stumble and F.
93	38	having redeemed man from the F.
97	19	surely Zion cannot F.
109	25	who diggeth a pit for them shall F.
	40	let not thy judgments F. upon that city
	52	and thine indignation F. upon them
122	6	if thine enemies F. upon thee
124	124	sealed up that ye may not F.
133	32	they shall F. *down* and be crowned

FALLEN

| 20 | 9 | contains a record of a F. people |

Sec.	Vs.	
	20	man became a F. man
76	27	he is F.! is F., even a son of
86	3	after they have F. asleep
88	105	she is F. who made all nations drink; she is F., is F.
101	53	watched and not have F. asleep
113	10	return from whence they have F.
118	1	supply place of those who are F.—6
132	39	he hath F. from his exaltation

FALLETH

| 88 | 87 | as a fig that F. from off a fig-tree |
| 124 | 7 | as the flower thereof which soon F. |

FALLS

| 117 | 13 | and when he F. he shall rise again |

FALSE

50	2	many spirits which are F. spirits
122	5	if in peril among F. brethren
	6	with all manner of F. accusations
130	3	an old sectarian notion and is F.

FALSEHOOD

| 127 | 1 | pretensions are all founded in F. |

FALSELY

| 121 | 18 | those who swear F. against my |

FAME

| 110 | 10 | F. of this house shall spread |
| 135 | 3 | and left a F. that cannot be slain |

FAMILIES

42	71	are to have their F. supported
48	6	begin to be gathered with your F.
52	36	let them labor with their F.
57	14	be planted with their F.
	15	make preparations for those F.
58	25	let them bring their F. to this land
75	24	assist in supporting F. of those, and F. of
	25	obtain places for your F.—26
84	103	inasmuch as they have F.
	104	let all those who have not F.
90	25	let your F. be small; those who do not belong to your F.
98	23	I speak concerning your F.; if men will smite you or your F.
100	1	your F. are well; they are in mine
105	21	those who have F. in the east
109	71	remember all their F.—72
118	3	I will provide for their F.
136	8	in taking the F. of those who
	11	ye shall be blessed in your F.

FAMILY

19	34	all save the support of thy F.
	36	when thou shalt desire to see thy F.
20	47	attend to all F. duties—51
23	3	and this because of thy F.
	6	pray in your F.

Sec.	Vs.	
31	2	many afflictions because of your F.; will bless you and your F.
	5	your F. shall live
42	32	sufficient for himself and F.
48	6	every man according to his F.
51	3	every man equal according to his F.
	14	reserve for the wants of his F.
75	28	to provide for his own F.
90	19	provided for the F. of thy
	20	continue with his F. upon the place
93	48	your F. must needs repent
	50	hath need to set in order his F.
98	28	that he come no more upon your F.
124	76	let his F. rejoice and turn
	83	let him not take his F.
	87	cease to fear concerning his F.
	105	let him locate his F. in
	108	let him not remove his F.
126	1	no more required to leave your F.
	3	take especial care of your F.

FAMINE

87	6	and with F., plague and earthquakes
89	13	not be used only in times of F.—15

FAMINES

43	25	by the voice of F., pestilences

FAR

38	29	ye hear of wars in F. countries; soon be great wars in F. countries
57	3	which is not F. from the courthouse
88	69	cast excess of laughter F. from you
90	18	keep uncleanness F. from you
103	3	I have suffered them thus F.
105	19	brought thus F. for a trial of
123	3	as F. as they can get hold of them
132	16	who are worthy of a F. more

FAR WEST

115	7	let city of F. be a holy and consecrated
	17	city of F. should be built up speedily
117	10	preside in midst of my people in F.
118	5	take leave of my saints in F. on 26th

FAREWELL

135	5	I bid F. unto the Gentiles

FARM

63	38	which dwell upon this F.
64	20	commandment that his F. should be sold
	21	F. G. Williams should not sell his F.

Sec.	Vs.	

FARMING

136	7	take teams and F. utensils

FARMS

38	37	that have F. that cannot be sold

FAST

9	14	stand F. in the work
54	2	stand F. in the office
104	68	as F. as you receive moneys
111	11	as F. as ye are able to receive them

FASTER

10	4	do not run F. than you have strength

FASTING

59	13	that thy F. may be perfect
	14	this is F. and prayer
88	76	continue in prayer and F. from this
119		establish a house of F.—109:8
95	16	dedicated unto me for your F.
109	16	that this house may be a house of F.

FASTINGS

95	7	that your F. might come up into ears

FAT

58	8	that feast of F. things might be prepared; of F. things, of wine

FATHER (Deity)

14	8	ask the F. in my name—18:18; 50:31; 88:64
15	6	in the kingdom of my F.—16:6; 18:15, 16, 25, 44, 46; 27:4; 132:49
18	23	name which is given of the F.—24
	40	fall down and worship the F.
19	2	accomplished the will of the F.
	19	glory be to the F.
	24	I came by the will of the F.
20	24	sit down on right hand of the F.; according to the will of the F.—66:12; 76:20
	27	which beareth record of the F.—42:17
	28	F., Son and Holy Ghost are one God
	29	all men must worship the F.
	73	I baptize you in the name of the F.—68:8
	76	call upon the F. in solemn prayer
	77	O God, the Eternal F.—79
21	1	through the will of God, the F.
27	2	remembering unto the F. my body
	14	those whom my F. hath given me
29	5	I am your advocate with the F.—32:3; 45:3; 110:4
	8	decree hath gone forth from F.—12
	27	ashamed to own before the F.
31	13	these words are by will of F.

Father 157 Fatherless

Sec.	Vs.	
35	2	one in the F. as the F. is one in me
38	4	I pleaded before the F. for them
	39	riches it is the will of the F. to give
42	3	as ye are agreed and have asked the F.
45	4	F. behold the sufferings and death
	5	F. spare these my brethren
50	27	sent forth by the will of the F.
	35	kingdom is given you of the F.
	41	you are of them my F. hath given me
	42	none of them my F. hath given me
	43	F. and I are one; I am in the F. and the F. in me—93:3
59	2	a crown in the mansions of my F.—106:8; 135:5
63	34	will come down from presence of F.
67	9	cometh down from the F. of lights
68	12	as many as the F. shall bear record
72	4	mansions prepared of my F.—81:6
76	13	which were ordained of the F.: who was in the bosom of the F.—25:39
	23	the only begotten of the F.—35; 93:11
	25	the Son whom the F. loved
	42	whom the F. had put into his power
	43	who glorifies the F.; son, after the F. has revealed him
	53	Spirit which the F. sheds forth
	55	into whose hands the F. has given
	71	have received the fulness of the F.
	77	but not of the fulness of the F.
	92	where God, even the F. reigns
	107	present it unto the F. spotless
78	4	espoused to the glory of your F.
	17	how great blessings the F. hath
84	22	no man can see the face of the F.
	37	receiveth me receiveth my F.
	38	receiveth my F. receiveth F's kingdom; all that my F. hath shall be given
	40	this oath and covenant of my F.
	47	cometh unto God even the F.
	48	the F. teacheth him of the covenant
	63	ye are they my F. hath given me
	74	kingdom where my F. and I am
	83	your F. knoweth that you have need
	92	bear testimony of it unto your F.
88	19	crowned with the presence of the F.
	75	that I may testify unto your F.
89	5	neither meet in the sight of your F.
93	4	F. because he gave me of his fulness
	5	I was in the world and received of my F.
	16	received fulness of the glory of the F.
	17	glory of the F. was with him
	19	that you may come unto the F.
	20	be glorified as I am in the F.
	21	I was in the beginning with the F.
	23	ye were also in the beginning with the F.
95	9	this is the promise of the F.—108:5; 132:63
	12	the love of the F. shall not continue
98	18	where my F. and I am there ye shall
99	4	rejecteth you shall be rejected of my F.
101	65	shall come in the kingdom of my F.
107	19	communion and presence of God the F.
109	4	now we ask thee Holy F.—10, 14, 22, 24, 29, 47
123	6	is enjoined on us by our heavenly F.
130	3	appearing of F. and Son is a personal; the idea that F. and Son dwell in
	22	F. has a body of flesh and bones
132	11	I and my F. ordained unto you—28
	12	no man shall come unto the F. but by me
	31	the continuation of the works of my F.—63
	33	ye cannot receive the promise of my F.
	59	if a man be called of my F.

FATHER

27	11	Michael, or Adam, the F. of all
29	34	neither Adam, your F., whom I created
68	21	priesthood descending from F. to son—107:40
84	16	by the hand of his F. Adam
104	28	the lot upon which his F. resides—43
	44	a blessing upon him and upon his F.
	45	reserved an inheritance for his F.
107	42	received the promise of God by his F.
	43	was the express likeness of his F.; he seemed like his F. in all things
109	64	lands thou gave to Abraham, their F.
122	6	tear thee from the society of thy F.; my F. my F., why can't you stay with us; O my F.
124	91	appointed unto him by his F.
128	21	chamber of old F. Whitmer
132	49	with Abraham, thy F.—57

FATHER-IN-LAW

84	6	which he received under the hand of his F.

FATHERLESS

123	9	imperative duty we owe to the F.
136	8	bear equal proportion in taking the F.; that cries of the F. came not up

Sec.	Vs.		Sec.	Vs.	
		FATHERS			**FAVOR**
2	2	plant the promises made to the F.; children shall turn to their F.—27:9; 98:16; 110:15; 128:17	105	25	I will give unto you F. and grace
				26	in this way you may find F. in
			109	21	repent and find F. in thy sight
3	17	through the testimony of their F.		56	that thy people may obtain F. in
	18	because of the iniquity of their F.	124	6	the set time has come to F. her
	20	might come to the knowledge of their F.			**FAYETTE**
27	10	with Jacob, Isaac, Abraham, your F.	24	3	go speedily unto church in F. and
29	48	required at the hands of their F.	128	20	in wilderness of F., Seneca Co.
45	16	promises that I have made unto your F.—96:7		21	in chamber of father Whitmer in F.
					FEAR
74	4	gave heed to traditions of their F.—93:39	1	7	therefore F. and tremble
			6	33	F. not to do good, my sons
77	15	Jerusalem in the land of their F.		34	F. not, little flock; do good—35:27
83	1	who have lost their husbands or F.		36	doubt not, F. not
84	14	through the lineage of his F.—15; 86:8	10	55	need not F. for such shall inherit
				56	it is they who do not F. me
	99	by the faith and covenants of their F.	25	9	thou needest not F. for thy husband
85	5	neither the names of the F.	30	5	F. not, but give heed unto the words
	7	names of their F., and of their children	38	15	F. not, for the kingdom is yours
98	32	law I gave unto your F. Joseph and		30	if ye are prepared ye shall not F.
	47	wherewith their F. have trespassed and their father's F.	40	2	F. of persecution caused him to reject
103	18	as your F. were led at the first	45	74	that F. may seize upon them and they
	19	I say not as I said unto your F.	50	41	F. not, little children, for you are mine
109	54	Constitution defended by our F.			
112	32	keys have come down from the F.	60	2	hide their talent because of F. of man
123	7	strongly riveted the creeds of the F.	63	6	let the rebellious F. and tremble
	9	whose husbands and F. have been murdered		16	shall deny the faith and shall F.
127	2	this day has the God of my F. delivered me		33	F. shall come upon every man
			64	43	nations shall F. because of her terrible
128	15	as Paul says concerning the F.	68	6	do not F. for I am with you
	18	welding link between the F. and the	76	5	gracious unto them who F. me
132	55	an hundred-fold of F. and mothers	79	4	servant Jared Carter, and F. not
136	21	even the God of your F., the God of	88	91	F. shall come upon all people
		FATHER'S		104	F. God and give glory to him who—133:38
27	4	yea, in this my F. kingdom	98	1	F. not, let your hearts be comforted
30	4	your home shall be at your F. house	101	36	F. not, even unto death
84	38	receiveth my Father receiveth my F. kingdom		84	though I F. not God, nor regard man
	58	fruit meet for their F. kingdom	122	9	F. not what man can do for God shall
	74	shall not come into my F. kingdom			
98	18	in my F. house are many mansions	124	87	cease to F. concerning his family
	47	fathers have trespassed and their F. fathers	136	17	F. not thine enemies; for they—30
133	18	his F. name written on their foreheads			**FEARED**
			3	7	you should not have F. man more than God
		FATNESS			
56	18	the F. of the earth shall be theirs	9	11	but you F. and the time is past
61	17	they may partake the F. thereof	30	1	you have F. man and have not relied
		FAULT			
20	80	any member overtaken in a F.	101	82	there was a judge which F. not God
88	124	cease to find F. one with another			**FEARETH**
		FAULTS	45	39	he that F. me shall be looking
6	19	admonish him in his F.			

Sec.	Vs.		Sec.	Vs.	
		FEARFUL	49	6	to put all enemies under his F.—58:22; 76:61, 106
63	17	the F. and the unbelieving, and liars	59	3	whose F. stand upon the land of Zion
		FEARING	60	15	shake off the dust of thy F.; wash thy F. as a testimony against—75:20; 84:92; 99:4
30	11	not F. what man can do for I am			
124	7	F. them not for they are as grass	78	16	who hath established his F. and set
		FEARS	84	109	let not the head say to the F. it hath no need of the F., for without the F.
67	3	there were F. in your hearts and this is			
	10	strip yourselves from jealousies and F.	88	74	cleanse your hands and F. before me
		FEAST		139	by the ordinance of washing of F.—140
58	8	that a F. of fat things, a F. of wine	94	4	55 by 65 F. in the width thereof—11; 95:15
		FEBRUARY	101	40	trodden under the F. of men
76	11	being in the spirit on the 16th of F.		86	let them importune at the F. of—87, 88
135	6	Hyrum Smith was 44 years old, F., 1844	103	7	kingdoms subdued under my F.
		FEEBLE	110	2	under his F. was a paved work of pure
81	5	strengthen the F. knees	128	19	how beautiful upon mountains are F.
		FEED			**FEIGNED**
84	89	the same *will* F. you and clothe you	104	4	broken the covenants with F. words—52
112	14	take up my cross and F. my sheep			**FELICITY**
		FEEDS	77	3	in enjoyment of their eternal F.
84	90	he who F. you or clothes you shall			**FELL**
		FEEL	135	1	Hyrum was shot first and F.
9	8	you shall F. that it is right			**FELLOW-BEINGS**
87	6	shall the inhabitants be made to F.	81	4	do the greatest good unto thy F.
101	8	in day of trouble they F. after me			**FELLOW-MAN**
109	13	that all people may F. thy power and F. constrained to	1	10	measure which he has measured to his F.
112	13	I the Lord *will* F. after them		19	man should not counsel his F.
127	2	I F. like Paul, to glory in tribulation			**FELLOW-MEN**
129	5	he will do so and you will F. his hand	109	43	delight not in destruction of our F.
					FELLOWS
	8	offer you his hand and you *will* not F.	133	34	upon the head of Ephraim and his F.
		FEELINGS			**FELLOW-SERVANTS**
9	9	but you shall have no such F.	13	1	upon you my F., in the name of Messiah
105	24	consistently with the F. of the people			**FELLOWSHIP**
128	1	subject seems to press upon my F.	83	2	they shall have F. in the church
		FEET		3	they shall not have F. in the church
6	37	prints of the nails in my hands and F.	88	133	in which I receive you to F.
24	15	casting off the dust of your F., cleansing your F. by the—75:20; 84:92; 99:4	104	75	but so long as he is in full F.
			134	10	provided that such dealings be for F.; and withdraw from them their F.
27	16	F. shod with the preparation of the—112:7			
35	14	their enemies shall be under their F.			
45	51	what are these wounds in thy F.			

Sec.	Vs.		Sec.	Vs.	
		FEMALE			**FIERY**
20	18	he created man, male and F. created	3	8	against the F. darts of the adversary
		FERVENT	27	17	quench the F. darts of the wicked
101	25	element shall melt with F. heat			**FIFTEEN**
		FETTERS	128	13	as Paul hath declared, I Cor. F:46-48
123	8	they are the shackles and F. of hell		16	quotation of Paul, I Cor. F.:29
		FEW			**FIFTEEN THOUSAND**
5	30	hast translated a F. more pages	124	64	be permitted to receive F.—65, 72
23	1	I speak unto you a F. words—3, 4, 5			**FIFTH**
33	4	none doeth good save it be a F.	76	15	29th verse of F. chapter of John
59	4	and with commandments not a F.	88	103	which is the F. trump, which is the F. angel
63	31	F. shall stand to receive inheritance	113	1	in the third, fourth and F. verses
64	18	after a F. weeks should return	128	17	Malachi, last chapter, verses F. and 6th
72	24	a F. words in addition to the laws			**FIFTIES**
95	5	many called but F. of them are chosen—121:34, 40	103	30	by tens, or by twenties or by F.
99	7	after a F. years thou mayest	104	68	receive moneys by hundreds, or by F.
112	2	there have been some F. things in thine	136	3	organized with captains of F., and
117	10	be faithful over a F. things and he—124:113		15	appoint presidents and captains of F.
128	2	I wrote a F. words of revelation; I have had a F. additional views			**FIFTY**
132	22	and F. there be that find it	104	69	if he obtain ten, or twenty, or F.
	53	he hath been faithful over F. things		73	if it be ten talents or F.
		FIELD	124	64	shall not receive less than F.—66
4	4	F. is white already to harvest—6:3; 11:3; 12:3; 14:3; 31:4; 33:3, 7		72	not under F. dollars, neither can
49	19	the beasts of the F. and the—59:16; 89:14, 17; 101:24			**FIFTY-FIVE**
84	82	consider the lilies of F.	94	4	it shall be built F. by 65 feet—11
86	2	I say that the F. was the world	95	15	the size thereof shall be F. feet in
	7	the F. remaineth to be burned			**FIFTY-SECOND**
88	51	having a F., sent forth servants into F. to dig in the F.	113	7	what is meant by Isaiah, F. chapter
	52	go ye and labor in the F.			**FIG**
	53	go ye also into the F. and in the	88	87	as a F. that falleth from a fig-tree
	56	the Lord of the F. went unto the first			**FIGHT**
128	23	let all the trees of the F. praise	35	14	they shall F. manfully for me
		FIELDS	88	115	Michael shall F. their battles
24	3	after thou hast sowed thy F.	98	37	the Lord would F. their battles
86	5	ready and waiting to reap down the F.	105	14	do not require at their hands to F.; I will F. your battles....
136	9	let each company prepare F. for	109	28	thou wilt F. for thy people
	11	ye shall be blessed in your F.	121	38	he is left to F. against God
		FIERCE			**FIG-TREE**
87	6	and the F. and vivid lightning also	35	16	learn the parable of the F.
101	90	in his F. anger in His time	88	87	as a fig that falleth from a F.
122	4	more terrible than the F. lion			**FIG-TREES**
	7	if F. winds become thine enemy	45	37	look and behold the F.
		FIERCENESS			**FIGURATIVE**
76	107	the wine-press of the F. of the wrath—88:106	77	2	they are F. expressions used by
					FILL
			11	13	which shall F. your soul with joy

Sec.	Vs.	
61	9	that they may F. their mission
	22	if so be that they F. their mission
84	5	the glory which shall F. the house
	107	and F. appointments you are not able to F.
88	12	of God, to F. the immensity of space
102	4	would F. their office according to
103	3	F. up the measure of their iniquities
107	38	to F. the several calls for preaching
109	72	great mountain and F. the whole earth
	74	that thy glory may F. the earth
118	6	F. places of those who have fallen
124	144	you should F. all these offices

FILLED

27	7	should be F. with the spirit of Elias
33	8	open your mouths and they shall be F.—10
49	17	be F. with the measure of man
65	2	until it has F. the whole earth
75	21	you shall be F. with joy and
84	27	being F. with the Holy Ghost
	32	F. with the glory of the Lord
	98	be F. with the knowledge of the Lord
88	19	hath F. the measure of its creation
	67	your whole bodies shall be F. with light; that which is F. with light comprehendeth
	107	saints shall be F. with his glory
101	9	my bowels are F. with compassion
102	8	it shall be F. by nomination
109	37	let thy house be F. with thy glory
123	7	which has F. the world with confusion
133	33	F. with songs of everlasting joy

FILLETH

88	25	it F. the measure of its creation

FILTHY

88	35	they must remain F. still—102

FINAL

107	80	this is a F. decision on controversies

FIND

6	11	thou mayest F. out mysteries
42	8	inasmuch as ye shall F. them that
	75	if ye shall F. that any persons
45	14	obtained promise that they should F. it
54	10	they shall F. rest to their souls
76	2	extent of his doings none can F. out
85	9	shall F. none inheritance in—11
88	63	seek diligently and ye shall F. me —83
89	19	and shall F. wisdom and great
97	1	to learn wisdom and to F. truth

Sec.	Vs.	
98	13	shall F. it again even life eternal— 103:27
105	26	in this way you may F. favor
109	21	return and F. favor in thy sight
123	3	as far as they can F. them out
	4	a committee to F. out these things
	12	they know not where to F. it
124	9	that ye may F. grace in their eyes
	23	that weary traveler may F. health
109		seek to F. safety and refuge
128	6	as you will F. recorded in Revelations
132	22	and few there be that F. it
136	26	if thou shalt F. that which thy

FINE

131	7	but it is more F. or pure

FINGER

84	3	appointed by the F. of the Lord

FINISH

124	19	that when he shall F. his work

FINISHED

5	4	no other gift until it is F.
9	1	until you have F. this record
19	2	I having F. the will of him whose
	19	I partook and F. my preparations
73	4	work of translation until it be F.
76	85	until the Lamb shall have F. his work
77	12	on the seventh day he F. his work
88	60	until his hour was F.
	106	angel saying: It is F.; It is F.
90	13	when you have F. the translation
102	18	on the case, have F. their remarks
115	12	labor diligently until it shall be F.; not anything remain that is not F.
128	24	holy temple when it is F.

FINISHING

10	3	continue on unto the F. of the
77	12	the preparing and F. of his work
121	32	reserved unto the F. and the end

FIRE

7	6	I will make him as flaming F.
19	31	by baptism and F., even the Holy— 20:41
29	12	day of my coming in a pillar of F.
	21	shall be cast down by devouring F.
	28	depart ye cursed into everlasting F.
33	11	then cometh the baptism of F.— 39:6
35	14	by the F. of mine indignation
36	6	come forth out of the F., hating even
43	32	earth shall pass away so as by F.
	33	shall go away into unquenchable F.
45	41	they shall behold blood, and F.

Sec.	Vs.		Sec.	Vs.	
	50	hewn down and cast into the F.—97:7		56	the Lord went unto the F. in the F. hour
	57	not be hewn down and cast into the F.		57	he withdrew from the F. that he
63	17	lake which burneth with F. and brimstone—76:36		59	beginning at the F., from last unto F. and from the F. to
	34	consume wicked with unquenchable F.—54		70	who are the F. laborers in this last—74
76	44	where the F. is not quenched		85	those who are not the F. elders
	105	suffer the vengeance of eternal F.		98	the F. fruits; who shall descend with him F., who are F. caught up
97	26	visit with vengeance, with devouring F.		108	F. angel shall sound his trump; works of God in F. thousand years
101	66	burned with unquenchable F.			
109	36	even cloven-tongues as of F.		129	he shall be F. in the house of God
110	3	his eyes were as a flame of F.		130	he should be F. in the house
128	24	for he is like a refiner's F.	90	9	unto the Gentiles F. and then unto
130	7	on a globe like a sea of glass and F.	93	12	received not of the fulness at F.—13, 14
133	41	as a melting F. that burneth and as the F.		44	F. set in order thy house
135	6	if the F. can scathe a green tree	94	3	let the F. lot on the south be
				14	the F. and second lots on the north
		FIRM	95	7	the creator of the F. day
5	22	be F. in keeping the commandments	98	34	should F. lift standard of peace
29	12	it hath gone forth in a F. decree		39	enemy has come upon thee the F. time
		FIRMAMENT		41	if he repent not the F. time
76	70	whose glory the sun of the F. is	102	12	who of the twelve shall speak F.
	71	differs from the sun in the F.		22	the F. decision shall stand
	81	glory of the moon in the F.		34	ascertain who should speak F.
	109	innumerable as the stars in the F.	103	18	as your fathers were led at the F.
			105	7	who are the F. Elders of my church
		FIRST		31	but F. let my army become great
5	4	this is the F. gift that I have		33	the F. elders of my church should
10	45	translate this F. part of engravings	107	2	why the F. is called Melchizedek
11	21	but F. seek to obtain my word		33	F. unto the Gentiles, secondly—34, 35, 97
20	2	to be the F. elder of this church		95	other seventy beside the F.
	5	was manifested unto this F. elder	108	4	remembered with the F. of mine elders
21	11	he being the F. unto you			
	12	and the F. preacher of the church	110	4	I am the F. and the last
27	8	to ordain you unto the F. priesthood	112	26	F. among those among you
29	30	F. shall be last and the last shall be F.	113	1	spoken of in the F. verse of the 11th—3
	32	F. spiritual, secondly temporal; again F. temporal		7	Isaiah, 52nd chapter and F. verse
	41	which is the F. death even that same	124	124	F. I give unto you Hyrum Smith
42	4	I give unto you this F. commandment	128	13	Paul hath declared, F. Corinthians —16
	33	after this F. consecration		14	that was not F. which is spiritual; the F. man is of the earth, earthy
45	54	shall have part in the F. resurrection—76:64; 132:19, 26	132	19	if it be after the F. resurrection
53	6	these are the F. ordinances that you		61	and the F. give her consent
58	10	F. the rich and the learned	133	8	F. upon the Gentiles, then upon the Jews
63	18	not have part in the F. resurrection			
68	14	to minister even according to the F.	135	1	Hyrum was shot F. and fell
77	7	F. seal contains things of F. thousand years			**FIRST-BORN**
	8	7th chapter and F. verse of	68	16	the F. among the sons of Aaron
84	16	Adam who was the F. man		17	F. holds the right of presidency
86	7	ye shall F. gather out the wheat		18	literal descendant and the F. of
88	52	said unto the F., in the F. hour I	76	54	they are the church of the F.—94; 78:21; 93:22

Sec.	Vs.		Sec.	Vs.	
	67	general assembly and church of F.—107:19			**FLAMING**
	71	differs from the church of the F.	7	6	I will make him as F. fire
	102	caught up to the church of the F.			**FLATTERED**
77	11	as many as will come to the church of the F.	121	20	despised by those that F. them
88	5	the glory of the church of the F.			**FLATTERETH**
93	21	I am the F.	10	25	and thus he F. them—26, 29
		FIRST PRESIDENCY			**FLED**
68	15	they shall be appointed by the F.	101	51	servants were affrighted and F.
	19	ordained under the hands of the F.			**FLEE**
	22	tried, save it be before the F.	42	64	converted to F. to the west
102	26	High Council of the seat of the F.—27	45	68	must F. unto Zion for safety
			54	7	go to now and F. the land lest
	33	presidents of the F. shall	124	106	warn the inhabitants to F. the wrath
112	20	whosoever receiveth the F.			
	30	for unto you and the F. is the	133	12	let them F. unto Zion
117	13	let him contend for redemption of F.		13	let them who be of Judah F. unto
120	1	by a council composed of the F.			**FLESH (All)**
124	126	these may constitute a quorum and F.	1	34	make these things known unto all F.
		FIR-TREE	38	11	all F. is corrupted before me
124	26	the box-tree, and the F., and the pine	16		all F. is mine and I am no respecter
			61	6	all F. is in mine hand and he—101:16
		FISH	63	6	all F. shall know that I am God
101	24	the F. of the sea shall be consumed	95	4	may pour out my spirit upon all F.
117	6	have I not the F. of the sea	98	17	and all F. be consumed before me
133	68	their F. stink and die for thirst	101	23	all F. shall see me together
		FISHES		26	the enmity of all F. shall cease
29	24	F. of the sea shall pass away		77	rights and protection of all F.
		FIT	112	23	all F. has become corrupt before me
10	37	until I shall see F. to make all	133	25	and shall reign over all F.
		FIVE		60	but now are to go forth unto all F.
64	21	land in Kirtland for space of F. years		61	the Lord who ruleth over all F.
104	69	if a man obtain F. talents let him			**FLESH**
	73	if it be F. talents or ten, or	1	19	neither trust in the arm of F.
135	1	about F. p. m., by an armed mob	18	11	the Lord suffered death in the F.
		FIVE HUNDRED	20	1	since the coming of our Savior in the F.
103	30	have obtained to number of F. of the		26	after he came in the F.
	32	if you cannot obtain F., seek 300		40	the emblems of the F. and blood
		FIVES	29	18	flies which shall eat their F.
104	68	receive by twenties, by tens, by F.		19	their F. shall fall from off their bones
		FIXED	36	6	the garments spotted with the F.
88	43	and their courses are F.	45	14	they should see it in their F.
133		in a determination that is F.		16	I stood before them in the F.
128	17	who had his eye F. on restoration	49	16	they twain shall be one F.
		FLAME		21	that wasteth F. and hath no need
110	3	his eyes were as a F. of fire	61	15	no F. shall be safe on the waters
			67	11	no man has seen God, in the F.
			76	73	judged according to men in the F.—88:99
				74	received not testimony of Jesus in the F.
			118		while in the F. they may be able to
			84	21	is not manifest unto men in the F.

| Flesh | | 164 | | Food |

Sec.	Vs.		Sec.	Vs.	
86	9	lawful heirs according to the F.			**FOES**
89	12	F. also of beasts and of the fowls	121	8	thou shalt triumph over all thy F.
93	4	I made F. my tabernacle			**FOLD**
	11	he dwelt in the F. and dwelt among us	10	59	other sheep have I which are not of this F.
129	1	having bodies of F. and bones			**FOLLIES**
	2	spirit hath not F. and bones	111	1	not displeased, notwithstanding your F.
130	22	Father has a body of F. and bones; Holy Ghost has not a body of F. and	124	48	on your own heads, by your F.
132	26	they shall be destroyed in the F.			**FOLLOW**
		FLIES	38	22	hear my voice and F. me
29	18	I will send forth F. upon the	56	2	that will not take up his cross and F. me—112:14
		FLIGHT	58	3	glory which shall F. much tribulation
58	56	be not in haste, nor by F.—101:68		5	and receive that which is to F.
63	37	declare both by word and by F.	59	2	their works shall F. them—63:15, 48
133	15	let not your F. be in haste	63	9	but signs F. those that believe—84:65
	58	two shall put tens of thousands to F.	82	11	judgment shall immediately F.
		FLOCK	100	2	F. me and listen to the counsel
6	34	fear not little F., do good—35:27	105	37	inasmuch as they F. the counsel
		FLOCKS	124	98	these signs shall F. him
88	72	I will take care of your F.			**FOLLOWING**
136	11	ye shall be blessed in your F.	20	72	administered in the F. manner
		FLOOD	58	64	with signs F. them that believe
109	70	swept away as with a F.	68	10	shall be blest with signs F.
		FLOOR	102	34	and the F. was the result
135	7	blood on the F. of Carthage jail	107	41	and came down by lineage in the F. manner
		FLOURISH	115	9	let there be a beginning this F. summer
35	24	rejoice upon the hills and F.—39:13	127	10	addressed them on the F. Sabbath
49	24	Jacob shall F. in the wilderness	130	14	I heard a voice repeat the F.
	25	Zion shall F. upon the hills—64:41	135	4	he read the F. paragraph:
		FLOW			**FOLLOWS**
109	48	our hearts F. out with sorrow	3	4	F. after the dictates of his own will
	74	cause the mountains to F. *down* at —133:40, 44	76	15	which was given unto us as F.
111	8	spirit that shall F. unto you	102	5	the number were 43, as F.
121	46	it shall F. unto thee forever and ever			**FOLLY**
128	23	rivers and rills F. *down* with gladness	35	7	their F. shall be made manifest—63:15; 136:19
133	26	ice shall F. *down* at their presence	45	49	that have laughed shall see their F.
		FLOWER	124	116	let him repent of all his F.
124	7	as the F. thereof which soon falleth			**FONT**
		FLOWING	124	29	a baptismal F. there is not upon the
38	18	a land F. with milk and honey	128	13	the baptismal F. was instituted as a
		FLY			**FOOD**
88	92	angels shall F. through the midst of	24	18	what thou needest for F. and raiment
		FLYING	42	43	nourished with herbs and mild F.
88	103	angel F. through the midst of heaven—133:36	43	13	provide for him F. and raiment
			49	19	ordained for use of man for F. and
			51	8	provide F. and raiment according to

| Food | 165 | Forever |

Sec.	Vs.	
59	13	let thy F. be prepared with singleness
	17	whether for F. or for raiment—19; 70:16
89	16	all grain is good for F. of man

FOOLISH

| 63 | 54 | there will be F. virgins among the |

FOOLS

| 122 | 1 | F. shall have thee in derision |

FOOT

| 45 | 48 | Lord shall set his F. upon this mount |
| 103 | 10 | cast out and trodden under F. of men |

FOOTSTOOL

| 38 | 17 | the earth is my F., wherefore again I |

FORASMUCH

| 127 | 1 | F. as the Lord has revealed unto me |

FORBIDDEN

29	40	he partook the F. fruit and transgressed
63	31	as you are F. to shed blood
64	27	it is F. to get in debt to thine enemies

FORBIDDETH

| 49 | 15 | whoso F. to marry is not ordained of God |
| | 18 | whoso F. to abstain from meats |

FORCE

84	75	this revelation is in F. from this
132	7	are of no efficacy, virtue or F.
	15	marriage not of F. when dead
	18	it is not valid neither of F.
	19	shall be of full F. when they are out
135	5	and their testament is now in F.

FOREFATHERS

| 121 | 27 | which our F. have awaited with |

FOREGOING

| 102 | 12 | organized according to F. pattern |
| | 24 | council after the manner of the F. |

FOREHEADS

| 77 | 9 | sealed servants of God in their F. |
| 133 | 18 | Father's name written on their F. |

FOREIGN

45	63	ye hear of wars in F. lands
110	10	fame of this house shall spread to F. lands
133	8	send forth into F. lands

Sec.	Vs.	

FORESEE

| 5 | 32 | I F. the lying in wait to destroy; I F. he will fall |

FOREST

| 29 | 20 | the beasts of the F. and the fowls |

FOREVER

1	39	truth abideth F. and ever
20	4	to whom be glory F.—16; 76:119; 84:102; 88:104
	12	same God yesterday, today and F.—35:1
23	2	preach the truth from henceforth and F.
	3	thy duty is unto the church F.
	5	this is thy duty henceforth and F.
38	20	for the inheritance of your children F.
56	20	their generations shall inherit earth F.
65	6	thine is the honor, power and glory F.
69	8	land of Zion to possess it F.
76	21	angels who worship him F. and ever
	62	they shall dwell in presence of God F.—133:35
	92	where God reigns upon his throne F.
	93	all things give him glory F. and ever
	108	throne of his power to reign F.—110
82	24	kingdom is yours and shall be F.
84	18	which priesthood continueth F.
88	20	celestial kingdom may possess it F.
	41	all things are by him F. and ever
	133	blameless, in thanksgiving F. and ever
92	2	you shall be blessed F.
97	28	multiply blessings upon her F.
103	7	given unto the saints to possess it F.
107	55	thou art a prince over them F.
108	8	to bless you and deliver you F.
109	34	and let them be blotted out F.
	54	constitution of our land be established F.
117	12	be had in sacred remembrance F.—124:96
	15	let blessings of my people be on him F.
119	4	shall be a standing law unto them F.
121	6	servant's will rejoice in thy name F.
	46	it shall flow unto thee F. and ever
122	4	thy God shall stand by thee F.
	9	God shall be with you F. and ever
124	59	from generation to generation F.
	101	him that sitteth upon the throne F.
	118	it shall be well with him F.
126	3	take special care of your family F.
128	23	let the creations declare his name F.
132	17	not Gods, but angels of God F.

Sec.	Vs.		Sec.	Vs.	
	19	a continuation of the seeds F.			**FORM**
133	52	according to his loving kindness F.	49	22	cometh not in the F. of woman
	56	sing the song of the Lamb F.	93	15	descended in the F. of a dove
		FOREWARN	102	13	according to the F. above written
61	18	you shall F. your brethren concerning	107	22	they F. a quorum—24, 26, 36, 37
				28	a majority may F. a quorum
89	4	I have warned you and F. you	111	3	F. acquaintance with men in this
		FORGAVE	124	63	they shall F. a constitution
64	8	and F. not one another in their hearts	128	12	was instituted to F. a relationship
					FORMED
		FORGET	71	9	no weapon F. against you shall prosper—109:25
9	9	that shall cause you to F. the thing	77	12	F. man out of the dust of the earth
133	2	upon all nations that F. God			
		FORGIVE			**FORMER**
42	25	he that repents thou shalt F.	56	8	let him obey the F. commandment—84:57
61	2	I F. sins and am merciful			
64	7	I F. sins unto those who confess	61	9	let them take their F. company
	9	ye ought to F. one another	82	7	who sinneth shall the F. sins return
	10	I F. whom I *will* F., but of you it is required to F. all	84	76	shall repent of their F. evil works
	13	not because ye F. not	92	2	faithful in keeping all F. commandments
75	8	he sinned, nevertheless I F. him	101	10	hath gone forth by a F. commandment
82	1	even so I, the Lord, F. you		68	said unto you in a F. commandment—103:12; 105:14
84	61	I *will* F. you of your sins			
98	39	thou shalt F. him—40, 41, 42, 43, 45	102	27	according to the F. pattern
	44	thou shalt not F. him		31	from the decision of the F. there can
109	34	F. the transgressions of thy people	104	24	in exchange for his F. inheritance
124	76	for I *will* F. all his sins—78; 132:50	128	2	it was declared in my F. letter
132	56	let mine handmaid F. my servant	135	2	the F. was wounded in a savage manner
		FORGIVEN			**FORMS**
1	32	he that repents shall be F.—58:42	134	4	nor dictate F. for public devotion
25	3	thy sins are F. thee—29:3; 31:5; 36:1; 50:36; 60:7; 61:2; 62:3; 64:3; 90:1, 6; 108:1; 110:5; 112:3			**FORNICATION**
			35	11	drink of the wine of the wrath of her F.—88:94, 105
42	26	he shall not be F. but shall be cast out	42		put away their companions because of F.
50	39	let him repent and he shall be F.—64:17; 68:24			**FORSAKE**
64	16	I have F. my servant Isaac Morley	35	22	F. him not, and surely these things—66:8
82	•1	as you have F. one another	53	2	you shall F. the world
95	1	chasten, that their sins may be F.	58	43	he will confess them and F. them
132	27	which shall not be F. in this world	66	10	F. all unrighteousness
	56	then shall she be F. her trespasses	93	37	light and truth F. that evil one
				48	repent and F. some things
		FORGIVENESS	98	11	F. all evil and cleave unto all good
42	18	he that kills shall not have F.		20	they do not F. their sins
	79	remember that he hath no F.			**FORSAKEN**
64	7	who confess their sins and ask F.			
76	34	there is no F. in this world nor—84:41	61	36	I have not F. you
			88	83	he that seeketh me shall not be F.
98	39	if he come unto thee praying thy F.	124	90	bless him that he shall not be F.
		FORGIVETH			
64	9	he that F. not his brother			

Sec.	Vs.	
		FORSAKETH
42	25	repents with all his heart and F. it
93	1	every soul who F. his sins
		FORTH
30	9	thou shalt commence from this time F.
31	4	begin to preach from this time F.
88	76	prayer and fasting from this time F.
115	10	from that time F. let my people—12
124	94	from this time F. I appoint unto him
128	3	the date, and names and so F.

(See *Break, Brought, Bring, Bringeth, Bringing, Call, Called, Come, Coming, Go, Goes, Goeth, Going, Gone, Hold, Holding, Looking, Poured, Proceedeth, Put, Putteth, Roll, Send, Sent, Set, Setting, Shed, Sheds, Shine, Shoot, Show, Showing, Shown, Speak, Stand, Streak, Stretch, Utter.*)

		FORTIETH
107	45	in the F. year of his age
		FORTY
104	43	which is F. rods long and 12 wide
		FORTY-EIGHT
107	87	to preside over F. priests
128	13	I Cor. xv:46, 47, F.
		FORTY-FOUR
135	6	Hyrum Smith was F. years old
		FORTY-SEVEN
128	13	I Cor. xv: 46, F., 48
		FORTY-SIX
128	13	I Cor. xv: F., 47, 48
		FORTY-THREE
102	5	the number; were F. as follows
		FORWARD
128	22	go F. and not backward
134	8	all men should step F. and use their
		FOSTER, JAMES
124	138	I give you Joseph Young, etc., and F. to
		FOSTER, ROBERT D.
124	115	if my servant F. will obey my voice
		FOSTERED
134	9	whereby one religious society is F.
		FOSTERING
109	69	and preserved by thy F. hand

Sec.	Vs.	
		FOUND
18	39	and when you have F. them you shall
19	5	those who are F. on my left hand
37	2	church whithersoever it is F.
43	19	lest ye be F. among the wicked
45	12	they F. it not because of wickedness
51	19	whoso is F. a faithful steward
68	19	when no literal descendant can be F.—107:17
	20	must be F. worthy and annointed
	23	inasmuch as he is F. guilty
83	2	if they are not F. transgressors
85	4	to be had where it may be F.
	5	their names shall not be F.
	7	the saints whose names are F.
	9	all they who are not F. written—11
	11	or that are F. to have apostatized
	12	as will be F. recorded in the 2nd
88	100	who are F. under condemnation
	102	there are F. among those who are to
	128	shall be F. standing in his place
	134	he that is F. unworthy of this
98	14	that you may be F. worthy—109:11
101	12	all who are F. upon the watchtower
	21	when there is F. no more room for them
	41	they were F. transgressors
104	5	any man F. a transgressor—10
	8	inasmuch as you are F. transgressors
	55	and ye are F. hypocrites
	74	until he be F. a transgressor
	77	in case the treasurer is F. unfaithful
109	50	if repentance is to be F.
119	5	they shall not be F. worthy to abide
124	28	there is not a place F. on the earth
	90	nor his seed be F. begging bread
133	22	the valleys shall not be F.
		FOUNDATION
1	30	power to lay the F. of the church
18	4	concerning the F. of my church
	5	upon the F. of my gospel
21	2	being inspired to lay the F. thereof
29	46	children are redeemed from the F.
35	18	things which were from the F. of
45	1	him who laid the F. of the earth
48	6	to lay the F. of the city—94:1
52	33	shall not build upon another's F.
58	7	honored by laying the F.
64	33	ye are laying F. of a great work
78	13	the F. and the ensample which I
94	6	dedicated unto the Lord from the F.—12
101	47	while they were yet laying the F.
115	9	let there be a F. this summer
	11	re-commence laying the F. of my house

Sec.	Vs.		Sec.	Vs.	
					FOUR HUNDRED NINETY-SIX
119	2	for the laying of the F. of Zion—124:39	107	46	Mahalaleel was F. years and 7 days old
124	33	instituted before the F. of the world—132:5			**FOUR HUNDRED THIRTY**
	41	kept hid from before the F. of the	107	49	making him F. years old when he was
118		called to lay the F. of Zion			**FOUR-FOLD**
127	2	I was ordained from before the F.	98	26	your reward shall be doubled F.
128	5	prepared before the F. of the world—8		44	and reward thee F. in all things
	18	never been revealed from the F. of		47	restore F. for all their trespasses
132	63	given by my Father before the F.	124	71	and do not repay F. for the stock
136	38	which F. he did lay and was faithful			**FOURTEEN**
		FOUNDATIONS	130	3	John F., verse 23. The appearing of
78	15	established the F. of Adam-ondi-Ahman			**FOURTH**
130	20	decreed in the heavens before the F.	20	1	in the F. month, and on the sixth day—21:3
		FOUNDED	77	1	spoken of by John. F. chapter
127	1	all F. in falsehood of the blackest	88	55	unto the F. and so on to the 12th
135	3	F. a great city and left a fame		57	and the third, and the F. and so on
		FOUNDERS	102		trump shall sound which is the F.
111	9	ancient inhabitants and F. of this city	98	28	children unto third and F. generation—29, 30, 46
		FOUNTAIN		37	enemies to the third and F. generation—103:26; 105:30
85	7	his bowels shall be a F. of truth		44	if he trespass against thee the F. time
		FOUNTAINS	113	1	Stem of Jesse spoken of in F. verse
133	39	that made the sea and the F. of water	115	10	let beginning be made on F. day of
		FOUR	124	50	who hindered my work, to third and F.
33	6	gather mine elect from F. quarters		52	on their heads unto third and F.
45	46	shall come forth from F. quarters of			**FOWLS**
77	2	to understand by the F. beasts spoken of	29	20	and the F. of the *air* shall
	3	are the F. beasts limited to; they are limited to F.		24	F. of the *air* and the fishes
	8	to understand by the F. angels; they are F. angels sent forth and given power over F. parts of earth	49	19	beasts of the field and the F. of the *air*—59:16
	9	he crieth unto the F. angels	77	2	things, and the F. of the *air*
102	5	17 elders, F. priests, and 13 members	89	12	flesh of beasts and the F. of the *air*
	14	if thought to be difficult F. shall be		14	and the F. of heaven—101:24; 117:6
	17	who draw even numbers, two, F., six		17	rye for the F. and for swine
107	44	at the age of 134 years, F. months			**FRAMED**
110	11	gathering of Israel from the F. parts	134	2	except such laws are F. and held
124	3	proclamation to the F. corners thereof			**FRAMER**
	128	my kingdom upon F. corners of earth	20	17	God the F. of heaven and earth
133	7	from the F. winds, from end of			**FRAUD**
135	1	and both received F. balls	57	8	that he may sell goods without F.
	2	wounded in savage manner with F. balls			**FREE**
	3	to the F. quarters of the earth	10	51	that it might be F. unto all
			24	11	have glory whether in bonds or F.
			38	22	you shall be a F. people
			43	20	call upon both bond and F.
			58	27	do many things of their own F. will

Sec.	Vs.	
88	86	liberty wherewith ye are made F.
98	8	I make you F., therefore ye are F.; the law also maketh you F.
124	69	out of their hands by their own F. will
128	22	for the prisoners shall go F.
134	2	secure the F. exercise of conscience
	7	in F. exercise of their religious belief
136	27	for it is a F. gift of the Lord

FREEDOM

98	5	supporting that principle of F.
106	1	in the land of F. and the regions
134	4	but never suppress the F. of the soul
	5	holding sacred the F. of conscience

FREELY

10	66	partake of the waters of life F.
19	26	impart it F. to the printing of
	37	and speak F. to all

FREQUENT

107	4	to avoid the too F. repetition of

FRIEND

88	133	to be your F. and brother
128	25	I am your never deviating F.

FRIENDLY

121	9	with warm hearts and F. hands

FRIENDS

23	6	pray vocally among your F.
45	52	wounded in the house of my F.
82	22	make unto yourselves F. with the
84	63	ye are my F.
	77	F., for from henceforth I shall call you F., even as my F. in days
88	3	I send another comforter upon you my F.
	62	I say unto you my F.—117; 93:51; 94:1; 97:1; 98:1; 100:1; 103:1; 104:1; 105:26
93	45	I will call you F., for you are my F.
109	6	in a revelation calling us thy F.
121	9	thy F. do stand by thee
	10	thy F. do not contend against thee
134	11	justified in defending their F.

FRUIT

6	31	joy in the F. of your labors
27	5	I will drink of the F. of the vine
29	40	he partook the forbidden F.
52	34	the same shall be blessed with much F.
84	58	that they may bring forth F. meet —101:100
89	11	every F. in the season thereof
	16	the F. of the vine, that which yieldeth F.
97	7	tree that bringeth not forth good F.
	9	that yieldeth much precious F.

Sec.	Vs.	
101	45	and take unto themselves the F. of my
	101	and they shall eat the F. thereof
132	30	his seed and the F. of his loins

FRUITFUL

97	9	a very F. tree that is planted in

FRUITS

52	17	he shall bring forth F. of praise
	18	he that bringeth not forth F. is not
88	98	they are Christ's; the first F.

FRUSTRATED

3	1	the purposes of God cannot be F.
	3	it is not the work of God that is F.

FULFILL

45	16	to F. the promises that I have made
85	10	as the Lord speaketh he *will* also F.
88	75	that I may F. this promise
105	14	as I said so *will* I F.
	28	sent wise men to F. that which
109	23	to F. that which thou hast spoken
124	47	neither F. the promises which ye
132	63	to F. the promise which was given

FULFILLED

1	7	have decreed in them shall be F.
	18	all this that it might be F.
	37	promises which are in them shall be F.—45:35; 49:10
	38	not pass away but shall all be F. —45:23; 56:11
3	19	that the promises of the Lord might be F.
5	4	until my purpose is F. in this
18	7	he hath F. the thing which I have
24	14	that the scriptures might be F.
29	10	spoken by mine apostles must be F.
	30	even so shall they be F.
35	22	surely these things shall be F.
42	39	mouths of my prophets shall be F.
45	25	until the times of the Gentiles be F.—30
	56	at that day shall the parable be F.
52	36	that the prophecies may be F.
58	31	have promised and have not F.
	33	for his promises are not F.
62	6	that the promise might be F.
74	3	law of Moses which law was F.
98	3	immutable covenant that they shall be F.
101	19	that the prophets might be F.
	62	after many days all things were F.
	64	my word must needs be F.
105	22	whatsoever he shall appoint shall be F.
	34	and her law be executed and F.
108	6	shall be F. upon you in that day
109	36	let it be F. upon them
	44	but thy word must be F.

Sec.	Vs.	
133	63	shall be F. that which was written

FULFILLING

Sec.	Vs.	
132	34	this therefore was F. the promises

FULFILMENT

Sec.	Vs.	
103	40	in obtaining the F. of these
109	11	to secure a F. of the promises
128	20	declaring the F. of the prophets

FULL

Sec.	Vs.	
10	21	their hearts are F. of wickedness
12	8	except he shall be humble, F. of love
17	1	which if you do with F. purpose of heart—18:27, 28
29	17	the cup of mine indignation is F.—43:26
42	57	until ye have received them in F.
56	17	whose eyes are F. of greediness—68:31
59	13	in other words that thy joy may be F.
62	2	your mission is not yet F.
66	12	my Father who is F. of grace and truth—93:11
77	4	that is, they are F. of knowledge
84	102	for he is F. of mercy, justice
87	6	hath made a F. end of all nations
101	11	when the cup of their iniquity is F.
	36	in this world your joy is not F., but in me your joy is F.
102	26	with a F. statement of testimony
103	3	that their cup might be F.
104	17	for the earth is F. and there is enough
	75	so long as he is in F. fellowship
105	3	but are F. of all manner of evil
107	56	Adam being F. of the Holy Ghost
109	32	we plead before thee for a F. deliverance
121	20	their basket shall not be F.
	45	let thy bowels be F. of charity
132	19	shall be of F. force when they are out

FULLER, EDSON

Sec.	Vs.	
52	28	let F. and Jacob Scott take their

FULLER'S

Sec.	Vs.	
128	24	refiner's fire and like F. soap

FULLMER, DAVID

Sec.	Vs.	
124	132	viz., F., Alpheus Cutler, and

FULLY

Sec.	Vs.	
59	9	more F. keep thyself unspotted from
86	7	until the harvest be F. ripe
110	14	behold, the time has F. come
123	6	before we can F. and completely claim
127	1	when I learn that storm is F. blown over.

FULNESS

Sec.	Vs.	
1	23	that F. of my gospel might be
14	10	F. of my gospel from the Gentiles to
20	9	which contains the F. of the gospel—27:5
27	13	dispensation, for the F. of times
29	24	and all the F. thereof, both men and
35	12	those who are ready to receive the F.
17	1	have sent forth the F. of my—133:57
39	11	thou shalt preach the F. of my gospel
	18	inasmuch as they receive the F. of my
42	12	in the which is the F. of my gospel
	15	until F. of my scriptures is given
45	28	it shall be the F. of the gospel
59	16	the F. of the earth is yours
63	21	of which account the F. ye have not
66	2	blessed are you for receiving F. of my
76	14	the record we bear is the F. of the
	20	and received of his F.
	56	they who have received of his F.
	71	who have received the F. of the Father
	76	receive of his glory but not of his F.
	77	the presence, but not F. of the Father
	86	they who receive not of his F. in the
	94	having received of his F. and grace
	106	until F. of times when Christ shall
84	24	which rest is the F. of his glory
88	29	shall receive of the same even a F.—30, 31
90	11	the F. of the gospel in his own tongue
93	4	because he gave me of his F.
	6	bore record of F. of my glory, and F. of John's record is
	12	he received not of F. at first—13, 14
	13	grace to grace until he received a F.—16
	18	shall receive F. of the record of John
	19	in due time receive of his F.—20
	26	he received a F. of truth
	27	no man receiveth a F. unless he
	33	spirit and element receive F. of joy
	34	when separated man cannot receive F.
104	58	to print F. of my scriptures
109	15	and receive a F. of the Holy Ghost
	65	converted to the F. of the gospel
	77	enthroned with an infinity of F.

| Fulness | | 171 | | Gates |

Sec.	Vs.		Sec.	Vs.	
112	30	the dispensation of F. of times—121:31; 124:41; 128:18, 20	57	16	F. directions shall be given hereafter
118	4	and there promulgate the F. thereof	58	34	F. directions concerning this land
121	27	as held in reserve for the F. of their	73	5	pattern unto elders until F. knowledge
124	28	even the F. of the priesthood	124	88	and await patiently F. instructions
132	6	instituted for F. of my glory; he that receiveth a F. there	128	6	F., I want you to remember that
	19	which glory shall be a F. and			**FURY**
135	3	has sent the F. of the gospel to the	101	89	and in his F. vex the nation
			121	5	in the F. of thine heart avenge us
		FUNDS	133	51	I have trampled them in my F.
72	10	to receive the F. of the church			**FUTURE**
	21	that they also may obtain F.	5	9	made known unto F. generations
		FURTHER	130	7	where all things, past, present and F.
6	22	if you desire a F. witness, cast			
30	4	until I give you F. commandments			**FUTURITY**
45	60	not given unto you to know *any* F.	101	78	act in principle pertaining to F.
47	1	until he is called to F. duties	123	15	there is much which lieth in F.

G

Sec.	Vs.		Sec.	Vs.	
		GABRIEL	42	40	let all thy G. be plain
128	121	the voice of G., and of Raphael, and		42	nor wear the G. of the laborer
			61	34	they shall rid their G.
		GAD	82	14	arise and put on her beautiful G.
84	10	and Jeremy under the hand of G.	88	85	their G. are not clean from the blood
	11	and G. under the hand of Esaias	109	76	that our G. may be pure
		GAIN	112	33	cleanse your hearts and your G.
10	56	build up churches to get G.	122	6	shall cling to thy G. and say
82	18	that every man may G. other talents	133	46	from God in heaven with dyed G.
		GAINS		48	his G. like him that treadeth in the
130	19	if a person G. more knowledge and		51	their blood have I sprinkled on my G.
		GALLAND, ISAAC	135	5	wherefore thy G. are clean; all men shall know that my G. are not
124	78	let G. put stock into that house			
	79	let G. be appointed among you and be			**GARNERS**
			101	65	that the wheat may be secured in the G.
		GAPE			
122	7	if the jaws of hell shall G. open			**GARNISH**
		GARDEN	121	45	let virtue G. thy thoughts unceasingly
29	41	cast out from the G. of Eden			
		GARDENS			**GATE**
59	17	for orchards, or for G., or for	22	2	cannot enter in at straight G. by
		GARMENT		4	enter ye in at the G. as I have
42	54	shalt not take thy brother's G.	43	7	shall come in at the G. and be
		GARMENTS	132	22	for strait is the G. and narrow
20	6	whose G. were pure and white		25	broad is the G. and wide the way
36	6	hating the G. spotted with the flesh			**GATES**
			10	69	G. of hell shall not prevail—17:8; 18:5; 21:6; 33:13; 98:22; 128:10

Sec.	Vs.	
		GATHER
10	65	*will* G. them as a hen gathereth her—29:2
27	13	G. together in one all things
33	6	G. mine elect from the four quarters
38	12	G. the tares that they may be burned
45	64	G. ye out from the eastern lands
	65	G. *up* your riches that ye may purchase
77	9	this is Elias which was to come to G.
	14	for him to G. the tribes of Israel
86	7	G. out the wheat from among the tares
88	111	that he may G. together his armies
	112	archangel shall G. his armies
	113	the devil shall G. his armies
101	22	it is my will that they should G.
	55	go and G. residue of my servants
	58	as they G. together against you
	65	I must G. together my people
	67	continue to G. to the places which
	72	let churches G. their moneys
	74	they may buy lands and G. together
103	22	G. yourselves unto the land of Zion
105	16	G. together for the redemption of
	24	carefully G. as much in one region
	27	time to G. *up* the strength of my
109	39	that they may G. out of that city
	58	may G. out the righteous to build a
111	2	whom I *will* G. out in due time
119	5	those who G. shall be tithed
122	7	if the heaven G. blackness
123	4	to G. up the libelous publications
125	2	let them G. themselves together
133	4	G. ye together, O ye people of my
	7	G. ye out from among the nations
		GATHERED
6	32	where two or three are G. together
29	8	they shall be G. into one place
	27	righteous shall be G. on my right
31	8	against the time when they shall be G.
38	31	G. unto me a righteous people
	38	all these things shall be G. unto
39	22	they shall be G. unto me in time
42	9	that ye may be G. in one
	36	that my covenant people may be G.
43	24	G. you together as a hen gathereth
45	25	but they shall be G. again
	43	the remnant shall be G. unto this
	69	be G. unto it out of every nation
	71	righteous shall be G. from all nations
48	6	then shall ye begin to be G.
76	102	they who will not be G. with the saints
77	15	after they are G. and have built the city

Sec.	Vs.	
84	100	the Lord hath G. all things in one
101	13	that have been scattered shall be G.
135	3	G. many thousands of Latter Day Saints
		GATHERETH
10	65	gather them as a hen G.—29:2; 43:24
		GATHERING
29	7	bring to pass the G. of mine elect
57	1	is the land I have appointed for G.
	15	and now concerning the G.
58	56	let work of G. be not in haste—101:68
84	2	for the G. of his saints—101:20
	4	built by the G. of his saints
86	7	and after the G. of the wheat
101	64	that work of G. my saints may continue
	70	for the beginning of the G. of my
105	15	lands consecrated for the G. of my
109	59	that the G. of thy people may roll
110	11	the keys of the G. of Israel
113	6	G. of my people in the last days
115	6	that G. together upon the land of Zion
	8	build a house unto me for the G.
	17	be built up speedily by the G.
123	1	G. up a knowledge of all the facts
		GAVE
1	17	and G. him commandments—20:7, 19
	18	also G. commandments to others
3	10	contrary to commandment which I G.
10	48	that my gospel which I G. unto them
20	8	and G. him power to translate
	21	the Almighty God G. his Only Begotten
	22	temptations but G. no *heed* unto them
27	7	he (Elias) visited and G. promise
29	35	I G. unto him that he should be an agent; I G. unto him commandment but no temporal commandment G. I
	42	I G. unto Adam and unto his seed
34	3	he G. his own life that as many as
38	32	for this cause I G. unto you the
39	4	as many as received me G. I power—45:8
45	8	G. I power to obtain eternal life
61	13	I G. unto you a commandment—95:7, 8
64	20	I G. commandment that his farm
74	4	G. *heed* to the traditions of their
75	6	I revoke the commission which I G.
93	4	the Father, because he G. me of his fulness
98	32	this is the law I G. unto my servant

Sec.	Vs.		Sec.	Vs.	
	33	this is the law I G. unto mine ancients	14	8	declare repentance unto this G.
103	4	commandments which I G. unto them	20	11	his holy work in this G.
132	34	Sarah G. Hager to Abraham to wife	31	3	declare glad tidings of joy to this G.
	39	for I G. them unto another	33	2	unto a crooked and perverse G.—34:6
	40	I G. unto thee an appointment	35	12	which I have sent forth unto this G.

GAVEST

45	4	the blood of him whom thou G. that	36	6	save yourselves from this untoward G.—109:41
			45	19	desolation shall come upon this G.
				21	this G. of Jews shall not pass away

GAZELAM

				30	in that G. shall the times of the
78	9	and my servant G., or Enoch, and		31	there shall be men standing in that G.
82	11	and my servant G., (Joseph Smith)—104:26, 43, 45, 46	56	20	inherit the earth from G. to G.
			69	8	Zion, to possess it from G. to G.

GEMS

			84	4	temple shall be reared in this G.—31
135	6	go down to posterity as G. for the		5	this G. shall not all pass away
			88	75	clean from the blood of this G.—138

GENEALOGY

				85	not clean from blood of this G.
85	4	neither is their G. to be kept	98	28	children's children unto third and fourth G.—29, 30, 37, 46; 103:26; 105:30

GENERAL

20	67	by direction of a G. conference	107	56	befall his posterity unto latest G.
	83	blotted out of G. church record	109	33	rise up in the midst of this G.
76	67	to the G. assembly and church of		71	be had in remembrance from G. to G.—117:12; 124:96; 127:9
85	1	keep a history and G. church record			
102	1	this day a G. council of 24 High	112	33	lest the blood of this G. be
	8	sanctioned by voice of a G. council	121	21	nor their posterity from G. to G.
	32	by the G. authorities of the church		23	a G. of vipers shall not escape
107	19	to commune with the G. assembly	123	11	that we owe to all the rising G.
	32	it may be brought before a G. assembly	124	50	unto the third and fourth G.—52
124	88	further instructions at my G. conference		56	his house have a place therein from G. to G.—59
	144	disapprove of them at my G. conference		69	for his G. after him from G. to G.—74, 77, 81, 82, 117
128	4	let there be a G. recorder; then the G. church recorder can enter on G. church book; his knowledge of the G. character; this is done on the G. church record; record of same on G. church book		78	interest in that house from G. to G.
				80	for himself and his G. from G. to G.

GENERATIONS

134	8	and the breach of the G. peace	5	9	shall be made known to future G.
			20	11	as well as in G. of old

GENERATION

			56	20	their G. shall inherit the earth
5	8	this unbelieving and stiffnecked G.	69	8	for the good of rising G.
	10	this G. shall have my word through you	70	8	shall be consecrated unto their G.
	14	this same testimony among this G.	76	8	show them even things of many G.
	18	unto the condemnation of this G.	84	17	continueth in church of God all G.
	25	then he shall say to this G.		18	his seed throughout all their G.—107:13
6	8	means of doing much good in this G.—11:8	97	28	upon her and her G. forever
	9	say nothing but repentance to this G.—11:9	109	24	standing in this thy house to all G.
10	33	overpower your testimony in this G.; that work may not come forth in this G.	110	12	all G. after us should be blessed

GENTILE

	53	if this G. harden not their hearts	18	26	both unto G. and unto Jew
11	22	grant unto children of men in this G.	19	27	which is my word to the G.
			57	4	running directly between Jew and G.

Sec.	Vs.	
		GENTILES
14	10	from the G. unto the house of Israel
18	6	stirred up to repentance both the G. and
20	9	gospel of Jesus Christ to the G.
21	12	before the world, yea before the G.
35	7	great work even among the G.
42	39	those who embrace my gospel among G.
45	9	standard for my people and for the G.
	25	until times of G. be fulfilled
	28	when the times of the G. is come in
	30	shall the times of the G. be fulfilled
86	11	continue a light unto the G.
87	5	shall vex the G. with a sore vexation
88	84	to go forth among the G. for the last
90	8	for the salvation of the G.
	9	unto the G. first and then to the Jews—107:33, 34, 35, 97; 133:8
107	25	to be especial witnesses unto the G.
109	60	who are identified with the G.
112	4	not only to the G. but also to the
113	10	their scattered condition among the G.
124	9	and the G. to the exaltation and
133	12	who are among the G. flee to Zion
135	5	that he would give unto the G. grace; now I bid farewell unto the G.

GENTLENESS

| 121 | 41 | only by long-suffering, G., meekness |

GEORGE

| 124 | 21 | let no man despise my servant G. |
| | 22 | let my servant G., and, build a house |

GET

10	15	to G. thee to tempt the Lord thy God—29
	19	that we may G. glory of the world
	56	build up churches to G. gain
64	27	forbidden to G. in debt to enemies
101	57	G. ye straightway unto my land
115	13	not G. in debt any more for building
121	39	as soon as they G. a little authority
123	3	as far as they can G. hold of them

GETTING

| 127 | 1 | in G. *up* their persecutions against me |

GHOST

(See Holy Ghost)

Sec.	Vs.	
		GIFT
3	11	as other men and have no more G.—5:31
5	4	you have a G. to translate; this is the first G. that I bestowed; you should pretend to no other G.; I will grant you no other G. until
6	10	thou hast a G. and blessed art thou because of thy G.
	11	thou shalt exercise thy G.
	12	make not thy G. known unto any save
	13	no G. greater than G. of salvation
	25	I grant unto you a G. if you desire
	27	in bringing to light with your G.
	28	I give unto you the keys of this G.
8	4	therefore this is thy G.
	5	remember this is your G.
	6	this is not *all* thy G.; you have another G. which is the G. of Aaron
	7	power of God that can cause this G.
	8	doubt not for it is the G. of God
10	2	you also lost your G. at the same time
	7	he has sought to destroy your G.
	18	we will say that he has no G.
11	10	thou hast a G. or shalt have a G.
14	7	which G. is the greatest of all
17	7	received the same G. like unto him
20	26	inspired by the G. of the Holy Ghost
	35	by the G. and power of Holy Ghost
33	15	I will bestow the G. of the Holy Ghost
39	23	they shall receive the G. of the Holy—49:14
43	4	none else shall be appointed to this G.
46	11	all have not every G. given unto; every man is given a G. by the spirit
51	5	he shall not retain the G.
68	25	baptism and the G. of the Holy Ghost
84	103	and receive money by G.
88	33	what doth it profit a man if a G., and he receives not the G.; neither rejoices in the giver of the G.
109	36	let the G. of tongues be poured out
121	26	by the unspeakable G. of the Holy
135	3	translated by the G. and power of God
136	27	for it is a free G. of the Lord

GIFTS

6	13	the greatest of *all* the G. of God—14:7
18	32	according to callings and G. of God—20:60
20	27	who should believe in the G. and

Sec.	Vs.		Sec.	Vs.	
46	8	seek ye earnestly the best G.	18	1	I G. unto you these words
	10	retain in your mind what those G. are		37	I G. unto you, Oliver Cowdery
	11	for there are many G. and to every		45	the blessings which I G. unto you
	26	all these G. come from God	19	32	last commandment which I shall G.
	27	given unto them to discern all G.	21	4	G. heed unto all his words which he shall G.—30:5
	29	that some may have all those G.	23	7	G. your language to exhortation
107	92	having all the G. of God which he	24	12	I will G. unto him strength
124	95	he may ask and receive the same G.		18	church shall G. unto thee in the hour

GILBERT, SIDNEY

			25	2	a revelation I G. unto you concerning
53	1	G., I have heard your prayers	28	3	the things which I shall G. unto him
57	6	let G. stand in the office I have	29	5	is his good will to G. you the kingdom
	8	let G. plant himself in this place		36	saying, G. me thine honor which is my
	9	let G. obtain a license, here is wisdom	30	4	until I G. you further commandments
61	7	expedient that G., and, be in haste		8	G. heed unto these things
	9	let G. and, take their former company	32	4	and they shall G. heed—5
	12	let G. take that which is not needful	36	4	this calling and commandment G. I
64	18	G. after a few weeks, shall return	38	18	to G. unto you greater riches
	26	not meet that G. and, should sell		19	I will G. it to you for the land of
90	35	not well pleased with my servant G.		32	there I will G. you my' law
101	96	contrary to my will that G. should sell		34	I G. unto the church in these parts
				39	the will of the Father to G. unto you; the riches of earth are mine to G.

GIRD

27	15	G. up your loins—36:8; 38:9; 43:19; 61:38; 73:6; 75:22; 106:5; 112:7, 14.	41	10	in the day that I shall G. them
35	14	I will G. up their loins	42	2	obey the law which I shall G.
88	141	G. himself according to the pattern		55	thou shalt G. it into my storehouse
				68	I will G. him liberally and upbraid not

GIRT

27	16	having your loins G. about with truth	43	1	G. an ear to the words which—58:1

GIVE

				6	this I G. unto you that you may not
1	14	neither G. heed to the words		16	that ye may G. even as I have spoken
5	13	I will G. them power—9:2; 100:10, 11; 104:10; 111:5	45	1	G. ear to him who laid foundation
6	2	G. heed unto my words—11:2; 12:2, 9; 14:2		61	I G. unto you that ye may now translate
	28	I G. unto you the keys of this gift	46	32	ye must G. thanks unto God
7	2	Lord, G. unto me power over death	50	1	G. ear to the voice of living God
	7	unto you three I will G. this power		31	if he G. you not that spirit then it
9	7	you supposed that I would G. it to you	51	1	and G. unto him directions
10	16	he will also G. him power again		4	G. unto him a writing that shall
	34	G. unto you commandment—18:3; 27:3; 35:6, 20; 37:3; 38:16, 40; 41:2, 9; 42:4, 5, 58; 43:8; 49:1, 11; 53:2; 58:50; 59:5; 60:13; 61:18; 68:33; 70:2, 6, 15; 75:25; 78:11; 82:15; 84:43, 73, 77; 88:62, 74, 76, 77; 90:12; 93:43; 94:1; 98:11; 100:7; 101:67; 103:34; 104:1, 11, 47, 54; 105:20; 124:144; 132:12, 51	52	14	I will G. unto you a pattern
			55	3	have power to G. the Holy Spirit
			56	5	I G. a new commandment—82:8
				16	that will not G. your substance to the
			58	34	I G. unto you further directions
			61	26	you shall G. unto all your brethren
			63	1	open your hearts and G. ear
				13	I G. commandments and many have turned
11	11	I G. these words unto thee		23	I will G. mysteries of the kingdom
	30	I G. power to become sons of God—39:4		41	I will G. unto my servant Joseph—124:125; 132:53

Sec.	Vs.		Sec.	Vs.	
66	8	G. him thine instructions	103	1	I *will* G. unto you a revelation
67	2	riches of eternity are mine to G.		5	counsel which I shall G. unto them
	4	I G. unto you a testimony	104	12	that every man may G. an account
	10	a promise I G. unto you—89:21; 100:8; 104:83; 118:3		63	I G. it unto you from this hour
70	1	hear the word which I G. unto my		73	the treasurer shall G. unto him
	3	which I shall hereafter G. unto—104:58		82	I *will* G. you the victory
	6	not G. these things unto the church		86	I G. unto you this privilege
71	3	this is a mission which I G. unto you	105	25	I *will* G. unto you favor and grace
72	16	every elder must G. an account of his	106	3	holy calling which I now G. him
	19	every elder who shall G. an account		8	I *will* G. him grace and assurance
73	6	I G. no more unto you at this time—94:17	109	56	that their prejudices may G. way
75	7	I G. unto him a new commission		64	lands which thou didst G. to Abraham
76	1	hear O ye heavens and G. ear O earth	111	4	I *will* G. this city into your hands
	22	this is the testimony which we G. of him	112	10	and G. thee answer to thy prayers
	93	and G. him glory forever and ever	113	10	or G. them revelation
78	7	G. unto you a place in the celestial	121	26	God shall G. unto the saints
	13	the ensample that I G. unto you	122	7	these things shall G. thee experience
80	2	I *will* G. unto you my servant Eden	124	6	G. *heed* to the light and glory
82	4	revelations and I G. them unto you; keep not my sayings which I G.		46	my holy words which I G.
	9	I G. unto you directions how you		49	when I G. a commandment
83	5	if their parents have not wherewith to G.		97	and shall G. him in the very hour
84	43	G. diligent *heed* to words of eternal	123	1	G. unto you the officers
	89	clothe you and G. you money	124	I	G. unto you Hyrum Smith
	105	if any man shall G. you a coat	126	I	G. unto you him for counselors
88	4	promise which I G. unto you	127	I	G. unto you my servant Brigham
	43	the stars also G. their light	131	I	G. unto you a High Council
	44	they G. light to each other	133	I	G. unto you Don C. Smith
	87	sun shall refuse to G. light	136	I	G. unto him Amasa Lyman
	104	fear God and G. glory to him—133:38	137	I	G. unto you John A. Hicks
	137	the spirit shall G. utterance	138	I	G. unto you Joseph Young
92	1	I G. unto the united order organized	141	I	G. unto you Vinson Knight
93	19	I G. unto you these sayings	127	5	I G. unto you a word in relation
	48	G. more earnest *heed* to your sayings	128	1	and G. you information in relation
	51	as I shall G. him utterance		10	I will G. unto thee the keys
94	16	until I G. you a commandment		16	I *will* G. you another quotation—17
95	13	I G. not unto you to live after manner	132	3	instructions which I am about to G.
96	6	to whom I G. promise of eternal life		28	I *will* G. unto thee the law
97	4	until I shall G. him other commandments		44	take her and G. her unto him that
98	1	in everything G. thanks		48	whatsoever you G. on earth; to whomsoever you G. any one
	12	he *will* G. unto the faithful		55	and G. unto him an hundred-fold
	36	I would G. unto them a commandment		61	and the first G. her consent
100	2	listen to the counsel which I shall G.		65	whatsoever I will G. unto him
	13	I G. unto you a word concerning	135	5	that he would G. unto the Gentiles grace
102	19	the president shall G. a decision			

GIVEN

Sec.	Vs.	
1	6	which I have G. them to publish
	8	power G. to seal both on earth and
	24	G. to my servants in their weakness
	30	to whom these commandments were G.
3	12	deliveredst up that which God had G.
5	2	I have G. these things unto you
	11	my words that are G. through you
	33	I have G. these commandments—43:8
6	31	the testimony which shall be G.

Sec.	Vs.		Sec.	Vs.	
9	9	save it be G. you from me	42	5	be G. by my spirit when they
	12	I have G. to my servant Joseph		11	not to be G. to any to go forth to
10	1	power G. to you to translate		14	spirit shall be G. by prayer of faith
	16	we will see if God has G. him power		15	until fulness of my scriptures is G.
	39	a more particular account was G. of		28	my laws are G. in my scriptures—59
15	5	my words which I have G.—16:5		65	to you it is G. to know the mysteries; to the world it is not G. to know them
17	1	which were G. to the Brother of Jared; directors which were G. to Lehi		69	the keys of the church have been G.
	8	commandments which I have G. you—20:77; 28:1; 70:3; 72:7; 75:4; 78:13; 84:57; 95:3; 101:10; 103:35, 40; 105:34	45	1	to whom the kingdom has been G.—72:11; 84:76
				58	earth shall be G. them for inheritance
				60	it shall not be G. to you to know
18	23	Jesus Christ is the name which is G.; there is none other name G. whereby	46	2	always has been G. to the elders
				8	remembering for what they are G.
	24	the name which is G. of the Father		9	they are G. for the benefit of those
	35	they are G. by my spirit—25:7; 61:27		10	what those gifts are that are G.
				11	all have not every gift G.; every man is G. a gift
19	10	punishment G. by my hand is endless		12	G. one and to some is G. another
				13	it is G. by the Holy Ghost to know—15, 16
20	2	which commandments were G.		14	it is G. to believe on their words
	10	which was G. by inspiration		16	G. to every man to profit withal
	21	scriptures which have been G.		17	to some is G. the word of wisdom
21	9	G. him through me by the Comforter		18	to some is G. the word of knowledge
24	5	writing the things which shall be G.		19	to some it is G. to have faith—20
	6	be G. thee in the very moment—84:85; 100:6		21	to some is G. the working of miracles
25	8	thy time shall be G. to writing		22	to others it is G. to prophecy
	11	be G. thee to make selection of hymns, as it shall be G. thee		24	it is G. to some to speak with tongues
27	14	those whom my Father hath G. me—50:41; 84:63		25	is G. interpretation of tongues
				27	G. unto them to discern all gifts
28	1	it shall be G. thee—88:64; 93:52; 101:27; 132:40		29	some may be G. to have all gifts
			47	1	transcribing all things G.
	7	have G. him the keys of the mysteries—35:18	48	5	it shall be G. to know the place
			49	20	not G. that one man should possess
	9	it shall be G. hereafter—53:4	50	1	words of wisdom which shall be G.
29	30	all my judgments are not G. to men		7	which has G. the adversary power
	33	it is G. that ye may understand		30	be G. you what you shall ask
	34	not at any time have I G. you a law		32	shall be G. power over that spirit
				35	kingdom is G. you of the Father
	47	power is not G. Satan to tempt		42	none that my Father hath G. shall be lost
	48	it is G. unto them			
30	2	you have not G. heed to my spirit	51	10	and G. unto another church
	6	I have G. unto him power		17	the hour and the day is not G.
31	11	it shall be G. by the Comforter—34:10; 35:19; 47:4; 124:5	52	17	according to the truths I have G.
				21	the commandment is G. to all
33	16	scriptures are G. for your instruction	56	5	revoke the commandment G. unto—6
35	20	scriptures shall be G.—42:56			
	23	G. him to prophecy; prove his words as they shall be G.		8	obey the former commandment G. him
	25	by the keys which I have G.	57	16	further directions shall be G.
36	7	this commandment shall be G.	58	16	his mission is G. him; it shall not be G. again
38	27	I have G. unto you a parable			
41	6	G. to them who are not worthy—90:26		18	laws of the kingdom which are G.
	12	these words are G. unto you			

Sec.	Vs.		Sec.	Vs.	
	38	other directions shall be G.	107	85	as it is G. according to covenants—86, 87
59	20	he hath G. all these things			
60	2	they hide the talent which I have G.	109	5	we have G. of our substance
	10	impart the money which I have G.		6	in a revelation G. to us—11, 60
61	27	G. power to command the waters: it is G. by the spirit to know		68	commandments thou hast G. to him
			111	3	as you shall be led and as G. you
	29	to you is G. the course to journey	112	15	keys which I have G. unto him—115:19
	33	inasmuch as it is G.			
64	4	I have G. unto you the kingdom		30	to you is power of this priesthood G.
68	8	acting in the authority G. you	124	141	knowledge of said bishopric is G. in
	11	G. to know the signs of the times		143	the above offices I have G. unto you
	12	G. power to seal them up to eternal	128	9	when the Lord has G. a dispensation; this power has always been G.
70	7	shall be G. into my storehouse			
71	1	power which shall be G. you			
	6	it shall be G. more abundantly		11	him to whom these keys are G.
72	9	in addition to the law G.	130	11	a white stone is G. to each
75	2	who have G. your names to—23	132	16	neither marry nor are G. in marriage
76	15	which was G. unto us as follows		37	because they were G. unto him
	18	it was G. us of the spirit		39	concubines were G. of me
	22	after the many testimonies G. of him		51	your wife whom I have G. you
	51	according to the commandment of G.—92:1; 94:15		52	receive all those G. my servant Joseph
	55	into whose hands the Father has G.		62	if he have ten virgins G. him; they are G. unto him—61, 63
77	8	to whom is G. power over four parts		63	fulfill promise G. by my Father
	9	to whom is G. seal of living God	133	60	for this cause commandments were G., in the day that they were G.
	11	to whom is G. power over the nations		62	shall be G. eternal life
78	16	and G. him the keys of salvation	134	6	and divine laws G. of heaven
81	2	I have G. the keys of the kingdom	136	37	keeping all the words I have G.
82	3	to whom much is G. much is required			**GIVER**
84	28	in whose hand is G. all power	88	33	neither rejoices in G. of the gift
	38	all shall be G. unto him			**GIVES**
	42	I have G. the heavenly. hosts	84	90	clothes you or G. you money
	73	these things are G. for your profit			**GIVETH**
85	3	to his law which he has G.—88:21	10	17	if God G. him power again
88	33	rejoices not in that which is G.	14	8	Holy Ghost which G. utterance
	36	all kingdoms have a law G.—38	46	7	ask of God who G. liberally
	42	he hath G. a law unto all things	84	46	the spirit G. light to every man
	141	according to the pattern G.—94:2, 5, 6, 12; 97:10	88	11	light which G. you light is through him
89	3	G. for a principle with a promise		13	which G. life to all things
90	2	keys of the kingdom G. unto you		45	the sun G. his light by day; the moon G. her light by night
	4	through you shall the oracles be G.			
98	20	words of wisdom which I have G.	98	3	he G. this promise unto you
101	15	they who have G. their lives for my name			**GIVING**
	49	might not this money be G.	20	43	and the G. of the Holy Ghost
	69	observe the commandments G.—103:29; 104:42	50	35	by G. *heed* and doing these things
			74	5	G. unto them a commandment
	78	according to moral agency G. them	89	4	by G. unto you this word of wisdom
102	22	if no additional light is G.	104	85	by G. your names by common consent
103	7	and the earth is G. to the saints			
	21	the parable which I have G.	128	3	G. the date and names and history
104	17	G. to children of men to be agents unto		21	G. line upon line, precept upon precept; G. us consolation by holding forth
	58	revelations which I have G. you—124:119			
105	29	according to the laws I have G.			

Sec.	Vs.	
		GLAD
19	29	thou shalt declare G. tidings—31:3; 62:5; 79:1
29	5	lift up your hearts and be G.—35:26
59	15	but with a G. heart and cheerful
76	40	this is the gospel, the G. tidings
79	4	let your heart be G. my servant
88	56	he was made G. with the light of
114	1	bear G. tidings to all the world
127	3	rejoice and be exceedingly G.—128:22
128	19	G. tidings for the dead; G. tidings of great joy; the feet of those that bring G. tidings
	20	G. tidings from Cumorah
		GLADDEN
59	18	to please the eye and G. the heart
		GLADNESS
19	39	lifting up thy heart for G.
40	2	he received the word with G.
75	21	shall be filled with joy and G.
128	19	a voice of G., for the living and dead
	23	brooks and rills flow down with G.
		GLASS
77	1	what is the sea of G. spoken of
130	7	on a globe like a sea of G. and fire
		GLOBE
130	7	on a G. like a sea of glass and fire
		GLORIES
43	12	if ye desire G. of the kingdom
66	2	be made partakers of the G. which—133:57
121	31	all their G., laws and set times
128	17	G. to be revealed in last days
	18	welding together of keys and G. and
		GLORIFIED
3	20	and be G. through faith
45	4	that thyself might be G.
64	13	this ye shall do that God may be G.
65	6	that thou mayest be G.
88	60	that his Lord might be G. in him; that they all might be G.
93	20	you shall be G. in me
	28	until he is G. in truth
132	63	that he may be G.
		GLORIFIES
76	43	who G. the Father and saves all the works
		GLORIFIETH
132	31	wherein he G. himself

Sec.	Vs.	
		GLORIOUS
20	16	the words of the G. majesty
42	45	have not hope of a G. resurrection
78	19	he shall be made G.
97	18	she shall become very G.
101	31	his rest shall be G.
109	23	bear exceedingly great and G. tidings
110	13	another great and G. vision burst upon us
128	17	this most G. of all subjects
	23	how G. is the voice we hear
133	46	clothed in his G. apparel
		GLORY
4	5	with an eye single to his G.—27:2; 55:1; 59:1; 82:19; 88:67
6	30	you shall dwell with me in G.
7	3	shalt tarry until I come in my G.
10	19	that we may get G. of the world
19	7	altogether for my name's G.—21:6; 98:3
	19	G. be to the Father, I partook and
20	4	to whom be all G. forever—16
	36	G. be rendered to his holy name
24	11	in me he shall have G.
25	14	the G. which shall come upon him
29	11	from heaven with power and great G.—34:7
	12	clothed in G., even as I am
43	10	G. shall be added to the kingdom
	25	by the voice of G., and honor, and riches
45	16	come in G. in clouds of heaven
	44	clothed with power and great G.
	56	when I shall come in my G.
	59	his G. shall be upon them
	67	the G. of the Lord shall be there
49	6	on the right hand of his G.
56	18	coming in G. unto their deliverance
58	3	G. which shall follow much tribulation
	4	ye shall be crowned with G.—75:5
63	12	for the good of men unto my G.
	66	more exceeding and eternal weight of G.—132:16
64	3	for this once, for mine own G.
	41	G. of the Lord shall be upon her
65	5	clothed in the brightness of his G.
	6	thine is the honor, power and G.
76	6	eternal shall be their G.
	19	G. of the Lord shone round about
	20	we beheld the G. of the Son
	39	through the triumph and G. of the Lamb
	56	who have received of his fulness and G.
	61	let no man G. in man but rather let him G. in God
	70	whose G. is that of the sun, even the G. of God, whose G. the sun

Glory   Glory

Sec.	Vs.	
	71	whose G. differs from that of
	76	who receive of his G. but not of fulness
	78	differ in G. as the moon differs
	81	we saw the G. of the telestial, which G. is of the lesser; as the G. of the stars differs from the G. of
	89	G. of telestial which surpasses all understanding
	91	we saw the G. of the terrestrial, which excels G. of telestial, in G., power
	92	we saw the G. of the celestial
	93	bow and give him G. forever
	96	G. of the celestial is one, as G. of the sun
	97	G. of the terrestrial is one, as G. of the moon
	98	G. of the telestial is one; as G. of the stars is one; differs from another star in G., so differs one from another in G.
	108	crowned with the crown of his G.
	109	we saw the G. and the inhabitants
	114	surpasses all understanding in G.
	118	bear his presence in the world of G.
	119	to God and the Lamb be G., honor
,,	3	represent the G. of the classes of
78	4	to the G. of your Father who is in
	8	that all things be done unto my G.
81	4	thou wilt promote the G. of him who
84	5	G. of the Lord shall fill the house
	24	which rest is the fulness of his G.
	32	shall be filled with the G. of the Lord
	82	in all their G. are not arrayed like
	101	clothed with the G. of her God
	102	G., honor, power and might be
88	4	the G. of the celestial kingdom
	5	which G. is that of the church
	18	may be prepared for celestial G.
	19	earth shall be crowned with G.
	22	cannot abide a celestial G.
	23	cannot abide a terrestrial G.
	24	cannot abide a telestial G.; he is not meet for a kingdom of G.; which is not a kingdom of G.
	28	your G. shall be that G. by which
	29	quickened by a portion of celestial G.
	30	quickened by a portion of terrestrial G.
	31	quickened by a portion of telestial G.
	45	they roll upon their wings in their G.
	104	fear God and give G. to him—133:38

Sec.	Vs.	
	107	angels shall be crowned with the G.; saints shall be filled with his G.
	116	this is the G. of God
	119	a house of G., a house of order—109:8, 16
93	6	record of the fulness of my G.
	7	I saw his G.
	11	I beheld his G. as the G. of the Only
	16	he received a fulness of the G.
	17	the G. of the Father was with him
	22	are partakers of the G. of
	36	the G. of God is intelligence
94	8	my G. shall be there
	9	my G. shall not be there—97:17
97	15	my G. shall rest upon it
101	25	knowledge and G. may dwell upon
	35	they shall partake of all this G.
	65	and be crowned with celestial G.
103	36	all victory and G. is brought to pass
104	7	a crown of G. at my right hand
109	12	that thy G. may rest down
	22	and thy G. be round about them
	37	rushing mighty wind with thy G.
	74	that thy G. may fill the earth
	76	crowns of G. upon our heads
	77	thou sittest enthroned with G.
121	27	in reserve for fulness of their G.
124	6	give heed to light and G. of Zion
	7	their G. as the flower which falleth
	17	I will crown him with great G.
	18	he shall beget G. and honor
	34	that you may receive honor and G.
	39	for the G. and endowment of all her
	60	contemplate the G. of Zion and the G. of
	87	the sickness shall redound to your G.
	95	and be crowned with the same G.
127	2	I feel to G. in tribulation
128	12	herein is G., and honor
	21	their keys, their majesty and G.
	23	proclaiming in our ears G. and
129	3	not resurrected but inherit same G.
	6	he will come in his G.
130	2	coupled with eternal G., which G. we do not
	7	all things for their G. are manifest
131	1	in celestial G. there are three heavens
132	4	and be permitted to enter my G.
	6	instituted for the fulness of my G.
	18	they cannot inherit my G.—27
	19	to their exaltation and G. in all; which G. shall be a fulness
	21	ye cannot attain to this G.
	57	even unto his exaltation and G.
133	32	and shall be crowned with G.

Sec.	Vs.	
	49	so great shall be the G.
135	6	scathe a green tree for G. of God; they lived for G., they died for G., and G. is their
136	31	be prepared to receive the G. even the G. of Zion
	37	ye cannot yet bear my G.

GNASHING

Sec.	Vs.	
19	5	weeping, wailing and G. of teeth—85:9; 101:91; 124:8, 52; 133:73

GO

Sec.	Vs.	
6	35	G. your ways and sin no more—24:2; 82:7
18	28	called to G. into all the world
19	27	that soon it may G. to the Jew
20	72	shall G. down into the water
24	3	G. speedily unto the church in
	17	whosoever shall G. to law with thee
25	6	thou shalt G. with him at the time
26	1	you shall G. to the west to hold
28	8	you shall G. unto the Lamanites
	15	from the time thou shalt G. until
30	10	until I command you to G. hence
31	6	G. from them only for a little time
	11	G. your way whithersoever I will; and whither you shall G.
32	2	he shall G. with my servants
	3	Ziba Peterson shall G. with them; I myself *will* G. with them
37	1	until ye shall G. to the Ohio—38:32; 39:14
	2	ye shall not G. until ye have
38	40	G. to with his might with the labor
	42	G. ye out from among the wicked
39	12	I *will* G. before thy face—49:27; 84:88
	14	not called to G. into eastern countries
43	33	wicked shall G. away into unquenchable
45	70	let us not G. up to battle
49	1	you shall G. and preach my Gospel
	11	G. among this people and say unto them
51	16	and command them to G. hence
52	10	let them G. two by two
54	7	G. to now and flee the land
56	5	Selah J. Griffin shall G. with him
	7	as many as *will* G. may G.
	9	to G. to the land of Missouri
59	9	thou shalt G. to the house of prayer
61	16	none is able to G. *up* to Zion
	22	whether they G. by water or land
	24	G. *up* unto the land of Zion—63: 41; 64:26; 72:24, 26; 90:28, 30; 103:34
63	39	shall not G. until I command them

Sec.	Vs.	
64	22	that shall G. with an open heart *up* to
66	6	G. not *up* to the land of Zion—103:34
	7	G. unto the eastern lands
	8	let Samuel H. Smith G. with you; I the Lord *will* G. with you
68	8	G. ye into all the world—80:1, 3; 84:62; 112:28
69	1	except one G. with him who will be true
	2	John Whitmer should G. with my
72	24	privileged to G. *up* unto Zion
75	6	to G. unto the eastern countries—79:1; 99:1
	8	G. ye into the south countries
	9	let Luke Johnson G. with him
	26	not fail to G. into the world
	27	made known whither they shall G.—79:2
76	36	they who shall G. away into lake of
	44	they shall G. away into everlasting
80	3	ye cannot G. amiss
84	62	whatsoever place ye cannot G. into; that the testimony may G. from you
	80	any man that shall G. and preach; they shall not G. hungry, neither
	92	G. away from him alone by yourselves
	105	G. your way rejoicing
	114	let the bishop G. unto the city of
88	52	G. ye and labor in the field—53
	92	Bridegroom cometh, G. ye out to meet—133:10, 19
93	51	let Sidney Rigdon G. his journey
98	33	not G. out to battle against
99	6	not G. until your children are provided for
	7	thou mayest G. *up* to the goodly land
101	44	G. ye unto my vineyard
	55	G. and gather the residue of my
	56	G. ye straightway unto the land—60
103	19	mine angel shall G. *up* before you—20
	30	until they have obtained companies to G.—34
	35	Baurak Ale may G. with you
104	63	see that ye G. to and make use of the
105	8	we *will* not G. *up* unto Zion
109	38	that when they G. out and proclaim
	56	when thy servants G. out from this
112	19	G. ye and I will be with you
117	5	let them G. saith the Lord
118	4	let them depart and G. over the waters

Sec.	Vs.	
124	49	and those sons G. with all their might
	79	to G. with my servant Hyrum
	85	let no man G. from this place
	88	G. and proclaim my gospel
128	22	shall we not G. on in so great a cause; G. forward and not backward; the prisoners shall G. free
132	25	many there are that G. in thereat
	32	G. ye therefore and do the works of
	50	G., and I make a way for your escape
133	5	G. ye out from Babylon—7, 14
	14	G. ye out from among the nations
	73	these shall G. away into outer darkness
135	4	after Hyrum had made ready to G.
	6	their names shall G. down to posterity
136	6	let them G. to with their might
	7	decide how many can G. next spring; to G. as pioneers to prepare
	16	G. and teach this my will; be ready to G. to a land of peace
	17	G. thy way and do as I have told
	25	G. straightway and tell thy neighbor

GO FORTH

1	5	they shall G.—5:11; 38:33; 42:5; 44:3
	8	they who G.
3	16	my work shall G.
5	6	G. and deliver my words
	18	their testimony shall G.
	19	a desolating scourge shall G.
11	26	you shall G.—42:4, 6, 8
19	5	but woes shall G.
39	15	men shall G. into all nations
	19	G. crying with a loud voice
	20	G. baptizing with water—42:7
42	11	not given to anyone to G. to preach
45	64	G. ye into the western countries
49	26	G. as I have commanded you
50	37	G. among the churches
58	13	that testimony might G. from Zion
	64	the sound must G. from this place
65	5	that his kingdom may G.—6
68	2	is appointed unto them to G.
72	21	that the revelations may G.
75	2	G. to proclaim my Gospel
	3	you should G. and not tarry
84	97	plagues shall G.
	117	G. ye as your circumstances will
88	84	to G. among the Gentiles
90	9	the word may G. unto the ends
96	5	my word should G. to the children
109	22	that thy servants may G. from this
112	5	let thy warning voice G.
	25	from my house shall it G.

Sec.	Vs.	
133	9	G. ye f. unto the land of Zion; that Zion may G. f. unto the regions
	10	let the cry G. among the people; G. to meet the bridegroom
	38	servants of God shall G.
	60	are to G. unto all flesh

GOD

1	9	when the wrath of G. shall be poured
	16	after the image of his own G.
	20	speak in the name of G.
	24	I am G.—5:2; 6:2; 11:2; 12:2; 14:2; 35:8; 49:5; 63:6; 101:16; 124:54, 71; 132:2, 12, 28, 40, 47, 49, 53, 54, 57; 136:21
	29	through the mercy of G.; by the power of G.—5:25, 26; 17:3
	39	the Lord is G.—76:1
3	1	purposes of G. cannot be frustrated
	2	G. doth not walk in crooked paths
	3	not the work of G. that is frustrated
	4	sets at naught the counsels of G.; incur the vengeance of a just G.—7, 13
	6	you have transgressed the laws of G.
	7	not have feared man more than G.
	10	G. is merciful
	12	deliveredst up that which G. had given
	13	sacred promises made before G.
4	2	ye that embark in the service of G.; ye may stand blameless before G.
	3	if ye have desires to serve G.
	5	eye single to glory of G.—82:19
6	3	salvation in the kingdom of G.—11:3; 12:3; 14:3
	4	the same is called of G.—11:4; 12:4; 14:4
	7	mysteries of G. shall be unfolded—11:7
	13	be saved in the kingdom of G.; the greatest of all the gifts of G. 14:7; 20:29
	16	there is none else save G. that
	20	faithful in keeping commandments of G.
	21	I am Jesus Christ, the Son of G.—10:57; 11:28; 14:9; 35:2; 36:8; 42:1; 45:52; 52:44; 55:2; 68:6
	23	what greater witness than from G.
8	1	as the Lord liveth who is your G.
	7	no other power save the power of G.
	8	it is the gift of G.; it is the work of G.

Sec.	Vs.		Sec.	Vs.	
	11	you may know the mysteries of G.			135, 140, 145; 132:6, 8, 13, 18, 26, 27, 52, 60, 64; 133:1
10	15	get thee to tempt the Lord, thy G.—29	22	4	seek not to counsel your G.
	16	see if G. has given him power	24	5	continue in calling upon G.
	17	if G. giveth him power again	25	1	hearken to the voice of your G.—33:1; 35:1; 41:1; 50:1; 81:1
	23	thinking to destroy the work of G.	29	18	I, G., will send forth flies
	28	not exempt from the justice of G.		22	men again begin to deny their G.
	70	your Redeemer your Lord and your G.—18:47	41	1.	G. caused that he should be cast out
11	21	you shall have the power of G.	42	1,	G. gave unto Adam and his seed; until G. should send angels
	23	seek the kingdom of G.		43	G. appointed to man the days of his
	30	give power to become the sons of G.—45:8	34	1	what I, G., shall say unto you
17	6	as your G. liveth it is true		3	might become the sons of G.—35:2
	9	I, Jesus Christ, your Lord and your G.—18:33, 47; 27:1	42	6	declaring my word like angels of G.
18	10	worth of souls is great in sight of G.		9	be my people and I will be your G.
	32	according to the gifts of G.—20:60		81	dealt with according to law of G.
19	4	I, G., am endless		87	delivered unto law, even that of G.—91
	16	I, G., have suffered these things		92	confess in secret and to G.
	18	which suffering caused myself, even G.	43	18	the trump of G. shall sound
	26	contains the truth and word of G.		23	hear the words of that G. who made you
	37	blessed be the name of the Lord G.—36:3; 39:19		27	these are the words of your G.
20	1	by the commandment of G.—94:15	45	11	whom ye say is the G. of Enoch
	2	Joseph Smith who was called of G.		18	which ye call the house of G.
	3	who was also called of G.		32	and curse G. and die
	6	G. ministered unto him by an angel		66	for the saints of the most high G.
	11	G. does inspire men and call them	46	7	ask of G. who giveth liberally
	12	same G. yesterday, today and forever		11	given by the spirit of G.—17
	16	the Lord G. has spoken it—36; 34:10; 49:7; 127:2; 133:74		13	to know that Christ is the Son of G.
	17	there is a G. in heaven, the same unchangeable G.		16	to know whether they be of G.
	19	the only living and true G.		26	all gifts come from G. for benefit of children of G.
	21	G. gave his Only Begotten Son		27	unto such as G. shall appoint; professing and yet be not of G.
	27	believe in gifts and callings of G.		30	according to the will of G.
	28	Father, Son, and Holy Ghost are one G.		32	ye must give thanks unto G.—59:7
	31	who serve G. with all their mights	49	15	not ordained of G.; for marriage is ordained of G.—18
	32	may fall and depart from living G.	50	15	and received them to be of G.
	35	nor diminishing from revelations of G.; which shall come by the voice of G.		18	if some other way it be not of G.—20
	37	who humble themselves before G.		23	which doth not edify is not of G.
	45	according to revelations of G.		24	that which is of G. is light; he that continueth in G.
	71	years of accountability before G.		26	he that is ordained of G.
	73	the person who is called of G.		31	you may know it is not of G.
	77	O G., the Eternal Father—79		32	shall proclaim that it is not of G.
21	1	through the willl of G. the Father		34	he that receiveth of G. let him account it of G.; accounted of G. worthy to receive
	6	G. will disperse the powers of	52	16	the same is of G. if he obey
	7	thus saith the Lord G.—12; 36:1; 38:1; 41:1; 51:1; 56:1, 10; 57:1, 3; 62:1; 64:1; 66:13; 69:1; 78:1, 2, 15; 82:7; 97:28; 98:30, 48; 101:95; 121:15; 124:32, 50, 51, 52, 53, 69, 71, 101, 119, 120,	53	1	made known unto you of the Lord, your G.
			56	18	they shall see the kingdom of G.

Sec.	Vs.		Sec.	Vs.	
58	3	cannot behold the design of your G.		66	come unto the city of the living G.
	7	upon which the Zion of G. shall stand		68	where G. and Christ are the judge of all
	13	the heritage of G.—17		70	even the glory of G., the highest
	18	laws given by the prophets of G.		79	not the crown over kingdom of our G.
	20	let G. rule him that judgeth		90	except him to whom G. has revealed it
	21	he that keepeth the laws of G.		92	where G. reigns upon his throne
	50	write a statement of the will of G.		107	fierceness of the wrath of G.—88:106
	51	inheritance for the children of G.		112	where G. and Christ dwell they cannot
	54	to labor for the saints of G.		116	Holy Spirit which G. bestows
59	5	thou shalt love the Lord, thy G. with		119	to G. and the Lamb be glory and
	8	shalt offer a sacrifice unto thy G.	77	2	in describing heaven the paradise of G.; every creature which G. has created
	20	it pleaseth G. that he hath given		5	who were then in the paradise of G.
	21	in nothing doth man offend G. save		6	it contains the mysteries of G.
60	4	know what bespeaketh the power of G.		8	they are four angels sent from G.
61	28	as the spirit of G. commandeth him		9	to whom is given seal of living G.; till we have sealed servants of G.
	31	lift up their voices to G. against		11	ordained unto holy order of G.
63	6	shall know that I am G.—101:16		12	as G. made the world in six days; will the Lord G. sanctify the earth
	10	signs come by the will of G.	82	6	anger of G. kindleth against the
	11	without faith no man pleaseth G.: with whom G. is angry he is not well pleased		18	for benefit of church of living G.
	24	this is the will of G.—72:8; 75:12	84	12	Esaias received it under hand of G.
64	11	let G. judge between me and thee		16	received priesthood by commandment of G.
	13	that G. may be glorified—65:6		17	continueth in church of G.
65	2	keys of kingdom of G. are committed		18	which is after holiest order of G.
	5	to meet the kingdom of G.		19	even the key of the knowledge of G.
	6	may kingdom of G. go forth		22	no man can see the face of G.
67	11	no man has seen G. at any time; except quickened by the spirit of G.		23	that they might behold the face of G.
	12	neither abide the presence of G.—13		27	until John whom G. raised up
68	1	by the spirit of the living G.		28	he was ordained by angel of G.
	4	the power of G. unto salvation		34	they become the elect of G.
	25	faith in Christ, the son of living G.		44	proceedeth forth from the mouth of G.—98:11
70	5	this is their business in church of G.		47	cometh unto G. even the Father
	10	who belong to church of the living G.		86	faithful who are called of G.
75	1	Alpha and Omega, your Lord, your G.		101	she is clothed with glory of her G.
76	12	so as to understand things of G.		102	power and might be ascribed to our G.
	21	before his throne, worshiping G.	85	3	it is contrary to the will of G.; names enrolled with the people of G.
	23	saw him on the right hand of G.		5	written in the book of the law of G.—7
	24	are begotten sons and daughters of G.		7	I, the Lord G. will send one mighty; to set in order the house of G.
	25	an angel of G. in authority; in presence of G., who rebelled; was thrust down from presence of G.		8	that man who was called of G.; to steady the ark of G.
	28	who rebelled against G., and sought to take kingdom of our G.	86	9	have been hid from the world in G.
	29	he maketh war with the saints of G.	88	5	even of G. the holiest of all
	33	doomed to suffer wrath of G.—104, 106; 87:6		12	proceedeth forth from presence of G.
	58	they are gods, even the sons of G.			
	61	rather let him glory in G.			
	62	shall dwell in the presence of G.			

Sec.	Vs.		Sec.	Vs.	
	13	G. who sitteth upon his throne	101	7	slow to hearken to G.; therefore their G. is slow to
	19	even in the presence of G.		82	a judge which feared not G.
	41	all things are by him, even G.		84	though I fear not G., nor regard man
	44	all these are one year with G.	102	4	according to the grace of G.
	45	roll, in the midst of the power of G.	103	5	the counsel which I, G., shall give
	47	hath seen G. moving in his majesty		7	observe the words which I, the Lord their G. shall speak
	49	when you shall comprehend even G.	105	8	who say, Where is their G.?
	61	according to decree G. hath made		32	that Zion is the kingdom of our G.
	68	that your minds become single to G.	107	3	after the order of the Son of G.
	75	may testify to your G. and my G.		19	enjoy communion and presence of G.
	78	that pertain to the kingdom of G.		42	Seth received the promise of G.
	85	souls may escape the wrath of G.		45	G. called upon Cainan
	92	sounding the trump of G.; the judgment of our G. is come		49	he walked with G. 365 years
	94	that persecuteth the saints of G.		80	is highest council of church of G.
	98	sounding the trump of angel of G.		84	none is exempted from laws of G.
	104	fear G. and give glory to him—133:38		92	having all the gifts of G.
	106	the Lamb of G. hath overcome	109	1	thanks be to thy name, O Lord G.
	108	works of G. in first thousand years		68	and vowed to thee, O mighty G.
	109	works of G. in second thousand years		70	and know that thou art G.
	114	cometh the battle of the great G.		77	O Lord G. Almighty, hear us in these
	116	this is the glory of G.		79	Hosanna to G. and the Lamb
	119	prepare a house of G.—109:8, 16	111	1	I, your G., am not displeased
	129	he shall be first in house of G.	112	10	the Lord thy G. shall lead thee
	130	when he cometh into house of G.	113	8	he had reference to those whom G.
	131	upon his knees before G.		10	bands of her neck are the curses of G.
	133	your brother through the grace of G.; walk in all commandments of G.	117	16	remember the Lord their G.
	136	for a salutation in house of G.	121	1	O G., where art thou?
89	2	will of G. in temporal salvation of		4	O Lord G. Almighty, Maker of heaven
	10	all wholesome herbs G. hath ordained		6	remember thy suffering saints, O our G.
	15	these hath G. made for the use of man		8	G. shall exalt thee on high
90	5	they who receive the oracles of G.		12	G. hath set his hand and seal to
	22	a man of G. and of strong faith		26	G. shall give unto you, knowledge by
93	14	he was called the Son of G.		28	whether there be one G. or many
	26	the spirit of truth is of G.		32	the eternal G. of all other gods
	29	man was in beginning with G.		38	left to himself to fight against G.
	30	that sphere in which G. placed it		45	wax strong in the presence of G.
	35	elements are the tabernacle of G.; man is the tabernacle of G.; G. shall destroy that temple	122	4	thy G. shall stand by thee
				9	for G. shall be with you forever
	36	the glory of G. is intelligence	123	7	imperative duty that we owe to G.
	38	G. having redeemed man from the fall; men became again innocent before G.		17	stand still to see salvation of G.
			124	24	or your G. will not dwell therein
	53	obtain knowledge of laws of G.		54	I am the Lord your G.—71; 132: 2, 12, 28, 40, 47, 49, 53, 54, 57; 136:21
97	14	pertaining to kingdom of G. on earth		104	the Lord your G. will heal him
	16	all the pure in heart shall see G.	127	2	G. knoweth all these things; the G. of my fathers has delivered me
	19	surely Zion is the city of our G.; for G. is there and the hand of		3	for Israel's G. is their G.
98	8	I, the Lord G., make you free		12	my prayer to G. is that you all
	47	if the children turn to their G.	128	5	only to answer the will of G.
				6	I saw the dead stand before G.

Sec.	Vs.		Sec.	Vs.	
	8	according to the ordinance which G.	76	59	they are Christ's and Christ is G.
	19	Zion, behold! thy G. reigneth; so shall knowledge of G. descend	84	63	for you are G. high priests
			130	4	is not the reckoning of G. time
	21	the voice of G. in the chamber of			**GODS**
	23	let all the sons of G. shout for joy			
129	4	saying he has a message from G.	76	58	they are G., even the sons of God
	9	whether any administration is from G.	121	28	whether there be one God or many G.
130	7	they reside in the presence of G.		32	eternal God of all other G.
	8	where G. resides is a great Urim and	132	17	henceforth are not G. but angels of
	12	I prophesy in the name of G.		18	because the angels and G. are appointed
	21	when we obtain any blessing from G.		19	pass by the angels and the G.
132	17	are not gods, but are angels of G.		20	then shall they be G.
	24	to know the only wise and true G.		37	and are not angels but are G.
	34	G. commanded Abraham, and Sarah gave			**GOES**
	56	and I, thy G., will bless her	84	103	every man who G. *forth*
	65	whatsoever I, his G., will give unto			**GOETH**
133	2	upon all nations that forget G.			
	3	shall see the salvation of their G.	10	27	thus he G. *up* and down in the earth
	17	G. hath sent forth the angel crying	42	64	let him that G. to the east teach
	34	is the blessing of the everlasting G.	52	14	he G. *forth* deceiving the nations
	38	servants of G. shall go forth	84	86	that G. *forth* to proclaim the gospel
	45	neither hath any eye seen, O G.	88	40	judgment G. before the face of him
	46	that cometh down from G. in heaven	133	15	he that G. let him not look back
134	1	governments were instituted of G.			**GOING**
	4	religion is instituted of G.	20	84	if G. to a church where they are not
135	1	exclaiming, "O Lord my G."	25	6	go with him at time of his G.
	2	through the providence of G. escaped	45	72	keep these things from G. abroad
	3	translated by gift and power of G.; he died great in the eyes of G.	65	1	whose G. *forth* is unto the ends of
			75	18	G. from house to house, village to
	4	I have a conscience void of offense towards G.	98	36	justify them in G. out to battle
			122	6	what are these men G. to do with you
	6	a green tree for the glory of G.	135	4	I am G. like a lamb to the slaughter
136	2	keep all the commandments of our G.			**GOLD**
	21	the G. of your fathers, the G. of Abraham	110	2	a paved work of pure G., in color like
	27	the free gift of the Lord thy G.	111	4	its wealth pertaining to G. shall be yours
	29	call on thy G. with supplication			
	32	calling upon the Lord his G.	124	11	come ye with all your G. and silver—26
		GODLINESS	128	24	and purge them as G. and silver
4	6	remember faith, virtue, G., charity			**GOLDEN**
19	10	behold the mystery of G.			
84	20	the power of G. is manifest	124	84	he setteth *up* a G. calf for worship
	21	the power of G. is not manifest			**GONE**
107	30	the decisions are to be made in G.	3	6	have G. on in persuasions of men
		GODLY	10	10	which have G. out of your hands 30:38
20	69	manifested by a G. walk and	11	22	study my word which has G. *forth*
		GOD'S	29	8	the decree hath G. *forth*—12; 101:10
19	11	eternal punishment is G. punishment		30	as the words have G. *forth*
	12	endless punishment is G. punishment	50	1	spirits which have G. abroad—2

Sec.	Vs.	
62	2	those who have not as yet G. up
82	6	all have G. out of the way
136	8	those who have G. into the army

GOOD

Sec.	Vs.	
6	8	shall be means of doing much G.—11:8
	13	if thou wilt do G. thou shalt
	27	if you have G. desires then shall
	33	fear not to do G. my sons; if ye sow G. ye shall reap G.—34
7	5	this was a G. desire
10	20	iniquity against that which is G.
11	12	that spirit which leadeth to do G.
	27	unto all who have G. desires
20	84	regular members in G. standing
21	6	cause heavens to shake for your G.—35:24
	7	in mighty power for G.
29	5	his G. will to give you the kingdom
33	4	there is none that doeth G.—35:12; 82:6
38	37	as seemeth them G.—48:3; 61:35
40	3	as seemeth me G.—42:16; 52:6; 56:4; 84:103; 100:1
41	8	as seemeth him G.—58:38, 51; 64:28; 124:72, 77, 80, 81
42	71	for the G. of the poor and for
50	44	I am the G. Shepherd
51	17	shall turn unto them for their G.
57	8	for the G. of the saints—12
58	27	be anxiously engaged in a G. cause
	28	inasmuch as men do G.
59	3	receive for their reward the G. things
	17	the herb and the G. things which
60	5	as seemeth you G.—62:5; 104:85
	9	all this for G. of the churches—69:8
61	13	for your G. I gave unto you a
	36	be of G. cheer—68:6; 78:18; 112:4
63	12	sought signs not for the G. of men
64	34	obedient shall eat G. of the land
72	12	consecrated to G. of the church
76	7	make known to them the G. pleasure
	17	they who have done G., in resurrection
81	4	thou wilt do the greatest G.
82	16	here is wisdom in me for your G.
89	5	it is not G., neither meet in
	8	tobacco is not G. for man
	16	all grain is G. for the food of
90	15	become acquainted with all G. books
	24	shall work together for your G.—98:3; 100:15; 105:40
96	5	subduing the hearts of, for your G.
97	7	that bringeth not forth G. fruit
98	10	G. and wise men ye should uphold
	11	cleave unto all G.

Sec.	Vs.	
101	40	it is thenceforth G. for nothing—103:10
111	11	I will order all things for your G.
122	7	these things shall be for thy G.
124	9	and soften many of them for your G.
	23	let it be a G. house, worthy of all
127	2	ordained for some G. end or bad; whether it be G. or bad
128	19	who bring glad tidings of G. things
134	1	for the G. and safety of society
	8	bringing offenders against G. laws
	10	provided such dealings be for G. standing

GOODLY

Sec.	Vs.	
97	9	fruitful tree planted in a G. land
99	7	thou mayest go up to the G. land
103	20	in time ye shall possess the G. land
	24	to drive you from my G. land

GOODNESS

Sec.	Vs.	
86	11	if ye continue in my G.
133	52	bestowed according to his G.

GOODS

Sec.	Vs.	
56	17	laying hold upon other men's G.
57	8	that he may sell G. without fraud
	9	that he may send G. also
134	10	to take from them this world's G.

GOSPEL

Sec.	Vs.	
1	23	that the fulness of my G. might
3	20	that they may believe the G.—19:27
6	26	records which contain much of my G.
	29	if they reject this part of my G.
10	45	throw greater views upon my G.
	46	contain all those parts of my G.
	48	this was their faith, that my G. might
	49	that this G. should be made known
	50	whosoever should believe in this G.
	52	bring this part of my G. to knowledge
	62	I will bring to light my G.
	63	that I may establish my G.
11	16	wait until you shall have my G.
	24	build on my rock, which is my G.
13	1	holds the keys of the G. of repentance
14	10	must bring forth fulness of my G.
18	4	all things written concerning my G.
	5	upon the foundation of my G.
	17	you have my G. before you
	26	who are called to declare my G.
	28	go into all the world to preach my G.—68:8; 80:1; 112:28
	32	to declare my G. according to power

Sec.	Vs.		Sec.	Vs.	
20	9	which contains fulness of my G.—27:5; 42:12		15	proclaim my G. as I have commanded
24	12	declare my G. with the voice of		24	sent unto world to proclaim the G.
25	1	those who receive my G. are sons	76	14	bear record of the fulness of the G.
27	13	dispensation of G. for the last times		40	this is the G., the glad tidings
	16	feet shod with preparation of the G.		50	this is the testimony of the G.
28	8	go to Lamanites and preach my G.		73	whom the Son visited and preached G.
	16	declaring my G. with sound of rejoicing—29:4		82	these are they who received not the G.
30	5	open your mouth to declare my G.—71:1		101	but received not the G., neither
	9	proclaim my G. with voice of trump	77	8	they who have the everlasting G. to
32	1	declare my G. and learn of me		9	the four angels having everlasting G.
33	2	declare my G. unto a crooked and		11	ordained to administering everlasting G.
	12	I say unto you, this is my G.—39:6; 76:40	79	1	proclaiming the everlasting G.
34	5	you are called to preach my G.—36:1	80	3	go ye and preach my G.
			81	3	in thy ministry in proclaiming the G.
35	12	who receive the fulness of my G.	84	19	greater priesthood administereth the G.
	15	poor and meek shall have G. preached		26	holdeth the key of preparatory G.
	17	I have sent forth fulness of my G.		27	which G. is the G. of repentance
	23	thou shalt preach my G.—39:11		75	G. is unto all who have not received it
36	5	to preach everlasting G. among nations		77	traveling to preach G. in my power
37	2	not go until you have preached my G.		80	any man that shall go and preach this G.—103
39	5	he that receiveth my G. receiveth me; he that receiveth not my G. receiveth		86	that goeth forth to proclaim this G.
				114	warn people of those cities with the G.
	18	as they receive fulness of my G.	88	78	instructed in the law of my G.
42	6	preaching my G. two by two		99	that they might receive the G.
	11	not be given anyone to preach my G.		103	the fifth angel who committeth the G.
	12	shall teach principles of my G.; which is the fulness of my G.		123	impart one to another as G. requires
	39	who embrace my G. among Gentiles	90	10	convincing heathen nations of the G.
45	28	light shall be fulness of my G.		11	shall hear the G. in his own tongue
49	1	preach my G. unto the Shakers	93	51	Rigdon proclaim G. of salvation
	3	to preach the G. unto them	99	1	proclaim mine everlasting G.—124:88
50	14	preach my G. by the spirit—68:1		8	continue proclaiming my G.
57	10	that my G. may be preached to those	101	22	worship me according to my G.
58	46	let them preach G. in the regions		39	when men are called unto my G.
	63	preaching the G. by the way	104	18	according to the law of my G.
	64	G. must be preached unto every creature	106	2	should preach my everlasting G.
59	3	blessed are they who have obeyed my G.	107	20	the letter of the G.—the baptism
				25	seventy are called to preach the G.
60	13	preached my G. among congregations of—68:1		35	open the door by proclamation of G.
65	2	G. shall roll forth unto ends of		38	to fill several calls for preaching G.
66	2	blessed for receiving fulness of G.	108	6	you shall have right to preach my G.
	5	proclaim my G. from land to land—68:1	109	29	will not repent when everlasting G.
				65	converted to fulness of everlasting G.
72	14	labors in administering the G.	110	12	dispensation of G. of Abraham
73	1	should continue preaching the G.	118	4	and there promulgate my G.
74	2	the Jews who believed not the G.	121	29	who have endured valiantly for G.
	4	the children believed not the G. of	124	2	make solemn proclamation of my G.
75	2	given your names to proclaim my G.			

Sec.	Vs.		Sec.	Vs.	
128	5	who should die without knowledge of G.			**GOVERNOR**
	17	most glorious of subjects of G.	101	87	let them importune at feet of G.
	18	without those who have died in the G.		88	if the G. heed them not let them
			124	24	if the G. which shall be appointed
	19	what do we hear in the G. received	135	7	the broken faith as pledged by the G.
133	36	angel having the everlasting G.			
	37	this G. shall be preached to every nation			**GOVERNORS**
			124	3	proclamation to the G. of the nation
	57	Lord sent forth fulness of his G.			
134	12	we believe it just to preach the G.; neither preach G. to, nor baptize them			**GRACE**
			17	8	my G. is sufficient for you—18:31
135	3	he has sent forth fulness of G.	20	4	according to the G. of our Lord—102:4
	7	their blood is witness to everlasting G.		30	justification through G. of our Lord
		GOT		31	sanctification through G. of our Lord
5	1	testimony that you have G. the plates		32	possibility that man may fall from G.
10	44	they have only G. a part of the account	21	1	through the G. of our Lord
90	22	let it be a man who has G. riches	50	40	ye must grow in G.
		GOULD, JOHN	66	12	my Father who is full of G. and truth—93:11
100	14	thy brethren, G. and, are in my hands	76	94	having received of his fulness and G.
		GOVERN	84	99	according to the election of G.
31	9	G. your house in meekness		102	he is full of mercy, justice, G.
38	36	to G. the affairs of the property	88	78	teach ye diligently and my G. shall
41	3	that ye may know how to G. my church		133	friend and brother through G. of God
42	59	to be my law to G. my church	93	12	but received G. for G.—13
		GOVERNED		20	you shall receive G. for G.
88	13	the law by which all things are G.	105	25	I *will* give unto you favor and G.
	34	that which is G. by law is also	106	8	I *will* give him G. and assurance
		GOVERNETH	109	10	we ask thee to assist us with thy G.
88	40	who G. and executeth all things		44	help thy servants to say, with thy G.
		GOVERNMENT	124	9	that ye may find G. in their eyes
102	8	removal from boundaries of church G.	135	5	that he would give to the Gentiles G.
123	6	present them to the heads of G.			**GRACIOUS**
134	2	no G. can exist in peace except	76	5	I am merciful and G. unto those who
	8	punished by laws of that G. in which	109	53	thou art G. and merciful
	9	to mingle religious influence with G.			**GRAIN**
	11	justified in defending the G.	89	14	all G. is ordained for use of man
	12	dangerous to peace of every G.	.	16	all G. is good for food of man
		GOVERNMENTS		17	mild drinks, as also other G.
124	143	above offices given for helps and G.	136	9	each company prepare fields for G.
134	1	believe that G. were instituted of God			**GRAND**
	3	all G. require civil officers	107	6	there are two divisions or G. heads
	5	all men bound to uphold G.; while protected by laws of such G.; all G. have right to enact laws—7	128	11	now the great and G. secret of
			129	9	these are three G. keys whereby
					GRANGER, OLIVER
			117	12	I remember my servant G., behold
				15	let no man despise my servant G.

Sec.	Vs.		Sec.	Vs.	
		GRANT		13	how G. is his joy in the soul that
5	3	no power over them except I G. it		15	G. shall be your joy with him
	4	I *will* G. unto you no other gift		16	if your joy will be G. with one soul, how G. will your joy be if you should
	14	to none else *will* I G. this power			
	22	I G. unto you eternal life	19	3	and the last G. day of judgment
	24	then *will* I G. unto him a view of		10	mystery of godliness how G. is it
	28	I *will* G. unto him no views		32	this is a G. and last commandment
6	25	I G. unto you a gift if you desire		38	G. shall be your blessing
8	9	whatsoever you shall ask that *will* I G.	20	13	therefore, having so G. a witness
			29	1	listen to the G. I Am—38:1; 39:1
11	22	until you have obtained all I shall G.		11	from heaven with power and G. glory
51	15	I G. unto this people a privilege of		14	before this G. day shall come—34:9
109	14	do thou G., Holy Father, that all		16	there shall be a G. hailstorm sent
124	31	I G. unto you sufficient time to build		21	that G. and abominable church
				48	that G. things may be required
		GRANTED	31	3	glad tidings of G. joy—79:1; 128:19
7	1	if ye shall ask it shall be G.			
10	47	it should be G. them according to	34	7	come in cloud with power and G. glory—45:44
98	2	the Lord hath decreed they shall be G.		8	it shall be a G. day at time of my
128	8	wherein it is G. that what you bind		9	G. destructions await the wicked
			35	4	thou shalt do G. things
		GRANTS		7	there shall be a G. work in the land
76	117	to whom he G. this privilege of seeing		10	G. things are to be shown forth
			38	5	until the judgment of the G. day
		GRAPE		12	angels are waiting the G. command to
89	6	pure wine of the G. of the vine		29	you say there will soon be G. wars
		GRASS		33	I have a G. work laid up in store
124	7	fearing them not, for they are as G.	39	8	I have bestowed G. blessings on thy.
		GRATIFY		9	thou hast seen G. sorrow
121	37	when we undertake to G. our pride		10	a blessing so G. as you never have known
		GRAVE		12	thou shalt have G. faith
128	13	baptismal font as similitude of the G.	43	17	the G. day of the Lord is nigh
				20	prepare for G. day of Lord—21, 22; 58:11; 133:10
		GRAVES		21	repent for G. day of the Lord—22
29	26	for their G. shall be opened—88:97		25	by the voice of G. hailstorms; by the G. sound of a trump
88	97	they who have slept in their G.			
	98	who are on earth and in their G.		30	for the G. Millennium shall come
128	12	the dead in coming forth out of G.	45	39	looking forth for the G. day of Lord
133	56	the G. of the saints shall be opened		44	clothed with power and G. glory
		GREAT		62	G. things await you
1	16	even Babylon the G., which shall fall	49	24	but before the G. day of the Lord
			56	18	kingdom of God coming in G. glory
2	1	before coming of the G. and dreadful—110:14; 128:17	64	33	ye are laying foundation for G. work; of small things proceedeth that which is G.
6	1	a G. and marvelous work is about—11:1; 12:1; 14:1			
	11	mysteries which are G. and marvelous	74	3	there arose a G. contention among
			76	2	G. is his wisdom
10	20	Satan has G. hold upon their hearts		9	their wisdom shall be G.
	64	I *will* unfold this G. mystery		114	G. and marvelous are the works of
14	11	G. shall be your reward—42:65; 76:6	78	17	have not understood how G. blessings
18	10	the worth of souls is G. in sight of	84	117	unto the G. and notable cities
			86	3	the G. persecutor of the church

Sec.	Vs.	
88	69	remember the G. and last promise
	75	fulfil this G. and last promise
	93	shall appear a G. sign in heaven
	94	that G. church the mother of
	102	to remain until that G. and last day
	114	then cometh battle of G. God
89	19	shall find wisdom and G. treasures
95	3	ye have not considered the G. commandment
97	18	Zion shall become very G.
101	52	what is the cause of this G. evil
105	12	I have prepared a G. endowment
	26	until army of Israel becomes very G.
	31	let my army become very G.
107	2	because Melchizedek was such a G.
108	3	be blessed with exceeding G. blessings
109	5	have done this work through G. tribulation
	23	they may bear G. and glorious tidings
	55	remember the G. ones of the earth
	59	that gathering may roll on in G. power
	61	thou hast a G. love for children of
	72	kingdom may become a G. mountain
110	3	as the sound of rushing of G. waters
	13	another G. and glorious vision burst
	16	G. and dreadful day of Lord is near
112	6	I have a G. work for thee to do
	33	behold, how G. is your calling
118	4	depart to go over the G. waters
123	14	should be attended to with G. earnestness
124	13	he shall be G. in mine eyes
	17	for his love he shall be G.; crown him with blessings and G. glory
	88	proclaim my gospel with G. joy
127	10	I desired with exceedingly G. desire
128	6	I saw the dead, small and G., stand
	9	according to decrees of the G. Jehovah
	11	now the G. and grand secret of the
	22	shall we not go on in so G. a cause
	24	the G. day of the Lord is at hand
130	8	where God resides is a G. Urim and
133	20	he shall stand upon the G. deep
	22	as the voice of G. thunder
	23	he shall command the G. deep
	27	highway shall be cast up in G. deep
	45	neither hath eye seen how G. things
	49	so G. shall be glory of his presence
135	3	he has founded a G. city; he lived G., and he died G.
136	35	their sorrow shall be G. unless they

Sec.	Vs.	
		GREAT BRITAIN
87	3	even the nation of G. as it is called
		GREATER
6	13	there is no gift G. than of salvation
	23	what G. witness can you have than
7	5	that he might do more or a G. work
	6	he has undertaken a G. work
10	43	my wisdom is G. than cunning of the
	45	which throw G. views upon my gospel
29	14	there shall be G. signs in heaven
35	3	I have prepared thee for a G. work —39:11
38	18	I deign to give unto you G. riches
58	2	the reward of the same is G. in
63	66	otherwise a G. condemnation
64	9	there remaineth in him the G. sin
82	3	who sins against G. light shall receive G. condemnation
84	19	this G. priesthood administereth gospel
88	37	either a G. or a lesser kingdom
107	14	it is an appendage to the G. priesthood
122	8	art thou G. than he
		GREATEST
6	13	which is the G. of all the gifts of —14:7
19	18	which caused myself, the G. of all
41	1	whom I delight to bless with G.
50	26	the same is appointed to be the G.
81	4	thou wilt do the G. good to thy
84	98	all shall know me, from the least to the G.
107	64	High Priesthood which is G. of all
		GREATNESS
133	46	traveling in G. of his strength
		GREATLY
109	48	they have been G. oppressed
110	9	hearts of thousands shall G. rejoice
121	42	which shall G. enlarge the soul
124	79	they shall be G. blessed
		GREEDINESS
56	17	whose eyes are full of G.—68:31
		GREEN
135	6	if the fire can scathe a G. tree
		GREETING
89	2	to be sent G., not by commandment
90	32	say to the brethren, in love G.
		GRIEF
123	7	who have been made to bow down with G.

Sec.	Vs.	
		GRIEVANCES
134	11	appeal for redress of all wrongs and G.
		GRIEVED
63	55	received not counsel but G. the spirit
121	37	the spirit of the Lord is G.
		GRIEVOUS
95	3	have sinned against me a very G. sin—6, 10
	10	which was very G. unto me
101	98	this is a very sore and G. sin
103	4	chastened with a G. chastisement
104	4	I have cursed them with a G. curse
109	48	because of their G. burdens
		GRIFFIN, SELAH J.
52	32	let my servants Knight and G. be ordained
56	5	my servant G. shall also go with him
	6	I revoke commandment given to G.
		GROANETH
84	49	the whole world G. under darkness
	53	the whole world G. under sin
		GROANINGS
88	89	earthquakes that shall cause G. in
		GROANS
123	7	the whole earth G. under its iniquity
		GROSS
112	23	darkness covereth earth and G. darkness
		GROUND
8	3	through the Red Sea on dry G.
84	80	hairs of his head shall not fall to G.—116
88	89	men shall fall upon the G. and shall
89	16	fruit, whether in the G. or above G.
104	34	all save G. reserved for the building
115	7	G. upon which thou standest is holy
133	29	parched G. shall no longer be thirsty
136	36	blood which crieth from the G.
		GROUNDS
124	46	because they pollute mine holy G.
		GROVER, THOMAS
124	132	viz., Charles C. Rich, G., and

Sec.	Vs.	
		GROW
45	58	their children shall G. *up* without sin
50	40	ye must G. in grace and knowledge
63	51	children shall G. *up* until old
69	8	that shall G. *up* on land of Zion
84	82	consider the lilies how they G.
86	7	let the wheat and tares G. together
109	15	that they may G. *up* in thee
		GROWETH
50	24	that light G. brighter and brighter
		GROWING
68	31	their children are G. up in wickedness
107	21	of necessity there are offices G. out of
123	7	influence been G. stronger and stronger
		GRUDGINGLY
70	14	be equal, and this not G., otherwise
		GUIDE
19	40	run about longer as a blind G.
45	57	taken the Holy Spirit for their G.
		GUIDED
46	2	as they are G. by the Holy Spirit
101	63	inasmuch as they are willing to be G.
		GUILE
41	11	in whom there is no G.
121	42	which shall enlarge the soul without G.
124	20	my servant Geo. Miller is without G.
	97	let him be humble and without G.
		GUILT
134	4	should punish G. but never suppress
		GUILTLESS
58	30	who am I that will hold him G. who
105	30	I will hold army of Israel G. in
		GUILTY
38	14	some of you are G. before me
64	22	I will not hold any G. that will go
68	23	inasmuch as he is found G.
104	7	that the G. may not escape
134	6	protection of innocent and punishment of G.

H

Sec.	Vs.	
		HABITATION
109	77	answer us from heaven thy holy H.
112	6	let thy H. be known in Zion
124	24	this house shall be a healthful H.
	60	let it be a delightful H. for man
	108	but let him change their H.
		HAD
10	60	I H. other sheep that were a branch
17	2	by that faith H. by prophets of old
	5	it is because he H. faith
25	11	sacred hymns to be H. in my church
31	2	you have H. many afflictions
38	13	a thing which is H. in secret chambers
72	6	these things shall be H. on record
74	2	law of circumcision was H. among Jews
	6	it was H. among the Jews
85	4	neither is their genealogy to be H.
101	44	a nobleman H. a spot of land
104	64	avails shall be H. in treasury
107	82	he shall be H. in remembrance before
109	71	that their names may be H. in remembrance
113	7	what people H. Isaiah reference to
	8	he H. reference to those whom God
117	12	his name shall be H. in remembrance—124:96
123	3	all persons who have H. a hand in
127	9	let all records be H. in order
128	2	I have H. a few additional views
132	39	prophets who H. the key of this power
		HAGAR
132	34	Sarah gave H. to Abraham to wife; from H. sprang many people
	65	I commanded Abraham to take H. to wife
		HAIL
109	30	and be swept away by the H.
121	9	thy friends shall H. thee again
		HAILSTORM
29	16	there shall be a great H. sent
		HAILSTORMS
43	25	by the voice of earthquakes and H.
		HAIR
9	14	a H. of your head shall not be lost

Sec.	Vs.	
29	25	not one H. neither mote shall be lost
84	80	an H. of his head shall not fall—116
110	3	the H. of his head was white like
		HALF
88	95	silence in heaven for H. an hour
		HANCOCK, LEVI
52	29	let H. and Coltrin take their journey
124	138	I give unto you H. and, to preside
		HANCOCK, SOLOMON
52	27	let H. and Carter take their journey
		HAND
1	35	hour is not yet but nigh at H.—58:4
2	1	by the H. of Elijah the prophet
3	2	neither doth he turn to the right H.
5	1	has desired a witness at my H.
	32	and receive a witness from my H.
19	5	to those who are found on my left H.
	10	the punishment given from my H. is
	13	received by the H. of my servant
20	3	ordained under his H.—25:7
	24	to sit down on right H. of the Father—66:12; 76:20
	82	or send by the H. of some priest
21	11	you are an elder under his H.
29	9	hour is nigh and the day soon at H.
	12	shall stand at my right H. in the day
	25	it is the workmanship of my H.
	27	righteous shall be gathered on my right H.; and the wicked on my left H.
	48	great things required at H. of fathers
30	3	inquire for yourself at my H.
31	7	I will establish a church by your H.
33	10	the kingdom of heaven is at H.—39:19; 42:7
34	7	the time is soon at H. that I shall
35	15	it is nigh at H.—104:59
	17	by the H. of my servant Joseph
36	2	I will lay my H. upon you by the H. of
38	22	what can stay my H.
	33	no power shall stay my H.

Hand 194 Hands

Sec.	Vs.
39	16 thinking I will stay my H. in judgment
	18 I will stay my H. in judgment
	21 for the time is at H.—78:3
42	43 and that not by the H. of an enemy
43	2 to receive revelations from my H.
	17 great day of the Lord is nigh at H.—128:24
45	37 that summer is now nigh at H.
49	6 taken his power on the right H. of his; which time is nigh at H.
55	2 shalt be ordained by H. of
58	23 the laws received from my H.
59	21 those who confess not his H. in all
61	6 all flesh is in mine H.
62	7 if he receive it from H. of the Lord
63	53 these things are now nigh at H.
72	3 required at the H. of every steward
76	3 who can stay his H.
	23 even on the right H. of God
84	3 dedicated by the H. of Joseph Smith
	6 received under the H. of his father-in-law
	7 received under the H. of Caleb
	8 received under the H. of Elihu
	9 Elihu under the H. of Jeremy
	10 Jeremy under the H. of Gad
	11 Gad under the H. of Esaias
	12 received it under the H. of God
	16 by the H. of his father Adam
	28 in whose H. is given all power
	88 I will be on your right H.
	119 I have put forth my H. to exert
85	7 holding the sceptre of power in his H.
	8 putteth forth his H. to steady the ark
87	6 feel chastening H. of Almighty God
90	30 receive an inheritance from H. of
97	19 for the H. of the Lord is there
101	71 and leave the residue in mine H.
104	7 promised a crown of glory on my right H.
107	44 was ordained by H. of Adam—46, 47, 48, 50
	51 was ordained under the H. of Seth
	52 ordained under the H. of Methuselah
109	23 thou hast put forth thy H. to fulfil
	69 preserved by thy fostering H.
	71 that thy right H. may exalt them
112	10 God shall lead thee by the H.
	15 my H. shall be over him
121	2 how long shall thy H. be stayed
	4 stretch forth thine H.
	12 God hath set his H. and seal to
122	2 blessings constantly from under thy H.
123	3 that have had a H. in their oppressions
	7 under most damning H. of murder

Sec.	Vs.
	9 have been murdered under its iron H.
124	19 who sitteth with Abraham at his right H.
126	1 it is no more required at your H. to
129	4 offer him your H. and request him to
	5 if he be an angel you will feel his H.
	8 he will offer his H. but you will not feel
132	1 as you have inquired of my H.
	39 by the H. of Nathan my servant
	51 I require an offering at your H.
133	56 stand on the right H. of the Lamb
	70 this shall ye have of my H.

HANDCUFFS
| 123 | 8 they are the very H. of hell |

HANDED
72	6 to be H. to the bishop in Zion
	13 an account shall be H. to the bishop
107	40 confirmed to be H. down from father
	78 it shall be H. over to the Council
128	4 to whom these records can be H.

HANDIWORK
| 104 | 14 built the earth as a very H. |

HANDLE
| 129 | 2 H. me and see, for a spirit hath not |

HANDLED
| 121 | 36 powers of heaven cannot be H. only on |

HANDMAID
90	28 my H. Vienna Jaques should receive
132	51 commandment I give unto mine H.
	52 let mine H. Emma Smith receive all
	54 I command mine H. to cleave unto
	56 let mine H. forgive my servant

HANDS
3	12 sacred, into H. of a wicked man—10:1
6	37 prints of the nails in my H. and feet
8	4 deliver you out of H. of your enemies
	8 you shall hold it in your H.; to take it away out of your H.
10	5 that you may escape H. of the
	8 delivered the writings into his H.
	10 which have gone out of your H.—30, 38
	23 I will require this at their H.

Hands   Hands

Sec.	Vs.	
18	7	been baptized by H. of my servant
	44	by your H. I will work a marvelous
20	41	by the laying on of H.—43, 68; 24: 9; 33:15; 35:6; 49:14; 52:10; 53: 3; 55:1; 68:25, 27; 76:52; 107:67
	58	authority to lay on H.
	70	who are to lay their H. upon them
24	16	lay their H. upon you by violence
25	8	he shall lay his H. upon thee
38	40	with the labor of his H.
39	23	on as many as ye baptize ye shall lay your H.
42	33	properties in the H. of the church
	40	the beauty of the work of thine own H.
	44	shall pray and lay their H. upon
	81	the church shall lift up their H. against
43	15	things which I have put into your H.
45	51	what are these wounds in thine H.
51	13	be kept in the H. of the bishop
52	39	let them labor with their own H. —58:60; 124:12
55	3	on whomsoever you shall lay your H.
56	17	whose H. are not stayed from laying hold; who will not labor with your own H.
58	51	moneys to be put in H. of the bishop
60	7	lifting up holy H. upon them
63	25	Zion, I holdeth it in mine own H.
	37	take righteousness in his H.
	44	these things are in his own H.
65	2	cut out of the mountain without H.
66	9	lay your H. upon the sick
67	2	heavens and earth are in mine H.
	14	conferred upon you by the H. of
68	19	ordained under the H. of—20, 21; 107:17
72	13	that which the Lord shall put into his H.
76	43	who saves all the works of his H.
	55	they are they into whose H. the
78	17	blessings the Father hath in his H.
81	5	lift up the H. which hang down
84	96	I have laid my H. upon the nations
88	74	cleanse your H. and your feet
	86	let your H. be clean until the Lord
	120	with uplifted H. unto the Most High—109:9, 19
	132	with uplifted H. to heaven—135
91	2	interpolations by the H. of men
97	12	which I require at their H.—105:3, 10
98	29	delivered thine enemy into thine H.
	31	thine enemy is in thine H.

Sec.	Vs.	
100	1	they are in mine H.—136:30
	14	thy brethren are in my H.
101	16	for all flesh is in mine H.
	54	saved mine vineyard from the H. of
	76	by the H. of those who are placed
	80	by the H. of wise men whom I raised up
	96	into the H. of mine enemies
103	2	smitten by the H. of mine enemies
	40	leave the residue in my H.
104	85	properties which I have put into your H.
105	14	I do not require at their H. to fight
109	4	the workmanship of the H. of us
	28	delivered out of H. of their enemies
	42	deliver thy servants from their H.
	72	kingdom set up without H.
	76	with palms in our H.
	78	the work of our H. which we have built
110	16	this dispensation committed into your H.
111	4	I will give this city into your H.
112	33	lest the blood, be required at your H.
113	4	it is a servant in the H. of Christ
115	15	I will not accept it at their H.
	16	I will accept it at their H.
117	5	let it remain in your H. saith the
119	1	surplus property to be put into the H.
121	9	with warm hearts and friendly H.
122	7	cast into the H. of murderers
123	10	the H. of the very devil to tremble
124	14	his stewardship will I require at his H.
	47	promises which ye expect at my H.
	49	require that work no more at H. of
	53	hindered by the H. of their enemies
	67	shall pay his stock into their H.
	68	in proportion to stock he pays into H. of; but if he pays nothing into their H.
	69	if any pay stock into their H.; convey the stock out of their H.
	70	receive any stock into their H.
	72	let Joseph pay stock into their H.
	73	they have asked it at my H.
	111	let Amos Davies pay stock into the H.
	117	and pay stock also into the H. of
129	4	request him to shake H. with you
	7	ask him to shake H. with you
	8	when you ask him to shake H.
132	5	who will have a blessing at my H.
	10	will I receive at your H. that which
	57	put his property out of his H.

Sec.	Vs.		Sec.	Vs.	
	60	the sacrifice which I require at his H.	58	35	my servant H. should be an example
133	32	crowned by the H. of the servants		38	other directions concerning H. shall
		HANG	70	1	word of Lord I give unto H. and
81	5	lift up the hands which H. down	82	11	expedient for H. and, to be bound
		HANGED	102	3	H., and, chosen standing High Council
121	22	that a millstone had been H. about		34	John Smith, H., etc., (signatures)
		HAPPINESS	104	24	let H. have appointed unto him his
77	2	in describing the H. of man and of		26	let H. devote his moneys for the
		HARD			**HARVEST**
19	15	how H. to bear you know not	4	4	the field is white already to H.—6:3; 11:3; 12:3; 14:3; 33:3, 7
124	116	lay aside all his H. speeches	45	2	summer shall be past and the H. ended—56:16
		HARDEN	86	7	until the H. is fully ripe, then ye
5	18	if they H. their hearts against	101	64	for the time of H. is come
10	32	Satan *will* H. their hearts			**HAS**
	53	if this generation H. not their hearts	10	18	will say that he H. no gift, that he H. no power
	65	if they *will* not H. their hearts—112:13		20	Satan H. great hold upon their hearts
20	15	those who H. their hearts in unbelief	20	73	and H. authority from Jesus Christ
29	7	mine elect H. not their hearts	42	11	by some one who H. authority
38	6	but H. their hearts, and wo, wo, wo		33	that every man who H. need may be amply
45	6	and H. not your hearts	61	1	voice of him who H. all power
	33	yet men *will* H. their hearts against	63	39	my servant who H. the care thereof
		HARDENED	68	18	no man H. a legal right to—107:16
84	24	but they H. their hearts and could		19	a High Priest H. authority to officiate
		HARDENETH	102	11	he H. power to preside over Council
82	21	the soul that H. his heart against	107	8	H. power and authority over all—107:17
		HARDLY		11	an elder H. a right to officiate
63	34	the saints also shall H. escape		14	H. power in administering outward
		HARDNESS		76	H. a legal right to the presidency
20	54	neither H. with each other	113	8	priesthood which she H. a right to
		HARM	129	4	saying he H. a message from God
10	25	behold, this is no H.	130	22	the Father H. a body of flesh and bones; Holy Ghost H. not a body of flesh and
42	27	thou shalt not do him *any* H.			
84	72	shall not have power to H. them	134	10	no religious society H. authority to
		HARMONY			**HAST**
128	20	between H., Susquehanna Co., and	6	10	thou H. a gift—11:10
134	6	peace and H. would be supplanted by	42	30	that which thou H. to impart
		HARRIS, EMER	109	61	thou H. great love for children of Jacob
75	30	let Carter and H. be united in the	136	27	be diligent in preserving what thou H.
		HARRIS, GEORGE W.			**HASTE**
124	132	viz., H. G. Sherwood, H., and	58	56	let work of gathering be not in H. nor—101:68
		HARRIS, MARTIN	60	8	preach the word, not in H.
5	1	as H. has desired a witness at my		14	not in H., neither in wrath
	26	I command H. that he shall say no more	61	7	let them be in H. upon their errand
	32	if H. humbleth not himself, he will		9	take their journey in H.—21
52	24	let Partridge and H. take their			

Sec.	Vs.		Sec.	Vs.	
63	24	not in H. lest there be confusion		11	become as other men and H. no more gift
93	51	let him go his journey and make H.	4	3	if ye H. desires to serve God
	52	let my servant make H. also	5	3	you H. no power over them except I grant it
101	72	be done in their time, be not in H.		4	you H. a gift to translate
133	15	let not your flight be in H.		10	this generation shall H. my word through you

HASTEN

				28	he shall H. no such views, for I will
52	43	I *will* H. the City in its time		31	thou shalt H. no more gift
88	73	I *will* H. my work in its time	6	23	what greater witness can you H. than
93	53	H. to translate my scriptures		27	if you H. good desires

HATE

				31	ye shall H. joy in fruit of your labors
43	21	if I call on you to repent and ye H. me	7	8	ye shall both H. according to desires
98	46	on fourth generation of them that H. me—103:26; 105:30	8	9	you shall H. knowledge concerning it
124	50	as they repent not, and H. me—52	9	2	other records H. I that I will give

HATH

				9	you shall H. no such feelings; you shall H. stupor of thought
6	7	he that H. eternal life is rich—11:7	10	4	or labor more than you H. strength
29	50	he that H. no understanding, it		59	other sheep H. I which are not of this
42	48	he that H. faith to be healed	11	16	wait until you shall H. my word
	49	he who H. faith to see shall see		21	you shall H. my spirit and my word
	50	he who H. faith to hear shall hear		27	I speak unto all who H. good desires—12:7
	51	the lame who H. faith to leap	14	7	you shall H. eternal life—101:38
	79	remember that he H. no forgiveness	17	1	you shall H. a view of the plates
49	21	or that wasteth flesh and H. no need	18	17	you H. my gospel before you
58	21	H. no need to break the laws of the land		18	you shall H. the Holy Ghost which
	41	he H. need to repent for he seeketh		19	if you H. not faith, hope and charity
72	13	he who H. not wherewith to pay		25	they cannot H. place in kingdom of
78	17	blessings the Father H. in his own hands		30	you H. that which is written before you
84	38	all that my Father H. shall be given		35	save by my power you could not H. them
	109	let not head say it H. no need of feet		37	search out Twelve who shall H. desires
	110	the body H. need of every member	19	23	and you shall H. peace in me
88	40	mercy H. compassion on mercy	20	26	all who believed should H. eternal life
	66	truth abideth and H. no end		58	nor deacons H. authority to baptize
93	42	that wicked one H. power over you		77	that they may always H. his spirit —79
	50	a bishop of my church H. need to be chastened	24	7	in this thou shalt H. strength
101	47	what need H. my Lord of this tower—48		8	patient in afflictions, for thou shalt H. many
127	11	cometh, but he H. nothing in me		9	in temporal labors thou shalt not H. strength; thou shalt H. wherewith to magnify
129	2	a spirit H. not flesh and bones as ye		11	in me he shall H. glory

HATING

			27	7	gave promise that he should H. a son
36	6	H. even the garments spotted with the flesh	28	8	thou shalt H. revelations but write not

HAVE

			29	29	cannot come for they H. no power
1	29	might H. power to translate through		39	if they never should H. bitter, they
	30	might H. power to lay the foundation			
	35	devil shall H. power over his own			
	36	Lord shall H. power over his saints			
3	4	a man may H. many revelations and H. power to do mighty works			

Sec.	Vs.	
33	12	they shall H. faith in me or they can
38	20	ye shall H. it for land of inheritance
	22	ye shall H. no laws but my laws
	33	I H. a great work laid up in store
	37	they that H. farms that cannot be sold
	39	ye shall H. the riches of eternity
39	12	thou shalt H. great faith
42	23	deny the faith and shall not H. spirit—63:16
	33	to administer to those who H. not
	43	whosoever are sick and H. not faith
	45	those that H. not hope of a glorious
	52	they who H. not faith to do these; but H. power to become my sons
	70	the teachers shall H. their stewardships
	92	that he may H. opportunity to confess
43	4	he shall not H. power except to appoint
44	5	that your enemies may not H. power
45	1	which live and move and H. a being
	5	come unto me and H. everlasting
46	14	that they also might H. eternal life
	18	taught to be wise and H. knowledge
	19	is given to H. faith to be healed
	20	it is given to H. faith to heal
	29	that some may H. all those gifts
48	2	as ye H. lands ye shall impart
	3	as ye H. not lands let them buy; necessary that they H. places to live
49	19	that he might H. in abundance
51	5	he shall not H. power to claim that
55	1	you shall H. a remission of your sins
	3	you shall H. power to give Holy spirit
56	14	you H. many things to repent of
	15	but H. pleasure in unrighteousness
60	3	taken away, even that which they H.
63	17	shall H. their part in that lake which
	18	they shall not H. part in the first
	27	that you may H. advantage of the world; that you may H. claim on the world
64	2	I *will* H. compassion
66	2	that they might H. life and be made
	12	you shall H. a crown of
68	16	they H. a legal right to the bishopric
	25	inasmuch as parents H. children in Zion
72	11	inasmuch as they H. wherewith to pay

Sec.	Vs.	
	20	let my servants H. claim for assistance
75	29	the idler shall not H. place in church
76	37	on whom second death shall H. power
77	8	these are they who H. everlasting Gospel
81	6	thou shalt H. a crown of immortality
83	2	women H. claim on their husbands; they shall H. fellowship in church
	3	they shall not H. fellowship in church
	4	all children H. claim upon parents
	5	after that, they H. claim upon church; if parents H. not wherewith
84	41	shall not H. foregiveness of sins
	72	poison of serpent shall not H. power
	78	I suffered them not to H. purse or scrip
	83	knoweth you H. need of these
	103	that inasmuch as they H. families
	104	let all those who H. not families
88	114	not H. power over saints any more
	118	and as all H. not faith seek ye—109:7
93	45	ye shall H. an inheritance with me
	49	lest that wicked one H. power in you
95	11	you shall H. power to build it
99	2	you shall H. power to declare my word
100	3	I H. much people in this place
101	21	then I H. other places which I will
	28	Satan shall not H. power to tempt
102	6	High Council can not H. power to act
	7	these seven shall H. power to appoint
	11	presidents H. power to preside in his
	18	the accused shall H. a privilege of
	19	understanding which he shall H. of case
	20	the case shall H. a rehearing
	24	High Priests H. power to call and organize
	25	shall H. power to appoint one of their
	27	they may appeal and H. a rehearing
	29	H. power to say whether it is necessary
	33	H. power to determine whether such case
104	10	not H. power to bring evil upon you
	27	H. the place upon which he now dwells
	28	H. the lot which is set off joining

Sec.	Vs.	
	29	H. the printing office and all things
	34	H. the house in which he now lives
105	10	that my people may H. experience
	21	those who H. families in the east
	37	they shall H. power after many days
107	9	H. right to officiate in all offices—12
	10	H. right to officiate in own standing
	19	to H. privilege of receiving mysteries
	74	necessary to H. other bishops and judges
	79	shall H. power to call other High Priests; shall H. power to decide upon testimony
	93	they should H. seven presidents to
108	6	shall H. right to preach my Gospel
109	5	that the Son of man might H. a place
	22	and thine angels H. charge over them
	34	O Jehovah, H. mercy upon this people
	50	H. mercy upon that wicked mob
	54	H. mercy upon all nations of the earth; H. mercy upon the rulers of our land
	62	H. mercy upon children of Jacob
	69	H. mercy upon his wife and children
	70	H. mercy upon all their connections
111	2	I H. much treasure in this city
	4	you shall H. power over it
112	6	I H. a great work for thee to do
	21	shall H. power to open the door of my
117	6	for H. I not the fowls of heaven; H. I not made the earth
121	21	they shall not H. right to priesthood
	24	I H. in reserve a swift judgment
124	26	all who H. knowledge of antiquities
	49	with their might and with all they H.
	59	his seed after him H. place in that house
	112	this let him do if he *will* H. interest
	121	let the quorum H. a just recompense
127	1	and H. not the least shadow of justice; all those with whom I H. business
128	13	that all things may H. their likeness
	25	I H. many things to say to you
129	2	not flesh and bones as ye see me H.
130	19	he *will* H. so much advantage in world
131	4	he cannot H. an increase
132	5	all who *will* H. a blessing at my
	20	be gods because they H. no end; be gods because they H. all power

Sec.	Vs.	
	44	you shall H. power to take her and give
	64	if any man H. a wife, who holds the keys
133	70	and this shall ye H. of my hand
134	5	all governments H. right to enact laws—7
	10	religious societies H. right to deal
135	5	prayed that they might H. charity; if they H. not charity it mattereth not
136	17	not H. power to stay my work
	31	to receive the glory that I H. for them

HAVING

12	8	full of love, H. faith, hope and
20	13	H. so great a witness, by them shall
	37	H. a determination to serve to the end
	70	every member H. children is to bring
	73	H. been commissioned of Jesus Christ
27	15	H. done all ye may be able to stand
	16	H. your loins girt about with truth; H. on breastplate of
29	49	whoso H. knowledge have I not commanded
33	4	priestcrafts, all H. corrupt minds
	15	whoso H. faith you shall confirm in my
	17	H. your lamps trimmed and burning
38	26	what man among you H. twelve sons
63	62	and use it in vain H. not authority
64	13	because ye forgive not, H. not compassion
77	8	H. power to shut up the heavens
	9	four angels H. the everlasting gospel
88	51	liken these kingdoms to a man H. a field
102	22	majority of Council H. power to
107	71	H. a knowledge of them by the spirit of
	92	H. all the gifts of God which he bestows
129	1	H. bodies of flesh and bones
132	1	doctrine of their H. many wives and their
133	18	H. his Father's name written on
	36	midst of heaven, H. everlasting gospel

HAWS, PETER

124	62	let H., and, organize themselves
	70	if H., and, receive any stock into

HEAD

9	14	a hair of your H. shall not be lost—84:80, 116

Sec.	Vs.		Sec.	Vs.	
28	6	who is at thy H. and at H. of church			**HEAL**
39	8	have bestowed great blessings on thy H.	35	9	they shall H. the sick
			46	20	to others it is given to have faith to H.
46	29	that there may be a H. in order that	84	68	in my name they shall H. the sick
50	30	and as ye are appointed to the H.	112	13	be converted and I *will* H. them
52	37	and placed upon the H. of Simonds Ryder	124	98	he shall H. the sick
			104		I *will* H. him that he shall be healed
84	109	let not the H. say to the feet			**HEALED**
107	55	I have set thee to be the H.			
83		their decision upon his H. shall be	42	43	are sick, and have not faith to be H.
92		which he bestows upon H. of the church		48	that hath faith in me to be H. shall be H.
110	3	the hair of his H. was white like the	46	19	to some is given to have faith to be H.
124	21	I seal upon his H. office of bishopric	124	104	I *will* heal him that he shall be H.
	57	this anointing have I put upon his H.; also be put upon H. of his posterity			**HEALING**
			24	13	except casting out devils, H. the sick
133	34	richer blessings upon H. of Ephraim			
136	3	a president and two counselors at H.			**HEALTH**
			89	18	shall receive H. in their navel, and
		HEADS	124	23	that the weary traveler may find H.
25	12	answered with a blessing upon their H.			**HEALTHFUL**
29	12	with crowns upon their H., in glory	124	24	this house shall be a H. habitation
39	15	it shall be poured forth upon their H.			**HEAR**
42	11	regularly ordained by H. of the church	1	2	neither ear that shall not H.
			11		that all that *will* H. may H.
56	4	to be answered upon H. of the rebellious	14		they who *will* not H. the voice of Lord
66	11	songs of everlasting joy upon their H.	14	8	witness of things which you shall H. and
68	25	the sin be upon the H. of the parents	24	6	they shall H. it or I will send them
70	15	manifestation of my blessings on their H.	29	7	mine elect H. my voice and harden not
82	2	lest sore judgments fall upon your H.	17		blood shall not cleanse them if they H. not
88	82	their sins are upon their own H.	34	1	my son, hearken and H. and behold
107	6	there are two divisions or grand H.	35	9	they shall cause the deaf to H.
109	76	and crowns of glory upon our H.		21	they *will* H. my voice and shall see me
110	5	therefore lift up your H. and rejoice	38	6	that *will* not H. my voice but harden
	10	poured out upon the H. of my people	22		H. my voice and follow me
121	33	knowledge upon H. of Latter-day Saints	29		H. of wars in far countries, but—45:63
123	6	present them to the H. of government	41	1	hearken and H., O ye my people; with the greatest blessings ye that H. me; ye that H. me not will I curse—133:16
124	21	blessings upon H. of the poor			
	48	bring judgments upon your own H.	42	2	hearken and H. and obey the law
	50	I will visit upon H. of those who		50	he who hath faith to H. shall H.
	52	and gnashing of teeth upon their H.	43	22	and make the ears of all tingle that H.
	92	patriarchial blessings upon H. of all my		23	H. the words of that God who made you
127	3	upon the H. of all their oppressors			
132	19	as hath been sealed upon their H.			
133	41	it shall be answered upon their H.			

Sec.	Vs.	
45	6	H. my voice while it is called today
	49	and all the ends of the earth shall H. it
	63	ye H. of wars in foreign lands; ye shall H. of wars in your own lands
50	45	you shall H. my voice and see me
63	1	H. the word of the Lord and his will—133:1
	2	H. the word of him whose anger is kindled
64	1	hearken ye and H. and receive my will
70	1	H. the word of the Lord which I give
	2	hearken and H. for thus saith the
76	1	H., O ye heavens and give ear
	16	concerning those who shall H. the voice
84	60	I say unto you who now H. my words
88	66	that which you H. is as the voice of
	94	long and loud and all nations shall H. it
	104	every ear shall H. it and every knee; while they H. sound of the trump
	129	that congregation may H. his words
90	11	every man shall H. fulness of gospel
101	94	that wise men and rulers may H. that
109	77	H. us in these our petitions
	78	O H., O H., O H. us O Lord and answer
127	6	let him H. with his ears that he may—128:2
128	9	this is a faithful saying! Who can H. it
	19	what do we H. in the gospel which we
	20	and again, what do we H.
	23	how glorious is the voice we H. from
133	16	hearken and H. O ye inhabitants
	26	their prophets shall H. his voice
136	32	and his ears opened that he may H.

HEARD

Sec.	Vs.	
18	36	you can testify that you have H. my
20	16	we have H. and bear witness to the
21	7	his diligence I know, his prayers I have H.
28	1	thou shalt be H. by the church
30	10	wherever you can be H. until I
35	3	I have H. thy prayers—38:16; 53:1; 112:1, 11
45	26	in that day shall be H. of wars and
52	36	declaring that which they have seen and H.
64	19	that which they have seen and H.

Sec.	Vs.	
67	1	ye elders whose prayers I have H.—96:6
76	10	which eye hath not seen, nor ear H.
	23	we H. the voice bearing record that
	49	we H. the voice saying, write the vision
	50	we saw and H. and this is the testimony
	110	and H. the voice of the Lord, saying
80	4	declare the things which ye have H.
102	18	after the evidences are H.—19
105	10	I have H. their prayers
109	57	we thy servants have H. thy voice
128	3	saw with his eyes and H. with his ears—4
130	14	I H. a voice repeat the following
133	21	his voice shall be H. among all people
	45	have not men H. nor perceived by
	50	his voice shall be H., I have trodden

HEARING

Sec.	Vs.	
50	36	blessed are you who are now H. the
102	20	after H. the evidences and pleadings

HEARKEN

Sec.	Vs.	
1	1	H. ye people of my church; H. ye people from afar—41:1; 45:1, 6; 46:1; 56:1; 63:1; 133:1; 136:41
5	5	if they will not H. to my words—124:46
15	1	H. my servant John
16	1	H. my servant Peter
25	1	H. unto the voice of the Lord—33:1; 39:1; 72:1
29	2	as many as will H. to my voice—33:6
34	1	H. and hear and behold what I
39	10	if thou wilt H. to my voice
41	2	H. O ye elders of my church—42:1; 43:1, 15; 50:1; 57:1; 58:1; 62:1; 64:1; 67:1
42	2	H. and hear and obey the law
43	17	H. ye, for behold the great day of
	23	H., O ye nations of the earth
	34	H. ye to these words, I am Jesus Christ
45	1	H. ye and give ear to him that
	2	H. unto my voice lest death overtake you
	11	H. ye together and let me show it unto
	15	H. and I will reason with you
49	1	H. unto my words my servant
51	1	H. unto me saith the Lord—69:1; 78:1
61	1	H. unto voice of him who has all power

Sec.	Vs.		Sec.	Vs.	
64	1	H. ye and hear and receive my will	17	1	which if you do with full purpose of H.
65	1	H. and lo, a voice as of one from on	18	27	take my name with full purpose of H.—28
70	1	H., O ye inhabitants of Zion	19	28	pray vocally as well as in thy H.
	2	H. and hear for thus saith the		39	and lifting up thy H. for gladness
75	2	H., O ye who have given your names	21	9	remission of sins unto the contrite H.
81	1	H. to the calling wherewith you are	23	2	thy H. shall be opened to preach truth
101	7	they were slow to H., therefore their God is slow to H.		3	thy H. is opened and thy tongue loosed
	74	if they *will* H. unto this counsel	25	12	my soul delighteth in song of the H.
	75	were the churches willing to H. to my		13	lift up thy H. and rejoice—31:3
103	4	they did not H. altogether to the	30	6	lifting up your H. to me in prayer
	5	inasmuch as they H. from this very hour	32	1	be meek and lowly of H.
	8	and H. not to observe all my words	33	1	discerner of thoughts and intents of H.
112	22	H. to the voice of my spirit	36	7	embrace it with singleness of H.
124	13	let him H. to your counsel—89, 112	39	8	thine H. is now right before me
	45	if my people *will* H. to my voice	40	1	the H. of my servant James Covill was
	110	even now if he *will* H. to my voice	41	11	this because his H. is pure before me
	118	H. to the counsel of my servants	42	22	love thy wife with all thy H.
133	16	H. ye inhabitants of the earth; H. to the voice of the Lord		25	he that repents with all his H.
	63	them that H. not to the voice of the Lord		40	thou shalt not be proud in thy H.
				74	testify before you in lowliness of H.
		HEARKENED	45	65	with one H. and with one mind gather
101	50	they H. not unto the commandments	46	7	that ye should do in holiness of H.
105	17	strength of mine house have not H. to	56	18	blessed are the poor who are pure in H.
	18	there are those who have H. unto my	58	5	that you may lay it to H. and receive
		HEARKENETH		15	which are unbelief and blindness of H.
84	46	that H. to the voice of the spirit—47		29	receiveth commandment with doubtful H.
		HEARKENING	59	5	thou shalt love the Lord with all thy H.
103	7	by H. to observe all the words which		8	even that of a broken H. and contrite
		HEART		13	let food be prepared with singleness of H.
1	2	neither H. that shall not be penetrated		15	with a glad H. and cheerful countenance
4	2	see that ye serve him with all your H.		18	both to please the eye and gladden the H.
5	24	humble himself in sincerity of his H.	61	16	upon the waters, but he that is upright in H.
6	16	that knowest the intents of thy H.	62	7	if he receive it with a thankful H.
	20	treasure these words in thy H.	63	55	he exalted himself in his H.
	22	night that you cried to me in your H.	64	22	that shall go with an open H. up to
8	1	ask in faith with an honest H.—11:10		34	the Lord requireth the H. and a
	2	I will tell you in your mind and H.; and which shall dwell in your H.	75	7	chasten him for murmurings of his H.
11	19	cleave unto me with all your H.	76	10	nor yet entered into H. of man
	26	treasure up in your H. until the time	79	4	let your H. be glad my son

Sec.	Vs.		Sec.	Vs.	
81	3	in prayer always vocally and in thy H.		63	Satan doth stir up the H. of the
82	21	and hardeneth his H. against it		65	if they will not harden their H.—112:13
97	16	all the pure in H. shall see God	19	7	that it might work upon the H. of
	21	this is Zion—the pure in H.	20	15	those who harden their H. in unbelief
98	14	I have decreed in my H. saith the Lord—104:5		37	with broken H. and contrite spirits
	45	thou shalt forgive him with all thine H.	27	9	turning H. of the fathers to children and H. of children to—98:16; 110:15
100	7	declare in my name in solemnity of H.		15	lift up your H. and rejoice—42:69; 128:22
101	18	they that remain and are pure in H.	29	5	lift up your H. and be glad—35:26
105	27	as I did the H. of Pharaoh		7	mine elect harden not their H.
106	7	notwithstanding the vanity of his H.		8	to prepare their H. and be prepared
107	30	in holiness and lowliness of H.	31	7	I will open the H. of the people
112	2	there have been some few things in thine H.	38	6	not hear my voice but harden their H.
	4	let thy H. be of good cheer		14	your iniquity, neither your H. of unbelief
	11	I know thy H. and have heard thy		19	if you seek it with all your H.
118	3	if they do this in lowliness of H.		29	ye know not the H. of men in your own
121	3	before thine H. shall be softened	43	34	treasure these things up in your H.
	4	let thine H. be softened and thy bowels	45	6	harden not your H.
	5	and in the fury of thine H. avenge		26	men's H. shall fail them and they—88:91
122	2	while the pure in H. shall seek counsel		29	they turn their H. from me because of
123	11	that we owe to all the pure in H.		33	men will harden their H. against me
124	15	because of the integrity of his H.—20		55	he shall have no place in the H. of
	54	save all those who have been pure in H.	56	15	your H. are not satisfied
	75	not fail, neither let his H. faint		17	whose H. are not broken and whose
128	17	turn the H. of fathers to children and the H. of children		18	whose H. are broken and whose spirits
130	3	that Father and Son dwell in man's H.	58	6	that your H. might be prepared
132	3	prepare thy H. to receive and obey		33	then they say in their H.
	56	I will make her H. to rejoice		52	children of men should open their H.
133	51	day of vengeance which was in my H.	59	15	with cheerful H. and countenances
136	11	if ye do this with a pure H. you shall	61	2	who confess their sins with humble H.
		HEARTS	63	1	open your H. and give ear from afar
2	2	he shall plant in H. of the children; H. of the children shall turn to their—27:9; 98:16; 110:15		16	if any shall commit adultery in their H.
5	18	if they harden their H. against them		57	those who desire in their H. in meekness
10	10	Satan hath put it into their H.—63:28	64	8	forgave not one another in their H.
	13	he hath put into their H. to do this		11	ye ought to say in your H., let God
	15	put it into their H. to get thee to tempt		16	they sought evil in their H.
	16	they say and think in their H., we will		22	I require the H. of the children of men
	20	Satan has great hold upon their H.	67	1	whose H. I know, whose desires I
	21	their H. are corrupt and full of		3	there were fears in your H.
	24	he stirreth up their H. to anger		5	you have sought in your H. knowledge
	32	Satan will harden the H. of the people	75	25	as brethren are willing to open their H.
	53	if this generation harden not their H.	78	10	Satan seeketh to turn their H.

Sec.	Vs.		Sec.	Vs.	
					HEATHEN
84	1	as they united their H. and lifted	45	54	then shall H. nations be redeemed
	24	they hardened their H. and could not	75	22	it shall be more tolerable for the H.
	76	upbraided for their evil H. of unbelief	90	10	convincing the nations, the H. nations
	88	my spirit shall be in your H.			**HEAVEN**
86	3	in whose H. the enemy sitteth to reign	1	8	to seal both on earth and in H.
				13	his sword is bathed in H.
88	3	that it may abide in your H.		17	I spake unto him from H.
	62	to ponder in your H. with this	5	12	for from H. will I declare it unto
	71	ponder the warning in your H.	6	27	lay up treasures for yourself in H.
	74	purify your H. and cleanse your hands		37	ye shall inherit the kingdom of H.
	109	the thoughts and intents of their H.	10	55	such shall inherit the kingdom of H.
89	4	will exist in the H. of conspiring men	20	17	we know that there is a God in H.; the framer of H. and earth and all
96	5	for the purpose of subduing the H.		24	and ascended into H. to sit down on
97	8	who know their H. are honest	27	13	both which are in H. and which are on
98	1	let your H. be comforted—100:15; 101:16	29	11	I will reveal myself from H. with
	17	the H. of the Jews unto the prophets		14	the stars shall fall from H.; there shall be greater signs in H.—45:42
	18	let not your H. be troubled		23	the H. and earth shall be consumed; there shall be a new H. and a new earth
	20	do not forsake the pride of their H.			
	47	and turn unto the Lord with all their H.		24	all things shall become new even the H.
100	5	the thoughts that I shall put into your H.		36	a third part of the hosts of H. turned
	12	continue your journey and let your H. rejoice	33	10	the kingdom of H. is at hand—39:19; 42:7
103	19	therefore let not your H. faint	38	1	looked upon all the seraphic hosts of H.
104	80	I will soften the H. of those—81; 105:27		11	in presence of all the hosts of H.
109	1	uprightly before thee with all their H.	43	18	the Lord shall utter his voice out of H.—23
	38	prepare the H. of thy saints for all	45	16	come in my glory in the clouds of H.
	48	our H. flow out with sorrow		44	they shall see me in the clouds of H.
	56	that their H. may be softened		69	gathered out of every nation under H.—64:42
110	6	let the H. of your brethren rejoice; and H. of my people rejoice	49	7	no man knoweth not even angels in H.
	9	yea the H. of thousands and tens of	50	27	subject unto him, both in H. and on
112	28	but purify your H. before me	56	11	though the H. and earth pass away
	33	cleanse your H. and your garments	58	2	reward is greater in kingdom of H.
121	9	they shall hail thee again with warm H.	62	3	the testimony is recorded in H.
	13	also because their H. are corrupted	63	34	I will come down in H. from presence
	35	because their H. are set so much upon	65	5	Son of man shall come down in H.
123	7	who have inherited lies, upon the H. of		6	that the kingdom of H. may come; mayest be glorified in H.
124	9	I will visit and soften their H.	76	9	and their understanding reach to H.
	76	turn away their H. from affliction		63	when he shall come in the clouds of H.
135	7	that will touch the H. of honest men		68	they whose names are written in H.
		HEAT			
84	92	pure water, whether in H. or cold			
101	25	that of element shall melt with fervent H.			

Sec.	Vs.	
	109	innumerable as stars in firmament of H.
77	2	used by the Revelator in describing H.
78	4	to glory of your Father who is in H.
84	83	for your Father who is in H. knoweth
	92	testimony to your Father which is in H.
	119	put forth my hand to exert powers of H.
87	6	with earthquakes and thunder of H. shall
88	79	of things both in H. and earth
	92	angels shall fly through midst of H.
	93	there shall appear a great sign in H.
	95	there shall be silence in H. for space; after shall curtain of H. be unfolded
	97	to meet him in midst of the pillar of H.
	103	flying through the midst of H.—133:36
	104	saying to all people both in H. and
	112	shall gather his armies even hosts of H.
	132	arise and with uplifted hands to H.
	135	salute with uplifted hands to H.
89	14	beasts of field and fowls of H.
93	15	there came a voice out of H. saying
	17	he received all power both in H. and
101	34	things that are upon earth and in H.
102	4	act in that office according to law of H.
106	3	seeking diligently the kingdom of H.
	6	there was joy in H. when my servant
107	19	receiving mysteries of the kingdom of H.
	33	agreeable to the institution of H.
109	52	that they may be wasted away from under H.
	77	these our petitions and answer us from H.
110	13	who was taken to H. without tasting
112	32	being sent down from H. unto you
117	6	have I not the fowls of H. and also
121	4	Maker of the H., earth and seas
	15	their posterity shall be swept from under H.
	33	pouring down knowledge from H.
	36	inseparably connected with powers of H.; powers of H. cannot be controlled
	45	distil upon thy soul as the dews from H.
123	13	they are truly manifest from H.

Sec.	Vs.	
124	93	what he shall bind on earth shall be bound in H.; loose on earth shall be loosed in H.—127:7; 128:8, 10; 132:46
127	4	for all this there is a reward in H.
	7	that it may be recorded in H.—128:7
128	7	the record which is kept in H.
	8	record on earth shall be recorded in H.; not record on earth, not be recorded in H.
	9	which records on earth and binds in H.; it became a law on earth and in H.
	10	I give thee the keys of kingdom of H.; shalt bind on earth shall be bound in H.; loose on earth shalt be loosed in H.
	14	second man is the Lord from H.; truly made out so are records in H.
	19	a voice of mercy from H.
	20	Moroni, an angel from H. declaring
	23	how glorious the voice we hear from H.
129	1	there are two kinds of beings in H.
	7	contrary to order of H. for a just man
130	20	law, irrevocably decreed in H.
132	16	but are appointed angels in H.
	46	sins you retain on earth, be retained in H.
	48	without condemnation on earth and in H.
133	7	from one end of H. to the other
	17	angel crying through midst of H.
	39	worship him that made H. and earth
	46	cometh down from God in H. with dyed
134	6	and divine laws given of H., prescribing

HEAVENLY

76	14	with whom we conversed in H. vision
	66	the H. place the holiest of all
	89	thus we saw in the H. vision, the glory
78	5	equal in bonds of H. things; for obtaining of H. things
	6	cannot be equal in obtaining H. things
84	42	I have given the H. hosts charge
123	6	which is enjoined on us by our H. Father
128	13	earthly conforming to that which is H.
	14	as is the H.; such are they that are H.

Sec.	Vs.	
		HEAVENS
1	38	though the H. and earth pass away
14	9	who created the H. and the earth
21	6	cause the H. to shake for your good —35:24
43	18	H. shall shake and earth tremble
45	1	who made the H. and all the hosts thereof
	22	the H. and the earth shall pass away
	40	shown forth in the H. above
	48	reel to and fro and the H. shall shake
49	6	and now reigneth in H. and will
	23	looking for the H. to be shaken
52	19	spirits in all cases under the whole H.
60	4	I the Lord rule in the H. above
67	2	the H. and earth are in mine hands
76	1	hear O ye H. and give ear O earth
	26	called perdition, for H. wept over him
	40	voice out of H. bore record unto us
77	8	having power to shut up the H.
84	42	by mine own voice out of the H.
	101	the H. have smiled upon her
	118	but the starry H. shall tremble
88	43	even the courses of the H. and earth
93	15	the H. were opened and the Holy Ghost
101	24	or of the fowls of the H., or of
104	14	I stretched out the H. and built the
107	19	to have the H. opened unto them
109	74	when thou shalt unveil the H. and
110	11	the H. were again opened unto us
121	2	thine eye behold from the eternal H.
	30	if there be bounds set to the H.
	33	what power shall stay the H.
	37	behold, the H. withdraw themselves
122	7	if the H. gather blackness and all
131	1	in celestial glory there are three H.
132	46	shall be eternally bound in the H.; shall be remitted eternally in the H.
133	40	O that thou wouldst rend the H.
	69	I clothe the H. with blackness
	71	when I called to you out of the H.
136	37	by mine own voice out of the H.
		HEAVIEST
41	1	curse with the H. of all cursings
		HEAVING
88	90	waves of the sea H. themselves beyond
		HEDGE
101	46	planted olive-trees and built a H.
	51	enemy came and broke down the H.

Sec.	Vs.	
	53	and built the H. round about
	54	kept the enemy from breaking down the H.
122	7	elements combine to H. up the way
		HEED
101	87	if he H. them not, let them importune
	88	if the Governor H. them not, let them
	89	if the President H. them not, then will
		(See Gave, Give, Given, Giving, Take)
		HEEL
121	16	all those that shall lift up the H. against
124	99	where serpent cannot lay hold upon his H.
		HEIGHT
76	48	the H., the depth, the misery thereof
		HEIGHTS
132	19	and shall inherit all H. and depths
		HEIRS
7	6	those who shall be H. of salvation
52	2	who are H. according to the covenant
70	8	as they become H. according to the laws
76	88	they shall be H. of salvation
86	9	ye are lawful H. according to the flesh
124	69	so long as he and his H. shall hold
		HELD
20	81	to attend the several conferences H.
46	3	meetings which are H. before the world
52	2	conference which shall be H. in Missouri
58	62	direct the conference which shall be H.
118	1	let a conference be H. immediately
121	27	as H. in reserve for the fulness of
127	9	to be H. in remembrance from generation
134	2	except laws are framed and H. inviolate
	12	allowing human beings to be H. in
		HELL
6	34	let earth and H. combine against you
10	26	until he draggeth their souls down to H.
	69	gates of H. shall not prevail against —17:8; 18:5; 21:6; 33:13; 98:22; 128:10

Sec.	Vs.	
29	38	there is a place prepared which place is H.
63	4	is able to cast the soul down to H.
76	84	they who are thrust down to H.—106
88	113	his armies, even the hosts of H.
104	18	lift up his eyes in H. being in torment
121	23	vipers shall not escape damnation of H.
122	1	and H. shall rage against thee
	7	if the very jaws of H. shall gape open
123	8	they are the very shackles and fetters of H.
	10	are enough to make H. itself shudder

HELLISH

123	6	in all their dark and H. hue

HELM

123	16	benefited very much by a very small H.

HELMET

27	18	take the H. of salvation and sword of

HELP

104	72	I have need of this to H. me in my
	73	to H. him in his stewardship
109	44	H. thy servants to say, Thy will be done
	79	H. us by the power of thy spirit
124	11	come with your gold and silver to the H.
	12	let my servant H. you to write this
	16	let my servant H. you in your labor

HELPS

124	143	for H. and governments, for the work of

HEN

10	65	I will gather them as a H. gathereth—29:2
43	24	gathered you together as a H.

HENCE

30	10	until I command you to go from H.—51:16
45	63	not many years H. ye shall hear of wars
88	87	not many days H. and the earth shall
105	15	not many years H. they shall not be
121	15	not many years H. they and their posterity
	40	H. many are called but few are chosen

Sec.	Vs.	
128	9	H. whatsoever those men did in authority
	12	H. this ordinance was instituted to

HENCEFORTH

23	2	preach the truth from H. and forever
	5	this is thy duty from H. and forever
30	11	be in Zion with all your soul from H.
38	15	therefore be ye strong from H.
63	49	dead that die in the Lord from H.
82	2	beware from H. and refrain from sin
84	77	for from H. I shall call you friends
90	2	thou art blessed from H. that bear
96	6	as he keepeth my commandments from H.
108	3	arise up and be more careful H.
	6	wheresoever I shall send you from H.
118	3	an effectual door shall be opened from H.
124	13	let him be true in all things from H.
	89	let him from H. hearken to the counsel
	92	from H. he shall hold the keys of
126	3	from this time H. and forever
127	2	and will deliver me from H.
132	17	from H. are not Gods but are angels
	53	from H. I will strengthen him

HENCEFORWARD

135	6	H. their names will be classed among

HERB

59	17	the H. and the good things which
89	8	is an H. for bruises and sick cattle
	11	every H. in the season thereof

HERBS

42	43	with all tenderness, with H. and mild
89	10	all wholesome H. God hath ordained for

HERDS

136	11	blessed in your flocks and your H.

HERE

10	34	behold H. is wisdom—37:4; 57:3, 9, 12; 58:23, 53; 82:16; 95:13; 96:1; 101:41; 107:92
	35	marvel not that I said H. is wisdom
38	26	clothed in robes, and sit thou H.
42	67	sufficient to establish you both H. and
64	26	sell their store and possessions H.

Sec.	Vs.	
93	31	H. is the agency of man and H. is the
94	1	Stake of Zion H. in land of Kirtland
110	7	my name shall be H. and I will manifest
124	85	who has come H. essaying to keep
	86	if they live H. let them live unto me; they shall rest from all their labors H.
128	21	H. a little and there a little
130	2	sociality which exists among us H.

HEREAFTER

Sec.	Vs.	
5	6	H. you shall be ordained and go forth
20	13	as many as shall H. come to knowledge
	35	which shall come H. by the gift and
28	9	no man knoweth, but it shall be given H.
42	35	New Jerusalem which is H. to be
	67	ye shall H. receive church covenants
45	65	inheritance which shall H. be appointed
48	6	laws which ye shall H. receive—50:35
50	16	he that is weak H. shall be made strong
53	4	commandments which shall be given H.
55	6	the residue shall be made known H.
57	16	further directions shall be given H.
58	3	concerning things which shall come H.
60	17	the residue H.
61	4	upon the waters and more especially H.
	22	according to the judgments H.
	28	as it remaineth with me to do H.
63	14	others that H. shall be revealed
68	14	there remain H., in due time of the
70	3	which I shall H. give unto them—104:58
	9	or shall H. appoint unto any man
93	6	John's record is H. to be revealed
94	5	pattern which shall be given you H.—6
115	1	who are and shall be appointed H.
124	102	the remainder I will show unto you H.
132	66	I will reveal unto you H.

HEREIN

Sec.	Vs.	
128	12	H. is glory and honor and immortality
132	63	H. is the work of my Father continued

HEREWITH

Sec.	Vs.	
98	12	I will try you and prove you H.

HERITAGE

Sec.	Vs.	
58	13	from mouth of city of H. of God
	17	to divide the lands of the H. of God
105	15	they shall not be left to pollute mine H.

HERRIMAN, HENRY

Sec.	Vs.	
124	138	I give unto you H., and, to preside

HERSELF

Sec.	Vs.	
20	73	who has presented H. for baptism
97	18	she shall prosper and spread H.
113	9	loosing H. from bands of her neck
132	51	commandment I give that she stay H.

HEWN

Sec.	Vs.	
45	50	shall be H. *down* and cast into fire—97:7
	57	shall not be H. *down* and cast into fire

HICKS, JOHN A.

Sec.	Vs.	
124	137	I give unto you H., and, to preside over

HID

Sec.	Vs.	
8	11	ancient records which have been H. up
14	9	a light which cannot be H. in darkness
86	9	ye have been H. from the world with
124	38	which had been H. from before the world
	41	kept H. from before the foundation
128	18	kept H. from the wise and prudent

HIDDEN

Sec.	Vs.	
6	27	scriputres which have been H. because
76	7	will I reveal all the H. mysteries
77	6	the H. things of his economy
89	19	treasures of knowledge, even H. treasures
101	33	the H. things which no man knew
123	13	in bringing to light the H. things of

HIDE

Sec.	Vs.	
58	60	and he thinketh to H. them
60	2	but H. the talent which I have given
88	87	the sun shall H. his face—33:49

HIDETH

Sec.	Vs.	
101	23	in my tabernacle which H. the earth

HIDING

Sec.	Vs.	
101	89	and come forth out of his H. place
121	1	where is pavilion that covereth thy H. place

Sec.	Vs.		Sec.	Vs.	
	4	let thy H. place no longer be covered			**HIGH COUNCIL**
123	6	which shall call him forth from his H. place	20	67	by the direction of a H.
			42	34	shall be appointed by the H. of the
		HIGBEE, ELIAS	102	1	proceeded to organize the H. of
113	7	questions by H.		2	the H. was appointed by revelation
		HIGH		6	the H. cannot have power to act
1	1	the voice of him who dwells on H.		12	whenever a H. of the church of
	28	be made strong and blessed from on H.		26	accompanying their decision to the H.
19	29	publish it upon every H. place		27	they may appeal to the H. of the seat
20	8	and gave him power from on H.		30	there is a distinction between the H. abroad and H. composed of
	16	the words of the glorious majesty on H.	107	33	Twelve are a traveling presiding H.
36	3	blessed be the name of the most H. God—39:19		34	the Twelve or the traveling H.
38	32	endowed with power from on H. —38; 105:11		36	the Presidency, or to the traveling H.
42	9	when it shall be revealed from on H.		37	the H. in Zion form a quorum equal
43	16	ye are to be taught from on H.		38	it is the duty of the traveling H.
45	66	place of safety for saints of Most H.	115	3	my faithful servants who are of the H.
58	47	call upon the rich, the H. and the low	120	1	bishop and his council, and by my H.
59	10	pay thy devotions to the Most H.	124	131	I give unto you a H. for the
	12	offer thine sacraments to the Most H.		139	wherever the traveling H. shall send
62	4	offer a sacrament to the Most H.			**HIGH COUNCILOR**
64	37	sitting on a hill or in a H. place	20	67	every H. is to be ordained by the
65	1	lo, a voice as of one from on H.			**HIGH COUNCILORS**
75	27	made known from on H. even by Comforter	20	66	the H. may have the privilege of of
76	57	and are priests of the Most H.			**HIGH COUNCILS**
	112	they shall be servants of the Most H.	107	36	standing H. form a quorum equal in
78	2	who has ordained you from on H.			**HIGHER**
	16	established his feet and set him on H.	94	5	a lower court and a H. court.—11
82	13	benefit of the saints of the Most H.	95	17	let the H. part of the inner court
84	1	united hearts and lifted voices on H.	107	12	when there are no H. authorities present
85	11	an inheritance among saints of Most H.		18	the authority of the H. or Melchizedek
88	6	he that ascended up on H. as also he	130	10	pertaining to H. order of kingdoms
	120	with uplifted hands to the Most H. —109:9			**HIGHEST**
95	8	I have chosen with power from on H.	76	70	the glory of God, the H. of all
			107	80	this is the H. council of the church
97	20	to be her salvation and her H. tower	131	2	and in order to obtain the H. a man
105	33	receive their endowment from on H.			**HIGH-MINDED**
106	3	his whole time in this H. and holy	124	3	and the H. governors of the nation
107	98	they may hold as H. and responsible			**HIGH-MINDEDNESS**
109	19	hands uplifted to the Most H.	90	17	be admonished in all your H. and pride
	35	sealed upon them with power from on H.			**HIGH PRIEST**
112	8	by thy word many H. ones shall be	20	67	every H. is to be ordained by the
121	8	God shall exalt thee on H.			the
124	27	for the Most H. to dwell therein			

Sec.	Vs.		Sec.	Vs.	
68	19	as a H. has authority to officiate		24	the H. when abroad have power
	22	no bishop or H. who shall be set		25	the said council of H. shall have
81	1	even to be a H. in my church		28	council of H. abroad is only to be
106	1	ordained a presiding H. over my		29	located H. abroad have power to say
107	2	Melchizedek was such a great H.		30	distinction between traveling H. and
	11	in his stead when H. is not present	107	10	H. have a right to officiate in
	12	the H. and elder are to administer		22	three presiding H. chosen by the
	17	as a H. has authority to officiate		53	and Methuselah, who were all H.
	66	in other words the presiding H.		79	shall have power to call other H.
	71	a H. may be set apart unto the	124	133	to be president over a quorum of H.
				136	they may preside over quorum of H.

HIGH PRIESTHOOD

20	67	every president of the H. is to be
78	1	who are ordained unto the H. of my
81	2	belongeth unto the presidency of the H.
84	29	necessary appendages belonging to H.
85	11	they who are of the H. whose names
107	9	presidency of H. have a right to
	64	then comes the H. which is the greatest
	65	be appointed of the H. to preside; shall be called president of the H.
	66	in other words 'presiding High Priest over H.
	69	a bishop must be chosen from H.
	73	but has been ordained to the H.
	76	except in case where a president of H.
	78	carried up before presidency of H.
	79	presidency of the H. shall have power
	82	as a president of H. shall transgress; assisted by twelve counselors of the H.
	91	duty president of H. is to

HIGH PRIESTS

20	66	the H. may have privilege of ordaining
42	31	before two of the elders or H.
	71	the elders or H. who are appointed to
68	15	they shall be H. who are worthy
72	1	ye who are the H. of my church
77	11	those who are sealed are H. ordained
84	63	you are mine apostles, even God's H.
	111	the H. should travel and also the
88	127	beginning at the H. even down to the
89	1	for the benefit of the Council of H.
102	1	a general council of twenty-four H.; to consist of twelve H.
	3	H. were chosen to be a standing
	5	nine H., seventeen elders, four
	7	seven shall have power to appoint other H.; to consist of twelve H.
	8	by the voice of a general council of H.

HIGHWAY

| 133 | 27 | an H. shall be cast up in the midst |

HILL

| 64 | 37 | like unto a judge sitting on a H. |

HILLS

35	24	Zion shall rejoice upon the H. and
39	13	that it may rejoice upon the H. and
49	25	Zion shall flourish upon the H.
133	31	the everlasting H. shall tremble at

HIMSELF

5	24	he exalts H., does not humble H., but if he will humble H.
	28	except he humble H. and acknowledge
	32	if Martin Harris humbleth not H.
20	6	after repenting and humbling H.
	73	who has presented H. for baptism
24	11	in me he shall have glory, not of H.
29	35	that he should be an agent unto H.
37	4	let every man choose for H. until I
38	24	let every man esteem his brother as H.—25
42	32	inasmuch as is sufficient for H. and
51	14	reserve unto H. for his own wants
57	8	let Sidney Gilbert plant H. in this
58	51	of H. or the agent as seemeth him good
63	55	he exalted H. in his heart
72	19	may render H. and his accounts approved
74	5	commandment not of the Lord but of H.
88	131	let him offer H. in prayer
	141	he is to gird H. according to pattern
101	42	he that exalteth H. shall be abased; he that abaseth H. shall be exalted
	84	but afterward he said within H.
102	10	after same manner that he H. was appointed
	11	in case that he H. is absent, the
106	6	and separated H. from crafts of men
	7	inasmuch as he will humble H. before

Sec.	Vs.	
107	100	he that shows H. not approved shall
109	5	a place to manifest H. to his people
	25	who diggeth a pit shall fall into same H.
114	1	in company with others including H.
121	38	ere he is aware he is left unto H. to
124	18	he shall beget glory and honor unto H.
	69	shall be for stock in that house for H.
	74	let him put stock in that house for H.
	77	for H. and his generation after him —69, 80, 81, 82, 117
	103	let him humble H. before me
	113	when he shall prove H. faithful in all
	114	let him therefore abase H.
	116	and clothe H. with charity
132	31	works of my Father wherein he glorifieth H.
133	62	unto him that sanctifieth H. before
135	4	to Carthage to deliver H. up to the
136	19	if any man shall seek to build up H.
	32	let him learn wisdom by humbling H.

HINDER

50	38	let no man H. them of doing that which
121	33	as to H. the Almighty from pouring down
124	49	and their enemies H. them from

HINDERED

90	27	thereby you be H. in accomplishing
124	50	upon the heads of those who H. my work
	51	and were H. by their enemies
	53	and have been H. by the hands of their

HIRE

31	5	the laborer is worthy of his H.— 84:79; 106:3
70	12	the same is worthy of his H.
111	9	this place you may obtain by H.

HISTORIES

123	5	and all the libelous H. that are

HISTORY

47	1	should write and keep a regular H.
	3	to keep church record and H. continually
69	3	continue in writing and making a H.
85	1	whom he has appointed to keep a H.

Sec.	Vs.	
	4	found on any of the records or H. of
93	53	to obtain a knowledge of H. and countries
128	3	and the H. of the whole transaction

HITHER

58	14	for this cause I have sent you H.
60	1	it pleaseth me that you have come up H.
105	20	that as many as have come up H.
108	1	you obeyed my voice in coming up H.
117	9	come up H. unto the land of my people
	14	let him come up H. speedily

HITHERTO

5	20	verified as it has H. been verified

HOAR-FROST

121	11	shall melt away as the H. melteth

HOLD

6	13	H. out faithful to the end
8	8	you shall H. it in your hands
10	20	Satan has great H. on their hearts
	37	H. your peace until I shall see fit
11	18	H. your peace, appeal unto my spirit
	22	H. your peace, study my word
26	1	to the west to H. the next conference
29	18	which shall take H. of the inhabitants
38	18	I H. forth and deign to give unto you
41	12	beware how you H. them for they are to
42	57	thou shouldst H. thy peace concerning
51	4	he shall H. this right and inheritance
56	17	from laying H. upon other men's goods
58	23	in this light ye shall H. them forth
	30	that will H. him guiltless that obeys
	61	also H. a conference upon this land
62	4	H. a meeting and rejoice together
63	6	let the unbelieving H. their lips
	25	I, the Lord, H. it in mine own hand
64	21	I will to retain a strong H. in the
	22	I will not H. any guilty that shall go
68	18	to H. the keys of this priesthood— 107:16
90	5	let them beware how they H. them lest they
98	39	thou shalt H. it no more as a testimony

Sec.	Vs.	
101	99	H. claim upon that which I appointed
105	30	I will H. the armies of Israel guiltless
107	18	to H. keys of all spiritual blessings
	20	to H. keys of ministering of angels
	70	he cannot H. keys of that priesthood
	98	they may H. as high and responsible
109	24	to honorably H. a name and standing
112	16	chosen to H. keys of my kingdom
	31	which power you H. in connection with
113	8	who should H. the power of priesthood
117	6	do I not H. the destinies of all the
122	9	H. on thy way, and Priesthood shall
123	3	as far as they can get H. of them
124	69	so long as he shall H. that stock
	92	he shall H. keys of the patriarchal
	99	where poisonous serpent cannot lay H.
	123	that ye may H. the keys thereof
	124	to H. sealing blessings of my church
	128	which Twelve H. the keys to open up
132	7	appointed on earth to H. this power; my servant Joseph to H. this power

HOLDETH

Sec.	Vs.	
84	19	and H. the key of the mysteries of
	26	which priesthood H. key of ministering

HOLDING

Sec.	Vs.	
63	32	I am H. my spirit from inhabitants
85	7	H. the sceptre of power in his hand
90	6	in H. the keys of this last kingdom
107	35	H. the keys to open the door by the
128	21	giving us consolation by H. forth that
134	5	H. sacred the freedom of conscience

HOLDS

Sec.	Vs.	
13	1	which H. the keys of the ministering
68	17	the firstborn H. the right of presidency
107	8	Melchizedek priesthood H. the right of
	15	and H. the keys or authority of same
132	64	man, who H. the keys of this power
134	1	he H. men accountable for their acts

HOLE

Sec.	Vs.	
135	2	without even a H. in his robe

HOLIEST

Sec.	Vs.	
76	66	the heavenly place, the H. of all
84	18	which is after the H. order of God
88	5	even God, the H. of all

HOLINESS

Sec.	Vs.	
20	69	walking in H. before the Lord
21	4	walking in all H. before me
38	24	practice virtue and H. before me—46:33
43	9	bind yourselves to act in all H.
46	7	that ye should do in all H. of heart
82	14	Zion must increase in H.
107	30	the decisions are to be made in H.
109	13	that it is thy house, a place of thy H.
133	35	after their pain, shall be sanctified in H.

HOLY

Sec.	Vs.	
10	46	which my H. prophets desired in their
20	6	God ministered unto him by an H. angel
	11	God does call them to his H. work
	20	by transgression of these H. laws
	25	believe and be baptized in his H. name
	26	who believed in the words of the H. prophets
	36	power and glory be rendered to his H. name
21	2	to build it up unto the most H. faith
27	6	by the mouth of all the H. prophets—86:10
35	23	call on H. prophets to prove his words
45	12	a day sought for by all H. men
	32	my disciples shall stand in H. places
	44	great glory with all the H. angels
49	8	H. men that ye know not of
	13	according to the H. commandment
59	9	offer up thy sacraments on my H. day
60	7	lifting up H. hands upon them; for I am able to make you H.
63	49	shall receive an inheritance in H. city
65	4	call upon his H. name, make known his
68	29	observe the Sabbath day to keep it H.
74	1	children unclean but now are they H.
	7	but little children are H., being
76	21	and saw the H. angels and they who are
77	11	ordained unto the H. order of God
84	59	shall the children pollute my H. land

Sec.	Vs.	
87	8	stand ye in H. places and be not
94	12	to be H., undefiled, according to
95	16	offering up your most H. desires
96	2	I design to build mine H. house
101	22	gather together and stand in H. places
	64	build them up to my name upon H. places
	77	according to just and H. principles
104	65	for sacred and H. purposes—68
	66	that it may be H. and consecrated
	68	save it be the H. and sacred writings
106	3	whole time in this H. calling
107	29	and were righteous and H. men
109	12	to be H. and that thy H. presence may
	19	with H. hands uplifted to the Most High
	58	to build a H. city to thy name
	77	from heaven, thy H. habitation
110	8	and do not pollute this H. house
115	7	let the city Far West be a H. land; it shall be called most H.; the ground upon which thou standest is H.
117	16	to keep and preserve it H.
119	6	observe not this law to keep it H.; kept thereon, that it may be most H.
124	19	blessed and H. is he for he is mine
	24	it shall be H. or the Lord will not
	39	your oracles in your most H. places; by the ordinance of my H. house; commanded to build unto my H. name
	44	consecrate that spot that it be made H.
	46	because they pollute mine H. grounds, mine H. ordinances, my H. words
	50	the transgression of my H. laws
	89	publish new translation of my H. word
127	9	in the archives of my H. temple
128	4	the record shall be just as H. as if
	24	let us present in his H. temple a book
132	7	for all eternity, and that too most H.
	41	appointed unto her by the H. annointing
133	3	he shall make bare his H. arm
	55	and the H. apostles, with Abraham
	56	he shall stand upon the H. city

See *Holy Father, Holy Ghost, Holy One, Holy Priesthood, Holy Scriptures, Holy Spirit.*

Sec.	Vs.	
		HOLY FATHER
109	4	we ask thee H.—10, 22, 24, 29, 47
	14	do thou grant H.
		HOLY GHOST
8	2	I will tell you by the H.
14	8	you shall receive the H.—25:8; 35:6; 36:2; 39:23; 49:14
18	18	you shall have the H.
	32	according to the power of the H.
19	31	by baptism and by fire, even the H.
20	26	inspired by the gift of the H.
	27	gifts and callings of God by the H.
	28	Father, Son and H. are one God
	35	by the gift and power of the H.—124:4
	41	for the baptism of fire and the H.—33:11; 39:6
	43	of the hands and the giving of the H.
	45	conduct meetings as led by the H.
	60	to be ordained by the power of the H.
	73	in the name of the Father, Son and H.—68:8
21	2	being inspired of the H. to lay
33	15	I will bestow the gift of the H.
34	10	given by the power of the H.
35	5	but they received not the H.
	6	they shall receive the H.—39:23; 49:14
	19	it shall be given by the H.—124:5
46	13	to some it is given by the H.—15, 16
68	3	as they are moved upon by H.—4; 121:43
	25	and of baptism and the gift of H.
84	27	filled with H. from him mother's
	64	remission of sin, shall receive H.
	74	that they may receive the H.
93	15	the H. descended upon him in form of
100	8	the H. shall be shed forth in
107	56	being full of the H., predicted
109	15	and receive a fulness of the H.
121	26	by the unspeakable gift of the H.
	46	the H. shall be thy constant companion
130	22	H. has not a body of flesh and bones; the H. could not dwell in us
	23	a man may receive the H. and it may
132	27	the blasphemy against the H.
		HOLY ONE
78	15	the Lord God, the H. of Zion
	16	under counsel and direction of the H.

Sec.	Vs.		Sec.	Vs.	
		HOLY PRIESTHOOD	61	23	while journeying to their H.
84	6	according to the H. which he		35	not separated until they return to H.
	25	took Moses out of their midst and H.			**HONEST**
107	3	before his day it was called the H.	8	1	shall ask in faith with an H. heart
119	4	standing law unto them for my H.	11	10	desire of me in faith with H. heart
			97	8	among them who know their hearts are H.
124	34	for therein are the keys of the H.	98	10	H. men should be sought for diligently
128	11	consists in obtaining powers of the H.	135	7	that will touch the hearts of H. men
131	5	through the power of the H.—132:44			**HONESTLY**
132	28	will give unto thee law of my H.	51	9	let every man deal H.
		HOLY SCRIPTURES			**HONEY**
20	11	proving to world that H. are true	38	18	a land flowing with milk and H.
	35	nor diminishing from the H.			**HONOR**
	69	works and faith agreeable to H.	20	36	and H. be rendered to his holy name
33	16	Book of Mormon and H. are given for	29	36	give me thine H. which is my power
		HOLY SPIRIT	43	25	and by the voice of glory and H. and
45	57	and have taken H. for their guide	65	6	thine is the honor, power and glory
46	2	as directed and guided by H.	75	5	ye shall be crowned with H. and glory
53	3	reception of H. by laying on of—55:1	76	5	I delight to H. those who serve me
55	3	you shall have power to give the H.		119	and to God and the Lamb be glory and H.
72	24	they that are appointed by H. to go	84	102	glory and H., and power, and might, be
76	35	having denied the H. after having	97	19	the nations of earth shall H. her
	52	receive H. by laying on of hands	109	10	that it may be done to thy H.
	53	who are sealed by H. of promise—132:7		77	where thou sittest enthroned with H.
	83	these are they who deny not the H.	122	4	thou shalt be had in H.
	86	but of the H. through ministration of	124	18	he shall beget glory and H. to
	116	only understood by power of the H.		21	my servant George for he shall H. me
88	3	abide in your hearts even H. of		34	that you may receive H. and glory
	137	a tabernacle of H. to your edification		39	for the glory and H. of her municipals
99	2	in the demonstration of my H.		55	that I may crown you with H. and
121	26	God shall give knowledge by his H.		95	and be crowned with the same H. and
124	124	to hold even the H. of promise	128	12	herein is glory, and H., and immortality
132	18	and is not sealed by H. of promise		23	proclaiming in our ears salvation, H.
	19	it is sealed unto them by H. of			**HONORABLE**
	26	they are sealed by H. of promise	76	75	these are they who are H. men of earth
		HOME	101	73	let H. men be appointed, even wise men
19	36	leave thy house and H. except when	124	3	to the H. president-elect
30	4	your H. shall be at your father's		96	his name may be had in H. remembrance
63	65	seek them a H. as they are taught			
88	79	things which are at H., things which			
93	50	more diligent and concerned at H.			
124	102	let my servant Joseph tarry at H.			
		HOMES			
52	3	leave their H. and journey to			
58	46	after that let them return to their H.			

Sec.	Vs.		Sec.	Vs.	
		HONORABLY	36		a third part of the H. of heaven turned
109	24	and H. hold a name and standing in this	38	1	which looked upon all the seraphic H.
	54	principles which were so H. defended		11	in the presence of all the H. of heaven
		HONORED	45	1	who made the Heaven and *all* H. thereof
58	7	that you might be H. in laying foundation	64	24	for I am the Lord of H.
124	76	he shall be H. in midst of his house	84	42	I have given heavenly H. charge concerning
134	6	every man should be H. in his station	88	112	and Michael shall gather the H. of
136	39	that he might be H. and the wicked be		113	the devil shall gather H. of hell
		HONORS	107	60	verily, says the Lord of H.
121	35	they aspire to the H. of men and do not	135	7	blood will cry unto the Lord of H.
128	21	declaring their keys, their H., their			**HOT**
		HOPE	89	9	H. drinks are not for the body or belly
4	5	and faith, H., charity and love, with	101	90	in his H. displeasure and anger
6	19	have patience, faith, H. and charity			**HOUR**
12	8	except he shall be humble, having H.	1	35	the H. is not yet but is nigh—58:4
18	19	if you have not faith, H., and charity	24	18	church shall give unto you in very H.
42	45	that have not H. of glorious resurrection	27	5	the H. cometh that I will drink of the
121	11	their H. shall be blasted and their	29	9	for the H. is nigh—10 .
128	21	that which is to come, confirming our H.	31	3	for the H. of your mission is come
		HOPES	33	3	it is the eleventh H. and for last time
121	14	that their H. may be cut off	39	21	the day nor the H. no man knoweth—49:7
		HORAH	45	2	in an H. when ye think not, summer is
82	11	and H. and Olihah, and, be bound		38	then shall they know that H. is nigh
		HORSE	51	17	the H. and the day is not given
89	11	corn for the ox and oats for the H.		20	cometh quickly in an H. you think not
		HORSES	61	38	for he cometh in an H. you think not
62	7	if you desire to ride upon H. or	63	54	until that H. there will be foolish virgins; at that H. cometh an entire separation
		HOSANNA	84	75	is in force from this very H. upon all
19	37	crying H., H., blessed be the name of—39:19		85	it shall be given you in the very H.—100:6
36	3	saying H., blessed be the name of the		86	let no man from this H. take purse or scrip
109	79	singing H. to God and the Lamb		115	the H. of their judgment is nigh
		HOSANNAS	88	52	in the first H. I will come unto you
124	101	and with H. to him that sitteth upon		53	in the second H. I will visit you with
		HOSTS		56	Lord went unto first in first H. and tarried all that H.
1	33	saith the Lord of H.—29:9; 56:10; 85:5; 121:23; 127:4, 8, 9; 133:64		58	every man in his H.
29	11	from heaven with all the H. thereof		60	in his own order until his H. was
	15	weeping and wailing among the H. of men			

Sec.	Vs.	
	61	every kingdom in its H. and in its time
	84	for the H. of the judgment which is to
	95	silence in heaven for space of half H.
	104	for the H. of his judgment is come—133:38
103	5	inasmuch as they hearken from this H.
	6	prevail against mine enemies from this H.
104	10	give unto you power from this very H.
	53	you are not bound only up to this H.
	63	I give it unto you from this very H.
109	62	that Jerusalem from this H. may begin
118	3	continue to preach from that H.
124	10	speedily in an H. ye think not of
	16	stand by you in the H. of affliction
	97	and shall give him in the very H. what
	124	notwithstanding the H. of temptation
133	11	for ye know neither the day nor the H.
	17	for the H. of his coming is nigh

HOURS

88	44	they give light in their minutes, in their H.

HOUSE

Sec.	Vs.	
10	60	they were a branch of H. of Jacob
14	10	from the Gentiles unto H. of Israel
18	6	both the Gentiles and also H. of Israel
19	36	leave thy H. and home, except when
20	47	visit the H. of each member and —51
29	12	to judge the whole H. of Israel
30	4	your home shall be at your father's H.
31	9	govern your H. in meekness, and be
39	11	my people which are of H. of Israel —42:39
41	7	have a H. built in which to live and
45	18	this temple which ye call H. of God; enemies say this H. shall never fall
	52	I was wounded in the H. of my friends
58	9	yea a supper of the H. of the Lord
	37	and also for the H. of the printing
59	9	thou shalt go to the H. of prayer
75	18	going from H. to H., village to —99:1

Sec.	Vs.	
	19	whatsoever H. ye enter and they receive you, leave your blessing on that H.
	20	whatsoever H. ye enter and they receive you not, depart speedily from that H.
	21	you shall be judges of that H.
	22	more tolerable for heathen than that H.
81	6	mansions prepared in H. of my Father
84	5	until an H. shall be built unto Lord; glory of Lord which shall fill the H.
	27	which Lord caused to continue with H. of Aaron
	31	offer a sacrifice in H. of the Lord; which H. shall be built in this generation
	32	upon Mount Zion in the Lord's H.
	94	woe unto that H. or that village —95
	115	their H. shall be left unto them desolate
85	7	to set in order the H. of God
88	119	establish a H. of prayer, a H. of fasting, a H. of faith, a H. of learning, a H. of glory, a H. of order, a H. of God—109:8
	127	the order of H. prepared for presidency
	128	this shall be the order of the H.; in the H. which shall be prepared for
	129	he shall be first in H. of God; that the congregation in the H. may—130
	130	when he cometh into the H. of God
	134	not suffer that mine H. be polluted by
	136	salutation to one another in H. of God
	137	in all your doings in the H. of God
90	5	rains descend and beat upon their H.
	10	in convincing the H. of Joseph of
93	43	you shall set in order your own H.; many things that are not right in your H.
	44	first, set in order thy H.
94	1	in land of Kirtland beginning at my H.
	3	for building of a H. for Presidency
	10	for the building of a H. unto me
	12	this H. shall be wholly dedicated unto
95	3	concerning the building of mine H.
	8	you should build a H. in the which H.
	11	it is my will that you should build a H.—97:10

House

Sec.	Vs.	
	13	let the H. be built, not after manner of
96	2	I design to build mine holy H.
	9	take away incumbrances upon the H.
97	12	that there may be a H. built unto me
	15	inasmuch as my people build a H. unto
98	18	in my Father's H. are many mansions
99	4	shall be rejected of Father and his H.
101	55	take all the strength of mine H.
	58	I may come with residue of mine H.
	61	a wise steward in midst of mine H.
102	1	24 High Priests assembled at H. of
103	22	say unto the strength of my H.—105:16
	30	to number of 500 of strength of my H.
	34	until obtained 100 of strength of my H.
104	28	the lot which is set off joining the H., Laneshine H.
	34	let Zombre have H. in which he lives
	43	which is laid off for building of my H.
	45	he shall be reckoned in H. of my
	46	I will multiply blessings upon H. of my
	57	appointed you to be stewards over mine H.
	86	master will not suffer his H. to be broken up
105	17	strength of mine H. have not hearkened
	27	have time to gather strength of mine H.
	33	their endowment from on high in my H.
109	2	commanded thy servants to build a H.
	4	we ask thee O Lord to accept this H.
	5	we have given our substance to build a H.
	12	that thy glory may rest upon this thy H.; that thy holy presence may be in this H.
	13	who shall enter upon threshold of Lord's H.; feel to acknowledge that it is thy H.
	14	all those who shall worship in this H.
	16	that this H. may be a H. of prayer, a H. of fasting, a H. of faith, a H. of glory, thy H.
	17	that all incomings into this H. may
	18	outgoings from this H. may be in name of
	20	that no unclean thing shall come into thy H.
	21	those who shall reverence thee in thy H.
	22	that thy servants may go forth from this H.
	24	hold a name and standing in this thy H.
	26	on whom thy name shall be put in this H.
	37	let thy H. be filled as with rushing
	56	when thy servants shall go out of thy H.
	63	be broken off from the H. of David
	78	accept the dedication of this H. unto
110	6	who have with their might built this H.
	7	I have accepted this H.; I will manifest myself in this H.
	8	and do not pollute this holy H.
	9	have been endowed in this H.
	10	the fame of this H. shall spread to
112	6	remove not thy H., for I have a great
	25	upon my H. shall it begin; from my H. shall it go forth
	26	blasphemed against me in midst of my H.
113	4	a descendant of the H. of Joseph
115	8	I command you to build a H. unto me
	10	labor diligently to build a H. unto
	11	recommence laying foundation of my H.
	13	not get in debt any more for building a H.
	14	but let a H. be built unto my name
117	16	remember their God and mine H. also
118	5	on the building-spot of my H.
119	2	for the building of mine H. and for
121	19	shall be severed from ordinances of my H.
124	11	to the H. of the daughters of Zion
	21	receive consecrations of mine H.
	22	let my servant George build a H.
	23	it shall be for a H. for boarding, a H.; therefore let it be a good H.
	24	this H. shall be a healthful habitation
	27	and build a H. to my name
	30	this ordinance belongeth to my H.; wherein ye are not able to build a H.
	31	all ye my saints build a H. unto me; I grant you a sufficient time to build a H.
	33	have had sufficient time to build a H.

Sec.	Vs.		Sec.	Vs.	
	37	except ye perform them in a H. which		122	accounted unto them for stock in that H.
	38	to build a H. in land of promise		145	rooms for all these offices in my H.
	39	ordained by ordinance of my holy H.	132	8	mine H. is a H. of order and not a H. of confusion—18
	40	let this H. be built unto my name	133	13	flee unto the mountains of Lord's H.
	42	will show all things pertaining to H.			**HOUSEHOLD**
	47	if you build a H. unto my name	121	45	full of charity to H. of faith
	51	those whom I commanded to build a H.			**HOUSES**
	55	I command you again to build a H.	42	35	for purpose of building H. of worship
	56	as pertaining to my boarding H.; let my servant Joseph and his H. have	59	17	for food, or for raiment, or for H.—70:16
	59	his seed after him have place in that H.	90	18	set in order your H.
			94	15	to be a committee to build mine H.
	60	let name of that H. be called Nauvoo H.		16	these two H. are not to be built until
	62	for the purpose of building that H.	104	34	reserved for building of my H.
	63	receive stock for building of that H.		39	have appointed to him the H. and lot
	64	$50 for a share of stock in that H.; from any one man for stock in that H.		68	appointed unto you in H., in lands, in
	66	from any one man in that H.	121	20	their H. and their barns shall perish
	67	any man as stockholder in this H.	132	55	give unto him an hundred-fold in H.
	68	he shall receive stock in that H.; he shall not receive any stock in that H.	136	9	let each company prepare H. and fields
	69	it shall be for stock in that H.		11	ye shall be blessed in your fields, H.
	70	to any other purpose, only in that H.			**HOUSETOPS**
	71	stock anywhere else, only in that H.	1	3	iniquities shall be spoken upon the H.
	72	let Joseph pay stock for building H.; cannot pay over $15,000 stock in that H.			**HOWBEIT**
			128	14	H. that was not first which is spiritual
	74	let him put stock in that H. for himself			**HUE**
	76	shall be honored in the midst of his H.	123	6	in all their dark and hellish H.
	77	let Hyrum put stock in that H. as			**HUMAN**
	78	let Isaac Galland put stock in that H.; remembered for an interest in that H.	134	4	we do not believe that H. law has right
				6	H. laws instituted for purpose of
	80	let William Marks pay stock into that H.		12	every government allowing H. beings to
	81	let H. G. Sherwood pay stock into that H.			**HUMBLE**
	82	let William Law pay stock into that H.	1	28	as they were H. they might be made
	111	appointed to build a H. for boarding, even the Nauvoo H.	5	24	he does not H. himself sufficiently; if he will H. himself in mighty prayer
	115	let him build a H. for my servant Joseph		28	except he H. himself and acknowledge
	117	into hands of the quorum of Nauvoo H.	12	8	assist in this work except he be H. and
	119	pay stock to quorum of Nauvoo H. unless	19	20	repent lest I H. you with my power
	121	let quorum of Nauvoo H. have a just; which they do in building Nauvoo H.		41	canst thou be H. and meek and conduct

Sec.	Vs.		Sec.	Vs.	
20	37	all those who H. themselves before God			**HUNDRED-FOLD**
29	2	as many as will H. themselves before me	78	19	added unto him even an H.
54	3	let them become truly H. before me	82	18	gain other talents, even an H.
61	2	those who confess their sins with H. hearts	98	25	your reward shall be an H.
				45	avenge thee of thine enemy an H.
67	10	inasmuch as ye H. yourselves, for ye are not sufficiently H.	132	55	I will give unto him an H. in this
76	93	all things bow in H. reverence			**HUNDREDS**
97	1	many of whom are truly H. and seeking	104	68	receive moneys by H., or by fifties
				84	loan money by H., or thousands
104	23	inasmuch as he shall be H. before me—106:7	136	3	with captains of H., of fifties, and —15
	79	is my will that you should H. yourselves			**HUNGER**
	80	inasmuch as you are diligent and H.	89	15	only in times of famine and excess of H.
	82	inasmuch as ye are H. and faithful			**HUNGRY**
105	23	let all my people be prayerful and H.	84	80	they shall not go H., neither athrist
112	10	be thou H. and the Lord thy God			**HUNTINGTON, WILLIAM**
	22	inasmuch as they shall H. themselves	124	132	viz., Alpheus Cutler, H., etc.
124	97	let him be H. and without guile			**HURLED**
	103	let him arise and come up and H. himself	133	49	the stars shall be H. from their places
128	25	I am, as ever, your H. servant			**HURT**
136	33	spirit to enlighten the H. and contrite	64	20	and counsel wrongfully to your H.
			77	9	saying, H. not the earth, neither the sea
		HUMBLED	84	71	administer poison it shall not H. them
61	37	inasmuch as you have H. yourselves			**HUSBAND**
		HUMBLETH	25	5	a comfort unto my servant, thy H.
5	32	if Martin Harris H. not himself he will		9	thy H. shall support thee in the church
		HUMBLING		14	let thy soul delight in thy H.
20	6	but after repenting and H. himself	74	1	unbelieving H. is sanctified by wife; unbelieving wife is sanctified by the H.
84	112	administer to their wants by H. the rich			
136	32	let him learn wisdom by H. himself		3	unbelieving H. was desirous that his
		HUMBLY	132	43	if her H. be with another woman
11	12	to do justly, to walk H., to judge			**HUSBANDS**
		HUMILITY	83	1	who have lost their H. and fathers
4	6	remember godliness, charity, H.		2	women have claims on their H. until their H. are taken
19	30	thou shalt do it with all H.			
104	79	obtain this blessing by your H.	123	9	whose H. and fathers have been murdered
105	12	inasmuch as they continue in H.			
118	3	if they will do this in all H.			**HYDE, ORSON**
		HUMPHREY, SOLOMON	68	1	H. was called by his ordination
52	35	let Wakefield and H. take their journey		7	this is the word of the Lord unto you H.
		HUNDRED	75	13	let H. and Smith take their journey
22	2	should be baptized an H. times it	100	14	thy brethren H. and, are in my hands
103	30	by fifties, or by an H.			
	34	until you have obtained one H.	102	3	H. and, to be standing High Council
104	69	or an H., let him do likewise			
	73	or an H., the treasurer shall give			

Sec.	Vs.		Sec.	Vs.	
	34	John Johnson, H., etc., (signatures); Oliver Cowdery, H., Clerks	124	8	appoint portion of the oppressor among H.
103	40	let H. journey with Orson Pratt			**HYRUM**
124	129	they are—Heber C. Kimball, H., etc.	11	23	H., my son, seek the kingdom of God
		HYMNS	23	3	I speak unto you H., a few words
25	11	also to make selection of sacred H.	112	17	where my servant Joseph and H. cannot come
		HYPOCRISY	115	13	neither my servant H. get in debt
121	42	which greatly enlarge the soul without H.	124	77	let H. put stock into that house
				79	go with my servant H. to accomplish
		HYPOCRITES		91	in the room of my servant H., that H. may take
50	6	wo unto them that are deceivers and H.		96	that H. may bear record of the things
	7	there are H. among you who have		102	I have a mission for my servant H.
	8	the H. shall be detected and shall be		118	let Joseph. H.. and Wm. Law lay the
64	39	liars and H. shall be proved by them	135	1	H. was shot first and fell calmly
101	90	appoint them their portion among H.		3	with his own blood, so has his brother H.
104	55	your faith is vain and ye are found H.		4	after H. had made ready to go

I

Sec.	Vs.		Sec.	Vs.	
		I		16	I have suffered these things for all
1	24	I am God—5:2; 6:2; 11:2; 12:2; 14:2; 35:8; 49:5 101:16; 124:71; 132:57		17	they must suffer even as I
				24	I came by the will of the Father
	35	I am no respecter of persons—38:16	21	7	him have I inspired
6	21	I am Jesus Christ—10:57; 11:28; 14:9; 19:24; 35:2; 36:8; 43:34; 49:28; 51:20; 52:44; 63:60	24	8	I am with thee to the end—10; 75:11; 100:12; 105:41
			25	15	where I am you cannot come—29:29
	21	I am the same that came unto my own—10:57; 11:29; 45:8; I am the light which shineth—10:58; 11:11; 45:7	27	18	where I am ye shall be also—132:23
			29	1	your Redeemer, the great I AM—38:1; 39:1
	32	so am I in the midst of you		5	I am in your midst—38:7; 49:27; 50:44; 61:36
8	12	it is I that have spoken it—11:11; 17:9; 18:33, 47; 49:7; 58:12; 59:24; 90:37; 97:7		12	being clothed in glory even as I am
				13	to be clothed upon even as I am
	12	I am the same that spake—38:3		43	thus did I appoint unto man
10	59	I am he who said, other sheep have I	30	11	for I am with you—31:13; 33:9; 34:11; 63:34; 108:8
11	28	I am the life and light—12:9; 45:7	32	3	I myself will go with them; I am their advocate with the Father—110:4
19	1	I am Alpha and Omega; I am He, the beginning and the end—38:1; 45:7; 63:60; 68:35; 84:120; 112:34; 132:66			
			33	18	I come quickly—34:12; 35:27; 39:24; 41:4; 49:28; 54:10; 68:35; 88:126; 99:5; 112:34
	2	I, having accomplished and finished the will; that I might subdue all things	34	12	I am your Lord and your Redeemer
			35	2	one in me as I am in the Father
	4	for I, God, am endless—10		21	purified even as I am pure

Sec.	Vs.		Sec.	Vs.	
36	8	I will suddenly come to my temple		12	I am not pleased with those among you
38	4	I am the same which have taken Zion	63	5	I utter my voice and it shall be obeyed
	10	with whom I am well pleased—50:37; 51:3; 61:35; 124:1, 12		17	I have said that the fearful, all liars
	16	the rich have I made		19	I say that ye are not justified
	22	for I am your lawgiver		23	I will give mysteries of my kingdom
	27	a parable, and it is even as I am		25	I hold it (Zion) in my own hands
39	12	I will be with thee—61:10		26	I render unto Cæsar the things
45	34	when I had spoken these words unto my		27	I will that you should purchase lands
	52	shall they know that I am the Lord; wounds with which I was wounded; I am he who was lifted up; I am Jesus who was crucified; I am the Son of God		32	I am angry with the wicked; I am holding my spirit from inhabitants
49	27	I will go before you		33	I have sworn in my wrath
50	13	I ask you this question		36	I have decreed all these things
	43	the Father and I are one; I am in the Father; ye are in me and I in you—93:3		55	I am not pleased with my servant—90:35
				58	I am not to be mocked in the last days—104:6; 124:71
	44	I am the Good Shepherd and Stone of Israel		59	I am from above; I am over all
	45	you shall know that I am—67:10; 84:119; 88:50; 93:1		63	and I will own them—101:3
52	2	land which I will consecrate unto my	64	7	I forgive sins unto those who confess
	43	I will hasten the City in its time		10	I will forgive whom I will forgive
	44	I will lift them up at the last day		15	I was angry with Ezra Booth
53	1	I have heard your prayers; this church which I have raised up		16	I withheld my spirit; I have forgiven my
	2	I, who was crucified for the sins of		21	I will retain a strong hold in the land; I will not overthrow wicked; I may save some
56	12	I will pay it unto him again			
58	30	who am I that made man			
	31	who am I that have promised and not fulfilled		22	I will not hold any guilty; I require the hearts of children of men
	42	I remember them no more			
60	4	I rule in the heavens above; when I shall make up my jewels—101:3	66	8	I will go with you
			67	4	I give unto you a testimony of truth
61	2	I forgive sins and am merciful	68	6	I am with you; I am Son of living God; bear record that I was, I am and I am to come
	5	I have decreed in my anger			
	13	I will reason with you as with men			
	14	I in the beginning blessed the waters; I cursed the waters		31	I am not pleased with inhabitants of
	17	I in the beginning cursed the land; in the last days have I blessed it	69	2	I will that John Whitmer should go
			70	3	I have appointed them stewards over
	19	I have decreed and the destroyer rideth		9	in his stewardship as I have appointed
	20	I was angry with you yesterday		16	whatsoever circumstances I shall place, or I shall send them
	24	I have appointed a way for journeying of		18	I am merciful and I will bless—76:5
	36	what I say unto one I say unto all; I have not forsaken you—82:5	75	7	I chasten him for murmurings of
62	6	I have brought you together; I promised the faithful and cannot lie		25	I give unto you this commandment 132:12
			76	47	I show it by vision unto many
	7	I am willing if any of you desire to ride	82	1	your trespasses, even so I forgive you
	9	I am with the faithful always		7	I will not lay any sin to your charge
				10	I am bound when ye do what I say

Sec.	Vs.		Sec.	Vs.	
84	74	kingdom where my Father and I am		13	I will feel after them
				15	I am with him and my hand—132:57
	96	I have laid my hands upon the nations	117	1	before I send again the snows
	119	I have put forth my hand to exert powers		2	for I command it—132:35
			124	15	I love him because of the integrity of—20
85	7	I will send one mighty and strong		54	I am the Lord your God—132:2, 12, 28, 40, 47, 49, 53, 54, 56, 57; 136:21
88	50	I am the light that is in you—93:2			
89	12	I have ordained for use of man			
	21	I give unto them a promise—118:3		78	I love him for the work he hath done
90	36	I will contend with Zion		83	I will build up Kirtland, but I have a scourge
93	4	I was in the world—5			
	20	glorified in me as I am in the Father		104	I will heal him
			127	8	I am about to restore many things
	21	I was in the beginning with the Father	132	1	I justified my servants, Abraham, Isaac
	26	I am the spirit of truth		24	whom he hath sent, I am he
	45	I will call you friends		65	whatsoever I will give unto him
94	15	the work which I have appointed	133	47	I am he who spake in righteousness
97	2	I show mercy to all the meek			
	3	I am pleased there should be a school	135	1	"I am a dead man"
				4	"I am going like a lamb to the slaughter; I am calm as summer's morning; I have a conscience void of offense; I shall die innocent
	6	I am willing to show mercy			
	8	every sacrifice which I shall command			
	9	I will cause them to bring forth			
	12	this is the sacrifice I require			
98	6	I justify you and your brethren	136	22	I am he who led the children of Israel
	8	I make you free, therefore ye are free			

ICE

Sec.	Vs.	
133	26	the I. shall flow down at their presence

| | 18 | I have prepared a place for you; where my Father and I am, there shall ye |

IDEA

Sec.	Vs.	
130	3	I. that Father and Son dwell in a man's

	19	I am not pleased with many who are
	21	I will chasten them
	22	I will turn away all wrath

IDENTIFIED

Sec.	Vs.	
109	60	us, who are I. with the Gentiles

| | 33 | save I commanded them |
| | 36 | I would give unto them a commandment |

IDLE

Sec.	Vs.	
42	42	thou shalt not be I.; he that is I.
60	13	thou shalt not I. away thy time
75	3	should not tarry neither be I.
88	69	cast away your I. thoughts
124		cease to be I.
90	31	and not be I. in her days

	37	I would fight their battles—105:14
	45	I will avenge thee of thine enemy
100	4	I have suffered you to come to this place
101	2	I have suffered the affliction to come
103	5	I have decreed a decree—6
104	5	I have decreed in my heart
	7	I have promised unto you a crown of glory

IDLER

Sec.	Vs.	
68	30	the I. shall be had in remembrance
75	29	the I. shall not have a place in church

	13	I should make every man accountable
	14	I stretched out the heavens
	16	this is the way I have decreed
	22	this stewardship I confer upon

IDLERS

Sec.	Vs.	
68	31	for there are I. among them

IDOL

Sec.	Vs.	
1	16	whose substance is that of an I.

| 110 | 4 | I am the first and last; I am he who liveth; I am he who was slain |
| 111 | 1 | I am not displeased with your coming |

IDOLATRY

Sec.	Vs.	
52	39	that there be no I. practiced

| 112 | 6 | I have a great work for thee to do |

Sec.	Vs.		Sec.	Vs.	
		IDUMEA			**IMMORTALITY**
1	36	in judgment upon I. or the world	29	43	be raised in I. unto eternal life
		IGNORANCE	75	5	crowned with honor and glory and I.—124:55
131	6	impossible for man to be saved in I.	81	6	thou shalt have a crown of I.
		IGNORANT	128	12	herein is glory, and honor, and I.
136	32	let him that is I. learn wisdom		23	proclaiming in our ears glory and
		ILLINOIS			**IMMOVABLE**
135	7	on escutcheon of State of I.	88	133	in a determination that is fixed, I.
		IMAGE			**IMMUTABLE**
1	16	walketh after I. of his own God, whose I. is in likeness of the world	98	3	with an I. covenant that they shall
			104	2	with promise I. and unchangeable
					IMPART
20	18	he created man after his own I.	11	13	I will I. unto you of my spirit
		IMAGINATION	19	26	I. it freely to the printing of the Book
124	99	mount up in I. of his thoughts		34	I. a portion of thy property
		IMMANUEL	42	30	that which thou hast to I. unto them
128	22	of eternal praise to the King I.		31	inasmuch as ye I. of your substance
		IMMATERIAL	48	2	ye shall I. to the eastern brethren
131	7	there is no such thing as I. matter	60	10	I. of the money I have given him
		IMMEDIATE	63	43	let him I. all the money he can I.
109	70	have mercy upon all their I. connections—71, 72.	88	123	learn to I. one to another as gospel requires
			104	18	if any man I. not his portion
134	11	where I. appeal cannot be made	105	3	they do not I. of their substance as
		IMMEDIATELY			**IMPARTIALLY**
82	11	except judgment shall I. follow	102	20	after hearing evidences and pleadings I.
88	93	I. there shall appear a great sign			
	95	I. after shall the curtain of heaven			**IMPEACH**
102	26	transmit I. a copy of the proceedings	135	7	is a witness that all the world cannot I.
118	1	let a conference be held I.			**IMPEACHED**
121	39	they will I. begin to exercise dominion	68	23	guilty by testimony that cannot be
					IMPERATIVE
124	2	called I. to make solemn proclamation	123	7	it is an I. duty we owe to God —9, 11
		IMMENSITY			**IMPERFECTIONS**
88	12	light proceedeth to fill I. of space	67	5	his I. you have known
		IMMERSE			**IMPORTANT**
20	74	then shall he I. him or her in water	69	3	making history of all the I. things
		IMMERSED	102	2	for the purpose of settling I. difficulties
128	12	to be I. therein to answer to likeness; to be I. in the water and come forth	107	78	the most I. business of the Church
					IMPORTUNE
		IMMERSION	101	76	should continue to I. for redress
13	1	and of baptism by I. for remission	86		let them I. at the feet of the judge
		IMMORTAL	87		let them I. at feet of the governor
77	1	it is the earth in its I. state—130:9	88		let them I. at feet of the president
121	32	when every man shall enter into I. rest			**IMPOSITIONS**
			123	5	murderous I. that have been practiced

Sec.	Vs.		Sec.	Vs.	
		IMPOSSIBLE	67	10	I. as you strip yourselves from
107	28	when circumstances render it I.	68	23	I. as he is found guilty
131	6	I. for a man to be saved in ignorance		25	I. as parents have children in Zion
				30	I. as they are appointed to labor
		IMPROVE	70	7	I. as they receive more than is
82	18	that every man may I. his talent		8	I. as they become heirs
				17	I. as they have not sinned
		IMPROVING	72	11	I. as they have wherewith to pay
104	68	by I. upon properties I have appointed	73	4	I. as it is practicable to preach
			75	25	I. as your brethren are willing
		IMPURE	80	2	I. as you desire a companion
121	33	how long can rolling waters remain I.	82	1	I. as ye have forgiven one another
				4	I. as ye keep not my sayings
		INALIENABLE		17	I. as his wants are just
134	5	while protected in their I. rights		20	I. as you sin not
			84	60	I. as you receive these things
		INASMUCH		103	I. as they have families
1	25	I. as they erred it might be made	89	5	I. as any man drinketh wine
	26	I. as they sought wisdom they	90	31	I. as she is faithful
	27	I. as they sinned they might	93	52	I. as ye keep my sayings
	28	I. as they were humble—104:23	97	4	I. as he continueth to abide in me
3	16	I. as the knowledge of a Savior		15	I. as mine people build a house
28	8	I as they receive thy teachings	101	58	I. as they gather together
35	23	and I. as ye do not write		63	I. as they are willing to be guided
39	15	I. as my people shall assemble		100	I. as they bring forth fruit
	18	I. as they do not repent	103	5	I. as they hearken from this hour
41	8	I. as he keepeth my commandments—96:6; 100:14		8	I. as they keep not my commandments
42	1	I. as they believe on my name		10	I. as they are not the Saviors
	8	I. as ye shall find them that will		24	I. as my enemies come
	31	I. as ye impart of your substance	104	2	I. as those whom I commanded
	38	for I. as ye do it unto the least of		3	I. as they were not faithful
	52	I. as they break not my laws		4	I. as some of my servants have
43	10	I. as ye do this—59:15, 16; 61:34; 75:11; 100:8		5	I. as any man belonging to the order
	10	I. as ye do it not		8	I. as you are found transgressors
44	2	I. as they are faithful—52:4, 5; 61:10; 71:7; 75:13; 79:3; 81:3; 92:2; 104:25, 31, 33, 35, 38, 42, 46; 105:12		9	I. as ye are cut off for transgression
				36	I. as it shall be made known
				80	I. as you are diligent and—82
				84	I. as you obtain a chance to loan
45	64	I. as they do repent—58:48; 109:53	105	18	I. as there are those who have hearkened
47	4	I. as he is faithful, it shall be		21	I. as my servant Joseph shall
48	2	I. as ye have lands ye shall		37	I. as they follow the counsel
	3	I. as ye have not lands, let them	106	7	I. as he will humble himself
50	43	I. as ye have received me, ye are	107	75	I. as there are other bishops
52	6	I. as they are not faithful, they shall		78	I. as there is not satisfaction
57	5	I. as my disciples are enabled		82	I. as a president of the High
	6	I. as can be in righteousness	112	3	I. as thou hast abased thyself
58	28	I. as men do good they shall in nowise	114	2	I. as there are those among you
	54	I. as there is land obtained	127	1	I. as they pursue me without a cause; I. as their pretensions are founded in
61	24	by land, I. as they are commanded			
	33	I. as it is given		10	I. as it is out of my power to do so
	37	I. as you have humbled yourselves—112:22	132	1	I. as you have inquired of my hand
					INCLINED
64	5	I. as he obeyeth my ordinances	121	4	let thine ear be I.
66	1	I. as you have turned away from			**INCLUDING**
	6	I. as you can send, send	107	1	I. the Levitical Priesthood

Sec.	Vs.		Sec.	Vs.	
114	1	I. himself, to testify of my name	134	6	of regulating our interests as I.
		INCOMINGS			**INFANT**
88	120	that your I. may be in the name of the Lord—109:9	93	38	men become in their I. state innocent
109	17	that all the I. of thy people	101	30	in that day an I. shall not die
		INCREASE			**INFERIOR**
1	21	that faith also might I.	130	9	all things pertaining to I. Kingdom
82	14	for Zion must I. in beauty			**INFINITE**
117	13	more sacred to me than his I.	20	17	there is a God in heaven who is I.
121	43	showing forth an I. of love		28	are one God, I. and eternal without end
131	4	he cannot have an I.			
		INCUMBRANCES			**INFINITY**
96	9	seek diligently to take away I.	109	77	enthroned with an I. of fulness
		INCUR			**INFIRMITIES**
3	4	he must fall and I. the vengeance	42	52	thou shalt bear their I.
		INDEPENDENCE			**INFLICT**
57	3	the place which is now called I.	134	10	neither to I. physical punishment
58	37	there should be lands purchased in I.			**INFLICTED**
			134	11	redress where personal abuse is I.
		INDEPENDENT			**INFLUENCE**
78	14	that Church may stand I. above	121	41	no power or I. can be maintained
93	30	all truth is I. in that sphere	122	4	though their I. shall cast thee into
		INDEPENDENTLY	123	7	upheld by the I. of that spirit which
107	76	to act in the office of bishop I.	134	9	not just to mingle religious I. with civil
		INDIGNATION		12	not to I. them in the least to cause
29	17	the cup of mine I. is full—43:26	136	10	let every man use all his I. and property
35	14	by the fire of mine I. will I			
56	1	they shall know mine arm and I.			**INFORMATION**
	16	your lamentation in the day of I.	128	1	give you I. in relation to many subjects
87	6	made to feel the wrath and I. of			
88	88	then cometh wrath and I.			**INFRINGE**
97	24	the I. of the Lord is kindled	134	4	unless their opinions prompt them to I.
98	22	I will turn away all I. from you			
	47	thine I. shall be turned away			**INFRINGED**
101	10	let fall the sword of mine I.	134	11	where right of property is I.
	11	mine I. is soon to be poured out			**INHABITANTS**
109	52	may thine I. fall upon them	1	6	O I. of the earth—34; 133:16, 36
124	48	ye, by your own works, bring I.		8	bearing these tidings unto the I. of
	52	I will answer judgment and I.		13	anger shall fall upon the I.
		INDIVIDUAL		17	calamity which should come upon I.
77	3	are limited to four I. beasts	5	5	woe shall come unto the I.
130	10	Thummim to each I. who receives one		19	scourge shall go forth among I. until I. thereof are consumed
134	2	laws which will secure to each I.	19	3	judgment which I shall pass upon I.
	9	I. rights of its members denied	29	18	flies shall take hold of I. thereof
		INDIVIDUALLY	43	28	for the last time call upon the I.
1	30	speaking collectively and not I.	45	64	call upon the I. to repent
		INDIVIDUALS		70	for the I. of Zion are terrible
42	33	properties in the hands of *any* I.	58	48	inasmuch as the I. will repent
102	17	who draw even numbers are the I.	61	3	whilst I. are perishing in unbelief
105	2	concerning the Church and not I.	62	5	declare glad tidings unto the I.
128	3	naming also some three I. that			

Sec.	Vs.	
63	32	I am withholding my spirit from I.
	37	lift a warning voice unto I.
64	38	I. of Zion shall judge all things
65	5	that the I. thereof may receive it
68	26	this shall be a law unto the I.
	29	the I. of Zion shall observe the Sabbath
	30	I. of Zion shall remember their labors
	31	I am not well pleased with I. of Zion
70	1	O ye I. of Zion
	8	benefits shall be consecrated unto I.
71	4	call upon the I. of the earth
76	1	and rejoice ye I. thereof
	24	I. thereof are begotten sons and
	109	we saw I. of the telestial world
82	6	anger of God kindleth against I.
87	6	the I. of the earth shall mourn; shall I. be made to feel the wrath
88	61	all these kingdoms and the I.
	92	prepare ye, prepare ye, O I. of
99	1	proclaim mine everlasting gospel to I.
107	74	a common judge among the I. of
109	38	in thy wrath, upon I. of the earth
	47	driven by I. of Jackson County
111	9	concerning the more ancient I. of City
112	5	let not the I. slumber because of
	24	vengeance cometh speedily upon I.
124	83	I have a scourge prepared for I. of
	88	proclaim my gospel to I. of Warsaw, I. of Carthage, I. of Burlington, I. of Madison
	89	publish the new translation to the I.
	106	warn the I. of the earth to flee
130	9	a Urim and Thummim unto I. who

INHERENT

| 134 | 5 | while protected in their I. rights |

INHERIT

6	37	ye shall I. the kingdom of heaven
10	55	for such shall I. the kingdom of
50	5	they shall I. eternal life—51:19
56	20	their generations shall I. the earth
59	2	for those that live shall I. the earth
64	35	rebellious shall not I. the land
72	4	accounted worthy to I. the mansions
78	22	a wise steward shall I. all things
88	17	poor and meek of earth shall I. it
	21	they must I. another kingdom
	26	and the righteous shall I. it
101	101	shall build, and another shall not I.
129	3	not resurrected, but I. same glory
132	18	they cannot, therefore, I. my glory
	19	and shall I. thrones, kingdoms and
	39	he shall not I. them out of the world

Sec.	Vs.	
		INHERITED
123	7	creeds of fathers, who have I. lies
		INHERITANCE
25	2	thou shalt receive an I. in Zion
38	19	I give it you for land of your I.
	20	land of I. and for I. of your children
45	58	earth shall be given them for I.
	65	that ye may purchase an I.
48	4	enabled to purchase land for an I.—58:51
51	4	that he shall hold this I. in church
52	5	made known unto them the land of your I.
	42	Missouri, which is the land of your I.
55	5	may be planted in land of your I.—57:8, 15
56	13	receive even in lands for their I.
57	5	obtain it for an everlasting I.
	7	to divide the Saints their I.
58	36	cometh unto this land to receive an I.
	38	that he may receive his I.—40
	44	time not yet come to receive their I.
	53	lest they receive none I.
63	20	shall receive an I. upon earth—48, 49; 94:13
	29	otherwise there is none I. for you
	31	but few shall stand to receive an I.
64	30	obtain an I. in the land of Zion
70	16	for food, for raiment; for an I.
72	17	answereth all things for an I.
85	3	who receive not an I. by consecration
	9	shall find none I. in that day—11
88	107	receive their I. and be made equal
90	30	an I. from the hand of the bishop
93	45	ye shall have an I. with me
99	7	go up also to possess thine I.
101	1	cast out from the land of their I.
104	24	in exchange for his former I.
	34	have the house and the I.; my houses, which pertains to that I.
	43	the I. upon which his father resides
	45	I have reserved an I. for his father
109	47	driven from the lands of their I.
125	4	take up their I. in the same
		INHERITANCES
83	3	they may remain upon their I.
	5	have not wherewith to give them I.
85	1	receive their I. legally from bishop
	2	who apostatize after receiving their I.
	7	to arrange by lot the I.
94	14	shall my servants receive their I.
96	3	for the benefit of those who seek I.
101	6	by these things they polluted their I.
	18	pure in heart shall return to their I

Sec.	Vs.		Sec.	Vs.	
103	11	shall return to the land of their I.	136	36	they have shed l. blood which crieth
	14	if they pollute their I. they shall be			**INNUMERABLE**
		INIQUITIES	76	67	have come to an I. company of
1	3	their I. shall be spoken upon housetops	109		they were as I. as the stars in the
3	18	because of their I. and abominations	132	30	should they continue as I. as stars
45	53	then shall they weep because of their I.			**INQUIRE**
66	1	as you have turned away from your I.	6	11	if thou wilt I. thou shalt know
			30	3	you are left to I. for yourself
103	3	that they might fill up measure of l.	102	23	the President may I. and obtain the
		INIQUITY	111	9	I. diligently concerning the more ancient
3	18	dwindled in unbelief because of l.	122	1	ends of the earth shall I. after thy
6	27	scriptures, hidden because of I.			**INQUIRED**
10	20	he stirreth them up to I.	6	14	for thou hast I. of me; as often as thou hast I. thou hast
	29	he flattereth them away to do I.			
18	6	the world is ripening in I.		15	thou knowest that thou hast l. of me
20	54	see that there is no I. in Church			
38	14	blessed, not because of your I.	132	1	inasmuch as you have I. of my hand
42	87	and if she do any manner of I.			**INQUIRY**
43	11	purge ye out the I. which is among you	42	76	be watchful and careful with all I.
45	27	I. shall abound			**INSEPARABLY**
	50	they that have watched for I. shall	93	33	spirit and element, I. connected
101	11	will I do when cup of their I. is	121	36	rights of priesthood are I. connected
123	7	whole earth groans under weight of its I.			**INSOMUCH**
124	50	the I. and transgression of my laws	42	45	I. that thou shalt weep for loss of
		INJURIES	44	4	I. that ye shall obtain power to
123	2	damages both of character and personal I.	45	67	I. that the wicked will not come unto
		INJUSTICE	107	43	I. that he seemed to be like his father
102	15	to prevent insult or I.—17			
		INNER	111	4	I. that they shall not discover your
94	4	in the I. court—11; 95:15			**INSPIRATION**
95	16	let the lower part of the I. court be	20	10	which was given by I. and is confirmed
	17	let the higher part of the I. court			
		INNOCENT			**INSPIRE**
93	38	every spirit of man was I. in beginning; man became again I. before God	20	11	proving that God does I. men
					INSPIRED
104	7	that the I. may not be condemned	20	7	gave him commandments which I.
109	31	thy servants have been I. before thee		26	who spake as they were I. by gift
	49	the cries of the I. ones to ascend up	21	2	being I. of the Holy Ghost to lay the
132	19	no murder whereby to shed I. blood—26		7	him have I I. to move the cause of
	27	commit murder wherein ye shed I. blood			**INSTANCE**
	44	not committed adultery but is I.	129	2	for I., Jesus said, "Handle me and see"
134	6	being placed for protection of the I.			
135	4	I shall die I. and it shall yet be said			**INSTANCES**
	7	they were I. of any crime; their I. blood on floor of; their I. blood on escutcheon; their I. blood on banner of liberty; their I. blood with the I. blood of all martyrs	18	2	I have manifested unto you in many I.
			33	4	they err in many I. because of

Sec.	Vs.		Sec.	Vs.	
		INSTEAD		36	the glory of God is I.
24	4	I will send a cursing I. of a blessing —6	130	18	whatever principles of I. we attain
	15	ye shall leave a cursing I. of a		19	if a person gains more knowledge and I.
107	38	call upon seventy I. of any others			**INTENT**
124	48	for I. of blessings ye bring cursings	60	9	for this I. have I sent them
	84	he aspireth to establish his counsel I.	88	20	for this I. was it made; for this I. are they sanctified
		INSTITUTED			**INTENTS**
88	139	the ordinance of washing of feet I.	6	16	none save God knoweth I. of thy heart
107	41	this order was I. in days of Adam			
124	33	for which the same was I. from	33	1	is a discerner of the I. of the heart
	134	which ordinance is I. for the	88	109	reveal the thoughts and I. of their
	137	quorum is I. for standing ministers			**INTEREST**
	139	quorum is I. for traveling elders	82	19	every man seeking the I. of his neighbor
128	12	hence this ordinance was I. to			
	13	the baptismal font was I. as a	119	4	shall pay one-tenth of all their I.
132	5	the conditions thereof which were I.	124	78	let him be remembered for an I. in
	6	it was I. for fulness of my glory		89	and with his I. support cause of poor
134	1	governments were I. of God for			
	4	believe that religion is I. of God		112	this let him do if he will have an I.
	6	human laws being I. for regulating	134	5	best calculated to secure public I.
		INSTITUTION			**INTERESTS**
107	33	agreeable to the I. of heaven	134	6	regulating our I. as individuals
		INSTRUCT			**INTERFERE**
43	8	ye shall I. and edify each other	134	4	to I. in prescribing rules of worship
		INSTRUCTED		12	not right to I. with bond servants
1	26	sought wisdom they might be I.			**INTERFERENCE**
43	9	ye shall become I. in the law	134	12	such I. we believe to be unlawful
88	78	may be I. more perfectly in theory			**INTERPOLATIONS**
		INSTRUCTION	91	2	which are I. by the hands of men
6	14	thou hast received I. of my spirit			**INTERPRETATION**
33	16	scriptures are given of me for your I.	46	25	to another is given the I. of tongues
55	4	that little children may receive I.	95	7	Lord of Sabaoth, by I., Creator of the first day
88	127	established for their I. in all things			
97	13	for a place of I. for all those who	109	36	tongues as of fire and the I. thereof
		INSTRUCTIONS			**INVIGORATED**
66	8	give him thine I.	88	124	that your bodies and minds may be I.
124	88	await patiently for further I.			
132	3	prepare thy heart to obey the I.			**INVIOLATE**
135	3	many other wise documents and I.	134	2	except such laws are framed and held I.
		INSTRUMENTALITY			
111	2	for benefit of Zion through your I.			**INVITE**
112	1	ordained through I. of my servants	20	59	they are to I. all to come unto Christ
		INSULT			
102	15	to prevent I. or injustice—17			**INVITED**
		INTEGRITY	58	9	supper to which all nations shall be I.
124	15	I love him because of I. of his heart			
	20	he may be trusted because of I. of			**IOWA**
		INTELLIGENCE	125	1	concerning saints in territory of I.
88	40	for I. cleaveth unto I.			
93	29	I. was not created or made			
	30	all truth is independent as all I. also			

Sec.	Vs.		Sec.	Vs.	
		IRON	45	17	the restoration of the scattered I.
123	8	it is an I. yoke, a strong band	50	44	am the Good Shepherd and Stone of I.
	9	been murdered under its I. hand	58	17	is appointed to be a judge in I.
124	27	and with I., with copper and with	61	25	shall do like unto children of I.
		IRREVOCABLY	77	9	seal of living God over 12 tribes of I.; to gather the tribes of I.
130	20	there is a law, I. decreed in heaven		11	144,000 out of all the tribes of I.
		ISAAC		14	for him to gather the tribes of I.
27	10	also with Joseph, Jacob and I.	84	23	this Moses plainly taught children of I.
98	32	the law I gave to Joseph, Jacob and I.		27	among the children of I. until John.
132	1	justified Abraham, I. and Jacob		99	the Lord hath redeemed his people I.
	36	commanded to offer his son I.	86	11	and a savior unto my people I.
	37	he abode in my law as I. also	89	21	shall pass by them as the children of I.
	50	the offering of Abraham of his son I.	90	8	for salvation of the nations of I.
133	55	with Abraham, I. and Jacob, shall be	101	12	all mine I. shall be saved
136	21	the God of Abraham, I. and Jacob	103	16	as Moses led children of I.
		ISAIAH		17	for ye are the children of I..
76	100	some of Esaias, some of I. and some	105	26	until army of I. becomes very great
113	1	4th and 5th verses of 11th Chapter of I.		30	I will hold the armies of I. guiltless
	3	in 1st verse of 11th chapter of I.	107	72	and also to be a judge in I.
	7	what is meant by the command in I.; what people has I. reference to		76	is tried, to sit as a judge in I.
		ISHMAELITES	109	1	thanks be to thy name O God of I.
3	18	Lamanites, and Lemuelites and the I.		67	may all scattered remnants of I.
		ISLANDS		70	may be converted and redeemed with I.
1	1	ye that are upon the I. of the sea	110	11	unto us the keys of gathering of I.
88	94	who sitteth upon the I. of the sea	113	8	and the redemption of I.
33	8	elders unto the I. of the sea		10	remnants of I. in scattered condition
	20	he shall stand upon I. of the sea	133	34	blessing of God upon the tribes of I.
	23	the I. shall become one land	136	1	concerning Camp of I. in their
		ISRAEL		22	who led children of I. out of; in last days to save my people I.
8	3	brought children of I. through Red Sea			**ISRAEL'S**
14	10	from Gentiles to the house of I.	127	3	for I. God is their God, and he will
18	6	both the Gentiles and house of I.			**ITEMS**
29	12	to judge the whole house of I.	68	13	now concerning the I. in addition
35	25	I. shall be saved in mine own due time			**ITSELF**
36	1	Lord God, the Mighty One of I.	49	10	exalted of I. shall be laid low
38	33	for I. shall be saved, and I will lead		84	let the morrow take thought for I.
39	11	my people which are of the house of I.—42:39	88	35	but seeketh to become a law unto I.
			93	30	truth is independent to act for I.
			123	10	enough to make hell I. shudder
			128	1	the subject seems to press I. upon my

J

Sec.	Vs.		Sec.	Vs.	
		JACKSON	109	47	by the inhabitants of J. county, Mo.
101	71	land be purchased in J. county	124	51	unto my name in J. county, Mo.
105	28	purchasing all lands in J. county			

Sec.	Vs.	
		JACOB
10	60	they were a branch of the house of J.
27	10	also with Joseph, J., and Isaac
49	24	J. shall flourish in the wilderness
52	2	my people, which are a remnant of J.
98	32	the law I gave to Nephi, Joseph and J.
109	58	thy servants, the sons of J., may gather
	61	thou hast great love for children of J.
	62	have mercy on the children of J.
	65	cause that the remnants of J. who
	68	O mighty God of J.
132	1	I justified Abraham, Isaac and J.
	37	and J. did none other things than
133	55	with Abraham, Isaac and J., shall be
136	21	the God of Abraham, Isaac and J.
		JACOBITES
3	17	to the Nephites, and the J. and the
		JAIL
135	1	They were shot in Carthage J.
	7	only confined in J. by conspiracy of; on the floor of Carthage J.
		JAMES
7	7	minister for him and thy brother J.
27	12	also with Peter, J. and John
39	7	my servant J., I have looked upon
128	20	the voice of Peter, J. and John
		JAMES, GEORGE
52	38	and also J. be ordained a priest
		JAQUES, VIENNA
90	28	my handmaid, J., should receive money
		JARED
17	1	which were given to the brother of J.
107	47	J. was 200 years old when ordained
	53	Adam called Seth, Enos, J., into the
		JARRINGS
101	6	there were J. and contentions, and
		JAWS
122	7	if the very J. of hell shall gape open
		JEALOUSIES
67	10	strip yourselves from J. and fears
		JEHOVAH
109	34	O J., have mercy upon this people
	42	but deliver thou, O J., we beseech
	56	shall go out from thy house, O J.
	68	how he has covenanted with J.

Sec.	Vs.	
110	3	even the voice of J. saying
128	9	according to decrees of the great J.
		JEOPARDIZING
134	12	thereby J. the lives of men
		JEOPARDY
134	10	to put them in J. of life or limb
		JEREMY
84	9	and Elihu under the hand of J.
	10	and J. under the hand of Gad
		JERUSALEM
5	20	told people of the destruction of J.
29	12	were with me in ministry at J.
33	8	who journeyed from J. in the
45	18	this temple which is in J., which
	24	this I have told you concerning J.
77	15	gathered and build the city of J.
95	9	even as mine apostles at J.
109	62	that J., from this hour, may begin to
124	36	and in her stakes and in J.
133	13	let them of Judah flee unto J.
	21	and he shall speak from J.
	24	and the land of J. shall be

See New Jerusalem

		JESSE
113	1	what is the Stem of J. spoken of
	3	rod that should come of Stem of J.
	4	partly descendant of J. as well as of
	5	what is the root of J. spoken of
	6	it is a descendant of J. as well as
		JESUS
20	75	in remembrance of the Lord J.
21	9	J. was crucified by sinful men
45	52	I am J. that was crucified
49	12	believe on the name of the Lord J.
50	29	ask whatsoever you will in the name of J.
	31	ask of the Father in the name of J.
76	41	he came in the world, even J.
	51	they who received testimony of J.
	69	just men made perfect through J.
	74	who received not the testimony of J.
	79	not valiant in the testimony of J.
	82	who received neither testimony of J.—76:101
107	19	J. the Mediator of the new covenant
129	2	J. said, "Handle me and see
135	3	has done more, save J. only, for
136	37	from Moses to J. and his apostles; from J. to Joseph Smith
		JESUS CHRIST
3	20	rely upon the merits of J.

Sec.	Vs.		Sec.	Vs.	
6	21	I am J.—10:57; 11:28; 14:9; 19:24; 35:2; 36:8; 43:34; 49:28; 51:20; 52:44; 63:60	127	12	prophet and seer of church of J.
			128	8	by the revelation of J. wherein
				21	tribulations of this church of J.
11	10	believing in the power of J.	132	24	to know the only true God and J.
15	1	listen to the words of J.—16:1	135	7	an ambassador for religion of J.
17	9	I, J., your Lord, have spoken it—18:33, 47	136	2	let all people of church of J.
18	22	baptized in my name which is J.—49:13			**JETHRO**
			84	6	under hand of his father-in-law, J.
	23	J. is the name given of the Father		7	J. received it under hand of Caleb
	41	be baptized in the name of J.			**JEW**
20	1	since the coming of J. in flesh	18	26	both unto Gentile and unto J.
	2	who was ordained an apostle of J.	19	27	to the Gentile, that soon it may go to the J.
	3	also called an apostle of J.			
	4	according to the grace of J.	57	4	running directly between J. and Gentile
	9	fulness of the Gospel of J.			
	29	all must believe on the name of J.			**JEWELS**
	30	justification through J. is just	60	4	in day when I shall make up my J.—101:3
	31	sanctification through J. is just			
	37	willing to take upon them name of J.			**JEWISH**
	70	lay hands upon them in name of J.	77	15	to the J. nation in the last days
	73	who has authority from J.; having been commissioned of J.			**JEWS**
			3	16	through the testimony of the J.
	77	we ask thee in the name of J.—79	20	9	to the Gentiles and to the J. also
21	1	thou shalt be called an apostle of J.; by the grace of your Lord, J.	21	12	thus saith the Lord, lo, to the J. also
27	1	listen to the voice of J.—29:1	45	21	this generation of J. shall not pass
31	13	these words are of me, even J.		51	then shall the J. look upon me and
	34	1 hearken unto what I say unto J.	74	2	circumcision was had among the J.
38	1	thus saith the Lord, even J.—66:13		6	are unholy, for it was had among the J.
39	1	listen to the Great I Am, J.	77	15	to prophecy to the J. after they
42	1	who have assembled in my name, J.	84	28	to overthrow the kingdom of the J.
46	13	given to know that J. is the Son	90	9	lo, they shall turn unto the J.
50	27	sent forth through J, his son	98	17	hearts of the J. to the prophets, and the prophets to the J.
55	2	by baptism in the name of J.			
59	5	in name of J. thou shalt serve	107	33	first to the Gentiles, secondly to J.—34, 35, 97; 133:8
62	1	hearken saith your God even J.			
68	6	ye shall bear record of me, J	112	4	not only to Gentiles, but also to the J.
74	2	who believed not the Gospel of J.			
	7	sanctified through atonement of I.			**JOB**
76	14	fulness of the gospel of J.	121	10	thou art not yet as J.; charge thee with transgression, as they did J.
79	4	fear not saith the Lord, even J.			
80	5	this is will of your Redeemer, J.			**JOHN**
81	7	these are the words of J.	7	1	J., my beloved, what desirest thou
84	1	a revelation of J. unto his	15	1	hearken, my servant J., and listen
	45	whatsoever is light is spirit of J.	20	35	and according to revelations of J.
88	5	glory of God through J. his son	27	7	also J., son of Zacharias, and his name should be J.
	133	I salute you in name of J.			
90	11	shed forth for the revelation of J.		8	which J. I have sent unto you
95	17	Omegus, even J. your Lord		12	and with Peter, James and J.
107	35	by proclamation of Gospel of J.	30	9	I say unto you my servant J.
109	4	now we ask thee in the name of J.	35	4	thou was sent forth even as J.
115	3	people of my church of J. of	47	1	my servant J. should write and keep
	4	called the church of J. of			
121	29	endured valiantly for gospel of J.			

Sec.	Vs.	
61	14	by the mouth of J. I cursed the waters
76	15	we came to the fifth chapter of J.
	100	some of J., and some of Moses, and
77	1	sea of glass spoken of by J.
	2	expressions used by Revelator J.
	3	four beasts, which were shown to J.
	5	by the 24 elders spoken of by J.; these elders whom J. saw
	6	understand by book which J. saw
	14	by the little book eaten by J.
84	27	among children of Israel until J.
88	3	as recorded in testimony of J.
93	6	J. saw and bore record of fulness
	11	I, J., bear record I beheld his glory
	12	I, J., saw he received not the fulness
	15	I, J., bear record the heavens were
	16	I, J., bear record he received fulness
	18	the fulness of the record of J.
	26	I am Spirit of truth and J. bore record
128	6	J. the Revelator was contemplating
	20	the voice of Peter, James and J.
130	3	J. xiv:23. The appearing of the
133	55	from Moses to Elijah; Elijah to J.
135	7	martyrs under the altar that J. saw

JOHN'S

88	141	13th chapter of J. testimony
93	6	fulness of J. record is hereafter to

JOHNSON, AARON

124	132	let my servant, J., be ordained

JOHNSON, JOHN

96	6	my servant Zombre (J.) whose offering
102	3	J., and, were chosen standing High Council
	34	Smith, J., etc., (signatures)
104	24	lot of land which J. obtained
	34	let J. have the house in which he

JOHNSON, LUKE

68	7	word of the Lord unto J. and unto
75	9	let J. go with him and proclaim
102	3	J., and, were chosen standing High Council
	34	Smith, J., etc. (signatures)

JOHNSON, LYMAN

68	7	word of the Lord unto J. and unto
75	14	let J. and O. Pratt take their journey

JOINED

78	8	you who are J. together in this order
132	18	because they are not J. by me

JOINING

104	28	J. the house which is to be for

Sec.	Vs.	

JOINT

84	80	neither in body, limb, nor J.

JOINTS

6	2	dividing asunder of both J. and marrow—11:2; 12:2; 14:2; 33:1

JOSEPH

3	9	thou art J. and wast chosen
5	7	they would not believe my servant J.
	9	which I have entrusted unto you J.
	21	I command you J. to repent
	23	I speak unto you J. concerning the man
	29	I command you J. that you shall say
	30	J., when thou hast translated a few more
6	18	stand by my servant J. faithfully
	25	to translate even as my servant J.
	28	I give unto you and unto J. the keys
9	4	is to write for my servant J.
	12	I have given J. sufficient strength
18	8	unto eternal life and his name is J.
23	5	I speak a few words unto you J.
27	10	and also with J., Jacob and Isaac
28	10	J. shall be appointed to preside
35	17	by the hand of my servant J.
47	1	assist you my servant J. in transcribing
78	4	the city of Enoch, (J.) for permanent
90	10	convincing house of J. of the gospel
96	7	for he is a descendant of Seth, (J.)
98	32	and thy fathers, J., Jacob, and Isaac
100	1	my friends, Sidney and J., your families
	9	to be a spokesman to my servant J.
105	21	inasmuch as J. shall appoint unto
112	15	rebel not against my servant J.
	17	where my servant J. cannot come
113	4	or of the house of J. on whom there
	6	descendant of Jesse as well as of J.
115	13	let not my servant J. get in debt any
	16	even my servant J. and counselors
	18	as they shall be manifest unto J.
124	22	such an one as J. shall show unto
	42	I will show unto J. all things
	56	let J. and his house have place therein
	58	J., in thee and thy seed shall all
	59	let J. and his seed after him have
	72	let J. pay stock into their hands; but J. cannot pay over
	79	the work that J. shall point out to
	89	hearken to counsel of my servant J.
	91	and anointed as counselor unto J.
	94	a revelator as well as my servant J.
	95	that he may act in concert with J. and shall receive counsel from J.

Sec.	Vs.		Sec.	Vs.	
	102	let J. tarry at home for he is needed		23	shall not come upon the waters to J.
	103	be a counselor to my servant J.		24	they shall J. by land, to J. to the land of Zion
	105	in neighborhood in which J. resides		29	the way for the Saints to J.
	107	let him assist my servant J.; let Law assist J.		32	let them J. for the congregations
	112	to counsel of J., and labor with his		33	let them J. and declare the word
	115	let him build a house for J.		35	let them J. together, two by two
	118	hearken unto counsel of J., Hyrum and	62	4	and now continue your J.
	125	I give unto you J. to be a presiding	63	39	in coming spring to take his J. *up*
125	2	unto places I shall appoint by J.	75	13	take their J. into eastern countries —14
130	15	J., my son, if thou livest until thou		15	take their J. into western countries
132	1	J., inasmuch as you have inquired		17	take their J. into south country
	7	I have appointed J. to hold this power		18	let all those take their J. as I
	30	from whose loins ye are namely J.	93	51	let Sidney Rigdon go on his J.
	40	I gave unto thee, J., an appointment	100	12	continue your J. and let your hearts
	44	I reveal it unto you my servant J.	103	37	let Parley P. Pratt J. with
	48	J., whatsoever you give on earth		38	let Lyman Wight J. with
	52	that have been given unto my servant J.		39	let Hyrum Smith J. with
	53	I give unto J. that he shall be made		40	let Orson Hyde J. with
	54	to abide and cleave unto my servant J.	111	1	not displeased with your coming this J.
	55	then shall my servant J. do all things	117	1	speedily J. from Kirtland
	56	let mine handmaid forgive J. his	136	2	let those who J. with them
	57	let not J. put his property out of		5	and other necessaries for the J.

JOURNEYED

Sec.	Vs.	
	60	let no one set on my servant J.
135	1	J. leaped from the window and was
	4	when J. went to Carthage to deliver
33	8	even as Nephi who J. from Jerusalem

JOSEPHITES

JOURNEYING

3	17	and to the Nephites, Jacobites and J.	54	9	after you have done J. I say
			61	18	waters, that they come not in J.

JOURNEY

				23	while J. unto their homes
28	14	take thy J. among the Lamanites		24	have appointed a way for J. of my
30	5	Peter, take your J. with Oliver	107	45	Cainan met Adam in J. to the
35	22	tarry with him and he shall J. with			

JOURNEYINGS

52	3	let my servants take their J. as soon; and J. to land of Missouri	124	106	and in all his J. let him lift up
	7	let my servant, take J. speedily	126	2	have seen your labor and toil in J.
	8	let John Murdock take J. same way	136	1	concerning Camp of Israel in their J.
	9	let them J. from thence preaching			

JOY

	22	let my servants take their J.—23, 24, 25, 26, 27, 28, 29, 30, 31, 32	6	31	then shall ye have J. in the fruit
	33	let all these take their J., and J. not in another's track	7	8	for ye both J. in that which ye
	35	let my servants, take J. in eastern	11	13	which shall fill your soul with J.
53	5	take your J. with Joseph Smith, and—55:5	18	13	great is his J. in soul that repenteth
54	7	take your J. and appoint whom ye		15	great shall be your J. with him
	8	take your J. into regions westward		16	if J. will be great with one soul, how great will be your J.
55	6	let Joseph Coe take his J. with	31	3	declare tidings of great J.
56	5	he shall take up his J. speedily	42	61	mayest know that which bringeth J.
60	5	will speak concerning your J.; take J. speedily for St. Louis	45	71	with songs of everlasting J.—66:11; 101:18; 109:39; 133:33
	6	take their J. for Cincinnati	51	19	shall enter into the J. of his Lord
	8	let residue take J. from St. Louis	52	43	I will crown the faithful with J.
61	9	let them take their J. in haste—21	59	13	fasting, that thy J. may be full
			70	18	shall enter into the J. of these
			75	21	shall be filled with J. and gladness
			79	1	proclaiming tidings of great J.

Joy   234   Judgments

Sec.	Vs.	
88	52	behold the J. of my countenance—53
93	33	spirit, element receiveth fulness of J.
	34	separated man cannot receive fulness of J.
101	36	in this world J. is not full, but in me your J. is full
106	6	there was J. in heaven when my
109	76	reap eternal J. for all sufferings
	80	thy saints shout aloud for J.
124	88	proclaim gospel with great J
	101	cry aloud with J. and rejoicing
128	19	glad tidings of great J.
	23	let the mountains shout for J.; solid rocks weep for J.; let all sons of God shout for J.

JOYFUL

136	29	that your souls may be J.

JUDAH

109	64	the children of J. begin to return
133	13	let them who be of J. flee to
	35	also the tribe of J. after their pain

JUDGE

10	37	cannot always J. the righteous
11	12	walk humbly, J. righteously
29	12	to J. whole House of Israel
58	17	is appointed to be a J. in Israel
	18	to J. his people by his testimony
64	11	let God J. between me and thee
	37	like a J. sitting on a hill to J.
	38	inhabitants of Zion shall J. all
	40	even the bishop, who is a J. shall
68	33	be had in remembrance before the J.
72	17	a certificate from the J. or bishop
76	68	where God and Christ are J. of all
77	12	complete salvation of man and J. all
101	81	parable of woman and the unjust J.
	82	there was in the city a J. which
	86	let them importune at feet of the J.
107	72	also to be a J. in Israel, to do
	74	thus shall he be a J., a common J.
	76	is tried, to sit as a J. in Israel
127	2	J. ye for yourselves

JUDGED

20	13	by them shall the world be J.
76	73	might be J. according to men in flesh—88:99
	111	shall be J. according to their works
88	100	spirits of men who are to be J.
128	6	dead were J. out of those things—7
	8	out of books shall your dead be J.

JUDGES

75	21	you shall be J. of that house
107	74	have other bishops or J. in Zion
	78	upon decision of the bishops or J.

Sec.	Vs.	

JUDGETH

58	20	let God rule him that J.

JUDGING

19	3	J. every man according to his

JUDGMENT

1	36	come down in J. upon Idumea
3	13	has depended upon his own J.
10	23	condemnation in the day of J.
19	3	and the last great day of J.
38	5	until the J. of the great day
39	16	thinking I will stay my hand in J.
	18	I will stay my hand in J.
41	12	answered on your souls in day of J.
43	25	called upon you by voice of J.
	29	will I come upon the earth in J.
	33	until they come before me in J.
50	6	I will bring them to J.
52	11	I will send forth J. unto victory
56	16	in day of J. and of indignation
59	20	to be used with J. not to excess
60	15	against them in the day of J.
62	8	according to J. and directions
63	15	lest J. shall come upon them
70	4	stewardship will I require in day of J.
75	21	in day of J. you shall be judges
	22	tolerable for heathen in day of J.
82	4	justice and J. are the penalty
	11	except J. shall immediately follow
	23	leave J. alone with me
84	58	there remaineth a scourge and a J.
	87	teach them of a J. to come
	115	the hour of their J. is nigh
88	35	neither by mercy, justice nor J.
	40	J. goeth before the face of him
	84	hour of J. which is to come
	92	the J. of our God is come
	104	for the hour of his J. is come—133:38
89	8	to be used with J. and skill
97	2	I shall bring them into J.
98	28	if he be not brought into J.
99	5	I come quickly to J.
101	78	for his own sins in day of J.
105	25	execute J. and justice for us
107	72	to sit in J. upon transgressors
109	77	enthroned with glory, J. mercy
121	24	I have in reserve a swift J.
124	52	and I will answer, J., wrath
133	2	upon the world with a curse to J.
	50	and have brought J. upon all people

See Judgment-Seat.

JUDGMENTS

19	5	I revoke not the J. which I
29	30	all my J. are not given unto men
61	22	known according to their J.
82	2	lest sore J. fall upon your heads

Sec.	Vs.		Sec.	Vs.	
88	79	the J. which are on the land			**JUSTICE**
105	24	talk not of J. neither boast of faith	10	28	not exempt from the J. of God
109	30	by the J. which thou wilt send—38	82	4	J. and judgment are the penalty
	40	let not thy J. fall upon that city	84	102	he is full of mercy, J., grace
	45	pour out thy J. without measure	88	35	cannot be sanctified by J., nor
119	6	that my J. may be kept thereon		40	J. continueth its course, and
124	39	and your statutes and J. for the	102	16	speak according to equity and J.
	48	ye bring cursings and J. on your	105	25	execute judgment and J. for us
134	5	as in their J. are best calculated	107	84	none exempted from J. of God
136	42	keeping my commandments lest J.	109	77	enthroned with glory, J., and
			127	1	without least coloring of J.
		JUDGMENT-SEAT	134	3	administer law in equity and J.
58	20	or him that sitteth upon the J.		7	have no right in J. to deprive
135	5	until we shall meet before the J.			**JUSTIFIABLE**
		JULY	98	5	that law is J. before me
115	10	let beginning be made on 4th of J.			**JUSTIFICATION**
		JUNE	20	30	J. through grace of our Lord
135	1	shot in Carthage jail on 27th of J.	98	38	this is an ensample for J. before me
		JUST			**JUSTIFIED**
3	4	incur the vengeance of a J. God	50	15	and, in this are ye J.
11	23	added according to that which is J.		39	in this my servant, is not J.
20	30	justification is J. and true	63	19	I say that ye are not J.
	31	sanctification is J. and true	64	13	that ye may be J. in the eyes of
38	26	looketh on his sons and saith I am J.	67	7	then ye are J. in saying that ye
42	72	are to receive a J. remuneration	88	39	who abide not in, are not J.
	73	his support or a J. remuneration	97	2	that I may be J., when I shall bring
51	19	whoso is found a J. steward	98	31	according to his works thou art J.; if he has sought thy life thou art J.
58	18	judge by testimony of the J.			
76	17	in the resurrection of the J.— 50, 65	132	1	wherein I J. my servants Abraham
76	53	upon all those who are J. and true		62	they are given him, therefore is he J.—61
	69	they who are J. men made perfect	134	11	all men are J. in defending themselves
82	17	inasmuch as his wants are J.			**JUSTIFY**
98	24	accounted as a J. measure unto you	98	6	I J. you and your brethren in
101	77	according to J. and holy principles		36	J. them in going out to battle
107	26	to that of the apostles J. named	132	59	by word, I *will* J. him
124	121	let quorum, have a J. recompense		60	my servant Joseph, I *will* J. him
127	3	he will meet out a J. recompense	134	7	such opinions do not J. sedition
128	4	the record shall be J. as holy, J. as if he had seen			**JUSTLY**
129	3	spirits of J. men made perfect—6	11	12	leadeth to do J., to judge
	7	contrary for a J. man to deceive	102	33	appealed, is J. entitled to re-hearing
134	9	not J. to mingle religious influence			
	12	believe it J. to preach the gospel			

K

Sec.	Vs.		Sec.	Vs.	
		KEEP	10	56	they who K. not my commandments
5	28	K. my commandments—6:6, 9, 37; 8:5; 11:6, 9, 18, 20; 12:6; 14:6, 7; 18:43; 25:15; 42:29; 43:35; 71:11	18	46	if you K. not my commandments
			19	13	repent and K. the commandments
			20	77	always remember him and K. his
			33	14	remember the covenants to K. them

Sec.	Vs.		Sec.	Vs.	
35	24	K. all commandments and covenants—136:2	70	11	agent who K. the Lord's storehouse
42	1	believe on my name, and K. my	93	1	obeyeth my voice and K. my
	78	shall observe to K. all the		27	no fulness unless he K. his
44	5	may be enabled to K. my laws		28	he that K. his commandments receiveth
45	72	K. these things from going abroad	96	6	eternal life inasmuch as he K. my
46	9	who love me and K. all my			
47	1	should write and K. a regular history		**KEEPING**	
	3	to K. the church record and history	5	22	be firm in K. the commandments
56	2	he that will not K. my commandments		35	if thou art faithful in K. my—104:42
58	24	have appointed to K. my storehouse	6	20	be faithful and diligent in K. the
			18	8	if he shall be diligent in K. my—30:8
59	9	more fully K. thyself unspotted	76	52	that by K. the commandments they
63	22	many who observe not to K. my	92	2	as you are faithful in K. all former
66	11	K. these sayings for they are true	136	37	if ye are faithful in K. all my words
68	29	observe Sabbath day to K. it holy		42	be diligent in K. all my
72	10	to K. the Lord's storehouse			
82	4	as ye K. not my sayings which I		**KEPT**	
85	1	K. a history and general church	6	26	records have been K. back because
89	18	who remember to K. and do these	20	82	of whole church may be K. in a book
90	18	K. slothfulness and uncleanness far			
93	20	if you K. my commandments you shall—95:11	21	1	there shall be a record K. among
	52	inasmuch as you K. my sayings	29	12	as many as have K. my commandments
95	12	if you K. not my commandments you—103:8	38	5	the wicked have I K. in chains of
100	14	as they K. my commandments they shall		6	so will I cause the wicked to be K.
	17	all that K. his commandments shall be	39	15	I have K. in store a blessing
			41	4	ye shall see that my law is K.
103	29	preparing the churches to K. the	42	33	it shall be K. to administer to
104	61	appoint one to K. the treasury		34	residue shall be K. in my
	67	treasurer appointed to K. the	44	6	poor and needy that they may be K.
105	8	many will say, we *will* K. our moneys	51	13	be K. in the hands of the bishop
			52	34	he that is faithful shall be K. and
110	8	if my people *will* K. my commandments	54	6	blessed are they who have K. covenant
117	16	mine house, to K. and preserve it holy	58	19	my law shall be K. on this land
			63	13	have turned away and not K. them
119	6	observe not this law to K. it holy		50	he that has K. the faith, blessed
124	85	come here, essaying to K. my	64	15	for they K. not the law, neither
	87	if ye love me, K. my commandments	76	73	spirits of men K. in prison
			83	6	storehouse shall be K. by consecrations
125	2	if they will do my will and K. my	84	110	that the system may be K. perfect
136	20	seek to K. all your pledges one with	85	4	neither is their genealogy to be K.
	21	K. yourselves from evil	93	44	he hath not K. the commandments
				47	you have not K. the commandments
	KEEPEST		101	54	could have made ready and K. enemy
109	1	who K. covenant and showest mercy	104	4	some of my servants have not K.
	KEEPETH			66	and a seal shall be K. upon it
41	8	inasmuch as he K. my commandments	119	6	that my judgments may be K. thereon
58	2	blessed is he that K. my commandments	123	12	who are only K. from the truth because
	21	he that K. the laws of God hath no		16	by being K. workways with the wind
	29	and K. it with slothfulness, the			
63	23	unto him that K. my commandments I	124	41	reveal things that have been K. hid

Sec.	Vs.		Sec.	Vs.	
128	7	the records which are K. on earth; is the record which is K. in heaven	113	6	unto whom rightly belongs the K.
	8	which they have K. concerning the dead	115	19	have I given the K. of this kingdom
	9	and K. a proper and faithful record	124	34	for therein are the K. of the holy
	18	have been K. hid from the wise and		92	he shall hold K. of the patriarchal
133	60	commanded to be K. from the world		95	K. by which he may ask and receive
				97	let William Law also receive the K.
		KEY		123	my priesthood, that ye may hold K.
84	19	K. of mysteries of the kingdom, even the K. of		128	which Twelve hold the K. to open
	26	K. of the ministering of angels and		143	the K. for helps and governments
128	14	which consist in the K. of knowledge	128	10	I will give unto thee the K. of the
130	11	the new name is the K. word		11	for him to whom these K. are given
				14	this is the sealing power, the K.
		KEYS		18	welding together of K. and powers
6	28	I give unto you K. of this gift		20	as possessing the K. of the kingdom
7	7	unto you three will I give the K.		21	declaring their rights, their K.
13	1	which holds the K. of the ministering	129	9	these are three grand K. whereby
27	5	have committed the K. of the record	132	7	never but one on whom the K. are
	6	K. of bringing to pass restoration		19	appointed this power and the K. of
	9	K. of the power of turning hearts	132	39	prophets who had K. of this power
	12	and bear the K. of your ministry		45	I have conferred upon you the K.
	13	committed the K. of the kingdom—81:2		59	I have endowed him with the K. and
28	7	given him the K. of the mysteries—35:18		64	if any man who holds K. of this power
35	25	by K. I have given shall they be led			**KICK**
42	69	the K. of the church have been given	121	38	to K. against the pricks, to
64	5	K. shall not be taken from my			**KILL**
65	2	K. of the kingdom of God are	42	18	thou shalt not K.—19
68	17	and the K. or authority of the same		79	if any persons shall K.
	18	to hold the K. of this priesthood	45	33	and they *will* K. one another
78	16	given him the K. of salvation	59	6	neither commit adultery, nor K.
90	2	to bear the K. of the kingdom	132	36	it was written, thou shalt not K.
	3	K. of this kingdom shall never be taken			**KILLED**
	6	equal with thee in holding the K.	136	36	for they K. the prophets
	7	K. of the school of the prophets			**KILLETH**
97	14	the K. of which have been conferred	42	19	but he that K. shall die
107	15	holds K. and authority of the same			**KILLS**
	16	no man has right to hold the K.	42	18	he that K. shall not have forgiveness
	18	to hold K. of spiritual blessings			**KIMBALL, HEBER C.**
	20	hold K. of the ministering of angels	124	129	they are—K., Parley P. Pratt, etc.
	35	holding the K. to open the door			**KIND**
	70	cannot hold the K. of that priesthood	43	25	of famines and pestilences of every K.
	76	has a legal right to the K. of this	128	18	a welding link of some K. or other
110	11	the K. of the gathering of Israel			**KINDLED**
	16	K. of this dispensation are committed	1	13	the anger of the Lord is K.
112	15	the K. which I have given unto him	5	8	my anger is K. against them—60:2; 84:24
	16	thou art the man to hold the K.	56	1	anger is K. against the rebellious—63:2
	32	K. of dispensation ye have received	59	21	against none is his wrath K. save
			61	31	anger is K. against their wickedness
			97	24	is K. against their abominations

Sec.	Vs.	
109	27	thine anger be K. against them
	52	may thine anger be K. and thine
121	5	let thine anger be K. against our

KINDLETH

Sec.	Vs.	
82	6	anger of God K. against the

KINDLY

Sec.	Vs.	
99	6	and K. sent up unto the bishop

KINDNESS

Sec.	Vs.	
4	6	remember patience, brotherly K.
107	30	godliness, brotherly K. and charity
121	42	by K. and pure knowledge which
133	52	the loving K. of their Lord; according to his loving K.

KINDRED

Sec.	Vs.	
10	51	whatsoever nation, K., tongue or
77	8	gospel to commit to every nation, K.
	11	ordained out of every nation, K.
98	33	not go out unto battle against any K.
124	58	in thee and thy seed shall the K.
133	37	preached unto every nation, K. and

KINDREDS

Sec.	Vs.	
7	3	shalt prophesy before nations, K.
42	58	taught unto all nations, K., tongues
88	103	unto all nations, K., tongues and
112	1	send it abroad among all nations, K.
124	58	concerning the K. of the earth

KINDS

Sec.	Vs.	
58	54	workmen sent forth of all K.
129	1	are two K. of beings in heaven

KING

Sec.	Vs.	
10	41	till you come to reign of K. Benjamin
38	21	ye shall have no K., nor ruler, for I will be your K.
45	53	because they persecuted their K.
	59	he will be their K. and lawgiver
128	22	eternal praise to the K. Immanuel
	23	the wonders of your eternal K.

KINGDOM

Sec.	Vs.	
6	3	everlasting salvation in the K. of God—11:3; 12:3; 14:3
	13	thou shalt be saved in the K. of God
	37	ye shall inherit the K. of heaven
7	4	speedily come unto me in my K.
10	55	for such shall inherit the K.
	56	and build up the K. of the devil
11	23	my son, seek the K. of God
15	6	may rest with them in K. of my—16:6
18	15	your joy with him in the K. of my
	16	brought unto me into the K. of my

Sec.	Vs.	
	25	cannot have place in the K. of my
	44	that they may come into the K. of
	46	ye cannot be saved in the K. of—20:29
25	1	are sons and daughters in my K.
27	4	in this my Father's K.
	13	have committed keys of my K.
29	5	his good will to give you the K.
33	10	the K. of heaven is at hand—39:19; 42:7
35	27	K. is yours until I come
36	2	teach peaceable things of the K.—39:6
38	9	behold the K. is yours—15
41	6	which belong to children of the K.
42	65	to know mysteries of the K.
	69	for unto you the K., or in other words
43	10	glory shall be added to the K.
	12	if ye desire glories of the K.
	13	if ye desire mysteries of the K.
45	1	to whom the K. has been given
46	5	who are earnestly seeking the K.—6
50	35	K. is given you of the Father
56	18	they shall see the K. of God
58	2	is greater in the K. of heaven
	18	according to the laws of the K.
61	37	blessings of the K. are yours
62	9	the K. is yours—78:18; 82:24
63	23	I will give the mysteries of my K.
64	4	I have given unto you the K.
	5	keys of K. shall not be taken from
65	2	keys of the K. are committed to man
	5	that his K. may go forth; to meet the K. of God which
	6	may K. of God go forth, that K. of heaven may come
70	8	according to the laws of the K.
71	1	proclaiming the things of the K.
72	1	to whom the K. and power have
	14	administering in things of the K.
	24	in addition to the laws of the K.
76	7	all hidden mysteries of my K.; all things pertaining to K.
	28	devil sought to take the K. of
	79	they obtain not the crown over K.
	107	when he shall deliver up the K.
	114	marvelous are mysteries of his K.
81	2	have given the keys of the K.
84	19	holdeth key of the mysteries of the K.
	28	to overthrow K. of the Jews
	34	they become the church and the K.
	38	receiveth my Father, receiveth my Father's K.
	58	bring forth fruit for Father's K.
	59	shall the children of the K. pollute
	74	shall not come into my Father's K.

Sec.	Vs.	
	76	those to whom the K. has been given
	80	preach the gospel of the K.
	86	to proclaim this gospel of the K.
88	4	even the glory of the celestial K.
	20	bodies who are of the celestial K.
	21	must inherit another K., even that of a terrestrial K., or a telestial K.
	22	abide a law of the celestial K.
	23	abide the law of a terrestrial K.
	24	abide the law of a telestial K.; not meet for K. of glory; must abide K. which is not a K. of glory
	25	earth abideth law of celestial K.
	37	no space in which there is no K.; no K. in which there is no space, either a greater or a lesser K.
	38	unto every K. is given a law
	61	every K. in its hour and its time
	70	first laborers in this last K.—74
	77	teach one another doctrine of the K.
	78	teach all things that pertain to K.
90	2	that bear keys of the K.; K. is coming forth for last time
	3	keys of this K. shall never be taken
	6	holding keys of this last K.
	14	unfold the mysteries of this K.
	16	set in order all affairs of this K.
94	3	work in all things pertaining to K—97:14; 100:11
97	14	keys of which K. have been conferred
99	3	as a little child, receiveth my K.
101	61	in mine house, a ruler in my K.
	65	when I shall come in the K. of
	100	bring forth fruit meet for my K.
103	35	organize my K. upon earth
104	59	building up my church and K.
105	4	union required by law of celestial K.
	5	built up on law of celestial K.
	32	K. of Zion is in very deed the K.
106	3	seeking diligently the K. of
107	19	receiving the mysteries of the K.
109	72	that the K. which thou hast set up
112	16	thou art the man to hold keys of K.
	17	to unlock the door of the K.
	21	power to open the door of my K.
113	6	belongs the keys of the K.
115	19	keys of the K. and ministry
124	128	to open up the authority of my K.
128	10	will give unto thee the keys of the K.
	14	in one sense the keys of the K.
	20	possessing the keys of the K.
130	9	pertaining to an inferior K.
	11	those who come into the celestial K.
131	4	that is the end of his K.
132	49	a throne for you in the K. of

Sec.	Vs.	
136	31	is not worthy of my K.
	41	you have received my K.

KINGDOMS

78	15	be made rulers over many K.
84	82	K. of the world in all their glory
	118	I will rend their K.
88	36	all K. have a law given
	37	and there are many K.
	46	unto what shall I liken these K.
	47	all these are K.
	51	I will liken these K. unto a man
	61	will I liken all these K.
	79	knowledge of countries and of K.—93:53
103	7	until K. of the world are subdued
	8	K. of the world shall prevail
105	32	K. of this world may be constrained
128	23	K., principalities and powers
130	9	or all K. of a lower order
	10	to a higher order of K.
132	19	shall inherit thrones, K. and

KINGS

1	23	declared before K. and rulers
76	56	they are they who are priests and K.
109	55	remember the K., the princes
124	3	proclamation shall be made to all K.
	5	my will concerning those K.
	11	awake, O K. of the earth
	16	in sending my word to the K.
	107	making solemn proclamation to K.

KIRTLAND

63	38	let my disciples in K. arrange
64	21	will to retain a strong hold in K.
82	12	in the land of Shinehah, (K.)
	13	have consecrated land of Shinehah, (K.)
89	1	High Priests assembled in K.
94	1	the stake of Zion in land of K.
98	19	not pleased with many in church at K.
104	21	which dwell in land of Shinehah, (K.)
	40	my stake in land of Shinehah, (K.)
	48	United Order of city of Shinehah, (K.)
105	33	be built unto my name in land of K.
109	2	build a house to thy name in this place, (K.)
117	1	and journey from the land of K.
	5	let properties of K. be turned out for
	16	let all my servants in land of K.
124	83	even unto K., I will build up K.

KNEE

76	110	these shall all bow the K.
88	104	and every K. shall bow

Sec.	Vs.		Sec.	Vs.	
		KNEEL		15	how sore you K. not; how exquisite you K. not; how hard to bear you K. not
20	76	he shall K. with the church		22	they must not K. these things lest
		KNEES	20	17	we K. that there is a God in heaven
81	5	strengthen the feeble K.		29	we K. that all men must repent
88	131	himself in prayer upon his K.		30	we K. that justification through
		KNEW		31	we K. that sanctification through
38	13	and ye K. it not		35	we K. that these things are true
45	54	and they that K. no law shall	21	7	and his diligence I K.
101	33	hidden things which no man K.		29	39 they could not K. the sweet
		KNEWEST		31	2 they will believe and K. the truth
35	4	and thou K. it not		38	8 ye shall see me and K. that I am— 50:45
		KNIGHT, JOSEPH		29	ye know not the hearts of men in your
23	6	I manifest unto you, K., by these words	39	7	looked on thy works and I K. thee
		KNIGHT, NEWEL		23	of my coming and shall K. me
52	32	let K., and Griffin both be ordained	41	3	that ye may K. how to govern
54	2	my servant K., you shall stand fast	42	61	that thou mayest K. the mysteries
56	6	I revoke commandment given to K. and		65	to K. the mysteries of the kingdom; world is not given to K. them
	7	let K. remain with them and as many	43	3	shall K. assuredly none other
124	132	viz., Thomas Grover, K., etc.		6	that you may K. they are not of me
		KNIGHT, VINSON		8	ye may K. how to act and direct
				33	their end no man ever shall K.
124	74	my servant K., if he will do my will	45	22	ye K. the end of the world cometh; ye K. that the heavens
	141	I give unto you, K., if he will		35	ye may K. that the promises
		KNOCK		38	they K. that the hour is nigh
4	7	K. and it shall be opened unto you —6:5; 11:5; 12:5; 14:5; 49:26; 66:9; 75:27; 88:63		46	as you now behold me and K. that I
				52	then shall they K. that I am the
				60	not be given you to K. any further
		KNOW		72	that they may not know your works
1	35	K. that the day speedily cometh		73	that when they shall K. it, they
3	20	that they might K. the promises	46	13	to K. that Jesus Christ is the Son
5	12	K. of a surety these things are true —25		15	to K. differences of administration
				16	to K. the diversities of operation
6	11	thou shalt K. mysteries which	48	5	shall be given to K. the place
	15	that thou mayest K. that thou	49	2	they desire to K. truth in part
	16	mayest K. that there is none else		7	nor shall they K. until he comes
	22	might K. concerning the truth of		8	holy men that ye K. not of
8	11	that you might K. the mysteries	50	21	why is it that ye cannot K. that
11	14	then shall ye K. or by this shall you K. all		25	I say it that ye may K. the truth
				30	but K. this, it shall be given
	16	K. of a surety of my doctrine		31	then you may K. it is not of God
15	4	many times you have desired to K.—16:4	52	19	by this pattern ye shall K. the spirits
18	1	you have desired to K. of me	56	1	they shall K. mine arm and mine
	2	wherefore you K. that they are true	58	8	that earth may K. the mouths of the
	3	and if you K. that they are true		43	by this ye may K. if a man repenteth
	25	if they K. not the name by which	60	4	all men shall K. what it is that
	36	have heard my voice and K. my words	61	27	it is given to K. all his ways
	38	by their works you shall K. them	63	6	all flesh shall K. that I am God
19	8	to K. even as mine apostles	67	1	and whose hearts I K.

Know   241   Knowledge

Sec.	Vs.	
	5	beyond his language; this you K.
	7	ye do not K. that they are true
	9	ye K. that there is no unrighteousness
	10	shall see me and K. that I am
	14	ye shall K. that which was conferred
68	11	be given to K. sign of the times
69	3	which he shall observe and K.
75	21	and K. this, you shall be judges
	23	that you might K. his will concerning
76	8	wonders of eternity shall they K.
	31	all those who K. my power and have
	94	they K. as they are known
80	4	declare the things ye K. to be true
84	50	you may K. they are under bondage
	53	you may K. the righteous from the
	91	by this you may K. my disciples
	98	all shall K. me who remain
	119	ye shall see it and K. that I am
88	50	shall ye K. that ye have seen me
93	1	shall see my face and K. that I am
	19	and K. how to worship; and K. what you worship
96	1	ye may K. how to act concerning
97	8	them who K. their hearts are honest
100	11	that thou mayest K. the certainty
101	16	be still and K. that I am God
	43	that you may K. my will concerning
	94	that rulers may hear and K. that
103	1	may K. how to act in discharge of
105	10	may K. more perfectly concerning
109	23	that they may K. this is thy work
	45	we K. that thou hast spoken by the
	57	that the ends of the earth may K.
	70	that they may K. that thou art God
110	16	ye may K. the great and dreadful day
112	11	I K. thy heart and have heard thy
	26	who have professed to K. my name
121	24	mine eyes see and K. all their works
	44	that he may K. thy faithfulness
122	7	K. thou, my son, that all these things
123	12	because they K. not where to find it
	13	things of darkness wherein we K. them
	16	you K., brethren, that a large ship
124	5	given you by Holy Ghost to K. my
	73	others who wish to K. my will
128	18	it is sufficient to K. in this

Sec.	Vs.	
129	9	may K. whether any administration is
130	14	once praying earnestly to K. the time
132	1	to K. and understand wherein I
	22	ye receive me not, neither do ye K. me
	23	if ye receive me, then shall ye K. me
	24	this is eternal lives to K. the
133	11	for ye K. neither the day nor the hour
135	5	all men shall K. that my garments

KNOWEST

6	15	thou K. that thou hast inquired
	16	save God that K. thy thoughts
42	28	thou K. my laws concerning
109	5	thou K. we have done this work
	31	thou K., O Lord that thy servants
	48	thou K. they have been oppressed
	61	thou K. thou hast great love for

KNOWETH

6	24	told you things which no man K.
15	3	will tell you that which no man K.—16:3
28	9	no man K. where the city shall be
35	19	Holy Ghost that K. all things
38	2	the same which K. all things
39	21	the day nor the hour no man K.—49:7
42	17	the Comforter K. all things
43	33	their end no man K. on earth
62	1	who K. the weakness of man
84	83	your Father K. you have need of
93	28	he is glorified and K. all things
127	2	God K. all these things
130	11	new name which no man K. save he
132	44	not broken her vow and she K. it

KNOWING

1	17	I, the Lord, K. the calamity
76	117	this privilege of K. for themselves
131	5	means a man's K. that he is sealed up

KNOWLEDGE

1	28	receive K. from time to time
3	16	as K. of a Savior has come to. so shall K. come to
	18	come to K. of the Lamanites
	20	might come to K. of their fathers
4	6	remember faith, virtue, K.
6	11	mayest bring many to a K. of the
8	1	so surely shall you receive a K.; believing you shall receive a K.

Sec.	Vs.		Sec.	Vs.	
	9	you shall have K. concerning it	26	1	shall be made K. what you shall do
	11	receive K. of those ancient records	39	10	blessing so great as you never have K.
10	40	K. of the people in this account		15	as is not K. among the children of
	52	bring gospel to K. of my people	42	11	K. to the church he has authority
20	13	as many as shall come to a K. of	45	60	in it all these things shall be made K.
29	49	whoso having K. have I not	52	2	make K. unto you what I will
42	61	receive K. upon K.		4	made K. unto them what they shall do
46	18	given word of K., and to have K.		5	made K., land of your inheritance
50	40	ye must grow in grace and in K.	53	1	made K. concerning your calling
58	56	according to K. which they receive		6	the residue shall be K. in a time— 55:6
67	5	you have sought in your hearts K.	58	50	shall be made K. by the spirit
69	7	may more easily obtain K.		55	privileges of the lands be made K.
73	5	pattern unto the elders until further K.	60	13	thy talent that it may not be K.
77	4	representation of light and K.; they are full of K.		17	made K. concerning Sidney Rigdon
84	19	even the key of the K. of God	61	22	as it is made K. unto them
	98	shall be filled with the K. of the Lord	63	22	make K. my will, I will make it K.
88	79	and a K. of countries and kingdoms	64	17	but when these things are made K.
89	19	shall find great treasures of K.		19	which he hath heard may be made K.
93	24	truth is K. of all things as they		39	who are not prophets shall be K.
	53	obtain a K. of history and countries	65	4	make K. his wonderful works among
101	25	that my K. and glory may dwell	67	5	his language you have K.; his imperfections you have K.
107	30	decisions made in virtue, K.			
	31	they shall not be unfruitful in K.	71	2	until it shall be made K. unto you
	71	having K. of them by the spirit of	72	7	duty of bishops shall be made K.
109	67	may come to a K. of the truth		9	making K. the duty of the bishop
121	26	God shall give unto you K. by his holy	73	2	then it shall be made K.
	33	pouring down K. from heaven	75	27	shall be made K. from on high
	42	by kindness and pure K., which	76	7	make K. good pleasure of my will
123	1	gathering up a K. of all facts		10	make K. the secrets of my will
124	26	will all who have K. of antiquities		94	they know as they are K.
	141	a K. of said bishopric is given in		116	neither is man capable to make them K.
128	4	records to be true from his K.	97	6	their works shall be made K.
	5	who should die without a K. of	104	36	as it shall be made K. to him
	11	there is no difficulty in obtaining a K.	112	6	let thy habitation be K. in Zion
	14	which consist in the key of K.		26	who have professed and have not K. me
	19	so shall the K. of God descend	122	9	thy days are K. and thy years
130	19	if a person gains more K. in this	130	10	order of kingdoms, will be made K
			132	45	make K. unto all things in due
		KNOWN	133	36	that these things might be K. among
1	25	as they erred it might be made K.		42	make thy name K. to thine adversaries
	34	make these things K. unto all flesh		46	from the regions which are not K.
5	9	shall be made K. unto future			
6	12	make not thy gift K. unto any			**KNOWS**
9	10	if you had K. this you could have	58	59	bear record of that which he K.
10	37	shall see fit to make all things K.	76	45	end, nor their torment no man K.
	49	this gospel should be made K.		90	no man K. it except him to whom
18	8	which purpose is K. in me			
20	84	members, where they are not K. may			
23	2	make K. thy calling			
24	12	strength such as is not K. among			

L

Sec.	Vs.	
		LABAN
17	1	the breastplate, the sword of L.
		LABOR
10	4	do not run faster or L. more
18	15	if you should L. all your days
21	9	I will bless all those who L.
30	10	and your L. shall be at your brother
	11	your whole L. shall be in Zion
38	40	go to with the L. of his hands—124:112
39	13	called to L. in my vineyard—43:28; 50:38; 71:4
52	36	let them L. with their families
	39	let them L. with their own hands
53	6	according to your L. in my vineyard
56	17	who *will* not L. with your own hands
58	54	to L. for the saints of God
	60	and L. with your own hands, until he is
64	25	ye *will* L. while it is called today
68	30	inasmuch as they are appointed to L.
72	14	faithful who L. in spiritual things
75	3	neither be idle but L. with your
	28	and let him L. in the church
84	109	every man L. in his own calling
88	52	go ye and L. in the field
	84	tarry ye and L. diligently
107	96	if the L. in vineyard requires it
115	10	L. diligently to build a house
	12	let them from that time forth L.
124	16	let Bennett help you in your L.
	44	if ye L. with all your might
126	2	I have seen your L. and toil
		LABORER
23	7	you may receive reward of the L.
31	5	for the L. is worthy of his hire—84:79; 106:3
42	42	idle shall not eat bread of the L.
72	17	to be received as a faithful L.
		LABORERS
33	3	last time that I shall call L. in
39	17	call faithful L. into my vineyard
88	70	the first L. in this kingdom—74
		LABORING
104	20	for his support while he is L.
		LABORS
6	31	have joy in the fruit of your L.
24	9	in temporal L. thou shalt not have
26	1	performing your L. on the land
41	9	spend all his time in L. of church
59	2	those that die shall rest from their L.
	10	appointed unto you to rest from your L.
61	32	L., even now, are wanted more
68	30	shall remember their L.
72	14	L. of the faithful who labor
	19	by the church in which he L.
124	86	they shall rest from all their L.
	121	recompense of wages for their L.
	122	L. shall be accounted for stock
		LACKETH
42	68	he that L. wisdom let him ask
		LADEN
31	5	you shall be L. with sheaves—33:9; 75:5
		LADY
25	3	thou art an elect L. whom I
		LAID
10	23	thus he has L. a cunning plan
27	2	my body which was L. down for you
38	33	I have a great work L. up in
42	31	they shall be L. before the bishop
	32	after they are L. before the bishop
45	1	who L. the foundation of the earth
49	10	exalted of itself shall be L. low
84	96	I have L. my hands on the nations
97	7	ax is L. at the root of the trees
104	36	lots L. off for the building up—43
	86	things which I have L. before you
107	72	L. before him according to the laws
112	18	for on them have I L. the burden
113	4	on whom there is L. much power
		LAKE
63	17	in that L. which burneth with fire
76	36	into the L. of fire and brimstone
		LAMANITES
3	18	shall come to knowledge of the L.
	20	and that the L. might come to the
10	48	the L., and also all that had become L.
19	27	may go to the Jew of whom the L. are a
28	8	you shall go unto the L. and preach

Sec.	Vs.		Sec.	Vs.	
	9	it shall be on the borders by the L.	48	4	purchase L. for an inheritance
	14	take thy journey among the L.	51	16	I consecrate unto them this L.
30	6	to build up my church among the L.		17	let them act upon this L. as for
32	2	go into the wilderness among the L.	52	2	the L. which I will consecrate
49	24	and the L. shall blossom as the rose		3	journey to the L. of Missouri
54	8	land of Missouri, unto borders of L.		14	Satan is abroad in the L.
				22	preaching the word unto this L.—
		LAMB			23, 25, 26, 27
58	11	in unto the marriage of the L.		42	L. of Missouri, now the L. of your
65	3	prepare ye the supper of the L			enemies
76	21	worshiping God and the L.	54	7	flee the L. lest your enemies
	39	triumph and glory of the L.		8	unto the L. of Missouri—56:5
	85	the Lord, even Christ, the L.	55	5	you may be planted in L. of your
	119	to God and the L. be glory	56	7	and be led by him to the L.
88	106	the L. of God hath overcome		9	no division made upon the L.,
	115	upon the throne, even the L.			appointed to L. of Missouri
109	79	singing Hosanna to God and the L.		12	will pay it in the L. of Missouri
122	6	like wolves for the blood of the L.	57	1	L. which is L. of Missouri; L.
133	18	when the L. shall stand on Mount			which I have appointed
	55	shall be in the presence of the L.		2	this is the L. of promise
	56	stand on the right hand of the L.;		4	L. should be purchased by saints
		sing the song of the L.		6	buy L. in all the regions
135	6	I am going like a L. to the		14	be planted in the L of Zion
		slaughter		15	commanded to come to this L.
			58	1	this L. to which I have sent you
		LAMB'S		7	bearing record of the L. upon
132	19	written in the L. Book of Life		14	appointed him his mission in this L.
				19	the law shall be kept on this L.
		LAME		21	let no man break laws of the L.;
35	9	cause the L. to walk			no need to break laws of L.
42	51	the L. who hath faith to leap		24	this L. is the L. of his residence,
58	11	then shall the poor, the L. and the			and also the L.
				25	bring their families to this L.
		LAMECH		34	directions concerning this L.
107	51	L. was 32 years old when ordained		36	every man that cometh to this L.
				40	receive his inheritance in the L.
		LAMENT		44	in this L. except they desire it
45	53	then shall they L., because they		46	not appointed to stay in this L.
				50	write a description of the L. of
		LAMENTATION		54	as there is L. obtained send work-
56	16	this shall be your L. in the day			men unto this L.
112	24	a day of weeping and of L.		57	consecrate and dedicate this L.
				58	appointed them in their own L.
		LAMPS		59	let no man return from this L.
33	17	your L. trimmed and burning		61	let elders coming to this L. hold
					conference upon this L.
		LAND	59	1	unto this L. with an eye single
10	49	other nations should possess this L.		3	whose feet stand upon the L. of
	50	did leave a blessing on this L.; be-			Zion
		lieve in this gospel in this L.	60	1	return speedily to the L.
26	1	performing your labors on the L.		5	unto the L. from whence ye came
29	8	to one place upon the face of this L.		12	residue who are to come to this L.
35	7	shall be a great work in the L.		14	after thou hast come up unto the L.
38	18	a L. of promise, a L. flowing with	61	16	none is able to go up unto the L.
	19	for the L. of your inheritance—		17	I in the beginning cursed the L.
		20; 52:5, 42		22	whether they go by water or by L.
	29	the hearts of men in your own L.		24	they shall journey by L. unto the
42	79	according to the laws of the L.—			L. of Zion
		84, 85, 86; 51:6; 83:3		28	whether upon the L. or the waters
45	31	desolating sickness shall cover the L.			
	66	a L. of peace, a city of refuge			

Sec.	Vs.	
62	2	who have not yet gone up to the L.
	4	assemble yourselves upon the L.
	6	rejoice together in the L.
63	24	unto the L. not in haste
	25	the L. of Zion I holdeth in mine
	29	L. of Zion shall not be obtained
	36	should be assembled upon the L.
	39	dispose of the L. that he may take journey to L.
	40	let moneys be sent up unto the L. —43
	41	who shall go up to the L.
	48	sendeth up treasures unto the L.
64	18	to his agency in the L. of Zion
	21	to retain a strong hold in the L.
	22	go with an open heart to the L.
	26	until residue shall go up to the L.
	30	obtain an inheritance in the L.
	34	obedient shall eat the good of the L
	35	shall be cut off out of the L.; rebellious shall not inherit L.
66	5	proclaim my gospel from L. to L.— 68:1
	6	go not up to the L. of Zion as yet
68	32	carry these sayings unto the L.
69	1	the moneys he shall carry unto the L.
	5	their stewardships to the L. of
	6	the L. of Zion shall be a seat
	8	grow up on the L. of Zion
72	23	in whatsoever L. they shall be
	26	he who shall go up unto the L.
77	15	Jerusalem in L. of their fathers
78	3	both in this place and in the L.
81	3	the gospel in L. of the living
82	12	both in L. of Zion and in L. of
	13	I have consecrated the L. of
84	59	shall the children pollute my holy L.
87	5	remnant left of the L. shall
88	79	the judgments that are on the L.
	110	he shall stand forth upon the L.
90	28	and go up unto the L. of Zion
	30	she should go up unto the L. of Zion
94	1	here in the L. of Kirtland
97	1	your brethren in the L. of Zion
	4	over the school in L. of Zion
	9	which is planted in a goodly L.
	10	built unto me in L. of Zion
98	4	concerning the laws of the L.
	5	law of the L. which is constitutional
	6	befriending constitutional law of L.
99	7	go up also unto the goodly L.
100	3	round about in this eastern L.
101	1	cast out from the L. of their
	44	a nobleman had spot of L., choice piece of L.
	45	that one may overlook the L.

Sec.	Vs.	
	56	go ye unto the L. of my vineyard —57
	58	that I may go and possess the L.
	70	round about the L. I have appointed to be the L.
	71	all the L. which can be purchased
	80	I established constitution of this L. and redeemed L. by shedding of blood
103	1	who have been scattered on the L.
	13	even their restoration to the L.
	20	in time ye shall possess the L.
	22	gather yourselves together to the L.; upon the L.
	24	to drive you from my goodly L. consecrated to be the L. of Zion
	30	should not return to the L. until; companies to go up unto the L.
	34	ye shall not go up unto the L. until
	35	my kingdom upon the consecrated L.
104	21	which dwell in the L. of Shinehah
	24	the lot of L. which my servant
	40	for my stake in L. of Shinehah.
105	33	to my name in the L. of Kirtland
106	1	in the L. of freedom and the regions
107	59	church of Christ in L. of Zion
109	54	have mercy upon rulers of our L.; the constitution of our L.
110	11	ten tribes from L. of the north
115	6	gathering together upon the L.
	7	let Far West be a consecrated L.
117	1	journey from L. of Kirtland
	8	or the L. where Adam dwelt
	9	up hither unto L. of my people
	11	to L. of Adam-ondi-Ahman
	14	speedily unto the L. of Zion
	16	my servants in L. of Kirtland
118	2	remain for a season in L. of Zion
119	5	those who gather to L. of Zion
	6	sanctify L. of Zion, it shall not be a L. of Zion
121	30	or to the dry L., or to the sun
122	5	if in perils by L. or by sea
124	38	to build a house in the L. of
	54	who have been slain in L. of
	87	because of the sickness of the L.; sickness of the L. shall redound to
125	3	upon the L. opposite Nauvoo
133	4	sanctify yourselves upon the L. of
	9	go ye forth unto the L. of Zion
	20	he shall stand upon the L. of
	23	the islands shall become one L.
	24	L. of Jerusalem and L. of Zion shall be turned back
	29	shall no longer be a thirsty L.
136	16	be ready to go to a L. of peace
	22	Israel out of the L. of Egypt

Sec.	Vs.	
		LANDS
19	34	impart a portion, even part of thy L.
42	35	for the purpose of purchasing L.
45	63	ye hear of wars in foreign L.; shall hear of wars in your own L.
	64	gather ye out from the eastern L.
48	2	as ye have L. ye shall impart to the
	3	as ye have not L. let them buy for the
	6	be appointed to purchase the L.
52	35	take their journey into the eastern L.
56	13	shall receive L. for their inheritance
57	5	as are enabled to buy L.
	8	may obtain money to buy L.
58	17	to divide the L. of the heritage
	37	should be L. purchased in Independence
	49	moneys to purchase L. in Zion
	51	purchase L. for an inheritance
	55	let privileges of the L. be made known
63	27	purchase the L. that you may have
66	7	go unto the eastern L.
70	16	for houses and for L. in whatsoever
101	70	purchase all the L. by money
	73	send them to purchase these L.
	74	they may buy L. and gather together
103	11	shall return to the L. of their
	23	purchase L. as I have commanded
	24	even from your own L.
104	68	in houses, or in L., or in cattle
105	15	the L. which I have consecrated
	28	purchasing all L. in Jackson County
	29	it is my will that these L.
	30	after these L. are purchased I; taking possession of their own L.
109	47	driven from the L. of their inheritance
	64	Judah may begin to return to L.
110	10	the fame, shall spread to foreign L.
124	83	not take his family to eastern L.—108
128	23	all ye seas and dry L. tell the
132	55	a hundred-fold of houses and L.
133	8	send forth unto foreign L.
		LANESHINE HOUSE
104	28	which is to be for the L. (printing office)
	29	let Olihah have the L. and all
		LANGUAGE
1	24	after the manner of their L.
23	7	give your L. to exhortation
52	16	whose L. is meek and edifieth
67	5	his L. you have known; that you might expresss beyond his L.
90	11	in his own tongue and his own L.

Sec.	Vs.	
		LANGUAGES
90	15	become acquainted with L., tongues
		LARGE
107	39	in all L. branches of the church
123	16	a very L. ship is benefited very much
		LAST
1	4	whom I have chosen in these L. days
4	2	blameless before God at the L. day
5	35	shall be lifted up at the L. day—9:14; 17:8; 52:44; 75:16, 22
17	8	if you do these L. commandments
18	24	shall they be called at the L. day
19	3	the L. great day of judgment
	32	this is a great and L. commandment
20	1	rise of the church in these L. days
	82	with the church since L. conference
22	3	I have caused this L. covenant
24	19	mighty pruning even for the L. time
27	6	spoken concerning the L. days—109:23
	13	dispensation of Gospel for L. time
29	30	first shall be L. and the L. shall
	32	spiritual, which is the L. of my work
	41	same death which is the L. death
33	3	for L. time that I shall call laborers
39	11	have sent forth in these L. days
	17	that it may be pruned for the L. time—95:4
43	28	for L. time; for the L. time call upon the
52	1	called and chosen in these L. days
53	1	have raised up in these L. days
61	14	in the L. days I cursed the waters
	17	so in the L. days have I blessed it
63	58	am not to be mocked in the L. days
64	30	provide for his saints in L. days
	34	the land of Zion in these L. days
	37	have made my church in these L. days
66	2	glories revealed in the L. days—128:17
76	22	this is the testimony L. of all
	85	redeemed until the L. resurrection
102		L. of all, these are they
77	15	to the Jewish nation in the L. days
84	2	church established in L. days
	117	desolation of abomination in the L.
86	4	in the L. days, while the Lord is
88	59	at the first, so to the L., from L. unto first and first unto L.
	69	remember the great and L. promise—75
	70	the first laborers in the L.—74

Sec.	Vs.	
	84	go forth among Gentiles for L. time
	102	remain until that great and L. day
89	2	salvation of all saints in L. days
	4	conspiring men in the L. days
90	2	kingdom is coming forth for L. time
	6	holding keys of this L. kingdom
107	53	bestowed upon them his L. blessing
109	45	concerning the wicked in the L. days
110	4	I am the first and the L.
112	30	given for L. days and for L. time
	32	L. of all being sent down from heaven
113	6	gathering of my people in L. days
	8	whom God should call in the L. days
115	4	shall my church be called in L. days
121	27	to be revealed in the L. times
123	6	as the L. effort enjoined on us
128	17	Malachi says, L. chapter, verses
132	7	Joseph to hold this power in L. days
136	22	my arm is stretched out in the L. days

LASTS

6	3	reap while the day L.—11:3; 12:3; 14:3

LATEST

107	56	posterity until the L. generation

LATTER

102	31	but from decision of the L. there
	32	the L. can only be called in question
135	2	the L. through the providence of God

LATTER-DAY

115	3	Church of Jesus Christ of L. Saints—4; 127:12; 128:21; 136:2
121	33	upon the heads of the L. Saints
128	24	as L. Saints offer unto the Lord an
135	3	gathered many thousands of the L. Saints

LAUGHED

45	49	they that L. shall see their folly

LAUGHTER

59	15	not with much L. for this is sin
88	69	cast away your excess of L.
	121	cease from all L., from all your

LAW

22	2	in at straight gate by L. of Moses
24	17	go to L. with thee shall be cursed by L.
29	34	given you a L. which was temporal
38	32	there I will give unto you my L.
41	3	by faith ye shall receive my L.

Sec.	Vs.	
	4	ye shall see that my L. is kept
	5	he that receiveth my L. and doeth it
42	2	hearken and hear and obey the L.
	59	for a L. to be my L. to govern
	81	dealt with according to the L. of
	84	he shall be delivered up to the L. of the land—85, 86
	87	delivered up to the L., even that of God—91
43	2	have received a commandment for a L.
	5	and this shall be a L. unto you
	8	how to act on the points of my L.
	9	ye shall become instructed in the L.
44	6	may be done according to my L.
45	54	they that knew no L. shall have a
58	19	my L. shall be kept on this land
	36	this is a L. unto every man that; do with his moneys as the L.
59	22	is according to L. and the prophets
64	13	may be justified in eyes of the L.
	15	for they kept not the L. neither
68	26	this shall be a L. unto inhabitants
70	10	none are exempt from this L.
72	9	in addition to the L. which has been
	15	according to the L. every man that
74	2	the L. of circumcision was had among
	3	contention concerning L. of circumcision; subject to L. of Moses which L. had been fulfilled
	4	in subjection to the L. of Moses
	5	except L. of Moses should be done away
76	72	these are they who died without L.
82	4	penalty which is affixed unto my L.
84	27	the L. of carnal commandments
85	3	consecration, agreeably to his L.
	5	written in the book of the L. of God—7, 11
88	13	L. by which all things are governed
	21	sanctified through the L.; the L. of Christ
	22	not able to abide L. of celestial
	23	who cannot abide L. of terrestrial
	24	who cannot abide L. of telestial
	25	the earth abideth L. of celestial, and transgresseth not the L.
	34	governed by L. is also preserved by L.
	35	which breaketh a L., abideth not by L.; a L. unto itself; cannot be sanctified by L.
	36	all kingdoms have a L. given
	38	unto every kingdom is given a L.; unto every L. there are certain bounds
	42	he hath given L. unto all things

Sec.	Vs.	
	78	instructed in L. of the gospel
	84	to bind up the L. to seal up the
98	5	that L. of the land which is constitutional
	6	justify you in befriending that L., the constitutional L.
	7	and as pertaining to L. of man
	8	and the L. also maketh you free
	32	this is the L. I gave unto Nephi
	33	this is the L. I gave unto mine
102	4	act according to the L. of heaven
104	18	according to the L. of my Gospel
105	4	required by L. of celestial kingdom
	5	principles of the L. of the celestial
	25	execute justice according to L.
	34	let her L. be executed
109	38	that they may seal *up* the L.
	46	enable thy servants to seal *up* the L.
119	4	this shall be a standing L.
	5	shall observe this L. or they shall
	6	if my people observe not this L., and by this L. sanctify
128	9	it became a L. on earth and in
130	20	there is a L., irrevocably decreed
	21	it is by obedience to that L.
132	3	all those who have this L. revealed
	5	all shall abide the L. appointed
	6	must and shall abide the L.
	7	the conditions of this L. are these
	11	and will I appoint; except it be by L.
	12	by my word, which is my L.—18, 19, 48
	15	they are not bound by any L.
	17	these angels did not abide my L.
	21	except ye abide my L. ye cannot attain
	24	receive ye therefore my L.
	25	neither do they abide in my L.
	27	he that abideth not this L.
	28	the L. of my Holy Priesthood
	31	by this L. are the continuation of
	32	enter into my L. and ye shall be
	33	if ye enter not into my L. ye cannot
	34	because this was the L., and from
	37	given unto him and he abode in my L.
	54	destroy her if she abide not my L.
	58	as touching L. of the priesthood—61
	59	in my name and according to my L.
	62	virgins given unto him by this L.
	64	teaches her the L. of my priesthood: are those who abide in my L.
	65	if she receive not this L.: he is exempt from the L. of Sarah: according to the L. when I
	66	as pertaining to this L. I will reveal

Sec.	Vs.	
133	72	sealed up testimony and bound up the L.
134	3	such as will administer L. in equity
	4	do not believe human L. has a right
	11	appeal to the civil L. for redress
135	4	pretended requirements of the L.

LAW, WILLIAM

124	82	let L. pay stock into that house
	97	let L. also receive the keys by which
	107	let L. assist my servant Joseph
	118	hearken unto counsel of Joseph and L.
	126	for counselors Sidney Rigdon and L.

LAWFUL

49	16	it is L. that he should have one
76	115	it is not L. for man to utter
86	9	for ye are L. heirs according to
132	65	it shall be L. in me if she receive

LAW GIVER

38	22	for I am your L.
45	59	he will be their King and their L.
64	13	not offend him who is your L.

LAWS

3	6	you have transgressed L. of God
20	1	agreeable to L. of our country
	20	by transgressions of Holy L.
38	22	ye shall have no L. but my L.
41	10	my L. in the day that I shall give
42	28	thou knowest my L. concerning these
	52	inasmuch as they break not my L.
	66	ye shall observe the L. which ye
	79	dealt with according to the L. of: it shall be proven according to L.
44	4	organize according to L. of man
	5	may be enabled to keep my L.
48	6	according to L. and commandments
51	2	be organized according to my L.
	4	according to L. of my church
	6	made sure according to the L. of
	15	organizing themselves according to my L.
58	18	according to the L. of the kingdom
	21	let no man break L. of land; he that keepeth L. of God hath no need to break L. of land
	23	L. which ye have received are L. of church
64	27	is said in my L., or forbidden to
70	8	heirs according to L. of kingdom
72	24	a few words in addition to the L.
82	15	done according to the L. of the Lord
	21	dealt with according to the L. of
83	1	in addition to the L. of church

Sec.	Vs.		Sec.	Vs.	
	3	according to L. of the land	101	35	called to L. down their lives for
93	53	obtain a knowledge of L. of God and	103	27	let no man be afraid to L. *down* his
98	4	concerning the L. of the land		28	whoso is not willing to L. *down* his
101	77	according to L. and constitution	105	15	destroy and L. waste mine enemies
103	35	establish children of Zion upon L.	109	66	that they may L. *down* their weapons
105	29	according to L. of consecration	124	99	serpent cannot L. hold upon his heel
	32	let us become subject unto her L.		116	L. aside all his hard speeches
107	59	church laws respecting church business		118	to L. the foundation of Zion
	72	upon testimony according to the L.—79	136	38	which foundation he did L. and I

LAYETH

Sec.	Vs.	
	84	none exempted from L. of God
4	4	the same L. *up* in store that he
109	15	be organized according to thy L.
98	13	whoso L. *down* his life in my—103:27
121	31	all their glories, L. and set times
124	50	the transgressions of my holy L.

LAYING

Sec.	Vs.	
134	1	either in making L. or administering
20	41	by the L. on of hands for the
	2	except such L. are framed and held
	43	confirmed by the L. on of hands—68; 33:15
	3	and enforce the L. of the same
	5	protected in their rights by the L., have a right to enact such L. as
24	9	continue in L. on of hands
35	6	Holy Ghost by the L. on of hands—49:14; 53:3; 55:1; 68:25; 76:52
	6	to the L. all men owe respect; human L. being instituted for the; divine L. given of heaven
52	10	L. on of the hands by the water's
56	17	L. hold upon other men's goods
58	7	be honored in L. the foundation
	7	bound to enact L. for protection; so long as reverence is shown for L.
	35	in L. his moneys before the bishop
64	33	ye are L. foundation of a great work
	8	by the L. of that government, and bringing offenders against good L. to
68	27	and receive the L. on of hands
94	1	L. out and preparing a beginning
101	47	while yet L. the foundation thereof
107	67	blessings upon church by the L. on
	11	where such L. exist as will protect; where appeal cannot be made to L.
115	11	recommence L. the foundation of my
119	2	for the L. of the foundation of Zion

LAY

LEAD

Sec.	Vs.	
1	30	power to L. foundation of this
10	22	he may L. their souls to destruction
6	27	a desire to L. *up* treasures for
20	44	and to take L. of all meetings
10	12	devil has sought to L. cunning plan
	49	take L. of meetings when there is—56
20	58	to baptize or L. on hands
	70	who are to L. their hands upon them
38	33	I *will* L. them whithersoever I will
21	2	inspired to L. the foundation thereof
78	18	for I *will* L. you along
24	16	whosoever shall L. hands upon you
103	16	a man who shall L. them like Moses
25	8	for he shall L. his hands upon thee
105	7	who are appointed to L. my people—124:45
10	L. aside the things of this world
36	2	I *will* L. my hand upon you by
112	10	thy God shall L. thee by the hand
39	17	L. to with your might and call

LEADER

| 23 | ye shall L. your hands and they |
| 54 | 7 | appoint whom you will to be your L. |

LEADERS

42	44	shall pray for and L. their hands
	81	shall L. the case before the church
112	30	to be your counselors and your L.
48	6	to L. the foundation of the city
55	3	on whomsoever you shall L. hands

LEADETH

58	5	remember, that you may L. it to heart
10	26	thus he flattereth and L. them along
66	9	L. your hands upon the sick and they
11	12	that spirit which L. to do good
72	15	must L. all things before bishop
82	7	I *will* not L. any sin to your charge

Sec.	Vs.		Sec.	Vs.	
132	22	the way that L. to exaltation	127	1	have not L. shadow of justice
	25	wide the way that L. to the deaths	134	12	nor to meddle with them in the L.

LEADING

110	11	L. of the ten tribes from the land

LEAF

135	4	and turned down the L. upon. it

LEAP

42	51	lame who hath faith to L. shall L.

LEAPED

135	1	Joseph L. from the window

LEARN

19	23	L. of me and listen to my words
32	1	declare my gospel and L. of me
35	16	L. the parable of the fig-tree
53	7	I would that ye should L. that
58	1	give ear to my word and L. of me
59	23	but L. that he who doeth the works
88	123	L. to impart one to another
90	15	study and L. and become acquainted
97	1	seeking diligently to L. wisdom
105	1	that you may L. my will concerning
	6	chastened until they L. obedience
107	99	now let every man L. his duty
121	35	that they do not L. this one lesson
127	1	when I L. the storm is fully blown
136	32	let him L. wisdom by humbling himself

LEARNED

58	10	first, the rich and the L.
105	3	they have not L. to be obedient
121	39	we have L. by sad experience that

LEARNING

25	8	given to writing and to L. much
46	1	were spoken for your profit and L.
88	118	seek L. even by study and by faith—109:7, 14
	119	establish a house of L., a house—109:8

LEARNS

107	100	he that L. not his duty and shows

LEAST

1	31	upon sin with L. degree of allowance
19	20	even in L. degree you have tasted
42	38	as ye doeth unto the L. of these
50	26	notwithstanding he is L. and the
67	6	seek even the L. that is among them
84	98	even from the L. unto the greatest
88	47	who hath seen any or the L. of these

LEAVE

10	50	thus they did L. a blessing
19	36	L. thy house and home, except
24	15	ye shall L. a cursing instead of
28	10	thou shalt not L. this place until
41	9	L. his merchandise and spend all
52	3	as preparations can be made to L.
56	10	otherwise he shall L. the place
61	24	after they L. the canal they shall
75	19	L. your blessing upon that house
82	23	L. judgment alone with me
88	62	I L. these sayings with you
101	71	and L. the residue in mine hand—103:40
118	5	let them take L. of my saints
126	1	no more required to L. your family
127	1	thought it wisdom to L. the place
133	64	shall L. them neither root nor branch

LEAVES

45	37	and their L. are yet tender

LEAVING

128	7	previous to L. my place

LED

20	45	conduct meetings as they are L.
28	4	if thou art L. by the Comforter
35	25	by the keys shall they be L.
56	7	be L. by him to the land which I
103	16	as Moses L. the children of Israel
	17	ye must needs be L. out of bondage
	18	as your fathers were L. at the first
111	3	shall be L. as it shall be given
124	99	he shall be L. in paths where the
136	22	I am he that L. children of Israel

LEES

58	5	of wine on the L. well refined

LEFT

3	2	turn to the right nor to the L.
19	5	those who are found on my L. hand
29	27	the wicked on my L. hand will I be
30	3	you are L. to inquire for yourself
38	37	let them be L. or rented as seemeth
42	75	have L. their companions for sake
45	20	not be L. one stone upon another
51	8	money which is L. unto this people
84	88	I will be on your right hand and your L.
	115	their house shall be L. desolate
87	5	remnants who are L. of the land
88	82	they are L. without excuse

Sec.	Vs.	
101	93	that all men may be L. without excuse
105	15	they shall not be L. to pollute
121	15	not one of them is L. to stand by
	38	he is L. unto himself to kick
123	6	whole nation may be L. without excuse
124	7	they may be L. also without excuse
	10	refuge for those who shall be L.
127	1	I have L. my affairs with agents
128	1	in my letter before I L. my place
130	16	I was L. thus without being able
135	3	L. a fame and name that cannot
136	40	I have L. a witness of my name

LEGAL

68	16	they have a L. right to bishopric
	18	no man has a L. right to this—107:16
107	76	literal descendant has a L. right

LEGALLY

68	20	otherwise they are not L. authorized
85	1	receive inheritances L. from the .

LEHI

17	1	miraculous directors given to L.

LEMAN

49	1	hearken unto my word, Sidney, and L.
	4	my servant L. shall be ordained for

LEMUELITES

3	18	come to the knowledge of the L. and

LENGTH

94	4	the L. thereof in the inner court—11
95	15	let it be sixty-five feet in L.

LESS

10	68	declareth more or L. than this—93:25; 98:7, 10; 124:120
122	9	thy years shall not be numbered L.
124	64	shall not receive L. than fifty

LESSER

68	19	in all the L. offices
76	81	which glory is that of the L.
84	26	and the L. priesthood continued
	30	appendages belonging to the L.
107		ordained to the L. priesthood
111		and also the L. priests
85	11	as well as the L. priesthood
88	37	either a greater or a L. kingdom
107	14	why it is called the L. priesthood
	17	authority to officiate in all L.
	20	the authority of the L., or Aaronic

Sec.	Vs.	

LESSON

121	35	because they do not learn this one L.

LEST

19	15	L. I smite you by the rod of my
	20	L. I humble you with my almighty: L. you suffer these punishments
	22	not know these things L. they perish
20	33	L. they fall into temptation
23	1	L. thou should enter into temptation—31:12
29	3	L. perils shall come upon you
38	30	L. the wickedness of men reveal
	39	L. ye become as the Nephites of old
43	19	L. ye be found among the wicked
45	2	L. death shall overtake you
46	8	beware, L. ye are deceived
27		L. there shall be any among you
50	9	L. he do that which is not in truth
	33	boasting, L. you be seized therewith
54	7	L. your enemies come upon you
58	15	let him take heed L. he fall
	53	L. they receive none inheritance
60	15	L. thou provoke them
61	18	L. their faith fail them and they
63	15	L. judgment shall come upon them
	24	L. there should be confusion
82	2	L. sore judgments fall upon your
86	6	L. you destroy the wheat also
90	5	L. they are accounted as a light thing
93	49	pray always L. that wicked one
98	17	L. I come and smite the whole earth—128:17
101	53	L. the enemy should come upon you
	84	L. by continual coming she weary me
110	15	L. the whole earth be smitten with
112	33	L. the blood of this generation be
121	43	L. he esteem thee to be his enemy
132	57	L. an enemy come and destroy him
133	15	L. sudden destruction shall come
136	25	tell thy neighbor L. he condemn
	42	be diligent L. judgment come upon

LET

6	3	L. him thrust in his sickle—11:3; 12:3; 14:3
	34	L. earth and hell combine against
20	33	L. the church take heed and pray
	34	L. those who are sanctified take heed
25	14	L. thy soul delight in thy husband
26	1	you shall L. your time be devoted

Sec.	Vs.		Sec.	Vs.	
35	14	I *will* L. fall the sword in their	56	7	L. my servant Newel Knight remain
37	4	L. every man choose for himself	57	6	L. my servant, stand in the office—7; 58:40
38	24	L. every man esteem his brother as himself—25		8	L. my servant, plant himself in this—11
	37	L. them be left or rented as seemeth		9	L. my servant, obtain a license; whoso readeth L. him understand
	41	L. your preaching be the warning voice		12	L. him obtain whatsoever he can
42	40	L. all thy garments be plain		13	L. my servant, assist him as I shall
	41	L. all things be done in cleanliness		14	L. those of whom I have spoken be
	64	L. him that goeth to the east teach		15	L. the bishop and the agent make
	68	L. him ask of me and I will give	58	15	L. him take heed lest he fall
43	34	L. solemnities of eternity rest upon		20	L. no man think he is ruler, but L. God rule
45	11	L. me show unto you my wisdom		21	L. no man break laws of the land
	70	L. us not go up to battle against		25	L. them bring their families to this
46	4	L. him not partake until he makes		39	L. him repent of his sins for he
48	3	L. them buy for the present time		46	L. them preach the gospel in; after that L. them return
50	9	L. every man beware lest he do that		47	L. them preach by the way and bear
	10	L. us reason together that ye may		48	L. them build up churches inasmuch
	11	L. us reason even as a man reasoneth		53	L. them do this lest they receive
	34	L. him account it of God and L. him		54	L. there be workmen sent forth
	37	L. my servant Joseph Wakefield		55	L. all these things be done in order; L. the privileges of the lands
	38	and L. them labor in the vineyard: L. no man hinder them of doing		56	L. the gathering be not in haste: L. it be done as shall be counseled
	39	nevertheless L. him repent		57	L. my servant, dedicate this land
51	3	L. my servant Edward Partridge—4		58	L. a conference meeting be called: after that L. my servants, return
	7	L. that which belongs to this people—10		59	L. no man return from this land except
	8	L. there be an agent appointed—58:49		60	L. that which has been bestowed; L. him stand as a member in church
	9	L. every man deal honestly		61	L. the residue of the elders hold
	11	L. them pay unto this church		62	L. my servant, direct the conference
	13	L. the bishop appoint a storehouse; L. all things, both in money and meat		63	L. them also return, preaching by
	14	L. him also reserve unto himself	59	13	L. thy food be prepared with singleness
	17	L. them act upon this land as for	60	5	L. there be a craft made, or bought
52	3	L. my servants, take their journey		7	L. them lift up their voice and
	9	L. them journey from thence preaching—7, 22, 23, 24. 25, 26. 27, 28, 29, 30, 31, 32, 35; 55:6; 60:6; 75:13, 17, 18		8	L. the residue journey, two by two—61:35
	10	L. them go two by two; L. them preach by the way		10	L. my servant, impart of the money
	12	L. my servant, beware for Satan		11	L. him return it by way of the agent
	33	L. all these take their journey unto	61	9	L. my servants, take their former; L. them take their journey in haste—21
	36	L. them labor with their families		11	L. residue take that which is needful—12
	37	L. that which was bestowed upon H. Bassett be taken		21	L. those concerning whom I have spoken
	38	L. Jared Carter be ordained a priest			
	39	L. residue of the elders watch over; L. them labor with their own hands			
	41	L. my servants take with them recommend, and L. there be one			
54	3	L. them repent of all their sins			

Sec.	Vs.		Sec.	Vs.	
	22	L. this be as it is made known		106	L. him take with him he that is weak
	23	L. them come not again upon the waters		109	L. every man stand in his own office; L. not the head say to the feet
	28	L. him do as the spirit commandeth		114	L. the bishop go unto city of New York
	32	L. them journey for the congregations		116	L. him trust in me and he shall not
	33	L. them declare the word among	86	7	L. the wheat and the tares grow
	35	L. my servant Reynolds Cahoon	88	71	L. those whom they have warned in
63	6	L. the wicked take heed; L. the rebellious fear; L. the unbelieving hold their lips		85	L. those who are not the first elders
				86	L. your hands be clean until the Lord
	15	L. such beware and repent speedily		122	L. not all be spokesmen at once; L. one speak at a time, and L. all listen
	38	L. my disciples in Kirtland arrange			
	39	L. my servant, dispose of the land		131	L. him offer himself in prayer
	40	L. all moneys which can be spared		132	L. the teacher arise, and, with
	42	L. my servant retain his store	90	5	L. them beware how they hold them
	43	L. him impart all the money he can		19	L. there be a place provided
	44	L. him do according to wisdom		20	L. my servant, continue with his; L. it not be sold
	45	L. him be ordained as an agent; L. him be ordained to this power		21	L. my counselor remain where he now
	57	L. them be ordained to this power		22	L. the bishop obtain an agent; L. it be a man who has got riches
	61	L. all men beware how they take my name		25	L. your families be small, especially
	63	L. the church repent of their sins		33	L. them cease wearying me concerning
	65	L. my servants, seek them a home			
64	11	L. God judge between me and thee	93	51	L. my servant, journey and make haste
66	8	L. my servant, go with thee and		52	L. my servants, make haste also
67	14	L. not your minds turn back, and	94	3	L. the first lot on the south be
68	32	L. my servant, carry these sayings	95	13	L. the house be built, not after
	33	L. him be had in remembrance before		14	L. it be built after the manner
				15	L. it be sixty-five feet in length
69	7	L. my servant, travel many times		16	L. the lower part of the inner court
71	5	whoso readeth, L. him understand —91:4		17	L. the higher part of the inner court
	8	L. them bring forth their strong	96	2	L. my servant, take charge of the
72	19	L. every elder be recommended		3	L. it be divided in lots according
	20	L. my servants, appointed as stewards	97	11	L. it be built speedily by tithing
				21	L. Zion rejoice, for this is Zion
	25	L. them carry up to the bishop		27	L. it be read this once into her ears
73	5	L. this be a pattern until further	98	1	L. your hearts be comforted—100: 15; 101:16
75	9	L. my servant, go with him and proclaim			
				18	L. not your hearts be troubled
	26	L. all such as can obtain places	100	12	L. your hearts rejoice
	27	L. them ask and they shall receive	101	10	that I would L. fall the sword
	28	L. him provide and he shall; and L. him labor in the church		68	L. not your gathering be in haste; L. all things be prepared
	29	L. every man be diligent in all		72	L. the churches gather all their moneys; L. these things be done in their time
	30	L. my servants, be united in ministry			
				73	L. honorable men be appointed
76	61	L. no man glory in man, rather L. him glory in God		86	L. them importune at the feet of —87, 88
78	9	L. my servant, sit in council with			
79	4	L. your heart be glad and fear not		97	L. not that which I have appointed
84	84	L. the morrow take thought for itself			
	86	L. no man among you from this hour			
	104	L. all those who have not families			

Sec.	Vs.		Sec.	Vs.	
103	19	L. not your hearts faint for I		10	L. the beginning be made on the 4th; L. my people labor diligently to build
	22	L. my servant, say unto the strength			
	23	L. the churches send up wise men			
	27	L. no man be afraid to lay down his		11	L. them recommence laying foundation
	37	L. my servant, journey with my— 38, 39, 40		12	L. them from that time forth labor
				13	L. not my servant, get in debt any more
104	20	L. my servant, have appointed unto —24, 39, 43		14	L. a house be built unto my name
	21	L. all things be done according to	117	1	L. them settle up their business
	26	L. my servant, devote his moneys for		2	L. them awake, and arise, and come
				4	L. them repent of all their sins
	27	L. my servant, have the place upon		5	L. properties of Kirtland be turned out; L. them go; L. it remain
	28	L. my servant, have the lot which is			
	29	L. my servants, have the Laneshine house		10	L. my servant, be faithful over a few; L. him preside in the midst; L. him be blessed
	34	L. my servant, have the house in			
	69	L. him cast them into the treasury; L. him do likewise		11	L. my servant, be ashamed of the
				13	L. him contend earnestly for the
	70	L. not any man among you say that		14	L. him come up hither speedily
105	20	that can stay, L. them stay		15	L. no man despise my servant, but L. the blessings of
	21	L. them tarry for a little season			
	23	L. all my people who dwell in the		16	L. all my servants remember the Lord
	31	L. my army become very great, and L. it be sanctified			
			118	1	L. a conference be held; L. the Twelve be organized and L. men be
	32	L. us become subject to her laws			
	34	L. those commandments be executed		2	L. my servant, remain for a season
				3	L. the residue continue to preach
	35	L. those be chosen that are worthy		4	L. them depart to go over the great
107	99	now L. every man learn his duty		5	L. them take leave of my saints in
108	2	L. your soul be at rest concerning		6	L. my servants, be appointed to fill
109	34	L. them be blotted out forever	121	4	L. thine eye pierce; L. thy pavilion be taken up; L. thy hiding-place; L. thine ear; L. thine heart be
	35	L. the anointing of thy ministers			
	36	L. it be fulfilled upon them as upon; L. gift of tongues be poured out			
				5	L. thine anger be kindled against
	37	L. thy house be filled as with a		45	L. thy bowels be full of charity; L. virtue garnish thy thoughts
	39	L. thy peace and salvation be upon			
	40	L. not thy judgments fall upon that	123	15	L. no man count them small things
	41	L. it be upon that city according to		17	L. us cheerfully do all things
	80	L. these thine anointed ones be clothed	124	4	L. it be written in the spirit of
				12	L. my servant, help you write this
110	6	L. the hearts of your brethren; L. the hearts of my people rejoice		13	L. him hearken to your counsel; L. him be faithful
				14	L. him remember his stewardship
112	4	L. thy heart be of good cheer		16	L. my servant, help you in your labor
	5	L. thy warning voice go forth; L. not the inhabitants slumber			
				21	L. no man despise my servant George
	6	L. thy habitation be known in Zion			
	7	L. thy feet be shod also		22	L. my servant, and others build a
	9	L. the tongue of the slanderer cease		23	L. it be a good house, worthy of all
	11	L. thy love be for them; L. thy love abound unto all men			
				25	L. all my saints come from afar
	12	L. them be admonished for their sins		40	L. this house be built unto my name
115	7	L. the city, Far West, be a holy		56	L. it be built unto my name; L. my name be upon it, and L. my
	9	L. there be a beginning of this work			
				59	L. my servant, and his seed after him

Sec.	Vs.		Sec.	Vs.	
	60	L. the name be called Nauvoo House; L. it be a delightful habitation		4	L. all those who come from the east
			127	3	L. all the saints rejoice, and be
	62	L. my servants, organize themselves		4	L. the work of my temple be continued; L. your diligence and perseverance
	72	L. my servant, pay stock in their hand		6	L. there be a recorder; L. him be eye witness; L. him hear
	74	L. him put stock into that house —77, 78, 80, 81, 82, 111		9	L. all the records be had in order
	75	L. him lift up his voice long and loud; L. him not fail, neither L. his heart faint	128	3	L. him be very particular and precise
				4	then L. there be a general recorder
	76	L. his family rejoice and turn away		5	but L. me tell you that it is only to
	78	L. him be remembered for an interest		15	L. me assure you that these are principles
	79	L. my servants, be appointed among you		22	L. your hearts rejoice and be exceeding glad: L. the earth; L. the dead speak forth;
	83	L. him not take his family into eastern		23	L. the mountains shout for joy; L. the woods and all the trees; L. the sun, moon; L. the sons of God shout for joy; L. the eternal creations declare his name.
	85	L. no man go from this place			
	86	if they live L. them live unto me; if they die L. them die unto me			
	87	L. my servant, put his trust in me		24	L. us therfeore, as a church and people; L. us present in his holy temple
	88	L. my servant go and proclaim my			
	89	L. him from henceforth hearken to			
	91	L. my servant, be appointed, ordained	130	15	L. this suffice and trouble me no more
	97	L. my servant, receive the keys by; L. him be humble before me	132	52	L. mine handmaid, Emma Smith receive
	100	L. him not withhold his voice		56	L. mine handmaid forgive my servant
	101	L. my servant, cry aloud and spare not		57	L. not my servant Joseph put his property
	102	L. my servant, tarry at home for he		60	L. no one set on my servant, for I
	103	L. him arise, and come up and stand		66	L. this suffice for the present
	105	L. him come and locate his family	133	6	L. every man call upon the Lord
	106	L. him lift up his voice with the sound		10	L. the cry go forth among all people
	107	L. him assist my servant Joseph; L. Law assist		12	L. them who are among the Gentiles
	108	L. him not remove his family unto; but L. him change their habitation		13	L. them who be of Judah flee unto
				15	L. not your flight be in haste; L. all things be prepared; L. him not look back lest sudden
	112	this L. him do and L. him hearken to			
	114	L. him therefore abase himself	136	2	L. all people of church be organized
	115	L. him build a house for my servant		3	L. companies be organized with captains
	116	L. him repent of all his folly		5	L. each company provide themselves
	119	L. no man pay stock to the quorum		6	L. them go to with their might
	121	L. the quorum of the Nauvoo House; L. their wages be as shall be agreed		7	L. each company decide how many can
				8	L. each bear an equal proportion
	122	L. every man who pays stock bear		9	L. each prepare houses and fields
	132	L. my servant, be ordained in his stead		10	L. every man use his influence and
				12	L. my servants, organize a company. —13, 14
125	2	L. them gather themselves together			
	3	L. them build up a city unto my name; L. the name of Zarahemla be		16	L. my servants teach this my will
				24	L. your words tend to edifying one
				32	L. him that is ignorant learn wisdom

Sec.	Vs.	
		LETTER
20	84	all members may take a L., certifying; if the member receiving the L.
44	1	called together by L. or some other
107	20	the L. of the gospel, the baptism
127	11	I now close my L. for the present,
128	1	as I stated to you in my L.
	2	it was declared in my former L. that
	7	revelation contained in the L. which
		LEVI
13	1	until sons of L. do offer again an
124	39	your sacrifices by the sons of L.
128	24	and he shall purify the sons of L.
		LEVITICAL
107	1	and Aaronic, including L. priesthood
	6	the other is the L. priesthood
	10	of a priest (of the L. order)
		LIAR
93	25	who was a L. from the beginning
		LIARS
63	17	all L. and whosoever loveth and
64	39	L. and hypocrites shall be proved
76	103	these are they who are L. and sorcerers
		LIBELOUS
123	4	gather up the L. publications that
	5	and all L. histories that are published
		LIBERALLY
42	68	I will give him L. and upbraid him not
46	7	to ask of God who giveth L.
		LIBERTIES
134	4	to infringe upon the rights and L.
		LIBERTY
88	86	abide ye in the L. wherewith ye are
135	7	their innocent blood on banner of L.
		LICENSE
20	64	which shall entitle him to a L.
57	9	let my servant obtain a L.
		LICENSES
20	63	elders are to receive their L. from
		LIE
5	33	there are many that L. in wait to
10	25	deceive and L. in wait to catch; it is no sin to L., that they may catch a man in a L.
42	21	thou shalt not L.
	86	and if he or she shall L., he
62	6	I promised the faithful and cannot L.

Sec.	Vs.	
63	17	whosoever loveth and maketh a L.—76:103
123	12	whereby they L. in wait to deceive
	17	do all things that L. in our power
133	70	ye shall L. *down* in sorrow
		LIED
10	18	will say that he has L. in his words
	31	they will say that you have L.
		LIETH
10	28	wo unto him that L. because he supposeth another L.
42	21	he that L. and will not repent
49	20	wherefore the word L. in sin
63	59	from above, and my power L. beneath
84	49	the whole world L. in sin
112	7	thy path L. among the mountains
123	15	there is much which L. in futurity
		LIES
123	7	of the fathers who have inherited L.
		LIFE
5	22	I grant unto you eternal L.
6	7	he that hath eternal L. is rich.—11:7
10	50	in this gospel might have eternal L.
	66	partake of the waters of L. freely
	70	who is the L. and light of the world 11:28; 12:9; 34:2; 39:2; 45:7
14	7	you shall have eternal L. which gift
18	8	he shall be blessed unto eternal L.—30:8
19	25	nor seek thy neighbor's L.
	32	even unto the end of thy L.
20	14	shall receive crown of eternal L.—66:12; 81:6
	26	in all things, should have eternal L.
25	2	I will preserve thy L. and thou
29	27	on my right hand unto eternal L.
	43	in immortality unto eternal L.
34	3	loved the world that he gave his L.
42	61	that which bringeth L. eternal
43	25	and the riches of eternal L.
45	5	come unto me and have everlasting L.
	8	gave I power to obtain eternal L.
46	14	that they also might have eternal L.
50	5	whether in L. or death, for they shall inherit eternal L.
	8	shall be cut off either in L. or
	27	the L., the light, the spirit
51	19	and shall inherit eternal L.
58	2	whether in L., or in death.—61:39; 76:59
59	23	and eternal L. in the world to come
63	3	and preserveth in L. them whom he
	23	springing up unto everlasting L.
66	2	that they might have L.
68	12	to seal them up unto eternal L.

Sec.	Vs.	
75	5	glory, immortality and eternal L.—128:23
77	8	to save L. and to destroy; to seal up unto L. or to cast down
78	16	without beginning of days or end of L.
84	43	give heed to the words of eternal L.
	85	treasure up continually the words of L.
85	2	also their manner of L. their faith
86	10	your L. and priesthood have remained
88	4	which I give unto you of eternal L.
	13	which giveth L. unto all things
89	14	to be the staff of L.
93	9	and in him was the L. of men
96	6	I give a promise of eternal L.
98	13	whoso layeth down his L. shall find it again even L. eternal 103:27
	20	observe words of wisdom and eternal L.
	31	if he has sought thy L. and thy L. is
101	30	his L. shall be as the age of a tree
	37	care not for body, neither the L. of, but for L. of the soul
	38	and ye shall have eternal L.
	65	in the garners to possess eternal L.
103	27	afraid to lay down his L. for my sake
	28	whoso is not willing to lay down his L.
104	5	he shall be cursed in his L.
124	55	and crown you with honor and eternal L.
127	2	common lot all the days of my L.
128	6	which was the Book of L.—7
	12	herein is glory and eternal L.
130	18	intelligence we attain unto in this L.
	19	gains more intelligence in this L.
131	5	that he is sealed up unto eternal L.
132	19	written in the Lamb's Book of L.
133	62	repenteth, shall be given eternal L.
134	2	property and the protection of L.
	10	to try men on right of property or L.; in jeopardy of L. or limb
	12	dissatisfied with situations in L.
135	3	in L. they were not divided, and in

LIFT

Sec.	Vs.	
25	13	L. *up* thy heart and rejoice—27:15; 31:3; 42:69
29	5	L. *up* your hearts and be glad.—35:26
33	2	L. *up* your voices as with the sound 34:6; 124:106
34	10	L. *up* your voice and spare not.—43:20
42	16	L. *up* your voices by the Comforter
	81	the church shall L. *up* their hands
43	21	if I who am a man, L. *up* my voice
45	32	men shall L. *up* their voices and curse
47	2	he can L. *up* his voice in meetings
52	44	I *will* L. them *up* at the last day
60	7	in this place let them L. *up* their
61	31	they shall L. *up* their voice unto
63	37	L. a warning voice unto inhabitants
71	10	if any man L. his voice against you
81	5	L. *up* the hands that hang down
84	98	shall L. *up* their voice and sing
98	34	first L. a standard of peace
100	5	L. *up* your voices unto this people
103	29	L. *up* his voice unto the congregations
104	18	shall L. *up* his eyes in hell
105	39	L. *up* an ensign of peace
106	2	L. *up* his voice and warn the people
	7	I *will* L. him *up* inasmuch as he
110	5	L. *up* your heads and rejoice
121	16	cursed are all those that shall L. *up*
124	75	let him L. *up* his voice long and loud
	104	shall L. *up* his voice on the mountains

LIFTED

Sec.	Vs.	
5	35	shalt be L. *up* at the last day—9:14; 17:8; 75:16, 22
24	1	have L. thee *up* out of afflictions
45	52	I am he who was L. *up*
84	1	as they L. their voices on high

LIFTING

Sec.	Vs.	
19	39	and L. *up* thy heart for gladness
30	6	ever L. *up* thy heart in prayer
42	6	L. *up* your voices as with the voice
60	7	L. *up* holy hands upon them
75	4	L. *up* your voices as with the sound
124	9	to the exaltation or L. up of Zion

LIGHT

Sec.	Vs.	
1	33	shall be taken even the L. which he
6	21	I am the L. which shineth in darkness—10:58; 11:11; 34:2; 39:2; 45:7
	27	than shall you assist in bringing to L.—11:19
	28	which shall bring to L. this ministry
10	21	they love darkness rather than L. —29:45
	61	will bring to L. their marvelous
	62	will also bring to L. my gospel; bring to L. the true points
	70	who is the L. and life of the world —11:28; 12:9; 34:2; 39:2; 45:7
14	9	a L. which cannot be hid in darkness
45	9	to be a L. to the world
	28	a L. shall break forth among them

| Light | 258 | Like |

Sec.	Vs.	
	29	they perceive not the L. and they
	36	when the L. shall begin to break
50	24	that which is of God is L.; he that receiveth L., receiveth more L., and that L. groweth
	27	the life and the L., the
58	23	in this L. ye shall hold them forth
77	4	a representation of L. and knowledge
82	3	he who sins against the greater L.
84	45	whatever is truth is L., and whatsoever is L. is
	46	the Spirit giveth L. to every man
85	7	clothed with L. for a covering
86	11	if you continue a L. to the Gentiles
88	6	through all things the L. of truth
	7	this is the L. of Christ. He is in the sun and the L. of the sun
	8	and is the L. of the moon
	9	and also the L. of the stars
	11	and the L. which now shineth, which giveth you L., which is the same L.
	12	which L. proceedeth forth from the
	13	the L. which is in all things
	40	L. cleaveth unto L.
	44	they give L. to each other in their
	45	the sun giveth his L. by day, the moon giveth her L. by night, and the stars their L.
	49	the L. shineth in darkness and the
	50	that I am the true L. which is in you
	56	made glad with the L. of the countenance
	58	all received the L. of the countenance
	67	your whole bodies shall be filled with L.; that body which is filled with L.
	87	and shall refuse to give L.
	121	cease from all your L. speeches
90	5	lest they are accounted a L. thing
93	2	I am the true L. that lighteth
	9	the L. and Redeemer of the world; in him was the life and L. of men
	28	receiveth truth and L. until he is
	29	the L. of truth was not created or
	31	unto them, and they receive not the L.
	32	whose spirit receiveth not the L.
	36	or in other words, L. and truth
	37	L. and truth forsake that evil one
	39	wicked one taketh away L. and truth
	40	bring up your children in L. and
	42	ye have not taught your children L.
102	16	is examined in its true L.

Sec.	Vs.	
	21	if any additional L. is shown
	22	in case no additional L. is given
103	9	were set to be a L. unto the world
106	5	that ye may be the children of L.
	8	if he continue to be a faithful witness and a L. to the church
115	5	that thy L. may be a standard for
123	13	in bringing to L. the hidden things
124	6	give heed to the L. and glory of Zion
	9	that they may come to the L. of truth
128	20	devil appeared as an angel of L.
129	8	the devil as an angel of L. when you
133	49	and the moon shall withhold its L.

LIGHTETH

| 93 | 2 | that L. every man that cometh into |

LIGHTLY

84	54	you have treated L. the things
101	8	they esteemed L. my counsel
128	15	that cannot be L. passed over

LIGHT-MINDEDNESS

| 88 | 121 | cease from all your pride and L. |

LIGHTNING

20	6	whose countenance was as L.
85	8	smitten by vivid shaft of L.
87	6	the fierce and vivid L. also

LIGHTNINGS

43	22	L. shall streak forth from the east
	25	called upon you by the voice of L.
88	90	the voice of L. and the voice of

LIGHTS

| 67 | 9 | cometh down from the Father of L. |

LIKE

17	7	and the same gift L. unto him
41	11	for he is L. unto Nathaniel of old
42	6	declaring my word L. unto angels
45	36	L. unto a parable that I will show
49	11	L. unto mine apostle of old
54	9	seek ye a living L. unto men
58	17	L. as it was in ancient days
59	6	nor kill, nor do anything L. unto it
61	25	do L. unto the children of Israel
64	37	L. unto a judge sitting on a hill
67	7	if any among you shall make one L. it
	8	but if ye cannot make one L. unto it
84	82	are not arrayed L. one of these
85	8	L. as a tree that is smitten by
97	10	L. unto the pattern which I have given
103	16	who shall lead them L. as Moses led

Sec.	Vs.		Sec.	Vs.	
107	43	he seemed to be L. unto his father			**LIMB**
	62	in L. manner, and also the deacons	84	80	neither in body, L. or joint
	91	whole church and be L. unto Moses	134	10	in jeopardy of either life or L.
110	2	in color L. amber			**LIMITED**
	3	hair of his head was white L. the	77	3	are the four beasts L.; they are L. to four individual
122	6	prowl around thee L. wolves			
124	21	L. unto my servant Edward Partridge			**LINE**
127	2	and I feel L. Paul, to glory in	57	4	unto the L. running directly between
128	24	he is L. a refiner's fire and L. fuller's soap	98	12	L. upon L., precept upon precept—128:21
130	1	we shall see he is a man L. ourselves			**LINEAGE**
	6	do not reside on a planet L. this earth	68	21	if at any time they can prove their L.
	7	on a globe L. a sea of glass	84	14	through the L. of his fathers
	9	earth will be made L. unto crystal		15	through the L. of their fathers
133	24	earth shall be L. as it was in days	86	8	continued through L. of your fathers
	48	his garments L. him that treadeth		10	needs remain through you and your L.
135	3	L. most of the Lord's anointed he has	107	41	came down by L. in the following
	4	I am going L. a lamb to the slaughter	113	8	which Zion has a right to by L.
136	35	L. a woman that is taken in travail			**LINK**
		LIKEN	128	18	unless there is a welding L. of some
88	46	unto what shall I L. these kingdoms			**LION**
	51	I *will* L. these kingdoms unto a man	122	4	more terrible than the fierce L.
	61	unto this parable *will* I L. all			**LIPS**
101	81	to what shall I L. children of Zion; I *will* L. them unto	63	6	let the unbelieving hold their L.
	85	thus *will* I L. the children of Zion		61	how they take my name in their L.
		LIKENED			**LIST**
103	21	the man to whom I L. the servant	20	82	with a L. of the names, so that a regular L.
		LIKENESS	29	45	their wages of whom they L. to obey
1	16	whose image is in L of the world	98	21	I will do what I L. if they do not
20	18	after his own image and in his own L.			**LISTED**
77	2	in the L. of that which is temporal; in the L. of that which is spiritual; spirit of man in L. of his person	49	6	done unto Son of man as they L.
					LISTEN
			1	1	ye upon the islands of the sea, L.
107	43	his L. was the express L. of his father	15	1	L. to the words of Jesus Christ— 16:1; 27:1; 29:1
128	12	to answer to the L. of the dead; in the L. of the resurrection; being in the L. of the dead	19	23	learn of me and L. to my words
			35	1	L. to the voice of the Lord—72:1
			39	1	L. to the voice of him who is from
	13	that all things may have their L.	45	3	L. to him who is the advocate with
		LIKEWISE		6	and ye elders, L. together
04	93	in whatsoever village ye enter do L.	63	1	L., you that call yourselves the
104	69	if he obtain an hundred let him do L.	78	2	L. to the counsel of him who
			81	1	L. to the voice of him who speaketh
		LILIES	88	122	let all L. unto his sayings
84	82	consider the L. of the field	100	2	L. to the counsel which I shall give

Sec.	Vs.		Sec.	Vs.	
133	16	L. ye elders of my church together		39	as soon as they get a L. authority
136	41	people of my church and ye elders L.	128	21	here a L. and there a L.
			133	58	and the L. one become a strong nation

LITERAL

68	15	except they be L. descendants of—18; 107:16
	16	and if they be L. descendants of
	19	when no L. descendant of Aaron can be—107:17
	20	a L. descendant must be designated
107	40	to the L. descendants of the chosen
	69	unless he is a L. descendant of
	70	for unless he is a L. descendant
	73	bishop who is not a L. descendant
	76	a L. descendant has the legal right of

LITTLENESS

117	11	and all his L. of soul before me

LIVE

7	2	that I may L. and bring souls unto
29	21	but surely will, as I L.—32:1
31	5	wherefore, your family shall L.
41	7	in which to L. and translate
	8	Rigdon should L. as seemeth him good
42	44	and if they L. they shall L. unto me
	45	thou shalt L. together in love
43	18	ye Saints, arise, and L.
	21	speaking to the ears of all that L.
	22	utter forth their voice to all that L.
45	1	which L., and move, and have a being
	46	come unto me and your souls shall L.
48	3	that they have places to L.
59	2	those that L. shall inherit the earth
84	22	no man can see the face of God and L.
	44	you shall L. by every word that—98:11
88	101	the rest of the dead L. not again
95	13	that ye shall L. after manner of the
124	3	of the nation in which you L.
	86	if they L. here let them L. unto me

LITERARY

72	20	as stewards over the L. concerns of

LITTLE

5	17	you must wait yet a L. while
6	34	fear not, L. flock, do good—35:27
11	16	wait a L. longer until you shall
29	22	spare the earth for but a L. season
	46	L. children are redeemed from the
	47	not given Satan to tempt L. children
31	2	bless your family, yea, your L. ones
	6	go from them only for a L. time
42	5	they shall go forth for a L. season
43	31	he shall only reign for a L. season
50	40	ye are L. children, ye cannot bear
	41	fear not, L. children, for you are
51	16	this land for a L. season until I
55	4	that L. children may receive instruction
61	22	it mattereth not to me, after a L.
	36	be of good cheer L. children, for I
63	40	mattereth not whether it be L. or much
	42	retain the store yet for a L. season
74	6	which saith L. children are unholy
	7	L. children are holy, being sanctified
77	14	the L. book which was eaten by John
78	17	ye are L. children and have not yet
84	119	yet a L. while and ye shall see it
88	71	which they have received for L. season
	111	he shall be loosed for a L. season
99	3	whoso receiveth you as a L. child
100	13	though she is chastened for L. season
103	4	they may be chastened for L. season
105	9	wait a L. season for redemption of—13
	21	let them tarry for a L. season
112	18	burden of all churches for L. season
121	19	for they have offended my L. ones

LIVED

84	13	Esaias also L. in the days of
135	3	than any other man that L. in it; he L. great and he died great
	6	they L. for glory; they died for

LIVELY

92	2	you shall be a L. member in this

LIVES

38	28	the enemy seeketh your L.
90	16	your mission in all your L.
101	15	who have given their L. for my name
	35	though called to lay down their L.
104	8	cannot escape my wrath in your L.
123	13	that we should wear out our L.
132	22	unto the continuation of the L.
	24	this is eternal L. to know the
	55	and crowns of eternal L. in the
134	12	thereby jeopardizing the L. of men

LIVES (verb)

56	8	concerning the place upon which he L.
76	22	testimony last of all that He L.

Sec.	Vs.		Sec.	Vs.	
90	20	the place where he now L.		16	having your L. girt about with truth
104	34	have the house in which he L.	35	14	and I will gird up their L.
		LIVEST	63	37	should take faithfulness upon his L.
130	15	if thou L. until thou art 85 years	112	7	gird up thy L. for the work
		LIVETH		14	gird up your L., take your cross
8	1	as the Lord L. who is your God	132	30	his seed, and the fruit of his L., from whose L. ye are
17	6	as your Lord L. it is true			
43	32	and he that L. in righteousness			**LONG**
63	50	he that L. when the Lord shall come	29	13	a trump shall sound both L. and loud—34:6; 43:18; 88:94
64	5	shall not be taken from, while he L.	34	6	lift up your voice, both L. and loud—124:75
110	4	I am he who L., I am he who was	43	18	trump of God shall sound both L.
		LIVING		25	by voice of mercy all the day L.
1	30	the only true and L. church upon	45	17	looked upon L. absence of your spirits
14	9	the L. God who created the heavens	101	48	and consulted for a L. time, saying
20	19	the only true and L. God	104	43	which is forty rods L.
	32	man may fall and depart from L. God		75	but so L. as he is in fellowship
42	1	Christ, the Son of the L. God—55:2; 68:25	109	49	how L. wilt thou suffer this people
				61	scattered on mountains for a L. time
	75	if ye find their companions are L.	121	2	how L. shall thy hand be stayed
50	1	give ear to voice of the L. God		3	how L. shall they suffer these wrongs
54	9	seek ye a L. like unto men		33	how L. can rolling waters remain impure
61	28	as spirit of L. God commandeth him			
63	23	a well of L. water springing up to	124	50	so L. as they repent not—52
68	1	by the spirit of the L. God		69	so L. as he and his heirs shall
	6	I am the Son of the L. God	132	15	with her so L. as he is in the world
70	10	to the church of the L. God—82:18		30	so L. as they were in the world
76	66	unto the city of the L. God	134	7	so L. as a regard and reverence are
77	9	is given the seal of the L. God			**LONGER**
81	3	proclaiming gospel in land of the L.	11	16	wait a little L. until you shall
88	108	his trump in the ears of all L.	19	40	canst thou run about L. as a blind
128	11	as well for the dead as the L.	21	8	he shall mourn for her no L.
	13	where the L. are wont to assemble, to show forth the L. and the dead	63	56	he standeth no L. in the office
			84	100	Satan is bound and time is no L.
	15	in relation to the dead and the L.	88	110	that there shall be time no L.
	19	a voice of gladness for the L.		124	cease to sleep L. than is needful
133	29	shall come forth pools of L. water	104	47	no L. be bound as a United Order
		LOAN	121	4	let thy hiding-place no L. be covered
104	53	by L. as shall be agreed by this			
	84	obtain a chance to L. money; you shall L. enough to deliver	133	26	and shall no L. stay themselves
				29	parched ground shall no L. be a thirsty
		LOCATE			**LONG-SUFFERING**
124	105	let him come and L. his family	107	30	in meekness and L. and in faith
136	10	where the Lord shall L. a stake, of	118	3	in meekness, and humility and L.
		LOCATED	121	41	only by persuasion, by L., by
102	29	the traveling or L. High Priests			**LOOK**
		LODGE	1	31	I the Lord cannot L. upon sin with
124	23	may come from afar to L. therein	6	36	L. unto me in every thought
		LOINS	19	27	and L. not for a Messiah to come
27	15	gird up your L.—36:8; 38:9; 43:19; 61:38; 73:6; 75:22; 106:5	38	35	they shall L. to the poor and needy

Sec.	Vs.	
45	37	ye L. and behold the fig-trees
	44	and then they shall L. for me and
	51	then shall the Jews L. upon me and
62	3	recorded in heaven for angels to L.
63	53	these are the things ye must L. for
133	15	he that goeth let him not L. back
	43	terrible things, things they L. not for

LOOKED

Sec.	Vs.	
35	3	I have L. upon thee and thy works
38	1	which L. upon the wide expanse of
39	7	have L. upon thy works and know thee
45	17	ye have L. upon the long absence of
50	4	I have L. and have seen abominations

LOOKEST

Sec.	Vs.	
109	53	when thou L. upon the face of thine

LOOKETH

Sec.	Vs.	
38	26	and L. upon his sons and saith, I am just
42	23	L. upon a woman to lust after her—63:16

LOOKING

Sec.	Vs.	
35	15	L. *forth* for the time of my coming—39:23
45	39	L. *forth* for the great day of the Lord
49	23	L. *forth* for the heavens to be shaken
61	38	L. *forth* for the coming of the Son

LOOSE

Sec.	Vs.	
88	94	made strong, no man can L. them
124	93	whatsoever he shall L. on earth—127:7; 128; 8, 10

LOOSED

Sec.	Vs.	
11	21	then shall your tongue be L.
23	3	thy heart is opened, thy tongue L.
31	3	and your tongue shall be L.
43	31	and when he is L. again
88	110	not be L. for a thousand years
	111	then he shall be L. for a little
104	64	neither shall the seal be L. which
124	93	loose on earth shall be L. in—127:7; 128:8, 10

LOOSING

Sec.	Vs.	
113	9	Zion's L. herself from the bands

LORD

Sec.	Vs.	
1	2	voice of the L. is unto all men
	5	I the L. have commanded them
	7	what I the L. have decreed in them
	10	the L. shall come to recompense—56:19
	11	voice of the L. to ends of the earth
	12	for the L. is nigh
	13	anger of the L. is kindled and his
	14	arm of the L. shall be revealed; who will not hear voice of the L.
	16	they seek not the L. to establish
	17	I the L., knowing the calamity
	20	might speak in the name of God the L.
	30	with which I, the L., am well pleased
	31	the L. cannot look upon sin with
	32	and does the commandments of the L.
	33	saith the L. of Hosts—29:9
	34	I the L. am willing to make these
	36	the L. shall have power over his saints
	38	what I the L. have spoken I have
	39	the L. is God and the spirit beareth
2	1	the great and dreadful day of the L.—110:14, 16; 128:17, 24
3	9	chosen to do the work of the L.
	18	whom the L. has suffered to destroy
	19	that the promises of the L. might be
	20	that they might know promises of the L.
5	2	I, the L., am God and have given
	25	the things which the L. hath shown
	26	I the L. command him that he shall
7	1	the L. said unto me, John, my
	2	L. give me power over death that
	3	the L. said unto me, verily, because
	4	for this cause the L. said unto Peter
8	1	assuredly, as the L. liveth, who is
10	15	to get to tempt the L. thy God—29
	70	your Redeemer, your L. and God—15:1; 16:1
13	1	offering unto the L. in righteousness—128:24
17	1	when he talked with the L. face to
	6	as your L. and God liveth it is true
	9	Jesus Christ, your L. and your God—18:33, 47
18	11	the L. suffered death in the flesh
19	1	am Alpha and Omega, Christ the L.—75:1
	37	blessed be the name of the L.
20	1	since the coming of our L.
	4	the grace of our L. and Savior—30, 31; 21:1
	16	for the L. God has spoken it—36; 49:7; 58:12; 59:24; 64:43; 90:37; 97:7; 127:2
	69	walking in holiness before the L.
	75	in remembrance of the L. Jesus

Sec.	Vs.	
21	3	in the year of our L.
	6	the L. God will disperse the powers
	7	thus saith the L. God—12; 36:1; 38:1; 44:1; 49:5; 50:6; 52:1, 11; 54:1; 55:1; 56:14; 57:3; 60:1; 61:2; 64:1; 66:1, 13; 70:2; 71:1, 9; 72:2; 73:1; 75:13, 23; 76:5, 31; 78:8; 86:8; 87:1; 88:1; 89:4; 90:1; 91:1; 92:1; 93:1; 95:1; 97:21; 99:1; 100:1; 108:1; 112:1; 113:2, 4, 6; 114:1, 2; 115:1; 117:1; 118:1; 119:1; 120:1; 124:1; 126:1; 127:4, 6; 132:1
25	1	hearken unto the voice of the L.—33:1
27	1	listen to the voice of your L.—35:1; 72:1
29	18	f the L. will send forth flies
	41	I the L. caused that he should be cast
	42	the L. God gave unto Adam and his seed; until the L. should send forth angels
	43	thus did I the L. appoint unto man
33	10	prepare ye the way of the L.—65:1, 3
34	1	what I the L. shall say unto you
	6	preparing the way of the L.
	10	for the L. God hath spoken
	12	I am the L. and your Redeemer
38	18	no more curse when the L. cometh
	42	be ye clean that bear vessels of the L.—133:5
41	1	saith the L.—56:1, 4, 10; 57:1; 58:30, 31; 59:1; 62:1; 66:1, 3; 69:1; 73:3; 78:1, 2, 15; 79:4; 80:1; 82:7; 83:1; 84:35; 85:5; 86:1; 87:8; 95:10, 16; 97:28; 98:3, 14, 38, 48; 112:24, 25, 26, 27; 117:4, 5, 7, 11, 12, 13, 14, 16; 118:5; 119:4; 120:1; 121:16, 23; 124:15, 17, 21, 32, 35, 47, 48, 50, 51, 52, 53, 54, 59, 69, 71, 72, 75, 76, 88, 101, 119, 120, 122, 135, 136, 137, 140, 145; 125:4; 127:4, 6, 8, 9; 132:6, 8, 9, 11, 12, 13, 18, 26, 27, 29, 39, 46, 47, 48, 51, 52, 54, 60, 64; 133:1, 36, 64
43	17	great day of the L. is nigh at hand
	18	the L. shall utter his voice out of—23; 45:49
	20	prepare for the great day of the L.—21, 22; 45:39
	27	these are the words of the L.
45	34	when I the L. hath spoken these words

Sec.	Vs.	
	42	before the day of the L. shall come—49:24
	45	before the arm of the L. shall fall
	47	then shall arm of the L. fall
	48	the L. shall set his foot upon this
	52	then shall they know I am the L.
	59	the L. shall be in their midst
	64	I the L. have said, gather ye out
	67	the glory of the L. shall be there: the terror of the L. shall
	74	when the L. shall appear he shall be
	75	the terror of the L. and the power
46	15	the same L., according as the L. will
49	12	believe on the name of the L. Jesus
50	4	I, the L., have looked upon you
	10	come, saith the L., and let us reason
	12	so will I the L., reason with you
	13	I the L. ask you this question
51	1	hearken unto me, saith the L.
	16	until the L. shall provide for them
	19	shall enter into the joy of his L.
52	2	I, the L., will make known unto you
	43	the L. will hasten the city in its
53	1	make known unto you of the L.; which I the L., have raised up
	2	I, the L., who was crucified
55	1	yea, even the L. of the whole earth
56	3	I, the L., command and he that will not
	4	I, the L., command and revoke as it
	12	I, the L., will pay it unto him
58	9	a supper of the house of the L.
	11	partake of the supper of the L.
	33	this is not the work of the L.
	41	the L. is not well pleased with him
	42	the L. remembereth them no more
	44	as it shall be appointed of the L.
	52	the L. willeth that the disciples
	57	the spot for the temple unto the L.
59	5	thou shalt love the L. thy God with
	7	thou shalt thank the L. thy God
	8	thou shalt offer a sacrifice to the L.
	12	confessing thy sins before the L.
60	4	I, the L., rule in the heavens above
61	2	I, the L., forgive sins and am
	5	I, the L., have decreed in mine anger
	10	I, the L., will be with them
	13	the L. will reason with you as with men
	14	the L. in beginning blessed the waters
	17	the L. in beginning cursed the land
	19	I, the L., decreed and the destroyer
	20	the L. was angry with you yesterday
	24	I, the L., have appointed a way for
	29	the camp of the L. to journey

Sec.	Vs.		Sec.	Vs.	
62	6	the L. have brought you together; the Lord promised the faithful		8	I, the L., will go with you
	7	the L. am willing if any among you; if he receive it from hand of the L.		9	return not till I, the L., shall send
			67	4	I, the L., give you a testimony
63	1	that call yourselves people of L., hear the word of the L.	68	4	shall be the will of the L., the mind of the L., the word of the L., the voice of the L.
	5	I, the L. utter my voice and it shall		5	this is the promise of the L.
	12	I, the L., am not pleased with those		6	I the L., am with you
				7	this is the word of the L. unto you
	17	I, the L., have said that the fearful and		14	in the due time of the L.
				21	ascertain it by revelation from L.
	19	I, the L., say unto you ye are not		30	be had in remembrance before the L.
	24	this is the will of the L. your God			
	25	Zion, the L. holdeth in mine own		31	L. not well pleased with inhabitants
	26	the L. render unto Caesar the		33	observeth not prayers before L.
	27	the L. will that you should purchase	69	2	I, the L., will that my servant
			70	1	I hear the word of the L. which I
	32	the L. am angry with the wicked		3	the L. have appointed them
	34	the L. am with them and will come		9	the L. requires of every man in his; as the L. has appointed
	36	the L. have decreed these things			
	41	the L. will give unto my servant power		16	in circumstances the L. shall place them, and the L. shall send them
	49	blessed are dead that die in the L., when the L. shall come; receive an inheritance before the L.		18	the L. am merciful and will bless
			71	8	their strong reasons against the L.
	50	that liveth when the L. shall come	72	3	for it is required of the L. your God
	53	speaking after manner of the L.— 64:24		8	this is the will of the L.—75:12
	55	the L. is not pleased with S. Rigdon		9	the word of the L. in addition to
	56	his writing not acceptable unto L.; if the L. receive it not		13	which the L. shall put into his hands
			74	5	commandment, not of the L. but of
	58	I, the L., am not to be mocked— 104:6; 124:71	75	7	I, the L., chasten him for murmurings
	62	use the name of the L. in vain		10	calling on the name of the L.
	63	I, the L., will own them, otherwise		25	the L., give unto you this commandment
64	7	the L. forgive sins unto those who			
	9	standeth condemned before the L.	76	1	the L. is God and beside him there
	10	L. will forgive whom I will, but		5	the L. am merciful and gracious
	15	the L. was angry with him who was		11	in the year of our L., 1832
				15	which the L. had appointed unto us
	16	and I, the L., withheld my spirit		19	L. touched eyes of our; glory of the L. shone round
	21	the L. will to retain a strong hold			
	22	I, the L., will not hold any guilty; I, the L., require the hearts of —34		28	L. commanded that we should write
				30	thus came the voice of the L. unto us
	24	I am the L. of Hosts		38	in the due time of the L.
	28	the L. should not take when he please		47	I, the L., show it by vision to many
				80	vision the L. commanded us to write
	29	do according to will of the L.			
	31	I, the L., declare unto you		85	until the L. shall have finished his
	34	L. requireth the heart and willing		110	heard the voice of the L. saying
	37	I, the L., have made my church in		114	marvelous are the works of the L.
	41	the glory of the L. shall be upon her	77	12	will the L. sanctify the earth
			81	1	listen to the word of the L.
65	4	pray unto the L., call upon his		4	promote the glory of him who is your L.
	5	call upon L. that his kingdom may			
66	3	for the L. will show them unto you —4	82	1	even so, I, the L., forgive you
				7	L. will not lay any sin to your

Sec.	Vs.		Sec.	Vs.	
	10	L. am bound when ye do what I say		120	incomings may be in name of L.;; outgoings may be in name of L..; salutations may be in name of L.—109:9, 17, 18, 19
	15	according to the laws of the L.		133	I salute you in name of the L.
84	2	word of L. concerning his church		137	all your doings in house of the L.
	3	appointed by the finger of the L.; with whom the L. was well pleased	89	12	fowls of air I, the L. have ordained
				21	I, the L., give unto them a promise—118:3
	4	this is the word of the L.	90	10	arm of the L. shall be revealed
	5	until an house shall be built unto L.; even the glory of the L. which		20	until mouth of the L. shall name. —21
	18	the L., confirmed a priesthood also		23	that the storehouse of the L. may
	24	therefore the L. in his wrath		36	the L. will contend with Zion
	27	which the L. in his wrath caused	93	47	must stand rebuked before the L.
	28	make straight the way of the L.; prepare for the coming of the L.		51	proclaim the acceptable year of the L.
	31	and sacrifice in house of the L., which shall be built unto the L.	94	6	it shall be dedicated unto the L.
				7	dedicated unto the L. for the work. —12
	32	shall be filled with glory of the L.		15	which I, the L., have given unto you
	45	for the word of the L. is truth			
	98	be filled with the knowledge of the L.	95	13	here is wisdom and mind of the L.
	99	the L. hath brought again Zion; the L. hath redeemed his people —100		17	even Jesus Christ, your L.
			97	2	I, the L., show mercy unto the meek
	100	L. hath gathered all things in one; L. hath brought Zion from above; L. hath brought Zion from beneath		3	I, the L., am well pleased that there
				6	the L. am willing to show mercy
				8	every sacrifice which the L. shall
	103	as the L. shall direct them, for		9	the L. will cause them to bring forth
	118	with you, saith the L. almighty, I			
	119	I the L. have put forth my hand		12	which I the L. require at their
85	7	I the L. will send one mighty and		15	build a house in name of the L.
	10	as the L. speaketh he will fulfill		19	and the hand of the L. is there
86	4	the L. is beginning to bring forth		23	shall not be stayed until L. come
	5	the angels are crying unto the L.		24	indignation of the L. is kindled
	6	but the L. saith unto them, pluck not		27	L. have accepted her offering
			98	2	waiting patiently on the L.; entered into the ears of the L.; the L. hath sworn and decreed
	11	the L. hath said it			
87	7	into ears of the L. of Sabaoth— 88:2; 95:7; 98:2		6	I, the L., justify you and your
				8	I, the L. God, make you free
	8	be not removed until day of L. come		19	the L. am not well pleased with many
88	2	this is pleasing unto your L.			
	56	the L. of the field went unto the		21	I, the L., will chasten them
	58	light of the countenance of their L.—56		22	I, the L., will turn away all wrath
				33	save I, the L., commanded them
	60	according as his L. had commanded; that his L. might be glorified in him and he in his L.		35	bring these testimonies before the L. —44
				36	the L. would justify them in
	71	call on the L. and ponder the warning		37	the L. would fight their battles
				45	I, the L., will avenge thee of thine
	84	as many as the mouth of the L. shall		47	and turn to the L. their God
				48	as a testimony before the L.
	85	until the mouth of the L. shall call	100	4	I, the L., have suffered you to come
	86	let your hands be clean until L. comes		17	all that call on the name of the L.
	95	face of the L. shall be unveiled	101	2	the L. have suffered the affliction

Sec.	Vs.		Sec.	Vs.	
	7	slow to hearken to voice of the L.; the L. is slow to hearken unto their		69	have mercy, O. L., upon his wife
				71	remember, O. L., the presidents of
				72	remember all thy church, O L.
	32	in that day when the L. shall come		75	that we may ever be with the L.
	38	seek the face of the L. always		77	O L., God Almighty, hear us in these
	46	went and did as their L. commanded		78	O hear, O hear, O hear us, O L.
	47	what need have my L. of this tower —48	110	2	saw the L. standing upon breastwork
	50	hearkened not unto commandments of L.	111	1	I the L. am not displeased with your
	52	and the L. of the vineyard said—55	112	2	with which I, the L., was not pleased
	59	and the servant said unto his L.		6	for I, the L., have a great work
	62	whatsoever his L. commanded him		10	the L. thy God shall lead thee
	89	then will the L. arise and come		13	I, the L., will feel after them
102	23	and obtain mind and will of the L.	113	10	exhorted to return to the L.; the promise of the L. is that he
103	5	unto the counsel which I, the L.
	7	observe all words which I, the L.	117	1	before I, the L., send again the snows
	21	to whom the L. of the vineyard spake
				2	not tarry, for I, the L., command it
104	5	I, the L., have decreed in my heart		16	let all my servants remember the L.
	7	I, the L., have promised a crown of	121	3	O L., how long shall they suffer
	13	the L. should make every man accountable		4	O L., maker of the heaven, earth and
	14	the L. stretched out the heavens		37	spirit of the L. is grieved
	16	this is the way that I, the L., have	124	15	I, the L., love him because of the
	22	and this blessing I, the L., confer		20	for the love he has for, I, the L., love
	66	be called the sacred treasury of the L.; holy and consecrated unto the L.
				23	shall contemplate word of the L.
				24	or the L. *will* not dwell therein
106	4	coming of the L. draweth nigh		54	for I am the L. your God
107	31	not be unfruitful in knowledge of L.		78	I, the L., love him for the work he
			124	83	I, the L., have a great scourge prepared
	33	to officiate in the name of the L.
	34	to act in the name of the L.		104	I, the L., will heal him that he
	42	posterity should be chosen of the L.	125	1	what is will of the L. concerning
	49	saw the L. and walked with him	127	1	the L. has revealed unto me that my
	54	and the L. appeared unto them		10	I will write the word of the L. from
	55	the L. administered unto Adam		12	subscribe myself your servant in the L.
	60	I say unto you saith the L. of Hosts
	80	had in remembrance no more before L.	128	2	make record of a truth before the L.
				5	and preparation that L. prepared
109	1	thanks be to thy name, O L.		9	whenever the L. has given dispensation; in authority, in name of L.
	3	and now thou beholdest, O L.
	4	we ask thee, O L. to accept of this		14	second man is the L. from heaven
	31	for thou knowest, O L. that thy—48		20	voice of the L. in the wilderness
	33	break it off, O L., from the necks —47		23	the trees of the field praise the L.
				24	great day of the L. is at hand
	43	O L. we delight not in destruction	130	7	and are continually before the L.
	44	Thy will be done, O L., and not ours		12	I prophesy in name of the L. God
			132	1	wherein I, the L., justified my
	46	O L. deliver thy people from the		2	I am the L. and will answer thee
	49	O L. how long wilt thou suffer this		12	I am the L. thy God and I give unto—28, 40, 47, 49, 53, 54, 57; 136:21
	50	have mercy, O L., on that wicked mob
	51	make bare thy arm, O L.		35	Nay, for I, the L., commanded it
	54	have mercy, O L., upon the nations		56	and I, the L., will bless her
	60	these words, O L., we have spoken		65	whatsoever I, the L., will give unto
	68	O L. remember Thy servant	133	1	hear word of the L. concerning you

Sec.	Vs.	
	2	L. who shall suddenly come to his; L. who shall come down upon the world
	6	called upon the name of the L.
	7	when the voice of L. is unto you
	9	the voice of the L. unto all people
	10	prepare for the great day of the L.
	16	and hear the voice of the L.
	17	the L. hath sent forth the angel; prepare ye the way of the L.
	25	and the L. shall stand in the midst
	26	shall come in remembrance before L.
	32	by the hands of servants of the L.
	35	in holiness before the L.
	40	calling upon name of L. day and night
	41	for the presence of the L. shall be
	42	O L. thou shalt come down to make
	48	the L. shall be red in his apparel
	52	the loving kindness of their L.
	57	the L. sent forth fulness of his
	59	the L. all thrash the nations
	61	the L. who ruleth over all flesh
	62	him that repenteth before the L.
	63	them that hearken not to voice of the L.
	65	this shall be the answer of the L.
	74	the L. your God hath spoken it
135	1	exclaiming, O L., my God
	3	the prophet and seer of the L.
	5	I prayed unto the L. that he would the L. said unto me, if they have not
	7	will cry unto the L. of Hosts
136	1	word and will of the L. concerning —9
	2	and statutes of the L. our God
	4	we will walk in all ordinances of the L.
	8	into ears of the L. against this
	10	where L. shall locate a stake of
	21	to take the name of the L. in vain
	27	the free gift of the L. thy God
	28	praise the L. with singing
	29	call on the L. with supplication
	32	and calling upon the L. his God

LORD'S

Sec.	Vs.	
59	12	remember that on the L. day
64	29	and ye are on the L. errand; is the L. business
70	11	agent who keepeth the L. storehouse
72	2	in this part of the L. vineyard
	10	to keep the L. storehouse
82	18	be cast into the L. storehouse
83	5	have claim upon the L. storehouse
84	32	upon Mount Zion in the L. house
85	1	it is the duty of the L. clerk
97	23	the L. scourge shall pass over

Sec.	Vs.	
109	13	upon the threshold of the L. house
133	13	unto the mountain of the L. house
	58	prepare the weak for the L. errand
135	3	like most of the L. anointed

LOSE

31	12	enter into temptation and L. your
58	28	they shall in nowise L. their reward
75	28	he shall in nowise L. his crown
78	12	shall L. his office and standing
84	90	shall in nowise L. his reward— 127:4
101	40	if salt of the earth L. its savor

LOSS

42	45	weep for the L. of them that die

LOST

3	14	this is reason that thou hast L.
9	14	a hair of your head shall not be L.
10	1	a wicked man, you have L. them
	2	you also L. your gift at same time
29	25	not one hair neither mote shall be L.
50	42	and none of them shall be L.
83	1	who have L. their husbands or
103	10	as salt that has L. its savor
113	8	return to power which she had L.
124	28	restore again that which was L.
136	26	find that which thy neighbor has L.

LOT

57	3	upon a L. which is not far from
84	3	beginning at the temple L.
85	7	arrange by L. the inheritance of
94	3	let the first L. on the south
	10	the second L. on the south shall be
	13	and on the third L. shall my servant
104	20	and the L. of the tannery
	24	the L. of land which my servant
	28	have the L. which is set off joining; which is L. number one; and also the L. upon
	39	and L. where he now resides, and the L. and building; and also the L.; and also the L. on which
	43	the L. which is laid off for the
127	2	been my common L. all the days of

LOTS

94	14	on first and second L. on north
96	3	let it be divided in L. according
102	12	duty to cast L. by numbers
	34	then proceeded to cast L. or ballot
104	34	and those L. which have been named
	36	he should sell the L. that are laid

LOUD

19	37	declare truth with a L. voice

Sec.	Vs.		Sec.	Vs.	
29	13	trump shall sound, long and L.—34:6; 43:18; 88:94	135	5	and also unto you my brethren whom I L.
36	3	declare it with a L. voice			**LOVED**
39	19	go forth, crying with a L. voice	29	12	as many as have L. me and kept my
50	32	against that spirit with a L. voice	34	3	who so L. the world that he gave
60	7	declare my word with L. voices	76	25	Begotten Son whom the Father L.
84	114	warn the people with a L. voice	95	1	and I have L. you
88	92	midst of heaven, crying with a L.			**LOVES**
	129	and distinctly, not with L. speech	76	103	whosoever L. and makes a lie
124	7	call upon them with L. proclamation			**LOVEST**
	75	let him lift up his voice long and L.	42	29	if thou L. me thou shalt serve me
	88	my everlasting gospel with L. voice			**LOVETH**
133	38	saying with a L. voice, fear God and	63	17	whosoever L. and maketh a lie
			88	40	virtue L. virtue
		LOUDER	124	15	because he L. that which is right
38	30	speak with a voice L. than that			**LOVING**
		LOVE	133	52	the L. kindness of the Lord; his L. kindness
4	5	and faith, hope, charity and L.			**LOW**
6	20	encircle thee in the arms of my L.	49	10	itself shall be laid L. of power
10	21	they L. darkness rather than light		23	for the mountains to be made L.
12	8	be humble and full of L.	58	47	call upon the rich, the high and the L.
20	19	that they should L. and serve him	104	16	in that the rich are made L.
	31	to all those who L. and serve God	112	8	many high ones shall be brought L.; many L. ones shall be exalted
29	45	for they L. darkness rather			**LOWER**
42	22	thou shalt L. thy wife with all thy	94	5	there shall be a L. court—11
	45	thou shalt live together in L.	95	16	let the L. part of the inner
45	27	the L. of men shall wax cold	130	9	all kingdoms of a L. order
46	9	for the benefit of those who L. me			**LOWLINESS**
59	5	thou shalt L. the Lord thy God	42	74	shall testify before you in all L.
	6	thou shalt L. thy neighbor as thyself	107	30	in holiness and L. of heart
76	116	which God bestows on those who L. him	118	3	if they will do this in all L.
88	123	see that ye L. one another			**LOWLY**
	133	grace of God, in the bonds of L.	32	1	and be meek and L. of heart
90	32	your brethren in Zion, in L. greeting			**LUCIFER**
95	1	and whom I L., I also chasten	76	26	he was L., a son of the morning
	12	the L. of the Father shall not continue			**LURKETH**
109	61	hast a great L. for the children	58	33	for their reward L. beneath
112	11	be not partial in L.; let thy L. be for them; let thy L. abound unto all men, unto all who L. my name			**LUST**
			42	23	looketh upon a woman to L. after her—63:16
121	13	because they L. to have others suffer			**LUSTS**
	41	except by meekness and L. unfeigned	46	9	that he may consume it on his own L.
	43	showing forth an increase of L. lest			
124	15	I L. him because of the integrity of			
	17	and for his L. he shall be great			
	20	for the L. he has to my testimony I L. him			
	78	I L. him for the work he hath done			
	87	if ye L. me keep my commandments			
133	53	and in his L. he redeemed them			

Sec.	Vs.	
		LUSTFUL
88	121	cease from all your L. desires
101	6	L. and covetous desires among them
		LYING
5	32	the L. in wait to destroy thee
10	13	that by L. they may say they have
	31	designs in L. against those words
20	54	neither L., backbiting, nor evil
57	3	a spot for the temple is L. westward
	4	and also every tract L. westward
67	4	of these commandments L. before you
109	29	those have spread L. reports
128	11	the whole subject L. before us

Sec.	Vs.	
		LYINGS
109	30	may be an end to L. and slanders
		LYMAN
108	1	my servant L., your sins are forgiven
124	22	let my servant L., and, build a house
		LYMAN, AMASA
124	136	give him L. and Packard for counselors
136	14	let L. and Smith organize a company

M

Sec.	Vs.	
		MADE
1	25	they erred, it might be M. known
	28	were humble they might be M. strong
2	2	promises M. to the fathers—45:16; 96:7
3	5	promises which were M. to you—45:35
	13	promises M. before God
	19	promises which he M. to his people
5	9	M. known unto future generations
6	7	then shall you be M. rich—11:7
9	12	strength whereby it is M. *up*
10	49	this gospel should be M. known
25	13	the covenants which thou hast M. 104:55
26	1	then it shall be M. known unto you
27	4	except it is M., new among you
35	7	their abominations shall be M. manifest
	11	which has M. all nations drink of —88:94, 105
38	1	before the world was M.
	3	which spake and the world was M.—49:17; 76:39
	16	and the rich have I M. and all
	17	I have M. the earth rich
42	32	every man shall be M. accountable
43	23	the words of that God who M. you
45	1	who M. the heavens, and by whom all things were M. which live
	60	in it all these things shall be M. known
49	23	for the mountains to be M. low
50	16	he that is weak shall be M. strong

Sec.	Vs.	
51	6	thus all things shall be M. sure
52	3	as preparations can be M. to leave
	4	it shall be M. known unto them—53:1, 6; 71:2; 73:2; 104:36
	5	M. known unto them the land of
	13	faithful shall be M. ruler over
	17	under my power shall be M. strong
54	4	covenant which they M. unto me
55	6	the residue shall be M. known
56	9	there shall be no divisions M.
58	30	who am I that M. man, that will
	50	it shall be M. known by the spirit
	55	privileges of the land be M. known
59	18	all things are M. for benefit and use
	20	unto this end were they M.
60	5	let there be a craft M.
	17	shall be M. known concerning Sidney
61	22	as it is M. known unto them
63	15	their folly shall be M. manifest—136:19
64	17	when these things are M. known unto
	19	may be M. known unto my disciples
	37	I have M. my church in these last
66	2	and be M. partakers of the glories
	8	that is faithful shall be M. strong
71	7	their shame shall be M. manifest
72	7	duty of bishop shall be M. known
75	27	shall be M. known from on high
76	30	with whom he M. war and overcame
	31	and have been M. partakers thereof
	42	put into his power and M. by him

Sec.	Vs.
	46 except to them who are M. partakers
	69 they who are just men M. perfect—129:3, 6
77	12 as God M. the world in six days
78	15 and be M. rulers over many kingdoms
	19 shall be M. glorious
87	6 be M. to feel the wrath and; hath M. full end of all nations
88	7 power thereof by which it was M.—8, 9
	14 through redemption which is M. for you
	20 for this intent was it M. and created
	56 he was M. glad with the light
	61 to the decree which God hath M.
	69 last promise which I have M. unto —75
	86 liberty wherewith ye are M. free
	94 her bands are M. strong
	107 and be M. equal with him
89	15 these hath God M. for the use of
93	4 and M. flesh my tabernacle
	9 because the world was M. by him
	10 the worlds were M. by him; men were M. by him; all things were M. by him
	29 intelligence was not created or M.
96	1 that this stake should be M. strong
	7 promise M. unto his father
97	6 their works shall be M. known
101	33 of the earth by which it was M.
	54 then ye could have M. ready
	66 and their bands M. strong
102	27 though no such decision had been M.
104	13 earthly blessings which I have M.
	16 in that the rich are M. low
	18 of the abundance which I have M.
107	27 every decision M. by either
	30 are to be M. in all righteousness
	32 any decision M. in unrighteousness
	40 to whom the promises were M.
108	3 your vows which you have M.
109	11 promises which thou hast M. unto us
	74 and the rough places M. smooth
112	20 whom I have M. counselors
115	10 let the beginning be made on the fourth
117	6 have I not M. the earth
	14 he shall be M. a merchant unto me
123	7 have been M. to bow down with grief
124	1 acknowledgments which you have M.

Sec.	Vs.
	3 proclamation shall be M. to all kings
	44 that it shall be M. holy
	113 he shall be M. ruler over many—132:44, 53
	115 the contract which he has M. with him
128	4 the record they have M. is true; and M. a record of same on
	14 records which are truly M. out
	15 they without us cannot be M. perfect; we without our dead cannot be M. perfect—18
130	9 earth *will* be M. like unto crystal
	10 higher order of kingdoms will be M. known
132	7 all covenants not M., and all contracts not M. unto this end
	9 offering, that is not M. in my name
	31 the promise was M. unto Abraham
	33 the promise which he M. unto
133	39 worship him that M. heaven and
	57 that men might be M. partakers
134	11 where immediate appeal cannot be M.
135	4 after Hyrum had M. ready to go
	5 thou shalt be M. strong

MADISON

| 124 | 88 also to inhabitants of M. |

MAGAZINES

| 123 | 5 all that are in the M. |

MAGGOTS

| 29 | 18 shall cause M. to come in upon them |

MAGISTRATE

| 134 | 4 that civil M. should restrain crime |

MAGISTRATES

| 134 | 3 require civil officers and M. |
| | 6 rulers and M. as such being placed |

MAGNA CHARTA

| 135 | 7 innocent blood on the M. of the |

MAGNIFY

24	3 M. thine office
	9 wherewith to M. thine office
66	11 thou shalt M. thine office
88	80 when I shall send you again to M.
132	64 for I *will* M. my name upon all

MAGNIFYING

| 84 | 33 and the M. their calling, are |

MAHALALEEL

82	11 it is expedient that M., and, be bound
107	46 M. was 496 years when ordained
	53 Adam called Seth, M., and, into the

Sec.	Vs.	
		MAHEMSON
82	11	that M. (Martin Harris), and, be bound
104	24	let M. have appointed unto him
	26	let M. devote his moneys for the
		MAIL
127	10	and send it to you by M.
		MAIN
111	8	that you should tarry, for the M.
		MAINSPRING
123	7	now the very M. of all corruption
		MAINTAINED
101	77	should be M. for the rights and
121	41	no influence ought to be M. by
		MAINTAINING
98	5	in M. rights and privileges belongs
		MAINTENANCE
83	2	have claim on husbands for their M.
	4	children have claim on parents for M.
		MAJESTY
20	16	words of the glorious M. on high
88	47	hath seen God moving in his M. and
109	59	may roll on in great power and M.
	77	with glory, honor, power and M.
128	21	their keys, their honors, their M.
		MAJORITY
102	22	the M. of the Council having power
107	28	a M. may form a quorum
		MAKE
1	34	am willing to M. these things known
6	12	M. not thy gift known to any, save
7	6	I *will* M. him as flaming fire
	7	I *will* M. thee to minister for him
10	37	until I see fit to M. all things
23	2	M. known thy calling unto church
25	11	to M. selection of sacred hymns
33	10	M. his paths straight—65:1; 133:17
43	22	M. the ears of all tingle that hear
48	6	M. a commencement to lay foundation
52	2	*will* M. known unto you what I will
56	20	now I M. an end of speaking unto
57	15	let the agent M. preparations
60	4	when I shall M. *up* my jewels—101:3
	7	for I am able to M. you holy
6	22	I would M. known my will unto you; *will* M. known my will
	56	not acceptable, he shall M. another
65	3	M. ready for the bridegroom
.	4	M. known his wonderful works
67	7	that shall M. one like unto it
	8	if ye cannot M. one like unto it
72	23	now I M. an end of my sayings
76	7	M. known unto them the good pleasure
	10	M. known unto them the secrets of
116		neither capable to M. them known
82	22	M. friends with the Mammon of
84	28	to M. straight the way of the Lord
103		M. use of it for their benefit
107		send them before you to M. appointments
88	74	that I may M. you clean
89	6	grape of the vine of your own M.
93	51	go his journey and M. haste
	52	let my servants M. haste also
98	8	I, the Lord, M. you free
102	23	if there is not, to M. case clear
104	13	that I should M. every man accountable
	63	go to and M. use of the stewardship
105	39	M. a proclamation for peace
	40	and M. proposals for peace
107	27	in order to M. their decisions of
108	3	vows you have made and do M.
109	49	and not M. a display of thy
	51	M. bare thine arm O Lord and redeem
114	1	M. a disposition of his merchandise
117	7	*will* I not M. solitary places bud
123	10	are enough to M. hell itself shudder
124	2	called to M. a solemn proclamation
	47	perform the oath which I M. unto you
	53	this I M. an example unto you
128	2	that he might M. record of a truth
132	18	and M. covenant with her for time
	45	M. known unto you all things in due
	50	and I M. a way for your escape
	56	and M. her heart to rejoice
133	3	he shall M. bare his holy arm
	42	M. thy name known to thine adversaries
	68	I M. the rivers a wilderness
	69	and M. sackcloth their covering
136	26	thou shalt M. diligent search till
		MAKER
30	2	than on the things of me, your M.
121	4	M. of the heaven, earth and seas
134	6	both to be answered by man to his M.
		MAKES
46	4	until he M. reconciliation

Sec.	Vs.	
76	95	he M. them equal in power and
	103	whosoever loves and M. a lie

MAKETH

Sec.	Vs.	
63	17	whosoever loveth and M. a lie
76	29	he M. war with the saints
85	6	M. my bones to quake while it M.
86	3	that M. all nations to drink of her
98	8	the law also M. you free

MAKING

Sec.	Vs.	
69	3	in writing and M. a history
72	9	M. known the duty of the bishop
107	49	M. him 430 years old when he was
124	107	in M. a solemn proclamation unto
134	1	in M. laws and administering them

MALACHI

Sec.	Vs.	
110	14	spoken of by the mouth of M.
128	17	for M. says, last chapter, verses
133	64	also that written by the prophet M.

MALE

Sec.	Vs.	
20	18	he created man, M. and female

MAMMON

Sec.	Vs.	
82	22	friends with the M. of unrighteousness

MAN

Sec.	Vs.	
1	10	unto every M. according to his work; measure to every M. according to—19:3
	16	every M. walketh in his own way
	19	that M. should not counsel his
	20	that every M. might speak in name
	33	spirit shall not always strive with M.
3	4	although a M. may have revelations
	7	you should not have feared M.
	12	into the hands of a wicked M.—10:1
5	23	the M. that desires the witness
	25	by the power of God and not of M.
6	24	things which no M. knoweth
10	6	even the M. in whom you trusted
	7	I said he is a wicked M.
	25	that they may catch a M. in a lie
15	3	tell you that which no M. knoweth—16:3
18	23	name given whereby M. can be saved
	34	these words are not of M. but are of me; you shall testify they are not of M.—31:13
19	4	every M. must repent or suffer
20	18	he created M., male and female
	20	M. became fallen M.
	32	M. may fall from grace
22	2	although a M. should be baptized
28	9	no M. knoweth where the city shall be
29	34	neither *any* M. nor the children
	43	thus did I appoint unto M. the days
30	1	you have feared M. and have not
	11	not fearing what M. can do for I am
36	7	that every M. which will embrace it
37	4	let every M. choose for himself
38	24	let every M. esteem his brother as —25
	26	what M. among you having twelve sons
	40	that every M. go to with his might
	41	warning voice, every M. to his neighbor
39	21	the day nor the hour no M. knoweth—49:7
42	32	every M. shall be made accountable
	33	that every M. who has need may be
80		if *any* M. or woman shall commit
84		if a M. or woman shall rob
43	21	if I who am a M. lift up my voice
	33	their end *no* M. knoweth on earth
44	4	organize according to laws of M.
45	39	signs of the coming of the Son of M.—68:11
	68	every M. that will not take his sword
46	11	to every M. is given a gift
	16	given to every M. to profit withal
48	6	every M. according to his family
49	6	they have done unto the Son of M. as
	15	marriage is ordained of God unto M.
	17	be filled with the measure of M.
	18	that M. should not eat the same
	19	is ordained for the use of M.
	20	not given that one M. should possess
	21	wo be unto M. that sheddeth blood
	22	Son of M. cometh not in form of woman; neither of a M. traveling on the
	23	reel to and fro as a drunken M.—88:87
50	9	let every M. beware lest he do
	11	let us reason even as a M. reasoneth
	12	now when a M. reasoneth he is understood of M.; because he reasoneth as a M.
	28	*no* M. is possessor of all things
	38	let *no* M. hinder them of doing
51	3	every M. equal according to his
	4	he shall appoint a M. his portion
	9	let every M. deal honestly
52	33	one M. shall not build upon another's
56	19	and he shall reward every M.
58	20	let *no* M. think he is ruler
	21	let *no* M. break the laws of land

Man   273   Man

Sec.	Vs.	
	30	who am I that made M. that will
	36	this is a law unto every M. that
	43	by this ye may know if a M. repenteth
	59	let *no* M. return from this land
	65	behold, the Son of M. cometh
59	18	made for the benefit and use of M.
	20	he hath given all these things unto M.
	21	and in nothing doth M. offend God
60	2	hide talent because of fear of M.
61	38	look for the coming of Son of M.
62	1	who knoweth the weakness of M.
63	11	for without faith *no* M. pleaseth God
	33	and fear shall come upon every M.
	37	every M. should take righteousness
	50	appointed to him to die at age of M.
	53	in the day of the coming of Son of M.
64	23	until coming of the Son of M.
65	2	committed unto M. on the earth
	5	Son of M. shall come down in
67	11	*no* M. has seen God at any time
	12	neither can *any* natural M. abide
68	18	*no* M. has a legal right to this
70	9	every M. in his stewardship; shall hereafter appoint unto *any* M.
71	10	if *any* M. lift his voice against you
72	8	is the M. who shall be appointed
	15	every M. that cometh *up* to Zion
	17	rendereth every M. acceptable
75	28	every M. who is obliged to provide
	29	let every M. be diligent in all things
76	10	nor yet entered into heart of M.
	16	shall hear the voice of the Son of M.
	45	nor their torment *no* M. knows
	46	neither will it be revealed unto M.
	48	neither *any* M. except those who are
	61	let *no* M. glory in M.
	90	*no* M. knows it except him to whom
	111	every M. shall receive according
	115	are not lawful for a M. to utter
	116	neither is M. capable to make them
77	2	in describing the happiness of M.; spirit of M. in likeness of his person
	12	formed M. out of the dust of the earth; complete the salvation of M.
78	4	have espoused, to the salvation of M.
	21	and appoint every M. his portion
82	17	every M. according to his wants
	18	that every M. may improve his talent; that every M. may gain other talents
	19	every M. seeking interest of his
84	16	his father Adam, who was the first M.

Sec.	Vs.	
	22	without this *no* M. can see the face
	46	spirit giveth light to every M.; spirit enlightened every M.
	71	if *any* M. shall administer poison
	80	*any* M. that shall go and preach
	85	that shall be meted unto every M.
	86	let *no* M. among you take purse
	92	and return not again unto that M.
	103	every M. who goes forth to proclaim
	105	if *any* M. shall give a coat, or
	106	if *any* M. among you be strong, let
	109	let every M. stand in his own office
85	8	while that M. who was called of God
88	15	spirit and body are the soul of M.
	33	what doth it profit a M. if a gift
	44	one year with God, but not with M.
	47	*any* M. who hath seen the least of
	51	liken these kingdoms unto a M.
	58	every M. in his hour and in his
	60	every M. in his own order
	81	every M. who hath been warned, to
	94	made strong, *no* M. can loose them
	122	that every M. may have equal privilege
89	5	inasmuch as *any* M. drinketh wine
	8	tobacco is not good for M.
	10	for constitution, nature and use of M.
	12	have ordained for the use of M.
	14	all grain ordained for the use of M., not only for M. but
	15	hath God made for the use of M.
	16	all grain is good for food of M.
	17	wheat for M., corn for the ox
90	11	every M. shall hear the fulness
	22	let him be a M. who has got riches, a M. of God
93	2	lighteth every M. that cometh into
	27	*no* M. receiveth a fulness
	29	M. was also in beginning with God
	31	here is the agency of M. and the condemnation of M.
	32	every M. whose spirit receiveth
	33	for M. is spirit
	34	M. cannot receive a fulness of joy
	35	M. is the tabernacle of God
	38	spirit of M. was innocent in beginning; God having redeemed M.
	53	knowledge of laws of God and M.
98	7	and as pertaining to law of M.
101	24	every corruptible thing, both of M.
	26	the enmity of M. shall cease
	27	whatsoever *any* M. shall ask it shall
	28	Satan shall not have power to tempt *any* M.
	33	hidden things which *no* M. knew
	65	reward every M. according as his work

Sec.	Vs.		Sec.	Vs.	
	78	that every M. may act in doctrine, that every M. may be accountable		12	previous to coming of Son of M.
	79	not right that any M. should be in bondage		14	time of the coming of Son of M.
	82	feared not God, neither regarded M.		15	thou shalt see the face of Son of M.
	84	I fear not God, nor regard M. yet		17	coming of Son of M. will not be sooner
102	16	every M. to speak according to equity		23	a M. may receive the Holy Ghost and
103	16	a M. who shall lead them like as Moses	131	2	a M. must enter into this order of
	21	is the M. to whom I likened the		6	impossible for M. to be saved in ignorance
	27	let *no* M. be afraid to lay down his	132	12	*no* M. shall come unto the Father but
104	5	inasmuch as *any* M. belonging to—10		15	if a M. marry him a wife—18, 19, 26
	11	appoint every M. his stewardship		41	if a M. receiveth a wife in the new
	12	that every M. may give an account		42	and she be with another M.—41
	13	I should make every M. accountable		59	if *any* M. be called of my Father
	18	if *any* M. shall take of the abundance		61	if *any* M. espouse a virgin; and have vowed to no other M.
	62	*no* M. shall call it his own		63	if one shall be with another M.
	69	if *any* M. obtain five talents		64	if *any* M. have a wife, who holds
	72	that *any* M. say I have need of this	133	6	let every M. call upon the name of
107	16	*no* M. has a legal right to this office		36	and have committed it unto M.
	43	he, Seth, was a perfect M.		66	*no* M. among you received me
	99	now let every M. learn his duty	134	1	instituted of God for benefit of M.
109	5	that Son of M. might have a place		6	every M. should be honored in his; between M. and M.; to be answered by M. to his
112	16	thou art the M. I have chosen			
	34	to recompense every M. according	135	1	exclaiming, "I am a dead M."
117	15	let *no* M. despise my servant Oliver		3	than *any* other M. that lived in it
121	25	a time appointed for every M.	136	10	let every M. use his influence and
	32	every M. shall enter into his eternal		19	if *any* M. seek to build up himself
	33	as well might a M. stretch forth his puny			

	37	amen to the priesthood of that M.	**MANAGE**		
122	8	Son of M. hath descended below them	70	5	to M. them and the concerns thereof
	9	fear not what M. can do, for God	82	12	to M. the affairs of the poor

MANAGING

123	15	let *no* M. count them as small things	82	17	M. the concerns of your stewardships
124	21	let *no* M. despise my servant George			

MANCHESTER

	60	a delightful habitation for M.	24	3	go speedily to the church in M. and

MANFULLY

	64	from *any* one M. for stock in that	35	14	they shall fight M. for me
	65	dollars stock from *any* one M.—66			

MANIFEST

	67	not receive *any* M. as stockholder	20	37	and truly M. by their works that
	72	neither can *any* other M.		69	members shall M. before the church
	85	let *no* M. go from this place	23	6	I M. unto you Joseph Knight, by
119	14	let *no* M. pay stock to the quorum	35	7	their abominations shall be made M.
122		let every M. who pays stock	63	15	and their folly shall be made M.
130		his priesthood *no* M. taketh from him—132	71	7	their shame shall be made M.
127	2	envy and wrath of M. have been my	84	20	the power of godliness is M.
128	9	to *any* M. by actual revelation		21	the power of godliness is not M.
	14	the first M. is of earth, earthy; the second M. is the Lord from heaven	85	6	while it maketh M., saying
			93	5	and the works of him were plainly M.
129	6	spirit of a just M. made perfect			
	7	contrary for a just M. to deceive			
130	1	we shall see he is a M. like ourselves			
	11	which no M. knoweth save he who			

Sec.	Vs.		Sec.	Vs.	
	31	which was from beginning is plainly M.	95	13	built, not after M. of the world; live after M. of the world
102	20	they can M. it, and the case shall		14	let it be built after the M. which
104	74	until it is M. before the Council	102	10	appointed after same M. that he
105	36	it shall be M. unto my servant, by		24	organize a council after the M. of
109	5	a place to M. himself to his people	105	3	but are full of all M. of evil
110	7	I *will* M. myself to my people	107	41	down by lineage in following M.
121	28	or many Gods, they shall be M.		62	in like M. and also the deacons
123	13	they are truly M. from heaven	109	11	in a M. that may be found worthy
124	97	which shall M. unto him the truth	122	6	with all M. of false accusations
130	7	where all things for their glory are M.	127	1	in a prompt and proper M.
	9	will be M. to those who dwell upon it	128	17	in an especial M. this most glorious
			132	26	and all M. of blasphemies
136	19	and his folly shall be made M.	135	1	were both shot in a brutal M.
				2	former was wounded in a savage M.

MANIFESTATION

5	16	them will I visit with the M. of my			**MAN'S**
8	1	spoken by M. of my spirit	130	3	that Father and Son dwell in a M. heart
70	15	for a M. of my blessings upon him		4	is not the reckoning of M. time
76	118	that through power and M. of the		22	Father has a body as tangible as M.
			131	5	means a M. knowing that he is sealed

MANIFESTATIONS

21	8	the M. of my blessings upon his works			**MANSIONS**
46	16	that the M. of the spirit may	59	2	shall receive a crown in the M. of
70	13	through the M. of the spirit	72	4	accounted worthy to inherit the M.
	14	the M. of the spirit shall be withheld	76	111	in the M. which are prepared
			81	6	in the M. which I have prepared
			98	18	in my Father's house are many M.

MANIFESTED

			106	8	prepared a crown in M. of my Father
18	2	I have M. unto you by my spirit	135	5	a place prepared in M. of my Father
20	5	after it was truly M. unto this			
50	31	if you behold a spirit M. that you			**MANTLE**
90	14	as shall be M. by the Comforter	88	125	bonds of charity as with a M.
115	18	as they shall be M. unto my servant			**MANY**

MANIFESTETH

			3	4	a man may have M. revelations, and power to do M. mighty works, yet
18	18	Holy Ghost which M. all things	5	33	there are M. that lie in wait to
21	9	which M. that Jesus was crucified	6	11	bring M. to the knowledge of the truth
91	4	for the spirit M. truth	8	6	behold it has told you M. things

MANKIND

			10	45	are M. things engraven on the plates
98	5	and that law belongs to all M.		59	M. there were that understood me not

MANNER

			11	30	as M. as receive me to them will I
1	24	after the M. of their language	15	4	M. times you have desired to know —16:4
9	6	that I have dealt with you after this M.	18	2	manifested unto you in M. instances
20	37	concerning the M. of baptism		16	joy if you should bring M. souls
	72	baptism administered in following M.		22	as M. as repent and are baptized
	76	after this M. shall he administer it		44	convincing of M. of their sins
	78	M. of administering the wine	20	13	even as M. as shall hereafter come
38	30	in a M. which shall speak in your ears		25	that as M. as would believe—29:43; 33:6; 34:3; 35:2; 38:4; 66:1; 90:8
42	87	if he do any M. of iniquity			
63	53	speaking after the M. of the Lord— 64:24			
76	51	baptized after M. of his burial			
85	2	also their M. of life, their faith			

Sec.	Vs.		Sec.	Vs.	
	26	even as M. as were before he came	91	1	M. things contained therein that—2
24	8	for thou shalt have M. afflictions	93	43	are M. things that are not right
29	2	even as M. as will hearken to my	95	5	there are M. that have been ordained
	12	even as M. as have loved me and kept	97	1	M. of whom are truly humble
31	2	you have had M. afflictions	98	18	in my Father's house are M. mansions
33	4	and they err in M. instances		19	not well pleased with M. who are
36	5	as M. as shall come up before my	101	41	even M. but not all
39	4	as M. as received me gave I power; give unto as M. as will receive me—45:8		62	after M. days all things were fulfilled
	9	thou hast rejected me M. times because	105	8	are M. who will say, where is their
				15	not M. years hence they shall not
	23	as M. as ye shall baptize with water		20	as M. as have come up hither
42	90	if thy brother offend M. he shall be chastened before M.		37	power after M. days to accomplish
			111	2	I have M. people in this city whom I
44	4	and M. shall be converted	112	7	thy path lies among M. nations
45	8	power to do M. miracles		8	M. high ones shall be brought low and M. low ones be exalted
	33	there shall be M. desolations			
	63	not M. years hence ye shall hear		11	be not partial in love above M. others
46	11	for there are M. gifts, and to every			
50	2	there are M. which are false spirits	117	10	and he shall be ruler over M.—124: 113; 132:44, 53
	38	as M. as are ordained unto this			
52	13	shall be made ruler over M. things	121	15	and not M. years hence they and their
56	7	as M. as will go may go			
	14	you have M. things to repent of		28	whether there be one God or M. Gods
58	27	do M. things of their own free will			
	44	time has not yet come for M. years		34	there are M. called but few are chosen
61	4	there are M. dangers upon the waters			
				40	hence, M. are called but few are chosen
	5	decreed M. destructions upon the			
	63	not M. years hence ye shall hear	123	12	for there are M. yet on the earth who
	22	there are M. who observe not to keep			
			124	9	will soften their hearts, M. of them
	58	of warning and not of M. words		84	M. things with which I am not pleased
	62	M. are under this condemnation			
66	6	tarry not M. days in this place	127	8	I am about to restore M. things
	11	and push M. people to Zion		10	by mail, as well as M. other things
68	12	of as M. as the Father shall bear	128	1	information in relation to M. subjects
69	7	travel M. times from place to place			
70	17	they have been faithful over M.		25	I have M. things to say to you
75	5	ye shall be laden with M. sheaves	132	1	having M. wives and concubines
76	8	even the things of M. generations		25	and M. there are that go in thereat
	22	after the M. testimonies which have		34	and from Hagar sprang M. people
	47	I show it by vision unto M.		38	David also received M. wives; as also M. others of my servants
77	11	to bring as M. as will come to the			
78	15	be made rulers over M. kingdoms		58	are M. things pertaining thereunto
84	32	also M. whom I have called	133	22	as the voice of M. waters
	66	they shall do M. wonderful works		36	shall appear unto M. that dwell on
87	1	in death and misery of M. souls	135	3	and M. other wise documents and; gathered M. thousands of Saints
	4	after M. days slaves shall rise up			
88	37	and there are M. kingdoms	136	7	decide how M. can go this spring
	84	as M. as the mouth of the Lord shall		39	M. have marveled because of his death
	87	not M. days hence and the earth shall			

MARKS, WILLIAM

Sec.	Vs.	
	94	who sitteth upon M. waters
117	1	saith the L. to M. and Whitney
90	35	not well pleased with M. things; others have M. things to repent of
	10	let M. be faithful over a few things

Sec.	Vs.		Sec.	Vs.	
124	79	and be ordained by my servant M.			**MARVELED**
	80	let M. pay stock into that house	136	39	many have M. because of his death
		MARRIAGE			**MARVELOUS**
49	15	M. is ordained of God unto man	4	1	a M. work is about to come forth 6:1; 11:1; 12:1; 14:1
58	11	come in unto the M. of the Lamb	6	11	know mysteries which are great and M.
131	2	meaning new and everlasting covenant of M.	8	8	shall hold it, and do M. works
132	15	their covenant and M. are not of force	10	61	I will bring to light their M. works
	16	neither marry nor are given in M.	18	44	by your hand I will work a M. work
		MARRIED	76	2	great is his wisdom, M. are his
42	76	receive none such if they are M.	114		M. are the works of the Lord
	77	and if they are not M. they shall	121	12	may not understand his M. workings
		MARROW			**MASTER**
6	2	asunder of both joints and M.— 11:2; 12:2; 14:2; 33:1	104	86	the M. will not suffer his house to be
89	18	health in their navel and M. to their			**MASTERS**
		MARRY	87	4	slaves shall rise up against their M.
49	15	whoso forbiddeth to M. is not ordained	134	12	contrary to will and wish of their M.
132	15	if a man M. him a wife, and M. her not by me			**MATTER**
	16	they neither M., nor are given in marriage	5	29	nor trouble me concerning this M. —59:22; 90:33; 130:15
	18	if a man M. a wife and make covenant	6	23	peace to your mind concerning the M.
	19	if a man M. a wife by my word —26	10	37	make all things known concerning the M.
		MARSH, THOMAS B.	19	32	give unto you concerning this M.
52	22	let M. and; take their journey	96	1	how to act concerning this M.
56	5	I revoke commandment given to M. and		4	take heed that ye see to this M.
75	31	also my servants Ezra Thayre and M.	105	22	will counsel him concerning this M.
		MARSHAL	128	2	additional views in relation to this M.
87	5	remnants *will* M. themselves and		3	now, in relation to this M.
		MARSHALED		11	now, the great secret of the whole M.
87	4	shall be M. and disciplined for war	131	7	no immaterial M.; all spirit is M.
		MARTYRDOM		8	we shall see that it is all M.
135	1	we announce the M. of Joseph Smith	132	2	will answer thee as touching this M.
		MARTYRS			**MATTERETH**
135	6	classed among the M. of religion	27	2	it M. not what ye shall eat or what
	7	blood of all the M. under the altar	60	5	as seemeth you good, it M. not to me
		MARVEL	61	22	it M. not whether they go by water
10	35	M. not that I said unto you	62	5	it M. not to me, only be faithful
18	8	M. not that I have called him	63	40	it M. not to me if it be little or
27	5	M. not for the hour cometh that	80	3	it M. not, for ye cannot go amiss
76	18	this caused us to M. for it was	135	5	if they have not charity it M. not
136	37	M. not at these things for ye are not			**MATTERS**
			30	7	concerning church M.
			102	28	most difficult cases of church M.
			107	80	upon controversies in spiritual M.
			117	8	and neglect the more weighty M.

Sec.	Vs.	
		MATTHEW
128	10	again for the precedent, M. xvi:18
		MAY
131	5	(M. 17, 1843.) The more sure word of prophecy
		MAYEST
5	30	then thou M. translate again
	34	thou M. accomplish the thing which
6	11	thou M. find out mysteries; thou M. bring many to knowledge
	15	thou M. know thou hast been enlightened
	16	thou M. know there is none else save
42	61	that thou M. know the peaceable things
59	9	thou M. keep thyself unspotted
65	6	that thou, O God, M. be glorified
99	7	thou M. go up to the goodly land
100	11	thou M. be a spokesman unto him
112	17	thou M. be my servant to unlock
136	27	that thou M. be a wise steward
		M'LELLIN, WILLIAM E.
66	1	saith the Lord to M., blessed are you
68	7	word of the Lord to my servant M.
75	6	unto M., I revoke commission I gave
90	35	not well pleased with my servant M. See also, *William*
		MEAN
74	7	this is what the scriptures M.
		MEANING
21	4	wherefore, M. the church, thou shalt
131	2	M. new and everlasting covenant of
		MEANS
5	34	I will provide M. whereby thou
6	8	shall be the M. of doing much good—11:8
8	9	whatsoever you shall ask by that M.
10	1	by the M. of the Urim and Thummim
	4	do not labor more than you have M. provided
20	8	by the M. which were before prepared
64	5	through the M. I have appointed
104	80	until I shall send M. unto you for
121	46	and without compulsory M. it shall flow
128	8	or by M. of their own agents
131	5	more sure word of prophecy M. a man's
135	3	has been the M. of publishing it
		MEANT
113	7	what is M. by the command in Isaiah

Sec.	Vs.	
		MEASURE
1	9	upon the wicked without M.
	10	M. to every man according to the M.
49	17	might be filled with the M. of man
58	61	exceedingly blessed even above M.
88	19	after it hath filled M. of its creation
	25	for it filleth the M. of its creation
98	24	being meted out a just M. unto you
101	11	poured out without M. upon all
103	2	pour out my wrath without M. in mine
	3	fill up the M. of their iniquities
109	45	pour out thy judgments without M.
		MEASURED
1	10	which he has M. to his fellow-man
		MEAT
19	22	they cannot bear M. now, but milk
51	13	let all things, both in money and M.
		MEATS
49	18	whoso forbiddeth to abstain from M.
		MEDDLE
134	12	nor to M. with, or influence them
		MEDIATOR
76	69	Jesus, the M. of the new covenant 107:19
		MEDITATED
76	19	and while we M. upon these things
		MEDIUM
132	7	through the M. of mine anointed
		MEEK
19	41	canst thou be humble and M.
32	1	and be M. and lowly of heart
35	15	the poor and M. shall have the gospel
52	16	whose language is M. and edifieth
58	41	he is not sufficiently M. before me
88	17	poor and M. of earth shall inherit it
97	2	I show mercy unto all the M.
109	72	with all the poor and M. of earth
		MEEKNESS
19	23	walk in M. of my spirit
25	5	consoling words in spirit of M.
	14	continue in the spirit of M.
31	9	govern your house in M.
38	41	to his neighbor in mildness and M.
63	57	those who desire in M. to warn
84	106	that he may be edified in all M.
100	7	in spirit of M. in all things
107	30	decisions in M. and long-suffering
118	3	if they will do this in M. and humility

Sec.	Vs.		Sec.	Vs.	
121	41	only by persuasion, by M. and love	76	57	priests of the Most High after order of M.
124	4	written in spirit of M. and by	84	14	Abraham received priesthood from M.
	18	in spirit of M., confessing me before	107	1	two priesthoods, the M. and Aaronic

MEET

				2	why first is called M.. is because M. was such a great
19	8	it is M. unto you to know even as		4	in ancient days called priesthood after M., or M. priesthood
20	55	that the church M. together often —75		6	one is the M. priesthood, the other
	61	are to M. in conference once in		7	an elder comes under priesthood of M.
41	6	it is not M. that things which belong		8	M. priesthood holds right of presidency
	7	it is M. that Joseph Smith should		9	presidency after order of M. have a
	8	it is M. that Sidney Rigdon should		10	high priests after order of M. have a
45	45	come forth to M. me in the cloud		14	is an appendage to M. priesthood
58	26	not M. that I should command in all		17	a high priest of the M. priesthood has; ordained under hands of presidency of M.
64	26	not M. that my servants should sell		18	power and authority of M. priesthood is to
65	5	to M. the kingdom of God on earth		22	of the M. priesthood, three presiding
71	7	call upon them to M. you both in public		29	were ordained after order of M.
84	58	bring forth fruit M. for their— 101:100		71	a high priest after order of M. may be
88	24	he is not M. for kingdom of glory		73	ordained after order of M.
	92	Bridegroom cometh, go ye out to M. —133:10, 19		76	where a president after order of M. is
	96	and be caught up to M. him—97	124	123	order of M. which is after order of my
	98	who are first to be caught up to M. him			

MELT

89	5	neither M. in the sight of your	101	25	element shall M. with fervent heat
90	30	it is M. in mine eyes that she should	121	11	and their prospects shall M. away
109	75	caught up in the cloud to M. thee			

MELTETH

121	16	but have done that which was M. in	121	11	as the hoarfrost M. before the
133	44	thou shalt M. him who rejoiceth and			

MELTING

135	5	until we shall M. before judgmentseat	133	41	shall be as the M. fire that burneth

MEMBER

MEETING

42	89	and it shall be done in a M.	20	47	and visit the house of each M.—51
58	58	let a conference M. be called		70	every M. of the church of Christ
62	4	hold a M. and rejoice together		80	any M. of church of Christ transgressing

MEETINGS

				84	if the M. is personally acquainted
20	44	and to take lead of all M.	38	40	and also M., go to with his might
	45	conduct the M. as they are led by	46	29	that every M. may be profited
	49	take lead of M. when there is no Elder	58	60	let him stand as a M. in the church
	56	take lead of M. in absence of	84	110	the body hath need of every .M.
46	2	conduct all M. as directed by	92	2	you shall be a lively M. in this order
	3	never cast any one out from your M.	96	8	he should become a M. of the order
	4	not cast any one out of sacrament M.—5	107	10	in office of a teacher, deacon and M.
	6	concerning your confirmation M.		27	every M. in each quorum must be
47	2	lift up his voice in M. whenever it			

MELCHIZEDEK

MEMBERS

68	15	by the First Presidency of the M. —19	20	38	the duty of M. of the church
	19	a High Priest of the M. priesthood			

Sec.	Vs.		Sec.	Vs.	
	55	see that all M. do their duty	21	9	Jesus was crucified by sinful M.
	68	duty of M. after they are received	24	12	strength such as it not known among M.
	69	M. shall manifest before the church	29	11	dwell in righteousness with M. on earth
	82	list of names of the M. uniting		15	weeping and wailing among hosts of M.
	84	all M. removing from the church; certifying that they are regular M.		22	and M. again begin to deny their God
42	70	have stewardships even as the M.		24	fulness thereof, both of M. and
	89	deliver up to the church and not to M.		30	all my judgments are not given unto M.
57	16	unto elders and M. further directions	36	4	commandment concerning all M.
72	24	laws respecting the M. of the church	38	29	ye know not the hearts of M. in your
85	11	M. in that day shall not find an		30	lest the wickedness of M. reveal
102	5	four priests and thirteen M.		34	certain M. shall be appointed
134	9	individual rights of its M. denied		38	when M. are endowed with power
	10	have a right to deal with their M.	39	15	from thence M. shall go forth into
		MEMORIAL	42	58	then ye shall teach them unto all M.
112	1	have come up as a M. before me	45	10	I will reason as with M. in days of old—15; 61:13
		MEMORIALS		12	a day sought for by all holy M.
124	39	and your M. for your sacrifices		27	the love of M. shall wax cold
		MEN		29	because of the precepts of M.
		See *Children of*		31	shall be M. standing in that generation
		MEN		32	among the wicked, M. shall lift up
1	1	whose eyes are upon all M.		33	yet M. will harden their hearts
	2	the voice of the Lord is unto all M.	46	7	not be seduced by commandments of M.; for some are of M.
	35	I will that all M. shall know	48	5	there are to be certain M. appointed
3	3	not work of God is frustrated but work of M.	49	8	all M. shall repent, except holy M. ye know not of
	6	you have gone on in persuasions of M.	54	9	seek ye a living like unto M.
	7	although M. set at naught the counsels	56	16	wo unto you rich M. that will not give
	11	be delivered up and become as other M.		17	wo unto you poor M. whose hearts are
5	21	yield to persuasions of M. no more	58	27	M. should be anxiously engaged in a
7	5	might do a greater work yet among M.		28	inasmuch as M. do good they shall in
10	8	wicked M. have taken them from you		32	I command and M. obey not
	27	seeking to destroy the souls of M.	60	4	all M. shall know what it is that
11	21	power of God unto convincing of M.	63	10	signs come by faith, not by will of M.
18	9	I command all M. everywhere to repent		12	and not for good of M. unto my glory
	11	suffered pain of all M. that all M. might repent		51	until they become old; old M. shall die
	12	that he might bring all M. unto him		61	let all M. beware how they take my name
	24	all M. must take upon them the name	64	10	of you it is required to forgive all M.
	32	according to gifts of God unto M.	65	1	yea, whose voice is unto M.
	34	these words are not of M. nor of man—31:13	76	69	they who are just M. made perfect—129:3
	42	all M. must repent and be baptized, not only M. but			
20	11	God does inspire M. and call them			
	29	all M. must repent and believe			

Sec.	Vs.		Sec.	Vs.	
	73	the spirits of M. kept in prison; judged according to M. in flesh —88:99		39	nature and disposition of almost *all* M.
	75	honorable M. of earth who were blinded by craftiness of M.		45	full of charity towards *all* M.
84	21	godliness not manifest unto M. in flesh	122	6	what are the M. going to do with you
88	89	and M. shall fall upon the ground	123	12	blinded by subtle craftiness of M.
	100	the spirits of M. who are to be judged	124	46	will not hearken to voice of these M.
	108	and reveal the secret acts of M. —109		49	commandment to any of the sons of M.; and those sons of M. go with all their; require no more of those sons of M.
89	4	exist in the hearts of conspiring M.			
91	2	interpolations by the hand of M.			
93	4	and dwelt among the sons of M.		112	that he may obtain the confidence of M.
	9	in him was the life and light of M.			
	10	M. were made by him	127	4	persecuted the righteous M. before you
	38	M. became again in their infant state	128	4	appointment of those M. by Church
98	10	honest and wise M. should be sought; good and wise M. ye should uphold		9	has given priesthood to any set of M., whatever those M. did in authority
	23	if M. will smite you once and ye	132	7	have an end when M. are dead
100	5	shall not be confounded before M.		13	ordained of M.; shall not remain after M. are dead
101	39	when M. are called to my gospel, accounted as the savor of M.		63	that they may bear the souls of M.
	40	they are called to be the savor of M.; and trodden under the feet of M.—103:10	133	16	he calleth upon *all* M. to repent
				45	have not M. heard nor perceived by
				57	that M. might be made partakers of
	55	which are my warriors, my young M.	134	1	that he holds M. accountable
				4	and that M. are amenable to him; to bind the consciences of M.
	73	and let honorable M. be appointed, even wise M.		5	*all* M. are bound to sustain and
	80	established constitution by wise M.		6	to the laws *all* M. owe respect and
	81	for M. ought always to pray and not		8	their tendency to evil among M.; *all* M. should step forward and use
	93	that *all* M. may be left without excuse			
	94	that wise M. and rulers may hear		10	to try M. on right of property or
	95	that M. may discern between the righteous		11	we believe that M. should appeal to; *all* M. justified in defending
103	9	for they are to be saviors of M.		12	thereby jeopardizing the lives of M.
	10	as they are not saviors of M. they; trodden under foot of M.	135	3	more for salvation of M. in this world
	22	my young M. and the middle-aged —105:16		4	void of offence towards *all* M.
	23	send up wise M. with their moneys		5	where *all* M. shall know my garments
	31	but M. do not always do my will		7	conspiracy of traitors and wicked M.; touch the hearts of honest M. - among
104	1	for salvation of M. until I come			
105	28	and to have sent wise M. to fulfill	136	7	expert M. to take teams and seeds
106	6	separated himself from crafts of M.			**MEND**
107	29	and were righteous and holy M.	75	29	except he repent and M. his ways
109	34	and as *all* M. sin, forgive the			**MEN'S**
	48	oppressed and afflicted by wicked M.	45	26	and M. hearts shall fail them
			52	20	according to M. faith it shall be done
111	3	form acquaintance with M. in this city	56	17	laying hold upon other M. goods
112	11	let thy love abound unto *all* M.	88	91	surely M. hearts shall fail them; for
118	1	let M. be appointed to supply the			**MENTION**
121	35	and aspired to the honors of M.	133	52	they shall M. the loving kindness of

Sec.	Vs.	
		MENTIONED
42	71	for other purposes as before M.
77	12	sounding of the trumpets M. in
	14	book eaten by John as M. in
107	24	three presidents previously M.
124	144	approve those names which I have M.
130	10	the white stone M. in Revelation
		MERCANTILE
104	39	on which the Ozondah, (M establishment)—40, 41
		MERCHANDISE
41	9	to leave his M. and spend all his time
114	1	and make a disposition of his M.
		MERCHANT
117	14	he shall be made a M. to my name
		MERCIES
46	15	suiting his M. according to the
		MERCIFUL
3	10	but remember, God is M.
38	14	I *will* be M. unto your weakness
50	16	I *will* be M. unto you.—64:4
61	2	M. unto those who confess their sins
70	18	I am M. and will bless them
76	5	I am M. and gracious unto those who
101	92	that I may be M. unto them
109	53	thou art gracious and M. and wilt
		MERCIFULLY
111	6	for I will deal M. with her
		MERCY
1	29	translate through the M. of God
29	1	whose arm of M. hath atoned for
43	25	by the voice of M. all the day long
54	6	for they shall obtain M.
84	102	for he is full of M., justice, and
88	35	cannot be sanctified by M., justice,
	40	M. hath compassion on M. and claimeth
97	2	I, the Lord, show M. unto all the meek
	6	I am willing to show M., nevertheless
99	3	blessed are they for they shall obtain M.
101	9	in day of wrath I will remember M.
106	7	will have M. on him, notwithstanding
109	1	who keepest covenant and showest M.
	34	have M. upon this people
	50	have M. upon that wicked mob
	54	have M. upon all the nations; have M. upon the rulers of our land

Sec.	Vs.	
	62	have M. upon the children of Jacob
	69	have M. upon his wife and children
	70	have M. upon all their connections
	77	where thou sittest enthroned in M.
110	7	will manifest myself to my people in M.
128	19	a voice of M. from heaven, a voice
		MERIDIAN
20	26	he came in the M. of time
39	3	same which came in the M. of
		MERITS
3	20	rely upon the M. of Jesus Christ
		MERRY
136	28	if thou art M. praise the Lord with
		MESSAGE
129	4	saying he has a M. from God, offer him
	7	but he will still deliver his M.
		MESSENGER
45	9	to be a M. before my face
93	8	even the M. of salvation
129	4	when a M. comes saying he has a
		MESSENGERS
124	26	send ye swift M., even chosen M.
		MESSIAH
13	1	in name of M.] confer the priesthood
19	27	and look not for a M. to come
109	67	believe in the M. and be redeemed
		MET
107	45	and he M. Adam in journeying to
		METE
127	3	he *will* M. out a just recompense
		METED
84	85	portion that shall be M. unto every man
98	24	as being M. out a just measure
		METHUSELAH
107	50	M. was 100 years old when ordained
	52	Noah was ten years old when ordained by M.
	53	Adam called Jared, Enoch and M. into the
		MICHAEL
27	11	also with M., or Adam, the father
29	26	before earth shall pass away M., mine
78	16	who hath appointed M. your prince
88	112	and M. the seventh angel, even

| Michael | 283 | Might |

Sec. Vs.
- 113 come up to battle against M. and his
- 115 for M. shall fight their battles
- 107 54 and blessed Adam and called him M.
- 128 20 the voice of M. on the banks of the
- 21 and the voice of M. the archangel; from M. or Adam down to

MIDDLE
- 101 55 and they that are of M. age

MIDDLE-AGED
- 103 22 my young men and the M.—105:16

MIDST
- 1 36 and shall reign in their M.
- 6 32 there will I be in the M. of them; even so am I in the M. of you
- 29 5 I am in your M. and am the advocate—32:3
- 32 3 will go with them and be in their M.
- 38 7 I am in your M. and ye cannot see me
- 45 59 the Lord shall be in their M. and his
- 49 27 will be in your M. and you shall not
- 50 44 I am in your M. and am the good
- 61 36 I am in your M. and have not forsaken
- 84 25 therefore he took Moses out of their M.
- 101 for he stands in the M. of his people
- 88 13 who is in the M. of all things
- 45 in the M. of the power of God
- 89 shall cause groanings in the M. of her
- 92 angels shall fly through the M. of
- 97 caught up to meet him in the M.
- 103 angel flying through the M. of
- 99 1 in the M. of persecution and wickedness
- 101 61 wise steward in the M. of mine house
- 103 35 and preside in the M. of my people—117:10
- 107 56 Adam stood up in M. of congregation
- 109 33 may rise up in M. of this generation
- 112 26 blasphemed against me in M. of my house
- 121 32 in the M. of the council of God
- 122 4 more terrible in M. of thine enemies
- 124 75 long and loud in M. of the people
- 76 he shall be honored in M. of his house
- 133 14 go ye out from M. of wickedness
- 17 crying through the M. of heaven

Sec. Vs.
- 25 shall stand in the M. of his people
- 27 highway shall be cast up in M. of
- 36 flying through the M. of heaven

MIGHT
- 1 18 all this that it M. be fulfilled
- 20 that every man M. speak in the name
- 21 that faith M. increase in the earth
- 22 everlasting covenant M. be established
- 23 that fulness of gospel M. be proclaimed
- 24 that they M. come to understanding
- 25 as they erred it M. be made known
- 26 as they sought wisdom they M. be
- 27 as they sinned they M. be chastened, that they M. repent
- 28 as they were humble they M. be made
- 29 M. have power to translate through
- 30 M. have power to lay foundation of
- 3 19 that promises of Lord M. be fulfilled
- 20 that Lamanites M. come to knowledge of; that they M. know the promises; through repentance M. be saved
- 4 2 serve him with all your heart, M. and
- 4 thrusteth in his sickle with his M—6:3; 11:3;. 12:3; 14:3; 33:7
- 6 22 that you M. know concerning the truth
- 7 4 he desired that he M. bring souls unto me
- 5 has desired that he M. do more
- 10 48 that they M. preach in their days, M. come unto their
- 50 whosoever, M. have eternal life
- 51 that it M. be free unto all
- 11 20 keep my commandments with all your M.
- 12 9 therefore give heed with your M.
- 17 9 that I M. bring about my righteous
- 18 11 that all men M. repent and come
- 12 that he M. bring all men unto him
- 19 2 that I M. subdue all things
- 7 that it M. work upon the hearts of
- 16 that they M. not suffer if they
- 18 that I M. not drink the bitter cup
- 21 11 that you M. be an elder unto this
- 24 14 that the scriptures M. be fulfilled
- 25 9 that all things M. be revealed
- 27 8 that you M. be called and ordained
- 29 43 he M. be raised in immortality unto
- 34 3 that as many, M. become the sons of God
- 38 31 that ye M. escape power of the enemy

Sec.	Vs.		Sec.	Vs.	
	40	go to with his M. with the labor of		4	M. be chastened for a little season
39	17	lay to with your M. and call faithful	105	2	they M. have been redeemed even now
45	4	that thyself M. be glorified	109	5	that the Son of Man M. have a place
	75	afraid because of power of his M.		77	enthroned, with glory, honor, M.
46	14	that they also M. have eternal life	110	6	who have with their M. built this house
49	16	that earth M. answer the end of its			
	17	that it M. be filled with measure of	121	18	that they M. bring them into bondage
	19	and that he M. have in abundance		33	as well M. man stretch forth his puny
50	3	deceive you, that he M. overthrow you	124	1	that I M. show forth my wisdom
58	6	sent you, that you M. be obedient, that your hearts M. be prepared		38	that those ordinances M. be revealed
	7	that you M. be honored of laying		44	if ye labor with all your M.
	8	feast of fat things M. be prepared		49	when those sons of men go with all their M.
	13	the testimony M. go forth from Zion			
59	5	love the Lord with all thy M.	128	2	that he M. make a record of a truth
61	4	suffered it that ye M. bear record		12	that one principle M. accord with the
	8	that you M. be one, that you M. not perish		18	I M. have rendered plainer translation
62	6	that the promise M. be fulfilled			
66	2	that they M. have life and be made	132	51	that I M. require an offering at your
67	5	that you M. express beyond his language	133	36	that these things M. be known among
74	6	children M. remain without circumcision; that tradition M. be done away		40	that the mountains M. flow down at
				57	that men M. be made partakers of
75	3	and labor with your M.	135	5	that they M. have charity
	23	that you M. know his will concerning	136	6	let them go to with their M.
76	42	that through him all M. be saved		39	that he M. be honored and the wicked M. be condemned

MIGHTEST

	52	they M. be washed and cleansed	7	4	that thou M. speedily come into my
	73	M. be judged according to men in the			

MIGHTS

	91	in glory, and in power, and in M.	20	31	serve God with all their M., minds and
	95	makes them equal in power and M.			
	114	surpasses all understanding in M. and			

MIGHTY

84	23	that they M. behold the face of God	1	19	break down the M. and strong ones
	102	glory, honor and power and M.	3	4	have power to do many M. works, yet
88	6	that he M. be in all things			
	32	to enjoy that which they M. have received	5	24	and humble himself in M. prayer
	57	that he M. visit the second also, and	21	7	inspired in M. power for good
	60	that his Lord M. be glorified, that all M. be glorified		9	in my vineyard with a M. blessing
	99	that they M. receive the gospel and be	24	19	prune my vineyard with a M. pruning
	107	crowned with the glory of his M.	29	2	and call upon me in M. prayer
95	7	that your mourning M. come into the ears	36	1	the Lord God, the M. One of Israel
97	20	hath sworn by the power of his M.	63	11	signs come by faith, unto M. works
98	47	and turn to the Lord with all their M.	65	1	from on high, who is M. and powerful
101	19	that the prophets M. be fulfilled	85	7	I will send one M. and strong
	49	M. not this money given to the	88	108	and reveal the M. works of God— 109
102	1	as the case M. require			
	2	difficulties which M. arise in church	100	10	power to be M. in testimony
103	3	M. fill up measure of their iniquities, that their cup M. be full		11	M. in expounding all scriptures

Sec.	Vs.	
105	24	neither boast of M. works
109	37	as with a M. rushing wind
	68	O M. God of Jacob
123	6	send forth the power of his M. arm
133	20	he shall stand upon the M. ocean
	47	he who spake in righteousness, M. to save

MILD

| 42 | 43 | nourished with herbs and M. food |
| 89 | 17 | all useful animals, and for M. drinks |

MILDNESS

| 38 | 41 | every man to his neighbor in M. |

MILES, DANIEL

| 124 | 138 | I give unto M. and, to preside over |

MILK

| 19 | 22 | cannot bear meat now, but M. they must |
| 38 | 18 | land flowing with M. and honey |

MILLENNIUM

| 43 | 30 | for the great M. shall come |
| 130 | 16 | referred to the beginning of the M. |

MILLER, GEORGE

124	20	my servant M. is without guile
	62	let my servant M. and, organize themselves
	70	let M. and, receive stock into their

MILLSTONE

| 121 | 22 | better that a M. had been hanged |

MIND

4	2	serve him with all your M., might
6	15	and I did enlighten thy M.
	22	cast your M. upon the night that you
	23	did I not speak peace to your M.
8	2	I will tell you in your M.
9	8	you must study it out in your M.
10	2	lost your gift, and your M. became
11	13	which shall enlighten your M.
	20	with all your M., might and strength—33:7; 59:5; 98:47
30	2	your M. has been on things of earth
45	65	and with one heart and one M. gather
64	34	Lord requireth the heart and willing M.
67	10	not with the natural M. but with
	12	neither after the carnal M.
68	4	shall be the M. of the Lord
84	80	shall not be weary in M., neither
95	13	here is wisdom and the M. of the Lord

Sec.	Vs.	
102	23	inquire and obtain the M. of the Lord
128	1	that subject seems to occupy my M.
133	61	according to M. and will of the Lord

MINDS

20	31	serve God with all their mights, M. and
33	4	all having corrupt M.
43	34	let solemnities of, rest upon your M.
46	10	and always retain in your M. what
67	14	let not your M. turn back, and ye
84	54	your M. have been darkened
	61	that you may remain steadfast in your M.
	85	treasure up in your M. continually
88	68	that your M. become single to God
124		that bodies and M. may be invigorated
102	23	to make case clear to the M. of the
104	81	out of their M. to bring affliction
110	1	the veil was taken from our M.
112	23	gross darkness the M. of the people
121	12	to blind their M. that they may not
	27	which their M. were pointed to

MINGLE

| 109 | 79 | that we may M. our voices with those |
| 134 | 9 | not just to M. religious influence with |

MINISTER

7	6	he shall M. for those who shall be
	7	I will make thee to M. for him
68	14	to M. even according to the first
76	88	who are appointed to M. for them
130	5	no angels who M. to this earth but those
132	16	to M. to those who are worthy of a

MINISTERED

| 10 | 62 | my gospel which was M. unto them |
| 20 | 6 | God M. unto him by an holy angel |

MINISTERING

7	6	make him as flaming fire and a M. angel
13	1	keys of the M. of angels
20	10	confirmed to others by M. of angels
	35	voice of God or the M. of angels
43	25	called upon you by the M. of angels
67	13	neither the M. of angels
76	88	appointed to be M. spirits to
84	26	holdeth the key of the M. of angels —107:20
107	71	set apart unto the M. of temporal
132	16	which angels are M. servants to
136	37	call upon by mine angels, my M. servants

Sec.	Vs.	
		MINISTERS
84	111	to be standing M. to church—124:137
107	39	duty to ordain evangelical M.
	97	seventy are to be traveling M. unto
109	35	let the anointing of thy M. be
		MINISTRATION
76	86	through the M. of the terrestrial
	87	terrestrial through M. of celestial
		MINISTRY
6	28	which shall bring to light this M.
	29	this part of my gospel and M.
7	7	give this power and keys of this M.
24	1	thou wast called and chosen to my M.
27	12	and bear the keys of your M.
29	12	Twelve which were with me in my M. at
30	2	the M. where unto you have been called
	4	shall attend to the M. in the church
67	10	you that have been ordained unto this M.
68	22	who shall be set apart for this M.
75	30	be united in the M.
77	5	who had been faithful in work of M.
81	3	in thy M. in proclaiming gospel
84	86	who are called in the church unto M.
88	84	that ye may be perfected in your M.—90:8; 97:14
	127	those who are called to the M.
90	12	continue in the M. and presidency
94	3	for the work of the M. of the
97	13	work of the M. in their several
107	74	where he shall be set apart unto this M.
	76	legal right to the keys of this M.
115	19	given keys of this kingdom and M.
124	143	the work of the M. and perfecting
		MINUTES
88	44	in their M., in their hours, in their
128	3	qualified for taking accurate M.
		MIRACLES
24	13	require not M., except I shall
35	8	I will show M., signs, and wonders
45	8	gave I power to do many M.
46	21	to some it is given the working of M.
		MIRACULOUS
17	1	the M. directors given to Lehi
		MISERY
19	33	and M. thou shalt receive

Sec.	Vs.	
76	48	and the M. thereof they understand not
87	1	in the death and M. of many souls
		MISSION
31	3	for the hour of your M. is come
58	14	appointed unto him his M. in this land
	16	his M. is given unto him
	17	whoso standeth in his M. is
61	7	be in haste upon their errand and M.
	9	that they may fill their M.
	22	if it so be that they fill their M.
62	2	wherefore your M. is not yet full
68	2	whose M. is appointed unto them
71	3	this is a M. for a season
77	14	it was a M. and an ordinance
88	80	the M. with which I have commissioned
90	16	this shall be your business and M.
114	1	that he may perform a M. next spring
124	102	I have a M. in store for my servant
135	3	sealed his M. with his own blood
		MISSIONS
73	2	shall be made known their several M.
		MISSOURI
52	2	conference which shall be held in M.
	3	leave their homes and journey to M.
	42	to rejoice upon the land of M.
54	8	regions westward, unto land of M.
56	5	journey speedily to land of M.
	9	appointed still to go to land of M.
	12	will pay it unto him again in land of M.
57	1	the land of M., which is the land
62	6	and rejoice together in the land of M.
84	3	in western boundaries of State of M.
109	47	by inhabitants of Jackson Co., M.
121	33	to stop M. river in its decreed course
124	51	a house unto my name in Jackson County, M.
	54	and have been slain in land of M.
127	1	my enemies both in M. and this state
		MIXTURE
115	6	shall be poured out without M.
		MOB
109	50	have mercy upon that wicked M.
135	1	they were shot by an armed M.
		MOCKED
63	58	I am not to be M. in the last days

Sec.	Vs.	
104	6	I am not to be M. in these things—124:71

MOCKER

45	50	calamity shall cover the M.

MOMENT

24	6	shall be given thee in the very M.
100	6	in the very hour, yea in the very M.
121	7	thine afflictions shall be but a M.
122	4	and but for a small M. thy voice

MONEY

24	18	for shoes, and for M. and for script
48	4	that ye save all the M. that ye can
51	8	and the M. which is left to this; agent appointed to take the M.
	11	if another church would receive M. of
	13	let all things, both in M. and in meat
56	10	he shall receive the M. which he
	12	and if my servant must needs pay the M.
57	8	that he may obtain M. to buy lands
60	10	impart of the M. I have given him
63	43	let him impart all the M. he can
84	89	feed and clothe you and give you M.
	90	he who feeds, clothes or give you M.
	103	inasmuch as they receive M. by gift
	104	let all those who receive M. send it
90	28	should receive M. to bear her expenses
	29	and the residue of the M. may be
101	49	might not this M. be given to
	56	I have bought it with M.
	70	purchase all the lands by M. which can be, for M.
103	22	the land which I have bought with M.
104	84	as you obtain a chance to loan M.

MONEY-CHANGERS

117	16	to overthrow the M. in mine own due time

MONEYS

54	7	be your leader and pay M. for you
57	6	which I have appointed to receive M.
58	35	example in laying his M. before the
	36	he shall do with his M. as the law
	49	to receive M. to purchase lands
	51	a subscription to obtain M. to be put
63	40	let all the M. which can be spared
	46	obtaining M. even as I have directed
69	1	and the M. which he shall carry to
101	72	churches gather together all their M.
103	23	let churches send up wise men with M.

Sec.	Vs.	
104	26	devote his M. for the proclaiming of
	68	all M. you receive in your stewardships, as fast as you receive M.
105	8	otherwise we will keep our M.
	30	lands previously purchased with their M.
124	70	receive stock in M., where receive real value of M.

MONTH

20	1	in the fourth M. and on the sixth day; of the M. which is called April—21:3

MONTHS

20	61	meet in conference once in three M.
88	44	their weeks, in their M., in their
107	44	ordained at age of 134 years, four M.
121	31	days, M. and years, and all the days of their days, M. and

MOON

5	14	clear as the M. and fair as the sun
29	14	the M. shall be turned into blood—34:9; 45:42
76	71	as that of the M. differs from the sun—78
	81	stars differs from that of glory of M.
	97	even as the glory of the M. is one
88	8	he is in the M. and the light of the M.
	45	the M. giveth her light by night
	87	the M. shall be bathed in blood
105	31	fair as the sun and clear as the M.
109	73	fair as the M. and clear as the sun
121	30	or to the dry land, the sun, the M.
128	23	let sun, M. and morning stars sing
133	49	and the M. shall withhold its light

MORAL

101	78	according to M. agency I have given

MORE

3	7	should not have feared man M. than God
	11	and shall have *no* M. gift—5:31
5	21	walk more uprightly before me; yield to persuasions of men *no* M.
	26	say *no* M. to them concerning
	29	do *no* M. nor trouble me *any* M. concerning—59:22; 130:15
	30	when translated a few M. pages
6	29	they can do *no* M. unto you than unto me
	35	go your ways and sin no M.—82:7
7	5	has desired that he might do M.
10	4	do not labor M. than you have strength
	39	that a M. particular account was

Sec.	Vs.		Sec.	Vs.	
	40	plates of Nephi is M. particular		75	waste places *no* M. to be thrown down
	68	whosoever declareth M. or less than	102	14	if M. difficult, six; but in no case shall M.
19	7	it is M. express than other scripture			
	38	even M. than if you should obtain	103	13	established, *no* M. to be thrown down
20	81	to send one or M. teachers			
24	2	go thy way and sin *no* M.	105	10	that people may be taught M. perfectly
29	3	remember to sin *no* M.			
	50	I declare *no* M. unto you at this— —73:6; 94:17	107	80	it shall be had in remembrance *no* M.
30	2	on things of earth M. than on me	108	2	resist *no* M. my voice
34	5	M. blessed are you because you are		3	arise and be M. careful henceforth
35	25	and *no* M. to be confounded at all	111	9	concerning M. ancient inhabitants
37	1	should translate *any* M. until ye go to		10	for there are M. treasures than one
			115	13	get in debt *any* M. for the building
	2	and M. especially in Colesville	117	8	and neglect the M. weighty matters
38	20	*no* M. to pass away		13	his sacrifice shall be M. sacred
42	25	forsaketh it and doeth it *no* M.	122	4	thy voice shall be M. terrible
	33	M. than is necessary for their support	124	49	require that work *no* M. at the hands
	44	elders of the church, two or M.	126	1	it is *no* M. required at your hand
	45	M. especially for those who have not	127	11	close my letter, for want of M. time
			130	19	if a person gains M. knowledge in
	55	if thou obtainest M. than that which	131	5	the M. sure word of prophecy
				7	spirit is matter but it is M. fine
	80	before two elders of the church or M.; if there are M. than two witnesses	132	16	who are worthy of a far M. and
				66	I will reveal M. unto you hereafter
			135	3	Joseph Smith has done M., save Jesus only
50	24	continueth in God, receiveth M. light			
			136	42	so *no* M. at present

MORLEY, ISAAC

			Sec.	Vs.	
51	13	which are M. than is needful—70:7	52	23	let M. and Ezra Booth take their
58	42	I the Lord remember them *no* M.	64	15	angry with M. for they kept not the law
59	9	that thou mayest M. fully keep thyself		16	I have forgiven my servant M.
60	3	if they are not M. faithful unto me		20	that M. may not be tempted above that
61	4	and M. especially hereafter			

MORMON, BOOK OF

See: *Book of Mormon*

MORMONISM

135	7	is a broad seal affixed to M.

MORNING

76	26	he was Lucifer, a son of the M.
	27	fallen, fallen, even a son of the M.
108	1	in coming up hither this M.
112	5	contend thou, therefore M. by M.
128	23	let the M. stars sing together
135	4	but I am calm as a summer's M.; the same M. after Hyrum had made

	32	their labors wanted M. abundantly
63	66	a M. exceeding and eternal weight of
69	7	may the M. easily obtain knowledge
70	13	yea, even M. abundantly
71	6	it shall be given M. abundantly
75	22	shall be M. tolerable for heathen
78	19	even a hundred-fold, yea M.
88	78	instructed M. perfectly in theory
	114	power over the saints *any* M. at all
	116	and they shall not *any* M. see death
93	25	whatsoever is M. or less than this— —98:7; 124:120
	48	give M. earnest heed unto your
	50	see that they are M. diligent
97	27	if she sin *no* M., none of these
98	28	that he come *no* M. upon you
	39	shall hold it *no* M. as a testimony— 48
	48	vengeance shall no M. come upon
101	21	when there is found *no* M. room for them

MORONI

27	5	with you on the earth and with M.
128	20	M., an angel from heaven declaring

MORROW

84	81	take no thought for the M., for

Sec.	Vs.	
	84	let the M. take thought for the things

MOSES

Sec.	Vs.	
8	3	spirit by which M. brought children of
22	2	by law of M., neither by your dead works
28	2	for he receiveth them even as M.
74	3	and become subject to the law of M.
	4	brought up in subjection to law of M.
	5	except the law of M. should be done away
76	100	some of John, some of M. some of Elias
84	6	sons of M. according to priesthood
	23	this M. plainly taught the children of
	25	he took M. out of their midst and the
	31	concerning the sons of M., for the sons of M.
	32	the sons of M. shall be filled with
	34	they become sons of M. and of Aaron
103	16	a man who shall lead them as M. led
107	91	over whole church and be like unto M.
110	11	opened unto us and M. appeared before us
124	38	commanded M. he should build a
132	1	justified M., David and Solomon
	38	and concubines, as also M. and
133	54	and M. also and they who were before
	55	and from M. to Elijah; and from
	63	which was written by the prophet M.
136	37	from Abraham to M.; from M. to Jesus

MOST

3	13	has broken the M. sacred promises
15	4	which would be of M. worth unto you—16:4
	6	the thing that will be of M. worth —16:6
21	2	build it up unto the M. holy faith
36	3	blessed be the name of the M. high —39:19
45	66	for the saints of the M. high
52	36	seen and heard and M. assuredly believe—58:59
59	10	pay thy devotions to the M. high
	12	oblations and thy sacraments to the M. High—62:4
67	6	appoint him that is the M. wise
76	57	and are priests of the M. high

Sec.	Vs.	
	112	they shall be servants of the M. High
82	13	benefit of saints of the M. High
85	11	among the saints of the M. High
88	120	with uplifted hands unto the M. High—109:9, 19
95	16	offering up your M. holy desires
96	5	this is the M. expedient in me
101	34	things M. precious, things that are
102	28	only to be called on M. difficult cases—107:78
107	78	the M. important business of the church
115	7	it shall be called M. holy
119	6	that it may be M. holy
123	7	under the M. damning hand of murder
124	27	for the M. High to dwell therein
	39	oracles in your M. holy places
128	17	this M. glorious of all subjects
132	7	and that too M. holy
135	3	and like M. of the Lord's anointed

MOSTLY

91	1	it is M. translated correctly

MOTE

29	25	not one hair, neither M., shall be lost

MOTHER

88	94	that great church, the M. of abominations
122	6	from society of thy father and M.

MOTHERS

132	55	of fathers and M., brothers and

MOTHER'S

84	27	with Holy Ghost. from his M. womb

MOUNT

17	1	given to brother of Jared upon the M.
45	48	shall the Lord set his foot upon this M.
63	21	shown unto mine apostles upon the M.
76	66	who are come unto M. Zion
84	2	to stand upon M. Zion—133:56
	32	filled with glory of Lord upon M. Zion
124	99	M. *up* in the imagination of his thoughts
133	18	the Lamb shall stand upon M. Zion
	20	he shall stand upon the M. of Olivet

MOUNT SINAI

29	13	even as upon M., and all the earth

Sec.	Vs.		Sec.	Vs.	
		MOUNTAIN	58	13	yea, from the M. of the city of
65	2	is cut out of the M. without hands	60	17	and by the M. of my servant, Joseph
109	72	may become a great M. and fill the	61	14	by M. of my servant John I cursed
		MOUNTAINS	84	2	has spoken by M. of his prophets
19	29	publish it upon the M.		44	that proceedeth from the M. of God—98:11
49	23	for the M. to be made low	85	7	whose M. shall utter eternal words
	25	and rejoice upon the M.	88	84	as many as the M. of the Lord shall name
109	61	who have been scattered upon the M.		85	until the M. of the Lord shall call them
	74	M. to flow down at thy presence—133:44	90	20	let it not be sold until the M. of
112	7	and thy path lieth among the M.		21	remain where he now resides until M.
117	6	have I not the beasts of the M.	109	45	by M. of holy prophets terrible things
	8	is there not room enough upon the M.	110	14	spoken of by the M. of Malachi
124	104	lift up his voice again on the M.	122	7	hell shall gape open the M. wide after
128	19	how beautiful upon the M. are the feet	128	3	that in M. of two or three witnesses
	23	let the M. shout for joy			**MOUTHS**
133	13	unto the M. of the Lord's house	1	4	by the M. of my disciples
	22	which shall break down the M.	33	8	open your M. and they shall be filled
	40	that the M. might flow down		9	open your M. and spare not
		MOURN		10	open your M. saying, repent, repent
21	8	he shall M. for her no longer	42	39	which I spake by the M. of my prophets
45	49	the nations of the earth shall M.	58	8	that the M. of the prophets shall not fail
87	6	the inhabitants of the earth shall M.	60	2	they will not open their M. but hide
97	21	while all the wicked shall M.	61	30	shall not open their M. in congregation
98	9	when the wicked rule the people M.	71	1	open your M. proclaiming my gospel
		MOURNED	86	10	spoken by M. of all holy prophets—109:23, 41
101	14	they who have M. shall be comforted			**MOVE**
		MOURNING	21	7	him have I inspired to M. cause of Zion
95	7	that your M. might come up into the	45	1	which live, M. and have a being
112	24	a day of desolation, of weeping, of M.	77	4	a representation of power, to M., to
		MOUTH	88	42	by which they M. in their times and
6	28	in M. of two or three witnesses	129	7	shake hands with him, he will not M.
19	15	lest I smite you by rod of my M.			**MOVED**
21	5	shall receive, as if from mine own M.	45	32	stand in holy places and shall not be M.
24	12	he shall open his M. and declare	68	3	as M. upon by the Holy Ghost—121:43
27	6	spoken by the M. of all the holy		4	M. upon by the Holy Ghost shall be
28	16	thou must open thy M. at all times	84	40	cannot break, neither can it be M.
29	21	as spoken by the M. of Ezekiel	87	8	be not M., until the day of the Lord
	29	from my own M. that they should return	97	19	Zion cannot fall, neither be M.
	30	as words have gone forth out of my M.	101	17	Zion shall not be M. out of her place
30	5	open your M. to declare my gospel			
	11	you shall ever open your M. in my			
42	81	shall be condemned by M. of two			
43	25	called upon you by M. of my servants			
	30	which I have spoken by the M. of			
50	36	words of mine from the M. of my			

Sec.	Vs.		Sec.	Vs.	
121	3	and thy bowels be M. with compassion—4			**MULTIPLY**
124	45	they shall not be M. out of their place	45	58	they shall M. and wax strong
	71	and shall be M. out of their place	97	28	and M. a multiplicity of blessings—104:38
	88	as he shall be M. upon by my spirit	104	23	I *will* M. blessings upon—25, 31, 33, 35, 42, 46
		MOVING	132	55	I *will* bless him and M. him
61	3	to be M. swiftly upon the waters		56	I *will* bless her and M. her
88	47	hath seen God M. in his majesty and		63	given him to M. and replenish the earth
		MUCH			**MULTITUDE**
1	3	shall be pierced with M. sorrow	107	55	a M. of nations shall come of thee
6	8	be the means of doing M. good—11:8			**MUNICIPALS**
	26	which contain M. of my gospel	124	39	and endowment of all her M.
10	63	that there may not be so M. contention			**MURDER**
25	8	given to writing and to learning M.	121	23	that discomfort my people and M.
26	2	by M. prayer and faith	123	7	under the most damning hand of M.
37	2	they pray unto me in M. faith—39:16	132	19	he shall commit no M. whereby to shed; abide in my covenant and commit no M.
42	32	as M. as is sufficient for		26	if they commit no M. wherein they
52	34	kept and be blessed with M. fruit		27	blasphemy is in that ye commit M.
58	3	shall follow after M. tribulation	134	8	that M., treason, robbery, should be
	4	after M. tribulation come the; ye shall be crowned with M. glory—103:12			**MURDERED**
			123	9	whose husbands and fathers have been M.
	27	and bring to pass M. righteousness	135	4	he was M. in cold blood
59	15	not with M. laughter for this is sin			**MURDERERS**
63	40	money, whether it be little or M.	122	7	cast into the hands of M.
82	3	unto whom M. is given M. is required			**MURDEROUS**
97	9	that yieldeth M. precious fruit	123	5	and nefarious and M. impositions
100	3	I have M. people in this place			**MURDOCK, JOHN**
105	24	gather together as M. in one region	52	8	let my servant M. and, take their
111	2	I have M. treasure in this city	99	1	M., thou art called to go into the
112	13	after M. tribulation I will feel			**MURMUR**
113	4	on whom there is laid M. power	9	6	do not M., my son, for it is wisdom
121	35	hearts are set so M. upon the	25	4	M. not because of the things which
123	15	there is M. which lieth in futurity			**MURMURINGS**
	16	ship benefited very M. by small	75	7	chasten him for the M. of his heart
130	12	which shall cause M. bloodshed previous			**MUSIC**
	19	he will have so much the advantage	136	28	praise the Lord with singing, with M.
		MULES			**MUST**
62	7	to ride upon horses, or upon M.	3	4	he M. fall and incur the vengeance
		MULTIPLICITY	5	17	you M. wait yet a little while
97	5	bless him with a M. of blessings—124:13, 90	9	8	M. study it out in your mind, then you M. ask
	28	multiply a M. of blessings upon—104:38, 42, 46	14	10	I M. bring forth fulness of my
104	2	they should be blessed with a M. of	17	1	you M. rely upon word
	33	even a M. of blessings	18	6	M. *needs* be that children of men are
		MULTIPLIED			
70	13	which abundance is M. unto them			

Sec.	Vs.		Sec.	Vs.	
	24	all men M. take upon them the name	75	24	and M. needs be sent unto the world
	30	wherefore you M. perform it according	77	14	Elias M. come and restore all things
	31	you M. walk uprightly before	78	3	M. needs be that an organization
	41	you M. preach unto the world; you M. repent and be baptized		7	you M. prepare yourselves by doing
	42	all men M. repent and be baptized	82	14	Zion M. increase in beauty; her borders M. be enlarged; her stakes M. be strengthened; Zion M. put on her beautiful garments
	43	you M. keep my commandments in all	84	76	from you it M. be preached unto them
19	4	surely every man M. repent or suffer	86	-10	priesthood M. needs remain through you
	17	would not repent they M. suffer even as I	88	18	M. needs be sanctified from all
	22	but milk they M. receive; they M. not know these things		21	they M. inherit another kingdom
20	29	we know all men M. repent and believe		24	he M. abide a kingdom which is not
23	6	you M. take up your cross, you M. pray		35	they M. remain filthy still
28	13	all things M. be done in order		79	things which M. shortly come to pass
	16	thou M. open thy mouth at all times	93	47	and M. needs stand rebuked before the Lord
29	10	spoken by mine apostles M. be		48	your family M. needs repent
	21	not come to pass but surely M.	94	2	it M. be done according to the pattern
	39	M. needs be that devil should tempt	95	2	ye M. needs be chastened—101:4, 41
38	39	M. needs be that riches of earth are	97	6	there are those who M. be chastened
44	6	ye M. visit the poor and needy	101	64	my word M. needs be fulfilled
45	68	M. needs flee unto Zion for safety		65	I M. gather together my people
46	31	all things M. be done in name of Christ		93	what I have said unto you M. needs be
	32	ye M. give thanks unto God	103	15	redemption of Zion M. needs come by power
	33	and ye M. practice virtue and holiness		17	ye M. needs be led out of bondage
48	3	it M. needs be that they have places	104	16	it M. needs be done in my own way
	4	it M. needs be that ye save all the	105	6	my people M. needs be chastened; learn obedience if it M. needs be by
49	2	not right before me and M. needs repent	107	27	M. be by unanimous voice of same; M. be agreed to its decisions
50	40	ye M. grow in grace and knowledge		60	there M. needs be presiding elders
51	1	M. receive directions how to organize		65	it M. needs be that one be appointed
	2	M. be organized according to my laws		69	a bishop M. be chosen from
56	8	M. repent of his pride and selfishness	109	44	but thy word M. be fulfilled
	12	if my servant M. pay the money	124	122	if it M. needs be, for their support
58	64	the sound M. go forth from this place; Gospel M. be preached to every creature	128	7	books spoken of M. be the books
			131	2	a man M. enter into this order of the
63	53	these are things ye M. look for	132	3	revealed unto them M. obey the same
	64	sacred, and M. be spoken with care		6	fulness thereof, M. and shall abide the law
64	32	all things M. come to pass in time	136	31	my people M. be tried in all things
68	20	a literal descendant M. be designated			**MYSELF**
	32	and M. be done away from among them	1	38	I have spoken and excuse not M.
			19	2	might subdue all things unto M.
72	15	M. lay all things before the bishop		18	which suffering caused M. even God
	16	M. give an account of his stewardship	29	11	I will reveal M. from heaven
				33	unto M. my works have no end
			32	3	I M. will go with them and be with
			43	14	reserve unto M. a pure people

Sec.	Vs.		Sec.	Vs.	
45	12	who were received unto M.		65	to you it is given to know the M.
49	8	except them which I have reserved unto M.	43	13	if ye desire the M. of the kingdom
63	39	excepting those I shall reserve unto M.	63	23	I will give the M. of my kingdom
85	10	these things I say not of M.	64	5	keys of M. of kingdom shall not be taken
88	126	come quickly and receive you unto M.	71	1	expounding the M. thereof out of the
100	16	will raise up unto M. a pure people	76	7	I will reveal all M., all hidden M.
104	68	writings which I have reserved unto M.	114		marvelous are the M. which he showed
105	5	otherwise I cannot receive her unto M.	77	6	contains the revealed will, M.
110	7	I will manifest M. unto my people	84	19	priesthood holdeth the key of the M.
124	19	that I may receive him unto M.	90	14	revelations to unfold the M. of the
	130	I have taken unto M.—132	97	5	expounding all scriptures and M.
127	12	I subscribe M. your servant in the Lord	107	19	have privilege of receiving the M.

MYSTERIOUS

Sec.	Vs.	
136	38	was faithful, and I took him to M.	127	2	for what cause it seems M.

MYSTERIES

MYSTERY

Sec.	Vs.		Sec.	Vs.	
6	7	the M. of God shall be unfolded—11:7	10	64	I will unfold unto them this great M.
	11	thou shalt know M. which are great; thou mayest find out M.	19	8	I will explain unto you this M.
8	11	that you may know the M. of God		10	the M. of Godliness, how great is it
28	7	have given him the keys of the M.	35	18	have given unto him the keys of the M.
42	61	that thou mayest know the M.	38	13	I show unto you a M., had in secret

N

Sec.	Vs.		Sec.	Vs.	
		NAILS		25	if they know not the N. by which called
6	37	prints of the N. in my hands and feet		27	they shall take upon them my N.; desire to take upon them my N.—28
		NAME		29	ordained to baptize in my N.
1	20	speak in the N. of God, the Lord		40	you shall worship the Father in my N.
3	20	glorified through faith in his N.		41	be baptized in the N. of
6	32	where two or three are gathered in my N.	19	10	for endless is my N.
10	61	works which they did in my N.		13	Joseph Smith, Jun., in my N.
11	30	even to them that believe on my N.		37	blessed be the N. of the Lord God
13	1	in the N. of Messiah I confer the	20	25	believe and be baptized in his N.
14	8	if you shall ask the Father in my N.—18:18; 42:3; 88:64		29	all men must believe on the N.; worship Father in his N., and endure in faith on his N.
18	8	and his N. is Joseph		36	and glory be rendered to his holy N.
	21	take upon you the N. of Christ		37	are willing to take upon them the N.
	22	repent and are baptized in my N.—49:13		70	lay their hands upon them in the N. of, and bless them in his N.
	23	Jesus Christ is the N. that is given: none other N. given whereby man can			
	24	all men must take upon them the N., for in that N. shall they be called			

Sec.	Vs.		Sec.	Vs.	
	73	calling him or her by N.; I baptize you in the N. of		69	in my N. they shall open the eyes
	77	we ask thee in the N. of thy Son; are willing to take upon them the N.—79		74	not baptized in water in my N.
			88	84	as many as the mouth of the Lord shall N.
21	11	unto this church, bearing my N.		110	and swear in the N. of him who
24	5	calling upon God in my N.		120	that your incomings may be in the N.: that your outgoings may be in the N.; that your salutations may be in N.—109:9, 17, 18, 19
	10	bearing my N. before the world
	15	and they receive you not in my N.
	16	command them to be smitten in my N.
27	7	and his N. should be John and he		133	I salute you in the N. of the Lord
	12	and especial witnesses of my N.—107:23	90	20	until the mouth of the Lord shall N.—21
29	42	through faith on the N. of mine Only	93	1	every soul that calleth on my N.
				19	come unto the Father in my N.
35	2	as many as will believe on my N.—38:4; 66:1	97	15	build an house unto me in the N. of
			98	28	see to it that ye warn him in my N.
	8	unto all those who believe on my N.	100	7	whatsoever ye declare in my N.
	9	whoso shall ask it in my N.		17	all that call on the N. of the Lord
36	3	blessed be the N. of the Most High —39:19	101	15	who have given their lives for my N.
38	4	in mine own N. have I pleaded		22	all they who call on my N. and worship
39	10	calling on my N. and you shall
41	1	ye that have professed my N.		35	who suffer persecution for my N.
42	1	assembled themselves in my N.; inasmuch as they believe on my N.		64	I may build them up unto my N.
				75	churches who call themselves after my N.—97; 103:4; 125:2
	4	ye shall go forth in my N.	102	5	who voted in the N. and for the
	6	in my N. lifting up your voices		8	to act in the N. of the church
	44	shall lay their hands upon them in my N.	104	49	organized in their own N., do business in own N.—50
45	5	spare my brethren that believe on my N.—8		60	consecrate it unto my N.
				82	inasmuch as ye call upon my N.
46	31	all things must be done in the N.	105	15	not be left to blaspheme my N.
49	11	mine apostle of old, whose N. was Peter		33	commanded to be built unto my N.
			107	4	out of respect or reverence to the N.; too frequent repetition of his N.
	12	believe on the N. of the Lord Jesus
50	4	the church that profess my N.
	29	ask whatsoever you will in N. of		33	to officiate in the N. of the Lord
	31	ask of the Father in N. of Jesus		34	seventy are to act in N. of the Lord
55	2	by way of baptism in the N. of	109	1	thanks be to thy N., O Lord God
56	1	O ye people who profess my N.—112:26		2	commanded to build a house to thy N.—5
59	5	in N. of Jesus thou shalt serve him		4	we ask thee, in the N. of Jesus Christ; in whose N. alone salvation can be
63	61	beware how they take my N. upon their
	62	who use N. of the Lord in vain		22	that thy N. may be upon them
65	4	call upon his holy N.		24	honorably hold a N. and standing
68	8	baptizing in the N. of the Father, and		26	upon whom thy N. shall be put in this
75	10	calling on the N. of the Lord		31	innocent in bearing record of thy N.
76	51	who believed on his N. and were baptized; buried in the water in his N.
				56	to bear testimony of thy N.
82	4	ye call upon my N. for revelations		58	to build a holy city unto thy N.
84	66	in my N. they shall do many wonderful		78	which we have built unto thy N.
				79	also this church to put upon it thy N.
	67	in my N. they shall cast out devils
	68	in my N. they shall heal the sick	110	6	their might, built this house to my N.

Sec.	Vs.		Sec.	Vs.	
	7	I have accepted this house and my N.		42	make thy N. known to thine adversaries
112	1	chosen to bear testimony of my N.	135	3	left a fame and a N. that cannot be slain
	4	thou shalt bear record of my N.—118:4; 124:139	136	21	to take N. of the Lord in vain
	6	in publishing my N. among the children		40	only I have left a witness of my N.

NAMED

(See also "Above-named")

Sec.	Vs.	
	11	and unto all who love my N.
	12	be faithful before me unto my N.
	19	ye shall proclaim my N.
	21	whosoever ye shall send in my N.
114	1	to testify of my N. and bear glad
	2	there are those among you who deny my N.
115	10	to build a house unto my N.—124:22, 27, 47, 51, 55, 56, 145
	13	in debt, for building a house to my N.
	14	built unto my N. according to pattern
117	11	be a bishop, not in N. but in deed
	12	his N. shall be held in sacred
	14	shall be made a merchant unto my N.
121	6	will rejoice in thy N. forever
122	1	ends of earth shall enquire after thy N.
124	18	honor to himself and unto my N.
	24	if it be built unto my N.
	37	which you have built to my N.
	39	commanded to build to my holy N.
	40	let this house be built unto my N.
	49	to do a work unto my N., and those
	56	let my N. be named upon it
	60	let the N. of that house be called
	96	that his N. may be held in honorable
125	2	build up cities unto my N.
	3	let them build a city unto my N.; let the N. of Zarahemla be named upon
126	2	and toil in journeyings for my N.
128	9	whatsoever those men did in N. of Lord
	23	let eternal creations declare his N.
130	11	whereon is a new N. written; new N. is the key word
	12	I prophecy in the N. of the Lord
132	9	offering, that is not made in my N.
	13	or things of N., whatsoever they may be
	46	what you bind on earth in my N.
	59	if he do anything in my N.
	64	I will magnify my N. upon all those
133	6	let every man call upon the N. of
	18	having his Father's N. written upon
	40	calling upon the N. of the Lord day

Sec.	Vs.	
96	2	the place which is N. among you
	9	that are upon the house N. among you
104	34	lots which have been N. for my servant
107	26	special witnesses or apostles just N.
124	56	let my name be N. upon it
125	3	let name of Zarahemla be N. upon it

NAMELY

Sec.	Vs.	
102	34	and the following was the result, N.
107	1	are in the church two priesthoods, N.
109	54	N., the Constitution of our land
128	17	N., baptism for the dead
129	1	two kinds of beings in heaven, N.
124	132	N., Samuel Bent, etc.
132	30	from whose loins ye are, N., my servant

NAMES

Sec.	Vs.	
20	82	with a list of N. of the several; of all the N. of the whole church
	83	so that their N. may be blotted out of record of N.
75	2	ye who have given your N.—23
76	68	these are they whose N. are written
85	3	should have their N. enrolled with
	5	their N. shall not be found, neither N. of the fathers, nor N. of the children
	7	the saints whose N. are found and the N. of
	11	whose N. are not found written
88	2	the book of the N. of the sanctified
104	49	organized in their own N. and do business in their own N.—50
	85	by giving your N. by common consent
109	71	that their N. may be perpetuated
123	3	N. of all persons that have had a hand
124	144	approve of those N. I have mentioned
128	3	giving the dates and N., etc.
135	6	henceforward their N. will be blessed; their N. will go down to posterity

Sec.	Vs.		Sec.	Vs.	
		NAME'S	36	5	to preach the gospel among the N.
19	7	altogether for my N. glory—98:3	38	33	shall go forth among all N.
21	6	for your good and his N. glory	39	15	from thence men shall go into all N.
98	13	layeth down his life for my N. sake		16	stay my hand in judgment upon the N.
112	12	admonish them sharply for my N. sake	42	58	for they shall be taught unto all N.
	20	whom I have made counselors for my N. sake	43	18	and shall say to the sleeping N.
		NAMING		20	call upon the N. to repent
128	3	N. also some three individuals that		23	hearken, O ye N. of the earth
		NARROW		24	O ye N., how often would I have
132	22	for strait is the gate and N. the way	45	19	destroyed and scattered among all N.
		NASHVILLE		24	a remnant be scattered among all N.
125	4	as well as in the city of N., or in	47		shall arm of the Lord fall upon the N.
		NATHAN		49	and the N. of the earth shall mourn
132	39	by the hand of N. my servant		54	shall the heathen N. be redeemed
		NATHANIEL		71	gathered out from among all N.
41	11	for he is like N. of old in whom		75	all N. shall be afraid of the terror
		NATION	49	10	the N. of the earth shall bow to it
10	51	free unto all of whatsoever N.	52	14	he goeth forth deceiving the N.
45	69	shall be gathered out of every N.	56	1	day of visitation and wrath upon N.
64	42	shall come unto her out of every N.	58	9	unto which all N. shall be invited
77	8	the gospel to commit to every N.	64	37	or in a high place to judge the N.
	11	ordained out of every N., kindred	77	11	to whom is given power over the N.
	15	to be raised up to the Jewish N.	84	96	I have laid my hands upon the N.
87	3	even the N. of Great Britain	87	2	war will be poured out upon all N.—3
98	33	not go out unto battle against any N.		3	and will call on other N. even the; and they shall also call upon other N. to defend against other N.
	34	if any N. should proclaim war; lift up standard of peace to that N.	88	79	wars and perplexities of the N.
	36	justify, to battle against that N.		94	and all N. shall hear it
101	89	and in his fury vex the N.		103	flying through midst of heaven unto all N.
112	21	open door of my kingdom unto any N.	90	8	salvation of Zion and N. of Israel
123	6	that the N. may be left without excuse		10	in convincing the N., the heathen N.
124	3	the governor of the N. in which you live	97	19	the N. of the earth shall honor her
133	37	gospel shall be preached unto every N.	101	11	poured out without measure upon all N.
	58	the little one become a strong N.		98	and are soon to befall the N.
135	6	reader in every N. will be reminded	105	31	her banners may be terrible to all N.
136	34	even the N. that has driven you out	107	33	and regulate the affairs in all N.—34
		NATIONS		55	a multitude of N. shall come of thee
7	3	thou shalt prophecy before many N.		98	under responsibility to travel among all N.
10	49	other N. should possess this land	109	54	have mercy upon all the N.
34	8	for all N. shall tremble—64:43; 133:42	112	1	send it abroad among all N.
35	11	has made all N. drink of the wine —86:3; 88:94, 105		7	and thy path lieth among many N.
	13	to thresh the N. by power of my spirit—133:59		16	hold the keys abroad among all N.

Sec.	Vs.		Sec.	Vs.	
115	5	thy light may be a standard for the N.		4	of Nashville or in the city of N.
117	6	all the armies of the N. of the earth	124	60	let that house be called N.
124	3	and to *all* the N. of the earth			**NAUVOO HOUSE**
133	2	upon *all* the N. that forget God	111		a house for boarding, even the N.
	3	make bare his arm in eyes of *all* N.	117		into hands of the quorum of the N.—119
	7	gather ye out from among the N.	121		let quorum of N. have just recompense; which they do in building N.
	8	send forth elders unto the N.; call upon *all* N.			
	14	go ye out from among the N. even from			**NAVEL**
134	6	regulating our interests as N.	89	18	health in their N. and marrow to their
	12	believe it just to preach to the N.			**NAY**
135	7	touch hearts of honest men among *all* N.	84	59	verily I say unto you, N.—132:35
					NEAR
		NATURAL	88	62	ye shall call upon me while I am N.
29	35	they are not N. nor temporal		63	draw N. unto me and I will draw N.
	43	that by his N. death he might be	110	16	great and dreadful day of Lord is N.
58	3	ye cannot behold with your N. eyes	135	4	N. close of twelfth chapter of Ether
67	10	not with the N. mind but with spiritual			**NECESSARIES**
	12	neither can any N. man abide in the	136	5	and other N. for the journey
88	28	receive same body which was a N. body			**NECESSARILY**
128	14	but that which is N., afterward that	134	3	all governments N. require civil
					NECESSARY
		NATURALLY	20	62	to do whatever church business is N.
29	33	speaking that you may N. understand	42	33	more than is N. for their support
				82	it is N. that the bishop is present
		NATURE	48	1	it is N. that ye should remain for
89	10	for constitution, N. and use of man		3	for it must needs be N. that they have
121	39	the N. and disposition of almost all men		4	N. that ye save all the money ye can
127	2	it all has become second N. to me	71	1	N. that you should open your mouths
128	8	the N. of this ordinance consists in	84	29	elder and bishop are N. appendages
134	8	punished according to N. of offense		30	teacher and deacon are N. appendages
		NAUGHT	96	4	that is N. to benefit mine order
3	1	neither can they come to N.	102	29	whether N. to call such a council
	4	and sets at N. the counsels of God	106	3	all things N. shall be added thereunto
	7	although men set at N. the counsels	107	74	and it becomes N. to have other bishops
	13	who has set at N. the counsels of	128	15	for their salvation is N. and essential
19	21	command that you preach N. but repentance		18	is N. in ushering in the dispensation
76	9	understanding of prudent shall come to N.			**NECESSITIES**
109	30	that their works may be brought to N.	70	7	more than is needful for their N.
		NAUVOO			**NECESSITY**
124	109	appointed unto you, even the city of N.	101	8	in day of trouble, of N. they feel after
125	3	the land opposite to city of N.			

Sec.	Vs.		Sec.	Vs.	
107	21	of N. there are presidents or			**NEEDS**
	96	if labor in vineyard of N. requires it			(See *Must*)
		NECK	18	6	it must N. be—29:39; 38:39; 45:68; 48:3, 4; 49:2; 51:1, 2; 56:12; 75:24; 78:3; 86:10; 88:18; 93:47, 48; 95:2; 97:6; 101:4, 41, 64, 93; 103:15, 17; 104:16; 105:6; 107:60, 65; 124:122
113	9	loosing herself from bands of her N.
	10	bands of her N. are the curses of God
		NECKS
109	33	break if off from the N. of thy			**NEEDS**
112	13	if they stiffen not their N. against	51	3	according to their wants and N.—82:17
121	22	millstone hanged about their N.
		NEED			**NEEDY**
10	55	belongeth to my church N. not fear	38	35	they shall look to the poor and N.
11	15	N. not suppose you are called to preach	42	34	to administer to the poor and N.
			37		has consecrated to the poor and N.—51:5; 72:12
42	33	that every man who has N. may be amply	44	6	ye must visit the poor and N.
49	21	that wasteth flesh and hath no N.	52	40	remember the poor and the N.—109:55
57	8	whatsoever the disciples N. to plant
58	21	hath no N. to break laws of land	104	18	impart not his portion unto the N.
41		also he hath N. to repent	124	75	plead the cause of the poor and N.
84	83	knoweth you have N. of all these			**NEFARIOUS**
109		it hath no N. of the feet	123	5	and N. and murderous impositions
110		the body hath N. of every member			**NEGLECT**
93	50	my servant hath N. to be chastened	117	8	and N. the more weighty matters
101	47	what N. hath my Lord of this tower—48			**NEIGHBOR**
49		for there is no N. of these things	38	41	every man to his N. in mildness
104	72	I have N. of this to help me in my	42	27	thou shalt not speak evil of thy N.
107	38	when they N. assistance to fill the	45	68	will not take up his sword against his N.
		NEEDED	59	6	thou shalt love thy N. as thyself
124	102	tarry at home for he is N.	82	19	every man seeking interest of his N.
		NEEDEST	88	81	who hath been warned to warn his N.
24	18	in the very hour what thou N. for food	136	25	if thou borrowest of thy N.; go straightway and tell thy N.
25	9	thou N. not fear, for thy husband		26	find that which thy N. has lost
		NEEDETH			**NEIGHBORHOOD**
43	13	whatsoever he N. to accomplish the work	124	105	let him locate his family in the N.
		NEEDFUL			**NEIGHBOR'S**
51	13	which is more than is N. for the wants	19	25	shalt not covet thy N. wife, nor seek thy N. life
61	3	it is not N. for this whole company			**NEITHER**
	11	take that which is N. for clothing	1	2	N. ear that shall not hear, N. heart
	12	take that which is not N. with him		14	N. the voice of his servants, N. give heed
70	7	more than is N. for their necessities
88	119	prepare every N. thing—109:8		19	N. trust in the arm of flesh
	124	cease to sleep longer than is N.	3	1	N. can they come to naught
91	3	not N. that Apocrypha should be		2	N. doth he turn to the right, N. doth he vary
	6	not N. that it should be translated
109	15	be prepared to obtain every N. thing	9	12	and N. of you have I condemned
136	39	it was N. he should seal his testimony	10	56	do not fear me, N. keep my commandments

Sec.	Vs.	
20	35	N. adding to, nor diminishing from
	54	N. hardness, N. lying, backbiting
	58	N. teachers nor deacons have authority
22	2	N. by your dead works
24	18	take no purse nor scrip, N. staves, N. two
27	3	not purchase wine, N. strong drink
28	12	N. shall anything be appointed unto
29	25	not one hair, N. mote shall be lost
	33	my works have no end, N. beginning
.	34	N. any man, N. Adam your father
	35	nor temporal, N. carnal, nor sensual
38	14	N. your hearts of unbelief
49	7	no man knoweth, N. the angels in
	22	N. of a man traveling on the earth
50	33	N. with boasting, nor rejoicing, lest
52	33	N. journey in another's track
59	6	N. commit adultery, nor kill
	20	not to excess, N. by extortion
60	13	N. shalt thou bury thy talent
	14	not in haste, N. in wrath
64	15	kept not the law, N. the commandment
67	10	not with the carnal, N. natural mind
	12	N. can any natural man abide presence; N. after the carnal
	13	N. the ministering of angels
68	34	transgress them not, N. take therefrom
70	6	not unto the church, N. unto the world
	11	N. the bishop, N. the agent, N. he
75	3	N. be idle, but labor with your might
76	3	N. are there any who can stay his
	45	the end thereof, N. the place thereof
	46	N. was it revealed, N. is, N. will
	48	they understand not, N. any man
	82	N. the testimony of Jesus—101
	101	N. the prophets. N. the everlasting
	116	N. is man capable to make them known
77	9	hurt not the earth, N. the sea
84	40	which he cannot break, N. can it be
	73	N. speak of them before the world
	78	not to have purse or scrip, N. two coats
	80	not be weary in mind, N. darkened, N. in body, N. athirst
	82	they toil not, N. do they spin
	85	N. take ye thought beforehand what
85	4	N. is their genealogy to be kept
	5	N. the names of the fathers, nor

Sec.	Vs.	
88	33	N. rejoices in him who is the giver
	35	N. by mercy, justice nor judgment
	101	N. again until the end of the earth
89	5	N. meet in the sight of your Father
	8	not for the body, N. for the belly
90	3	N. in the world to come
	17	be not ashamed, N. confounded
	35	N. with my servant Sidney Gilbert
93	29	intelligence not created, N. can be
97	19	Zion cannot fall, N. be moved out of
98	23	revile not against them, N. seek revenge
	28	come no more upon you, N. your family
	35	N. the second nor the third time
101	20	N. shall there be any other place
	37	care not for the body, N. the life
	82	feared not God, N. regarded man
104	64	N. shall the seal be loosed
105	24	N. boast of faith nor of mighty works
107	98	not unto the Twelve, N. to the seventy
115	13	N. my servant Sidney, N. my servant
121	10	N. charge thee with transgression
124	47	N. fulfill the promises ye expect
	72	N. can any other man
	75	N. let his heart faint
128	15	N. can we without our dead be made—18
132	13	N. in nor after the resurrection
	16	they N. marry nor are given in
	18	then it is not valid, N. of force; N. by my word
	22	receive me not; N. do ye know me
	25	N. do they abide in my law
133	11	for ye know N. the day nor the hour
	45	N. hath any eye seen, O God,
	64	shall leave them N. root nor branch
	67	I could not redeem, N. my power to
134	12	N. preach the gospel to, nor baptize

NEPHI

10	38	engraven upon the plates of N.
	39	given of these things upon plates of N.
	40	the account upon the plates of N.
	41	which are upon the plates of N.
	42	shall publish it as the record of N.
	44	have only got a part of account of N.
	45	many things on plates of N. which do; this first part of engravings of N.
33	8	you shall become as N. of old
98	32	this is the law I gave unto N.

Sec.	Vs.		Sec.	Vs.	
		NEPHITES		34	N., I am with them and will come
1	29	having received the record of the N.		43	N., let him impart all the money
3	17	and to the N. and the Jacobites and		50	N., it is appointed to him to die at
	18	suffered to destroy their brethren the N.	64	7	N., he has sinned, but verily I say
38	39	lest ye become as the N. of old		16	N., I have forgiven my servant
		NEVER	69	7	N., let my servant travel many times
13	1	this shall N. be taken again from	70	7	N., as they receive more than is
29	29	N. at any time have I declared that		14	N., in your temporal things you shall
	39	if they N. should have bitter, they	75	8	he sinned; N.. I forgive him
39	10	blessing so great as you N. have	76	47	N., I show it by vision to many
45	18	enemies say this house shall N. fall	78	18	N., be of good cheer for I will
46	3	N. to cast anyone out from your	82	2	N., there are those who have sinned
50	44	built upon this rock shall N. fall	84	94	N., search diligently and spare not
76	4	and his years N. fail		114	N., let the bishop go unto the city of
	32	better for them N. to have been born	88	32	N., they shall return again to their own
90	3	keys of this kingdom shall N. be taken		48	N., he who came unto his own was not
98	48	their trespasses shall N. be brought		49	N., the day shall come when you shall
101	94	that which they have N. considered	89	12	N., they are to be used sparingly
103	7	they shall N. cease to prevail		17	N., wheat for man, corn for the ox
122	3	thy people shall N. be turned against	90	4	N., through you shall the oracles be
128	18	those things which N. have been revealed		35	N., I am not well pleased with many
	25	humble servant and N. deviating friend	95	10	N., my servants sinned a very grievous
132	7	there is N. but one on earth at a time	97	6	N., there are those that must be
				25	N., Zion shall escape if she observe
134	4	but N. control conscience; but N. suppress freedom of the soul		27	N., let it be read this once in their
		NEVERTHELESS	98	9	N., when the wicked rule the people
1	32	N., he that repents and does the		31	N., thine enemy is in thine hands
3	16	N., my work shall go forth		41	N., thou shalt forgive him—42
9	10	N., it is not expedient that you	101	68	N., let not your gathering be in haste
10	3	N., it is now restored unto you again		100	N., I do not say they shall not dwell
19	6	N., it is not written that there	103	14	N., if they pollute their inheritances
	19	N., glory be to the Father, I partook	107	69	N., a bishop must be chosen from
24	2	N., thou art not excusable in thy; N., go thy way and sin no more		71	N., a High Priest after the order
31	2	N., I will bless you and your family	112	3	N., as thou hast abased thyself
39	9	N., thou hast seen great sorrow	124	83	N., I will build up Kirtland, but
46	3	N., ye are commanded never to cast		137	standing ministers, N. they may travel
	4	N., if any have trespassed let him	127	2	N., deep water is what I am wont to
50	16	N., I will be merciful unto you	128	9	N., in all ages of the world, whenever
	39	N., let him repent and he shall be	132	36	N., it was written thou shalt not kill
59	11	N., thy vows shall be offered up			**NEW**
61	4	N., I suffered it that ye might	22	1	a N. and everlasting covenant—131:1; 132:4, 6, 19, 26, 27, 41, 42
	6	N., all flesh is in my hand			
	8	N., I would not suffer that ye should			
	27	N., unto whom it is given power to	27	4	partake of none except it be made N.
62	3	N., ye are blessed for the testimony			
63	13	N., I give commandments and many			
	20	N., he that endureth in faith			
	26	N., I render unto Caesar the things			

Sec.	Vs.		Sec.	Vs.	
29	23	shall be a N. heaven and a N. earth	49	6	which time is N. at hand
	24	and all things shall be N.—63:49; 101:25	63	53	they are now N. at hand
56	5	wherefore I give a N. commandment—82:8	84	115	the hour of their judgment is N.
			104	3	they were N. unto cursing
75	7	I give unto him a N. commission and a N. commandment		59	when I shall dwell with them, which is N.
76	69	the mediator of the N. covenant—107:19	106	4	the coming of the Lord draweth N.
			133	17	for the hour of his coming is N.

NIGHT

84	57	remember the N. covenant even the	6	22	cast your mind upon the N. you cried
	98	shall sing this N. song saying	24	12	with voice of a trump, both day and N.
124	89	and publish the N. translation of my			
130	11	whereon is a N. name written; the N. name is the key word	45	19	desolation shall come as a thief in the N.
131	1	meaning N. and everlasting covenant	86	5	crying unto the Lord day and N.
			88	45	the moon giveth her light by N.

NEW JERUSALEM

42	9	when city of N. shall be prepared	97	23	scourge shall pass over by N. and by day
	35	building up of the N. which is	101	51	enemy came by N. and broke down the
	62	where the N. shall be built			
	67	establish you both here and in N.	106	4	overtaketh world as a thief in the N.
45	66	it shall be called the N.			
84	2	which shall be the city of N.	112	5	and when N. cometh let not inhabitants
	4	N. shall be built by gathering of			
133	56	stand upon the holy city, the N.	133	35	dwell in his presence day and N.
				40	upon name of Lord, day and N.

NEW TESTAMENT

45	60	until the N. shall be translated		56	sing song of the Lamb, day and N.

NEW YORK

NINE

84	114	let bishop go to the city of N.	102	5	forty-three as follows: N. High Priests
104	81	write speedily to Cainhannock, (N.)			

NEXT

NINETEEN

26	1	until you shall go to hold N. conference	128	10	for the precedent, Matthew xvi:18, N.
52	2	N. conference which shall be held in			

NINETEENTH

114	1	perform a mission unto me N. spring	135	6	costs the best blood of the N. century
115	10	be made on the 4th day of July N.			
118	4	N. spring let them depart to go			
	5	on the 26th of April N.			

NINTH

132	19	in the N. resurrection	77	13	written in N. chapter of Revelations
136	7	decide how many can go N. spring			

NICOLAITANE

NINETY-SIX

117	11	let Whitney be ashamed of the N. band	107	89	is to preside over N. elders

NIGH

NO

1	12	for the Lord is N.—43:17	1	2	there is N. eye that shall not see
	35	the hour is not yet, but is N. at hand—58:4		35	I am N. respecter of persons—38:16
			5	3	you have N. power over them except I
29	9	the hour is N. and the day soon—10		28	he shall have N. such views; I will grant unto him N. views
35	15	my coming is N. at hand			
	16	for even now already summer is N.—45:37	6	13	there is N. gift greater than the
			8	8	N. power shall be able to take it away
	26	your redemption draweth N.			
45	38	shall they know that the hour is N.	9	7	you took N. thought save it was to
	63	they are N. even at your doors		13	be faithful and yield to N. temptation.

Sec.	Vs.		Sec.	Vs.	
10	18	that he has N. gift, has N. power		109	say, it hath N. need of the feet
	25	this is N. harm; it is N. sin to lie	88	37	N. space in which there is N. kingdom; N. kingdom in which there is N. space
18	20	contend against N. church			
19	6	that there shall be N. end to this		66	truth abideth and hath N. end
20	22	suffered temptations but gave N. heed		67	and there shall be N. darkness in you
	49	when there is N. elder present		110	that there shall be time N. longer
	54	that there is N. iniquity in the church	93	30	otherwise there is N. existence
	65	N. person is to be ordained to any	101	29	N. sorrow because there is N. death
	66	where there is N. branch of the church		49	for there is N. need of these things
21	8	he shall mourn for her N. longer	102	14	in N. case shall more than six be
23	1	thou art under N. condemnation—3, 4, 5		22	in case N. additional light is given
24	18	thou shalt take N. purse nor scrip		28	N. common or ordinary case is to be
29	29	cannot come; for they have N. power	104	47	you shall N. longer be bound as an
	33	my works have N. end		56	otherwise ye are N. stewards
	35	but N. temporal commandment gave I	107	12	when there are N. higher authorities
	50	he that hath N. understanding		32	otherwise there can be N. appeal
38	18	upon which there shall be N. curse	109	20	N. unclean thing shall be permitted
	21	ye shall have N. king nor ruler		26	N. combination of wickedness shall
	22	ye shall have N. laws but my laws	121	4	let thy hiding place be N. longer
	26	having twelve sons and is N. respecter		41	N. power or influence can be maintained
	33	N. power can stay my hand	124	130	his priesthood N. man taketh from him—132
41	11	in whom there is N. guile			
42	79	remember he hath N. forgiveness		140	the other has N. responsibility of
45	4	and death of him who did N. sin	128	11	there is N. difficulty in obtaining
	54	they that knew N. law shall have	130	5	are N. angels who minister to this
	55	Satan shall have N. place in hearts	132	7	are of N. efficacy, virtue or force
49	21	that wasteth flesh and hath N. need		19	he shall commit N. murder whereby—26
52	39	that there be N. idolatry nor		20	shall be gods because they have N. end
56	9	there shall be N. divisions made			
58	21	let N. man break laws of the land; hath N. need to break laws of land	133	26	and shall N. longer stay themselves
				29	parched ground shall N. longer be a
	26	wherefore he receiveth N. reward	134	2	N. government can exist in peace, except
61	15	N. flesh shall be safe upon the waters			
63	11	he showeth N. signs only in	136	19	he shall have N. power, and his folly
	56	he standeth N. longer in the office			
	64	in this there is N. condemnation			See *Man*.
64	16	that thing in which there was N. evil			

NO ("More")

3:11; 5:21, 29, 31; 6:29, 35; 24:2; 29:3, 50; 35:25; 38:20; 42:25; 58:42; 59:22; 73:6; 82:7; 94:17; 97:27; 98:28, 39, 48; 101:21, 75; 103:13; 107:80; 108:2; 124:49; 126:1; 130:15; 136:42

67	9	there is N. unrighteousness in them
68	19	when N. literal descendant of Aaron—107:17
	22	N. bishop or High Priest who shall be
71	9	N. weapon formed against you shall—109:25
76	1	and beside him there is N. Savior
	34	there is N. forgiveness in this world
82	10	when ye do not what I say, ye have N.
84	81	take N. thought for the morrow
	100	Satan is bound and time is N. longer

NO ("One")

12:8; 20:71; 25:6; 28:2; 132:4, 60

NO ("Other")

5:4; 8:7; 32:4; 132:61

Sec.	Vs.		Sec.	Vs.	
		NO ("Such")		21	against N. is his wrath kindled save
		9:9; 102:27; 131:7	61	16	N. is able to go up to land of Zion
		NOAH	63	29	otherwise there is N. inheritance
84	14	through lineage of fathers even till N.	70	10	N. are exempt from this law who belong
	15	and from N. till Enoch, through	76	2	extent of his doings N. can find out
107	52	N. was 10 years old when ordained	82	6	N. doeth good for all have gone out of
133	54	N. also and they who were before	85	9	shall find N. inheritance in that day
		NOBLE	97	27	N. of these things shall come upon her
58	10	first, the learned, the wise and the N.	101	20	there is N. other place appointed
122	2	while the pure in heart, the N., and	107	84	N. shall be exempted from justice of
		NOBLEMAN	132	37	Jacob did N. other things than that
101	44	a certain N. had a spot of land		39	in N. of these things did he sin
	46	the servants of the N. went and did		54	cleave unto my servant and to N. else
	51	the servants of the N. fled	133	50	and N. were with me
	52	the N., Lord of the vineyard, called		67	there was N. of you to answer
		NOBLES		71	there are N. to deliver you
109	55	remember the kings, the N., the great			**NOON-DAY**
		NOBLY	95	6	they are walking in darkness at N.
109	54	which were so honorably and N. defended			**NORTH**
		NOMINATION	42	63	sent forth to the N. and to the south
102	8	it shall be filled by the N. of the	44	1	called together from the N. and from
		NONE	75	26	go into the world whether to the N. or
1	2	there is N. to escape	80	3	preach my gospel whether to the N. or
	5	shall go forth and N. shall stay them	94	14	first and second lots on the N.
5	14	to N. else will I grant this power	110	11	ten tribes from the land of the N.
6	16	there is N. else save God that knowest	125	4	let all those who come from the N. and
18	23	there is N. other name given whereby	133	23	shall be driven back into N. countries
27	4	you shall partake of N. except it be		26	they who are in the N. countries
29	12	as many as have loved me, and N. else			**NORTHERN STATES**
30	7	N. have I appointed to be his counselor	87	3	N. shall be divided against the Southern
33	4	there is N. which doeth good— 35:12			**NORTHROP**
38	10	N. else with whom I am well pleased	33	1	N. open ye your ears and hearken to
42	22	shalt cleave unto her and N. else			**NOTABLE**
	76	receive N. such among you	84	117	to the great and N. cities and
43	3	there is N. other appointed unto you			**NOTHING**
	4	N. else shall be appointed unto this	6	9	say N. but repentance unto this— 11:9
50	42	and N. of them shall be lost	8	10	without faith you can do N.
52	9	saying N. other things than that	18	19	if you have not faith, you can do N.
	36	declaring N. other things than that	22	2	baptized a hundred times, availeth N.
54	4	it has become void and of N. effect	32	3	and N. shall prevail
58	53	lest they receive N. inheritance	59	21	and in N. doth man offend God, save
59	13	on this day thou shalt do N. other thing			

Sec.	Vs.	
101	40	it is thenceforth good for N.—103:10
121	28	in the which N. shall be withheld
124	68	but if he pays N. into their hands
127	11	prince of this world cometh, but he hath N. in me
132	38	but in N. did they sin, save in

NOTIFIED
118	6	and be officially N. of appointment

NOTION
130	3	is an old sectarian N. and is false

NOTWITHSTANDING
46	2	N. those things which are written
50	26	N. he is least and the servant of all
78	14	N. the tribulation which shall descend
88	26	N. it shall die, it shall be quickened
	27	for N. they die they also shall rise
101	9	N. their sins my bowels are
	17	N. her children are scattered
106	7	and N. the vanity of his heart
107	56	and N. he was bowed down with age
	98	N. they may hold as high offices
111	1	am not displeased N. your follies
124	124	N. the hour of temptation that may

NOURISHED
42	43	shall be N. with all tenderness

NOWISE
33	12	or they can in N. be saved
58	28	they shall in N. lose their reward—84:90; 127:4
75	28	he shall in N. lose his crown
132	27	can in N. enter into my glory

NUMBER
102	5	the N. composing the council
	12	commencing with N. one and so to N. twelve
	25	power to appoint one of their own N.
103	30	obtained to the N. of 500
104	28	which is lot N. one
107	93	chosen out of the N. of the seventy
132	30	ye could not N. them
136	7	choose out a sufficient N.

NUMBERED
122	9	and thy years shall not be N. less

NUMBERS
102	12	to cast lots by N. and thereby
	17	those councilors who draw even N.

O

Sec.	Vs.	
		OATH
84	39	according to the O. and covenant
	40	receive this O. and covenant of my
124	47	I will not perform the O. which I

OATHS
132	7	all covenants, O., vows, that are not

OATS
89	17	corn for the ox, O. for the horse

OBEDIENCE
89	18	walking in O. to the commandments
105	6	chastened until they learn O.
130	19	through his diligence and O. than
	21	it is by O. to the law upon which
132	50	have seen your sacrifices in O. to

OBEDIENT
28	3	thou shalt be O. unto the things
58	6	sent you that you might be O.
64	34	the willing and O. shall eat the good
105	3	they have not learned to be O.

OBEDIENTLY
38	26	and they serve him O., and he saith

OBEY
29	45	their wages of whom they list to O.
40	1	he covenanted that he would O. my word
42	2	hearken and O. the law which I
52	15	if he O. mine ordinances—16
56	3	he that *will* not O. shall be cut off
	8	and O. the former commandment
	15	ye O. not the truth but have pleasure
58	32	I command and men O. not
59	21	save those who O. not his commandments
124	115	if Robert D. Foster *will* O. my voice

Sec.	Vs.	
132	3	prepare thy heart to receive and O., for all must O. the same
	53	I am the Lord and ye shall O. my voice

OBEYED

59	3	who have O. my gospel, for they
63	5	I utter my voice and it shall be O.
108	1	you have O. my voice in coming up
133	71	ye O. not my voice when I called

OBEYETH

64	5	inasmuch as he O. mine ordinances
93	1	calleth on my name and O. my voice

OBEYS

58	30	that O. not my commandments

OBLATIONS

59	12	thou shalt offer thine O. and

OBLIGATIONS

132	7	all covenants, O., that are not made

OBLIGED

75	28	every man who is O. to provide for

OBSCURITY

1	30	to bring it forth out of O.

OBSERVE

42	13	they shall O. the covenants and
	15	this ye shall O. to do as I have
	65	thou shalt O. all these things
	66	ye shall O. the laws which ye have
	78	shall O. to keep all commandments
63	22	there are many who O. not to keep
68	29	O. the Sabbath day to keep it holy
69	3	which he shall O. and know
97	8	to O. their covenants by sacrifice
	25	Zion shall escape if she O. to do
	26	but if she O. not to do whatsoever
98	4	my people should O. to do all things
	10	wise men ye should O. to uphold
	20	O. the words of wisdom and eternal life
	21	if they do not repent and O. all things
	22	if ye O. to do whatsoever I command
101	69	O. the commandments which I have
	72	O. to have all things prepared before
103	7	by hearkening to O. all the words
	8	hearken not to O. all my words, the
119	5	and shall O. this law or they shall
	6	if my people O. not this law to keep

Sec.	Vs.	
		OBSERVED
54	6	have kept the covenant and O. the
		OBSERVETH
68	33	he that O. not his prayers
		OBSERVING
108	3	more careful in O. your vows
		OBTAIN
11	21	first seek to O. my word
17	2	you shall O. a view of them
19	38	more than if you should O. treasures
44	4	ye shall O. power to organize
45	8	gave I power to O. eternal life
48	4	O. all that ye can in righteousness
54	6	for they shall O. mercy
57	5	may O. it for an everlasting inheritance
	8	that he may O. money to buy lands; O. whatsoever things
	9	let my servant O. a license
	12	let him O. whatsoever he can O. in
58	51	to O. moneys to be put into the hands
64	30	that they may O. an inheritance in
	31	my words are sure that they shall O. it
69	7	may the more easily O. knowledge
72	21	O. funds that shall benefit the church
75	25	O. places for your families
	26	let all such as can O. places for
76	79	wherefore they O. not the crown
90	22	search diligently to O. an agent
91	5	the Spirit, shall O. benefit therefrom
93	53	O. a knowledge of history and countries
97	2	blessed are such for they shall O.
99	3	blessed are they for they shall O. mercy
102	23	inquire and O. mind of the Lord
103	32	cannot O. 500, you may O. 300
	33	cannot O. 300, you may O. 100
104	69	if any man among you O. five talents; or if he O. ten
	79	and O. this blessing by your diligence
	84	as you O. a chance to loan money
109	15	be prepared to O. every needful thing
	56	and thy people O. favor in the sight
111	9	this place you may O. by hire
124	112	that he may O. confidence of men
130	21	when we O. any blessing from God
131	2	and in order to O. the highest
	3	if he does not he cannot O. it

Sec.	Vs.	
		OBTAINED
11	22	until you have O. all which I shall
17	3	after that you have O. faith
45	14	but O. a promise that they should find it
52	41	let there be one O. for my servant
58	54	inasmuch as there is land O.
63	29	land not be O. but by purchase
103	30	until they have O. companies to go up; O. to number of 500
	34	until you have O. 100 of the strength
104	24	O. in exchange for former inheritance
		OBTAINEST
42	55	if thou O. more than that which
		OBTAINING
63	46	O. moneys even as I have directed
69	8	O. all things which shall be for the
78	5	for the O. of heavenly things
	6	ye cannot be equal in O. heavenly
84	33	unto O. these two priesthoods
94	3	for the Presidency in O. revelations
103	40	in O. the fulfillment of these
128	11	consists in O. the powers of the Holy; no difficulty in O. a knowledge
		OBVIATE
128	3	to O. this difficulty, there can be a
		OCCASION
20	52	assist the elder if O. requires
	57	by the deacons if O. requires
64	6	those who have sought O. against
	8	sought O. against one another
		OCCUPY
128	1	that subject seems to O. my mind
		OCCUR
102	8	whenever any vacancy shall O.
		OCEAN
133	20	he shall stand upon the mighty O.
		O'CLOCK
135	1	they were shot about five O. p. m.
		OFFEND
42	88	if thy brother or sister O. thee
	90	if thy brother or sister O. many
	91	and if any O. openly, he or she
	92	and if any shall O. in secret
59	21	in nothing doth man O. God, save
64	13	may not O. him who is your lawgiver

Sec.	Vs.	
		OFFENDED
42	92	whom he or she has O.
121	19	they have O. my little ones
		OFFENDERS
42	75	and they themselves are the O.
134	8	in bringing O. to punishment
		OFFENSE
54	5	wo to him by whom this O. cometh
134	8	according to nature of O.; government in which the O. is committed
135	4	I have a conscience void of O.
		OFFER
13	1	until the sons of Levi do O. again
59	8	thou shalt O. a sacrifice unto the
	9	O. up thy sacraments on my holy day
	12	thou shalt O. thine oblations and thy
62	4	O. a sacrament to the Most High
84	31	shall O. an acceptable offering and
88	131	let him O. himself in prayer upon his
89	5	to O. up your sacraments before him
101	4	commanded to O. up his only son
124	104	if he *will* O. unto me an acceptable
128	24	that they may O. unto the Lord an; let us therefore O.
129	4	O. him your hand and request him to
	8	he *will* O. you his hand and you will
132	36	Abraham was commanded to O. his son
	51	that which I commanded you to O. her
		OFFERED
59	11	thy vows shall be O. up on all days
67	3	receive the blessing which was O. you
		OFFERING
13	1	sons of Levi do offer again an O.
84	31	shall offer an acceptable O. and
95	16	dedicated for your sacrament O.; O. *up* your most holy desires
96	6	whose O. I have accepted
97	27	I have accepted of her O.
98	35	if that people did not accept the O.
105	19	their prayers, and will accept their O.
124	1	I am well pleased with your O.
	104	if he will offer an acceptable O.
126	1	for your O. is acceptable unto me
128	24	they may offer an O. in righteousness
132	9	will I accept an O. not made in my name

Sec.	Vs.	
	50	as I accepted the O. of Abraham
	51	that I might require an O. at your

OFFERINGS

Sec.	Vs.	
124	49	it behooveth me to accept of their O.
	51	for this cause have I accepted of the O.
	75	and I will accept of his O.; shall not be as O. of Cain

OFFICE

Sec.	Vs.	
20	65	no person is to be ordained to any O.
24	3	magnify thine O.
	9	shalt have with which to magnify thine O.
25	5	the O. of thy calling shall
38	23	teach one another according to the O.
42	10	my servant shall stand in the O.—57:6, 7; 58:40
47	3	Cowdery I have appointed to another O.
50	38	as many as are ordained to this O.
54	2	you shall stand fast in the O.
63	56	he standeth no longer in the O.
66	11	thou shalt magnify thine O.
68	18	no man has a legal right to this O.—107:16
	19	he may officiate in O. of bishop—107:17
78	12	he who breaketh it shall lose his O.
81	3	in the O. which I have appointed
	5	stand in the O. which I have appointed
84	109	let every man stand in his own O.
102	4	act in that O. according to law of
	8	by removal from O. for transgression
	10	it is according to the dignity of his O.
104	28	Laneshine-house (printing O.)—29
107	7	the O. of an elder comes under the
	10	and also in the O. of an elder, priest
	22	appointed and ordained unto that O.
	60	preside over those of the O. of an elder
	61	preside over those of the O. of a priest
	62	preside over those of the O. of a teacher
	68	the O. of a bishop is not equal unto it; O. of a bishop is in
	75	they shall act in the same O.
	76	to act in O. of a bishop independently
	85	duty of President over O. of a deacon

Sec.	Vs.	
	86	duty of a president over O. of teachers; teaching them duty of their O.
	87	to teach them the duties of their O.
	89	duty of President over O. of elders
	91	duty of president of O. of High Priesthood
	99	let man learn his duty and act in O.
124	21	I seal upon his head the O. of a
	91	that my servant Hyrum may take O. of
	103	let him stand in O. of his calling
	135	this is the O. of their calling

OFFICERS

Sec.	Vs.	
88	127	even for all the O. of the church
107	21	there are presiding O. growing out of
	23	thus differing from other O. in the—25
	58	set in order all the other O. of the
	98	whereas other O. of the church, who
124	123	I now give unto you the O. belonging
134	3	all governments require civil O.

OFFICES

Sec.	Vs.	
68	19	may officiate in all lesser O.
84	29	the O. of elder and bishop are
	30	the O. of teacher and deacon are
97	13	in their several callings and O.
102	4	would fill their O. according to
107	5	all other O. in church are appendages
	8	has authority over all the O.
	9	a right to officiate in all the O—12
	17	authority to officiate in all lesser O.
	21	who are ordained to the several O.
	98	may hold as high and responsible O.
124	143	the above O. I have given unto you
	144	you should fill all these O.
	145	prepare rooms for all these O. in my

OFFICIALLY

Sec.	Vs.	
118	6	and be O. notified of their appointment

OFFICIATE

Sec.	Vs.	
68	19	High Priest has authority to O. in all; he may O. in office of a bishop—107:17
	20	are not legally authorized to O.
107	9	have a right to O. in all offices
	10	have a right to O. in their own standing
	11	an elder has a right to O. in his
	12	they have a right to O. in all these
	33	to O. in the name of the Lord, under

Sec.	Vs.		Sec.	Vs.	
		OFFSPRING		15	speak unto you as unto men in days of O.
122	6	tear thee from bosom of thy wife and thine O.	49	11	like unto mine apostle of O. whose name
		OFT	63	51	children shall grow up until O., O. men shall die
3	6	how O. you have transgressed the	64	8	disciples, in days of O., sought occasion
43	25	how O. have I called upon you by mouth of	66	2	as written by the prophets of O.
98	40	as O. as thine enemy repenteth thou		25	laying on of hands when eight years O.
		OFTEN	68	27	shall be baptized when eight years O.
6	14	as O. as thou hast inquired thou hast	76	7	from days of O., and for ages to come
20	55	see that the church meet together O.		28	we beheld Satan that O. serpent
	75	expedient that church meet together O.	84	28	at the time he was eight days O.
43	24	how O. would I have gathered you together		105	take the O. and cast it to the poor
85	6	O. times it maketh my bones to quake	88	110	Satan shall be bound, that O. serpent
133	6	and speak O. one to another	101	30	an infant shall not die until he is O.
135	7	as they had O. been proved before	107	45	he was 87 years O. when he received
		OHIO		46	Mahalaleel was 496 years O. when
37	1	until ye shall go to the O.		47	Jared was 200 years O. when he
	3	assemble together at the O.		48	Enoch was 25 years O. when he was
38	32	commandment that ye should go to the O.		49	making him 430 years O. when he was
39	14	but thou art called to go to the O.		50	Methuselah was 100 years O. when he
	15	shall assemble themselves to the O		51	Lamech was 32 years O. when he was
	16	people of O. call upon me in much faith		52	Noah was 10 years old when he was
58	49	an agent appointed unto church in O.	128	21	voice of God in chamber of O. father
84	104	send it unto the bishop in O.	130	3	is an O. sectarian notion and is false
		OIL		15	if thou livest until thou art 85 years O.
33	17	lamps trimmed and burning and O. with you	133	53	and carried them all the days of O.
		OLAHA SHINEHAH	135	6	Hyrum Smith was 44 years O.
117	8	and upon the plains of O., the land			**OLIHAH**
		OLD	82	11	expedient for O. (Oliver Cowdery). and
1	16	an idol which waxeth O. and shall	104	28	let my servant O. have the lot
8	1	concerning engravings of O. records		29	let O. and, have the Laneshine house
17	2	by that faith had by prophets of O		34	which have been named for my servant O.
20	11	as well as in generations of O.			**OLIVER**
22	1	O. covenants have I caused to be done away	6	20	thou art O. and I have spoken unto thee
	3	even as in days of O.	23	1	I speak unto you O. a few words
29	24	for all O. things shall pass away—63:49	24	10	thy brother, O., shall continue in
33	8	you shall become as Nephi of O.	28	1	O., it shall be given unto thee
35	6	even as the apostles of O.			
38	39	lest ye become as the Nephites of O.			
41	11	for he is like unto Nathaniel of O.			
43	20	call upon nations to repent, both O. and			
45	10	will reason as with men in days of O.—61:13			

Sec.	Vs.	
30	5	take your journey with your brother O.

OLIVET

133	20	he shall stand upon Mount O.

OLIVE TREES

101	44	piece of land and plant twelve O.
	45	that mine O. may not be broken
	46	planted the O. and built a
	51	and enemy broke down the O.

OMEGA

See *Alpha and Omega*

OMEGUS

95	17	in other words, O., even Jesus Christ

ONCE

20	61	meet in conference O. in three months
64	3	for this O., for mine own glory, I
88	122	let not all be spokesmen at O.
97	27	let it be read this O. to her ears
98	23	if men smite you or your families O.
104	83	you shall be delivered this O. out of
	85	and pledge the properties this O.
	86	I give unto you this privilege this O.
124	95	that O. were put on him that was my
130	14	I was O. praying very earnestly to know

ONE

3	2	his course is O. eternal round—35:1
6	32	in my name as touching O. thing
12	8	no O. can assist in this work
18	15	and bring save it be O. soul unto me
	16	if your joy will be great with O. soul
	35	you can read them O. to another
19	9	you that are chosen, even as O.
20	28	which are O. God, infinite and
	60	which is in the O. who ordains him
	71	no O. can be received into church
	81	to send O. or more of their teachers
	82	kept in a book by O. of the elders
25	6	while there is no O. to be a scribe
27	13	gather together in O. all things
28	2	no O. shall be appointed to
29	8	they shall be gathered unto O. place
	13	to be with me that we may be O.
	25	not O. hair, neither mote shall be lost
31	2	and be O. with you in my church
33	11	repent and be baptized every O. of you

Sec.	Vs.	
35	2	even O. in me, as I am O. in the Father; as the Father is O. in me, that we may be O.
36	1	Lord God, the Mighty O. of Israel
38	23	teach O. another according to the
	26	he saith unto the O. be thou clothed
	27	be O., if ye are not O., ye are not mine
42	3	you are agreed as touching this O. thing
	4	go forth in my name, every O. of you
	9	that ye may be gathered in O.—36
	11	shall not be given to *any* O. to go; except he be ordained by some O. who
	91	if *any* O. offend openly he shall be
45	20	shall not be left O. stone upon another
	33	take up the sword O. against the other, and kill O. another
	65	with O. heart and with O. mind
	69	only people not at war O. with another
46	3	never cast *any* O. out of your meetings
	4	also commanded not to cast *any* O. out
	12	to some it is given O. and to some
49	16	lawful he should have O. wife, they twain shall be O. flesh
	20	not given that O. man should possess
50	11	as a man reasoneth O. with another
	22	understandeth O. another and both are
	43	the Father and I. are O.
51	9	that ye may be O. as I have commanded
52	33	take their journey unto O. place; O. man shall not build upon another's
	41	and let there be O. obtained for
61	8	that you might be O., and not perish
	18	what I say unto O. I say unto all —36; 82:5; 92:1; 93:49
64	8	sought occasion against O. another; forgave not O. another
	9	ye ought to forgive O. another, for he
65	1	lo, a voice as of O. from on high
67	7	or that shall make O. like unto it
	8	but if ye cannot make O. like unto it
69	1	except O. go with him who will be true
76	96	glory of celestial is O. as glory of sun is O.

Sec.	Vs.		Sec.	Vs.	
	97	glory of terrestrial is O. as glory of moon is O.	107	6	one is the Melchizedek Priesthood
	98	glory of telestial is O. as glory of stars is O., and as O. star differs, so differs O. from another in glory		27	same validity O. with the other
				65	needs be that O. be appointed
				85	edifying O. another as it is given
				88	for this is O. of the duties of
	100	they are some of O. and some of		90	this presidency is a distinct O.
82	1	as ye have forgiven O. another	109	59	appoint other stakes besides this O.
84	47	every O. that hearkeneth to the voice	111	10	there are more treasures than O. in
			115	11	in O. year from this day let them
	82	are not arrayed like O. of these	121	15	not O. of them is left to stand
	100	the Lord hath gathered all things in O.		28	whether there be O. God or many gods
85	7	I will send O. mighty and strong		35	they do not learn this O. lesson
88	44	all these are O. year with God	124	22	such an O. as my servant Joseph
	66	as voice of O. crying in the wilderness		62	appoint O. of them to be a president
				64	from *any* O. man for stock in that
	77	teach O. another the doctrine		65	15,000 dollars stock from *any* O. man
	118	teach O. another words of wisdom —109:7		66	for a share of stock from *any* O. man
	122	let O. speak at a time		140	O. is to travel continually, the other; O. has responsibility of presiding
	123	see that ye love O. another; impart O. to another			
	124	cease to find fault O. with another	128	3	very difficult for O. recorder to be
	136	for a salutation to O. another		12	that O. principle might accord with
90	24	ye have covenanted O. with another		13	that they may accord O. with another
93	3	and the Father and I are O.		14	in O. sense of the word, the keys
	25	is the spirit of that wicked O.		17	a quotation from O. of the prophets
	37	light and truth forsaketh that evil O.	130	10	to each individual who receives O.
	39	wicked O. cometh and taketh away light	132	4	for *no* O. can reject this covenant
				7	there is never but O. on the earth
	42	that wicked O. hath power over you		48	to whomsoever you give *any* O. on earth
	49	lest that wicked O. have power		60	let *no* O. therefore set on my servant
	51	by your prayer of faith with O. consent		61	belongeth unto him and to *no* O. else
101	45	that O. may overlook the land			
	50	were at variance O. with another		63	but if O. or either of the ten virgins
	55	the lord said unto O. of his servants	133	6	speak often O. to another
				7	from O. end of heaven to the other
	79	that man should be in bondage, O. to another		23	and the islands shall become O. land
102	1	O. or three presidents as the case		58	and the little O. become a strong nation
	8	any O. of the above-named councilors	134	9	whereby O. religious society is fostered
	11	in case of the absence of O. or both			
	12	commencing with number O. and so in	136	20	keep your pledges O. with another
				23	cease to contend O. with; cease to speak evil O. of another
	13	consider whether it is a difficult O.		24	let your word tend to edifying O. another
	20	who have not spoken or *any* O. of them			See *No One, Holy One*
	25	power to appoint O. of their own number			**ONE-HALF**
104	28	which is lot number O.	102	15	has a right to O. of the Council
	61	appoint O. among you to keep the			**ONE HUNDRED**
	62	shall belong to you all with O. accord	103	33	peradventure you may obtain O. —34
	64	not taken out of treasury by *any* O.			
105	24	as much in O. region as can be			

Sec.	Vs.		Sec.	Vs.	
107	50	Methuselah was O. years old when he was			**ONLY**
		ONE HUNDRED FIFTY	1	30	the O. true and living church on
135	1	by an armed mob, of from O. to 200	10	44	they have O. got a part of the account
		ONE HUNDRED FORTY-FOUR THOUSAND		62	the O. doctrine which is in me
77	11	what are we to understand by sealing of O.—133:18	18	42	not O. men, but women and children
		ONE HUNDRED THIRTY-FOUR	20	19	the O. living and true God; O. being whom they should worship
107	44	Enos was ordained at the age of O. years		26	not O. those who believed after he came
		ONES		50	he is O. to preach, teach, expound
1	19	break down the mighty and strong O.	31	6	go from them O. for a little time
31	2	bless your family, yea your little O.	43	31	he shall O. reign for little season
64	43	and shall fear because of her terrible O.	45	69	the O. people that shall not be at war
76	37	the only O. on whom the second death	51	5	shall O. have claim on that portion
	38	the only O. who shall not be redeemed	53	7	he O. is saved who endureth unto end
90	36	and plead with her strong O.	58	44	O. as it shall be appointed unto them
109	49	and the cries of their innocent O.	59	13	O. let thy food be prepared with
	55	remember the great O. of the earth, and the afflicted O.	61	35	O. let my servant Reynolds Cahoon and
	72	with all their sick and afflicted O.	62	5	O. be faithful and declare glad
	80	let these thine anointed O. be	63	11	O. in wrath to their condemnation
112	8	many high O. shall be brought low, and many low O. shall	76	37	the O. ones on whom second death
121	19	they have offended my little O.		38	the O. ones who shall not be redeemed
		ONE-TENTH		116	O. to be seen and understood by the
119	4	shall pay O. of all their interest	84	48	and not for your sakes O., but for
		ONE THOUSAND EIGHT HUNDRED FORTY-FOUR		57	not O. to say, but to do according
135	1	in Carthage jail, 27th of June, O.		118	I will not O. shake the earth but
	6	Hyrum Smith was 44 years old Feb., O.	89	5	O. in assembling yourselves together
		ONE THOUSAND EIGHT HUNDRED FORTY-THREE		13	used O. in times of winter, or cold
131	5	May 17th, O. The more sure word of		14	not O. for man, but for the beasts
135	6	Joseph Smith was 38 years in Dec. O.		15	O. in times of famine and excess of
		ONE THOUSAND EIGHT HUNDRED THIRTY	101	4	commanded to offer up his O. son
20	1	being O. years since coming of our Lord		40	O. to be cast out and trodden under
21	3	organized in the year of our Lord, O.		55	save those O. whom I have appointed
		ONE THOUSAND EIGHT HUNDRED THIRTY-TWO	102	13	two O. of the councilors shall speak
76	11	on the 16th of Feb. in the year O.		28	is O. to be called on the most difficult
130	13	praying earnestly on the subject, Dec. 25, O.		32	the latter can O. be called in question
			104	47	brethren in Zion, O. on this wise
				53	not bound O. up to this hour, O. on this wise,
				64	O. by the voice of the order—71
			105	38	not O. the people that have smitten you
			106	2	not O. in his own place, but in the
			107	43	distinguished from him O. by his age
			112	4	not O. unto the Gentiles but also
			121	36	handled O. upon principles of righteousness

Sec.	Vs.		Sec.	Vs.	
	41	O. by persuasion, by long-suffering by	61	30	shall not O. their mouths in congregations
123	6	may not O. publish to all the world	63	1	O. your hearts and give ear from afar
	9	not O. to our own wives and children	64	22	go with an O. heart to the land of
	12	and who are O. kept from the truth	71	1	O. your mouths in proclaiming my
124	30	O. in the days of your poverty	75	25	as brethren are willing to O. their
	70	to any other purpose, O. in that house—71	76	35	crucified him and put him to an O. shame
128	5	it is O. to answer the will of God	84	69	they shall O. the eyes of the blind
	18	and not O. this, but those things	107	35	holding the keys to O. the door by
129	6	for that is the O. way he can appear	112	21	shall have power to O. the door of my
130	2	O. it will be coupled with eternal glory	122	7	if the very jaws of hell gape O. after
131	7	and can O. be discerned by purer eyes	124	115	as the door shall be O. to him from
132	24	the O. wise and true God and Jesus	128		hold the keys to O. *up* authority of
134	4	amenable to him and to him O.			

OPENED

4	7	knock and it shall be O. unto you—6:5; 11:5; 12:5; 14:5; 49:26; 66:9; 75:27; 88:63.
23	2	thy heart shall be O. to preach the
	3	thy heart is O. and thy tongue loosed
29	26	for their graves shall be O. and they.—88:97; 133:56
76	12	our eyes were O. and our
	19	they were O. and the glory of the
93	15	and lo, the heavens were O. and the
100	3	an effectual door shall be O.—112:19; 118:3
101	92	pray ye that their ears may be O.
107	19	to have the heavens O. unto them
110	1	eyes of our understanding were O.
	11	the heavens were again O. unto us
128	6	and the books were O.: and another book was O.—7
136	32	that his eyes may be O., that his ears may be O.

OPENING

77	10	or the O. of the sixth seal
	13	after the O. of the seventh seal

OPENLY

42	91	and if any offend O., he or she shall be rebuked O.

OPERATIONS

46	16	to know the diversities of O.

OPINIONS

134	4	unless their religious O. prompt them
	7	or proscribe them in their O.; and their O. do not justify sedition

OPPORTUNITY

42	92	may have an O. to confess in secret

ONLY BEGOTTEN

20	21	God gave his O. Son, as it is
29	42	through faith on name of mine O. Son
	46	are redeemed through mine O.
49	5	I have sent mine O. Son into the
76	13	ordained of the Father through his O.
	23	he is the O. of the Father
	25	who rebelled against the O. Son
	35	having denied the O. Son
	57	after the order of the O. Son
93	11	as the glory of the O. of the Father—124:123

OPEN

24	12	he shall O. his mouth and declare
28	16	thou must O. thy mouth at all times
30	5	you shall O. your mouth to declare my
	11	you shall ever O. your mouth in my cause
31	7	I *will* O. the hearts of the people
33	1	O. ye your ears and hearken to the
	8	O. your mouths and they shall be filled.—10
	9	O. your mouths and spare not and you
58	52	children of men should O. their hearts
60	2	they *will* not O. their mouths but hide
100	11	I will give unto T. power; he shall

Sec.	Vs.		Sec.	Vs.	
		OPPOSITE		65	no person is to be O. to any office
125	3	upon the land O. to city of Nauvoo		67	to be O. by direction of High Council
		OPPRESSED	21	10	he should be O. by you, mine apostle
109	48	they have been greatly O. and afflicted	24	19	and also those whom thou hast O.
		OPPRESSION	25	7	thou shalt be O. under his hand
109	67	and be redeemed from O. and rejoice	27	8	be called and O. even as Aaron
123	7	the most damning hand of O.		12	by whom I have O. and confirmed you
124	53	hindered by their enemies and by O.	36	5	shall be O. and sent forth to preach
		OPPRESSIONS		7	every man may be O. and sent forth
121	3	suffer these wrongs and unlawful O.	41	9	be O. a bishop unto the church
123	3	that have had a hand in their O.	42	11	except he be O. by some one who has been regularly O.
		OPPRESSOR	43	7	he that is O. of me; shall come in at the gate and be O.
124	8	to appoint the portion of the O.	49	4	my servant shall be O. unto this work
		OPPRESSORS		15	forbiddeth to marry is not O. of God, for marriage is O. of
127	3	a just reward on heads of all their O.		18	to abstain from meats is not O. of God
		ORACLES		19	for the beasts, etc., are O. for use
90	4	through you shall O. be given another	50	13	unto what were ye O.
	5	all they who receive the O. of God		17	he that is O. of me and sent forth —26
124	39	for your O. in your most holy places		35	all things which are not O. of him
	126	to receive the O. for the whole church		38	as many of my servants as are O.
		ORCHARDS	52	32	let my servants both be O. and take
59	17	for houses, or for barns, or for O.		38	let Jared Carter be O. a priest and also George James be O.
		ORDAIN	55	2	thou shalt be O. by the hand of my
5	11	servants whom I shall call and O.		4	you shall be O. to assist my servant
18	32	to O. priests and teachers	63	45	let him be O. as an agent; and be O. unto this power
20	39	and to O. other elders, priests and		57	let them be O. unto this power
	48	also O. other priests, teachers and	67	10	that have been O. unto this ministry
27	8	to O. you unto this first priesthood	68	2	an ensample unto all who were O. unto
46	27	unto such as God shall appoint and O.		19	provided he is called, set apart and O.—107:17
95	14	whom ye shall appoint and O. unto		20	O. under the hands of this presidency
96	9	ye shall O. him unto this blessing	70	3	O. them to be stewards over the
100	9	I *will* O. you unto this calling	72	8	is the man who shall be O. unto this
107	39	duty to O. evangelical ministers		9	the duty of the bishop who has been O.
	58	duty to O. and set in order all other	76	13	which were O. of the Father through
		ORDAINED		48	who are O. unto this condemnation
5	6	you shall be O. and go forth		52	who is O. and sealed unto this power
	17	wait a while for ye are not yet O.	77	11	are High Priests O. unto holy order of; O. out of every nation
18	29	O. of me to baptize in my name			
	32	you are O. of me to ordain priests	78	1	who are O. unto the high priesthood
20	2	and O. an apostle of Jesus Christ			
	3	second elder, and O. under his hand			
	60	is to be O. according to gifts and; to be O. by the power			
	64	each priest O. by a priest may take			

Sec.	Vs.		Sec.	Vs.	
	2	him who has O. you from on high			**ORDAINS**
79	1	ordination wherewith he has been O.	20	60	which is in the one who O. him
84	28	and was O. by an angel of God at			**ORDER**
107		take with you those who are O.	20	68	so that all things may be done in O.—28:13; 58:55; 107:84
89	10	all wholesome herbs God has O. for	46	29	in O. that every member may be profited
	12	flesh also of beasts I have O. for use	76	57	are priests after the O. of Melchizedek, which was after O. of Enoch, which was after O. of the Only Begotten; 124:123
	14	all grain is O. for the use of man			
90	11	through those O. unto this power			
95	5	many have been O. among you whom I	77	3	in their destined O. or sphere
				11	ordained unto the holy O. of God
104	61	he shall be O. unto this blessing	78	4	everlasting establishment and O. unto
106	1	O. a presiding High Priest over my			
107	21	who are O. to the several offices		8	who are joined together in this O.
	22	chosen by the body, appointed and O.	82	20	this O. I have appointed to be an everlasting O.
	29	who were O. after the order of	84	18	which is after the holiest O. of God
	42	Seth, who was O. by Adam at the age	85	7	to set in O. the house of God
	44	Enos was O. at the age of 134 years	87	3	in O. to defend themselves against
	46	Mahalaleel was 496 years old when O.	88	60	every man in his own O.
				119	establish a house of O., a house of God—109:8
	47	Jared was 200 years old when O.			
	48	Enoch was 25 years old when O.		127	the O. of the house prepared for
	50	Methuselah was 100 years old when O.		128	this shall be the O. of the house of
	51	Lamech was 32 years old when O.	89	2	showing forth the O. and will of God
	52	Noah was ten years old when O.	90	15	set in O. the churches
	73	but has been O. to High Priesthood		16	set in O. all the affairs of this
109	21	blessings which thou hast O. to be		18	set in O. your houses—93:43, 44
112	1	O. through instrumentality of my	92	1	I give unto the United O.; a revelation, that ye shall receive him into the O.
121	32	according to that which was O. in			
124	34	O. that you may receive honor and		2	you shall be a lively member of this O.
	36	it is O. that in Zion shall be			
	39	are O. by the ordinances of my Holy	93	50	set in O. his family
	79	let my servant, Isaac Galland, be O.	94	6	according to the O. of the priesthood
	84	instead of the counsel I have O.			
	91	let my servant William be O. and	96	4	that portion necessary to benefit my O.
	132	let my servant, be O. in his stead			
	135	but rather be O. for standing ministers		8	he should become a member of the O.
			101	69	in O. that all things be prepared
	137	yet they are O. to be standing ministers	104	1	properties which belong to the O.; to be a united O., and everlasting O.
127	2	unless I was O. from before the			
128	5	O. and prepared before foundation of		5	inasmuch as any man belonging to the O.—10
	22	who hath O. before the world was		19	concerning the properties of the O.
132	11	as I and my Father O. unto you before		21	done according to counsel of the O.; united consent or voice of the O.—36
	13	whether it be O. of men, by thrones or			
	28	as was O. by me and my Father before		40	for benefit of the Ozondah of my O.
				47	shall no longer be bound as a United O.
		ORDAINING		48	you shall be called the United O.
20	66	may have the privilege of O. where			

Sec.	Vs.	
	53	you are dissolved as a United O.; as agreed by this O. in council
	64	only by the voice of the O. or by —71, 72, 76, 77
	74	manifest before council of the O.
107	3	after the O. of the Son of God
	9	after the O. of Melchizedek—10, 29, 71, 73, 76; 124:123
	10	of the Levitical O.
	27	in O. to make their decisions of same
	40	the O. of this priesthood was confirmed
	41	this O. was instituted in days of Adam
	58	to ordain and set in O. all the other
	93	vision, showing the O. of the seventy
111	11	] will O. all things for your good
124	123	after O. of mine Only Begotten
127	9	let all the records be had in O.
128	5	you may think this O. of things to be
	12	in O. to answer likeness of the dead
129	7	it is contrary to O. of heaven for a
130	9	or all kingdoms of a lower O.
	10	pertaining to a higher O. of kingdoms
131	2	and in O. to obtain the highest, must enter into this O. of
132	8	for mine house is a house of O.—18

See *United Order*

ORDERS

77	3	or do they represent classes or O.

ORDINANCE

21	11	this being an O. unto you, that you
77	14	it was a mission and an O.
88	139	received by O. of washing of feet, for unto this end was O. of
	140	O. of washing feet is to be administered
124	30	for this O. belongeth to my house
	33	wherein the O. of baptizing for dead
	39	ordained by the O. of my holy house
	134	which O. is instituted for purpose of
128	4	and shall answer the O. just the same
	5	by conforming to the O. and preparation
	8	the nature of this O. consists in; according to O. which God has prepared
	12	the O. of baptism by water, to be; hence this O. was instituted, with the O. of

Sec.	Vs.	
		ORDINANCES
1	15	they have strayed from mine O.
52	15	if he obey mine O.—16
53	6	these are the first O. which you
64	5	inasmuch as he obeyeth mine O.
84	20	in the O. thereof, the power of
	21	without the O. thereof, the power
107	14	power in administering outward O. —20
	67	from same comes administering of O.
121	19	they shall be severed from the O.
124	38	that those O. might be revealed
	40	that I may reveal mine O. therein
	46	because they pollute mine holy O.
128	8	attended to the O. in their own *propria*
136	4	that we will walk in all the O. of

ORDINARY

102	28	no common or O. case is to be sufficient

ORDINATION

53	3	take upon you mine O.
68	1	Orson Hyde was called by his O. to
79	1	in the power of the O. wherewith he
107	45	87 years old when he received his O.
108	4	then you shall receive right by O.

ORGANIZATION

78	3	that there be an O. of my people

ORGANIZE

44	4	obtain power to O. yourselves
51	1	directions how to O. this people
78	11	prepare and O. yourselves by a bond
88	74	O., and prepare and sanctify yourselves
	119	O. yourselves, prepare every needful —109:8
102	1	proceeded to O. the High Council
	24	have power to O. a Council
103	35	O. my kingdom upon consecrated land
104	11	O. yourselves and appoint every man his
	58	I have commanded you to O. yourselves
124	62	let my servants O. themselves
136	12	let my servant O. a company—13, 14

ORGANIZED

20	1	regularly O. and established agreeable to
	65	where there is a regularly O. branch
21	3	which church was O. and established

Sec.	Vs.	
51	2	be O. according to my laws
68	25	in any of her stakes that are O.—26
90	7	which I have commanded to be O.
92	1	United Order, O. agreeable to the
102	12	whenever a High Council is regularly O.
104	1	order which I commanded to be O.
	48	after you are O. you shall be called; after they are O.
	49	they shall be O. in their own names
109	15	and be O. according to thy laws
118	1	let the Twelve be O. and let men be
136	2	be O. into companies, with covenant
	3	companies be O. with captains
	6	when the companies are O. let them

ORGANIZING

Sec.	Vs.	
51	15	grant privilege of O. themselves

ORPHANS

Sec.	Vs.	
83	6	widows and O. shall be provided for

ORSON

Sec.	Vs.	
34	1	my son, O., hearken and hear and

OTHER

Sec.	Vs.	
3	11	become as O. men and have no more gift
5	4	should pretend to *no* O. gift; will grant unto you *no* O.
8	7	there is *no* O. power save the
9	2	O. records have I that I will give
10	17	in O. words, if he bringeth forth
	49	that O. nations should possess this
	59	O. sheep have I which are not of this
	60	I will show that I had O. sheep
18	23	none O. name given whereby man can be
19	7	it is more express than O. scriptures
20	6	white above all O. whiteness
	39	to ordain O. elders, priests
	48	ordain O. priests, teachers and
	54	neither hardness with each O.
	63	receive their license from O. elders
	82	whomsoever the O. elders shall appoint
32	4	and pretend to *no* O. revelation
38	26	to the O., be thou clothed in rags
42	37	or, in O. words—69, 74; 58:20; 59:13, 14; 61:23; 63:42; 78:4, 9; 82:9, 17; 83:5; 88:127; 93:36, 45; 95:17; 101:12; 104:5, 69; 107:66; 128:8
	71	for good of the poor and for O. purposes
43	3	none O. appointed unto you to receive
44	1	by letter or some O. way
50	17	by spirit of truth, or some O. way—18
	18	and if it be by some O. way, it be not of God—20
51	18	an example, in O. places, in all churches
52	9	saying none O. things than that—36
56	17	laying hold upon O. men's goods
58	38	and O. directions shall be given
59	13	on this day thou shalt do none O. thing
68	14	remaineth O. bishops to be set apart
77	2	every O. creature which God has created
78	14	independent above all O. creatures
82	18	that every man may gain O. talents
87	3	Southern states will call on O. nations; they shall call on O nations, to defend themselves against O. nations
88	3	which O. Comforter is the same that
	44	give light to each O. in their times and
89	17	for mild drinks, as also O. grain
97	4	until I shall give him O. commandments
101	20	there is none O. place appointed; neither shall there be any O.
	21	then I have O. places which I will
102	7	have power to appoint O. High Priests—107:79
	10	to be assisted by two O. presidents
	11	the O. presidents have power to
107	5	all O. authorities or offices are
	6	the O. is the Levitical Priesthood
	23	thus differing from O. officers—25
	27	of the same validity one with the O.
	58	to set in order all the O. officers
	74	becomes necessary to have O. bishops
	75	as there are O. bishops appointed they
	95	presidents are to choose O. seventy
	96	and also O. seventy until seven
	98	O. officers are not under responsibility
109	59	to appoint unto Zion O. stakes
115	18	O. places should be appointed for stakes
121	32	the Eternal God of all O. gods
124	70	to *any* O. purpose, only in that house
	72	neither can *any* O. man
	140	the O. is to preside over the churches; the O. has no responsibility of
127	10	by mail, as well as many O. things

Other		317			Out

Sec.	Vs.		Sec.	Vs.	
128	4	to whom these O. records can be handed		66	O. a greater condemnation
	12	that one principle might accord with the O.	66	6	O. think not of thy property
			68	20	O. they are not legally authorized
	18	a welding link of some kind or O.; upon some subject or O.	70	14	O. the abundance of manifestations
			72	18	O. he shall not be accepted of the
131	4	he may enter into the O., but that is		26	O. he who shall go up to the land
			78	10	O. Satan seeketh to turn their hearts
132	34	fulfilling, among O. things the promises	84	58	O. there remaineth a scourge and a
			88	50	O. ye could not abound
	37	did none O. things than that which they; because they did none O.	93	30	O. there is no existence
			98	10	O. whatsoever is less than these cometh
	61	and they have vowed to no O. man			
133	7	from one end of heaven to the O.	99	8	O. thou shalt continue proclaiming
135	3	done more than any O. man; and many O. wise documents and	104	56	O. ye are no stewards
				85	or O. as it shall seem good unto you
136	5	and O. necessaries for the journey			
		OTHERS	105	5	O. I cannot receive her unto myself
1	18	also gave commandments to O. that they		8	O. we will not go up unto Zion
			107	28	when circumstances render it O.
18	26	there are O. who are called to		32	O. there can be no appeal from
20	10	and confirmed to O. by ministering	109	52	and if it cannot be O., may thine
46	7	for some are of men and O. of devils	124	122	O. their labors shall be accounted
			127	1	by turning out property or O.
	14	to O. is given to believe on their			**OUGHT**
	20	and to O. is given faith to heal	8	10	do not ask for that which you O. not to
	22	and to O. it is given to prophesy			
	23	and to O. the discerning of spirits	30	1	have not relied on me as you O.
63	14	and O. remain with you	64	9	ye O. to forgive one another
64	40	and O. shall be planted in their stead		11	ye O. to say in your hearts, let God
			68	32	these things O. not to be
69	4	from Oliver Cowdery and O.	101	53	O. ye not to have done as I commanded
84	3	dedicated by the hand of, and O.			
90	35	and O. have many things to repent of		81	men O. always to pray and not to faint
107	38	call upon the seventy instead of any O.	121	41	no power can or O. to be maintained
112	11	be not partial to them above O.			**OURSELVES**
114	1	in company with O., even Twelve	123	7	duty that we owe to O., our wives
	2	O. shall be planted in their stead	130	1	shall see that he is a man like O.
121	13	bring upon O., and love to have O. suffer			**OUT**
124	22	let my servant, and O., build a house	1	30	to bring it forth O. of obscurity, O. of darkness
	73	there are O. who wish to know my will	5	14	my church O. of the wilderness
			6	11	that thou mayest find O. mysteries
132	38	also many O. of my servants		13	and hold O. faithful to the end
	39	and O. of the prophets who had the keys	8	4	shall deliver you O. of hands of
				8	not able to take it away O. of your
134	4	to infringe on rights and liberties of O.	9	8	you must study it O. in your mind
			10	10	words which have gone O. of your hands—30, 38
		OTHERWISE	18	37	you shall search O. the Twelve
42	72	either a stewardship or O.	20	74	and come forth again O. of the water
49	4	O. he shall not prosper			
51	2	if O., they will be cut off—63:63		83	their names may be blotted O. of
	16	until I shall provide for them O.	24	1	lifted thee up O. of thy afflictions
56	10	O. he shall receive the money		13	except casting O. devils, healing— 35:9
63	29	O. there is none inheritance for you			

Out

Sec.	Vs.
27	14 those whom my Father hath given me O. of
29	4 ye are chosen O. of the world to
	30 words gone forth O. of my mouth
33	5 called forth O. of the wilderness —109:73
36	6 come forth O. of the fire, hating the
38	42 go ye O. from among the wicked
42	71 families supported O. of the property
43	11 purge ye O. the iniquity which is
	18 Lord shall utter his voice O. of heaven—23
45	64 gather ye O. from the eastern lands
	69 gathered unto it O. of every nation
	71 gathered O. from among all nations
56	10 shall be cut off O. of my church
63	54 to pluck O. the wicked and cast them
64	33 O. of small things proceedeth that
	35 the rebellious shall be cut off O. of
	36 they shall be plucked O.
	42 come unto her O. of every nation
65	2 cut O. of the mountain without hands
67	6 seek ye O. of the book of commandments
71	1 expounding mysteries O. of scriptures
72	13 shall pay the debt O. of that which
	15 thus it cometh O. of the church
76	2 extent of his doings none can find O.
	40 which the voice O. of the heavens
	69 who wrought O. this perfect atonement
77	11 O. of all the tribes of Israel; twelve thousand O. of every tribe; ordained O. of every nation
	12 formed man O. of the dust of the earth
82	6 for all have gone O. of the way
84	25 he took Moses O. of their midst
	42 by my own voice O. of heavens
	79 I send you O. to prove the world —87
86	7 first gather O. the wheat from among
88	81 send you O. to testify and warn the
	92 Bridegroom cometh, go ye O. to meet—133:10, 19
	118 seek O. of the best books words of —109:7, 14
90	37 she shall not be removed O. of her place
93	15 there came a voice O. of heaven, saying

Sec.	Vs.
	48 or be removed O. of their place—49, 50
94	1 commence work of laying O. and preparing
95	1 their deliverance O. of temptation
97	19 Zion cannot be moved O. of her place—101:17
98	11 proceedeth forth O. of the mouth
	24 as being meted O. a just measure
	27 and shall not be blotted O.—44
	33 they should not go O. unto battle
	36 justify them in going O. to battle
101	89 come forth O. of his hiding place
103	17 ye must needs be led O. of bondage
104	14 I stretched O. the heavens
	64 shall not be taken O. of the treasury—71
	77 shall be removed O. of his place
	81 it shall be taken away O. of their
	83 be delivered this once O. of bondage
107	4 but O. of respect or reverence for
	21 presiding officers growing O. of
	35 the Twelve being sent O. to open the
	93 chosen O. of the number of seventy
109	5 O. of our poverty we have given of
	34 let them be blotted O. forever
	38 when they go O. and proclaim thy word
	39 that they may gather O. of that city
	48 and our hearts flow O. with sorrow
	56 when thy servants go O. from thy house
	58 may gather O. the righteous to build
111	2 whom I will gather O. in due time
117	5 properties be turned O. for debts
123	3 get hold of them and find them O.
	4 be appointed to find O. these things
	13 that we should waste and wear O. our
124	45 they shall not be moved O. of their
	69 or convey the stock away O. of their
	71 they shall be moved O. of their place
	79 work that my servant shall point O. to
	109 find safety and refuge O. of the city
127	1 by turning O. property, or
	2 has delivered me O. of them all
	3 he will mete O. a just recompense
	10 as it is O. of my power to do so
128	6 dead were judged O. of those things —7

Sec.	Vs.	
	8	for O. of the books shall your dead be
	12	and come forth O. of the water is in likeness; coming forth O. of their graves
	14	records which are truly made O.
	19	the voice of truth O. of the earth
	22	to redeem them O. of their prison
132	15	are not bound when O. of the world —18
	16	when they are O. of the world they
	19	of full force when they are O. of the
	27	not forgiven in this world, nor O. of
	30	O. of the world they should continue, both in the world and O.
	39	he shall not inherit them O. of the
	57	put his property O. of his hands, lest
133	5	go ye O. from Babylon—7, 14
	7	gather ye O. from among the nations
	21	he shall utter his voice O. of Zion
	71	when I called to you O. of the heavens
136	7	then choose O. a sufficient number
	22	led the children of Israel O.; my arm is stretched O. to save
	37	by my own voice O. of the heavens

See Cast, Driven, Pour, Poured

OUTER

101	91	even in O. darkness, where there is
133	73	these shall go away into O. darkness

OUTGOINGS

88	120	that your O. may be in the name of—109:9, 18

OUTWARD

107	14	in administering O. ordinances—20

OVEN

133	64	day cometh that shall burn as an O.

OVER

1	35	devil shall have power O. his own
	36	Lord shall have power O. his saints
5	3	you have no power O. them except as I
7	2	give unto me power O. death
10	15	in asking to translate it O. again
15	2	mine arm is O. all the earth—16:2
20	42	to baptize, and watch O. the church
	53	teacher's duty is to watch O. the church
28	10	to preside O. the conference by voice
30	2	not given heed to those set O. you
	7	his counselor O. him in church
35	19	watch O. him that his faith fail not
38	21	I will be your king and watch O. you
42	32	a steward O. his own property
44	5	that enemies may not have power O. you
46	27	appoint and ordain to watch O. church
50	32	given you power O. that spirit
52	13	faithful shall be made ruler O. many
	39	let the elders watch O. the churches
62	3	they rejoice O. you and your
63	59	I am O. all, and in all, and
68	17	right of presidency O. this
70	3	to be stewards O. the revelations
	11	in a stewardship O. temporal things
	17	they have been faithful O. many
72	6	to be handed O. to the bishop in —13
	20	as stewards O. the literary concerns
76	26	for the heavens wept O. him
	63	to reign on the earth O. his people
	79	obtain not the crown O. the kingdom
77	8	to whom is given power O. four parts of
	9	seal of living God O. the twelve tribes
	11	to whom is given power O. the nations
78	12	delivered O. to buffetings of Satan —82:21; 104:10
	15	made rulers O. many kingdoms
84	111	to watch O. the church, to be
88	2	and the angels rejoice O. you— 90:34
	114	shall not have power O. the saints any
90	13	preside O. affairs of the church
	32	have called you to preside O. Zion
93	42	that wicked one hath power O. you
97	4	shall continue to preside O. school
	23	the Lord's scourge shall pass O. by night
101	76	as rulers and in authority O. you
102	10	he should preside O. the council
	11	he has power to preside O. the
	25	to preside O. such council for the time
104	13	as a steward O. earthly blessings
	57	unto you to be stewards O. mine house
106	1	a presiding High Priest O. my church
107	8	has power and authority O. all offices
	55	thou art a prince O. them forever

Sec.	Vs.		Sec.	Vs.	
	60	to preside O. those of the office of —61, 62	50	8	the same are O. of the world
	65	one to preside O. the Priesthood		33	that ye be not O.
	66	the presiding High Priest over the		35	and power to O. all things
	78	it shall be handed O. unto		41	I have O. the world
	85	president O. office of deacon to preside O.	52	18	he that is O. and bringeth not forth
			61	9	and through faith they shall O.
	86	president O. office of teachers to preside O.	63	20	the same shall O. and shall receive
				47	he that is faithful shall O. the world
	87	president O. priesthood of Aaron to preside O.		66	these things remain to O. through
	89	president O. office of elders to preside O.	64	2	I will that ye should O. the world
			75	16	who is faithful shall O. all things
	91	is to preside O. the whole church		22	ye shall O. all things
	93	seven presidents to preside O. them	76	31	and suffered themselves to be O.
	94	and the seventh is to preside O. the		53	and who O. by faith
	95	seventy, and are to preside O. them		60	and they shall O. all things
109	22	and thine angels have charge O. them		107	I have O. and have trodden the
			88	106	the Lamb of God hath O. and trodden
	26	to rise up and prevail O. thy people		115	Michael shall O. him who seeketh the
	29	spread lying reports O. the world			
111	4	that you shall have power O. it		**OVERCOMES**	
112	15	and my hand shall be O. him	90	36	until she O. and is clean
117	10	let my servant be faithful O. a few things—124:113; 132:44, 53		**OVERFLOWING**	
			45	31	until they shall see an O. scourge
118	4	let them depart and go O. the great waters		**OVERLOOK**	
			101	45	that one may O. the land round about
121	8	thou shalt triumph O. all thy foes			
124	62	to be a president O. their quorum		**OVERPOWER**	
	65	not permitted to receive O. $15,000 —72	10	33	thus Satan thinketh to O. your
	125	to be a presiding elder O. all my		**OVERTAKE**	
	127	to be a president O. the Twelve	45	2	lest death shall O. you
	133	to be president O. quorum of High Priests	106	5	that day shall not O. you as a thief
				OVERTAKEN	
	134	presidents O. different stakes	20	80	any member being O. in a fault
	136	that they may preside O. the quorum—137		**OVERTAKETH**	
			106	4	it O. the world as a thief in the night
	138	to preside O. the quorum of seventies			
	140	the other is to preside O. the churches		**OVERTHROW**	
			50	3	that he might O. you
	141	to preside O. the bishopric	64	21	in the which I will not O. the wicked
127	1	when the storm is fully blown O.			
	2	I shall triumph O. all my enemies	84	28	to O. the kingdom of the Jews
128	4	with certificates O. their signatures	117	16	and to O. the money-changers in mine
	15	principles cannot be lightly passed O.		**OWE**	
133	25	and he shall reign O. all flesh	123	7	it is an imperious duty that we O. to—9, 11
	61	the Lord who ruleth O. all flesh			
	72	ye were delivered O. unto darkness	134	6	to the laws all men O. respect and
136	42	and your enemies triumph O. you		**OWN**	
	OVERCAME		1	16	every man walketh in his O. way, after image of his O. God
76	30	with whom he made war and O.			
	OVERCOME				
38	9	and the enemy shall not O.			

Own   321   Own

Sec.	Vs.
	35 devil shall have power of O. dominions
	38 whether by my O. voice or by the voice
3	4 yet if he boasts in his O. strength; after dictates of his O. will
	13 depended on his O. judgment, boasted in his O. wisdom
6	21 I came unto my O. and my O. received me not—10:57; 11:29; 39:3; 45:8
10	26 to catch themselves in their O. snare
18	8 I have called him unto my O. purpose
19	26 thou shalt not covet thy O. property
20	15 it shall turn to their O. condemnation
	18 after his O. image and his O. likeness
21	5 as if from mine O. mouth, in patience
24	16 in mine O. due time—35:25; 42:62; 43:29; 56:3; 67:14; 71:10; 82:13; 90:29, 32; 117:16; 136:18
29	27 *will* I be ashamed to O. before the Father
	29 have I declared from my O. mouth that
	48 according to my O. pleasure
34	3 so loved the world that he gave his O.
35	20 even as they are in my O. bosom; to salvation of my O.
38	4 have taken Zion into my O. bosom; in mine O. name have I
	29 know not hearts of men in your O. land
42	32 a steward over his O. property
	40 their beauty the work of thine O. hands
43	25 called upon you by mine O. voice
45	63 ye shall hear of wars in your O. lands
51	14 let him also reserve for his O. wants
52	39 let them labor with their O. hands
56	14 ye seek to counsel in your O. ways
	17 who will not labor with your O. hands
58	20 according to counsel of his O. will
	27 and do many things of their O. free will
	58 appointed them in their O. land
	60 and labor with his O. hands
63	4 who buildeth up at his O. will and 25 Zion I hold in mine O. hands
	44 these things are in his O. hands
	63 I, the Lord, *will* O. them, otherwise

Sec.	Vs.
64	3 for this once, for my O. glory
75	28 obliged to provide for his O. family
76	69 through the shedding of his O. blood
	111 receive according to his O. works, his O. dominion
78	17 hath in his O. hands and prepared for
84	42 by mine O. voice out of the heavens—136:37
	109 let every man stand in his O. office; labor in his O. calling
88	32 they shall return again to their O.
	40 mercy claimeth her O.; justice claimeth its O.
	48 who came unto his O., was not comprehended
	60 every man in his O. order
	68 shall be in his O. time, in his O. way, and his O. will
	82 their sins are upon their O. heads
	114 shall be cast away into their O. place
89	6 grape of the vine, of your O. make
90	11 hear fulness of gospel in his O. tongue, his O. language
93	43 you shall set in order your O. house
101	3 I *will* O. them and they shall be mine
	78 may be accountable for his O. sins
102	25 to appoint one of their O. number
103	2 without measure in mine O. time
	24 to drive you even from your O. lands
104	16 it must be done in mine O. way
	49 organized in their O. names, their O. name—50
	50 do business in their O. name, their O. names
	62 no man among you shall call it his O.
	70 let not any among you say it is his O.
105	30 in taking possession of their O. lands
106	2 not only in his O. place but in the
107	10 to officiate in their O. standing
110	8 I will speak with mine O. voice
120	1 and by mine O. voice unto them
121	12 and take them in their craftiness
123	9 not only to our O. wives and children
124	48 ye, by your O. works, bring cursings upon your O. heads
	69 by their O. free will and act
	112 labor with his O. hands that he may
127	1 for my O. safety and the safety of
128	4 certificates over their O. signatures; with his O. statement

Sec.	Vs.		Sec.	Vs.	
	8	according to their O. works, in their O. *propria persona;* by means of their O. agents	135	3	has sealed his mission with his O. blood
					OX
132	59	if a man be called by mine O. voice	89	17	wheat for man, and corn for the O.
					OZONDAH
133	24	shall be turned back into their O. place	104	39	on which the O., (mercantile establishment) stands; on corner south of the O.
	66	when I came unto my O. no man among		40	for benefit of the O.
134	5	such laws as in their O. judgments		41	even this whole O., him and his

P

Sec.	Vs.		Sec.	Vs.	
		PACKARD, NOAH			**PARABLE**
124	136	I give him A. Lyman and P. for counselors	35	16	they shall learn the P. of the fig-tree
		PAGE, HIRAM	38	27	this I have given unto you a P.
28	11	take thy brother P. and tell him	45	36	like unto a P. which I will show you
		PAGE, JOHN E.		56	shall the P. be fulfilled which I spake
118	6	let my servant P. be appointed to	86	1	concerning P. of the wheat and tares—101:65
124	129	they are Orson Pratt, P., and			
		PAGES	88	61	unto this P. will I liken all kingdoms
5	30	hast translated a few more P.	101	43	I will show unto you a P.
		PAID		81	P. of the woman and unjust judge
56	10	shall receive the money he has P.	103	21	in the P. which I have given
		PAIN			**PARADISE**
18	11	he suffered the P. of all men	77	2	the P. of God, the happiness of man
19	18	to tremble because of P. and to bleed		5	and were then in P. of God
133	35	also the tribe of Judah, after their P.			**PARAGRAPH**
		PAINED	135	4	he read the following P.
38	12	and all eternity is P.			**PARCHED**
		PAINTED	133	29	the P. ground shall no longer be a
135	1	by an armed mob, P. black			**PARDONED**
		PALACE	56	14	behold, your sins are not P.
124	2	after similitude of a P.			**PARENTS**
		PALE	68	25	inasmuch as P. have children in Zion! the sin be upon the heads of the P.
123	10	and to stand aghast and P.			
		PALMS	83	4	all children have claim upon their P.
109	76	with P. in our hands and crowns of		5	if the P. have not wherewith to give
		PALSY			**PARLEY**
123	10	hands of the devil to tremble and P.	49	1	my servants Sidney and P., I give
				3	I send you, P. and, to preach the

Sec.	Vs.		Sec.	Vs.	
		PART			**PARTIAL**
6	29	if they reject this P. of my gospel	112	11	be not P. to them in love above many
10	44	they have only got a P. of the account			**PARTICULAR**
	45	you should translate this first P.	10	39	a more P. account was given
	52	will I bring this P. of my gospel to		40	Nephi is more P. concerning
17	6	even that P. which I have commanded	128	3	let him be very P. and precise
				5	you may think this order very P.
19	34	yea, even P. of thy lands, and all			**PARTIES**
29	36	a third P. of the hosts of heaven	102	2	settled to satisfaction of the P.
45	54	shall have P. in the first resurrection—76:64		24	to settle difficulties when P. request
				27	should the P. or either of them be
49	2	they desire to know the truth in P.	123	12	there are many among all sects, P. and
61	8	not suffer that ye should P. until chastened			**PARTLY**
	9	it behooveth me that ye should P.	113	4	who is P. a descendant of Jesse
63	17	shall have their P. in that lake			**PARTOOK**
	18	shall not have P. in first resurrection	19	19	I P. and finished my preparations
72	2	in this P. of the Lord's vineyard.—5, 9, 10, 16, 17, 19	29	40	he P. the forbidden fruit and transgressed
88	99	received their P. in that prison			**PARTRIDGE, EDWARD**
95	16	let lower P. of the inner court	41	9	I have called my servant P. and give
	17	let the higher P. of the inner court	42	10	I say unto you, P., stand in the office—57:7
104	62	shall call it his own or any P. of it.—70	50	39	in this thing P. is not justified
	71	there shall not any P. of it be used	51	1	unto P., and give him directions
		PARTAKE		3	let P. and those whom he has chosen
10	66	P. of the waters of life freely		4	let P., when he shall appoint a man his
20	75	meet often to P. of bread and wine		18	this shall be an ensample to P.
	77	to the souls of those who P. of it	52	24	let P. and Martin Harris take their
27	2	when ye P. of the sacrament		41	let P., and, take with them a recommend
	4	wherefore you shall P. of none except	58	14	and have selected my servant P.
46	4	not partake until he makes reconciliation		24	P., this land is land of his residence
58	11	and P. of the supper of the Lord		62	let P. direct the conference which
61	17	that they may P. of the fatness thereof	60	10	let P. impart the money which I have
101	35	yet shall they P. of all this glory	64	17	and also P., behold he hath sinned
132	51	that she stay herself and P. not of	115	2	and my servant P. and counselors
		PARTAKER	124	19	and also my aged servant P. and
96	7	a P. of the blessings of the promise		21	like unto my servant P., that he may
		PARTAKERS			**PARTS**
66	2	and be made P. of the glories	6	27	those P. of my scriptures which have
76	31	my power and have been made P. thereof	8	1	which contain those P. of my scripture
	46	except them who are made P. thereof	10	46	does contain all those P. of my Gospel
93	22	are P. of the glory of the same	37	2	ye have preached my gospel in those P.
133	57	that men might be made P. of the glories	38	34	I give unto my church in these P.
		PARTAKING	58	64	unto the uttermost P. of the earth
20	68	previous to P. of the sacrament	77	8	power over the four P. of the earth
88	141	and after P. of bread and wine	110	11	gathering Israel from four P. of the
			111	4	they shall not discover your secret P.

Sec.	Vs.		Sec.	Vs.	
		PASS			**PAST**
1	38	though heaven and earth P. away, my word shall not P. away—56:11	9	11	but you feared and the time is P.
			45	2	the summer shall be P. and the harvest
19	3	which I shall P. upon inhabitants	56	16	the harvest is P., summer is ended
	5	revoke not judgments which I shall P.	84	54	your minds in times P. have been darkened
27	6	bringing to P. the restoration of all	126	1	to leave your family as in times P.
29	7	bring to P. gathering of mine elect	130	7	their glory are manifest, P., present and
	23	heaven and earth shall P. away.—45:22			**PATH**
	24	for all things shall P. away	112	7	thy P. lieth among the mountains
	26	before the earth shall P. away			**PATHS**
	36	and it came to P.—40; 74:3, 4; 135:5	3	2	God doth not walk in crooked P.; his P. are straight and
38	13	to bring to P. even your destruction	25	2	and walk in P. of virtue before me
	20	in eternity no more to P. away	33	10	way of the Lord, and make his P. straight—65:1; 133:17
43	32	the earth shall P away so as by fire	124	99	he shall be led in P. where the poisonous
45	21	this generation of Jews shall not P. away			**PATIENCE**
	23	not P. away until all shall be fulfilled	4	6	remember faith, virtue, knowledge, P.
	31	shall not P. until they shall see an	6	19	have P., faith, hope, charity
	35	all these things shall come to P.	21	5	his word ye shall receive in all P.
56	11	these words shall not P. away	63	66	things remain to overcome through P.
58	27	and bring to P. much righteousness	67	13	continue in P. until ye are perfected
63	49	when old things shall P. away			
64	32	but all things must come to P. in their	101	38	that in P. ye may possess your souls
84	5	generation shall not all P. away	107	30	in P., Godliness, brotherly kindness
	99	which was brought to P. by the faith	127	4	let your P. be redoubled
87	1	the wars which shall shortly come to P.			**PATIENT**
88	14	is brought to P. the resurrection of	6	19	be P.; be sober; be temperate
	79	things which must shortly come to P.	9	3	be P. my son, for it is wisdom
89	21	the destroying angel shall P. by them	11	19	be P. until you shall accomplish it
90	26	to bring to P. my work, are not taken	24	8	be P. in afflictions.—31:9; 66:9
95	4	that I may bring to P. my strange act.—101:95	54	10	be P. in tribulation
					PATIENTLY
97	23	the Lord's scourge shall P. over by night	98	2	waiting P. on the Lord.
103	36	all victory and glory is brought to P.		23	bear it P. and revile not
				24	if ye bear it not P.
105	11	cannot be brought to P. until mine		25	and bear it P. your reward shall be—26
122	5	if thou art called to P. through			
	9	their bounds are set, they cannot P.	108	4	wait P. until the solemn assembly
127	2	perils which I am called to P. through	124	88	await P. further instructions
132	18	angels of God, by whom they cannot P.			**PATRIARCH**
			124	91	Hyrum may take the office of P.
	19	they shall P. by the angels and gods	134	1	I give Hyrum Smith to be a P. to you
		See *Came* and *Come*	135	1	the prophet, and Hyrum Smith, the P.
		PASSED			**PATRIARCHAL**
101	33	things which have P., and hidden	124	92	he shall hold keys of P. blessings
122	7	and sentence of death be P. upon thee			
128	15	principles cannot be lightly P. over			

Sec.	Vs.		Sec.	Vs.	
		PATTEN, DAVID W.	119	4	shall P. one-tenth of interest annually
114	1	wisdom in my servant P. that he	124	67	the same shall P. his stock into hands
124	19	as my servant P. who is with me		69	and if any P. stock into their hands
130		P. I have taken unto myself		72	let my servant P. stock into their; but he cannot P. over, nor under —111
		PATTERN		80	let my servant P. stock into that house—81, 82
24	19	shall do according to this P.	117		P. stock also into hands of the quorum
52	14	I will give unto you a P. in all	119		let no man P. stock to the quorum unless
	18	bringeth not fruits according to this P.			
	19	by this P. ye shall know the spirits			**PAYS**
63	21	transfigured according to the P.	124	68	of stock he P. into their hands, but if he P. nothing
73	5	let this be a P. unto the elders	122		let every man who P. stock
88	141	gird himself according to the P. given			
94	2	must be done according to the P.			**PEACE**
	5	according to P. which shall be given —6, 12	1	35	when P. shall be taken from the earth
97	10	like unto the P. which I have given	6	23	did I not speak P. to thy mind
102	12	organized according to foregoing P.	10	37	hold your P. until I shall see fit
	27	according to former P. written	11	18	hold your P.; appeal unto my spirit
115	14	house he built according to P.		22	hold your P.; study my word which
	15	if build it not according to P.	19	23	and you shall have P. in me
	16	but if, build it according to P.	27	16	with preparation of Gospel of P.
		PAUL	42	57	thou shouldst hold thy P. concerning
18	9	I speak unto you, even as unto P.	45	46	if ye have slept in P. blessed are you
76	99	these are they who are of P. and of		66	the New Jerusalem, a land of P.
127	2	I feel like P. to glory in tribulation	59	23	even P. in this world and eternal life
128	13	which is heavenly as P. hath declared	82	23	P. be with you; my blessings
	15	as P. says concerning the fathers	84	102	justice, grace and truth, and P.
	16	give you another quotation of P.	88	125	which is bond of perfectness and P.
		PAVED	90	31	that she may settle down in P.
110	2	under his feet was a P. work of pure	98	16	renounce war and proclaim P.
				34	should first lift a standard of P.
		PAVILION		35	did not accept the offering of P.
121	1	where is the P. that covereth thy	101	8	in day of their P. they esteemed lightly
	4	let thy P. be taken up		48	seeing this is a time of P.
		PAY	105	25	that you may rest in P. and safety
19	35	P. the debt thou hast contracted with		38	sue for P., not only the people that
42	54	thou shalt P. for that which thou		39	lift up an ensign of P., make a proclamation of P.
51	11	let them P. unto this church again		40	make proposals of P. unto those
54	7	be your leader and to P. moneys for you	109	39	let thy P. and salvation be upon that
56	12	if my servant must P. the money, I will P. it unto him again	111	8	let the P. and power of my spirit
59	10	and P. thy devotions to the Most High	121	7	my son, P. be unto thy soul
64	28	and P. as seemeth him good	134	2	no government can exist in P.
72	11	shall P. for that they receive, as they have wherewith to P.		6	without them P. would be supplanted
	13	who hath not wherewith to P., bishop shall P.		8	the breach of the general P., and for the public P.
104	78	my will you shall P. all your debts			
111	5	I will give you power to P. them			

Sec.	Vs.	
	12	dangerous to P. of every government
136	16	may be ready to go to a land of P.

PEACEABLE

Sec.	Vs.	
36	2	teach you the P. things of the kingdom
39	6	which teacheth the P. things of the
42	61	that thou mayest know the P. things

PEARLS

41	6	or the P. to be cast before swine

PELAGORAM

78	9	let P., (Sidney Rigdon), sit in council
82	11	that P., and Gazelam, and, be bound
104	20	let P. have appointed unto him the
	22	this stewardship I confer upon P.

PENALTY

82	4	justice and judgment are the P.

PENETRATED

1	2	neither heart that shall not be P.
121	2	and thine ear be P. with their cries

PENTECOST

109	36	as upon those on the day of P.

PEOPLE

1	1	hearken, O ye P. of my church; hearken, ye P. from afar—41:1; 45:1, 6; 46:1; 56:1; 63:1; 133:1; 136:41
	4	voice of warning shall be unto all P.
	7	fear and tremble, O ye P.
	14	shall be cut off from among the P.
3	16	knowledge of Savior come unto my P.
	19	promises which he made to his P.
5	20	as I told the P. of the destruction
	25	shall say unto P. of this generation
6	26	because of wickedness of the P.
7	3	before nations, kindreds, tongues and P.—42:58; 77:8, 11; 88:103; 98:33; 112:1; 133:37
10	32	Satan will harden hearts of the P.
	40	to knowledge of the P.—52
	46	which should come forth unto this P.
	51	that it might be free unto all P.
	60	I will show unto this P.
	63	Satan doth stir up hearts of P.
15	6	declare repentance unto this P.—16:6; 18:14; 44:3
18	15	in crying repentance unto this P.
19	29	publish it among every P.
20	9	contains a record of a fallen P.

Sec.	Vs.	
29	2	who will gather his P. as a hen
31	7	I will open the hearts of the P.
35	7	manifest in the eyes of all P.
38	22	and you shall be a free P.
	31	be gathered unto me a righteous P.
	39	ye shall be the richest of all P.
39	11	to recover my P. which are of the house
	15	my P. shall assemble themselves at
	16	P. in Ohio call upon me in much faith
42	9	may be my P. and I will be your God
	36	that my covenant P. may be gathered; for salvation of my P.
	39	my P. who are of the house of Israel
43	14	reserve unto myself a pure P.
	29	my P. shall be redeemed and shall
44	5	wherewith enemy seeketh to destroy my P.
45	9	to be a standard for my P.
	19	this P. shall be destroyed
	69	the only P. that shall not be at war
	72	accomplish this work in eyes of the P.
49	11	go among this P. and say unto them
51	1	directions how to organize this P.
	3	appoint unto this P. their portion
	7	which belongs to this P., be appointed unto this P.
	8	money which is left unto this P.; an agent appointed unto this P.; according to the wants of this P.
	9	let every man be alike among this P.
	10	let that which belongeth to this P. not
	13	more than is needful for wants of P.
	15	I grant unto this P. a privilege of
52	2	which I will consecrate unto my P.
56	6	stiff-neckedness of my P. in Thompson
	14	thus saith the Lord unto my P.
57	9	that he may send goods unto the P.
58	18	to judge his P. by the testimony of
	45	they shall push the P. together
61	31	lift up their voices against that P.; a P. well nigh ripened for destruction
63	1	you that call yourselves the P. of the
	15	their works shall follow them in eyes of P.
64	23	a day for the tithing of my P.
	42	she shall be an ensign to the P.

Sec.	Vs.	
65	4	make known his wonderful works among P.
66	7	bear testimony unto every P., reasoning with the P.
	11	thou shalt push many P. to Zion
68	1	from P. to P. and from land to land
	33	in remembrance before judge of my P.
70	1	all P. of my church who are far off
74	3	a great contention among the P.
76	63	to reign on the earth over his P.
78	3	that there be an organization of my P.; storehouse for the poor of my P.
84	2	for the restoration of his P.
	23	sought diligently to sanctify his P.
	28	way of the Lord before face of his P.
	99	the Lord has redeemed his P.—100
	101	for he stands in the midst of his P.
	114	and warn the P. of those cities
	119	I will come and reign with my P.
85	3	that he may tithe the his P.; their names enrolled with P. of God
86	11	a savior unto my P. Israel
88	81	I sent you out to testify and warn P.
	88	cometh wrath and indignation upon the P.
	91	for fear shall come upon *all* P.
	93	and *all* P. shall see it together
	104	saying to *all* P. in heaven and earth
90	15	and with languages, tongues and P.
	23	into disrepute before eyes of P.
97	11	built speedily by the tithing of my P. •
	15	inasmuch as my P. build a house
	23	the report thereof shall vex *all* P.
98	4	my P. should observe to do all things
	9	when the wicked rule the P. mourn
	34	if *any* P. should proclaim war; lift standard of peace to that P.
	35	if that P. did not accept offering
	36	justify going out to battle that P.
	38	this is an ensample unto *all* P.
100	3	I have much P. in this place
	5	lift up your voices unto this P.
	9	you should be spokesman unto this P.
	16	I will raise up unto myself a pure P.
101	10	let fall the sword in behalf of my P.
	65	I must gather together my P.
	77	according to constitution of the P.
	96	storehouse which I have appointed to my P.
	98	this is a grievous sin against my P.
	99	is my will that my P. should claim
103	5	a decree which my P. shall realize
	16	I will raise up unto my P. a man

Sec.	Vs.	
	35	and preside in the midst of my P.
104	59	and to prepare my P. for the time
105	1	the redemption of mine afflicted P.
	2	were it not for transgressions of my P.—9
	6	my P. must needs be chastened
	7	those who are appointed to lead my P.
	10	that my P. may be taught more perfectly
	16	together for the redemption of my P.
	23	let *all* my P. who dwell in the
	24	consistently with feelings of the P.
	25	saying unto the P., execute judgment
	26	you may find favor in the eyes of the P.
	27	I will soften the hearts of the P.
	38	sue for peace, not only the P. that have; but also all P.
106	2	warn the P. not only in his own place
109	5	a place to manifest himself to his P.
	10	we ask thee to assist us, thy P.
	11	promises made unto us, thy P.
	12	thy glory may rest down upon thy P.
	13	that *all* P. who shall enter upon the
	17	that all the incomings of thy P.
	21	when thy P. transgress they may repent
	24	establish the P. that shall worship
	26	no combination shall prevail over thy P.
	27	if *any* P. shall rise against this P.
	28	and if they shall smite this P.; thou wilt fight for thy P.
	30	end to lyings and slanders against thy P.
	34	have mercy upon this P.; forgive transgressions of thy P.
	36	gift of *tongues* be poured out on thy P.
	38	that thy P. may not faint in day of trouble
	39	and P. of that city receive their
	41	and P. of that city receive not the
	46	deliver thy P. from calamity of wicked
	49	how long wilt thou suffer this P. to
	50	wicked mobs who have driven thy P.
	51	thou didst appoint a Zion to thy P.
	52	that the cause of thy P. may not fail
	55	remember *all* P. and the churches and *all* the
	56	and thy P. obtain favor in the sight

Sec.	Vs.	
	59	that gathering of thy P. may roll on
110	6	let hearts of *all* my P. rejoice
	7	I will manifest myself to my P.
	8	if my P. will keep my commandments
	10	blessing poured out on heads of my P.
111	2	many P. in this city whom I will gather
112	23	gross darkness the minds of the P.
113	6	for gathering of my P. in last days
	7	what P. had Isaiah reference to
115	3	unto all the elders and P. of my church
	10	let my P. labor diligently to build
	15	if my P. build not according to pattern
	16	if my P. build according to pattern, I will accept it of my P.
	19	I will sanctify him before the P.
116	1	where Adam came to visit his P.
117	9	come hither unto land of my P.
	10	preside in the midst of my P.; with the blessings of my P.
	11	and be a bishop unto my P.
	14	for the benefit of my P.
	15	let the blessings of my P. be upon him
119	3	shall be beginning of tithing of my P.
	6	if my P. observe not this law to keep it
121	2	behold the wrongs of thy P.
	23	wo to those that discomfort my P.
122	3	thy P. shall never be turned against thee
123	1	abuses put on them by P. of this state
	5	and impositions practiced upon this P.
124	10	where shall be safety of my P.
	11	come ye, to the help of my P.
	16	to the kings of the P. of the earth
	21	upon the heads of the poor of my P.
	39	which my P. are always commanded to
	40	reveal mine ordinances unto my P.
	45	if my P. will hearken unto my voice; my P. shall not be moved out of their
	75	long and loud in the midst of the P.
	84	golden calf for the worship of my P.
	92	patriarchal blessings upon *all* my P.
	104	if he will remain with my P.
127	1	my own safety and safety of this P.
128	24	let us therefore as a church and a P.
132	34	from Hagar sprang many P.

Sec.	Vs.	
133	4	prepare ye O. my P., O ye P. of my church
	9	the voice of the Lord unto *all* P.; that borders of my P. may be enlarged
	10	let the cry go forth among *all* P.
	21	his voice shall be heard among *all* P.
	25	Savior shall stand in midst of his P.
	50	I have brought judgment upon *all* P.
	63	they should be cut off among the P.
134	3	and upheld by the voice of the P.
135	3	he died great in eyes of God and his P.
136	2	let all the P. of the church be
	8	into the ears of the Lord against this P.
	9	will of the Lord concerning his P.
	10	use all his influence to remove this P.
	22	in the last days to save my P. Israel
	31	my P. must be tried in all things

PERADVENTURE

Sec.	Vs.	
103	32	that P. you may obtain 300
	33	that P. you may obtain 100
	35	pray earnestly that P. my servant may go

PERCEIVE

Sec.	Vs.	
45	29	for they P. not the light and they turn

PERCEIVED

Sec.	Vs.	
133	45	have not men heard nor P. by the ear

PERDITION

Sec.	Vs.	
76	26	and was called P., he was Lucifer
	32	they who are the sons of P.
	43	except those sons of P. who deny

PERFECT

Sec.	Vs.	
50	24	brighter and brighter until P. day
59	13	that thy fasting may be P.
76	69	they who are just men made P.: who wrought this P. atonement
84	110	that the system may be kept P.
107	43	because he, (Seth) was a P. man
128	15	they without us cannot be made P., neither can we without our dead be made P.—18
	18	that a whole and P. union
129	3	the spirits of just men made P.
	6	if he be the spirit of a just man made P.

Sec.	Vs.	
		PERFECTED
45	46	your redemption shall be P.
67	13	continue in patience until ye are P.
76	106	and shall have P. his work
88	34	by law, and P. and sanctified by the same
	84	that you may be P. in your ministry—90:8
97	14	P. in understanding of their ministry
		PERFECTING
124	143	the ministry, and the P. of my saints
		PERFECTLY
88	78	that you may be instructed more P.
105	10	that my people may be taught more P. and know more P.
		PERFECTNESS
88	125	which is the bond of P. and peace
		PERFORM
6	35	P. with soberness the work I have
18	30	P. it according to the words which
20	64	shall authorize him to P. the duties
101	95	and P. my work, my strange work
114	1	that he may P. a mission next spring
124	37	except ye P. them in a house
	47	I will not P. the oath which I made
	49	to P. that work, and enemies come upon
		PERFORMANCES
132	7	all covenants, contracts, bonds, and P.
		PERFORMING
26	1	P. your labors on the land, such as
124	49	hinder them from P. that work
		PERHAPS
123	4	P. a committee can be appointed to
		PERILS
29	3	lest P. shall come upon you
122	5	if thou art in P. among false brethren; P. among robbers; P. by land or by sea
127	2	as for the P. I am called to pass
		PERISH
1	16	waxeth old and shall P. in Babylon
19	22	must not know these things lest they P.
61	6	you shall not P. by the waters
	8	that you might not P. in wickedness

Sec.	Vs.	
64	19	known unto my disciples that they P. not
76	9	the wisdom of the wise shall P.
121	20	their houses and their barns shall P.
		PERISHETH
4	4	layeth up in store that he P. not
		PERISHING
61	3	whilst inhabitants are P. in unbelief
		PERMANENT
78	4	for a P. and everlasting establishment
		PERMIT
58	52	as soon as time will P.
84	117	go forth as circumstances shall P.
		PERMITTED
19	29	among every people thou shalt be P. to see
101	99	though they should not be P. to dwell
109	20	no unclean thing shall be P. to come
124	64	they shall be P. to receive $15,000
	65	they shall not be P. to receive over
	66	they shall not be P. to receive under
	67	shall not be P. to receive any man as a
132	4	and be P. to enter into my glory
		PERPETUATED
109	71	that their names may be P.
		PERPLEXITIES
88	79	the wars and the P. of the nations
		PERSECUTE
121	38	to P. the saints, and fight against God
127	4	and if they P. you, so persecuted they
		PERSECUTED
45	53	lament because they P. their king
101	1	who have been afflicted and P.
127	4	so P. they the prophets and righteous
		PERSECUTETH
88	94	that P. the saints of God, that shed
		PERSECUTION
40	2	the fear of P. and cares of the world
99	1	in the midst of P. and wickedness
101	35	all they who suffer P. for my name

Sec.	Vs.	
		PERSECUTIONS
109	68	and all his afflictions and P.
		PERSECUTOR
86	3	the great P. of the church, the whore
		PERSEVERANCE
127	4	let your diligence and P. be redoubled
		PERSON
20	65	no P. is to be ordained to any office
	73	the P. who is called of God shall go down with the P.
42	78	every P. who belongeth to this church
77	2	spirit of man in likeness of his P.
107	81	is not *any* P. exempt from this council
130	19	if a P. gains more knowledge in this life
		PERSONAGE
130	22	Holy Ghost is a P. of spirit
		PERSONAGES
129	1	angels who are resurrected P.
		PERSONAL
132	2	both of character and P. injuries
130	3	father and son, in that verse, is a P.
134	1	where P. abuse is inflicted
		PERSONALLY
20	84	if the member is P. acquainted with
		PERSONS
1	35	for I am no respecter of persons—38:16
5	3	not show them except to those P.
42	74	P. having put away their companions
	75	but if ye shall find out that *any* P.
	79	if *any* P. among you shall kill
123	3	names of all P. that have had a hand
134	11	unlawful assaults of all P. in times
135	1	of from 150 to 200 P.
	2	were the only P. in the room at the time
		PERSUADED
30	2	been P. by those whom I have not
		PERSUASION
121	41	only by P., by long-suffering, by
		PERSUASIONS
3	6	and have gone on in the P. of men
5	21	yield to the P. of men no more

Sec.	Vs.	
		PERTAIN
88	78	all things that P. to the kingdom
104	29	and all things that P. to it
124	41	things that P. to the dispensation
		PERTAINING
11	14	P. to things of righteousness
64	38	shall judge all things P. to Zion
76	7	all things P. to my kingdom—100:11
82	12	all things P. to the bishopric, both in
90	25	as P. to those who do not belong to your
94	3	in all things P. to church and kingdom
97	14	perfected in all things P. to the
98	7	and as P. to law of man, whatsoever is
101	78	act in doctrine and principle P. to futurity
105	37	to accomplish all things P. to Zion
111	4	and its wealth P. to gold and silver
112	16	keys of kingdom, as P. to the Twelve
123	15	much lieth in futurity P. to the Saints
124	42	show all things P. to this house
	56	as P. to my boarding house
	121	as P. to the price thereof
127	8	about to restore many things P. to
128	15	as P. to our salvation
130	9	whereby all things P. to inferior
	10	whereby things P. to a higher order
132	6	as P. to new and everlasting covenant
	58	there are many things P. thereto
	61	as P. to the law of the priesthood
	64	law of my priesthood as P. to these
	66	as P. to this law I will reveal more
		PERTAINS
104	34	which P. to that inheritance and those
		PERVERSE
33	2	to a crooked and P. generation—34:6
		PERVERSENESS
112	9	let tongue of the slanderer cease its P.
		PESTILENCE
63	24	lest there be confusion which bringeth P.
97	26	will visit her with P., with plague
		PESTILENCES
43	25	by the voice of famine and P.

Sec.	Vs.	
		PETER
7	4	said unto P., if I will that he tarry
	5	I say unto thee P. this was a good
16	1	hearken my servant P. and listen to
27	12	and also with P., James and John
30	5	I say unto you P. you shall take
49	11	unto mine apostle of old whose name was P.
128	10	I say unto thee, that thou art P.
	20	the voice of P., James and John
		PETERSON, ZIBA
32	3	and P. shall go with them, and I
58	60	let that bestowed on P. be taken from
		PETITION
90	1	sins are forgiven thee according to thy P.
		PETITIONS
109	77	hear us in these P. and answer us from
	78	answer these P. and accept dedication
		PHARAOH
105	27	as I did the heart of P. from time to
		PHELPS, WILLIAM W.
57	11	let P. be planted in this place and be
58	40	let P. stand in the office which I
61	7	let P. and, be in haste upon their
	9	let P. and, take their former company
70	1	unto P. by way of commandment
		PHYSICAL
134	10	neither to inflict any P. punishment
		PHYSICIAN
31	10	you shall be a P. unto the church
		PIECE
101	44	even upon this very choice P. of land
		PIERCE
121	4	stretch forth thy hand; let thine eye P.
		PIERCED
1	3	rebellious shall be P. with much sorrow
6	37	the wounds which P. my side
		PIERCETH
85	6	which whispereth through and P. all

Sec.	Vs.	
		PILGRIMS
45	13	and confessed they were strangers and P.
		PILLAR
29	12	in the day of my coming in a P. of fire
88	97	to meet him in midst of the P. of heaven
		PINE-TREE
124	26	the box-tree, the fir-tree and the P
		PIONEERS
136	7	to go as P. to prepare for putting in
		PIT
109	25	he who diggeth a P. for them shall fall
122	7	if thou shouldst be cast into the P.
		PITCHING
61	25	P. their tents by the way
		PITY
133	53	in his love and P. he redeemed them
		PLACE
6	14	thou wouldst not have come to the P.
18	25	they cannot have P. in the kingdom
19	29	publish it on every high P.
24	15	in whatsoever P. ye shall enter
28	10	thou shalt not leave this P. until
29	8	they shall be gathered in unto one P.
	38	there is a P. prepared for them, which P. is hell
31	6	I will prepare a P. for them
38	35	send them forth to the P. which I
42	8	from this P. ye shall go into regions
	53	thou shalt stand in the P. of thy
45	43	remnant shall be gathered unto this P.
	55	he shall have no P. in hearts of
	66	a P. of safety for the saints of
48	5	the P. is not yet to be revealed; shall be given to know the P.
49	25	unto the P. which I have appointed
52	8	take their journey unto the same P.—33
53	4	to be an agent in the P. which shall
54	9	until I prepare a P. for you
56	8	concerning the P. upon which he lives
	10	shall leave the P. and shall be cut
57	2	this is the P. for the city of Zion

Place

Sec.	Vs.	
	3	the P. which is now called Independence
	8	let my servant plant himself in this P.
	11	let Wm. Phelps be planted in this P.
	13	in whatsoever P. I shall appoint
58	37	for the P. of the storehouse
	64	the sound must go forth from this P.
60	5	take your journey speedily for the P.
	7	in this P. let them lift up their voice—61:31
64	26	until residue which remaineth in this P.
	37	sitting on a hill, or in a high P.
66	6	tarry not many days in this P.
	7	bear testimony in every P.
	8	shall be made strong in every P.
69	6	a P. to receive and do all these things
	7	travel many times from P. to P.
70	16	whatsoever circumstances I shall P. them
75	29	the idler shall not have P. in the
76	45	and the end thereof, neither the P.
	66	the heavenly P., the holiest of all
78	3	both in this P., and in land of Zion
	7	if I give you a P. in celestial world
79	1	go into eastern countries from P. to P.
84	4	by the gathering beginning at this P.; the P. of the temple
	62	whatsoever P. ye cannot go into ye
87	2	upon all nations beginning at that P.
88	32	they shall return again to their own P.
	70	tarry ye in this P., and call a
	114	shall be cast away into their own P.
	128	shall be found standing in his P.
	129	in a P. that the congregation may hear
	134	he shall not have P. among you
90	19	let there be a P. provided for the
	20	continue with his family upon the P.
	37	she shall not be removed out of her P.
93	48	or be removed out of their P.—49, 50
96	2	take charge of the P. which is named
97	13	for a P. of thanksgiving for all saints; for a P. of instruction
	19	Zion cannot be moved out of her P.—101:17
98	18	I have prepared a P. for you

Sec.	Vs.	
100	3	I have much people in this P.
	4	I have suffered you to come to this P.
101	20	there is none other P. appointed; neither shall there be any other P.
	89	and come forth out of his hiding P.
102	7	capable to act in the P. of absent
104	20	the P. where he now resides
	27	the P. upon which he now dwells
	77	shall be removed out of his P.
106	2	not only in his own P. but in
107	45	in journeying to the P. Shedolamak
109	2	build a house to thy name in this P.—124:55
	5	that the Son of man might have a P.
	13	that it is thy house a P. of holiness
	23	from this P. they may bear glorious
111	7	tarry in this P. and in regions
	8	the P. where it is my will that you
	9	this P. you may obtain by hire
112	19	in whatsoever P. ye shall proclaim
	27	the affairs of my church in this P.
116	1	the P. where Adam shall come to visit
118	1	to supply the P. of those who are fallen
121	1	where is pavilion that covereth thy hiding P.
	4	let thy hiding P. no longer be covered
123	6	which shall call him forth from his hiding P.
124	22	upon the P. which he shall show
	28	there is not a P. found on earth that he
	42	and the P. whereon it shall be built
	43	ye shall build it on the P.
	45	they shall not be moved out of their P.
	56	let my servant and his house have a P.
	59	his seed after him have a P. in that
	71	they shall be moved out of their P.
	85	let no man go from this P. who has
127	1	wisdom to leave the P. for a short season
128	1	as I stated before I left my P.
	7	previously to leaving my P.
	13	in a P. underneath where the living
	18	welding of powers and glories should take P.
130	8	the P. where God resides is a great
133	24	shall be turned back into their own P.

| Place | 333 | Planted |

Sec.	Vs.	
135	5	sitting down in the P. I have prepared
136	10	to remove this people to the P. I See Center-place.

PLACED

Sec.	Vs.	
52	37	taken from him and P. upon head of
93	30	that sphere in which God has P. it
101	76	hands of those who are P. as rulers
104	64	seal which shall be P. upon it
	67	and a seal shall be P. upon it
134	6	rulers and magistrates being P. for the

PLACES

23	6	pray among your friends and in all P.
24	12	at all times, in all P. he shall open
45	32	my disciples shall stand in holy P.
	33	shall be earthquakes also in divers P.
48	1	remain for present time in your P.
	3	necessary that they have P. to live
49	23	the rough P. to become smooth—109:74
51	18	be an example, in other P., in all
58	47	bear testimony of truth in all P.
75	25	obtain P. for your families
	26	let all such as can obtain P.
87	8	wherefore, stand ye in holy P.
99	4	cleanse your feet in the secret P.
101	18	build up waste P. of Zion—103:11
	21	then I have other P. which I will
	22	and stand in holy P.
	64	up unto my name upon holy P.
	67	gather together unto the P. which I
	75	establish her waste P.
109	39	her stakes, the P. of thine appointment
112	17	unlock door of the kingdom in all P.
115	18	other P. should be appointed for stakes
117	7	make solitary P. to bud and blossom
118	6	be appointed to fill the P. of those
124	36	those P. appointed for refuge, shall be the P. for your baptisms
	39	your oracles in your most holy P.
125	2	let them gather themselves to the P.
128	21	at sundry times, and in divers P.
133	49	the stars shall be hurled from their P.

PLAGUE

87	6	and with famine, and P., and earthquake
97	26	with sore affliction, pestilence, P.

PLAGUES

Sec.	Vs.	
84	97	and P. shall go forth, and shall not

PLAIN

42	40	let thy garments be P.
128	18	but it is sufficiently P. to suit my

PLAINER

128	18	I might have rendered a P. translation

PLAINLY

45	16	I will show it P. as I showed it to
84	23	this Moses P. taught to the children
93	5	and the works of him were P. manifest
	31	from the beginning is P. manifest unto
104	74	manifest before council of the order P.

PLAINNESS

133	57	reasoning in P. and simplicity

PLAINS

117	8	upon the P. of Olaha Shinehah

PLAN

10	12	devil has sought to lay a cunning P.
	23	thus he has laid a cunning P. thinking

PLANET

130	4	according to the P. on which they reside
	6	angels do not reside on P. like this

PLANETS

88	43	which comprehend the earth and all P.

PLANT

2	2	he shall P. in the hearts of the children
35	18	if not, another *will* I P. in his stead
57	8	let my servant P. himself in this; to P. them in their inheritance —15
101	44	and P. twelve olive trees
	101	they shall P. vineyards and shall eat

PLANTED

55	5	that you may be P. in land of your
57	11	let Wm. Phelps be P. in this place
	14	let those be P. in land of Zion
64	40	others shall be P. in their stead—114:2
97	9	a fruitful tree P. in a goodly land
101	46	P. the olive tree and built a hedge
	53	after ye had P. the vineyard and
124	2	this stake which I have P. to be a

Sec.	Vs.	
		PLANTS
124	61	whom I have set to be as P. of renown
		PLATES
3	19	for this purpose are these P. reserved
5	1	that you my servant have got the P.
	4	you have a gift to translate the P.
10	38	engraven upon the P. of Nephi
	39	was given of these things upon the P.
	40	because the account engraven on P. of
	41	translate engravings on the P. of Nephi
	45	there are many things on P. of Nephi
17	1	you shall have a view of the P.
		PLEAD
90	36	I will P. with her strong ones
109	32	therefore, we P. before thee a full
124	75	and P. the cause of the poor and needy
		PLEADED
38	4	have I P. before the Father for them
		PLEADING
45	3	who is P. your cause before him
		PLEADINGS
102	20	hearing the evidences and P. impartially
		PLEASE
59	18	both to P. the eye and gladden the
63	10	nor as they P. but by the will of God
64	28	that the Lord should not take when he P.
		PLEASED
1	30	with which I, the Lord, am well P.
38	10	none else with whom I am well P.
45	4	in whom thou wast well P.
50	37	let my servant in whom I am well P.—51:3; 61:35
58	41	I am not well P. with him, for he
60	2	with some I am not well P. for they
63	11	with whom God is angry he is not well P.
	12	I am not P. with those among you who
	55	I am not P. with my servant Sidney
68	31	am not P. with inhabitants of Zion
84	3	with whom the Lord was well P.
90	35	I am not P. with many things, not well P. with my servant
97	3	well P. that there should be a school
98	19	not well P. with many at Kirtland
112	2	with which I the Lord was not well P.
124	1	I am well P. with your offering
	12	for I am well P. with him
	84	many things with which I am not well P.
		PLEASES
63	4	who destroyeth when he P. and is able to
		PLEASETH
59	20	it P. God that he hath given all these
60	1	it P. me that you have come up hither
63	11	without faith no man P. God
		PLEASING
25	11	sacred hymns, which is P. unto me
46	15	as it will be P. unto the same Lord
55	4	receive instruction before me as is P.
66	3	things which are not P. in my sight
88	2	this is P. unto your Lord
89	13	it is P. unto me that they should not
		PLEASURE
29	48	as I will, according to my own P.
56	15	but have P. in unrighteousness
63	4	who buildeth up at his own will and P.
76	7	make known unto them good P. of my will
136	30	and I will do my P. with them
		PLEDGE
104	85	and P. the properties I have put into
		PLEDGED
135	7	broken faith of State as P. by governor
		PLEDGES
136	20	seek and keep all your P. one with
		PLUCK
63	54	send mine angels to P. out the wicked
86	6	P. not *up* the tares while the blade
		PLUCKED
64	36	wherefore they shall be P. out
		POINT
124	79	the work my servant shall P. out to

Sec.	Vs.	
		POINTED
121	27	which their minds were P. to
		POINTS
10	62	bring to light true P. of my doctrine
	63	contention concerning P. of my doctrine
43	8	how to act upon the P. of my law
		POISON
84	71	and if any man shall administer P.
	72	the P. of a serpent shall not have
124	98	who would administer deadly P.
		POISONOUS
24	13	and against P. serpents
124	99	where the P. serpent cannot lay hold
		POISONS
24	13	and against deadly P.
		POLISHED
124	2	which shall be P. with the refinement.
		POLLUTE
84	59	shall the children of the kingdom P.
103	14	if they P. their inheritances, I will
105	15	they shall not be left to P. mine
109	20	permitted to come into thy house to P. it
110	8	and do not P. this holy house
124	46	because they P. mine holy grounds
		POLLUTED
88	134	shall not suffer that mine house be P.
101	6	by these things they P. their inheritances
	97	let not that be P. by mine enemies
		POLLUTION
124	24	shall not suffer any P. to come upon it
		PONDER
30	3	inquire for yourself and P. upon the
88	62	leave these sayings with you to P. in
	71	and P. the warning in their hearts
		POOLS
133	29	there shall come forth P. of living
		POOR
35	15	the P. and meek shall have the gospel
38	16	the P. have complained before me
	35	they shall look to the P. and needy
42	30	thou wilt remember the P. and
	31	impart of your substance unto the P.

Sec.	Vs.	
	34	to administer to the P. and needy
	37	that which he has consecrated to the P.—51:5
	39	unto the P. of my people, who are of
	71	for the good of the P. and other purposes
44	6	ye must visit the P. and needy
52	40	remember the P. and the needy, the sick
56	16	that will not give your substance to P.
	17	wo unto you P. men whose hearts are
	18	blessed are the P. who are pure in
	19	and the P. shall rejoice
58	8	feast of fat things prepared for the P.
	11	then shall the P., the lame and the blind
	47	call upon high and low and P. to repent
72	12	to the good of the church, the P.
78	3	storehouse for the P. of my people
82	12	to manage the affairs of the P.
83	6	shall be provided for, as also the P.
84	105	take the old and cast it to the P.
	112	searching after the P. to administer
88	17	P. and meek of earth shall inherit it
104	16	that the P. shall be exalted
	18	and impart not his portion to the P.
105	3	to the P. and afflicted among them
109	55	remember all the P., the needy, and
	72	with all the P. and meek of the earth
124	21	upon the heads of the P. of my people
	75	to plead the cause of the P. and needy
	89	with his interest support cause of P.
136	8	in taking the P., the widows, the
		PORE
19	18	and to bleed at every P. and suffer
		PORTION
19	34	impart a P. of thy property
51	4	when he shall appoint a man his P.; that shall secure unto him his P.
	5	he shall not have power to claim that P., only claim on that P.
60	10	impart a P. unto mine elders
71	1	according to that P. of spirit and
78	21	and appoint every man his P.
84	85	be given you in the very hour that P.
85	9	their P. shall be appointed them among

Sec.	Vs.	
88	29	quickened by a P. of the celestial
	30	quickened by a P. of the terrestrial
	31	quickened by a P. of the telestial
96	4	that P. necessary to benefit my order
101	90	appoint them their P. among hypocrites
104	18	and impart not his P. he shall with
124	8	to appoint the P. of the oppressor
	70	they shall not appropriate *any* P.
	71	and if they do appropriate *any* P.
132	39	from his exaltation and received his P.

PORTIONS

51	3	appoint unto this people their P.

POSSESS

10	49	that other nations should P. this land
38	20	ye shall P. it again in eternity
49	20	not given that one man should P. that
69	8	to P. it from generation to generation
88	20	may P. it forever and ever—103:7
99	7	to P. thine inheritance
101	38	that in patience ye may P. your souls
	58	with residue of mine house and P. the
	65	in the garners to P. eternal life
103	20	in time ye shall P. the goodly land
105	29	should P. them according to the laws

POSSESSING

128	20	P. the keys of the kingdom and of the

POSSESSION

105	30	in taking P. of their own lands

POSSESSIONS

64	26	should sell their store and their P. here

POSSESSOR

50	27	wherefore he is P. of all things
	28	but no man is P. of all things, except

POSSIBILITY

20	32	but there is a P. that man may fall

POSSIBLE

5	7	if it were P. that you could show
10	49	if it were P. that other nations
57	15	come to this land as soon as P.
90	19	let a place be provided as soon as P.

POSSIBLY

114	1	settle his businesss as soon as he own P.

POSTERITY

107	42	his P. should be chosen of the Lord
	53	with the residue of his P. who were
	56	predicted whatsoever should befall his P.
121	15	they and their P. shall be swept
	21	nor their P. after them
124	57	shall be put upon the head of his P.
135	6	their names shall go down to P. as gems

POUR

19	38	I *will* P. *out* my Spirit upon you —44:2
27	18	my spirit, which I *will* P. *out* upon you
95	4	that I may P. *out* my spirit on all flesh
103	2	on whom I *will* P. *out* my wrath
109	45	that thou wilt P. *out* thy judgment

POURED

1	9	when the wrath of God shall be P. *out*
5	19	scourge continue to be P. *out*
39	15	it shall be P. forth upon their heads
84	58	a judgment to be P. *out* upon children
87	2	war *will* be P. *out* upon all nations—3
101	11	mine indignation is soon to be P. *out*
105	12	endowment and blessing to be P. *out*
109	21	which thou hast ordained to be P. *out*
	36	let gift of tongues be P. *out* upon
110	9	blessings that shall be P. *out*
	10	beginning of blessing which shall be P.
115	6	from wrath when it shall be P. *out*

POURING

121	33	hinder Almighty from P. down knowledge

POVERTY

109	5	out of our P. we have given our
124	30	acceptable only in the days of your P.

POWER

1	8	P. given to seal both on earth and
	29	P. to translate, by P. of God, the Book of Mormon
	30	have P. to lay foundation of this church
	35	the devil shall have P. over his own
	36	the Lord shall have P. over his saints

Sec.	Vs.		Sec.	Vs.	
3	4	and have P. to do many mighty works		30	I have created by word of my P., which is P. of my spirit
	12	had given thee sight and P. to translate		31	by the P. of my spirit I created them
5	3	you have no P. over them except I		36	give me thine honor, which is my P.
	13	I will give them P. that they may		47	P. is not given Satan to tempt little
	14	to none else will I grant this P.	30	6	given him P. to build up my church
	25	shown unto me by the P. of God —26	33	16	P. of my spirit quickeneth all things
7	2	give unto me P. over death that I	34	7	I shall come in a cloud with P.
	7	and unto you three will I give this P.	35	13	thresh nations by P. of my spirit
8	7	no P. save P. of God than can cause	38	31	ye might escape the P. of the enemy
	8	no P. shall be able to take it away		32	there you shall be endowed with P.
9	2	I will give unto you P. that you may		33	and no P. shall stay my hand
10	1	you had P. given you to translate		38	when men are endowed with P. from
	16	if God has given him P. to translate, he will give him P. again	39	4	gave I P. to become my sons
	17	and if God giveth him P. again we		12	come to pass that P. shall rest upon thee
	18	we will say that he has no gift, no P.	42	5	shall be given by the P. of my spirit
11	10	believing in the P. of Jesus Christ, or in my P. which		6	shall go forth in P. of my spirit
	11	by my P. I give these words unto thee		52	have P. to become my sons
	21	yea, the P. of God unto convincing	43	4	shall not have P. except to appoint
	30	will I give P. to become sons of God		15	put into your hands by P. of my spirit
15	2	speak unto you with sharpness and P.—16:2		16	ye shall be endowed with P.
17	3	you shall testify of them by P. of	44	4	shall obtain P. to organize yourselves
	5	for it is by my P. he has seen them		5	that your enemies may not have P.
	7	you have received the same P. and	45	8	gave I P. to do many miracles; gave I P. to obtain eternal life
18	32	according to P. of the Holy Ghost		44	clothed with P. and great glory
	35	by my P. you can read them one to; save it were by my P. you could not		75	terror of the Lord, and P. of his might
	47	by P. of my spirit I have spoken it	49	6	has taken his P. on right hand
19	3	retaining all P. even to destroying		10	of itself shall be laid low of P.
	14	by my almighty P. you have received	50	7	which has given the adversary P.
	20	lest I humble you with my almighty P.		27	the light, the spirit and the P.
20	8	and gave him P. from on high		32	given you P. over that spirit
	24	to reign with almighty P. according		35	and P. to overcome all things
	35	by gift and P. of the Holy Ghost —34:10	51	5	he shall not have P. to claim that
	36	honor, P. and glory be rendered	52	17	he that trembleth under my P.
	60	to be ordained by P. of Holy Ghost	55	3	you shall have P. to give the Holy
21	7	to move cause of Zion in mighty P.	56	18	see the kingdom of God coming in P.
27	9	committed keys of P. of turning hearts	58	11	after that cometh day of my P.
28	3	with P. and authority unto the church		28	for the P. is in them wherein they
29	11	from heaven, with P. and great glory	60	4	what it is that bespeaketh P. of God
	29	they cannot come for they have no P.	61	1	voice of him who has all P.
				27	is given P. to command the waters
			63	41	P. that he shall be enabled to discern
				45	let him be ordained unto this P. —57
				59	I am from above, my P. lieth beneath
			65	6	thine is the honor, P. and glory
			68	4	the P. of God unto salvation

Sec.	Vs.		Sec.	Vs.	
	12	you shall be given P. to seal them up		45	in their glory, in midst of P. of God
	19	provided he is called unto this P.		47	hath seen God moving in majesty and P.
71	1	that portion of spirit and P. which		114	they shall not have P. over the saints
	6	shall be given more abundantly, even P.	90	10	be revealed in P. in convincing the
72	1	to whom kingdom and P. have been given		11	through those ordained unto this P.
	8	Whitney shall be ordained unto this P.	93	17	he received all P. both in heaven and
76	10	by my P. will I make known the secrets		42	that wicked one hath P., as yet, over
	12	by P. of the spirit our eyes were opened		49	lest that wicked one have P. in you
	31	concerning all those who know my P.; through P. of the devil to be overcome; deny truth and defy my P.	95	8	whom I have chosen with P. from on high
				11	you shall have P. to build it
				14	whom ye shall appoint unto this P.
	37	on whom second death shall have any P.	97	20	he hath sworn by the P. of his might
	42	whom the Father had put into his P.	99	2	you shall have P. to declare my word
	52	who is ordained or sealed unto this P.	100	1	for in me there is all P.
	91	even in glory, and P. and might		10	give him P. to be mighty in testimony
	95	he makes them equal in P. and in might		11	P. to be mighty in expounding all
	108	to sit on the throne of his P.	101	28	Satan shall not have P. to tempt any man
	116	only to be understood by P. of the	102	6	the High Council cannot have P.
	118	that through the P. and manifestation		7	these seven shall have P. to appoint
77	4	their wings are a representation of P.		11	he has P. to preside over the council; the other presidents have P. to preside
	8	to whom is given P. over four parts of; having P. to shut up the heavens		22	the Council having P. to determine same
				24	have P. to call and organize a council
	11	to whom is given P. over the nations		25	have P. to appoint one of own number
	12	that which he hath not put into his P.		29	have P. to say whether it is necessary
79	1	in the P. of the ordination wherewith		33	P. to determine whether any such case
84	20	the P. of godliness is manifest	103	15	redemption of Zion must come by P.
	21	without Priesthood, P. of godliness is not		17	must be led out of bondage by P.
	28	ordained unto this P. to overthrow; in whose hand is given all P.	104	10	give you P. from this very hour; he shall not have P. to bring evil
	72	shall not have P. to harm them	105	11	until elders are endowed with P.
	77	traveling to preach the gospel in my P.		37	they shall have P. after many days
			107	8	and has P. over all the offices
	102	glory, honor and P. be ascribed to		14	has P. in administering outward
85	7	holding the sceptre of P. in his hand		17	ordained unto this P. by the hands of
88	7	and the P. thereof by which it was made—8, 9		18	of the P. and authority of the higher
				20	the P. and authority of the lesser
	10	and the earth also, and the P. thereof		24	they form a quorum equal in P.
	13	even the P. of God who sitteth upon		27	decisions of the same P. and validity
	26	and shall abide the P. by which it		79	shall have P. to call other High Priests; shall have P. to decide upon testimony
			109	13	that all people may feel thy P.

Sec.	Vs.		Sec.	Vs.	
	22	go from this house, armed with thy P.		67	could not redeem, neither my P. to deliver
	26	that no combination shall have P. to	135	3	translated by gift and P. of God
	33	break it off by thy P.	136	17	they shall not have P. to stop my work
	35	be sealed upon them with P. from on		19	he shall have no P. and his folly
	59	gathering of thy people may roll on in P.			**POWERFUL**
	77	enthroned with glory, honor, P.	6	2	my word which is quick and P.—11:2; 12:2; 14:2; 27:1; 33:1
	79	and help us by the P. of thy spirit	65	1	voice of one who is mighty and P.
111	4	that you shall have P. over it			**POWERS**
	5	I will give you P. to pay them	21	6	God will disperse the P. of darkness
	8	by the peace and P. of my spirit	24	1	been delivered from the P. of Satan
112	21	shall have P. to open door of my kingdom	38	11	P. of darkness prevail upon the earth
	30	is the P. of this priesthood given	58	22	be subject to the P. that be
	31	which P. you hold in connection with	84	119	to exert the P. of heaven
113	4	on whom there is laid much P.	121	29	all thrones, dominions and P.
	8	who should hold the P. of the priesthood; to return to that P. which she had lost		36	inseparably connected with P. of heaven; P. of heaven cannot be controlled only
121	33	what P. shall stay the heavens	128	11	consists in obtaining P. of the Holy
	41	no P. can be maintained by virtue of		18	welding together keys and P. and glories
123	6	before he can send P. of his mighty arm		23	kingdoms, principalities and P.
	17	let us do all things that lie in our P.	132	13	thrones, principalities and P.—19
124	4	let it be written by P. of the Holy			**PRACTICABLE**
127	10	as it is out of my P. to do so	73	4	inasmuch as it is P., to preach in
128	8	consists in P. of the priesthood			**PRACTICE**
	9	a P. which records or binds on earth; this P. has always been given	38	24	P. virtue and holiness before me —46:33
	14	this is the sealing and binding P.	124	48	abominations you P. before me
	21	their majesty and glory, and the P. of			**PRACTICED**
131	5	through the P. of the Holy Priesthood	52	39	there be no idolatry nor wickedness P.
132	7	appointed on earth to hold this P.; have appointed Joseph to hold this P.; on whom this P. and keys	123	5	murderous impositions P. upon this
					PRAIRIES
			57	5	every tract bordering by the P.
					PRAISE
	18	whom I have appointed unto this P.—19	52	17	and shall bring forth fruits of P.
	20	be Gods, because they have all P.	58	39	for he seeketh the P. of the world
	39	prophets who had keys of this P.	109	79	with acclamations of P., singing Hosanna
	44	shall you have P. by P. of my Holy	128	22	let dead speak forth anthems of P.
	45	conferred upon you keys and P. of the		23	let the trees of the field P. the Lord
	48	it shall be visited by my P.	136	28	P. the Lord with singing, with music, with prayer of P.
	59	have endowed him with keys and P. of			**PRATT, ORSON**
	64	if any man who holds keys of this P.	52	26	let P. and, take their journey—75:14
133	59	thresh nations by P. of his spirit	103	40	let Orson Hyde journey with P.
			124	129	they are Parley P. Pratt, P., and
			136	13	let P., and, organize a company

Sec.	Vs.		Sec.	Vs.	
	PRATT, PARLEY P.		46	7	doing all things with P. and thanksgiving
32	1	now, concerning my servant P.	52	9	taught them by the Comforter through P.
50	37	let P. go forth among the churches	58	44	except they desire it through P. of
52	26	let P. and Orson Pratt, take their	59	9	go to the house of P. and offer up
97	3	with P., for he abideth in me		14	this is fasting and P.; rejoicing and P.
103	30	my will that P. should not return to	63	64	and ye receive the spirit through P.
	37	let P. journey with Joseph Smith, Jr.		65	as taught through P. by the spirit
124	29	they are Heber C. Kimball, P., and	81	3	in P. always vocally and in thy heart
	PRAY		84	61	in solemnity and spirit of P.
10	5	P. always that you may come off conqueror	88	76	ye shall continue in P. and fasting
19	28	thou shalt P. vocally as well as in		119	establish a house even a house of P.—109:8
	38	P. always and I will pour out my spirit		131	let him offer himself in P. upon his
20	33	P. always lest they fall into temptation—31:12; 61:39		135	with the same P. and covenant
	47	exhort them to P. vocally and in secret—51		137	ye are called to do this by P. and
23	6	P. vocally before the world		141	it is to be commenced with P.
32	4	P. always that I may unfold them to	93	51	and by your P. and faith, with one —52
37	2	they P. unto me in much faith	102	34	after P. the conference adjourned
42	44	shall P. and lay their hands upon them	104	79	by your humility, and the P. of faith
65	4	P. unto the Lord, call upon his holy		80	inasmuch as you exercise P. of faith
68	28	they shall teach their children to P.	107	22	upheld by confidence and P. of church
88	126	P. always that ye may not faint	109	16	that this house may be a house of P.
90	24	P. always and be believing	127	12	my P. to God is that you all may be saved
93	49	P. always lest that wicked one have	136	28	with a P. of praise and thanksgiving
	50	P. always or they shall be removed.		**PRAYERFUL**	
101	81	men ought always to P. and not to faint	105	23	let all my people be faithful and P.
	92	P. ye therefore that their ears may		**PRAYERS**	
103	35	P. earnestly that peradventure my	10	46	which my disciples desired in their P.
112	12	and P. for thy brethren of the Twelve		47	according to their faith in their P. —52
	PRAYED			49	their faith in their P. was that Gospel
135	5	I P. unto the Lord that he would give		50	a blessing upon this land in their P.
	PRAYER		21	7	and his P. I have heard
5	24	humble himself in mighty P. and faith	35	3	I have heard thy P. and have prepared
20	76	call upon the Father in solemn P.	38	16	I have heard your P. and the poor have
25	12	song of the righteous is a P. unto me		30	I tell these things because of your P.
26	2	all things shall be done by much P.	53	1	I have heard your P. concerning your
28	13	in the church, by P. of faith	67	1	whose P. I have heard and whose hearts
29	2	and call upon me in mighty P.	68	33	he that observeth not his P. before
	6	being united in P. according to my	88	2	the alms of your P. have come into
30	6	ever lifting up your heart unto me in P.	90	1	thy P. and the P. of thy brethren
41	3	by the P. of faith ye shall receive			
42	14	spirit shall be given you by P. of			
43	12	uphold him before me by P. of faith			

Sec.	Vs.		Sec.	Vs.	
96	6	and whose P. I have heard, unto whom		25	take their journey and P. by the way—26, 27
98	2	your P. have entered into the ears	53	3	to P. faith and repentance, and remission
101	7	God is slow to hearken unto their P.	55	2	P. repentance and remission of sins
103	36	through your diligence and P. of faith	58	46	let them P. the gospel in the regions
105	19	have heard their P. and will accept		47	let them P. by the way and bear testimony
108	7	strengthen your brethren in your P.	60	8	P. the word, not in haste, among the
112	1	Thomas, I have heard thy P.		13	to P. among congregations of wicked
	10	and give thee answer to thy P.	68	8	P. gospel unto every creature—80:1; 112:28
	11	heard thy P. concerning thy brethren	73	4	P. in the regions round about
124	2	your P. are acceptable before me	80	3	P. my gospel, whether to the north or

PRAYETH

			84	77	traveling to P. the gospel in my
52	15	he that P., whose spirit is contrite		80	that shall go and P. this gospel and

PRAYING

			106	2	and should P. my everlasting gospel
33	17	be faithful, P. always, having your	107	25	seventy are called to P. the gospel
75	11	P. always that they faint not	108	6	you shall have right to P. my gospel
95	16	for your fasting and for your P.	118	3	continue to P. from that hour
98	39	come unto thee P. thy forgiveness	134	12	we believe it just to P. the gospel; but, neither P. the gospel to, nor baptize
130	13	while I was P. earnestly on the subject			
	14	I was once P. very earnestly to know			

PREACHED

			35	15	the meek shall have the gospel P.

PREACH

			37	2	until ye have P. my gospel in those parts
10	48	gospel, that they might P. in their days	50	21	receiveth it as it is P. by spirit of
11	15	not called to P. until you are called	57	10	P. unto those who sit in darkness
18	28	to P. my gospel unto every creature	58	64	must be P. unto every creature
	41	you must P. unto the world saying	63	52	for this cause P. the apostles unto
19	21	that you P. naught but repentance	76	73	whom the Son visited and P. gospel
	37	P., exhort, declare the truth	84	76	from you it must be P. unto them
20	46	Priest's duty is to P., teach	133	37	gospel shall be P. to every nation
	50	he is only to P., teach, expound			
23	2	shall be opened to P. the truth			

PREACHER

			21	12	and the first P. of this church
	4	thou art not yet called to P. before			
28	8	go to Lamanites and P. my gospel			
31	4	you shall begin to P. from this time			

PREACHETH

			50	22	he that P. and he that rejoiceth
34	5	you are called of me to P. my gospel			

PREACHING

35	23	thou shalt P. my gospel and call on	26	1	time be devoted to P. and confirming
36	1	P. my gospel as with the voice of a	38	41	let your P. be the warning voice
	5	ordained and sent forth to P.	42	6	P. my gospel, two by two
39	11	thou shalt P. fulness of my gospel	52	9	journey from thence, P. word by the way—22, 23
42	11	not be given to any one to P. my gospel	58	63	let them return, P. gospel by the way
44	3	P. repentance unto the people	69	8	P. and expounding, writing, copying
49	1	and P. my gospel unto the Shakers			
	3	I send you to P. the gospel unto them	73	1	they should continue P. the gospel
50	14	to P. my gospel by the spirit	95	16	for your P., and your fasting, and
	17	he that is sent forth to P. the word; doth he P. it by the spirit of truth	107	38	to fill the several calls for P.
			124	18	Wight should continue P. for Zion
52	10	let them P. by the way in every			

Sec.	Vs.		Sec.	Vs.	
		PRECEDENT	33	10	repent and P. ye the way of the Lord
128	10	again for the P., Matthew xvi:18	35	4	even as John, to P. the way before
		PRECEPT	38	40	to P. and accomplish the things
98	12	line upon line, P. upon P.—128:21	43	20	P. yourselves for the great day of —133:10
		PRECEPTS		21	repent, and P. for the great day
45	29	from me because of the P. of men	45	9	a messenger before my face to P. the
103	4	they did not hearken unto the P.	54	9	until I P. a place for you
		PRECIOUS	65	1	P. ye the way of the Lord—3; 133:17
97	9	that yieldeth much P. fruit		3	P. ye the supper of the Lamb
101	34	things most P., things that are above	71	4	and P. the way for the commandments
109	43	their souls are P. before thee	78	7	you must P. yourselves by doing the
124	26	with all your silver and P. stones; with all the P. trees of the earth		11	P. and organize yourselves by a bond
	27	with zinc, and with all your P. things		13	this is preparation wherewith I P. you
		PRECISE	84	28	to P. them for coming of the Lord
128	3	let him be very particular and P.	107		to P. the way and fill appointments
		PRECISELY	85	3	to P. them against day of vengeance
128	7	the principles agreeing P. with the	88	74	organize, and P. and sanctify yourselves
		PREDICATED		84	to P. the saints for hour of judgment
130	20	upon which all blessings are P.		92	P. ye, P. ye, O inhabitants of earth
	21	obedience to law upon which it is P.		119	P. every needful thing, establish—109:8
		PREDICTED	95	1	with the chastisement I P. a way for
107	56	Adam P. whatsoever should befall his		4	wherewith I design to P. mine apostles
		PREFACE	101	23	P. for the revelation which is to
1	6	this is my P. unto the book of my	104	59	to P. my people for the time when I
		PREJUDICES		60	ye shall P. a treasury
109	56	that their P. may give way before	109	38	and P. the hearts of thy saints for
	70	that their P. may be broken up	124	139	to P. a way before my face
		PREPARATION		145	ye should P. rooms for all these
27	16	your feet shod with P. of the gospel	132	3	P. thy heart to receive and obey
78	13	this is the P. wherewith I prepare		49	and P. a throne for you in the
95	4	the P. wherewith I design to prepare	133	4	P. ye, P. ye O my people
128	5	conforming to the ordinance and P.		19	P. ye for the coming of the bridegroom
		PREPARATIONS		58	to P. the weak for those things
19	19	I partook and finished my P. unto	136	6	to P. for those who are to tarry
52	3	as soon as P. can be made to leave		7	to P. for putting in spring crops
57	15	let bishop and the agent make P. for		9	let each company P. houses and fields
		PREPARATORY			**PREPARED**
84	26	ministering of angels and P. gospel	20	8	by the means which were before P.
115	9	let there be a beginning, a P. work	29	8	be P. in all things against the day
		PREPARE		28	P. for the devil and his angels
1	12	P. ye, P. ye for that which is to come		38	there is a place P. for them from
29	8	to P. their hearts and be	35	3	and P. thee for a greater work—39:11
31	6	and I *will* P. a place for them			
	8	you shall strengthen and P. them			

Sec.	Vs.	
38	9	gird' up thy loins and be P.
	30	if ye are P. ye shall not fear
42	9	when New Jerusalem shall be P.
45	61	that ye may be P. for things to come—65:5
58	6	that your hearts be P. to bear testimony
	8	that feast of fat things might be P.
	9	supper of the house of the Lord well P.
	11	partake of supper of the Lord, P.
59	2	mansions, which I have P. for them—81:6
	13	let thy food be P. with singleness
63	39	be P. in the coming spring to take
72	4	mansions P. for them of my Father —76:111
78	10	understand not the things P. for
	15	come up unto the crown ·P. for you
	17	in his own hands and P. for you
88	18	it may be P. for celestial glory
	80	that ye may be P. in all things when
	99	in that prison which is P. for them
	127	the house P. for the presidency
	128	in the house which shall be P. for
98	18	and I have P. a place for you
101	68	let all things be P. before you— · 133:15
	69	in order that all things be P. before you
	72	observe to have all things P. before
104	13	which I have P. for my creatures
	17	yea, 1 P. all things and have given
	67	there shall be another treasury P.
105	10	that they themselves may be P.
	12	I have P. a great endowment—18
106	8	I have P. a crown for him in the
109	15	be P. to obtain every needful thing
	46	may be P. against day of burning
124	83	have a scourge P. for the inhabitants
125	2	may be P. for that which is in store
128	5	P. before foundation of the world
	8	which God has P. for their salvation
133	45	the great things thou hast P. for him
135	5	which I have P. in the mansions of
136	31	that they may be P. to receive the glory

PREPARETH

| 78 | 20 | who P. all things before he taketh you |

PREPARING

34	6	P. way of the Lord for his second
39	20	P. the way before· my face for the
77	12	the P. and finishing of his work; P. the way before the time

Sec.	Vs.	
94	1	P. a beginning and foundation of
103	29	in P. the churches to keep the

PRESCRIBING

| 134 | 4 | to interfere in P. rules of worship |
| | 6 | P. rules on spiritual concerns |

PRESENCE

29	41	he should be cast out from my P.
38	11	in P. of all the hosts of heaven
60	15	not in their P. lest thou provoke them
63	34	in heaven, from P. of my Father
67	12	neither can natural man abide in P.
	13	ye are not able to abide the P. of
76	25	who was in authority in P. of God; was thrust down from P. of God
	62	these shall dwell in · the P. of God
	77	they who receive P. of the Son
	94	they who dwell in his P. are the
	118	they may be able to bear his P. in
84	24	and could not endure his P.
88	12	which light proceedeth from P. of
	19	even with the P. of God the Father
94	8	and my P. shall be there—97:16
	9	and my P. shall not come into it
103	19	shall go before you but not my P.
	20	shall go before you and also my P.
	26	my P. shall be with you even in
107	19	to enjoy communion and P. of God
109	12	that thy holy P. may be continually
	69	they may be exalted in thy P.
	74	mountains flow down at thy P.— 133:40, 44
121	32	man shall enter into his eternal P.
	45	shall wax strong in P. of God
130	7	but they reside in the P. of God
133	26	the ice shall flow down at their P.
	31	hills shall tremble at their P.
	35	to dwell in his P. day and night
	41	for the P. of the Lord shall be as
	42	all nations shall tremble at thy P.
	49	great shall be the glory of his P.
	53	and the angel of his P. saved them
	55	and Jacob, shall be in P. of the Lamb

PRESENT

9	3	that you should translate at P. time
20	49	when there is no elder P.
	50	but when there is an elder P.
38	2	all things are P. before mine eyes
42	82	necessary that bishop is P. also
48	1	ye should remain for the P. time
	3	let them buy for the P. time; have places to live for the P.
58	3	ye cannot behold, for P. time, the
76	59	whether life or death, or things P.
107		and P. it to the Father spotless

Sec.	Vs.		Sec.	Vs.	
84	42	confirm upon you who are P. this day	97	4	he shall continue to P. over school
102	6	or regularly appointed successors are P.	102	10	he should P. over the council
	16	to P. the case after the evidence is		11	he has power to P. over council; other presidents have power to P.
107	11	when the High Priest is not P.		25	to P. over such council for the
	12	when there are no higher authorities P.	103	35	and P. in the midst of my people
123	5	and P. the whole concatenation of	107	60	P. over those who are of—61, 62
	6	but P. them to the heads of governments		65	to P. over the priesthood and he
127	11	I now close my letter for the P.		85	to P. over twelve deacons
128	3	difficult for one recorder to be P.; some three individuals that are P., if there be any P.		86	to P. over twenty-four teachers
				87	to P. over forty-eight priests
				89	to P. over ninety-six elders
				91	is to P. over the whole church
	18	from Adam even to the P. time—21		93	have seven presidents to P. over them
	24	let us P. in his holy temple		94	the seventh is to P. over the six
	25	but shall now close for the P.		95	to whom they belong and are to P. over
130	7	glory are manifest, past, P. and	117	10	let him P. in the midst of my people
132	66	let this suffice for the P.	124	136	they may P. over quorum of High Priests
136	42	so no more at P.		137	to P. over the quorum of elders
				138	to P. over the quorum of seventies

PRESENTED

				140	to P. over the churches from time
20	64	certificate when P. to an elder		141	to P. over the bishopric
	73	who has P. herself for baptism			
58	51	epistle to be P. to all churches			**PRESIDENCY**
78	2	in that you have P. before me	48	6	as appointed unto him by the P.
			68	17	holds the right of the P. over the

PRESERVE

				20	must be designated by this P.; ordained under hands of this P.
25	2	I *will* P. thy life and thou		21	under hands of above-named P.
35	14	by fire of mine indignation *will* I P.		23	if found guilty before this P.
63	3	in life them whom he *will* P.	81	2	always under P. of high priesthood
104	65	thus shall ye P. the avails of the	88	127	of the house prepared for the P.
117	16	to keep and P. it holy, and to		128	the house of the P. of the school
			90	12	continue in ministry and P.

PRESERVED

			94	3	building an house for the P.; for work of the P.; for ministry of P.
3	19	for this purpose are these plates P.		7	dedicated for the work of the P.
10	35	show it not that you may be P.	107	8	Melchizedek Priesthood holds right of P.
38	38	see that all things are P.			
42	56	and they shall be P. in safety		9	P. of High Priesthood have right
44	5	that you may be P. in all things		10	under the direction of the P.—33
61	10	as they are faithful they shall be P.		15	bishopric is the P. of this
62	6	faithful among you should be P.		17	unto this power by P. of the
88	34	governed by law is also P. by law		22	form a quorum of the P. of the church
107	42	should be P. unto end of earth		36	equal in authority to the P.
109	69	and P. by thy fostering hand		76	has a legal right to the P. of this
				78	before P. of the High Priesthood

PRESERVETH

				79	and the P. of the council of; thus the P. of the
63	3	and P. in life them who he will		90	this P. is a distinct one from

PRESERVING

			115	15	which I shall show unto their P.—16
136	27	thou shall be diligent in P. what	119	2	and for the debts of the P.

PRESIDE

			124	84	which I have ordained, even the P. See *First Presidency*.
28	10	shall be appointed to P. over conference			
90	13	P. over the affairs of the church			
	16	to P. in council and set in order			
	32	to P. over Zion in mine own due time			

Sec.	Vs.	
		PRESIDENT
20	67	every P. of the High Priesthood is to be
88	128	he that is appointed to be P., shall
	135	they shall salute the P. or teacher
	140	to be administered by the P.
101	88	let them importune at feet of P.
	89	and if the P. heed them not then
102	8	filled by nominations of the P.
	9	P. of the church, who is also P. of council
	19	the P. shall give a decision according
	20	discover an error in decision of P.
	23	the P. may inquire and obtain
	33	resolved, that P. shall have power
107	65	shall be called P. of High Priesthood
	76	where a P. of the High Priesthood is
	82	inasmuch as a P. shall transgress
	85	duty of the P. over office of deacon
	86	duty of P. over office of teachers
	87	duty of P. over Priests
	88	this P. is to be a bishop
	89	duty of P. over the office of elders
	91	duty of P. of the High Priesthood is
	94	the seventh P. is to preside over
124	62	appoint one of them to be P. of the
	127	to be P. over the twelve traveling
	133	to be P. over a quorum of High Priests
	142	and P. of teachers, and P. of deacons, and the P. of the Stake
136	3	with a P. and his two counselors

PRESIDENT-ELECT

124	3	proclamation made to the P.

PRESIDENTS

102	1	and one or three P. as the case
	3	were acknowledged P. by voice of
	8	filled by nomination of the P.
	10	to be assisted by two other P.
	11	the other P. have same power
	33	resolved that the P. shall have power
107	21	of necessity there are P. or
	24	equal in authority to the three P.
	29	decisions of a quorum of three P.
	93	they should have seven P. to preside
	94	the seventh of these P. shall preside
	95	these seven P. are to choose other
109	71	remember, O Lord, the P. even all P. of
124	134	who shall be appointed standing P.
	135	but rather be ordained for standing P.

Sec.	Vs.	
136	7	each company with their captains or P.
	15	and appoint P. or captains of hundreds

PRESIDING

20	66	the P. elders may have privilege
	67	every P. elder is to be ordained
88	140	to be administered by P. elder
106	1	should be ordained a P. High Priest
107	21	of necessity there are P: offices
	22	three P. High Priests, chosen by the
	33	Twelve are traveling P. High Council
	60	there must needs be P. elders to
	66	in other words, the P. High Priest
124	125	to be P. elder over all my church
	140	one has the responsibility of P.; the other has no responsibility of P.

PRESS

128	1	and P. itself upon my feelings

PRETEND

5	4	you should P. to no other gift
32	4	and P. to no other revelation

PRETENDED

10	13	which you have P. to translate
	31	that you have P. to translate, but that
135	4	to the P. requirements of the law

PRETENSIONS

127	1	as their P. are founded in falsehood

PREVAIL

6	34	built upon my rock, they cannot P.
10	69	gates of hell shall not P.—17:8; 18:5; 21:6; 33:13; 98:22; 128:10
32	3	I am their advocate, and nothing shall P.
38	11	powers of darkness P. upon the earth
103	6	they shall begin to P. against mine
	7	they shall never cease to P.
	8	kingdoms of world shall P. against
109	26	power to rise up and P. over thy

PREVENT

102	15	to P. insult or injustice—17

PREVIOUS

20	68	P. to partaking of the sacrament
107	42	three years P. to his (Adam's) death
	53	three years P. to death of Adam, he
128	7	which I wrote to you P. to my
130	12	bloodshed, P. to coming of Son of Man

	16 the Millennium or some P. appearing
135	4 three days P. to his assassination

PREVIOUSLY

92	1 agreeable to commandment P. given
105	30 which they have P. purchased with
107	24 to the presidents P. mentioned

PREY

133	28 their enemies shall become a P. unto

PRICE

124	121 as pertaining to the P. thereof

PRICKS

121	38 left to himself to kick against the P.

PRIDE

23	1 beware of P. lest thou shouldst
25	14 continue in meekness and beware of P.
38	39 beware of P. lest ye become as Nephites
39	9 rejected me many times because of P.
56	8 must repent of his P. and of his
88	121 cease from all your P. and
90	17 in all your high-mindness and P.
98	20 they do not forsake the P. of their
121	37 to cover our sins or to gratify our P.

PRIEST

20	52 the P. is to assist the elder
	56 in the absence of the elder or P.
	60 every elder, P., teacher, or deacon
	64 each P. who is ordained by a P.
	76 the elder or P. shall administer it
	82 or send by the hand of some P.
	84 certificate may be signed by any P.; if personally acquainted with the P.
38	40 commandment that every P., and
52	38 Carter be ordained a P. and James be ordained a P.
85	12 as unto the children of the P.
107	10 in office of a P. (of Levitical order)
	61 over those of the office of a P.
	63 from teacher to P. and from P. to See *High Priest*.

PRIESTCRAFTS

33	4 they err, because of P., all having

PRIESTHOOD

2	1 I will reveal unto you the P., by
13	1 I confer the P. of Aaron, which
27	8 to ordain you unto this first P.
68	2 those who were ordained unto this P.

Sec.	Vs.
	15 First Presidency of the Melchizedek P.—19
	17 the right of presidency over this P.
	18 to hold the keys of this P. except he—107:16
	19 High Priest of the Melchizedek P.
	20 not authorized to officiate in their P.
	21 right of P. descending from father
84	14 Abraham received the P. from
	16 to Abel who received the P. by
	17 which P. continueth in the church
	18 Lord confirmed a P. upon Aaron; which P. continueth; with the P. after holiest
	19 this greater P. administereth
	21 without ordinances and authority of P.
	26 lesser P. continued, which P. holdeth
	30 belonging to lesser P., which P. was
	35 all they who receive this P.—40
	39 covenant which belongeth to the P.
	42 all those who come not to this P.
107	those ordained to the lesser P.
85	11 as well as the lesser P.
86	8 with whom the P. hath continued
	10 your life and the P. hath remained
	11 through this P., a savior unto my people
94	6 according to the order of the P.
107	1 including the Levitical P.
	2 the first is called Melchizedek P.
	4 called that P. the Melchizedek P.
	5 other offices are appendages to this P.
	6 one is the Melchizedek P., the other Aaronic P.
	7 an elder comes under P. of Melchizedek
	8 Melchizedek P. holds right of presidency
	10 after order of Melchizedek P.
	13 second P. is called P. of Aaron
	14 why it is called lesser P.; it is an appendage to the greater P.
	15 bishopric is the presidency of this P.
	17 High Priest of Melchizedek P. has; set apart by presidency of Melchizedek P.
	18 power of higher P. is to hold
	20 power of the lesser P. is to hold
	22 of the Melchizedek P., three presiding
	40 the order of this P. was confirmed
	65 to preside over the P.
	70 he cannot hold keys of that P.
	76 legal right to presidency of this P.
	87 duty of president over P. of Aaron
	88 this is one of the duties of this P.

Sec.	Vs.	
112	30	unto you is power of this P. given
113	6	unto whom rightly belongs the P.
	8	who should hold Power of P. to bring; to put on the authority of the P.
119	2	for foundation of Zion and for the P.
121	21	shall not have the right to the P.
	36	rights of the P. are inseparably
	37	amen to the P. of that man
	41	to be maintained by virtue of the P.
	45	the doctrine of the P. shall distil
122	9	and the P. shall remain with thee
124	28	taken away, even fulness of the P.
	42	pertaining to this house and P. thereof
	91	Hyrum may take the office of P. and
	95	and P. and gifts of the P.
	123	officers belonging to my P.; even the P. which is
	130	his P. no man taketh from him
	132	no man taketh his P., but another may be appointed to same P.
	137	which P. is to preside over the
127	8	restore many things pertaining to P.
128	8	consists in the power of the P.
	9	has given a dispensation of the P.
	17	eye fixed on restoration of the P.
	21	declaring the power of their P.
131	2	man must enter into this order of P.
132	7	but one on whom keys of this P. are
	19	appointed this power and keys of P.
	45	upon you the keys of this P.
	58	as touching the law of the P.—61
	59	I have endowed him with power of this P.
	64	and teaches unto her law of my P. See *High Priesthood, Holy Priesthood*

PRIESTHOODS

84	33	faithful to the obtaining these two P.
107	1	there are in the church two P.
	21	the several offices in these two P.

PRIESTS

18	32	to ordain P. and teachers
20	38	duty of the elders, P., teachers
	39	and to ordain other elders, P.
	48	he may also ordain other P.
	68	the P. are to have a sufficient time
42	12	the P. shall teach principles of my
	70	the P. shall have their stewardships
76	56	they are they who are P. and kings
	57	and are P. of the Most High
84	111	should travel, and also the lesser P.

Sec.	Vs.	
102	5	four P. and thirteen Elders
107	61	and also P. to preside over those
	87	to preside over forty-eight P.
124	142	Rolfe and his counselors for P. See *High Priests.*

PRIEST'S

20	46	the P. duty is to preach, teach

PRINCE

27	11	the father of all, the P. of all
78	16	who hath appointed Michael your P.
107	54	and called him Michael, the P., the
	55	thou art a P. over them forever
127	11	the P. of this world cometh but he

PRINCES

109	55	Remember the kings, the P., the nobles

PRINCIPALITIES

121	29	all thrones, dominions, P. and powers
128	23	eternal life; kingdoms, P. and powers
132	13	ordained of men, by thrones, P.
	19	and shall inherit thrones, P. and

PRINCIPLE

88	78	instructed in P., in doctrine, in
89	3	given for a P. with promise, adapted
97	14	in theory, in P. and in doctrine
98	5	supporting that P. of freedom
101	78	that every man may act in doctrine and P.
102	23	cases of difficulty respecting P.
128	7	the P. agreeing precisely with
	12	that one P. might accord with the other
130	18	whatever P. of intelligence we attain
132	1	as touching the P. and doctrine of

PRINCIPLES

42	12	shall teach the P. of my gospel
101	77	according to just and holy P.
105	5	unless by the P. of the celestial
109	54	may those P. which were so honorably
121	36	handled only upon P. of righteousness
128	15	these are P. in relation to the dead

PRINT

104	58	organize yourselves to P. my words

PRINTER

19	35	pay debt contracted with the P.
57	11	be established as a P. to the church

PRINTING

19	26	impart it freely to P. of the Book

Sec.	Vs.	
55	4	to do the work of P., and selecting
58	37	and also for the house of P.
84	104	the revelations and the P. thereof
94	10	the P. of the translation of my
	12	for the work of the P., in all things
104	28	which is to be for the P. office
	29	let my servants have the P. office
	63	for the purpose of P. these sacred
88	99	who have received their part in that P.

PRINTS
6	37	the P. of the nails in my hands and

PRISON
76	73	who are the spirits of men kept in P.
88	99	who have received their part in that P.
122	6	and thou be dragged to P.
128	22	to redeem them out of their P.

PRISONERS
128	22	for the P. shall go free

PRIVATE
19	28	pray in public as well as in P.—81:3
71	7	to meet you in public and P.
134	4	dictate forms for public or P. devotion

PRIVILEGE
9	5	I have taken away this P. from you
20	66	may have the P. of ordaining
51	15	grant this people P. of organizing
67	10	it is your P. and a promise
76	117	this P. of seeing and knowing for
88	122	every man may have an equal P.
102	10	it is his P. to be assisted by two
	18	accused shall have P. of speaking
104	84	from bondage, it is your P.
	86	I give unto you this P., this once
107	19	to have the P. of receiving the
134	7	to deprive citizens of this P.

PRIVILEGED
72	24	they who are P. to go up unto Zion

PRIVILEGES
3	14	is reason that thou hast lost thy P.
58	55	let P. of the lands be made known
98	5	in maintaining rights and P.
134	9	another proscribed in its spiritual P.

PROBABLY
130	13	may P. arise through slave question

PROBATION
29	43	appoint unto man the days of his P.

PROCEED
101	95	that I may P. to bring to pass my act
104	86	if you P. to do the things which I

PROCEEDED
102	1	P. to organize the High Council
	34	then P. to cast lots, or ballot

PROCEEDETH
64	33	out of small things P. that which
84	44	shall live by every word that P. forth—98:11
88	12	which light P. *forth* from presence

PROCEEDINGS
102	26	transmit a copy of their P.
128	3	be precise in taking the whole P.

PROCESS
38	13	even your destruction in P. of time

PROCLAIM
1	18	they should P. these things unto
30	9	P. my gospel as with the voice of a—124:88
50	32	you shall P. against that spirit with
66	5	P. my gospel from land to land
68	1	P. everlasting gospel by the spirit
71	2	P. unto the world in the regions
75	2	go forth to P. my gospel and to prune
	9	P. the things which I have commanded—13, 15
	24	sent unto the world to P. the Gospel
84	86	that goeth forth to P. the gospel
103		every man who goes forth to P. mine
93	51	P. the acceptable year of the Lord
98	16	renounce war and P. peace
	34	if any nation should P. war against
99	1	to go from city to city to P. mine
109	38	that when they go out and P. thy word
112	19	in whatsoever place ye shall P. my

PROCLAIMED
1	23	that fulness of my gospel might be P.
60	14	after thou hast P. my word, thou
66	5	those regions where it has not been P.
109	29	when the everlasting Gospel shall be P.

PROCLAIMING
60	14	speedily return P. my word
71	1	open your mouths in P. my gospel
75	4	P. the truth according to revelations

| Proclaiming | 349 | Promises |

Sec.	Vs.	
79	1	P. glad tidings of great joy
81	3	also in thy ministry in P. the
99	8	P. my gospel until thou be taken
104	26	devote his moneys for the P. of my
128	23	P. in our ears glory, and salvation

PROCLAMATION

Sec.	Vs.	
105	39	make a P. for peace unto ends of
107	35	open the door by P. of Gospel
124	2	immediately to make a solemn P.
	3	this P. shall be made to all kings
	7	call upon them with a loud P.
	12	let my servant help to write this P.
107		assist in making a solemn P. unto the

PROFESS

| 50 | 4 | in the church that P. my name |
| 56 | 1 | O ye people who P. my name |

PROFESSED

| 41 | 1 | will I curse, that have P. my name |
| 112 | 26 | you who have P. to know my name |

PROFESSING

| 46 | 27 | lest there shall be any among you P. |

PROFIT

46	1	spoken unto you for your P. and
	16	may be given to every man to P.
84	73	are given unto you for your P. and
88	33	what doth it P. a man if a gift is

PROFITED

| 46 | 12 | that all may be P. thereby |
| | 29 | in order that every member may be P. thereby |

PROLONGED

| 5 | 33 | that thy days may be P. |

PROMISE

27	7	and gave P. that he should have a son
38	18	a land of P., a land flowing with
45	14	but obtained a P. that they should
57	2	this is a land of P., the place for
62	6	that the P. might be fulfilled; I, the Lord, P. the faithful
67	10	a P. I give unto you that have been
68	5	this is the P. of the Lord
76	53	sealed by the Holy Spirit of P.—132:7, 18, 19, 26
82	10	when ye do not what I say ye have no P.
88	3	even the Holy Spirit of P.—124:124
	4	this Comforter is the P. which I give
	69	remember the great and last P.
	75	that I may fulfill this P., this great and last P.

Sec.	Vs.	
89	3	given for a principle with a P.
	21	I the Lord give unto them a P.
95	9	this is the P. of the Father
96	6	unto whom I give a P. of eternal life
	7	partaker of the blessings of the P.
98	3	therefore he giveth this P. unto you
100	8	I give unto you this P.
104	2	with P. immutable and unchangeable
	83	a P. that you shall be delivered
107	31	the P. is, if these things abound in them
	42	and received the P. of God by his
108	5	this is the P. of the Father unto
113	10	P. of the Lord is that he will speak
118	3	give unto them a P. I will provide
123	6	before we can fully claim that P.
124	38	to build a house in the land of P.
132	31	this P. is yours also, because, and the P. was made unto
	33	ye cannot receive the P. of my Father
	63	and to fulfill the P. given by my
136	2	with a covenant and a P. to keep

PROMISED

49	10	that which I have P. I have fulfilled
58	31	who am I that have P. and have not
88	3	which Comforter is the same that I P.
103	13	this is the blessing I have P.
104	7	I have P. you a crown of glory

PROMISES

1	37	P. in them shall all be fulfilled
2	2	plant in hearts of the children the P.
3	5	also the P. which were made to you
	13	has broken the most sacred P.
	19	that P. of the Lord might be fulfilled
	20	that they might know P. of the Lord
27	10	your fathers, by whom P. were made
45	16	to fulfill the P. I have made
	35	ye may know that the P. which have
58	33	then they say his P. are not fulfilled
107	40	chosen seed to whom the P. were made
109	11	to secure fulfillment of P. which
124	47	neither fulfill the P. ye expect
132	30	Abraham received P. concerning his seed
	34	this, therefore, was fulfilling the P.

Sec.	Vs.	
	37	entered into exaltation according to P.

PROMOTE
81	4	and *will* P. glory of him who is your

PROMPT
127	1	transact all business in a P. and
134	4	unless religious opinions P. them

PROMULGATE
118	4	and there P. my gospel, the fulness

PRONOUNCED
29	41	which shall be P. upon the wicked

PROPER
101	63	be guided in a right and P. way
127	1	transact all business in a P. manner
128	9	and kept a P. and faithful record

PROPERTIES
42	30	consecrate of thy P. for their support
	32	concerning consecration of the P. of
	33	if there shall be P. in hands of
82	17	are to have equal claims on the P.
85	1	and of all those who consecrate P.
104	1	concerning all the P. which belong
	19	concerning the P. of the order
	55	all these P. are mine, or else your
	56	if P. are mine, then are ye stewards
	68	by improving upon the P. which I have
	85	and pledge the P. which I have put
117	5	let the P. of Kirtland be turned out
119	5	shall be tithed of their surplus P.
124	70	require any stock, in moneys or P.

PROPERTY
19	26	thou shalt not covet thy own P.
	33	even the destruction of thyself and P.
	34	impart a portion of thy P.
38	36	to govern the affairs of the P. of
42	32	a steward over his own P.
	71	have their families supported out of P.
66	6	otherwise think not of thy P.
82	18	to become common P. of the whole church
117	4	for what is P. unto me saith the Lord
119	1	I require all their surplus P.
123	2	of all the P. and amount of damages; as well as real P.
127	1	by turning out P. or otherwise
132	57	let Joseph put his P. out of his hands
134	2	the right and control of P.

Sec.	Vs.	
	10	to try men on the right of P. or life
	11	or right of P. infringed; justified in defending themselves and P.
136	8	according to dividend of their P.
	10	use influence and P. to remove this

PROPHECIES
1	37	P. and promises shall all be fulfilled
52	36	that the P. may be fulfilled

PROPHECY
11	25	deny not the spirit of P.
20	35	nor diminishing from the P. of his
131	5	the more sure word of P. means; by revelation and Spirit of P.

PROPHESY
7	3	thou shalt P. before nations, kindreds and
34	10	therefore P. and it shall be given
35	23	it shall be given him to P.
42	16	ye shall speak and P. as seemeth me
45	15	I will speak unto you and P. as unto
46	22	and to others it is given to P.
77	15	two prophets are to P. to the Jews
130	12	I P. in the name of the Lord God

PROPHET
2	1	by the hand of Elijah the P.
21	1	thou shalt be called a seer, a P.
29	21	as spoken by mouth of Ezekiel the P.
107	92	to be a seer, a revelator, a P.
110	13	Elijah, the P., stood before us
116	1	as spoken of by Daniel, the P.
124	94	that he may be a P., a seer, a revelator—125
127	12	your servant, P., seer and
128	17	I will send you Elijah, the P., before
133	63	that which was written by the P. Moses
	64	also that written by the P. Malachi
135	1	martyrdom of Joseph Smith the P., and
	3	Joseph Smith, the P. and Seer

PROPHETS
1	14	neither give heed to words of the P.
	18	which was written by the P.—66:2
10	46	which my holy P. desired in their
17	2	that faith which was had by P. of old
20	26	who believed in words of the holy P.
27	6	spoken by the mouth of the holy P.—84:2; 86:10; 109:23, 41, 45

Sec.	Vs.	
35	23	and call on the holy P. to prove his
42	39	which I spake by mouths of my P.
52	9	which the P. and apostles have written
	36	declaring none other things than the P.
58	8	the mouths of the P. shall not fail
	18	which are given by P. of God
59	22	this is according to law and the P.
64	39	they who are not apostles and P. shall
76	101	received not the Gospel, neither the P.
77	15	they are two P. to be raised up
88	127	presidency of the school of the P.
	136	salutation in school of the P.
	137	all your doings in school of the P.
90	7	the keys of the school of the P.
	13	finished translation of the P.
95	10	contention arose in school of the P.
98	17	hearts of the Jews to the P. and the P. to the Jews
	32	and all mine ancient P. and apostles
101	19	that the P. might be fulfilled
127	4	so persecuted they the P. before you
128	17	give you a quotation from one of the P.
	20	declaring fulfillment of the P.
132	39	given by Nathan and others of the P.
133	26	their P. shall hear his voice
	54	Enoch and the P. before him
136	36	for they killed the P. and them

PROPHET'S

| 130 | 4 | is not P. time, man's time, according to |

PROPORTION

124	68	in P. to amount of stock he pays
	122	bear his P. of their wages, if it
136	8	let each company bear an equal P.

PROPOSALS

| 105 | 40 | and make P. for peace unto those who |

PROPRIA PERSONA

| 128 | 8 | attended ordinances in their own P. |

PROPRIETY

| 123 | 1 | we suggest the P. of all the saints |

PROSCRIBE

| 134 | 7 | or P. them in their opinions, so long |

PROSCRIBED

| 134 | 9 | and another P. in its spiritual |

Sec.	Vs.	
		PROSECUTIONS
127	1	in getting up their P. against me
		PROSPECTS
121	11	and their P. shall melt away
		PROSPER
9	13	do this thing and thou shalt P.
49	4	otherwise he shall not P.
71	9	no weapon against you shall P.—109:25
97	18	if Zion do these things she shall P.
		PROTECT
134	11	where such laws exist as *will* P.
		PROTECTED
134	5	while P. in their inherent rights; unbecoming every citizen while thus P.
		PROTECTION
101	77	should be maintained for rights and P.
134	2	of property, and P. of life
	6	for the P. of the innocent
	7	are bound to enact laws for the P. of
		PROUD
29	9	all the P. and they that do wickedly—64:24; 133:64
42	40	thou shalt not be P. in thy heart
84	112	by humbling the rich and the P.
		PROVE
35	23	call on holy prophets to P. his words
68	21	if at any time they can P. their lineage
84	79	I send you out to P. the world
98	12	I will try you and P. you herewith
	14	that I *will* P. you in all things
121	12	that he may P. them also and take them
124	55	that you may P. yourselves unto me
	113	when he shall P. himself faithful
132	51	I did it to P. you all as I did
		PROVED
42	79	and it shall be P. according to laws
57	13	as it shall be P. by the spirit
64	39	liars and hypocrites shall be P. by
135	7	as they had often been P. before
		PROVIDE
5	34	I *will* P. means whereby thou mayest
45	13	P. for him food and raiment
51	8	take the money to P. food and raiment

Sec.	Vs.		Sec.	Vs.	
	16	until I shall P. for them otherwise			**PUBLIC**
57	10	and thus P. for my saints	19	28	in P. as well as in private
64	30	he hath set you to P. for his saints	42	35	for the P. benefit of the church
75	28	who is obliged to P. for his own family, let him P.	46	3	cast out any one from your P. meetings
104	15	it is my purpose to P. for my saints	71	7	call on them to meet you both in P. and
	16	have decreed to P. for my saints	81	3	in prayer, in P. and in private
118	3	I *will* P. for their families	134	4	nor dictate forms for P. devotion
136	5	let each company P. for themselves		5	calculated to secure P. interest
		PROVIDED		8	and for the P. peace and tranquility
10	4	than you have strength or means P.			**PUBLICATIONS**
68	19	P. he is called and set apart— 107:17	123	4	to gather up the libelous P. afloat
83	6	widows and orphans shall be P. for			**PUBLISH**
90	19	let there be a place P. as soon	1	6	which I have given to P. unto you
	26	that those things that are P. for you	10	32	they *will* P. this and Satan will harden
99	6	until your children are P. for		42	you shall P. it as the record of Nephi
134	10	P. such dealings be for fellowship	19	29	P. it upon the mountains and upon
		PROVIDENCE	118	2	in land of Zion to P. my words
78	14	that through my P. the church may	123	6	that we may not only P. to the world
135	2	the latter, through P. of God escaped	124	89	and P. new translation of my word
		PROVING			**PUBLISHED**
20	11	P. to the world that Holy Scriptures	72	21	that the revelations may be P.
		PROVISIONS	123	5	all the libelous histories that are P.
136	5	with all the teams, wagons and P.			**PUBLISHING**
		PROVOKE	112	6	in P. my name among the children of
60	15	not in their presence lest thou P. them	135	3	been the means of P. it on two continents
		PROWL			**PULPIT**
122	6	and thine enemies P. around thee	110	2	standing on the breastwork of the P.
		PRUDENCE			**PULSIPHER, ZERA**
89	11	these to be used with P. and	124	138	I give unto you P., and, to preside
		PRUDENT			**PUNISH**
76	9	understanding of the P. shall come to	134	4	should P. guilt but never suppress
128	18	kept hid from the wise and P.			**PUNISHED**
		PRUNE	134	5	and should be P. accordingly
24	19	thou art called to P. my vineyard		8	P. according to naure of offense; P. according to their criminality
75	2	proclaim my gospel and P. my vineyard			**PUNISHMENT**
95	4	prepare mine apostles to P. my	19	10	P. from my hand is endless P.
		PRUNED		11	eternal P. is God's P.
39	17	that it may be P. for the last time		12	endless P. is God's P.
		PRUNING	76	44	go away into everlasting P., which is endless P., which is eternal P.
24	19	prune my vineyard with a mighty P.	134	6	and the P. of the guilty
				8	offenders against good laws to P.
				10	neither to inflict any physical P.

Sec.	Vs.	
		PUNISHMENTS
19	20	lest you suffer these P. of which I
		PUNY
121	33	as well might man stretch forth his P.
		PURCHASE
27	3	shall not P. wine, neither strong
45	65	that ye may P. an inheritance
48	4	to P. land for an inheritance—58:51
	6	P. the lands and make a commencement
58	49	to receive moneys to P. lands in Zion
	52	to P. this whole region of country
63	27	P. lands that you may have advantage
	29	not obtained but by P. or by blood
	30	if by P., behold you are blessed
101	70	P. all the lands which can be purchased
	73	and send them to P. these lands
103	23	P. lands even as I have commanded
		PURCHASED
57	4	land should be P. by the saints
58	37	should be lands P. in Independence
101	70	purchase all the land which can be P.
	71	which can be P. in Jackson County
105	28	lands in Jackson Co., that can be P.
	29	these lands should be P., and after they are P.
	30	after lands are P. I will hold the; which they have previously P.
		PURCHASING
42	35	and for the purpose of P. lands
105	28	concerning the P. of all lands in
		PURE
20	6	whose garments were P. and white
35	21	shall be purified even as I am P.
41	11	because his heart is P. before me
	12	and they are P. before me
43	14	reserve unto myself a P. people
56	18	blessed are the poor who are P. in heart
84	92	cleanse your feet with P. water
89	6	this should be P. wine of grape
97	9	in a goodly land, by a P. stream
	16	and all the P. in heart shall see God
	21	this is Zion, the P. in heart

Sec.	Vs.	
100	16	will raise up unto myself a P. people
101	18	they that remain and are P. in heart
109	76	that our garments may be P.
110	2	paved work of P. gold in color like
	3	his head was white like the P. snow
121	2	and thine eye, yes thy P. eye, behold
	42	by kindness and P. knowledge
122	2	while the P. in heart and the wise
123	11	that we owe to all the P. in heart
124	54	your brethren who have been P. in heart
131	7	spirit is matter but is more fine or P.
132	52	and who are virtuous and P. before me; who are not P. and have said they were P.
136	11	if ye do this with a P. heart
	37	marvel not at these things for ye are not P.
		PURER
131	7	and can only be discerned by P. eyes
		PURGE
43	11	P. ye out iniquity among you
128	24	and P. them as gold and silver
		PURIFIED
35	21	they shall be P. even as I am pure
38	8	he that is not P. shall not abide
50	28	except he be P. and cleansed from
	29	if ye are P. and cleansed from all
131	8	when our bodies are P. we shall see
		PURIFIER
128	24	he shall sit as a refiner and P. of
		PURIFY
76	116	who love him and P. themselves
88	74	P. your hearts and cleanse your
112	28	but P. your hearts before
128	24	and he shall P. the sons of Levi
135	6	to P. the vineyard of corruption
		PURPOSE
3	19	for this very P. are these plates
5	4	until my P. is fulfilled in this
	9	entrusted unto you for a wise P.
17	1	which if you do with full P. of heart
18	8	called him unto my own P. which P. is known in me
	27	my name with full P. of heart—28

Sec.	Vs.	
42	31	appointed and set apart for that P.
	35	for the P. of purchasing lands
61	35	and this for a wise P. in me
96	4	for the P. of bringing forth my word
	5	for the P. of subduing hearts of the
101	33	and the P. and the end thereof
	80	for this P. have I established constitution; wise men raised up unto this very P.
102	2	for the P. of settling important
	8	convened for that P. to act
104	15	it is my P. to provide for my saints
	58	for this P. I have commanded you
	59	for the P. of building up my church
	63	for the P. of printing these sacred
124	62	for the P. of building that house
	70	portion of that stock to any other P.
	134	for the P. of qualifying those
128	18	sufficiently plain to suit my P.
134	6	for P. of regulating our interest

PURPOSES

Sec.	Vs.	
3	1	the P. of God cannot be frustrated
17	4	may bring about my righteous P.—9
42	71	for good of poor and for other P.
76	3	his P. fail not, neither are there
104	65	treasury for sacred and holy P.
	68	reserved unto myself for holy P.

PURSE

Sec.	Vs.	
24	18	thou shalt take no P. nor scrip
84	78	I suffered them not to have P. or
	86	no man from this hour take P. or scrip

PURSUE

Sec.	Vs.	
127	1	they P. me without a cause, and have not

PURSUED

Sec.	Vs.	
128	1	since I have been P. by my enemies

PURSUIT

Sec.	Vs.	
127	1	enemies were again in P. of me

PUSH

Sec.	Vs.	
58	45	they shall P. the people together
66	11	and shall P. many people to Zion

PUT

Sec.	Vs.	
10	10	Satan has P. it into their hearts—13, 15
11	12	P. your trust in that spirit which

Sec.	Vs.	
42	74	having P. away their companions
43	15	the things which I have P. into your
49	6	to P. all enemies under his feet
58	51	to be P. into the hands of the bishop
72	13	that which the Lord shall P. into his
76	35	and P. him to an open shame
	42	whom the Father had P. into his power
77	12	except that which he hath not P. into his
82	14	Zion must P. on her beautiful garments
84	119	have P. forth my hand to exert the powers
100	5	speak the thoughts I shall P. into
104	85	pledge properties I have P. into your
109	23	that thou hast P. forth thy hand to
	26	upon whom thy name shall be P. in
	38	P. upon thy servants the testimony
	47	yoke of affliction that has been P.
	79	this church, to P. upon it thy name
113	7	P. on thy strength, O Zion
	8	to P. on her strength is to P. on authority of
119	1	surplus property to be P. into hands
123	1	abuses P. upon them by the people of
124	57	this anointing have I P. upon his head; also be P. upon head of his posterity
	74	let him P. stock into that house—77, 78
	87	let my servant P. his trust in me
	95	that once were P. upon him who was my
127	9	that they may be P. in the archives of
132	19	whatsoever my servant hath P. upon them
	57	let my servant P. his property out of his
133	58	two should P. their thousands to flight
134	10	or to P. them in jeopardy of life or

PUTTETH

Sec.	Vs.	
63	28	for Satan P. it into their hearts to
85	8	P. forth his hand to steady the ark

PUTTING

Sec.	Vs.	
136	7	to prepare for P. in spring crops

Q

Sec.	Vs.	
		QUAKE
29	13	and all the earth shall Q.
85	6	it maketh my bones to Q.
		QUALIFIED
128	3	who is well Q. for taking minutes
		QUALIFY
4	5	glory of God, Q. him for the work
		QUALIFYING
124	134	for purpose of Q. those who shall be
		QUARTERS
33	6	from the four Q. of the earth—45:46; 135:3
		QUENCH
27	17	able to Q. all the fiery darts of the
		QUENCHED
76	44	worm dieth not, and fire is not Q.
		QUESTION
50	13	I asketh you this Q., unto what were
	16	ye shall answer this Q. yourselves
102	32	the latter can only be called in Q.
130	4	in answer to the Q., "is not the
	13	probably arise through the slave Q.
		QUESTIONS
113	7	Q., by Elias Higbee, as follows:
		QUICK
6	2	my word which is Q. and powerful—11:2; 12:2; 14:2; 27:1; 33:1
		QUICKENED
67	11	except Q. by the spirit of God
88	26	shall be Q. again, and abide power by which it is Q.
	28	glories by which your bodies are Q.
	29	ye who are Q. by a portion of celestial
	30	who are Q. by portion of terrestial
	31	who are Q. by portion of telestial
	32	they who remain shall also be Q.

Sec.	Vs.	
	49	being Q. in him and by him
	96	who are alive shall be Q.
		QUICKENETH
33	16	the power of my spirit Q. all things
88	11	light that Q. your understanding
	17	through him that Q. all things
		QUICKLY
33	18	I come Q.—34:12; 35:27; 39:24; 41:4; 49:28; 54:10; 68:35; 88:126; 99:5; 112:34
51	20	who cometh Q. in an hour you think not
87	8	day of the Lord cometh Q.
		QUORUM
107	22	form a Q. of the Presidency of the
	24	form a Q. equal in authority—26, 36, 37
	27	every member in each Q. must be agreed
	28	a majority may form a Q.
	29	a Q. of three presidents were anciently
	36	equal to the Q. of the presidency
124	62	to be a president over their Q.
	117	the Q. of the Nauvoo House—119, 121
	126	these may constitute a Q. and First Presidency
	133	be president over Q. of high priests
	136	preside over Q. of high priests
	137	over Q. of elders, which Q. is
	138	to preside over Q. of seventies
	139	which Q. is instituted for
	140	difference between this Q. and Q. of elders
		QUORUMS
107	27	every decision by these Q. must be
	30	decisions of these Q. are to be made
	32	in case any decision of these Q is; assembly of several Q.
		QUOTATION
128	7	you will discover from this Q.
	16	I will give you another Q.
	17	in connection with this Q. I give you a Q.

R

Sec.	Vs.	
		RAGE
122	1	and hell shall R. against thee
		RAGS
38	26	to the other, be thou clothed in R.
		RAILING
50	33	not with R. accusation, that ye be
		RAIMENT
24	18	what thou needest for food and R.
43	13	provide for him food and R.
49	19	for use of man for food and for R.
51	8	take the money to provide food and R.
59	17	whether for food or for R., or for
	19	for food and for R., for taste and
70	16	for food and for R.; for an inheritance
133	51	and stained all my R.
		RAINS
90	5	and the R. descend and beat upon
		RAISE
88	72	I *will* R. up elders and send unto
100	16	*will* R. *up* unto myself a pure people
103	16	I *will* R. *up* unto my people a man
124	100	if I will that he shall R. the dead
		RAISED
29	43	that he might be R. in immortality
53	1	church I have R. *up* in these last days
77	15	they are two prophets to be R. *up*
84	27	until John, whom God R. *up*
101	80	wise men whom I R. *up* for this very
124	1	for unto this end have I R. you *up*
		RAISING
136	9	prepare fields for R. grain for those
		RAPHAEL
128	21	the voice of Gabriel and R. and of
		RASCALITY
123	5	whole concatenation of diabolical R.
		RAYS
121	11	before burning R. of rising sun

Sec.	Vs.	
		REACH
76	9	and their understanding R. to heaven
		READ
10	11	they R. contrary from that you translated
18	35	by my power you can R. them one to
19	39	canst thou R. this without rejoicing
97	27	let it be R. this once to her ears
135	4	he R. the following paragraph
		READER
135	6	the R. in every nation will be reminded
		READETH
57	9	whoso R. let him understand—71:5; 91:4
		READY
33	17	be R. at coming of the Bridegroom
35	12	those R. to receive the fulness of
50	46	watch therefore, that ye may be R.
65	3	make R. for the Bridegroom
86	5	who are R. to be sent forth to reap down
88	94	therefore she is R. to be burned
101	54	then ye could have made R. and kept
135	4	had made R. to go to the slaughter
136	16	may be R. to go to a land of peace
		REAL
123	2	personal injuries as well as R. property
124	70	wherein they receive the R. value
		REALIZE
103	5	a decree which my people shall R.
		REAP
6	3	therefore whoso desireth to R., let him R. while day lasts—11:3; 11:3; 12:3, 4; 14:3, 4
	4	thrust in his sickle and R.—11:3; 12:3, 4; 14:3, 4
	33	whatsoever ye sow that shall ye R.; if ye sow good ye shall R. good
11	27	who have thrust in their sickle to R.
31	4	to R. in the field which is white
33	7	thrust in your sickles and R. with all
38	12	angels are waiting to R. *down* the

Sec.	Vs.		Sec.	Vs.	
86	5	ready to be sent forth to R. *down*		4	to be answered on the heads of the R.
109	76	R. eternal joy for all our sufferings	63	6	let the R. fear and tremble
		REARED	64	35	and the R. shall be cut off
84	4	temple shall be R. in this generation		36	the R. are not of the blood of Ephraim
		REARWARD			**REBUKE**
49	27	will go before you and be your R.	112	9	thy voice shall be a R. to the; at thy R. let tongue of
		REASON	133	68	at my R. I dry up the sea
3	14	this is R. thou hast lost thy privileges			**REBUKED**
45	10	I *will* R. as with men in days of old—61:13	42	91	he or she shall be R. openly
				92	he or she shall be R. in secret
	15	hearken and I *will* R. with you	93	47	you must stand R. before the Lord
49	4	ordained, that he may R. with them	95	2	wherefore you must be chastened and R.
50	10	let us R. together that ye may			
	11	let us R. even as a man reasoneth			**RECEIVE**
	12	I *will* R. that you may understand	1	28	and R. knowledge from time to time
67	3	this is the R. ye did not receive	4	7	ask and ye shall R.—6:5; 11:5; 12:5; 14:5; 49:26; 66:9; 75:27; 88:63; 103:31, 35
		REASONETH			
50	11	reason even as a man R. one with			
	12	when a man R. he is understood. because he R. as a man	5	14	to R. this testimony
				32	and R. a witness from my hand
		REASONING	6	19	and also R. admonition of him
45	10	I will show you my strong R.	8	1	so surely shall you R. a knowledge
66	7	in their synagogues, R. with the people		11	R. knowledge from those ancient records
68	1	R. and expounding all scriptures	11	14	believing in me that you shall R.—18:18
133	57	R. in plainness and simplicity		30	as many as R. me *will* I give
		REASONS	14	8	you shall R. the Holy Ghost—25:8
71	8	bring forth their strong R. against	19	22	cannot bear meat, but milk they must R.
		REBEL			
112	15	R. not against my servant Joseph		33	misery thou shalt R. if thou slight
		REBELLED	20	14	those who R. it in faith, shall R. a crown
29	36	for he R. against me, saying, give me		63	the elders are to R. their licenses
76	25	who R. against the Only Begotten		64	or he may R. it from a conference
	28	even the devil who R. against God	21	5	his word ye shall R. as if from mine
		REBELLION	23	7	that you may R. reward of the laborer
84	76	your brethren in Zion for their R.	24	4	if they R. thee not I will send upon
87	1	beginning at R. of South Carolina		15	and they R. you not in my name
134	5	sedition and R. are unbecoming	25	1	those who R. my gospel are sons and
		REBELLIONS			
56	6	of my people in Thompson and their R.		2	thou shalt R. an inheritance in
				15	a crown of righteousness thou shalt R.
109	66	lay down their weapons and cease their R.	26	2	for all things you shall R. by faith
		REBELLIOUS	28	2	one shall be appointed to R. commandments
1	3	the R. shall be pierced with much		8	inasmuch as they R. thy teachings
	8	to seal the unbelieving and R.	29	3	therefore ye R. these things
56	1	mine anger is kindled against the R.—63:2		6	whatsoever ye shall ask in faith ye shall R.

Sec.	Vs.		Sec.	Vs.	
	13	to R. a crown of righteousness		57	12 if the world R. his writings
	45	R. their wages of whom they list to obey		58	5 lay it to heart and R. that which
31	7	and they *will* R. you		32	I revoke and they R. not the blessing
	10	unto the world for they *will* not R. you		36	to this land to R. an inheritance
35	6	and they shall R. the Holy Ghost—39:23		38	that he may R. his inheritance
	9	cause the blind to R. their sight		40	and R. his inheritance in the land
	12	to R. the fulness of my gospel		44	for them to R. their inheritance
36	2	and you shall R. my spirit—39:10		49	to R. moneys to purchase lands in Zion
39	4	give unto as many as *will* R. me		53	lest they R. none inheritance save by
	18	as they do repent and R. fulness of		56	knowledge which they R. from time to
41	3	by faith ye shall R. my law		59	2 shall R. a crown in the mansions
42	3	even so ye shall R.			3 they shall R. for their reward
	8	as you find them that *will* R. you			23 shall R. his reward, even peace in
	14	if ye R. not the spirit ye shall not teach		60	15 against those who R. thee not
	33	and R. according to his wants		62	7 he shall R. this blessing, if he R. it
	37	shall not R. again that which he has		63	20 shall R. an inheritance on the earth
	54	pay for that thou shalt R. of thy			31 but few shall stand to R. an inheritance
	61	thou shalt R. revelation upon			40 whom I have appointed to R.
	67	ye shall hereafter R. church covenants			48 shall R. an inheritance in this world
	72	they are to R. a just remuneration			49 shall R. an inheritance before the Lord
	73	bishop also shall R. his support			56 and if the Lord R. it not he shall
	76	that ye R. none such among you			64 ye R. the spirit through prayer
	77	they shall repent or ye shall not R.			66 may R. a more exceeding and eternal
43	2	to R. commandments and revelations		64	1 and R. my will concerning you
	3	none other appointed to R. commandments		65	5 that inhabitants thereof may R. it
	5	that ye R. not the teachings of any		67	3 ye endeavored to believe ye should R.; this is reason ye did not R.
	7	R. through him whom I have appointed		68	27 and R. the laying on of hands
45	29	but they R. it not, for they		69	4 that he R. counsel and assistance from
46	28	he that asketh in spirit shall R. in			6 place to R. and do all these things
48	6	which ye shall hereafter R.		70	7 as they R. more than is needful
49	14	whoso doeth this shall R. the gift		71	5 let him understand and R. also
50	19	doth he R. it by the spirit of truth		72	10 to R. the funds of the church in this
	31	and ye R. not that spirit, ye shall			11 who shall pay for that which they R.
	34	accounted of God worthy to R.		75	19 and they R. you, leave your blessing
	35	and which ye shall hereafter R.			20 and they R. you not, depart speedily
51	1	it must be that he R. directions how		76	52 and R. the Holy Spirit by the laying
	9	be alike among this people and R. alike			76 who R. of his glory but not of his
	11	if another church would R. money			77 who R. of the presence of the Son
53	6	the first ordinances which you shall R.			86 who R. not of his fulness in eternal
55	4	that little children may R. instruction			88 telestial R. it of the administering
56	10	otherwise he shall R. the money			111 every man shall R. according to his own
	12	that those of whom he shall R.		77	9 and if you *will* R. it, this is Elias
	13	according to that they do they shall R.		82	3 shall R. the greater condemnation
57	3	if you *will* R. wisdom, here is wisdom		84	35 they who R. this priesthood R. me
	6	to R. moneys, to be an agent			40 those who R. this priesthood R. this oath
					60 blessed are you as ye R. these things

Sec.	Vs.	
	64	shall R. the Holy Ghost
	74	that they may R. the Holy Ghost
	103	and R. money by gift they should send
	104	who R. moneys, send it to the bishop
85	1	and R. inheritances legally from the
	3	R. not their inheritance by consecration
88	1	to R. his will concerning you
	28	shall R. the same body which was a; ye shall R. your bodies
	29	shall then R. of the same, a fulness—30, 31
	32	to enjoy that they are willing to R.
	33	and he R. not the gift
	99	that they might R. the Gospel and be
	107	R. their inheritance and be made equal
	126	I come quickly and R. you unto myself
	133	in which covenant I R. into fellowship
	138	ye shall not R. any among you into
89	18	shall R. health in their navel and
90	5	all they who R. the oracles of God
	9	that they may R. the word
	14	R. revelations to unfold the mysteries
	28	should R. money to bear her expenses
	30	R. an inheritance from the hand of the
92	1	ye shall R. him into the order
93	18	if you are faithful you shall R. fulness
	19	and in due time R. of his fulness
	20	you shall R. of his fulness and be; you shall R. grace for grace
	31	and they R. not the light
	33	spirit and elements R. fulness of joy
	34	when separated man cannot R. fulness
94	13	shall Hyrum Smith R. his inheritance
	14	and Jared Carter R. an inheritance
104	68	all moneys you R. in your stewardships; as fast as you R. moneys
105	5	otherwise I cannot R. her unto myself
	33	should R. their endowment from on high
	37	follow the counsel which they R.
108	1	to R. counsel of him whom I have
	4	and R. right by ordination with the
109	15	and R. a fulness of the Holy Ghost
	39	and people of that city R. their testimony
	41	and people of that city R. not the

Sec.	Vs.	
111	11	as fast as ye are able to R. them
112	19	that they may R. my word
114	2	in their stead, and R. their bishopric
124	16	reward shall not fail if he R. counsel
	19	that I may R. him unto myself
	21	that he may R. the consecrations
	34	that you may R. honor and glory
	39	wherein you R. conversations and
	61	that he may R. also the counsel
	63	whereby they may R. stock for the
	64	they shall not R. less than fifty, and permitted to R. $15,000
	65	they shall not be permitted to R.—66, 67
	68	he shall R. stock in that house; he shall not R. any stock in that
	70	R. any stock into their hands, wherein they R. real value
	95	that he shall R. counsel from my; whereby he may ask and R.
	97	also R. the keys by which he may R. blessings; he shall R. of my spirit
	126	to R. oracles for the whole church
	141	if he *will* R. it, to preside over
130	23	a man may R. the Holy Ghost, and it
132	3	prepare thy heart to R. and obey
	10	*will* I R. at your hands that which I
	22	because ye R. me not in the world
	23	but if ye R. me in the world; shall R. your exaltation
	24	R. ye therefore my law
	25	because they R. me not, neither
	33	ye cannot R. the promise of my Father
	52	let mine handmaid R. all those that
	64	upon all those who R. and abide in
	65	if she R. not this law, for him to R.
136	31	may be prepared to R. the glory that

RECEIVED

1	29	having R. the record of the Nephites
	33	shall be taken the light he has R.
5	1	borne record that you have R. of me
6	14	thou hast R. instruction of my spirit
	21	and my own R. me not—10:57; 11:29; 39:3; 45:8
	24	behold, you have R. a witness; have you not R. a witness
10	52	to destroy that they have R., but
	62	shall not deny that which you have R.

Sec.	Vs.		Sec.	Vs.	
17	7.	you have R. the same power		71	who have R. the fulness of the Father
18	43	now, after you have R. this—46		74	who R. not the testimony of Jesus, but afterwards R. it
19	13	the commandments which you have R.		82	these are they who R. not the gospel
	14	it is by my power you have R. them		94	having R. of his fulness and grace
20	5	he had R. a remission of his sins		101	but R. not the Gospel
	37	that they have R. of the spirit of Christ shall be R. by baptism		102	firstborn and R. into the cloud
	68	duty after they are R. by baptism	84	6	which he R. under hand of Jethro
	71	no one can be R. into the church unless		7	Jethro R. it under hand of Caleb
27	8	first priesthood which you have R.		8	Caleb R. it under hand of Elihu
30	3	ponder upon things which you have R.		12	Esaias R. it under hand of God
35	5	but they R. not the Holy Ghost		14	which Abraham R. the priesthood, who R. it through lineage
39	4	to as many as R. me gave I power		16	who R. priesthood by commandment
40	2	he R. the word with gladness, but		41	breaketh this covenant after he R. it
42	32	after he has R. these testimonies; a steward over property R.		42	this priesthood which ye have R.
	57	not teach until you have R. them in full		54	treated lightly the things you R.
	59	take the things which thou hast R.		75	gospel is unto all who have not R. it
	66	observe the laws ye have R.	88	32	to enjoy that they might have R.
43	2	ye have R. a commandment for a law		58	they all R. the light of his countenance
	7	those revelations which you have R.		71	which they have R. for little season
	9	sanctified by that which ye have R.		99	who have R. their part in that prison
	10	added to kingdom which ye have R.; shall be taken that ye have R.		139	R. by ordinance of washing of feet
	14	remain unto them that have R. him	93	5	I was in the world and R. of my Father
44	6	according to my law which ye have R.		12	R. not the fulness at first, but R. grace for grace
45	8	but unto as many as R. me gave I		13	R. not of fulness at first, but continued until he R.
	12	who were R. unto myself		14	because he R. not of the fulness at first
	57	that are wise and have R. the truth		16	he R. a fulness of the glory
48	6	according to laws ye have R.		17	he R. all power both in heaven and
49	1	preach my gospel which ye have R., as ye have R. it		26	he R. a fulness of truth, all truth
	4	not according to that he has R. of them	107	42	and R. promise of God by his father
50	15	then R. ye spirits which ye could not understand and R. them to be of God		45	87 years old when he R. his ordination
	35	giving heed to things you have R.	112	28	unto every creature who has not R.
	43	inasmuch as ye have R. me ye are in me		31	all those who have R. a dispensation
58	23	laws which ye have R. from my hand		32	keys of dispensation ye have R.
63	21	the fulness ye have not yet R.	128	19	what do we hear in gospel we have R.
	55	he R. not counsel but grieved the	132	18	it cannot be R. there, because angels
66	1	inasmuch as ye have R. my truths		27	after ye have R. my covenant
72	17	and to be R. as a wise steward		29	Abraham R. all things whatsoever he R.,
76	20	and R. of his fulness		30	Abraham R. promises concerning his seed
	35	denied the Holy Spirit after having R.		37	Abraham R. concubines and they
	51	who R. the testimony of Jesus			
	56	who have R. of his fulness and glory			

Sec.	Vs.	
	38	David also R. many wives; and in nothing did they sin save that they R. not of me
	39	fallen from his exaltation and R. his
133	66	no man among you R. me
	71	when they were sent ye R. them not
135	1	and both R. four balls
136	41	you have R. my kingdom

RECEIVES

Sec.	Vs.	
124	67	at the time he R. stock
130	10	to each individual who R. one

RECEIVETH

Sec.	Vs.	
21	4	give unto you as he R. them
28	2	for he R. them even as Moses
39	5	that R. my gospel R. me, he that R. not my gospel R. not me
	22	he that R. these things R. me
41	5	he that R. my law and doeth it; he that saith he R. it and doeth it not
49	5	he that R. him shall be saved, he that R. him not
50	19	he that R. the word of truth
	21	he that R. word by spirit of truth, R. it as it is
	22	he that preacheth and he that R.
	24	he that R. light, and continueth, R. more light
	34	he that R. of God, let him rejoice
58	26	wherefore he R. no reward
	29	R. commandment with doubtful heart
71	6	unto him that R. shall be given more
78	19	he who R. all things with thankfulness
84	36	he that R. my servants R. me
	37	he that R. me R. my Father
	38	he that R. my Father R. my Father's
	52	whoso R. not my voice is not of me
	88	whoso R. you there will I be also
	89	whoso R. you R. me—99:2
	92	he that R. you not, go away from him
88	40	wisdom R. wisdom
91	6	whoso R. not by the spirit
93	27	no man R. a fulness unless
	28	R. truth and light until he is glorified
	32	man whose spirit R. not the light
99	3	whoso R. you as a little child, R. my kingdom
112	20	whosoever R. my word R. me, and whosoever R. me R. those
130	11	no man knoweth save he that R. it

Sec.	Vs.	
132	6	he that R. a fulness thereof
	41	if a man R. a wife in the new and

RECEIVING

Sec.	Vs.	
20	84	if the member R. the letter is
66	2	blessed are you for R. mine everlasting
85	2	apostatize after R. their inheritances
107	19	have privilege of R. the mysteries

RECEPTION

Sec.	Vs.	
53	3	and the R. of the Holy Spirit—55:1

RECKONED

Sec.	Vs.	
104	45	he shall be R. in the house of

RECKONING

Sec.	Vs.	
130	4	is not the R. of God's time, angel's time

RECLAIMED

Sec.	Vs.	
50	7	but behold, such shall be R.

RE-COMMENCE

Sec.	Vs.	
115	11	let them R. laying foundation of my

RECOMMEND

Sec.	Vs.	
52	41	take with them a R. from the church

RECOMMENDED

Sec.	Vs.	
72	19	be R. by the church, or churches
112	21	duly R. and authorized by you

RECOMPENSE

Sec.	Vs.	
1	10	Lord shall come to R. every man
56	19	his R. shall be with him
112	34	my reward is with me to R. every man
124	121	have a just R. for wages for all their
127	3	he will meet out a just R. of reward

RECONCILED

Sec.	Vs.	
42	88	if he or she confess thou shalt be R.

RECONCILIATION

Sec.	Vs.	
46	4	let him not partake until he makes R.

RECORD

Sec.	Vs.	
1	29	after having received the R. of the
	39	the spirit beareth R. and the R. is true
5	1	of which you have testified and borne R.
9	1	continue until you have finished this R.
10	42	you shall publish it as R. of Nephi

Sec.	Vs.		Sec.	Vs.	
20	9	which contains a R. of a fallen people		7	which contained the R. of their works; is the R. which is kept in heaven
	27	which beareth R. of Father and the Son—42:17		8	whatsoever you R. on earth; whatsoever you do not R. on earth
	83	be blotted out of general church R.		9	and kept a proper and faithful R.
21	1	there shall be a R. kept among you		20	witnesses to bear R. of the book
27	5	the R. of the stick of Ephraim			**RECORDED**
47	3	to keep the church R. and history	62	3	the testimony is R. in heaven for
58	7	bearing R. of the land upon which	85	12	as will be found R. in second chapter
	59	except he bear R. by the way of that	88	2	your prayers are R. in the book of
	63	bearing R. of the things revealed		3	as is R. in the testimony of John
59	24	and the spirit beareth R.	98	2	your prayers are R. with this seal
61	4	I suffered it that ye might bear R.	127	7	that it may be R. in heaven—128:7
62	5	then you may return to bear R.	128	6	as you will find R. in Revelation
67	8	if ye do not bear R. that they are true		8	whatsoever you record on earth shall be R. in heaven; whatsoever you do not record on earth shall not be R. in
68	6	you shall bear R. of me, Jesus Christ			**RECORDER**
	12	of as many as the Father shall bear R.	127	6	let there be a R. and let him be eye
71	4	bear R. and prepare the way	128	2	I wrote a few words concerning a R.; there should be a R. who should be
72	6	these things shall be had on R.		3	very difficult for one R. to be present; there can be a R. appointed in each
76	14	of whom we bear R. and the R. we bear		4	then let there be a general R., then the general church R. can
	23	and we heard the voice bearing R.			**RECORDINGS**
	25	this we saw also and bear R.	127	7	that in all your R. it may be recorded in heaven—128:7
	40	which voice out of heavens bore R.			**RECORDS**
	50	we bear R. for we saw and heard	3	19	these plates which contain these R.
85	1	to keep a history and general church R.	6	26	there are R. which contain much
93	6	John saw and bore R., John's R. is hereafter to be revealed	8	1	concerning the engravings of old R.
	7	and he bore R. saying, I saw his glory		11	receive knowledge from those ancient R.
	11	I bear R. that I beheld his glory	9	2	other R. have I that I will give
	15	and I bear R. the heavens were opened	85	4	or to be found on any of the R.
	16	I bear R. he received a fulness of	127	9	let all the R. be had in order
	18	you shall receive fulness of R. of John	128	4	to whom these other R. can be handed; verily believes the above R. to be true
	26	John bore R. of me saying		7	and refer to R. kept on the earth
100	8	in bearing R. unto all things		8	according to the R. which they have kept
109	31	innocent before thee in bearing R.		9	a power which R. and binds on earth
112	4	thou shalt bear R. of my name		14	and as are the R. on earth so also are R. in heaven
118	4	promulgate gospel and bear R. of my		24	a book containing the R. of our dead
124	96	Hyrum may bear R. of the things			
	139	to bear R. of my name in all the world			
128	2	that he might make a R. of truth			
	3	certifying in his R. that he saw			
	4	certifying that R. made is true; enter the R. on the general church books; the R. shall be just as holy as if he had seen and made a R. of			

Sec.	Vs.		Sec.	Vs.	
		RECOVER	19	1	I am He, the R. of the world
39	11	covenant sent forth to R. my people	29	1	Jesus Christ, your R., the Great I AM
66	9	lay hands upon the sick; they shall R.	31	13	Jesus Christ, your R. by the will of
			66	1	saith the Lord, your R., the Savior
		RECOVERED	78	20	saith your R., even the Son Ahman
135	2	wounded, but has since R.	80	5	your R. even Jesus Christ
		RED	93	9	the light and the R. of the world
133	48	the Lord shall be R. in his apparel			**REDEMPTION**
		RED SEA	29	42	declare unto them repentance and R.
8	3	children of Israel through the R.	35	26	your R. draweth nigh
17	1	in the wilderness on borders of the R.	45	17	how the day of R. shall come
				46	and your R. shall be perfected
		REDEEM	49	5	have sent my Son for R. of the world
77	12	and shall R. all things except that	78	12	buffetings of Satan until day of R.—82:21; 104:9; 132:26
101	56	R. my vineyard for it is mine			
	75	to R. Zion and establish her waste	88	14	through the R. which is made for you
109	51	and R. that which thou didst appoint		16	resurrection is R. of the soul
128	22	to R. them out of their prison		17	R. of the soul is through him who
133	67	my arm not shortened that I could not R.		99	then cometh the R. of those who are
		REDEEMED	101	43	my will concerning R. of Zion
29	44	cannot be R. from their spiritual fall		76	to importune for redress and R.
	46	little children are R. from foundation of	103	1	the salvation and R. of your brethren
43	29	my people shall be R. and shall reign		13	your R. and the R. of your brethren
45	54	than shall heathen nations be R.		15	R. of Zion must needs come by power
76	38	the only ones who shall not be R.		18	even so shall the R. of Zion be
	85	they who shall not be R. from the devil		29	concerning restoration and R. of Zion
84	99	the Lord hath R. his people, Israel—100	105	1	the R. of mine afflicted people
93	38	God having R. man from the fall		9	wait for a little season for R. of —13
100	13	Zion shall be R. although she is		16	gather together for R. of my people
101	80	and R. land by the shedding of blood		34	executed and fulfilled after her R.
105	2	they might have been R. even now	113	8	to bring again Zion and the R. of
109	62	that Jerusalem may begin to be R.	117	13	let him contend earnestly for the R.
	67	and be R. from oppression	124	124	ye are sealed up unto the day of R.
	70	that they may be converted and R.			**REDOUBLED**
133	52	now the year of my R. is come	127	4	let your works be R. and you shall
	53	and in his pity he R. them			**REDOUND**
136	18	Zion shall be R. in mine own due time	124	87	sickness of the land shall R. to your
		REDEEMER			**REDRESS**
8	1	who is your God and your R.—34:12	101	76	continue to importune for R.
10	70	your R., your Lord and your God—18:47; 66:13; 72:8	105	25	execute justice and R. us of our wrongs
15	1	Jesus Christ, your Lord and your R.—16:1; 18:47; 27:1; 34:1	134	11	appeal to the civil law for R.
					REEL
18	11	your R. suffered death in the flesh	45	48	earth shall tremble and R. to and fro—49:23; 88:87

Sec.	Vs.	
		REFER
128	7	and R. to the records which are kept.
		REFERENCE
113	7	what people had Isaiah R. to
	8	he had R. to those whom God should
		REFERRED
130	16	whether this coming R. to beginning
		REFINED
58	8	of wine on the lees well R.
		REFINEMENT
124	2	shall be polished with that R. which
		REFINER
128	24	he shall sit as a R. and purifier
		REFINER'S
128	24	for he is like a R. fire and like
		REFRAIN
82	2	R. from sin, lest sore judgments
		REFUGE
45	66	a city of R., a place of safety
115	6	and for a R. from the storm
124	10	and R. for those who shall be left
	36	those places I have appointed for R.
	109	he shall seek to find safety and R.
		REFUSE
34	9	the stars shall R. their shining
88	87	and shall R. to give light
132	36	Abraham, however, did not R. and it
		REGARD
101	84	though I fear not God, nor R. man
134	7	so long as a R. and reverence is shown
		REGARDED
101	82	which feared not God, neither R. man
		REGION
30	10.	and in that R. round about
42	8	ye shall build up my church in every R.
57	10	who sit in the R. and shadow of death
58	52	to purchase this whole R. of country
101	70	in the R. round about the land which
105	20	that can stay in the R. round about

Sec.	Vs.	
	24	together, as much in one R. as can be
		REGIONS
30	4	and in the R. round about—44:3; 48:3; 52:39; 57:6; 58:46; 66:5; 71:2; 73:1. 4: 100:3; 105:23; 106:1; 111:7; 115:18; 133:9
42	8	go forth into the R. westward
54		take your journey in the R. westward
77	8	to cast down to R. of darkness
133	46	yea, from the R. which are not known
		REGULAR
20	82	so that a R. list of all the names
	84	certifying that they are R. members
47	1	write and keep a R. history
		REGULARLY
20	1	it being R. organized and established
	65	where there is a R. organized branch
42	11	except he has been R. ordained by
102	6	or their R. appointed successors
	12	whenever a high council is R. organized
		REGULATE
107	33	and R. all the affairs of the same
		REGULATING
78	3	in R. and establishing the affairs of
107	34	in R. all the affairs of the same
134	6	for express purpose of R. our interests
		REGULATIONS
134	10	according to rules and R. of such
		RE-HEARING
102	20	and the case shall have a R.
	21	if after careful R. any additional
	27	they may appeal and have a R.
	33	whether such case is justly entitled to R.
		REIGN
1	36	and shall R. in their midst
10	41	till you come to the R. of King
20	24	to R. with almighty power according
29	21	for abominations shall not R.
38	12	which causeth silence to R. and
43	29	my people shall R. with me on earth
	31	Satan shall only R. for little season
49	6	and *will* R. till he descends
58	22	until he reigns whose right it is to R.
76	44	to R. with devil and his angels

Sec.	Vs.		Sec.	Vs.	
	63	to R. on earth over his people	62	3	angels look upon, and R. over you
	108	throne of his power to R. forever		4	hold a meeting and R. together
84	119	I will come and R. with my people		6	and R. together in land of Missouri
86	3	the enemy, even Satan, sitteth to R.	76	1	and R. ye inhabitants thereof
133	25	the Savior shall R. over all flesh	88	2	and the angels R. over you
		REIGNETH	90	34	your brethren begin to repent and angels R.
49	6	and now R. in the heavens, and will	97	21	let Zion R. for this is Zion, the pure; let Zion R. while all the wicked
82	5	spreadeth his dominions and darkness R.	98	1	R. and in everything give thanks
128	19	and that say unto Zion thy God R.	100	12	continue your journey, let your heart R.
		REIGNS	109	67	be redeemed from oppression and R.
58	22	until he R. whose right it is to reign	110	6	let hearts of your brethren R., let all my people R.
76	92	where God R. upon his throne forever		9	the hearts of thousands shall greatly R.
		REJECT	121	6	thy servants *will* R. in thy name
6	29	if they R. my words, blessed are ye	124	76	let his family R. and turn away their
	31	but if they R. not my words, blessed	127	3	let all the saints R. therefore
20	15	but those who R. it, it shall turn to	128	22	let your hearts R. and be exceedingly glad
40	2	fear of persecution caused him to R.	132	56	will multiply her and make her heart R.
84	114	which await them if they do R. these			**REJOICES**
	115	for if they do R. these things the hour	88	33	he R. not in that which is given, neither R. in the giver
124	8	if they R. my servants and my testimony			**REJOICETH**
132	4	for no one can R. this covenant and enter	133	44	thou shalt meet him who R.
		REJECTED			**REJOICING**
39	9	thou hast R. me many times because of	19	37	with a loud voice, with a sound of R.
99	4	whoso R. you shall be rejected of my		39	canst thou read this without R.
124	32	ye shall be R. as a church with your dead	21	8	for his days of R. are come
135	7	that cannot be R. by any court on earth	28	16	declaring my gospel with sound of R.—29:4
136	34	thy brethren have R. you and your	50	33	neither with boasting nor R. lest ye
		REJECTETH	52	43	crown the faithful with joy and R.
84	94	wo unto that house that R. you— 95	59	14	or in other words, R. and prayer
99	4	whoso R. you shall be rejected of my	84	105	cast it to the poor and go your way R.
		REJOICE	124	101	cry aloud with joy and R.
25	13	lift up thy heart and R.—27:15; 31:3; 42:69; 110:5			**RELATION**
35	24	Zion shall R. upon the hills and	127	5	a word in R. to baptism for the dead—128:16
39	13	bring forth Zion that it may R.	128	1	information in R. to many subjects
49	25	Zion shall R. upon the mountains		2	additional views in R. to this matter
50	22	both are edified and R. together		3	in R. to this matter it would be very
	34	let him R. that is accounted worthy		6	this very subject in R. to the dead
52	42	to R. upon the land of Missouri		11	facts in R. to salvation of the
56	19	and the poor shall R.		14	records on earth in R. to your dead
				15	these are principles in R. to your dead
			134	1	accountable for their acts in R. to

Sec.	Vs.	
		RELATIONSHIP
128	12	instituted to form R. with ordinance
		RELEASE
19	35	R. thyself from bondage
		RELIED
30	1	have not R. on me for strength
		RELIEF
38	35	administer to their R. that they—44:6
134	11	appeal to the laws and R. afforded
		RELIGION
134	4	we believe R. is instituted of God
135	6	classed among the martyrs of R.
	7	is an ambassador for the R. of Jesus
		RELIGIOUS
134	4	unless their R. opinions prompt them
	7	in free exercise of their R. belief; such R. opinions do not justify sedition
	9	not just to mingle R. influence with civil; whereby one R. society is fostered
	10	all R. societies have a right to deal; do not believe any R. society has
		RELY
3	20	and R. upon merits of Jesus Christ
17	1	you must R. upon my word with full
18	3	that you R. upon the things which are
		REMAIN
27	10	by whom the promises R.
43	14	he shall R. unto them that have
45	25	shall R. until times of the Gentiles
48	1	necessary that ye should R. for present
56	7	let my servant R. with them
62	8	these things R. with you to do
63	14	some have turned away and others R.
	66	these things R. to overcome
64	24	I will not spare any that R. in Babylon
68	14	there R. hereafter, other bishops
70	15	for their benefit while they R.
74	6	children might R. without circumcision
83	3	yet they may R. upon their inheritances
84	57	they shall R. under this condemnation
	61	that you may R. steadfast in your

Sec.	Vs.	
	98	until all shall know me who R.
86	10	priesthood must R. through you and
88	32	they who R. shall also be quickened
	35	therefore they must R. filthy still
	102	there are found among those to R. those that shall R. filthy still
90	21	let Rigdon R. where he now resides
101	18	they that R. and are pure in heart
115	12	not anything R. that is not finished
117	5	let it R. in your hands
118	2	let my servant R. for a season
121	33	how long can rolling waters R. impure
122	9	the Priesthood shall R. with thee
124	104	if he will R. with my people
132	13	and shall not R. after men are dead
	14	whatsoever things R. are by me
	17	but R. separately and singly
136	9	for those who R. behind this season
		REMAINDER
10	3	finishing the R. of the work of
	46	the R. of this work does contain all
124	102	the R. I will show unto you hereafter
		REMAINED
86	10	your life and the priesthood hath R.
		REMAINETH
29	50	it R. in me to do according as it
40	3	it R. with me to do as seemeth me
61	28	as it R. with me to do hereafter
63	64	without this there R. condemnation
64	9	there R. in him the greater sin
	26	the residue which R. in this place
84	58	there R. a scourge and a judgment
86	7	and the field R. to be burned
117	5	whatsoever R. let it remain in your
		REMAINING
102	20	but should the R. councilors discover
		REMARKS
102	18	and councilors have finished their R.
		REMEMBER
3	3	R., R. it is not work of God that is
	5	R. the promises that were made to you
	10	but R., God is merciful
4	6	R. faith, virtue, knowledge
6	10	R. it is sacred and cometh from above
8	5	R. these words; R. this is your gift
	10	R., without faith you can do nothing
10	39	you R. it was said in those writings
	70	R. words of him who is the life and

Sec.	Vs.	
18	10	R. the worth of souls is great in the
20	77	and always R. him and keep his
	79	that they do always R. him, that they
29	3	R. to sin no more
	30	R. that all my judgments are not given
33	12	and R. that they shall have faith
	14	R. the church articles and covenants
42	30	thou wilt R. the poor and consecrate
	79	for R. that he hath no forgiveness
46	10	I would that ye should always R.
52	40	R. the poor and the needy, the sick
58	5	R. this, which I tell you before
	42	and I, the Lord, R. them no more
59	12	R. that on this the Lord's day thou
63	64	R. that which cometh from above is sacred
68	30	the inhabitants shall R. their labors
84	57	until they repent and R. the covenant
88	69	R. the great and last promise
89	18	all saints who R. to keep and do
90	24	R. the covenant with which ye have
101	9	in the day of wrath I *will* R. mercy
109	47	R. those who have been driven from their
	55	R. the kings, the princes, the nobles
	68	O Lord, R. thy servant Joseph Smith
	71	R. the presidents of thy church
	72	R. all thy church, with their
117	12	I R. my servant Oliver Granger
	16	let all my servants R. the Lord
121	6	R. thy suffering saints, O our God
124	14	let him R. that his stewardship will
128	6	I want you to R. that John the

REMEMBERED

108	4	then you shall be R. with the first
124	78	let him be R. for an interest in

REMEMBERETH

133	44	who R. thee in thy ways

REMEMBERING

27	2	R. unto the Father my body which was
46	8	always R. for what they are given

REMEMBRANCE

20	75	in R. of the Lord Jesus
	77	that they may eat in R. of the body
	79	that they may do it in R. of the blood
68	30	the idler shall be had in R. before

Sec.	Vs.	
	33	let him be had in R. before the judge
85	9	who are not found written in the book of R.
88	131	in token or R. of the everlasting—133
107	80	it shall be had in R. no more before
	82	he shall be had in R. before council
109	71	in everlasting R. from generation to
117	12	his name shall be had in sacred R.
124	96	that his name may be had in honorable R.
127	9	archives, to be held in R. from generation
133	26	they in the north countries shall come in R.

REMINDED

135	6	the reader in every nation *will* be R.

REMISSION

13	1	by immersion for R. of sins
19	31	R. of sins by baptism and by fire
20	5	that he had received a R. of his sins
	37	Spirit of Christ unto R. of their sins
21	8	days of rejoicing have come unto R. of
	9	for R. of sins unto the contrite heart
27	2	which was shed for R. of your sins
33	11	repent and be baptized for R. of—49:13
53	3	preach faith, repentance and R. of
55	1	you shall have a R. of sins
	2	to preach repentance and R. of sins
68	27	children shall be baptized for R. of
84	27	Gospel of repentance, baptism and R.
	64	baptized by water for R. of sins
	74	and are not baptized for R. of their
107	20	baptism of repentance for R. of

REMIT

132	46	whosesoever sins you R. on earth shall

REMITTED

132	46	whatsoever sins you remit on earth shall be R.

REMNANT

19	27	the Jew, of whom the Lamanites are a R.
45	24	shall a R. be scattered among all
	43	the R. shall be gathered unto this place
52	2	my people which are a R. of Jacob

Sec.	Vs.	
		REMNANTS
87	5	R. who are left of the land will marshal
109	65	and cause that the R. of Jacob, who
	67	may all the scattered R. of Israel
113	10	the scattered R. are exhorted to; or the R. of Israel in scattered condition
		REMOVAL
102	8	by death, R. from office, or R. from
		REMOVE
93	49	lest that wicked one R. you out of
112	6	R. not thy house for I, the Lord, have
124	108	let him not R. his family unto the
136	10	to R. this people to the place where
		REMOVED
90	37	she shall not be R. out of her place
93	48	repent, or be R. out of their place
	50	or they shall be R. out of their
104	77	and shall be R. out of his place
		REMOVING
20	84	all members R. form the church, may
		REMUNERATION
42	72	they are to receive a just R. for all
	73	the bishop shall receive a just R.
		REND
84	118	with you I *will* R. their kingdoms
133	40	O that thou wouldst R. the heavens
		RENDER
63	26	I R. unto Cæsar the things which are
72	3	to R. an account of his stewardship
	5	shall R. an account of their stewardship
	19	he may R. himself and his accounts
	22	they also may R. themselves approved
107	28	when circumstances R. it impossible
		RENDERED
20	36	and glory be R. to his holy name
128	18	I might have R. a plainer translation
		RENDERETH
72	17	R. every man acceptable
		RENEWED
84	48	the covenant which he has R. and
		RENEWING
84	33	unto the R. of their bodies

Sec.	Vs.	
		RENOUNCE
98	16	R. war and proclaim peace
		RENOWN
124	61	whom I have set as plants of R.
		RENT
38	8	for the veil of darkness shall soon be R.
67	10	the veil shall be R. and you shall see
		RENTED
38	37	let them be left or R. as seemeth
		REPAY
82	23	judgment is mine and I *will* R.
124	71	and do not R. fourfold for the stock
136	25	if thou canst not R. then go and tell
		REPEAT
130	14	when I heard a voice R. the following
		REPENT
1	27	be chastened that they might R.
3	10	therefore R. of that which thou hast
5	19	to be poured out if they R. not
	21	command my servant Joseph to R.
18	9	I command all men everywhere to R.
	11	that all men might R. and come unto
	22	as many as R. and are baptized
	41	saying, you must R. and be baptized
	42	for all men must R. and be baptized
19	4	surely every man must R. or suffer
	13	I command you to R. and keep the
	15	R., R., lest I smite you by the rod
	16	that they might not suffer if they R.
	17	but if they would not R. they must
	20	wherefore, I command you again to R.
20	29	we know that all men must R.
	72	baptism, unto all those who R.
29	17	upon the wicked, for they *will* not R.
	44	from spiritual fall, because they R. not
	49	whoso have I not commanded to R.
33	10	R., R., and prepare the way of the Lord
	11	yea, R. and be baptized every one
39	18	inasmuch as they do R. I will stay
42	7	R., R. ye for kingdom of heaven is
	20	he that stealeth and *will* not R.
	21	he that lieth and *will* not R.
	77	they shall R. of all their sins
43	20	call upon the nations to R.

Sec.	Vs.	
	21	if I call upon you to R. and ye hate me; R. and prepare for the great day of
	22	R. ye for the great day of the Lord is come
45	64	call on the inhabitants to R.; and as they do R. build up
49	2	they are not right before me and must R.
	8	I will that all men shall R.
	13	R. and be baptized in the name of
	26	R. of all your sins, ask and ye
50	39	let him R. and he shall be forgiven
54	3	let them R. of all their sins
56	8	my servant must R. of his pride
	14	you have many things to R. of
58	15	if he R. not of his sins which are
	39	let him R. of his sins, for he seeketh
	41	and also he hath need to R.
	47	call upon the rich and poor to R.
	48	inasmuch as the inhabitants *will* R.
63	15	let such beware and R. speedily
	63	let the church R. of their sins
64	17	and they R. of the evil they shall be
66	3	R. therefore of those things which are
75	29	except he R. and mend his ways
84	57	under this condemnation until they R.
	76	they shall R. of their former evil works
90	34	your brethren in Zion begin to R.
	35	and others have many things to R. of
93	48	your family must need R. and forsake
98	21	if they do not R. and observe all
	27	against your enemy if he R. not
	39	if he R. and come unto thee praying
	41	and R. not the first time
	42	against thee the second time and R. not
	43	against thee the third time and R. not
	44	not blotted out until he R. and reward
	47	but if the children shall R.
109	21	they may speedily R. and return unto
	29	shame and confusion if they *will* not R.
	50	that they may R. of their sins
	53	inasmuch as they *will* R. thou art
117	4	R. of all their sins and covetous
124	50	so long as they R. not and hate me—52
	116	and let him R. of all his folly

Sec.	Vs.	
133	16	commandeth all men everywhere to R.
136	35	unless they speedily R., yea, speedily

REPENTANCE

3	20	through their R. they might be saved
6	9	say nothing but R. to this generation—11:9
13	1	and of the Gospel of R.
14	8	that you may declare R. unto this
15	6	to declare R. unto this people—16:6
18	6	that children of men are stirred up to R.
	12	on conditions of R.
	14	you are called to cry R. unto this
	15	labor all your days in crying R.
	44	that they may come unto R.
19	21	that you preach naught but R.
	31	thou shalt declare R. and faith
20	71	before God, and is capable of R.
29	42	to declare unto them R. and redemption
34	6	cry R. unto a crooked and perverse
35	5	thou didst baptize by water unto R.
36	6	crying R., saying, save yourselves
39	6	this is my gospel: R. and baptism by
44	3	and preach R. unto the people
53	3	to preach faith, and R. and remission
55	2	to preach R. and remission of sins
63	57	to warn sinners to R., let them be
68	25	to understand doctrine of R., faith in
84	27	which gospel is the gospel of R.
107	20	letter of the gospel—baptism of R.
109	50	if R. is to be found

REPENTED

20	37	that they have truly R. of their sins
58	42	he who has R. of his sins, the same

REPENTETH

10	67	whosoever R. and cometh unto me
18	13	great is his joy in soul that R.
42	24	committeth adultery and R. not
	28	he that sinneth and R. not—37
58	43	by this ye may know if a man R.
64	12	he that R. not of his sins ye shall
98	40	and as often as thine enemy R.
104	10	is found a transgressor and R. not
133	62	unto him that R. and sanctifieth

REPENTING

20	6	but, after R. and humbling himself

Sec.	Vs.	
		REPENTS
1	32	he that R. and does the commandments
	33	he that R. not from him shall be taken
42	23	if he R. not he shall be cast out
	25	he that R. with all his heart and
68	24	and if he R. he shall be forgiven
		REPETITION
107	4	to avoid too frequent R. of his name
		REPLENISH
132	63	given him to multiply and R. the earth
		REPORT
97	23	the R. thereof shall vex all people
		REPORTS
109	29	who have spread lying R. abroad, over
		REPRESENT
77	3	or do they R. classes or orders; to R. the glory of
		REPRESENTATION
77	4	their eyes are a R. of light, their wings a R. of power
		REPROACHFULLY
42	92	that the church may not speak R. of him
		REPROVE
84	87	I send you out to R. the world
		REPROVED
121	43	toward him whom thou hast R., lest
		REPROVING
84	117	R. the world in righteousness
121	43	R. betimes with sharpness when moved
		REPUBLIC
134	3	the voice of the people if a R.
		REQUEST
102	24	when the parties or either of them shall R.
129	4	R. him to shake hands with you
		REQUIRE
10	23	but I *will* R. this at their hands
24	13	R. not miracles, except I shall
64	22	I R. the hearts of the children of men
70	4	an account of this stewardship *will* I R.
97	12	this is the sacrifice which I R.

Sec.	Vs.	
102	1	as the case might R.
105	10	the things which I R. at their hands
	14	I do not R. at their hands to fight
119	1	I R. all their surplus property to be
124	14	his stewardship *will* I R. at his hands
	49	it behooveth me to R. that work no more
127	1	or otherwise as the case may R.
132	51	that I might R. an offering at your
	60	he shall do the sacrifice which I R.
134	3	all governments necessarily R. civil
		REQUIRED
24	14	except it be R. of you by them who
26	1	your labors on the land such as is R.
29	48	that great things may be R. of their
60	11	he that is not, of him it is not R.
64	10	but of you it is R. to forgive all men
72	3	it is R. of the Lord of every steward
78	7	which I have commanded and R. of you
82	3	unto whom much is given much is R.
105	3	not obedient to the things I R.
	4	according to the union R. by law of
112	33	lest blood of this generation be R. at
126	1	it is no more R. at your hands to leave
		REQUIREMENTS
135	4	deliver himself up to the pretended R.
		REQUIRES
20	52	assist the elder if occasion R.
	57	assisted by the deacons if occasion R.
70	9	the Lord R. of every man in his
88	123	impart one to another as gospel R.
104	73	give unto him the sum which he R.
107	96	if the labor in the vineyard R. it
		REQUIRETH
64	34	the Lord R. the heart and a willing
		RESERVE
43	14	may R. unto myself a pure people
51	14	let him R. unto himself for his own
63	39	excepting those whom I shall R. for
121	24	and I have in R. a swift judgment
	27	held in R. for the fulness of their
		RESERVED
5	9	I have R. those things which I have
45	12	a city R. until a day of righteousness
49	8	except them which I have R. unto
104	34	which has been R. for the building of

Sec.	Vs.		Sec.	Vs.	
	45	I have R. an inheritance for his father		71	and leave the R. in mine hand—103:40
	68	and sacred writings which I have R. unto	107	53	with the R. of his posterity who were
121	32	that should be R. for the finishing	118	3	let R. continue to preach from that hour

RESIDE

RESIST

20	84	removing from the church where they R.	108	2	and R. no more my voice

RESOLVED

130	4	according to planet on which they R.	102	33	R. that the president or presidents
	6	angels do not R. on a planet like this			

RESPECT

	7	but they R. in the presence of God	107	4	but out of R. or reverence to the name
134	5	uphold the governments in which they R.	134	6	to the laws all men owe R. and

RESIDENCE

RESPECTS

58	24	this land is the land of his R. and the land of the R. of him	134	8	breach of the peace, in all R.

RESIDES

RESPECTER

90	21	let Sidney Rigdon remain where he now R.—104:20	1	35	for I am no R. of persons, and will—38:16
104	28	also the lot upon which his father R.	38	26	having twelve sons and is no R. of

RESPECTING

	39	the houses and lot where he now R.	72	24	a few words R. members of the church
	43	the inheritance upon which his father R.	102	23	in cases of difficulty R. doctrine
124	105	in which my servant Joseph R.	107	59	the church laws R. church business
130	8	where God R. is a great Urim and			

RESPECTIVE

RESIDUE

			134	5	and uphold the R. governments
38	5	the R. of the wicked have I kept in			

RESPONSIBLE

42	33	which is a R. to be consecrated	107	98	they may hold as high and R. offices
	34	the R. shall be kept in my storehouse			

RESPONSIBILITY

52	39	let the R. of the elders watch over	107	98	are not under the R. to travel among
53	6	the R. shall be known in a time			
55	6	the R. shall be made known hereafter	124	140	one has R. of presiding, the other has no R.
57	16	unto the R., further directions shall			
58	44	concerning the R. of the elders of			

REST

	58	to accomplish R. of the work, and the R. as shall be	15	6	that you may R. with them in kingdom—16:6
	61	let R. of elders of this church also	19	9	that you may enter into my R.
60	8	let the R. take their journey	39	12	power shall R. upon thee
	12	I speak of the R. who are to come to	43	34	let solemnities of eternity R. upon
	17	the R. hereafter	54	10	they shall find R. to their souls
61	11	let the R. take that which is needful	59	2	them that die shall R. from all their
	33	concerning the R., let them journey		10	this is a day appointed unto you to R.
64	26	until the R. shall go up unto the			
90	29	R. of the money may be consecrated	76	39	for all the R. shall be brought forth
97	6	to the R. of the school I am willing	84	5	and a cloud shall R. upon it
101	55	gather the R. of my servants and take		24	they should not enter into his R. while; which R. is the
	58	I may come with the R. of mine house	117	1	say unto you, the R. of my servants

Sec.	Vs.	
88	101	these are the R. of the dead
97	15	my glory shall R. upon it
101	31	caught up, and his R. shall be glorious
105	25	that you may R. in peace and safety
108	2	let your soul be at R. concerning
	4	by ordination with R. of mine elders
109	12	that thy glory may R. down upon thy
121	32	shall enter into his immortal R.
124	86	for they shall R. from all their

RESTETH

Sec.	Vs.	
84	56	this condemnation R. upon the children

RESTING-PLACE

Sec.	Vs.	
124	60	a R. for the weary traveler

RESTORATION

Sec.	Vs.	
27	6	bringing to pass R. of all things
45	17	also the R. of the scattered Israel
77	15	in last days at the time of the R.
84	2	for the R. of this people
86	10	until the R. of all things
103	13	even their R. to the land of Zion
	29	concerning R. and redemption of Zion
128	17	his eye fixed on R. of the priesthood

RESTORE

Sec.	Vs.	
77	9	which was to come and R. all things
	14	who must come and R. all things
98	47	and R. fourfold all their trespasses
124	28	and R. again that which was lost
127	8	I am about to R. many things
132	40	gave an appointment and R. all things
	45	priesthood, wherein I R. all things
136	25	thou shalt R. that thou hast borrowed

RESTORED

Sec.	Vs.	
10	3	it is now R. unto you again
109	21	and be R. to the blessings which

RESTRAIN

Sec.	Vs.	
134	4	should R. crime but never control

RESULT

Sec.	Vs.	
102	34	the following was the R., namely

RESUME

Sec.	Vs.	
128	1	I now R. subject of baptism for dead

RESURRECTED

Sec.	Vs.	
129	1	angels who are R. personages
	3	they who are not R. but inherit

RESURRECTION

Sec.	Vs.	
42	45	who have not hope of a glorious R.
45	54	shall have part in the first R.—76:64
63	18	they shall not have part in the first R.
	52	for this cause preached apostles R. of
76	16	speaking of the R. of the dead
	17	done good, in R. of the just; done evil, in R. of the unjust
	39	the rest shall be brought forth by R.
	50	who come forth in R. of the just —65
	85	not redeemed until last R.
88	14	is brought to pass the R. from the
	16	R. is the redemption of the soul
128	12	in likeness of R. of the dead
130	18	it will rise with us in the R.
132	7	of no efficacy or force after the R.
	13	neither in nor after the R.
	19	ye shall come forth in first R., and if after first R., in the next R.
	26	yet shall they come forth in first R.
133	55	who were with Christ in his R.

RETAIN

Sec.	Vs.	
46	10	always R. in your minds what gifts
51	5	he shall not R. the gift, but shall
63	42	R. his store yet for a little
64	21	I will to R. a strong hold in the land
132	46	whosoever sins you R. on earth, shall

RETAINED

Sec.	Vs.	
10	41	which you have translated, which you have R.
132	46	sins you retain on earth shall be R. in

RETAINING

Sec.	Vs.	
19	3	R. all power, even to destroying of

RETIRE

Sec.	Vs.	
88	124	R. to thy bed early that ye may not

RETURN

Sec.	Vs.	
28	15	until the time thou shalt R., what
29	29	never have I declared that they should R.
37	3	against the time Cowdery shall R.
42	5	of my spirit when they shall R.
58	46	after that let them R. to their homes
	58	let my servants R. with them
	59	let no man R. from this land

Sec.	Vs.		Sec.	Vs.	
	63	let them also R. preaching the gospel	31	4	things which have been R. to my servant
60	1	who are to R. speedily to the land	42	9	it shall be R. unto you from on high
	8	until they R. to the churches from		35	New Jerusalem hereafter to be R.
	10	unto mine elders who are commanded to R.		62	it shall be R. unto you in mine own
	11	let him R. it by way of the agent	48	5	the place is not yet to be R. but, to them it shall be R.
	14	thou shalt speedily R., proclaiming			
61	35	be not separated until they R. to their	58	63	bearing record of things R. unto them
62	5	then you may R. to bear record	63	14	that hereafter shall be R.
64	18	should R. upon his business	66	2	glories which are to be R. in last days
66	9	R. not till I the Lord shall send			
82	7	to soul that sinneth shall former sins R.	76	43	deny the Son after Father has R. him
84	92	and R. not again to that man		46	neither was it R., neither *will* be R. except to them
88	32	they shall R. again unto their own			
101	18	they that are pure in heart shall R.		90	except him to whom God has R. it
103	11	shall R. to their inheritances and	77	6	it contains the R. will, mysteries
	30	should not R. to land of their brethren	90	10	arm of the Lord shall be R. in power
109	21	may speedily repent and R. unto thee	93	6	John's record is hereafter to be R.
			105	23	which I have R. unto them, until it is wisdom in me they should be R.
	64	children of Judah may begin to R.			
113	8	to R. to that power which she had lost	121	26	that has not been R. since the world
	10	scattered remnants exhorted to R		27	to be R. in the last times
127	1	then I will R. unto you again		29	all dominions and powers shall be R.
		REVEAL		31	all their glories and set times shall be R.
2	1	I *will* R. unto you the priesthood			
27	5	whom I have sent unto you to R. the	123	17	salvation of God, and for his arm to be R.
	18	my word which I R. unto you	124	8	my testimony which I have R.
29	11	for I will R. myself from heaven		38	that those ordinances might be R.
38	30	lest wickedness of men R. these things	127	1	Lord has R. to me that my enemies
			128	17	the glories to be R. in the last days
76	7	to them *will* I R. all mysteries		18	and be R. from the days of Adam; things which never have been R., shall be R. to babes
88	108	and R. the secret acts of men— 109			
101	32	when the Lord shall come, he shall R. all		20	declaring the book to be R.
105	23	and R. not the things which I have	132	3	all those who have this law R. must obey
124	40	that I may R. mine ordinances therein			
			133	57	the glories which were to be R.
	41	for I deign to R. unto my church			**REVELATION**
132	4	I R. unto you a new and everlasting	8	3	behold, this is the spirit of R.
	44	and I R. it unto my servant Joseph	11	25	deny not the spirit of R.
	66	I *will* R. more unto you hereafter	25	2	a R. I give unto you concerning my
		REVEALED	32	4	and pretend to no other R.
1	3	and their secret acts shall be R.	42	61	thou shalt receive R. upon R.
	14	the arm of the Lord shall be R.	64	12	either by commandment or by R.
25	9	that all things might be R. unto them	68	21	or ascertain it by R. from the Lord
			77	1	spoken of by John, 4th chapter, 6th verse of R.
27	12	the same things which I R. unto them	84	1.a	R. of Jesus Christ to his servant
				75	and this R. is in force from this
28	9	it is not R. where the city	89	2	not by constraint but by R.

Sec.	Vs.		Sec.	Vs.	
	4	giving you this Word of Wisdom by R.	94	3	work of the presidency in obtaining R.
90	11	for the R. of Jesus Christ	104	58	to print the R. which I have given
92	1	I give unto the united order, a R. and	109	11	promises made unto us in the R. given
101	23	prepare for R. which is to come		60	concerning the R. and commandments
102	1	assembled at the house of, by R.	124	39	for the beginning of the R. and foundation
	2	the High Council was appointed by R.	119		unless he shall be a believer in the R.
	9	President of the church is appointed by R.	135	3	has brought forth the R. and commandments
	23	and obtain the mind of the Lord by R.			**REVELATOR**
103	1	I will give unto you a R. and	77	2	figurative expressions used by the R.
107	39	they shall be designated by R.	100	11	he shall be a R. unto thee
	58	agreeable to the R. which says	107	92	to be a seer, a R., a translator
109	6	and as thou hast said in a R. given	124	94	that he may be a prophet, seer, and a R.—125
113	10	promise of the Lord is he will give them R.	128	6	remember John the R. was contemplating
128	2	I wrote a few words of R. to you			**REVENGE**
	6	as you will find recorded in R. 20:12	98	23	revile not against them neither seek R.
	7	which is commanded you in the R.			**REVERENCE**
	8	power of the priesthood by R. of	76	93	all things bow in humble R. and give
	9	given to any man by actual R.	107	4	but out of respect or R. to the name
130	10	than the white stone mentioned in R. 2:17	109	21	those who shall R. thee in thy house
131	5	sealed up unto eternal life, by R.	134	7	so long as regard and R. are shown
132	7	and sealed by R. and commandment			**REVILE**
	29	Abraham received all things by R.	31	9	R. not against those that R.
		REVELATIONS	98	23	and R. not against them neither seek
3	4	although a man may have many R.		25	and you R. not against your enemy
20	35	are true and according to R. of John, or the R. of God			**REVILERS**
	45	according to the commandments and R.	19	30	reviling not against R.
28	1	concerning R. I have given			**REVILING**
	2	no one shall be appointed to receive R.	19	30	R. not against revilers
	3	to declare faithfully the R.			**REVOKE**
	7	and the R. which are sealed	19	5	I R. not the judgment which I pass
	8	thou shalt have R. but write them not	56	4	I command and R. as seemeth me good
43	2	whom I have appointed to receive R.		5	wherefore I R. the commandment given
	3	none other appointed to receive R.		6	I R. the commandment which was given to
	5	any that shall come before you as R.	58	32	I R. and they receive not the blessing
	7	to teach those R. which you have	61	19	and I R. not the decree
52	17	according to the R. and truths	75	6	I R. the commission I gave unto **him**
59	4	and with R. in their time			
70	3	to be stewards over the R.			
71	4	prepare the way for the R. to come			
72	21	that the R. may be published			
75	4	according to the R. and commandments			
82	4	ye call upon my name for R.			
84	104	for the bringing forth of the R.			
90	14	receive R. to unfold the mysteries			

Sec.	Vs.		Sec.	Vs.	
		REVOLUTIONS			**RICH, CHARLES C.**
121	31	all the times of their R.	124	132	viz., Geo. W. Harris, R., and
		REWARD			**RICHARDS, WILLARD**
6	33	ye shall also reap good for your R.	118	6	and R., be appointed to fill places
14	11	and great shall be your R.—42:65; 76:6	124	129	they are Wilford Woodruff, R., and
23	7	that you may receive R. of laborer	135	2	John Taylor and R., were the only
31	12	into temptation and lose your R.			**RICHER**
54	10	I come quickly and my R. is with me—112:34	133	34	and the R. blessing upon the head of
56	19	and he shall R. every man			**RICHES**
58	2	the R. of the same is greater in the	6	7	seek not for R. but for wisdom—11:7
	26	wherefore he receiveth no R.	38	18	I deign to give unto you greater R.
	28	they shall in nowise lose their R.—84:90; 127:4		39	seek the R. which it is the will of the Father; for ye shall have R. of eternity; R. of earth are mine to give
	33	their R. lurketh beneath and not from			
59	3	shall receive for their R. the good	42	39	will consecrate the R. of those
	23	shall receive his R., even peace in this	43	25	and the R. of eternal life
63	48	and also a R. in the world to come	45	65	and with one mind gather up your R.
64	11	and R. thee according to thy deeds	56	16	for your R. will canker your souls
70	15	a R. for their diligence and for their	67	2	the R. of eternity are mine to give
98	25	your R. shall be an hundredfold	68	31	they seek not earnestly R. of eternity
	26	your R. shall be doubled unto you	78	18	the R. of eternity are yours
	44	until he repent and R. thee fourfold	90	22	let it be a man who has got R.
101	65	to R. every man according as his work			**RICHEST**
124	16	his R. shall not fail if he receive	38	39	ye shall be the R. of all people
127	3	R. upon the heads of all their oppressors			**RID**
	4	for all this there is a R. in heaven	61	34	as they do this they shall R. their garments
135	6	and glory is their eternal R.			**RIDE**
		REWARDED	62	7	if any desireth to R. upon horses
56	12	that those may be R. again			**RIDETH**
90	29	and she be R. in mine own due time	61	19	the destroyer R. upon the face thereof
98	23	neither seek revenge, ye shall be R.			**RIGDON, SIDNEY**
	30	thou shalt be R. for thy righteousness	36	2	by the hand of my servant R.
		REWARDEST		5	shall come before my servants R. and
98	31	if thou R. him according to his works	41	8	R. shall live as seemeth him good
		RICH	42	4	excepting Joseph Smith, Jr. and R.
6	7	then shall you be made R.; he that hath eternal life is R.—11:7	52	3	let Joseph Smith and R. take their
38	16	the R. have I made and all flesh is		24	take their journey with R. and
	17	and I have made the earth R.		41	let R. and, take with them a recommend
56	16	wo unto you R. men, that will not	53	5	you shall take your journey with R.—55:5; 60:6
58	10	firstly, the R. and the learned	58	50	R. shall write a description of
	47	call upon the R., the high and the low		57	let R. consecrate and dedicate this
84	112	by humbling the R. and the proud		58	let conference be called, and R. and
104	16	in that the R. are made low	60	17	it shall be made known concerning R.
133	30	they shall bring forth their R. treasures			

Sec.	Vs.	
61	23	now concerning my servants R. and
	30	R. and, shall not open their mouths in
63	55	I am not pleased with my servant R.
	65	let R. and, seek them a home as they
70	1	also unto R., by way of commandment
71	1	and R., that the time has verily come
73	3	Joseph Smith and R., it is expedient to
76	11	we, Joseph Smith and R. being in the spirit
78	9	let R. and, sit in council with
82	11	that R. and, be bound together by a
90	6	thy brethren, R., and their sins are
	21	let R. remain where he now resides
93	44	R. in some things hath not kept the
	51	let R. go his journey and make haste
102	3	R. and, were acknowledged presidents
103	29	R. shall lift up his voice in the
	38	let Lyman Wight journey with R.
104	20	let R. have appointed to him the place
	22	this stewardship I confer on R.
115	1	thus saith the Lord to R. and
124	126	give to him for counselors, R. and

RIGGS, BURR

75	17	let Ashley and R. take their journey

RIGHT

3	2	neither doth he turn to the R. hand
9	8	ask me if it be R., and if it is R. I will cause, that you shall feel it is R.
	9	but if it be not R. you shall have no
20	24	to sit down on the R. hand of the
29	12	shall stand at my R. hand
	27	righteous shall be gathered on my R.
39	8	thine heart is now R. before me
40	1	heart of my servant was R. before me
41	3	and have all things R. before me
49	2	for they are not R. before me
	6	he has taken his power on the R. hand
51	4	even this R. and this inheritance
57	13	that all things may be R. before me
58	22	until he reigns whose R. it is to
66	12	eternal life at R. hand of my Father
68	16	they have a legal R. to the bishopric
	17	first born holds the R. of presidency

Sec.	Vs.	
	18	no man has a legal R. to this office —107:16
	21	their R. of the priesthood descending
76	20	glory of the Son on R. hand of the
	23	for we saw him on the R. hand of the
84	88	I will be on your R. hand and on your
93	43	there are many things that are not R. in
101	63	willing to be guided in R. and proper
	79	it is not R. that any man should be in
102	15	the accused has a right to one half
104	7	a crown of glory at my R. hand
107	8	priesthood holds R. of presidency
	9	have a R. to officiate in all the other
	10	have a R. to officiate in their own
	11	an elder has a R. to officiate in his
	12	they have a R. to officiate in all
	76	a literal descendant has a legal R.
108	4	and receive R. by ordination
	6	you shall have R. to preach my gospel
109	71	that thy R. hand may exalt them
113	8	which she (Zion) has a R. to by
121	21	they shall not have R. to priesthood
124	15	he loveth that which is R. before me
	19	sitteth with Abraham at his R. hand
	91	appointed by blessing and also by R.
127	1	have not the least coloring of justice or R.
133	56	and stand on the R. hand of the Lamb
134	2	the R. and control of property
	4	that human law has R. to interfere
	5	all governments have the R. to enact laws—7
	7	we do not believe they have a R. to
	10	all religious societies have R. to deal; not authority to try men on R. of
	11	or the R. of property infringed
	12	not R. to interfere with bond servants

RIGHTEOUS

10	36	shall not show it unto the R.
	37	you cannot always judge the R., or tell wicked from R.

Sec.	Vs.	
17	4	that I may bring about my R. purposes—9
25	12	the song of the R. is a prayer unto me
29	27	R. shall be gathered on my right
38	31	be gathered unto me a R. people
45	71	that the R. shall be gathered
63	54	an entire separation of the R. and
67	9	that which is R. cometh down from above
84	53	by this you may know the R. from the
88	26	and the R. shall inherit it
101	95	that men may discern between the R.
107	29	and who were R. and holy men
	53	residue of his posterity who were R.
109	39	may gather out of that city the R.
	58	may gather out the R. to build a holy
127	4	so persecuted they the R. men that
134	12	and warn the R. to save themselves

RIGHTEOUSLY

11	12	to walk humbly, to judge R.

RIGHTEOUSNESS

1	16	they seek not to establish his R.
11	14	which are pertaining unto things of R.
13	1	an offering unto the Lord in R.
20	14	who receive it in faith and work R.
25	15	a crown of R. thou shalt receive
27	16	having on the breastplate of R.
29	11	and dwell in R. with men on earth
	12	being clothed with robes of R.
	13	to receive a crown of R.
43	32	he that liveth in R. shall be changed
45	12	city reserved until a day of R. shall
48	4	obtain all that ye can in R.
50	9	which is not in truth and R. before
52	11	I will cut my work short in R.
57	6	inasmuch as can be done in R.
	12	whatsoever he can obtain in R.
58	27	and bring to pass much R.
59	8	unto the Lord thy God in R.
	11	vows shall be offered up in R. on all
	23	he who doeth the works of R.
63	37	every man should take R. in his hands
76	5	delight to honor those who serve me in R.
84	97	which shall be cut short in R.

Sec.	Vs.	
117		reproving the world in R.
98	30	thou shalt be rewarded for thy R.
100	16	a people that will serve me in R.
106	3	kingdom of heaven and its R.
107	30	decisions are to be made in all R.
	84	in order, according to truth and R.
109	59	that thy work may be cut short in R.
	76	may be clothed upon with robes of R.
121	36	handled only upon principles of R.
	46	unchanging sceptre of R. and truth
122	4	than the fierce lion, because of thy R.
128	24	may offer the Lord an offering in R.
132	36	it was accounted unto him for R. —37
133	44	meet him who rejoiceth and worketh R.
	47	I am he who spake in R.

RIGHTLY

107	40	and R. belongs to literal descendants
113	6	unto whom R. belongs the priesthood

RIGHTS

98	5	in maintaining R. and privileges
101	77	maintained for the R. and protection
121	36	the R. of Priesthood are inseparably
128	21	declaring their dispensation, their R.
134	4	to infringe upon R. and liberties
	5	while protected in their inherent R.
	9	and individual R. of its members denied

RILLS

128	23	ye rivers and R. flow down with gladness

RIPE

29	9	day soon at hand when the earth is R.
86	7	grow together until harvest is fully R.

RIPENED

61	31	a people well nigh R. for destruction

RIPENING

18	6	the world is R. in iniquity

RISE

20	1	the R. of the Church of Christ in
63	49	they shall R. from the dead and shall

Sec.	Vs.		Sec.	Vs.	
87	4	slaves shall R. *up* against their masters		24	build upon my R. which is my gospel
88	27	they also shall R. again a spiritual	18	4	my church, my gospel, my R.
109	26	shall have power to R. *up* and prevail		5	upon foundation of my gospel, my R.
	27	and if any people shall R. against		17	my gospel, my rock and my salvation
	33	that we may R. *up* in the midst of	33	13	upon this R. will I build my church; upon this R. ye are built —128:10
117	13	and when he falls he shall R. again			
128	16	if the dead R. not at all, why are	50	44	that buildeth on this R. shall never fall
130	18	it *will* R. with us in resurrection			

RISEN

ROCKS

18	12	he hath R. again from the dead	128	23	and ye solid R. weep for joy
			133	26	they shall smite the R. and the ice

RISING

ROD

5	14	in this the beginning of the R. *up*	19	15	lest I smite you by the R. of my mouth
69	8	for good of the R. generations			
121	11	before burning rays of the R. sun	113	3	what is the R. spoken of in Isaiah
123	11	duty we owe to the R. generation			

RODS

RIVER

121	33	to stop the Missouri R. in its course	104	43	which is forty R. long, twelve wide
128	20	on the Susquehanna R.			

ROLFE, SAMUEL

RIVERS

128	23	and ye R. and brooks, and rills flow	124	142	and R. and counselors for priests
133	68	I make the R. a wilderness; their fish			

ROLL

RIVETED

123	7	which hath so strongly R. the creeds	65	2	from thence shall gospel R. *forth*, as stone shall R. *forth*
			88	45	as they R. upon their wings in glory

ROB

42	84	if a man or woman shall R.	109	59	that gathering of thy people may R. on

ROBBERS

ROLLED

122	5	if thou art in perils among R.	88	95	as scroll is unfolded after it is R. *up*

ROBBERY

ROLLING

134	8	that R., theft, and, should be punished	121	33	how long can R. waters remain impure

ROBE

ROLLS

135	2	without even a hole in his R.	88	45	the earth R. upon her wings, and the

ROBES

ROOM

29	12	being clothed with R. of righteousness —109:76	101	21	when there is no more R. for them
38	26	be thou clothed in R. and sit thou here	117	8	is there not R. enough upon mountains
			124	91	in the R. of my servant Hyrum
			135	2	were the only persons in the R. at

ROCK

ROOMS

6	34	for if ye are built upon my R.	124	145	ye should prepare R. for all these
10	69	him will I establish upon my R.			
11	16	until you shall have my word, my R.			

Sec.	Vs.	
		ROOT
97	7	the ax is laid at the R. of the trees
109	52	they may be wasted away, R. and branch
113	5	what is the R. of Jesse spoken of
133	64	it shall leave them neither R. nor

ROSE

20	23	he died and R. again the third day
49	24	Lamanites shall blossom as the R.
107	54	and they R. *up* and blessed Adam

ROUGH

49	23	for the R. places to be made smooth —109:74

ROUND

3	2	his course is one eternal R.—35:1

ROUND (About)

30	4	in the regions R. about.—30:10; 44:3; 48:3; 52:39; 57:6; 58:46; 66:5; 71:2; 73:1, 4; 100:3; 101: 70; 105:20, 23; 106:1; 111:7; 115:18; 133:9
76	19	glory of the Lord shone R. about
	29	encompasses the saints R. about
84	88	and my angels R. about you
	112	the bishop should travel R. about
88	41	all things are R. about him, and he is R. about all things
101	45	set watchmen R. about them and overlook the land R. about
	46	built a hedge R. about and set— 101:53
	71	and the counties R. about.—105: 28
109	22	and thy glory be R. about them

ROUNDY, SHADRACH

124	141	I give unto you R., if he will receive it

RUINED

135	6	bring *forth* for salvation of a R. world

RULE

58	20	but let God R. him that judgeth
60	4	I the Lord, R. in the heavens above
98	9	when the wicked R. the people mourn

RULED

58	58	the residue shall be R. by the conferences

RULER

38	21	in time ye shall have no king nor R.
41	4	and I *will* be your R. when I come
52	13	shall be made R. over many things
58	20	let no man think he is R. but let
101	61	in mine house, a R. in my kingdom
117	10	faithful over few things shall be R. over
124	113	he shall be made R. over many— 132:44, 53

RULERS

1	23	and before kings and R.
78	15	and be made R. over many kingdoms
101	76	by those who are placed as R.
	94	that wise men and R. may hear and
109	54	have mercy upon the R. of our land
134	,6	R. and magistrates as such, being
	7	we believe that R. have a right and

RULES

134	4	in prescribing R. of worship
	6	prescribing R. on spiritual concerns
	10	according to R. and regulations of

RULETH

133	61	will of the Lord who R. over all flesh

RUMORS

45	26	be heard of wars and R. of wars

RUN

10	4	do not R. faster or labor more than
19	40	or canst thou R. about longer as a blind
89	14	wild animals that R. or creep on earth
	20	shall R. and not be weary, shall walk

RUNNING

57	4	even to the line R. directly between

RUSHING

109	37	let thy house be filled as with a R. wind
110	3	as the sound of R. of great waters

RYDER, SIMONDS

52	37	taken from him and placed on R.

RYE

89	17	and R. for the fowls and for swine

S

Sec.	Vs.		Sec.	Vs.	
		SABAOTH		13	for his sacrifice shall be more S.
87	7	into the ears of the Lord of S.—88:2; 95:7; 98:2	134	5	holding S. the freedom of conscience
		SABBATH			**SACRIFICE**
68	29	observe the S. to keep it holy	59	8	thou shalt offer a S. unto the Lord
127	10	to have addressed them the following S.	64	23	it is a day of S. and a day of tithing
		SACKCLOTH	84	31	shall offer an acceptable S. in the
133	69	and make S. their covering	97	8	willing to observe covenants by S.; yea, every S. which the Lord
		SACRAMENT		12	this is the tithing and S. which I
20	46	to baptize and administer the S.	117	13	his S. shall be more sacred unto me
	58	nor deacons have authority to administer S.	132	51	that I might require an offering and S.
	68	previous to their partaking of the S.		60	he shall do S. which I require
27	2	what ye shall drink when ye partake the S.			**SACRIFICES**
46	4	not to cast out any one from your S.	124	39	and your memorials for your S.
	5	nor cast any out of your S. meetings	132	50	I have seen your S. and will forgive; I have seen your S. in obedience
62	4	and offer a S. to the Most High			**SAD**
95	16	be dedicated unto me for your S. offering	121	39	we have learned by S. experience
		SACRAMENTS			**SAFE**
59	9	and offer up thy S. on my holy day	61	15	no flesh shall be S. upon the waters
	12	offer thine oblations and S. unto			**SAFETY**
89	5	assembling to offer up your S.	42	56	and they shall be preserved in S.
		SACRED	45	66	a place of S. for the saints of the
3	12	thou deliveredst up that which was S.		68	must needs flee unto Zion for S.
	13	has broken the most S. promises	105	25	that you may rest in peace and S.
6	10	remember it is S. and cometh from	124	10	and where shall be the S. of my people
	12	trifle not with S. things		23	that weary traveler may find health and S.
8	11	records hid up that are S.		109	not my will that he shall seek S. out of
9	9	you cannot write that which is S.	127	1	for my own S. and the S. of this people
10	9	yea, that which was S. to wickedness	134	1	for the good and S. of society
25	11	to make a selection of S. hymns			**SAID**
63	64	that which cometh from above is S.	3	2	neither doth he vary from that he hath S.
104	62	all the S. things shall be delivered	5	2	he who spake unto you S. unto you
	63	exclusive of the S. things for the purpose of printing the S. things		34	for this cause have I S. stop and
	64	and the avails of the S. things	6	32	say unto you as I S. to my disciples
	65	and thus preserve the avails of S.; for S. and holy purposes	7	1	and the Lord S. unto me, John
	66	this shall be called the S. treasury		2	and I S. unto him, give me power
	68	save it be the holy and S. writings, reserved for S. purposes		3	and the Lord S. unto me, thou shalt tarry
117	12	his name shall be had in S. remembrance		4	for this cause the Lord S. unto Peter

Sec.	Vs.	
10	7	I S. that he is a wicked man
	35	I S. unto you, here is wisdom, for I S. show it not to the world
	39	remember it was S. in those writings
	47	I S. unto them it should be granted
	53	for this cause have I S.
	59	I am he who S. other sheep have I
20	61	as S. conferences shall direct or
	62	and S. conferences are to do whatever
42	55	done according to that I have S.
45	35	and I S. unto them, be not troubled
	64	I have S. gather out of the eastern
	70	and it shall be S. among the wicked
52	42	I have S. if ye are faithful
61	16	it shall be S. in days to come
63	16	as I have S. before, he that looketh
	17	I have S. that the fearful and unbelieving
	22	as I would make known my will
64	27	it is S. in my laws, or forbidden
	28	it is not S. that the Lord should not take
76	34	I have S. here is no forgiveness
84	31	I S. concerning the sons of Moses
	63	and as I S. unto mine apostles—64
86	11	the Lord hath S. it
88	52	and he S. unto the first, go ye and
	53	and he S. unto the second, go ye also
98	21	whatsoever I have S. unto them
101	10	as I have S., it shall come to pass
	44	and he S. unto his servants, go ye
	52	and S. unto them, what is the cause of
	55	Lord of the vineyard S. unto one of
	59	the servant S. unto his lord, when
	60	and he S. unto his servant, when I
	68	as I have S. in former commandment—103:12; 105:14
	84	afterward he S. within himself
	93	what I have S. unto you must needs be
102	25	and S. Council of High Priests
	26	it shall be the duty of S. council to
	27	dissatisfied with decision of S.
103	19	not unto you as I S. to your fathers
	35	as I S. unto you, ask and ye shall
104	53	only on this wise, as I S., by loan
	63	printing these sacred records as I have S.
107	55	comfort unto Adam, and S. unto him
109	6	and as thou hast S. in a revelation
	14	and also by faith, as thou hast S.
110	13	Elijah stood before us and S.
116	1	because, S. he, it is the place where

Sec.	Vs.	
124	58	and as I S. unto Abraham concerning
	107	even as I have before S. unto you
	108	change their habitation even as I have S.
	141	a knowledge of S. bishopric is given
127	11	as the Savior S., the prince of this
129	2	Jesus S., Handle me and see, for a
132	19	and it shall be S. unto them, ye
	52	who are not pure and have S. they were
	55	do all things for her even as he hath S.
133	46	it shall be S., who is this that
135	4	Joseph S., I am going like a lamb to the slaughter; it shall yet be S. of me, he was; shall it be S. to the slaughter
	5	it came to pass that the Lord S. unto

SAINTS

Sec.	Vs.	
1	36	Lord shall have power over his S.
43	18	ye S., arise and live, ye sinners
45	45	the S. that have slept shall come forth
	46	S. shall come forth from four quarters
	66	a place of safety for the S.
57	1	consecrated for gathering of the S.
	4	the land should be purchased by the S.
	7	to divide the S. their inheritance
	8	for the good of the S.—12
	10	and thus provide for my S.
58	54	to labor for the S. of God
61	17	for the use of my S.
	24	away for the journeying of my S.
	29	the course for the S. or the way for the S.
63	24	will of the Lord concerning his S.
	34	the S. also shall hardly escape
	36	I will that my S. should be assembled
64	30	he hath set you to provide for S.
76	29	he maketh war with the S.
	102	they who will not be gathered with S.
78	9	sit in council with the S. which
82	13	for benefit of the S. of the Most
84	2	for the gathering of his S.
	4	built by the gathering of the S.
85	7	by lot the inheritances of the S.
	11	shall not find inheritance among the S.
87	7	that the cry of the S. and blood of the S.

Sec.	Vs.	
88	84	to prepare S. for the hour of judgment
	94	that persecuteth the S. of God
	96	and the S. that are upon the earth
	107	the S. shall be filled with his glory
	114	not have power over the S. any more
89	1	for benefit of the S. in Zion
	2	in temporal salvation of all S.
	3	the weakest of all S. who are or can be called S.
	18	all S. who remember to keep
97	13	a place of thanksgiving for all S.
101	20	for the gathering of my S.—105:15; 115:8
	64	that work of gathering my S. may
	70	for beginning of gathering my S.
103	7	and the earth is given to the S.
104	15	it is my purpose to provide for my S.
	16	I have decreed to provide for my S.
	36	building up the city of my S.
105	3	impart of their substance as becometh S.
	29	that my S. should possess them
109	38	and prepare the hearts of thy S.
	80	and thy S. shout aloud for joy
115	3	Church of Jesus Christ of Latter-day S.—127:12; 128:21; 136:2
	4	for thus shall my church be called, Church of Jesus Christ of Latter-day S.
	17	built up speedily by gathering of my S.
118	5	let them take leave of my S.
121	6	remember thy suffering S., O. God
	33	upon the heads of the Latter-day S.
	38	to persecute the S., to fight against
123	1	propriety of all the S. gathering
	15	much pertaining to the S. which
124	25	let all my S. come from afar
	29	that my S. may be baptized for
	31	all ye my S. to build a house unto
	143	and the perfecting of my S.
125	1	concerning the S. in territory of Iowa
	2	and are essaying to be my S.
127	3	let all the S. rejoice therefore.
	10	I will say to all the S.
128	24	as a people and as Latter-day S.
133	56	the graves of the S. shall be opened
135	3	many thousands of the Latter-day S.
136	16	go and teach this my will to the S.

SAITH

1	1	S. the voice of him who dwells
	33	S. the Lord of Hosts. 29:9
10	25	he S. unto them, deceive and lie in

Sec.	Vs.	
	29	Satan S. he hath deceived you
21	7	thus S. the Lord God—12; 36:1; 38:1; 44:1; 49:5; 50:6; 52:1, 11; 54:1; 55:1; 56:14; 57:3; 60:1; 61:2; 64:1; 66:1, 13; 70:2; 71:1, 9; 72:2; 73:1; 75:13, 23; 76:5, 31; 78:8; 80:1; 83:1; 86:1, 8; 87:1; 88:1; 89:4; 90:1; 91:1; 92:1; 93:1; 95:1; 97:21; 99:1; 100:1; 108:1; 112:1; 113:2, 4, 6; 114:1, 2; 115:1; 117:1; 118:1; 119:1; 120:1; 124:1; 125:2; 126:1; 127:4, 6; 132:1; 133:15
28	10	what he S. to thee thou shalt tell
38	26	and he S. to the one; and looketh upon his sons and S. I am just
39	10	my voice which S. unto thee, arise
41	1	S. the Lord—50:10; 51:1; 56:1, 4, 10; 57:1; 58:30, 31; 59:1; 62:1; 66:1, 3; 69:1; 73:3; 78:1, 2, 15; 79:4; 82:7; 84:35; 85:5; 87:8; 95:10, 16; 97:28; 98:3, 14, 38, 48; 107:60; 112:24, 25, 26, 27; 117:4, 5, 7, 11, 12, 13, 14, 16; 118:5; 119:4; 120:1; 121:16, 23; 124:15, 17, 21, 32, 35, 47, 48, 50, 51, 52, 53, 54, 59, 69, 71, 72, 75, 76, 88, 101, 119, 120, 122, 135, 136, 137, 140, 145; 125:4; 127:4, 6, 8, 9; 132: 6, 8, 9, 11, 12, 13, 18, 26, 27, 29, 39, 46, 47, 48, 51, 52, 54, 60, 64; 133:1, 36, 64
	5	he that S. he receiveth it and doeth
64	12	do with him as the scripture S.
74	6	which S. little children are unholy
78	20	S. your Redeemer even the Son of
84	118	with you S. the Lord Almighty I will
85	6	thus S. the still small voice
86	6	the Lord S. unto them, pluck not up
101	70	which S. or teacheth to purchase all
	81	parable of unjust judge, which S.
	95	between righteous and wicked, S. your God
113	7	which S.: Put on thy strength, O Zion
121	15	swept from under heaven, S. God

SAKE

6	18	circumstances he may be for world's S.
42	75	left companions for S. of adultery
69	1	for my servant Oliver Cowdery's S.
84	48	but for the S. of the whole world

Sec.	Vs.		Sec.	Vs.	
93	46	I called you servants for world's S.; ye are their servants for my S.	77	12	and complete the S. of man
			78	2	that S. may be unto you in that thing
98	13	layeth down his life for my S.— 101:35; 103:27		4	have espoused to the S. of man
				16	given unto him the keys of S.
103	27	be afraid to lay down his life for my S.	82	9	that it may turn to you for your S.
	28	not willing to lay down his life for my S.	84	73	given for your profit and for S.
			89	2	in temporal S. of all saints
112	12	admonish them sharply for my name's S.	90	8	in their ministry for S. of Zion
				10	of the gospel of their S.
	20	made counselors for my name's S.	93	8	the Word, even the messenger of S.
				51	and proclaim the gospel of S.
		SAKES		53	and all this for the S. of Zion
37	1	because of the enemy and for your S.	97	12	be a house built for S. of Zion
				20	to be her S. and her high tower
84	48	confirmed upon you for your S. and not for your S. only	100	4	expedient in me for the S. of souls
			101	63	a right and proper way for their S.
		SALT	103	1	concerning S. and redemption of your
101	39	they are accounted as S. of the earth			
	40	if that S. loses its savor it is good for	104	1	for the S. of men until I come
				51	done for your S., and also for their S.
103	10	they are as S. that has lost its savor	109	4	in whose name alone S. can be
		SALUTATION		39	let thy peace and S. be upon that
88	134	he that is found unworthy of this S.		80	let anointed ones be clothed with S.
	136	this is a sample unto you for a S.	123	17	to see the S. of God, and for his arm
		SALUTATIONS	128	5	for S. of the dead who should
88	120	that all your S. may be in name of —109:9, 19		8	which God has prepared for their S.
				11	in relation to S. of children of men
		SALUTE		15	as pertaining to our S.; for their S. is necessary to our S.
88	132	S. his brethren with these words			
	133	I S. you in the name of the Lord		23	proclaiming in our ears glory and S.
	135	they shall S. the president or teacher	133	3	and shall see the S. of their God
			135	3	has done more for S. of men in this
		SALVATION		6	forth for the S. of a ruined world
4	4	but bringeth S. to his soul			**SAME**
6	3	everlasting S. in kingdom of God— 11:3; 12:3; 14:3	1	38	or by voice of my servants, it is the S.
	13	no gift greater than gift of S.	4	4	the S. layeth up in store
7	6	for those who shall be heirs of S.	5	14	to receive this S. testimony among
18	17	and my rock and my S.	6	4	the S. is called of God—11:4; 12:4; 14:4
27	18	and take the helmet of S.			
35	20	to the S. of mine own elect		21	I am the S. that came unto my own—11:29
38	16	for your S. I give a commandment			
42	36	I do this for the S. of my people	8	12	I am the S. that spake unto you
43	25	would have saved you with everlasting S.	10	2	you also lost your gift at S. time
				17	if he bringeth forth the S. words, we have the S. with us
45	58	children grow up without sin unto S.		31	if you should bring forth the S. words
46	7	considering the end of your S.			
63	7	shall see signs but not unto S.		67	and cometh unto me the S. is my church
64	3	for mine own glory and S. of souls		68	the S. is not of me, but against me
68	4	and the power of God unto S.	17	7	you have received the S. power, the S. faith, the S. gift
76	88	for they shall be heirs of S.			

Sec.	Vs.		Sec.	Vs.	
18	9	you are called even with that S. calling	93	22	are partakers of the glory of the S.
	22	the S. shall be saved	102	10	after S. manner that he was appointed
20	12	the S. God, yesterday, today and—35:1		19	to. sanction the S. by their vote
	17	the S. unchangeable God, the framer		22	majority having power to determine S.
	65	regularly organized branch of the S.	107	27	by unanimous voice of the S.; decisions of the S. power and
27	12	the S. things I revealed unto them		29	are not entitled to the S. blessings
29	41	even that S. death which is the last		33	and regulate all the affairs of the S.—34
32	4	unfold the S. to their understanding		67	from the S. comes the administering
35	11	the S. which has made all nations		75	they shall act in the S. office
38	1	the S. which looked upon the wide	109	25	shall fall into the S. himself
	2	the S. which knoweth all things	124	4	at the time of the writing of the S.
	3	I am the S. which spake and the world		33	and for which the S. was instituted
	4	I am the S. which have taken Zion		67	except the S. shall pay his stock
39	3	the S. which came in meridian of		95	crowned with the S. blessings
41	5	and doeth it, the S. is my disciple; the S. is not my disciple		130	another may be appointed unto S.—132
46	15	as it will be pleasing to S. Lord	125	4	take up their inheritance in the S.
49	18	that man should not eat the S.	128	3	when called upon, certify to the S.
50	8	the S. are overcome of the world		4	shall answer the ordinance just the S.; and made a record of the S.
	26	the S. is appointed to be the greatest		9	kept a proper and faithful record of S.
52	8	take their journey to the S. place	129	3	but inherit the S. glory
	15	the S. is accepted of me if he obey	130	2	and that S. sociality which exists
	16	the S. is of God if he obey mine	132	3	who have this law revealed must obey S.
	22	by the way unto this S. land—23, 25, 26, 27	134	3	to enforce laws of the S.
	34	the S. shall be kept and blessed		5	secure public interest at the S. time
	40	the S. is not my disciple		11	where such laws exist as will protect S.
56	2	the S. shall not be saved	135	4	the S. morning, after Hyrum had
58	2	the S. is greater in the kingdom			**SAMUEL**
	26	the S. is a slothful and not a wise	23	4	I speak a few words unto thee S.
	29	keepeth it with slothfulness the S. is damned			**SANCTIFICATION**
	42	repented of his sins, the S. is forgiven	20	31	know also, that S. through the grace
63	20	doeth my will the S. shall overcome	100	15	walk uprightly to S. of the church
	23	the S. shall be in him a well of living			**SANCTIFIED**
68	17	and the keys and authority of the S.—107:15	20	34	let those who are S. also take heed
70	12	the S. is worthy of his hire	39	18	as they do repent and become S.
76	4	from eternity to eternity he is the S.	43	9	thus ye shall become instructed and S.
77	2	four beasts spoken of in S. verse	74	1	unbelieving husband is S. by the wife; and unbelieving wife is S. by
84	89	the S. will feed you and clothe you		7	little children being S. through
88	3	other Comforter is S. that I promised	76	21	they who are S. before his throne
	11	the S. light that quickeneth your	77	1	it is the earth in its S. state
	28	the S. body which was a natural body		12	he finished his work and S. it
	29	shall receive of the S. even a fulness—30, 31	84	33	are S. by the spirit unto renewing of
	34	perfected and sanctified by the S.	88	2	in the book of the names of the S.
	135	with the S. prayer and covenant; in token of the S.		18	must be S. from all unrighteousness

Sanctified   385   Save

Sec.	Vs.	
	20	for this intent are they S.
	21	and they who are not S. through
	26	wherefore it shall be S.
	34	and perfected and S. by the same
	35	cannot be S. by law, by mercy
	116	this is the glory of God and the S.
101	5	not endure chastening cannot be S.
105	31	let it be S. before me
	36	those chosen and they shall be S.
109	12	that it may be S. and consecrated
	13	to acknowledge that thou hast S. it
130	9	this earth in its S. state will be
133	35	the tribe of Judah shall be S.
135	6	go down to posterity as gems for the S.

SANCTIFIETH

133	62	unto him that repenteth and S.

SANCTIFY

20	77	we ask thee to bless and S. this bread
	79	we ask thee to bless and S. this wine
43	11	S. yourselves before me
	16	S. yourselves and ye shall be endowed
76	41	to bear the sins and to S. the world
77	12	even so will the Lord S. the earth
84	23	Moses sought diligently to S. his people
88	68	S. yourselves that your minds
	74	prepare yourselves and S. yourselves
115	9	I *will* S. him before the people
119	6	and by this law S. land of Zion
133	4	prepare ye, O my people, S. yourselves

SANCTION

102	19	to S. the same by their vote

SANCTIONED

102	8	and S. by voice of a general council

SANCTUARY

88	137	that it may become a S. of the spirit

SAND

76	109	or as the S. upon the sea shore
132	30	or if ye were to count the S. upon

SARAH

132	34	S. gave Hagar to Abraham for wife
	65	and he is exempt from the law of S.

SAT

93	15	in form of dove and S. upon him

SATAN

10	5	that you may conquer S.; escape the servants of S.

Sec.	Vs.	
	10	S. has put it into their hearts
	14	I will not suffer that S. shall
	20	S. has a great hold upon their hearts
	22	S. stirreth them up that he may lead
	29	S. saith unto them, he hath deceived
	32	S. will harden hearts of the people
	33	S. thinketh to overpower your testimony
	63	S. doth stir up the hearts of the
19	3	even to destroying of S. and his
24	1	hast been delivered from powers of S.
28	11	are not of me, and S. deceiveth
29	47	power not given S. to tempt little
35	24	S. shall tremble and Zion rejoice
40	2	but straightway S. tempted him
43	31	for S. shall be bound, and when he
45	55	S. shall be bound that he shall have
50	3	S. hath sought to deceive you
53	12	for S. desireth to sift him as chaff
	14	for S. is abroad in the land
63	28	for S. putteth it into their hearts
64	17	he hath sinned and S. seeketh to
76	28	for we beheld S. that old serpent
78	10	S. seeketh to turn their hearts
	12	to buffetings of S. until day of—82:21; 104:9, 10; 132:26
84	100	S. is bound and time is no longer
86	3	in whose hearts even S. sitteth to
88	110	S. shall be bound, that old serpent
101	28	S. shall not have power to tempt any
132	57	for S. seeketh to destroy

SATISFACTION

102	2	settled to the S. of the parties
107	78	as there is not S. upon the decision

SATISFIED

56	15	and your hearts are not S.
	17	whose bellies are not S.

SAVAGE

109	65	converted from their wild and S. condition
135	2	the former was wounded in a S. manner

SAVE

6	12	S. it be to those of thy faith
	16	there is none else S. God that knowest
8	7	no other power S. the power of God
9	7	you took no thought S. it was to ask me
	9	S. it be given you from me

Save   386   Saw

Sec.	Vs.	
15	3	no man knoweth S. me and thee alone—16:3
18	15	and bring S. it be one soul unto me
	20	S. it be the church of the devil
	35	S. it were by my power you could not
19	34	and all S. the support of thy family
33	4	none which doeth good S. it be a few
36	6	S. yourselves from this generation
38	42	S. yourselves, be ye clean
48	4	that ye S. all the money that ye can
58	53	S. it be by the shedding of blood
59	21	S. those who confess not his hand
61	23	come not upon the waters, S. on the canal
64	21	that thereby I may S. some
68	22	S. it be before the First Presidency
77	8	to S. life and to destroy
88	138	S. he is clean from the blood of this
98	33	S. I, the Lord, commanded them
101	55	S. those only whom I have appointed
104	34	all S. the ground which has been
	68	S. it be the holy and sacred writings
109	41	warn them to S. themselves from
124	54	and *will* S. all those of your brethren
130	11	which no man knoweth S. he that
132	38	in nothing did they sin, S. in those
	39	in none of these things did he sin S.
133	47	who spake in righteousness, mighty to S.
134	12	to S. themselves from corruption of
135	3	has done more, S. Jesus only, for the
136	22	in the last days to S. my people

SAVED

3	20	through repentance they might be S.
6	13	thou shalt be S. in kingdom of God
18	22	endure to the end the same shall be S.
	23	none other name whereby man can be S.
	46	keep not commandments cannot be S.
20	25	endure in faith to end should be S.
	29	or they cannot be S. in kingdom
33	12	or they can in nowise be S.
35	25	Israel shall be S. in mine own due
38	33	for Israel shall be S.
42	60	doeth according to these shall be S.
43	25	and would have S. you with an
45	2	harvest ended and your souls not S
49	5	he that receiveth him shall be S.
53	7	he only is S. who endureth

Sec.	Vs.	
56	2	the same shall not be S.
	16	summer is ended and my soul is not S.
68	9	he that is baptized shall be S.—112:29
76	42	that through him all might be S.
100	14	as they keep commandments they shall be S.—17
101	12	all mine Israel shall be S.
	54	and S. my vineyards from the hands
127	12	my prayer is that you all may be S.
131	6	impossible for man to be S. in ignorance
132	17	remain in S. condition to eternity
	32	enter into my law and ye shall be S.
133	53	and the angel of his presence S. them

SAVES

76	43	and S. all the works of his hands
	44	wherefore he S. all except them

SAVIOR

1	20	speak in name of S. of the world
3	16	knowledge of S. has come into the world, so shall knowledge of S. come unto
19	31	declare repentance and faith on S.
	41	yea, come unto me thy S.
20	1	since the coming of our Lord and S.
	4	according to grace of our Lord and S.
	30	justification through grace of our S.
	31	sanctification through grace of our S.
42	1	in my name, the S. of the world
43	34	I am Jesus Christ, the S. of the world
66	1	saith the Lord, your Redeemer, the S.
76	1	and beside him there is no S.
86	11	a S. unto my people Israel
127	11	as the S. said, the prince of this
130	1	when the S. shall appear, we shall see
133	25	the S. shall stand in the midst of

SAVIORS

103	9	they were set to be the S. of men
	10	as they are not the S. of men, they are

SAVOR

101	39	as salt of the earth and S. of men
	40	they are called to be the S. of men; if salt of the earth lose its S.
103	10	as salt that has lost its S.

SAW

76	14	the Son whom we S. and with whom we

Sec.	Vs.
	21 and S. the holy angels and they
	23 for we S. him even on the right hand
	25 and this we S. also and bear record
	30 and we S. a vision of the sufferings
	50 we bear record, for we S. and heard
	71 we S. the terrestrial world, and lo
	80 is the end of the vision we S. of
	81 we S. the glory of the telestial
	89 and thus we S. in the heavenly vision
	91 thus we S. the glory of terrestrial
	92 and we S. the glory of the celestial
	109 we S. the glory and the inhabitants of
	113 this is the end of the vision we S.
77	5 that these elders whom John S., were
	6 understand by the book which John S.
93	6 John S. and bore record of fulness
	7 I S. his glory that he was in the
	12 John S. he received not of fulness
107	49 he S. the Lord and walked with him
110	2 we S. the Lord standing on breastwork
128	3 that he S. with his eyes and heard
	6 and I S. the dead, small and great
135	7 martyrs under the altar that John S.

SAY

Sec.	Vs.
1	8 I S. unto you—1, 34; 5:1, 5, 9, 24, 28; 6:6, 8, 14, 22, 26, 29, 32; 7:3, 5, 8; 8:1; 9:1, 8; 10:1, 11, 14, 20, 28, 30, 37, 38, 56; 11:6, 12, 13, 30; 12:6; 15:6; 16:6; 17:1; 22:1; 25:1, 10, 16; 26:1; 27:2; 28:1, 2, 8, 9; 29:3, 4, 12, 14, 22, 26, 29, 34, 42, 46, 49; 30:1, 5, 9; 31:6, 10; 32:1; 33:1, 2, 5, 7, 12, 18; 34:7, 12; 35:3, 22; 36:1; 37:1, 2; 38:4, 7, 10, 21, 23, 25, 27, 28, 40; 39:5, 7, 8, 14, 16; 40:1; 42:2, 3, 4, 10, 11, 74, 76; 43:2, 4, 7, 13, 27; 44:6; 45:2, 7, 19, 57, 60, 62, 63, 72; 46:1, 5, 6, 9, 10, 17, 31; 47:2, 3; 49:1, 2, 9, 15, 22, 26; 50:2, 7, 17, 25, 36; 51:20; 52:3, 7, 22, 33, 35, 38; 53:1, 5; 54:2, 9; 55:5; 56:8; 57:8, 11; 58:2, 6, 19, 27, 44, 52; 59:16; 61:3, 9, 21, 30, 36; 63:2, 6, 8, 16, 18, 19, 22, 45, 55, 57, 62; 64:2, 3, 7, 9, 14, 18, 20, 24, 36, 41; 66:2, 3, 5; 67:3, 10; 71:2; 72:5, 8, 16, 19; 73:3; 75:1, 3, 6, 14, 15, 17, 24, 28; 78:3, 17; 79:1; 81:1; 82:1, 2, 7, 8, 11, 14, 22; 84:59, 60, 63, 64, 74, 76, 77, 103, 117; 86:2, 5; 88:14, 25, 34, 42, 48, 62, 85, 117, 136; 89:10; 90:1, 3, 6, 12, 19, 28, 30, 32, 34, 36; 91:3; 93:20, 21, 41, 44, 45, 47, 51, 53; 94:1, 4, 10; 95:5, 8, 11; 96:1, 5, 6. 8; 97:1, 2, 3, 8, 10; 98:1, 4, 21, 22, 28, 39; 99:6; 100:5; 101:1, 6, 9, 32, 63, 72, 76, 96; 103:1, 5, 11, 15, 19, 20, 21. 34; 104:1, 19, 57, 78; 105:1, 2, 20, 26, 33, 38; 106:4, 6; 107:60, 78, 85; 112:2, 14, 15, 16, 21, 23, 32, 33; 115:5, 13, 17; 117:12, 16; 119:5, 6; 124:2, 12, 15, 18, 20, 21, 25, 33, 37, 39, 40, 45, 49, 55, 56, 62, 70, 72, 74, 77, 91, 102, 103, 110, 111, 115, 119, 121, 123, 130, 131, 132, 137, 141, 142; 125:2; 128:10; 132:7, 18, 19, 21, 26, 35, 41, 46, 47, 48, 51, 56, 64, 66; 133:7
5	2 now this shall you S. unto him
	25 he shall S. unto the people of this
	26 he shall S. no more, except he shall S. I have seen; these are the words he shall S.
	29 that you shall S. unto him
	30 I S., when thou hast translated
6	9 S. nothing but repentance to this—11:9
10	13 that by lying they may S. they have
	16 they S. and think in their hearts
18	we *will* S. that he has lied in his
31	they *will* S. that you have lied
36	I do not S. you shall not show it
54	I do not S. this to destroy my church but do S. it to build up
20	73 and shall S., calling him by name
	78 he shall take the cup also and S.
24	10 shall not suppose that he can S. enough
29	28 I *will* S. unto them, depart from me
	41 when I shall S., depart ye cursed
34	1 what I the Lord God shall S. unto you
38	29 you S. there will soon be great wars
42	19 I S., thou shalt not kill
43	18 and shall S. to the sleeping nations
	21 what *will* ye S. when the day cometh
45	11 him whom ye S. is the God of Enoch
	18 enemies S. this house shall never
	22 ye S. ye know that the end; ye S. also that ye know the heavens
	23 in this ye S. truly, for so it is

Sec.	Vs.		Sec.	Vs.	
	26	they shall S. Christ delayeth his			**SAYING**
	37	ye S. when they begin to shoot forth	18	41	S., you must repent and be baptized
	51	Jews shall S., what are these wounds	20	76	upon the Father in solemn prayer, S.
	52	I *will* S. unto them these wounds are	29	36	S., Give me thine honor, which is my
49	11	S. unto them like mine apostle of old	33	10	S., repent, repent, and prepare the
50	25	I S. it that you may know	36	3	S., Hosanna, blessed be the name
58	33	then they S. in their hearts, This is not		6	crying repentance, S. save yourselves
61	18	what I S. unto one I S. unto all—61:36; 82:5; 92:1; 93:49; 112:14	39	19	S., the kingdom of heaven is at hand
64	11	ye ought to S. in your hearts, let God	42	7	baptizing with water, S. repent ye
75	8	I S. unto him again, go into the south	43	20	S. prepare for the great day of the —21, 22
76	32	of whom I S. it had been better for		23	S. Hearken. O ye nations of the
	100	they who S. they are some of one and	45	4	S. Father behold the sufferings of
82	10	I am bound when ye do what I S., when ye do not what I S.		16	S., as ye have asked of me concerning
84	57	not only to S. but to do according	52	2	S., I the Lord will make known
85		neither take thought what ye shall S.		9	S. none other things than that
	109	let not the head S. unto the feet	59	5	S., thou shalt love the Lord with all
85	10	these things I S. not of myself	67	7	then ye are justified in S. that ye
90	32	I S. unto you, your brethren in Zion	76	49	heard the voice, S., write the vision
97	19	and shall S., surely Zion is the city		107	S., I have overcome and have trodden
100	6	in the very moment what ye shall S.		110	S., these all shall bow the knee and
	8	unto all things whatsoever ye shall S.	77	9	S., hurt not the earth neither the sea
101	31	shall not sleep, that is to S. in the	78	1	S., hearken unto me saith the Lord
	47	they began to S. among themselves	84	98	and sing this new song, S.
	100	I do not S. they shall not dwell	85	6	quake, while it maketh manifest, S.
102	29	have power to S. whether it is necessary	88	54	unto the third, S., I will visit you
103	22	S. unto the strength of my house—105:16		92	sounding the trump, S., prepare ye
104	70	let not any man among you S. that it		94	S., that great church the mother of
	72	any man among you S. unto treasurer		102	S., there are found among those
105	8	many who *will* S., where is their God		104	S. to all people both in heaven and; S. fear God and give glory—133:38
109	44	help thy servants to S., Thy will		105	S. she is fallen who made all nations
122	6	and shall S., My father, why can't		106	S., it is finished, it is finished
124	26	and S. unto them: come ye with all		135	by S. amen, in token of the same
	47	and do not the things that I S., I will	93	7	S., I saw his glory that he was in
	58	so I S. unto my servant Joseph		15	S., this is my beloved Son
	97	give him in the very hour what he shall S.		26	S., he received a fulness of truth
127	1	I would S. to all those with whom	101	48	S. among themselves, what need have
	10	I *will* S. to all the Saints that I		83	S., avenge me of mine adversary
128	19	that S. unto Zion, behold, thy God	105	25	while we are S. unto the people
	23	again I S. how glorious is the voice	109	6	S., call your solemn assembly
	25	I have many things to S. to you on	110	3	even the voice of Jehovah, S.
133	47	and he shall S., I am he who		12	S. that in us and our seed all
			128	9	this is a faithful S., who can hear it
			129	4	when a messenger comes S. he has a
			133	17	S., prepare ye the way of the Lord
				40	S., O that thou wouldst rend the

Sec.	Vs.	
		SAYINGS
66	11	keep these S. for they are true
68	32	carry these S. to the land of Zion
	34	these S. are true and faithful
72	23	and now I make an end of my S.
82	4	and inasmuch as ye keep not my S.
88	62	I leave these S. with you to ponder
	122	and let all listen unto his S.
89	18	all saints who remember to do these S.
93	19	I give unto you these S.
	48	give more earnest heed unto your S.
	52	inasmuch as you keep my S.
		SAYS
107	58	agreeable to the revelation which S.
	77	agreeable to commandment which S.
128	15	as Paul S. concerning the fathers
	17	for Malachi S., I will send you Elijah
		SCATHE
135	6	if fire can S. a green tree for
		SCATTER
101	57	and S. their watchmen—105:16
		SCATTERED
45	17	and restoration of the S. Israel
	19	destroyed and S. among all nations
	24	shall a remnant be S. among all
101	13	have been S. shall be gathered
	17	notwithstanding her children are S.
	76	those who have been S. by enemies
103	1	who have been S. on land of Zion
	11	your brethren which have been S.
109	61	who have been S. on the mountains
	67	and may all the S. remnants of
113	10	the S. remnants are exhorted to; remnants of Israel in their S. condition
115	3	S. abroad in all the world
124	3	to all nations of earth S. abroad
	35	baptisms by those S. abroad are not
134		over different stakes S. abroad
		SCATTERING
105	30	S. their watchmen and avenging
		SCEPTRE
85	7	mighty and strong, holding the S. of
106	6	when my servant bowed to my S.
121	46	and thy S. an unchanging S. of
		SCHOOL
88	127	for presidency of the S. of prophets
	128	order of house of presidency of S.
	136	in the S. of the prophets
	137	in all your doings in S. of the
	138	not receive any among you in this S.
90	7	the keys of the S. of the prophets

Sec.	Vs.	
	13	preside over the affairs of the S.
95	10	contentions arose in S. of prophets
	17	dedicated for the S. of mine apostles
97	3	concerning the S. in Zion, I am pleased that there should be a S.
	4	he shall continue to preside over S.
	5	to the edification of the S.
	6	and to the residue of the S. I, the
		SCHOOLS
55	4	and writing books for S. in this
		SCORNER
45	50	and the S. shall be consumed
		SCOTT, JACOB
52	28	let Edson Fuller and S. take their
		SCOURGE
5	19	for a desolating S. shall go forth
45	31	until they shall see an overflowing S.
84	58	otherwise there remaineth a S.
	96	to S. them for their wickedness
97	23	the Lord's S. shall pass over by night
124	83	but I have a S. prepared for the
		SCOURGED
63	31	ye shall be S. from city to city
		SCRIBE
25	6	and be unto him for a S., while there is no one to be a S.
90	19	for family of thy counselor and S.
		SCRIP
24	18	thou shalt take no purse nor S.; for shoes, for money, for S.
84	78	I suffered them not to have purse or S.
	86	no man from this hour take purse or S.
		SCRIPTURE
8	1	which contain those parts of my S.
64	12	and do with him as the S. saith
68	4	by the Holy Ghost shall be S.
		SCRIPTURES
6	27	those parts of my S. which have been
10	63	they do wrest the S. and do not
19	7	it is more express than other S.
20	21	as it is written in those S.
	41	and the Holy Ghost according to the S.
	80	shall be dealt with as the S. direct
24	5	expounding all S. to the church
	9	magnify thine office, expound all S.
	14	that the S. might be fulfilled
25	7	shall be ordained to expound S.

Sec.	Vs.	
35	20	the S. shall be given even as
26	1	devoted to the studying of the S.
42	15	until fulness of S. is given
	28	these things are given in my S.
	56	thou shalt ask and my S. shall be
	59	which have been given thee in my S.
68	1	expounding all S. unto them
71	1	expounding mysteries thereof out of S.
74	7	and this is what the S. mean
93	53	should hasten to translate my S.
94	10	printing the translation of my S.
97	5	expounding all S. and mysteries
100	11	mighty in expounding all S.
104	58	print the fulness of my S.

(See Holy Scriptures.)

SCROLL

88	95	as a S. is unfolded after it is

SEA

1	1	that are upon the islands of the S.
29	24	and the fishes of the S.
54	5	that he had been drowned in depth of S.—121:22
77	1	what is the S. of glass spoken of
	9	hurt not the earth neither the S.
88	90	and the voice of the waves of the S.
	94	who sitteth upon islands of the S.
	110	shall stand upon the land and the S.
101	24	fowls of heaven or fish of the S.
117	6	also the fish of the S., and beasts
122	5	if thou art in perils by land or by S.
130	7	on a globe like a S. of glass
133	8	send forth elders to the islands of the S.
	20	shall stand upon islands of the S.
	39	that made heaven, and earth and S.
	68	at my rebuke I dry up the S.

SEAL

1	8	power given to S. both on earth
	9	to S. them *up* unto the day when wrath
68	12	power to S. them *up* to eternal life
77	7	the first S. contains the things
	8	to S. *up* unto life or cast down
	9	to whom is given S. of the living God
	10	or the opening of the sixth S.
	13	after the opening of the seventh S.
88	84	to bind up the law and S. *up* the
98	2	recorded with this S. and testament
101	61	this shall be my S. and blessing
104	62	there shall be a S. upon treasury
	64	and a S. shall be upon it, neither shall the S. be loosed

Sec.	Vs.	
	66	a S. shall be kept upon it that
	67	and a S. shall be placed upon it
109	38	they may S. *up* the law and prepare
	46	enable thy servants to S. *up* the law
121	12	that God hath set to his hand and S.
124	21	I S. upon his head the office
132	46	whatsoever you S. upon earth in my
	49	I will S. upon you your exaltation
135	1	to S. the testimony of this book
	7	is a broad S. affixed to Mormonism
136	39	that he should S. his testimony

SEALED

28	7	and the revelations which are S.
35	18	mystery of those things that have been S.
76	52	who is ordained and S. unto this
	53	and are S. by the Holy Spirit of— 132:7, 19, 26
77	6	book which was S. on the back with
	7	the seven seals with which it was S.
	9	till we have S. the servants of God
	11	those who are S. are High Priests
	12	when he shall have S. all things
109	35	let anointing of thy ministers be S.
124	124	ye are S. *up* unto day of redemption
131	5	knowing that he is S. *up* unto eternal
132	18	and is not S. by Holy Spirit of
	19	S. by the Holy Spirit; as hath been S. upon their heads
	46	S. up earth shall be S. in heaven
133	72	they S. *up* the testimony and bound up
135	3	has S. his mission and his works

SEALING

77	11	by S. of the 144,000 out of all
124	124	to hold the S. blessings of the church
128	14	this is the S. and binding power

SEALS

77	6	was sealed on the back with seven S.
	7	by the seven S. with which it was

SEARCH

1	37	S. these commandments for they are
18	37	you shall S. out the twelve
63	59	I am over all and S. all things
84	94	S. diligently and spare not
90	22	S. diligently to obtain an agent
	24	S. diligently, pray always and be
136	26	make diligent S. till thou shalt

SEARCHING

84	112	S. after the poor to administer to

Sec.	Vs.	
		SEAS
121	4	maker of the heaven, earth and S.
	30	bounds set to the heavens or the S.
128	23	and all the S. and dry lands, tell
		SEASHORE
76	109	or as the sand upon the S.
132	30	were to count the sand upon the S.
		SEASON
3	14	thou hast lost thy privileges for a S.
5	30	thou shalt stop for a S.
29	22	will I spare the earth for a little S.
42	5	they shall go forth for a little S.
43	31	he shall only reign for a little S.
51	16	unto them this land for a little S.
59	18	come of the earth in the S. thereof
63	42	retain his store yet for a little S.
68	33	prayers before Lord in S. thereof
71	2	proclaim for the space of a S.
	3	this is a mission for a S.
88	58	every man in his hour, in his S.
	61	kingdom in its time and in its S.
	71	which they have received for little S.
	111	he shall be loosed for a little S.
89	11	every herb in S., every fruit in S.
100	13	although chastened for a S.—103:4
105	9	mine elders should wait for a little S.—13
	21	let them tarry for a little S.
112	18	burden of churches for a little S.
118	2	let my servant remain for a S.
121	24	a swift judgment in the S. thereof
127	1	wisdom to leave place for short S.
136	9	who are to remain behind this S.
		SEASONS
88	42	by which they move in their times and S.
	44	light to each other in times and S.
121	12	to change the times and S.
		SEAT
69	6	land of Zion shall be a S. to receive
102	26	of the S. of the First Presidency—27, 33
		(See Judgment-seat.)
		SECOND
20	3	to be the S. elder of this church
34	6	way of the Lord for his S. coming
63	17	brimstone, which is the S. death
76	37	the only one on whom the S. death
77	7	and the S. also of the S. thousand
	9	Revelation, 7th Chapter, S. verse
85	12	in the S. chapter of Ezra, 61st and S. verses
88	53	and said unto the S. go ye also; and in the S. hour

Sec.	Vs.	
	57	that he might visit the S. also
	99	which is the S. trump
	109	then shall the S. angel sound his; in the S. thousand years
94	10	the S. lot on the south
	14	and on the first and S. lots
98	25	if your enemy smite you S. time
	35	neither the S. nor the third time
	40	and so on to the S. and third time
	42	if he trespass against thee the S. time
107	13	the S. priesthood is called the
113	1	spoken of in the first, S. verses
	9	bands of her neck; S. verse
127	2	it all has become a S. nature to me
128	14	the S. man is the Lord from heaven
132	61	and if he espouse the S.
		SECONDLY
29	32	S. temporal, and again, S., spiritual
107	33	and S. unto the Jews
129	3	S. the spirits of just men made perfect
		SECRET
1	3	their S. acts shall be revealed—88:108, 109
19	28	before the world as well as in S.
20	47	to pray vocally and in S.—51; 23:6
38	13	a thing which is had in S. chambers
	28	enemy in S. chambers seeketh your lives
42	64	on the earth and of S. combinations
	92	if any offend in S., he shall be rebuked in S.; to confess in S.
60	15	but in S., and wash thy feet
99	4	you shall cleanse your feet in S. places
111	4	they shall not discover your S.
117	11	and of all their S. abominations
128	11	the grand S. of the whole matter
		SECRETS
76	10	make known to them S. of my will
		SECTARIAN
130	3	is an old S. notion and is false
		SECTS
123	12	among all S., parties and denominations
		SECULAR
84	113	to do his S. business as he shall
		SECURE
51	4	that shall S. unto him his portion
109	11	to S. fulfillment of the promises

Sec.	Vs.		Sec.	Vs.	
134	2	as *will* S. to each individual	84	22	no man can S. the face of God
	5	best calculated to S. public interest		98	and shall S. eye to eye
				119	ye cannot S. it now, yet a little while and ye shall S.

SECURED

			88	66	in the wilderness because you cannot S.
24	3	sowed thy fields and S. them, go		68	days will come that you shall S. him
101	65	that wheat may be S. in the garners		93	all people shall S. it together
				116	they shall not any more S. death
				123	S. that ye love one another

SECURITY

			93	1	shall S. my face and know that I am
70	15	a reward for their S.		50	and S. that they are more diligent
			96	4	take heed that ye S. to this matter

SEDITION

			97	16	the pure in heart shall S. God
134	5	S. and rebellion are unbecoming	98	28	S. to it that ye warn in my name
	7	religious opinions do not justify S.	101	23	and all flesh shall S. me together
			104	63	now S. to it that ye go to and make
			112	27	S. to it that ye trouble not

SEDUCED

			113	10	S. the 6th, 7th and 8th verses
46	7	that ye may not be S. by evil spirits	121	24	mine eyes S. and know all their works

SEE

1	2	there is no eye that shall not S.	123	17	to S. the salvation of God
4	2	S. that ye serve him with all your heart	127	1	*will* S. that all my debts are
5	24	a view of things he desires to S.	129	2	handle me and S. for a spirit hath not, as ye S. me have
10	3	S. that you are faithful and continue	130	1	we shall S. him as he is; we shall S. that he is a man like
	16	we *will* S. if God has given him power		15	thou shalt S. the face of the Son
	37	until I shall S. fit to make known		16	whether I should die and thus S. his
14	8	witness of things you shall hear and S.	131	8	we cannot S. it; we shall S. it is all matter
19	29	that thou shalt be permitted to S.	133	3	ends of earth shall S. salvation of
	36	when thou shalt desire to S. thy	136	32	eyes may be opened that he may S.
20	54	and S. that there is no iniquity			

SEED

	55	and S. that the church meet together often; S. that all members do their duty	29	42	God gave unto Adam and unto his S.
35	21	hear my voice and shall S. me	84	18	also upon Aaron and his S.—107:13
38	7	I am in your midst and ye cannot S. me		34	they become the S. of Abraham
	8	day soon cometh that ye shall S. me	86	2	the apostles were the sowers of the S.
	38	S. that all things are preserved	103	17	ye are of the S. of Abraham
41	4	ye shall S. that my law is kept	104	22	upon him and his S. after him
	10	to S. to all things as it shall be		24	inheritance for him and his S.
42	49	he who hath faith to S. shall S.		25	blessings upon him and his S.—37, 40, 41, 42
45	14	they should find it and S. it in		32	for them and their S. after them
	20	this temple which ye now S. shall		33	blessings upon them and their S.
	31	they shall S. an overflowing scourge	107	40	literal descendants of chosen S.
	37	behold the fig-trees and ye S. them	110	12	in us and our S. all generations
	38	when they shall S. all these things	124	58	in thee and thy S. shall the kindred
	40	they shall S. signs and wonders		59	let my servant and his S. after him
	44	they shall S. me in the clouds of		81	for himself and his S. after him—82
	49	they that have laughed shall S. their		90	forsaken, or his S. found begging bread
50	45	you shall hear my voice and S. me	132	30	received promises concerning his S. and as touching Abraham and his S.
56	18	for they shall S. the kingdom of God			
63	7	seeketh signs shall S. signs but not			
67	10	veil shall be rent and you shall S. me			
	14	ye shall S. and know that which was			
76	12	so as to S. and understand the			
	94	they S. as they are seen and know			

Sec.	Vs.		Sec.	Vs.	
		SEEDS			**SEEKETH**
132	19	continuation of the S. forever and	38	28	in secret chambers S. your lives
136	7	to take teams, S., and farming	44	5	wherewith the enemy S. to destroy
		SEEING	46	9	and him that S. so to do
63	36	S. I have decreed all these things	58	39	for he S. the praise of the world
76	117	privilege of S. and knowing for		41	for he S. to excel and is not
101	48	S. this is a time of peace	63	7	he that S. signs shall see signs, but
		SEEK	64	17	and Satan S. to destroy his soul
1	16	they S. not the Lord to establish his	78	10	Satan S. to turn their hearts
6	6	S. to bring forth and establish—	88	35	but S. to become a law unto itself
		11:6; 12:6; 14:6		83	he that S. me early shall find me
	7	S. not for riches but for wisdom—	115		overcome him who S. the throne of him
		11:7	132	57	for Satan S. to destroy
11	21	S. not to declare my word, but S.	136	19	build up himself and S. not my counsel
	23	S. the kingdom of God and all things			**SEEKING**
19	25	nor S. thy neighbor's life	10	27	S. to destroy the souls of men
22	4	and S. not to counsel your God	46	5	who are earnestly S. the kingdom—6
25	10	and S. for the things of a better	82	19	every man S. interest of his neighbor
38	19	if you S. it with all your hearts	97	1	S. diligently to learn wisdom
	39	if ye S. the riches which it is	106	3	S. diligently the kingdom of heaven
45	9	and for the Gentiles to S. to it			**SEEM**
46	8	S. ye earnestly the best gifts	104	85	as it shall S. good unto you
	9	that all may be benefited that S.	127	2	they S. but a small thing to me
54	9	S. ye a living like unto men	128	9	it may S. to some to be a bold doctrine
56	14	you S. to counsel in your own ways			**SEEMED**
63	8	there are those among you who S. signs	107	43	that he S. to be like unto his father
	65	S. them a home as they are taught			**SEEMETH**
66	10	S. not to be cumbered	38	37	let them be left or rented as S. good
67	6	S. ye out of the book of commandments	40	3	to do with him as S. me good
68	31	they also S. not the riches of eternity	41	8	Rigdon should live as S. him good
88	63	S. me diligently and ye shall find me	42	16	ye shall speak and prophecy as S. me
	118	S. ye diligently and teach one; S. ye out of the best books; S. learning even by study—109:7	48	3	let them buy as S. them good
			52	6	they shall be cut off as S. me good
96	3	benefit of those who S. inheritances	56	4	I command and revoke as S. me good
	9	S. diligently to take away incumbrances	58	38	may receive his inheritance as S. him
98	16	S. diligently to turn the hearts of		51	as S. him good or as he shall direct
	23	neither S. revenge shall be rewarded	60	5	be a craft made or bought as S. you good
101	38	S. the face of the Lord always	61	35	let them journey together as S. them
103	32	S. diligently that peradventure you—33	62	5	you may return altogether as S. you
109	14	that they may S. learning even by study	64	28	should take and pay as S. him good
			84	103	as Lord shall direct for thus it S. me
122	2	shall S. counsel and authority and	100	1	I will do with them as S. me good
124	109	not my will he shall S. safety out	124	72	for building of that house as S. him
136	19	if any man shall S. to build up himself		77	pay stock into that house as S. him good—80, 81
	20	S. ye and keep all your pledges			

Sec.	Vs.	
		SEEMS
127	2	and for what cause S. mysterious
128	1	as that subject S. to occupy my mind
		SEEN
5	25	I have S. the things the Lord has shown; they are true for I have S. them
	26	except he shall say I have S. them
17	3	and have S. them with your eyes
	5	ye shall testify that you have S. them; as Joseph has S. them; he has S.
21	8	his weeping for Zion I have S.
25	4	because of things thou hast not S.
39	9	thou hast S. great sorrow
50	4	I have S. the abominations in the church
52	36	declaring that which they have S.
64	19	that which he hath S. and heard
67	11	for no man has S. God at any time
76	10	those things which eye hath not S.
94		and they see as they are S.
116		they are only to be S. and understood
88	47	any man who hath S. the least of these, hath S. God moving
	48	I say unto you he hath S. him
	50	then shall ye know that ye have S. me
101	54	the watchman would have S. the enemy
124	17	I have S. the work he hath done
126	2	I have S. your labor and toil
128	4	just the same as if he had S. with his
132	50	I have S. your sacrifices and will
133	45	neither hath any eye S., O God, how
135	5	because thou hast S. thy weakness
		SEER
21	1	thou shalt be called a S., a translator
107	92	yea, to be a S., a revelator, a
124	94	that he may be a prophet and a S.
	125	to be a revelator, a S. and prophet
127	12	your servant, prophet and S. of the
135	3	Joseph Smith, the prophet and S.
		SEIZE
45	74	that fear may S. upon them
		SEIZED
50	33	neither with rejoicing lest you be S.
		SELECT
57	13	to copy, and to correct and S.

Sec.	Vs.	
		SELECTED
58	14	and have S. my servant Edward
		SELECTING
55	4	and of S. and writing books for
69	8	expounding, writing, S. and obtaining
		SELECTION
25	11	to make a S. of sacred hymns as it
		SELFISHNESS
56	8	must repent of his pride and S.
		SELL
57	8	that he may S. goods without fraud
64	21	I will not that my servant should S.
	26	should not S. their store and possessions
101	96	should S. my storehouse which I have
104	36	is my will that he should S. lots
124	69	and do not S. or convey the stock
		SEND
5	15	three witnesses *will* I S. *forth* of
10	45	engravings of Nephi and S. *forth* in
20	81	to S. one or more of their teachers
	82	or S. by the hand of some priest
24	24	I *will* S. upon them a cursing—6
25	6	that I may S. my servant Oliver
29	18	I *will* S. *forth* flies upon the face
	42	until I should S. *forth* angels
38	35	and S. them *forth* to the place
49	3	wherefore I S. you to preach the
52	11	I *will* S. *forth* judgment unto victory
57	9	that he may S. goods unto the people
63	54	in that day *will* I S. mine angels
66	6	inasmuch as you can S., S.
	9	return not until I shall S. you
69	5	S. *forth* accounts of their stewardships
70	16	whithersoever I shall S. them
79	2	I *will* S. upon him the Comforter
84	62	place ye cannot go ye shall S.
79		I S. you out to prove the world
87		I S. you out to reprove the world
103		that they should S. it unto them
104		S. it *up* unto the bishop in Zion
107		S. them before you to make appointments
85	7	I *will* S. one mighty and strong
88	3	I now S. upon you another Comforter
	72	and will raise up elders and S. unto
	80	when I shall S. you again to magnify

Sec.	Vs.		Sec.	Vs.	
101	73	and S. them to purchase these lands	38	38	when men are endowed and S. forth
103	23	S. *up* wise men with their moneys	39	11	gospel which I have S. *forth* in; S. *forth* to recover my people
104	80	until I shall S. means unto you			
108	6	preach my gospel wheresoever I shall S.	42	63	my servants shall be S. *forth* to the
109	30	by the judgments which thou wilt S.	43	15	ye are not S. *forth* to be taught but to
	38	those judgments thou art about to S.	45	9	I have S. mine everlasting covenant —49:9
112	1	and to S. it abroad among all nations	49	5	I have S. mine only begotten Son
	4	thou shalt S. *forth* my word unto ends	50	14	which was S. *forth* to teach the truth
	19	whithersoever they shall S. you		17	S. *forth* to preach the word of truth
	21	whosoever ye shall S. in my name; whithersoever ye shall S.		26	he that is ordained and S. *forth*
117	1	before I S. again the snows		27	the spirit and the power S. *forth* by
123	6	before he can S. *forth* the power	58	1	this land unto which I have S. you
124	26	and S. ye swift messengers		6	I have S. you that you might be
	128	to S. my word to every creature		14	for this cause I have S. you hither
	139	shall S. them to prepare a way before		54	let there be workmen S. *forth* of all
126	3	command you to S. my word abroad	60	9	for this intent have I S. them
127	10	and S. it to you by mail		13	they have been S. to preach my
128	17	I *will* S. you Elijah the prophet		16	and the will of him who hath S. you
133	8	S. *forth* the elders of my church; S. *forth* unto foreign lands	63	40	let all moneys be S. *up* unto land —43

SENDETH

			64	35	shall be S. away and shall not inherit
63	48	he that S. *up* treasures to the land	65	1	as one S. *down* from on high

SENDING

			66	2	S. *forth* unto the children of men
124	16	in S. my word to the kings of the	75	24	who must needs be S. into the world

SENECA

			77	8	they are four angels S. *forth* from God
128	20	in wilderness, Fayette, S. County	84	32	many whom I have called and S. *forth*
	21	in S. county and at sundry times		76	rebellion against you at time I S. you

SENSE

128	14	and in one S. of the word, the keys	86	5	ready and waiting to be S. *forth* to reap

SENSUAL

			88	51	he S. *forth* his servants into the field
20	20	man became S. and devilish,		81	I S. you out to testify and warn the
29	35	they are not temporal, neither S.	89	2	to be S. greeting—not by commandment

SENT

27	5	whom I have S. unto you to reveal the	95	10	I S. them forth to be chastened
	8	John, whom I have S. unto you	99	6	and kindly S. *up* unto the bishop
	12	and James and John whom I have S.	105	15	the destroyer I have S. forth to
	16	which I have S. mine angels to commit		28	and to have S. wise men to fulfil
29	8	desolation are S. *forth* upon wicked	107	35	the Twelve being S. out holding keys
	16	hailstorm S. *forth* to destroy crops	109	57	thy servants, and that thou hast S. us
35	4	thou wast S. *forth* even as John			
	12	my gospel which I have S. forth	110	14	Elijah should be S. before the great
	17	I have S. *forth* fulness of my Gospel	112	20	receiveth those whom I have S.
36	5	shall be ordained and S. *forth*		32	being S. down from heaven unto you
	7	every man may be ordained and S. *forth*			

Sec.	Vs.		Sec.	Vs.	
132	24	and Jesus Christ whom he hath S.		26	I command my S. Martin Harris, he
	59	and by the voice of him that S. me		29	if this be the case I command you my S.
133	17	the Lord hath S. forth the angel		32	I foresee that if my S. Martin Harris
	36	I have S. *forth* my angel flying			
	57	the Lord S. *forth* fulness of Gospel	6	18	stand by my S. Joseph faithfully
	71	when they were S. you received them not		25	to translate even as my S. Joseph
135	3	has S. fulness of everlasting gospel		28	I give unto my S. Joseph the keys
136	33	my spirit is S. *forth* into the world	9	1	and did commence again to write for my S.
	36	they killed them that were S. unto them		4	work is to write for my S. Joseph
		SENTENCE		12	I have given to my S. sufficient strength
122	7	and the S. of death passed upon thee	15	1	hearken my S. John and listen
		SEPARATED	16	1	hearken my S. Peter and listen
45	12	who were S. from the earth and were	17	4	that my S. may not be destroyed
61	35	be not S. until they return		5	even as my S. has seen them
93	34	and when S. man cannot receive a	18	1	because of the thing that you my S.
106	6	when my servant S. himself from the		7	been baptized by hand of my S.
135	3	and in death they were not S.	19	13	received by hand of my S.
		SEPARATELY	25	5	shall be for a comfort of my S.
132	17	but remain S. and singly, without		6	that I may send my S. whithersoever
		SEPARATION	28	2	no one shall be appointed excepting my S.
63	54	at that hour cometh entire S. of the		10	my S. shall be appointed to preside
		SERAPHIC	30	9	my S. John, thou shalt commence from
38	1	and all the S. hosts of heaven.	31	4	things which have been revealed to my S.
		SERAPHS	32	1	now concerning my S. Parley P. Pratt
109	79	shining S. around thy throne	35	3	my S. Sidney, I have looked upon thee
		SERPENT		17	fulness of my Gospel by hand of my S.
76	28	for we beheld Satan, that old S.			
84	72	and the poison of a S. shall not	36	1	my S. Edward you are blessed and
88	110	Satan shall be bound, that old S.		2	by the hand of my S. Sidney Rigdon
124	99	where the poisonous S. can not lay hold	37	3	against the time my S. Oliver shall
		SERPENTS	39	7	my S. James I have looked upon thy
24	13	healing sick and against poisonous S.	40	1	heart of my S. Coville was right
111	11	be ye wise as S. and yet without sin	41	7	my S. Joseph should have a house built
		SERVANT		8	my S. Sidney should live as seemeth
1	17	I called upon my S. Joseph Smith		9	I have called my S. Edward, and give
	29	my S. might have power to translate	42	10	my S. Edward shall stand in his office
5	1	as my S. has desired a witness that my S. Joseph have	43	12	appoint ye my S. and uphold him
	2	have given these things unto you my S.	47	1	my S. John should write and keep a; assist my S. Joseph
	7	they would not believe my S.	49	4	and my S. Leman should be ordained
	9	which I have entrusted unto you my S.	50	26	notwithstanding he is least and S. of all
	21	I command you my S. to repent		36	words of mine from the mouth of my S.
	23	again I speak unto you my S. Joseph			

Sec.	Vs.	
	37	let my S. Joseph Wakefield, in whom; and my S. Parley
	38	and also my S. John Corrill, or
	39	in this thing my S. is not justified
51	1	I will speak unto my S. Edward
	3	let my S. and those he has chosen
	4	let my S. give unto him a writing
	18	this shall be an example unto my S.
52	7	let my S. Lyman Wight and my S. Corrill
	8	and my S. John Murdock and my S. Hyrum
	12	let my S. Lyman Wight beware for
	22	let my S. Thos. B. Marsh and my S. Ezra
	23	let my S. Isaac Morley and my S. Ezra
	41	let there be one obtained for my S.
53	1	my S. Sidney Gilbert, I have heard your
54	2	my S. Newel Knight, you shall stand fast
55	1	my S. William, thou are called and
	2	thou shalt be ordained by hand of my S.
	4	you shall be ordained to assist my S.
	6	let my S. Joseph Coe take his journey
56	5	a new commandment to my S. Thomas and my S. Selah
	7	let my S. Newel Knight remain with them
	8	my S. Ezra Thayre must repent of pride
	12	and if my S. must needs pay the money
57	6	let my S. stand in the office— 7; 58:40
	8	let my S. plant himself in this place
	9	let my S. obtain a license, here is
	11	let my S. be planted in this place
	13	let my S. assist him as commanded
58	14	I have selected my S. Edward
	24	as I spake concerning my S. Edward
	26	is a slothful and not a wise S.
	35	my S. Martin Harris should be an example
	38	other directions concerning my S.
	50	my S. Sidney shall write a description
	57	let my S. Sidney consecrate this land
	62	let my S. Edward direct the conference
60	10	let my S. Edward impart of the money
	17	by mouth of my S. it shall be made

Sec.	Vs.	
61	7	expedient that my S. Sidney and my S. William be in haste
	12	let my S. Sidney take that which is not
	14	by mouth of my S. John I cursed the
	35	let my S. Reynolds and my S. Samuel be not
63	39	let my S. Titus who has the care thereof
	41	I will give unto my S. Joseph power
	42	let my S. Newel K. retain his store
	46	visit the churches with my S. Oliver
	55	I am not pleased with my S. Sidney
64	5	the keys shall not be taken from my S.
	15	who was my S. Ezra Booth and also my S. Isaac Morley
	16	I have forgiven my S. Isaac Morley
	17	my S. Edward, he hath sinned
	18	it is expedient that my S. Sidney
	20	that my S. Isaac may not be tempted
	21	will not that my S. Frederick should sell
66	1	unto my S. William E., blessed are you
	3	my S. William, you are clean but not all
	8	let my S. Samuel H. go with you
67	5	your eyes have been upon my S. Joseph
	14	conferred upon you by my S. Joseph
68	1	my S. Orson Hyde was called by his
	7	this is the word of the Lord unto my S. Orson, and my S. Luke, and my S. Lyman, and my S. William E.
	32	let my S. Oliver carry these sayings
69	1	for my S. Oliver Cowdery's sake
	2	my S. John should go with my S. Oliver
	4	assistance from my S. Oliver
	7	let my S. John travel many times from
70	1	word which I give my S. Joseph, my S. Martin, my S. Oliver, my S. John, my S. Sidney, and my S. William W.
72	8	my S. Newel K. is the man who shall be
75	6	I say unto my S. William E., I revoke
	9	let my S. Luke go with him and
	13	let my S. Orson and my S. Samuel H. take their

Sec.	Vs.		Sec.	Vs.	
	14	I say unto my S. Lyman and my S. Orson	101	59	the S. said unto his Lord. When shall
	15	I say unto my S. Asa and my S. Calves		60	and he said to his S.: when I will, go
	17	I say unto my S. Major and my S. Burr		62	and his S. went straightway and did
	30	let my S. Simeon and my S. Emer be united in ministry		96	that my S. Gilbert should sell my
	31	and also my S. Ezra and my S. Thomas B.	103	21	my S. Baurak Ale, is the man to whom I likened the S.
	32	and also my S. Hyrum and my S. Reynolds		22	then let my S. Baurak say unto my house
	33	and also my S. Daniel and my S. Seymour		29	my S. Sidney shall lift up his voice
	34	and also my S. Sylvester and my S. Gideon		30	my S. Parley P. and my S. Lyman, should not return
	35	and also my S. Ruggles and my S. Stephen		35	my S. Baurak Ale. may go with you
	36	and also my S. Micah and my S. Eden		37	let my S. Parley P. journey with my S. Joseph
78	9	let my S. Ahashdah, and my S. Gazelam, and my S. Pelagoram		38	let my S. Lyman journey with my S. Sidney
79	1	my S. Jared should go again into the		39	let my S. Hyrum journey with my S. Frederick G.
	4	let your heart be glad my S. Jared		40	let my S. Orson, journey with my S. Orson Pratt, whithersoever my S. Joseph
80	1	my S. Stephen, go ye into the world	104	20	let my S. Pelagoram have the place
	2	I will give unto you my S. Eden		22	I confer upon my S. Pelagoram a blessing
81	1	my S. Frederick G., listen to the voice; and a counselor to my S. Joseph		24	let my S. Mahemson have the lot which my S. Zombre
82	11	it is expedient for my S. Gazelam, etc., to be bound together		26	let my S. Mahemson devote his moneys as my S. Gazelam shall
84	1	a revelation unto his S. Joseph and six		27	let my S. Shaderlaomach have the place
90	20	let my aged S. Joseph continue with		28	let my S. Olihah have the lot which is
	25	especially my aged S. Joseph		34	let my S. Zombre have the house, save those lots named for my S. Olihah
	35	not well pleased with my S. William E., neither my S. Sidney		39	let my S. Ahashdah have appointed unto
92	1	concerning my S. Shaderlaomach —2		40	all this I have appointed to my S. Ahashdah—41
93	41	my S. Frederick G., you have continued		43	let my S. Gazelam have appointed unto him
	44	my S. Sidney in some things hath not		45	in the house of my S. Gazelam
	45	I say unto my S. Joseph, ye shall have		46	blessings upon house of my S. Gazelam
	50	my S. Newel K. need to be chastened	105	16	have commanded my S. Baurak Ale
	51	let my S. Sidney go his journey		21	inasmuch as my S. Joseph shall appoint
94	13	on the third lot shall my S. Hyrum		27	until my S. Baurak Ale shall have time
96	2	let my S. Ahashdah take charge of		36	it shall be manifest unto my S.
	6	my S. Zombre, whose offering I have	106	1	my S. Warren A. should be appointed
97	3	my S. Parley P., for he abideth in me		6	when my S. Warren bowed to my sceptre
98	32	the law I gave unto my S. Nephi		7	blessed is my S. Warren, for I will
99	1	my S. John, thou art called to go			
100	9	my S. Sidney should be a spokesman unto my S. Joseph			

Sec.	Vs.	
108	1	my S. Lyman, your sins are forgiven
109	29	spread lying reports against thy S.
	68	O Lord, remember thy S. Joseph
112	1	my S. Thomas, I have heard thy prayers
	15	rebel not against my S. Joseph
	16	my S. Thomas, thou art the man
	17	thou mayest be my S. to unlock, where my S. Joseph, and my S. Sidney, and my S. Hyrum cannot come
113	4	it is a S. in the hands of Christ
114	1	that my S. David W. settle up all his
115	1	thus saith the Lord to my S. Joseph, and my S. Sidney, and my S. Hyrum—13
	2	and also to my S. Edward
	16	which I shall show unto my S. Joseph
	18	they shall be manifest unto my S. Joseph
117	1	saith the Lord to my S. William and my S. Newel K., let them
	10	let my S. William be faithful over a few
	11	let my S. Newel K. be ashamed of the
	12	I remember my S. Oliver and say
	15	let no man despise my S. Oliver
118	2	let my S. Thomas remain for a season
	6	let my S. John, and my S. John E., and my S. Wilford, and my S. Willard, be appointed
124	1	my S. Joseph, I am well pleased
	12	let my S. Robert B. help you to write
	15	blessed is my S. Hyrum for he
	16	let my S. John C. help you in your labor; my S. Joseph in hour of affliction
	18	my S. Lyman should continue in
	19	as I did my S. David, and my S. Edward, and my aged S. Joseph
	20	my S. George is without guile
	21	bishopric like unto my S. Edward; let no man despise my S. George
	22	let my S. George, my S. Lyman, my S. John build as my S. Joseph shall
	42	I will show unto my S. Joseph all
	56	let my S. Joseph and his house have
	58	so I say unto my S. Joseph, in thee
	59	let my S. Joseph and his seed after
	62	let my S. George, my S. Lyman, my S. John, and my S. Peter organize—70

Sec.	Vs.	
	72	let my S. Joseph pay stock into their; but my S. cannot pay over
	74	say unto you concerning my S. Vinson
	77	let my S. Hyrum put stock into that
	78	let my S. Isaac put stock into that
	79	let my S. Isaac be appointed among you, be ordained by my S. William, and blessed by my S. Hyrum to accomplish work that my S. Joseph shall
	80	let my S. William pay stock into that
	81	let my S. Henry G. pay stock into
	82	let my S. William pay stock into
	84	with my S. Almon I am not well pleased
	87	let my S. William put his trust in me
	88	let my S. William go and proclaim
	89	hearken to the counsel of my S. Joseph
	91	let my S. William be ordained counselor to my S. Joseph, in room of my S. Hyrum, that my S. Hyrum may take
	94	revelator as well as my S. Joseph
	95	that he may act in concert with my S. Joseph, receive counsel from my S. Joseph; once were upon him that was my S. Oliver
	96	that my S. Hyrum may bear record
	97	let my S. William receive the keys
	101	let my S. William cry aloud
	102	I have a mission for my S. William, and my S. Hyrum; let my S. Joseph tarry at home
	103	if my S. Sidney will serve me and be counselor to my S. Joseph
	105	in which my S. Joseph resides
	107	let him assist my S. Joseph; and let my S. William assist my S. Joseph
	108	if my S. Sidney will do my will let
	111	let my S. Amos pay stock into the
	112	hearken to counsel of my S. Joseph
	115	if my S. Robert D. will obey my voice, let him build a house for my S. Joseph
	125	my S. Joseph to be a presiding elder
	126	for counselors my S. Sidney and my S. William
	127	I give unto you my S. Brigham

Sec.	Vs.		Sec.	Vs.	
	132	let my S. Aaron be ordained unto his		24	let my S. Edward and Martin take journey with my S.
125	2	which I shall appoint by my S. Joseph		25	let my S. David and Harvey take
126	1	saith the Lord unto you my S. Brigham		26	let my S. Parley and Orson take
127	12	I subscribe myself your S. in the Lord		27	let my S. Solomon and Simeon take
				28	let my S. Edson and Jacob take
128	25	I am as ever your humble S.		29	let my S. Levi and Zebedee take
132	1	saith the Lord unto my S. Joseph		30	let my S. Reynolds and Samuel take
	7	appointed my S. Joseph to hold this		31	let my S. Wheeler and William take
	19	whatsoever my S. hath put upon them		32	let my S. Newel and Selah also take
	30	from whose loins ye are, my S. Joseph		35	let my S. Joseph and Solomon take
	39	by the hand of Nathan my S.		41	let my S. Joseph, Sidney and Edward take recommend
	40	I gave unto thee my S. Joseph	53	5	take your journey with my S. Joseph and—55:5
	44	and I reveal it unto you my S. Joseph	56	5	revoke commandment given my S. —6
	48	I say unto you my S. Joseph	58	58	let my S. Sidney and Joseph return
	52	receive all those given my S. Joseph	60	6	let my S. Sidney, Joseph and Oliver take
	53	my S. Joseph shall be made ruler	61	9	let my S. Sidney and William W. take their
	54	to abide and cleave unto my S. Joseph		23	concerning my S. Sidney, Joseph and Oliver
	55	then shall my S. Joseph do all things.		30	my S. Sidney, Joseph and Oliver shall not
	56	forgive my S. Joseph his trespasses	63	65	let my S. Joseph and Sidney seek them a home
	57	let not my S. Joseph put his property; for I am the Lord and he is my S.	64	26	not meet that my S. should sell their store
	60	let no one set upon my S. Joseph	68	5	the promise of the Lord unto you my S.
		SERVANTS	69	5	my S. should send forth the accounts
1	6	this is the authority of my S.	70	15	this commandment I give unto my S.
	14	neither the voice of his S.	71	1	my S. Joseph and Sidney, the time has come
	24	these commandments were given unto my S.	72	20	let my S. appointed as stewards
	38	whether by mine own voice or my S.	73	3	my S., it is expedient to translate
5	11	the testimony of three of my S.	76	112	they shall be S. of the Most High
10	5	may escape hands of S. of Satan	77	9	sealed the S. of God in their foreheads
27	8	which John I have sent you my S.	82	1	I say unto you my servants
32	2	he shall go with my S. Oliver and		11	expedient for my S. Alam and
33	1	my S. Ezra and Northrop, open your ears	84	36	he that receiveth my S. receiveth me
36	5	as many as shall come before my S.		117	I say unto the rest of my S. go ye
42	4	excepting my S. Joseph and Sidney	86	1	unto you my S. concerning parable of
	63	my S. shall be sent forth to the east	88	51	he sent forth his S. into the field
43	25	called upon you by mouth of my S.	93	46	I called you S. for world's sake, and you are their S. for my sake.
	30	spoken by the mouth of my S.		52	let my S. Joseph and, make haste
44	1	thus saith the Lord unto you my S.	94	14	on first and second lots shall my S.
49	1	hearken my S. Sidney, Parley and Leman	95	10	my S. sinned a grievous sin
	3	I send you my S. Sidney and Parley			
	4	which shall be taught him by you my S.			
50	38	as many of my S. as are ordained			
52	3	let my S. Joseph and Sidney take			

Sec.	Vs.		Sec.	Vs.	
100	14	my S. Orson and John are in my hands		38	as also Solomon and Moses my S., as also many others of my S.
101	44	he said unto his S., go unto my	133	30	unto children of Ephraim, my S.
	46	the S. of the nobleman went and did		32	by the hands of the S. of the Lord
	51	S. of the nobleman arose and fled		38	and the S. of God shall go forth
	52	he called upon his S. and said unto		71	ye believed not my S. and when they
	55	said unto one of his S. go and gather residue of my S.; also among all my S.	136	12	let my S. organize a company—
104	4	some of my S. have not kept the		13, 14	
	29	let my S. have the printing office		16	let my S. that have been appointed go
108	4	solemn assembly shall be called of my S.		37	mine angels, my ministering S.
109	1	and showest mercy unto thy S.			**SERVE**
	2	who hast commanded thy S. to build	4	2	see that ye S. him with all your heart
	3	thy S. have done according to thy		3	if ye have desires to S. God ye are
	4	workmanship of the hands of thy S.	20	19	that they should love and S. him
	22	that thy S. may go forth from this		31	who love and S. God with all their
	29	have spread lying reports against thy S.		37	having a determination to S. him
	31	thy S. have been innocent before thee	38	26	twelve sons, and they S. him obediently
	33	break it off from necks of thy S.	42	29	thou shalt S. me and keep all my
	38	put upon thy S. the testimony of the	59	5	in name of Jesus Christ thou shalt S. him
	39	whatsoever city thy S. shall enter—	76	5	delight to honor those who S. me
	41		100	16	a people that *will* S. me in righteousness
	41	receive not testimony of thy S. and thy S. warn them	124	103	if my servant Sidney *will* S. me
	42	deliver thou thy S. from their hands			**SERVICE**
	44	helps thy S. to say, thy will be done	4	2	O ye that embark in the S. of God
	46	enable thy S. to seal up the law	24	7	shalt devote all thy S. in Zion
	56	when thy S. shall go out of thy house	57	9	as clerks employed in his S.
	57	that we thy S. have heard thy voice			**SERVICES**
	58	that thy S. may gather out the	42	72	just remuneration for all their S.
110	8	yea I will appear unto my S.		73	the bishop also for all his S.
	9	endowment with which thy S. have been			**SERVITUDE**
112	1	through instrumentality of my S.	134	12	allowing human beings held in S.
115	3	and also unto my faithful S. who			**SET**
117	16	let all my S. in land of Kirtland	3	7	although men S. at naught the counsel
121	2	wrongs of thy people and of thy S.		13	who has S. at naught the counsels
	6	thy S. will rejoice in thy name	30	2	and to those who were S. over you
	17	because they are the S. of sin	42	31	appointed and S. apart for that
	18	who swear falsely against my S.	45	48	shall the Lord S. his foot upon this
124	8	if they reject my S. and my testimony	64	30	he hath S. you to provide for his
	45	hearken unto the voice of my S.	65	5	kingdom which is S. *up* on the earth
	118	hearken to the counsel of my S.	68	14	other bishops to be S. apart unto
	134	presidents or S. over different stakes		19	provided he is called and S. apart— 107:17
132	1	wherein I justified my S. Abraham, Isaac, etc., my S.		22	no High Priest who shall be S. apart
	16	which angels are ministering S. to	78	16	established his feet and S. him on
			85	7	to S. in order the house of God
			90	15	and S. in order the churches
				16	and S. in order all the affairs of

Sec.	Vs.		Sec.	Vs.	
	18	S. in order your houses	117	1	let them S. *up* their business speedily
93	43	you shall S. in order your own house			**SETTLED**
	44	therefore, first, S. in order thy	102	2	which could not be S. by the church
	50	and S. in order his family and see			**SETTLING**
96	1	that I have S. for the strength of	102	2	for purpose of S. important difficulties
101	45	and S. watchmen round about them			**SEVEN**
	46	and S. watchmen and began to build	77	5	who belonged to the S. churches
	53	and S. watchmen upon the walls thereof, and S. a		6	sealed on back with S. seals
103	9	they were S. to be a light unto		7	by the S. seals with which it was
104	28	have the lot which is S. off joining		12	sounding of trumpets of the S. angels
107	55	I have S. thee to be at the head	98	40	forgive him until seventy times S.
	58	to ordain and S. in order all the	102	6	cannot have power to act without S.
	71	may be S. apart unto ministering of		7	these S. shall have power to appoint
	74	where he shall be S. apart unto this	107	46	Mahalaleel was 496 years and S. days old
109	72	the kingdom which thou hast S. up		93	they should have S. presidents to
121	12	God hath S. to his hand and seal		95	these S. presidents are to choose
	29	shall be revealed and S. forth upon		96	until S. times seventy if the labor
	30	if there be bounds S. to the heavens			*(See Seven Thousand.)*
	31	all their glories, laws and S. times			**SEVENTEEN**
	35	their hearts are S. so much upon the	102	5	as follows: nine high priests, S. elders
122	9	for their bounds are S. they cannot	130	10	stone mentioned in Revelation 2:S.
124	6	for the S. time has come to favor her			**SEVENTEENTH**
	61	whom I have S. to be as plants	131	5	May S., 1843: The more sure word
128	9	to *any* man or *any* S. of men			**SEVENTH**
132	19	angels and Gods which are S. there	77	7	and so on until the S.
	60	let no one S. on my servant Joseph		8	spoken of in the S. chapter, 1st verse
		SETH		9	Revelation S. chapter. 2nd verse
96	7	for he is a descendant of S. (Joseph)		12	and on the S. day he finished his work, so in the beginning of the S. thousand; finishing his work in beginning of S.
107	42	from Adam to S., who was ordained by		13	after the opening of the S. seal
	43	because he, S., was a perfect man	88	106	which is the S. angel, saying
	51	when he was ordained under hand of S.		110	and so on until S. angel shall sound
	53	Adam called S., Enos, and, into the		112	and Michael, the S. angel, even the
		SETS	107	94	and the S. president of these is to
3	4	and S. at naught the counsels of God	113	10	see the sixth, S. and eighth verses
		SETTETH			**SEVEN THOUSAND**
124	84	he S. *up* a golden calf for worship	77	6	during the S. years of its continuance
		SETTING			**SEVENTIES**
84	117	S. *forth* clearly and understandingly	124	138	to preside over the quorum of S.
		SETTLE			**SEVENTY**
28	14	thou shalt assist to S. all these	98	40	thou shalt forgive until S. times
90	31	that she may S. down in peace	107	25	the S. are also called to preach
102	24	to S. difficulties when the parties		34	the S. are to act in the name of
114	1	that he S. *up* all his business as soon			

Sec.	Vs.	
	38	call upon the S. when they need
	90	is a distinct one from that of the S.
	93	vision, showing the order of the S., chosen out of the S.
	95	are to choose other S. besides the first S.
	96	and also other S. until seven times S.
	97	these S. are to be traveling ministers
	98	belong not to Twelve neither to the S.

SEVERAL

Sec.	Vs.	
20	61	the S. elders composing this church
	81	be the duty of the S. churches; teacher to attend the S. conferences
	82	with list of the names of the S.
52	33	journey into their S. courses
73	2	by voice of conference their S. missions
82	11	together in your S. stewardships
84	117	go ye forth in your S. callings
97	13	work of ministry in their S. callings
107	21	to the S. offices in these priesthoods
	32	a general assembly of the S. quorums
	38	to fill the S. calls for preaching

SEVERALLY

Sec.	Vs.	
107	63	S. as they are appointed

SEVERED

Sec.	Vs.	
121	19	they shall be S. from ordinances of

SHACKLES

Sec.	Vs.	
123	8	they are the very S. and fetters of hell

SHADOW

Sec.	Vs.	
57	10	who sit in the region and S. of death
127	1	have not the least S. of justice

SHAFT

Sec.	Vs.	
85	8	shall fall by the S. of death, as tree by S. of lightning

SHAKE

Sec.	Vs.	
10	56	cause them to tremble and S. to the
21	6	cause heavens to S. for your good —35:24
38	30	louder than that which S. the earth
43	18	heavens shall S. and earth shall tremble
45	48	and the heavens also shall S.

Sec.	Vs.	
60	15	S. off the dust of thy feet against —75:20
84	118	I *will* not only S. the earth, but
129	4	request him to S. hands with you
	7	ask him to S. hands with you, but he
	8	when you ask him to S. hands he will

SHAKEN

Sec.	Vs.	
49	23	for the heavens to be S. and the
132	14	shall be S. and destroyed

SHAKERS

Sec.	Vs.	
49	1	even as ye have received it, unto the S.

SHALEMANASSEH

Sec.	Vs.	
82	11	and S. and Mahemson, to be bound

SHAME

Sec.	Vs.	
10	23	and it shall turn to their S.
71	7	their S. shall be made manifest
76	35	crucified him and put him to an open S.
109	29	and bring to S. and confusion
133	49	sun shall hide his face in S.

SHARE

Sec.	Vs.	
124	64	not less than fifty dollars for a S.
	66	under fifty dollars for a S.

SHARPER

Sec.	Vs.	
6	2	than a two-edged sword—11:2; 12:2; 14:2; 33:1

SHARPLY

Sec.	Vs.	
112	12	admonish them S. for my name's sake

SHARPNESS

Sec.	Vs.	
15	2	I speak unto you with S. and power —16:2
121	43	reproving betimes with S. when moved

SHEAVES

Sec.	Vs.	
31	5	you shall be laden with S. upon your—33:9
75	5	ye shall be laden with many S.
79	3	I will crown him again with S.

SHED

Sec.	Vs.	
20	79	the blood which was S. for them
27	2	and my blood which was S. for
45	4	behold the blood of thy Son which was S.
63	31	as you are forbidden to S. blood
88	94	saints of God, that S. their blood
90	11	S. *forth* upon them for the revelation
100	8	the Holy Ghost shall be S. *forth*

Sec.	Vs.	
132	19	whereby to S. innocent blood; S. innocent blood.—26, 27
136	36	and they have S. innocent blood

SHEDDETH

Sec.	Vs.	
49	21	wo unto the man that S. blood

SHEDDING

58	53	save it be by the S. of blood
63	28	anger against you and to S. of blood
76	69	through the S. of his own blood
101	80	redeemed the land by S. of blood

SHEDERLAOMACH

92	1	my servant, S. (Frederick G. Williams)
104	2	I say unto you, S., you shall be a
	27	let S. have the place upon which
	29	let S. and, have the Laneshine house

SHEDOLAMAK

107	45	he met Adam in journeying to S.

SHEDS

76	53	which the Father S. *forth* upon all

SHEEP

10	59	other S. have I which are not of this
	60	I had other S. that were a branch
112	14	follow me and feed my S.

SHEOL

121	4	and benighted dominion of S.

SHEPHERD

50	44	I am the good S.

SHERWOOD, HENRY G.

124	81	let S. pay stock into that house
132		viz., Samuel Bent, S., etc.,

SHIELD

27	17	taking the S. of faith wherewith
35	14	I will be their S. and buckler

SHINE

109	73	and S. *forth* as fair as the moon
115	5	arise and S. *forth*, that thy light

SHINEHAH

82	12	and in the land of S., (Kirtland)
	13	have consecrated the land of S.
104	21	the order which dwell in land of S.
	40	for my stake in the land of S.
	48	the stake of Zion, the city of S.

SHINELAH

104	58	even to S. (print) my words

SHINELANE

104	63	for the purpose of S. (printing) my

SHINETH

Sec.	Vs.	
6	21	I am the light which S. in darkness—10:58; 11:11; 39:2; 45:7; 88:49
34	2	a light which S. in darkness and the
88	7	which truth S. This is the light
	11	the light which S. is through him

SHINING

34	9	the stars shall refuse their S.
109	79	with those bright S. seraphs

SHIP

123	16	you know that a very large S. is

SHOD

27	16	and your feet S. with the preparation
112	7	let thy feet be S. also, for thou

SHOES

24	18	for food and raiment, and for S.

SHONE

76	19	the glory of the Lord S. round about
110	3	his countenance S. above brightness

SHOOT

45	37	ye say when they begin to S. *forth*

SHORT

52	11	will cut my work S. in righteousness—84:97; 109:59
127	1	to leave the place for a S. season
135	3	in the S. space of twenty years

SHORTENED

35	8	I am God and mine arm is not S.
133	67	yet my arm was not S. at all

SHORTLY

87	1	concerning wars that will S. come
88	79	things which must S. come to pass

SHOT

135	1	they were S. in Carthage jail; Hyrum was S. first; Joseph was S. dead in; they were both S. after

SHOULDST

23	1	lest thou S. enter into temptation
42	57	thou S. hold thy peace concerning
122	7	if thou S. be cast into the pit

SHOUT

109	80	let thy Saints S. aloud for joy
128	23	let the mountains S. for joy; let all the sons of God S.

Sec.	Vs.	SHOW
5	3	you should not S. them except to
	7	if it were possible that you could S.
	11	unto whom I *will* S. these things
10	34	because I S. unto you wisdom, S. it not to the world—35
	36	I do not say that you shall not S. it
	43	I *will* S. unto them my wisdom is greater
	60	and I *will* S. unto this people that
18	39	you shall S. these things unto them
19	21	S. not these things unto world
35	8	I *will* S. miracles, signs and
38	13	now I S. unto you a mystery
45	10	I *will* S. unto you my strong reasoning
	11	let me S. it unto you, my wisdom
	16	and I *will* S. it plainly as I showed
	17	I *will* S. unto you how the day of
	36	like unto parable which I *will* S.
66	3	for I *will* S. them unto you
	4	I *will* S. unto you what I will
76	8	things to come *will* I S. them
	47	I S. it by vision unto many, but
95	14	built after manner which I shall S.
97	1	that I may S. unto you my will
	2	for I S. mercy unto all the meek
	6	I the Lord am willing to S. mercy
101	43	I *will* S. unto you a parable
	63	I *will* S. unto you wisdom in me
115	14	according to pattern I *will* S.—15, 16
124	1	that I might S. *forth* my wisdom
	22	as my servant Joseph shall S. unto them on the place he shall S.
	42	I *will* S. unto my servant Joseph
	95	who shall S. unto him the keys
	96	bear record of the things I shall S.
	102	the remainder I *will* S. unto you
128	13	to S. *forth* the living and the dead

SHOWED

| 45 | 16 | will show it plainly as I S. it to |
| 76 | 114 | mysteries of kingdom which he S. us |

SHOWEST

| 109 | 1 | and S. mercy unto thy servants |

SHOWETH

| 39 | 6 | the Comforter which S. all things |
| 63 | 11 | wherefore unto such he S. no sign |

SHOWING

20	12	thereby S. he is the same God
89	2	S. *forth* the order and will of God
107	93	S. the order of the seventy
121	43	then S. *forth* an increase of love

Sec.	Vs.	SHOWN
5	25	which the Lord has S. unto Joseph, for they have been S. unto me
	26	say, they have been S. unto me
35	10	great things are to be S. *forth*
	11	without faith shall not anything be S. *forth*
45	40	they shall be S. *forth* in heavens
63	21	pattern S. unto mine apostles
77	3	beasts which were S. to John
102	21	if any additional light is S.
134	7	as regard and reverence are S. to

SHOWS

| 107 | 100 | that S. himself not approved shall |

SHRINK

| 19 | 18 | not drink the bitter cup and S. |

SHUDDER

| 123 | 10 | enough to make hell itself S. |

SHULE

| 104 | 39 | in which the S. (ashery) is situated |

SHUT

| 76 | 47 | but straightway S. it *up* again |
| 77 | 8 | having power to S. *up* the heavens |

SICK

24	13	except healing the S.
35	9	they shall heal the S.
42	43	among you are S. and have not fait'
52	40	remember the poor, the needy, th S.
66	9	lay your hands upon the S. and they
84	68	in my name they shall heal the S.
89	8	herb for bruises and S. cattle
109	72	with all their S. and afflicted ones
124	98	he shall heal the S., he shall cast

SICKLE

4	4	he that thrusteth in his S. with his
6	3	let him thrust in his S. with his —4; 11:3, 4; 12:3, 4; 14:3, 4
11	27	and have thrust in their S. to reap
31	5	thrust in your S. with all your soul

SICKLES

| 33 | 7 | thrust in your S. and reap with your |

SICKNESS

| 45 | 31 | a desolating S. shall cover the land |
| 124 | 87 | because of the S. of the land, the S. shall redound to |

SIDE

| 6 | 37 | the wounds which pierced my S. |
| 52 | 10 | laying on of hands by water's S. |

Sec.	Vs.		Sec.	Vs.	
61	3	inhabitants on either S. are perishing		8	there are those among you who seek S.
127	1	not the least right on their S.		9	faith cometh not by S. but S. follow
		SIDNEY		10	S. come by faith not by will of
35	3	S. I have looked upon thy works		11	S. come by faith unto mighty works; unto such he showeth no S.
49	1	hearken unto my words, S. and		12	those who have sought after S.
	3	I send you, S., and Parley to preach	68	10	believeth shall be blest with S.
100	1	my friends, S. and Joseph, your families		11	to know the S. of the times and S. of the coming
	9	S. should be a spokesman to this	84	65	these S. shall follow them that believe
112	17	where my servants S. and Hyrum cannot	124	98	and these signs shall follow him
115	13	let not my servant S. get in debt any			**SILENCE**
124	103	if my servant S. will serve me	38	12	which causeth S. to reign
	108	if my servant S. will do my will	88	95	there shall be S. in heaven for
		SIFT			**SILVER**
52	12	Satan desireth to S. him as chaff	111	4	pertaining to gold and S. shall be
		SIGHT	124	11	come with your gold and your S. —26
3	12	God had given thee S. and power to	128	24	shall sit as a refiner of S. and purge them as gold and S.
18	10	worth of souls is great in S. of God			**SIMILITUDE**
35	9	the blind to receive their S.	124	2	which is after the S. of a palace
66	3	things which are not pleasing in my S.	128	13	baptismal font as S. of the grave
89	5	neither meet in S. of your Father			**SIMPLE**
109	11	that we may be found worthy in thy S.	1	23	proclaimed by the weak and the S.
	21	and find favor in thy S.			**SIMPLICITY**
	56	thy people may obtain favor in their S.	133	57	reasoning in plainness and S.
		SIGN			**SIN**
46	9	and asketh not for a S. that he may	1	31	look upon S. with least degree of
88	93	there shall appear a great S. in heaven	6	35	go your ways and S. no more.— 24:2; 82:7
		SIGNALIZED	10	25	telleth them it is no S. to lie
111	8	the place shall be S. by the peace	18	31	walk uprightly before me and S. not
		SIGNATURES	29	3	remember to S. no more lest perils
128	4	with certificates over their own S.		47	they cannot S. for power is not given
		SIGNED	45	4	death of him who did no S.
20	84	certificate may be S. by any elder, or it may be S. by		58	children shall grow up without S.
		SIGNS	49	8	men shall repent for all are under S.
29	14	there shall be greater S. in heaven		20	wherefore the world lieth in S.
35	8	will show miracles, S. and wonders	50	28	except he be cleansed from all S.
39	23	looking forth for S. of my coming —45:39		29	if ye are cleansed from all S. ye
45	16	concerning the S. of my coming	59	15	not with much laughter for this is S.
	40	they shall see S. and wonders	64	9	there remaineth in him the greater S.
58	64	with S. following them that believe	68	25	the S. be upon the head of parents
63	7	he that seeketh S. shall see S. but	82	2	from henceforth refrain from S.
				7	I will not lay any S. to your charge
				20	inasmuch as you S. not

Sec.	Vs.	
84	49	the whole world lieth in S., und(the bondage of S.
	50	they are under the bondage of S.
	51	who cometh not unto, is under S.
	53	whole world groaneth under S.
88	35	and willeth to abide in S., and abideth in S. cannot be
	86	entangle not yourselves in S.
95	3	have sinned against me a grievous S.—6, 10
97	27	if she S. no more none of these
101	98	this is a very sore and grievous S.
109	34	and as all men S. forgive
111	11	wise as serpents and yet without S.
121	17	because they are the servants of S.
132	26	he or she shall commit *any* S.
	38	and in nothing did they S. save in
	39	in none of these things did he S. against
	59	if by my word he will not commit S.

SINCE

20	1	S. the coming of our Lord and Savior
	82	with the church S. last conference
27	6	all the holy prophets S. world began.—86:10
121	26	has not been revealed S. the world was
128	1	S. I have been pursued by my enemies
133	45	S. the beginning of the world have not men
135	2	with four balls, but has S. recovered

SINCERELY

20	6	after humbling himself S.
109	68	and that he has S. striven to do

SINCERITY

5	24	in the S. of his heart

SINFUL

21	9	Jesus was crucified by S. men

SING

84	98	and S. this new song saying
128	23	and the morning stars S. together
133	56	they shall S. the song of the Lamb

SINGING

46	71	shall come to Zion S. with songs of
109	79	with acclamations of praise S. Hosanna
128	22	let the earth break forth into S.
136	28	praise the Lord with S., with music

SINGLE

4	5	with an eye S. to the glory of God
27	2	do it with an eye S. to my glory—55:1; 59:1; 82:19
88	67	if your eye be S. to my glory your
	68	that your minds may become S. to God

SINGLENESS

36	7	which will embrace it with S. of heart
59	13	let thy food be prepared with S.

SINGLY

132	17	but remain separately and S.

SINNED

1	27	inasmuch as they S. they might be
64	3	are those among you who have S.
	7	nevertheless he has S., but I forgive those who have not S. unto death
	17	also my servant Edward he has S.
70	17	inasmuch as they have not S.
75	8	he S., nevertheless I forgive him
82	2	among you who have S. exceedingly, yea even all of you have S.
95	3	ye have S. against me a grievous sin—6, 10
121	16	and cry they have S. when they have not S.

SINNERS

43	18	ye S. stay and sleep until I shall
63	57	in meekness to warn S. to repentance

SINNETH

42	28	he that S. and repenteth not—37
82	7	but unto that soul who S. shall the

SINS

13	1	by immersion for remission of S.
18	44	unto convincing many of their S.
.19	20	that you confess your S. lest you
	31	remission of S. by baptism and by
20	5	he had received a remission of his S.
	37	that they have repented of all their S., unto remission of their S.
21	8	unto the remission of his S.
	9	crucified by sinful men for S. of the; yea for remission of S.
25	3	thy S. are forgiven thee
27	2	shed for the remission of your S.
29	1	whose arm of mercy hath atoned for your S.
	3	at this time your S. are forgiven
31	5	your S. are forgiven you—36:1; 50:36; 60:7; 62:3; 108:1; 110:5
33	11	for a remission of your S.
35	2	who was crucified for S. of the world—46:13; 53:2; 54:1
39	10	be baptized and wash away your S.

Sec.	Vs.		Sec.	Vs.	
42	77	they shall repent of all their S.	132	46	whosoever S. you remit shall be; whosoever S. you retain
49	13	be baptized for remission of S.			**SISTER**
	26	repent of all your S.	42	88	if thy brother or S. offend thee
53	3	preach repentance and remission of S.—55:2		90	if thy brother or S. offend many
54	3	let them repent of their S. and			**SISTERS**
55	1	you shall have a remission of your S.	122	6	from society of brethren and S.
			128	15	dearly beloved brethren and S.
56	14	your S. have come up unto me	132	55	of fathers, mothers, brothers and S.
58	15	if he repent not of his S. which are			**SIT**
	39	let him repent of his S., for he	20	24	to S. down on right hand of Father
	42	he who has repented of his S. is	38	26	and saith, S. thou here, and S. thou there
	43	ye may know if a man repenteth of S.	45	28	among them that S. in darkness
	60	until he is chastened for all his S.	57	10	preached unto those who S. in
59	12	confessing thy S. unto thy brethren	76	108	to S. on the throne of his power
61	2	whose S. are now forgiven you, for I forgive S., to those who confess their S.	78	9	S. in council with the saints
			107	72	to S. in judgment on transgressors
	8	until chastened for all your S.	76		to S. as a judge in Israel
63	63	let the church repent of their S.		85	to S. in council with them—86, 87, 89
64	3	I have forgiven you your S.	116	1	where the Ancient of Days shall S.
	7	I forgive S. unto those who confess S.	128	24	he shall S. as a refiner and purifier
	12	he that repenteth not of his S.	132	37	and S. upon thrones and are not angels
68	27	for remission of S. when eight years			**SITS**
76	41	crucified, to bear the S. of the world	76	110	to him who S. upon the throne forever
	52	to be washed and cleansed from their S.			**SITTEST**
82	3	he who S. against the greater light	109	77	where thou S. enthroned in glory
	7	soul who sinneth shall former S. return			**SITTETH**
	21	the soul that S. against this covenant	58	20	him that S. upon the judgment-seat
84	27	gospel of repentance and remission of S.—107:20			**SLEEP**
	41	shall not have forgiveness of S. in this	43	18	ye sinners stay and S. until I call
	61	I will forgive you of your S.	63	51	but they shall not S. in the dust
	64	for remission of S. shall receive	88	124	cease to S. longer than is needful
	74	in water for remission of their S.	101	31	and when he dies he shall not S.
88	82	their S. are upon their own heads			**SLEEPING**
90	1	my son, thy S. are forgiven thee	43	18	and shall say to the S. nations
	6	their S. are forgiven them also			**SLEPT**
93	1	every soul who forsaketh his S.	45	45	saints that have S. shall come forth
95	1	I chasten that their S. may be		46	if ye have S. in peace, blessed are
98	20	for they do not forsake their S.	88	97	they who have S. in their graves
101	9	notwithstanding their S. my bowels			**SLIGHT**
	78	may be accountable for his own S.	19	33	if thou wilt S. these counsels
109	50	that they may repent of their S.			**SLOTHFUL**
112	3	all thy S. are forgiven thee	58	26	the same is a S. and not wise servant
	12	let them be admonished for their S.	101	50	they became very S. and hearkened not
117	4	let them repent of all their S.	107	100	he that is S. shall not be counted
121	37	when we undertake to cover our S.			
124	76	for I will forgive all his S.—78; 132:50			

Sec.	Vs.	
		SLOTHFULNESS
58	29	and keepeth it with S. is damned
90	18	keep S. and uncleanness far from you
		SLOW
101	7	they were S. to hearken, therefore the Lord is S. to
		SLUMBER
112	5	let not inhabitants S. because of thy
		SMALL
64	33	out of S. things proceedeth that
85	6	thus saith the still S. voice
90	25	let your families be S.
121	7	afflictions shall be but a S. moment
122	4	and but for a S. moment thy voice
123	15	let no man count them as S. things
	16	benefited very much by a S. helm
127	2	they seem but a S. thing to me
128	6	and I saw the dead, S. and great
		SMALLEST
19	20	which in S. degree you have tasted
		SMELL
59	19	for raiment, for taste and for S.
		SMILED
84	101	and the heavens have S. upon her
		SMITE
19	15	lest I S. you with the rod of my
24	16	I *will* S. them according to your words
98	17	and S. the whole earth with a curse
	23	if men *will* S. you or your families
	25	if your enemy S. you second time
	26	if he shall S. you the third time
109	28	if they shall S. this people, thou wilt S. them
128	17	lest I come and S. the earth with
133	26	they shall S. the rocks and the ice
		SMITH, DON C.
124	133	S. to be president over a quorum of
		SMITH, EDEN
75	36	also Micah B. Welton, and S.
80	2	I will give unto you my servant S.
		SMITH, EMMA
25	1	while I speak unto S., my daughter
132	51	I give unto mine handmaid, S., your wife
	52	let S. receive all those that have been
	54	I command S. to abide and cleave unto

Sec.	Vs.	
		SMITH, GEORGE A.
124	129	they are—Heber C. Kimball, S., and
136	14	let Amasa Lyman and S. organize a company
		SMITH, HYRUM
52	8	also John Murdock and S. take their
75	32	also S. and Reynolds Cahoon
94	13	on the third lot shall S. receive his
103	39	let S. journey with F. G. Williams
115	1	thus saith the Lord to my servant S.
124	15	my servant S., I the Lord love him
124		I give unto you S. to be a patriarch
135	1	martyrdom of S. the patriarch
	6	S. was 44 years old, February, 1844
		SMITH, JOHN
102	3	S., and, were chosen standing High Council
	34	Joseph Smith, Sr., S., etc. (signatures)
		SMITH, JOSEPH, JR.
1	17	called upon S. and spake unto him
	29	S. might have power to translate
5	1	witness that you, S., have the plates
	2	I have given these things unto S.
	25	seen the things which Lord has shown to S.
9	1	commence again to write for S.
17	4	that S. may not be destroyed
	5	that you have seen them as S. has seen
18	7	thou hast been baptized by S.
19	13	keep commandments received by S.
20	2	which commandments were given to S.
25	5	thy calling shall be for a comfort to S.
27	8	which John I have sent unto you S. and
28	2	to receive revelations excepting S.
30	7	concerning church matters except S.
31	4	shall declare the things revealed to S.
36	5	as many as shall come before S.
41	7	it is meet that S. should have a
42	4	every one of you, excepting S. and
43	12	appoint ye my servant S., and uphold
52	3	let S. and, take their journey as soon—60:6
	24	take their journey with S. and—53:5; 55:5
	41	let S. and, take with them a recommend
55	2	shalt be ordained under hand of S.

Sec.	Vs.		Sec.	Vs.	
56	12	if my servant S. needs pay the money		16	my servant S. in the hour of affliction
58	58	and after that let S. and, return	127	12	Smith, Joseph, (signature—128:25
60	17	by the mouth of S. shall it be made	135	1	announce martyrdom of S. the prophet
61	23	concerning S. and, let them come not		3	S. has done more, save Jesus only
	30	S. and, shall not open their mouths in		6	S. was 38 in December, 1843
63	41	S. shall be able to discern by the spirit	136	37	from Jesus and his apostles to S.
					SMITH, JOSEPH, SR.
	65	let S. and, seek them a home as they	90	20	let my aged servant S., continue with
64	5	the kingdom shall not be taken from S.		25	let your families be small, especially S.
67	5	your eyes have been upon S., and	102	3	S., and, chosen as standing High Council
	14	conferred upon you by the hands of S.		34	Jared Carter, S., and (signatures)
70	1	word of the Lord which I give unto S.	124	19	also my aged servant S., who sitteth
71	1	thus saith the Lord unto S. and—115:1			**SMITH, SAMUEL H.**
73	3	S. and, it is expedient to translate again	52	30	let Cahoon and S. take their journey
76	11	we, S. and, being in the spirit	61	35	let S. and, be not separated until
78	1	the Lord spoke unto Enoch (S.)	66	8	let S. go with you and forsake him not
	9	my servant Gazelam, or Enoch, (S.)	75	13	let Hyde, and S. take their journey
81	1	called to be a counselor to S.	102	3	S., and, chosen as standing High Council
82	11	expedient that S., and, be bound together		34	Joseph Coe, S., and, (signatures)
84	1	a revelation to S., and six elders	124	141	I give unto you S., if he will receive it
	3	and dedicated by the hand of S.			**SMITH, SYLVESTER**
93	45	my servant S., I will call you friends	75	34	also my servant S. and Gideon Carter
	47	unto S., you have not kept the commandments	102	3	S. and, chosen as standing High Council
	52	let S., and, make haste and it shall be		34	John S. Carter, S., and, (signatures)
102	1	assembled at house of S., by revelation			**SMITH, WILLIAM**
	3	S. and, were acknowledged presidents	124	129	they are—Heber C. Kimball, S., and
103	21	Baurak Ale, (S.) is the man to whom			**SMITTEN**
	22	let Baurak Ale, (S.) say unto strength of—105:16	24	16	ye shall command to be S. in my name
	35	that peradventure S. may go with you	27	9	that whole earth be not S. with curse—110:15
	37	Parley P. Pratt to journey with S.	85	8	like as a tree S. by vivid shaft of
	40	whithersoever S. shall counsel them	103	2	being driven and S. by hands of
104	26	according as my servant S. shall direct	105	38	not only people that have S. you
	43	let S. have appointed unto him the lot		40	of peace to those who have S. you
	45	he shall be reckoned in house of S.	109	65	who have been cursed and S. because
	46	I will multiply blessings on house of S.	128	18	the earth *will* be S. with a curse
105	27	until my servant S. shall have time to			**SMOKE**
109	68	O Lord, remember thy servant S.	.45	41	shall behold fire and vapors of S.
124	1	S., I am well pleased with your			**SMOOTH**
			49	23	for the rough place to be made S.—109:74

Sec.	Vs.	
		SNARE
10	26	to catch themselves in their own S.
63	15	shall come upon them as a S.
90	17	for it bringeth a S. upon your souls
		SNARES
61	18	and they are caught in S.
		SNIDER, JOHN
124	22	let S., and others build a house unto
	62	let S., and, organize themselves
	70	if S., and, receive stock into their
		SNOW
110	3	his head was white like the pure S.
		SNOW, ERASTUS
136	12	let S. and Benson, organize a company
		SNOWS
117	1	before I send again the S. upon
		SOAP
128	28	a refiner's fire and like fuller's S.
		SOBER
6	19	be patient, be S., be temperate
43	35	be S., keep all my commandments
61	38	be watchful and be S.
73	6	gird up your loins and be S.
		SOBERNESS
6	35	perform with S. the work which I
18	21	speak the truth in S.
		SOCIALITY
130	2	same S. which exists among us here
		SOCIETIES
134	10	religious S. have right to deal with, according to rules of such S.
		SOCIETY
122	6	if they tear thee from the S. of thy
134	1	for the good and safety of S.
	9	whereby one religious S. is fostered
	10	do not believe religious S. has right to, only to excommunicate from S.
		SOCKETS
29	19	and their eyes from their S.
		SOFTEN
104	80	and I *will* S. the hearts of—81; 105:27; 124:9
		SOFTENED
109	56	that their hearts may be S. when
121	3	before thine heart shall be S. towards
	4	let thine heart be S. and thy bowels

Sec.	Vs.	
		SOLD
38	37	that have farms that cannot be S.
64	20	commandment that his farm should be S.
90	20	let it not be S. until the mouth of
		SOLEMN
20	76	call upon the Father in S. prayer
88	70	call a S. assembly of those
117		call your S. assembly as commanded—109:6
95	7	commandment that you should call S.
108	4	wait patiently until S. assembly
109	10	in calling our S. assembly
124	2	called to make a S. proclamation
	39	and your S. assemblies, wherein
	107	making S. proclamation to kings of
133	6	call your S. assemblies, speak often
		SOLEMNITIES
43	34	let S. of eternity rest upon your
		SOLEMNITY
84	61	in S. and the spirit of prayer
100	7	in S. of heart, in spirit of meekness
107	84	may be done in order and in S.
		SOLID
128	23	and ye S. rocks weep for joy
		SOLITARY
117	7	make S. places to bud and blossom
		SOLOMON
132	1	as also Moses, David and S., as
	38	and concubines, as also S. and Moses
		SOME
20	82	or send by the hand of S. priest
34	9	refuse their shining and S. shall fall
38	14	S. of you are guilty before me
42	11	except he be ordained by S. one who
44	1	by letter or S. other way
46	7	for S. are of men and others of devils
	12	to S. is given one and to S. another
	13	to S. it is given to know that
	15	to S. is given to know difference
	16	given to S. to know diversities
	17	to S. is given the word of wisdom
	19	to S. is given to have faith to be
	21	to S. is given the working of miracles
	24	given to S. to speak with tongues
	29	to S. may be given to have all these
50	7	hypocrites who have deceived S.

Sec.	Vs.		Sec.	Vs.	
	17	by Spirit of truth or S. other way —19	46	13	to know that Jesus Christ is the S.
	18	if by S. other way it is not of God —20	49	5	have sent mine Only Begotten S.
				6	they have done unto the S. of man
58	61	S. of whom are exceedingly blessed		22	S. of man cometh not in form of woman
60	2	with S. I am not well pleased	50	27	through Jesus Christ his S.—88:5
63	14	S. of whom have turned away from you	58	65	behold the S. of man cometh
64	21	and thereby I may save S.	61	38	looking forth for coming of S. of man
76	100	who say they are S. of one and S. of another; S. of Christ, S. of John, S. of Moses and S. of Elias, S. of Esaias, S. of Isaiah and S. of Enoch	63	53	in day of coming of the S. of man
			64	23	until the coming of the S. of man
			65	5	S. of man shall come down in heaven
93	44	in S. things he has not kept the	68	6	record that I am S. of the living God
	48	must repent and forsake S. things		8	baptizing in name of Father and S.
104	4	as S. of my servants have not kept		21	priesthood descending from father to S.
112	2	there have been S. few things in			
127	2	unless ordained for S. good end or	76	13	through his only begotten S.
128	3	naming also S. three individuals		14	Jesus Christ who is the S., whom we
	9	it may seem to S. to be a very bold		16	those who shall hear voice of the S.
	18	a welding link of S. kind upon S. subject or		20	and we beheld the glory of the S.
130	16	or to S. previous appearance		25	rebelled against the only begotten S.; from the presence of God and the S.
133	36	angel who hath appeared unto S.		26	he was Lucifer, S. of the morning
		SON		27	he is fallen, fallen, even a S. of
6	21	I am Jesus Christ, the S. of God— 10:57; 11:28; 14:9; 35:2; 36:8; 45:52; 52:44		35	having denied the only begotten S.
				43	who deny the S. after Father has
				57	after the order of only begotten S.
9	1	I say unto you my S.—90:1		73	kept in prison whom the S. visited
	3	be patient, my S., for it is wisdom		77	who receive of the presence of the S.
	6	do not murmur my S., for it is wisdom	78	20	your Redeemer, even the S. Ahman
11	23	thou art Hyrum, my S., seek the	93	4	the S. because he was in the world
20	21	God gave his only begotten S.		14	thus he was called the S. of God
	27	beareth record of Father and the S.		15	this is my beloved S.
	28	which Father, S. and, are one God	95	17	school of mine apostles, saith S. Ahman
	73	in the name of the Father, the S. and	101	4	commanded to offer up his only S.
	77	we ask thee in the name of thy S.; in remembrance of the body of thy S.; to take upon them the name of thy S.—79	107	3	after the order of the S. of God
				40	handed down from father to S.
			109	4	Jesus Christ, the S. of thy bosom
				5	that S. of man might have a place
	79	in remembrance of blood of thy S.	121	7	my S., peace be unto thy soul
27	7	John the S. of Zacharias, that he should have a S.	122	6	and thine elder S. shall cling to
				7	my S., all these things shall give thee
29	42	through faith on mine only Begotten S.		8	the S. of man hath descended below
31	1	Thomas, my S., blessed are you	124	123	after order of mine only begotten S.
34	1	my S. Orson, hearken and hear	130	3	appearing of Father and Son, was a; idea that Father and S. dwell in a
	3	wherefore you are my S.			
42	1	Jesus Christ the Son of the living God—55:2; 68:25		12	previous to coming of the S. of man
	17	beareth record of the Father and S.		14	to know time of coming of S. of man
45	4	behold the blood of thy S. which			
	39	signs of the coming of the S. of man—68:11		15	Joseph, my S., if thou livest until, thou shalt see face of S.

Sec.	Vs.	
	17	coming of S. of Man will not be any
	22	Father has a body of flesh; the S. also
132	36	commanded to offer his S. Isaac
	50	offering of Abraham, of his S.

SONG

25	12	my soul delighted in S. of heart; S. of righteous is a prayer
84	98	and sing this new S. saying
133	56	they shall sing the S. of the Lamb

SONGS

45	71	singing S. of everlasting joy—66:11; 101:18; 109:39; 133:33

SONS

6	33	fear not to do good, my S.
11	30	will I give power to become S. of God—39:4; 45:8
13	1	until the S. of Levi do offer again
25	1	are S. and daughters in my kingdom
34	3	as believe might become S. of God
35	2	that they may become the S. of God
38	26	for what man having twelve S.; and and looketh upon his S. and saith I am just
42	52	they have power to become my S.
68	16	the firstborn among S. of Aaron
76	24	are begotten S. and daughters unto
	32	they who are the S. of perdition
	43	saves all except those S. of perdition
	58	they are gods, even the S. of God
84	6	and the S. of Moses, according to
	30	confirmed upon Aaron and his S.
	31	concerning S. of Moses, for S. of Moses, and S. of Aaron shall offer
	32	and S. of Moses and of Aaron shall be filled; whose S. ye are
	34	they become S. of Moses and of Aaron
93	4	and dwelt among S. of men
109	58	that the S. of Jacob may gather
124	39	your sacrifices, by the S. of Levi
	49	give commandment to any S. of men; and those S. go with all might; to require that work no more of those S.
128	23	let all S. of God shout for joy
	24	and he shall purify the S. of Levi

SOON

19	27	that S. it may go to the Jew
29	9	day S. at hand when the earth is ripe
34	7	time is S. at hand that I shall come
38	8	day S. cometh that ye shall see me; veil of darkness shall S. be rent

Sec.	Vs.	
	29	there will S. be great wars in far
52	3	as S. as preparations can be made
57	15	make preparations as S. as possible
58	52	as S. as time will permit
90	19	let there be a place provided as S. as
101	11	indignation is S. to be poured out
	98	and are S. to befall the nations
114	1	settle up his business as S. as
121	39	as S. as they get a little authority
124	7	as flower thereof which S. falleth

SOONER

130	17	will not be any S. than that time

SORCERER

63	17	whoremonger and S. shall have their

SORCERERS

76	103	they who are liars and S. and

SORE

19	15	and your sufferings be S., how S., ye know not
82	2	lest S. judgments fall upon your
87	5	shall vex Gentiles with S. vexation
97	26	I will visit her with S. affliction
101	98	this is a very S. and grievous sin
103	4	with a S. and grievous chastisement
104	4	with a very S. and grievous curse

SORELY

64	8	they were afflicted and S. chastened

SORROW

1	3	rebellious pierced with much S.
39	9	thou hast seen great S. for thou
101	29	there shall be no S. because there
109	48	and our hearts flow out with S.
123	7	made to bow down with grief and S.
133	70	ye shall lay down in S.
136	35	even the days of S.; and their S. shall be great

SORROWFUL

136	29	if thou art S. call upon the Lord

SOUGHT

1	26	as they S. wisdom they might be
10	6	they have S. to destroy you; in whom you trusted has S. to
	7	he has S. to take away the things; has S. to destroy your gift
	12	devil has S. to lay a cunning plan
45	12	a day S. for by all holy men
50	3	Satan hath S. to deceive you
54	10	who have S. me early shall find rest
63	12	you who have S. after signs
64	6	those who have S. occasion against him

Sec.	Vs.		Sec.	Vs.	
	8	in days of old S. occasion against	41	12	they are to be answered on your S.
	16	they S. evil in their hearts	45	2	harvest ended and your S. not saved
67	5	ye have S. in your hearts that you		46	come unto me and your S. shall live
76	28	S. to take kingdom of our God			
84	23	S. diligently to sanctify his people	54	10	sought me early shall find rest to S.
98	10	wise men should be S. for diligently	56	16	your riches will canker your S.
	31	if he has S. thy life, thine enemy is	64	3	for salvation of S. I have forgiven
134	3	should be S. for and upheld by	87	1	in the death and misery of many S.
			88	85	that their S. may escape the wrath
			90	17	it bringeth a snare upon your S.

SOUL

Sec.	Vs.	
		100 4 expedient for salvation of S.
4	4	but bringeth salvation to his S.
6	3	that he may treasure up for his S.
		—11:3; 12:3; 14:3
8	4	and bring your S. to destruction
11	13	which shall fill your S. with joy
18	13	great is his joy in S. that repenteth
	15	and bring save it be one S. unto me
	16	if your joy will be great with one S.
25	12	my S. delighteth in the song of
	14	let thy S. delight in thy husband
30	11	with all your S. from henceforth
31	5	thrust in your sickle with all your S.
33	1	the joints and marrow, S. and spirit
56	16	summer is ended and my S. is not saved
59	19	strengthen the body and enliven the S.
63	4	and is able to cast S. down to hell
64	17	Satan seeketh to destroy his S.
82	7	but unto that S. who sinneth
	21	the S. that sins against this covenant
84	64	every S. who believeth on your words
88	15	spirit and body is the S. of man
	16	the resurrection is redemption of S.
	17	redemption of S. is through him
93	1	every S. who forsaketh his sins
101	37	care for the S. and the life of the S.
108	2	let your S. be at rest concerning
117	11	and of all his littleness of S.
121	7	my son, peace be unto thy S.
	42	greatly enlarge S. without hypocrisy
	45	shall distil upon thy S. as dews
134	4	but never suppress freedom of the S.

Sec. Vs.
101 38 that in patience ye may possess your S.
109 43 their S. are precious before thee
121 37 or compulsion upon the S. of men
132 63 that they may bear the S. of men
136 29 that your S. may be joyful

SOUND

Sec.	Vs.	
19	37	with a S. of rejoicing—28:16; 29:4
29	13	a trump shall S. both long and
	26	mine archangel shall S. his trump
33	2	lift your voices as with S. of a— 34:6; 75:4; 124:106
42	6	as with the S. of a trump
43	18	the trump of God shall S. both
	25	and by the great S. of a trump
45	45	an angel shall S. his trump and the
49	23	and all this when the angel shall S.
58	64	the S. must go forth from this place
80	1	that cometh under S. of your voice
84	114	warn people with the S. of the gospel
88	94	another angel shall S. his trump; shall S. his trump both long and loud
	99	and another angel shall S.
	100	another trump shall S. which is the—102, 103, 105, 106
	104	and this shall be the S. of his; while they hear the S. of
	108	and then shall the angel again S.—109, 110
109	75	when the trump shall S. for dead
110	3	his voice was as S. of rushing waters

SOULS

Sec.	Vs.	
7	2	that I may live and bring S. unto
	4	he desired that he might bring S.
10	22	he may lead their S. to destruction
	26	he draggeth their S. down to hell
	27	seeking to destroy S. of men
15	6	that you may bring S. unto me— 16:6
18	10	worth of S. is great in sight of
	16	your joy if you should bring many S.
20	77	sanctify this bread to the S. of all
	79	sanctify this wine to the S. of all

SOUNDING

Sec.	Vs.	
77	12	what are we to understand by S. of; the S. of the trumpets are the
88	92	S. the trump of God saying, prepare
	98	S. of the trump of angel of. God

SOUTH

Sec.	Vs.	
42	63	to the west, to the north and the S.—44:1; 75:26; 80:3; 125:4
75	8	go ye into the S. countries
	17	journey also into the S. country

Sec.	Vs.	
94	3	let the first lot on the S. be
	10	the second lot on the S. shall be
104	39	and also the lot on the corner S.

SOUTH CAROLINA

Sec.	Vs.	
87	1	beginning at rebellion of S.
130	12	much bloodshed will be in S.

SOUTHERN STATES

87	3	the S. shall be divided against the, and the S. will call on

SOVEREIGN

134	3	by the people or will of the S.

SOW

6	33	whatsoever ye S. ye shall reap; if ye S. good ye shall

SOWED

24	3	after thou hast S. thy fields

SOWERS

86	2	the apostles were the S. of the seed

SOWETH

86	3	the enemy, Satan, S. the tares

SPACE

Sec.	Vs.	
64	21	for the S. of five years
71	2	for the S. of a season until it
88	12	presence of God to fill immensity of S.
	37	no S. where there is no kingdom; no kingdom where there is no S.
	95	silence for the S. of half an hour
	110	not loosed for S. of a thousand years
135	3	in the short S. of twenty years

SPAKE

Sec.	Vs.	
1	17	and S. unto him from heaven
5	2	he who S. unto you said unto you
8	12	I am the same that S. unto you
20	26	who S. as they were inspired by the
38	3	I am the same which S. and the world
42	39	that which I S. by mouth of my
45	16	I S. unto them saying, as ye have
	56	which I S. concerning the ten virgins
58	24	as I S. concerning my servant
78	1	the Lord S. unto Enoch, (Joseph
103	21	Lord · of the vineyard S. in the parable
133	47	I am he who S. in righteousness

SPARE

Sec.	Vs.	
29	22	then *will* I S. the earth but for
33	9	open your mouths and S. not
34	10	lift up your voice and S. not— 43:20

Sec.	Vs.	
45	5	S. these my brethren that believe
64	24	I *will* not S. any that remain in
84	94	search diligently and S. not
98	30	then if thou wilt S. him thou shalt
103	14	I *will* not S. them if they pollute
104	17	earth is full, there is enough to S.
124	101	cry aloud and S. not, with joy

SPARED

63	40	let all the moneys that can be S.

SPARINGLY

89	12	nevertheless they are to be used S.

SPEAK

Sec.	Vs.	
1	20	that every man might S. in name of God
5	23	I S. unto you my servant Joseph
6	23	did I not S. peace to your mind
11	11	for behold, it is I that S.
	27	I S. unto all who have good desires
12	7	I S. unto you and also to all
	9	life of the world that S. these words
15	2	I S. unto you with sharpness—16:2
18	9	Oliver Cowdery, I S. unto you and also, and I S. even as unto Paul
	21	and S. the truth in soberness
	31	now I S. unto you the Twelve
19	9	I S. unto you that are chosen
	37	and S. freely to all, preach and
23	1	I S. unto you a few words—3, 4, 5
24	6	in the very moment what thou shalt S.
25	1	while I S. unto you Emma Smith
28	4	if thou art led to S. or teach
35	9	and cause the dumb to S.
38	30	in a manner which shall S. in your
42	16	ye shall S. and prophesy as seemeth
	18	and now I S. unto the church
	27	thou shalt not S. evil of thy neighbor
	92	that the church may not S. reproachfully
43	1	give an ear to the words I shall S.
45	15	I *will* S. unto you and prophesy
46	5	I S. this concerning those who
	24	given to some to S. with tongues
51	1	I *will* S. unto my servant Edward
60	5	S. unto you concerning your journey
	12	I S. of the residue who are to come
68	3	S. as they are moved upon by the
	4	whatsoever they shall S. when moved
75	1	I S. even by the voice of my spirit
78	2	S. in your ears the words of wisdom
84	70	the tongue of the dumb shall S.
	73	neither S. them before the world
88	122	let one S. at the time
97	1	I S. unto you with my voice

Sec.	Vs.		Sec.	Vs.	
98	23	now I S. concerning your families	52	7	take their journey S.—56:5; 60:5
100	5	S. the thoughts that I shall put into	57	14	as S. as can be with their families
102	12	who of the twelve shall S. first	60	1	who are to return S. unto the land
	13	two only of the councilors shall S.		14	thou shalt S. return, proclaiming
	14	in no case more than six to S.	63	15	let such beware and repent S.
	16	the councilors appointed to S.; every man to S. according to equity —18		46	now S. visit the churches
			75	20	ye shall depart S. from that house
			97	11	let it be built S. by tithing of
	34	to ascertain who should S. first		22	vengeance cometh S. upon the ungodly
103	7	the Lord their God shall S. unto			
105	7	I S. not concerning those who are	104	81	therefore write S. unto New York
	8	I S. concerning my churches abroad	109	21	they may S. repent and return
110	8	and S. unto them with my own voice	112	24	vengeance cometh S. upon inhabitants
113	10	the promise is that he *will* S. to	115	17	Far West should be built up S. by
128	22	let the dead S. *forth* anthems of	117	1	let them settle up their business S.
133	6	and S. often one to another		14	let him come up hither S.
	21	he shall S. from Jerusalem and	124	10	the day of my visitation cometh S.
136	23	cease to S. evil one of another	136	35	unless they S. repent, yea very S.

SPEAKETH

11	10	or in my power which S. unto thee			

SPEND

41	9	to S. all his time in labors of the

18	35	it is my voice which S. them
52	16	he that S., whose spirit is contrite
81	1	listen to the voice of him who S.
85	10	as the Lord S., he will also fulfill

SPHERE

77	3	in destined order or ·S. of creation
93	30	all truth is independent in that S.

SPEAKING

SPILT

38	4	of the blood which I have S.

1	30	S. unto the church collectively
15	5	for S. my words which I have given—16:5
20	54	neither backbiting nor evil S.
29	33	S. that you may naturally understand
43	21	S. to the ears of all that live
56	20	now I make an end of S. unto you
63	53	S. after the manner of the Lord—64:24
76	16	S. of the resurrection of the dead
102	18	have a privilege of S. for themselves
105	2	S. concerning the church and not

SPIN

84	82	they toil not neither do they S. ·

SPIRIT

1	33	my S. shall not always strive with man
	39	the Lord is God and S. beareth record
5	16	with manifestation of my S.; even of water and of the S.
6	14	hast received instruction of my S.
	15	hast been enlightened by S. of truth
8	1	spoken by manifestation of my S.
	3	this is the S. of revelation; this is the S. by which Moses
11	12	put your trust in the S. which leadeth; this is my S.
	13	I will impart unto you of my S.
	18	hold your peace; appeal unto my S.
	21	you shall have my S. and my word
	25	deny not the S. of revelation, nor the S. of prophecy
18	2	by my S. in many instances
	35	for they are given by my S.
	47	by power of my S. I have spoken it
19	18	and to suffer both body and S.
	20	you tasted at time I withdrew my S.
	23	walk in meekness of my S.
	38	I will pour out my S. upon you—44:2

SPECIAL

107	23	or S. witnesses of the name of
	26	to that of the twelve S. witnesses

SPEECH

88	129	carefully, not with loud S.
112	5	not slumber because of thy S.

SPEECHES

88	121	cease from all your light S.
124	116	and lay aside all his hard S.

SPEEDILY

1	35	shall know that the day S. cometh
7	4	that thou mightest S. come unto me
24	3	go S. unto the church in Colesville
35	10	time S. cometh that great things

Sec.	Vs.		Sec.	Vs.	
20	37	that they have received of S. of Christ	57	13	as it shall be proved by the S.
	77	that they may always have his S. to—79	58	38	directions shall be given him of the S.
25	5	with consoling words, in S. of meekness		50	as it shall be made known by the S.
	7	as it shall be given thee by my S.	59	8	that of a broken heart and contrite S.
	14	continue in the S. of meekness		24	I have spoken and S. beareth record
27	7	he should be filled with S. of Elias	61	27	given by the S. to know all his ways
	18	and take the sword of my S.		28	let him do as the S. commandeth
29	30	which is the power of my S.	62	8	according to directions of the S.
	31	by power of my S. created] them	63	32	I am holding my S. from inhabitants
30	2	you have not given heed to my S.		41	he shall be enabled to discern by S.
33	1	joints and marrow, soul and S.		55	received not counsel but grieved the S.
	16	power of my S. quickeneth all things		64	spoken by constraint of S.; receive the S. through prayer
35	13	thrash nations by power of my S.—133:59		65	taught through prayer by the S.
36	2	and you shall receive my S.—39:10	64	16	I, the Lord, withheld my S.
42	5	shall be given by power of my S.	67	11	except quickened by the S.
	6	shall go forth in power of my S.	68	1	by the S. of the living God
	13	as they shall be directed by the S.	70	13	through the manifestations of the S.
	14	S. shall be given you by prayer; if ye receive not the S. ye shall not teach		14	manifestations of S. shall be withheld
	23	and shall not have the S.—63:16	71	1	according to that portion of S.
43	15	into your hands by power of my S.	75	1	I who speak by voice of my S.—97:1
46	7	that which the S. testifies unto you	76	10	for by my S. will I enlighten them
	11	to every man is given a gift by the S.		11	we, being in the S. on the 16th of
	16	that manifestations of S. may be		12	by power of the S. our eyes were opened
	17	by the S. of God the word of wisdom		18	for it was given unto us of the S.
	28	he that asketh in S. shall receive in S.		28	and while we were yet in the S.
	30	he that asketh in S. asketh according		80	to write while we were yet in the S.—113, 115
	31	whatsoever you do in the S.		118	through power and manifestation of S.
	32	ye must give thanks unto God in the S.	77	2	S. of man in likeness of his person and also S. of the beast
50	10	now come, saith the Lord, by the S.	84	33	are sanctified by the S. unto the
	14	preach my Gospel by the S.		45	whatsoever is light is S., even the S. of
	17	in S. of truth, doth he preach it by S. of truth or some		46	the S. giveth light to every man; the S. enlightened every man that hearkeneth to the S.
	19	doth he receive it by the S. of truth		47	that hearkeneth to S. cometh unto
	21	he that receiveth by S. of truth, receiveth it as preached by S. of truth		61	in solemnity and S. of prayer
	27	the light, the S. and the power		88	and my S. shall be in your hearts
	31	a S. manifested you cannot understand; receive not that S.; if he give you not that S.		106	if any man be strong in the S.
	32	given unto you power over that S.; you shall proclaim against that S.	88	15	the S. and the body are the soul of man
52	1	in these last days by voice of his S.		28	they who are of a celestial S.
	15	he that prayeth whose S. is contrite		66	my voice is S.; my S. is truth
	16	he that speaketh whose S. is contrite		137	as the S. shall give utterance
			91	4	for the S. manifesteth truth
				5	whoso is enlightened by the S.
				6	whoso receiveth not by the S.
			93	9	the S. of truth, who came into the
				11	full of grace and truth, even S. of

| Spirit | 418 | Spoken |

Sec.	Vs.		Sec.	Vs.	
	23	that which is S., even the S. of truth		41	which is the last death, which is S.
	25	is the S. of that wicked one		44	cannot be redeemed from S. fall
	26	S. of truth is of God; I am the S. of	67	10	not with the natural mind, but the S.
	32	whose S. receiveth not the light			
	33	for man is S., and S. and element	70	12	appointed to administer S. things
	38	S. of man was innocent in beginning	72	14	the faithful who labor in S. things
95	4	may pour out my S. upon all flesh	77	2	that which is S. in likeness of temporal, and temporal in likeness of S.
100	7	in S. of meekness in all things			
104	36	made known to him by voice of the S.	88	27	they shall rise again a S. body
	81	write that which is dictated by my S.	107	8	to administer in S. things—10, 12
				18	to hold keys of all S. blessings
105	36	shall be manifest by voice of my S.		32	which constitute S. authorities
	40	the voice of the S. which is in you		80	a final decision in S. matters
107	71	knowledge of them by S. of truth	108	2	at rest concerning your S. standing
109	79	help us by the power of thy S.	128	14	that was not first which is S.; afterward that which is S.
111	8	power of my S., that shall flow unto			
112	22	and hearken to voice of my S.	133	14	of wickedness, which is S. Babylon
121	37	S. of the Lord is grieved, and when	134	6	prescribing rules on S. concerns
123	7	by influence of that S. which hath		9	another proscribed in S. privileges
124	4	let it be written in S. of meekness			**SPIRITUALLY**
	18	preaching for Zion in S. of meekness	14	11	shall be blessed both S. and
	88	as he shall be moved by my S.	24	3	I will bless them both S. and
	97	as he shall receive of my S.	29	41	wherein they became S. dead
129	2	a S. hath not flesh and bones as			**SPOIL**
	6	if he be a S. of a just man made	101	45	when the enemy shall come to S.
130	22	but is a personage of S.	109	50	that they may cease to S.
131	5	by revelation and S. of prophecy			**SPOKE**
	7	all S. is matter but it is more fine	29	10	for as they S. so shall it come to
136	33	my S. is sent forth into world		21	who S. of these things which have not
		SPIRITS			**SPOKEN**
20	37	with broken hearts and contrite S.	1	3	their iniquities shall be S. upon
45	17	long absence of your S. from your		24	I am God and have S. it
46	7	ye may not be seduced by evil S.		38	what I have S. I have S.
	23	and to others the discerning of S.	5	28	of the things of which I have S.
50	1	and the S. which have gone abroad	6	20	I have S. unto thee because of thy
	2	there are many S. which are false S.	8	1	scripture of which I have S. by
	15	then received ye S. ye could not		12	it is I that have S. it
	30	the S. shall be subject unto you	11	19	those things of which has been S.
52	19	by this pattern ye shall know the S.	17	9	I have S. it unto you—18:33
56	17	whose S. are not contrite	18	37	have the desires of which I have S.
	18	whose S. are contrite		47	by power of my spirit have S. it
76	73	who are the S. of men kept in prison	19	20	suffer punishments of which I have S.
	88	appointed to be ministering S. for	20	16	the Lord God has S. it—36; 34:10; 49:7; 58:12; 59:24; 64:43; 90:37; 97:7; 127:2; 133:74
88	100	then cometh S. of men who are to be			
97	8	hearts are broken and S. contrite	27	6	S. by the mouth of all the holy— 84:2; 86:10; 109:23, 41, 45
129	3	S. of just men made perfect			
		SPIRITUAL	29	10	that which was S. by mine apostles
29	31	created all things both S. and temporal		21	as it is S. by the mouth of Ezekiel
	32	first S., secondly temporal; again first temporal, secondly S.	36	7	sent forth even as I have S.
			43	16	that ye may give even as I have S.
	34	all things unto me are S.		30	great Millennium of which I have S.
	35	for my commandments are S.			

Sec.	Vs.		Sec.	Vs.	
45	34	when I had S. these words to my	110	10	the fame of this house shall S. to
46	1	were S. unto you for your profit			**SPREADETH**
57	14	let those of whom I have S. be planted, as I have S.	82	5	the adversary S. his dominions
					SPRING
61	21	those concerning whom I have S.	63	39	may be prepared in coming S.
63	64	sacred and must be S. of with care	114	1	perform a mission unto me next S.
64	19	for this cause have I S. these things	118	4	next S. let them depart to go
77	1	sea of glass S. of by John	136	7	decide how many can go next S., to prepare for putting in S. crops
	2	four beasts S. of in the same verse			
	5	four and twenty elders S. of by			**SPRINGING**
	8	the four angels S. of in the	63	23	a well of living water S. *up* unto
	10	what time are the things S. of to be	86	14	blade is S. *up* and is yet tender
84	33	two priesthoods of which I have S.			**SPRINKLED**
88	122	that when all have S. all may be	133	51	their blood have I S. on my garments
102	19	the accuser and accused have S.			
	20	councilors who have not S.			**STAFF**
109	60	those words we have S. before thee	89	14	to be the S. of life not only for man
110	14	S. of by mouth of Malachi			**STAINED**
113	1	who is the stem of Jesse S. of	133	51	and S. all my raiment
	3	what is the rod S. of in first			**STAKE**
	5	what is the root of Jesse S. of	82	13	and for a S. to Zion
116	1	where Adam shall sit as S. of by Daniel	94	1	foundation of the city of the S. of
			96	1	it is expedient in me that this S.
128	7	the books S. of must be the books	104	40	established for my S. in the land
		SPOKESMAN		48	the United Order of the S. of Zion
100	9	should be S. unto this people, even to be a S. unto my	107	74	a common judge in a S. of Zion
			124	2	and of this S. which I have planted
	11	that thou mayest be a S. unto him	142		president of the S. and counselors
124	104	and be a S. before my face	136	10	where the Lord shall locate a S. of
		SPOKESMEN			**STAKES**
88	122	let not all be S. at once, but let	68	25	in any of her S. which are organized—26
		SPOT			
38	31	without S. and blameless	82	14	her S. must be strengthened
57	3	a S. for the temple is lying westward	101	21	and they shall be called S. for the
			107	36	High Councils at the S. of Zion
58	57	and the S. of the temple unto the		37	to Councils of the Twelve at the S.
61	2	elders who are assembled on this S.	109	39	come forth to Zion or to her S.
84	31	the consecrated S. I have appointed		59	we ask thee to appoint other S.
101	44	a nobleman had a S. of land	115	6	gathering together upon her S.
124	43	for that is the S. I have chosen		18	be appointed for S. in the regions
	44	I will consecrate that S. that it	119	7	an ensample unto all S. of Zion
		SPOTLESS	124	36	ordained that in Zion and her S.
61	34	and they shall be S. before me	134		servants over different S. scattered
76	107	present it to the Father S., saying	125	4	and in all the S. I have appointed
		SPOTTED	133	9	and that her S. may be strengthened
36	6	hating the garments S. with the flesh			**STAND**
			4	2	that ye may S. blameless before God
135	5	my garments are not S. with your blood	5	2	you should S. as a witness of these
				34	stop and S. still until I command
		SPRANG	6	18	S. by my servant Joseph faithfully
132	34	and from Hagar S. many people	9	14	S. fast in the work wherewith I
		SPREAD	14	8	that you may S. as a witness of the
97	18	she shall prosper and S. herself			
109	29	all those who have S. lying reports			

Sec.	Vs.	
27	15	having done all ye may be able to S.
	16	S., having your loins girt about
29	11	and the wicked shall not S.
	12	the Twelve shall S. at my right hand
38	17	wherefore again I *will* S. upon it
	20	while the earth shall S.
42	10	Edward Partridge shall S. in the office
	53	shalt S. in place of thy stewardship
45	32	my disciples shall S. in holy places
	70	are terrible, wherefore we cannot S.
	74	and they shall S. afar off and
54	2	you shall S. fast in the office
57	6	let Sidney Gilbert S. in the office
	7	let my servant Edward S. in the office
58	7	upon which the Zion of God shall S.
	40	let my servant William S. in office
	60	let him S. as a member in the church
59	3	blessed are they whose feet S. upon
63	31	but few shall S. to receive inheritance
68	6	I am with you and *will* S. by you
78	14	that the church may S. independent
81	5	S. in the office which I have
84	2	his saints to S. upon Mount Zion
	109	let every man S. in his own office; how shall the body be able to S.
87	8	S. ye in holy places and be not
88	10	even the earth upon which you S.
	89	and shall not be able to S.
	110	he shall S. *forth* upon the land
93	47	must needs S. rebuked before the Lord
95	2	chastened and S. rebuked before my
98	27	the three testimonies shall S.
101	22	gather together and S. in holy places
102	17	to S. *up* in behalf of the accused
	22	the first decision shall S.
106	8	assurance wherewith he may S.
107	100	shall not be counted worthy to S.
121	9	thy friends do S. by thee
	15	not one of them left to S. by wall
122	4	and thy God shall S. by thee
123	7	with whom we shall be brought to S.
	10	make hell shudder and to S. aghast
	17	then may we S. still with utmost
124	16	let John C. Bennet S. by you in
	103	and S. in the office of his calling
127	10	to have addressed them from the S.
128	6	I saw the dead S. before God
	24	who can S. when he appeareth
133	18	the Lamb shall S. upon Mount Zion
	20	he shall S. upon Mount Olivet

Sec.	Vs.	
	25	shall S. in the midst of his people
	56	they shall come forth and S. on right hand, when he shall S. upon Mount

STANDARD
45	9	to be a S. for my people
98	34	should first lift a S. of peace
115	5	that thy light may be a S. for the

STANDEST
115	7	the ground upon which thou S. is

STANDETH
58	17	whoso S. in his mission is appointed
63	56	he S. no longer in the office
64	9	S. condemned before the Lord

STANDING
20	84	regular members in good S.
45	31	shall be men S. in that generation
78	12	shall lose his S. in the church
84	111	to be S. ministers unto the church
88	128	shall be found S. in his place
102	3	were chosen to be a S. council
107	10	a right to officiate in their own S.
	36	the S. High Councils at the Stakes
108	2	be at rest concerning spiritual S.
109	24	a name and a S. in this thy house
110	2	saw the Lord S. on the breastwork
119	4	this shall be a S. law unto them
124	134	who shall be appointed S. presidents
	135	but be ordained for S. presidents
	137	quorum instituted for S. ministers; ordained to be S. ministers
134	10	be for fellowship and good S.

STANDS
84	101	for he S. in the midst of his people
104	39	the lot on which the Ozondah S.
128	18	it is sufficiently plain as it S.

STANTON, DANIEL
75	33	also my servant S., and Brunson

ST. LOUIS
60	5	speedily for the place called S.
	8	let residue take journey from S.

STAR
76	98	as one S. differs from another S.

STARRY
84	118	but the S. heavens shall tremble

STARS
29	14	the S. shall fall from heaven—45:42
34	9	the S. shall refuse their shining
76	81	even as the glory of the S. differs
	98	the glory of the S. is one, for as one

Sec.	Vs.		Sec.	Vs.	
	109	they were as innumerable as the S.—132:30		58	46 who are not appointed to S. in this
88	9	and also the light of the S.		76	3 neither are there any who can S. his hand
	45	and the S. giveth their light		105	20 that can S. in the region round about, let them S.
	87	the S. shall become exceedingly angry			21 and those who cannot S. who have
121	30	or to the sun, moon or S.		121	33 what power shall S. the heavens
128	23	let the morning S. sing together		122	6 father, why can't you S. with us
133	49	the S. shall be hurled from their		132	51 that she S. herself and partake not
				133	26 and shall no longer S. themselves

STATE

STAYED

77	1	the earth in its eternal S.		29	19 and their tongues shall be S.
84	3	western boundaries of the S. of		56	17 whose hands are not S. from laying
93	38	men became in their infant S. innocent		97	23 it shall not be S. until the Lord
123	1	abuses by the people of this S.		121	2 how long shall thy hand be S.
127	1	both in Missouri and this S.			

STEAD

130	9	earth in its immortal S. will be made		28	7 appoint unto them another in his S.
135	7	on escutcheon of S. of Illinois, with broken faith of the S.		35	18 if not, another will I plant in his S.
				42	10 another shall be appointed in his S.—104:77
				43	4 except to appoint another in his S.
				64	40 others shall be planted in their S.—114:2

STATED

128	1	as I S. in my letter before I left

STATEMENT

58	50	and a S. of the will of God		102	11 have power to preside in his S.
102	26	with a full S. of the testimony		107	11 has a right to officiate in his S.
128	4	with his own S. that he verily believes the S. to be true		124	132 appointed unto priesthood in his S.; unto this calling in his S.

STATEMENTS

STEADFAST

102	33	after examining S. accompanying it		31	9 govern in meekness and be S.
123	4	to take S. and affidavits		84	61 remain S. in your minds in solemnity

STATES

STEADFASTNESS

134	7	we believe rulers, S., governments have		49	23 continue in S., looking forth for
				82	24 if you fall not from your S.

STATION

STEADY

134	6	every man should be honored in his S.		85	8 putteth forth his hand to S. the ark

STATUTES

STEAL

119	6	that my S. may be kept thereon		42	20 thou shalt not S.—59:6
124	39	and your S. and judgments		85	and if he or she shall S.
136	2	keep all the commandments and S.			

STEALETH

42	20	he that S. and will not repent

STAVES

STEM

24	18	take no purse nor scrip, neither S.		113	1 who is the S. of Jesse spoken of
					3 rod that should come of the S. of

STAY

STEP

1	5	and none shall S. them		134	8 all men should S. forward and use
38	22	your lawgiver, and who can S. my hand			

STEWARD

	33	and no power shall S. my hand		42	32 a S. over his own property
39	16	thinking I *will* S. my hand in		51	19 a faithful, just and a wise S.
	18	I *will* S. my hand in judgment		72	3 required at hand of every S.
43	18	ye sinners S. and sleep until I			17 to be received as a wise S.
					26 shall not be accounted a wise S.

Sec.	Vs.		Sec.	Vs.	
78	22	a wise S. shall inherit all things			**STIFFEN**
101	61	upon you a faithful and wise S.	112	13	and S. not their necks against me
104	13	make every man accountable as a S.			**STIFFNECKED**
	74	is an unfaithful and an unwise S.—77	5	8	this unbelieving and S. generation
136	27	that thou mayest be a wise S.; and thou art his S.			**STIFFNECKEDNESS**
			56	6	in consequence of the S. of my people

STEWARDS

					STILL
70	3	have ordained them to be S.	3	10	thou art S. chosen and art again
72	20	who are appointed S. over literary	5	34	stop, and stand S. until I command
	22	and be accounted as wise S.	56	9	be appointed S. to go to land of
101	90	cut off those wicked and unfaithful S.	85	6	thus saith the S. small voice
104	56	then ye are S. otherwise ye are no S.	88	35	they must remain filthy S.
	57	have appointed you to be S., even S. indeed	102		who shall remain filthy S.
	86	these things are mine and ye are my S.	101	16	be S. and know that I am God
			123	17	then may we stand S. with utmost
			129	7	but he will S. deliver his message

STEWARDSHIP

					STINK
42	53	stand in the place of thy S.	133	68	their fish S. and die for thirst
	72	to receive either a S. or otherwise			**STIR**
70	4	an account of this S. will I require	10	32	to S. them *up* to anger against you
	9	requires of every man in his S.		63	yea Satan doth S. *up* the hearts of
	11	in a S. over temporal things			**STIRRED**
	12	those appointed to a S.	18	6	be S. *up* unto repentance
72	3	render an account of his S.	63	27	that they may not be S. *up* unto anger
	5	shall render an account of their S.			**STIRRETH**
	16	must give an account of his S.	10	20	he S. them *up* to iniquity against
104	11	appoint every man his S.		22	Satan S. them *up* that he may lead
	12	of his S. which is appointed unto him		24	he S. *up* their hearts to anger
	20	lot of the tannery for his S.			**STOCK**
	22	this S. and blessing I confer	124	63	they may receive S. for building
	24	for his S. a lot of land which my		64	fifty dollars for a share of S.; from any one man for S.
	30	this shall be their S.		65	over fifteen thousand dollars S.
	32	this is the beginning of the S. I—37, 44		66	under fifty dollars for share of S.
	40	appointed unto Ahashdah for his S.		67	shall pay his S. at the time he receives S.
	41	this is the S. I have appointed		68	in proportion to amount of S. he shall receive S.; he shall not receive any S.
	54	a commandment concerning your S.		69	if any pay S. it shall be for S. as long as they hold that S. and do not sell the S.
	63	make use of the S. I have appointed			
	72	need of this to help in my S.			
	73	which he requires to help in his S.		70	if my servants receive any S., they shall not appropriate that S. to any
	75	so long as he is wise in his S.			
124	14	his S. will I require at his hands		71	if they appropriate any S. without consent, and do not repay fourfold for the S. they shall be

STEWARDSHIPS

42	70	priests and teachers shall have their S.
64	40	if they are not faithful in their S.
69	5	send forth accounts of their S.
82	11	bound together in your several S.
	17	managing the concerns of your S.
104	68	moneys that you receive in your S.

STICK

27	5	keys of record of the S. of Ephraim

Sec.	Vs.		Sec.	Vs.	
	72	let my servant Joseph pay S.; but cannot pay over, for S., nor under	78	3	establishing the affairs of the S,
	74	let him put S. into that house for —77, 78, 80, 81, 82, 111	82	18	to be cast into the Lord's S.
	117	and pay S. also into the quorum of	83	5	they have claim upon the Lord's S.
	119	let no man pay S. to the quorum unless		6	S. shall be kept by consecrations
	122	let every man who pays S. bear proportion of: shall be accounted to them for S.	90	23	discharge every debt that the S. of
			101	96	should sell my S. which I have

STOCKHOLDER

STORM

124	67	not receive any man as a S. except	115	6	and for a refuge from the S.
71	without the consent of the S.	123	16	how a very small helm in time of S.
		127	1	when I learn the S. is blown over

STONE

STORMS

28	11	written from that S. are not of me	90	5	and stumble and fall when the S.
45	20	not be left one S. upon another
50	44	and I am the S. of Israel

STRAIGHT

65	2	as the S. cut out of the mountain	3	2	therefore his paths are S.
130	10	the white S. mentioned in Revelation	33	10	way of the Lord, make his paths S.—65:1; 133:17
	11	a white S. is given to each of those	84	28	to make S. the way of the Lord

STONES

STRAIGHTWAY

| 124 | 26 | come ye with all your precious S. | 40 | 2 | but S. Satan tempted him |
| | | 76 | 47 | but S. shut it up again |

STOOD

101	56	go ye S. unto the land of my
45	16	as I S. before them in the flesh		57	get ye S. unto my land
107	56	and Adam S. up in the midst of the		60	when I will, go ye S. and do
110	13	Elijah the prophet S. before us and		62	his servant went S. and did all
		136	25	go S. and tell thy neighbor lest

STOP

STRAIT

5	30	thou shalt S. for a season until I	22	2	ye cannot enter in at the S. gate
	34	S. and stand still until I command	132	22	for S. is the gate and narrow the way
121	33	to S. the Missouri river in its course
136	17	they shall not have power to S.

STRANGE

STORE

95	4	may bring to pass my S. act— 101:95
4	4	the same layeth up in S. that he	101	95	perform my work, my S. work
38	33	I have a great work laid up in S.
39	15	I have kept in S. a blessing

STRANGERS

57	8	in this place and establish a S.	45	13	confessed they were S. and pilgrims
63	42	retain his S., or the S. for a little	124	23	that S. may come from afar to lodge
64	26	not sell their S. and possessions here		56	to build for the boarding of S.
90	22	a man who has got riches in S.

STRAYED

101	75	is even now already in S. sufficient	1	15	they have S. from mine ordinances
124	102	I have a mission in S. for my
125	2	may be prepared for that which is in S.

STREAK

| 43 | 22 | when the lightnings shall S. forth |

STOREHOUSE

STREAM

42	34	the residue shall be kept in my S.	97	9	in a goodly land, by a pure S.
	55	give it into my S. that all things	121	33	decreed course, or to turn it up S.
51	13	let the bishop appoint a S.

STRENGTH

58	24	whom I appointed to keep my S.	3	4	yet if he boasts in his own S.
	37	for the place of my S. and also	4	2	see that ye serve him with all your S.
70	7	it shall be given into my S.
	11	the agent who keepeth the Lord's S.	9	12	given unto my servant sufficient S.
72	10	to keep the Lord's S.	10	4	do not run faster than you have S.
		11	20	with all your mind, might and S.

Sec.	Vs.	
20	31	serve God with all their mights and S.
24	7	in this thou shalt have S.
	9	in temporal labors, not have S.
	11	whether in weakness or in S.
	12	I will give unto him S. such as is
30	1	and have not relied on me for S.
33	7	reap with all your mind, might and S.
59	3	it shall bring forth in its S.
	5	love the Lord with all thy, and S.
84	101	travailed and brought forth its S.
96	1	that I have set for S. of Zion
98	47	with all their might, mind and S.
101	21	for the curtains or S. of Zion
	55	take all the S. of mine house, who are the S. of mine
103	22	say unto the S. of my house—105:16
	30	five hundred of the S. of my house
	34	one hundred of the S. of my house
105	17	but S. of mine house have not hearkened
	27	time to gather up S. of my house
113	7	put on thy S., O Zion
	8	to put on her S. is to put on the
133	46	traveling in greatness of his S.

STRENGTHEN

Sec.	Vs.	
20	53	and be with them and S. them
23	3	thy calling is to S. the church—4, 5
31	8	you shall S. them and prepare them
50	37	S. them by word of exhortation
59	19	to S. body and enliven the soul
81	5	and S. the feeble knees
108	7	S. your brethren in all your
132	53	from henceforth I *will* S. him

STRENGTHENED

Sec.	Vs.	
37	2	and have S. *up* the church
82	14	her stakes must be S.
133	9	and that her stakes may be S.

STRETCH

Sec.	Vs.	
121	4	S. *forth* thy hand, let thine eye
	33	as well might man S. *forth* his puny arm

STRETCHED

Sec.	Vs.	
104	14	the Lord S. out the heavens
136	22	my arm is S. out in the last days

STRETCHED-OUT

Sec.	Vs.	
103	17	by power and a S. arm

STRICT

Sec.	Vs.	
3	5	but how S. were your commandments

Sec.	Vs:	

STRIFE

60	14	neither in wrath nor with S.

STRIFES

101	6	there were jarrings and envyings and S.

STRIP

67	10	S. yourselves of jealousies and fears

STRIVE

1	33	my spirit shall not always S. with man

STRIVEN

109	68	he hath sincerely S. to do thy will

STRONG

1	19	break down the mighty and S. ones
	28	as they were humble they might be made S.
27	3	neither S. drink of your enemies
38	15	be ye S. from henceforth
45	10	I will show unto you my S. reasoning
	58	they shall multiply and wax S.
50	16	weak among you shall be made S.
52	17	he that trembleth shall be made S.
64	21	I will to retain a S. hold in
66	8	he that is faithful shall be made S.
71	8	bring forth their S. reasons against
84	106	if any man be S. in the spirit, that he may become S. also
85	7	I will send one mighty and S.
88	94	her bands are made S., no man can
89	5	any man drinketh wine or S. drink
	7	S. drinks are not for the belly
90	22	a man of God and of S. faith
	36	that I will plead with her S. ones
96	1	that this Stake should be made S.
101	66	bound in bundles and bands made S.
121	45	then shall thy confidence wax S.
123	8	it is an iron yoke, it is a S. band
133	58	and the little one become a S. nation
135	5	thou shalt be made S. even to the

STRONGER

121	44	that thy faithfulness is S. than
123	7	and has been growing S. and S.

STRONGEST

128	1	press itself upon my feelings the S.

STRONGLY

123	7	hath so S. riveted the creeds of the

STUBBLE

29	9	they that do wickedly shall be as S.—64:24; 133:64

Sec.	Vs.		Sec.	Vs.	
		STUDY			**SUBJECTION**
9	8	you must S. it out in your mind	74	4	brought up in S. to law. of Moses
11	22	S. my word which hath gone forth, S. my word which shall come forth			**SUBJECTS**
			128	1	information in relation to many S.
88	118	seek learning by S. and by faith— 109:7, 14		17	this most glorious of all S.
					SUBSCRIBE
90	15	S. and learn and become acquainted	127	12	I S. myself your servant in the Lord
		STUDYING			**SUBSCRIPTION**
26	1	devoted to the S. of the Scriptures	58	51	an epistle and S. to be presented
		STUMBLE			**SUBSTANCE**
90	5	and S. and fall when the storms	1	16	and whose S. is that of an idol
		STUPOR	42	31	as ye impart of your S. to the poor
9	9	you shall have a S. of thought	56	16	that will not give your S. to the poor
		SUBDUE	105	3	and do not impart of their S.
19	2	that I might S. all things to	109	5	we have given of our S. to build
76	61	who shall S. all enemies under his			**SUBTLE**
		SUBDUED	123	12	blinded by the S. craftiness of men
65	6	that thy enemies may be S.			**SUCCESSION**
76	106	shall have S. all enemies under	102	12	and so in S. to number twelve
103	7	kingdoms of the world are S.			**SUCCESSORS**
		SUBDUES	82	20	everlasting order unto you and your S.
58	22	and S. all enemies under his feet	102	6	or regularly appointed S. are present
		SUBDUING			**SUCCOR**
96	5	for the purpose of S. the hearts	62	1	how to S. them who are tempted
		SUBJECT	81	5	S. the weak, lift up the hands of
29	40	he became S. to will of the devil			**SUCH**
50	27	for all things are S. unto him	5	28	he shall have *no* S. views
	30	the spirits shall be S. unto you	9	9	you shall have *no* S. feelings
58	22	be S. to the powers that be	10	28	S. are not exempt from justice of God
63	59	that all things shall be S. unto me		55	for S. shall inherit the kingdom
74	3	and become S. to the law of Moses	24	12	strength S. as is not known among men
104	76	treasurer shall be S. to the council			
	77	he shall be S. to the voice of the	26	1	labors on land S. as is required
105	32	let us become S. to her laws	39	15	a blessing S. as is not known among
127	10	on S. of baptism for the dead; I will write on that S.	42	31	S. as he shall or has appointed
128	1	I now resume the S. of baptism for dead, as that S. seems		67	S. as shall be sufficient to
				76	that ye receive none S. among you
	6	this very S. in relation to dead	46	27	and unto S. as God shall appoint
	11	the *summum bonum* of the whole S.	50	7	but behold S. shall be reclaimed
	18	welding link upon some S. or other, and what is that S.	58	33	wo unto S. for their reward lurketh
			60	2	wo unto S. for mine anger is
25	2	I have many things to say on the S., but shall continue S. another time	63	8	there have been S. even from
				11	unto S. he showeth no signs, only in
130	13	while praying earnestly on the S.		15	let S. beware and repent speedily
132	20	because all things are S. unto them; angels are S. unto them		66	that S. may receive a more exceeding
			75	26	let all S. as can obtain places
		SUBJECTEST	97	2	blessed are S. for they shall
121	4	who controllest and S. the devil	102	25	to preside over S. council for

Sec.	Vs.		Sec.	Vs.	
	27	as though *no* S. decision had been made		13	and they love to have others S.
	28	sufficient to call S. council	124	24	shall not S. any pollution to come
	29	whether *necessary* to call S. council			**SUFFERED**
	33	determine whether any S. case is	3	15	thou hast S. the counsel of thy
107	2	Melchizedek was S. a great High Priest		18	whom the Lord has S. to destroy
124	22	S. a one as my servant Joseph shall	18	11	your Redeemer S. death in the flesh; he S. the pain of all men
128	14	as is the earthy S. are they; as is the heavenly S. are	19	16	I have S. these things for all
131	7	is *no* S. thing as immaterial matter	20	22	he S. temptations but gave no heed
134	2	except S. laws are framed and held	61	4	I S. it that ye might bear record
	3	S. as will administer the law in equity	76	31	and S. themselves to be overcome
	5	protected by laws of S. governments; a right to enact S. laws as	84	78	I S. them not to have purse or scrip
	6	magistrates, as S., being placed	100	4	I have S. you to come to this place
	7	and S. religious opinions do not	101	2	I have S. the affliction to come
	10	rules and regulations of S. societies; that S. dealings be for fellowship		77	which I have S. to be established
	11	where S. laws exist as will protect	103	3	for I have S. them thus far
	12	S. interference we believe unlawful	109	31	for which they have S. these things
		SUCKLINGS			**SUFFERING**
128	18	shall be revealed unto babes and S.	19	18	which S. caused myself, even God
		SUDDEN	121	6	remember thy S. saints, O God
133	15	lest S. destruction shall come			**SUFFERINGS**
		SUDDENLY	19	15	and your S. be sore, how sore you
36	8	I *will* S. come to my temple	45	4	behold the S. and death of him who
133	2	the Lord who shall S. come to his	76	30	we saw a vision of the S. of those
		SUE		38	after the S. of his wrath
105	38	I say unto you, S. for peace		49	the vision of the S. of the ungodly
		SUFFER	109	76	reap eternal joy for all our S.
10	14	I *will* not S. that Satan shall	123	1	gather up knowledge of the S. put
	43	I *will* not S. that they shall destroy			**SUFFICE**
19	4	every man must repent or S.	19	32	for this shall S. for thy daily walk
	16	that they might not S. if they	130	15	let this S. and trouble me no more
	17	if they would not repent they must S.	132	66	therefore, let this S. for the present
	18	and to S. both body and spirit			**SUFFICIENCY**
	20	lest you S. these punishments	102	23	if there is not a S. written
38	35	to relief, that they shall not S.			**SUFFICIENT**
61	8	I would not S. that ye should part	9	12	have given unto my servant S. strength
76	33	doomed to S. the wrath of God	17	8	for my grace is S. for you—18:31
104		these are they who S. the wrath	20	68	are to have S. time to expound
105		who S. the vengeance of eternal fire	42	32	as is S. for himself and family
106		to S. the wrath of Almighty God		67	as shall be S. to establish you
88	134	ye shall not S. that mine house	60	16	this is S. for you and the will of
94	8	ye shall not S. any unclean thing—97:15	101	75	is even now already in store a S.
			102	28	is to be S. to call such a council
101	35	they who S. persecution for my name	124	31	I grant unto you a S. time to build
104	86	the master *will* not S. his house to		33	after you have had S. time to build
105	6	if needs be by the things they S.	128	18	S. to know that the earth will be
109	49	how long wilt thou S. this people	136	7	then choose a S. number of men
121	3	how long shall they S. these wrongs			**SUFFICIENTLY**
			5	24	does not humble himself S. before me
			58	41	he is not S. meek before me
				60	until he is S. chastened for all

Sec.	Vs.	
67	10	for ye are not S. humble
128	18	it is S. plain to suit my purpose

SUGGEST

Sec.	Vs.	
123	1	we would S. for your consideration

SUIT

84	105	give unto you a coat or a S.
128	18	sufficiently plain to S. my purpose

SUITABLE

48	1	as it shall be S. to circumstances

SUITING

46	15	S. his mercies according to the

SUM

104	73	give unto him the S. he requires

SUMMER

35	16	even now already S. is nigh
45	2	when ye think not, S. shall be past
	37	that S. is now nigh at hand
56	16	S. is ended and my soul is not saved
115	9	a preparatory work this following S.

SUMMER'S

135	4	I am calm as a S. morning

SUMMUM BONUM

128	11	the S. of the whole subject

SUN

5	14	clear as the moon and fair as the S.—105:31; 109:73
29	14	the S. shall be darkened and the moon—34:9; 45:42
76	70	whose glory is that of the S., whose glory the S. of the
	71	as that of the moon differs from the S.—78
	96	even as the glory of the S. is one
88	7	he is in the S. and the light of the S.
	45	the S. giveth his light by day
	87	the S. shall hide his face and shall
110	3	shone above the brightness of the S.
121	11	before burning rays of the rising S.
	30	or to the S., moon or stars
128	23	let S., moon and morning stars sing
133	49	the S. shall hide his face in shame

SUNDRY

128	21	at S. times and in divers places

SUPPER

58	9	yea a S. of the house of the Lord
	11	and partake of the S. of the Lord
65	3	prepare ye the S. of the Lamb

SUPPLANTED

Sec.	Vs.	
134	6	would be S. by anarchy and terror

SUPPLICATION

136	29	call on the Lord with S.

SUPPLIED

42	33	that every man may be amply S.

SUPPLY

118	1	let men be appointed to S. the place

SUPPORT

19	34	and all save the S. of thy family
24	3	and they shall S. thee
25	9	for thy husband shall S. thee
42	30	consecrate of thy properties for their S.
	33	more than is necessary for their S.
	55	more than would be for thy S.
	73	bishop also shall receive his S.
75	24	also to S. the families of those
	26	obtain places for their families and S.
104	20	for his S. while he is laboring
	45	inheritance for his father, for his S.
124	89	with his interest S. the cause
122		if it must needs be for their S.

SUPPORTED

3	8	extended his arm and S. you against
42	71	to have their families S. out of
123	7	and oppression S. and urged on

SUPPORTING

75	24	assist in S. the families of those
98	5	S. that principle of freedom in

SUPPOSE

11	15	you need not S. that you are called
24	10	he shall not S. that he can say enough
121	39	a little authority as they S.

SUPPOSED

9	7	you have S. that I would give it to

SUPPOSETH

10	28	because he S. that another lieth to

SUPPRESS

134	4	but never S. freedom of the soul

SUPREME

107	4	reverence to the name of the S. Being

Sec.	Vs.	
		SURE
51	6	and thus all things shall be made S.
64	31	my words are S. and shall not fail
131	5	the more S. word of prophecy means
		SURELY
8	1	so S. shall you receive a knowledge
19	4	S. every man must repent or suffer
29	21	have not come to pass but S. must
35	22	and S. these things shall be fulfilled
39	21	no man knoweth, but it S. shall come
88	91	and S. men's hearts shall fail them
97	19	S. Zion is the city of our God, S. Zion cannot fall
		SURETY
5	12	they shall know of a S. that these
	25	I know of a S. that they are true
11	16	that you may know of a S. of my doctrine
		SURGE
122	7	if the billowing S. conspire against
		SURPASSES
76	89	which S. all understanding—114
		SURPLUS
119	1	I require all their S. property
	5	shall be tithed of their S. properties
		SUSQUEHANNA
128	20	voice of Michael on the banks of the S.; between Harmony, S. County, and Colesville on S. river
		SUSTAIN
134	5	all men bound to S. and uphold
		SUSTAINED
123	2	amount of damages they have S.
		SWEAR
88	110	and S. in the name of him who sitteth
121	18	and those who S. falsely against
		SWEET
29	39	bitter, they could not know the S.
42	46	for it shall be S. unto them
		SWEPT
109	30	and be S. away by the hail
	70	and S. away as with a flood
121	15	shall be S. from under heaven

Sec.	Vs.	
		SWIFT
121	24	I have in reserve a S. judgment
124	26	and send ye S. messengers, yea, chosen
		SWIFTLY
61	3	to be moving S. upon the waters
		SWIM
127	2	deep water is what I am wont to S. in
		SWINE
41	6	or the pearls be cast before S.
89	17	rye for the fowls and for S.
		SWORD
1	13	his S. is bathed in heaven
6	2	sharper than a two-edged S.—11:2; 12:2; 14:2; 33:1
17	1	also the breastplate, the S. of Laban
27	18	take the S. of my Spirit which I
35	14	I will let fall the S. in their
45	33	they will take up the S. against
	68	that will not take his S. against his
87	6	thus with the S. and by bloodshed
97	26	with S., with plague, with vengeance
101	10	let fall the S. of mine indignation
121	5	with thy S. avenge us of our wrongs
122	6	if with drawn S. thine enemies tear; shall be thrust from thee by the S.
		SWORE
84	24	Lord S. they should not enter into
		SWORN
63	33	I have S. in my wrath and decreed
97	20	he hath S. by power of his might
98	2	the Lord hath S. and decreed that
101	10	I have S. and the decree hath gone forth
		SYNAGOGUE
63	31	scourged from city to city, from S. to S.
		SYNAGOGUES
66	7	bear testimony in their S.
68	1	in their S. reasoning with them
		SYSTEM
84	110	that the S. may be kept perfect

T

Sec.	Vs.		Sec.	Vs.	
		TABERNACLE		88	T. him or her between thee and him
88	137	a T. of the Holy Spirit for your	45	33	they *will* T. *up* the sword one against
93	4	I was in the world and made flesh my T.		68	that *will* not T. his sword against
	35	the elements are the T. of God; man is the T. of God	51	8	to T. money to provide food and
101	23	covering of my temple in my T.	52	3	T. their journey as soon as preparations
124	38	Moses that he should build a T.		7	T. their journey.—8:22, 23, 24, 25, 26, 27, 28, 29, 30, 31, 32, 33, 35; 53:5; 54:7, 8; 55: 5, 6; 60: 5, 6, 8; 63:39; 75:13, 14, 15, 17, 18
		TAHHANES			
104	20	and the lot of T. (the tannery) for			
		TAKE		41	T. with them a recommend from the
5	31	I *will* T. away the things I have			
8	8	no power shall be able to T. it away	53	3	T. upon you mine ordination
10	7	he has sought to T. away the things	56	2	he that *will* not T. *up* his cross
18	21	T. upon you the name of Christ		5	T. *up* his journey speedily
	24	all men must T. upon them the name	58	15	let him T. *heed* lest he fall
	27	they shall T. upon them my name: who shall desire to T. upon them	61	9	T. their former company and T. their journey in haste.—61:21
	28	if they desire to T. upon them my name		11	T. that which is needful for clothing
20	33	let church T. *heed* and pray always		12	T. that which is not needful
	34	let those who are sanctified T. *heed*	63	3	T. even them whom he will T.
	37	and willing to T. upon them the name.—20:77		6	let the wicked T. *heed*
	44	and to T. the lead of all meetings		37	T. righteousness in his hands
	49	to T. lead of meetings when there		61	how they T. my name in their lips
	56	to T. lead of meetings in absence	64	28	that the Lord should T. them when he
	64	each priest may T. a certificate	68	34	transgress them not neither T. therefrom
	78	he shall T. the cup also and say			
	84	members removing may T. a letter	72	11	T. an account of the elders
23	6	that you must T. *up* your cross	76	28	sought to T. the kingdom of our God
24	18	thou shalt T. no purse nor scrip	78	21	he will T. you *up* in a cloud and
27	15	T. upon you my whole armor	84	81	T. no thought for the morrow
	18	T. the helmet of salvation		84	let the morrow T. thought for the
28	11	thou shalt T. thy brother Hiram		85	neither T. ye thought beforehand
	14	T. thy journey among the Lamanites		86	from this hour T. purse and scrip
				105	T. the old and cast it to the poor
29	17	I *will* T. vengeance upon wicked		106	let him T. with him he that is weak
	18	which shall T. hold of the inhabitants		107	T. with you those who are ordained
				113	employ an agent to T. charge
30	5	you shall T. your journey with your	88	72	lo, I *will* T. care of your flocks
			96	2	T. charge of the place which is named
42	54	shall not T. thy brother's garment		4	T. *heed* that ye see to this matter
	59	T. the things which thou hast received		9	seek diligently to T. away incumbrances

Sec.	Vs.		Sec.	Vs.	
101	45	and T. to themselves the fruit of my	112	15	shall not be T. from him till I come
	55	T. all the strength of mine house	121	4	let thy pavilion be T. *up*
104	18	if any man shall T. of the abundance	124	28	lost, or which he hath T. away
				130	David Patten I have T. unto myself
112	14	T. *up* your cross, follow me		132	Seymour Brunson I have T. unto myself
118	5	let them T. leave of saints in Far West	136	35	like a woman T. in travail

TAKETH

Sec.	Vs.	
121	12	and T. them in their own craftiness
123	4	to T. statements and affidavits
24	83	let him not T. his family to the
	91	Hyrum may T. office of Patriarch
125	4	T. *up* their inheritances in the same
126	3	T. special care of your family
128	18	that a perfect union should T. place
132	44	to T. her and give unto him that hath
	65	when I commanded Abraham to T. Hagar
134	10	to T. from them this world's goods
136	7	to T. teams, seeds, farming utensils
	21	to T. the name of the Lord in vain

Sec.	Vs.	
78	20	prepareth all things before he T. you
93	39	wicked one cometh and T. away light
124	130	his priesthood no man T. from him
	132	no man T. his priesthood, but

TAKING

Sec.	Vs.	
27	17	T. the shield of faith wherewith ye
105	30	guiltless in T. possession of lands
128	3	qualified for T. accurate minutes; precise in T. whole proceedings
	8	T. a different view of the translation
136	8	in T. the poor, the widows and the

TAKEN

Sec.	Vs.	
1	33	from him shall be T. even the light
	35	when peace shall be T. from earth
9	5	I have T. away this privilege from you
10	8	wicked men have T. them from you
13	1	shall never be T. again from earth
38	4	I have T. the Zion of Enoch into
42	32	they cannot be T. from the church
43	3	receive revelations until he be T.
	4	for if it be T. from him
	10	as ye do it not it shall be T.
45	57	have T. Holy Spirit for their guide
49	6	he has T. his power on right hand
51	10	not be T. and given to another church
52	37	bestowed on Basset be T. from him
58	60	bestowed on Peterson be T. from him
60	3	if not more faithful it shall be T.
64	5	the keys shall not be T. from my
72	13	an account shall be T. and handed over
83	2	until their husbands are T.
84	97	they shall not be T. from the earth
90	3	keys of this kingdom shall never be T.
	26	be not T. from you and given to
99	8	proclaiming gospel until thou be T.
101	23	when the veil shall be T. off and
104	64	it shall not be used or T. out of —71
	81	it shall be T. out of their minds
110	1	the veil was T. from our minds
	13	who was T. to heaven without tasting

TALENT

Sec.	Vs.	
60	2	but hide the T. which I have given
	13	neither shalt thou bury thy T.
82	18	that every man may improve his T.

TALENTS

Sec.	Vs.	
82	18	that every man may gain other T.
104	69	if any man obtain five T. let him
	73	if it be five T., or ten T.

TALK

Sec.	Vs.	
19	31	and of tenets thou shalt not T.
105	24	T. not of judgment, neither boast of
128	9	seems very bold doctrine that we T. of

TALKED

Sec.	Vs.	
17	1	when he T. with the Lord face to face

TANGIBLE

Sec.	Vs.	
130	22	flesh and bones as T. as man's

TANNERY

Sec.	Vs.	
104	20	lot of the T. for his stewardship

TARES

Sec.	Vs.	
38	12	to gather the T. that they may be
86	1	the parable of the wheat and the T.—101:65
	3	he soweth the T. wherefore the T. choke
	6	pluck not up the T. while
	7	let wheat and T. grow together, gather the wheat from the T.; the T. bound in
88	94	she is the T. of the earth
101	66	while the T. shall be bound in bundles

Sec.	Vs.	
		TARRIED
88	56	and T. with him all that hour
		TARRY
7	3	thou shalt T. until I come
	4	if I will that he T. till I come
35	22	T. with him and he shall journey
63	41	those of my disciples who shall T.
	45	agent to the disciples that shall T.
66	6	T. not many days in this place
75	3	you should go forth and not T.
88	70	T. ye, T. ye, in this place
	84	T. ye and labor diligently
95	9	T., even as mine apostles at Jerusalem
101	55	save those I have appointed to T.
105	21	let them T. for a little season
111	7	T. in this place and in regions
	8	where it is my will you should T.
117	2	arise and come forth and not T.
	3	if they T. it shall not be well with
124	102	let Joseph T. at home for he is needed
130	23	it may descend upon him and not T.
133	4	that have not been commanded to T.
136	6	to prepare for those who are to T.
		TASTE
42	46	those that die shall not T. of death
59	19	for raiment, for T. and for smell
		TASTED
19	20	which in the least degree you have T.
		TASTING
110	13	taken to heaven without T. death
		TAUGHT
42	58	for they shall be T. unto all nations
43	15	not sent forth to be T. but to teach
	16	ye are to be T. from on high
46	18	that all may be T. to be wise
49	4	according to that which shall be T. him
52	9	which is T. them by the Comforter
63	65	as they are T. through prayer
84	23	now this Moses plainly T. to children
93	42	you have not T. your children light
105	10	that my people may be T. more perfectly
109	14	may be T. words of wisdom out of best
		TAYLOR, JOHN
118	6	let T., and, be appointed to fill the
124	129	they are—Heber C. Kimball, T., and
135	2	T. and Willard Richards, were the only

Sec.	Vs.	
		TEACH
20	42	to T., expound, exhort, baptize—46, 50, 59
28	1	whatsoever thou shalt T. them
	4	to speak, or T., or at all times
36	2	T. you the peaceable things of the
38	23	T. one another according to the office
42	12	shall T. the principles of my gospel
	14	if ye receive not the spirit shall not T.
	57	not T. them until received in full
	58	ye shall T. them unto all men
	64	T. them that shall be converted to flee
43	7	to T. those revelations which you
	15	not sent forth to be taught but to T.
50	14	which was sent forth to T. the truth
68	25	that T. them not to understand doctrine
	28	T. their children to pray and walk
75	10	Comforter which shall T. them all
79	2	Comforter which shall T. him the truth
84	87	T. them of the judgment which is to come
88	77	T. one another the doctrine of the
	78	T. diligently and my grace shall
	118	T. one another words of wisdom—109:7
107	85	to T. them their duty—87
	89	to T. them according to the covenants
136	16	go and T. this my will to the saints
		TEACHER
20	60	every T. is to be ordained
	64	each T. who is ordained by a priest
38	40	elder, priest, T. go to with his
84	30	offices of T. and deacon are necessary
88	122	appoint among yourselves a T.
	128	T. shall be found standing in his
	132	let the T. arise and with uplifted
	135	they shall salute the president or T.
107	10	also in the office of a T.
	62	over those of the office of a T.
	63	from deacon to T. and from T. to priest
		TEACHERS
18	32	to ordain priests and T.
20	38	duty of the elders, priests, T.
	39	ordain other priests, T. and—48
	58	neither T. nor deacons have authority
	81	to send one or more of their T. to
	84	or it may be signed by the T.

Sec.	Vs.	
42	12	T. of this church shall teach principles
	70	T. shall have their stewardships
84	111	T. should be appointed to watch
107	62	T. to preside over those who are
	86	president of T. to preside over 24 T.
124	142	say unto president of the T. and

TEACHER'S

20	53	the T. duty is to watch over the

TEACHES

132	64	T. unto her law of my priesthood

TEACHETH

39	6	and T. peaceable things of the
84	48	the Father T. him of the covenant
101	70	which T. to purchase all the lands

TEACHING

42	15	I have commanded concerning your T.
107	86	T. them the duties of their office

TEACHINGS

28	8	inasmuch as they receive thy T.
42	13	and these shall be their T.
43	5	that ye receive not the T. of any

TEAMS

136	5	provide themselves with all the T.
	7	to take T., seeds and farming

TEAR

122	6	if they T. thee from society of; and thine enemies T. thee from the

TEETH

19	5	weeping and wailing and gnashing of T.—101:91; 133:73
85	9	where are wailing and gnashing of T.
124	8	where there is gnashing of T.
	52	wailing and anguish and gnashing of T.

TELESTIAL

76	81	we saw the glory of the T.
	88	the T. receive it of the administering
	89	glory of T. which surpasses all
	91	excels in all things glory of T.
	98	glory of T. is one even as; so differs one from another in the T.
	109	saw the glory of inhabitants of T.
88	21	must inherit that of a T. kingdom
	24	who cannot abide law of T. cannot abide T. glory
	31	quickened by a portion of the T.

Sec.	Vs.	
		TELL
5	20	I T. you these things as I told
6	15	I T. thee these things that thou
	16	I T. thee that thou mayest know
	17	I T. thee these things as a witness
8	2	I *will* T. you in your mind and heart
	9	whatsoever you shall ask me to T. you
10	37	you cannot always T. wicked from the
15	3	*will* T. you that which no man knoweth—16:3
28	10	what he saith to thee thou shalt T.
	11	T. him these things are not of me
38	14	I T. it unto you and ye are blessed
	30	T. you these things because of prayers
58	5	remember this which I T. you before
128	5	let me T. you it is only to answer
	23	T. the wonders of your eternal king
136	25	go straightway and T. thy neighbor

TELLETH

10	25	and T. them it is no sin to lie

TEMPERANCE

4	6	remember faith, virtue, knowledge, T.
107	30	in faith, knowledge, T., patience

TEMPERATE

6	19	be patient; be sober; be T.
12	8	being T. in all things

TEMPESTS

43	25	and by the voice of T.—88:90

TEMPLE

36	8	I will suddenly come to my T.
42	36	when I shall come to my T.
45	18	behold this T. which is in Jerusalem
	20	this T. shall be thrown down
57	3	a spot for the T. is lying westward
58	57	the spot of the T. unto the Lord
84	3	beginning at the T. lot
	4	even the place of the T., which shall be reared in
93	35	whatsoever T. is defiled God shall destroy that T.
101	23	when the veil of the covering of my T.
127	4	let the work of my T. and all the
	9	put in the archives of my Holy T.
128	24	let us present in this holy T.
133	2	the Lord who shall suddenly come to his T.

Sec.	Vs.	
		TEMPLES
93	35	tabernacle of God, even T.
97	17	I will not come into unholy T.
		TEMPORAL
24	9	in T. labors thou shalt not have strength
29	31	all things both spiritual and T.
	32	first spiritual, secondly T., first T.
	34	have I given a law which was T.
	35	but no T. commandment gave I unto him; they are not natural nor T.
	42	should not die as to the T. death
63	38	arrange their T. concerns
70	11	in a stewardship over T. things
	12	a stewardship to administer T.
	14	in your T. things you shall be equal
77	2	spiritual in likeness of T. and T. in likeness of
	6	during its T. existence
89	2	will of God in T. salvation of all
107	68	in administering all T. things
	71	set apart to the ministering of T.
		TEMPORALLY
14	11	be blessed both spiritually and T.
24	3	I will bless them spiritually and T.
		TEMPT
10	15	to get thee to T. the Lord thy God —29
29	39	the devil should T. children of men
	47	not given Satan to T. little children
101	28	shall not have power to T. any man
		TEMPTATION
9	13	be faithful, yield to no T.
20	33	lest they fall into T.
23	1	lest thou shouldst enter into T.
29	40	because he yielded unto T.
31	12	lest you enter into T.
61	39	pray that you enter not into T.
66	10	a T. with which thou hast been troubled
95	1	way for their deliverance out of T.
124	124	notwithstanding the hour of T. may
		TEMPTATIONS
20	22	he suffered T. but gave no heed
112	13	after their T. and much tribulation
		TEMPTED
29	36	Adam being T. of the devil
	40	the devil T. Adam and he partook
40	2	but straightway Satan T. him
62	1	how to succor them that are T.
64	20	that my servant may not be T. above

Sec.	Vs.	
		TEN
45	56	which I spake concerning the T. virgins
102	17	who draw even number, 6, 8, T.
104	69	or if he obtain T., or 20, or 50
	73	or if it be T. talents, or 20, or 50
107	52	Noah was T. years old when ordained
110	11	and leading the T. tribes from the
132	62	and if he have T. virgins given him
	63	if one or either of the T. virgins
		TEND
136	24	let your words T. to edify one another
		TENDENCY
134	8	their T. to evil among men
		TENDER
45	37	and their leaves are yet T.
86	4	while the blade is yet T.—6
		TENDERNESS
42	43	shall be nourished with all T.
		TENETS
19	31	of T. thou shalt not talk
		TENS
103	30	to go up to Zion by T. or by twenties
104	68	as you receive moneys by T. or fives
110	9	yes the hearts of thousands and T. of
133	58	two should put T. of thousands to flight
136	3	with captains of fifties and T.
	15	and appoint captains of fifties and T.
		TENTH
77	14	as mentioned in the T. chapter of
113	5	root of Jesse spoken of in T. verse
		TENTS
61	25	pitching their T. by the way
		TERMINATE
87	1	will eventually T. in death of many
		TERRESTRIAL
76	71	we saw the T. world; these are they who are of the T.
	78	they are bodies T. and not
	80	end of the vision of the T.
	86	through the ministration of the T.
	87	and the T. through the ministration
	91	thus we saw glory of the T.
	97	the glory of the T. is one even
88	21	inherit that of a T. kingdom

Sec.	Vs.		Sec.	Vs.	
	23	who cannot abide law of T. cannot abide T. glory	98	27	and these three T. shall stand
	30	quickened by a portion of the T.		35	should bring these T. before the —44
		TERRIBLE	103	24	after these T. brought against them
5	14	and T. as an army with banners— 109:73			**TESTIMONY**
45	70	for the inhabitants of Zion are T.	3	16	through the T. of the Jews
	74	when the Lord appears he shall be T.		17	through the T. of their fathers
				18	this T. shall come to knowledge of
64	43	shall fear because of her T. ones	5	11	in addition to your T., the T. of three
97	18	very glorious, very great and T.		14	to receive this same T. among this
105	31	that her banners may be T. unto all		15	the T. of three witnesses will I send
109	45	T. things concerning the wicked		18	and their T. shall also go forth
122	4	thy voice shall be more T. in midst	6	31	shall be established by the T.
133	43	when thou doest T. things	10	33	Satan thinketh to overpower your T.
		TERRITORY	24	15	dust of your feet against them as a T.—75:20
125	1	concerning saints in the T. of Iowa	58	6	might be prepared to bear T.
		TERROR		13	that T. might go forth from Zion
45	67	and the T. of the Lord shall be there		18	judge his people by T. of the just
				47	bear T. of truth in all places
	75	afraid because of T. of the Lord	60	15	as T. against them in day of
134	6	supplanted by anarchy and T.	62	3	blessed for T. ye have borne
		TESTAMENT	66	7	bear T. in every place
98	2	are recorded with this seal and T.	67	4	I give unto you a T. of the truth
135	5	dead, and their T. is in force	68	23	by T. that cannot be impeached
			76	22	this is the T. last of all
		(See New Testament.)		50	this is the T. of the Gospel
		TESTATORS		51	who received the T. of Jesus
135	5	the T. are now dead and their		74	who received not T. of Jesus
				79	not valiant in the T. of Jesus
		TESTIFIED		82	received neither the T. of Jesus— 101
5	1	of which you have T. and borne record	84	61	in bearing T. to all the world
20	26	who truly T. of him in all things		62	that the T. may go from you into
107	57	and are to be T. of in due time		92	bear T. of it unto your Father
		TESTIFIES		94	that rejecteth you or your T.—95
46	7	that which the Spirit T. unto you	88	3	as is recorded in T. of John
		TESTIFY		84	bind up the law and seal up the T.
17	3	you shall T. of them by power of		88	after your T. cometh wrath
	5	ye shall T. that you have seen them		89	after your T. cometh T. of earthquakes
18	34	you shall T. they are of me		90	also the T. of the voice of thunderings
	36	you can T. that you have heard my		141	given in John's T. concerning me
42	74	if they shall T. before you in all	98	39	no more as a T. against thine enemy
88	75	that I may T. unto your Father		48	never be brought any more as a T.
	81	I sent you out to T. and warn	99	4	by the way, for a T. against them
114	1	to T. of my name and bear glad	100	10	give him power to be mighty in T.
121	23	and T. against them, saith the Lord	102	26	with a full statement of the T.
127	6	that he may T. of a truth	107	72	upon T. as it shall be laid before
		TESTIFYING		79	upon T. according to laws of the
110	14	T. that Elijah should be sent before	109	38	put upon thy servants the T. of the
		TESTIMONIES		39	and people of that city receive their T.
42	32	after he has received these T.		41	and the people receive not the T.
76	22	after the many T. which have been		46	seal up the law and bind *up* the T.

Sec.	Vs.		Sec.	Vs.	
	49	and their blood come up in T.; make a display of thy T.		16	I tell T; that thou mayest know
	56	to bear T. of thy name		17	I tell T. as a witness unto T.
112	1	who were chosen to bear T. of thy name		20	I have spoken unto T.; I will encircle T. in the arms of
122	3	turned against thee by T. of traitors	7	2	I may live and bring souls unto T.
124	7	call upon them with your T.		4	what is that to T.
	8	if they reject my servants and my T.		7	I will make T. to minister for him
	20	for the love which he has to my T.	10	15	to get T. to tempt the Lord—29
133	72	they sealed up the T. and bound *up*	11	10	my power which speaketh unto T.
135	1	to seal the T. of this book and the		11	I give these words unto T.
136	34	have rejected you and your T.	15	3	no man knoweth save me and T.—16:3
	39	it was needful he should seal his T.	19	25	I command T.—26, 28
		THANK	20	77	we ask T. in the name of thy Son; and witness unto T., O God—79
59	7	thou shalt T. the Lord in all things	24	1	I have lifted T. up out of thy afflictions; I have counseled T.
		THANKFUL		3	and they shall support T.
62	7	with a T. heart in all things		4	but if they receive T. not
		THANKFULNESS		5	writing the things given T.
78	19	he who receiveth all things with T.		6	shall be given T. in the very moment
		THANKS		8	I am with T. even unto the end
46	32	ye must give T. unto God		17	whosoever shall go to law with T.
98	1	and in everything give T.		18	Church shall give unto T. what
109	1	T. be to thy name, O Lord, God	25	3	thy sins are forgiven T.—90:1; 112:3
		THANKSGIVING		4	for they are withheld from T.
46	7	doing all things with prayer and T.		7	as it shall be given T. by Spirit
59	15	as ye do these things with T.		8	for he shall lay his hands on T.
88	133	blameless, in T., forever and ever		9	thy husband shall support T
	137	called to do this by prayer and T		11	it shall be given T. to make selection; as it shall be given T.
89	11	to be used with prudence and T.	28	1	it shall be given unto T.
	12	for the use of man with T.		10	what he saith to T. thou shalt tell
97	13	a place of T. for all saints		11	take thy brother between him and T.
136	28	with a prayer of praise and T.		15	it shall be given T. from the time
		THAYRE, EZRA	35	3	I have looked upon T. and thy works and prepared T. for a greater work
52	22	let Marsh and T., take their journey		6	I give unto T. a commandment—20
56	5	I revoke commandment given to T. and	39	7	have looked upon thy works and know T.
	8	T. must repent of his pride		10	my voice which saith unto T.
75	31	also my servants T. and Marsh		11	prepared T. for a greater work
		THEE		12	that power shall rest upon T.; I will be with T.
3	12	given T. sight and power to translate	42	59	given T. in my scriptures
5	30	I say unto T., Joseph; until I command T. again		88	if thy brother offend T., take him between him and T.
	31	things which I have entrusted with T.	60	15	against those who receive T. not
	32	the lying in wait to destroy T.—33	64	11	Let God judge between me and T. and reward T.
	33	have given unto T. these commandments	81	3	I will bless him and also T.
	34	stand still until I command T.; the thing I have commanded T.	90	6	they are accounted equal with T.
6	14	I say unto T.—7:3, 5; 11:12; 25:10; 28:1, 2; 39:8, 14; 128:10	98	39	enemy has come upon T. first time; come unto T. praying forgiveness
	15	now I tell T. these things			

Sec.	Vs.		Sec.	Vs.	
	40	wherewith he has trespassed against T.		6	if thy enemies fall upon T.; tear T. from society of; tear T. from bosom of; shall be thrust from T.; enemies prowl around T.
	41	if he trespass against T. and— 42, 43, 44		7	sentence of death passed upon T.; surge conspire against T.; gape open mouth wide after T.; these things shall give T.
	44	until he repent and reward T.; wherewith he has trespassed against T.		9	the priesthood shall remain with T.
	45	I will avenge T. of thy enemy	124	58	in T. and thy seed shall the
100	11	I will give unto T. power; he shall be a revelator unto T.	128	10	I will give unto T. the keys
107	55	I have set T. to be at the head; a multitude of nations shall come of T.	132	2	I will answer T. as touching this
				28	will give unto T. the law of my Holy
109	1	have walked uprightly before T.		40	I gave unto T. an appointment
	4	now we ask T. Holy Father—22, 24, 29, 47		49	I will be with T. unto the end
			133	44	who remembereth T. in thy ways
	10	we ask T. to assist us		45	hath any eye seen beside T.; prepared for him that waiteth for T.
	12	which we now dedicate to T.	135	5	it matereth not unto T.
	15	that they may grow up in T.	136	25	tell thy neighbor lest he condemn T.
	21	speedily repent and return unto T.; who shall reverence T. in thy			**THEFT**
	31	have been innocent before T.	134	8	that murder, treason, robbery, T.
	32	we plead before T. for a full deliverance			**THEMSELVES**
	42	deliver thou, we beseech T., thy	10	26	to catch T. in their own snare
	43	their souls are precious before T.		56	but build up churches unto T.
	49	blood come up in testimony before T.	20	37	all those who humble T. before— 29:2; 112:22
	52	cause of thy people not fail before T.		82	the several members uniting T.
	59	we ask T. to appoint unto Zion	29	39	could not be agents unto T.
	60	these words we have spoken before T.	39	15	my people shall assemble T. to the
			42	75	and they T. are the offenders
	62	we ask T. to have mercy	44	2	that they assemble T. together— 63:24
	67	be redeemed and rejoice before T.			
	68	he has covenanted and vowed to T.	49	10	if not of T., they shall come down
	75	caught up in a cloud to meet T.	51	15	organizing T. according to my laws
	78	the dedication of this house unto T.	58	25	as they shall counsel between T.
112	2	things in thy heart and with T.		28	wherein they are agents unto T.
	6	have a great work for T. to do	72	22	that they may render T. approved
	10	thy God shall lead T. by the hand, and give T. answer to thy prayer	76	31	and suffered T. to be overcome
				35	having crucified him unto T.
121	8	God shalt exalt T. on high	116	4	and purify T. before him
	9	thy friends do stand by T.; they shall hail T. again	117		privilege of seeing and knowing for T.
	10	thy friends do not contend against T., nor charge T. with	84	73	they shall not boast T. of these
			87	3	in order to defend T. against
	11	they who charge T. with transgression		5	who are left will marshal T.
	43	lest he esteem T. to be his enemy	88	87	and shall cast T. down as a fig
	46	it shall flow unto T. forever		90	heaving T. beyond their bounds
122	1	fools shall have T. in derision; hell shall rage against T.	98	37	avenged T. on all their enemies
			101	45	take unto T. fruit of my vineyard
	3	thy people shall never be turned against T.		47	they began to say among T.
				48	consulted for long time among T.
	4	their influence shall cast T. into; thy God shall stand by T.		75	who call T. after my name—97; 103:4; 125:2
			102	18	have privilege of speaking for T.
			104	17	children of men to be agents unto T.

Sec.	Vs.		Sec.	Vs.	
105	10	that they T. may be prepared		18	T. be diligent
109	41	warn them to save T. from this		20	T. treasure up these words
121	13	may come upon T. to uttermost		33	T., if ye sow good ye shall also
	17	the children of disobedience T.		34	T., fear not little flock
	20	they T. shall be despised by those	7	6	T. I will make him as flaming fire
	37	the heavens withdraw T.	8	4	T. this is thy gift
124	62	organize T. and appoint one of		8	T., doubt not, it is the gift
	121	as shall be agreed among T.		9	T., whatsoever you shall ask me to
125	2	let them gather T. together unto		10	T. ask in faith
128	8	whether they T. have attended to	9	8	T., you shall feel that it is right
	20	declaring T. as possessing keys		9	T., you cannot write that which is
133	26	and shall no longer stay T.	10	3	T. see that you are faithful and
134	11	men are justified in defending T.		9	T., you have delivered them up
	12	warn the righteous to save T.		18	T. they will not agree
136	5	let each company provide T. with		19	T. we will destroy him
				21	T. they will not ask of me
		THENCE		37	T. I say unto you, hold your peace
38	33	and from T. shall go forth		41	T., you shall translate the
39	15	and from T. men shall go forth		45	T., it is wisdom in me that you
52	9	and let them journey from T.		55	T., whosoever belongeth to my church
60	6	from T. let my servants take		64	T., I will unfold to them
61	32	from T. let them journey for the		68	T. he is not of my church
65	2	from T. shall the Gospel roll forth	11	26	T., treasure up in your heart
		THENCEFORTH	12	9	T. give heed with your might
90	13	shall from T. preside over affairs	19	15	T. I command you to repent
	31	not be idle in her days from T.	20	13	T. having so great witnesses
101	40	it is T. good for nothing—103:10		33	T. let the church take heed
		THEORY	27	16	stand, T., having your loins girt
88	78	instructed more perfectly in T.	29	3	T. ye receive these things
97	14	perfected in T., in principle	31	5	T., thrust in your sickle with all
		THEREAT	34	10	T. prophesy, and it shall be given
132	25	and many there are that go in T.	38	15	T., be ye strong from henceforth
		THEREBY	42	34	T., the residue shall be kept
20	12	T. showing he is the same God		68	T., he that lacketh wisdom let him
46	12	that all may be profited T.—29	50	21	T. why is it ye cannot understand
64	21	that T. I may save some		46	watch. T., that ye may be ready
90	5	are brought under condemnation T.	51	5	T. he shall not retain the gift
	8	that T. they may be perfected	66	3	repent, T., of those things which
	23	T. he may be enabled to discharge	75	6	T., I revoke the commission
	27	T. you are hindered in accomplishing		22	T., gird up your loins—106:5; 112:7
102	12	and T. ascertain who of the twelve	80	4	T., declare the things ye have heard
134	12	T. jeopardizing the lives of men	81	3	T., I acknowledge him and will bless
		THEREFORE	82	5	T., what I say unto one I say unto all
3	2	T. his paths are straight		11	T., it is expedient for my servant
	10	T. repent of that which thou hast		15	T. I give unto you this commandment
4	2	T. O ye that embark in service of	84	20	T., in the ordinances thereof
	3	T., if ye have desires to serve God		24	T., the Lord in his wrath swore
6	2	T., give heed to my words—11:2; 12:2; 14:2; 30:5		25	T., he took Moses out of their midst
	3	T., whoso desireth to reap let him —11:3; 12:3; 14:3		31	T., concerning the sons of Moses
	5	T., if you will ask of me you shall —11:5; 12:5; 14:5; 103:35		38	T. all that my Father hath shall
	11	T. thou shalt exercise thy gift		40	T., all who receive this priesthood
				62	T., go ye into all the world

Sec.	Vs.		Sec.	Vs.	
	64	T., every soul who believeth	101	4	T., they must needs be chastened —41
	81	T., take no thought for the morrow		6	T. by these things they polluted
	84	T., let the morrow take thought		7	T., the Lord is slow to hearken unto
	86	T., let no man among you take purse		37	T., care not for the body, neither
	107	T., take with you those ordained		40	T., if that salt lose its savor
	109	T., let every man stand in his own		57	T., get ye straightway to my land
85	10	T. as the Lord speaketh, he will also		65	T., I must gather together my people
	12	T. it shall be done unto them as		67	T., a commandment I give unto all
86	7	T., let the wheat and the tares grow		79	T., it is not right that any man
	8	T., thus saith the Lord unto you		92	pray ye, T., that their ears may be
	10	T. your life and the priesthood		99	T., it is my will that my people
	11	T., blessed are ye if ye continue	103	16	T., I will raise up unto my people
88	18	T., it must needs be sanctified		19	T., let not your hearts faint
	24	T. he is not meet for kingdom of glory; T. he must abide a kingdom		22	T., let my servant say unto strength of
	35	T., they must remain filthy still		32	T., if you cannot obtain 500, seek
	61	T., unto this parable will I liken	104	4	T., as some of my servants have not
	68	T., sanctify yourselves that your		8	T., as you are found transgressors
	82	T., they are left without excuse		11	T., a commandment I give unto you
	84	T., tarry ye and labor diligently		18	T., if any man shall take of the
	94	T., she is ready to be burned		45	T. he shall be reckoned in the house
	117	T., call your solemn assembly		53	T. you are dissolved as United Order
	121	T., cease from all your light speeches		81	T. write speedily to New York
	129	T., he shall be first in the house	105	9	T., in consequence of transgression
90	2	T., thou art blessed from henceforth		13	T. it is expedient in me that mine
	33	T., let them cease wearying me		32	T., let us become subject to her laws
91	4	T., whoso readeth, let him understand		41	T., be faithful; and behold, I am
	6	T. it is not needful that it	106	7	T., blessed is my servant Warren
93	8	T., in the beginning the Word was	108	2	T., let your soul be at rest
	20	T., you shall receive grace for grace		7	T., strengthen your brethren in
	44	T., first set in order thy house	109	32	T. we plead before thee a full
95	9	T., I command you to tarry		46	T. deliver thy people from the
	10	T. I sent them forth to be chastened		62	we T. ask thee to have mercy
	12	T. you shall walk in darkness	110	5	T., lift up your heads and rejoice
	14	T. let it be built after the manner		16	T., the keys of this dispensation
96	2	T. let my servant take charge	111	3	T., it is expedient that you should
	4	T., take heed that ye see to this		11	T., be ye wise as serpents and yet
	9	T. ye shall ordain him unto this	112	3	T., all thy sins are forgiven thee
97	21	T., let Zion rejoice for this is Zion; T. let		5	contend thou, T., morning by morning
98	3	T., he giveth this promise unto you		27	T., see to it that ye trouble not
	6	T., I justify you and your brethren	115	8	T., I command you to build an house
	8	make you free, T. ye are free indeed	117	3	T., if they tarry it shall not be
	14	T., be not afraid of your enemies		7	T., will I not make solitary places
	16	T., renounce war and proclaim peace		9	T., come up hither unto the land
100	2	T., follow me, and listen to		13	T., let him contend earnestly for
	4	T., I have suffered thee to come to		14	T., let him come up hither speedily
	5	T., lift up your voices to this		15	T. let no man despise my servant
	12	T., continue your journey and let	122	9	T., hold on thy way and the priesthood; T., fear not what man can do
	15	T. let your hearts be comforted— 101:16	123	9	T., it is an imperative duty that we
				13	T., that we should waste and wear
				17	T., let us cheerfully do all things

Sec.	Vs.		Sec.	Vs.	
124	7	call, T., upon them with loud		27	for the Most High to dwell T.
	13	let him, T., hearken to your counsel		34	for T. are the keys of the Holy
	21	I T. say unto you, I seal upon his		40	that I may reveal mine ordinances T.
	23	T. let it be a good house, worthy		56	Joseph and his house have place T.
	39	T., that your anointings and washings	125	4	that have desires to dwell T.
	51	T., for this cause have I accepted	128	12	to be immersed. T. in order to answer
	59	T., let my servant, and his seed			
	74	T., I say unto you concerning my			**THEREOF**
	78	T., let him be remembered for an	5	19	and the inhabitants T. consumed
	87	T., let my servant put his trust in me	19	3	which I shall pass on inhabitants T.
	101	T., let my servant cry aloud		38	and corruptibleness to the extent T.
	114	let him T. abase himself that he	21	2	to lay the foundation T.
126	3	I T. command you to send my word	29	11	with all the hosts T.
				18	which shall take hold of inhabitants T.
127	3	let all the saints rejoice, T., and be		24	the earth and all the fulness T.
128	14	this, T., is the sealing and binding	45	1	who made the heavens and hosts T.
	24	let us, T., as a church and people	59	18	which come of the earth in season T.
129	8	you may T. detect him	61	17	that they may partake the fatness T.
130	15	T. let this suffice and trouble me		19	the destroyer rideth upon face T.
132	3	T., prepare thy heart to receive	63	39	my servant, who has the care T.; that dwell upon the face T.
	15	T., if a man marry him a wife; T., they are not bound by	65	5	that inhabitants T. may receive it
	16	T., when they are out of the world	68	33	prayers before the Lord in season T.
	17	T. they cannot be enlarged, but	70	5	to manage them and the concerns T.; yea, the benefits T.
	18	they cannot, T., inherit my glory	71	1	expounding the mysteries T.
	20	T. they shall be from everlasting	76	1	and rejoice ye inhabitants T.
	24	receive ye, T., my law		24	the inhabitants T. are begotten
	32	go ye, T., and do the works of Abraham		31	and have been made partakers T.
	34	this, T., was fulfilling the promises		45	and the end T. neither the place T.
	35	was Abraham, T., under condemnation		46	except to them made partakers T.
	39	and, T., he hath fallen from his		48	the height, the depth, the misery T.
	50	go, T. and I make a way for escape	78	18	kingdom is yours and blessings T.
	60	let no one, T., set on my servant	84	20	in the ordinances T., the power
	62	given unto him, T. is he justified		21	and without the ordinances T.
	65	it shall be lawful in me	104		the revelations and printing T.
	66	T., let this suffice for the present	88	7	light of the sun and the power T.
133	11	watch, T., for ye know neither the		8	light of the moon and the power T.
	12	let them, T., who are among the Gentiles		9	light of the stars and power T.
136	37	T., marvel not at these things		10	the earth also and the power T.
	41	now, T., hearken, O ye people of my		61	these kingdoms and inhabitants T.
			89	11	every herb in the season T.; every fruit in the season T.
		THEREFROM	94	4	fifty-five feet in the width T. and in the length T.—11
68	34	transgress them not, neither take T.		6	unto the Lord from foundation T. —12
84	41	and altogether turneth T.		11	sixty-five feet in the length T.
91	5	by the spirit shall obtain benefit T.	95	15	and the size T. shall be; in the inner court T.
		THEREIN	97	23	the report T. shall vex all people
91	1	are many things T. that are true	99	1	mine gospel unto inhabitants T.
	2	many things T. that are not true	101	33	and the purposes and end T.
96	9	that he may dwell T.		47	while laying the foundation T.
104	14	and all things T. are mine		53	set watchmen upon the walls T.
124	23	that strangers may come to lodge T.		54	from breaking the hedge T.
	24	or the Lord your God will not dwell T.			

Sec.	Vs.		Sec.	Vs.	
	101	and they shall eat the fruit T.		42	3 agreed as touching this one T.
109	36	as of fire and interpretation T.		43	13 and whatsoever T. he needeth
115	12	from cornerstone T. unto the top T.		50	39 wherefore in this T. my servant is not
118	4	promulgate my gospel, the fulness T.		59	13 thou shalt do none other T.
121	24	a swift judgment in the season T.		64	16 they condemned for evil that T. in
	32	unto the finishing and the end T.		72	3 in this T. ye have done wisely
124	3	to the four corners T.		78	2 in that T. which you have presented
	7	all their glory as the flower T.		88	119 prepare every needful T.—109:8
	42	pertaining to this house and priesthood T.		90	5 lest they are counted a light T.
	60	the glory of this cornerstone T.		94	8 shall not suffer any unclean T.
	83	scourge prepared for inhabitants T.			9 if there shall come into it any unclean T.
	121	as pertaining to the price T.		97	15 do not suffer any unclean T. to
	123	that ye may hold the keys T.		101	24 and every corruptible T. shall be
	143	the above offices and the keys T.		100	7 whatsoever T. ye declare in my name
132	5	for that blessing and conditions T.		109	15 be prepared to obtain every needful T.
	6	he that receiveth a fulness T.			20 no unclean T. shall be permitted

THEREON

101	99	though not permitted to dwell T.	127	2	they seem but a small T. to me
	100	I do not say they shall not dwell T.; they shall dwell T.	131	7	there is no such T. as immaterial

THINGS

119	6	that my judgments may be kept T.
130	9	to inhabitants who dwell T.

THERETO

11	22	then shall all things be added T.

THEREUNTO

106	3	all things necessary shall be added T.
132	58	there are many things pertaining T.

THEREWITH

50	33	with boasting, lest you be seized T

THIEF

45	19	desolation shall come as a T. in the night
106	4	overtaketh the world as a T. in the
	5	that day shall not overtake you as a T.

THING

5	34	mayest accomplish the T. which I—45:72
6	32	in my name as touching one T.
9	9	to forget the T. which is wrong
	13	do this T. which I have commanded
10	14	his evil design in this T.
14	11	which T. if ye do and are faithful
15	5	blessed are you for this T.—16:5
	6	the T. which will be of most worth—16:6
18	1	the T. which you have desired to know
	7	he hath fulfilled the T. I commanded
19	9	you that are chosen in this T.
22	1	caused to be done away in this T.
38	13	a T. which is had in secret chambers

1	18	should proclaim these T. to world
	19	weak T. of the world shall come
	34	willing to make these T. known
3	5	you have been entrusted with these T.
5	2	and have given these T. unto you; as a witness of these T.
	9	those T. which I have entrusted
	11	unto whom I will show these T.
	12	of a surety these T. are true
	13	behold and view these T. as they are
	20	I tell you these T. even as
	24	will grant unto him view of the T.
	25	I have seen the T. which the Lord
	26	say no more concerning these T.
	28	acknowledge the T. he has done; will grant him no views of the T.
	31	I will take away the T. which I
6	12	trifle not with sacred T.
	15	I tell thee these T. that thou
	17	I tell thee these T. as a witness
	22	know concerning truth of these T.
	24	I have told you T. no man knoweth
8	1	receive knowledge of whatsoever T.
	6	it has told you many T.
	10	trifle not with these T.
10	7	he sought to take away the T.
	34	commandments concerning these T.
	38	an account of those T. written
	39	given of the T. upon the plates
	40	is more particular concerning the T.
	45	are many T. engraven on the plates
	63	in these T. they do err for they wrest

Sec.	Vs.		Sec.	Vs.	
11	14	pertaining to T. of righteousness		62	I say, great T. await you
	19	in bringing to light those T.		72	keep these T. from going abroad
	25	wo unto him that denieth these T.		73	that they may consider these T.
14	8	that you may stand as witness of these T.	46	1	these T. were spoken unto you
				2	notwithstanding those T. written, it
18	2	the T. you have written are true	47	4	given by Comforter to write these T.
	3	rely upon the T. which are written	50	35	by giving heed and doing these T.
	39	you shall show these T. unto them	52	9	saying none other T. than that
19	16	I have suffered these T. for all		13	be made ruler over many T.—
	21	show not these T. unto the world			, 132:53
	22	they must not know these T. lest they		36	declaring none other T. than the
				40	for he that doeth not these T. is
20	17	by these T. we know there is a God	56	14	you have many T. to do and repent of
	35	we know that these T. are true			
21	6	by doing these T. the gates of hell	57	8	obtain whatsoever T. disciples may need
24	5	writing the T. which shall be given			
	14	these T. ye shall not do except		14	to do those T. as I have spoken
25	4	murmur not because of the T. thou	58	3	concerning T. which shall come hereafter
	10	lay aside the T. of this world; seek for T. of a better		6	bear testimony of the T. to come
27	12	the same T. I revealed unto them		8	that a feast of fat T. might be
28	3	be obedient to the T. I shall give		27	do many T. of their own free will
	11	tell him those T. he hath written		63	bearing record of the T. revealed
	12	these T. have not been appointed unto	59	3	for their reward the good T. of earth
29	3	therefore ye receive these T.		15	as ye do these T. with thanksgiving
	21	Ezekiel who spoke of these T.		17	the herb and the good T. which come
	48	that great T. might be required of			
30	2	your mind has been on T. of earth more than on T. of me	61	13	gave commandment concerning these T.
	3	ponder upon the T. which you have	62	8	these T. remain with you to do
	8	give heed unto these T. and be	63	19	not justified because these T. are
31	4	you shall declare the T. which		26	rendereth unto Cæsar the T. which
35	4	thou shalt do great T.		44	these T. are in his own hands
	10	great T. are to be shown forth		46	expounding these T. unto them
	13	I have called upon weak T. of the		53	these T. are the T. ye must look for
	18	the keys of the mystery of those T., T. from the foundation; T. which shall come		66	these T. remain to overcome
			64	14	for this cause ye shall do these T.
	22	surely these T. shall be fulfilled		17	but when these T. are made known
36	2	the peaceable T. of the kingdom—39:6		19	for this cause have I spoken these T.
				33	out of small T. proceedeth that which
38	30	I tell you these T. because of: lest wickedness of men reveal these T.	66	3	repent of those T. not pleasing in
	40	to accomplish the T. I have commanded		12	continue in these T. even unto
			68	32	these T. ought not to be and must be
39	22	he that receiveth these T. receiveth	69	3	making history of all important T.
41	6	not meet that T. which belong to the	70	6	shall not give these T. to church
42	28	knowest my laws concerning these T.		11	appointed in stewardship over temporal T.
	52	who have not faith to do these T.			
	59	thou shalt take the T. which thou		12	appointed to administer spiritual T.; to administer in temporal T.
	60	he that doeth according to these T.			
	61	know the mysteries and peaceable T.		14	in your temporal T. you shall be equal
43	15	to teach children of men the T.		17	have been faithful over many T.
	34	treasure these T. up in your hearts		18	shall enter into the joy of these T.
45	23	T. which I have told you shall not	71	1	in proclaiming the T. of the kingdom
	61	be prepared for the T. to come	72	6	these T. shall be had on record

Sec.	Vs.		Sec.	Vs.	
	14	the faithful who labor in spiritual T., administering the T. of the kingdom	98	20	do not forsake all their detestable T.
			100	11	pertaining to T. of my kingdom
75	9	go with him and proclaim the T.	101	6	by these T. they polluted their
	13	proclaim the T. I have commanded		33	T. which have passed, hidden T., T. of the earth
76	8	T. to come will I show them; T. of many generations		34	T. most precious, T. that are above, T. that are beneath, T. that are in the earth
	10	those T. which eye has not seen			
	12	to see and understand T. of God		49	for there is no need of these T.
	13	even those T. from the beginning		59	when shall these T. be
	19	while we meditated upon these T.		69	given you concerning these T.
77	2	and of creeping T. and the fowls of		72	let these T. be done in their time
	6	the hidden T. of his economy		92	that these T. may not come upon them
	7	first seal contains the T. of the			
	10	what time are the T. spoken of in		98	in consequence of those T. I have
	13	when are the T. to be accomplished	104	6	I am not to be mocked in these T.—124:71
78	5	be equal in bands of heavenly T., and earthly T. also; for obtaining of heavenly T.		62	all the sacred T. shall be delivered
				63	exclusive of the sacred T., for purpose of printing T.
	6	if not equal in earthly T. ye cannot be equal in obtaining heavenly T.		64	the sacred T. shall be had in treasury
	7	prepare yourselves by doing the T.		65	preserve the avails of the sacred T.
	10	blinded and understand not the T.		86	if you proceed to do the T. I have
	19	T. of this earth shall be added	105	3	not learned to be obedient to the T.
	20	do the T. which I have commanded		6	if needs be by the T. they suffer
80	4	declare the T. which ye have heard		10	the T. which I require at their hands
81	4	in doing these T. thou wilt do the		23	reveal not the T. I have revealed
84	54	treated lightly the T. you have	107	8	to administer in spiritual T.—12
	60	inasmuch as you receive these T.		10	in administering spiritual T
	61	testimony to all world of those T.		31	if these T. abound in them
	73	shall not boast themselves of these T.; these T. are given for your profit		57	these T. were all written in the book
				71	unto the ministering of temporal T.
	84	let morrow take thought for T. of itself	109	31	for which they have suffered these T.
	91	he that doeth not these T. is not		45	spoken terrible T. concerning wicked
	114	await them if they reject these T.			
	115	if they do reject these T. the hour	112	2	there have been some few T. in thine
85	10	these T. I say not of myself			
88	79	T. both in heaven and in earth; T. which have been; T. which are, T. which must shortly come to pass; T. at home, T. abroad	117	10	let my servant be faithful over few T.
			121	13	T. they are willing to bring upon
				35	hearts set so much upon T. of this
			123	4	appointed to find out these T.
90	26	that those T. that are provided for you		13	bringing to light all hidden T.
				15	let no man count them as small T. for much depends upon these T.
	27	hindered in accomplishing those T.			
	35	not pleased with many T.; have many T. to repent of	124	1	through the weak T. of the earth
				27	and with all your precious T.
91	1	many T. contained therein are true		32	if you do not these T. at the end
	2	many T. contained therein are not true		41	which have been kept hid; T. that pertain to dispensation
93	24	truth is knowledge of T. as they are		47	and do not do the T. that I say
	43	many T. are not right in your house		84	many T. with which I am not pleased
	44	in some T. he hath not kept the			
	48	needs repent and forsake some T.		96	Hyrum may bear record of the T.
97	18	if Zion do these T. she shall prosper		113	faithful in even a few T.
	27	if she sin no more none of these T.			

Sec.	Vs.	
127	8	I am about to restore many T.
	10	as well as many other T.
128	5	you may think this order of T. very
	6	judged out of those T. written in the—7
	18	but those T. which never have been
	19	that bring glad tidings of good T.
	25	I have many T. to say to you
130	10	whereby T. pertaining to higher order
132	13	whether powers or T. of name
	14	whatsoever T. remain are by me; whatsoever T. are not by me
	34	fulfilling among other T. the promises
	37	Jacob did none other T. than that; because they did none other T. than
	38	save in those T. they received not of me
	39	in none of these T. did he sin
	53	he hath been faithful over a few T.
	58	there are many T. pertaining thereunto
	64	teaches her law pertaining to these T.
133	36	that these T. might be known among you
	43	when thou doest terrible T., T. they
	45	how great T. thou hast prepared for
	58	to prepare the weak for those T. that
	59	by weak T. of the earth, Lord shall
136	37	marvel not at these T. for ye are

THINGS, (All)

Sec.	Vs.	
5	7	if you could show them all these T.
10	37	make all T. known unto the world
11	14	by this you shall know all T.
	22	all T. shall be added thereunto
	23	all T. shall be added according
12	8	being temperate in all T.
14	6	keep my commandments in all T. 18:43
18	4	in them are all T. written
	18	which manifesteth all T. which are
	45	I give unto you are above all T.
19	2	that I might subdue all T.
20	17	heaven and earth and all T. which are
	26	who testified of him in all T.
	68	expound all T. concerning the church; that all T. may be done in order
25	9	that all T. might be revealed unto
26	2	all T. shall be done by common consent; all T. you shall receive by faith
27	6	restoration of all T. spoken by the

Sec.	Vs.	
	13	gather together in one all T. both
	18	be agreed as touching all T.
28	1	thou shalt be heard in all T.
	13	all T. must be done in order, and by
	14	shalt assist to settle all these T.
29	8	be prepared in all T. against the
	24	all old T. shall pass away; all T. shall become new—63:49; 101:25
	30	the last shall be first in all T.
	31	all T. both spiritual and temporal
	34	all T. unto me are spiritual
33	16	my spirit quickeneth all T.
35	19	Holy Ghost that knoweth all T.
38	2	the same which knoweth all T., for all T.
	3	world was made, and all T. came by me
	38	see that all T. are preserved; all these T. shall be gathered unto
39	6	Comforter which showeth all T.
41	3	and have all T. right before me:— 57:13
	10	see to all T. as it shall be
42	17	the Comforter knoweth all T.
	41	let all T. be done in cleanliness
	55	that all T. may be done according
	65	thou shalt observe all these T.
	71	assist as counselors in all T.
	93	thus ye shall conduct in all T.
44	5	that you may be preserved in all T.
	6	that they may be kept until all T.
45	1	by whom all T. were made which live
	35	when all these T. shall come to pass
	38	when they shall see all these T.
	60	in it all these T. shall be made known
46	7	commanded in all T. to ask of God; doing all T. with prayer, thanksgiving
	31	all T. must be done in the name of
47	1	assist in transcribing all T.
50	27	for he is possessor of all T., for all T. are subject to
	28	no man is possessor of all T.
	35	power to overcome all T. that
	40	ye cannot bear all T. now.—78:18
51	6	thus all T. shall be made sure.
	13	let all T both in money and meat
52	14	I will give you a pattern in all T.
	40	remember in all T. the poor
58	26	that I should command in all T.; he that is compelled in all T.
	55	let all T. be done in order.— 107:84
59	7	thank the Lord in all T.

Sec.	Vs.		Sec.	Vs.	
	18	all T. which come of the earth		17	through him who quickeneth all T.
	20	he hath given all these T. unto		40	judgment governeth all T.
	21	who confess not his hand in all T.		41	He comprehendeth all T.; all T. are before him; all T. are round about him; he is above all T. and in all T.; he is through all T. and round about all T.; all T. are by him and of him.—93:10
62	7	with a thankful heart in all T.			
63	36	I have decreed all these T. upon			
	59	through all and search all T.; all T. shall be subject unto me			
64	32	all T. must come to pass in their		42	he hath given a law unto all T.
	38	inhabitants of Zion shall judge all T.		67	filled with light comprehendeth all T.
69	6	place to receive and do all these T.		78	all T. that pertain unto the kingdom
	8	obtaining all T. which shall be		80	that ye may be prepared in all T.
72	15	must lay all T. before the bishop		91	all T. shall be in commotion
	17	acceptable, and answereth all T.		125	above all T. clothe yourselves with
	19	accounts approved in all T.		127	in all T. that are expedient for
	20	have claim for assistance in all T.	90	24	all T. shall work together for your good.—100:15; 105:40
	21	benefit of the church in all T.			
	22	render themselves approved in all T.	93	28	until he knoweth all T.
75	10	which shall teach them all T.	94	3	all T. pertaining to the church
	16	shall overcome all T.—22; 76:60		10	all T. whatsoever I shall command.—94:12
	29	every man be diligent in all T.			
76	7	concerning all T. pertaining to my kingdom		12	according to the pattern in all T.
	55	whose hands the Father has given all T.	95	1	their deliverance in all T.
				3	the great commandment in all T.
	59	all T. are theirs whether life or death, or T. present, or T. to come	97	14	all T. pertaining to the kingdom
				25	if she observe to do all T.
	91	which excels in all T.—76:92	98	3	all T. wherewith you have been
	93	before whose throne all T. bow		4	observe to do all T. whatsoever.—98:21
77	9	Elias came to restore all T.—77:14		14	I will prove you in all T.
	12	judge all T. and redeem all T.; sealed all T. unto the end of all T.		44	reward thee four-fold in all T.
			100	7	spirit of meekness in all T.
				8	bearing record unto all T.
78	8	it is expedient that all T. be done		11	certainty of all T. pertaining to the
	19	he who receiveth all T. with	101	19	all these T. that the prophets
	20	who prepareth all T. before he		32	shall come, he shall reveal all T.
	22	wise steward shall inherit all T.		60	go ye straightway and do all T.
82	12	all T. pertaining to the bishopric		62	went straightway and did all T.; many days, all T. were fulfilled
	19	doing all T. with an eye single to			
84	80	continue faithful in all T.		68	let all T. be prepared before you.—101:69, 72; 133:15
	83	you have need of all these T.			
	100	the Lord hath gathered all T. in	104	14	all T. therein are mine.—104:15; 86
85	1	general church record of all T.		17	I prepared all T. and have given
	6	whispereth through and pierceth all T.		21	let all T. be done according to the
				29	printing office and all T. that
86	10	until restoration of all T.		68	all T. save it be the holy and
88	6	he descended below all T.; he comprehended all T; that he might be in all T. and through all T.—88:41		86	all these T. are mine and ye are
			105	22	counsel him concerning all T.
				37	accomplish all T. pertaining to
			106	3	all T. necessary shall be added
	13	light which is in all T.; which giveth life to all T.; law by which all T. are governed; who is in the midst of all T.—88:41	107	43	like unto his father in all T.
				68	administering all temporal T.
			111	11	I will order all T. for your good

Sec.	Vs.	
121	4	of all T. that in them are and who
122	7	all these T. shall give thee experience
123	17	do all T. that lie in our power
124	13	be faithful and true in all T.
	42	all T. pertaining to this house
	55	prove that ye are faithful in all T.
	97	shall manifest the truth of all T.
	113	prove himself faithful in all T.
127	2	God knoweth all these T.
128	13	that all T. may have their likeness
130	7	all T. for their glory are manifest
	9	all T. pertaining to an inferior
132	19	shall be done unto them in all T.; their exaltation and glory in all T.
	20	because all T. are subject unto them
	29	Abraham received all T.
	40	and restore all T.—132:45
	45	make known unto you all T.
	55	shall my servant do all T. for her
	65	lawful for him to receive all T.
136	31	my people must be tried in all T.

THINK

10	16	they T. in their hearts we will see
45	2	in an hour when ye T. not, summer is
51	20	quickly, in an hour you T. not
58	20	let no man T. he is ruler
61	38	he cometh in an hour you T. not.—124:10
66	6	otherwise T. not of thy property
128	5	you may T. this order of things very

THINKETH

10	33	Satan T. to overpower your testimony
58	60	and he T. to hide them

THINKING

10	23	T. to destroy the work of God
39	16	T. I will stay my hand in judgment

THIRD

20	23	died and rose again the T. day
29	36	a T. part of the hosts of heaven
88	54	unto the T. saying I will visit
	57	visit the second, also the T.
	100	which is the T. trump
94	13	on the T. lot shall my servant
98	26	if he shall smite you the T. time
	28	unto the T. and fourth generation.—29, 30, 37, 46; 103: 26; 105:30; 124:50, 52

Sec.	Vs.	
	35	neither the second nor the T. time
	40	and so on to the second and T. time
	43	if he trespass against thee T. time
113	1	who is son of Jesse spoken of in T.

THIRST

133	68	fish stink and die for T.

THIRSTY

133	29	shall no longer be a T. land

THIRTEEN

102	5	as follows: four priests, T. members and

THIRTEENTH

88	141	given in T. chapter of John's

THIRTY-EIGHT

135	6	Joseph Smith was T. in December, 1843

THIRTY-TWO

107	51	Lamech was T. years old when ordained

THOMAS

31	1	T., blessed are you because of your
56	5	my servant T. shall take up his
112	1	T., I have heard thy prayers
	16	T., thou art the man I have chosen
118	2	let my servant T. remain for a season

THOMPSON

56	6	stiff-neckedness of my people in T.

THOMPSON, ROBERT B.

124	12	let T. help you to write this proclamation

THOUGHT

6	36	look unto me in every T.
9	7	you took no T. save it was to ask
	9	you shall have a stupor of T.
42	72	as may be T. best or decided
84	81	take no T. for the morrow
	84	let the morrow take T. for itself
	85	neither take ye T. beforehand
102	14	but if it is T. to be difficult
127	1	I have T. it expedient and wisdom

THOUGHTS

6	16	none else save God knowest thy T.
33	1	a discerner of the T. and intents
88	69	cast away your idle T. and your
	109	and reveal the T. and intents of
100	5	speak the T. that I shall put into
121	45	let virtue garnish thy T. unceasingly
124	99	up in the imagination of his T.

Sec.	Vs.	
		THOUSAND
29	11	with men on earth a T. years
	22	when the T. years are ended
77	6	this earth during the seven T. years
	7	the first T. years, the second T.
	10	accomplished in the sixth T. years
	12	in the beginning of the seventh T.
88	101	live not again until the T. years
	108	works of God in the first T. years
	109	works of God in the second T. years
	110	shall not be loosed for space of a T.
124	64	permitted to receive fifteen T.
	65	not permitted to receive over fifteen T.
	72	servant cannot pay over fifteen T.
		THOUSANDS
104	84	to loan money by hundreds or T.
110	9	the hearts of T. and tens of T.
133	58	two shall put tens of T. to flight
135	3	gathered many T. of Latter-day Saints
		THRASH
35	13	to T. nations by power of my Spirit. —133:59
		THREE
5	11	testimony of T. of my servants
	15	testimony of T. witnesses will I
6	28	in the mouth of two or T. witnesses
	32	where two or T. are gathered together
7	7	unto you T. I will give this power
20	61	meet in conference once in T. months
72	25	a certificate from T. elders of the
95	14	manner which I shall show unto T. of
98	27	these T. testimonies shall stand
102	1	consists of one or T. presidents
107	22	T. presiding high priests, chosen
	24	equal in authority to the T. presidents
	29	decisions of a quorum of T. presidents
	42	blessed by him T. years previous to
	53	T. years previous to the death of Adam
128	3	some T. individuals that are present; that in mouth of two or T. witnesses
	20	declaring the T. witnesses to bear
129	9	these are T. grand keys whereby
131	1	in celestial glory there are T. degrees
135	4	T. days previous to assassination

Sec.	Vs.	
		THREE HUNDRED
103	32	peradventure you may obtain T.
	33	if you cannot obtain T., seek that
		THREE HUNDRED SIXTY-FIVE
107	49	he walked with God T. years,
		THRESHOLD
109	13	that all who enter on T. of Lord's
		THRONE
76	21	who are sanctified before his T.
	92	reigns upon his T. forever
	93	before whose T. all things bow in
	108	to sit on the T. of his power
	110	who sits upon the T. forever
88	13	of God who sitteth upon his T.—40, 104, 110, 115; 124:101
	115	who seeketh the T. of him who
109	79	shining seraphs around thy T.
132	29	his exaltation and sitteth upon his T.
	49	and prepare a T. for you in kingdom
		THRONES
121	29	all T. and dominions, and powers
132	13	by T. or principalities or powers
	19	shall inherit T., kingdoms and
	37	and sit upon T. and are not angels
		THROUGH
1	29	power to translate T. the mercy of
3	16	T. the testimony of the Jews
	17	T. the testimony of their fathers
	20	be glorified T. faith in his name, that T. repentance
5	10	shall have my word T. you
	11	my words that are given T. you
8	3	T. the Red Sea on dry ground
20	6	T. faith God ministered to him
	30	justification T. the grace of our
	31	sanctification T. the grace of our Lord
21	1	elder of the church T. will of God
	9	which are given him T. me by the
29	42	redemption T. faith on the name
	46	children redeemed T. mine Only Begotten
43	2	T. him whom I have appointed—7
	4	unto this gift except it be T. him
50	27	by will of the Father T. Jesus Christ
51	12	this shall be done T. the bishop
52	9	taught by the Comforter T. prayer
57	13	as shall be proved by Spirit T. him
58	44	except they desire it T. prayer of
61	9	T. faith they shall overcome
63	59	I am over all, in all and T. all
	64	and ye receive the spirit T. prayer
	65	as they are taught T. prayer
	66	things remain to overcome T. patience

Sec.	Vs.	
64	5	T. the means I have appointed
70	13	T. the manifestations of the Spirit
74	7	being sanctified T. the atonement
76	13	ordained T. his only Begotten Son
	24	that by him, and T. him and of him
	31	T. the power of devil to be overcome
	39	T. triumph and glory of the Lamb
	42	that T. him all might be saved
	69	just men made perfect T. Jesus; T. shedding of his own blood
	86	T. ministration of the terrestrial
	87	T. ministration of the celestial
	118	that T. power and manifestation
78	14	that T. my providence, the church
84	14	received it T. the lineage of—15
	46	spirit enlighteneth every man T.
85	6	which whispereth T. and pierceth
86	8	T. the lineage of your fathers
	10	remain T. you and your lineage
	11	T. this priesthood a savior unto my
88	5	holiest of all T. Jesus Christ
	6	and T. all things the light of truth
	11	light which now shineth is T. him
	14	T. the redemption which is made
	17	redemption of the soul is T. him
	21	who are not sanctified T. the law
	41	he is in all things and T. all things
	92	angels shall fly T. midst of—103; 133:17, 36
	133	be your friend and brother T. grace
90	4	T. you shall the oracles be given
	7	T. your administration the keys
	9	T. your administration they may; and T. their administration the word
	11	T. those who are ordained unto
93	10	all things were made by him and T.
	22	all those who are begotten T. me
	39	light and truth, T. disobedience
103	36	T. your diligence, faithfulness and
104	4	broken covenant T. covetousness
	52	covenants broken T. transgression
109	5	done this work T. great tribulation
111	2	gather out T. your instrumentality
112	1	T. instrumentality of my servants
122	5	art called to pass T. tribulation
124	1	show my wisdom T. the weak things
127	2	as for perils I am called to pass T.
128	21	T. all the travels and tribulations
130	13	probably arise T. slave question
	19	T. his diligence and obedience
131	5	T. the power of the Holy Priesthood
132	7	T. the medium of mine anointed
	18	T. him whom I have anointed
	19	in time and T. all eternity
	49	unto end of world and T. all eternity
135	2	the latter, T. providence of God

Sec.	Vs.	

THROUGHOUT

| 84 | 18 | their seed T. all their generations—107:13 |

THROW

10	45	T. greater views upon my gospel
101	57	T. *down* their tower and scatter
105	16	T. *down* the towers of mine enemies

THROWING

| 105 | 30 | and of T. *down* the towers of mine |

THROWN

45	20	this temple shall be T. *down*
101	75	no more to be T. *down*—103:13
103	14	pollute inheritances they shall be T.
132	13	shall be T. *down* and shall not remain

THRUST

6	3	let him T. in his sickle with his might—11:3; 12:3; 14:3; 33:7
	4	*will* T. in his sickle and reap—11:4; 12:4; 14:4
11	27	and have T. in their sickle to reap
29	37	and they were T. *down* and thus came
31	5	T. in your sickle with all your soul
76	25	was T. *down* from presence of God
84		these are they who are T. down to hell
122	6	if then he shall be T. from thee by

THRUSTETH

| 4 | 4 | he that T. in his sickle with his |

THUMMIM

(See *Urim and Thummim*.)

THUNDER

| 87 | 6 | the T. of heaven and the fierce and |
| 133 | 22 | as the voice of a great T. |

THUNDERINGS

| 43 | 25 | called upon you by voice of T. |
| 88 | 90 | cometh testimony of voice of T. |

THUNDERS

| 43 | 21 | when the T. shall utter their voices |

THYSELF

19	33	even the destruction of T. and
	35	release T. from bondage
	41	and conduct T. wisely before me
45	4	whom thou gavest that T. might be
59	6	thou shalt love thy neighbor as T.
	9	fully keep T. unspotted from the world
112	3	as thou hast abased T. thou shalt
	11	let thy love be for them as for T.

Sec.	Vs.	
		TIDINGS
1	8	they who go forth bearing these T.
19	29	thou shalt declare glad T.
31	3	declare glad T. of great joy
62	5	declare glad T. to inhabitants
76	40	the glad T. which the voice out of the
79	1	proclaiming glad T. of great joy
109	23	bear exceedingly glorious T.
114	1	and bear glad T. unto all the world
128	19	glad T. for the dead; glad T. of great joy; that bring glad T. of good things
	20	glad T. from Cumorah
		TIME
1	28	receive knowledge from T. to T.
3	8	been with you in every T. of trouble
5	19	to be poured out from T. to T.
	20	word shall be verified at this T.
6	14	the place where thou art at this T.
9	3	should translate at this present T.
	11	but you feared and the T. is past
10	2	you lost your gift at the same T.
11	26	until the T., in my wisdom that
19	20	you tasted at the T. I withdrew my
20	26	after he came in the meridian of T.
	61	or from T. to T. as said conferences
	62	business necessary to be done at the T.
	64	take certificate from him at the T.
	68	the elders are to have sufficient T.
	82	whomsoever elders shall appoint from T. to T.
24	16	in mine own due T.—35:25; 42:62; 43:29; 56:3; 67:14; 71:10; 82:13; 90:29, 32; 103:2; 117:10; 136:18
	19	with a mighty pruning for last T.
25	4	is wisdom in me in a T. to come
	6	go with him at T. of his going
	8	thy T. shall be given to writing
26	1	let your T. be devoted to studying
28	4	if thou art led at any T. to speak
	15	from the T. thou shalt go to the T.
29	3	at this T. your sins are forgiven
	29	never at any T. have I declared
	34	not at any T. have I given a law
	50	I declare no more to you at this T.
30	5	for the T. has come that it is
	9	thou shalt commence from this T. forth
31	4	begin to preach from this T. forth
	6	go from them only for a little T.
	8	prepare them against the T. when
33	3	the last T. I shall call laborers
34	7	the T. is soon at hand that I shall
	8	a great day at the T. of my coming
35	10	the T. speedily cometh that great
	15	looking forth for T. of my coming

Sec.	Vs.	
	18	shall come from this T. until T. of my
37	3	against the T. that my servant Oliver
38	13	your destruction in process of T.
	21	in T. ye shall have no king nor ruler
39	3	which came in the meridian of T.
	8	thine heart is now right at this T.
	17	it may be pruned for last T.
	20	preparing for the T. of my coming —77:12
	21	for the T. is at hand; the day nor
	22	gathered unto me in T. and eternity
41	9	spend all his T. in labors of church
42	9	until T. shall come it shall be
	33	to those who have not from T. to T.
43	28	labor in my vineyard for last T.; for last T. call upon inhabitants of
48	1	you should remain for the present T.
	3	let them buy for the present T.; places to live for the present T.
	4	that in T. ye may be enabled to
49	6	under his feet, which T. is nigh
52	2	what ye shall do from this T. until
	43	I will hasten the city in its T.
53	6	the residue shall be known in a T.
58	3	ye cannot behold for the present T.
	44	the T. has not yet come for many years
	52	this whole region as soon as T. will
	55	of lands be made known from T. to T.
	56	knowledge they receive from T. to T.
59	4	and with revelations in their T.
60	13	thou shalt not idle away thy T.
61	17	blessed it in its T. for use of my
63	53	and in a. T. to come, even in the day
64	28	not said at any T. that the Lord
	32	all things must come to pass in their T.
67	11	no man has seen God at any T.
68	14	in the due T. of the Lord other
	21	if at any T. they can prove their
71	1	the T. has come that it is expedient
72	3	of his stewardship both in T. and in
	4	he who is faithful and wise in T.
73	6	I give no more unto you at this T.—94:17
76	38	not be redeemed in due T. of the
77	10	what M. are the things spoken of
	15	in last days at T. of restoration
78	3	the T. has come and is now at hand
84	28	ordained at the T. he was eight days
	76	rebellion against you at the T. I
	100	Satan is bound and T. is no longer
87	2	the T. will come that war shall
88	58	in his T. and in his season
	61	every kingdom in its hour, in its T.

Time 449 Times

Sec.	Vs.	
	68	and it shall be in his own T.
	73	I will hasten my work in its T.
	76	in prayer and fasting from this T.
	84	among the Gentiles for the last T.
	85	for their T. is not yet come
	110	that there shall be T. no longer
	122	but let one speak at a T.
90	2	kingdom is coming forth for last T.
	14	from T. to T. as shall be manifested by
93	19	and in due T. receive of his fulness
95	4	to prune my vineyard for last T.
98	25	enemy shall smite you second T.
	26	if he shall smite you the third T.
	35	neither the second nor the third T.
	39	enemy has come upon thee the first T.
	40	and so on unto the second and third T.
	41	and repent not the first T.
	42	if he trespass against thee second T.
	43	if he trespass against thee third T.
	44	if he trespass against thee fourth T.
101	48	and consulted for a long T. saying, seeing this is a T. of peace
	64	for the T. of harvest is come
	72	let these things be done in their T.
	90	in his T., will cut off those wicked
102	25	preside over such council for T. being
103	20	in T. ye shall possess the goodly
104	58	I shall from T. to T. give unto you
	59	for the T. when I shall dwell with
105	8	he will deliver them in T. of trouble
	27	will soften the hearts from T. to T.; shall have T. to gather up the strength
	35	T. has come for a day of choosing
106	3	and devote his whole T. to this high
107	57	and are to be testified of in due T.
108	6	from henceforth from that T.
109	61	scattered on mountains for long T
110	14	the T. has fully come spoken of by
111	2	will gather out in due T. for benefit
	4	it shall come to pass in due T.
112	30	for the last days and for last T.
	31	have received dispensation at *any* T.
115	10	let them from that T. labor—12
	18	manifested unto my servant from T. to T.
117	14	in due T. he shall be made merchant
120	1	T. is now come that it shall be disposed
121	25	a T. appointed for every man according
	28	a T. to come in which nothing shall'
123	16	by a very small helm in T. of storm
124	4	at the T. of writing the same

Sec.	Vs.	
	5	what shall befall them in T. to come
	6	for the set T. has come to favor her
	19	David Patten who is with me at this T.
	31	grant unto you sufficient T. to build; during this T. your baptisms
	33	after you have sufficient T. to build
	35	after this T. your baptisms for
	67	pay at the T. he receives stock
	94	from this T. forth I appoint unto him
	115	door shall be open to him from T. to T.
	140	to preside over the churches from T. to T.; responsibility of presiding from T. to T.
125	2	which is in store for a T. to come
126	3	care of your family from this T.
127	1	that my debts are cancelled in due T.
	10	will write word of Lord from T. to T.—128:1
	11	close my letter for want of more T.
128	3	who can at *any* T. certify to same
	18	from days of Adam to present T.
	25	and continue the subject another T.
130	4	is not reckoning of God's T., angel's T., prophet's T. and man's T. according to
	14	to know T. of coming of Son
	17	will not be any sooner than that T.
132	7	as well for T. and for eternity; never but one on earth at a T.
	18	covenant for T. and all eternity
	19	in T. and through all eternity
	38	from beginning of creation till this T.
	45	and make known all things in due T.
133	7	T. has come when voice of Lord is
134	5	at the same T. holding sacred the
135	2	only persons in room at the T.

TIMES

15	4	many T. you have desired of me to know—16:4
22	2	although baptized a hundred T., it
24	12	at all T. he shall open his mouth
27	13	dispensation of Gospel for last T.; and for fulness of T.
28	4	or at all T. by way of commandment
	16	thou must open thy mouth at all T.
39	9	thou hast rejected me many T.
45	25	remain until T. of Gentiles be
	28	when the T. of the Gentiles is come
	30	in that generation shall T. of Gentiles
59	11	offered up on all days, at all T.

Sec.	Vs.		Sec.	Vs.	
68	11	given to know signs of the T.		24	for after T. cometh the burning
69	7	let my servant travel many T.		25	ye will labor while it is called T.
76	106	until the fulness of T. when Christ			**TOGETHER**
84	54	your minds in T. past have been	1	1	ye on the islands of the sea listen T.
85	6	and often T. it maketh my bones to	6	32	where two or three are gathered T.
88	42	by which they move in their T. and	20	55	see that church meet T. often
	44	give light to each other in their T.		75	expedient that church meet T. often
89	13	not be used only in T. of winter	27	13	I will gather T. in one all things
	15	only in T. of famine and excess of	37	3	assemble yourselves T. — 45:64; 52:42; 58:46; 63:24; 88:74
98	40	thou shalt forgive until seventy T.	41	2	ye shall assemble yourselves T.
107	96	until seven T. seventy	42	1	who have assembled yourselves T. —3; 57:1; 67:1; 72:1; 78:1; 88:1; 105:1
112	30	which is the dispensation of fulness of T.
121	12	his hand, to change T. and seasons		45	thou shalt live T. in love
	27	to be revealed in the last T.	43	8	when ye are assembled T.
	31	all the T. of their revolutions; all their glories and set T.; in dispensation of fulness of T.		24	gathered you T. as a hen gathereth
			44	1	elders of my church should be called T.
124	41	that pertain to dispensation of fulness of T.		2	in the day they assemble themselves T.
126	1	to leave your family as in T. past	45	6	ye elders listen T.—136:41
128	3	for one recorder to be present at all T.		11	hearken ye T. and let me show
	18	dispensation of fulness of T.—20	49	25	assembled T. unto the place
	21	at sundry T. and in divers places	50	10	let us reason T. that ye may
134	11	in T. of exigency when immediate		22	both are edified and rejoice T.
135	3	of Lord's anointed in ancient T.	58	45	push the people T. from ends of
		TINGLE	61	35	let them journey T.
43	22	and make the ears of all T. that hear	62	4	hold meeting and rejoice T.
				6	I have brought you T. that; be preserved and rejoice T.
		TITHE	77	9	to gather T. the tribes of Israel
85	3	that he may T. his people	78	8	who are joined T. in this order
		TITHED	82	11	to be bound T. by a bond that
64	23	he that is T. shall not be burned	84	98	and with the voice T. sing this
119	4	those who have thus been T.	110		that all may be edified T.
	5	shall be T. of their surplus properties	86	7	let wheat and tares grow T. until
			88	93	and all people shall see it T.
		TITHING		111	that he may gather T. his armies
64	23	this is a day for T. of my people		112	Michael shall gather T. his armies
97	11	built by the T. of my people		113	devil shall gather T. his armies
	12	this is the T. and sacrifice which	89	5	only in assembling yourselves T.
119	3	be the beginning of T. of my people	90	24	shall work T. for your good—98:3; 100:15; 105:40
		TO AND FRO	101	22	shall gather T. and stand in holy
10	27	he goeth T. in the earth seeking		23	and all flesh shall see me T.
45	48	earth shall tremble and reel T.— 49:23; 88:87		55	go and gather T. the residue of
				58	inasmuch as they gather T. against
		TOBACCO		64	the work of gathering T. of my
89	8	T. is not for the body neither for		65	I must gather T. my people
		TODAY		67	shall continue to gather T.
20	12	the same God, yesterday, T. and— —35:1		72	gather T. all their moneys
				74	buy lands and gather T. upon them
45	6	hear my voice while it is called T.	103	22	gather yourselves T. unto Zion— 115:6
61	20	T. mine anger is turned away	105	15	for gathering T. of my saints— 115:8
64	23	now it is called T. until coming		16	gather T. for the redemption
				24	but carefully gather T. as much

Sec.	Vs.	
124	26	T. with all the precious trees
125	2	let them gather themselves T. unto
128	18	and welding T. of dispensations
	23	let the morning stars sing T. for joy
133	4	gather ye T. O ye people of my
	16	listen ye elders of my church T.

TOIL

Sec.	Vs.	
84	82	they T. not, neither do they spin
126	2	I have seen your labor and T. in

TOKEN

Sec.	Vs.	
88	131	in T. of the everlasting covenant—133
	135	by saying, Amen, in T. of the same
104	75	this shall be his T. unto treasurer

TOLD

Sec.	Vs.	
5	20	as I T. the people of the destruction
6	24	I have T. you things which no man
8	6	it has T. you many things
38	33	it shall be T. them what they shall
43	7	be ordained as I have T. you
45	21	every desolation which I have T. you
	23	these things which I have T. you
	24	I have T. you concerning Jerusalem
132	50	in obedience to that I have T. you
136	17	do as I have T. you and fear not

TOLERABLE

Sec.	Vs.	
45	54	and it shall be T. for them
75	22	shall be more T. for the heathen

TOMORROW

Sec.	Vs.	
64	24	T. all the proud and they that do

TONGUE

Sec.	Vs.	
10	51	whatsoever nation, kindred, T. or
11	21	then shall your T. be loosed—31:3
23	3	heart is opened and thy T. loosed
76	110	bow the knee and every T. confess—88:104
77	8	gospel to commit to every nation, T.
	11	ordained out of every kindred, T. and
84	70	and the T. of the dumb shall speak
90	11	hear gospel in his own T.
98	33	battle against any nation, T. or
	34	and if any nation, T. or people; standard of peace to that nation, T.
	36	in going to battle against that T.
112	9	let the T. of the slanderer cease
133	37	preached unto every nation, T. and

TONGUES

Sec.	Vs.	
7	3	prophesy before nations, T. and
29	19	their T. shall be stayed that they
42	58	taught to all nations, T. and
46	24	given to some to speak with T.
	25	to another interpretation of T.
88	103	gospel unto all nations, T. and

Sec.	Vs.	
90	15	become acquainted with languages, T.
109	36	let gift of T. be poured out, even cloven T. as of fire
112	1	send it abroad among nations, T. and

TOOK

Sec.	Vs.	
9	7	when you T. no thought save it was
84	25	he T. Moses out of their midst and
136	38	he was faithful and I T. him to myself

TOP

Sec.	Vs.	
115	12	from corner stone to T. thereof

TORMENT

Sec.	Vs.	
19	6	no end to this T., but written endless T.
76	44	not quenched, which is their T.
	45	nor their T., no man knows
104	18	lift up his eyes in hell being in T.

TOUCH

Sec.	Vs.	
135	7	that *will* T. the hearts of honest men

TOUCHED

Sec.	Vs.	
76	19	the Lord T. eyes of our understanding

TOUCHING

Sec.	Vs.	
6	32	in my name as T. one thing
27	18	and be agreed as T. all things—42:3
50	1	and are agreed as T. the church
132	1	as T. the principle and doctrine
	2	I will answer thee as T. this matter
	30	and as T. Abraham and his seed
	58	now as T. the law of the priesthood

TOWARD

Sec.	Vs.	
121	3	before thine heart shall be softened T. them
	4	be moved with compassion T. us—3
	43	an increase of love T. him whom

TOWARDS

Sec.	Vs.	
101	9	bowels filled with compassion T.
112	11	be not partial T. them in love above
121	45	full of charity T. all men
135	4	void of offence T. God and T. all men

TOWER

Sec.	Vs.	
97	20	to be her salvation and her high T.
101	45	and build a T. that one might; to be a watchman on the T.
	46	and began to build a T.
	47	what need hath my lord of this T.—48
	53	and built a T. also and set a watchman upon the T.

Sec.	Vs.		Sec.	Vs.	
	54	watchman upon the T. would have seen			**TRANSGRESSES**
	57	throw *down* their T. and scatter	51	4	until he T. and is not accounted
		(See *Watch Tower*)			**TRANSGRESSETH**
		TOWERS	88	25	the earth, T. not the law
105	16	throw down the T. of mine enemies			**TRANSGRESSING**
	30	and of throwing down the T. of mine	20	80	any member T. or being overtaken
		TRACK			**TRANSGRESSION**
52	33	neither journey in another's T.	3	9	but because of T., if thou art not
		TRACT	5	32	I foresee he will fall into T.
57	4	and also every T. lying westward	20	20	by T. of these holy laws
	5	every T. bordering by the prairies	29	41	from my presence because of his T.
		TRADITION	52	37	in consequence of T., let that
74	6	that the T. might be done away	82	11	covenant that cannot be broken by T.
93	39	because of the T. of their fathers	102	8	removal from office for T.
		TRADITIONS		32	by authorities of church in case of T.
74	4	children gave heed to T. of fathers	104	9	inasmuch as ye are cut off for T.
		TRAITORS		52	covenants being broken through T.
122	3	against thee by testimony of T.		76	in case of T., the treasurer
135	7	by conspiracy of T. and wicked	109	65	smitten because of their T.
		TRAMPLED	121	10	neither charge thee with T.
3	15	to be T. upon from the beginning		11	they who charge thee with T.
133	51	I have T. them in my fury		17	but those who cry T. do it
		TRANQUILITY	124	50	the iniquity and T. of my laws
134	8	and for the public peace and T.	132	26	and he shall commit any sin or T.
		TRANSACT			**TRANSGRESSIONS**
127	1	who *will* T. all business in a prompt	24	2	thou art not excusable in thy T.
		TRANSACTION	101	2	afflicted in consequence of their T.
128	3	and the history of the whole T.	105	2	were it not for T. of my people
		TRANSCRIBING		9	in consequence of T. of my people
47	1	in T. all things which shall be	109	34	forgive the T. of thy people
		TRANSFIGURATION		38	upon inhabitants because of their T.
63	20	when the day of T. shall come	132	60	he shall do the sacrifice for his T.
		TRANSFIGURED			**TRANSGRESSOR**
63	21	when the earth shall be T.	104	5	as any man shall be found a T.—10
		TRANSGRESS		74	until he be found a T.
3	5	promises, if you did not T. them	112	9	voice shall be a rebuke to the T.
42	10	if he T., another shall be appointed	132	65	and she then becomes the T.
51	5	if he shall T. and is not accounted			**TRANSGRESSORS**
68	34	T. them not, neither take therefrom	82	4	ye become T. and justice and
107	82	as a president of, shall T., he	83	2	and if they are not found T.
109	21	and when thy people T., any of them	101	41	they were found T., therefore they
		TRANSGRESSED	104	8	as you are found T. ye cannot escape
3	6	you have T. the commandments and	107	72	to sit in judgment upon T. upon
29	40	partook forbidden fruit and T.			**TRANSLATE**
			1	29	might have power to T. through
			3	12	God had given thee power to T.—10:1, 16
			5	4	you have a gift to T. the plates
				30	then thou mayest T. again
			6	25	to T. even as my servant Joseph
			8	11	that you may T. and receive
			9	1	because you did not T. according
				2	power that you may assist to T.

Sec.	Vs.	
	3	not expedient that you should T. at—10
	5	as you commenced when you began to T.
10	4	means provided to enable you to T.
	13	words which you have pretended to T.
	15	in asking to T. it over again
	39	you shall not T. again those words
	31	that you have pretended to T. but
	41	you shall T. the engravings which
	45	you should T. this first part of
20	8	to T. the Book of Mormon
37	1	not expedient ye should T. any more
41	7	house in which to live and T.
45	61	I give unto you that ye may now T.
73	3	it is expedient to T. again
93	53	hasten to T. my scriptures

TRANSLATED

5	30	when thou hast T. a few more pages
9	10	if you had known this you could have T.
10	10	or which you have T.
	11	that which you T. and caused to be
	41	you come to that which you have T.
17	6	and he has T. the book
45	60	until the New Testament be T.
91	1	it is mostly T. correctly
	3	that the Apocrypha should be T.
	6	not needful that it should be T.
107	49	430 years old when he was T.
135	3	Book of Mormon which he T. by

TRANSLATES

10	17	or if he T. again, or in other words

TRANSLATING

11	22	or that which is now T.

TRANSLATION

10	3	finishing remainder of the work of T.
	34	until you have accomplished work of T.
11	19	yea, the T. of my work
73	4	continue work of T. until finished
76	15	while we were doing the work of T.
90	13	when you have finished the T.
94	10	for the work of printing the T.
124	89	and publish the new T. of my holy
128	8	taking a different view of the T.
	18	I might have rendered a plainer T.

TRANSLATOR

21	1	thou shalt be called a seer, a T.
107	92	to be a seer, a revelator, a T.
124	125	to be a T., a revelator, a seer

TRANSMIT

102	26	said council to T. immediately a

TRANSPIRE

85	1	all things that T. in Zion

TRAVAIL

136	35	like a woman taken in T.

TRAVAILED

84	101	the earth hath T. and brought forth

TRAVEL

69	7	T. many times from place to place
84	111	the High Priests should T. and
	112	the bishop also should T. about
107	90	for those who do not T. into all
	98	not under responsibility to T., but to T. as their circumstances
124	135	and they may T. also if they choose
	137	nevertheless they may T., yet
	140	one is to T. continually

TRAVELER

124	23	that the weary T. may find health
	60	a resting place for the weary T.

TRAVELING

20	66	the T. bishops and elders may
49	22	neither of a man T. on the earth
84	77	T. to preach the Gospel
88	71	whom they have warned in their T.
102	29	the T. or located High Priests
	30	distinction between T. High Priests and T.
107	23	the twelve T. counselors are called
	33	Twelve are a T. presiding High
	34	of the Twelve or T. High Council
	36	or to the T. High Council
	38	it is the duty of T. High Council
	97	seventy are to be T. ministers
124	127	be president over the T. Council
	139	quorum is instituted for T. elders; wherever the T. High Council shall
133	46	T. in greatness of his strength

TRAVELS

128	21	through all the T. and tribulations

TREAD

133	51	I did T. upon them in mine anger

TREADETH

133	48	like him that T. in the wine vat

TREASON

134	8	that murder, T., robbery, and

TREASURE

6	3	that he may T. up for his soul— 11:3; 12:3; 14:3
	20	T. up these words in thy heart
11	26	T. up in your heart until the time
38	30	T. up wisdom in your bosoms

| Treasure | 454 | Tribulation |

Sec. Vs.
43 34 T. these things *up* in your hearts
84 85 T. *up* in your minds continually
111 2 I have much T. in this city

TREASURER
104 67 and a T. appointed to keep the
    72 say unto the T. I have need of this
    73 the T. shall give unto him the
    75 his token unto the T. that T. shall not withhold
    76 in case of transgression, T. shall be
    77 in case T. is found unfaithful.

TREASURES
6   27 to lay up T. for yourself in
19 38 more than if you should obtain T. of
63 48 he that sendeth up T. to the land
89 19 great T. of knowledge, even hidden T.
111 10 more T. than one for you in this
133 30 they shall bring forth their T.

TREASURY
104 60 prepare for yourselves a T.
    61 appoint one among you to keep the T.
    62 there shall be a seal upon the T.; shall be delivered into the T.
    64 the sacred things shall be had in T.; shall not be taken out of T.
    65 preserve the avails in the T.
    66 this shall be called the sacred T.
    67 there shall be another T. prepared; to keep the T.
    68 shall be cast into T. as fast as
    69 let him cast them into the T.
    71 not any part taken out of T. only

TREATED
84 54 you have T. lightly the things

TREE
85   8 like a T. smitten by vivid shaft
97   7 every T. that bringeth not forth
     9 as a very fruitful T. planted in a
101 30 his life shall be as age of a T.
135 6 if fire can scathe a green T. for

TREES
59 16 that which climbeth upon the T. and
77   9 hurt not the earth nor the T. until
97   7 ax is laid at root of the T.
124 26 with all the precious T. of earth
128 23 and all T. of the field praise the
135 6 how easy it will be to burn dry T.

TREMBLE
1   7 fear and T. O ye people
10 56 to T. and shake to the center
19 18 to T. because of pain, and bleed

Sec. Vs.
34   8 for all nations shall T.
35 24 Satan shall T. and Zion rejoice
43 18 heavens shall shake and earth T.
45 48 earth shall T. and reel to and fro— 49:23; 88:87
    74 they shall stand afar off and T.
63   6 let the rebellious fear and T.
64 43 nations of earth shall T. because of
84 118 but the starry heavens shall T.
123 10 hands of the very devil to T. and
133 31 everlasting hills shall T. at their
    42 all nations shall T. at thy

TREMBLETH
52 17 he that T. under my power shall

TRESPASS
98 40 repenteth of the T. wherewith he
    41 if he T. against thee and repent not
    42 if he T. against thee second time
    43 if he T. against thee third time
    44 if he T. against thee fourth time

TRESPASSED
46   4 if *any* have T. let him not partake
98 40 wherewith he has T. against thee —44
    47 wherewith they have T. and their fathers have T.
132 56 wherein she has T. against me

TRESPASSES
64   9 forgiveth not his brother his T.
82   1 forgiven one another your T.
98 47 restore four-fold all their T.
    48 their T. shall never be brought
132 56 forgive my servant his T. then shall she be forgiven her T.

TRIAL
105 19 brought thus far for T. of faith

TRIBE
77 11 12,000 out of every T.
133 35 and they also of the T. of Judah

TRIBES
77   9 over the T. of Israel; to gather the T. of Israel
    11 144,000 out of all T. of Israel
    14 for him to gather the T. of Israel
110 11 leading of the ten T. from the north
133 34 of God upon the T. of Israel

TRIBULATION
29   8 prepared against day when T. and
54 10 be patient in T. until I come
58   2 he that is faithful in T.
     3 glory which shall follow after T.
     4 after much T. come the blessings— 103:12
78 14 notwithstanding the T. which shall

Sec.	Vs.		Sec.	Vs.	
		Tribulation			**TRUE**
109	5	we have done this work through great T.	1	30	the only T. and living church
112	13	after their temptations and much T.		37	for they are T. and faithful
122	5	if thou art called to pass through T.		39	spirit beareth record, record is T.
127	2	I feel to glory in T.	5	12	know of a surety these things are T.
		TRIBULATIONS		25	I know of a surety they are T.
103	13	after your T., and T. of your brethren	6	17	that which thou hast been writing is T.—18:2
128	21	through all the travels and T. of	10	62	the T. points of my doctrine
		TRIED	17	6	as your God liveth it is T.
			18	2	you know that they are T.
42	80	he shall be T. before two elders		3	and if you know that they are T.
68	22	no bishop or High Priest shall be T.	20	11	proving the Holy Scriptures are T.
101	4	therefore they must needs be T.		19	serve him the only living and T. God
107	76	except where a president is T.		30	that justification is just and T.
136	31	my people must be T. in all things		31	that sanctification is just and T.
		TRIFLE		35	and we know that these things are T.
6	12	T. not with sacred things	23	7	your duty to unite with the T. church
8	10	T. not with these things	66	11	keep these sayings for they are T.
32	5	give heed to these words and T. not	67	7	saying ye do not know they are T.
		TRIMMED		8	if ye do not bear record they are T.
33	17	having your lamps T. and burning	68	34	these sayings are T. and faithful
		TRIUMPH	69	1	except one go with him who will be T.
76	39	through T. and glory of the Lamb	71	11	my commandments are T. and faithful
121	8	thou shalt T. over all thy foes	76	53	upon all those who are just and T.
127	2	I shall T. over all my enemies	80	4	which ye believe and know to be T.
136	42	lest your faith fail and enemies T.	88	50	I am the true light—93:2
		TRODDEN	91	1	things contained therein that are T.
76	107	have T. the wine-press alone—133:50		2	contained therein that are not T.
88	106	hath overcome and T. the wine-press	102	16	evidence examined in its T. light
101	40	cast out and T. under feet of men—103:10	121	37	that they may be conferred is T.
104	5	shall be T. down by whom I will	124	13	let him be faithful and T.
		TROUBLE	128	4	certifying the record made is T.; above statement to be T.
3	8	been with you in every time of T.	132	24	the only wise and T. God, and Jesus
5	29	nor T. me any more concerning this—59:22; 130:15			**TRULY**
101	7	slow to answer them in day of their T.	20	5	after it was T. manifested to
	8	in day of their T. of necessity they		26	who T. testified of him in all
105	8	he will deliver them in time of T.		37	that they have T. repented of their; and T. manifest by their works
109	38	may not faint in the day of T.	45	23	and in this ye say T., for so it is
112	27	T. not yourselves concerning the	54	3	become T. humble before me and contrite
122	4	their influence shall cast thee into T.	97	1	many of whom are T. humble
		TROUBLED	123	13	they are T. manifest from heaven
45	34	unto my disciples, they were T.	128	9	and did it T. and faithfully
	35	be not T., for when all these things		14	the records that are T. made out
66	10	temptation with which thou hast been T.			**TRUMP**
98	18	let not your hearts be T.	24	12	with the voice of a T.—29:4; 30:9; 36:1; 42:6
		TROUBLETH	29	13	for a T. shall sound
101	84	yet because this widow T. me I		26	Michael shall sound his T.

Sec.	Vs.		Sec.	Vs.	
33	2	your voices as with the sound of a T.—75:4	23	2	to preach the T. from henceforth
34	6	voice as with the sound of a T.—124:106	27	16	having your loins girt about with T.
43	18	the T. of God shall sound	31	2	they will believe and know the T.
	25	and by the great sound of a T.	45	57	that are wise and have received the T.
45	45	an angel shall sound his T.	49	2	they desire to know the T. in part
88	92	sounding the T. of God, saying	50	9	that which is not in T. and righteousness
	94	another angel shall sound his T.; he shall sound the T. both long and loud		14	which was sent forth to teach the T.
				17	to preach word of T. by the Comforter, in the Spirit of T.; doth he preach it by Spirit of T. or
	98	sounding of the T. of the angel		19	he that receiveth word of T. doth he receive it by Spirit of T. or
	99	angel shall sound which is the second T.		21	he that receiveth word by the Spirit of T. receiveth it as preached by Spirit of T.
	100	another T., which is the third T.			
	102	another T., which is the fourth T.		25	I say it that you may know the T.
	103	another T., which is the fifth T.		40	grow in grace and knowledge of the T.
	104	this shall be the sound of his T., while they hear the T.			
	105	shall sound his T. which is the sixth	56	15	ye obey not the T. and have pleasure
	106	shall sound his T., which is the seventh	58	47	bear testimony of T. in all places
			66	12	who is full of grace and T.
	108	then shall the first angel sound his T.	67	4	I give unto you a testimony of the T.
	109	shall the second angel sound his T.	75	4	proclaiming the T. according to
	110	until the seventh angel shall sound his T.	76	5	who serve me in T. unto the end
				31	to deny the T. and defy my power
109	75	when the T. shall sound for the dead	78	10	to turn their hearts away from T.
		TRUMPET	79	2	Comforter which shall teach him the T.
49	23	when the angel shall sound his T.	84	45	for word of the Lord is T.; whatsoever is T. is light
		TRUMPETS			
77	12	to understand by sounding of the T.; the T. of the seven angels		101	and T. is established in her bowels
				102	he is full of mercy, grace and T.
		TRUST	85	7	his bowels shall be a fountain of T.
1	19	neither T. in the arm of flesh	88	6	that he might be the light of T.
11	12	put your T. in that spirit which		7	which T. shineth, this is the light
84	116	let him T. in me and he shall not		40	T. embraceth T., virtue loveth virtue
124	87	let my servant put his T. in me	66		my Spirit is T.; T. abideth
		TRUSTED	91	4	for the spirit manifesteth T.
10	6	the man in whom you have T.	93	9	Spirit of T. who came into the world
124	20	he may be T. because of his integrity		11	full of grace and T., even the spirit of T.
		TRUSTING		23	that which is Spirit, even spirit of T.
19	30	do it with all humility T. in me		24	T. is knowledge of things as they are
		TRUTH		26	spirit of T. is of God; I am the spirit of T.; received fulness of T., even all T.
1	39	the T. abideth forever			
6	11	bring many to knowledge of the T.		28	keepeth commandments receiveth T. until glorified in T.
	15	been enlightened by spirit of T.			
	22	know concerning the T. of these		29	the light of T. was not created
18	21	and speak the T. in soberness		30	all T. is independent in that sphere
19	26	Book of Mormon which contains the T.		36	or in other words light and T.
	37	preach, exhort, declare the T.		37	light and T. forsake that evil one

Sec.	Vs.		Sec.	Vs.	
	39	that wicked one taketh away T.	61	20	today mine anger is T. away
	40	bring up children in light and T.	63	13	many have T. away from my commandments
	42	have not taught your children T.		14	some of whom have T. away from you
97	1	to learn wisdom and to find T.	66	1	as you have T. from your iniquities
107	71	having knowledge of them by spirit of T.	98	47	then thine indignation shall be T. away
	84	according to T. and righteousness	117	5	properties be T. out for debts
109	23	glorious tidings, in T., unto ends of	122	3	thy people shall never be T. against thee
	56	that prejudices may give way before T.	133	24	shall be T. back into their own place
	67	may Israel come to knowledge of the T.	135	4	and T. down the leaf upon it
	77	thou sittest enthroned with glory, T.			**TURNETH**
121	46	unchanging sceptre of righteousness and T.	84	41	and altogether T. therefrom shall
123	12	who are only kept from the T.			**TURNING**
124	9	that they may come to light of T.	27	9	T. the hearts of the fathers to the
	97	which shall manifest unto him the T.	127	1	by T. out property or otherwise
127	6	that he may testify of a T.			**TWAIN**
128	2	make record of T. before the Lord	45	48	and it shall cleave in T.
	19	a voice of T. out of the earth	49	16	and the T. shall be one flesh
135	7	is a witness of the T. of the gospel			**TWELFTH**
		TRUTHS	88	55	and so on unto the T.—57
52	17	according to revelations and T.	135	4	near the close of the T. chapter of Ether
66	1	as you have received my T.			**TWELVE**
		TRY	18	27	yea, even T., the T. shall be my disciples; the T. are they who
98	12	I *will* T. you and prove you herewith		31	now I speak unto you, the T.
134	10	has authority to T. men on the right		37	that you shall search out the T.
		TURN	29	12	mine apostles, the T., who were with me
2	2	hearts of children shall T. to their	38	26	what man among you having T. sons
3	2	neither doth he T. to the right hand	77	9	seal of living God over the T. tribes
10	23	and it shall T. to their shame	101	44	and plant T. olive-trees
20	15	it shall T. to their condemnation	102	1	to consist of T. High Priests
45	29	they T. their hearts from me		12	duty of the T. councilors; who of the T. shall speak first; so in succession to number T.
51	17	shall T. unto them for their good			
67	14	let not your minds T. back			
78	10	Satan seeketh to T. their hearts		13	the T. councilors shall consider
82	9	may T. to you for your salvation		17	who draw even numbers, ten, T.
88	65	it shall T. to your condemnation		19	call on the T. councilors to sanction
90	9	then they shall T. unto the Jews		30	High Council composed of the T.
98	16	to T. the hearts of their children		34	the T. councilors then proceeded to
	22	I will T. away all wrath and	104	43	which is forty rods long and T. wide
	47	if the children shall T. to the Lord	107	23	the T. traveling councilors are called to be the T. apostles
109	53	and wilt T. away thy wrath			
110	15	to T. the hearts of the fathers to— 128:17		26	equal in authority to that of the T.
				33	the T. are a traveling presiding
121	33	or to T. it up stream, as to hinder		34	under direction of the T.
124	76	T. away their hearts from affliction		35	the T. being sent out holding the keys
		TURNED		37	equal to the councils of the T.
29	14	and the moon shall be T. into blood —34:9; 45:42			
	36	a third part of the hosts of heaven T. he			

Sec.	Vs.	
	39	it is the duty of the T. in branches
	58	it is the duty of the T. to ordain
	79	to call other High Priests, even T.
	82	who shall be assisted by T. counselors
	85	to preside over T. deacons, to sit in
	98	who belong not to the T. neither to
112	12	and pray for thy brethren of the T.
	14	I say unto all the T., arise and
	16	keys of my kingdom as pertaining to the T.
	21	by voice of your brethren, the T.
	30	for unto you, the T., and those
114	1	in company with others, even T.
118	1	let the T. be organized and men be
124	127	to be president over the T.
	128	which T. hold the keys to open
128	6	recorded in Revelation xx:T.
135	2	two of the T. were the only persons
136	3	under direction of the T. apostles

TWELVE THOUSAND

77	11	T. out of every tribe

TWENTIES

103	30	by tens, or by T. or by fifties
104	68	by T., or by tens or by fives

TWENTY

104	69	or if he obtain ten, or T. or fifty
	73	if it be five talents, or ten or T.
128	6	find recorded in Revelation T:12
135	3	in the short space of T. years

TWENTY-FIFTH

130	13	while I was praying, December T., 1832

TWENTY-FIVE

107	48	Enoch was T. years old when ordained

TWENTY-FOUR

77	5	to understand by the T. elders
102	1	a general council of T. High Priests
107	86	to preside over T. of the teachers

TWENTY-NINE

128	16	I Corinthians, xv:T, "Else what shall they

TWENTY-NINTH

76	15	we came to the T. verse of the fifth

TWENTY-SEVENTH

135	1	shot on the T. of June, 1844

TWENTY-SIXTH

118	5	in Far West on the T. of April next

Sec.	Vs.	

TWENTY-THREE

103	3	(John xiv:T) The appearing of the Father

TWINKLING

43	32	shall be changed in the T. of an eye—63:51; 101:31

TWO

6	28	in mouth of T. or three witnesses—128:3
	32	where T. or three are gathered
24	18	neither staves, neither T. coats
42	6	preaching my gospel T. by T.
	31	his counselors, T. of the elders
	44	elders of the church, T. or more
	80	shall be tried before T. elders of; every word established by T. witnesses; if more than T. witnesses it is better
	81	be condemned by mouth of T. witneses
52	10	let them go T. by T. and preach by
60	8	journey from St. Louis, T. by T.
61	35	let them journey together, or T. by T.
62	5	even altogether, or T. by T. as
77	15	to be understood by the T. witnesses; they are T. prophets to be raised
84	33	unto obtaining of these T. priesthoods
	78	to have purse or scrip, neither T. coats
94	16	these T. houses are not to be built
102	10	to be assisted by T. other presidents
	13	T. only of the councilors shall speak
	17	who draw even numbers, that is T., four
107	1	there are in the church T. priesthoods
	6	but there are T. divisions or
	21	several offices in these T. priesthoods
129	1	are T. kinds of beings in heaven
130	10	mentioned in Revelation T., verse 17
133	58	T. shall put their tens of thousands
135	2	T. of the Twelve were the only persons
	3	means of publishing it on T. continents
	4	T. days previous to assassination
136	3	with a president and T. counselors

TWO-EDGED

6	2	sharper than a T. sword—11:2; 12:2; 14:2; 33:1

Sec.	Vs.		Sec.	Vs.	
		TWO HUNDRED			**TYPICAL**
107	47	Jared was T. years old when ordained	76	70	whose glory is written of as being T.
					TYRANNY
135	1	by an armed mob of 150 to T. persons	123	7	the most damning hand of murder, T.

U

Sec.	Vs.		Sec.	Vs.	
		UNANIMOUS			**UNCLEAN**
102	3	by U. voice of the council	74	1	else were your children U.
107	27	must be by the U. voice of the same	88	124	cease to be U.; cease to find fault
		UNBECOMING	94	8	not suffer any U. thing to come
134	5	sedition and rebellion are U.		9	if there shall come into it any U.
		UNBELIEF	97	15	and do not suffer any U. thing to
3	18	who dwindled in U. because of their	109	20	no U. thing shall be permitted to come
20	15	who harden their hearts in U.			**UNCLEANNESS**
38	14	neither your hearts of U.	90	18	keep slothfulness and U. far from you
58	15	his sins, which are U. and blindness			
61	3	whilst inhabitants are perishing in U.			**UNDEFILED**
84	54	have been darkened because of U.	94	12	this house to be holy, U., according
	55	which vanity and U. hath brought			**UNDER**
	76	upbraided for their hearts of U.	10	65	gathereth her chickens U. her wings—29:2; 43:24
		UNBELIEVER	20	3	and ordained U. his hand
74	5	believer should not be united to an U.	21	11	that you are an elder U. his hand
			23	1	thou art U. no condemnation—3, 4, 5
		UNBELIEVERS	25	7	thou shalt be ordained U. his hand
85	9	shall be appointed them among U.	35	14	their enemies shall be U. their feet
101	90	their portion among hypocrites and U.	45	69	out of every nation U. heaven
			49	6	to put all enemies U. his feet
		UNBELIEVING		8	shall repent, for all are U. sin
1	8	to seal the U. and rebellious	52	17	he that trembleth U. my power
5	8	this U. and stiffnecked generation		19	ye shall know the spirits U. whole heavens
63	6	let the U. hold their lips			
	17	the fearful, the U., and all liars	58	22	and subdues all enemies U. his feet—76:61, 106
74	1	else were your children Z. wife and the U. wife	63	62	many there be U. this condemnation
	3	for the U. husband was desirous	64	42	unto her out of every nation U. heaven
		UNCEASINGLY	67	8	ye are U. condemnation if ye do not
121	45	let virtue garnish thy thoughts U.	68	19	ordained U. hands of—20, 21
		UNCHANGEABLE	78	16	U. counsel and direction of the Holy One
20	17	the same U. God, the framer of	80	1	that cometh U. sound of your voice
88	133	a determination that is fixed and U.	84	6	which he received U. the hand of —7, 8, 9, 10, 11, 12
104	2	with promises immutable and U.			
		UNCHANGING		49	groaneth U. darkness and U. bondage of sin
121	46	and thy sceptre an U. sceptre			

Sec.	Vs.		Sec.	Vs.	
	50	they are U. bondage of sin because		21	why is it that ye cannot U.
	51	whoso cometh not unto me is U. the		22	he that preacheth and that receiveth U.
	53	whole world groaneth U. sin and		31	a spirit manifested that ye cannot U.
	55	brought the whole world U. condemnation	57	9	whoso readeth let him U.—71:5; 91:4
	57	they shall remain U. this condemnation	68	25	that teach them not to U. the
88	79	of things in heaven and earth and U.	76	12	so as to see and U. things of God
100		who are found U. condemnation		48	the misery thereof they U. not
104		in earth and that are U. the earth	77	2	what are we to U. by—4, 5, 6, 7, 8, 9, 11, 12, 14; 113:9
90	5	and are brought U. condemnation		5	we are to U. that these elders
93	32	receiveth not light is U. condemnation		6	we are to U. that it contains the
	41	you have continued U. this condemnation		7	we are to U. that the first seal
				8	we are to U. they are four angels
101	40	and trodden U. the feet of men—103:10		9	we are to U. the angel ascending
				11	we are to U. those who are sealed are
103	7	until, are subdued U. my feet		12	we are to U. that as God made world
105	7	they are not all U. this condemnation		14	we are to U. that it was a mission
107	7	an elder comes U. the priesthood of	78	10	they become blinded and U. not the
	10	U. the direction of the presidency—33	82	8	that you may U. my will concerning
	34	U. the direction of the Twelve—136:3	88	46	unto what shall I liken, that ye may U.
	47	ordained U. the hand of—48, 50, 51, 52		78	that are expedient for you to U.
	98	are not U. responsibility to travel	93	19	that ye may U. how to worship
109	32	complete deliverance from U. this yoke	113	10	we are to U. that scattered remnants
	52	may be wasted away from U. heaven	121	12	that they may not U. his marvelous
110	2	U. his feet was a paved work of	132	1	to U. wherin I justified Abraham
121	15	their posterity shall be swept from U.			**UNDERSTANDING**
122	2	blessings constantly from U. thy hand	1	24	that they might come to U.
123	7	U. the most damning hand of murder; whole earth groans U. weight of its	20	68	expound all things to their U.
			29	50	he that hath no U. it remaineth
			32	4	I may unfold them to their U.
	9	have been murdered U. its iron hand	76	9	and their U. reach to heaven; the U. of the prudent shall come to naught
124	66	not permitted to receive U. fifty		89	which surpasses all U.—114
	72	in that house, nor U. fifty dollars	97	14	perfected in U. of their ministry
132	35	was Abraham U. condemnation	102	19	decision according to U. which he
	43	and he was U. a vow, he hath broken	110	1	eyes of our U. were opened
135	7	and all the martyrs U. the altar			**UNDERSTANDINGLY**
		UNDERNEATH	84	117	setting forth clearly and U. the
128	13	a place U. where the living are wont			**UNDERSTANDINGS**
		UNDERSTAND	76	12	our eyes were opened and our U. were
10	63	wrest the scriptures and do not U. them		19	the Lord touched the eyes of our U.
29	33	that you may naturally U.; given unto you that ye may U.	88	11	same light that quickeneth your U.
					UNDERSTOOD
50	10	let us reason together that ye may U.	9	7	behold, you have not U.
	12	reason with you that you may U.	10	59	many there were that U. me not
	15	received ye spirits ye could not U.	50	12	when a man reasoneth he is U. of man
			76	116	they are only to be seen and U.

Sec.	Vs.	
77	15	what is to be U. by the witnesses
78	17	ye have not yet U. how great blessings

UNDERTAKE

Sec.	Vs.	
121	37	but when we U. to cover our sins

UNDERTAKEN

| 7 | 6 | he has U. a greater work, therefore |

UNFAITHFUL

101	90	will cut off those wicked, U. and
104	74	that he is an U. steward
	77	if treasurer is found an U. steward

UNFEIGNED

| 121 | 41 | by gentleness, meekness and love U. |

UNFOLD

10	64	I *will* U. this great mystery
32	4	I may U. the same to their understanding
90	14	to U. the mysteries of the kingdom

UNFOLDED

| 6 | 7 | the mysteries of God shall be U.—11:7 |
| 88 | 95 | shall the curtain of heaven be U. as a scroll is U. |

UNFRUITFUL

| 107 | 31 | they shall not be U. in knowledge of |

UNGODLY

76	49	end of the vision of suffering of U.
84	117	of all their unrighteous and U. deeds
97	22	vengeance cometh speedily upon the U.
99	5	to convince all of their U. deeds
133	2	and upon all the U. among you
136	33	and to the condemnation of the U.

UNHOLY

74	4	wherein they became U.
	6	which saith that little children are U.
97	17	I will not come into U. temples

UNION

| 105 | 4 | not united according to the U. |
| 128 | 18 | a whole and complete and perfect U. |

UNITE

| 23 | 7 | your duty to U. with true church |

UNITED

29	6	ask in faith, being U. in prayer
74	5	a believer should not be U. to an
75	30	be U. in the ministry
84	1	as they U. their hearts and lifted
104	21	and U. consent or voice of the
105	4	and are not U. according to the

UNITED ORDER

92	1	I give unto you the U., organized
104	1	established to be a U. and an
	47	shall no longer be bound as a U.
	48	you shall be called the U. of, and your brethren, the U. of
	53	you are dissolved as an U. with

UNITED STATES

| 135 | 7 | and on the *magna charta* of the U. |

UNITING

| 20 | 82 | members U. themselves with the church |

UNJUST

76	17	in the resurrection of the U.
101	81	parable of the woman and U. judge.
	90	those wicked, and U. stewards
104	7	may not be condemned with the U.
134	12	such interference we believe to be U.

UNLAWFUL

121	3	suffer these wrongs and U. oppressions
134	11	from U. assaults and encroachments
	12	such interference we believe to be U.

UNLEARNED

| 35 | 13 | those who are U. and despised |

UNLESS

20	71	U. he has arrived to the years of
93	27	U. he keepeth his commandments
105	5	Zion cannot be built up U. it is
107	29	U. this is the case their decisions
	69	U. he is a literal descendant—70
124	119	U. he shall be a believer in the
127	2	U. I was ordained from before the
128	18	U. there is a welding link of some
134	4	U. their religious opinions prompt
136	35	their sorrow shall be great U. they

UNLOCK

| 112 | 17 | to U. the doors of the kingdom |

UNNOTICED

| 84 | 80 | shall not fall to ground U.—116 |

UNQUENCHABLE

43	33	wicked shall go away into U. fire
63	34	consume the wicked with U. fire
	54	and cast them into U. fire
101	66	they may be burned with U. fire

UNRIGHTEOUS

| 84 | 87 | reprove the world of their U. deeds —117 |
| 121 | 39 | begin to exercise U. dominion |

UNRIGHTEOUSNESS

| 56 | 15 | but have pleasure in U. |
| 66 | 10 | forsake all U. |

Unrighteouness   Until

Sec.	Vs.	
67	9	ye know there is no U. in them
76	41	and to cleanse it from all U.
82	22	make friends with the mammon of U.
88	18	must needs be sanctified from all U.
107	32	in case any decision is made in U.
121	37	in any degree of U.

UNSPEAKABLE

121	26	by the U. gift of the Holy Ghost

UNSPOTTED

59	1	keep thyself U. from the world

UNSTOP

84	69	and U. the ears of the deaf

UNTIL

Sec.	Vs.	
5	4	U. my purpose is fulfilled; no other gift U. it is finished
	19	U. the earth is empty and the
	30	even U. I command thee again
	34	stop and stand still U. I command
7	3	thou shalt tarry U. I come in my
	7	the keys of this ministry U. I come
9	1	continue U. you have finished this
10	26	U. he dragged their souls down to
	34	U. you have accomplished the work of
	37	hold your peace U. I shall see fit
	41	U. you come to that you have translated
11	15	nor called to preach U. you are
	16	wait a little longer U. you shall have
	19	be patient U. you shall accomplish
	22	U. you have obtained all which I
	26	treasure up in your heart U. the time
13	1	U. the sons of Levi do offer again
19	21	show not these things U. it is wisdom
26	1	U. after you shall go to the west
27	18	and be faithful U. I come—112:34
28	7	U. I shall appoint unto them another
	10	not leave U. after the conference
	15	U. the time that thou shalt return
29	42	they should not die U. I the Lord
	47	U. they begin to become accountable
30	4	U. I give unto you further
	10	U. I command you to go from hence
34	11	I am with you U. I come
35	18	U. the time of my coming
	27	kingdom is yours U. I come
37	1	U. ye shall go to the Ohio
	2	U. ye have preached my gospel in
	4	every man choose for himself U.]
38	5	U. the judgment of the great day
42	9	U. the time shall come it shall be
	15	U. fulness of my scriptures is

Sec.	Vs.	
	57	not teach them U. ye have received
43	3	U. he be taken if he abide in me
	18	stay and sleep U. I shall call again
	33	U. they come before me in judgment
44	6	U. all things shall be done
45	12	U. a day of righteousness shall
	21	U. every desolation that I have
	23	not pass away U. all be fulfilled
	25	remain U. the time of Gentiles be
	26	delayeth his coming U. end of the
	31	U. they shall see an overflowing
	60	U. New Testament is translated
	72	U. it is expedient in me; U. ye have accomplished the thing
46	4	not partake U. he makes reconciliation
47	1	U. he is called to further duties
49	7	nor shall they know U. he comes
50	24	brighter and brighter U. perfect day
51	4	U. he transgresses and is not
	16	U. I shall provide for them otherwise
52	2	from this time U. next conference
54	9	U. I prepare a place for you
	10	patient in tribulation U. I come
58	22	U. he reigns whose right it is to
	29	doeth not anything U. commanded
	60	U. he is sufficiently chastened
60	8	U. they return to the churches whence
61	8	U. chastened for all your sins
	30	U. they arrive at Cincinnati
	35	not separated U. they return to
63	39	that shall not go U. I command
	51	shall grow up U. they become old
	54	U. that hour there will be foolish
64	23	U. the coming of the Son of Man
	26	U. the residue of the church shall
65	2	U. it has filled the whole earth
67	13	continue in patience U. perfected
71	2	U. it shall be made known unto you
73	1	in regions round about U. conference—4
	4	U. it is finished
	5	pattern unto elders U. further
76	85	U. the last resurrection, U. the Lord
	106	U. the fulness of times when Christ
77	7	and so on U. the seventh
78	12	U. the day of redemption—82:21; 104:9
83	2	U. their husbands are taken
	4	for their maintenance U. they are
84	5	U. an house shall be built
	27	among children of Israel U. John •
	57	under this condemnation U. they repent
	97	U. I have completed my work
	98	U. all shall know me who remain

Sec.	Vs.		Sec.	Vs.	
86	7	U. the harvest is fully ripe			**UNVEIL**
	10	U. restoration of all things	88	68	for he *will* U. his face unto you
87	6	U. the consumption decreed hath made	109	74	thou shalt U. the heavens
			124	8	when I shall U. the face of my
	8	be not moved U. day of the Lord			**UNVEILED**
88	60	U. his hour was finished, according	88	95	the face of the Lord shall be U.
	85	U. the mouth of the Lord shall call			**UNWISE**
	86	let your hands be clean U. the Lord	104	74	is an unfaithful and U. steward
	101	live not again U. the thousand years, neither U. the end		77	in case he is found an U. steward
	102	to remain U. that great and last day			**UNWORTHY**
	110	and so on U. the seventh angel	88	134	he that is found U. of this salutation
	126	that ye may not faint U. I come			
90	20	let it not be sold U. the mouth—21			**UP**
	36	and chasten her U. she overcomes	See *Arise, Ascend, Ascended, Bear, Bind, Bound, Bring, Broken, Brought, Build, Buildeth, Building, Built, Burn, Carried, Carry, Cast, Caught, Come, Cometh, Coming, Deliver, Delivered, Deliveredst, Devour, Dry, Fill, Gather, Gathering, Getting, Gird, Go, Goeth, Gone, Grow, Growing, Hid, Laid, Lay, Layeth, Lift, Lifted, Lifting, Made, Make, Mount, Offer, Offered, Offering, Open, Pluck, Raise, Raised, Rise, Rising, Rose, Seal, Sealed, Send, Sendeth, Sent, Set, Setteth, Settle, Shut, Springing, Stand, Stir, Stirred, Stirreth, Stood, Strengthened.*		
93	13	U. he receiveth a fulness			
	28	U. he is glorified in truth and			
94	16	not to be built U. I give unto you			
97	4	U. I shall give other commandments			
	23	it shall not be stayed U. the Lord			
98	37	U. they had avenged themselves			
	40	forgive him U. seventy times seven			
	44	not blotted out U. he repent and			
99	6	go U. your children are provided for			
	8	proclaiming gospel U. thou be taken			
101	21	U. day cometh when there is found			**UPBRAID**
	30	infant shall not die U. he is old	42	68	give him liberally and U. him not
103	7	U. kingdoms of the world are subdued			**UPBRAIDED**
	30	U. they have obtained companies; U. obtained to number of	84	76	to be U. for their evil hearts
					UPHELD
	34	U. you have obtained a hundred	107	22	and U. by the confidence, faith and
104	1	for the salvation of men U. I come	123	7	U. by influence of that spirit
	74	U. he be found a transgressor	134	3	should be sought for and U. by the
	80	U. I shall send means unto you			**UPHOLD**
	84	U. you shall loan enough to deliver	10	5	servants of Satan that U. his work
105	6	chastened U. they learn obedience	43	12	U. him before me by the prayer of
	11	U. mine elders are endowed with power	93	51	with one consent, I *will* U. him
			98	10	wise men ye should observe to U.
	23	U. it is wisdom in me that they be	134	5	and U. the respective governments
	26	U. the army of Israel becomes great			**UPLIFTED**
	27	U. my servant shall have time to	88	120	with U. hands to the Most High—109:9, 19
107	74	U. the borders of Zion are enlarged			
	96	U. seven times seventy if the labor		132	arise, and with U. hands to heaven
108	4	wait patiently U. solemn assembly		135	salute the president with U. hands
109	40	U. this is accomplished, let not			**UPRIGHT**
115	12	labor diligently U. it shall be finished; U. there shall not anything	61	16	none but he that is U. in heart
					UPRIGHTLY
121	26	not revealed since the world was U. now	5	21	repent and walk more U. before me
130	15	if thou livest U. thou art 85	18	31	you must walk U. before me and sin not
132	38	from beginning of creation U. this			
135	5	U. we shall meet before the judgment seat	46	7	in holiness of heart, walking U.
		UNTOWARD			
36	6	save yourselves from this U. generation—109:41			

| Uprightly | 464 | Valiantly |

Sec. Vs.
68   28 children to pray and walk U. before
90   24 if ye walk U. and remember the
100 15 for good to them that walk U.
109   1 servants who walk U. before thee

URGED
123   7 U. on and upheld by the influence

URIAH
132 39 save in the case of U. and his wife

URIM AND THUMMIM
10   1 translate by the means of the U.
17   1 the breastplate, sword of Laban., the U.
130   8 where God resides is a great U.
      9 this earth will be a U. to the
    10 the white stone will become a U. to

USE
49 19 ordained for the U. of man for food
59 18 made for the benefit and U. of man
61 17 for the U. of my saints that they
63 62 who U. the name of the Lord and U. it in vain
84 103 send it to them or make U. of it
89 10 God hath ordained for the U. of man—12
    14 all grain is ordained for U. of man
    15 these hath God made for the U. of man
104 63 that ye go and make U. of stewardship
134   8 U. their ability in bringing offenders
136 10 let every man U. all his influence

USED
59 20 to be U. with judgment, not to excess
77   2 U. by the Revelator John in describing
89   8 to be U. with judgment and skill
    11 to be U. with prudence and thanksgiving
    12 they are to be U. sparingly
    13 not to be U. only in times of winter

Sec. Vs.
104 64 it shall not be U. or taken out of
    71 there shall not any part of it be U.

USEFUL
89 17 and barley for all U. animals

USHER
128 18 dispensation is now beginning to U. in

USHERING
128 18 in U. in the dispensation of

UTENSILS
136   7 take teams, seeds and farming U.

UTMOST
123 17 may we stand still with U. assurance

UTTER
29 19 that they shall not U. against me
43 18 the Lord shall U. his voice out of heaven—43:23
    21 when the thunders shall U. their voices
    22 lightnings shall U. forth their voices
45 49 the Lord shall U. his voice and all
63   5 I U. my voice and it shall be obeyed
76 115 and are not lawful for man to U.
84 114 of the desolation and U. abolishment
85   7 whose mouth shall U. words, eternal
133 21 he shall U. his voice out of Zion

UTTERANCE
14   8 the Holy Ghost which giveth U.
88 137 as the spirit shall give U.
93 51 as I shall give him U. and by your prayer

UTTERLY
2   3 the earth would be U. wasted at
5 19 consumed away and U. destroyed
101   9 I will not U. cast them away

UTTERMOST
58 64 unto the U. parts of the earth
121 13 may come upon themselves to the U.

V

Sec. Vs.
VACANCY
102   8 whenever any V. shall occur by death

VAIN
63 62 use the name of the Lord in V.
104 55 or else your faith is V.

Sec. Vs.
121 37 to cover our sins, our V. ambition
136 21 to take the name of the Lord in V.

VALIANT
76 79 who are not V. in testimony of Jesus

VALIANTLY
121 29 who have endured V. for gospel of

Sec.	Vs.	
		VALID
132	18	then it is not V., neither of force
		VALIDITY
107	27	same power or V. one with the other
		VALLEY
107	53	into the V. of Adam-ondi-Ahman
		VALLEYS
49	23	and for the V. to be exalted—109:74
128	23	shout for joy and all ye V. cry aloud
133	22	and the V. shall not be found
		VALUE
124	70	receive the real V. of moneys
		VANITIES
20	5	entangled again in V. of the world
		VANITY
84	55	which V. and unbelief have brought
106	7	notwithstanding the V. of his heart
		VAPORS
45	41	they shall behold blood and V. of smoke
		VARIANCE
101	50	while they were at V. one with another
		VARY
3	2	neither doth he V. from that which
		VEIL
38	8	V. of darkness shall soon be rent
67	10	the V. shall be rent and you shall
101	23	when the V. of covering of my temple
110	1	the V. was taken from our minds
		VENGEANCE
3	4	incur the V. of a just God upon him
29	17	I will take V. upon the wicked
76	105	who suffer the V. of eternal fire
85	3	against the day of V. and burning
97	22	V. cometh speedily upon the ungodly
	26	with sword, with V., with devouring fire
98	28	if that enemy shall escape my V.
	48	V. shall no more come upon them
112	24	V. cometh speedily upon inhabitants
133	51	this was the day of V. which was
		VERSE
76	15	we came to the 29th V. of the fifth
77	1	by John, 4th chapter, 6th V.
	2	four beasts spoken of in same V.
	8	spoken of in 7th chapter and 1st V.

Sec.	Vs.	
	9	Revelation, 7th chapter, 2nd V.
113	3	what is the rod spoken of in 1st V.
	5	root of Jesse spoken of in 10th V.
	7	in Isaiah, 52nd chapter, 1st V.
	9	from bands of her neck, 2nd V.
130	3	in that V. is a personal appearance
		VERSES
85	12	in 2nd chapter, 61st and 62nd V. of
113	1	spoken of in the 4th and 5th V. of
	10	see the 6th, 7th and 8th V.
128	17	Malachi says, last chapter, V. 5th and 6th
		VERIFIED
5	20	my word shall be V. at this time as it hath hitherto been V.
		VESSELS
38	42	be ye clean that bear the V. of—133:5
76	33	for they are V. of wrath doomed
		VEX
87	5	shall V. Gentiles with sore vexation
97	23	the report thereof shall V. all people
101	89	and his fury V. the nation
		VEXATION
87	5	vex the Gentiles with a sore V.
		VICTORY
52	11	I will send forth judgment unto V.
103	36	all V. and glory is brought to pass
104	82	behold I will give you the V.
128	22	and on, on to V.
		VIEW
5	13	and V. these things as they are
	24	I grant to him a V. of the things
17	1	you shall have a V. of the plates
	2	by your faith that you shall obtain a V.
128	8	or, taking different V. of translation
		VIEWS
5	28	he shall have no such V., I will grant him no V.
10	45	do throw greater V. upon my gospel
128	2	I have had a few additional V.
		VILLAGE
75	18	going from V. to V., city to city—99:1
84	93	whatsoever V. or city ye enter
	94	wo unto that V. or city that rejecteth—95
		VILLAGES
84	117	unto the great and notable cities and V.

Sec.	Vs.		Sec.	Vs.	
		VINE			**VIRTUE**
27	5	I will drink of the fruit of the V.	4	6	remember faith, V., knowledge
89	6	of the grape of the V. of your own	25	2	walk in the paths of V.
	16	as also the fruit of the V.	38	4	by V. of the blood I have spilt
		VINEYARD		24	practice V. and holiness before me —46:33
21	9	will bless those who labor in my V.	68	21	by V. of the decree concerning their
24	19	thou art called to prune my V.	88	40	V. loveth V.; light cleaveth unto
33	3	I shall call laborers in my V.	107	30	and in faith, V. and knowledge
	4	and my V. has become corrupted	121	41	be maintained by V. of priesthood
39	13	thou art called to labor in my V.		45	let V. garnish thy thoughts
	17	call faithful laborers into my V.	132	7	are of no efficacy, V. or force after
43	28	labor ye in my V. for last time			**VIRTUOUS**
50	38	and let them labor in the V.	122	2	the noble and V. shall seek counsel
53	6	according to your labor in my V.	132	52	and who are V. and pure before me
71	4	wherefore, labor ye in my V.			**VISION**
72	2	in this part of the Lord's V.	76	14	with whom we conversed in heavenly V.
	5	in this part of my V.—9, 19, 16, 17, 19		28	that we should write the V.
75	2	proclaim my Gospel and prune my V.		30	we saw a V. of the sufferings of
88	85	continue in the V. until the mouth		47	I show it by V. unto many but
95	4	to prune my V. for the last time		49	write the V. for this is the end of the V.
101	44	go ye unto my V. and plant		80	end of V. we saw of the terrestrial
	45	take unto themselves fruit of my V.		89	in heavenly V. the glory of telestial
	52	Lord of the V. called on his		113	the end of the V. which we saw
	53	after ye had planted the V., and watched for my V.	107	93	and it is according to the V.
	54	and saved my V. from the hands of	110	11	after this V. closed the heavens
	55	the Lord of the V. said unto one		13	after this V. had closed, another great and glorious V.
	56	go unto the land of my V., and redeem my V.			**VISIT**
103	21	to whom the Lord of the V. spake	5	16	them *will* I V. with the manifestation
104	20	while he is laboring in my V.	20	47	and V. the house of each member—51
107	96	if the labor in the V. requires	44	6	ye must V. the poor and needy
135	6	to purify the V. of corruption	63	46	now speedily V. the churches
		VINEYARDS	88	53	in the second hour I *will* V. you
59	17	for orchards, for gardens, for V.		54	unto the third, saying, I *will* V. you
101	101	they shall plant V. and shall eat		57	that he might V. the second and the
		VIOLENCE	97	26	I *will* V. her according to her works
24	16	shall lay their hands on you by V.	116	1	where Adam shall come to V. his
		VIPERS	124	8	that I may V. them in the day of
121	23	a generation of V. shall not escape		9	I *will* V. and soften their hearts
		VIRGIN		50	I *will* V. upon heads of those who
132	61	if any man espouse a V. and desire			**VISITATION**
		VIRGINS	56	1	in the day of V. and wrath
45	56	which I spake concerning the ten V.		16	your lamentation in the day of V.
63	54	until that hour there will be foolish V.	124	8	that I may visit them in day of V.
132	61	and they are V. and have vowed to no		10	the day of my V. cometh speedily
	62	and if he have ten V. given unto him			**VISITED**
	63	but if one or either of the ten V.	27	7	which Elias V. and gave promise
			76	73	kept in prison who the Son V.
			132	48	shall be V. with blessings not cursings

Sec.	Vs.	
		VIVID
85	8	smitten by the V. flash of lightning
87	6	and the fierce and V. lightning also
		VOCALLY
19	28	thou shalt pray V. as well as in thy
20	47	exhort them to pray V. and in secret—51
23	6	you must pray V. before the world
81	3	in prayer, always, V. and in thy heart
		VOICE
1.	1	saith the V. of him who dwells on high
	2	V. of the Lord unto all men
	4	V. of warning shall be unto all people
	11	V. of the Lord is unto ends of earth
	14	they who will not hear the V. of, neither the V. of his servants
	38	whether by mine own V., or V. of my servants
18	35	it is my V. which speaketh them
	36	you have heard my V. and know my words
19	37	declare the truth with a loud V.
20	35	by V. of God or ministering of angels
24	12	as with the V. of a trump—29:4; 30:9; 36:1; 42:6
25	1	hearken unto the V. of the Lord—33:1
	16	this is my V. unto all
27	1	listen to the V. of Jesus Christ—29:1
28	10	preside over conference by V. of it
29	2	as many as will hearken to my V.
	7	for mine elect hear my V. and harden not
33	6	believe on me and hearken to my V.
34	6	lift up your V. as with the sound —124:106
	10	lift up your V. and spare not
35	1	listen to the V. of the Lord—72:1
	21	they will hear my V. and shall see —50:45
36	3	you shall declare it with a loud V.
38	6	that will not hear my V. but harden
	22	hear my V. and follow me
	30	speak in your ears with a V. louder
	34	shall be appointed by V. of church
	41	let your preaching be warning V.
39	1	hearken and listen to V. of him—72:1
	10	if thou wilt hearken to my V.
	19	go forth crying with loud V. saying
41	9	he should be appointed by V. of
43	18	the Lord shall utter his V.—45:49
	21	for if I do lift up my V. and call
	23	the Lord shall utter his V. out of
	25	by mine own V., by V. of thunderings, by V. of lightnings, by V. of tempests, by V. of earthquakes, by V. of famines, by V. of judgment, and by V. of mercy, and V. of glory
45	2	hearken unto my V. lest death overtake
	6	hear my V. while it is called today
47	2	he can also lift up his V. in meetings
50	1	give ear to V. of the living God
	32	with a loud V. that it is not of God
51	4	not accounted worthy by V. of the
	12	be appointed by the V. of the church—58:49
52	1	chosen by the V. of his spirit
60	7	lift up their V. and declare my word
61	1	hearken unto V. of him who hath all
63	5	I utter my V. and it shall be obeyed
	37	lift a warning V. unto inhabitants
65	1	a V. as of one from on high, whose V. is unto man
	3	a V. crying, prepare ye the way
68	4	shall be the V. of the Lord, the
71	10	if any man lift his V. against you
72	7	made known by V. of the conference—73:2
75	1	I speak even by the V. of my spirit
76	16	concerning those who shall hear V. of Son
	23	and we heard the V. bearing record
	30	for thus came the V. of the Lord unto us
	40	which the V. out of heaven bore record
	49	we heard the V. saying, write the vision
	110	and heard the V. of the Lord saying
80	1	that cometh under sound of your V.
81	1	listen to the V. of him who speaketh
84	42	confirm upon you by mine own V.
	46	that hearkeneth to V. of the spirit —47
	52	whoso receiveth not my V. is not acquainted with my V.
	60	who now hear my words which are my V.
	98	shall lift up their V. and with the V.
	114	warn with a loud V. of the desolation
85	6	thus saith the still small V.
88	66	as the V. of one crying in wilderness; my V., because my V. is spirit

Sec.	Vs.		Sec.	Vs.	
	90	the V. of thunderings, V. of lightnings, the V. of tempests, and the V. of the waves		20	a V. of the Lord in the wilderness: the V. of Michael; the V. of Peter
	92	angels crying with a loud V., sounding		21	the V. of God in the chamber of; the V. of Michael; the V. of Gabriel and
	98	all this by the V. of the sounding		23	how glorious is the V. from heaven
93	1	who calleth on my name and obeyeth my V.	130	13	this a V. declared to me while praying
	15	there came a V. out of heaven saying		14	when I heard a V. repeat the following
97	1	I speak unto you with my V.. even V. of my spirit	132	53	I am the Lord and ye shall obey my V.
101	7	were slow to hearken to V. of the Lord		59	by mine own V., and by the V. of him
	75	were the churches willing to hearken to my V.	133	7	when the V. of the Lord is unto you
102	3	acknowledged presidents by V.; by the unanimous V. of the—107:27		9	and the V. of the Lord to all people
				16	listen and hear V. of the Lord
	8	sanctioned by V. of general council		21	he shall utter his V. out of Zion: and his V. shall be heard
	9	acknowledged by V. of the church		22	it shall be a V. as the V. of many waters, as V. of thunder
103	29	shall lift up his V. in congregations			
104	21	united consent or V. of the order		26	their prophets shall hear his V.
	36	by V. of my spirit and the V. of the order		38	saying with a loud V., fear God and
				50	his V. shall be heard, I have trodden
	53	will admit, and V. of the council direct		63	them that hearken not to V. of the
	64	only by the V. of the order——71		71	ye obeyed not my V. when I called you
	72	this shall be the V. and consent of			
	76	subject unto the V. of the order—77	134	3	and upheld by the V. of the people
105	36	shall be manifest by V. of my spirit	136	37	given by mine own V. out of heaven
	40	according to the V. of the spirit			
106	2	lift up his V. and warn the people			**VOICES**
108	1	you have obeyed my V. in coming up	33	2	called to lift up your V. as with
	2	and resist no more my V.	42	6	lifting up your V. as with voice of a
109	57	may know that we have heard thy V.		16	lift up your V. by the Comforter
110	3	his V. was as the sound of rushing waters: even the V. of Jehovah	43	20	lift up your V. and spare not
				21	when thunders shall utter their V. from
	8	speak unto them with my own V.		22	lightnings shall utter forth their V.
112	5	let thy warning V. go forth	45	32	men shall lift up V. and curse God
	9	thy V. shall be a rebuke to transgressor	60	7	declare my word with loud V. without
	21	shall send by V. of your brethren	61	31	in that place they shall lift up their V.
	22	and hearken to the V. of my spirit			
120	1	and by mine own V. unto them	75	4	lifting your V. as with the sound of
122	4	thy V. shall be more terrible in	84	1	united their hearts and lifted V. on high
124	45	will hearken unto my V. and V. of my	100	5	lift up your V. unto this people
	46	if they will not hearken to my V., nor V. of	109	79	that we may mingle our V. with those
	75	let him lift up his V. long and loud			**VOID**
	88	proclaim my gospel with a loud V.			
	100	let him not withhold his V.	54	4	so it has become V. and of none effect
	104	shall lift up his V. on the mountains			
	110	if he will hearken to my V. it	135	4	I have a conscience V. of offense
	115	if my servant will obey my V.			**VOLUME**
128	19	a V. of gladness; a V. of mercy from heaven; a V. of truth; a V. of gladness for living and dead	99	5	as it is written of me in the V. of

Sec.	Vs.		Sec.	Vs.	
		VOTE		44	is innocent and hath not broken her V.
20	63	by V. of the church to which they			
	65	without the V. of that church			**VOWED**
	66	branch of church that V. may be called	109	68	how he has covenanted and V. to thee
102	19	to sanction the same by their V.	132	61	and have V. to no other man
		VOTED			**VOWS**
102	5	who V. in the name and for church			
	6	V.: that High Council cannot have	59	11	thy V. shall be offered up on all days
	8	V.: that whenever any vacancy shall	108	3	in observing your V. which you have
		VOW			
132	43	if he was under a V. he hath broken his V.	132	7	all covenants, oaths, V. not made

W

Sec.	Vs.		Sec.	Vs.	
		WAGES			**WALK**
29	45	they receive their W. of whom they	3	2	God doth not W. in crooked paths
124	121	have a just recompense of W.; let their W. be as shall be agreed	5	21	repent and W. more uprightly before
	122	let every man bear proportion of W.	11	12	to W. humbly, to judge righteously
		WAGONS	18	31	you must W. uprightly before me
136	5	provide themselves with teams, W.	19	23	W. in the meekness of my spirit
		WAILING		32	this shall suffice for thy daily W.
19	5	weeping, W. and gnashing of teeth—85:9; 101:91; 124:52; 133:73	20	69	by a godly W. and conversation
			25	2	if thou W. in the paths of virtue
			35	9	shall cause the lame to W.
29	15	and there shall be weeping and W.	68	28	children to pray and to W. uprightly
		WAIT	88	133	to W. in all commandments of God
5	17	you must W. yet a little while for	89	20	and shall W. and not faint
	32	lying in W. to destroy thee	90	24	if ye W. uprightly and remember
	33	there are many that lie in W. to	95	12	therefore you shall W. in darkness
10	25	deceive and lie in W. to catch	100	15	for good, to them that W. uprightly
11	16	W. a little longer until you shall	109	1	thy servants who W. uprightly
105	9	mine elders should W. a little season—13	136	4	that we *will* W. in all the ordinances
108	4	W. patiently for solemn assembly			**WALKED**
123	12	whereby they lie in W. to deceive	107	49	he W. with him; he W. with God
		WAITETH			**WALKETH**
133	45	prepared for him that W. for thee	1	16	every man W. in his own way
		WAITING	59	16	upon the trees and W. upon the earth
38	12	angels are W. the great command to			
86	5	W. to be sent forth to reap down			**WALKING**
98	2	W. patiently on the Lord	20	69	W. in holiness before the Lord—21:4
		WAKEFIELD, JOSEPH	46	7	W. uprightly before me
50	37	let W., and Parley P. Pratt go forth	89	18	W. in obedience to the commandments
52	35	let W. and Humphrey take their journey	95	6	they are W. in darkness at noonday

Sec.	Vs.		Sec.	Vs.	
		WALL	89	4	I have W. and forewarn you
121	15	not one is left to stand by the W.			**WARNING**
		WALLS	1	4	voice of W. shall be unto all people
101	53	and set watchmen upon the W.	38	41	let your preaching be the W. voice
	57	break down the W. of mine enemies	63	37	lift a W. voice to inhabitants
122	4	into trouble and into bars and W.		58	for this is a day of W. and not of
124	61	and as watchmen upon her W.	88	71	and ponder the W. in their hearts
		WANT	112	5	day after day let thy W. voice
127	11	I now close for W. of more time			**WARREN**
128	6	and further, I W. you to remember	106	6	joy in heaven when my servant W.
		WANTED		7	blessed is my servant W. for I will
61	32	for their labors even now are W.			**WARRIORS**
		WANTS	101	55	which are my W., my young men
42	33	and receive according to his W.	105	16	even my W., my young men
51	3	according to their W. and needs			**WARS**
	8	according to the W. of this people	38	29	ye hear of W. in far countries; you
	13	more than needful for W. of this			say there will soon be great W.
	14	for his own W. and W. of his family	45	26	will be heard of W. and rumors of W.
70	7	for their necessities and their W.		63	ye hear of W. in foreign lands; ye
72	11	and to administer to their W.			shall hear of W. in your own lands
82	17	every man according to his W. inasmuch as his W. are just	63	33	have decreed W. upon face of the earth
84	112	administer to their W. by humbling	87	1	concerning W. that will shortly come
		WAR	88	79	the W. and perplexities of the nations
45	69	only people that shall not be at W.			**WARSAW**
76	29	for he maketh W. with the saints	124	88	proclaim to the inhabitants of W.
	30	those with whom he made W. and overcame			**WASH**
87	2	W. will be poured out upon all nations—3	39	10	be baptized and W. away thy sins
	4	slaves shall be marshaled for W.	60	15	and W. thy feet as a testimony
98	16	renounce W. and proclaim peace			**WASHED**
	34	if any nation should proclaim W.	76	52	be W. and cleansed from their sins
		WARD			**WASHING**
128	3	recorder appointed in each W. of	88	139	by the ordinance of W. the feet; was W. of feet instituted
		WARM		140	ordinance of W. of feet is to be
121	9	with W. hearts and friendly hands	89	7	but for the W. of your bodies
		WARN			**WASHINGS**
20	59	they are to W., expound, exhort and	124	37	how shall your W. be acceptable
63	57	those who desire to W. sinners to		39	your anointings and your W. and your
84	114	and W. people of those cities			**WASTE**
88	81	sent out to testify and W. the; W. his neighbor	101	18	to build up the W. places of Zion—103:11
98	28	see to it that ye W. him in my name		75	and establish her W. places, no more
106	2	lift up his voice and W. the people	105	15	to destroy and lay W. mine enemies
109	41	and thy servants W. them to save	123	13	that we should W. and wear out our
124	106	W. inhabitants of the earth to flee			**WASTED**
134	12	W. the righteous to save themselves	2	3	earth would be utterly W. at his coming
		WARNED			
88	71	whom they have W. in their traveling			
	81	becometh every man who hath been W. to			

Sec.	Vs.	
109	52	that they may be W. away, both root

WASTETH

Sec.	Vs.	
49	21	that W. flesh and hath no need

WATCH

Sec.	Vs.	
20	42	exhort, baptize and W. over church -
	53	teacher's duty to W. over the church
35	19	W. over him that his faith fail not
38	21	I will be your king and W. over you
46	27	and ordain to W. over the church
50	46	W. therefore that ye may be ready
52	39	let the elders W. over the churches
82	5	W., for the adversary spreadeth his
84	111	appointed to W. over the church
133	11	W. therefore, for ye know neither

WATCHED

Sec.	Vs.	
45	50	they that have W. for iniquity shall
101	53	and W. for my vineyard and not fallen

WATCHES

Sec.	Vs.	
45	44	he that W. not for me shall be cut off

WATCHFUL

Sec.	Vs.	
42	76	ye shall be W. with all inquiry
61	38	be W. and be sober, looking forth

WATCHMAN

Sec.	Vs.	
101	45	to be a W. upon the tower
	53	and set a W. upon the tower
	54	the W. upon the tower would have seen

WATCHMEN

Sec.	Vs.	
101	45	and set W. round about them
	46	set W. and began to build a tower
	53	ought ye not to have set W. on the
	57	and scatter their W.
105	16	of mine enemies and scatter their W.
	30	scattering their W. and avenging me
124	61	and as W. upon her walls

WATCH-TOWER

Sec.	Vs.	
101	12	all who are found upon the W.

WATER

Sec.	Vs.	
5	16	born of me even of W. and the spirit
20	73	shall go down into the W. with the
	74	immerse him or her in the W., and come out of the W.
33	11	yea, be baptized even by W.
35	5	thou didst baptize by W. unto
	6	now thou shalt baptize by W. and they
39	6	repentance and baptism by W. and then
	20	go forth baptizing with W.—42:7
	23	as ye shall baptize with W. ye shall

Sec.	Vs.	
52	10	baptizing by W. and the laying on
55	1	after thou hast been baptized by W.
61	22	whether they go by W. or by land
63	23	a well of living W. springing up
76	51	buried in the W. in his name
84	64	and is baptized by W. for the
	74	and are not baptized in W.
	92	cleanse your feet even with W., pure W.
127	2	deep W. is what I am wont to swim in
128	12	ordinance of baptism by W.; to be immersed in the W., and come forth out of the W.
133	29	shall come forth pools of living W.

WATERS

Sec.	Vs.	
10	66	and partake of the W. of life freely
61	3	to be moving swiftly upon the W.
	4	there are many dangers upon the W.
	5	I have decreed many destructions upon the W., especially these W.
	6	you shall not perish by the W.
	14	I in the beginning blessed the W. but in last days I cursed the W.
	15	no flesh shall be safe on the W.
	16	none able to go up to Zion on the W.
	18	forewarn your brethren concerning these W.
	23	let them come not again upon the W.; shall not come upon the W. to journey save
	27	given power to command the W.
	28	whether upon the land or the W.
88	94	her who sitteth upon many W.
110	3	as the sound of rushing of great W.
118	4	let them depart to go over the great W.
121	33	how long can rolling W. remain impure
133	22	as the voice of many W.
	39	made the sea and fountains of W.
	41	as the fire which causeth W. to boil

WATER'S

Sec.	Vs.	
52	10	laying on of hands by the W. side

WAVES

Sec.	Vs.	
88	90	and the voice of the W. of the sea
123	16	kept workways with the wind and W.

WAY

Sec.	Vs.	
1	16	every man walketh in his own W.
18	9	speak unto you by W. of commandment—70:1
20	37	by W. of commandment to the church—28:4
24	2	go thy W. and sin no more

Way 472 Weapon

Sec.	Vs.	
28	5	not write by W. of commandment—8
31	11	go your W. whithersoever I will
33	10	prepare ye the W. of the Lord—65:1, 3; 133:17
34	6	preparing W. of the Lord for his
35	4	sent to prepare the W. before me—45:9
39	20	preparing the W. before my face—124:139
44	1	from south by letter or some other W.
50	17	by spirit of truth or some other W.—19
	18	and if by some other W. it is not—20
52	8	unto the same place by W. of Detroit
	9	preaching the word by the W.—22, 23, 25, 26, 27,
	10	preach by the W. in every congregation
55	2	by W. of baptism in the name of
58	47	let them preach by the W.
	59	except he bear record by the W.
	63	preaching the Gospel by the W.
60	11	return it by the W. of the agent
61	24	I have appointed a W. for journeying; this is the W.
	25	pitching their tents by the W.
	29	unto you is given the W. for the
63	22	known unto you, not by W. of commandment
71	4	prepare the W. for the commandments
77	12	preparing the W. before the time of
79	2	teach him the W. whither he shall go
82	6	for all have gone out of the W.
84	28	to make straight the W. of the Lord
105		and go your W. rejoicing
107		to prepare the W. and fill appointments
	108	is the W. that mine apostles
88	68	in his own time and in his own W.
95	1	with chastisement I prepare a W.
99	4	in secret places by the W. for a
101	63	to be guided in a right and proper W.
	74	in this W. they may establish Zion
104	16	but it must be done in mine own W.; this is the W. that I
105	26	in this W. you may find favor in
109	56	that prejudices may give W. before
122	7	all elements combine to hedge up the W.
	9	therefore, hold on thy W. and the
129	6	that is the only W. he can appear
132	22	strait is the gate and narrow the W.
	25	broad is the gate and wide the W.

Sec.	Vs.	
	50	and I make a W. for your escape.
136	17	go thy W. and do as I have told you

WAYS

6	11	convince them of error of their W.
35		go your W. and sin no more—82:7
56	14	because ye seek to counsel in your own W.
61	27	given by the spirit to know all his W.
75	29	except he repents and mends his W.
76	2	great is his wisdom, marvelous his W.
98	20	they do not forsake their wicked W.
133	44	who remembereth thee in thy W.

WAYSIDE

24	15	cleansing your feet by the W.

WAX

45	27	and the love of men shall W. cold
	58	and they shall multiply and W. strong
121	45	then shall thy confidence W. strong

WAXETH

1	16	an idol which W. old and shall

WEAK

1	19	the W. things of the world shall
	23	that gospel might be proclaimed by the W.
35	13	I have called upon the W. things
50	16	he that is W. among you, hereafter
81	5	succor the W., lift up the hands
84	106	let him take with him he that is W.
86	6	for verily your faith is W.
89	3	adapted to capacity of the W.
124	1	through the W. things of the earth
133	58	to prepare the W. for those things, when the W. should confound the wise
	59	and by the W. things of the earth

WEAKEST

89	3	to the capacity of the weak and W.

WEAKNESS

1	24	given unto my servants in their W.
24	11	whether in W. or in strength
35	17	and in W. have I blessed him
38	14	I will be merciful unto your W.
62	1	your advocate who knoweth W. of man
135	5	because thou hast seen thy W., thou

WEALTH

111	4	its W. pertaining to gold and silver

WEAPON

71	9	no W. formed against you shall prosper—109:25

Sec.	Vs.		Sec.	Vs.	
		WEAPONS		41	I am not W. pleased with him
109	66	that they may lay down their W.	60	2	but with some I am not W. pleased
		WEAR	63	11	with whom God is angry, not W. pleased
42	42	nor W. garments of the laborer		23	a W. of living water springing up
123	13	we should W. out our lives in	68	31	not W. pleased with inhabitants
		WEARY	70	17	and have done W. inasmuch as they
64	33	be not W. in well-doing	85	11	as W. as the lesser priesthood
84	80	shall not be W. in mind	90	35	I am not W. pleased with many things
88	124	to thy bed early, that ye may not be W.	98	19	not W. pleased with many at Kirtland
89	20	and shall run and not be W.	100	1	your families are W.
101	84	lest by continual coming she W. me	112	2	with which I was not W. pleased
124	23	that the W. traveler may find health	113	4	of Jesse as W. as of Ephraim
	60	a resting place for the W. traveler		6	of Jesse as W. as of Joseph
		WEARYING	117	3	if they tarry it shall not be W.
90	33	cease W. me concerning this matter	121	8	and if thou endure it W. God shall
		WEEKS		33	as W. might man stretch forth his puny
64	18	Sidney Gilbert, after a few W. should	123	2	personal injuries as W. as real property
88	44	in their days, in their W., in their	124	94	a revelator as W. as my servant
		WEEP	110		if he will hearken it shall be W.
42	45	thou shalt W. for the loss of them	118		it shall be W. with him forever
45	53	shall W. because of their iniquities	125	4	as W. as in the city of Nashville
128	23	and the solid rocks W. for joy	127	10	by mail, as W. as many other things
		WEEPING	128	3	who is W. qualified for taking minutes
19	5	W., wailing and gnashing of teeth—101:91; 133:73		11	as W. for the dead as for the living
21	8	his W. for Zion I have seen	132	7	as W. for time as for all eternity
29	15	W. and wailing among hosts of men			**WELL-BELOVED**
112	24	a day of desolation, of W. and of	126	1	dear and W. brother Brigham Young
		WEIGHT			**WELL-DOING**
63	66	more exceeding and eternal W. of glory—132:16	64	33	be not weary in W. for ye are
123	7	earth groans under W. of iniquity			**WELL-NIGH**
		WEIGHTY	61	31	a people W. ripened for destruction
117	8	that you should neglect more W. matters			**WELTON, MICAH B.**
		WELDING	75	36	and also W., and my servant Eden Smith
128	18	unless there is a W. link of some kind, a W. together			**WENT**
		WELL	88	56	lord of the field W. unto the first
1	30	I am W. pleased—38:10; 50:37; 51:3; 61:35; 84:3; 97:3; 124:1, 12	101	46	servants of nobleman W. and did
19	28	pray vocally as W. as in thy heart; as W. as in secret; in public as W. as in private		62	and his servant went and did all
20	11	as W. as in generations of old	135	4	when Joseph W. to Carthage to
	27	as W. as those who should come after			**WEPT**
23	6	pray vocally as W. as in secret	76	26	for the heavens W. over him
45	4	in whom thou wast W. pleased			**WEST**
58	8	of wine on the lees W. refined	26	1	you shall go to the W. to hold next
	9	yea a supper W. prepared	42	63	shall be sent forth to east and to W.
				64	that shall be converted to flee to W.
			43	22	lightnings streak forth from east to W.
			44	1	be called together from east and from W.

Sec.	Vs.		Sec.	Vs.	
75	26	obtain places whether to east or W.		35	W. temple is defiled God shall destroy
80	3	preach my gospel to the east and to the W.	94	10	and all things W. I shall command —12; 97:25, 26; 98:4
125	4	let all who come from the east and the W.	98	21	I will do W. I list, if they do not observe W. I have said .
136	1	camp of Israel in journeyings to W.		22	if ye observe to do W. I command
			100	7	declare W. things ye declare in my
		WESTERN		8	unto all things W. ye shall say
45	64	go ye forth into the W. countries	101	27	in that day W. any man shall ask
75	15	take their journey unto W. countries		60	do all things W. I have commanded
84	3	in the W. boundaries of the state		62	did all things W. Lord commanded
			105	22	and all things W. he shall appoint
		WESTWARD	107	56	predicted W. should befall his posterity
42	8	shall go forth in the regions W.	109	39	W. city thy servants shall enter—41
54	8	take journey into the regions W.	112	19	in W. place ye shall proclaim my name
57	3	and a spot for the temple is lying W.	117	5	W. remaineth let it remain in your
	4	and also every tract lying W.	124	55	that ye are faithful in all things W.
				93	W. he shall bind on earth; W. he shall loose on earth—127:7; 128:8, 10
		WHATEVER			
20	62	to do W. church business is necessary	128	8	W. you record on earth; W. you do not record on earth
42	74	W. persons among you having put away		9	W. those men did in authority
64	29	W. ye do according to will of the	132	13	W. they may be, that are not of me
130	18	W. principle of intelligence we		14	W. things remain are by me; W. things are not by me shall
132	26	commit any sin or transgression W.		19	W. my servant hath put upon them
				29	Abraham received all things W. he
		WHATSOEVER		46	W. you seal on earth; W. you bind on earth
6	18	in W. difficult circumstances he may		48	W. you give on earth, and to whom
	33	W. ye sow that shall ye also reap		65	W. I the Lord, his God, will give
8	1	W. things you shall ask in faith— 29:6			**WHEAT**
	9	W. you shall ask me to tell you	86	1	the parable of the W. and tares
10	51	of W. nation, kindred, tongue or		3	wherefore the tares choke the W.
11	14	shall know all things W. you desire		6	lest you destroy the W. also
12	8	W. shall be entrusted to his care		7	let the W. and the tares grow together; ye shall first gather out the W.; after the gathering of the W.
24	15	in W. place ye shall enter and they—75:19, 20			
25	9	W. I will according to their faith	89	17	W. for man, corn for the ox
27	18	as touching all things W. ye ask	101	65	according to parable of the W. and, that the W. may be secured
28	1	W. thou shalt teach them by the			
29	30	in all things W. I have created			**WHENCE**
43	13	W. thing he needeth to accomplish	60	1	return to the land from W. they came
46	31	W. you do in the spirit		5	unto the land from W. you came
	32	for W. blessing ye are blessed with		8	return to churches from W. they came
50	29	ask W. you will in the name of	113	10	to the Lord from W. they have fallen
57	8	obtain W. things the disciples need			
	12	W. he can obtain in righteousness			**WHENEVER**
	13	in W. place I shall appoint unto	47	2	in meetings, W. it shall be expedient
68	4	W. they shall speak when moved upon	102	8	W. any vacancy shall occur
70	16	in W. circumstances I shall place		12	W. a High Council of the church
72	23	in W. land they shall be established			
84	45	W. is truth is light, and W. is light is spirit			
	62	W. place ye cannot go into, send			
	93	in W. village or city ye enter do			
88	64	W. ye ask the Father in my name			
93	25	and W. is more or less than this— 98:7, 10			

Sec.	Vs.		Sec.	Vs.	
	13	W. this Council convenes to act	22	2	W., although a man should be baptized
128	9	W. the Lord has given a dispensation		4	W., enter ye in at the gate as I have
		WHEREAS	23	3	W. thy duty is unto the church
107	98	W. other officers of the church	25	13	W., lift up thy heart and rejoice—27:15
		WHEREBY	27	3	W., a commandment I give, that you
5	34	W. thou mayest accomplish the thing		4	W., you shall partake of none except
9	12	sufficient strength, W. it is made up		5	W., marvel not, for the hour cometh
18	23	none other name given W. man can be	29	8	W. the decree hath gone forth
				18	W., I will send forth flies upon
78	13	W. you may accomplish the commandments		28	W. I will say unto them, Depart from
96	1	here is wisdom, W. ye may know		34	W., all things unto me are spiritual
123	12	W. they lie in wait to deceive		40	W., the devil tempted Adam and he
124	63	W. they may receive stock for the		41	W., I caused that he should be cast out
	95	the keys W. he may ask and receive		47	W.. they cannot sin. for power is not
	124	W. ye are sealed up unto the day of	30	3	W., you are left to inquire for
129	9	three grand keys W. you may know		8	W., give heed unto these things
130	9	W. all things pertaining to inferior	31	5	W., your family shall live
	10	W. things pertaining to a higher	33	7	W., thrust in your sickles and reap
132	19	no murder W. to shed innocent		17	W., be faithful, praying always
134	9	W. one religious society is fostered	34	3	W. you are my son
		WHEREFORE		10	W., lift up your voice and spare not
1	7	W., fear and tremble, O. ye people	35	13	W., I call upon the weak
	11	W. the voice of the Lord is unto		19	W., watch over him that his faith
	17	W., I, knowing the calamity	36	8	W., gird up your loins—38:9; 43:19
14	10	W., I must bring forth the fulness			
17	7	W., you have received same power	38	17	W., again I will stand upon it
18	2	W. you know that they are true		22	W., hear my voice and follow me
	5	W., if you shall build up my church		30	W., treasure up wisdom in your bosoms
	7	W., as thou hast been baptized		32	W., for this cause gave I unto you
	8	W., if he shall be diligent in keeping	39	17	W. lay to with your might and call
	11	W. he suffered the pain of all men		19	W., go forth crying with a loud
	14	W., you are called to cry repentance	40	3	W. he broke my covenant and it
	24	W., all men must take upon them	41	12	W., beware how you hold them
	25	W., if they know not the name by	43	28	W., labor ye in my vineyard—71:4
	30	W., you must perform it according to	45	5	W., Father, spare these my brethren
				10	W.. come ye unto it, and with him
	34	W., you shall testify they are of me		11	W., hearken ye together and let me
	36	W., you can testify that you have		15	W. hearken and I will reason with
	45	W., the blessings that I give unto		46	W., if ye have slept in peace
19	5	W., I revoke not the judgments which		61	W. ye may now translate it
				64	W. gather ye out from eastern lands
	7	W. it is more express than other		70	are terrible, W. we cannot stand
	8	W., I will explain this mystery	46	8	W., beware lest ye are deceived
	10	for endless is my name: W.		30	W. it is done even as he asketh
	13	W., I command you to repent and keep—20	47	4	W.. it shall be given him
			49	3	W., I send you my servant Sidney
	22	W., they must not know these things		8	W., I will that all men repent
20	21	W., the Almighty God gave his Only		9	W., I have sent unto you mine everlasting
21	4	W., thou shalt give heed to all his		11	W., I give unto you a commandment—59:5; 60:13; 70:6; 75:25; 78:11
	10	W. it behooveth me that he should be			
				16	W., it is lawful that he should have

Sec.	Vs.		Sec.	Vs.	
	20	W. the world lieth in sin		25	W., if ye believe me, ye will labor
	23	W., be not deceived, but continue		29	W., as ye are agents, and are on the
50	9	W., let every man beware lest he do		33	W., be not weary in well-doing
	13	W., I asketh you this question		36	W. they shall be plucked out
	22	W., he that preacheth and he that	65	6	W., may the kingdom of God go forth
	27	W., he is possessor of all things			
	31	W., if you behold a spirit manifested	67	13	W., continue in patience until perfected
	39	W., in this thing my servant is not			
	44	W., I am in your midst	68	6	W., be of good cheer and do not fear
51	3	W., let my servant and those he has			
	11	W., if another church would receive		15	W. they shall be High Priests
	17	W. let them act upon this land as		32	W., let my servant carry these sayings
52	3	W., let my servants take their journey			
				34	W.. transgress them not, neither
	15	W. he that prayeth whose spirit	69	2	W., I will that my servant should go
	19	W.. by this pattern ye shall know	70	2	W. hearken and hear for thus saith
54	7	W., go to now and flee the land		5	W., I have appointed unto them
56	4	W. I command and revoke as seemeth			
			71	7	W.. confound your enemies
	5	W., I revoke the commandment which		8	W., let them bring forth their
				11	W., keep my commandments
	7	W., let my servant remain with them	74	5	W., for this cause the apostle wrote
			75	30	W., let my servants be united in
57	2	W., this is the land of promise	76	29	W., he maketh war with the saints
	4	W., it is wisdom that the land		44	W.. he saves all except them
58	4	W. the day cometh that ye shall be crowned		48	W., the end, the width, the height
				58	W., as it is written, they are Gods
	22	W.. be subject to the powers that be		59	W., all things are theirs
	25	W., let them bring their families		61	W., let no man glory in man
	26	W., he receiveth no reward		78	W., they are bodies terrestrial
	46	W., assemble yourselves together		79	W.. they obtain not the crown
59	22	W. trouble me no more concerning	77	9	W., he crieth to the four angels
61	7	W.. it is expedient that my servant	78	20	W., do the things I have commanded
	9	W. let my servants take their former	79	4	W.. let your heart be glad
	15	W., the days will come that no flesh	80	3	W., go and preach my gospel
	21	W., let those concerning whom I have	81	5	W., be faithful and stand in the office
	28	W., let him do as the spirit of the	86	3	W., the tares choke the wheat
62	2	W. your mission is not yet full	87	8	W.. stand ye in holy places
63	6	W., let the wicked take heed and	88	3	W., I now send you another Comforter
	11	W., unto such he showeth no signs			
	12	W., I am not pleased with those		26	W., it shall be sanctified
	17	W., the fearful and unbelieving	95	2	W., ye must needs be chastened
	27	W., I will that you should purchase	98	10	W., honest men and wise men should
	29	W., the land of Zion shall not be			
	36	W., I have decreed all these things	101	36	W., fear not even unto death
	38	W., let my disciples in Kirtland	107	63	W., from deacon to teacher
	51	W., children shall grow up until they		65	W., it must needs be that one be
				68	W., the office of a bishop is not
	52	W.. for this cause preached the apostles		99	W., let every man learn his duty
			112	19	W., whithersoever they send you, go
	56	W. his writing is not acceptable	133	4	W., prepare ye O my people
	61	W., let all men beware how they take		19	W., prepare for coming of bridegroom
	63	W., let the church repent of their sins		65	W., this shall be the answer of
				72	W., they sealed up the testimony
	64	W., without this there remaineth condemnation	135	5	W. thy garments are clean

WHEREIN

Sec.	Vs.	
64	2	W. I will have compassion upon you
	9	W., ye ought to forgive one another
29	40	W. he became subject to will of devil

Sec.	Vs.	
	41	W. he became spiritually dead
58	28	W. they are agents unto themselves
74	4	W. they became unholy
123	13	things of darkness; W. we know them
124	30	W. ye are not able to build a house
	33	W. the ordinance of baptizing for
	39	W. ye receive conversations and
	70	W. they receive the real value of
128	8	W. it is granted that whatsoever you
132	1	W. I justified my servants Abraham
	26	no murder, W. they shed innocent blood—27
	31	W. he glorified himself
	45	W. I restore all things
	56	W. she has trespassed against me

WHEREON

124	42	and the place W. it shall be built
130	11	W. is a new name written

WHERESOEVER

108	6	preach my gospel W. I shall send you

WHEREUNTO

30	2	the ministry W. you have been called
	42	10 in office W. I have appointed him —54:2
88	80	magnify calling W. I have called you

WHEREVER

30	10	W. you can be heard until I command
124	139	W. the traveling High Council shall

WHEREWITH

5	22	W. I have commanded you—42:3
9	14	the work W. I have called you
10	7	things W. you have been entrusted
24	9	thou shalt have W. to magnify thine
27	17	W. ye shall be able to quench all
38	23	the office W. I have appointed you
43	13	the work W. I have commanded him
44	5	band may be broken W. enemy seeketh
72	11	inasmuch as they have W. to pay
	13	he who hath not W. to pay
78	13	the preparation W. I prepare you— 95:4
79	1	ordination W. he has been ordained
81	1	to the calling W. you are called
83	5	if their parents have not W. to give
88	86	in the liberty W. ye are made free
90	24	W. ye have covenanted one with another
98	3	all things W. you have been afflicted
	40	W. he has trespassed against thee
	44	in all things W. he has trespassed —47

Sec.	Vs.	
101	2	W. they have been afflicted
106	8	and assurance W. he may stand

WHEREWITHAL

84	81	or W. ye shall be clothed

WHILE

5	17	you must wait yet a little W.
6	3	and reap W. the day lasts—11:3; 12:3; 14:3
17	1	given to Lehi W. in the wilderness
25	1	W. I speak unto you Emma Smith
	6	W. there is no one to be a scribe
38	20	forever, W. the earth shall stand
45	6	hear my voice W. it is called today
61	23	W. journeying to their homes
64	5	taken from my servant W. he liveth
	25	ye will labor W. it is called today
70	15	for their benefit W. they remain
76	15	for W. we were doing the work of
	19	and W. we meditated upon these
	28	and W. we were yet in the spirit
	80	to write W. we were yet in the spirit—113
	115	commanded we should not write W. we
	118	manifestation of Spirit W. in the flesh
84	24	into his rest W. in the wilderness
	28	baptized W. yet in his childhood
	119	yet a little W. and ye shall see it
85	6	W. it maketh manifest, saying
	7	W. his bowels shall be fountain of
	8	W. that man who was called of God
86	4	even now W. the Lord is beginning
	6	pluck not up the tares W. the blade
88	62	ye shall call upon me W. I am near
104		W. they hear the sound of the trump
90	3	never be taken from you W. thou art
97	21	W. all the wicked shall mourn
101	47	W. they were yet laying foundation
	50	W. they were at variance one with
	54	seen the enemy W. yet afar off
	66	W. the tares shall be bound in
	84	he would not for a W. but afterward
104	20	W. he is laboring in my vineyard
105	25	W. you are saying unto the people
122	2	W. the pure in heart and the wise
124	23	W. he shall contemplate the word
130	13	W. I was praying earnestly on the
134	5	W. protected in their inherent rights

WHILST

61	3	W. inhabitants are perishing in

Sec.	Vs.	
		WHIRLWIND
63	6	shall come upon them as a W.
97	22	upon the ungodly as W.
112	24	day of lamentation and as a W.

WHISPERETH

Sec.	Vs.	
85	6	which W. through and pierceth all

WHIT

| 33 | 4 | vineyard has become corrupted every W. |

WHITE

4	4	the field is W. already to harvest— 6:3; 11:3; 12:3; 14:3; 33:3. 7
20	6	whose garments were pure and W.
31	4	the field which is W. already to be
110	3	hair of his head was W. like the pure
130	10	then the W. stone mentioned in
	11	a W. stone is given to each of these

WHITENESS

| 20 | 6 | pure and white above all other W. |

WHITHER

31	11	what you shall do and W. you shall go
75	27	by the Comforter W. they shall go
79	2	and the way W. he shall go

WHITHERSOEVER

25	6	that I may send my servant W. I will
31	11	go your way W. I will
37	2	strengthened church W. it is found
38	33	I will lead them W. I will
70	16	W. I the Lord shall send them
103	40	journey with my servant W. my
112	19	W. they shall send you, go ye
	21	unto any nation W. ye shall send

WHITLOCK, HARVEY

| 52 | 25 | let Whitmer and W. take their journey |

WHITMER

| 128 | 21 | voice of God in chamber of Father W. |

WHITMER, DAVID

18	9	I speak unto you and also W., by way of
	37	unto W., you shall search out the Twelve
52	25	let W., and Whitlock take their journey

WHITMER, JOHN

69	2	W. should go with my servant Oliver
	7	let W. travel many times from place to
70	1	also unto W., by way of commandment

WHITMER, PETER, JR.

| 32 | 2 | go with Cowdery and W., into wilderness |

WHITNEY, NEWEL K.

63	42	let W. retain his store for a little
64	26	not meet that W. and, should sell
72	8	W. is the man who shall be appointed
78	9	let my servant W., and, sit in council
82	11	expedient that W. and, be bound
84	112	the bishop, W., should travel round
93	50	W. hath need to be chastened and set
96	2	let W. take charge of the place
104	39	let W. have appointed unto him the house
	40	appointed unto W. for his stewardship
	41	unto W. even this whole Ozondah
117	1	let W. and, settle up their business
	11	let W. be ashamed of the Nicholaitane

WHOEVER

| 124 | 93 | that W. he blesses shall be blessed. W. he curses shall |

WHOLE

1	30	upon the face of the W. earth
2	3	the W. earth would be utterly wasted
20	82	list of the names of the W. church
27	9	that the W. earth may not be smitten
	15	and take upon you my W. armor
29	12	to judge the W. house of Israel
30	11	your W. labor shall be in Zion
45	26	the W. earth shall be in commotion
52	19	spirits in all cases under W. heavens
55	1	yea, even the Lord of the W. earth
58	52	even to purchase this W. region
61	3	not needful for this W. company to
65	2	until it has filled the W. earth
82	18	the common property of W. church
84	48	but for the sake of the W. world
	49	and the W. world lieth in sin
	53	the W. world groaneth under sin
	55	brought W. church under condemnation
88	67	W. bodies shall be filled with light
98	17	lest I smite W. earth with a curse
104	41	even this W. Ozondah, him and
106	3	devote his W. time in this high

Sec.	Vs.	
107	91	is to preside over the W. church
109	72	a great mountain and fill the W. earth
110	15	lest W. earth be smitten with a curse
115	6	without mixture upon W. earth
123	5	and present the W. concatenation of
	6	that W. nation be left without excuse
	7	W. earth groans under weight of its
124	126	receive oracles for the W. church
128	3	in taking the W. proceedings and the history of W. transaction
	11	the grand secret of W. matter, of the W. subject
	18	that a W., complete and perfect union

WHOLESOME

89	10	all W. herbs hath God ordained for

WHOLLY

94	7	it shall be W. dedicated to the Lord—12

WHOM

Sec.	Vs.	
1	4	mine apostle, W. I have chosen
	30	those to W. these commandments
3	18	W. the Lord has suffered to destroy
5	3	except to those persons to W. I
	11	W. I shall call and ordain, unto W. I will show
10	6	even the man in W. you have trusted
19	27	of W. the Lamanites are a remnant
20	4	to W. be all glory, both now and—16
	19	the only being W. they should worship
24	19	also all those W. thou hast ordained
25	3	thou art an elect lady W. I have called
27	5	Moroni W. I have sent unto you, to W. I have committed
	6	Elias to W. I have committed the
	9	Elijah to W. I have committed the
	10	your fathers by W. the promises remain
	12	W. I have sent unto you, by W. I have
	13	unto W. I have committed the keys—81:2
	14	all those W. my Father hath given me
29	34	neither Adam your father, W. I created
	45	receive their wages of W. they list
30	2	W. I have not commanded
38	10	none else with W. I am well pleased
41	1	ye W. I delight to bless

Sec.	Vs.	
	2	O ye elders of my church W. I have
	11	in W. there is no guile
42	92	to him or her W. he or she has
43	2	through him W. I have appointed —7
	15	ye elders of my church W. I have
45	1	to W. the kingdom has been given; by W. all things were made
	4	in W. thou wast well pleased; the blood of him W. thou gavest
	11	the wisdom of him W. ye say is the God
50	37	in W. I am well pleased—51:3; 61:35; 84:3
51	3	and those W. he has chosen
52	1	unto the elders W. I have called
	21	unto all the elders W. I have chosen
54	5	wo to him by W. this offence cometh
	7	appoint W. you will to be your leader
56	12	that those of W. he shall receive
57	7	those W. he has appointed to assist
	9	unto the people by W. he will
	14	let those of W. I have spoken be—61:21
58	24	W. he has appointed for counselors; W. I appointed to keep my storehouse
	61	some of W. are exceedingly blessed
61	27	unto W. it is given power to command
63	3	to take even them W. he will; them W. he will preserve
	11	with W. God is angry he is not well
	14	some of W. have turned away from
	39	excepting those W. I shall reserve
	40	them W. I have appointed to receive
64	10	I will forgive W. I will forgive
72	1	to W. kingdom and power has been given
76	14	of W. we bear record; and W. we saw and with W. we conversed
	25	Begotten Son W. the Father loved
	30	with W. he made war and overcame
	32	of W. I say it had been better for
	34	of W. I have said there is no
	37	only ones on W. the second death
	42	W. the Father had put into his power
	63	these are they W. he shall bring
	73	in prison, W. the Son visited
	90	except him to W. God has revealed it
	117	to W. he grants this privilege
77	5	these elders W. John saw were
	8	to W. is given power of the four parts

Sec.	Vs.		Sec.	Vs.	
	9	to W. is given the seal of the living		51	the offerings of those W. I
	11	to W. is given power over the nations		61	W. I have set to be as plants
				111	W. I have appointed to build a house
82	3	unto W. much is given much is required	127	1	all those with W. I have business
84	27	until John, W. God raised up, being	128	4	to W. these other records can be
	32	many W. I have called and sent forth		11	for him to W. these keys are given
			132	7	W. I have appointed on the earth, on W. this power is conferred
	63	ye are they W. my Father hath given me		18	sealed through him W. I have anointed; by W. they cannot pass
	76	those to W. kingdom has been given		19	unto W. I have appointed this power
85	1	W. he has appointed to keep history		24	and Jesus Christ W. he hath sent
86	8	with W. priesthood hath continued		51	your wife, W. I have given unto you
88	71	W. they have warned in traveling	135	5	also unto my brethren W. I love
95	1	you W. I love, and W. I love I chasten	136	37	W. I did call upon by mine angels
	5	W. I have called but few are chosen	**WHOMSOEVER**		
	8	to endow those W. I have chosen	20	82	W. the other elders shall appoint
	14	three of you W. ye shall appoint	55	3	on W. you shall lay your hands
96	6	to W. I give promise of eternal life	97	2	show mercy upon all W. I will
97	1	many of W. are truly humble	103	25	W. ye curse I will curse and ye—132:47
101	55	save those W. I have appointed to tarry	132	47	W. ye bless I will bless, and W. ye curse
	80	W. I raised up to this very purpose		48	to W. you give any one on earth
102	7	W. they may consider worthy	**WHORE**		
103	2	on W. I will pour out my wrath	29	21	abominable church which is the W.
	21	the man to W. I likened the servant to W. the Lord	86	3	persecutor of the church, the W.
104	2	as those W. I commanded were faithful	**WHOREMONGER**		
	5	be trodden down by W. I will	63	17	the W., and the sorcerer, shall have
	80	hearts of those to W. you are in debt—81	**WHOREMONGERS**		
105	27	mine elders W. I have appointed	76	103	these are they who are adulterers and W.
107	40	to W. the promises were made	**WHOSE**		
	72	his counselors W. he has chosen	1	1	W. eyes are upon all men
	95	the first seventy to W. they belong		16	W. image is in the likeness of world, and W. substance
108	1	receive counsel of him W. I have	19	2	finished the will of him W. I am
	4	rest of mine elders W. I have chosen	20	6	W. countenance was as lightning, W. garments were pure
109	26	upon W. thy name shall be put	27	1	W. word is quick and powerful—33:1
111	2	many people in this city W. I will gather	29	1	W. arm of mercy hath atoned for
112	16	thou art the man W. I have chosen	35	1	W. course is one eternal round
	20	receiveth those W. I have sent; W. I have made counselors	49	11	mine apostle of old, W. name was Peter
113	4	Joseph, on W. there is laid much power	52	15	he that prayeth, W. spirit is contrite
	6	unto W. rightly belongs the priesthood		16	he that speaketh, W. spirit is, W. language is meek
	8	reference to those W. God should	56	17	ye poor men W. hearts are not broken, W. spirits are not contrite, W. bellies are not satisfied; W. hands are not stayed, and W. eyes are full of
121	43	love towards him W. thou reproved			
123	5	published, and writing, and by W.			
	7	with W. we shall be brought to stand			
124	45	W. I have appointed to lead my people			
	46	voice of these men W. I have appointed			

Sec.	Vs.		Sec.	Vs.	
	18	W. hearts are broken, W. spirits are contrite		89	W. receiveth you receiveth me—99:2
58	22	until he reigns W. right it is to	91	5	W. is enlightened by the spirit
59	3	they W. feet stand upon the land		6	W. receiveth not by the spirit
61	2	W. sins are now forgiven you	98	13	W. layeth down his life in my cause—103:27
	31	W. anger is kindled against their	99	3	W. receiveth you as a little child
63	2	W. anger is kindled against the wicked		4	W. rejecteth you shall be rejected of
65	1	W. going forth is unto the ends of; W. voice is unto men	103	28	W. is not willing to lay down his life
67	1	W. prayers I have heard, W. hearts I know, W. desires have			**WHOSOEVER**
68	2	W. mission is appointed unto them	5	16	W. believeth on my words them will
76	55	into W. hands the Father hath given	6	4	W. will thrust in his sickle—11:4; 12:4; 14:4
	68	they W. names are written in heaven	10	50	that W. should believe in this
	70	they W. bodies are celestial, W. glory is that of the sun, W. glory the sun is written of		55	W. belongeth to my church need not
	71	W. glory differs from that of		67	W. repenteth and cometh unto me
	93	before W. throne all things bow		68	W. declareth more or less than this
84	28	in W. hand is given all power		69	W. is of my church and endureth
	32	the sons of Moses W. sons are ye	24	16	W. shall lay their hands upon you
85	7	W. mouth shall utter words, eternal; W. names are found		17	W. shall go to law with thee
	11	W. names are not found written in	38	33	W. I will shall go forth among
86	3	in W. hearts the enemy, even Satan	42	43	W. among you are sick and have not
88	17	in W. bosom it is decreed that	63	17	W. loveth and maketh a lie and—76:103
93	32	every man W. spirit receiveth not	112	20	W. receiveth my word receiveth me, and W. receiveth me
96	6	W. offering I have accepted, and W. prayers I have heard		21	W. ye shall send in my name
109	4	in W. name alone salvation can be			**WICKED**
123	9	W. husbands and fathers have been	1	9	shall be poured out upon the W.
132	30	Abraham, from W. loins ye are	3	12	into the hands of a W. man—10:1
		WHOSESOEVER	10	7	I said that he is a W. man
132	46	W. sins you remit on earth; and W. sins you retain		8	W. men have taken them from you
				37	you cannot always tell the W. from
		WHOSO	27	17	quench all the fiery darts of the W.
6	3	W. desireth to reap let him thrust—11:3; 12:3; 14:3	29	8	desolation sent forth upon the W.
				11	and the W. shall not stand
29	49	W. having knowledge have I not		17	I will take vengeance upon the W.
33	15	W. having faith you shall confirm		27	and the W. on my left hand will I
35	9	W. shall ask it in my name in faith		41	which shall be pronounced upon the W.
49	14	W. doeth this shall receive the	34	9	and great destruction await the W.
	15	W. forbiddeth to marry it is not	38	5	the residue of the W. have I kept in
	18	W. forbiddeth to abstain from meats		6	so will I cause the W. to be kept
51	19	W. is found a faithful, a just and	42	go ye out from among the W.
57	9	W. readeth let him understand—71:5; 91:4	43	19	lest ye be found among the W.
				33	the W. shall go away into unquenchable
58	17	W. standeth in his mission is	45	32	among the W. men shall lift up their
84	33	W. is faithful to obtaining these two		67	that the W. will not come unto it
	41	but W. breaketh this covenant		68	it shall come to pass among the W.
	51	for W. cometh not under me is under		70	it shall be said among the W., let us
	52	W. receiveth not my voice is not	60	8	among the congregations of the W.
	88	and W. receiveth you there will I			

Sec.	Vs.		Sec.	Vs.	
		—13, 14; 61:30, 32, 33; 62:5; 68:1	99	1	in the midst of persecution. and W.
63	2	anger is kindled against the W.	109	26	that no combination of W. shall
	6	I say, let the W. take heed	133	14	from the midst of W. which is Babylon
	32	I am angry with the W.			**WIDE**
	33	and the W. shall slay the W.	38	1	looked upon the W. expanse of eternity
	34	consume the W. with unquenchable fire	104	43	which is 40 rods long and 12 W.
	37	desolation shall come upon the W.	122	7	gape open the mouth W. after thee
	54	entire separation of W. and righteous; pluck out the W. and cast them	132	25	broad is the gate and W. the way
64	21	in which I will overthrow the W.			**WIDOW**
84	53	may know the righteous from the W.	101	83	there was a W. in that city and she
88	75	clean from blood of this W. generation		84	because this W. troubleth me I will
	85	the abomination which awaits the W.	136	8	that the cries of the W. and fatherless
	121	cease from all your W. doings			**WIDOWS**
93	25	is the spirit of that W. one	83	6	W. and orphans shall be provided for
	39	that W. one cometh and taketh away	123	9	but to the W. and fatherless whose
	42	that W. one hath power as yet over	136	8	in taking the poor, the W., the
	49	lest that W. one have power in you			**WIDTH**
97	21	while all the W. shall mourn	76	48	the end, the W., the height thereof
	24	kindled against all their W. works	94	4	shall be built 55 by 65 feet in W.
98	9	when the W. rule the people mourn			—11; 95:15
	20	they do not forsake their W. ways			**WIFE**
101	90	will cut off those W. stewards	19	25	shalt not covet thy neighbor's W.
	95	discern between the righteous and the W.	42	22	thou shalt love thy W. with all
104	18	he shall, with the W., lift up his	49	16	lawful that he should have one W.
109	45	terrible things concerning the W.	74	1	husband is sanctified by W. and unbelieving W. by
	46	from the calamity of the W.	109	69	have mercy on his W. and children
	48	oppressed and afflicted by W. men	122	6	enemies tear thee from bosom of thy W.
	50	have mercy upon that W. mob	132	15	if a man marry him a W. in the world—18, 19, 26
135	7	by conspiracy of traitors and W. men		34	gave Hagar to Abraham to W.
136	39	and the W. might be condemned		39	save in the case of Uriah and his W.
		WICKEDLY		41	if a man receiveth a W. in the new
10	56	and all those that do W.		51	mine handmaid, Emma Smith, your W.
29	9	they that do W. shall be as stubble— 64:24; 133:64		64	if any man has a W., who holds keys
		WICKEDNESS		65	commanded Abraham to take Hagar to W.
6	26	kept back because of W. of people			**WIGHT, LYMAN**
10	9	yea, that which was sacred unto W.	52	7	let W. and, take their journey speedily
	21	hearts are full of W. and abominations		12	let W. beware for Satan desireth to
29	9	that W. shall not be upon the earth	103	30	Pratt and W. should not return until
	17	because of the W. of the world I will		38	let W. journey with Sidney Rigdon
38	30	lest W. of men reveal these things by their W.	124	18	W. should continue in preaching
45	12	they found it not because of W.		62	let W., and, organize themselves
52	39	that there be no idolatry nor W.		70	if W., and, receive any stock in
61	8	that you might not perish in W.			
	31	anger is kindled against their W.			
68	31	children are also growing up in W.			
84	96	to scourge them for their W.			

Sec.	Vs.	
		WILD
89	14	and all W. animals that run or
109	65	converted from their W. and savage
		WILDERNESS
5	14	coming forth of my church out of the W.
17	1	given to Lehi while in the W.
32	2	into the W. among the Lamanites
33	5	and called forth out of the W.
	8	who journeyed from Jerusalem in W.
49	24	Jacob shall flourish in the W.
84	23	to the children of Israel in the W.
	24	not enter into his rest in the W.
86	3	and drive the church into the W.
88	66	voice of one crying in the W., in the W. because you
107	45	God called upon Cainan in the W.
109	73	that church may come forth out of W.
124	38	should bear it with them in the W.
128	20	in the W. of Fayette; in the W. between Harmony and Colesville
133	68	I make the rivers a W.
		WILL
1	35	I W. that all men shall know that
3	4	and follows dictates of his own W.
7	7	for if ye shall ask what you W.
	4	if I W. that he tarry till I come
19	2	having finished the W. of him
	24	I came by the W. of the Father and I do his W.
20	1	by the W. and commandments of God
	24	according to the W. of the Father
21	1	through the W. of God the Father
25	2	I give unto you concerning my W.
	6	send my servant whithersoever I W.
	9	revealed unto them whatsoever I W.
29	5	it is his good W. to give you the
	12	by the W. of the Father that mine
	40	became subject to the W. of the devil
	48	it is given to man even as I W
31	11	go whithersoever I W.
	13	your Redeemer, by W. of the Father
32	1	I W. that he shall declare my gospel
38	33	from thence, whomsoever I W. shall: W. lead whithersoever I W.
	39	riches which it is the W. of the
46	15	according as the Lord W.
	30	asketh according to the W. of God
49	8	I W. that all men shall repent
50	8	in life or death even as I W.
	27	sent forth by the W. of the Father
	29	ye shall ask whatsoever you W.
52	2	make known unto you what I W.
	6	they shall be cut off, even as I W.

Sec.	Vs.	
54	7	appoint whom you W. to be your leader
55	6	made known hereafter even as I W.
57	9	may send goods even by whom he W.
58	1	learn of me what I W. concerning
	20	according to the counsel of his own W.
	27	do many things of their own free W.
	50	and a statement of the W. of God
60	16	this is the W. of him who sent you
63	1	word of Lord and his W. concerning
	4	who buildeth up at his own W. and
	10	not by W. of men but by W. of
	20	endureth in faith and doeth my W.
	22	I would make known my W. unto you
	24	this is the W. of the Lord, your God—72:8; 75:12
	27	I W. that you should purchase
	36	I W. that my saints should be assembled
	46	behold, this is my W.—103:31
64	1	receive my W. concerning you
	2	I W. that ye should overcome world
	21	I W. not that my servant should sell; I W. to retain a strong hold
	29	ye do according to W. of the Lord
66	4	what I W.; what is my W; concerning you
	5	it is my W. that you should proclaim
68	4	shall be the W. of the Lord
69	2	I W. that my servant should go—79:1
71	1	which shall be given you, as I W.
75	3	it is my W. that you should go forth
	23	that you might know his W. concerning
76	7	make known good pleasure of my W.
	10	unto them the secrets of my W.
77	6	contains the revealed W., mysteries
78	7	if you W. that I give unto you a
80	5	this is the W. of him who hath called
82	8	that you may understand my W.
85	3	it is contrary to the W. of God—101:96
88	1	assembled yourselves to receive his W.
	68	in his own way according to his W.
	75	promise made unto you when I W.
89	2	the order and W. of God in the
90	28	it is my W. that my handmaid
93	53	it is my W. that you should hasten to translate

Will 484 Williams, Frederick, G.

Sec.	Vs.
95	11 it is my W. that you should build—97:10
97	1 that I may show unto you my W.
	2 show mercy on whomsoever I W.
98	4 it is my W. my people should observe
101	22 it is my W. that all who call on my
	43 that you may know my W.
	60 when I W., go ye straightway and
	76 it is my W. they should continue to—124:18
	99 it is my W. that my people should claim
103	29 my W. that my servant shall lift up
	30 my W. that my servant should not return
	31 men do not always do my W.
104	5 trodden down by whom I W.
	20 even as I W. when I shall command him
	36 it is my W. that he should sell lots
	78 it is my W. you shall pay your debts
	79 it is my W. you shall humble
105	1 that you may learn my W. concerning
	29 my W. that these lands should be
106	1 my W. that my servant be appointed
109	44 thy W. be done, O Lord, not ours
	68 hath sincerely striven to do thy W.
111	8 where it is my W. you should tarry
115	17 it is my W. that city of Far West
124	5 to know my W. concerning those kings
	69 by their own free W. and act; if you will do my W.
	73 who wish to know my W. concerning
	74 if he W. do my W.—83, 89, 108
100	if I W. that he should raise the dead
109	it is not my W. that he should seek
125	1 what is the W. concerning saints in
	2 if they W. do my W.
128	5 it is only to answer the W. of God
132	40 ask what ye W. and it shall
133	61 according to mind and W. of Lord
134	3 or the W. of the sovereign
	12 contrary to the W. of their masters
136	1 the W. of the Lord concerning Camp of
	9 the W. of the Lord concerning his people
	16 go teach this my W. to the saints

See *Abide, Accept, Administer, Admit, Agree, Answer, Appear,*

Sec.	Vs.

Appoint, Arise, Ask, Avenge, Bear, Become, Begin, Believe, Bestow, Bless, Bow, Break, Bring, Build, Burn, Call, Canker, Cast, Cause, Chasten, Choose, Come, Commit, Confess, Confound, Consecrate, Contend, Counsel, Crown, Cry, Curse, Cut, Deal, Deliver, Destroy, Discover, Disperse, Disturb, Do, Draw, Drink, Dwell, Embrace, Encircle, Endure, Enlighten, Establish, Exist, Explain, Fall, Feed, Feel, Fight, Find, Forgive, Fulfill, Gather, Gird, Give, Go, Grant, Harden, Hasten, Have, Heal, Hear, Hearken, Hold, Humble, Impart, Justify, Keep, Kill, Knock, Labor, Lay, Lead, Let, Lie, Lift, Liken, Love, Magnify, Make, Manifest, Marshal, Merciful, Mete, Move, Multiply, Obey, Offer, Open, Order, Ordain, Overthrow, Own, Pay, Perform, Permit, Plant, Pour, Prepare, Preserve, Promote, Protect, Prove, Provide, Publish, Raise, Reason, Receive, Reign, Rejoice, Remember, Rend, Repay, Repent, Require, Retain, Return, Reveal, Rise, Sanctify, Save, Say, Secure, See, Send, Serve, Shake, Show, Smite, Smitten, Soften,
- *Spare, Speak, Stand, Stay, Strengthen, Suffer, Take, Tell Terminate, Thrust, Touch, Transact, Try, Turn, Unfold, Unveil, Uphold, Visit, Walk, Work, Write.*

WILLETH

58	52 the Lord W. that the disciples
63	3 who W. to take even them whom he
88	35 and W. to abide in sin

WILLIAM

55	1 say unto you W. thou art called and
66	3 say unto you W. you are clean but not
124	87 let W. put his trust in me and cease
	88 let W. go and proclaim my Gospel
	91 let W. be appointed, ordained and
	101 let W. cry aloud and spare not
	102 I have a mission in store for W.

See also *Law, Marks, M'Lellin* and *Phelps.*

WILLIAMS, FREDERICK G.

64	21 I will not that W. should sell his farm
81	1 I say unto W., listen to voice of him
90	6 I say unto W. and their sins are forgiven

Sec.	Vs.	
	19	for family of thy counselor, even W.
92	1	W., that ye receive him into the order
	2	W., you shall be a lively member
93	41	W., you have continued under this condemnation
	52	let W., and, make haste also and it
102	3	W., and, were acknowledged as presidents
103	39	let Hyrum Smith journey with W.
104	27	let W. have the place upon which he now
	29	let W. and, have the Laneshine house

WILLIAMS, SAMUEL

124	137	I give unto you W., and, to preside

WILLING

1	34	I am W. to make these things known
20	37	W. to take upon them the name of—77
62	7	I am W. if any among you desire
64	34	the Lord requireth a W. mind; and the W. and obedient shall eat the
75	25	as your brethren are W. to open their
88	32	to enjoy that which they are W. to receive, because they were not W. to enjoy
97	6	I am W. to show mercy, nevertheless
	8	and are W. to observe their covenants
101	63	as they are W. to be guided in a
	75	were the churches W. to hearken
103	28	whoso is not W. to lay down his life
121	13	things which they are W. to bring upon

WILSON, CALVES

75	15	Asa Dobbs and W. shall take their journey

WILSON, DUNBAR

124	132	viz., W., Seymour Brunson, etc.

WIND

109	37	as with a mighty rushing W.
123	16	by being kept workways with the W.

WINDOW

135	1	Joseph leaped from the W. and was

WINDS

90	5	when the storms descend and W. blow
122	7	if fierce W. become thine enemy
133	7	gather out from the four W.

Sec.	Vs.	
		WINE
20	40	and to administer bread and W.
	75	meet often to partake of bread and W.
	78	the manner of administering the W.
	79	to bless and sanctify this W. to
27	3	you shall not purchase W. neither
35	11	made all nations drink of the W.——88:94, 105
58	8	of W. on the lees well refined
88	141	and after partaking of bread and W.
89	5	inasmuch as any man drinketh W.
	6	this should be W. yea, pure W.

WINE-PRESS

76	107	I have trodden the W. alone, even the W. of—88:106; 133:50

WINE-VAT

133	48	like him that treadeth in the W.

WINGS

10	65	gathereth her chickens under her W.—29:2; 43:24
77	4	what are we to understand by the W.; their W. are a representation of power
88	45	the earth rolls upon her W., as they roll upon their W.
124	18	I will bear him up as on eagle's W.
	99	mount up in his thoughts as on eagle's W.

WINTER

89	13	not to be used only in times of W.

WISDOM

1	26	as they sought W. they might be
3	13	and boasted in his own W.
6	7	seek not for riches but for W.—11:7
9	3	be patient, for it is W. in me
	6	it is W. in me that I have dealt
10	34	here is W. and because I show unto you W.
	35	marvel not that I said here is W.
	40	concerning the things which in my W.
	43	my W. is greater than the cunning
	45	it is W. that you should translate
11	26	until the time which in my W.
19	21	unto the world until it is W. in me
25	4	which is W. in me in a time to come
27	5	behold, this is W. in me
28	5	not by way of commandment but by W.
37	4	here is W. let every man choose for
38	30	treasure up W. in your bosoms
42	68	he that lacketh W. let him ask
45	11	even my W., the W. of him that
46	17	given by the spirit the word of W.

Sec.	Vs.	
50	1	and attend to the words of W.
52	17	bring forth fruits of praise and W.
57	3	if you will receive W. here is W.
	4	it is W. that the land should be purchased
	5	this is W. that they may obtain
	6	in righteousness and as W. shall
	9	obtain a license, here is W.
	12	here is W., let him obtain
58	23	behold, here is W.—53; 71:5; 82:16, 22; 96:1; 101:41; 107:92
	35	it is W. in me that my servant
	37	it is W. also that there should be
63	44	let him do according to W.
64	26	not sell their store, for this is not W.
69	1	not W. in me that he should be
76	2	great is his W., marvelous his ways
	9	their W. shall be great: the W. of the wise shall perish
78	2	speak in your ears the words of W.
88	40	W. receiveth W.
	118	teach one another words of W.; out of the best books words of W.—109:7
89	1	a word of W. for the benefit
	2	by revelation and the word of W.
	4	by giving unto you this word of W.
	19	and shall find W. and great treasures
95	13	here is W. and the mind of the Lord
96	3	divided in lots according to W.
	6	it is W. and expedient in me
97	1	to learn W. and find truth
98	20	observe the words of W. and eternal
101	63	I will show unto you W. in me
104	11	it is W. in me; therefore a commandment
105	23	until it is W. in me that they should
109	14	may be taught words of W.
114	1	it is W. in my servant David, that
124	1	show forth my W. through the weak
127	1	I have thought it W. in me to leave
136	32	let him that is ignorant learn W.

WISE

Sec.	Vs.	
5	9	for a W. purpose in me—61:35
10	12	and on this W. the devil has sought
45	57	they that are W. and have received
46	18	that all may be taught to be W.
51	19	whoso is a just and W. steward
58	10	first, the rich, the W. and the noble
	26	is a slothful and not a W. servant
63	54	will be foolish virgins among the W.
67	6	appoint him that is the most W.
72	4	for he who is faithful and W. in time
	17	as a W. steward and faithful laborer

Sec.	Vs.	
	22	and be accounted as W. stewards
	26	shall not be accounted as W. steward
76	9	the wisdom of the W. shall perish
78	22	a W. steward shall inherit all
98	10	W. men should be sought for diligently; W. men ye should uphold
101	61	a faithful and a W. steward
	73	even W. men and send them to purchase
	80	by the hands of W. men whom I raised
	94	that W. men and rulers may hear and
103	23	let all the churches send up W. men
104	47	to your brethren only on this W.
	53	only on this W. as I said, by loan
	75	and is W. in his stewardship
105	28	to send W. men to fulfill that which
111	11	be W. as serpents yet without sin
122	2	while the pure in heart and the W.
128	18	but have been kept hid from the W.
132	24	to know the only W. and true God
133	58	when the weak should confound the W.
135	3	and many other W. documents and
136	27	that thou mayest be a W. steward

WISELY

Sec.	Vs.	
19	41	and conduct thyself W. before me
72	3	in this thing ye have done W.

WISH

Sec.	Vs.	
124	73	others also who W. to know my will
134	12	contrary to the will and W. of their

WITHAL

Sec.	Vs.	
46	16	be given to every man to profit W.

WITHDRAW

Sec.	Vs.	
121	37	behold the heavens W. themselves
134	10	and W. from them their fellowship

WITHDRAWN

Sec.	Vs.	
121	37	and when it is W., Amen to the priesthood

WITHDREW

Sec.	Vs.	
19	20	at the time I W. my spirit
88	57	he W. from the first that he might

WITHHELD

Sec.	Vs.	
25	4	for they are W. from thee and from
64	16	and I the Lord W. my spirit
70	14	manifestations of Spirit shall be W.
121	28	in the which nothing shall be W.

WITHHOLD

Sec.	Vs.	
104	75	that the treasurer shall not W.
124	100	let him not W. his voice
133	49	and the moon shall W. its light

Sec.	Vs.	
		WITHIN
9	8	shall cause your bosom to burn W. you
101	84	afterward he said W. himself
		WITHOUT
1	9	upon the wicked W. measure
8	10	W. faith you can do nothing
19	39	canst thou read this W. rejoicing
20	28	one God infinite, eternal, W. end
	65	W. the vote of that church
35	11	W. faith shall not anything be shown
38	31	a righteous people W. spot and
45	58	chidren shall grow up W. sin unto
57	8	that he may sell goods W. fraud
60	7	with loud voices, W. wrath or doubting
63	11	for W. faith no man pleaseth God
	64	W. this there remaineth condemnation
64	6	sought occasion against thee W. cause
65	2	cut out of the mountain W. hands
74	6	children might remain W. circumcision
76	112	they cannot come worlds W. end
78	16	who is W. beginning of days or end—84:17
84	21	and W. the ordinances thereof
	22	for W. this no man can see the face
109		for W. the feet how shall the body
88	82	therefore they are left W. excuse
101	11	poured out W. measure on all nations
	93	that all men may be left W. excuse—124:7
102	6	cannot have power to act W. seven
	11	preside over the Council W. an
103	2	pour out my wrath W. measure
107	76	to act independently W. counselors
109	45.	pour out thy judgments W. measure
	72	which thou hast set up W. hands
110	13.	taken to heaven W. tasting death
111	11	be ye wise as serpents, yet W. sin
115	6	when it shall be poured out W. mixture
121	42	greatly enlarge the soul W. hypocrisy and W. guile
	46	W. compulsory means it shall flow
123	6	that nation may be left W. excuse
124	20	my servant George Miller is W. guile
	71	W. consent of the stockholder
	97	humble before me and be W. guile
127	1	as they pursue me W. a cause
128	5	who should die W. knowledge of Gospel
	15	they W. us cannot be made perfect, neither can we W. our dead—18
	18	W. those who have died in the Gospel

Sec.	Vs.	
130	16	W. being able to decide whether this
132	17	remain W. exaltation, in their saved
	48	and shall be W. condemnation on earth
134	6	as W. them peace and harmony would
135	2	W. even a hole in his robe
		WITHSTAND
27	15	that ye may be able to W. the evil
		WITNESS
5	1	has desired a W. at my hand
	2	you should stand as a W. of these
	23	concerning man that desires the W.
	32	and receive a W. from my hand
6	17	I tell these things as a W. unto
	22	if you desire a further W. cast your
	23	what greater W. can you have than from
	24	and now, you have received a W., have you not received a W.
14	8	that you may stand as a W. of
20	16	and bear W. to the words of the
	37	and W. before the church that they
	77	and W. unto thee, O. God, the eternal—79
106	8	to be a faithful W. and a light
135	7	is a W. to the truth of the gospel
136	40	only in that I have left a W. of my name
		WITNESSES
5	15	testimony of three W. will I send
6	28	in the mouth of two or three W.—128:3
20	13	having so great W. by them shall
27	12	and especial W. of my name
42	80	against him or her by two W., if more than two W. it is better
	81	shall be condemned by mouth of two W.
77	15	what is understood by the two W.
107	23	special W. of the name of Christ
	25	to be especial W. to the Gentiles
	26	equal to that of the Twelve W.
128	4	and all the attending W.
	20	declaring the three W. to bear record
		WIVES
123	7	also to ourselves, to our W. and
	9	duty we owe to our W. and children
132	1	of their having many W. and concubines
	38	David received many W., as also
	39	David's W. were given unto him by
	55	of fathers, mothers, W. and children

Sec.	Vs.	
		WO
10	28	W. be unto him that lieth to deceive
11	25	W. unto him that denieth these things
38	6	and W., W., W. is their doom
42	47	W. unto them for their death is bitter
49	21	W. be unto man that sheddeth blood
50	6	W. unto them that are deceivers
	8	W. unto them who are cut off from my
54	5	W. unto him by whom this offence
56	16	W. unto you rich men that will not give
	17	W. unto you poor men whose hearts
58	33	W. unto such for their reward
60	2	W. unto such for mine anger is kindled
84	94	W. unto that house that rejecteth
	—95	
121	19	W. unto them because they have offended
	23	W. unto all those that discomfort my
		WOE
5	5	W. shall come unto the inhabitants
		WOES
19	5	but W. shall go forth, weeping and
		WOLVES
122	6	enemies prowl around thee like W.
		WOMAN
42	23	that looketh upon a W. to lust after her—63:16
	80	any man or W. shall commit adultery
	84	if a man or W. shall rob he or she
49	22	cometh not in the form of a W.
101	81	parable of the W. and unjust judge
132	43	if her husband be with another W.
136	35	like a W. that is taken in travail
		WOMB
84	27	with the Holy Ghost from his mother's W.
		WOMEN
18	42	not only men but W. and children
83	1	concerning W. and children who belong
	2	W. have claim on their husbands
		WONDERFUL
65	4	make known his W. works among
84	66	they shall do many W. works
		WONDERS
35	8	will show miracles, signs and W.
45	40	and they shall see· signs and W.

Sec.	Vs.	
63	12	who have sought after signs and W.
76	8	the W. of eternity shall they know
128	23	tell the W. of your eternal king
		WONT
127	2	deep water is what I am W. to swim in
128	13	where the living are W. to assemble
		WOODRUFF, WILFORD
118	6	let W. and, be appointed to fill places
124	129	they are—Heber C. Kimball, W., and
136	13	let Pratt and W. organize a company
		WOODS
128	23	let the W. and all the trees of
		WORD
1	38	my W. shall not pass away
5	10	this generation shall have my W.
	15	three witnesses will I send forth my W.
	20	and my W. shall be verified at this
6	2	give heed unto my W.—11:2; 12:2; 14:2
	28	shall every W. be established
10	43	not suffer that they shall destroy my W.
11	16	until you shall have my W.
	21	seek not to declare my W. but to obtain my W., then you shall have my W.
	22	study my W. which has gone forth and my W. which shall go
17	1	you must rely upon my W.
19	26	which contains the truth and the W.
	27	which is my W. to the Gentile
21	5	for his W. ye shall receive as if
27	1	whose W. is quick and powerful—33:1
	18	and my W. which I reveal unto you
29	30	have created by W. of my power
31	6	declare my W. and I will prepare a
39	16	but I cannot deny my W.
40	1	he covenanted that he would obey my W.
	2	he received the W. with gladness, but fear caused him to reject my W.
41	2	assemble yourselves to agree upon my W.
42	6	declaring my W. like unto angels
	80	every W. shall be established against
46	17	given by spirit of God the W. of wisdom
	18	to another the W. of knowledge
49	1	hearken unto my W. my servant Sidney

Sec.	Vs.		Sec.	Vs.	
50	17	sent forth to preach the W. of truth		22	humble themselves and abide in my W.
	19	he that receiveth the W. of truth	118	2	let my servant remain to publish my W.
	21	he that receiveth W. by spirit of	124	16	in sending my W. to the kings of
	37	strengthen them by W. of exhortation		23	while he shall contemplate the W.
52	9	preaching the W. by the way—22, 23		89	the new translation of my holy W.
	39	declare the W. in the regions among	128	to send my W. to every creature
53	3	remission of sins according to my W.	126	3	command you to send my W. abroad
58	1	give ear to my W. and learn of me	127	5	I give unto you a W. in relation to
60	7	declare my W. with loud voices		10	I will write the W. of the Lord from
	8	two by two, preach the W., not in haste	128	3	in mouth of, every W. may be established
	14	after thou hast proclaimed my W., return proclaiming my W.		14	and, in one sense of the W., the
61	33	declare the W. among the congregations	130	11	the new name is the key W.
63	1	hear the W. of the Lord and his will	131	5	the more sure W. of prophecy means
	2	hear the W. of him whose anger is	132	12	or by my W. which is my law
	37	declare both by W. and by flight		13	that are not by me or by my W.
68	4	shall be the W. of the Lord		15	marry her not by me or by my W.
	7	this is the W. of the Lord—84:4		18	that covenant is not by me or by my W.; not joined by me or by my W.
70	1	hear the W. of the Lord which I give		19	if a man marry a wife by my W.
72	9	the W. of the Lord in addition to		26	if a man marry a wife according to my W.
81	1	listen to the W. of the Lord your God		29	Abraham received all things by my W.
84	2	W. of the Lord concerning his church		40	shall be given you according to my W.
	44	you shall live by every W. that		46	you bind on earth by my W.
	45	for the W. of the Lord is truth		48	you give any one on earth by my W.
86	4	is beginning to bring forth the W.		59	according to my law and by my W.
89	1	a W. of Wisdom for the benefit of		65	did not administer to him according to my W.
	2	by revelation and the W. of wisdom	133	1	hear the W. of the Lord concerning
	4	by giving unto you this W. of wisdom	136	1	the W. and will of the Lord concerning

WORDS

Sec.	Vs.	
90	9	that they may receive the W. and the W. go forth
93	8	in the beginning the W. was, for he was the W.
96	4	for purpose of bringing forth my W.
	5	that my W. should go forth unto the
	8	may assist in bringing forth my W.
98	11	ye shall live by every W. that
99	2	shall have power to declare my W.
100	13	I give unto you a W. concerning Zion
101	64	and my W. must needs be fulfilled
109	38	when they go out to proclaim thy W.
	44	but thy W. must be fulfilled
112	4	thou shalt send forth my W. unto ends
	8	by thy W. many high ones shall be, and by thy W. many low ones
	19	that they may receive my W.
	20	whosoever receiveth my W. receiveth

Sec.	Vs.	
1	14	neither give heed to W. of prophets
3	7	the counsels of God and despise his W.
5	5	if they will not hearken to my W.
	6	deliver my W. unto the children of
	7	if they will not believe my W.
	11	they shall go forth with my W.
	16	whosoever believeth on my W. them
	26	these are the W. he shall say
6	2	therefore give heed unto my W.
	17	the W. or the work thou hast been
	20	treasure up these W. in thy heart
	29	if they reject my W., and this
	31	but if they reject not my W.
8	5	remember these W. and keep my
10	10	alter the W. you have written
	11	because they have altered the W.
	13	say they have caught you in the W. which

Sec.	Vs.		Sec.	Vs.	
	17	or, in other W.—42:37, 69, 74; 58:20; 59:13, 14; 61:23; 63:42; 78:4, 9; 82:9, 17; 83:5; 88:127; 93:36, 45; 95:17; 101:12; 104:5, 69; 107:66; 128:8	63	58	a day of warning, not of many W.
			64	31	my W. are sure and shall not fail
			72	24	a few W. in addition to the laws
			78	2	speak in your ears, W. of wisdom
			81	7	these are the W. of Alpha and Omega
	17	if he bringeth forth the same W.	84	43	give diligent heed to the W. of
	18	we will say he has lied in his W.		60	say unto you who now hear my W.
	29	now, they have altered these W.		64	every soul who believeth on your W.
	30	you shall not translate again those W.		74	they who believe not on your W.
	31	evil designs in lying against those W.; if you should bring forth the same W.		85	in your minds continually W. of life
				94	that rejecteth you or your W.—95
	32	that they will not believe my W.	85	7	who shall utter W., eternal W.
	42	confound those who have altered my W.	88	118	teach one another W. of wisdom; seek out of best books W. of wisdom—109:7
	70	remember the W. of him who is the		129	that congregation may hear his W.
11	11	by my power I give these W. unto		132	salute his brethren with these W.
12	9	life of the world that speak these W.	98	20	they do not observe the W. of wisdom
15	1	listen to the W. of Jesus Christ—16:1			
	5	for speaking my W. which I have —16:5	103	7	hearkening to observe *all* the W.
				8	and hearken not to observe *all* my W.
18	1	I give unto you these W.			
	30	according to the W. which are written	104	4	broken the covenant with feigned W.—52
	34	these W. are not of men, nor of man—31:13		26	moneys for the proclaiming of my W.
	36	you have heard my voice and know my W.		58	organize yourselves to print my W.
19	23	learn of me and listen to my W.	105	17	have not hearkened unto my W.
20	16	and bear witness to the W. of the		18	are those who have hearkened to my W.
	26	who believed in W. of the holy prophets	109	14	may be taught W. of wisdom out of
21	4	thou shalt give heed to all his W.		60	these W., O Lord, we have spoken
	9	they shall believe on his W.	124	46	pollute my holy W. which I give
23	1	I speak unto you, a few W.—3, 4, 5	128	2	I wrote a few W. of revelation to you
	6	I manifest to you by these W.			
24	16	will smite them according to your W.	136	24	let your W. tend to edify one another
25	5	in his afflictions with consoling W.		37	if faithful in keeping all my W.
29	30	as the W. have gone forth out of my			**WORD'S**
30	5	give heed unto the W. and advice of	6	18	in circumstances he may be for W. sake
32	5	give heed to these W. and trifle not			
35	23	call on holy prophets to prove his W.			**WORK**
41	12	these W. are given unto you and they	1	10	unto every man according to his W.
			3	3	not the W. of God which is frustrated but W. of men
43	1	give an ear to the W. I shall speak		9	thou wast chosen to do the W. of the Lord
	22	saying these W., repent ye for			
	23	hear the W. of that God who made you		10	and art again called to the W.
	27	these are the W. of the Lord your God		16	nevertheless my W. shall go forth
			4	1	a marvelous W. is about to come forth—6:1; 11:1; 12:1; 14:1
	34	hearken ye to these W., I am Jesus			
45	34	when the Lord had spoken these W.		3	to serve God ye are called to the W.
46	14	it is given to believe on their W.		5	faith, hope and, qualify him for the W.
50	1	attend to the W. of wisdom which			
	36	you who are now hearing these W.	6	9	assist to bring forth my W.—11:9
56	11	these W. shall not pass away		17	that the W. which thou hast been

Sec.	Vs.		Sec.	Vs.	
	35	perform with soberness the W. I have	73	4	continue the W. of translation
7	5	that he might do more or a greater W.	76	15	while doing the W. of translation
	6	yea, he has undertaken a greater W.	85		until, the Lamb, shall have finished his W.
8	8	for it is the W. of God	106		and shall have perfected his W.
9	4	the W. which you are called to do	77	5	faithful in the W. of the ministry
	14	stand fast in the W. wherewith I		12	on the seventh day he finished his W.; the preparing and finishing his W.
10	3	the remainder of the W. of translation	88	73	I will hasten my W. in its time
	5	of Satan that do uphold his W.	90	24	shall W. together for your good—98:3; 100:15; 105:40
	12	plan, that he may destroy this W.		26	provided for you to bring to pass my W.
	19	we will destroy him and also the W.	94	1	commence a W. of laying out
	23	thinking to destroy the W. of God		3	for the W. of the presidency; for the W. of the ministry—124:143
	24	their hearts to anger against this W.		7	for the W. of the presidency
	33	that the W. may not come forth in		10	for the W. of the printing of the —12
	34	you have accomplished the W. of		15	that they may do the W. I have
	45	of Nephi, and send forth in this W.	97	13	who are called to W. of the ministry
	46	all the remainder of this W. does	101	20	for the W. of the gathering of my
11	19	yes, the translation of my W.		64	W. of gathering together my saints
	20	this is your W. to keep my commandments		65	reward every man according as his W.—112:34
12	7	to bring forth and establish this W.		95	and perform my W., my strange W.
	8	no one can assist in this W. except	109	5	thou knowest we have done this W.
17	4	unto the children of men in this W.		23	that they may know this is thy W.
18	44	I *will* W. a marvelous W. among the		33	that we may rise up and do thy W.
19	7	that it might W. on the hearts of		59	that thy W. may be cut short in
20	11	and call them to his holy W. in		78	and accept the W. of our hands
	13	as shall come to knowledge of this W.	110	2	under his feet was a paved W. of
	14	who receive it in faith and W.	112	6	I have a great W. for thee to do
29	32	which is the beginning of my W.; which is the last of my W.		7	gird up thy loins for the W.
31	1	because of your faith in my W.	115	9	let there be a beginning of this W., and a preparatory W.
35	3	and prepared thee for a greater W.—39:11	124	17	I have seen the W. he hath done
	7	there shall be a stage W. in the land		19	that when he shall finish his W.
38	33	for I have a great W. laid up in store		49	to do a W. unto my name; and to perform that W.; hinder them from performing that W.; require that W. no more
	36	and this shall be their W. to govern		50	on the heads of those who hindered my W.
42	40	the beauty of the W. of thine own hands		53	who have been commanded to do a W.
43	13	whatsoever he needeth to accomplish W.		78	I love him for the W. he hath done
45	72	that ye may accomplish this W. in eyes		79	to accomplish the W. that my servant
49	4	my servant shall be ordained to this W.	127	4	let the W. of my temple, and all
52	11	will cut my W. short in righteousness—84:97	132	63	herein is the W. of my Father continued
55	4	assist to do the W. of printing	136	17	shall not have power to stop my W.
	5	in land of your inheritance to do this W.		37	out of the heavens to bring my W.
58	33	this is not the W. of the Lord			**WORKETH**
	56	let the W. of the gathering be not	133	44	shalt meet him who W. righteousness
	58	to accomplish the residue of the W.			
64	33	are laying foundation of a great W.			

Sec.	Vs.		Sec.	Vs.	
		WORKING	101	51	and the enemy destroyed their W.
46	21	to some is given the W. of miracles	100	as they bring forth fruit and W. meet
		WORKINGS	105	24	do not boast of faith, nor mighty W.
121	12	may not understand his marvelous W.	109	30	that all their W. may be brought to
			121	24	mine eyes see and know all their W.
		WORKMANSHIP		25	every man according as his W. shall be
29	25	for it is the W. of mine hand	124	48	ye by your W. bring cursings, wrath
109	4	accept this house, the W. of the		86	and shall continue their W.
		WORKMEN	127	4	and all the W. I have appointed; and your W. be redoubled
58	54	let there be W. sent forth of all	128	6	written in the books according to their W.—7
		WORKS		7	contained the record of their W.
3	1	the W. and designs and purposes		8	judged according to their own W.
	4	and have power to do mighty W.	132	31	the continuation of the W. of my
8	8	in your hands, and do marvelous W.		32	go ye and do the W. of Abraham
10	61	bring to light their marvelous W.	135	3	sealed his mission and his W. with
18	38	by their desires and their W. you			**WORKWAYS**
19	3	destroying of Satan and his W.; judging every man according to his W.	123	16	being kept W. with the wind
					WORLD
20	37	truly manifest by their W. that	1	16	whose image is in likeness of the W.
	69	that there may be W. and faith		18	they should proclaim these things to W.
21	8	manifestations of my blessings on his W.		19	weak things of the W. shall come forth
22	2	neither by your dead W.		20	the Lord, even the Savior of the W.
	3	for it is because of your dead W.		23	proclaimed to the ends of the W.
29	33	unto myself my W. have no end		36	come down in judgment upon the W.
35	3	I have looked upon thee and thy W.			
39	7	I have looked upon thy W. and know	3	16	knowledge of Savior has come unto W.
45	72	that they may not know your W. until	10	19	that we may get glory of the W.
				34	show it not unto W. until you—35
59	2	and their W. shall follow them—63:15		37	to make all things known to the W.
	23	he who doeth the W. of righteousness		70	who is the life and light of the W.—11:28; 12:9; 34:2; 39:2; 45:7
63	11	signs come by faith unto mighty W.	18	6	the W. is ripening in iniquity
	48	his W. shall follow him		28	go into *all* the W. to preach my—68:8; 80:1; 84:62; 112:28
65	4	make known his wonderful W. among		41	you must preach unto the W. saying
76	43	and saves all the W. of his hands	19	1	I am the Redeemer of the W.
	111	shall be judged according to their W., according to his own W., his own dominion		3	destroying his works at end of the W.
				21	show not these things to the W. until
	114	marvelous are the W. of the Lord		28	before the W. as well as in secret
77	6	revealed will, mysteries and W. of	20	5	entangled again in vanities of the W.
84	66	they shall do many wonderful W.		10	and is declared unto the W. by them
	76	they shall repent of their evil W.		11	proving to the W. that the Holy
85	2	their manner of life, their faith and W.		13	by them shall the W. be judged
88	108	secret acts of men and W. of God —109	21	9	crucified for the sins of the W.—35:2; 46:13; 53:2; 54:1
93	5	the W. of him were plainly manifest		12	unto the church and before the W.—23:2; 30:4
97	6	and their W. shall be made known			
	24	against all their wicked W.			
	26	will visit her according to all her W.			
98	31	if thou reward him according to his W.			

Sec.	Vs.		Sec.	Vs.	
23	4	not yet called to preach before the W.		47	that endureth shall overcome the W.
	6	must pray vocally and before the W.		48	an inheritance in this W.; a reward in the W. to come
24	10	continue bearing my name before the W.		52	preached the apostles unto the W.
25	4	withheld from thee and from the W.	64	2	I will that ye should overcome the W.
	10	lay aside the things of the W.			
27	6	by holy prophets since the W. began—86:10	70	6	not to the church, neither to the W.
			71	2	proclaim unto the W. in the regions
	14	whom Father hath given me out of the W.	72	14	labor unto the church and unto the W.
29	4	ye are chosen out of the W.	75	24	sent unto the W. to proclaim gospel unto the W.
	17	because of the wickedness of the W.			
	46	redeemed from foundation of the W.		26	not fail to go into the W.
31	10	physician unto church but not the W.	76	13	from the beginning before the W. was
34	3	who so loved the W. that he gave his		41	he came into the W... to be crucified for the W., to bear sins of the W., to sanctify the W.
35	13	called upon weak things of the W.			
	18	sealed from the foundation of the W.		71	we saw the terrestrial W.
38	1	the hosts of heaven before W. was made		86	not of his fulness in eternal W.
				98	from another in glory in telestial W.
	3	which spake and the W. was made		109	the inhabitants of the telestial W.
39	9	because of pride and cares of the W.		118	to bear his presence in W. of glory
40	2	cares of the W. caused him to reject	77	12	as God made the W. in six days
42	1	the Savior of the W.—43:34; 66:1	78	7	give unto you a place in celestial W.
	18	not have forgiveness in this W. nor in the W. to come—76:34; 84:41		14	creatures beneath celestial W.
			84	46	light to every man that cometh into W., enlighteneth every man through the W.—93:2
	65	unto the W. it is not given to know			
	89	in a meeting and not before the W.		48	for sake of the whole W.
45	9	sent mine covenant into W. to be a light unto the W.		53	the whole W. groaneth under sin
				61	bearing testimony to all the W.
	22	ye know that the end of the W. cometh		62	go ye into all the W.; may go from you into all the W.
	72	keep these things from going to the W.		73	neither speak them before the W.
				75	is in force upon all the W.
46	3	meetings which are held before the W.		79	I send you out to prove the W.
				82	kingdoms of the W. in all their glory
49	5	mine only Begotten into the W., for redemption of the W.		87	I send you out to reprove the W.
				117	reproving the W. in righteousness
	17	according to his creation before the W.	86	2	I say the field was the W.
	20	wherefore the W. lieth in sin—84:49		9	have been hid from the W. in Christ
			88	2	even them of the celestial W.
50	2	gone forth in the earth deceiving the W.		85	both in this W. and in the W. to come
	8	for the same are overcome of the W.	90	3	while thou art in the W., neither in W. to come
	41	I have overcome the W.			
53	2	that you shall forsake the W.	93	4	I was in the W. and made flesh my
57	12	if the W. receiveth his writings		5	was in the W. and received of my Father
58	39	for he seeketh the praise of the W.			
	64	from this place into all the W.		7	was in beginning before the W. was
59	9	keep thyself unspotted from the W.		9	light and redeemer of the W., who came into the W. because the W. was made by him
	23	peace in this W., eternal life in the W. to come			
63	27	that you may have advantage of the W.; have claim on the W.		52	shall not be confounded in this W. nor in the W. to come

Sec.	Vs.		Sec.	Vs.	
95	13	built not after manner of the W.; not that ye shall live after manner of W.		55	give unto him an hundred-fold in this W.
101	36	for in this W. your joy is not full	133	2	shall come down upon the W. with a curse
103	7	until kingdoms of the W. are subdued		45	since beginning of W. have not men
	8	kingdoms of the W. shall prevail		60	to be kept from the W. in the day
	9	were set to be a light unto the W.	134	12	save themselves from corruptions of W.
105	32	that kingdoms of this W. may be	135	3	for salvation of men in this W.
106	4	and it overtaketh W. as a thief		6	for salvation of a ruined W.
107	8	in the church in all ages of W.		7	a witness that *all* the W. cannot impeach
	23	special witnesses in *all* the W.	136	33	my spirit is sent forth into the W.
	25	unto the Gentiles and in *all* the W.			**WORLDS**
	90	those who do not travel in *all* the W.	76	24	of him the W. are and were created
109	29	lying reports abroad over the W.		39	of the Father before the W. were made
114	1	bear glad tidings unto *all* the W.	112		they cannot come W. without end
115	3	saints scattered abroad in *all* the W.	93	10	the W. were made by him
121	26	not revealed since W. was until now	132	55	crowns of eternal lives in eternal W.
	32	of all other Gods before the W. was		63	for their exaltation in eternal W.
	35	are set so much upon this W.			**WORLD'S**
123	6	may not only publish to *all* the W.	93	46	called you servants for the W. sake
	7	and filled the W. with confusion	134	10	take from them this W. goods
124	3	shall be made to the kings of the W.			**WORM**
	18	confessing me before the W.	76	44	where their W. dieth not and the fire
	33	instituted before foundation of W.—132:5			**WORSHIP**
	38	which had been hid from before the W.—41	18	40	shall fall down and W. the Father
139		bear record of my name in *all* the W.	20	19	the only being whom they should W.
127	2	before foundation of W.—128:5, 8, 18; 130:20; 132:63		29	and W. the Father in his name
	11	the prince of this W. cometh but he	42	35	and building houses of W.
128	9	in all ages of the W. whenever	76	21	who W. him forever and ever
	22	ordained before W. was—132:11, 28	93	19	may understand and know how to W., and know what you W.
130	19	so much the advantage in W. to come	101	22	who call on my name and W. me
132	13	and everything that is in the W.	109	14	that all who shall W. in this house
	15	marry a wife in the W.; with her so long as he is in the W.; when they are out of the W.		24	to establish the people that shall W.
	16	when out of the W. they neither marry	115	8	that they may W. me
	18	not of force when out of the W.; when out of the W. it cannot be	124	84	setteth up a golden calf for the W.
	19	of full force when out of the W.	133	39	and W. him that made heaven and earth
	22	because ye receive me not in the W.	134	4	in prescribing rules of W. to bind
	23	but if ye receive me in the W.		6	prescribing rules for faith and W.
	27	not be forgiven in the W. nor out of the W.			**WORSHIPING**
	30	continue so long as they were in the W.; out of the W. they should continue; both in the W. and out of the W.	76	21	W. God and the Lamb, who worship
	39	shall not inherit them out of the W.			**WORTH**
	49	be with thee even unto end of W.	15	4	which would be of the most W.—16:4
				6	the thing which will be of the most W.—16:6
			18	10	the W. of souls is great in the sight
					WORTHY
			20	69	that they are W. of it

Sec.	Vs.	
31	5	for the laborer is W. of his hire—84:79; 106:3
41	6	given to them that are not W.—90:26
50	34	accounted of God W. to receive
51	4	is not accounted W. by the voice
	5	is not accounted W. to belong to
67	14	and when ye are W. in mine own due
68	15	shall be high priests who are W.
	20	by this Presidency and found W.
70	12	the same is W. of his hire
72	4	is accounted W. to inherit mansions
98	14	that you may be found W.
	15	ye are not W. of me
102	7	whom they consider W. and capable
105	35	and let those be chosen that are W.
107	100	shall not be counted W. to stand
109	11	that we may be found W. in thy sight
119	5	they shall not be found W. to abide
124	23	a house W. of all acceptation
128	24	records, W. of all acceptation
132	16	thee who are W. of a far more and
136	31	that will not bear chastisement is not W.

WOULDST

6	14	thou W. not have come to the place
133	40	O that thou W. rend the heavens, that thou W. come down

WOUNDED

45	52	wounds with which I was W. in house
135	2	former was W. in a savage manner

WOUNDS

6	37	behold the W. which pierced my side
45	51	what are these W. in thine hands and
	52	these W. are the W. with which I was

WRATH

1	9	unto the day when the W. of God
19	15	by the rod of my mouth and by my W.
35	11	wine of the W. of her fornication—88:94, 105
43	26	the cup of the W. of mine indignation
56	1	in day of visitation and W. upon
59	21	against none is his W. kindled save
60	7	with loud voices, without W. or
	14	neither in W. nor with strife

Sec.	Vs.	
63	6	the day of W. shall come upon them
	11	he showeth no signs only in W.
	33	I have sworn in my W. and decreed
76	33	for they are vessels of W. doomed to suffer the W.
	38	after the sufferings of his W.
	104	who suffer W. of God on the earth
	106	cast down to hell and suffer W. of
	107	fierceness of W. of Almighty God—88:106
84	24	therefore, the Lord in his W.
	27	which the Lord in his W. caused to
87	6	shall inhabitants be made to feel W.
88	85	that their souls may escape W. of
	88	after your testimony cometh W. and
98	22	I will turn away all W. and indignation
101	9	in day of W. I will remember mercy
103	2	I will pour out my W. without
104	8	ye cannot escape my W. in your lives
109	38	thou art about to send, in thy W.
	53	and wilt turn away thy W. when
112	24	a day of W., a day of burning
115	6	refuge from storm and from W.
124	48	by your own works bring cursings, W.
	52	I will answer judgment, W. and
106		the inhabitants to flee the W. to come
127	2	envy and W. have been my common lot

WREST

10	63	for they do W. the scriptures and

WRITE

9	1	and did commence again to W. for
	4	work is to W. for my servant Joseph
	9	you cannot W. that which is sacred
24	1	thou wast called and chosen to W.
	6	given thee what thou shalt speak and W.
28	5	shalt not W. by way of commandment—8
35	20	thou shalt W. for him
	23	inasmuch as ye do not W.
47	1	W. and keep a regular history
	4	by the Comforter to W. these things
58	50	W. a description of land of Zion
76	28	that we should W. the vision
	49	W. the vision for this is the end
	80	that the Lord commanded us to W.
113		which we were commanded to W. while

Sec.	Vs.	
	115	which he commanded us we should not W.
90	32	ye shall W. this commandment and say
104	81	W. speedily unto New York, and W. according to
124	12	help you to W. this proclamation
127	10	I *will* W. the word of the Lord
128	1	that I would W. you from time to time

WRITING

6	17	work which thou hast been W. is true
24	5	W. the things which shall be given
25	8	thy time shall be given to W.
51	4	give unto him a W. that shall
55	4	selecting and W. books for schools
63	56	his W. is not acceptable to the Lord
69	3	he shall continue in W. and making
	8	preaching, expounding, W., copying
123	5	that are published and are W.
124	4	at the time of W. the same

WRITINGS

10	1	because you delivered up those W. —8
	39	remember it was said in those W.
57	12	if the world receiveth his W.
104	68	save in the holy and sacred W.

WRITTEN

1	18	which was W. by he prophets
10	10	words which you have caused to be W.
	11	translated and caused to be W.
	38	an account of those things you have W.
18	2	the things you have W. are true
	3	rely upon the things which are W.
	4	for in them are all things W.
	29	according to that which is W.
	30	according to the words which are W.
19	6	not W. that there shall be no end, but is W. endless
	7	it is W. eternal damnation
20	21	as it is W. in those scriptures
24	14	do according to that which is W.
28	11	hath W. from that stone are not of me
29	6	as. it is W., ye shall ask in faith
	50	in me to do according as it is W.
32	4	give heed to that which is W.
46	2	notwithstanding things which are W.
52	9	which prophets and apostles have W.

Sec.	Vs.	
66	2	as W. by prophets and apostles in days
68	10	with signs following as it is W.
73	5	until further knowledge as it is W.
76	58	as it is W. they are Gods
	68	they whose names are W. in heaven
	70	the sun is W. of as being typical
77	13	which are W. in 9th chapter of
	14	who, as it is W., must come and
84	57	to do according to that I have W.
85	5	W. in the Book of the Law of God
	9	they who are not found W. in book of
	11	whose names are not found W. in the
99	5	as W. of me in the volume of the book
102	13	according to the form above W.
	23	if there is not a sufficiency W.
	27	according to the former pattern W.
107	57	were all W. in Book of Enoch
124	4	let it be W. in spirit of meekness
128	6	judged out of those things W. in
	7	things which were W. in books
130	11	whereon is a new name W.
132	19	then shall it be W. in the Lamb's book
	36	it was W. thou shalt not kill
133	18	Father's name W. on their foreheads
	63	shall be fulfilled that which was W.
	64	also that which was W. by Malachi

WRONG

5	28	things he has done which are W.
9	9	to forget the thing which is W.

WRONGFULLY

64	20	and counsel W. to your hurt

WRONGS

105	25	and redress us of our W.
121	2	behold the W. of thy people
	3	how long shall they suffer these W.
	5	with thy sword avenge us of our W.
134	11	to civil law for redress of all W.

WROTE

74	5	for this cause the apostle W. to
128	2	I W. a few words of revelation
	7	which I W. to you previously

WROUGHT

76	69	who W. out this perfect atonement

Y

Sec.	Vs.	
		YEAR
21	3	established in Y. of your Lord, 1830
76	11	in the Y. of our Lord, 1832
88	44	all these are one Y. with God
93	51	proclaim the acceptable Y. of the Lord
107	45	God called upon Cainan in the 40th Y.
115	11	in one Y. from this day let them
133	52	now the Y. of my redeemed is come
		YEARS
18	42	arrived to Y. of accountability—20:71
20	1	being 1830 Y. since coming of Lord
29	11	with men on earth a thousand Y.
	22	when the thousand Y. are ended
45	63	not many Y. hence ye shall hear of
51	17	act upon this land as for Y.
58	44	time has not yet come for many Y.
64	21	in Kirtland for space of five Y.
68	25	laying on of hands when eight Y. old
	27	shall be baptized when eight Y. old
76	4	and his Y. never fail
77	6	during the 7,000 Y. of its continuance
	7	the things of the first thousand Y.; also of the second thousand Y.
	10	to be accomplished in the 6,000th Y.
	12	in beginning of 7,000th Y.
84	17	without beginning of days or end of Y.
88	44	in their weeks, their months, their Y.
	101	until the thousand Y. are ended
	108	works of God in first thousand Y.
	109	works of God in second thousand Y.
	110	not be loosed for a thousand Y.
99	7	after a few Y. if thou desirest
105	15	not many Y. hence they shall not
107	42	by Adam at the age of 69 Y., blessed by him three Y.
	44	Enos ordained at age of 134 Y.
	45	he was 87 Y. old when he received
	46	Mahalaleel was 496 Y. and
	47	Jared was 200 Y. old when he was
	48	Enoch was 25 Y. old when he was
	49	walked with God 365 Y., making him 430 Y. old when
	50	Methuselah was 100 Y. old when he
	51	Lamech was 32 Y. old when he was
	52	Noah was ten Y. old when he was
	53	three Y. previous to death of Adam
121	15	not many Y. hence they and their
	31	all the appointed Y. and all the days of their days, months and Y.
122	6	thine elder son, but six Y. of age
	9	thy Y. shall not be numbered less
130	15	if thou livest until 85 Y. old
135	3	in short space of twenty Y. he
	6	Hyrum was 43 Y. and Joseph was 38 Y.
		YES
130	5	I answer, Y., but there are no angels
135	4	to the slaughter; Y., for so it was
		YESTERDAY
20	12	the same God Y., today and forever
35	1	the same today as Y. and forever
61	20	I the Lord, was angry with you Y.
		YET
1	35	the hour is not Y. but is nigh—58:4
3	4	Y. if he boasts in his own strength
	8	Y. you should have been faithful
5	17	you must wait Y. a little while, for ye are not Y. ordained
7	5	or a greater work Y. among men
23	4	thou art not as Y. called to preach
45	37	and the leaves are Y. tender
46	27	among you professing and Y. not of God
48	5	the place is not Y. to be revealed
58	44	time has not Y. come for many years
62	2	those who have not Y. gone up to; your mission is not Y. full
63	35	this is not Y., but by and by
	42	retain his store Y. for little season
66	6	go not up to land of Zion as Y.
76	10	nor Y. entered into heart of man
	28	and while we were Y. in the spirit —80, 113, 115

Sec.	Vs.		Sec.	Vs.	
78	17	ye have not as Y. understood			**YOUNG, JOSEPH**
82	24	for even Y. the kingdom is yours	124	138	I give unto you Y. and, to preside over
83	3	Y. they may remain upon their			**YOURSELF**
84	28	baptized while Y. in his childhood	6	27	a desire to lay up treasures for Y.
	119	ye cannot see it now, Y. a little while	10	31	but that you have contradicted Y.
86	4	blade is springing up and is Y. tender—6	30	3	you are left to inquire for Y.
88	85	for their time is not Y. come			**YOURSELVES**
93	42	wicked one hath power, as Y., over you	36	·6	save Y. from this generation—38:42
101	3	Y. I will own them and they shall	41	2	ye shall assemble Y. together—45:64; 52:42; 58:46; 88:74
	35	Y. shall they partake of this glory	42	1	who have assembled Y. together—3; 57:1; 67:1; 72:1; 78:1; 88:1; 105:1
	47	while they were Y. laying foundation	43	9	bind Y. to act in all holiness
	54	seen the enemy while Y. afar off		11	sanctify Y. before me—16; 88:68, 74; 133:4
	84	Y. because this widow troubleth me		20	prepare Y. for the great day—88:74; 133:10
111	11	wise as serpents, Y. without sin	44	4	organize Y. according to—88:119; 104:11, 58; 109:8
121	10	thou art not Y. as Job			
123	12	there are many Y. on the earth who	50	16	ye shall answer this question Y.
124	137	Y. they are ordained to be standing	61	37	as you have humbled Y. before me
132	26	Y. they shall come forth in the first	62	4	assemble Y. upon the land of
133	67	Y. my arm was not shortened	63	1	you that call Y. people of the Lord
135	4	and it shall Y. be said of me, he	67	10	as you strip Y. from jealousies, and humble Y.
136	37	for ye are not Y. pure; ye cannot Y. bear my glory	78	7	prepare Y. by doing the things
		YIELD		11	organize Y. by a bond or
5	21	Y. to persuasions of men no more	82	15	bind Y. by this covenant
9	13	be faithful and Y. to no temptation		22	make unto Y. friends with Mammon
		YIELDED	84	43	beware concerning Y.
29	40	because he Y. to temptation		92	go away from him alone by Y.
		YIELDETH		107	that you Y. are not able to fill
89	16	that which Y. fruit, whether in	88	74	assemble Y.; organize Y.; prepare Y.; sanctify Y.
97	9	that Y. much precious fruit		86	entangle Y. not in sin
		YOKE		122	appoint among Y. a teacher
109	32	complete deliverance from this Y.		125	clothe Y. with the bonds of charity
	47	break off, O Lord, this Y. of	89	5	only in assembling Y. together
	63	the Y. of bondage may begin to be	103	22	gather Y. together unto the land
123	8	it is an iron Y., it is a strong band	104	60	organize for Y. a treasury
		YOUNG		79	you shall humble Y. before me
43	20	call on nations to repent, both old and Y.		84	to deliver Y. from bondage
101	55	which are my warriors, my Y. men	111	5	concern not Y. about your debts
103	22	my Y. men and the middle-aged—105:16		6	concern not Y. about Zion
		YOUNG, BRIGHAM	112	15	exalt not Y.
124	127	I give unto you Y. to be president over		27	trouble not Y. concerning the affairs
			124	55	that you may prove Y. unto me
			127	2	judge ye for Y.
126	1	dear and well-beloved Brother Y.	136	21	keep Y. from evil
					YOUWARD
			112	15	given unto him and also to Y.

Z.

Sec.	Vs.		Sec.	Vs.	
		ZACHARIAS		26	until the residue shall go up to Z.
27	7	also John, the son of Z., which Z. he		30	obtain an inheritance in land of Z.
		ZARAHEMLA		34	shall eat the good of the land of Z.
125	3	let the name of Z. be named upon it		35	shall be cut off out of the land of Z.
		ZINC		38	inhabitants of Z. shall judge all things pertaining to Z.
124	27	with iron, copper, brass and Z.		41	Z. shall flourish and the glory
		ZION	66	6	go not up to land of Z. as yet
6	6	bring forth and establish cause of Z.—11:6; 12:6; 14:6		11	push many people to Z. with songs of
21	7	have I inspired to move cause of Z.	68	25	inasmuch as parents have children in Z.
	8	his weeping for Z. have I seen		26	be a law unto inhabitants of Z.
24	7	shalt devote all thy service in Z.		29	inhabitants of Z. shall observe Sabbath
25	2	shalt receive an inheritance in Z.		30	inhabitants of Z. shall remember their
28	9	no man knoweth where city of Z.		31	not well pleased with inhabitants of Z.
30	11	your whole labor shall be in Z.		32	carry these sayings to land of Z.
35	24	Z. shall rejoice upon the hills and —49:25	69	1	money he shall carry to land of Z.
38	4	have taken the Z. of Enoch into my		5	accounts of their stewardships in Z.
39	13	build up my church and bring forth Z.		6	land of Z. shall be a seat and place
45	67	and it shall be called Z.		8	that shall grow up on land of Z.
	68	must needs flee unto Z. for safety	70	1	hearken, O. ye inhabitants of Z.
	70	let us not go up to battle against Z.; inhabitants of Z.; are terrible		8	consecrated unto inhabitants of Z.
	71	shall come to Z. singing with songs	72	6	to he handed over to bishop in Z. —13
57	2	and the place for the city of Z.		14	answer the debt to the bishop in Z.
	14	be planted in land of Z. as speedily		15	every man that cometh to Z. must lay all things before bishop in Z.
58	7	upon which the Z. of God shall stand		17	a certificate unto the bishop in Z.
	13	that testimony might go forth from Z.		18	shall not be accepted of bishop in Z.
	49	receive moneys to purchase lands in Z.		24	appointed to go up unto Z.; who are privileged to go up unto Z.
	50	write a description of the land of Z.		26	otherwise he who shall go up to Z.
59	3	whose feet stand upon land of Z.	76	66	they who come unto Mount Z.
60	14	after thou hast come up unto Z.	78	3	both in this place and the land of Z.
61	16	none able to go up to land of Z.		9	sit in council with the saints in Z.
	24	to journey and go up to the land of Z.		15	saith the Lord God the Holy One of Z.
62	2	who have not as yet gone up to Z.	82	12	to the bishopric both in land of Z. and
	4	assemble yourselves upon land of Z.—63:24, 36		13	and for a stake to Z.
63	25	Z. I hold in mine own hands		14	for Z. must increase in beauty; Z. must arise and put on
	29	land of Z. shall not be obtained	84	2	to stand upon Mount Z., which
	39	take his journey to the land of Z.		32	the glory of the Lord upon Mount Z.
	40	money be sent up to land of Z.—43		56	condemnation resteth upon children of Z.
	41	those who shall go up to land of Z.		58	be poured out upon children of Z.
	48	sendeth up treasures to land of Z.		76	your brethren in Z. for their rebellion
64	18	and to his agency in land of Z.			
	22	shall go with an open heart to Z.			

Sec.	Vs.		Sec.	Vs.	
	99	the Lord hath brought again Z.—100		22	gather yourselves together on land of Z.
	104	send it unto bishop in Z.; printing thereof and establishing Z.		24	consecrated to be the land of Z.
				29	the restoration and redemption of Z.
85	1	of all things that shall transpire in Z.		30	companies to go up to land of Z.
				34	shall not go up to land of Z. until—to go with you to land of Z.
89	1	and also the saints in Z.		35	establish children of Z. upon laws
90	8	in their ministry for salvation of Z.	104	47	concerning Z.; shall no longer be bound with brethren of Z.
	28	and go up unto land of Z.			
	30	she should go up unto land of Z.		48	United Order of Stake of Z.; United Order of City of Z.
	32	say unto your brethren in Z.; to preside over Z. in			
	34	your brethren in Z. begin to repent	105	5	Z. cannot be built up unless it is
	36	I, the Lord, will contend with Z.		8	we will not go up unto Z. and will
93	53	all this for the salvation of Z.		9	a little season for redemption of Z.—13
94	1	foundation of city of the stake of Z.			
96	1	that I have set for the strength of Z.		14	do not require to fight battles of Z.
97	1	my will concerning your brethren in Z.		32	kingdom of Z. is in very deed the
				34	commandments given concerning Z.
	3	concerning the school in Z.; there should be a school in Z.		37	accomplish all things pertaining to Z.
	4	shall preside over the school in Z.	107	36	High Council at stakes of Z.
	5	edification of the church in Z.		37	High Council in Z. form a quorum; of the Twelve at the stakes of Z.
	10	house should be built in land of Z.			
	12	built unto me for salvation of Z.		59	to church of Christ in land of Z.
	18	if Z. do these things she shall prosper		74	judge among inhabitants of Z., or in a Stake of Z., until borders of Z. are enlarged, and necessary to have other judges in Z.
	19	surely Z. is the city of our God; surely Z. cannot fall			
	21	let Z. rejoice; for this is Z., the pure in heart; let Z.	109	39	that they may come forth to Z.
				51	didst appoint a Z. unto thy people
	25	Z. shall escape if she observe		59	we ask thee to appoint unto Z. other
99	6	sent up kindly unto bishop in Z.	111	2	for the benefit of Z.
100	13	a word concerning Z.; Z. shall be redeemed		6	concern not yourselves about Z.
			112	6	let thy habitation be known in Z.
101	16	hearts be comforted concerning Z.	113	7	put on thy strength O Z.
	17	Z. shall not be moved out of her place		8	power of priesthood to bring again Z.; which she (Z.) has
	18	to build up the waste places of Z.		9	by Z. loosing herself from the bands
	21	for the curtains or strength of Z.	115	3	of the High Council of my church in Z.
	41	wisdom concerning children of Z.			
	43	concerning redemption of Z.		6	that gathering upon land of Z. may be
	70	which I have appointed to be Z.			
	74	and in this way they may establish Z.	117	9	the land of my people, even Z.
				14	come up hither speedily unto Z.
	75	to redeem Z. and establish her waste	118	2	remain for a season in land of Z.
			119	1	into hands of bishop of my church in Z.
	81	unto what shall I liken children of Z.			
				2	for laying the foundation of Z.
	85	thus will I liken the children of Z.		5	those who gather unto land of Z.
103	1	who have been scattered on land of Z.		6	by this law sanctify land of Z., it shall not be a land of Z. unto you
	11	and build up the waste places of Z.			
	13	their restoration to land of Z.		7	an ensample unto all the stakes of Z.
	15	redemption of Z. must come by power	124	2	to be a cornerstone of Z.
				6	to the light and glory of Z.
	18	so shall the redemption of Z. be		9	to exaltation or lifting up of Z.
				11	to the house of the daughters of Z.

Sec.	Vs.		Sec.	Vs.	
	18	should continue in preaching for Z.		21	he shall utter his voice out of Z.
	23	cornerstone I have appointed for Z.		24	land of Z. shall be turned back
	36	for it is ordained that in Z.		32	be crowned with glory, even in Z.
	39	of revelations and foundation of Z.	136	10	where the Lord shall locate stake of Z.
	60	that he may contemplate glory of Z.		18	Z. shall be redeemed in mine own
	118	called to lay the foundation of Z.		31	I have for them, even the glory of Z.
	131	a High Council for cornerstone of Z.			
128	19	that say unto Z., thy God reigneth			**ZOMBRE (John Johnson)**
133	4	gather ye together upon land of Z.	96	6	Z., whose offering I have accepted
	9	go ye forth unto land of Z., that Z. may go forth unto	104	24	the lot of land which my servant Z.
	12	who are among the Gentiles flee to Z.		34	let Z. have the house in which he
	18	when Lamb shall stand upon Mount Z.—56			**ZORAMITES**
	20	upon islands of sea, upon land of Z.	3	17	to the Nephites, Josephites and the Z.

Printed in the United States
96573LV00006B/36/A